THE NORTON READER
Shorter Twelfth Edition

THE NORTON READER
An Anthology of Nonfiction

SHORTER TWELFTH EDITION

LINDA H. PETERSON, *General Editor*
Yale University

JOHN C. BRERETON
Boston Athenaeum

W·W·NORTON & COMPANY
NEW YORK · LONDON

W. W. Norton & Company has been independent since its founding in 1923, when William Warder Norton and Mary D. Herter Norton first published lectures delivered at the People's Institute, the adult education division of New York City's Cooper Union. The Nortons soon expanded their program beyond the Institute, publishing books by celebrated academics from America and abroad. By mid-century, the two major pillars of Norton's publishing program—trade books and college texts—were firmly established. In the 1950s, the Norton family transferred control of the company to its employees, and today—with a staff of four hundred and a comparable number of trade, college, and professional titles published each year—W. W. Norton & Company stands as the largest and oldest publishing house owned wholly by its employees.

Manufacturing by R. R. Donnelly & Sons, Inc.
Book design by Martin Lubin Graphic Design
Production manager: Diane O'Connor

ISBN 978-0-393-93173-0 (pbk.)

W. W. Norton & Company, Inc., 500 Fifth Avenue, New York, N.Y. 10110
www.wwnorton.com

W. W. Norton & Company Ltd., Castle House, 75/76 Wells Street, London W1T 3QT

2 3 4 5 6 7 8 9 0

BRIEF CONTENTS

Contents

HISTORY 464

POLITICS AND GOVERNMENT 512

SCIENCE AND TECHNOLOGY 562

LITERATURE, THE ARTS, AND MEDIA   625

PHILOSOPHY AND RELIGION   683

PREFACE

The Norton Reader brings together a wide selection of essays on a wide range of subjects—from Judith Ortiz Cofer recalling her grandmother's home in Puerto Rico to Barbara Tuchman describing the eruption of bubonic plague in medieval Europe to Nicholas D. Kristof analyzing the dress of Saudi women. With 206 selections in the Regular Edition and 123 in the Shorter Edition, *The Norton Reader* offers depth, breadth, and variety for instructors who wish to teach the essay in its many modes and forms—including the seminal experiments of Francis Bacon and John Donne, the modern classics of George Orwell, Virginia Woolf, and E. B. White, and contemporary examples by such diverse writers as Jamaica Kincaid, Terry Tempest Williams, Patricia Williams, and Al Gore.

Since its first edition, *The Norton Reader* has upheld a tradition of anthologizing excellent prose. Arthur Eastman, the founding editor, always insisted that essays be selected for their achievement. "Excellence would be their pillar of smoke by day, of fire by night," he wrote in the preface to the eighth edition. With this vision, the original editors of the *Reader* anthologized the classic essays that appeal to modern readers and that we now recognize as comprising the essay canon. Yet the *Reader* has also continued to adapt and renew itself by adding new writers who keep the essay alive (and lively) and whose writing appeals to new generations of student readers.

This new edition blends the new and the old, the innovative and the classic. Features that distinguish the *Reader* include:

- Both canonical and contemporary essays by authors as diverse as Mary Wollstonecraft and Toni Morrison, Henry David Thoreau and Richard Selzer, Martin Luther King Jr. and Patricia Williams.

- Coverage of important themes and influential styles of writing. Sections on education, ethics, language and communication, nature and the environment, history, and religion, among others, introduce students to important academic ideas and ongoing civic debates. Instructors have the flexibility to use these sections as they choose.

- Pedagogical apparatus to serve the instructors' and students' needs, but not too much to overwhelm the essays themselves. We provide contextual notes to indicate when, where, and why the essay was written; annotations to explain unfamiliar persons, events, and concepts; and study questions for all essays.

- A section called "Authors," located at the end of the volume, gives information about the men and women who wrote the essays, and allows readers to choose whether to find out about the authors before reading their essays or to encounter the authors as unknowns and let them identify themselves within their essays.

Among the new and expanded features in the twelfth edition, we have added materials to offer more guidance for students on critical reading and on writing, to extend the formal range of the essay, and to locate the essay within the larger context of visual culture:

- Thirty-three new selections, including essays that represent the work of American, Canadian, African, Indian, English, Irish, and Caribbean writers. New voices include Bill McKibben making a case for single-child families, Lauren Slater meditating on the meaning of love, Michael Pollan arguing for the greater rights of animals, and Anthony Lane analyzing the musical hit "The Sound of Music."

- A new, extensive introduction for students that offers advice on critical reading and on writing college essays. The introduction addresses key features of the "Outcomes Statement" of the Council of Writing Program Administrators and highlights rhetorical skills essential to college success.

- A new Genres Index locates readings in major genres, such as memoirs, profiles of people and places, visual and textual analysis, and argument. The Genres Index is designed to help instructors meet crucial goals of the WPA "Outcomes Statement," including teaching students to write in several genres, to identify conventions of format and structure, and to understand how genres shape reading and writing.

- Visual images—photographs, drawings, graphs, and other illustrations—that accompanied the essays are included, with original captions, for more than twenty selections, including a visual essay on the graphic novel, "Understanding Comics." We hope that these images will encourage readers to think about the ways in which the visual and the verbal interact in modern culture, and the ways in which images enrich, highlight, and sometimes challenge the written text.

- Contextual notes provide information about when and where the essay first appeared and, if it began as a talk, when and where it was delivered and to what audience.

- Study questions for all selections, emphasizing both individual response and collaborative effort, encourage students to become active critical readers and writers.

- *A Guide to The Norton Reader*, written by Anne Fernald, Melissa Goldthwaite, and Charles Hood, offers a wealth of suggestions for classroom discussion and writing assignments. A new twenty-five-page section provides invaluable practical classroom support, with suggested in-class activities, tips for planning a writing course (including five sample syllabi), advice for teachers of developmental writing, and more.

ACKNOWLEDGMENTS

Among our many critics, advisors, and friends, the following were of special help in the preparation of the twelfth edition, either by offering advice or by nominating essays to be included in this edition: Alan Ainsworth (Houston Community College), Greg Clark (Brigham Young University), Anne Fernald (Fordham University), Melissa Goldthwaite (St. Joseph's University), Paul Heilker (Virginia Polytechnic Institute and State University), Charles Hood (Antelope Valley Community College), Paul Matsuda (University of New Hampshire), Ira Nadel (University of British Columbia), Peggy Oliver (San Jacinto College South), Kate Ryan (University of Montana), Raul Sanchez (University of Florida), Linda Smith (Midlands Technical College). Our colleague and editor emerita Joan Hartman deserves our deep gratitude for her ongoing contributions to *The Norton Reader*.

The editors would like to express appreciation and thanks to the many teachers who provided reviews: Kathy Albertson (Georgia Southern University), David Anderson (Butler County Community College), Melissa Bader (Riverside Community College, Norco), Kim Ballerini (Nassau Community College), Maryam Barrie (Washtenaw Community College), Barbara Bengels (Hofstra University), Mark E. Bingham (Florida College), Joseph Bizup (Columbia University), Joseph Blaih (Youngstown State University), Monica Bosson (City College of San Francisco), Dawn Brickey (Charleston Southern University), Brock Brower (Dartmouth College), Cheryl Brown (Towson University), Danika M. Brown (University of Texas, Pan American), Sheree Brown (College of Mount St. Joseph), John C. Cabral (L.A. Mission College), David Calonne (Eastern Michigan University), Robert Carlton (Palomar College), William Carney (Texas Tech University), Shannon Carroll (Frank Phillips College), Lynn Casmier-Paz (University of Central Florida), Isaac Cates (Long Island University, C.W. Post Campus), Anthony Collins (Inver Hills Community College), Samuel Collins (Towson University), Keith Comer (Idaho State University), Richard Compean (City College of San Francisco), Sonni Cooper (Sierra College), Imraan Coovadia (Adelphi University), Walter Corbella (Kent State University), Kathleen Crosby (Hofstra University), Jennine Crucet (University of Minnesota), Robert E. Cummings (University of Georgia), Denise Curry (University of Saint Francis), Jill Cutler (Yale University), Laurie Dashnau (Houghton College), Laurie Dawson (Sonoma State University), Jackie DiSalvo (Baruch College), John Dudley (University of South Dakota), Richard Durocher (St. Olaf College), Anne Dvorak (Longview Community College), Olivia Edenfield (Georgia Southern University), Kim Edwards (Monroe County Community College), Jodi Egerton (The University of Texas at Austin), Jeff Ellis (Towson University), Breanne Ertmer (Texas A&M University), Kenneth D. Fisher (Pennsylvania State University, Wilkes-Barre), George Friend

(Millersville University), Kim Gainer (Radford University), Ann D. Garbett (Averett University), Stephen D. Gibson (Utah Valley State), Lisa Giles (Brandeis University), Tim Giles (Georgia Southern University), William Gillard (Farleigh Dickinson University), C. Herbert Gilliland (United States Naval Academy), Donald Gilzinger, Jr. (Suffolk County Community College), Karen Gocsik (Dartmouth College), Hazel Greenberg (San Jacinto College South), Alfred Guy (Yale University), Tami Haaland (Montana State University, Billings), Douglas Haneline (Ferris State University), Shona Harrison (Malaspina University-College), Judy Hart (Frank Phillips College), John Hartner (Community College of Allegheny County, North Campus), William Heath (University of Mary, Hardin-Baylor), Jacob Heller (SUNY College at Old Westbury), Sally Henschel (Midwestern State University), Marc Hewson (University of Ottawa), Suzanne Hill (Towson University), Will Hochman (Southern Connecticut State University), Melanie Hunter (Tulsa Community College), Sherrie Inness (Miami University), Sue Iseman (Ohio Northern University), Emily A. Bernhard Jackson (University of Arkansas), M.W. Jackson (St. Bonaventure University), Joanne Ciske Jacobs (Shenandoah University), Ann Jagoe (North Central Texas College), Allison James (Monterey Peninsula College), Emily Janda (Texas A&M University), Mary Ann Janda (Utica College), Michelle Jarenski (Loyola University), Scott Jarvis (Hofstra University), Trish Jenkins (University of Alaska, Anchorage), Margaret Johnson (Idaho State University), Gabriel Jones (San Diego State University), Stewart Justman (University of Montana), J. Kastely (University of Houston), Elaine M. Kauver (Baruch College), Karen Rae Keck (Texas Tech University), Paul Kellerman (Penn State University), Audrey Kerr (Southern Connecticut State University), Joy Kidwell (Boise State University), Lew Klatt (Calvin College), Michael J. Krozel (Central Connecticut State University), Celena Kusch (Merrimack College), Carol Kushner (Dutchess Community College), Ethna Lay (Hofstra University), Mary Levitt (Massachusetts College of Liberal Arts), Keming Liu (Medgar Evers College), Elise Maglio (Providence College), Julie Maia (West Valley College), David Malone (Union University), Joshua J. Mark (Marist College), Jim Martin (Mount Ida College), Sharan McBride (Houston Community College System), Thomas McConnell (University of South Carolina, Upstate), Margaret McKenzie (Diablo Valley College), Margaret A. McLaughlin (Georgia Southern University), Becky Jo McShane (Weber State University), Carla Mettling (Columbia College), Deborah Miller (University of Georgia), Susan J. Miller (Santa Fe Community College), Melaney Moisan (Chemeketa Community College), Albert S. Moorin (San Diego State University), Michael Moreau (Glendale College), Michael Mulvey (Central Connecticut State University), Joseph Musser (Ohio Wesleyan University), Nancy Nahra (Champlain College), Amy Nawrocki (Sacred Heart University), Vanita Neelakanta (Brandeis University), Beverley Neiderman (Kent State University), Nathan K. Nelson (Ferris State University), Tor Nielsen (Elmira College), Monica Norris (Texas Tech University), Nathan Oates (University of Missouri, Columbia), Peggy Oliver (San Jacinto College South), Corey Palmer (Mesa State College), John G. Parks (Miami University), Robert Piasecki (Norwich University), Phil Poulos (California State University, Los Angeles),

Patricia T. Price (Georgia Southern University), Dale Purvis (Georgia Southern University), Daniela Rugasa (Southern Connecticut State University), Cleatus Rattan (University of Mary, Hardin-Baylor), J. Lisa Ray (Thomas Nelson Community College), Doug Rice (Sacramento State University), Rich Rice (Texas Tech University), Charles Riley (Baruch College), Beth Ritter-Guth (Lehigh Carbon Community College), Aaron Ritzenberg (Yale University), Mark Roberts (California Polytechnic State University, San Luis Obispo), Susan Roberts (Central Connecticut State University), Juliet Rodeman (University of Missouri, Columbia), Kristina Rogers (American River College), Carl Rollyson (Baruch College), Kathy Roosa (San Jacinto College South), Rae Rosenthal (Community College of Baltimore County Essex), Jeff Runyon (University of Northern Colorado), Kara Russell (Central Connecticut State University), Mary A. Sadler (College of Charleston), Shelley Saltzman (Columbia University), Mike Sanders (Kent State University), Diane Scharper (Towson University), Andrew Schonebaum (Barnard College), Kreg Segall (Suffolk County Community College, Grant Campus), Eileen Seifert (DePaul University), M. P. A. Sheaffer (Millersville University of Pennsylvania), Audell Shelburne (University of Mary, Hardin-Baylor), Claude Clayton Smith (Ohio Northern University), Greg Smith (San Jacinto College South), Jeanne Smith (McPherson College), Whitney Womack Smith (Miami University, Hamilton), William Smith (Weatherford College), Margaret Spillane (Yale University), John Staines (Earlham College), Andrew Stambuk (Hofstra University), Katherine Staples (Austin Community College), Carla Steinberg (College of Marin), Rebecca Steinitz (Ohio Wesleyan University), Pamela Stinson (Northern Oklahoma College), Barbara Stuart (Yale University), Yuko Taniguchi (The University of Minnesota), Jonathan Taylor (Ferris State University), Victor H. Thompson (Thomas Nelson Community College), John Trimble (University of Texas), Brenda Tuberville (University of Texas, Tyler), Trevor Tucker (University of Ottawa), Deborah Uman (St. John Fisher College), Nicole B. Wallack (Columbia University), Carmen Walsh (Towson University), John Wang (Queens College), Denise C. White (Kennesaw State University), Patricia Whiting (Carleton University), Audrey Wick (University of Texas, Arlington), Jane E. Wohl (Sheridan College), Mark Wolzenburg (Champlain College), Deborah Workman (Myers University), and Scott D. Yarbrough (Charleston Southern University).

Special thanks goes to Carol Hollar-Zwick for her excellent editorial work on the introduction. At Yale University, we thank Abigail Deutsch for advice on annotations; Paula Resch, Margaret Spillane, Barbara Stuart, and Deborah Tenney for new essay suggestions; and Randi Saloman for her work on the biographical sketches. At Norton, we owe thanks to Katharine Ings for her copyediting; Diane O'Connor and Marian Johnson for their help with production; Nancy Rodwan and Margaret Gorenstein for their able help with permissions; and our editors past and present, Jennifer Bartlett, Carol Hollar-Zwick, Marilyn Moller, Nicole Netherton, and Julia Reidhead, for their new ideas and constant encouragement. A special thanks goes to our newest editor, Erin Granville, and to editorial assistants Catherine Spencer and Ana Cooke—their patience, intelligence, and commitment to the *Reader* have been exemplary.

INTRODUCTION
Reading and Writing with The Norton Reader

Reading with a Writer's Eye

During the coming term your writing instructor will ask you to read a selection of essays in *The Norton Reader*. Whether you read many essays or just a few, we hope that you will enjoy them. Reading essays in a college textbook may seem different from the reading you usually do in magazines, books, or on-line—and reading essays for a college course *is* different, even though you will find some aspects quite familiar. When you read on your own, you choose the topics and the formats, letting your personal interests guide you. When you read in a college writing course, you will discover essays that reflect your own interests, but your instructor will also introduce you to topics you've never before encountered, to forms of writing common in college but new to you, and to levels of difficulty that will prepare you for the reading in future college classes and the writing assigned in them.

In *The Norton Reader* you will find essays that address these various interests, forms, and goals. The 123 pieces collected here originally appeared in many different venues—from a daily newspaper in Baltimore to a beautifully produced book of art photographs, from a speech given publicly by a U.S. president to a collection of private meditations by a famous author. In an anthology like *The Norton Reader*, all of these selections appear in the same format, with the same typeface and layout; all have annotations to explain references and allusions; and all have questions to urge you to think about major issues and themes. In these visible ways, the essays in this collection differ from their originals.

Even so, we hope that the original pleasure, purpose, and power of each essay will come through. To help in the reading process, we provide you with information about the context in which the essay first appeared—including the readers for whom it was intended, the magazine, book, or newspaper in which it was published, and the knowledge that its original readers brought to their reading or listening. (See "Who is the audience?" p. xvi, and "What is the rhetorical context and purpose?" p. xix.) We also suggest, in this introduction, some ways of reading essays that will help you to analyze them. (See "What is the genre and its conventions?" p. xxi.) Finally, we provide strategies for writing your own essays. (See "Writing in College," p. xxxiv.) Among the goals of a college reader like this one are connecting reading and writing, linking the two processes as interactive, and making your reading enrich, inspire, and improve your writing.

Most of the essays in *The Norton Reader* originally appeared in magazines or books written for general readers—educated people but not specialists in the subject. The essays were read by people like you who wanted to know—or know more—about their subjects, who knew about—or were intrigued by—their authors, or who were tempted to launch into unfamiliar subjects because they encountered them in a magazine they ordinarily read. In the world outside the classroom, readers bring their own interests and motives to the essays they read. Although putting essays in a textbook might make them seem a little artificial, we hope to make your reading process more "real" by suggesting strategies that help you understand their contexts, purposes, and ongoing relevance.

When you begin reading an essay that your instructor assigns, ask yourself some or all of the following questions. These questions—about the audience for the essay, the author and his or her purpose in writing the essay, and the genre of the essay—will help you understand the essay, re-create its original context, analyze its meaning, recognize its organization and rhetorical strategies, and imagine how you might use similar strategies for your own writing.

WHO IS THE AUDIENCE?

An *audience* consists of those to whom the essay is directed—the people who read the article, listen to the speech, or view the text. The question about audience might be posed in related ways: For whom did the author write? What readers does the author hope to reach? What readers did he or she actually reach?

Sometimes that audience is a single reader, as in an entry in a private diary; sometimes the audience is national or international, as in an editorial for a newspaper like the *Washington Post* or the *New York Times*. Often, the audience shares a common interest, as the readers of an environmental magazine might do or the buyers of books of biography or history. To help you understand the original audience for each essay, we provide *contextual notes* at the bottom of the first page of each essay. Contextual notes give information about when and where the essay first appeared and, if it began as a talk, when and where it was delivered and to what audience. If we know, we try to give a sense of what the original audience was like or, at least, what we can gauge from the publishing context.

For example, the contextual note for Scott Russell Sanders's "Looking at Women" (p. 118) tells you that it appeared in the *Georgia Review*, a small-circulation magazine that attracts readers who enjoy fiction, essays, and poetry and who like essays with a literary feel. In contrast, Nicholas Kristof's "Saudis in Bikinis" (p. 200) appeared as an editorial in the *New York Times*, a daily newspaper with a huge national readership, where Kristof has a regular column on the Op-Ed page. Sanders could assume that his audience would like reading personal memoirs and biographical profiles, whereas Kristof knew that he needed to speak to a large, diverse national audience of people holding very different opinions on matters of education, politics, religion, and social questions like gender. Knowing these audiences gives a window into the writers' choices, strategies, and styles. Sanders's essays begins as if it were a story, in an intriguing yet leisurely way:

> On that sizzling July afternoon, the girl who crossed at the stoplight in front of our car looked, as my mother would say, as though she had been poured into her pink shorts.

Kristof, in contrast, gets down to business quickly, since he knows he has only 750 or so words to explain the issue to his readers and convince them of his position. Kristof may begin with an intriguing observation—"On my first evening in Riyadh, I spotted a surreal scene"—but by his fourth sentence, he has reached the issue under consideration:

> Saudi women may be regarded in the West as antique doormats covered in black veils, but the women themselves vigorously reject the stereotype. "It hurts when you hear what people say about us, that we're repressed."

The expectations of the two different audiences explain, in part, the writers' different approaches and styles.

Sometimes contextual notes give information about where the selection was published and how it was received—another way to understand the audience. Maya Angelou's "Graduation" (p. 12) comes from her autobiography, *I Know Why the Caged Bird Sings*, published in 1969; Angelou then continued writing her life story in five sequential volumes, most recently *A Song Flung Up to Heaven* (2002)—a sequence that testifies to her book's success and its appeal to a wide variety of readers. A different example of success with readers appears in the contextual note for David Baltimore's "Limiting Science: A Biologist's Perspective" (p. 601), which gives this information:

> Written by a Nobel Prize-winning scientist and originally published in *Daedalus* (Spring 1978), the professional journal of the American Academy of Arts and Sciences; the Academy re-published the essay in *Daedalus* (Fall 2005).

This note lets you know that the author, a world-class biologist, meant to reach a wide audience of educated men and women and had the clout to argue for the importance of freedom in research. Members of the Academy of Arts and Sciences were his immediate audience, but the author knew that his argument would extend beyond them to politicians and government officials, given his own stature and that of the Academy. The fact that Baltimore's essay was published a second time, twenty-five years later, reveals that the American Academy of Arts and Sciences believes his argument remains timely in today's debate over issues of cloning, genetic engineering, and organ research.

In each contextual note, we try to explain a little about the books, magazines, and newspapers that published these essays—the *New York Times Magazine*, a large-circulation weekly magazine included with the Sunday newspaper, or the *Georgia Review*, a small, but well-respected literary journal published three times a year by the University of Georgia, or *I Know Why the Caged Bird Sings*, a free-standing book. As editors, we could swamp you with information about publication and authorship, but we prefer to include more essays and keep contextual information focused on the original audience and publication context—that is, on where the essay appeared, who read it, and (if we know) what reaction it received.

WHO IS THE AUTHOR?

If the audience consists of those who read the essays, the *author* is the term we use for the person who writes them. Essayists, as authors, tend to introduce themselves to their audiences, revealing personal experiences, preferences, and beliefs that bear on the subject at hand and that help explain the essayist's point of view. The essayist's self-presentation—sometimes called *persona*, sometimes *ethos*—is more important than the essayist's actual name. In "We Do Abortions Here: A Nurse's Story" (p. 444), the title gives us an important fact about the author and her perspective: she is a nurse and has seen abortions up close. Knowing this fact is more important than knowing the essayist's name (Sallie Tisdale). In "Who Shot Johnny?" (p. 224), Debra Dickerson introduces herself directly to her readers in the opening paragraph:

> I am unrepentant and vocal about having gained admittance to Harvard through affirmative action; I am a feminist, stoic about my marriage chances as a well-educated, 36-year-old black woman who won't pretend to need help taking care of herself.

Who the author is—where she comes from, what her background is, what her educational and professional experience are—becomes part of Dickerson's story, and it influences her perspective on the random shooting of her nephew, about which she writes.

Not all authors are as direct as Tisdale or Dickerson. In "On Dumpster Diving" (p. 21) Lars Eighner doesn't tell us much about who he is—other than a homeless person who has learned to scavenge in Dumpsters with great success. But you don't need to know his past history or present status as an author to apprecate his account of salvaging useful items from trash others have thrown away. Nor do you need to know that David Guterson, the author of "Enclosed. Encyclopedic. Endured: The Mall of America" (p. 105), later became famous for the novel *Snow Falling on Cedars*. In his article about the largest mall in America, Guterson presents himself as a reporter, observing what he sees, shaping the information for his readers, and posing questions for himself and them about what the mall means and why it is so popular. His distance and objectivity as a reporter are important aspects of his self-presentation, of who he is as author of this essay.

Because we believe that essayists prefer to introduce themselves and reveal details of personality and experience that they consider most relevant, we do not preface each essay with a biographical note. We think they, as authors, should step forward and we, as editors, should stand back and let them speak. But if you want to learn more about the writer of an essay, you can check the *Authors* section at the end of the book. The entries there provide information about the men and women who wrote the essays. Putting this information at the end of the book gives you a choice. You may already know something about

an author and not wish to consult this section. You may wish to find out something about an author before you read his or her writing. Or you may just prefer to encounter the authors on their own terms, letting them identify
themselves within the essay. Sometimes knowing who authors are and where
their voices come from helps readers grasp what they say—but sometimes it
doesn't.

WHAT IS THE RHETORICAL CONTEXT AND PURPOSE?

The *rhetorical context*, sometimes called *rhetorical situation* or *rhetorical occasion*, refers to the context—social, political, biographical, historical—in
which writing takes place and becomes public. The term *purpose*, in a writing
class, refers to the author's goal—whether to inform, to persuade, to entertain, to analyze, or to do something else through the essay. We could also
pose this question as follows: What goals did the writer have in composing
and publishing the essay? What effect did the author wish to have on the
audience?

For some selections, the rhetorical context is indicated by the *title*. Abraham Lincoln's "Second Inaugural Address" (p. 537) and John F. Kennedy's "Inaugural Address" (p. 539) were presidential speeches made on the formal
occasion of their swearing in. An inauguration represents a significant moment in a leader's—and the nation's—life. The speech given on such an occasion requires a statement of the president's goals for the next four years. In
addition to the title, you can discover more about the rhetorical context of a
president's inaugural speech in the *opening paragraph* because he (so far it's
only *he*) will often refer to the historical context early on. Lincoln, for example, refers back to his first inaugural address and the "impending civil war";
then he acknowledges that the war continues and that he prays "this mighty
scourge of war may speedily pass away." In the midst of the American civil war,
Lincoln knows that he must, as president, address the political conflict that
faces the nation, offer hope for its resolution, and set the moral tone for the
aftermath. That's his purpose.

Like the presidential speech, many essays establish the rhetorical context
in their opening paragraphs. Editorials and Op-Eds begin with a "hook"—an
opening reference to the issue at hand or the news report under consideration.
You might even say that the editorial writer "creates" the rhetorical context
and shows us her purpose straight away. In her Op-Ed "Get a Knife, Get a
Dog, but Get Rid of Guns" (p. 198), Molly Ivins begins with "Guns. Everywhere guns"—letting her readers know that she's addressing the hot topic of
gun control and establishing her position right up front (she's pro-control).
Ivins's main purpose is to persuade others to adopt her position, but another
purpose is, through humor, to amuse her readers and laugh the anti-control
group out of court. Brent Staples's "Why Colleges Shower Their Students with
A's" (p. 260) reveals in its title the rhetorical purpose: to analyze the cause of
grade inflation. At the end of his opening paragraph Staples indicates the consumer context that informs his thinking:

> Faced with demanding consumers and stiff competition, colleges have sim-
> ply issued more and more A's, stoking grade inflation and devaluing degrees.

Even if you know nothing about grades at colleges other than your own, you can tell from this opening that the writer is identifying what he sees as a problem and proposing causes and possible cures.

Sometimes we provide information about the rhetorical context in the *contextual note* (described above) or in the *annotations* to each essay (described below). The contextual note for Martin Luther King Jr.'s "Letter from Birmingham Jail" (p. 548) explains that the letter was:

> Written on April 16, 1963, while King was jailed for civil disobedience.

The annotations (footnotes marked with small numerals) give further clues. For instance, note 1, written by King himself, explains the specific circumstances in which the "Letter" was composed:

> This response to a published statement by eight fellow clergymen from Ala-
> bama (Bishop C. C. J. Carpenter, Bishop Joseph A. Durick, Rabbi Milton L.
> Grafman, Bishop Paul Hardin, Bishop Holan B. Harrison, the Reverend
> George M. Murray, the Reverend Edward V. Ramage and the Reverend Earl
> Stallings) was composed under somewhat constricting circumstances. Be-
> gun on the margins of the newspaper in which the statement appeared
> while I was in jail, the letter was continued on scraps of writing paper sup-
> plied by a friendly Negro trusty, and concluded on a pad my attorneys were
> eventually permitted to leave me.

This annotation lets you know that King was answering his fellow clergymen, who objected to the demonstrations he led and argued, in their published statement, that "racial matters could properly be pursued in the courts." It also suggests the ways in which some religious authorities attempted to suppress King's political views.

Here is some additional information about *annotations* and how to use them as you read an essay: The annotations are explanatory footnotes—a common feature of a textbook. Commercial magazines and newspapers usually do not include footnotes, whereas academic writing often does. When the original authors wrote the footnotes themselves, we indicate that in square brackets, for example, [Angelou's note] or [Orwell's note]. This tells you that the author wished to cite an expert, add information, or send the reader to another source. In most cases, however, we the editors have written the footnotes to help with difficult words, allusions, and references. We provide information about people, places, works, theories, and other unfamiliar things that the original audience may have known. For example, for Maya Angelou's "Graduation" (p. 12) we give an annotation for Gabriel Prosser and Nat Turner, but not Abraham Lincoln and Christopher Columbus. Angelou's readers, many of them African American, would have known that Prosser and Turner were executed leaders of slave rebellions in the nineteenth century. But because not all readers today know (or remember) this part of American history, we add a footnote.

Here's a final important point: Annotation, while it facilitates the making of meaning in reading, can never take its place. Reading is an active process. Experienced readers take responsibility for that action—reading critically, constructing meaning, interpreting what they read. If our annotations help you read critically, then use them; if they interfere, then just continue reading the main text and skip over them.

WHAT IS THE GENRE AND ITS CONVENTIONS?

Genre is a term used by composition and literature teachers to refer to form—specifically, to forms that have common features and follow certain conventions of style, presentation, and subject matter. Literary genres include the short story and novel, the tragedy and comedy, the lyric and the epic poem. Essay genres include the memoir and the biographical profile, the visual analysis and Op-Ed, the literacy narrative and the parable. For the essay, *genre* partially determines the form's content and organization, but it should never do so in a "cookie-cutter" way.

Conventions are practices or customs commonly used in a genre—like a handshake for a social introduction or a eulogy at a funeral. Genre and convention are linked concepts, the one implying the other. Scientific articles (a genre) begin with a title and an abstract (conventions) and include sections about the methodology and the results (also conventions). Op-Eds, by convention, begin with a "hook"; profiles of persons or places include a physical description of the subject; literacy narratives include a key episode in the acquisition of reading or writing skills. But in reading and writing essays, conventions should not be treated in an automatic, rigid, or insincere way. They should be seen as guidelines, strategies, or special features, not as rules.

As you read an essay, think about its form: what it includes, how the writer presents the subject, what features seem distinctive. If you read a pair or group of essays assigned by your teacher, you might ask yourself whether they represent the same genre or are noticeably different. If they are the same, you will recognize similar features; if they are different, you will notice less overlap.

Below are some common genres included in *The Norton Reader* and some features to watch for as you read:

Narrative genres

Narrative genres tell a story, using vivid details, about people, events, and conflicts or crises. They also reflect on the meaning of the stories, offering the reader an interpretation or explanation of what occurred. Common narrative genres include the autobiographical essay, literacy narrative, historical narrative, and biographical narrative.

Autobiographical essay   The genre of *autobiography* focuses on a significant personal experience in the writer's past and draws out the meaning as the writer tells the story and reflects on the experience. Sometimes an autobiographical essay is called *memoir, personal narrative,* or *mini-autobiography.* Its key features include a dramatic event or episode; vivid details and narration; and an interweaving of narration with reflection on and interpretation of the essayist's experience.

If you are assigned Alice Walker's "Beauty: When the Other Dancer Is the Self" (p. 47) or George Orwell's "Shooting an Elephant" (p. 512), you will immediately spot the dramatic event. For Walker, it is the day a BB pellet strikes her eye and causes "a glob of whitish scar tissue, a hideous cataract." For Orwell, it is the day when he, a young British official in Burma, must shoot an elephant that has gone "must." Walker introduces the drama in two italicized sentences: *"It was great fun being cute. But then, one day, it ended."* In the remainder of the essay she reflects on how the injury affected her sense of self, her identity. Orwell builds up to the dramatic moment more slowly, taking us through the thoughts and events that lead to his pulling the trigger. As he tells his story, Orwell reflects on the motivations of his action and reaches a point of insight:

> And it was at this moment, as I stood there with the rifle in my hands, that I first grasped the hollowness, the futility of the white man's dominion in the East.

These two essayists handle the conventions of their autobiographical essays differently, with different narrative styles and different pacing, but they both focus on a significant event and draw out its significance in the course of the essay.

Literacy narrative   A subcategory of the autobiographical essay, the *literacy narrative* focuses on learning to read or write. Like other narrative genres, it uses personal experience, requires vivid details and a sharp narrative style, and gives a clear indication of the narrative's significance. Teachers frequently assign this genre in composition courses, for reading or writing or both.

If you read Frederick Douglass's "Learning to Read" (p. 228) or Ben Franklin's "Learning to Write" (p. 233), you will encounter two classic versions of the literacy narrative. For Douglass, a slave, reading was a forbidden, illegal activity, so to learn to read he was "compelled to resort to various stratagems," as he phrases it. Douglass's literacy narrative includes rich details about his life as a slave, the strategies he used to acquire literacy, and the essential value that reading held for someone who did not want to remain *"a slave for life."* For Franklin, a young man trained as a printer, writing became a means to raise himself in his social and professional world, and his narrative explains some of the tactics that allowed him to succeed. As you read Douglass or Franklin, watch for the details they choose to include and the anecdotes they recount as important to their stories. Other literacy narratives in *The Norton Reader* include Maxine Hong Kingston's "Tongue-Tied" (p. 282) and Richard Rodriguez's "Aria" (p. 286), both by modern American writers who tell of their educational experiences with fascinating, sometimes painful details and with serious reflection on the meaning of reading and writing in American culture.

Historical narrative   This genre also relies on narrative—on telling a story—but focuses on the larger social or political patterns that the story reveals. Like other narrative genres, *historical narrative* requires vivid details and an indication of the narrative's significance, but it may incorporate more than a single, dramatic event (though it will often begin by describing one) and offer multiple stories or episodes.

You will find several examples of historical narrative in the "History" section, including Barbara Tuchman's " 'This Is the End of the World': The Black Death" (p. 467) and Walt Whitman's "Death of Abraham Lincoln" (p. 491). Both writers know that vivid descriptions and compelling anecdotes are central to good historical narratives. In her opening paragraph, Tuchman shows us—in gory detail—what the "black death" (bubonic plague) looked like:

> The diseased sailors showed strange swellings about the size of an egg or an apple in the armpits and groin. The swellings oozed blood and pus and were followed by spreading boils and black blotches on the skin from internal bleeding.

A gruesome picture, but it captures the reader's attention and fascinates us enough to read on.

In contrast, Whitman does not emphasize the blood and gore of Abraham Lincoln's assassination. Instead, he sets the scene in a theater with "ladies in rich and gay costumes, officers in their uniforms"; describes the action on-stage as it unfolds in a conventional romantic drama; and builds suspense until the moment when the audience hears "the muffled sound of a pistol-shot" and a man cries out in "a firm and steady voice": *"Sic semper tyrannis."* Whitman's account is full of the precise details that American readers wished to know, but he also incorporates an analysis of the president's death and its significance in American history. He suggests that "the grand deaths of the race—the dramatic deaths of every nationality—are its most important inheritance-value"—a point expanded in the closing paragraphs.

Biographical narrative   The *biographical narrative* is a subcategory of the historical narrative discussed above, and it is related to the *biographical profile* described below. Sometimes writers choose to focus their accounts of historical events on a specific person, perhaps because that person was a "key player," the moving force in the event, or perhaps because that person allows a window into how a large historical event felt to an average citizen.

You will find both techniques—and variations on them—in essays throughout *The Norton Reader*. Walt Whitman tells the story of an American president's assassination in his "Death of Abraham Lincoln" (p. 491). Logically, Whitman focuses his narrative on the president, telling what happened on the day of the assassination but including other biographical details that he recalls from previous sightings of Lincoln and ending with his reflections on the significance of what he calls "a heroic-eminent life." In contrast, the authors of three mini-biographies included under the rubric "World War II: Victims, Villains, Heroes" (p. 503) focus on "little people"—ordinary or average men and women who, in the throes of war, took heroic stances or did heroic deeds that involved great danger. As you read historical and biographical narratives, compare their features and try to notice their conventions: people and places need to be described with accuracy and interest, stories need to be told with clarity and good pace, significance needs to emerge from the narrative, not just be tacked on at the end.

Descriptive genres

Descriptive genres let the reader know how a person, place, or thing looks, sounds, feels, or maybe even smells. But they do more: they give a dominant impression, interpret a person's actions, offer a reflection on the significance of place, or in some other way put the objective details into a larger framework. Descriptive genres in *The Norton Reader* include the profile of a person, profile of a place, and natural history.

Profile of a person   Also called a *biographical sketch* or a *mini-biography*, the *profile of a person* features an individual or a group of people and uses first-hand knowledge, interviews, and/or research to present its subject. Since readers like to read about interesting subjects, it is sometimes assumed that the person must be interesting beforehand. But, really, it's the writer who makes the person interesting by discovering special characteristics or qualities through interviews or observation, by finding an interesting angle from which to present the subject, and by including engaging details, anecdotes, or dialogue to enliven the portrait. These are the special features, or conventions, of the biographical profile.

Profiles can be free-standing essays or parts of books. Daniel Bergner's "Chasing Evil" (p. 509) is a portrait of Peter Malkin, the man who tracked and captured Adolf Eichmann, the Nazi engineer of Hitler's "final solution." Bergner begins with a sharp image of Malkin, wearing "fur-lined leather gloves," as he seizes Eichmann. The detail of the gloves allows the writer to crystallize Malkin's emotions: " 'the thought of placing my bare hands over the mouth that had ordered the death of millions, of feeling the hot breath and saliva on my skin, filled me with an overwhelming sense of revulsion.' " Other details in the portrait—the clean, well-ordered bedroom where Eichmann is kept hidden, the food and wine he is fed, and the sketches Malkin makes of his captive—allow the writer to analyze the relationship of captor to captive and to chart the complex, changing emotions.

Profiles about family members can be difficult. Even if an essayist loves his or her parents, not every reader will find someone else's parents distinctive, memorable, or worth reading about. So it takes vivid details, humorous (or chilling) stories, and a bit of distance to succeed in the family profile. Annie Dillard *makes* her mother memorable in "An American Childhood" (p. 70) by recalling idiosyncratic stories and sayings, including the line "Terwilliger bunts one" that amuses and annoys her mother. Scott Russell Sanders, perhaps unfortunately, remembers too many characteristic episodes about his father. His profile, titled "Under the Influence" (p. 59), begins: "My father drank." Both of these writers had ordinary parents, but they make them seem extraordinary by the vividness of their memories, the special angles they take, and the overarching perspective on their parents' character that they bring to the essay.

Profile of a place   Places can also become the focus of a profile, in a subcategory sometimes simply called a *place essay*. The features of this genre involve discovering the special characteristics or qualities of the place, finding an interpretive framework in which to present it, and including engaging details, anecdotes, or dialogue to enliven the essay. Since places can't speak, the essayist must speak for them and say enough about them to make them come alive.

Essayists re-create places in different ways. Margaret Atwood, writing about northern Canada in "True North" (p. 95), begins with a camp song that she—like lots of other Canadians and Americans—remembers from childhood:

> Land of the silver birch,
> Home of the beaver,
> Where still the mighty moose
> Wanders at will.
> Blue lake and rocky shore,
> I will return once more.

Atwood goes on to re-create the northern landscape that she loves so well, that brings "tears to our eyes, not for simple reasons." In contrast, David Guterson begins with hard facts in "The Mall of America" (p. 105):

> 140,000 hot dogs sold each week, 10,000 permanent jobs, 44 escalators and 17 elevators, 12,750 parking spaces, 13,300 short tons of steel, $1 million in cash dispersed weekly from 8 automatic-teller machines.

Guterson's facts give us the immense scale of the mall—details that boggle the imagination, but that speak to some deep-seated American desire for immensity. Both essayists bring their places to life, but in different ways and with different approaches to understanding the meaning of a place.

If a profile includes both person and place, it is what the writer Anne Fadiman calls a "Character in Context" piece. Many times, we learn about a person by seeing him or her in a characteristic space; the place defines the person, the person defines the place. N. Scott Momaday's "The Way to Rainy Mountain" (p. 88) gives us a sacred place of the Kiowas, an old landmark that they called "Rainy Mountain." Yet his profile is also about his grandmother, Abo, whom he associates with the sacred mountain:

> Her forebears came down from the high country in western Montana nearly three centuries ago. They were mountain people, a mysterious tribe of hunters whose language has never been positively classified in any major group.

To understand the significance of Momaday's return to Rainy Mountain, we must understand the mountain's associations with his grandmother. And vice versa: to understand Abo's significance to her grandson, we must understand the meaning of Rainy Mountain to the Kiowa.

Natural history   The term *natural history* can refer generally to any historical writing about nature, but it also designates a genre related to the profile: the life cycle or biography of a plant or animal. (Think of it as profiling not a person but a bear or a dragonfly or a weed like goldenrod.) You will find some of these essays in the "Nature and Environment" section of this book, and you may also encounter them in biology classes. They describe a plant or animal, take it through its life cycle, and sometimes explain its significance or relationship to the human species.

In "The Spider and the Wasp" (p. 358), Alexander Petrunkevitch describes the life cycle of two animals, starting with the tarantula, then moving to its archenemy, the digger wasp of the genus *Pepsis*. His essay raises a puzzling scientific question about "intelligence pitted against instinct—a strange situation in which the victim, though fully able to defend itself, submits unwittingly to its destruction." In "The Serpents of Paradise" (p. 352) Edward Abbey, too, incorporates elements of natural history—in this case of two gopher snakes, *Drymarchon corais couperi*. Abbey puzzles not over a scientific question, but over human issues of "sympathy, mutual aid, symbiosis, continuity." As he interprets the snakes' behavior in human terms, he wonders:

> How can I descend to such anthropomorphism? Easily—but is it, in this case, entirely false? Perhaps not. I am not attributing human motives to my snake and bird acquaintances. I recognize that when and where they serve purposes of mine they do so for beautifully selfish reasons of their own.

Both versions of natural history—raising scientific questions, raising questions about human actions—appear in *The Norton Reader*. Look for them in Henry David Thoreau's "The Battle of the Ants" (p. 464), and in Aldo Leopold's "Marshland Elegy" (p. 377), which gives a natural history of one of the writer's favorite places.

Analytic genres

Analytic genres carefully and methodically examine a text, an image, a cultural object, or a social trend by breaking it into parts, closely reading its components, and noting how the parts work in relation to the whole. In *The Norton Reader* you will find examples of textual analysis, visual analysis, and cultural analysis.

Textual analysis   Also called *close reading*, *textual analysis* focuses on written words. It examines words and phrases for explicit and implicit meanings; it looks for similes (comparisons using *like* or *as*) and metaphors (comparisons without explicit connectors) to reveal patterns of association and hidden meanings; and it interprets the whole text on the basis of these methodical, individual observations. The *text* may be anything from the Bible or Koran, to poems and novels, to ads, billboards, or official memos.

In "Politics and the English Language" (p. 317), for example, George Orwell analyzes five samples of modern prose that in his view represent "the mental vices from which we now suffer." Orwell criticizes the use of pretentious language and meaningless words—like *epoch-making, epic, historic, unforgettable*—that obscure meaning and result in vagueness. He points to dead and dying metaphors—*stand shoulder to shoulder with, play into the hands of, no axe to grind*—that once evoked a visual image but have now lost evocativeness and force. And he argues that politicians often use such language to obscure the meaning of their actions:

> People are imprisoned for years without trial, or shot in the back of the neck or sent to die of scurvy in Arctic lumber camps: this is called *elimination of unreliable elements.*

By improving our use of language we might, Orwell suggests, improve our political situation. By analyzing the language of politics—that is, by engaging in textual analysis—we can become shrewder readers of political rhetoric.

Visual analysis   Like textual analysis, *visual analysis* looks for explicit and implicit meanings; searches for patterns of association and hidden intentions; and interprets the whole object on the basis of these methodical, individual observations. Instead of a written text, visual analysis focuses on an image, a photograph, a painting, or another visual phenomenon.

Some visual analyses have as their goal the explanation of the image itself. For example, John Updike's "Moving Along" (p. 668) looks closely at two paintings—one by a sixteenth-century Indian artist, the other by a contemporary American "Funk Artist." Updike devotes a paragraph to each painting, describing what he sees, commenting on the little details, and connecting both works to the theme of "moving along" and the human desire to walk, run, ride, and fly. Other selections use visual analysis as part of a larger argument. In "A Century of Cinema" (p. 654) Susan Sontag uses movie stills to illustrate the two modes of expression that she finds throughout the history of this medium: "cinema as the transcription of real, unstaged life" and "cinema as invention, artifice, illusion, fantasy." As you read her essay, compare the stills from *The Arrival of a Train at La Ciotat Station* and *Persona* to visualize these modes.

In *The Norton Reader* you will find essays that combine textual and visual analysis or that use images to trigger both kinds of analysis. (Watch for essays that include photographs, drawings, graphs, and other visual material.) In writing "Strangers" (p. 75), Toni Morrison began by thinking about a book of photographs, interpreting the images, and pondering their significance, but her essay also analyzes the ethical implications of writing narratives, of creating life stories for people she does not know. In other essays, such as N. Scott Momaday's "The Way to Rainy Mountain" (p. 88) and Fred Strebeigh's "The Wheels of Freedom: The Bicycle in China" (p. 202), the authors provide images to accompany their prose: in Momaday's case, his father's drawings; in Strebeigh's, photographs he took during his travels in China at the time of the Tiananmen uprising. These images enrich the primary analyses of the authors by underscoring key points and adding visual evidence to their arguments.

Cultural analysis   This genre, called both *cultural analysis* and *cultural critique*, takes an object, trend, fad, or other phenomenon as the subject of its analysis. It uses the strategies of textual and visual analysis described above, adding personal response and library research, if desirable, to explain and interpret. Examples of this form appear in the section "Cultural Critique."

What kinds of cultural objects and trends do essayists analyze? Almost anything and everything, it seems. Nicholas Kristof analyzes the clothing—visible and invisible—of Saudi women in "Saudis in Bikinis" (p. 200). Fred Strebeigh analyzes the Chinese bicycle (p. 202), interviewing people who rely on them for work and play, giving us a history of their manufacture, reflecting on their names ("Forever," "Flying Pigeon"), and concluding that they represent "the wheels of freedom" to many Chinese people. Jessica Mitford looks at the American funeral industry in "Behind the Formaldehyde Curtain" (p. 186). Mitford engages many different strategies in making her analysis—from "the arrival of the corpse at the mortuary" to the process of embalming to the presentation of the body for open-casket viewing. Her goal is to debunk the "American way of death," as she calls it, and to show how the undertaker has assumed the place formerly held by the clergyman.

Argumentative genres

Forms of modern argument have their roots in classical Greece and Rome—that is, they go back at least 2,500 years. The Greek philosopher Aristotle held that there were really only two essential parts of an argument: (1) the statement of the case, and (2) the proof of the case. But he conceded that in practice most orators added two other parts: an introduction and a conclusion.

Roman rhetoricians like Quintillian refined and expanded this simple Aristotelian approach to include five or six parts:

(1) *exordium*: the introduction

(2) *narratio*: the statement or exposition of the case under discussion

(3) *divisio*: the outline of the points or steps in the argument

(4) *confirmatio*: the proof of the case (sometimes called *probatio*)

(5) *confutatio*: the refutation of opposing arguments

(6) *peroratio*: the conclusion

Yet Roman rhetoricians also acknowledged that, for any given argument, orators might want to omit parts. (They might, for example, omit *divisio* if the steps of the argument were simple.) And orators would often rearrange the parts of their speeches. They might, for instance, refute an opponent's arguments before advancing their own case.

Unless you participate in a debating society, you—like most modern college students—won't see this formal version of classical argument very often. Yet all Americans study it in civics class when they discuss the "Declaration of Independence" (p. 532) because Thomas Jefferson used the tactics of classical rhetoric as revived in the eighteenth century. Today, we hear its legacy in public speeches and see traces of it in newspaper editorials. The Greek and Roman philosophers weren't so much prescribing a genre as they were describing common argumentative practices. It makes sense that, if you want to argue your case effectively, you need to introduce it, outline the key points, present your evidence, and refute your opponent's position—all the steps they described. You will find these steps in the argumentative genres considered below: Op-Eds and editorials, public speeches and orations.

Op-Eds and editorials   This genre focuses on issues of public interest and encourages ordinary citizens to contribute their perspectives, opinions, and arguments to the public debate. *Op-Eds* and *editorials* begin with a "hook"—a link to a recent event or news article that grabs readers' attention—as the introduction. Specific features, or conventions, include a forthright statement of position, evidence in support, often a counterargument or rebuttal of the opposition, and sometimes a formal conclusion.

Brent Staples's "Why Colleges Shower Their Students with A's" (p. 260) features most of these conventions. Staples begins by citing the principle of a famous economist, Milton Friedman, to the effect that superior products flourish and shabby ones die out. But Staples refutes this principle when applied to colleges and argues that, in fact, colleges are giving too many A's and thus "stoking grade inflation and devaluing degrees." When you read Staples's Op-Ed, note how he puts forward his evidence, then rebuts a common argument of his opposition:

> The argument that grades are rising because students are better prepared is simply not convincing. The evidence suggests that students and parents are demanding—and getting—what they think of as their money's worth.

Staples wraps up with some proposals to remedy grade inflation and a final stab at parents and students who are "addicted to counterfeit excellence." Although he no doubt wrote from the evidence he had gathered and the conclusion he had independently reached, you will discover that Staples uses five of the six parts of the "formal" classical argument—all but number 3.

Public speeches and orations   Because *speeches* and *orations* derive directly, if also distantly, from the classical tradition of argument, they often show its formal features. Many speechwriters introduce the issue at hand, state their position, offer evidence in support and counterarguments against, and sum up—sometimes with a high rhetorical flourish. These modern tactics are based on the older classical conventions.

Elizabeth Cady Stanton shows her knowledge of public oratory in the "Declaration of Sentiments and Resolutions" (p. 535), presented at the first U.S. women's rights convention and modeled on the American Declaration of Independence. A century later, the Rev. Martin Luther King, one of the great civil rights leaders and orators of modern America, continues the tradition in "A Letter from Birmingham Jail" (p. 548). King makes the case for civil disobedience, taking his audience through the steps of his thinking and quietly refuting those who disagree. It is no coincidence that these important American speeches and documents use the formal conventions of argument: in so doing, the speakers demonstrate their education, ability, and right to debate the pressing issues of their day.

Mark Twain's "Advice to Youth" (p. 389) is not a formal oration, but instead a humorous speech given to an audience that asked for a talk "didactic, instructive, or something in the nature of good advice." His speech resembles the modern graduation address in its "advice to youth." For each major point, Twain uses a conventional form of the maxim—"Go to bed early, get up early," "Never handle firearms carelessly," and so on. But then he undercuts such conventional advice with a qualifying clause—"Always obey your parents, *when they are present*" or "Be respectful of superiors, *if you have any*." The result of Twain's humorous treatment is to question the conventional advice we offer to young people and to ask whether, in fact, adults live by it.

Parables   A *parable* is a story that illustrates a point, poses or answers a question, or suggests a lesson. A parable can imply an argument—though it does not make that argument directly or simply. The word *parable* means "thrown beside," and there's a sense in which any attempt to interpret a parable too specifically will always just miss the mark: the form is too complex to be reduced to a single meaning or simple moral. It is worth considering the parable as an alternative form of argument—a genre a writer might use when more formal arguments won't quite work. Feminists, for example, have sometimes turned to the parable when they find that masculine logic fails to grasp an issue. Native Americans, including Chief Seattle, have traditionally used the parable to refute the wrong-headed logic of white Americans.

Most religious traditions include parables—such as those told by Jesus or the Zen parables we include in the section on "Philosophy and Religion." In the Zen parable "Muddy Road" (p. 717) there's a literal-minded character, Ekido, who lives strictly by the rules, and a more knowing character, Tanzan, who has deeper wisdom. Ekido knows that a monk is supposed to avoid women, so he chastises Tanzan for picking up a "lovely girl in a silk kimono and sash" and carrying her across a muddy intersection. Tanzan responds with a question: "I left the girl there. Are you still carrying her?" Tanzan's question suggests that it's not the literal touching of a woman that matters. What matters is sexual desire. By carrying the image of the girl in his mind and brooding on it, Ekido is harboring desire within his heart, perhaps giving it space to grow. The parable is about the complexities of human desire—but it's hard to argue Tanzan's position without using many more words and perhaps being less effective. The parable—a narrative with a probing final twist—does the trick.

As you read arguments in various sections of *The Norton Reader*—whether in "Ethics," "Politics," or "Science and Technology"—consider where and why authors use formal techniques (conventions of argument) and where and why they turn to alternative strategies—strategies identified with other genres. In the end, the goal is to make an effective argument, to convince the reader of the validity of your evidence, or urge the listener to take a prescribed course of action.

STRATEGIES FOR CRITICAL READING

The previous pages have focused on reading specific kinds of essays and on strategies for recognizing genres and their conventions. Here we offer some general tips for approaching the reading your instructor assigns this semester.

Preview the essay

Think about the essay's title, read its opening paragraph, skim the topic sentences (usually, the first sentence of each paragraph). Look at the contextual note on the first page, and try to imagine the experience, issue, or debate that motivated the essayist to write. *Previewing* is a technique widely used for college reading, but not all writing teachers encourage it. Some teachers encourage previewing for academic writing, explaining that it helps readers focus on key issues; other teachers discourage previewing, pointing out that a good essay—like a good novel or movie—can be ruined by knowing the ending.

Write in the margin

As you read, note points that seem interesting and important, forecast issues that you think the writer will address, pose questions of your own. Talk back. Most essayists want active readers who think about what the essay says, implies, and urges as a personal response or course of action. Similarly, note points that you don't understand or that you find ambiguous. Puzzling over a sentence or a passage with your classmates can lead to crucial points of debate. Mark your queries and use them to energize class discussion.

Analyze the illustrations

Many of the essays in *The Norton Reader* include illustrations from their original publications. Think about how the essays and the images "speak" to each other. Consider whether the images enrich, highlight, or possibly challenge the essay. Does the image primarily illustrate the essay, or does it emphasize a feature unexplained by the essayist? Does the image enrich and make clearer one aspect of the writing, or does it minimize certain aspects of the subject, perhaps aspects you find important? What do you see in the images that the essayist discusses or explains? What do you see that he or she overlooks or minimizes? Thinking about images can help you clarify the author's argument or reveal points the author may have missed.

Summarize the essay

Write a summary of the essay. Begin by making a list of its key points and identifying the evidence used in support of each; then try to state briefly, in your own words, the "gist" or core of the essay. The goal is to condense the argument and evidence, while remaining faithful to the author's meaning. Your summary will be useful when you discuss the essay in class or write about it in a paper. For some genres, including the scientific report, a summary or *abstract* is included in the essay itself (see p. 575 for an example).

Keep a reading journal

Buy a class notebook or designate a special section of your college notebook for reflections on the essays you read. For each essay, take notes, record your responses, write questions about what puzzles you and what you want to discuss in class. Write down sentences or passages that you like and that you might want to use as models for your own essays. You may also want to list questions that the essayist raises and answers, as well as write down questions that you think the essayist has overlooked.

Use the study questions

Review the questions that follow each essay in *The Norton Reader*, and think about the issues—the subject, the structure, the language—that they pose. We include these questions to help you become an active reader, to focus attention on key issues, and sometimes to make suggestions for *doing* or *writing* something.

- Some questions ask you to locate or mark the essays' structural features, the patterns that undergird and clarify meaning. Narrative, description, exposition, persuasion, and argument follow conventional shapes—or distort them—and your ability to recognize these shapes will improve your comprehension.

- Other questions ask you to paraphrase meanings or extend them—that is, to express the meaning in your own words, to amplify points by providing your own examples, or to reframe points by connecting them with points in other essays.

- Still other questions ask you to notice special features or conventions that contribute to meaning: the author's choice of title, the author's voice (or persona), the author's assumptions about audience (and how the author speaks to the audience), and the author's choice of style and forms of expression.

- At least one question, usually the last, asks you to write. Sometimes we ask you to demonstrate comprehension by writing about something from your experience or reading that extends an essay and enforces its argument. Sometimes, we invite you to express disagreement or dissent by writing about something from your experience or knowledge that qualifies the author's argument or calls it into question. The final question may ask you to compare or contrast two authors' positions—especially when their positions seem opposed. Or we may ask you to adapt one of the essay's rhetorical strategies to a topic of your own choice and to make the essay even more your own by basing it on personal experience.

Re-read the essay

If possible, read the essay a second time before you discuss it in class. If you're short on time, re-read the key passages and paragraphs that you marked in marginal notes. Ask yourself what you see the second time that you didn't register on first reading.

As these tactics suggest, reading need not be only a private activity; it can also become communal and cooperative. Sharing reading journals in class helps to reveal points of ambiguity and to generate debate. Discussion, with the whole class or in smaller groups, can clarify your own and others' interpretation of the essays. What interests and motives does each reader bring to particular essays? Do some interests and motives yield better readings than others? What meanings do readers agree about? What meanings do they disagree about? Can we account for our differences? What are responsive and responsible readings? Are there irresponsible readings, and how do we decide? All these questions—and others—can emerge as private reading moves into the more public arena of the classroom.

Readers write, writers read. Making meaning by writing is the flip side of making it by reading, and we hope to engage you in both processes. But in neither process are meanings passed from hand to hand like nickels, dimes, and quarters. Instead, they are constructed—as a quilt or a house or an institution. We hope that these suggestions for reading will lead you to engaged and fruitful writing.

*W*riting in College

Much of the writing you will do in a composition course will start with an assignment from your instructor. Perhaps you will be asked to respond to some of the essays in *The Norton Reader*—to expand on something a writer has said, to agree or disagree with a claim a writer has made, or to do some research to extend an author's argument and say something new about it. Or, you may be assigned a particular genre or kind of writing—a literacy narrative, a profile of a person or place, a visual or textual analysis, or an argumentative paper—and asked to use selections in this book as models of these kinds of writing. We have selected the readings because they are full of important ideas you can react to, either by agreeing or disagreeing, and also because the essays represent excellent examples of good writers at their best, models for aspiring writers to follow.

What follows is a brief guide for writing with *The Norton Reader*. We'll look at discovering your purpose, addressing your audience, finding a subject, determining what genre to employ, using rhetorical strategies, and understanding the writing process.

KNOWING YOUR PURPOSE

Your *purpose* is, put simply, the goal for your writing. What do you want to achieve? What points do you want to make? What idea or cause motivates you to write? Anything you can do to sharpen your thinking and infuse your writing with a clear sense of purpose will be to the good: you will find it easier to stay focused and help your readers see your key point and main ideas about your subject.

What are some common purposes writers have? The authors of the essays in *The Norton Reader* had informing, persuading, entertaining, or expressing as some of their purposes. So, too, your writing will have a primary purpose, usually defined in an assignment by words such as "explain," "describe," "analyze," "argue." Each is a signal about the purpose for your writing.

For instance, if an assignment asks you to *analyze* the persuasiveness of Nicholas Kristof's Op-Ed "Saudis in Bikinis" (p. 200), then your purpose is to explain the claims Kristof makes, examine the evidence he uses to support them, discuss points or perspectives he misses, and develop a thesis about the reasons for the essay's persuasiveness. If an assignment asks you to *argue* for or against Kristof's claim about women in Saudi Arabia, then your purpose is to take a side, defending or refuting his claims and using evidence from your own knowledge and from reputable sources to support your argument.

Use these questions to think about your purpose for writing:

■ What does the assignment ask you to do? Is the goal to inform readers, entertain them, argue a point, or express an idea or feeling? Beyond a general purpose, what does the assignment require in terms of a specific purpose?

- How does your purpose affect your choice of a subject? What do you know about the subject? How can you find out more about this subject?

- How can you connect to your readers? What will they want or need to know? How do you want them to respond to your writing?

ADDRESSING YOUR AUDIENCE

Just as the authors in *The Norton Reader* aimed their essays at different *audiences*—readers of books, large newspapers, magazines, small journals, and scholarly publications, as well as activists, ordinary citizens, and churchgoers—so you need to imagine your audience as you write. Too wide an audience—"the general public"—and you run the risk of making your essay too diffuse, trying to reach everyone. Too narrow an audience—"my roommate Zach"—and you run the risk of being too specific.

How can you imagine an audience of your own? One way is to look around your writing classroom: that's your immediate audience, the people who are taking the course with you and your instructor. Another way is to think about your home community: your family, your neighbors, and the people of your town or city. Think of your audience as readers like yourself, with some of the same knowledge of the world and some of the same tastes. Consider your audience's range of reference: historical events they have witnessed first-hand, movies and TV shows they know about or have seen, and the books they have read or heard of. Think of them as willing to be convinced by whatever you write, but in need of good evidence.

Inevitably, some writers find that imagining an audience made only of class members seems too restrictive. That's fine; feel free to invoke another audience, say a group of people who share a certain passion, perhaps for a team, a sport, a game, or a type of music or film. (But remember to take into account your instructor, who may need some filling in about the special knowledge you share with your audience.)

Use these questions to guide you in thinking about audience:

- What readers are you hoping to reach with your writing?

- What information can you assume your readers know? What information do you need to explain?

- In what ways will you need to adjust the style of your writing—the language, tone, sentence structure and complexity, and examples—to meet the needs of your audience?

FINDING A SUBJECT

Like the audience and purpose for your writing, the *subject* of your writing—what you write about—will often be assigned by your instructor. Some assignments are very specific, such as this study question following Andrea Barrett's essay "A Hole in the Wall" (p. 3): "Write about how you react when Barrett speaks of her neighborhood's having become so international and multicultural. Is it anything like neighborhoods you have lived in or know? Can you imagine yourself living in such a neighborhood? What might attract you or repel you about such a neighborhood?" In this assignment you'll have to write about a neighborhood you know, and you'll have to give your opinion of it, your "take" on being there. Other assignments may be more general, such as the following study question on Scott Russell Sanders's profile of his father, "Under the Influence" (p. 59): "Drawing on your memories of a friend or family member, write an essay about some problem that person had and its effect on your life." This broader assignment requires you to determine the person you wish to discuss, the problem you wish to analyze, and the larger effect the person and problem had on your life.

Some assignments give you even more leeway in choosing a subject, leaving you with the inevitable question "What should I write about?" In this case, write about what you know or care about, drawing on knowledge you've already gleaned about a subject from personal experience, your reading, or research. Your knowledge does not have to be totally new, but your perspective on a subject needs to come from you—a real person writing about a subject that matters.

How do you find what you know or care about? One way is to raise questions about an essay you've read:

- What is the author's main point? Do you agree or disagree with the main point?

- Has the author said enough about the subject? What gaps or omissions do you see, if any? Are there sentences or paragraphs that you could expand into an essay of your own?

- Are the author's examples and evidence convincing? If not, why not? Can you provide a more compelling example, additional evidence, or a counter example?

- Does this reading "speak" to anything else you've read in *The Norton Reader*? Can you explain how this reading connects to the other? Do the readings agree or disagree?

- Is this reading true to your own experience? Has anything like this happened to you, or have you ever observed anything like this?

You can also choose a subject by reflecting on your own experience:

- Has someone you know affected your life in some way—by teaching you, by serving as an example (good or bad), or by changing your attitude?

- Is there a place that you can describe to others, telling them what makes it unique or special to you?

- Is there a subject you feel strongly about, something you believe others need to learn about—for example, a program on your campus or in your neighborhood, a controversial item of national significance, or a matter of global importance?

■ Have you had an experience that has taught you something valuable, influenced the way you live, or made you think differently about life, school, work, family, or friends? Readers will be interested in the details of the experience, including how it affected you and what you have learned.

DETERMINING GENRE

Like the purpose, audience, and subject of your writing, the *genre* or form of your writing may be prescribed in your instructor's assignment. *The Norton Reader* contains a variety of essay genres:

■ **Narrative genres**, which tell stories and include autobiographical essays, literacy narratives, historical narratives, and biographical narratives.

■ **Descriptive genres**, which give details about how a person, place, or thing looks, sounds, and feels, often in a larger framework. These include profiles of people and places and essays about nature and natural history.

■ **Analytic genres**, which examine texts, images, and cultural objects and trends.

■ **Argumentative genres**, which take stands and provide evidence to support them. These include Op-Eds, editorials, public speeches, and parables.

These genres are discussed on pp. xxi–xxxi and listed in the Genres Index on p. 763.

If you're assigned a literacy narrative, for example, your writing will tell a vivid, detailed story about an experience you've had with reading, writing, or schooling. To write a profile of a place, you will need to give a coherent impression of it by gathering and organizing detailed descriptions of how the place looks, smells, or even feels. If you're asked to take a stand on an important issue, you will write in an argumentative genre; if you choose an Op-Ed or editorial, you will need to focus on a central claim, support that claim with solid evidence, consider opposing views, and be brief. Or, if your assignment is a textual analysis of one of the readings in this book, you will need to examine features of the essay—its structure, style, key metaphors and phrases—paying close attention to rhetorical details.

If you have some leeway in choosing the genre in which you will write, consider what genre best fits your purpose, audience, and subject:

■ What goal do you have for your writing? What genre is most appropriate for that goal?

- Who will read your writing? What genre will best convey the point of your writing to your readers?

- What are you writing about? What genre is well-suited to your subject?

To gain more understanding of these genres, read plenty of examples, analyze the forms and strategies they use, and then try out a genre on your own. There's no better way to understand how a genre works than to try your hand at writing it.

USING RHETORICAL STRATEGIES

As you plan your essay, you will want to think about the *rhetorical strategies* by which you will present your ideas and evidence to readers. These strategies, sometimes called *rhetorical modes* or *techniques*, help a writer organize evidence, connect facts into a sequence, and provide clusters of information necessary for conveying a purpose or an argument. You might choose to *analyze* the cause of an outcome, *compare* one thing to another, *classify* your facts into categories, *define* a key term, *describe* a person, place, or phenomenon, *explain* how a process works, or *narrate* a pertinent event or experience.

Sometimes, the writing assignment that your instructor gives will determine the strategy: for example, an assignment that asks you to compare the approach described in Peter Singer's book *Animal Liberation* to Pollan's own approach (see p. 414) will require that you use a compare/contrast strategy. Similarly, a study question in this book might imply a strategy: for example, one of the questions following E. B. White's "Democracy" (p. 542) states, "Using White's technique, write a definition for an abstract term," and thus asks that you think about definition and how that strategy might work in an essay about "generosity" or "love" or "virtue."

Many essays use a mix of strategies. You might want to define a key term in an opening paragraph, narrate a story to make a point in the next paragraph, and analyze cause and effect in yet another. Except for very short pieces, most writers use several rhetorical strategies in an essay, choosing the one they think best fits their material. In "The Tyranny of the Majority" (p. 543), Lani Guinier uses a childhood story in her opening paragraph—an episode in which a girl in her Brownie troop wins a contest by having her mother make her entry. Guinier then follows this example of foul play with a definition of "fair play": "To me fair play means that the rules encourage everyone to play. They should reward those who win, but they must be acceptable to those who lose." Later she compares different ways of conceptualizing democracy, some that take only winners into account, others that allow the views of the minority to be included. The mix of rhetorical strategies keeps the reader involved, shows that the writer is engaged in complex thinking, and creates an effective argument.

Following are some rhetorical strategies that you will encounter in *The Norton Reader* and that you will want to use in your own writing.

Analyzing cause and effect

Focusing on causes helps a writer think about why something happened; focusing on effects helps a writer think about what might or could happen. Cause is oriented toward the future; effect looks back to the past. But you can use this strategy by working in either direction: from present to future, or from present to the past.

If you were writing about global warming and intending to show its harmful effects, you might lay out your evidence in this sequence:

Cause → leads to → these effects.

If you were writing about binge drinking and trying to identify the reasons for its rise among college students, you might reverse the direction:

Effect ← is the result of ← these causes.

Analyzing a cause (or causes) is a crucial strategy for genres such as cultural critique, Op-Ed, and historical narrative. But you can also use it in an autobiographical essay, where you might analyze the effects of a childhood trauma on your later life, or in a profile of a person, where you might seek the sources (the causes) of the person's adult personality or achievements.

Comparing and contrasting

Comparisons look for similarities between things; contrasts look for differences. In most uses of this rhetorical strategy, you will want to consider both similarities and differences—that is, you will want to compare *and* contrast. That's because most things worth comparing have something in common, even if they also have significant differences. You may end up finding more similarities than differences, or vice versa, but when using this strategy, think about both.

Comparison-contrast may be used for a single paragraph or for an entire essay. It tends to be set up in one of two ways: block or point-by-point. In the block technique, the writer gives all the information about one item and then follows with all the information about the other. Think of it as giving all the A's, then all the B's. Usually, the order of the information is the same for both. In the point-by-point technique, the writer focuses on specific points of comparison, alternating A, B, A, B, A, B, and so on until the main points have been covered.

Comparing and contrasting is an excellent strategy to use in writing a report, making an argument in an Op-Ed, or giving a speech to persuade your audience to take a specific course of action. You can set forth the pros and cons of different programs, political policies, or courses of action, leading up to the recommendation you endorse and believe is the more effective.

Classifying and dividing

Classifying and dividing involves either putting things into groups or dividing up a large block into smaller units. While this strategy might seem better suited to a biology lab than to a writing class, in fact it works well for organizing facts that seem chaotic or for handling big topics that at first glance seem overwhelming. Classifying and dividing allow the writer—and the reader—to get control of a big topic and break it into smaller units of analysis.

How does Lars Eighner explain his practice of dumpster diving? He begins by classifying the food he scavenges into two categories: food safe to eat (canned goods, dry foods "free of visible contaminates," raw fruits and vegetables "with intact skins," and candy) and unsafe food ("game, poultry, pork, and egg-based foods"). How does the composer Aaron Copland discuss "How We Listen" (p. 678)? He divides his essay—and the modes of listening to music—into three "planes" or levels of listening. This basic division helps the writer explain the different goals and experiences that listeners bring to a piece of music. Dividing goals into levels allows the writer to manage a difficult, abstract topic and to lead the reader from the simpler to the more complex level of listening.

You will find that classifying and dividing is helpful in writing all genres of analysis: textual, visual, and cultural. You will also find that it can help in argumentative genres because it enables you, as a writer or speaker, to break down a complex argument into parts or to group pieces of evidence into similar categories.

Defining

Defining involves telling your reader what something means—and what it does not. It involves saying what something is—and what it is not. As a strategy, defining means making sure you—and your readers—understand what you mean by a key term. It may mean re-defining a common term to have a more precise meaning or giving nuance to a term that is commonly used too broadly. Defining and re-defining are great strategies to use in argumentative writing: they help the writer reshape the thinking of the audience and see a concept in a new light.

This rhetorical strategy is not as simple as looking up a word in a dictionary, though often that is a good place to begin. If you look up your key word in a good collegiate dictionary, you may discover that it meant something one hundred years ago that it no longer means, or that it is used in technical writing in a specific sense, or that it has a range of meanings from which you must choose to convey *your* intention. Citing one of these definitions can help in composing your essay. But defining as a rhetorical strategy may also include giving examples or providing descriptions: What does *democracy* feel like to the citizen? (See E. B. White's "Democracy," p. 542.) What does *salvation* look like to the unconverted? (See Langston Hughes's "Salvation," p. 683.) What is a *postcard* in a literary sense? (See Garrison Keillor's "Postcards," p. 306.) In these versions of defining, the rhetorical strategy overlaps with the next one: describing.

Describing

When writers describe a person, place, or thing, they indicate what it looks like and often how it feels, smells, sounds, or tastes. As a strategy, describing involves showing rather than telling, helping readers see rather than giving them a formal definition, making the subject come alive rather than remaining abstract. When you describe, you want to choose precise verbs, specific nouns, vivid adjectives—unless your subject is dullness itself.

As a writer, you will use description in many kinds of assignments: in profiles of people and places to provide a key to their essence, in visual analysis to reveal the crucial features of a painting or photograph, in cultural critique to highlight the features of the object or phenomenon you will analyze, and in scientific lab reports to give details of an experiment. Almost no essay can be written without at least some description, and many essays rely on this strategy as a fundamental technique. In *The Norton Reader* you will find study questions in almost every section that begin with "Describe": "Describe a 'treasure' someone found and held on to," "Take a flower or tree and write a close-up description of it," "Describe some particular experience that raises a large social question"—these are just a few examples of writing assignments that ask for description.

Explaining a process

With this rhetorical strategy, the writer explains how something is done: from everyday processes like how to write a letter, how to play basketball, or how to make French fries, to unusual or extreme processes like how to embalm a corpse or how to face death. Sometimes, writers use this strategy in historical essays to show how something was done in the past. As these examples suggest, explaining a process can be useful in a range of genres: from a literacy narrative that explains learning to read, to a cultural analysis that treats the funeral industry, to a sermon or philosophical essay that explores the meaning and purpose of death and dying.

To make a process accessible to the reader, you will need to identify the main steps or stages and then explain them in order, one after the other. Sequence matters. In preparing to write a paragraph explaining a process, it might help to list the steps as a flow chart or as a cookbook recipe—and then turn your list into a paragraph (or more) of fully elaborated prose.

Narrating

This final rhetorical strategy—narrating—may be the most fundamental. We tell stories about ourselves, about our families, and about friends and neighbors. We tell stories to make a point, to illustrate an argument, to offer evidence or counter-evidence, and sometimes even to substitute for an argument. As these uses suggest, narrating appears in many genres: from memoirs and biographies, to Op-Eds, formal speeches, and parables. Narrating is basic to essay writing.

As you plan a paragraph or segment of narration, think about sequence: the order in which the events occurred (chronological order) or an order in which the events might be most dramatically presented (reverse chronological order or the present moment with flashback). Often, sequential order is easier for the reader to comprehend, but sometimes beginning *in medias res* (at the present moment *in the middle of things*) and then flashing back to the past creates a more compelling story. Consider incorporating time markers—not only dates, but also sequential phrases: early one evening, later that night, the next morning. And use transitions and transitional words: first, then, meanwhile, later, finally. When you've finished narrating your event or episode, re-read it and ask, What have I left out that the reader needs to know? What might I omit because the reader doesn't need to know it?

STRATEGIES FOR WRITING

If you were to watch a writer at work, you would observe that the task of writing often occurs in stages. Most writers generate ideas, write a draft, revise the draft (sometimes once, often many times), edit (make sentence- or word-level changes), and finally, proofread (check to see that the grammar, spelling, and formatting are correct). Along the way, writers develop a main point for their writing, find examples and evidence to support that point, and integrate the evidence into their work. You would be observing what teachers of writing call the *writing process,* a series of stages that writers use, though some omit a stage, some combine one or more of them, and others follow each one carefully. Your writing will benefit if you understand how the writing process works, and, even more important, how to make the process work for *you.*

Generate ideas

For many people, the hardest part of writing is looking at the blank page or empty screen. What can you say? How can you even get started? Sometimes your task is made easier when your instructor gives you a specific assignment or asks a particular question. In the next pages, we'll follow one student as she develops an essay responding to Brent Staples's "Why Colleges Shower Their Students with A's." Her instructor assigned the following study question (p. 260):

> How broad is Staples's range of examples? Would he need to adjust his position if he considered other colleges? Write an analysis of the situation at your college either to confirm or to contest Staples's argument.

The student knew she had to analyze Staples's range of examples and so began gathering ideas by rereading his essay. She noted that he cites only three colleges by name—the University of Pennsylvania, the University of Phoenix, and Duke University—and decided to do research on her own campus. Her instructor directed her to the Office of Institutional Research, which supplied her with a summary of grade distribution at her college. The summary showed that 30 percent of grades were A's, 45 percent were B's, and 25 percent were C's or below. The evidence her research produced did not seem particularly odd to her; it was about what she expected, and it refuted Staples's claim that "colleges shower their students with A's." Notice this student's process for generating ideas and getting started: she began with the question in *The Norton Reader*, reread the essay, conducted research, and discovered hard evidence that did not support Staples's claim. In fact, she developed a claim of her own, a counterclaim to Staples's.

Sometimes, the assignment your teacher gives or a study question in *The Norton Reader* is more open-ended, such as this one following Nancy Mairs's "On Being a Cripple" (p. 30):

> Mairs deliberately chooses to call herself a "cripple." Select a person or group that deliberately chooses its own name or description and explain the rationale behind the choice.

You can respond to this assignment by examining your own memory for stories you've heard, incidents you've witnessed, or people you've met, or you may need to do some research in order to have enough to say. Use one or more of the following techniques to mine your memory or generate ideas:

- Freewrite for several minutes to discover what you already know and think about a subject.

- Make a list of everything you know about the subject. Group or cluster related ideas.

- Read some articles about the subject. Take notes on what you read.

- Ask questions about the subject, starting with *who, what, when, why,* and *how.*

Different writers develop different ways of finding their material, so experiment with different techniques until you discover one or more that work for you.

Develop a main point or thesis

Most writing in college courses needs a central claim, often called a *thesis.* Most papers contain a thesis statement, often stated in the introduction, that tells readers the main point that will be supported, developed, and extended in the body of the paper.

Sometimes the thesis statement will be an arguable claim supported by evidence, such as Brent Staples's thesis, which falls at the end of the first paragraph of his Op-Ed: "Faced with demanding consumers and stiff competition, colleges have simply issued more and more A's, stoking grade inflation and devaluating degrees." The student who responded to Staples's essay also developed a thesis statement, narrowing a broad initial claim—"Staples is wrong about colleges showering their students with A's"—to a specific, arguable claim—"For most students at Central College, however, Staples is wrong: 70 percent of students on this campus are not being showered with A's." Her thesis statement is good because it is emerges from the research she has carried out on her own campus.

At other times, the main point of your writing won't be stated so plainly. Instead, it will be "in the air," or evident to the reader, but you won't be trying to argue a claim with evidence. If you're writing in a narrative or descriptive genre, for example, you'll have a main point, of course, particularly if you're writing a historical or biographical narrative or creating a profile of a person or place. You will make a claim about the reasons something happened or about the reasons for a person's or place's distinctive characteristics, as Margaret Atwood does in "True North" (p. 95):

> The north is another country. It's also another language. Or languages.

Those three sentences are main point, the guiding principle by which she thinks about the Canadian north.

Gather evidence

What counts as adequate evidence for your claim or thesis? The student whose response to Brent Staples's "Why Colleges Shower Students with A's" was not convinced by the evidence Staples used and found evidence that refuted his claim. Her argument would have been even stronger if she had looked for other sources, such as published survey results and reports of grade distribution at other colleges, to find out whether Staples's claim or her hunch was more accurate.

In other kinds of writing, evidence is drawn more often from personal experience than from secondary sources. In a literacy narrative, for example, the evidence will be in the examples and details of the story you tell about a formative time in your education. In a profile of a person, the evidence will also take the form of examples—the descriptive details about the person's personality, accomplishments, talents, weaknesses, looks, and behavior; anecdotes or stories about the person's life; or testimony from people who've observed the person closely. Evidence is also often drawn directly from reading. In a textual analysis, the evidence will be examples that demonstrate the text's structure, style, and language.

Organize your ideas

How you organize your ideas in a piece of writing depends to a large extent on your genre and purpose. Margaret Atwood organizes "True North" as a journey to the north, inching us there by describing her impressions of a trip, using the historical present tense ("A bunch of us are sitting around the table, at what is now a summer cottage in Georgian Bay"), and pausing occasionally to fill us in on what happens at different times, thus linking her impressions together loosely in her narrative. Similarly, David Guterson organizes "Enclosed, Encyclopedic, Endured: The Mall of America" (p. 105) as an answer to a question:

> Here was a new structure that had cost more than half a billion dollars to erect—what might it tell us about ourselves?

His essay proceeds as a narrative exploration of the Mall itself, over a number of days; he links his observations to stops he makes on his trip through the complex.

For many of the essays you write in college, you will use the familiar format of an introduction, body, and conclusion, with separate paragraphs in the body for each major piece of evidence. The introduction often connects your ideas to what your readers already know and seeks to interest them in what you have to say. For instance, the student writing in response to Brent Staples's Op-Ed began her essay this way:

> The notion of grade inflation has been in the air for the past decade. Critics have complained that today's students are receiving far too many A's and not enough C's, D's, and F's. Things were different in the past, these critics say; grades really meant something back when the critics went to college; today's college students have it far too easy. In his recent Op-Ed piece, Brent Staples struck the familiar theme when he claimed to explain why colleges nowadays "shower" their students with A's. For most students at Central College, however, Staples is wrong: 70 percent of students on this campus are not being showered with A's.

In the body of an essay, you may want to place your most compelling piece of evidence first, or you may want it to come last to tie matters up for the reader. (But don't hide your best bit of evidence by placing it in the middle.) The student who wrote in response to Staples decided to use the body of her essay to present anecdotal evidence from her roommates, informal survey results from classmates about their grades, and finally the results of her research at the Office of Institutional Research. Whatever type of organization you choose, try the ideas out and write a different outline for each type of placement to see which works more successfully.

In the conclusion, you try to wrap things up, finish off your line of reasoning, and send your readers off with a final thought. Brent Staples ends "Why Colleges Shower Their Students with A's" with a predication:

> Addicted to counterfeit excellence, colleges, parents and students are unlikely to give it up. As a consequence, diplomas will become weaker and more ornamental as the years go by.

That's a fine way to conclude. Our student writer, responding to Staples, takes a different approach in her conclusion:

> Those of us who work hard and study at Central College note that we have never been "showered" with A's. We study at a place where high grades remain difficult to earn, and our situation makes me wonder whether Staples

gathered only the evidence he wanted to find. Had he considered other colleges, he would not have made such a sweeping assertion.

Write multiple drafts

Even the most experienced writers know they can't do everything at once: find or invent material, assess its usefulness, arrange it in paragraphs, and write it out in well-formed sentences. If you try to produce a good essay at one sitting, in a single draft, you are likely to thin out your material, lock yourself into a structure that may not work and that you don't have time to change, and write jumbled paragraphs and clumsy sentences that won't fully convey your meaning or intention. In the end, writing a few drafts—in short periods spaced over more than a day—will produce a better essay, one that is thoughtful and deserving of a respectable grade. Here are some tips for drafting in stages:

- Get started by composing a rough draft or small sections of a draft. Don't feel obliged to start with the introduction and write straight through to the conclusion. If you don't know where to begin, write a section you know you want to include, then move to another. As you compose, you will begin to find out what you mean, what is important to your argument, what is missing, and what needs to be revised. Think of composing a rough draft as a way of discovering what you want to say.

- If you get stuck, try focused freewriting. That is, write all you can in response to a particular point or about a particular idea, not stopping for five minutes. After you're done, read what you've written looking for your thoughts on the subject. Much of what you've written won't be worthwhile, but you may have come up with key notions or put yourself in touch with useful ideas.

- Write a single paragraph for each key piece of evidence you have to support your thesis. Later on you can refine these paragraphs, combining some and breaking up others.

- At any point in this process, print out a clean version of your draft, read it through, and make changes. Add to, subtract from, rearrange, and revise the parts of your essay.

Acknowledge others' words and ideas

Your writing should reflect your own thinking, of course, but you'll often incorporate the ideas and actual words of others. Synthesizing and citing the work of others shows your readers that you have consulted reputable sources and, if you use sources honestly and skillfully, will make readers more open to your argument. It may help you to think of anything you write as part of a dialogue you are having with other writers and scholars; just be sure to credit the other writers and scholars whose words and ideas you borrow, so your readers can follow the dialogue and know who said what.

When you cite information from another source in your writing, you must credit the source. First, give the author credit by acknowledging his or her work in your text. If you cite someone's exact words, put them in quotation marks, or, if you quote more than five lines, indent them without quotation marks. Tell your readers where you got the words by including the author's name in your text and putting the page number of the book or article in parentheses right after the quote. Here is an example of a direct quotation with appropriate citation:

> Staples argues that the rise of part-time instructors is partially responsible for grade inflation: "Writing in the last issue of *Academe*, two part-timers suggest that students routinely corner adjuncts, threatening to complain if they do not turn C's into A's" (260).

If you paraphrase a source, that is, if you use another person's idea but not the exact words, you still need to cite the source of that idea, even though you have expressed it in your own words. Here is an example of a paraphrase:

> Staples dismisses the argument that grades are getting higher because of students' better preparation (261).

At the end of your paper on a separate page, list all the sources you have quoted and paraphrased. Many style guides provide directions for formatting source material. The guide used most frequently in English classes is the *MLA Handbook for Writers of Research Papers*, Sixth Edition (2003), published by the Modern Language Association.

Sometimes writers in a hurry are tempted to absorb others' writing wholesale into their papers. This is *plagiarism*. Plagiarism is unethical because it involves the theft of another writer's words and ideas; in college courses, it is a guarantee of failure when discovered. Avoid plagiarizing at all costs. If you have fallen behind on a writing assignment, tell your instructor. You will often find that he or she will accept a late submission, and even if you are graded down for submitting the paper late, that is better than stealing others' ideas and words.

Revise alone and with peers

Although writers can and often do compose and revise alone, we all need helpful responses, whether from professional editors, classmates, or friends. You, too, will need to become a good reviser, both of your own work and of the work of your peers. It is useful first to internalize another reader for yourself and revise your work on your own, and then to give your draft to an actual reader who can read and comment on it.

All writers need to try out their arguments and ideas before they produce a final draft. Many writing classes encourage that process, teaching students to draft and revise independently but also enabling them to put less-than-final drafts forward for responses from the instructor and fellow students. Examples and arguments that seem clear to the writer may seem forced or exaggerated to another reader. In peer groups, listen to readers who disagree with you, who find your position slanted, overstated, or not fully convincing. Be responsive to their comments, and qualify interpretations or further explain points that they do not understand.

Here are some all-purpose questions that you can use to review a draft on your own or in a peer group. The questions should probably be asked in the order below, since they move from larger elements to smaller ones.

Introduction   Treat the introduction as a promise by asking, "Does this essay keep the promises the introduction makes?" If it doesn't, either the introduction or the essay needs to be revised. Try to determine where the problem lies: Is the introduction off track? Does one or more of the paragraphs wander off the topic? Does the introduction promise an organization that isn't followed?

Content   Next ask yourself, "Does this essay include enough material?" You may feel that some of the essays in *The Norton Reader* are dense and overspecific; your instructor, on the other hand, may find your essays skimpy and underspecific, with too few details and examples. As you read your own work and that of your classmates, look for examples and details that transmit meaning and engage your interest, understanding, and imagination. Check for adequate and persuasive evidence and multiple illustrative examples that clarify main points. If you or your readers think you need more evidence, examples, or information, revise accordingly.

Evidence and source material   Then ask, "Does the essay interpret its material clearly and connect its examples to the main argument?" Your essay, and those you read as a peer reviewer, should specify the meanings of the examples you use; don't expect the examples to speak for themselves. A case in point is the use of quotations. How many are there? How necessary are they? How well are they integrated? What analysis or commentary follows each? Watch for quotations that are simply dropped in, without enough introduction or "placing" so that the reader can understand their significance. Quotations should be well integrated, clearly explaining who is speaking, where the voice is coming from, and what to attend to.

Organization and transitions   Then ask, "Are the main and supporting points of this essay well-organized?" Writing puts readers in possession of material in a temporal order: that is, readers read from start to finish. Sometimes material that appears near the end of an essay might work better near the beginning; sometimes material that appears near the beginning might better be postponed. Pay attention to transitions between and within paragraphs; if they are unclear, the difficulty may lie in the organization of the material.

Tone   Then ask, "Is the tone of the essay appropriate for its purpose and its audience?" Whether the tone is light-hearted, serious, reasoned, funny, enraged, thoughtful, or anything else, it needs to be appropriate to the purpose of the essay and sensitive to the expectations of the audience. Be aware of how formal your writing should be and whether contractions, abbreviations, and slang are acceptable.

Sentences Then ask, "Which sentences unfold smoothly and which sentences might cause readers to stumble?" If working in a group, ask your classmates to help you rephrase a sentence or write the thought in new words. Remember, you're trying to reach readers just like your peers, so take their questions and reactions seriously.

Learning to be a responsive reader of essays in *The Norton Reader* can teach you to respond helpfully to the essays of peer writers in your composition class—and to improve your own. Large and small elements of the composing process are reciprocal. Learn to work back and forth among wholes and parts, sections and paragraphs, introductions and conclusions. As shape and meaning come together, you can begin to refine smaller elements: sentences, phrases, specific words. You can qualify your assertions, complicate your generalizations, and tease out the implications of your examples.

Edit, proofread, and format the final draft

After you have revised the structure of your writing, you should devote time to pruning for excess, reviewing the words, and correcting errors in grammar, punctuation, and spelling—what experienced writers call editing and proofreading. This work is best done after giving the paper a rest and coming to it afresh. You may be tempted to move directly to the proofreading stage, thus shortchanging the larger, more important revision work described above. So long as the larger elements of an essay need repair, it's too soon to work on the smaller ones, so save the tinkering for last. When you're satisfied with the overall shape of your essay, turn to the work of tightening your writing by eliminating repetition and awkward phrases, correcting grammar, punctuation, and spelling, and putting your work in its final form. Be sure you know what style and format your work should take, be it that of an academic paper with set margins, double-spacing, and a title page, or some other format. Ask your instructor if you are unsure about any of these, and make the necessary changes. Then, like other writers, you will need to stop—not because there isn't more to be done but because you have other things to do.

PERSONAL REPORT

JOAN DIDION   *On Going Home*

I AM HOME for my daughter's first birthday. By "home" I do not mean the house in Los Angeles where my husband and I and the baby live, but the place where my family is, in the Central Valley of California. It is a vital although troublesome distinction. My husband likes my family but is uneasy in their house, because once there I fall into their ways, which are difficult, oblique, deliberately inarticulate, not my husband's ways. We live in dusty houses ("D-U-S-T," he once wrote with his finger on surfaces all over the house, but no one noticed it) filled with mementos quite without value to him (what could the Canton dessert plates mean to him? how could he have known about the assay scales, why should he care if he did know?), and we appear to talk exclusively about people we know who have been committed to mental hospitals, about people we know who have been booked on drunk-driving charges, and about property, particularly about property, land, price per acre and C-2 zoning and assessments and freeway access. My brother does not understand my husband's inability to perceive the advantage in the rather common real-estate transaction known as "sale-leaseback," and my husband in turn does not understand why so many of the people he hears about in my father's house have recently been committed to mental hospitals or booked on drunk-driving charges. Nor does he understand that when we talk about sale-leasebacks and right-of-way condemnations we are talking in code about the things we like best, the yellow fields and the cottonwoods and the rivers rising and falling and the mountain roads closing when the heavy snow comes in. We miss each other's points, have another drink and regard the fire. My brother refers to my husband, in his presence, as "Joan's husband." Marriage is the classic betrayal.

Or perhaps it is not any more. Sometimes I think that those of us who are now in our thirties were born into the last generation to carry the burden of "home," to find in family life the source of all tension and drama. I had by all objective accounts a "normal" and a "happy" family situation, and yet I was almost thirty years old before I could talk to my family on the telephone without crying after I had hung up. We did not fight. Nothing was wrong. And yet some nameless anxiety colored the emotional charges between me and the place that I

From Slouching towards Bethlehem (1966), *Didion's first volume of nonfiction, which includes both autobiographical essays and articles analyzing American culture of the 1960s.*

came from. The question of whether or not you could go home again was a very real part of the sentimental and largely literary baggage with which we left home in the fifties; I suspect that it is irrelevant to the children born of the fragmentation after World War II. A few weeks ago in a San Francisco bar I saw a pretty young girl on crystal[1] take off her clothes and dance for the cash prize in an "amateur-topless" contest. There was no particular sense of moment about this, none of the effect of romantic degradation, of "dark journey," for which my generation strived so assiduously. What sense could that girl possibly make of, say, *Long Day's Journey into Night*?[2] Who is beside the point?

That I am trapped in this particular irrelevancy is never more apparent to me than when I am home. Paralyzed by the neurotic lassitude engendered by meeting one's past at every turn, around every corner, inside every cupboard, I go aimlessly from room to room. I decide to meet it head-on and clean out a drawer, and I spread the contents on the bed. A bathing suit I wore the summer I was seventeen. A letter of rejection from *The Nation*, an aerial photograph of the site for a shopping center my father did not build in 1954. Three teacups hand-painted with cabbage roses and signed "E.M.," my grandmother's initials. There is no final solution for letters of rejection from *The Nation* and teacups hand-painted in 1900. Nor is there any answer to snapshots of one's grandfather as a young man on skis, surveying around Donner Pass in the year 1910. I smooth out the snapshot and look into his face, and do and do not see my own. I close the drawer, and have another cup of coffee with my mother. We get along very well, veterans of a guerrilla war we never understood.

Days pass. I see no one. I come to dread my husband's evening call, not only because he is full of news of what by now seems to me our remote life in Los Angeles, people he has seen, letters which require attention, but because he asks what I have been doing, suggests uneasily that I get out, drive to San Francisco or Berkeley. Instead I drive across the river to a family graveyard. It has been vandalized since my last visit and the monuments are broken, overturned in the dry grass. Because I once saw a rattlesnake in the grass I stay in the car and listen to a country-and-Western station. Later I drive with my father to a ranch he has in the foothills. The man who runs his cattle on it asks us to the roundup, a week from Sunday, and although I know that I will be in Los Angeles I say, in the oblique way my family talks, that I will come. Once home I mention the broken monuments in the graveyard. My mother shrugs.

I go to visit my great-aunts. A few of them think now that I am my cousin, or their daughter who died young. We recall an anecdote about a relative last seen in 1948, and they ask if I still like living in New York City. I have lived in Los Angeles for three years, but I say that I do. The baby is offered a horehound drop, and I am slipped a dollar bill "to buy a treat." Questions trail off, answers are abandoned, the baby plays with the dust motes in a shaft of afternoon sun.

1. A methamphetamine.
2. Tragedy by playwright Eugene O'Neill (1888–1952), based on the shame and deception that haunted his own family.

It is time for the baby's birthday party: a white cake, strawberry-marsh-mallow ice cream, a bottle of champagne saved from another party. In the evening, after she has gone to sleep, I kneel beside the crib and touch her face, where it is pressed against the slats, with mine. She is an open and trusting child, unprepared for and unaccustomed to the ambushes of family life, and perhaps it is just as well that I can offer her little of that life. I would like to give her more. I would like to promise her that she will grow up with a sense of her cousins and of rivers and of her great-grandmother's teacups, would like to pledge her a picnic on a river with fried chicken and her hair uncombed, would like to give her *home* for her birthday, but we live differently now and I can promise her nothing like that. I give her a xylophone and a sundress from Madeira, and promise to tell her a funny story.

QUESTIONS

1. Didion speaks of herself at home as "paralyzed by the neurotic lassitude engendered by meeting one's past at every turn" (paragraph 3). What about the essay helps explain these feelings?

2. What does Didion mean by "the ambushes of family life" (paragraph 6)? (Besides "ambushes" note Didion's other highly charged language: e.g., "betrayal" in paragraph 1 and "guerrilla war" in paragraph 3.)

3. In paragraph 6 Didion says she would like to give her daughter "*home* for her birthday, but we live differently now." In an essay, explain whether or not you think parents today can give their children "home." Include examples.

ANDREA BARRETT   *A Hole in the Wall*

July and August. After living in the same house for fifteen years, my husband and I moved from Rochester—upstate New York, a small city surrounded by farms—to Brooklyn. Our plan was to live for a year in the city, during which Barry would take a leave from his university teaching job, concentrating instead on his photography, and I'd hold a fellowship at the New York Public Library. Although Barry was excited and optimistic, I was mostly nervous: I'd written all my books in the same little room and feared my work might not weather the transplant.

Hopefully, foolishly, we'd signed a lease in May for a space behind a big hole in the wall of an industrial building in Williamsburg. Windows had filled

Published in The American Scholar *(Autumn 2002), a general-interest magazine published by the Phi Beta Kappa Society.*

the hole by the time we arrived on a hot July day; a floor had been laid, wall-board was up, appliances stood in the kitchen. But the appliances weren't connected, and neither was the gas; there was no hot water and no way to cook; no screens, no key for the door, no way to get mail; no phone lines or radiators or shelves or closet poles; no lights in the bathroom nor stair rails nor a thousand other things. An apologetic trickle of electricity flowed through an orange extension cord strung from a neighboring building: not enough to power an air-conditioner. Each time we entered or left we picked our way over rubble, unlocked a padlock, unwrapped a heavy chain binding the wire fence that caged us off from the street. At the stroke of eight each morning the polyglot crew arrived and began working loudly everywhere at once. We showered at the public pool and ate in the local bars, moaning and groaning all the while. At first it was funny, and then it wasn't.

Later it was funny again. Our first four weeks in Brooklyn were preposterous, ridiculous, a cosmic joke. In the muddy back courtyard three piglets appeared, wallowing and oinking and gaining weight until the night they were carried away, each one shrieking, to become someone's festival meal. By the end of that month—after the pigs and after the heat wave, which I spent largely immersed in a tub of cold water; after the bouts with no electricity at all and the weeks of jack-hammering; after the arrival of the giant spinning truck that submerged the pigs' former home (a garden-in-the-making, we'd believed) beneath a sea of red concrete—we were dining out on our disaster stories, our first-month-in-the-city tales. We joked that we'd moved to a third-world country: it was like Bosnia, like Beirut. What did we know? New York is a pit, I said cheerfully. I could say that because it wasn't true, because I had no idea what I was saying, because the worst was over.

• •

By the end of August we had a home: we could shower, hang up our clothes, cook dinner, phone our friends. Most of the workmen were gone most of the time. I was starting to notice that, although our neighborhood was untidy and loud, I was interested in everything around me. My neighbors were people new to me, who'd come here from much farther than Rochester. Some were Polish immigrants, most of them elderly; they moved, talking under their breath, through a sea of recent young colonizers: artists, photographers, writers, and filmmakers. Construction sites all over the neighborhood brought in crews of workmen—Russian, Ecuadoran, Mexican, and Polish—until five or six languages rose from the morning streets. Our dog, an ill-bred, ill-behaved, somewhat scruffy pound-mutt disliked in Rochester, where the owners of poodles and borzois and Yorkshire terriers would cross the park to avoid her, here found herself a model of daintiness among a pack of pit bulls, Dobermans, Rottweilers, Great Danes, and peculiar crosses.

The subway, I discovered, would take me safely anywhere, at almost any hour: what freedom! And there was music, too—on the L train platform, and also at the Union Square station I passed through each day, someone was always playing: bass and saxophone, solo accordion, a pair of percussionists, one on trap set and the other on white plastic buckets and big glass bottles. Both underground and above I was surrounded by faces: so much emotion, so much expression, so many different countenances registering so many different things. In Rochester everything had been hidden. Here much was played out in public, before my eyes—and to my surprise, I liked this. There might be, I was learning to think (during those ten or eleven days of real life, during what felt like a kind of flowering) some reason to put up with the expense and inconvenience of living here.

Tuesday. What kind of a city was this, where a plane—no, two planes—could crash into a building? I think I thought that: truly, everything that happened that day is muddled. I saw the second one hit, while I was walking home from the dogsitter's. The pilot had fallen asleep, the air-traffic system was down, someone had made an awful and clumsy mistake and something I couldn't imagine had happened: a hijacking never crossed my mind, I was to naïve to think that thought. But in a city where it sometimes seemed that nothing worked—in Brooklyn, I had told my family, everything is broken—a mistake of even this magnitude seemed possible.

It was my upstairs neighbor, leaning out the window and shouting down to me—I must have run to our building—who first used the word "they": some "they" had attacked the second tower. But who were "they"? Nothing he said made sense. My husband, now framed in our front window, looked similarly puzzled; I ran upstairs and we turned on the TV. Somewhere during those minutes we also first heard the words *terrorist* and *hijacking*. We looked out the window again. Then at the TV. Then we ran up to the roof.

In our part of Williamsburg, the East River is only a block and a half away and the buildings are low, a mixture of warehouses, three-and four-story tenements, and industrial buildings. Nothing impedes the view of the jagged wall of stone and metal across the river, so near it seems one can touch it. The other tenants—two young Brits, a photographer and a filmmaker; a ballet dancer from Mexico and her musician boyfriend; the older French photographer who'd called down to me—were already up on the roof, staring at what had always dominated the sky. Smoke rose from the towers; flames began to shoot from the sides; by then we were crying. The builder and a friend appeared, also some neighbors from next door, while the Brits, who had cell phones, called their families in London to say they were alive. All over the world, I realized, this must be on TV; in Florida, my mother would be terrified. I ran downstairs to call her.

When I returned, what I saw was impossible. Someone tried to explain it to me—the south tower had collapsed while I was gone—but I couldn't hear it; I turned again and again to the sight and each time covered my eyes and turned away. Where had the tower gone? Soon the builder said, in a low sad voice, "Shit. There goes the other one," and when I opened my eyes I saw the second tower unmaking itself, the sides curling away from the middle like skin peeling off a banana, the smoke spewing upward until everything was gone.

••

10   Why talk about the rest of that morning, the rest of that day? All of us
were glued alternately to the desecrated skyline and the television, watching
the same images again and again, each minute more deeply aware of the people who'd been inside those towers and what had happened to them. The
trains closed down, the city closed down. No one knew what to do or say. At
two that afternoon the L train opened; Barry took his camera and went into
Manhattan, working his way farther and farther downtown—so far that he was
uncomfortably close to building #7 when it came down. When he returned
that evening to fetch more film, he convinced me to go back in with him. I
should see this, he said: the way so much of daily life was still being lived; the
tremendous social momentum that keeps us moving through the forms of life
even after the heart has stopped. I would, he said, find the people and the
sight of what still stood consoling. While I didn't believe that, I knew that if I
didn't go into Manhattan soon, I would never go there again. I'd put the dog
and cat in the car and start driving and never stop—as if I could drive away
from this, or that it would matter, now, where I lived.

••

Below Houston, then below Canal: closed streets, tired cops, an endless
line of trucks and bulldozers and cranes and flatbed trailers mounded with
lights and generators, machines whose names I don't know parked end to end
with their engines running and their headlights on, a procession that stretched
for miles and seemed to pulse with longing to get going, to do something, to
move toward their grim tasks, prevented from that by the fires burning at what
was already being termed Ground Zero. But also, among the tired firemen
trudging toward the nearest open subway station, at West Fourth, between the
young police cadets and the Port Authority workers and the volunteer nurses
and EMTs, we saw people walking dogs, pushing babies in strollers, sitting in
bars and talking earnestly over supper and drinks. People on bikes. People holding hands. People unable not to do what they had always done, in the neighborhoods where they made their homes; people moving about, people living.
      Where North Moore intersects with West Street, volunteers had gathered.
Meaning to see what we could do, we joined the crowd. Cots and stretchers
filled a courtyard rimmed with face masks, bottled water, food, all sorts of supplies. No one walked or crawled or was carried from the rubble and there was
nothing for the rest of us to do. We could see the fire burning, still. The smoke
was lashing through the crowd, the trucks still waited helplessly. So did we.

Wednesday, Thursday, Friday. We watch the TV, we read the papers, we watch
the TV, we read the papers. We talk to people on the streets and in bars and
cafés. At dusk we stand on abandoned lots at the riverside along with everyone
else. We used to walk the dog here at night, in the silent but pleasant company
of others who, like us, had picked their way through the broken grass and the
holes in the fence, around the garbage and over the rocks, to get a taste of the
breeze blowing up the river and a sight of the city, so close. Now there are

hundreds of people here, faces glimpsed before at windows or on the subway platform or in the park. In silent ranks we watch the sun set over the smoking hole. The first night the cloud of smoke blew east, over Brooklyn Heights, and we could hardly smell it. But the wind has shifted since then, and, as the sun sets, the smoke drapes Manhattan like a scarf and slides across the water into our nostrils.

It rains on Thursday night, after bolts of lightning first strike so close by that sparks fly and our next-door neighbor's television and amplifier are fried: a steady, unrelenting rain pushed toward us by a strong wind blowing up the river. Before I think to close the front windows (which face the bridge, and used to face the towers), the rain pours through the screens, all over the sill and down the wall to the floor. I wipe up what I can. The next morning I head for the sill with a rag, having learned during my first city rainstorm that each drop coming through the screens leaves behind a dot of the filth it has carried from the air. Now the entire sill is dark gray, six linear feet of grime. What I dab comes up like ash and as I back away, the rag still in my hand, I realize that's what it is: ash of buildings, ash of planes. Ash of people.

Everything in the apartment is gritty, I now see. Table, floor, pillows and sheets; after that I can't stand to touch anything, and I can't sleep. Neither can Barry, who has processed his photos and is now obsessively editing them. He can't stop looking, and neither can I. We ought to stop looking, we ought to stop thinking like this, we ought to get in the car and go someplace, anyplace; we ought to do something to take care of everyone hurt, but we can't. We try to give blood and we can't do that either: for the moment every place is full. On the TV, banners run across the screen saying no more volunteers are needed, please don't come to these places to help, stop stop stop.

15

• •

The dog paces nervously, trying to understand why we're acting so strangely. If a dog can think, we think she thinks this: Why can't I run at the river now; who are all these people? Why do they have candles in their hands? The smells in the wind make her nervous, too, along with our frantic comings and goings and the way that we're perpetually staring at glowing screens. The TV (we still can't stop watching). The screen at which Barry edits the digital versions of his photographs (he can't stop that either). The computers on which we try to retrieve and answer scores of e-mail messages, everyone either of us has ever known asking: Are you all right? Are you all right?

We are, we write back. Knowing we aren't, exactly; and also that we've been extraordinarily lucky. We write and write and write and write, and the more we say the worse we feel until finally we decide we shouldn't say anything at all.

• •

What, then, are we supposed to say to all those people who ask, "Don't you want to go back to Rochester? Are you going back? You must want to go back." I *did* think of going, sometime after the first minutes, during the first hour; I was stopped not by courage or a sense of shared community but by the physical impossibility of leaving. The dog, the cat, two people, the car; I imagined us crammed with all the rest of Brooklyn onto the BQE,[1] that narrow, broken-down, torn-up excuse for a highway. A sea of vehicles trying, like red blood corpuscles in a wounded capillary, to squeeze their way through the construction bottlenecks and across the bridges to the thruway: who was I kidding? No one was getting out of here, I thought despairingly on that first day; if something else was going to happen, then it would just have to happen.

Now the roads are working again, some of them, some of the time. But now leaving seems impossible for other reasons, which I can feel but can't articulate, even to myself.

• •

On Thursday, when I go into my office nervously—the library remains open, like the museums; much is made of getting back to "normal life," of "not giving in to them" (whoever they are)—we all try to pretend we're working. No one is very convincing; less so after someone notices that people are stampeding down 42nd Street, in front of our windows, and that the street is now closed off. Uneasy minutes pass, during which we hear too many sirens and see too many police cars and too many running people, before learning that Grand Central and the Condé Nast building have been evacuated because of bomb threats.

President Bush is scheduled to visit Ground Zero on Friday. Traffic will be blocked, the trains will stop, security will be crazy everywhere: is going in worth it? I ponder staying home, feel like a coward, and solve the problem by waking Friday morning with an enormous migraine that I blame, in my bleary and delirious state, on the ash we are breathing: what is on my sills is also in my sinuses. Whatever the cause, I am sick. Certainly it's not my fault, then, that I don't go into Manhattan?

That evening, when I can see enough to walk, I return to the edge of the river with Barry, the dog, and a great many neighbors: the now-usual gathering, we stand and stare at the hole. Tonight we're joined by military transport helicopters flying low overhead, scanning us with their headlamps, and by fighter jets—four of them: F-16s, someone tells me—zooming back and forth in pairs, looping around the island. Since Tuesday the sky has been silent and empty, except for other ominous jets with their distinctive sound. These four extend their ellipses across the river and over us. Each time they pass us, I start to cry. Barry reminds me gently that they must be patrolling because of the president's visit; that they're American jets and won't attack us; that a war hasn't started, that *the* war hasn't started. A friend tells me I should welcome the sound: it means we are being protected.

Saturday. For twenty-four hours, what seems most relevant to me are the New York City newspapers from July 30 and 31, 1916, reporting the last huge ex-

---

1. Brooklyn–Queens Expressway.

plosion in New York: the munitions storage site at Black Tom Island, near Jersey City and the Statue of Liberty. For months I'd been meaning to look at these papers, as research for a novel I hoped to write. Now the stories seem to have an entirely different, and urgent, point. All day I hide in the library, reading microfilm, obsessed with this and determined to share it with others. How analogous, I think. German sabotage was blamed; a wave of anti-German hate crimes followed; the United States was not yet in the war, but this would be one of the factors swaying public opinion toward participation. I print out sheaves of pages.

Later, this will seem crazy. Reading through those fuzzy copies, I'll notice that although thousands of people were shaken up, windows were broken not only in Jersey City but all across lower Manhattan and Brooklyn, businesses were damaged and warehouses burned, and two hundred people were initially reported dead, only a few people really died. Property damage, not mass slaughter. The pages are meaningless.

Sunday, Monday. The jets continue, the helicopters continue; these start to seem almost normal. Months ago I accepted an invitation to visit a school a few hours north of the city and talk to the students about reading and writing. As the school has decided to go on with the planned event (miraculously, not a single student has lost a relative, and everyone is eager, the headmaster says, to "return to normal"), I gingerly board a train on Sunday afternoon. A few seats down from me, a firefighter who's clearly been working for days—his face is drawn, his clothes are filthy, his hat is covered with ash, or worse—falls asleep before we leave the station. Across from him a man in his fifties thumbs through a news magazine, a special edition devoted entirely to September 11. When I look at him next he is weeping silently as he stares at whatever photo occupies the last page. Meanwhile the woman next to me, who clutches a bag labeled "Baby Gap," keeps looking over my shoulder. (Of course I'm still reading about the events, and staring at the photographs: why can't I stop this?) When I offer her part of my paper she accepts and then confides that she can't stop this either, indeed has been reading my pages surreptitiously. Russian-born, a recent immigrant, she lives in the suburbs and has a baby who, when the planes came, was staying with her father near Coney Island. Everyone is all right—but oh, she says. How terrified I was!

As we talk, the landscape beyond the window changes. Trees, lush green grass. Flowers, hedges, marshes, birds—it looks like paradise. White houses. How starved I have been, I realize, for a glimpse of nature. For a few moments I am madly homesick.

And yet—although I stay in a guest room in a lovely house; although I walk across glistening fields that smell like hay, and gaze at old and beautiful trees; although the school's faculty members are immensely kind and the students are smart and attentive, as Monday passes I feel steadily odder, more disoriented, more unhappy. People here have seen the events on TV, rather than with their own eyes. They haven't smelled them or touched them or felt them. It's not their fault, they're not hard-hearted, they don't suffer from a failure of the imagination—it's simply that they are removed, and that their lives (of course!) are going on.

Don't I want them to go on? Don't I want the students studying, and necking in the corners, and worrying about their boy- and girlfriends, and if they have the right clothes and how volleyball practice will go and what will happen at the dance?

I do, and I also don't. I want to shriek at them and am horrified at my desire to shriek at them. I understand how unfair I am being. But all I can think about, by the end of the day, is how much I want to go home.

• •

30   By "home," I mean Brooklyn.

• •

I can't sleep, I can't work, I can't think. I can't afford to live here, nor can I do without the life and friends I left behind in Rochester. And so how, exactly, have I come to think of this place as home? When I walk the block and a half to the river now I see, instead of the giant towers that once filled the skyline, a hole that continues to smoke. Everything that fell into that hole, and everyone still living their lives around it, is what keeps me here and makes me feel that I can't bear to leave.

Later. If this were fiction, I would have stopped with the line above, on that note of muted adaptation. But the truth is this: the second week is harder than the first, and the third seems harder still. One night the first thing Barry tells me when I arrive home is that our car has been broken into and the CD player stolen. Without thinking, I ask, "Did they smash the windows?"

"No," he says.

"Then how did they get in?"

35   "I don't know. The doors are all locked, I checked."

We stare at each other, puzzled, until I remember that we have never *had* a CD player. When I point this out to Barry, he says, "But there's a big empty hole in the dash."

"That's always been there," I say carefully.

A long, silent minute later, he says, "I don't know. It just seemed like something was missing."

• •

We are, all of us, daily more exhausted and more distressed, battered not just by the constant grief and the new difficulties of daily life, but by the stories spreading through the city like a virus. In another context we might dismiss these as urban legends. Now there's no way of knowing whether they're true or false, unbearable fact or manifestation of what we most dread. They spread at the river shore, at the dog park, at dinner parties and hospitals, delineating the circles of damage and trauma: the friend who finds out, after days of ignorance, that an acquaintance was on one of the fatal planes. The young relative whose first day in New York includes a meeting with a friend who retrieved his car from Battery Park City and found the windshield spattered with blood and parts. The fellow dog owner whose journalist friend, walking through rubble near Ground Zero, saw a gun and holster on the ground and—thoughtfully, kindly, wanting no one else to be damaged—bent to pick it up and so, inadvertently, held for a second the fragment of torso it still enclosed. The medical students who, another acquaintance says, have volunteered at the morgue to help sort through and label the heaps of remains and whose lives are being reshaped by this experience.

Everyone has a story, or knows a story; they spread like shards of shrapnel,   40
hacking parts off the people who hear them. Yet we can't, despite that, keep from repeating them; only repetition seems to make the wounds bearable. At a lunch delayed, and then finally held, all any of us can talk about are the events of the past weeks. Where we were when it happened and what we first knew; who knows the person to whom this or that happened; who lived, who died, who saw what unspeakable thing: the stories, the stories, the stories. On the table, which is in a lovely room filled with congenial people, in a nice restaurant on a pretty day, a long wooden tray filled with rows of green apples sits glowing, demanding to be recognized as beautiful and worthy. All of us look at it, all of us are for a moment consoled and refreshed. A minute later, all of us are bent close to each other again, urgently telling more stories. This is home now, I realize once more. This is where I live. This is not going to get easier.

QUESTIONS

1. Barrett ends her essay with "This is not going to get easier." Do you think that in the years that have passed things might have become "easier" for her? Could writing this piece have been part of the process of making things "easier"?

2. What do you think transformed Barrett into a New Yorker? Can you point to specific details in her essay?

3. Write about how you react when Barrett speaks of her neighborhood's having become international and multicultural (paragraph 4). Is it anything like neighborhoods you have lived in or know? Can you imagine yourself living in such a neighborhood? What might attract you or repel you about such a neighborhood?

4. What is there about humans who insist on transforming their experience into stories, as Barrett emphasizes in her concluding paragraph? Do you find yourself similarly telling stories?

Maya Angelou *Graduation*

THE CHILDREN IN STAMPS[1] trembled visibly with anticipation. Some adults were excited too, but to be certain the whole young population had come down with graduation epidemic. Large classes were graduating from both the grammar school and the high school. Even those who were years removed from their own day of glorious release were anxious to help with preparations as a kind of dry run. The junior students who were moving into the vacating classes' chairs were tradition-bound to show their talents for leadership and management. They strutted through the school and around the campus exerting pressure on the lower grades. Their authority was so new that occasionally if they pressed a little too hard it had to be overlooked. After all, next term was coming, and it never hurt a sixth grader to have a play sister in the eighth grade, or a tenth-year student to be able to call a twelfth grader Bubba. So all was endured in a spirit of shared understanding. But the graduating classes themselves were the nobility. Like travelers with exotic destinations on their minds, the graduates were remarkably forgetful. They came to school without their books or tablets or even pencils. Volunteers fell over themselves to secure replacements for the missing equipment. When accepted, the willing workers might or might not be thanked, and it was of no importance to the pregraduation rites. Even teachers were respectful of the now quiet and aging seniors, and tended to speak to them, if not as equals, as beings only slightly lower than themselves. After tests were returned and grades given, the student body, which acted like an extended family, knew who did well, who excelled, and what piteous ones had failed.

Unlike the white high school, Lafayette County Training School distinguished itself by having neither lawn, nor hedges, nor tennis court, nor climbing ivy. Its two buildings (main classrooms, the grade school and home economics) were set on a dirt hill with no fence to limit either its boundaries or those of bordering farms. There was a large expanse to the left of the school which was used alternately as a baseball diamond or basketball court. Rusty hoops on swaying poles represented the permanent recreational equipment, although bats and balls could be borrowed from the P.E. teacher if the borrower was qualified and if the diamond wasn't occupied.

Over this rocky area relieved by a few shady tall persimmon trees the graduating class walked. The girls often held hands and no longer bothered to speak to the lower students. There was a sadness about them, as if this old world was not their home and they were bound for higher ground. The boys,

From I Know Why the Caged Bird Sings *(1970), the first volume of Angelou's autobiography of growing up in a segregated southern town. After its popular success, Angelou continued her life story in five sequential volumes, ending with* A Song Flung Up to Heaven *(2002), an account of the turbulent years of the civil rights movement and the assassinations of Malcolm X and Martin Luther King Jr.*

1. A town in Arkansas.

on the other hand, had become more friendly, more outgoing. A decided change from the closed attitude they projected while studying for finals. Now they seemed not ready to give up the old school, the familiar paths and class-rooms. Only a small percentage would be continuing on to college—one of the South's A & M (agricultural and mechanical) schools, which trained Negro youths to be carpenters, farmers, handymen, masons, maids, cooks and baby nurses. Their future rode heavily on their shoulders, and blinded them to the collective joy that had pervaded the lives of the boys and girls in the grammar school graduating class.

Parents who could afford it had ordered new shoes and readymade clothes for themselves from Sears and Roebuck or Montgomery Ward. They also en-gaged the best seamstresses to make the floating graduating dresses and to cut down secondhand pants which would be pressed to a military slickness for the important event.

Oh, it was important, all right. Whitefolks would attend the ceremony,   5
and two or three would speak of God and home, and the Southern way of life, and Mrs. Parsons, the principal's wife, would play the graduation march while the lower-grade graduates paraded down the aisles and took their seats below the platform. The high school seniors would wait in empty classrooms to make their dramatic entrance.

In the Store I was the person of the moment. The birthday girl. The center. Bailey[2] had graduated the year before, although to do so he had had to forfeit all pleasures to make up for his time lost in Baton Rouge.

My class was wearing butter-yellow piqué dresses, and Momma launched out on mine. She smocked the yoke into tiny crisscrossing puckers, then shirred the rest of the bodice. Her dark fingers ducked in and out of the lemony cloth as she embroidered raised daisies around the hem. Before she considered herself finished she had added a crocheted cuff on the puff sleeves, and a pointy crocheted collar.

I was going to be lovely. A walking model of all the various styles of fine hand sewing and it didn't worry me that I was only twelve years old and merely graduating from the eighth grade. Besides, many teachers in Arkansas Negro schools had only that diploma and were licensed to impart wisdom.

The days had become longer and more noticeable. The faded beige of for-mer times had been replaced with strong and sure colors. I began to see my classmates' clothes, their skin tones, and the dust that waved off pussy wil-lows. Clouds that lazed across the sky were objects of great concern to me. Their shiftier shapes might have held a message that in my new happiness and with a little bit of time I'd soon decipher. During that period I looked at the arch of heaven so religiously my neck kept a steady ache. I had taken to smil-ing more often, and my jaws hurt from the unaccustomed activity. Between the two physical sore spots, I suppose I could have been uncomfortable, but that was not the case. As a member of the winning team (the graduating class

2. The author's brother.

of 1940) I had outdistanced unpleasant sensations by miles. I was headed for
the freedom of open fields.

10   Youth and social approval allied themselves with me and we trammeled
memories of slights and insults. The wind of our swift passage remodeled my
features. Lost tears were pounded to mud and then to dust. Years of withdrawal were brushed aside and left behind, as hanging ropes of parasitic moss.

My work alone had awarded me a top place and I was going to be one of
the first called in the graduating ceremonies. On the classroom blackboard, as
well as on the bulletin board in the auditorium, there were blue stars and
white stars and red stars. No absences, no tardinesses, and my academic work
was among the best of the year. I could say the preamble to the Constitution
even faster than Bailey. We timed ourselves often: "We the people of the
United States in order to form a more perfect union . . ." I had memorized the
Presidents of the United States from Washington to Roosevelt in chronological as well as alphabetical order.

My hair pleased me too. Gradually the black mass had lengthened and
thickened, so that it kept at last to its braided pattern, and I didn't have to
yank my scalp off when I tried to comb it.

Louise and I had rehearsed the exercises until we tired out ourselves.
Henry Reed was class valedictorian. He was a small, very black boy with
hooded eyes, a long, broad nose and an oddly shaped head. I had admired him
for years because each term he and I vied for the best grades in our class.
Most often he bested me, but instead of being disappointed I was pleased that
we shared top places between us. Like many Southern Black children, he lived
with his grandmother, who was as strict as Momma and as kind as she knew
how to be. He was courteous, respectful and soft-spoken to elders, but on the
playground he chose to play the roughest games. I admired him. Anyone, I
reckoned, sufficiently afraid or sufficiently dull could be polite. But to be able
to operate at a top level with both adults and children was admirable.

His valedictory speech was entitled "To Be or Not to Be." The rigid tenth-
grade teacher had helped him write it. He'd been working on the dramatic
stresses for months.

15   The weeks until graduation were filled with heady activities. A group of
small children were to be presented in a play about buttercups and daisies and
bunny rabbits. They could be heard throughout the building practicing their
hops and their little songs that sounded like silver bells. The older girls (non-
graduates, of course) were assigned the task of making refreshments for the
night's festivities. A tangy scent of ginger, cinnamon, nutmeg and chocolate
wafted around the home economics building as the budding cooks made samples for themselves and their teachers.

In every corner of the workshop, axes and saws split fresh timber as the
woodshop boys made sets and stage scenery. Only the graduates were left out
of the general bustle. We were free to sit in the library at the back of the building or look in quite detachedly, naturally, on the measures being taken for our
event.

Even the minister preached on graduation the Sunday before. His subject was, "Let your light so shine that men will see your good works and praise your Father, Who is in Heaven." Although the sermon was purported to be addressed to us, he used the occasion to speak to backsliders, gamblers and general ne'er-do-wells. But since he had called our names at the beginning of the service we were mollified.

Among Negroes the tradition was to give presents to children going only from one grade to another. How much more important this was when the person was graduating at the top of the class. Uncle Willie and Momma had sent away for a Mickey Mouse watch like Bailey's. Louise gave me four embroidered handkerchiefs. (I gave her crocheted doilies.) Mrs. Sneed, the minister's wife, made me an undershirt to wear for graduation, and nearly every customer gave me a nickel or maybe even a dime with the instruction "Keep on moving to higher ground," or some such encouragement.

Amazingly the great day finally dawned and I was out of bed before I knew it. I threw open the back door to see it more clearly, but Momma said, "Sister, come away from that door and put your robe on."

I hoped the memory of that morning would never leave me. Sunlight was   20
itself young, and the day had none of the insistence maturity would bring it in a few hours. In my robe and barefoot in the backyard, under cover of going to see about my new beans, I gave myself up to the gentle warmth and thanked God that no matter what evil I had done in my life He had allowed me to live to see this day. Somewhere in my fatalism I had expected to die, accidentally, and never have the chance to walk up the stairs in the auditorium and gracefully receive my hard-earned diploma. Out of God's merciful bosom I had won reprieve.

Bailey came out in his robe and gave me a box wrapped in Christmas paper. He said he had saved his money for months to pay for it. It felt like a box of chocolates, but I knew Bailey wouldn't save money to buy candy when we had all we could want under our noses.

He was as proud of the gift as I. It was a soft-leather-bound copy of a collection of poems by Edgar Allan Poe, or, as Bailey and I called him, "Eap." I turned to "Annabel Lee" and we walked up and down the garden rows, the cool dirt between our toes, reciting the beautifully sad lines.

Momma made a Sunday breakfast although it was only Friday. After we finished the blessing, I opened my eyes to find the watch on my plate. It was a dream of a day. Everything went smoothly and to my credit, I didn't have to be reminded or scolded for anything. Near evening I was too jittery to attend to chores, so Bailey volunteered to do all before his bath.

Days before, we had made a sign for the Store, and as we turned out the lights Momma hung the cardboard over the doorknob. It read clearly: CLOSED. GRADUATION.

My dress fitted perfectly and everyone said that I looked like a sunbeam in   25
it. On the hill, going toward the school, Bailey walked behind with Uncle Willie, who muttered, "Go on, Ju." He wanted him to walk ahead with us because it embarrassed him to have to walk so slowly. Bailey said he'd let the ladies walk together, and the men would bring up the rear. We all laughed, nicely.

Little children dashed by out of the dark like fireflies. Their crepe-paper dresses and butterfly wings were not made for running and we heard more than one rip, dryly, and the regretful "uh uh" that followed.

The school blazed without gaiety. The windows seemed cold and un-friendly from the lower hill. A sense of ill-fated timing crept over me, and if Momma hadn't reached for my hand I would have drifted back to Bailey and Uncle Willie, and possibly beyond. She made a few slow jokes about my feet getting cold, and tugged me along to the now-strange building.

Around the front steps, assurance came back. There were my fellow "greats," the graduating class. Hair brushed back, legs oiled, new dresses and pressed pleats, fresh pocket handkerchiefs and little handbags, all homesewn. Oh, we were up to snuff, all right. I joined my comrades and didn't even see my family go in to find seats in the crowded auditorium.

The school band struck up a march and all classes filed in as had been re-hearsed. We stood in front of our seats, as assigned, and on a signal from the choir director, we sat. No sooner had this been accomplished than the band started to play the national anthem. We rose again and sang the song, after which we recited the pledge of allegiance. We remained standing for a brief minute before the choir director and the principal signaled to us, rather des-perately I thought, to take our seats. The command was so unusual that our carefully rehearsed and smooth-running machine was thrown off. For a full minute we fumbled for our chairs and bumped into each other awkwardly. Habits change or solidify under pressure, so in our state of nervous tension we had been ready to follow our usual assembly pattern: the American national anthem, then the pledge of allegiance, then the song every Black person I knew called the Negro National Anthem. All done in the same key, with the same passion and most often standing on the same foot.

30 Finding my seat at last, I was overcome with a presentiment of worse things to come. Something unrehearsed, unplanned, was going to happen, and we were going to be made to look bad. I distinctly remember being explicit in the choice of pronoun. It was "we," the graduating class, the unit, that con-cerned me then.

The principal welcomed "parents and friends" and asked the Baptist minister to lead us in prayer. His invocation was brief and punchy, and for a second I thought we were getting on the high road to right action. When the principal came back to the dais, however, his voice had changed. Sounds al-ways affected me profoundly and the principal's voice was one of my favorites. During assembly it melted and lowed weakly into the audience. It had not been in my plan to listen to him, but my curiosity was piqued and I straight-ened up to give him my attention.

He was talking about Booker T. Washington, our "late great leader," who said we can be as close as the fingers on the hand, etc. . . . Then he said a few vague things about friendship and the friendship of kindly people to those less fortunate than themselves. With that his voice nearly faded, thin, away. Like a river diminishing to a stream and then to a trickle. But he cleared his throat and said, "Our speaker tonight, who is also our friend, came from Texarkana to deliver the commencement address, but due to the irregularity of the train schedule, he's going to, as they say, 'speak and run.' " He said that we understood and wanted the man to know that we were most grateful for the time he was able to give us and then something about how we were willing always to adjust to another's program, and without more ado—"I give you Mr. Edward Donleavy."

Not one but two white men came through the door off-stage. The shorter one walked to the speaker's platform, and the tall one moved to the center seat and sat down. But that was our principal's seat, and already occupied. The dislodged gentleman bounced around for a long breath or two before the Baptist minister gave him his chair, then with more dignity than the situation deserved, the minister walked off the stage.

Donleavy looked at the audience once (on reflection, I'm sure that he wanted only to reassure himself that we were really there), adjusted his glasses and began to read from a sheaf of papers.

He was glad "to be here and to see the work going on just as it was in the   35
other schools."

At the first "Amen" from the audience I willed the offender to immediate death by choking on the word. But Amens and Yes, sirs began to fall around the room like rain through a ragged umbrella.

He told us of the wonderful changes we children in Stamps had in store. The Central School (naturally, the white school was Central) had already been granted improvements that would be in use in the fall. A well-known artist was coming from Little Rock to teach art to them. They were going to have the newest microscopes and chemistry equipment for their laboratory. Mr. Donleavy didn't leave us long in the dark over who made these improvements available to Central High. Nor were we to be ignored in the general betterment scheme he had in mind.

He said that he had pointed out to people at a very high level that one of the first-line football tacklers at Arkansas Agricultural and Mechanical College had graduated from good old Lafayette County Training School. Here fewer Amens were heard. Those few that did break through lay dully in the air with the heaviness of habit.

He went on to praise us. He went on to say how he had bragged that "one of the best basketball players at Fisk sank his first ball right here at Lafayette County Training School."

The white kids were going to have a chance to become Galileos and   40
Madame Curies and Edisons and Gauguins, and our boys (the girls weren't even in on it) would try to be Jesse Owenses and Joe Louises.

Owens and the Brown Bomber were great heroes in our world, but what school official in the white-goddom of Little Rock had the right to decide that those two men must be our only heroes? Who decided that for Henry Reed to become a scientist he had to work like George Washington Carver, as a bootblack, to buy a lousy microscope? Bailey was obviously always going to be too small to be an athlete, so which concrete angel glued to what country seat had decided that if my brother wanted to become a lawyer he had to first pay

penance for his skin by picking cotton and hoeing corn and studying correspondence books at night for twenty years?

The man's dead words fell like bricks around the auditorium and too many
settled in my belly. Constrained by hard-learned manners I couldn't look behind
me, but to my left and right the proud graduating class of 1940 had dropped
their heads. Every girl in my row had found something new to do with her
handkerchief. Some folded the tiny squares into love knots, some into triangles,
but most were wadding them, then pressing them flat on their yellow laps.

On the dais, the ancient tragedy was being replayed. Professor Parsons
sat, a sculptor's reject, rigid. His large, heavy body seemed devoid of will or
willingness, and his eyes said he was no longer with us. The other teachers examined the flag (which was draped stage right) or their notes, or the windows
which opened on our now-famous playing diamond.

Graduation, the hush-hush magic time of frills and gifts and congratulations and diplomas, was finished for me before my name was called. The accomplishment was nothing. The meticulous maps, drawn in three colors of
ink, learning and spelling decasyllabic words, memorizing the whole of *The
Rape of Lucrece*[3]—it was for nothing. Donleavy had exposed us.

45   We were maids and farmers, handymen and washerwomen, and anything
higher that we aspired to was farcical and presumptuous.

Then I wished that Gabriel Prosser and Nat Turner[4] had killed all white-
folks in their beds and that Abraham Lincoln had been assassinated before the
signing of the Emancipation Proclamation, and that Harriet Tubman[5] had
been killed by that blow on her head and Christopher Columbus had drowned
in the *Santa Maria*.

It was awful to be a Negro and have no control over my life. It was brutal
to be young and already trained to sit quietly and listen to charges brought
against my color with no chance of defense. We should all be dead. I thought
I should like to see us all dead, one on top of the other. A pyramid of flesh with
the whitefolks on the bottom, as the broad base, then the Indians with their
silly tomahawks and teepees and wigwams and treaties, the Negroes with their
mops and recipes and cotton sacks and spirituals sticking out of their mouths.
The Dutch children should all stumble in their wooden shoes and break their
necks. The French should choke to death on the Louisiana Purchase (1803)
while silkworms ate all the Chinese with their stupid pigtails. As a species, we
were an abomination. All of us.

Donleavy was running for election, and assured our parents that if he won
we could count on having the only colored paved playing field in that part of

3. A 1,855-line narrative poem by Shakespeare, which recounts the story of the daughter of a Roman prefect. When she was defiled, she stabbed herself in the presence of
her father and her husband.
4. Gabriel Prosser (c. 1776–1800) and Nat Turner (1800–1831), executed leaders of
slave rebellions in Virginia.
5. Black abolitionist (c. 1820–1913), known for her work as a "conductor" on the Underground Railroad.

Arkansas. Also—he never looked up to acknowledge the grunts of acceptance—also, we were bound to get some new equipment for the home economics building and the workshop.

He finished, and since there was no need to give any more than the most perfunctory thank-you's, he nodded to the men on the stage, and the tall white man who was never introduced joined him at the door. They left with the attitude that now they were off to something really important. (The graduation ceremonies at Lafayette County Training School had been a mere preliminary.)

The ugliness they left was palpable. An uninvited guest who wouldn't   50
leave. The choir was summoned and sang a modern arrangement of "Onward, Christian Soldiers," with new words pertaining to graduates seeking their place in the world. But it didn't work. Elouise, the daughter of the Baptist minister, recited "Invictus,"[6] and I could have cried at the impertinence of "I am the master of my fate, I am the captain of my soul."

My name had lost its ring of familiarity and I had to be nudged to go and receive my diploma. All my preparations had fled. I neither marched up to the stage like a conquering Amazon, nor did I look in the audience for Bailey's nod of approval. Marguerite Johnson, I heard the name again, my honors were read, there were noises in the audience of appreciation, and I took my place on the stage as rehearsed.

I thought about colors I hated: ecru, puce, lavender, beige and black.

There was shuffling and rustling around me, then Henry Reed was giving his valedictory address, "To Be or Not to Be." Hadn't he heard the white-folks? We couldn't *be,* so the question was a waste of time. Henry's voice came out clear and strong. I feared to look at him. Hadn't he got the message? There was no "nobler in the mind" for Negroes because the world didn't think we had minds, and they let us know it. "Outrageous fortune"? Now, that was a joke. When the ceremony was over I had to tell Henry Reed some things. That is, if I still cared. Not "rub," Henry, "erase." "Ah, there's the erase." Us.

Henry had been a good student in elocution. His voice rose on tides of promise and fell on waves of warnings. The English teacher had helped him to create a sermon winging through Hamlet's soliloquy. To be a man, a doer, a builder, a leader, or to be a tool, an unfunny joke, a crusher of funky toadstools. I marveled that Henry could go through with the speech as if we had a choice.

I had been listening and silently rebutting each sentence with my eyes   55
closed; then there was a hush, which in an audience warns that something unplanned is happening. I looked up and saw Henry Reed, the conservative, the proper, the A student, turn his back to the audience and turn to us (the proud graduating class of 1940) and sing, nearly speaking,

> "Lift ev'ry voice and sing
> Till earth and heaven ring
> Ring with the harmonies of Liberty . . ."

6. An inspirational poem by William Ernest Henley (1849–1903), once very popular for occasions such as this one.

It was the poem written by James Weldon Johnson. It was the music composed by J. Rosamond Johnson. It was the Negro national anthem. Out of habit we were singing it.

Our mothers and fathers stood in the dark hall and joined the hymn of encouragement. A kindergarten teacher led the small children onto the stage and the buttercups and daisies and bunny rabbits marked time and tried to follow:

> "Stony the road we trod
> Bitter the chastening rod
> Felt in the days when hope, unborn, had died.
> Yet with a steady beat
> Have not our weary feet
> Come to the place for which our fathers sighed?"

Each child I knew had learned that song with his ABC's and along with "Jesus Loves Me This I Know." But I personally had never heard it before. Never heard the words, despite the thousands of times I had sung them. Never thought they had anything to do with me.

On the other hand, the words of Patrick Henry had made such an impression on me that I had been able to stretch myself tall and trembling and say, "I know not what course others may take, but as for me, give me liberty or give me death."

And now I heard, really for the first time:

> "We have come over a way that with tears
>   has been watered,
> We have come, treading our path through
>   the blood of the slaughtered."

60   While echoes of the song shivered in the air, Henry Reed bowed his head, said "Thank you," and returned to his place in the line. The tears that slipped down many faces were not wiped away in shame.

We were on top again. As always, again. We survived. The depths had been icy and dark, but now a bright sun spoke to our souls. I was no longer simply a member of the proud graduating class of 1940; I was a proud member of the wonderful, beautiful Negro race.

Oh, Black known and unknown poets, how often have your auctioned pains sustained us? Who will compute the lonely nights made less lonely by your songs, or the empty pots made less tragic by your tales?

If we were a people much given to revealing secrets, we might raise monuments and sacrifice to the memories of our poets, but slavery cured us of that weakness. It may be enough, however, to have it said that we survive in exact relationship to the dedication of our poets (include preachers, musicians and blues singers).

QUESTIONS

1. Presumably, all of Angelou's readers would have witnessed a graduation ceremony and brought their memories to her essay. How does she fulfill the reader's expectations for what graduation includes? How does she surprise us with details we don't expect?

2. In paragraph 43 Angelou writes that "the ancient tragedy was being replayed." What does she mean? How does her essay help to resist the tragic script?

3. Write a personal essay about an event you anticipated hopefully but that did not fulfill your expectations, incorporating an explanation of your disappointment into your account, as Angelou does.

LARS EIGHNER   *On Dumpster Diving*

LONG BEFORE I began Dumpster diving I was impressed with Dumpsters, enough so that I wrote the Merriam-Webster[1] research service to discover what I could about the word *Dumpster*. I learned from them that it is a proprietary word belonging to the Dempster Dumpster company. Since then I have dutifully capitalized the word, although it was lowercased in almost all the citations Merriam-Webster photocopied for me. Dempster's word is too apt. I have never heard these things called anything but Dumpsters. I do not know anyone who knows the generic name for these objects. From time to time I have heard a wino or hobo give some corrupted credit to the original and call them Dipsy Dumpsters.

I began Dumpster diving about a year before I became homeless.

I prefer the word *scavenging* and use the word *scrounging* when I mean to be obscure. I have heard people, evidently meaning to be polite, use the word *foraging,* but I prefer to reserve that word for gathering nuts and berries and such, which I do also according to the season and the opportunity. *Dumpster diving* seems to me to be a little too cute and, in my case, inaccurate because I lack the athletic ability to lower myself into the Dumpsters as the true divers do, much to their increased profit.

I like the frankness of the word *scavenging,* which I can hardly think of without picturing a big black snail on an aquarium wall. I live from the refuse of others. I am a scavenger. I think it a sound and honorable niche, although if I could I would naturally prefer to live the comfortable consumer life, perhaps—and only perhaps—as a slightly less wasteful consumer, owing to what I have learned as a scavenger.

While Lizbeth[2] and I were still living in the shack on Avenue B as my sav-   5

From Travels with Lizbeth *(1993), an account of Eighner's life as a homeless person.*

1. A large publisher of dictionaries.
2. The author's dog.

ings ran out, I put almost all my sporadic income into rent. The necessities of daily life I began to extract from Dumpsters. Yes, we ate from them. Except for jeans, all my clothes came from Dumpsters. Boom boxes, candles, bedding, toilet paper, a virgin male love doll, medicine, books, a typewriter, dishes, furnishings, and change, sometimes amounting to many dollars—I acquired many things from the Dumpsters.

I have learned much as a scavenger. I mean to put some of what I have learned down here, beginning with the practical art of Dumpster diving and proceeding to the abstract.

What is safe to eat?

After all, the finding of objects is becoming something of an urban art. Even respectable employed people will sometimes find something tempting sticking out of a Dumpster or standing beside one. Quite a number of people, not all of them of the bohemian type, are willing to brag that they found this or that piece in the trash. But eating from Dumpsters is what separates the dilettanti from the professionals. Eating safely from the Dumpsters involves three principles: using the senses and common sense to evaluate the condition of the found materials, knowing the Dumpsters of a given area and checking them regularly, and seeking always to answer the question, "Why was this discarded?"

Perhaps everyone who has a kitchen and a regular supply of groceries has, at one time or another, made a sandwich and eaten half of it before discovering mold on the bread or got a mouthful of milk before realizing the milk had turned. Nothing of the sort is likely to happen to a Dumpster diver because he is constantly reminded that most food is discarded for a reason. Yet a lot of perfectly good food can be found in Dumpsters.

10   Canned goods, for example, turn up fairly often in the Dumpsters I frequent. All except the most phobic people would be willing to eat from a can, even if it came from a Dumpster. Canned goods are among the safest of foods to be found in Dumpsters but are not utterly foolproof.

Although very rare with modern canning methods, botulism is a possibility. Most other forms of food poisoning seldom do lasting harm to a healthy person, but botulism is almost certainly fatal and often the first symptom is death. Except for carbonated beverages, all canned goods should contain a slight vacuum and suck air when first punctured. Bulging, rusty, and dented cans and cans that spew when punctured should be avoided, especially when the contents are not very acidic or syrupy.

Heat can break down the botulin, but this requires much more cooking than most people do to canned goods. To the extent that botulism occurs at all, of course, it can occur in cans on pantry shelves as well as in cans from Dumpsters. Need I say that home-canned goods are simply too risky to be recommended.

From time to time one of my companions, aware of the source of my provisions, will ask, "Do you think these crackers are really safe to eat?" For some reason it is most often the crackers they ask about.

This question has always made me angry. Of course I would not offer my companion anything I had doubts about. But more than that, I wonder why he cannot evaluate the condition of the crackers for himself. I have no special knowledge and I have been wrong before. Since he knows where the food comes from, it seems to me he ought to assume some of the responsibility for deciding what he will put in his mouth. For myself I have few qualms about dry foods such as crackers, cookies, cereal, chips, and pasta if they are free of visible contaminates and still dry and crisp. Most often such things are found in the original packaging, which is not so much a positive sign as it is the absence of a negative one.

Raw fruits and vegetables with intact skins seem perfectly safe to me, ex- 15 cluding of course the obviously rotten. Many are discarded for minor imperfections that can be pared away. Leafy vegetables, grapes, cauliflower, broccoli, and similar things may be contaminated by liquids and may be impractical to wash.

Candy, especially hard candy, is usually safe if it has not drawn ants. Chocolate is often discarded only because it has become discolored as the cocoa butter de-emulsified. Candying, after all, is one method of food preservation because pathogens do not like very sugary substances.

All of these foods might be found in any Dumpster and can be evaluated with some confidence largely on the basis of appearance. Beyond these are foods that cannot be correctly evaluated without additional information.

I began scavenging by pulling pizzas out of the Dumpster behind a pizza delivery shop. In general, prepared food requires caution, but in this case I knew when the shop closed and went to the Dumpster as soon as the last of the help left.

Such shops often get prank orders; both the orders and the products made to fill them are called *bogus*. Because help seldom stays long at these places, pizzas are often made with the wrong topping, refused on delivery for being cold, or baked incorrectly. The products to be discarded are boxed up because inventory is kept by counting boxes: A boxed pizza can be written off; an unboxed pizza does not exist.

I never placed a bogus order to increase the supply of pizzas and I believe 20 no one else was scavenging in this Dumpster. But the people in the shop became suspicious and began to retain their garbage in the shop overnight. While it lasted I had a steady supply of fresh, sometimes warm pizza. Because I knew the Dumpster I knew the source of the pizza, and because I visited the Dumpster regularly I knew what was fresh and what was yesterday's.

The area I frequent is inhabited by many affluent college students. I am not here by chance; the Dumpsters in this area are very rich. Students throw out many good things, including food. In particular they tend to throw everything out when they move at the end of a semester, before and after breaks, and around midterm, when many of them despair of college. So I find it advantageous to keep an eye on the academic calendar.

Students throw food away around breaks because they do not know whether it has spoiled or will spoil before they return. A typical discard is a half jar of peanut butter. In fact, nonorganic peanut butter does not require refrigeration and is unlikely to spoil in any reasonable time. The student does not know that, and since it is Daddy's money, the student decides not to take a chance. Opened containers require caution and some attention to the question, "Why was this discarded?" But in the case of discards from student apartments, the answer may be that the item was thrown out through carelessness, ignorance, or wastefulness. This can sometimes be deduced when the item is found with many others, including some that are obviously perfectly good.

Some students, and others, approach defrosting a freezer by chucking out the whole lot. Not only do the circumstances of such a find tell the story, but also the mass of frozen goods stays cold for a long time and items may be found still frozen or freshly thawed.

Yogurt, cheese, and sour cream are items that are often thrown out while they are still good. Occasionally I find a cheese with a spot of mold, which of course I just pare off, and because it is obvious why such a cheese was discarded, I treat it with less suspicion than an apparently perfect cheese found in similar circumstances. Yogurt is often discarded, still sealed, only because the expiration date on the carton had passed. This is one of my favorite finds because yogurt will keep for several days, even in warm weather.

Students throw out canned goods and staples at the end of semesters and when they give up college at midterm. Drugs, pornography, spirits, and the like are often discarded when parents are expected—Dad's Day, for example. And spirits also turn up after big party weekends, presumably discarded by the newly reformed. Wine and spirits, of course, keep perfectly well even once opened, but the same cannot be said of beer.

My test for carbonated soft drinks is whether they still fizz vigorously. Many juices or other beverages are too acidic or too syrupy to cause much concern, provided they are not visibly contaminated. I have discovered nasty molds in vegetable juices, even when the product was found under its original seal; I recommend that such products be decanted slowly into a clear glass. Liquids always require some care. One hot day I found a large jug of Pat O'Brien's Hurricane mix. The jug had been opened but was still ice cold. I drank three large glasses before it became apparent to me that someone had added the rum to the mix, and not a little rum. I never tasted the rum, and by the time I began to feel the effects I had already ingested a very large quantity of the beverage. Some divers would have considered this a boon, but being suddenly intoxicated in a public place in the early afternoon is not my idea of a good time.

I have heard of people maliciously contaminating discarded food and even handouts, but mostly I have heard of this from people with vivid imaginations who have had no experience with the Dumpsters themselves. Just before the pizza shop stopped discarding its garbage at night, jalapeños began showing up on most of the thrown-out pizzas. If indeed this was meant to discourage me, it was a wasted effort because I am a native Texan.

For myself, I avoid game, poultry, pork, and egg-based foods, whether I find them raw or cooked. I seldom have the means to cook what I find, but when I do I avail myself of plentiful supplies of beef, which is often in very good condition. I suppose fish becomes disagreeable before it becomes dangerous. Lizbeth is happy to have any such thing that is past its prime and, in fact, does not recognize fish as food until it is quite strong.

Home leftovers, as opposed to surpluses from restaurants, are very often bad. Evidently, especially among students, there is a common type of personality that carefully wraps up even the smallest leftover and shoves it into the back of the refrigerator for six months or so before discarding it. Characteristic of this type are the reused jars and margarine tubs to which the remains are committed. I avoid ethnic foods I am unfamiliar with. If I do not know what it is supposed to look like when it is good, I cannot be certain I will be able to tell if it is bad.

No matter how careful I am I still get dysentery at least once a month, oftener in warm weather. I do not want to paint too romantic a picture. Dumpster diving has serious drawbacks as a way of life.

I learned to scavenge gradually, on my own. Since then I have initiated several companions into the trade. I have learned that there is a predictable series of stages a person goes through in learning to scavenge.

At first the new scavenger is filled with disgust and self-loathing. He is ashamed of being seen and may lurk around, trying to duck behind things, or he may try to dive at night. (In fact, most people instinctively look away from a scavenger. By skulking around, the novice calls attention to himself and arouses suspicion. Diving at night is ineffective and needlessly messy.)

Every grain of rice seems to be a maggot. Everything seems to stink. He can wipe the egg yolk off the found can, but he cannot erase from his mind the stigma of eating garbage.

That stage passes with experience. The scavenger finds a pair of running shoes that fit and look and smell brand-new. He finds a pocket calculator in perfect working order. He finds pristine ice cream, still frozen, more than he can eat or keep. He begins to understand: People throw away perfectly good stuff, a lot of perfectly good stuff.

At this stage, Dumpster shyness begins to dissipate. The diver, after all, has the last laugh. He is finding all manner of good things that are his for the taking. Those who disparage his profession are the fools, not he.

He may begin to hang on to some perfectly good things for which he has neither a use nor a market. Then he begins to take note of the things that are not perfectly good but are nearly so. He mates a Walkman with broken earphones and one that is missing a battery cover. He picks up things that he can repair.

At this stage he may become lost and never recover. Dumpsters are full of things of some potential value to someone and also of things that never have much intrinsic value but are interesting. All the Dumpster divers I have known come to the point of trying to acquire everything they touch. Why not take it, they reason, since it is all free? This is, of course, hopeless. Most divers come to realize that they must restrict themselves to items of relatively immediate utility. But in some cases the diver simply cannot control himself. I have met several of these pack-rat types. Their ideas of the values of various pieces of junk verge on the psychotic. Every bit of glass may be a diamond, they think, and all that glisters, gold.

I tend to gain weight when I am scavenging. Partly this is because I always find far more pizza and doughnuts than water-packed tuna, nonfat yogurt, and fresh vegetables. Also I have not developed much faith in the reliability of Dumpsters as a food source, although it has been proven to me many times. I tend to eat as if I have no idea where my next meal is coming from. But mostly I just hate to see food go to waste and so I eat much more than I should. Something like this drives the obsession to collect junk.

As for collecting objects, I usually restrict myself to collecting one kind of small object at a time, such as pocket calculators, sunglasses, or campaign buttons. To live on the street I must anticipate my needs to a certain extent: I must pick up and save warm bedding I find in August because it will not be found in Dumpsters in November. As I have no access to health care, I often hoard essential drugs, such as antibiotics and antihistamines. (This course can be recommended only to those with some grounding in pharmacology. Antibiotics, for example, even when indicated are worse than useless if taken in insufficient amounts.) But even if I had a home with extensive storage space, I could not save everything that might be valuable in some contingency.

40   I have proprietary feelings about my Dumpsters. As I have mentioned, it is no accident that I scavenge from ones where good finds are common. But my limited experience with Dumpsters in other areas suggests to me that even in poorer areas, Dumpsters, if attended with sufficient diligence, can be made to yield a livelihood. The rich students discard perfectly good kiwifruit; poorer people discard perfectly good apples. Slacks and Polo shirts are found in the one place; jeans and T-shirts in the other. The population of competitors rather than the affluence of the dumpers most affects the feasibility of survival by scavenging. The large number of competitors is what puts me off the idea of trying to scavenge in places like Los Angeles.

Curiously, I do not mind my direct competition, other scavengers, so much as I hate the can scroungers.

People scrounge cans because they have to have a little cash. I have tried scrounging cans with an able-bodied companion. Afoot a can scrounger simply cannot make more than a few dollars a day. One can extract the necessities of life from the Dumpsters directly with far less effort than would be required to accumulate the equivalent value in cans. (These observations may not hold in places with container redemption laws.)

Can scroungers, then, are people who must have small amounts of cash. These are drug addicts and winos, mostly the latter because the amounts of cash are so small. Spirits and drugs do, like all other commodities, turn up in Dumpsters and the scavenger will from time to time have a half bottle of a rather good wine with his dinner. But the wino cannot survive on these occasional finds; he must have his daily dose to stave off the DTs. All the cans he can carry will buy about three bottles of Wild Irish Rose.

I do not begrudge them the cans, but can scroungers tend to tear up the

Dumpsters, mixing the contents and littering the area. They become so specialized that they can see only cans. They earn my contempt by passing up change, canned goods, and readily hockable items.

There are precious few courtesies among scavengers. But it is common 45 practice to set aside surplus items: pairs of shoes, clothing, canned goods, and such. A true scavenger hates to see good stuff go to waste, and what he cannot use he leaves in good condition in plain sight.

Can scroungers lay waste to everything in their path and will stir one of a pair of good shoes to the bottom of a Dumpster, to be lost or ruined in the muck. Can scroungers will even go through individual garbage cans, something I have never seen a scavenger do.

Individual garbage cans are set out on the public easement only on garbage days. On other days going through them requires trespassing close to a dwelling. Going through individual garbage cans without scattering litter is almost impossible. Litter is likely to reduce the public's tolerance of scavenging. Individual cans are simply not as productive as Dumpsters; people in houses and duplexes do not move so often and for some reason do not tend to discard as much useful material. Moreover, the time required to go through one garbage can that serves one household is not much less than the time required to go through a Dumpster that contains the refuse of twenty apartments.

But my strongest reservation about going through individual garbage cans is that this seems to me a very personal kind of invasion to which I would object if I were a householder. Although many things in Dumpsters are obviously meant never to come to light, a Dumpster is somehow less personal.

I avoid trying to draw conclusions about the people who dump in the Dumpsters I frequent. I think it would be unethical to do so, although I know many people will find the idea of scavenger ethics too funny for words.

Dumpsters contain bank statements, correspondence, and other docu- 50 ments, just as anyone might expect. But there are also less obvious sources of information. Pill bottles, for example. The labels bear the name of the patient, the name of the doctor, and the name of the drug. AIDS drugs and anti-psychotic medicines, to name but two groups, are specific and are seldom prescribed for any other disorders. The plastic compacts for birth-control pills usually have complete label information.

Despite all of this sensitive information, I have had only one apartment resident object to my going through the Dumpster. In that case it turned out the resident was a university athlete who was taking bets and who was afraid I would turn up his wager slips.

Occasionally a find tells a story. I once found a small paper bag containing some unused condoms, several partial tubes of flavored sexual lubricants, a partially used compact of birth-control pills, and the torn pieces of a picture of a young man. Clearly she was through with him and planning to give up sex altogether.

Dumpster things are often sad—abandoned teddy bears, shredded wedding books, despaired-of sales kits. I find many pets lying in state in Dumpsters. Although I hope to get off the streets so that Lizbeth can have a long and comfortable old age, I know this hope is not very realistic. So I suppose when her time comes she too will go into a Dumpster. I will have no better place for her. And after all, it is fitting, since for most of her life her livelihood has come from the Dumpster. When she finds something I think is safe that has been spilled from a Dumpster, I let her have it. She already knows the route around the best ones. I like to think that if she survives me she will have a chance of evading the dog catcher and of finding her sustenance on the route.

Silly vanities also come to rest in the Dumpsters. I am a rather accomplished needleworker. I get a lot of material from the Dumpsters. Evidently sorority girls, hoping to impress someone, perhaps themselves, with their mastery of a womanly art, buy a lot of embroider-by-number kits, work a few stitches horribly, and eventually discard the whole mess. I pull out their stitches, turn the canvas over, and work an original design. Do not think I refrain from chuckling as I make gifts from these kits.

55   I find diaries and journals. I have often thought of compiling a book of literary found objects. And perhaps I will one day. But what I find is hopelessly commonplace and bad without being, even unconsciously, camp. College students also discard their papers. I am horrified to discover the kind of paper that now merits an A in an undergraduate course. I am grateful, however, for the number of good books and magazines the students throw out.

In the area I know best I have never discovered vermin in the Dumpsters, but there are two kinds of kitty surprise. One is alley cats whom I meet as they leap, claws first, out of Dumpsters. This is especially thrilling when I have Lizbeth in tow. The other kind of kitty surprise is a plastic garbage bag filled with some ponderous, amorphous mass. This always proves to be used cat litter.

City bees harvest doughnut glaze and this makes the Dumpster at the doughnut shop more interesting. My faith in the instinctive wisdom of animals is always shaken whenever I see Lizbeth attempt to catch a bee in her mouth, which she does whenever bees are present. Evidently some birds find Dumpsters profitable, for birdie surprise is almost as common as kitty surprise of the first kind. In hunting season all kinds of small game turn up in Dumpsters, some of it, sadly, not entirely dead. Curiously, summer and winter, maggots are uncommon.

The worst of the living and near-living hazards of the Dumpsters are the fire ants. The food they claim is not much of a loss, but they are vicious and aggressive. It is very easy to brush against some surface of the Dumpster and pick up half a dozen or more fire ants, usually in some sensitive area such as the underarm. One advantage of bringing Lizbeth along as I make Dumpster rounds is that, for obvious reasons, she is very alert to ground-based fire ants. When Lizbeth recognizes a fire-ant infestation around our feet, she does the Dance of the Zillion Fire Ants. I have learned not to ignore this warning from Lizbeth, whether I perceive the tiny ants or not, but to remove ourselves at Lizbeth's first pas de bourrée. All the more so because the ants are the worst in the summer months when I wear flip-flops if I have them. (Perhaps someone will misunderstand this. Lizbeth does the Dance of the Zillion Fire Ants when she recognizes more fire ants than she cares to eat, not when she is being bit-ten. Since I have learned to react promptly, she does not get bitten at all. It is the isolated patrol of fire ants that falls in Lizbeth's range that deserves pity. She finds them quite tasty.)

By far the best way to go through a Dumpster is to lower yourself into it. Most of the good stuff tends to settle at the bottom because it is usually weightier than the rubbish. My more athletic companions have often demon-strated to me that they can extract much good material from a Dumpster I have already been over.

To those psychologically or physically unprepared to enter a Dumpster, I recommend a stout stick, preferably with some barb or hook at one end. The hook can be used to grab plastic garbage bags. When I find canned goods or other objects loose at the bottom of a Dumpster, I lower a bag into it, roll the desired object into the bag, and then hoist the bag out—a procedure more eas-ily described than executed. Much Dumpster diving is a matter of experience for which nothing will do except practice.

Dumpster diving is outdoor work, often surprisingly pleasant. It is not en-tirely predictable; things of interest turn up every day and some days there are finds of great value. I am always very pleased when I can turn up exactly the thing I most wanted to find. Yet in spite of the element of chance, scavenging more than most other pursuits tends to yield returns in some proportion to the effort and intelligence brought to bear. It is very sweet to turn up a few dollars in change from a Dumpster that has just been gone over by a wino.

The land is now covered with cities. The cities are full of Dumpsters. If a member of the canine race is ever able to know what it is doing, then Lizbeth knows that when we go around to the Dumpsters, we are hunting. I think of scavenging as a modern form of self-reliance. In any event, after having sur-vived nearly ten years of government service, where everything is geared to the lowest common denominator, I find it refreshing to have work that rewards initiative and effort. Certainly I would be happy to have a sinecure again, but I am no longer heartbroken that I left one.

I find from the experience of scavenging two rather deep lessons. The first is to take what you can use and let the rest go by. I have come to think that there is no value in the abstract. A thing I cannot use or make useful, perhaps by trading, has no value however rare or fine it may be. I mean useful in a broad sense—some art I would find useful and some otherwise.

I was shocked to realize that some things are not worth acquiring, but now I think it is so. Some material things are white elephants that eat up the possessor's substance. The second lesson is the transience of material being. This has not quite converted me to a dualist, but it has made some headway in that direction. I do not suppose that ideas are immortal, but certainly mental things are longer lived than other material things.

Once I was the sort of person who invests objects with sentimental value. Now I no longer have those objects, but I have the sentiments yet.

Many times in our travels I have lost everything but the clothes I was wearing and Lizbeth. The things I find in Dumpsters, the love letters and rag dolls of so many lives, remind me of this lesson. Now I hardly pick up a thing without envisioning the time I will cast it aside. This I think is a healthy state of mind. Almost everything I have now has already been cast out at least once, proving that what I own is valueless to someone.

Anyway, I find my desire to grab for the gaudy bauble has been largely sated. I think this is an attitude I share with the very wealthy—we both know there is plenty more where what we have came from. Between us are the rat-race millions who nightly scavenge the cable channels looking for they know not what.

I am sorry for them.

QUESTIONS

1. How does Eighner organize his essay? What does such an organization imply?

2. Eighner's simple, understated tone suggests that anyone can adapt to Dumpster diving with a little practice. Why do you think he uses such a tone?

3. Write about someone who does what Eighner deplores in his closing paragraphs, "invests objects with sentimental value." Let your description reveal whether or not you agree with Eighner.

NANCY MAIRS   *On Being a Cripple*

> To escape is nothing. Not to escape is nothing.
> —LOUISE BOGAN

THE OTHER DAY I was thinking of writing an essay on being a cripple. I was thinking hard in one of the stalls of the women's room in my office building, as I was shoving my shirt into my jeans and tugging up my zipper. Preoccupied, I flushed, picked up my book bag, took my cane down from the hook, and unlatched the door. So many movements unbalanced me, and as I pulled the door open I fell over backward, landing fully clothed on the toilet seat with my legs splayed in front of me: the old beetle-on-its-back routine. Saturday afternoon, the building deserted, I was free to laugh aloud as I wriggled back to my feet, my voice bouncing off the yellowish tiles from all directions. Had anyone been there with me, I'd have been still and faint and hot with chagrin. I decided that it was high time to write the essay.

First, the matter of semantics. I am a cripple. I choose this word to name

From Plaintext *(1986), a collection of personal essays, many about Mairs's life with multiple sclerosis.*

me. I choose from among several possibilities, the most common of which are "handicapped" and "disabled." I made the choice a number of years ago, without thinking, unaware of my motives for doing so. Even now, I'm not sure what those motives are, but I recognize that they are complex and not entirely flattering. People—crippled or not—wince at the word "cripple," as they do not at "handicapped" or "disabled." Perhaps I want them to wince. I want them to see me as a tough customer, one to whom the fates/gods/viruses have not been kind, but who can face the brutal truth of her existence squarely. As a cripple, I swagger.

But, to be fair to myself, a certain amount of honesty underlies my choice. "Cripple" seems to me a clean word, straightforward and precise. It has an honorable history, having made its first appearance in the Lindisfarne Gospel[1] in the tenth century. As a lover of words, I like the accuracy with which it describes my condition: I have lost the full use of my limbs. "Disabled," by contrast, suggests any incapacity, physical or mental. And I certainly don't like "handicapped," which implies that I have deliberately been put at a disadvantage, by whom I can't imagine (my God is not a Handicapper General), in order to equalize chances in the great race of life. These words seem to me to be moving away from my condition, to be widening the gap between word and reality. Most remote is the recently coined euphemism "differently abled," which partakes of the same semantic hopefulness that transformed countries from "undeveloped" to "underdeveloped," then to "less developed," and finally to "developing" nations. People have continued to starve in those countries during the shift. Some realities do not obey the dictates of language.

Mine is one of them. Whatever you call me, I remain crippled. But I don't care what you call me, so long as it isn't "differently abled," which strikes me as pure verbal garbage designed, by its ability to describe anyone, to describe no one. I subscribe to George Orwell's thesis that "the slovenliness of our language makes it easier for us to have foolish thoughts."[2] And I refuse to participate in the degeneration of the language to the extent that I deny that I have lost anything in the course of this calamitous disease; I refuse to pretend that the only differences between you and me are the various ordinary ones that distinguish any one person from another. But call me "disabled" or "handicapped" if you like. I have long since grown accustomed to them; and if they are vague, at least they hint at the truth. Moreover, I use them myself. Society is no readier to accept crippledness than to accept death, war, sex, sweat, or wrinkles. I would never refer to another person as a cripple. It is the word I use to name only myself.

I haven't always been crippled, a fact for which I am soundly grateful. To be whole of limb is, I know from experience, infinitely more pleasant and use-

5

1. Illustrated manuscript of the four gospels of the New Testament done by Irish monks; English commentaries were added in the tenth century.

2. A quotation from "Politics and the English Language" (included in the section "Language and Communication") by Orwell (1903–1950), British essayist and novelist, famous for his political commentaries.

ful than to be crippled; and if that knowledge leaves one open to bitterness at my loss, the physical soundness I once enjoyed (though I did not enjoy it half enough) is well worth the occasional stab of regret. Though never any good at sports, I was a normally active child and young adult. I climbed trees, played hopscotch, jumped rope, skated, swam, rode my bicycle, sailed. I despised team sports, spending some of the wretchedest afternoons of my life, sweaty and humiliated, behind a field-hockey stick and under a basketball hoop. I tramped alone for miles along the bridle paths that webbed the woods behind the house I grew up in. I swayed through countless dim hours in the arms of one man or another under the scattered shot of light from mirrored balls, and gyrated through countless more as Tab Hunter and Johnny Mathis[3] gave way to the Rolling Stones, Creedence Clearwater Revival, Cream. I walked down the aisle. I pushed baby carriages, changed tires in the rain, marched for peace.

When I was twenty-eight I started to trip and drop things. What at first seemed my natural clumsiness soon became too pronounced to shrug off. I consulted a neurologist, who told me that I had a brain tumor. A battery of tests, increasingly disagreeable, revealed no tumor. About a year and a half later I developed a blurred spot in one eye. I had, at last, the episodes "disseminated in space and time" requisite for a diagnosis: multiple sclerosis. I have never been sorry for the doctor's initial misdiagnosis, however. For almost a week, until the negative results of the tests were in, I thought that I was going to die right away. Every day for the past nearly ten years, then, has been a kind of gift. I accept all gifts.

Multiple sclerosis is a chronic degenerative disease of the central nervous system, in which the myelin that sheathes the nerves is somehow eaten away and scar tissue forms in its place, interrupting the nerves' signals. During its course, which is unpredictable and uncontrollable, one may lose vision, hearing, speech, the ability to walk, control of bladder and/or bowels, strength in any or all extremities, sensitivity to touch, vibration, and/or pain, potency, coordination of movements—the list of possibilities is lengthy and, yes, horrifying. One may also lose one's sense of humor. That's the easiest to lose and the hardest to survive without.

In the past ten years, I have sustained some of these losses. Characteristic of MS are sudden attacks, called exacerbations, followed by remissions, and these I have not had. Instead, my disease has been slowly progressive. My left leg is now so weak that I walk with the aid of a brace and a cane; and for distances I use an Amigo, a variation on the electric wheelchair that looks rather like an electrified kiddie car. I no longer have much use of my left hand. Now my right side is weakening as well. I still have the blurred spot in my right eye. Overall, though, I've been lucky so far. My world has, of necessity, been circumscribed by my losses, but the terrain left me has been ample enough for me to continue many of the activities that absorb me: writing,

3. Tab Hunter (b. 1931), American actor and singer popular in the 1960s; Johnny Mathis (b. 1935), American singer popular in the 1950s and 1960s and well known for his love ballads.

teaching, raising children and cats and plants and snakes, reading, speaking publicly about MS and depression, even playing bridge with people patient and honorable enough to let me scatter cards every which way without sneaking a peek.

Lest I begin to sound like Pollyanna, however, let me say that I don't like having MS. I hate it. My life holds realities—harsh ones, some of them—that no right-minded human being ought to accept without grumbling. One of them is fatigue. I know of no one with MS who does not complain of bone-weariness; in a disease that presents an astonishing variety of symptoms, fatigue seems to be a common factor. I wake up in the morning feeling the way most people do at the end of a bad day, and I take it from there. As a result, I spend a lot of time *in extremis*[4] and, impatient with limitation, I tend to ignore my fatigue until my body breaks down in some way and forces rest. Then I miss picnics, dinner parties, poetry readings, the brief visits of old friends from out of town. The offspring of a puritanical tradition of exceptional venerability, I cannot view these lapses without shame. My life often seems a series of small failures to do as I ought.

I lead, on the whole, an ordinary life, probably rather like the one I would have led had I not had MS. I am lucky that my predilections were already solitary, sedentary, and bookish—unlike the world-famous French cellist I have read about, or the young woman I talked with one long afternoon who wanted only to be a jockey. I had just begun graduate school when I found out something was wrong with me, and I have remained, interminably, a graduate student. Perhaps I would not have if I'd thought I had the stamina to return to a full-time job as a technical editor; but I've enjoyed my studies.

In addition to studying, I teach writing courses. I also teach medical students how to give neurological examinations. I pick up freelance editing jobs here and there. I have raised a foster son and sent him into the world, where he has made me two grandbabies, and I am still escorting my daughter and son through adolescence. I go to Mass every Saturday. I am a superb, if messy, cook. I am also an enthusiastic laundress, capable of sorting a hamper full of clothes into five subtly differentiated piles, but a terrible housekeeper. I can do italic writing and, in an emergency, bathe an oil-soaked cat. I play a fiendish game of Scrabble. When I have the time and the money, I like to sit on my front steps with my husband, drinking Amaretto and smoking a cigar, as we imagine our counterparts in Leningrad and make sure that the sun gets down once more behind the sharp childish scrawl of the Tucson Mountains.

This lively plenty has its bleak complement, of course, in all the things I can no longer do. I will never run again, except in dreams, and one day I may have to write that I will never walk again. I like to go camping, but I can't follow George and the children along the trails that wander out of a campsite through the desert or into the mountains. In fact, even on the level I've learned never to check the weather or try to hold a coherent conversation: I need all my attention for my wayward feet. Of late, I have begun to catch my-

4. Latin for "in the last straits"—here it means "at the limits of endurance."

self wondering how people can propel themselves without canes. With only one usable hand, I have to select my clothing with care not so much for style as for ease of ingress and egress, and even so, dressing can be laborious. I can no longer do fine stitchery, pick up babies, play the piano, braid my hair. I am immobilized by acute attacks of depression, which may or may not be physiologically related to MS but are certainly its logical concomitant.

These two elements, the plenty and the privation, are never pure, nor are the delight and wretchedness that accompany them. Almost every pickle that I get into as a result of my weakness and clumsiness—and I get into plenty—is funny as well as maddening and sometimes painful. I recall one May afternoon when a friend and I were going out for a drink after finishing up at school. As we were climbing into opposite sides of my car, chatting, I tripped and fell, flat and hard, onto the asphalt parking lot, my abrupt departure interrupting him in mid-sentence. "Where'd you go?" he called as he came around the back of the car to find me hauling myself up by the door frame. "Are you all right?" Yes, I told him, I was fine, just a bit rattly, and we drove off to find a shady patio and some beer. When I got home an hour or so later, my daughter greeted me with "What have you done to yourself?" I looked down. One elbow of my white turtleneck with the green froggies, one knee of my white trousers, one white kneesock were blood-soaked. We peeled off the clothes and inspected the damage, which was nasty enough but not alarming. That part wasn't funny: The abrasions took a long time to heal, and one got a little infected. Even so, when I think of my friend talking earnestly, suddenly, to the hot thin air while I dropped from his view as though through a trap door, I find the image as silly as something from a Marx Brothers movie.

I may find it easier than other cripples to amuse myself because I live propped by the acceptance and the assistance and, sometimes, the amusement of those around me. Grocery clerks tear my checks out of my checkbook for me, and sales clerks find chairs to put into dressing rooms when I want to try on clothes. The people I work with make sure I teach at times when I am least likely to be fatigued, in places I can get to, with the materials I need. My students, with one anonymous exception (in an end-of-the-semester evaluation), have been unperturbed by my disability. Some even like it. One was immensely cheered by the information that I paint my own fingernails; she decided, she told me, that if I could go to such trouble over fine details, she could keep on writing essays. I suppose I became some sort of bright-fingered muse. She wrote good essays, too.

15   The most important struts in the framework of my existence, of course, are my husband and children. Dismayingly few marriages survive the MS test, and why should they? Most twenty-two- and nineteen-year-olds, like George and me, can vow in clear conscience, after a childhood of chicken pox and summer colds, to keep one another in sickness and in health so long as they both shall live. Not many are equipped for catastrophe: the dismay, the depression, the extra work, the boredom that a degenerative disease can insinuate into a relationship. And our society, with its emphasis on fun and its association of fun with physical performance, offers little encouragement for

a whole spouse to stay with a crippled partner. Children experience similar stresses when faced with a crippled parent, and they are more helpless, since parents and children can't usually get divorced. They hate, of course, to be different from their peers, and the child whose mother is tacking down the aisle of a school auditorium packed with proud parents like a Cape Cod dinghy in a stiff breeze jolly well stands out in a crowd. Deprived of legal divorce, the child can at least deny the mother's disability, even her existence, forgetting to tell her about recitals and PTA meetings, refusing to accompany her to stores or church or the movies, never inviting friends to the house. Many do.

But I've been limping along for ten years now, and so far George and the children are still at my left elbow, holding tight. Anne and Matthew vacuum floors and dust furniture and haul trash and rake up dog droppings and button my cuffs and bake lasagna and Toll House cookies with just enough grumbling so I know that they don't have brain fever. And far from hiding me, they're forever dragging me by racks of fancy clothes or through teeming school corridors, or welcoming gaggles of friends while I'm wandering through the house in Anne's filmy pink babydoll pajamas. George generally calls before he brings someone home, but he does just as many dumb thankless chores as the children. And they all yell at me, laugh at some of my jokes, write me funny letters when we're apart—in short, treat me as an ordinary human being for whom they have some use. I think they like me. Unless they're faking. . . .

Faking. There's the rub. Tugging at the fringes of my consciousness always is the terror that people are kind to me only because I'm a cripple. My mother almost shattered me once, with that instinct mothers have—blind, I think, in this case, but unerring nonetheless—for striking blows along the fault-lines of their children's hearts, by telling me, in an attack on my selfishness, "We all have to make allowances for you, of course, because of the way you are." From the distance of a couple of years, I have to admit that I haven't any idea just what she meant, and I'm not sure that she knew either. She was awfully angry. But at the time, as the words thudded home, I felt my worst fear, suddenly realized. I could bear being called selfish: I am. But I couldn't bear the corroboration that those around me were doing in fact what I'd always suspected them of doing, professing fondness while silently putting up with me because of the way I am. A cripple. I've been a little cracked ever since.

Along with this fear that people are secretly accepting shoddy goods comes a relentless pressure to please—to prove myself worth the burdens I impose, I guess, or to build a substantial account of goodwill against which I may write drafts in times of need. Part of the pressure arises from social expectations. In our society, anyone who deviates from the norm had better find some way to compensate. Like fat people, who are expected to be jolly, cripples must bear their lot meekly and cheerfully. A grumpy cripple isn't playing by the rules. And much of the pressure is self-generated. Early on I vowed that, if I had to have MS, by God I was going to do it well. This is a class act, ladies and gentlemen. No tears, no recriminations, no faintheartedness.

One way and another, then, I wind up feeling like Tiny Tim,[5] peering over the edge of the table at the Christmas goose, waving my crutch, piping down God's blessing on us all. Only sometimes I don't want to play Tiny Tim. I'd rather be Caliban,[6] a most scurvy monster. Fortunately, at home no one much cares whether I'm a good cripple or a bad cripple as long as I make vichyssoise with fair regularity. One evening several years ago, Anne was reading at the dining-room table while I cooked dinner. As I opened a can of tomatoes, the can slipped in my left hand and juice spattered me and the counter with bloody spots. Fatigued and infuriated, I bellowed, "I'm so sick of being crippled!" Anne glanced at me over the top of her book. "There now," she said, "do you feel better?" "Yes," I said, "yes, I do." She went back to her reading. I felt better. That's about all the attention my scurviness ever gets.

20   Because I hate being crippled, I sometimes hate myself for being a cripple. Over the years I have come to expect—even accept—attacks of violent self-loathing. Luckily, in general our society no longer connects deformity and disease directly with evil (though a charismatic once told me that I have MS because a devil is in me) and so I'm allowed to move largely at will, even among small children. But I'm not sure that this revision of attitude has been particularly helpful. Physical imperfection, even freed of moral disapprobation, still defies and violates the ideal, especially for women, whose confinement in their bodies as objects of desire is far from over. Each age, of course, has its ideal, and I doubt that ours is any better or worse than any other. Today's ideal woman, who lives on the glossy pages of dozens of magazines, seems to be between the ages of eighteen and twenty-five; her hair has body, her teeth flash white, her breath smells minty, her underarms are dry; she has a career but is still a fabulous cook, especially of meals that take less than twenty minutes to prepare; she does not ordinarily appear to have a husband or children; she is trim and deeply tanned; she jogs, swims, plays tennis, rides a bicycle, sails, but does not bowl; she travels widely, even to out-of-the-way places like Finland and Samoa, always in the company of the ideal man, who possesses a nearly identical set of characteristics. There are a few exceptions. Though usually white and often blonde, she may be black, Hispanic, Asian, or Native American, so long as she is unusually sleek. She may be old, provided she is selling a laxative or is Lauren Bacall. If she is selling a detergent, she may be married and have a flock of strikingly messy children. But she is never a cripple.

Like many women I know, I have always had an uneasy relationship with my body. I was not a popular child, largely, I think now, because I was peculiar: intelligent, intense, moody, shy, given to unexpected actions and inexplicable notions and emotions. But as I entered adolescence, I believed myself unpopular because I was homely: my breasts too flat, my mouth too wide, my hips too narrow, my clothing never quite right in fit or style. I was not, in fact, par-

5. A crippled, frail young boy saved by Scrooge's eventual generosity in Charles Dickens's novel *A Christmas Carol.*

6. The monstrous son of the witch Sycorax in Shakespeare's play *The Tempest.*

ticularly ugly, old photographs inform me, though I was well off the ideal; but I carried this sense of self-alienation with me into adulthood, where it regenerated in response to the depredations of MS. Even with my brace I walk with a limp so pronounced that, seeing myself on the videotape of a television program on the disabled, I couldn't believe that anything but an inchworm could make progress humping along like that. My shoulders droop and my pelvis thrusts forward as I try to balance myself upright, throwing my frame into a bony S. As a result of contractures, one shoulder is higher than the other and I carry one arm bent in front of me, the fingers curled into a claw. My left arm and leg have wasted into pipe-stems, and I try always to keep them covered. When I think about how my body must look to others, especially to men, to whom I have been trained to display myself, I feel ludicrous, even loathsome.

At my age, however, I don't spend much time thinking about my appearance. The burning egocentricity of adolescence, which assures one that all the world is looking all the time, has passed, thank God, and I'm generally too caught up in what I'm doing to step back, as I used to, and watch myself as though upon a stage. I'm also too old to believe in the accuracy of self-image. I know that I'm not a hideous crone, that in fact, when I'm rested, well dressed, and well made up, I look fine. The self-loathing I feel is neither physically nor intellectually substantial. What I hate is not me but a disease.

I am not a disease.

And a disease is not—at least not singlehandedly—going to determine who I am, though at first it seemed to be going to. Adjusting to a chronic incurable illness, I have moved through a process similar to that outlined by Elisabeth Kübler-Ross in *On Death and Dying*. The major difference—and it is far more significant than most people recognize—is that I can't be sure of the outcome, as the terminally ill cancer patient can. Research studies indicate that, with proper medical care, I may achieve a "normal" life span. And in our society, with its vision of death as the ultimate evil, worse even than decrepitude, the response to such news is, "Oh well, at least you're not going to *die*." Are there worse things than dying? I think that there may be.

I think of two women I know, both with MS, both enough older than I to have served me as models. One took to her bed several years ago and has been there ever since. Although she can sit in a high-backed wheelchair, because she is incontinent she refuses to go out at all, even though incontinence pants, which are readily available at any pharmacy, could protect her from embarrassment. Instead, she stays at home and insists that her husband, a small quiet man, a retired civil servant, stay there with her except for a quick weekly foray to the supermarket. The other woman, whose illness was diagnosed when she was eighteen, a nursing student engaged to a young doctor, finished her training, married her doctor, accompanied him to Germany when he was in the service, bore three sons and a daughter, now grown and gone. When she can, she travels with her husband; she plays bridge, embroiders, swims regularly; she works, like me, as a symptomatic-patient instructor of medical students in neurology. Guess which woman I hope to be.

At the beginning, I thought about having MS almost incessantly. And because of the unpredictable course of the disease, my thoughts were always terrified. Each night I'd get into bed wondering whether I'd get out again the next morning, whether I'd be able to see, to speak, to hold a pen between my fingers. Knowing that the day might come when I'd be physically incapable of killing myself, I thought perhaps I ought to do so right away, while I still had the strength. Gradually I came to understand that the Nancy who might one day lie inert under a bedsheet, arms and legs paralyzed, unable to feed or bathe herself, unable to reach out for a gun, a bottle of pills, was not the Nancy I was at present, and that I could not presume to make decisions for that future Nancy, who might well not want in the least to die. Now the only provision I've made for the future Nancy is that when the time comes—and it is likely to come in the form of pneumonia, friend to the weak and the old—I am not to be treated with machines and medications. If she is unable to communicate by then, I hope she will be satisfied with these terms.

Thinking all the time about having MS grew tiresome and intrusive, especially in the large and tragic mode in which I was accustomed to considering my plight. Months and even years went by without catastrophe (at least without one related to MS), and really I was awfully busy, what with George and children and snakes and students and poems, and I hadn't the time, let alone the inclination, to devote myself to being a disease. Too, the richer my life became, the funnier it seemed, as though there were some connection between largesse and laughter, and so my tragic stance began to waver until, even with the aid of a brace and a cane, I couldn't hold it for very long at a time.

After several years I was satisfied with my adjustment. I had suffered my grief and fury and terror, I thought, but now I was at ease with my lot. Then one summer day I set out with George and the children across the desert for a vacation in California. Part way to Yuma I became aware that my right leg felt funny. "I think I've had an exacerbation," I told George. "What shall we do?" he asked. "I think we'd better get the hell to California," I said, "because I don't know whether I'll ever make it again." So we went on to San Diego and then to Orange, up the Pacific Coast Highway to Santa Cruz, across to Yosemite, down to Sequoia and Joshua Tree, and so back over the desert to home. It was a fine two-week trip, filled with friends and fair weather, and I wouldn't have missed it for the world, though I did in fact make it back to California two years later. Nor would there have been any point in missing it, since in MS, once the symptoms have appeared, the neurological damage has been done, and there's no way to predict or prevent that damage.

The incident spoiled my self-satisfaction, however. It renewed my grief and fury and terror, and I learned that one never finishes adjusting to MS. I don't know now why I thought one would. One does not, after all, finish adjusting to life, and MS is simply a fact of my life—not my favorite fact, of course—but as ordinary as my nose and my tropical fish and my yellow Mazda station wagon. It may at any time get worse, but no amount of worry or anticipation can prepare me for a new loss. My life is a lesson in losses. I learn one at a time.

And I had best be patient in the learning, since I'll have to do it like it or   30
not. As any rock fan knows, you can't always get what you want. Particularly
when you have MS. You can't, for example, get cured. In recent years researchers and the organizations that fund research have started to pay MS
some attention even though it isn't fatal; perhaps they have begun to see that
life is something other than a quantitative phenomenon, that one may be very
much alive for a very long time in a life that isn't worth living. The researchers
have made some progress toward understanding the mechanism of the disease:
It may well be an autoimmune reaction triggered by a slowacting virus. But
they are nowhere near its prevention, control, or cure. And most of us want to
be cured. Some, unable to accept incurability, grasp at one treatment after another, no matter how bizarre: megavitamin therapy, gluten-free diet, injections
of cobra venom, hypothermal suits, lymphocytopharesis, hyperbaric chambers.
Many treatments are probably harmless enough, but none are curative.

The absence of a cure often makes MS patients bitter toward their doctors. Doctors are, after all, the priests of modern society, the new shamans,
whose business is to heal, and many an MS patient roves from one to another,
searching for the "good" doctor who will make him well. Doctors too think of
themselves as healers, and for this reason many have trouble dealing with MS
patients, whose disease in its intransigence defeats their aims and mocks their
skills. Too few doctors, it is true, treat their patients as whole human beings,
but the reverse is also true. I have always tried to be gentle with my doctors,
who often have more at stake in terms of ego than I do. I may be frustrated,
maddened, depressed by the incurability of my disease, but I am not diminished by it, and they are. When I push myself up from my seat in the waiting
room and stumble toward them, I incarnate the limitation of their powers. The
least I can do is refuse to press on their tenderest spots.

This gentleness is part of the reason that I'm not sorry to be a cripple. I
didn't have it before. Perhaps I'd have developed it anyway—how could I know
such a thing?—and I wish I had more of it, but I'm glad of what I have. It has
opened and enriched my life enormously, this sense that my frailty and need
must be mirrored in others, that in searching for and shaping a stable core in
a life wrenched by change and loss, change and loss, I must recognize the
same process, under individual conditions, in the lives around me. I do not
deprecate such knowledge, however I've come by it.

All the same, if a cure were found, would I take it? In a minute. I may be
a cripple, but I'm only occasionally a loony and never a saint. Anyway, in my
brand of theology God doesn't give bonus points for a limp. I'd take a cure; I
just don't need one. A friend who also has MS startled me once by asking, "Do
you ever say to yourself, 'Why me, Lord?'" "No, Michael, I don't," I told him,
"because whenever I try, the only response I can think of is 'Why not?'" If I
could make a cosmic deal, who would I put in my place? What in my life
would I give up in exchange for sound limbs and a thrilling rush of energy? No
one. Nothing. I might as well do the job myself. Now that I'm getting the hang
of it.

QUESTIONS

1. How does Mairs organize her essay? What connects the different parts to each other?

2. What stereotypes of "disabled" people does Mairs expect us to believe in? How does she set out to counter them?

3. Mairs deliberately chooses to call herself a "cripple." Select a person or group that deliberately chooses its own name or description and explain the rationale behind the choice.

RICHARD SELZER   *The Knife*

ONE HOLDS THE KNIFE as one holds the bow of a cello or a tulip—by the stem. Not palmed nor gripped nor grasped, but lightly, with the tips of the fingers. The knife is not for pressing. It is for drawing across the field of skin. Like a slender fish, it waits, at the ready, then, go! It darts, followed by a fine wake of red. The flesh parts, falling away to yellow globules of fat. Even now, after so many times, I still marvel at its power—cold, gleaming, silent. More, I am still struck with a kind of dread that it is I in whose hand the blade travels, that my hand is its vehicle, that yet again this terrible steel-bellied thing and I have conspired for a most unnatural purpose, the laying open of the body of a human being.

A stillness settles in my heart and is carried to my hand. It is the quietude of resolve layered over fear. And it is this resolve that lowers us, my knife and me, deeper and deeper into the person beneath. It is an entry into the body that is nothing like a caress; still, it is among the gentlest of acts. Then stroke and stroke again, and we are joined by other instruments, hemostats and forceps, until the wound blooms with strange flowers whose looped handles fall to the sides in steely array.

There is sound, the tight click of clamps fixing teeth into severed blood vessels, the snuffle and gargle of the suction machine clearing the field of blood for the next stroke, the litany of monosyllables with which one prays his way down and in; *clamp, sponge, suture, tie, cut*. And there is color. The green of the cloth, the white of the sponges, the red and yellow of the body. Beneath the fat lies the fascia, the tough fibrous sheet encasing the muscles. It must be sliced and the red beef of the muscles separated. Now there are retractors to hold apart the wound. Hands move together, part, weave. We are fully engaged, like children absorbed in a game or the craftsmen of some place like Damascus.

Deeper still. The peritoneum, pink and gleaming and membranous, bulges

Published in Selzer's first collection of autobiographical essays, Mortal Lessons: Notes on the Art of Surgery *(1976).*

into the wound. It is grasped with forceps, and opened. For the first time we can see into the cavity of the abdomen. Such a primitive place. One expects to find drawings of buffalo on the walls. The sense of trespassing is keener now, heightened by the world's light illuminating the organs, their secret colors revealed—maroon and salmon and yellow. The vista is sweetly vulnerable at this moment, a kind of welcoming. An arc of the liver shines high and on the right, like a dark sun. It laps over the pink sweep of the stomach, from whose lower border the gauzy omentum is draped, and through which veil one sees, sinuous, slow as just-fed snakes, the indolent coils of the intestine.

You turn aside to wash your gloves. It is a ritual cleansing. One enters this   5
temple doubly washed. Here is man as microcosm, representing in all his parts the earth, perhaps the universe.

I must confess that the priestliness of my profession has ever been impressed on me. In the beginning there are vows, taken with all solemnity. Then there is the endless harsh novitiate of training, much fatigue, much sacrifice. At last one emerges as celebrant, standing close to the truth lying curtained in the Ark of the body. Not surplice and cassock but mask and gown are your regalia. You hold no chalice, but a knife. There is no wine, no wafer. There are only the facts of blood and flesh.

And if the surgeon is like a poet, then the scars you have made on countless bodies are like verses into the fashioning of which you have poured your soul. I think that if years later I were to see the trace from an old incision of mine, I should know it at once, as one recognizes his pet expressions.

But mostly you are a traveler in a dangerous country, advancing into the moist and jungly cleft your hands have made. Eyes and ears are shuttered from the land you left behind; mind empties itself of all other thought. You are the root of groping fingers. It is a fine hour for the fingers, their sense of touch so enhanced. The blind must know this feeling. Oh, there is risk everywhere. One goes lightly. The spleen. No! No! Do not touch the spleen that lurks below the left leaf of the diaphragm, a manta ray in a coral cave, its bloody tongue protruding. One poke and it might rupture, exploding with sudden hemorrhage. The filmy omentum must not be torn, the intestine scraped or denuded. The hand finds the liver, palms it, fingers running along its sharp lower edge, admiring. Here are the twin mounds of the kidneys, the apron of the omentum hanging in front of the intestinal coils. One lifts it aside and the fingers dip among the loops, searching, mapping territory, establishing boundaries. Deeper still, and the womb is touched, then held like a small muscular bottle—the womb and its earlike appendages, the ovaries. How they do nestle in the cup of a man's hand, their power all dormant. They are frailty itself.

There is a hush in the room. Speech stops. The hands of the others, assistants and nurses, are still. Only the voice of the patient's respiration remains. It is the rhythm of a quiet sea, the sound of waiting. Then you speak, slowly, the terse entries of a Himalayan climber reporting back.

"The stomach is okay. Greater curvature clean. No sign of ulcer. Pylorus,[1]   10

1. The opening from the stomach to the duodenum, which is the first part of the small intestine.

duodenum fine. Now comes the gall-bladder. No stones. Right kidney, left, all right. Liver . . . uh-oh."

Your speech lowers to a whisper, falters, stops for a long, long moment, then picks up again at the end of a sigh that comes through your mask like a last exhalation.

"Three big hard ones in the left lobe, one on the right. Metastatic deposits. Bad, bad. Where's the primary? Got to be coming from somewhere."

The arm shifts direction and the fingers drop lower and lower into the pelvis—the body impaled now upon the arm of the surgeon to the hilt of the elbow.

"Here it is."

15   The voice goes flat, all business now.

"Tumor in the sigmoid colon, wrapped all around it, pretty tight. We'll take out a sleeve of the bowel. No colostomy. Not that, anyway. But, God, there's a lot of it down there. Here, you take a feel."

You step back from the table, and lean into a sterile basin of water, resting on stiff arms, while the others locate the cancer.

When I was a small boy, I was taken by my father, a general practitioner in Troy, New York, to St. Mary's Hospital, to wait while he made his rounds. The solarium where I sat was all sunlight and large plants. It smelled of soap and starch and clean linen. In the spring, clouds of lilac billowed from the vases; and in the fall, chrysanthemums crowded the magazine tables. At one end of the great high-ceilinged, glass-walled room was a huge cage where colored finches streaked and sang. Even from the first, I sensed the nearness of that other place, the Operating Room, knew that somewhere on these premises was that secret dreadful enclosure where *surgery* was at that moment happening. I sat among the cut flowers, half drunk on the scent, listening to the robes of the nuns brush the walls of the corridor, and felt the awful presence of *surgery*.

Oh, the pageantry! I longed to go there. I feared to go there. I imagined surgeons bent like storks over the body of the patient, a circle of red painted across the abdomen. Silence and dignity and awe enveloped them, these surgeons; it was the bubble in which they bent and straightened. Ah, it was a place I would never see, a place from whose walls the hung and suffering Christ turned his affliction to highest purpose. It is thirty years since I yearned for that old Surgery. And now I merely break the beam of an electric eye, and double doors swing open to let me enter, and as I enter, always, I feel the surging of a force that I feel in no other place. It is as though I am suddenly stronger and larger, heroic. Yes, that's it!

20   The operating room is called a theatre. One walks onto a set where the cupboards hold tanks of oxygen and other gases. The cabinets store steel cutlery of unimagined versatility, and the refrigerators are filled with bags of blood. Bodies are stroked and penetrated here, but no love is made. Nor is it ever allowed to grow dark, but must always gleam with a grotesque brightness. For the special congress into which patient and surgeon enter, the one must have his senses deadened, the other his sensibilities restrained. One lies

naked, blind, offering; the other stands masked and gloved. One yields; the other does his will.

I said no love is made here, but love happens. I have stood aside with lowered gaze while a priest, wearing the purple scarf of office, administers Last Rites to the man I shall operate upon. I try not to listen to those terrible last questions, the answers, but hear, with scorching clarity, the words that formalize the expectation of death. For a moment my resolve falters before the resignation, the *attentiveness*, of the other two. I am like an executioner who hears the cleric comforting the prisoner. For the moment I am excluded from the centrality of the event, a mere technician standing by. But it is only for the moment.

The priest leaves, and we are ready. Let it begin.

Later, I am repairing the strangulated hernia of an old man. Because of his age and frailty, I am using local anesthesia. He is awake. His name is Abe Kaufman, and he is a Russian Jew. A nurse sits by his head, murmuring to him. She wipes his forehead. I know her very well. Her name is Alexandria, and she is the daughter of Ukrainian peasants. She has a flat steppe of a face and slanting eyes. Nurse and patient are speaking of blintzes, borscht, piroshki—Russian food that they both love. I listen, and think that it may have been her grandfather who raided the shtetl where the old man lived long ago, and in his high boots and his blouse and his fury this grandfather pulled Abe by his side curls to the ground and stomped his face and kicked his groin. Perhaps it was that ancient kick that caused the hernia I am fixing. I listen to them whispering behind the screen at the head of the table. I listen with breath held before the prism of history.

"Tovarich," she says, her head bent close to his.

He smiles up at her, and forgets that his body is being laid open.

"You are an angel," the old man says.

25

One can count on absurdity. There, in the midst of our solemnities, appears, small and black and crawling, an insect: The Ant of the Absurd. The belly is open; one has seen and felt the catastrophe within. It seems the patient is already vaporizing into angelhood in the heat escaping therefrom. One could warm one's hands in that fever. All at once that ant is there, emerging from beneath one of the sterile towels that border the operating field. For a moment one does not really see it, or else denies the sight, so impossible it is, marching precisely, heading briskly toward the open wound.

Drawn from its linen lair, where it snuggled in the steam of the great sterilizer, and survived, it comes. Closer and closer, it hurries toward the incision. Ant, art thou in the grip of some fatal *ivresse*?[2] Wouldst hurtle over these scarlet cliffs into the very boil of the guts? Art mad for the reek we handle? Or in some secret act of formication engaged?

The alarm is sounded. An ant! An ant! And we are unnerved. Our fear of defilement is near to frenzy. It is not the mere physical contamination that we

---

2. French for "drunkenness."

loathe. It is the evil of the interloper, that he scurries across our holy place, and filthies our altar. He *is* disease—that for whose destruction we have gathered. Powerless to destroy the sickness before us, we turn to its incarnation with a vengeance, and pluck it from the lip of the incision in the nick of time. Who would have thought an ant could move so fast?

30 Between thumb and forefinger, the intruder is crushed. It dies as quietly as it lived. Ah, but now there is death in the room. It is a perversion of our purpose. Albert Schweitzer[3] would have spared it, scooped it tenderly into his hand, and lowered it to the ground.

The corpselet is flicked into the specimen basin. The gloves are changed. New towels and sheets are placed where it walked. We are pleased to have done something, if only a small killing. The operation resumes, and we draw upon ourselves once more the sleeves of office and rank. Is our reverence for life in question?

In the room the instruments lie on trays and tables. They are arranged precisely by the scrub nurse, in an order that never changes, so that you can reach blindly for a forceps or hemostat without looking away from the operating field. The instruments lie *thus!* Even at the beginning, when all is clean and tidy and no blood has been spilled, it is the scalpel that dominates. It has a figure the others do not have, the retractors and the scissors. The scalpel is all grace and line, a fierceness. It grins. It is like a cat—to be respected, deferred to, but which returns no amiability. To hold it above a belly is to know the knife's force—as though were you to give it slightest rein, it would pursue an intent of its own, driving into the flesh, a wild energy.

In a story by Borges,[4] a deadly knife fight between two rivals is depicted. It is not, however, the men who are fighting. It is the knives themselves that are settling their own old score. The men who hold the knives are mere adjuncts to the weapons. The unguarded knife is like the unbridled war-horse that not only carries its helpless rider to his death, but tramples all beneath its hooves. The hand of the surgeon must tame this savage thing. He is a rider reining to capture a pace.

So close is the joining of knife and surgeon that they are like the Centaur—the knife, below, all equine energy, the surgeon, above, with his delicate art. One holds the knife back as much as advances it to purpose. One is master of the scissors. One is partner, sometimes rival, to the knife. In a moment it is like the long red fingernail of the Dragon Lady. Thus does the surgeon curb in order to create, restraining the scalpel, governing it shrewdly, setting the action of the operation into a pattern, giving it form and purpose.

35 It is the nature of creatures to live within a tight cuirass that is both their constriction and their protection. The carapace of the turtle is his fortress and retreat, yet keeps him writhing on his back in the sand. So is the surgeon ren-

3. French doctor and philosopher (1875–1965) noted for his humanitarian work in Africa.
4. Jorge Luis Borges (1899–1986), Argentinean writer of poems and short stories that have a fantastical quality.

dered impotent by his own empathy and compassion. The surgeon cannot weep. When he cuts the flesh, his own must not bleed. Here it is all work. Like an asthmatic hungering for air, longing to take just one deep breath, the surgeon struggles not to feel. It is suffocating to press the feeling out. It would be easier to weep or mourn—for you know that the lovely precise world of proportion contains, just beneath, *there*, all disaster, all disorder. In a surgical operation, a risk may flash into reality: the patient dies . . . of *complication*. The patient knows this too, in a more direct and personal way, and he is afraid.

And what of that *other*, the patient, you, who are brought to the operating room on a stretcher, having been washed and purged and dressed in a white gown? Fluid drips from a bottle into your arm, diluting you, leaching your body of its personal brine. As you wait in the corridor, you hear from behind the closed door the angry clang of steel upon steel, as though a battle were being waged. There is the odor of antiseptic and ether, and masked women hurry up and down the halls, in and out of rooms. There is the watery sound of strange machinery, the tinny beeping that is the transmitted heartbeat of yet another *human being*. And all the while the dreadful knowledge that soon you will be taken, laid beneath great lamps that will reveal the secret linings of your body. In the very act of lying down, you have made a declaration of surrender. One lies down gladly for sleep or for love. But to give over one's body and will for surgery, to *lie down* for it, is a yielding of more than we can bear.

Soon a man will stand over you, gowned and hooded. In time the man will take up a knife and crack open your flesh like a ripe melon. Fingers will rummage among your viscera. Parts of you will be cut out. Blood will run free. Your blood. All the night before you have turned with the presentiment of death upon you. You have attended your funeral, wept with your mourners. You think, "I should never have had surgery in the springtime." It is too cruel. Or on a Thursday. It is an unlucky day.

Now it is time. You are wheeled in and moved to the table. An injection is given. "Let yourself go," I say. "It's a pleasant sensation," I say. "Give in," I say.

Let go? Give in? When you know that you are being tricked into the hereafter, that you will end when consciousness ends? As the monstrous silence of anesthesia falls discourteously across your brain, you watch your soul drift off.

Later, in the recovery room, you awaken and gaze through the thickness of drugs at the world returning, and you guess, at first dimly, then surely, that you have not died. In pain and nausea you will know the exultation of death averted, of life restored.   40

What is it, then, this thing, the knife, whose shape is virtually the same as it was three thousand years ago, but now with its head grown detachable? Before steel, it was bronze. Before bronze, stone—then back into unremembered time. Did man invent it or did the knife precede him here, hidden under ages of vegetation and hoofprints, lying in wait to be discovered, picked up, used?

The scalpel is in two parts, the handle and the blade. Joined, it is six inches from tip to tip. At one end of the handle is a narrow notched prong upon which the blade is slid, then snapped into place. Without the blade, the handle has a blind, decapitated look. It is helpless as a trussed maniac. But slide on the blade, click it home, and the knife springs instantly to life. It is headed now, edgy, leaping to mount the fingers for the gallop to its feast.

Now is the moment from which you have turned aside, from which you have averted your gaze, yet toward which you have been hastened. Now the scalpel sings along the flesh again, its brute run unimpeded by germs or other frictions. It is a slick slide home, a barracuda spurt, a rip of embedded talon. One listens, and almost hears the whine—nasal, high, delivered through that gleaming metallic snout. The flesh splits with its own kind of moan. It is like the penetration of rape.

The breasts of women are cut off, arms and legs sliced to the bone to make ready for the saw, eyes freed from sockets, intestines lopped. The hand of the surgeon rebels. Tension boils through his pores, like sweat. The flesh of the patient retaliates with hemorrhage, and the blood chases the knife wherever it is withdrawn.

45

Within the belly a tumor squats, toadish, fungoid. A gray mother and her brood. The only thing it does not do is croak. It too is hacked from its bed as the carnivore knife lips the blood, turning in it in a kind of ecstasy of plenty, a gluttony after the long fast. It is just for this that the knife was created, tempered, heated, its violence beaten into paper-thin force.

At last a little thread is passed into the wound and tied. The monstrous booming fury is stilled by a tiny thread. The tempest is silenced. The operation is over. On the table, the knife lies spent, on its side, the bloody meal smear-dried upon its flanks. The knife rests.

And waits.

QUESTIONS

1. This essay seems very revealing, but of what? What does Selzer want us to know? (He doesn't seem to reason with us or to persuade us of anything by means of well-reasoned argument.)

2. At one point, Selzer switches from straight exposition to second-person address, employing "you" (paragraph 36). What impact does this switch have on you as reader? What rationale can you give for this switch?

3. Selzer assumes his readers know about surgery from personal experience. Is this a correct assumption? Imagine how a person who has never had surgery might respond. Write about the impact Selzer's essay has upon you from your own perspective of someone familiar or unfamiliar with surgery.

ALICE WALKER   *Beauty: When the Other Dancer Is the Self*

I T IS A BRIGHT summer day in 1947. My father, a fat, funny man with beautiful eyes and a subversive wit, is trying to decide which of his eight children he will take with him to the county fair. My mother, of course, will not go. She is knocked out from getting most of us ready: I hold my neck stiff against the pressure of her knuckles as she hastily completes the braiding and then beribboning of my hair.

My father is the driver for the rich old white lady up the road. Her name is Miss Mey. She owns all the land for miles around, as well as the house in which we live. All I remember about her is that she once offered to pay my mother thirty-five cents for cleaning her house, raking up piles of her magnolia leaves, and washing her family's clothes, and that my mother—she of no money, eight children, and a chronic earache—refused it. But I do not think of this in 1947. I am two and a half years old. I want to go everywhere my daddy goes. I am excited at the prospect of riding in a car. Someone has told me fairs are fun. That there is room in the car for only three of us doesn't faze me at all. Whirling happily in my starchy frock, showing off my biscuit-polished patent-leather shoes and lavender socks, tossing my head in a way that makes my ribbons bounce, I stand, hands on hips, before my father. "Take me, Daddy," I say with assurance; "I'm the prettiest!"

Later, it does not surprise me to find myself in Miss Mey's shiny black car, sharing the back seat with the other lucky ones. Does not surprise me that I thoroughly enjoy the fair. At home that night I tell the unlucky ones all I can remember about the merry-go-round, the man who eats live chickens, and the teddy bears, until they say: that's enough, baby Alice. Shut up now, and go to sleep.

It is Easter Sunday, 1950. I am dressed in a green, flocked, scalloped-hem dress (handmade by my adoring sister, Ruth) that has its own smooth satin petticoat and tiny hot-pink roses tucked into each scallop. My shoes, new T-strap patent leather, again highly biscuit-polished. I am six years old and have learned one of the longest Easter speeches to be heard that day, totally unlike the speech I said when I was two: "Easter lilies/pure and white/blossom in/the morning light." When I rise to give my speech I do so on a great wave of love and pride and expectation. People in the church stop rustling their new crinolines. They seem to hold their breath. I can tell they admire my dress, but it is my spirit, bordering on sassiness (womanishness), they secretly applaud.

From In Search of Our Mother's Gardens: Womanist Prose *(1983), a collection of essays meditating on African American and feminist sources of inspiration, published the year after Walker's highly successful novel* The Color Purple.

5   "That girl's a little *mess*," they whisper to each other, pleased.

Naturally I say my speech without stammer or pause, unlike those who stutter, stammer, or, worst of all, forget. This is before the word "beautiful" exists in people's vocabulary, but "Oh, isn't she the *cutest* thing!" frequently floats my way. "And got so much sense!" they gratefully add . . . for which thoughtful addition I thank them to this day.

It was great fun being cute. But then, one day, it ended.

I am eight years old and a tomboy. I have a cowboy hat, cowboy boots, checkered shirt and pants, all red. My playmates are my brothers, two and four years older than I. Their colors are black and green, the only difference in the way we are dressed. On Saturday nights we all go to the picture show, even my mother; Westerns are her favorite kind of movie. Back home, "on the ranch," we pretend we are Tom Mix, Hopalong Cassidy, Lash LaRue (we've even named one of our dogs Lash LaRue); we chase each other for hours rustling cattle, being outlaws, delivering damsels from distress. Then my parents decide to buy my brothers guns. These are not "real" guns. They shoot "BBs," copper pellets my brothers say will kill birds. Because I am a girl, I do not get a gun. Instantly I am relegated to the position of Indian. Now there appears a great distance between us. They shoot and shoot at everything with their new guns. I try to keep up with my bow and arrows.

One day while I am standing on top of our makeshift "garage"—pieces of tin nailed across some poles—holding my bow and arrow and looking out toward the fields, I feel an incredible blow in my right eye. I look down just in time to see my brother lower his gun.

10   Both brothers rush to my side. My eye stings, and I cover it with my hand. "If you tell," they say, "we will get a whipping. You don't want that to happen, do you?" I do not. "Here is a piece of wire," says the older brother, picking it up from the roof; "say you stepped on one end of it and the other flew up and hit you." The pain is beginning to start. "Yes," I say, "Yes, I will say that is what happened." If I do not say this is what happened, I know my brothers will find ways to make me wish I had. But now I will say anything that gets me to my mother.

Confronted by our parents we stick to the lie agreed upon. They place me on a bench on the porch and I close my left eye while they examine the right. There is a tree growing from underneath the porch that climbs past the railing to the roof. It is the last thing my right eye sees. I watch as its trunk, its branches, and then its leaves are blotted out by the rising blood.

I am in shock. First there is intense fever, which my father tries to break using lily leaves bound around my head. Then there are chills: my mother tries to get me to eat soup. Eventually, I do not know how, my parents learn what has happened. A week after the "accident" they take me to see a doctor. "Why did you wait so long to come?" he asks, looking into my eye and shaking his head. "Eyes are sympathetic," he says. "If one is blind, the other will likely become blind too."

This comment of the doctor's terrifies me. But it is really how I look that bothers me most. Where the BB pellet struck there is a glob of whitish scar tissue, a hideous cataract, on my eye. Now when I stare at people—a favorite pastime, up to now—they will stare back. Not at the "cute" little girl, but at her scar. For six years I do not stare at anyone, because I do not raise my head.

Years later, in the throes of a mid-life crisis, I ask my mother and sister whether I changed after the "accident." "No," they say, puzzled. "What do you mean?"

What do I mean?

15

I am eight, and, for the first time, doing poorly in school, where I have been something of a whiz since I was four. We have just moved to the place where the "accident" occurred. We do not know any of the people around us because this is a different county. The only time I see the friends I knew is when we go back to our old church. The new school is the former state penitentiary. It is a large stone building, cold and drafty, crammed to overflowing with boisterous, ill-disciplined children. On the third floor there is a huge circular imprint of some partition that has been torn out.

"What used to be here?" I ask a sullen girl next to me on our way past it to lunch.

"The electric chair," says she.

At night I have nightmares about the electric chair, and about all the people reputedly "fried" in it. I am afraid of the school, where all the students seem to be budding criminals.

"What's the matter with your eye?" they ask, critically.

20

When I don't answer (I cannot decide whether it was an "accident" or not), they shove me, insist on a fight.

My brother, the one who created the story about the wire, comes to my rescue. But then brags so much about "protecting" me, I become sick.

After months of torture at the school, my parents decide to send me back to our old community, to my old school. I live with my grandparents and the teacher they board. But there is no room for Phoebe, my cat. By the time my grandparents decide there *is* room, and I ask for my cat, she cannot be found. Miss Yarborough, the boarding teacher, takes me under her wing, and begins to teach me to play the piano. But soon she marries an African—a "prince," she says—and is whisked away to his continent.

At my old school there is at least one teacher who loves me. She is the teacher who "knew me before I was born" and bought my first baby clothes. It is she who makes life bearable. It is her presence that finally helps me turn on the one child at the school who continually calls me "one-eyed bitch." One day I simply grab him by his coat and beat him until I am satisfied. It is my teacher who tells me my mother is ill.

My mother is lying in bed in the middle of the day, something I have never seen. She is in too much pain to speak. She has an abscess in her ear. I stand looking down on her, knowing that if she dies, I cannot live. She is being treated with warm oils and hot bricks held against her cheek. Finally a doctor

25

comes. But I must go back to my grandparents' house. The weeks pass but I am hardly aware of it. All I know is that my mother might die, my father is not so jolly, my brothers still have their guns, and I am the one sent away from home.

"You did not change," they say.

Did I imagine the anguish of never looking up?

I am twelve. When relatives come to visit I hide in my room. My cousin Brenda, just my age, whose father works in the post office and whose mother is a nurse, comes to find me. "Hello," she says. And then she asks, looking at my recent school picture, which I did not want taken, and on which the "glob," as I think of it, is clearly visible, "You still can't see out of that eye?"

"No," I say, and flop back on the bed over my book.

That night, as I do almost every night, I abuse my eye. I rant and rave at it, in front of the mirror. I plead with it to clear up before morning. I tell it I hate and despise it. I do not pray for sight. I pray for beauty.

"You did not change," they say.

I am fourteen and baby-sitting for my brother Bill, who lives in Boston. He is my favorite brother and there is a strong bond between us. Understanding my feelings of shame and ugliness he and his wife take me to a local hospital, where the "glob" is removed by a doctor named O. Henry. There is still a small bluish crater where the scar tissue was, but the ugly white stuff is gone. Almost immediately I become a different person from the girl who does not raise her head. Or so I think. Now that I've raised my head I win the boyfriend of my dreams. Now that I've raised my head I have plenty of friends. Now that I've raised my head classwork comes from my lips as faultlessly as Easter speeches did, and I leave high school as valedictorian, most popular student, and *queen,* hardly believing my luck. Ironically, the girl who was voted most beautiful in our class (and was) was later shot twice through the chest by a male companion, using a "real" gun, while she was pregnant. But that's another story in itself. Or is it?

"You did not change," they say.

It is now thirty years since the "accident." A beautiful journalist comes to visit and to interview me. She is going to write a cover story for her magazine that focuses on my latest book. "Decide how you want to look on the cover," she says. "Glamorous, or whatever."

Never mind "glamorous," it is the "whatever" that I hear. Suddenly all I can think of is whether I will get enough sleep the night before the photography session: if I don't, my eye will be tired and wander, as blind eyes will.

At night in bed with my lover I think up reasons why I should not appear on the cover of a magazine. "My meanest critics will say I've sold out," I say. "My family will now realize I write scandalous books."

"But what's the real reason you don't want to do this?" he asks.

"Because in all probability," I say in a rush, "my eye won't be straight."

"It will be straight enough," he says. Then, "Besides, I thought you'd made your peace with that."

And I suddenly remember that I have.

I remember:

I am talking to my brother Jimmy, asking if he remembers anything unusual about the day I was shot. He does not know I consider that day the last time my father, with his sweet home remedy of cool lily leaves, chose me, and that I suffered and raged inside because of this. "Well," he says, "all I remember is standing by the side of the highway with Daddy, trying to flag down a car. A white man stopped, but when Daddy said he needed somebody to take his little girl to the doctor, he drove off."

I remember:

I am in the desert for the first time. I fall totally in love with it. I am so overwhelmed by its beauty, I confront for the first time, consciously, the meaning of the doctor's words years ago: "Eyes are sympathetic. If one is blind, the other will likely become blind too." I realize I have dashed about the world madly, looking at this, looking at that, storing up images against the fading of the light. *But I might have missed seeing the desert!* The shock of that possibility—and gratitude for over twenty-five years of sight—sends me literally to my knees. Poem after poem comes—which is perhaps how poets pray.

40

On Sight

I am so thankful I have seen
The Desert
And the creatures in the desert
And the desert Itself.

The desert has its own moon
Which I have seen
With my own eye.
There is no flag on it.

Trees of the desert have arms
All of which are always up
That is because the moon is up
The sun is up

Also the sky
The stars
Clouds
None with flags.

If there were flags, I doubt
the trees would point.
Would you?

45   *But mostly, I remember this:*

I am twenty-seven, and my baby daughter is almost three. Since her birth I have worried about her discovery that her mother's eyes are different from other people's. Will she be embarrassed? I think. What will she say? Every day she watches a television program called "Big Blue Marble." It begins with a picture of the earth as it appears from the moon. It is bluish, a little battered-looking, but full of light, with whitish clouds swirling around it. Every time I see it I weep with love, as if it is a picture of Grandma's house. One day when I am putting Rebecca down for her nap, she suddenly focuses on my eye. Something inside me cringes, gets ready to try to protect myself. All children are cruel about physical differences, I know from experience, and that they don't always mean to be is another matter. I assume Rebecca will be the same.

But no-o-o-o. She studies my face intently as we stand, her inside and me outside her crib. She even holds my face maternally between her dimpled little hands. Then, looking every bit as serious and lawyerlike as her father, she says, as if it may just possibly have slipped my attention: "Mommy, there's a *world* in your eye." (As in, "Don't be alarmed, or do anything crazy.") And then, gently, but with great interest: "Mommy, where did you *get* that world in your eye?"

For the most part, the pain left then. (So what, if my brothers grew up to buy even more powerful pellet guns for their sons and to carry real guns themselves. So what, if a young "Morehouse man"[1] once nearly fell off the steps of Trevor Arnett Library because he thought my eyes were blue.) Crying and laughing I ran to the bathroom, while Rebecca mumbled and sang herself off to sleep. Yes indeed, I realized, looking into the mirror. There *was* a world in my eye. And I saw that it was possible to love it: that in fact, for all it had taught me of shame and anger and inner vision, I *did* love it. Even to see it drifting out of orbit in boredom, or rolling up out of fatigue, not to mention floating back at attention in excitement (bearing witness, a friend has called it), deeply suitable to my personality, and even characteristic of me.

That night I dream I am dancing to Stevie Wonder's[2] song "Always" (the name of the song is really "As," but I hear it as "Always"). As I dance, whirling and joyous, happier than I've ever been in my life, another bright-faced dancer joins me. We dance and kiss each other and hold each other through the night. The other dancer has obviously come through all right, as I have done. She is beautiful, whole and free. And she is also me.

1. A student at Morehouse College in Atlanta, Georgia.
2. African American singer, songwriter, and music producer (b. 1950).

QUESTIONS

1. Throughout her essay Walker refers to the "accident." Why does she put the word in quotation marks? Has Walker made her peace with the "accident" and its consequences?

2. Walker writes her essay by selecting particular moments in her life. What does each moment show? How do these moments relate to Walker's theme?

3. What is the effect of ending the essay by recounting a dream? How does the dream relate to the essay's title?

4. Write an essay comparing and contrasting Walker's essay and Mairs's "On Being a Cripple." Consider especially their responses to injury or illness and their attitudes toward those subjects.

E. B. WHITE   *Once More to the Lake*

ONE SUMMER, ALONG ABOUT 1904, my father rented a camp on a lake in Maine and took us all there for the month of August. We all got ringworm from some kittens and had to rub Pond's Extract on our arms and legs night and morning, and my father rolled over in a canoe with all his clothes on; but outside of that the vacation was a success and from then on none of us ever thought there was any place in the world like that lake in Maine. We returned summer after summer—always on August 1st for one month. I have since become a salt-water man, but sometimes in summer there are days when the restlessness of the tides and the fearful cold of the sea water and the incessant wind which blows across the afternoon and into the evening make me wish for the placidity of a lake in the woods. A few weeks ago this feeling got so strong I bought myself a couple of bass hooks and a spinner and returned to the lake where we used to go, for a week's fishing and to revisit old haunts.

I took along my son, who had never had any fresh water up his nose and who had seen lily pads only from train windows. On the journey over to the lake I began to wonder what it would be like. I wondered how time would have marred this unique, this holy spot—the coves and streams, the hills that the sun set behind, the camps and the paths behind the camps. I was sure the tarred road would have found it out and I wondered in what other ways it would be desolated. It is strange how much you can remember about places like that once you allow your mind to return into the grooves which lead back. You remember one thing, and that suddenly reminds you of another thing. I guess I remembered clearest of all the early mornings, when the lake was cool and motionless, remembered how the bedroom smelled of the lumber it was made of and of the wet woods whose scent entered through the screen. The partitions in the camp were thin and did not extend clear to the top of the rooms, and as I was always the first up I would dress softly so as not to wake

Originally appeared in "One Man's Meat," White's column for Harper's *Magazine (October 1941); later included in* One Man's Meat *(1942), a collection of his columns about life on a Maine saltwater farm, and then in* Essays of E. B. White *(1977).*

the others, and sneak out into the sweet outdoors and start out in the canoe, keeping close along the shore in the long shadows of the pines. I remembered being very careful never to rub my paddle against the gunwale for fear of disturbing the stillness of the cathedral.

The lake had never been what you would call a wild lake. There were cottages sprinkled around the shores, and it was in farming country although the shores of the lake were quite heavily wooded. Some of the cottages were owned by nearby farmers, and you would live at the shore and eat your meals at the farmhouse. That's what our family did. But although it wasn't wild, it was a fairly large and undisturbed lake and there were places in it which, to a child at least, seemed infinitely remote and primeval.

I was right about the tar: it led to within half a mile of the shore. But when I got back there, with my boy, and we settled into a camp near a farmhouse and into the kind of summertime I had known, I could tell that it was going to be pretty much the same as it had been before—I knew it, lying in bed the first morning, smelling the bedroom, and hearing the boy sneak quietly out and go off along the shore in a boat. I began to sustain the illusion that he was I, and therefore, by simple transposition, that I was my father. This sensation persisted, kept cropping up all the time we were there. It was not an entirely new feeling, but in this setting it grew much stronger. I seemed to be living a dual existence. I would be in the middle of some simple act, I would be picking up a bait box or laying down a table fork, or I would be saying something, and suddenly it would be not I but my father who was saying the words or making the gesture. It gave me a creepy sensation.

5   We went fishing the first morning. I felt the same damp moss covering the worms in the bait can, and saw the dragonfly alight on the tip of my rod as it hovered a few inches from the surface of the water. It was the arrival of this fly that convinced me beyond any doubt that everything was as it always had been, that the years were a mirage and there had been no years. The small waves were the same, chucking the rowboat under the chin as we fished at anchor, and the boat was the same boat, the same color green and the ribs broken in the same places, and under the floor-boards the same fresh-water leavings and débris—the dead helgrammite,[1] the wisps of moss, the rusty discarded fishhook, the dried blood from yesterday's catch. We stared silently at the tips of our rods, at the dragonflies that came and went. I lowered the tip of mine into the water, tentatively, pensively dislodging the fly, which darted two feet away, poised, darted two feet back, and came to rest again a little farther up the rod. There had been no years between the ducking of this dragonfly and the other one—the one that was part of memory. I looked at the boy, who was silently watching his fly, and it was my hands that held his rod, my eyes watching. I felt dizzy and didn't know which rod I was at the end of.

We caught two bass, hauling them in briskly as though they were mackerel, pulling them over the side of the boat in a businesslike manner without any landing net, and stunning them with a blow on the back of the head.

1. The larvae of the dobsonfly (usually spelled "hellgrammite").

When we got back for a swim before lunch, the lake was exactly where we had left it, the same number of inches from the dock, and there was only the merest suggestion of a breeze. This seemed an utterly enchanted sea, this lake you could leave to its own devices for a few hours and come back to, and find that it had not stirred, this constant and trustworthy body of water. In the shallows, the dark, water-soaked sticks and twigs, smooth and old, were undulating in clusters on the bottom against the clean ribbed sand, and the track of the mussel was plain. A school of minnows swam by, each minnow with its small individual shadow, doubling the attendance, so clear and sharp in the sunlight. Some of the other campers were in swimming, along the shore, one of them with a cake of soap, and the water felt thin and clear and unsubstantial. Over the years there had been this person with the cake of soap, this cultist, and here he was. There had been no years.

Up to the farmhouse to dinner through the teeming, dusty field, the road under our sneakers was only a two-track road. The middle track was missing, the one with the marks of the hooves and the splotches of dried, flaky manure. There had always been three tracks to choose from in choosing which track to walk in; now the choice was narrowed down to two. For a moment I missed terribly the middle alternative. But the way led past the tennis court, and something about the way it lay there in the sun reassured me; the tape had loosened along the backline, the alleys were green with plantains and other weeds, and the net (installed in June and removed in September) sagged in the dry noon, and the whole place steamed with midday heat and hunger and emptiness. There was a choice of pie for dessert, and one was blueberry and one was apple, and the waitresses were the same country girls, there having been no passage of time, only the illusion of it as in a dropped curtain—the waitresses were still fifteen; their hair had been washed, that was the only difference—they had been to the movies and seen the pretty girls with the clean hair.

Summertime, oh summertime, pattern of life indelible, the fade-proof lake, the woods unshatterable, the pasture with the sweetfern and the juniper forever and ever, summer without end; this was the background, and the life along the shore was the design, the cottagers with their innocent and tranquil design, their tiny docks with the flagpole and the American flag floating against the white clouds in the blue sky, the little paths over the roots of the trees leading from camp to camp and the paths leading back to the outhouses and the can of lime for sprinkling, and at the souvenir counters at the store the miniature birch-bark canoes and the post cards that showed things looking a little better than they looked. This was the American family at play, escaping the city heat, wondering whether the newcomers in the camp at the head of the cove were "common" or "nice," wondering whether it was true that the people who drove up for Sunday dinner at the farmhouse were turned away because there wasn't enough chicken.

It seemed to me, as I kept remembering all this, that those times and those summers had been infinitely precious and worth saving. There had been jollity and peace and goodness. The arriving (at the beginning of August) had been so big a business in itself, at the railway station the farm wagon drawn up, the first smell of the pine-laden air, the first glimpse of the smiling farmer, and the great importance of the trunks and your father's enormous authority in such matters, and the feel of the wagon under you for the long ten-mile haul, and at the top of the last long hill catching the first view of the lake after eleven months of not seeing this cherished body of water. The shouts and cries of the other campers when they saw you, and the trunks to be unpacked, to give up their rich burden. (Arriving was less exciting nowadays, when you sneaked up in your car and parked it under a tree near the camp and took out the bags and in five minutes it was all over, no fuss, no loud wonderful fuss about trunks.)

10   Peace and goodness and jollity. The only thing that was wrong now, really, was the sound of the place, an unfamiliar nervous sound of the outboard motors. This was the note that jarred, the one thing that would sometimes break the illusion and set the years moving. In those other summertimes all motors were inboard; and when they were at a little distance, the noise they made was a sedative, an ingredient of summer sleep. They were one-cylinder and two-cylinder engines, and some were make-and-break and some were jump-spark,[2] but they all made a sleepy sound across the lake. The one-lungers throbbed and fluttered, and the twin-cylinder ones purred and purred, and that was a quiet sound too. But now the campers all had outboards. In the daytime, in the hot mornings, these motors made a petulant, irritable sound; at night, in the still evening when the afterglow lit the water, they whined about one's ears like mosquitoes. My boy loved our rented outboard, and his great desire was to achieve singlehanded mastery over it, and authority, and he soon learned the trick of choking it a little (but not too much), and the adjustment of the needle valve. Watching him I would remember the things you could do with the old one-cylinder engine with the heavy flywheel, how you could have it eating out of your hand if you got really close to it spiritually. Motor boats in those days didn't have clutches, and you would make a landing by shutting off the motor at the proper time and coasting in with a dead rudder. But there was a way of reversing them, if you learned the trick, by cutting the switch and putting it on again exactly on the final dying revolution of the flywheel, so that it would kick back against compression and begin reversing. Approaching a dock in a strong following breeze, it was difficult to slow up sufficiently by the ordinary coasting method, and if a boy felt he had complete mastery over his motor, he was tempted to keep it running beyond its time and then reverse it a few feet from the dock. It took a cool nerve, because if you threw the switch a twentieth of a second too soon you would catch the flywheel when it still had speed enough to go up past center, and the boat would leap ahead, charging bull-fashion at the dock.

We had a good week at the camp. The bass were biting well and the sun shone endlessly, day after day. We would be tired at night and lie down in the accumulated heat of the little bedrooms after the long hot day and the breeze

2. Methods of ignition timing.

would stir almost imperceptibly outside and the smell of the swamp drift in through the rusty screens. Sleep would come easily and in the morning the red squirrel would be on the roof, tapping out his gay routine. I kept remembering everything, lying in bed in the mornings—the small steamboat that had a long rounded stern like the lip of a Ubangi, and how quietly she ran on the moonlight sails, when the older boys played their mandolins and the girls sang and we ate doughnuts dipped in sugar, and how sweet the music was on the water in the shining night, and what it had felt like to think about girls then. After breakfast we would go up to the store and the things were in the same place—the minnows in a bottle, the plugs and spinners disarranged and pawed over by the youngsters from the boys' camp, the fig newtons and the Beeman's gum. Outside, the road was tarred and cars stood in front of the store. Inside, all was just as it had always been, except there was more Coca-Cola and not so much Moxie and root beer and birch beer and sarsaparilla. We would walk out with a bottle of pop apiece and sometimes the pop would backfire up our noses and hurt. We explored the streams, quietly, where the turtles slid off the sunny logs and dug their way into the soft bottom; and we lay on the town wharf and fed worms to the tame bass. Everywhere we went I had trouble making out which was I, the one walking at my side, the one walking in my pants.

One afternoon while we were there at that lake a thunderstorm came up. It was like the revival of an old melodrama that I had seen long ago with childish awe. The second-act climax of the drama of the electrical disturbance over a lake in America had not changed in any important respect. This was the big scene, still the big scene. The whole thing was so familiar, the first feeling of oppression and heat and a general air around camp of not wanting to go very far away. In midafternoon (it was all the same) a curious darkening of the sky, and a lull in everything that had made life tick; and then the way the boats suddenly swung the other way at their moorings with the coming of a breeze out of the new quarter, and the premonitory rumble. Then the kettle drum, then the snare, then the bass drum and cymbals, then crackling light against the dark, and the gods grinning and licking their chops in the hills. Afterward the calm, the rain steadily rustling in the calm lake, the return of light and hope and spirits, and the campers running out in joy and relief to go swimming in the rain, their bright cries perpetuating the deathless joke about how they were getting simply drenched, and the children screaming with delight at the new sensation of bathing in the rain, and the joke about getting drenched linking the generations in a strong indestructible chain. And the comedian who waded in carrying an umbrella.

When the others went swimming my son said he was going in too. He pulled his dripping trunks from the line where they had hung all through the shower, and wrung them out. Languidly, and with no thought of going in, I watched him, his hard little body, skinny and bare, saw him wince slightly as he pulled up around his vitals the small, soggy, icy garment. As he buckled the swollen belt suddenly my groin felt the chill of death.

QUESTIONS

1. What has guided White in his selection of the details he gives about the trip? Why, for example, does he talk about the road, the dragonfly, the boat's motor?

2. White speaks of the lake as a "holy spot." What about it was holy?

3. White's last sentence often surprises first-time readers. Go back through the essay and pick out sections or words or phrases that seem to prepare for the ending.

4. Write about revisiting a place that has a special meaning for you.

PEOPLE, PLACES

SCOTT RUSSELL SANDERS *Under the Influence*

Y FATHER DRANK. He drank as a gut-punched boxer gasps for breath, as a starving dog gobbles food—compulsively, secretly, in pain and trembling. I use the past tense not because he ever quit drinking but because he quit living. That is how the story ends for my father, age sixty-four, heart bursting, body cooling and forsaken on the linoleum of my brother's trailer. The story continues for my brother, my sister, my mother, and me, and will continue so long as memory holds.

In the perennial present of memory, I slip into the garage or barn to see my father tipping back the flat green bottles of wine, the brown cylinders of whiskey, the cans of beer disguised in paper bags. His Adam's apple bobs, the liquid gurgles, he wipes the sandy-haired back of a hand over his lips, and then, his bloodshot gaze bumping into me, he stashes the bottle or can inside his jacket, under the workbench, between two bales of hay, and we both pretend the moment has not occurred.

"What's up, buddy?" he says, thick-tongued and edgy.

"Sky's up," I answer, playing along.

"And don't forget prices," he grumbles. "Prices are always up. And taxes." 5

In memory, his white 1951 Pontiac with the stripes down the hood and the Indian head on the snout jounces to a stop in the driveway; or it is the 1956 Ford station wagon, or the 1963 Rambler shaped like a toad, or the sleek 1969 Bonneville that will do 120 miles per hour on straightaways; or it is the robin's-egg blue pickup, new in 1980, battered in 1981, the year of his death. He climbs out, grinning dangerously, unsteady on his legs, and we children interrupt our game of catch, our building of snow forts, our picking of plums, to watch in silence as he weaves past into the house, where he slumps into his overstuffed chair and falls asleep. Shaking her head, our mother stubs out the cigarette he has left smoldering in the ashtray. All evening, until our bedtimes, we tiptoe past him, as past a snoring dragon. Then we curl in our fearful sheets, listening. Eventually he wakes with a grunt, Mother slings accusations at him, he snarls back, she yells, he growls, their voices clashing. Before long, she retreats to their bedroom, sobbing—

Originally published in Harper's Magazine *(November 1989), a monthly dedicated to discussing American politics, literature, and culture.*

not from the blows of fists, for he never strikes her, but from the force of words.

Left alone, our father prowls the house, thumping into furniture, rummaging in the kitchen, slamming doors, turning the pages of the newspaper with a savage crackle, muttering back at the late-night drivel from television. The roof might fly off, the walls might buckle from the pressure of his rage. Whatever my brother and sister and mother may be thinking on their own rumpled pillows, I lie there hating him, loving him, fearing him, knowing I have failed him. I tell myself he drinks to ease an ache that gnaws at his belly, an ache I must have caused by disappointing him somehow, a murderous ache I should be able to relieve by doing all my chores, earning A's in school, winning baseball games, fixing the broken washer and the burst pipes, bringing in money to fill his empty wallet. He would not hide the green bottles in his tool box, would not sneak off to the barn with a lump under his coat, would not fall asleep in the daylight, would not roar and fume, would not drink himself to death, if only I were perfect.

I am forty-two as I write these words, and I know full well now that my father was an alcoholic, a man consumed by disease rather than by disappointment. What had seemed to me a private grief is in fact a public scourge. In the United States alone some ten or fifteen million people share his ailment, and behind the doors they slam in fury or disgrace, countless other children tremble. I comfort myself with such knowledge, holding it against the throb of memory like an ice pack against a bruise. There are keener sources of grief: poverty, racism, rape, war. I do not wish to compete for a trophy in suffering. I am only trying to understand the corrosive mixture of helplessness, responsibility, and shame that I learned to feel as the son of an alcoholic. I realize now that I did not cause my father's illness, nor could I have cured it. Yet for all this grown-up knowledge, I am still ten years old, my own son's age, and as that boy I struggle in guilt and confusion to save my father from pain.

Consider a few of our synonyms for *drunk*: tipsy, tight, pickled, soused, and plowed; stoned and stewed, lubricated and inebriated, juiced and sluiced; three sheets to the wind, in your cups, out of your mind, under the table; lit up, tanked up, wiped out; besotted, blotto, bombed, and buzzed; plastered, polluted, putrified; loaded or looped, boozy, woozy, fuddled, or smashed; crocked and shit-faced, corked and pissed, snockered and sloshed.

10   It is a mostly humorous lexicon, as the lore that deals with drunks—in jokes and cartoons, in plays, films, and television skits—is largely comic. Aunt Matilda nips elderberry wine from the sideboard and burps politely during supper. Uncle Fred slouches to the table glassy-eyed, wearing a lamp shade for a hat and murmuring, "Candy is dandy but liquor is quicker." Inspired by cocktails, Mrs. Somebody recounts the events of her day in a fuzzy dialect, while Mr. Somebody nibbles her ear and croons a bawdy song. On the sofa with Boyfriend, Daughter giggles, licking gin from her lips, and loosens the bows in her hair. Junior knocks back some brews with his chums at the Leopard Lounge and stumbles home to the wrong house, wonders foggily why he

cannot locate his pajamas, and crawls naked into bed with the ugliest girl in school. The family dog slurps from a neglected martini and wobbles to the nursery, where he vomits in Baby's shoe.

It is all great fun. But if in the audience you notice a few laughing faces turn grim when the drunk lurches on stage, don't be surprised, for these are the children of alcoholics. Over the grinning mask of Dionysus,[1] the leering mask of Bacchus,[2] these children cannot help seeing the bloated features of their own parents. Instead of laughing, they wince, they mourn. Instead of celebrating the drunk as one freed from constraints, they pity him as one enslaved. They refuse to believe *in vino veritas*,[3] having seen their befuddled parents skid away from truth toward folly and oblivion. And so these children bite their lips until the lush staggers into the wings.

My father, when drunk, was neither funny nor honest; he was pathetic, frightening, deceitful. There seemed to be a leak in him somewhere, and he poured in booze to keep from draining dry. Like a torture victim who refuses to squeal, he would never admit that he had touched a drop, not even in his last year, when he seemed to be dissolving in alcohol before our very eyes. I never knew him to lie about anything, ever, except about this one ruinous fact. Drowsy, clumsy, unable to fix a bicycle tire, throw a baseball, balance a grocery sack, or walk across the room, he was stripped of his true self by drink. In a matter of minutes, the contents of a bottle could transform a brave man into a coward, a buddy into a bully, a gifted athlete and skilled carpenter and shrewd businessman into a bumbler. No dictionary of synonyms for *drunk* would soften the anguish of watching our prince turn into a frog.

Father's drinking became the family secret. While growing up, we children never breathed a word of it beyond the four walls of our house. To this day, my brother and sister rarely mention it, and then only when I press them. I did not confess the ugly, bewildering fact to my wife until his wavering walk and slurred speech forced me to. Recently, on the seventh anniversary of my father's death, I asked my mother if she ever spoke of his drinking to friends. "No, no, never," she replied hastily. "I couldn't bear for anyone to know."

The secret bores under the skin, gets in the blood, into the bone, and stays there. Long after you have supposedly been cured of malaria, the fever can flare up, the tremors can shake you. So it is with the fevers of shame. You swallow the bitter quinine[4] of knowledge, and you learn to feel pity and compassion toward the drinker. Yet the shame lingers in your marrow, and, because of the shame, anger.

For a long stretch of my childhood we lived on a military reservation in Ohio,   15
an arsenal where bombs were stored underground in bunkers, vintage air-

---

1. Greek god of wine and intoxication.
2. Roman god of wine and intoxication.
3. "In wine is truth."
4. Drug from the bark of the South American cinchona tree, used to treat malaria.

planes burst into flames, and unstable artillery shells boomed nightly at the dump. We had the feeling, as children, that we played in a mine field, where a heedless footfall could trigger an explosion. When Father was drinking, the house, too, became a mine field. The least bump could set off either parent.

The more he drank, the more obsessed Mother became with stopping him. She hunted for bottles, counted the cash in his wallet, sniffed at his breath. Without meaning to snoop, we children blundered left and right into damning evidence. On afternoons when he came home from work sober, we flung ourselves at him for hugs, and felt against our ribs the telltale lump in his coat. In the barn we tumbled on the hay and heard beneath our sneakers the crunch of buried glass. We tugged open a drawer in his workbench, looking for screwdrivers or crescent wrenches, and spied a gleaming six-pack among the tools. Playing tag, we darted around the house just in time to see him sway on the rear stoop and heave a finished bottle into the woods. In his good night kiss we smelled the cloying sweetness of Clorets, the mints he chewed to camouflage his dragon's breath.

I can summon up that kiss right now by recalling Theodore Roethke's[5] lines about his own father in "My Papa's Waltz":

> The whiskey on your breath
> Could make a small boy dizzy;
> But I hung on like death:
> Such waltzing was not easy.

Such waltzing was hard, terribly hard, for with a boy's scrawny arms I was trying to hold my tipsy father upright.

For years, the chief source of those incriminating bottles and cans was a grimy store a mile from us, a cinder block place called Sly's, with two gas pumps outside and a moth-eaten dog asleep in the window. A strip of flypaper, speckled the year round with black bodies, coiled in the doorway. Inside, on rusty metal shelves or in wheezing coolers, you could find pop and Popsicles, cigarettes, potato chips, canned soup, raunchy postcards, fishing gear, Twinkies, wine, and beer. When Father drove anywhere on errands, Mother would send us kids along as guards, warning us not to let him out of our sight. And so with one or more of us on board, Father would cruise up to Sly's, pump a dollar's worth of gas or plump the tires with air, and then, telling us to wait in the car, he would head for that fly-spangled doorway.

20   Dutiful and panicky, we cried, "Let us go in with you!"

"No," he answered. "I'll be back in two shakes."

"Please!"

"No!" he roared. "Don't you budge, or I'll jerk a knot in your tails!"

So we stayed put, kicking the seats, while he ducked inside. Often, when he had parked the car at a careless angle, we gazed in through the window and saw Mr. Sly fetching down from a shelf behind the cash register two green

---

5. American poet (1908–1963) whose father also drank too much.

pints of Gallo wine. Father swigged one of them right there at the counter, stuffed the other in his pocket, and then out he came, a bulge in his coat, a flustered look on his red face.

Because the Mom and Pop who ran the dump were neighbors of ours, liv-ing just down the tar-blistered road, I hated them all the more for poisoning my father. I wanted to sneak in their store and smash the bottles and set fire to the place. I also hated the Gallo brothers, Ernest and Julio, whose jovial faces shone from the labels of their wine, labels I would find, torn and curled, when I burned the trash. I noted the Gallo brothers' address, in California, and I studied the road atlas to see how far that was from Ohio, because I meant to go out there and tell Ernest and Julio what they were doing to my father, and then, if they showed no mercy, I would kill them.

25

While growing up on the back roads and in the country schools and cramped Methodist churches of Ohio and Tennessee, I never heard the word *alco-holism,* never happened across it in books or magazines. In the nearby towns, there were no addiction treatment programs, no community mental health centers, no Alcoholics Anonymous chapters, no therapists. Left alone with our grievous secret, we had no way of understanding Father's drinking except as an act of will, a deliberate folly or cruelty, a moral weakness, a sin. He drank be-cause he chose to, pure and simple. Why our father, so playful and competent and kind when sober, would choose to ruin himself and punish his family, we could not fathom.

Our neighborhood was high on the Bible, and the Bible was hard on drunkards. "Woe to those who are heroes at drinking wine, and valiant men in mixing strong drink," wrote Isaiah. "The priest and the prophet reel with strong drink, they are confused with wine, they err in vision, they stumble in giving judgment. For all tables are full of vomit, no place is without filthiness." We children had seen those fouled tables at the local truck stop where the no-torious boozers hung out, our father occasionally among them. "Wine and new wine take away the understanding," declared the prophet Hosea. We had also seen evidence of that in our father, who could multiply seven-digit numbers in his head when sober, but when drunk could not help us with fourth-grade math. Proverbs warned: "Do not look at wine when it is red, when it sparkles in the cup and goes down smoothly. At the last it bites like a serpent, and stings like an adder. Your eyes will see strange things, and your mind utter per-verse things." Woe, woe.

Dismayingly often, these biblical drunkards stirred up trouble for their own kids. Noah made fresh wine after the flood, drank too much of it, fell asleep without any clothes on, and was glimpsed in the buff by his son Ham, whom Noah promptly cursed. In one passage—it was so shocking we had to read it under our blankets with flashlights—the patriarch Lot fell down drunk and slept with his daughters. The sins of the fathers set their children's teeth on edge.

Our ministers were fond of quoting St. Paul's pronouncement that drunk-ards would not inherit the kingdom of God. These grave preachers assured us that the wine referred to during the Last Supper was in fact grape juice. Bible and sermons and hymns combined to give us the impression that Moses should have brought down from the mountain another stone tablet, bearing the Eleventh Commandment: Thou shalt not drink.

30   The scariest and most illuminating Bible story apropos of drunkards was the one about the lunatic and the swine. Matthew, Mark, and Luke each told a version of the tale. We knew it by heart: When Jesus climbed out of his boat one day, this lunatic came charging up from the graveyard, stark naked and filthy, frothing at the mouth, so violent that he broke the strongest chains. Nobody would go near him. Night and day for years this madman had been wailing among the tombs and bruising himself with stones. Jesus took one look at him and said, "Come out of the man, you unclean spirits!" for he could see that the lunatic was possessed by demons. Meanwhile, some hogs were conveniently rooting nearby. "If we have to come out," begged the demons, "at least let us go into those swine." Jesus agreed. The unclean spirits entered the hogs, and the hogs rushed straight off a cliff and plunged into a lake. Hearing the story in Sunday school, my friends thought mainly of the pigs. (How big a splash did they make? Who paid for the lost pork?) But I thought of the redeemed lunatic, who bathed himself and put on clothes and calmly sat at the feet of Jesus, restored—so the Bible said—to "his right mind."

When drunk, our father was clearly in his wrong mind. He became a stranger, as fearful to us as any graveyard lunatic, not quite frothing at the mouth but fierce enough, quick-tempered, explosive; or else he grew maudlin and weepy, which frightened us nearly as much. In my boyhood despair, I reasoned that maybe he wasn't to blame for turning into an ogre. Maybe, like the lunatic, he was possessed by demons. I found support for my theory when I heard liquor referred to as "spirits," when the newspapers reported that somebody had been arrested for "driving under the influence," and when church ladies railed against that "demon drink."

If my father was indeed possessed, who would exorcise him? If he was a sinner, who would save him? If he was ill, who would cure him? If he suffered, who would ease his pain? Not ministers or doctors, for we could not bring ourselves to confide in them; not the neighbors, for we pretended they had never seen him drunk; not Mother, who fussed and pleaded but could not budge him; not my brother and sister, who were only kids. That left me. It did not matter that I, too, was only a child, and a bewildered one at that. I could not excuse myself.

On first reading a description of delirium tremens—in a book on alcoholism I smuggled from the library—I thought immediately of the frothing lunatic and the frenzied swine. When I read stories or watched films about grisly metamorphoses—Dr. Jekyll becoming Mr. Hyde,[6] the mild husband changing into a werewolf, the kindly neighbor taken over by a brutal alien —I could not help seeing my own father's mutation from sober to drunk. Even today, knowing

6. London physician and his evil alter ego, in Robert Louis Stevenson's novel.

better, I am attracted by the demonic theory of drink, for when I recall my father's transformation, the emergence of his ugly second self, I find it easy to believe in possession by unclean spirits. We never knew which version of Father would come home from work, the true or the tainted, nor could we guess how far down the slope toward cruelty he would slide.

How far a man *could* slide we gauged by observing our back-road neighbors—the out-of-work miners who had dragged their families to our corner of Ohio from the desolate hollows of Appalachia, the tight-fisted farmers, the surly mechanics, the balked and broken men. There was, for example, whiskey-soaked Mr. Jenkins, who beat his wife and kids so hard we could hear their screams from the road. There was Mr. Lavo the wino, who fell asleep smoking time and again, until one night his disgusted wife bundled up the children and went outside and left him in his easy chair to burn; he awoke on his own, staggered out coughing into the yard, and pounded her flat while the children looked on and the shack turned to ash. There was the truck driver, Mr. Sampson, who tripped over his son's tricycle one night while drunk and got so mad that he jumped into his semi and drove away, shifting through the dozen gears, and never came back. We saw the bruised children of these fathers clump onto our school bus, we saw the abandoned children huddle in the pews at church, we saw the stunned and battered mothers begging for help at our doors.

Our own father never beat us, and I don't think he ever beat Mother, but he threatened often. The Old Testament Yahweh was not more terrible in his wrath. Eyes blazing, voice booming, Father would pull out his belt and swear to give us a whipping, but he never followed through, never needed to, because we could imagine it so vividly. He shoved us, pawed us with the back of his hand, as an irked bear might smack a cub, not to injure, just to clear a space. I can see him grabbing Mother by the hair as she cowers on a chair during a nightly quarrel. He twists her neck back until she gapes up at him, and then he lifts over her skull a glass quart bottle of milk, the milk running down his forearm; and he yells at her, "Say just one more word, one goddamn word, and I'll shut you up!" I fear she will prick him with her sharp tongue, but she is terrified into silence, and so am I, and the leaking bottle quivers in the air, and milk slithers through the red hair of my father's uplifted arm, and the entire scene is there to this moment, the head jerked back, the club raised. 35

When the drink made him weepy, Father would pack a bag and kiss each of us children on the head, and announce from the front door that he was moving out. "Where to?" we demanded, fearful each time that he would leave for good, as Mr. Sampson had roared away for good in his diesel truck. "Someplace where I won't get hounded every minute," Father would answer, his jaw quivering. He stabbed a look at Mother, who might say, "Don't run into the ditch before you get there," or, "Good riddance," and then he would slink away. Mother watched him go with arms crossed over her chest, her face closed like the lid on a box of snakes. We children bawled. Where could he go? To the truck stop, that den of iniquity? To one of those dark, ratty flophouses in town? Would he wind up sleeping under a railroad bridge or on a park bench or in a cardboard box, mummied in rags, like the bums we had seen on our trips to Cleveland and Chicago? We bawled and bawled, wondering if he would ever come back.

He always did come back, a day or a week later, but each time there was a sliver less of him.

In Kafka's[7] *The Metamorphosis,* which opens famously with Gregor Samsa waking up from uneasy dreams to find himself transformed into an insect, Gregor's family keep reassuring themselves that things will be just fine again, "When he comes back to us." Each time alcohol transformed our father, we held out the same hope, that he would really and truly come back to us, our authentic father, the tender and playful and competent man, and then all things would be fine. We had grounds for such hope. After his weepy departures and chapfallen returns, he would sometimes go weeks, even months without drinking. Those were glad times. Joy banged inside my ribs. Every day without the furtive glint of bottles, every meal without a fight, every bedtime without sobs encouraged us to believe that such bliss might go on forever.

Mother was fooled by just such a hope all during the forty-odd years she knew this Greeley Ray Sanders. Soon after she met him in a Chicago delicatessen on the eve of World War II and fell for his butter-melting Mississippi drawl and his wavy red hair, she learned that he drank heavily. But then so did a lot of men. She would soon coax or scold him into breaking the nasty habit. She would point out to him how ugly and foolish it was, this bleary drinking, and then he would quit. He refused to quit during their engagement, however, still refused during the first years of marriage, refused until my sister came along. The shock of fatherhood sobered him, and he remained sober through my birth at the end of the war and right on through until we moved in 1951 to the Ohio arsenal, that paradise of bombs. Like all places that make a business of death, the arsenal had more than its share of alcoholics and drug addicts and other varieties of escape artists. There I turned six and started school and woke into a child's flickering awareness, just in time to see my father begin sneaking swigs in the garage.

40   He sobered up again for most of a year at the height of the Korean War, to celebrate the birth of my brother. But aside from that dry spell, his only breaks from drinking before I graduated from high school were just long enough to raise and then dash our hopes. Then during the fall of my senior year—the time of the Cuban missile crisis, when it seemed that the nightly explosions at the munitions dump and the nightly rages in our household might spread to engulf the globe—Father collapsed. His liver, kidneys, and heart all conked out. The doctors saved him, but only by a hair. He stayed in the hospital for weeks, going through a withdrawal so terrible that Mother would not let us visit him. If he wanted to kill himself, the doctors solemnly warned him, all he had to do was hit the bottle again. One binge would finish him.

7. Franz Kafka (1883–1924), Prague-born novelist and short-story writer whose works raise puzzling moral, spiritual, and political dilemmas.

Father must have believed them, for he stayed dry the next fifteen years. It was an answer to prayer, Mother said, it was a miracle. I believe it was a reflex of fear, which he sustained over the years through courage and pride. He knew a man could die from drink, for his brother Roscoe had. We children never laid eyes on doomed Uncle Roscoe, but in the stories Mother told us he became a fairy-tale figure, like a boy who took the wrong turning in the woods and was gobbled up by the wolf.

The fifteen-year dry spell came to an end with Father's retirement in the spring of 1978. Like many men, he gave up his identity along with his job. One day he was a boss at the factory, with a brass plate on his door and a reputation to uphold; the next day he was a nobody at home. He and Mother were leaving Ontario, the last of the many places to which his job had carried them, and they were moving to a new house in Mississippi, his childhood stomping grounds. As a boy in Mississippi, Father sold Coca-Cola during dances while the moonshiners peddled their brew in the parking lot; as a young blade, he fought in bars and in the ring, seeking a state Golden Gloves championship; he gambled at poker, hunted pheasants, raced motorcycles and cars, played semiprofessional baseball, and, along with all his buddies—in the Black Cat Saloon, behind the cotton gin, in the woods—he drank. It was a perilous youth to dream of recovering.

After his final day of work, Mother drove on ahead with a car full of begonias and violets, while Father stayed behind to oversee the packing. When the van was loaded, the sweaty movers broke open a six-pack and offered him a beer.

"Let's drink to retirement!" they crowed. "Let's drink to freedom! to fishing! hunting! loafing! Let's drink to a guy who's going home!"

At least I imagine some such words, for that is all I can do, imagine, and I see Father's hand trembling in midair as he thinks about the fifteen sober years and about the doctors' warning, and he tells himself *God damnit, I am a free man,* and *Why can't a free man drink one beer after a lifetime of hard work?* and I see his arm reaching, his fingers closing, the can tilting to his lips. I even supply a label for the beer, a swaggering brand that promises on television to deliver the essence of life. I watch the amber liquid pour down his throat, the alcohol steal into his blood, the key turn in his brain.

Soon after my parents moved back to Father's treacherous stomping ground, my wife and I visited them in Mississippi with our five-year-old daughter. Mother had been too distraught to warn me about the return of the demons. So when I climbed out of the car that bright July morning and saw my father napping in the hammock, I felt uneasy, for in all his sober years I had never known him to sleep in daylight. Then he lurched upright, blinked his bloodshot eyes, and greeted us in a syrupy voice. I was hurled back helpless into childhood.

"What's the matter with Papaw?" our daughter asked.

"Nothing," I said. "Nothing!"

Like a child again, I pretended not to see him in his stupor, and behind

my phony smile I grieved. On that visit and on the few that remained before
his death, once again I found bottles in the workbench, bottles in the woods.
Again his hands shook too much for him to run a saw, to make his precious
miniature furniture, to drive straight down back roads. Again he wound up in
the ditch, in the hospital, in jail, in treatment centers. Again he shouted and
wept. Again he lied. "I never touched a drop," he swore. "Your mother's making
it up."

50   I no longer fancied I could reason with the men whose names I found on
the bottles—Jim Beam, Jack Daniels—nor did I hope to save my father by burning down a store. I was able now to press the cold statistics about alcoholism
against the ache of memory: ten million victims, fifteen million, twenty. And yet,
in spite of my age, I reacted in the same blind way as I had in childhood, ignoring biology, forgetting numbers, vainly seeking to erase through my efforts whatever drove him to drink. I worked on their place twelve and sixteen hours a day,
in the swelter of Mississippi summers, digging ditches, running electrical wires,
planting trees, mowing grass, building sheds, as though what nagged at him was
some list of chores, as though by taking his worries on my shoulders I could redeem him. I was flung back into boyhood, acting as though my father would not
drink himself to death if only I were perfect.

I failed of perfection; he succeeded in dying. To the end, he considered
himself not sick but sinful. "Do you want to kill yourself?" I asked him. "Why
not?" he answered. "Why the hell not? What's there to save?" To the end, he
would not speak about his feelings, would not or could not give a name to the
beast that was devouring him.

In silence, he went rushing off the cliff. Unlike the biblical swine, however, he left behind a few of the demons to haunt his children. Life with him
and the loss of him twisted us into shapes that will be familiar to other sons
and daughters of alcoholics. My brother became a rebel, my sister retreated
into shyness, I played the stalwart and dutiful son who would hold the family together. If my father was unstable, I would be a rock. If he squandered
money on drink, I would pinch every penny. If he wept when drunk—and only
when drunk—I would not let myself weep at all. If he roared at the Little
League umpire for calling my pitches balls, I would throw nothing but strikes.
Watching him flounder and rage, I came to dread the loss of control. I would
go through life without making anyone mad. I vowed never to put in my
mouth or veins any chemical that would banish my everyday self. I would
never make a scene, never lash out at the ones I loved, never hurt a soul.
Through hard work, relentless work, I would achieve something dazzling—in
the classroom, on the basketball floor, in the science lab, in the pages of
books—and my achievement would distract the world's eyes from his humiliation. I would become a worthy sacrifice, and the smoke of my burning would
please God.

It is far easier to recognize these twists in my character than to undo
them. Work has become an addiction for me, as drink was an addiction for my
father. Knowing this, my daughter gave me a placard for the wall: WORK-
AHOLIC. The labor is endless and futile, for I can no more redeem myself

through work than I could redeem my father. I still panic in the face of other people's anger, because his drunken temper was so terrible. I shrink from causing sadness or disappointment even to strangers, as though I were still concealing the family shame. I still notice every twitch of emotion in the faces around me, having learned as a child to read the weather in faces, and I blame myself for their least pang of unhappiness or anger. In certain moods I blame myself for everything. Guilt burns like acid in my veins.

I am moved to write these pages now because my own son, at the age of ten, is taking on himself the griefs of the world, and in particular the griefs of his father. He tells me that when I am gripped by sadness he feels responsible; he feels there must be something he can do to spring me from depression, to fix my life. And that crushing sense of responsibility is exactly what I felt at the age of ten in the face of my father's drinking. My son wonders if I, too, am possessed. I write, therefore, to drag into the light what eats at me—the fear, the guilt, the shame—so that my own children may be spared.

I still shy away from nightclubs, from bars, from parties where the solvent   55
is alcohol. My friends puzzle over this, but it is no more peculiar than for a man to shy away from the lions' den after seeing his father torn apart. I took my own first drink at the age of twenty-one, half a glass of burgundy. I knew the odds of my becoming an alcoholic were four times higher than for the sons of nonalcoholic fathers. So I sipped warily.

I still do—once a week, perhaps, a glass of wine, a can of beer, nothing stronger, nothing more. I listen for the turning of a key in my brain.

QUESTIONS

1. Sanders frequently punctuates his memories of his father with information from other sources—dictionaries, medical encyclopedias, poems and short stories, the Bible. What function do these sources perform? How do they enlarge and enrich Sanders's essay?

2. Why does Sanders include the final three paragraphs (53–55)? What effect do they create that would be lost without them?

3. Drawing on your memories of a friend or family member, write an essay about some problem that person had and its effect on your life.

ANNIE DILLARD　　from *An American Childhood*

ONE SUNDAY AFTERNOON Mother wandered through our kitchen, where Father was making a sandwich and listening to the ball game. The Pirates were playing the New York Giants at Forbes Field. In those days, the Giants had a utility infielder named Wayne Terwilliger. Just as Mother passed through, the radio announcer cried—with undue drama—"Terwilliger bunts one!"

"Terwilliger bunts one?" Mother cried back, stopped short. She turned. "Is that English?"

"The player's name is Terwilliger," Father said. "He bunted."

"That's marvelous," Mother said. " 'Terwilliger bunts one.' No wonder you listen to baseball. 'Terwilliger bunts one.' "

5　　For the next seven or eight years, Mother made this surprising string of syllables her own. Testing a microphone, she repeated, "Terwilliger bunts one"; testing a pen or a typewriter, she wrote it. If, as happened surprisingly often in the course of various improvised gags, she pretended to whisper something else in my ear, she actually whispered, "Terwilliger bunts one." Whenever someone used a French phrase, or a Latin one, she answered solemnly, "Terwilliger bunts one." If Mother had had, like Andrew Carnegie, the opportunity to cook up a motto for a coat of arms, hers would have read simply and tellingly, "Terwilliger bunts one." (Carnegie's was "Death to Privilege.")

She served us with other words and phrases. On a Florida trip, she repeated tremulously, "That . . . is a royal poinciana." I don't remember the tree; I remember the thrill in her voice. She pronounced it carefully, and spelled it. She also liked to say "portulaca."

The drama of the words "Tamiami Trail" stirred her, we learned on the same Florida trip. People built Tampa on one coast, and they built Miami on another. Then—the height of visionary ambition and folly—they piled a slow, tremendous road through the terrible Everglades to connect them. To build the road, men stood sunk in muck to their armpits. They fought off cottonmouth moccasins and six-foot alligators. They slept in boats, wet. They blasted muck with dynamite, cut jungle with machetes; they laid logs, dragged drilling machines, hauled dredges, heaped limestone. The road took fourteen years to build up by the shovelful, a Panama Canal in reverse, and cost hundreds of lives from tropical, mosquito-carried diseases. Then, capping it all, some genius thought of the word Tamiami: they called the road from Tampa to Miami, this very road under our spinning wheels, the Tamiami Trail. Some called it Alligator Alley. Anyone could drive over this road without a thought.

Hearing this, moved, I thought all the suffering of road building was worth it (it wasn't my suffering), now that we had this new thing to hang these new words on—Alligator Alley for those who liked things cute, and, for con-

From An American Childhood, *Dillard's 1987 memoir of growing up in Pittsburgh.*

noisseurs like Mother, for lovers of the human drama in all its boldness and terror, the Tamiami Trail.

Back home, Mother cut clips from reels of talk, as it were, and played them back at leisure. She noticed that many Pittsburghers confuse "leave" and "let." One kind relative brightened our morning by mentioning why she'd brought her son to visit: "He wanted to come with me, so I left him." Mother filled in Amy and me on locutions we missed. "I can't do it on Friday," her pretty sister told a crowded dinner party, "because Friday's the day I lay in the stores."

(All unconsciously, though, we ourselves used some pure Pittsburghisms. We said "tele pole," pronounced "telly pole," for that splintery sidewalk post I loved to climb. We said "slippy"—the sidewalks are "slippy." We said, "That's all the farther I could go." And we said, as Pittsburghers do say, "This glass needs washed," or "The dog needs walked"—a usage our father eschewed; he knew it was not standard English, nor even comprehensible English, but he never let on.)

"Spell 'poinsettia,' " Mother would throw out at me, smiling with pleasure. "Spell 'sherbet.' " The idea was not to make us whizzes, but, quite the contrary, to remind us—and I, especially, needed reminding—that we didn't know it all just yet.

"There's a deer standing in the front hall," she told me one quiet evening in the country.

"Really?"

"No. I just wanted to tell you something once without your saying, 'I know.' "

Supermarkets in the middle 1950s began luring, or bothering, customers by giving out Top Value Stamps or Green Stamps. When, shopping with Mother, we got to the head of the checkout line, the checker, always a young man, asked, "Save stamps?"

"No," Mother replied genially, week after week, "I build model airplanes." I believe she originated this line. It took me years to determine where the joke lay.

Anyone who met her verbal challenges she adored. She had surgery on one of her eyes. On the operating table, just before she conked out, she appealed feelingly to the surgeon, saying, as she had been planning to say for weeks, "Will I be able to play the piano?" "Not on me," the surgeon said. "You won't pull that old one on me."

It was, indeed, an old one. The surgeon was supposed to answer, "Yes, my dear, brave woman, you will be able to play the piano after this operation," to which Mother intended to reply, "Oh, good, I've always wanted to play the piano." This pat scenario bored her; she loved having it interrupted. It must have galled her that usually her acquaintances were so predictably unalert; it must have galled her that, for the length of her life, she could surprise everyone so continually, so easily, when she had been the same all along. At any rate, she loved anyone who, as she put it, saw it coming, and called her on it.

She regarded the instructions on bureaucratic forms as straight lines. "Do you advocate the overthrow of the United States government by force or violence?" After some thought she wrote, "Force." She regarded children, even babies, as straight men. When Molly learned to crawl, Mother delighted in buying her gowns with drawstrings at the bottom, like Swee'pea's,[1] because, as she explained energetically, you could easily step on the drawstring without the baby's noticing, so that she crawled and crawled and crawled and never got anywhere except into a small ball at the gown's top.

20   When we children were young, she mothered us tenderly and dependably; as we got older, she resumed her career of anarchism. She collared us into her gags. If she answered the phone on a wrong number, she told the caller, "Just a minute," and dragged the receiver to Amy or me, saying, "Here, take this, your name is Cecile," or, worse, just, "It's for you." You had to think on your feet. But did you want to perform well as Cecile, or did you want to take pity on the wretched caller?

During a family trip to the Highland Park Zoo, Mother and I were alone for a minute. She approached a young couple holding hands on a bench by the seals, and addressed the young man in dripping tones: "Where have you been? Still got those baby-blue eyes; always did slay me. And this"—a swift nod at the dumbstruck young woman, who had removed her hand from the man's— "must be the one you were telling me about. She's not so bad, really, as you used to make out. But listen, you know how I miss you, you know where to reach me, same old place. And there's Ann over there—see how she's grown? See the blue eyes?"

And off she sashayed, taking me firmly by the hand, and leading us around briskly past the monkey house and away. She cocked an ear back, and both of us heard the desperate man begin, in a high-pitched wail, "I swear, I never saw her before in my life. . . ."

On a long, sloping beach by the ocean, she lay stretched out sunning with Father and friends, until the conversation gradually grew tedious, when without forethought she gave a little push with her heel and rolled away. People were stunned. She rolled deadpan and apparently effortlessly, arms and legs extended and tidy, down the beach to the distant water's edge, where she lay at ease just as she had been, but half in the surf, and well out of earshot.

She dearly loved to fluster people by throwing out a game's rules at whim—when she was getting bored, losing in a dull sort of way, and when everybody else was taking it too seriously. If you turned your back, she moved the checkers around on the board. When you got them all straightened out, she denied she'd touched them; the next time you turned your back, she lined them up on the rug or hid them under your chair. In a betting rummy game called Michigan, she routinely played out of turn, or called out a card she didn't hold, or counted backward, simply to amuse herself by causing an uproar and watching the rest of us do double takes and have fits. (Much later, when serious suitors came to call, Mother subjected them to this fast card

---

1. The infant in the comic strip "Popeye" by Elzie Crisler Segar.

game as a trial by ordeal; she used it as an intelligence test and a measure of spirit. If the poor man could stay a round without breaking down or running out, he got to marry one of us, if he still wanted to.)

She excelled at bridge, playing fast and boldly, but when the stakes were low   25
and the hands dull, she bid slams for the devilment of it, or raised her opponents' suit to bug them, or showed her hand, or tossed her cards in a handful behind her back in a characteristic swift motion accompanied by a vibrantly innocent look. It drove our stolid father crazy. The hand was over before it began, and the guests were appalled. How do you score it, who deals now, what do you do with a crazy person who is having so much fun? Or they were down seven, and the guests were appalled. "Pam!" "Dammit, Pam!" He groaned. What ails such people? What on earth possesses them? He rubbed his face.

She was an unstoppable force; she never let go. When we moved across town, she persuaded the U.S. Post Office to let her keep her old address—forever—because she'd had stationery printed. I don't know how she did it. Every new post office worker, over decades, needed to learn that although the Doaks' mail is addressed to here, it is delivered to there.

Mother's energy and intelligence suited her for a greater role in a larger arena—mayor of New York, say—than the one she had. She followed American politics closely; she had been known to vote for Democrats. She saw how things should be run, but she had nothing to run but our household. Even there, small minds bugged her; she was smarter than the people who designed the things she had to use all day for the length of her life.

"Look," she said. "Whoever designed this corkscrew never used one. Why would anyone sell it without trying it out?" So she invented a better one. She showed me a drawing of it. The spirit of American enterprise never faded in Mother. If capitalizing and tooling up had been as interesting as theorizing and thinking up, she would have fired up a new factory every week, and chaired several hundred corporations.

"It grieves me," she would say, "it grieves my heart," that the company that made one superior product packaged it poorly, or took the wrong tack in its advertising. She knew, as she held the thing mournfully in her two hands, that she'd never find another. She was right. We children wholly sympathized, and so did Father; what could she do, what could anyone do, about it? She was Samson in chains.[2] She paced.

She didn't like the taste of stamps so she didn't lick stamps; she licked the   30
corner of the envelope instead. She glued sandpaper to the sides of kitchen drawers, and under kitchen cabinets, so she always had a handy place to strike a match. She designed, and hounded workmen to build against all norms, doubly wide kitchen counters and elevated bathroom sinks. To splint a finger, she stuck it in a lightweight cigar tube. Conversely, to protect a pack of cigarettes, she carried it in a Band-Aid box. She drew plans for an over-the-finger toothbrush for babies, an oven rack that slid up and down, and—the family

2. The Israelite champion against the Philistines, to whom he was betrayed by Delilah (see Judges 14–16).

favorite—Lendalarm. Lendalarm was a beeper you attached to books (or tools) you loaned friends. After ten days, the beeper sounded. Only the rightful owner could silence it.

She repeatedly reminded us of P. T. Barnum's dictum: You could sell anything to anybody if you marketed it right. The adman who thought of making Americans believe they needed underarm deodorant was a visionary. So, too, was the hero who made a success of a new product, Ivory soap. The executives were horrified, Mother told me, that a cake of this stuff floated. Soap wasn't supposed to float. Anyone would be able to tell it was mostly whipped-up air. Then some inspired adman made a leap: Advertise that it floats. Flaunt it. The rest is history.

She respected the rare few who broke through to new ways. "Look," she'd say, "here's an intelligent apron." She called upon us to admire intelligent control knobs and intelligent pan handles, intelligent andirons and picture frames and knife sharpeners. She questioned everything, every pair of scissors, every knitting needle, gardening glove, tape dispenser. Hers was a restless mental vigor that just about ignited the dumb household objects with its force.

Torpid conformity was a kind of sin; it was stupidity itself, the mighty stream against which Mother would never cease to struggle. If you held no minority opinions, or if you failed to risk total ostracism for them daily, the world would be a better place without you.

Always I heard Mother's emotional voice asking Amy and me the same few questions: Is that your own idea? Or somebody else's? *"Giant* is a good movie," I pronounced to the family at dinner. "Oh, really?" Mother warmed to these occasions. She all but rolled up her sleeves. She knew I hadn't seen it. "Is that your considered opinion?"

35   She herself held many unpopular, even fantastic, positions. She was scathingly sarcastic about the McCarthy hearings[3] while they took place, right on our living-room television; she frantically opposed Father's wait-and-see calm. "We don't know enough about it," he said. "I do," she said. "I know all I need to know."

She asserted, against all opposition, that people who lived in trailer parks were not bad but simply poor, and had as much right to settle on beautiful land, such as rural Ligonier, Pennsylvania, as did the oldest of families in the finest of hidden houses. Therefore, the people who owned trailer parks, and sought zoning changes to permit trailer parks, needed our help. Her profound belief that the country-club pool sweeper was a person, and that the department-store saleslady, the bus driver, telephone operator, and housepainter were people, and even in groups the steelworkers who carried pickets and the Christmas shoppers

3. The televised hearings in 1954 (the Army accused Wisconsin senator Joseph R. McCarthy [1908–1957] of improperly seeking preferential treatment for a former colleague then in the service; Senator McCarthy, widely known as a Communist-hunter, accused the Army of covering up certain espionage action) led to the senator's loss of public favor and contributed to his "condemnation" by the Senate in December 1954.

who clogged intersections were people—this was a conviction common enough in democratic Pittsburgh, but not altogether common among our friends' parents, or even, perhaps, among our parents' friends.

Opposition emboldened Mother, and she would take on anybody on any issue—the chairman of the board, at a cocktail party, on the current strike; she would fly at him in a flurry of passion, as a songbird selflessly attacks a big hawk.

"Eisenhower's going to win," I announced after school. She lowered her magazine and looked me in the eyes: "How do you know?" I was doomed. It was fatal to say, "Everyone says so." We all knew well what happened. "Do you consult this Everyone before you make your decisions? What if Everyone decided to round up all the Jews?" Mother knew there was no danger of cowing me. She simply tried to keep us all awake. And in fact it was always clear to Amy and me, and to Molly when she grew old enough to listen, that if our classmates came to cruelty, just as much as if the neighborhood or the nation came to madness, we were expected to take, and would be each separately capable of taking, a stand.

QUESTIONS

1. Dillard piles up examples in this excerpt, barely creating transitions between them. What do the many examples add up to? Is there an overall point she wishes to make about her mother? Try to state it in your own words.

2. When this piece was originally published in Dillard's *An American Childhood*, the chapter had no title. If you could title this piece, what would that title be? Why?

3. Do some freewriting about one of your own parents (or someone important in your life when you were a child). Like Dillard, use as many specific examples as possible to communicate that person's character and personality.

TONI MORRISON   *Strangers*

I AM IN THIS river place—newly mine—walking in the yard when I see a woman sitting on the seawall at the edge of a neighbor's garden. A homemade fishing pole arcs into the water some twenty feet from her hand. A feeling of welcome washes over me. I walk toward her, right up to the fence that separates my place from the neighbor's, and notice with pleasure the clothes she wears: men's shoes, a man's hat, a well-worn colorless sweater over a long black dress. The woman turns her head and greets me with an easy smile and

Morrison wrote this essay to introduce a book of photographs by Robert Bergman, A Kind of Rapture *(1998).*

a "How you doing?" She tells me her name (Mother Something) and we talk for some time—fifteen minutes or so—about fish recipes and weather and children. When I ask her if she lives there, she answers no. She lives in a nearby village, but the owner of the house lets her come to this spot any time she wants to fish, and she comes every week, sometimes several days in a row when the perch or catfish are running and even if they aren't because she likes eel, too, and they are always there. She is witty and full of the wisdom that older women always seem to have a lock on. When we part, it is with an understanding that she will be there the next day or very soon after and we will visit again. I imagine more conversations with her. I will invite her into my house for coffee, for tales, for laughter. She reminds me of someone, something. I imagine a friendship, casual, effortless, delightful.

She is not there the next day. She is not there the following days, either. And I look for her every morning. The summer passes, and I have not seen her at all. Finally, I approach the neighbor to ask about her and am bewildered to learn that the neighbor does not know who or what I am talking about. No old woman fished from her wall—ever—and none had permission to do so. I decide that the fisherwoman fibbed about the permission and took advantage of the neighbor's frequent absences to poach. The fact of the neighbor's presence is proof that the fisherwoman would not be there. During the months following, I ask lots of people if they know Mother Something. No one, not even people who have lived in nearby villages for seventy years, has ever heard of her.

I feel cheated, puzzled, but also amused, and wonder off and on if I have dreamed her. In any case, I tell myself, it was an encounter of no value other than anecdotal. Still. Little by little, annoyance then bitterness takes the place of my original bewilderment. A certain view from my windows is now devoid of her, reminding me every morning of her deceit and my disappointment. What was she doing in that neighborhood, anyway? She didn't drive, had to walk four miles if indeed she lived where she said she did. How could she be missed on the road in that hat, those awful shoes? I try to understand the intensity of my chagrin, and why I am missing a woman I spoke to for fifteen minutes. I get nowhere except for the stingy explanation that she had come into my space (next to it, anyway—at the property line, at the edge, just at the fence, where the most interesting things always happen), and had implied promises of female camaraderie, of opportunities for me to be generous, of protection and protecting. Now she is gone, taking with her my good opinion of myself, which, of course, is unforgivable.

Isn't that the kind of thing that we fear strangers will do? Disturb. Betray. Prove they are not like us. That is why it is so hard to know what to do with them. The love that prophets have urged us to offer the stranger is the same love that Jean-Paul Sartre[1] could reveal as the very mendacity of Hell. The signal line of "No Exit," "*L'enfer, c'est les autres*," raises the possibility that "other people" are responsible for turning a personal world into a public hell. In the admonition of a prophet and the sly warning of an artist, strangers as well as the beloved are understood to tempt our gaze, to slide away or to stake claims. Religious prophets caution against the slide, the looking away; Sartre warns against love as possession.

1. French existentialist philosopher (1905–1980). The line in Sartre's 1944 play *No Exit* is usually translated as "Hell is other people."

5   The resources available to us for benign access to each other, for vaulting
the mere blue air that separates us, are few but powerful: language, image,
and experience, which may involve both, one, or neither of the first two. Language (saying, listening, reading) can encourage, even mandate, surrender, the
breach of distances among us, whether they are continental or on the same
pillow, whether they are distances of culture or the distinctions and indistinc-
tions of age or gender, whether they are the consequences of social invention
or biology. Image increasingly rules the realm of shaping, sometimes becoming, often contaminating, knowledge. Provoking language or eclipsing it, an
image can determine not only what we know and feel but also what we believe
is worth knowing about what we feel.

These two godlings, language and image, feed and form experience. My instant embrace of an outrageously dressed fisherwoman was due in part to an image on which my representation of her was based. I immediately sentimentalized
and appropriated her. I owned her or wanted to (and I suspect she glimpsed it).
I had forgotten the power of embedded images and stylish language to seduce,
reveal, control. Forgot, too, their capacity to help us pursue the human project—
which is to remain human and to block the dehumanization of others.

But something unforeseen has entered into this admittedly oversimplified
menu of our resources. Far from our original expectations of increased intimacy and broader knowledge, routine media presentations deploy images and
language that narrow our view of what humans look like (or ought to look like)
and what in fact we are like. Succumbing to the perversions of media can blur
vision, resisting them can do the same. I was clearly and aggressively resisting
such influences in my encounter with the fisherwoman. Art as well as the market can be complicit in the sequestering of form from formula, of nature from
artifice, of humanity from commodity. Art gesturing toward representation has,
in some exalted quarters, become literally beneath contempt. The concept of
what it is to be human has altered, and the word *truth* needs quotation marks
around it so that its absence (its elusiveness) is stronger than its presence.

Why would we want to know a stranger when it is easier to estrange another? Why would we want to close the distance when we can close the gate?
Appeals in arts and religion for comity in the Common Wealth are faint.

It took some time for me to understand my unreasonable claims on that
fisherwoman. To understand that I was longing for and missing some aspect of
myself, and that there are no strangers. There are only versions of ourselves,
many of which we have not embraced, most of which we wish to protect ourselves from. For the stranger is not foreign, she is random, not alien but remembered; and it is the randomness of the encounter with our already
known—although unacknowledged—selves that summons a ripple of alarm.
That makes us reject the figure and the emotions it provokes—especially when
these emotions are profound. It is also what makes us want to own, govern,
administrate the Other. To romance her, if we can, back into our own mirrors.
In either instance (of alarm or false reverence), we deny her personhood, the
specific individuality we insist upon for ourselves.

10   Robert Bergman's radiant portraits of strangers provoked this meditation.

Occasionally, there arises an event or a moment that one knows immediately will forever mark a place in the history of artistic endeavor. Bergman's portraits represent such a moment, such an event. In all its burnished majesty his gallery refuses us unearned solace, and one by one by one the photographs unveil *us*, asserting a beauty, a kind of rapture, that is as close as can be to a master template of the singularity, the community, the unextinguishable sacredness of the human race.

QUESTIONS

1. In his book, *A Kind of Rapture*, Robert Bergman included people he encountered on the streets of America. Why does Morrison not dwell on that fact?

2. In the opening paragraphs (1–3) Morrison relates a story about a woman she sees fishing near her property; later in the essay she expresses regret, even guilt, that her story "sentimentalized and appropriated" the woman (paragraphs 6–7). What does Morrison mean by this self-criticism? Do you agree that it may be ethically wrong to create stories about the strangers we see?

3. What do you see in these photographs? More than Morrison does? Different things? Can you read these images the way Updike reads paintings in "Moving Along" (p. 668)?

JAMAICA KINCAID   *Sowers and Reapers*

WHY MUST PEOPLE INSIST that the garden is a place of rest and repose, a place to forget the cares of the world, a place in which to distance yourself from the painful responsibility that comes with being a human being?

The day after I spoke to a group of people at the Garden Conservancy's tenth-anniversary celebration, in Charleston, South Carolina, an American man named Frank Cabot, the chairman and founder of the organization and a very rich man, who has spent some of his money creating a spectacular garden in the surprisingly hospitable climate of eastern Canada, told me that he was sorry I had been invited, that he was utterly offended by what I had said and the occasion I had used to say it, for I had done something unforgivable—I had introduced race and politics into the garden.

There were three of us on a panel, and our topic was "My Favorite Garden." One of the speakers said that his favorite was Hidcote Manor, in England, created by an American Anglophile named Lawrence Johnston. (A very

First published in the New Yorker *(January 22, 2001), a magazine of literature and the arts. Kincaid is perhaps best known as a novelist, but as a staff writer for the* New Yorker *she has produced many essays like this one examining her own experiences.*

nice climbing yellow rose, which is sometimes available through the Wayside Gardens catalogue, is named after him.) There are at least a thousand gardens in every corner of the world, but especially in England, that should come before Hidcote as a choice for favorite garden. The garden of the filmmaker Derek Jarman, who succumbed to AIDS in 1994, is a particularly good example. Dramatically set in the shadow of a nuclear-power station in Dungeness, Kent, surrounding a one-story house that has been painted black, this garden, when I saw it, was abloom with poppies in brilliant shades and with *Crambe maritima* (sea kale) and pathways lined with pebbles, the kind found at the seashore, and all sorts of worn-down objects that looked as if they were the remains of a long-ago shipwreck just found. When you see it for the first time, it so defies what you expect that this thought really will occur to you: Now, what is a garden? And, at the same time, you will be filled with pleasure and inspiration.

Another man spoke of a garden he was designing in Chicago which would include a re-creation of a quadripartite garden made by prisoners in Auschwitz. (This way of organizing a garden is quite common, and it has a history that begins with Genesis 2:10—"A river issues from Eden to water the garden, and it then divides and becomes four branches.") The garden in Auschwitz was created over many years and by many people, all of whom were facing death, and it gave me a sharp pang to realize that, while waiting to be brutally murdered, some people had made a garden.

5   I had prepared a talk in which I was going to say that my favorite garden is the Garden of Eden, because every time I see a garden that I love it becomes my favorite garden until I see another garden that I love and completely forget the garden that so dominated my affections a short time before; and also because this garden, Eden, is described in the fewest words I have ever seen used to describe a garden, and yet how unforgettable and vivid the description remains: "And from the ground the Lord God caused to grow every tree that was pleasing to the sight and good for food, with the tree of life in the middle of the garden, and the tree of knowledge of good and bad."

But after that man spoke of the Holocaust garden, a nice speech on Eden was no longer possible.

I heard myself telling my audience that I had been surprised to see, on the way into my hotel, in the little park across the way, a statue of John Caldwell Calhoun,[1] that inventor of the rhetoric of states' rights and the evil encoded in it, who was elected Vice-President of the United States twice. I remarked on how hard it must be for the black citizens of Charleston to pass each day by the statue of a man who hated them, cast in a heroic pose. And then I wondered if anyone in the audience had seen the Holocaust memorial right next to the statue of John Caldwell Calhoun: a strange cryptlike, criblike structure, an-

1. Calhoun (1782–1850), senator from South Carolina, U.S. vice president 1825–32, and ardent segregationist and theoretician of States' Rights, the doctrine of limited federal power and individual states' choice in such matters as slavery.

other commemoration of some of the people who were murdered by the Germans. Then I said that John Caldwell Calhoun was not altogether so far removed from Adolf Hitler; that these two men seem to be more in the same universe than not.

It was all this and more that I said that made Frank Cabot angry at me, but not long after his outburst I joined a group of attendees to the conference who were going off to tour and have dinner at Middleton Place, the famous plantation. Middleton is a popular destination for Americans who are interested in gardens, garden history, or a whiff of the sweet stench that makes up so much of American history. It is, on the one hand, a series of beautiful rooms in the garden sense: there is a part for roses only, there is a part for azaleas, there is a part for camellias, and so on and so on. The most spectacular part of the garden is a grassy terrace made by human hands, and on the slope of the terrace are small and perfectly regular risings, so that when seen from below they look like stiff pleats in a skirt that has just been disturbed by a faint breeze. At the foot of the terrace are two small lakes that have been fashioned to look like a butterfly stilled by chloroform. It is all very beautiful, even slightly awesome; and then there is the awfulness, for those gardens and that terrace and those lakes were made by slaves. The water from the river adjacent to the plantation was channelled to flood the rice fields, and this was done by slaves, who had brought their rice-cultivation skills with them from Africa. For, as far as I know, there are no rice fields in England, Scotland, Ireland, or Wales. I was feeling quite sad about all this when I came upon a big rubble of bricks. It was all that remained of the main house on the plantation in the wake of the strategy, conceived by that ingenious pyromaniac and great general from the North, William Tecumseh Sherman,[2] which had helped to bring the traitorous South to its knees. As I walked toward a tent to have a dinner of black-eyed peas and rice, ribs and chicken and sweet potatoes, a dinner that I think of as the cuisine of black people from the American South, and where I would hear the Lester Lanin[3] orchestra accompany a white man imitating the voice of Louis Armstrong as he sang songs made famous by Louis Armstrong, I ran into Mr. Frank Cabot, and I kept from him a fact that I happen to know: Arthur Middleton, of Middleton plantation, was one of the signers of the Declaration of Independence.

Nowhere is the relationship between the world and the garden better documented than in Thomas Jefferson's "Garden and Farm Books," an obsessively detailed account of his domestic life. People like to say that Jefferson is an enigma, that he was a man of contradictions, as if those things could not be said of just about anybody. But you have only to read anything he wrote, and you will find the true man, Thomas Jefferson, who is always so unwittingly transparent, always most revealing when confident that he has covered his

2. Union Civil War general (1820–1891) famous for his scorched-earth policy designed to destroy the South's means of production.

3. Orchestra leader (1911–2004) associated with upper-class social events.

tracks. He tried to write an autobiography, but he stopped before he had written a hundred pages. In it he states that he was born, that his father's name was Peter, that he wrote the Declaration of Independence, that he went to France and witnessed the French Revolution. The whole thing reads as if it were composed by one of the many marble busts of him which decorate the vestibules of government buildings. The Jefferson to be found in the autobiography is the unwittingly transparent Jefferson. The Jefferson who is confident that he has covered his tracks is to be found in the "Garden and Farm Books." The first entry in the "Garden" book is so beautiful, and so simple a statement: "1766. Shadwell. Mar. 30. Purple hyacinth begins to bloom." It goes on: "Apr. 6. Narcissus and Puckoon open. [Apr.] 13. Puckoon flowers fallen. [Apr.] 16. a bluish colored, funnel-formed flower in low-grounds in bloom." (This must have been *Mertensia virginica*.) The entries continue in this way for years, until 1824: the peas are sown, the asparagus planted, the fruit trees planted, the vegetables reaped. Each entry reads as if it were a single line removed from a poem: something should come before, and something should come after. And what should come before and after is to be found in the "Farm" book, and it comes in the form of a list of names: Ursula, George, Jupiter, Davy, Minerva, Caesar, and Jamy; and the Hemings, Beverly, Betty, Peter, John, and Sally. (Why is it that people who readily agree that Jefferson owned Sally Hemings cannot believe that he slept with her?)[4] It is they who sowed the peas, dug the trenches, and filled them with manure. It is they who planted and harvested the corn. And when Jefferson makes this entry in his "Garden" book, on April 8, 1794—"our first dish of Asparagus"—it is they who have made it possible for him to enjoy asparagus. None of these names appear in the "Garden" book; the garden is free of their presence, but they turn up in the "Farm" book, and in painful, but valuable-to-know, detail. Little Beverly Hemings, Jefferson's son by Sally, must have been a very small boy the year that he was allotted one and a half yards of wool. One year, John Hemings, Sally's uncle, received, along with Sally's mother, seven yards of linen, five yards of blue wool, and a pair of shoes. On and on it goes: the garden emerging from the farm, the garden unable to exist without the farm, the garden kept apart from the farm, race and politics kept out of the garden.

10   But, you know, the garden Jefferson made at Monticello is not really very good. You don't see it and think, Now, there is something I would like to do. It is not beautiful in the way that the garden George Washington's slaves made at Mount Vernon is beautiful. (I owe this new appreciation of Mount Vernon to Mac Griswold and her excellent book "Washington's Gardens at Mount Vernon: Landscape of the Inner Man.") There is hardly anything featured in the garden at Monticello that makes you want to rush home, subdue a few people, and re-create it. And the reason might be that Jefferson was less interested in the garden than in the marvellous things grown there. Each year, I order packets of something he grew, *Dolichos lablab*, purple hyacinth

4. Sally Hemings (1773–1835) was Jefferson's slave and was rumored to be the mother of his child; recent DNA testing has confirmed a genetic link.

beans, something no garden should be without. What is beautiful about Monticello is the views, whether you are looking out from the house or looking at it from far away. Jefferson did not so much make a garden as a landscape. The explanation for this may be very simple: his father was a surveyor. This might also explain why he is responsible for some of the great vistas we know—the American West.

Not long after I returned from Charleston, a small amount of money that I had not expected came my way. In my ongoing conversation with my garden, I had for a very long time wanted to build a wall to add to its shape and character. So I immediately called Ron Pembroke, the maker of the most excellent landscapes in the area where I live. My house is situated on a little rise, a knoll, and I find the way it looks from many angles in the general landscape to be very pleasing, and so I had firmly in mind just the kind of wall I wanted. But Ron Pembroke, after walking me up and down and back and forth with a measuring tape in his hand, and taking me in his truck to see the other walls he had built, convinced me that my design was really quite ugly and that his was beautiful and superior.

And so began the building of two hundred-foot-long walls, one above the other, separated by a terrace eight feet wide. One day, four men arrived in the yard, and they were accompanied by big pieces of machinery, including, of course, an earthmover. The men began to rearrange the slope that fell away from the house, and by the end of the day my nice house looked as if it were the only thing left standing after a particularly disastrous natural event. The construction of the walls went on. Day after day, four men, whose names were Jared Clawson, Dan, Tony, and John, came and dug trenches and pounded stakes into the ground after they had looked through a surveyor's instrument many times. One day, truckloads of coarsely pummelled gray stone were deposited in the driveway and carefully laid at the bottom of the trenches. Another day, truckloads of a beautiful gray, blue, yellowish, and glistening stone were delivered and left on the lawn. This stone came from a quarry in Goshen, Massachusetts, Ron Pembroke told me. It is the stone he prefers to use when he builds walls, and it is more expensive than other kinds of stone, but it does display his work to best advantage. My two walls, he said, would most likely require a hundred tons of stone.

The walls started to take shape, at first almost mysteriously. The four men began by placing stones atop one another, in a staggered arrangement, so that always one stone was resting on top of two. In the beginning, each stone they picked up seemed to be just the perfect one needed. But then things began to get more difficult. Sometimes a stone would be carried to the wall with great effort and, after being pounded into place, it would not look quite right to Tony and Dan and John and Jared Clawson.

And did I say that all this was being done in the autumn? I do not know if that is the ideal time to build a wall, but I was so happy to see my walls being made that I became very possessive of the time spent on them and wanted the four men to be building only my walls. I didn't begrudge them lunchtime or

time taken to smoke a cigarette, but why did they have to stop working when
the day was at an end, and why did the day have to come to an end, for that
matter? How I loved to watch those men work, especially the man named
Jared Clawson. It was he who built the stairs that made it possible to walk
from the lower wall to the eight-foot-wide terrace, and then up to the level
ground of a patio, which was made flush with the top of the upper wall. And
the stairs were difficult to make, or so it seemed to me, for it took Jared Clawson ten days to make them.

15   One day, it was finished. The walls were built, and they looked fantastic.
My friend Paige had given me twelve bottles of champagne, a present for my
twentieth wedding anniversary. I loved the taste of this champagne so much
that I gave a bottle to each of the men who had helped build my walls. How
glad was my spirit when, at the end of all this, Ron Pembroke presented me
with a bill, and I in turn gave him a check for the complete amount, and there
was nothing between us but complete respect and admiration and no feeling
of the injustice of it all, no disgust directed toward me and my nice house,
beautifully set off by those dramatic walls, for he had his own house and his
own wall and his own spouse and his own anniversary.

          At the foot of the lower wall, I have planted five hundred daffodils, ranging
in shade from bright yellow to creamy white. In the terrace separating the lower
and the upper walls, I have planted two hundred *Tulipa* 'Mrs. J.T. Scheepers,'
which is perhaps my favorite tulip in the world. In the four beds on either side
of the patio, I have planted two hundred *Tulipa* 'Blue Diamond,' a hundred
Tulipa 'Angélique,' and only fifty of *Tulipa* 'Black Hero' because they were so expensive. Towering above these hundreds of bulbs, I planted the magnolias
'Woodsman' and 'Elizabeth' and 'Miss Honeybee'; and then *Magnolia zenii* and
Magnolia denudata. At the beginning of the woodland, which I can see from a
certain angle if I am standing on the upper wall, I planted a hundred *Fritillaria
meleagris* and fifty each of *Galanthus elwesii* and *Galanthus nivalis*.

          Ron Pembroke refilled the trenches with a rich topsoil, a mixture of com-
posted organic material and riverbank soil, but I did not see one earthworm
wriggling around in it, and this made me worry, for I have such a reverence for
earthworms, whose presence signifies that the soil is good. Their anxious, iri-
descent, wriggly form, when confronted with broad daylight, is very reassuring.
We may be made from dust (the dust of the garden, I presume), but it is not to
dust that we immediately return; first, we join the worms.

          The garden is not a place to lose your cares; the garden is not a place of
rest and repose. Even God did not find it so.

QUESTIONS

1. According to Kincaid, Frank Cabot, chairman of the Garden Conservancy, said she
did the "unforgivable—I had introduced race and politics into the garden" (paragraph
2). Can you imagine how race and politics could ever have been left out? What might
have led some garden people to ignore or suppress them?

2. The essay has two parts: the Charleston speech and the garden building project. What is the relationship between the two? Why does Kincaid spend so much time on her admiration for the workers?

3. Write an essay describing how you took on a task and completed it successfully. Or write about how someone you know did a good job on a difficult assignment. Go into the kind of detail Kincaid does about her wall.

JUDITH ORTIZ COFER *More Room*

M Y GRANDMOTHER'S HOUSE is like a chambered nautilus; it has many rooms, yet it is not a mansion. Its proportions are small and its design simple. It is a house that has grown organically, according to the needs of its inhabitants. To all of us in the family it is known as *la casa de Mamá.*[1] It is the place of our origin; the stage for our memories and dreams of Island life.

I remember how in my childhood it sat on stilts; this was before it had a downstairs. It rested on its perch like a great blue bird, not a flying sort of bird, more like a nesting hen, but with spread wings. Grandfather had built it soon after their marriage. He was a painter and housebuilder by trade, a poet and meditative man by nature. As each of their eight children were born, new rooms were added. After a few years, the paint did not exactly match, nor the materials, so that there was a chronology to it, like the rings of a tree, and Mamá could tell you the history of each room in her *casa,* and thus the genealogy of the family along with it.

Her room is the heart of the house. Though I have seen it recently, and both woman and room have diminished in size, changed by the new perspective of my eyes, now capable of looking over countertops and tall beds, it is not this picture I carry in my memory of Mamá's *casa.* Instead, I see her room as a queen's chamber where a small woman loomed large, a throne-room with a massive four-poster bed in its center which stood taller than a child's head. It was on this bed where her own children had been born that the smallest grandchildren were allowed to take naps in the afternoons; here too was where Mamá secluded herself to dispense private advice to her daughters, sitting on the edge of the bed, looking down at whoever sat on the rocker where generations of babies had been sung to sleep. To me she looked like a wise empress right out of the fairy tales I was addicted to reading.

Though the room was dominated by the mahogany four-posters, it also

From Cofer's 1990 book, Silent Dancing: A Partial Reminiscence of a Puerto Rican Childhood, *which won the 1991 PEN/Martha Albrand Special Citation for Nonfiction.*

1. Mama's house.

contained all of Mamá's symbols of power. On her dresser instead of cosmetics there were jars filled with herbs: *yerba buena, yerba mala,*[2] the making of purgatives and teas to which we were all subjected during childhood crises. She had a steaming cup for anyone who could not, or would not, get up to face life on any given day. If the acrid aftertaste of her cures for malingering did not get you out of bed, then it was time to call *el doctor.*

5   And there was the monstrous chifforobe she kept locked with a little golden key she did not hide. This was a test of her dominion over us; though my cousins and I wanted a look inside that massive wardrobe more than anything, we never reached for that little key lying on top of her Bible on the dresser. This was also where she placed her earrings and rosary at night. God's word was her security system. This chifforobe was the place where I imagined she kept jewels, satin slippers, and elegant sequined, silk gowns of heartbreaking fineness. I lusted after those imaginary costumes. I had heard that Mamá had been a great beauty in her youth, and the belle of many balls. My cousins had other ideas as to what she kept in that wooden vault: its secret could be money (Mamá did not hand cash to strangers, banks were out of the question, so there were stories that her mattress was stuffed with dollar bills, and that she buried coins in jars in her garden under rosebushes, or kept them in her inviolate chifforobe); there might be that legendary gun salvaged from the Spanish-American conflict over the Island. We went wild over suspected treasures that we made up simply because children have to fill locked trunks with something wonderful.

On the wall above the bed hung a heavy silver crucifix. Christ's agonized head hung directly over Mamá's pillow. I avoided looking at this weapon suspended over where her head would lay; and on the rare occasions when I was allowed to sleep on that bed, I scooted down to the safe middle of the mattress, where her body's impression took me in like a mother's lap. Having taken care of the obligatory religious decoration with a crucifix, Mamá covered the other walls with objects sent to her over the years by her children in the States. *Los Nueva Yores*[3] were represented by, among other things, a postcard of Niagara Falls from her son Hernán, postmarked, Buffalo, N.Y. In a conspicuous gold frame hung a large color photograph of her daughter Nena, her husband and their five children at the entrance to Disneyland in California. From us she had gotten a black lace fan. Father had brought it to her from a tour of duty with the Navy in Europe (on Sundays she would remove it from its hook on the wall to fan herself at Sunday mass). Each year more items were added as the family grew and dispersed, and every object in the room had a story attached to it, a *cuento*[4] which Mamá would bestow on anyone who received the privilege of a day alone with her. It was almost worth pretending to be sick, though the bitter herb purgatives of the body were a big price to pay for the spirit revivals of her story-telling.

2. Good herbs, bad herbs.
3. The New Yorkers.
4. Tale.

Mamá slept alone on her large bed, except for the times when a sick grandchild warranted the privilege, or when a heartbroken daughter came home in need of more than herbal teas. In the family there is a story about how this came to be.

When one of the daughters, my mother or one of her sisters, tells the *cuento* of how Mamá came to own her nights, it is usually preceded by the qualifications that Papá's exile from his wife's room was not a result of animosity between the couple, but that the act had been Mamá's famous bloodless coup for her personal freedom. Papá was the benevolent dictator of her body and her life who had had to be banished from her bed so that Mamá could better serve her family. Before the telling, we had to agree that the old man was not to blame. We all recognized that in the family Papá was as an *alma de Dios*,[5] a saintly, soft-spoken presence whose main pleasures in life, such as writing poetry and reading the Spanish large-type editions of *Reader's Digest,* always took place outside the vortex of Mamá's crowded realm. It was not his fault, after all, that every year or so he planted a babyseed in Mamá's fertile body, keeping her from leading the active life she needed and desired. He loved her and the babies. Papá composed odes and lyrics to celebrate births and anniversaries and hired musicians to accompany him in singing them to his family and friends at extravagant pig-roasts he threw yearly. Mamá and the oldest girls worked for days preparing the food. Papá sat for hours in his painter's shed, also his study and library, composing the songs. At these celebrations he was also known to give long speeches in praise of God, his fecund wife, and his beloved island. As a middle child, my mother remembers these occasions as a time when the women sat in the kitchen and lamented their burdens, while the men feasted out in the patio, their rum-thickened voice rising in song and praise for each other, *compañeros* all.[6]

It was after the birth of her eighth child, after she had lost three at birth or in infancy, that Mamá made her decision. They say that Mamá had had a special way of letting her husband know that they were expecting, one that had begun when, at the beginning of their marriage, he had built her a house too confining for her taste. So, when she discovered her first pregnancy, she supposedly drew plans for another room, which he dutifully executed. Every time a child was due, she would demand, *more space, more space.* Papá acceded to her wishes, child after child, since he had learned early that Mamá's renowned temper was a thing that grew like a monster along with a new belly. In this way Mamá got the house that she wanted, but with each child she lost in heart and energy. She had knowledge of her body and perceived that if she had any more children, her dreams and her plans would have to be permanently forgotten, because she would be a chronically ill woman, like Flora with her twelve children: asthma, no teeth, in bed more than on her feet.

And so, after my youngest uncle was born, she asked Papá to build a large room at the back of the house. He did so in joyful anticipation. Mamá had

10

5. Literally, "soul of god." A thoroughly good person.
6. Companions.

asked him special things this time: shelves on the walls, a private entrance. He thought that she meant this room to be a nursery where several children could sleep. He thought it was a wonderful idea. He painted it his favorite color, sky blue, and made large windows looking out over a green hill and the church spires beyond. But nothing happened. Mamá's belly did not grow, yet she seemed in a frenzy of activity over the house. Finally, an anxious Papá approached his wife to tell her that the new room was finished and ready to be occupied. And Mamá, they say, replied: "Good, it's for *you*."

And so it was that Mamá discovered the only means of birth control available to a Catholic woman of her time: sacrifice. She gave up the comfort of Papá's sexual love for something she deemed greater: the right to own and control her body, so that she might live to meet her grandchildren—me among them—so that she could give more of herself to the ones already there, so that she could be more than a channel for other lives, so that even now that time has robbed her of the elasticity of her body and of her amazing reservoir of energy, she still emanates the kind of joy that can only be achieved by living according to the dictates of one's own heart.

Questions

1. At the end of the essay, Cofer explains in fairly direct terms why her grandmother wanted "more room." Why do you think she uses narration as the primary mode in the rest of the essay? What does she gain by first narrating, then explaining?

2. Cofer uses many similes and metaphors—for example, in paragraph 1 she says that her grandmother's house was "like a chambered nautilus" and in paragraph 5 that her grandmother's Bible was "her security system." Discuss the use of one or two such comparisons that you find particularly effective.

3. What are the possible meanings of the title?

4. Write about a favorite or mysterious place you remember from childhood.

N. Scott Momaday *The Way to Rainy Mountain*

A SINGLE KNOLL RISES out of the plain in Oklahoma, north and west of the Wichita Range. For my people, the Kiowas, it is an old landmark, and they gave it the name Rainy Mountain. The hardest weather in the world is there. Winter brings blizzards, hot tornadic winds arise in the spring, and in summer the prairie is an anvil's edge. The grass turns brittle and brown, and it cracks be-

First published in 1967 in the Reporter, *a now defunct small-circulation American magazine; reprinted in* The Way to Rainy Mountain, *Momaday's 1969 book about the West. The illustrations were drawn by the author's father, Al Momaday.*

neath your feet. There are green belts along the rivers and creeks, linear groves of hickory and pecan, willow and witch hazel. At a distance in July or August the steaming foliage seems almost to writhe in fire. Great green and yellow grasshoppers are everywhere in the tall grass, popping up like corn to sting the flesh, and tortoises crawl about on the red earth, going nowhere in the plenty of time. Loneliness is an aspect of the land. All things in the plain are isolate; there is no confusion of objects in the eye, but *one* hill or *one* tree or *one* man. To look upon that landscape in the early morning, with the sun at your back, is to lose the sense of proportion. Your imagination comes to life, and this, you think, is where Creation was begun.

I returned to Rainy Mountain in July. My grandmother had died in the spring, and I wanted to be at her grave. She had lived to be very old and at last infirm. Her only living daughter was with her when she died, and I was told that in death her face was that of a child.

I like to think of her as a child. When she was born, the Kiowas were living the last great moment of their history. For more than a hundred years they had controlled the open range from the Smoky Hill River to the Red, from the headwaters of the Canadian to the fork of the Arkansas and Cimarron. In alliance with the Comanches, they had ruled the whole of the southern Plains. War was their sacred business, and they were among the finest horsemen the world has ever known. But warfare for the Kiowas was preeminently a matter of disposition rather than of survival, and they never understood the grim, unrelenting advance of the U.S. Cavalry. When at last, divided and ill-provisioned, they were driven onto the Staked Plains in the cold rains of autumn, they fell into panic. In Palo Duro Canyon they abandoned their crucial stores to pillage and had nothing then but their lives. In order to save themselves, they surrendered to the soldiers at Fort Sill and were imprisoned in the old stone corral that now stands as a military museum. My grandmother was spared the humiliation of those high gray walls by eight or ten years, but she must have known from birth the affliction of defeat, the dark brooding of old warriors.

Her name was Aho, and she belonged to the last culture to evolve in North America. Her forebears came down from the high country in western Montana nearly three centuries ago. They were a mountain people, a mysterious tribe of hunters whose language has never been positively classified in any major group. In the late seventeenth century they began a long migration to the south and east. It was a journey toward the dawn, and it led to a golden age. Along the way the Kiowas were befriended by the Crows, who gave them the culture and religion of the Plains. They acquired horses, and their ancient nomadic spirit was suddenly free of the ground. They acquired Tai-me, the sacred Sun Dance doll, from that moment the object and symbol of their worship, and so shared in the divinity of the sun. Not least, they acquired the sense of destiny, therefore courage and pride. When they entered upon the southern Plains they had been transformed. No longer were they slaves to the simple necessity of survival; they were a lordly and dangerous society of fighters and thieves, hunters and priests of the sun. According to their origin myth, they entered the world through a hollow log. From one point of view, their migration was the fruit of an old prophecy, for indeed they emerged from a sunless world.

5   Although my grandmother lived out her long life in the shadow of Rainy Mountain, the immense landscape of the continental interior lay like memory in her blood. She could tell of the Crows, whom she had never seen, and of the Black Hills, where she had never been. I wanted to see in reality what she had seen more perfectly in the mind's eye, and traveled fifteen hundred miles to begin my pilgrimage.

Yellowstone, it seemed to me, was the top of the world, a region of deep lakes and dark timber, canyons and waterfalls. But, beautiful as it is, one might have the sense of confinement there. The skyline in all directions is close at hand, the high wall of the woods and deep cleavages of shade. There is a perfect freedom in the mountains, but it belongs to the eagle and the elk, the badger and the bear. The Kiowas reckoned their stature by the distance they could see, and they were bent and blind in the wilderness.

Descending eastward, the highland meadows are a stairway to the plain. In July the inland slope of the Rockies is luxuriant with flax and buckwheat, stonecrop and larkspur. The earth unfolds and the limit of the land recedes. Clusters of trees, and animals grazing far in the distance, cause the vision to reach away and wonder to build upon the mind. The sun follows a longer course in the day, and the sky is immense beyond all comparison. The great billowing clouds that sail upon it are the shadows that move upon the grain like water, dividing light. Farther down, in the land of the Crows and Blackfeet, the plain is yellow. Sweet clover takes hold of the hills and bends upon itself to cover and seal the soil. There the Kiowas paused on their way; they had come to the place where they must change their lives. The sun is at home on the plains. Precisely there does it have the certain character of a god. When the Kiowas came to the land of the Crows, they could see the dark lees of the hills at dawn across the Bighorn River, the profusion of light on the grain shelves, the oldest deity ranging after the solstices. Not yet would they veer southward to the caldron of the land that lay below; they must wean their blood from the northern winter and hold the mountains a while longer in their view. They bore Tai-me in procession to the east.

A dark mist lay over the Black Hills, and the land was like iron. At the top of a ridge I caught sight of Devil's Tower upthrust against the gray sky as if in the birth of time the core of the earth had broken through its crust and the motion of the world was begun. There are things in nature that engender an awful quiet in the heart of man; Devil's Tower is one of them. Two centuries ago, because they could not do otherwise, the Kiowas made a legend at the base of the rock. My grandmother said:

> Eight children were there at play, seven sisters and their brother. Suddenly the boy was struck dumb; he trembled and began to run upon his hands and feet. His fingers became claws, and his body was covered with fur. Directly there was a bear where the boy had been. The sisters were terrified; they ran, and the bear after them. They came to the stump of a great tree, and the tree spoke to them. It bade them climb upon it, and as they did so it began to rise into the air. The bear came to kill them, but they were just beyond its reach. It reared against the tree and scored the bark all around with its claws. The seven sisters were borne into the sky, and they became the stars of the Big Dipper.

From that moment, and so long as the legend lives, the Kiowas have kinsmen in the night sky. Whatever they were in the mountains, they could be no more. However tenuous their well-being, however much they had suffered and would suffer again, they had found a way out of the wilderness.

My grandmother had a reverence for the sun, a holy regard that now is all but gone out of mankind. There was a wariness in her, and an ancient awe. She was a Christian in her later years, but she had come a long way about, and she never forgot her birthright. As a child she had been to the Sun Dances; she had taken part in those annual rites, and by them she had learned the restoration of her people in the presence of Tai-me. She was about seven when the last Kiowa Sun Dance was held in 1887 on the Washita River above Rainy Mountain Creek. The buffalo were gone. In order to consummate the ancient sacrifice—to impale the head of a buffalo bull upon the medicine tree—a delegation of old men journeyed into Texas, there to beg and barter for an animal from the Goodnight herd. She was ten when the Kiowas came together for the last time as a living Sun Dance culture. They could find no buffalo; they had to hang an old hide from the sacred tree. Before the dance could begin, a company of soldiers rode out from Fort Sill under orders to disperse the tribe. Forbidden without cause the essential act of their faith, having seen the wild herds slaughtered and left to rot upon the ground, the Kiowas backed away forever from the medicine tree. That was July 20, 1890, at the great bend of the Washita. My grandmother was there. Without bitterness, and for as long as she lived, she bore a vision of deicide.

Now that I can have her only in memory, I see my grandmother in the several postures that were peculiar to her: standing at the wood stove on a winter morning and turning meat in a great iron skillet; sitting at the south window, bent above her beadwork, and afterwards, when her vision failed, looking down for a long time into the fold of her hands; going out upon a cane, very slowly as she did when the weight of age came upon her; praying. I remember her most often at prayer. She made long, rambling prayers out of suffering and hope, having seen many things. I was never sure that I had the right to hear, so exclusive were they of all mere custom and company. The last time I saw her she prayed standing by the side of her bed at night, naked to the waist, the light of a kerosene lamp moving upon her dark skin. Her long, black hair, always drawn and braided in the day, lay upon her shoulders and against her breasts like a shawl. I do not speak Kiowa, and I never understood her prayers, but there was something inherently sad in the sound, some merest hesitation upon the syllables of sorrow. She began in a high and descending pitch, exhausting her breath to silence; then again and again—and always the same intensity of effort, of something that is, and is not, like urgency in the human voice. Transported so in the dancing light among the shadows of her room, she seemed beyond the reach of time. But that was illusion; I think I knew then that I should not see her again.

Houses are like sentinels in the plain, old keepers of the weather watch. There, in a very little while, wood takes on the appearance of great age. All colors wear soon away in the wind and rain, and then the wood is burned gray and the grain appears and the nails turn red with rust. The windowpanes are black and opaque; you imagine there is nothing within, and indeed there are many ghosts, bones given up to the land. They stand here and there against the sky, and you approach them for a longer time than you expect. They belong in the distance; it is their domain.

Once there was a lot of sound in my grandmother's house, a lot of coming and going, feasting and talk. The summers there were full of excitement and reunion. The Kiowas are a summer people; they abide the cold and keep to themselves, but when the season turns and the land becomes warm and vital they cannot hold still; an old love of going returns upon them. The aged visitors who came to my grandmother's house when I was a child were made of lean and leather, and they bore themselves upright. They wore great black hats and bright ample shirts that shook in the wind. They rubbed fat upon their hair and wound their braids with strips of colored cloth. Some of them painted their faces and carried the scars of old and cherished enmities. They were an old council of warlords, come to remind and be reminded of who they were. Their wives and daughters served them well. The women might indulge themselves; gossip was at once the mark and compensation of their servitude. They made loud and elaborate talk among themselves, full of jest and gesture, fright and false alarm. They went abroad in fringed and flowered shawls, bright beadwork and German silver. They were at home in the kitchen, and they prepared meals that were banquets.

There were frequent prayer meetings, and great nocturnal feasts. When I

was a child I played with my cousins outside, where the lamplight fell upon
the ground and the singing of the old people rose up around us and carried
away into the darkness. There were a lot of good things to eat, a lot of laughter and surprise. And afterwards, when the quiet returned, I lay down with my
grandmother and could hear the frogs away by the river and feel the motion of
the air.

Now there is a funeral silence in the rooms, the endless wake of some final word. The walls have closed in upon my grandmother's house. When I returned to it in mourning, I saw for the first time in my life how small it was. It
was late at night, and there was a white moon, nearly full. I sat for a long time
on the stone steps by the kitchen door. From there I could see out across the
land; I could see the long row of trees by the creek, the low light upon the
rolling plains, and the stars of the Big Dipper. Once I looked at the moon and
caught sight of a strange thing. A cricket had perched upon the handrail, only
a few inches away from me. My line of vision was such that the creature filled
the moon like a fossil. It had gone there, I thought, to live and die, for there,
of all places, was its small definition made whole and eternal. A warm wind
rose up and purled like the longing within me.

15   The next morning I awoke at dawn and went out on the dirt road to Rainy
Mountain. It was already hot, and the grasshoppers began to fill the air. Still,
it was early in the morning, and the birds sang out of the shadows. The long
yellow grass on the mountain shone in the bright light, and a scissortail hied
above the land. There, where it ought to be, at the end of a long and legendary
way, was my grandmother's grave. Here and there on the dark stones were ancestral names. Looking back once, I saw the mountain and came away.

QUESTIONS

1. Throughout this essay, Momaday uses similes (comparisons with "like" or "as") and
metaphors (comparisons without specific connectors). Which comparisons were most
helpful in aiding your understanding? Which comparison was most surprising?

2. Momaday connects personal and cultural history to a particular place. Find another
essay, either in "People, Places" or "Nature and the Environment," that makes similar
connections. Write a comparison of the two essays.

3. In paragraph 10, Momaday describes the roles that women played in his grandmother's Kiowa culture. Consider the roles women played in your grandmother's generation and culture; perhaps ask your mother or grandmother about their experiences. To
what extent have those roles remained the same or changed in your generation? Write
an account based on your conversations with older family members and your own personal knowledge.

MARGARET ATWOOD *True North*

> Land of the silver birch,
> Home of the beaver,
> Where still the mighty moose
> Wanders at will,
> Blue lake and rocky shore,
> I will return once more;
> Boom-diddy-boom-boom
> Boom-diddy-boom-boom
> Boo-OO-oo-oo-oom.
> —ARCHAIC SONG

WE SANG THIS ONCE, squatting around the papier-mâché Magic Mushroom in the Brownie pack, while pretending to be wolves in Cub Scouts, or while watching our marshmallows turn to melted Styrofoam on the ends of our sticks at some well-run, fairly safe summer camp in the wilds of Muskoka, Haliburton, or Algonquin Park. Then we grew up and found it corny. By that time we were into Jean-Paul Sartre[1] and the lure of the nauseous. Finally, having reached the age of nostalgia, we rediscovered it on a cassette in The Children's Book Store, in a haunting version that invested it with all the emotional resonance we once thought it possessed, and bought it, under the pretense of giving our children a little ethnic musical background.

It brought tears to our eyes, not for simple reasons. Whales get to us that way too, and whooping cranes, and other things hovering on the verge of extinction but still maintaining a tenuous foothold in the world of the actual. The beavers are doing all right—we know this because they just decimated our poplars—but the mighty moose is having a slimmer time of it. As for the blueness of the lakes, we worry about it: too blue and you've got acid rain.

Will we return once more, or will we go to Portugal instead? It depends, we have to admit, partly on the exchange rate, and this makes us feel disloyal. I am, rather quixotically, in Alabama, teaching, even more quixotically, a course in Canadian literature. Right now we're considering Marian Engel's novel *Bear*. Since everything in Canada, outside Toronto, begins with geography, I've unfolded a large map of Ontario and traced the heroine's route north; I've located the mythical house of the book somewhere on the actual shore of Georgian Bay, northern edge. I've superimposed a same-scale map of Alabama on this scheme, to give the students an idea of the distances. In the north, space is larger than you think, because the points of reference are farther apart.

Atwood wrote this piece for Saturday Night *(January 1987), Canada's oldest general circulation magazine, published from 1887 to 2001.*

1. French existentialist philosopher, novelist, playwright, essayist, literary critic, and political activist (1905–1980). One of his novels was entitled *Nausea*.

"Are there any words you came across that puzzled you?" I ask.

Blackfly comes up. A large black fly is proposed. I explain blackflies, their smallness, their multitude, their evil habits. It gives me a certain kick to do this: I'm competing with the local water moccasins.

Mackinaw. A raincoat? Not quite. Loon. Tamarack. Reindeer moss. Portage. Moose. Wendigo.

"Why does she make Lucy the old Indian woman talk so funny?" they ask. Lucy, I point out, is not merely Indian but a French-speaking Indian. This, to them, is a weird concept.

The north is another country. It's also another language. Or languages.

Where is the north, exactly? It's not only a place but a direction, and as such its location is relative: to the Mexicans, the United States is the north, to Americans Toronto is, even though it's on roughly the same latitude as Boston.

Wherever it is for us, there's a lot of it. You stand in Windsor and imagine a line going north, all the way to the pole. The same line going south would end up in South America. That's the sort of map we grew up with, at the front of the classroom in Mercator projection, which made it look even bigger than it was, all that pink stretching on forever, with a few cities sprinkled along the bottom edge. It's not only geographical space, it's space related to body image. When we face south, as we often do, our conscious mind may be directed down there, towards crowds, bright lights, some Hollywood version of fame and fortune, but the north is at the back of our minds, always. There's something, not someone, looking over our shoulders; there's a chill at the nape of the neck.

The north focuses our anxieties. Turning to face north, face the north, we enter our own unconscious. Always, in retrospect, the journey north has the quality of dream.

Where does the north begin?

Every province, every city, has its own road north. From Toronto you go up the 400. Where you cross the border, from here to there, is a matter of opinion. Is it the Severn River, where the Shield granite appears suddenly out of the earth? Is it the sign announcing that you're halfway between the equator and the North Pole? Is it the first gift shop shaped like a wigwam, the first town—there are several—that proclaims itself The Gateway to the North?

As we proceed, the farms become fewer, rockier, more desperate-looking, the trees change their ratios, coniferous moving in on deciduous. More lakes appear, their shorelines scraggier. Our eyes narrow and we look at the clouds: the weather is important again.

One of us used to spend summers in a cottage in Muskoka, before the road went in, when you took the train, when there were big cruise ships there, and matronly motor launches, and tea dances at the hotels, and men in white flannels on the lawns, which there may still be. This was not just a cottage but a Muskoka cottage, with boathouse and maid's quarters. Rich people went north in the summers then, away from cities and crowds; that was before the cure for polio, which has made a difference. In this sort of north, they tried to duplicate the south, or perhaps some dream of country life in England. In the living room there were armchairs, glass-fronted bookcases, family photos in silver frames, stuffed birds under glass bells. The north, as I said, is relative.

For me, the north used to be completely in force by the Trout Creek plan- ing mill. Those stacks of fresh-cut lumber were the true gateway to the north, and north of that was North Bay, which used to be, to be blunt, a bit of an armpit. It was beef-sandwich-on-white-bread-with-gravy-and-canned-peas country. But no more. North Bay now has shopping malls, and baskets of flow- ers hanging from lampposts above paving-stone sidewalks, downtown. It has a Granite Club. It has the new, swish, carpeted buildings of Laurentian Univer- sity. It has gourmet restaurants. And in the airport, where southbound DC-9s dock side by side with northbound Twin Otters, there's a book rack in the cof- fee shop that features Graham Greene and Kierkegaard,[2] hardly standard air- port fare.

The south is moving north.

We bypass North Bay, which now has a bypass, creeping southerliness, and do not go, this time, to the Dionne Quints Museum, where five little silhouettes in black play forever beside an old log cabin, complete with the basket where they were packed in cotton wool, the oven where they were warmed, the five prams, the five Communion dresses.

Beyond North Bay there is a brief flurry of eccentricity—lawns populated with whole flocks of wooden-goose windmills—and then we go for miles and miles past nothing but trees, meeting nothing but the occasional truck loaded with lumber. This area didn't used to be called anything. Now it's the Near North Travel Area. You can see signs telling you that. Near what, we wonder uneasily? We don't want to be near. We want to be far.

At last we see the Ottawa River, which is the border. There's a dam across   20
it, two dams, and an island between them. If there were a customs house it would be here. A sign faces us saying *Bienvenue;* out the back window there's one saying *Welcome.* This was my first lesson in points of view.

And there, across the border in Québec, in Témiscaming, is an image straight from my childhood: a huge mountain made of sawdust. I always wanted to slide down this sawdust mountain until I finally did, and discovered it was not like sand, dry and slippery, but damp and sticky and hard to get out of your clothes. This was my first lesson in the nature of illusion.

Continue past the sawdust mountain, past the baseball diamond, up the hill, and you're in the centre of town, which is remarkable for at least three things: a blocks-long public rock garden, still flourishing after more than forty-

2. Greene (1904–1991), English novelist; Søren Kierkegaard (1813–1855), Danish clergyman and philosopher who criticized Christianity and set the stage for modern existentialism.

five years; a pair of statues, one a fountain, that look as if they've come straight
from Europe, which I think they did; and the excellent, amazingly low-priced
hamburgers you can get at the Boulevard Restaurant, where the décor, featuring last year's cardboard Santa Claus and a stuffed twenty-three-pound pike, is
decidedly northern. Ask the owner about the pike and he'll tell you about one
twice as big, forty-five pounds in fact, that a fellow showed him strapped to the
tailgate of his van, and that long, too.

You can have this conversation in either French or English: Témiscaming
is a border town and a northern one, and the distinctions made here are as
likely to be north-south as French-English. Up in these parts you'll hear as
much grumbling, or more, about Québec City as you will about Ottawa, which
is, after all, closer. Spit in the river and it gets to Ottawa, eh?

For the north, Témiscaming is old, settled, tidy, even a little prosperous
looking. But it's had its crises. Témiscaming is the resource economy personified. Not long ago it was a company town, and when the company shut down
the mill, which would have shut down the town too, the workers took the unprecedented step of trying to buy it. With some help they succeeded, and the
result was Tembec, still going strong. But Témiscaming is still a one-industry
town, like many northern towns, and its existence is thus precarious.

25   Not so long ago, logging was a different sort of business. The men went
into the woods in winter, across the ice, using horse-drawn sledges, and set up
camp. (You still come across these logging camps now and then in your travels
through the lakes, abandoned, already looking as ancient as Roman aqueducts;
more ancient, since there's been no upkeep.) They'd cut selectively, tree by tree,
using axes and saws and the skills that were necessary to avoid being squashed
or hacked. They'd skid the trees to the ice; in the spring, after the ice went out,
there would be a run down the nearest fast river to the nearest sawmill.

Now it's done with bulldozers and trucks, and the result is too often a
blitzed shambles; cut everything, leave a wreck of dead and, incidentally, easily
flammable branches behind. Time is money. Don't touch the shoreline though,
we need that for tourists. In some places, the forest is merely a scrim along the
water. In behind it's been hollowed out.

Those who look on the positive side say it's good for the blueberries.

Sometimes we went the other way, across to Sudbury, the trees getting smaller
and smaller and finally disappearing as you approached. Sudbury was another
magic place of my childhood. It was like interplanetary travel, which we liked to
imagine, which was still just imagination in those days. With its heaps of slag
and its barren shoulders of stone, it looked like the moon. Back then, we tell
the children, before there were washer-dryers and you used something called a
wringer washer and hung the sheets out on something called a clothesline,
when there weren't even coloured sheets but all sheets were white, when Rinso
white and its happy little washday song were an item, and Whiter than White
was a catch phrase and female status really did have something to do with your
laundry, Sudbury was a housewife's nightmare. We knew people there; the windowsills in their houses were always grey.

Now the trees are beginning to come back because they built higher smokestacks. But where is all that stuff going now?

The Acid Rain Dinner, in Toronto's Sheraton Centre, in 1985. The first of these fund-raising events was fairly small. But the movement has grown, and this dinner is huge. The leaders of all three provincial parties are here. So is the minister of the environment from the federal government. So are several labour leaders, and several high-ranking capitalists, and representatives of numerous northerly chambers of commerce, summer residents' associations, tourist-camp runners, outfitters. Wishy washy urban professionals who say "frankly" a lot bend elbows with huntin', shootin', fishin', and cussin' burnt necks who wouldn't be caught dead saying "frankly." This is not a good place to be overheard saying that actually acid rain isn't such a bad thing because it gets rid of all that brown scum and leeches in the lake, or who cares because you can water-ski anyway. Teddy Kennedy, looking like a bulky sweater, is the guest speaker. Everyone wears a little gold pin in the shape of a rain drop. It looks like a tear.

Why has acid rain become the collective Canadian nightmare? Why is it— as a good cause—bigger than baby-seal bashing? The reasons aren't just economic, although there are lots of those, as the fishing-camp people and foresters will tell you. It's more than that, and cognate with the outrage aroused by the uninvited voyage of the American icebreaker *Polar Sea* through the Northwest Passage, where almost none of us ever goes. It's territorial, partly; partly a felt violation of some area in us that we hardly ever think about unless it's invaded or tampered with. It's the neighbours throwing guck into our yard. It's our childhood dying.

On location, in summer and far from the glass and brass of the Sheraton Centre, we nervously check our lakes. Leeches still in place? Have the crayfish, among the first to go, gone yet? (We think in terms of "yet.") Are the loons reproducing, have you seen any young? Any minnows? How about the lichen on the rocks? These inventories have now become routine, and that is why we're willing to fork out a hundred dollars a plate to support our acid-rain lobbyists in Washington. A summer without loons is unthinkable, but how do you tell that to people who don't know it because they've never had any to begin with?

We're driving through Glencoe, in the Highlands of Scotland. It's imposing, as a landscape: bleak, large, bald, apparently empty. We can see why the Scots took so well to Canada. Yet we know that the glens and crags round about are crawling with at least a thousand campers, rock climbers, and other seekers after nature; we also know that, at one end of this glen, the Campbells butchered the MacDonalds in the seventeenth century, thus propelling both of them into memorable history. Go walking here and you'll find things human: outlines of stone fences now overgrown, shards of abandoned crofts.

In Europe, every scrap of land has been claimed, owned, re-owned, fought

over, captured, bled on. The roads are the only no-man's-land. In northern
Canada, the roads are civilization, owned by the collective human *we*. Off the
road is *other*. Try walking in it, and you'll soon find out why all the early traffic
here was by water. "Impenetrable wilderness" is not just verbal.

35   And suppose you get off the road. Suppose you get lost. Getting lost, elsewhere and closer to town, is not knowing exactly where you are. You can always ask, even in a foreign country. In the north, getting lost is not knowing
how to get out.

You can get lost on a lake, of course, but getting lost in the forest is worse.
It's tangly in there, and dim, and one tree does begin to look remarkably like
another. The leaves and needles blot up sound, and you begin to feel watched:
not by anyone, not by an animal even, or anything you can put a name to, just
watched. You begin to feel judged. It's as if something is keeping an eye on you
just to see what you will do.

What will you do? Which side of the tree does moss grow on, and here,
where there are ferns and the earth is damp, or where it's dry as tinder, it
seems that moss grows everywhere, or does not grow at all. Snippets of Boy
Scout lore or truisms learned at summer camp come back to you, but scrambled. You tell yourself not to panic: you can always live off the land.

Easier said than done, you'd soon find. The Canadian Shield is a relatively
foodless area, which is why even the Indians tended to pass through it, did not
form large settlements except where there was arable land, and remained limited in numbers. This is not the Mekong delta.[3] If you had a gun you could
shoot something, maybe, a red squirrel perhaps; but if you're lost you probably
don't have a gun, or a fishing rod either. You could eat blueberries, or cattail
stems, or crayfish, or other delicacies dimly remembered from stories about
people who got lost in the woods and were found later in good health although
somewhat thinner. You could cook some reindeer moss, if you had matches.

Thus you pass on to fantasies about how to start a fire with a magnifying
glass—you don't have one—or by rubbing two bits of stick together, a feat at
which you suspect you would prove remarkably inept.

40   The fact is that not very many of us know how to survive in the north. Ru-
mour has it that only one German prisoner of war ever made it out, although
many made it out of the actual prisoner-of-war camps. The best piece of
northern survival advice is: *Don't get lost.*

One way of looking at a landscape is to consider the typical ways of dying in it.
Given the worst, what's the worst it could do? Will it be delirium from drinking salty water on the high seas, shrivelling in the desert, snakebite in the jungle, tidal waves on a Pacific isle, volcanic fumes? In the north, there are
several hazards. Although you're probably a lot safer there than you are on the
highway at rush hour, given the odds, you still have to be a little wary.

Like most lessons of this sort, those about the north are taught by precept

3. A vast plain in southeast Vietnam where the Mekong River empties into the South
China Sea.

and example, but also, more enjoyably, by cautionary nasty tale. There is death by blackfly, the one about the fellow who didn't have his shirt cuffs tight enough in the spring and undressed at night only to find he was running with blood, the ones about the lost travellers who bloated up from too many bites and who, when found, were twice the size, unrecognizable, and dead. There is death from starvation, death by animal, death by forest fire; there is death from something called "exposure," which used to confuse me when I heard about men who exposed themselves: why would they intentionally do anything that fatal? There's death by thunderstorm, not to be sneered at: on the open lake, in one of the excessive northern midsummer thunderstorms, a canoe or a bush plane is a vulnerable target. The north is full of Struwelpeter-like[4] stories about people who didn't do as they were told and got struck by lightning. Above all, there are death by freezing and death by drowning. Your body's heat-loss rate in the water is twenty times that in air, and northern lakes are cold. Even in a life jacket, even holding on to the tipped canoe, you're at risk. Every summer the numbers pile up.

Every culture has its exemplary dead people, its hagiography of landscape martyrs, those unfortunates who, by their bad ends, seem to sum up in one grisly episode what may be lurking behind the next rock for all of us, all of us who enter the territory they once claimed as theirs. I'd say that two of the top northern landscape martyrs are Tom Thomson, the painter who was found mysteriously drowned near his overturned canoe with no provable cause in sight, and the Mad Trapper of Rat River, also mysterious, who became so thoroughly bushed that he killed a Mountie and shot two others during an amazing wintertime chase before being finally mowed down. In our retelling of these stories, mystery is a key element. So, strangely enough, is a presumed oneness with the landscape in question. The Mad Trapper knew his landscape so well he survived in it for weeks, living off the land and his own bootlaces, eluding capture. One of the hidden motifs in these stories is a warning: maybe it's not so good to get *too* close to Nature.

I remember a documentary on Tom Thomson that ended, rather ominously, with the statement that the north had taken him to herself. This was, of course, pathetic fallacy[5] gone to seed, but it was also a comment on our distrust of the natural world, a distrust that remains despite our protests, our studies in the ethics of ecology, our elevation of "the environment" to a numinous noun, our save-the-tree campaigns. The question is, would the trees save us, given the chance? Would the water, would the birds, would the rocks? In the north, we have our doubts.

A bunch of us are sitting around the table, at what is now a summer cottage in Georgian Bay. Once it was a house, built by a local man for his family, which finally totalled eleven children, after they'd outgrown this particular

45

4. Like a person with long, thick, unkempt hair, from a character in a children's book by Heinrich Hoffman (1809–1894).
5. The attribution of human emotions to inanimate objects, often the landscape.

house and moved on to another. The original Findlay wood-burning cook stove is still in the house, but so also are some electric lights and a propane cooker, which have come since the end of the old days. In the old days, this man somehow managed to scrape a living from the land: a little of this, a little of that, some fishing here, some lumbering there, some hunting in the fall. That was back when you shot to eat. "Scrape" is an appropriate word: there's not much here between the topsoil and the rock.

We sit around the table and eat, fish among other things, caught by the children. Someone mentions the clams: there are still a lot of them, but who knows what's in them any more? Mercury, lead, things like that. We pick at the fish. Someone tells me not to drink the tap water. I already have. "What will happen?" I ask. "Probably nothing," they reply. "Probably nothing" is a relatively recent phrase around here. In the old days, you ate what looked edible.

We are talking about the old days, as people often do once they're outside the cities. When exactly did the old days end? Because we know they did. The old days ended when the youngest of us was ten, fifteen, or twenty; the old days ended when the oldest of us was five, or twelve, or thirty. Plastic-hulled superboats are not old days, but ten-horse-power outboard motors, circa 1945, are. There's an icebox in the back porch, unused now, a simple utilitarian model from Eaton's, ice chamber in the top section, metal shelves in the bottom one. We all go and admire it. "I remember iceboxes," I say, and indeed I can dimly remember them, I must have been five. What bits of our daily junk—our toasters, our pocket computers—will soon become obsolete and therefore poignant? Who will stand around, peering at them and admiring their design and the work that went into them, as we do with this icebox? "So this was a *toilet seat*," we think, rehearsing the future. "Ah! A *light bulb*," the ancient syllables thick in our mouths.

The kids have decided some time ago that all this chat is boring, and have asked if they can go swimming off the dock. They can, though they have to watch it, as this is a narrow place and speedboats tend to swoosh through, not always slowing down. Waste of gas, in the old days. Nobody then went anywhere just for pleasure, it was the war and gas was rationed.

"Oh, *that* old days," says someone.

50   There goes a speedboat now, towing a man strapped in a kneeling position to some kind of board, looking as if he's had a terrible accident, or is about to have one. This must be some newfangled variety of water-skiing.

"Remember Klim?" I say. The children come through, trailing towels. "What's Klim?" one asks, caught by the space-age sound of the word.

"Klim was 'milk' spelled backwards," I say. "It was powdered milk."

"Yuk," they say.

"Not the same as now," I say. "It was whole milk, not skim; it wasn't instant. You had to beat it with an eggbeater." And even then some of it wouldn't dissolve. One of the treats of childhood was the little nodules of pure dry Klim that floated on top of your milk.

55   "There was also Pream," says someone. How revolutionary it seemed.

The children go down to take their chances in the risky motorized water.

Maybe, much later, they will remember us sitting around the table, eating fish they themselves had caught, back when you could still (what? Catch a fish? See a tree? What desolations lie in store, beyond the plasticized hulls and the knee-skiers?). By then we will be the old days, for them. Almost we are already.

A different part of the north. We're sitting around the table, by lamplight—it's still the old days here, no electricity—talking about bad hunters. Bad hunters, bad fishers, everyone has a story. You come upon a campsite, way in the back of beyond, no roads into the lake, they must have come in by float plane, and there it is, garbage all over the place, beer cans, blobs of human poop flagged by melting toilet paper, and twenty-two fine pickerel left rotting on a rock. Business executives who get themselves flown in during hunting season with their high-powered rifles, shoot a buck, cut off the head, fill their quota, see another one with a bigger spread of antlers, drop the first head, cut off the second. The woods are littered with discarded heads, and who cares about the bodies?

New way to shoot polar bear: you have the natives on the ground finding them for you, then they radio the location in to the base camp, the base camp phones New York, fellow gets on the plane, gets himself flown in, they've got the rifle and the clothing all ready for him, fly him to the bear, he pulls the trigger from the plane, doesn't even get out of the g.d. *plane,* they fly him back, cut off the head, skin it, send the lot down to New York.

These are the horror stories of the north, one brand. They've replaced the ones in which you got pounced upon by a wolverine or had your arm chewed off by a she-bear with cubs or got chased into the lake by a moose in rut, or even the ones in which your dog got porcupine quills or rolled in poison ivy and gave it to you. In the new stories, the enemies and the victims of old have done a switch. Nature is no longer implacable, dangerous, ready to jump you; it is on the run, pursued by a number of unfair bullies with the latest technology.

One of the key nouns in these stories is "float plane." These outrages, this banditry, would not be possible without them, for the bad hunters are notoriously weak-muscled and are deemed incapable of portaging a canoe, much less paddling one. Among their other badnesses, they are sissies. Another key motif is money. What money buys these days, among other things, is the privilege of no-risk slaughter.

As for us, the ones telling the stories, tsk-tsking by lamplight, we are the good hunters, or so we think. We've given up saying we only kill to eat; Kraft dinner and freeze-dried food have put paid to that one. Really there's no excuse for us. However, we do have some virtues left. We can still cast a fly. We don't cut off heads and hang them stuffed on the wall. We would never buy an ocelot coat. We paddle our own canoes.

We're sitting on the dock at night, shivering despite our sweaters, in mid-August, watching the sky. There are a few shooting stars, as there always are at this time in August, as the earth passes through the Perseids. We pride ourselves on knowing a few things like that, about the sky; we find the Dipper, the

60

North Star, Cassiopeia's Chair, and talk about consulting a star chart, which we know we won't actually do. But this is the only place you can really *see* the stars, we tell each other. Cities are hopeless.

Suddenly, an odd light appears, going very fast. It spirals around like a newly dead firecracker, and then bursts, leaving a cloud of luminous dust, caught perhaps in the light from the sun, still up there somewhere. What could this be? Several days later, we hear that it was part of an extinct Soviet satellite, or that's what they say. That's what they would say, wouldn't they? It strikes us that we don't really know very much about the night sky at all any more. There's all kinds of junk up there: spy planes, old satellites, tin cans, man-made matter gone out of control. It also strikes us that we are totally dependent for knowledge of these things on a few people who don't tell us very much.

Once, we thought that if the balloon ever went up we'd head for the bush and hide out up there, living—we naively supposed—off the land. Now we know that if the two superpowers begin hurling things at each other through the sky, they're likely to do it across the Arctic, with big bangs and fallout all over the north. The wind blows everywhere. Survival gear and knowing which moss you can eat is not going to be a large help. The north is no longer a refuge.

65   Driving back towards Toronto from the Near North, a small reprise runs through my head:

> Land of the septic tank,
> Home of the speedboat,
> Where still the four-wheel-drive
> Wanders at will,
> Blue lake and tacky shore,
> I will return once more:
> Vroom-diddy-vroom-vroom
> Vroom-diddy-vroom-vroom
> Vroo-OO-oo-oom.

Somehow, just as the drive north inspires saga and tragedy, the drive south inspires parody. And here it comes: the gift shops shaped like teepees, the maple-syrup emporiums that get themselves up like olde-tyme sugaring-off huts; and, farther south, the restaurants that pretend to offer wholesome farm fare, the stores that pretend to be general stores, selling quilts, soap shaped like hearts, high-priced fancy conserves done up in frilly cloth caps, the way Grandma (whoever she might be) was fondly supposed to have made them.

And then come the housing developments, acres of prime farmland turning overnight into Quality All-Brick Family Homes; and then come the Industrial Parks; and there, in full anti-bloom, is the city itself, looming like a mirage or a chemical warfare zone on the horizon. A browny-grey scuzz hovers above it, and we think, as we always do when facing re-entry, we're going into *that*? We're going to breathe *that*?

But we go forward, as we always do, into what is now to us the unknown. And once inside, we breathe the air, not much bad happens to us, we hardly notice. It's as if we've never been anywhere else. But that's what we think, too, when we're in the north.

QUESTIONS

1. What context does Atwood set for the opening section? How does her need to explain to American Southerners in a college classroom help her communicate with the readers of this essay?

2. Beginning in paragraph 18, Atwood reenacts a journey to the "north." What does this journey, re-created for the reader, help her achieve?

3. Why does Atwood include a section about "typical ways of dying" in a northern landscape? What qualities about northern Canada can she present through this unusual approach?

4. Write an essay about a geographical region that appeals to you but that may be unknown or unappealing to others. Using techniques learned from Atwood or other writers in this section, try to communicate the region's appeal as you write.

DAVID GUTERSON   *Enclosed. Encyclopedic. Endured: The Mall of America*

L AST APRIL, on a visit to the new Mall of America near Minneapolis, I carried with me the public-relations press kit provided for the benefit of reporters. It included an assortment of "fun facts" about the mall: 140,000 hot dogs sold each week, 10,000 permanent jobs, 44 escalators and 17 elevators, 12,750 parking places, 13,300 short tons of steel, $1 million in cash disbursed weekly from 8 automatic-teller machines. Opened in the summer of 1992, the mall was built on the 78-acre site of the former Metropolitan Stadium, a five-minute drive from the Minneapolis–St. Paul International Airport. With 4.2 million square feet of floor space—including twenty-two times the retail footage of the average American shopping center—the Mall of America was "the largest fully enclosed combination retail and family entertainment complex in the United States."

Eleven thousand articles, the press kit warned me, had already been written on the mall. Four hundred trees had been planted in its gardens, $625 mil-

Published in Harper's Magazine *(August 1993), a monthly magazine that often prints critical accounts of American cultural phenomena.*

lion had been spent to build it, 350 stores had been leased. Three thousand bus tours were anticipated each year along with a half-million Canadian visitors and 200,000 Japanese tourists. Sales were projected at $650 million for 1993 and at $1 billion for 1996. Donny and Marie Osmond had visited the mall, as had Janet Jackson and Sally Jesse Raphael, Arnold Schwarzenegger, and the 1994 Winter Olympic Committee. The mall was five times larger than Red Square and twenty times larger than St. Peter's Basilica; it incorporated 2.3 miles of hallways and almost twice as much steel as the Eiffel Tower. It was also home to the nation's largest indoor theme park, a place called Knott's Camp Snoopy.

On the night I arrived, a Saturday, the mall was spotlit dramatically in the manner of a Las Vegas casino. It resembled, from the outside, a castle or fort, the Emerald City or Never-Never Land, impossibly large and vaguely unreal, an unbroken, windowless multistoried edifice the size of an airport terminal. Surrounded by parking lots and new freeway ramps, monolithic and imposing in the manner of a walled city, it loomed brightly against the Minnesota night sky with the disturbing magnetism of a mirage.

I knew already that the Mall of America had been imagined by its creators not merely as a marketplace but as a national tourist attraction, an immense zone of entertainments. Such a conceit raised provocative questions, for our architecture testifies to our view of ourselves and to the condition of our souls. Large buildings stand as markers in the lives of nations and in the stream of a people's history. Thus I could only ask myself: Here was a new structure that had cost more than half a billion dollars to erect—what might it tell us about ourselves? If the Mall of America was part of America, what was that going to mean?

5   I passed through one of the mall's enormous entranceways and took myself inside. Although from a distance the Mall of America had appeared menacing— exuding the ambience of a monstrous hallucination—within it turned out to be simply a shopping mall, certainly more vast than other malls but in tone and aspect, design and feel, not readily distinguishable from them. Its nuances were instantly familiar as the generic features of the American shopping mall at the tail end of the twentieth century: polished stone, polished tile, shiny chrome and brass, terrazzo floors, gazebos. From third-floor vistas, across vaulted spaces, the Mall of America felt endlessly textured—glass-enclosed ele-

vators, neon-tube lighting, bridges, balconies, gas lamps, vaulted skylights—and densely crowded with hordes of people circumambulating in an endless promenade. Yet despite the mall's expansiveness, it elicited claustrophobia, sensory deprivation, and an unnerving disorientation. Everywhere I went I spied other pilgrims who had found, like me, that the straight way was lost and that the YOU ARE HERE landmarks on the map kiosks referred to nothing in particular.

Getting lost, feeling lost, being lost—these states of mind are intentional features of the mall's psychological terrain. There are, one notices, no clocks or windows, nothing to distract the shopper's psyche from the alternate reality the mall conjures. Here we are free to wander endlessly and to furtively watch our fellow wanderers, thousands upon thousands of milling strangers who have come with the intent of losing themselves in the mall's grand, stimulating design. For a few hours we share some common ground—a fantasy of infinite commodities and comforts—and then we drift apart forever. The mall exploits our acquisitive instincts without honoring our communal requirements, our eternal desire for discourse and intimacy, needs that until the twentieth century were traditionally met in our marketplaces but that are not met at all in giant shopping malls.

On this evening a few thousand young people had descended on the mall in pursuit of alcohol and entertainment. They had come to Gators, Hooters, and Knuckleheads, Puzzles, Fat Tuesday, and Ltl Ditty's. At Players, a sports bar, the woman beside me introduced herself as "the pregnant wife of an Iowa pig farmer" and explained that she had driven five hours with friends to "do the mall party scene together." She left and was replaced by Kathleen from Minnetonka, who claimed to have "a real shopping thing—I can't go a week without buying new clothes. I'm not fulfilled until I buy something."

Later a woman named Laura arrived, with whom Kathleen was ac-

quainted. "I *am* the mall," she announced ecstatically upon discovering I was
a reporter. "I'd move in here if I could bring my dog," she added. "This place is
heaven, it's a *mecca.*"

"We egg each other on," explained Kathleen, calmly puffing on a cigarette.
"It's like, sort of, an addiction."

10   "You want the truth?" Laura asked. "I'm constantly suffering from megamall withdrawal. I come here all the time."

Kathleen: "It's a sickness. It's like cocaine or something; it's a drug."

Laura: "Kathleen's got this thing about buying, but I just need to *be* here.
If I buy something it's an added bonus."

Kathleen: "She buys stuff all the time; don't listen."

Laura: "Seriously, I feel sorry for other malls. They're so small and *boring.*"

15   Kathleen seemed to think about this: "Richdale Mall," she blurted finally.
She rolled her eyes and gestured with her cigarette. "Oh, my God, Laura. Why
did we even *go* there?"

There is, of course, nothing naturally abhorrent in the human impulse to
dwell in marketplaces or the urge to buy, sell, and trade. Rural Americans traditionally looked forward to the excitement and sensuality of market day; Native Americans traveled long distances to barter and trade at sprawling, festive
encampments. In Persian bazaars and in the ancient Greek agoras the very
soul of the community was preserved and could be seen, felt, heard, and
smelled as it might be nowhere else. All over the planet the humblest of people have always gone to market with hope in their hearts and in expectation of
something beyond mere goods—seeking a place where humanity is temporarily in ascendance, a palette for the senses, one another.

But the illicit possibilities of the marketplace also have long been acknowledged. The Persian bazaar was closed at sundown; the Greek agora was
off-limits to those who had been charged with certain crimes. One myth of the
Old West we still carry with us is that market day presupposes danger; the
faithful were advised to make purchases quickly and repair without delay to
the farm, lest their attraction to the pleasures of the marketplace erode their
purity of spirit.

In our collective discourse the shopping mall appears with the tract
house, the freeway, and the backyard barbecue as a product of the American
postwar years, a testament to contemporary necessities and desires and an invention not only peculiarly American but peculiarly of our own era too. Yet
the mall's varied and far-flung predecessors—the covered bazaars of the
Middle East, the stately arcades of Victorian England, Italy's vaulted and skylit
gallerias, Asia's monsoon-protected urban markets—all suggest that the rituals
of indoor shopping, although in their nuances not often like our own, are
nevertheless broadly known. The late twentieth-century American contribution has been to transform the enclosed bazaar into an economic institution
that is vastly profitable yet socially enervated, one that redefines in fundamental ways the human relationship to the marketplace. At the Mall of
America—an extreme example—we discover ourselves thoroughly lost among

strangers in a marketplace intentionally designed to serve no community needs.

In the strict sense the Mall of America is not a marketplace at all—the soul of a community expressed as a *place*—but rather a tourist attraction. Its promoters have peddled it to the world at large as something more profound than a local marketplace and as a destination with deep implications. "I believe we can make Mall of America stand for all of America," asserted the mall's general manager, John Wheeler, in a promotional video entitled *There's a Place for Fun in Your Life.* "I believe there's a shopper in all of us," added the director of marketing, Maureen Hooley. The mall has memorialized its opening-day proceedings by

producing a celebratory videotape: Ray Charles singing "America the Beautiful," a laser show followed by fireworks, "The Star-Spangled Banner" and "The Stars and Stripes Forever," the Gatlin Brothers, and Peter Graves. "Mall of America . . . ," its narrator intoned. "The name alone conjures up images of greatness, of a retail complex so magnificent it could only happen in America."

Indeed, on the day the mall opened, Miss America visited. The mall's logo—a red, white, and blue star bisected by a red, white, and blue ribbon—decorated everything from the mall itself to coffee mugs and the flanks of buses. The idea, director of tourism Colleen Hayes told me, was to position America's largest mall as an institution on the scale of Disneyland or the Grand Canyon, a place simultaneously iconic and totemic, a revered symbol of the United States and a mecca to which the faithful would flock in pursuit of all things purchasable.

On Sunday I wandered the hallways of the pleasure dome with the sensation that I had entered an M. C. Escher drawing—there was no such thing as up or down, and the escalators all ran backward. A 1993 Ford Probe GT was displayed as if popping out of a giant packing box; a full-size home, complete with artificial lawn, had been built in the mall's rotunda. At the Michael Ricker Pewter Gallery I came across a miniature tableau of a pewter dog peeing on a pewter man's leg; at Hologram Land I pondered 3-D hallucinations of the

20

Medusa and Marilyn Monroe. I passed a kiosk called The Sportsman's Wife; I stood beside a life-size statue of the Hamm's Bear, carved out of pine and available for $1,395 at a store called Minnesot-ah! At Pueblo Spirit I examined a "dream catcher"—a small hoop made from deer sinew and willow twigs and designed to be hung over its owner's bed as a tactic for filtering bad dreams. For a while I sat in front of Glamour Shots and watched while women were groomed and brushed for photo sessions yielding high-fashion self-portraits at $34.95 each. There was no stopping, no slowing down. I passed Mug Me, Queen for a Day, and Barnyard Buddies, and stood in the Brookstone store examining a catalogue: a gopher "eliminator" for $40 (it's a vibrating, anodized-aluminum stake), a "no-stoop" shoehorn for $10, a nose-hair trimmer for $18. At the arcade inside Knott's Camp Snoopy I watched while teenagers played Guardians of the 'Hood, Total Carnage, Final Fight, and Varth Operation Thunderstorm; a small crowd of them had gathered around a lean, cool character who stood calmly shooting video cowpokes in a game called Mad Dog McCree. Left thumb on his silver belt buckle, biceps pulsing, he banged away without remorse while dozens of his enemies crumpled and died in alleyways and dusty streets.

At Amazing Pictures a teenage boy had his photograph taken as a bodybuilder—his face smoothly grafted onto a rippling body—then proceeded to purchase this pleasing image on a poster, a sweatshirt, and a coffee mug. At Painted Tipi there was wild rice for sale, hand-harvested from Leech Lake, Minnesota. At Animalia I came across a polyresin figurine of a turtle retailing for $3,200. At Bloomingdale's I pondered a denim shirt with its sleeves ripped away, the sort of thing available at used-clothing stores (the "grunge look," a Bloomingdale's employee explained), on sale for $125. Finally, at a gift shop in Knott's Camp Snoopy, I came across a game called Electronic Mall Madness, put out by Milton Bradley. On the box, three twelve-year-old girls with good features happily vied to beat one another to the game-board mall's best sales.

At last I achieved an enforced self-arrest, anchoring myself against a bench while the mall tilted on its axis. Two pubescent girls in retainers and braces sat beside me sipping coffees topped with whipped cream and chocolate sprinkles, their shopping bags gathered tightly around their legs, their eyes fixed on the passing crowds. They came, they said, from Shakopee—"It's nowhere," one of them explained. The megamall, she added, was "a buzz at first, but now it seems pretty normal. 'Cept my parents are like Twenty Questions every time I want to come here. 'Specially since the shooting."

On a Sunday night, she elaborated, three people had been wounded when shots were fired in a dispute over a San Jose Sharks jacket. "In the *mall*," her friend reminded me. "Right here at megamall. A shooting."

25   "It's like nowhere's safe," the first added.

The sipped their coffees and explicated for me the plot of a film they saw as relevant, a horror movie called *Dawn of the Dead*, which they had each viewed a half-dozen times. In the film, they explained, apocalypse had come, and the survivors had repaired to a shopping mall as the most likely place to make their last stand in a poisoned, impossible world. And this would have been perfectly all right, they insisted, except that the place had also attracted hordes of the infamous living dead—sentient corpses who had not relinquished their attraction to indoor shopping.

I moved on and contemplated a computerized cash register in the infant's section of the Nordstrom store: "The Answer Is Yes!!!" its monitor reminded clerks. "Customer Service Is Our Number One Priority!" Then back at Bloomingdale's I contemplated a bank of televisions playing incessantly an advertisement for Egoïste, a men's cologne from Chanel. In the ad a woman on a wrought-iron balcony tossed her black hair about and screamed long and passionately; then there were many women screaming passionately, too, and throwing balcony shutters open and closed, and this was all followed by a bottle of the cologne displayed where I could get a good look at it. The brief, strange drama repeated itself until I could no longer stand it.

America's first fully enclosed shopping center—Southdale Center, in Edina, Minnesota—is a ten-minute drive from the Mall of America and thirty-six years its senior. (It is no coincidence that the Twin Cities area is such a prominent player in mall history: Minnesota is subject to the sort of severe weather that makes climate-controlled shopping seductive.) Opened in 1956, Southdale spawned an era of fervid mall construction and generated a vast new industry. Shopping centers proliferated so rapidly that by the end of 1992, says the National Research Bureau, there were nearly 39,000 of them operating everywhere across the country. But while malls recorded a much-ballyhooed success in the America of the 1970s and early 1980s, they gradually became less profitable to run as the exhausted and overwhelmed American worker inevitably lost interest in leisure shopping. Pressed for time and short on money, shoppers turned to factory outlet centers, catalogue purchasing, and "category killers" (specialty stores such as Home Depot and Price Club) at the expense of shopping malls. The industry, unnerved, reinvented itself, relying on smaller and more convenient local centers—especially the familiar neighborhood strip mall—and building far fewer large regional malls in an effort to stay afloat through troubled times. With the advent of cable television's Home Shopping Network and the proliferation of specialty catalogue retailers (whose access to computerized market research has made them, in the Nineties, powerful competitors), the mall industry reeled yet further. According to the International Council of Shopping Centers, new mall construction in 1992 was a third of what it had been in 1989, and the value of mall-construction contracts dropped 60 percent in the same three-year period.

Anticipating a future in which millions of Americans will prefer to shop in the security of their living rooms—conveniently accessing online retail companies as a form of quiet evening entertainment—the mall industry, after less than forty years, experienced a full-blown mid-life crisis. It was necessary for the industry to re-invent itself once more, this time with greater attentiveness to the qualities that would allow it to endure relentless change. Anxiety-ridden and sapped of vitality, mall builders fell back on an ancient truth, one capable of sustaining them through troubled seasons: they discovered what humanity had always understood, that shopping and frivolity go hand in hand and are inherently symbiotic. *If you build it fun, they will come.*

30   The new bread-and-circuses approach to mall building was first ventured in 1985 by the four Ghermezian brothers—Raphael, Nader, Bahman, and Eskandar—builders of Canada's $750 million West Edmonton Mall, which included a water slide, an artificial lake, a miniature-golf course, a hockey rink, and forty-seven rides in an amusement park known as Fantasyland. The complex quickly generated sales revenues at twice the rate per square foot of retail space that could be squeezed from a conventional outlet mall, mostly by developing its own shopping synergy: people came for a variety of reasons and to do a variety of things. West Edmonton's carnival atmosphere, it gradually emerged, lubricated pocketbooks and inspired the sort of impulse buying on which malls everywhere thrive. To put the matter another way, it was time for a shopping-and-pleasure palace to be attempted in the United States.

After selling the Mall of America concept to Minnesotans in 1985, the Ghermezians joined forces with their American counterparts—Mel and Herb Simon of Indianapolis, owners of the NBA's Indiana Pacers and the nation's second-largest developers of shopping malls. The idea, in the beginning, was to outdo West Edmonton by building a mall far larger and more expensive—something visionary, a wonder of the world—and to include such attractions as fashionable hotels, an elaborate tour de force aquarium, and a monorail to the Minneapolis–St. Paul airport. Eventually the project was downscaled substantially: a million square feet of floor space was eliminated, the construction budget was cut, and the aquarium and hotels were never built (reserved, said marketing director Maureen Hooley, for "phase two" of the mall's development). Japan's Mitsubishi Bank, Mitsui Trust, and Chuo Trust together put up a reported $400 million to finance the cost of construction, and Teachers Insurance and Annuity Association (the majority owner of the Mall of America) came through with another $225 million. At a total bill of $625 million, the mall was ultimately a less ambitious project than its forebear up north on the Canadian plains, and neither as large nor as gaudy. Reflecting the economy's downturn, the parent companies of three of the mall's anchor tenants—Sears, Macy's, and Bloomingdale's—were battling serious financial trouble and needed substantial transfusions from mall developers to have their stores ready by opening day.

The mall expects to spend millions on marketing itself during its initial year of operation and has lined up the usual corporate sponsors—Ford, Pepsi, US West—in an effort to build powerful alliances. Its public-relations representatives travel to towns such as Rapid City, South Dakota, and Sioux City, Iowa, in order to drum up interest within the Farm Belt. Northwest Airlines, another corporate sponsor, offers package deals from London and Tokyo and fare adjustments for those willing to come from Bismarck, North Dakota; Cedar Rapids, Iowa; and Kalamazoo or Grand Rapids, Michigan. Calling itself a "premier tourism destination," the mall draws from a primary tourist market that incorporates the eleven Midwest states (and two Canadian provinces) lying within a day's drive of its parking lots. It also estimates that in its first six months of operation, 5.3 million out of 16 million visitors came from beyond the Twin Cities metropolitan area.

The mall has forecast a much-doubted figure of 46 million annual visits by 1996—four times the number of annual visits to Disneyland, for example, and twelve times the visits to the Grand Canyon. The number, Maureen Hooley explained, seems far less absurd when one takes into account that mall pilgrims make far more repeat visits—as many as eighty in a single year—than visitors to theme parks such as Disneyland. Relentless advertising and shrewd promotion, abetted by the work of journalists like myself, assure the mall that visitors will come in droves—at least for the time being. The national media have comported themselves as if the new mall were a place of light and promise, full of hope and possibility. Meanwhile the Twin Cities' media have been shameless: on opening night Minneapolis's WCCO-TV aired a one-hour mall special, hosted by local news anchors Don Shelby and Colleen Needles, and the *St. Paul Pioneer Press* (which was named an "official" sponsor of the opening) dedicated both a phone line and a weekly column to answering esoteric mall questions. Not to be outdone, the *Minneapolis Star Tribune* developed a special graphic to draw readers to mall stories and printed a vast Sunday supplement before opening day under the heading A WHOLE NEW MALLGAME. By the following Wednesday all perspective was in eclipse: the local press reported that at 9:05 A.M., the mall's Victoria's Secret outlet had recorded its first sale, a pair of blue/green silk men's boxer shorts; that mall developers Mel and Herb Simon ate black-bean soup for lunch at 12:30 P.M.; that Kimberly Levis, four years old, constructed a rectangular column nineteen bricks high at the mall's Lego Imagination Center; and that mall officials had retained a plumber on standby in case difficulties arose with the mall's toilets.

From all of this coverage—and from the words you now read—the mall gains status as a phenomenon worthy of our time and consideration: place as celebrity. The media encourage us to visit our megamall in the obligatory fashion we flock to *Jurassic Park*—because it is there, all glitter and glow, a piece of the terrain, a season's diversion, an assumption on the cultural landscape. All of us will want to be in on the conversation and, despite ourselves, we will go.

Lost in the fun house I shopped till I dropped, but the scale of the mall eventually overwhelmed me and I was unable to make a purchase. Finally I met Chuck Brand on a bench in Knott's Camp Snoopy; he was seventy-two and, in his personal assessment of it, had lost at least 25 percent of his mind. "It's fun being a doozy," he confessed to me. "The security cops got me figured and keep their distance. I don't get hassled for hanging out, not shopping. Because the deal is, when you're seventy-two, man, you're just about all done shopping."

After forty-seven years of selling houses in Minneapolis, Chuck comes to the mall every day. He carries a business card with his picture on it, his company name and phone number deleted and replaced by his pager code. His wife drops him at the mall at 10:00 A.M. each morning and picks him up again at six; in between he sits and watches. "I can't sit home and do nothing," he

35

insisted. When I stood to go he assured me he understood: I was young and had things I had to do. "Listen," he added, "thanks for talking to me, man. I've been sitting in this mall for four months now and nobody ever said nothing."

The next day I descended into the mall's enormous basement, where its business offices are located. "I'm sorry to have to bring this up," my pre-arranged mall guide, Michelle Biesiada, greeted me. "But you were seen talking to one of our housekeepers—one of the people who empty the garbage? —and really, you aren't supposed to do that."

Later we sat in the mall's security center, a subterranean computerized command post where two uniformed officers manned a bank of television screens. The Mall of America, it emerged, employed 109 surveillance cameras to monitor the various activities of its guests, and had plans to add yet more. There were cameras in the food courts and parking lots, in the hallways and in Knott's Camp Snoopy. From where we sat, it was possible to monitor thirty-six locations simultaneously; it was also possible, with the use of a zoom feature, to narrow in on an object as small as a hand, a license plate, or a wallet.

While we sat in the darkness of the security room, enjoying the voyeuristic pleasures it allowed (I, for one, felt a giddy sense of power), a security guard noted something of interest occurring in one of the parking lots. The guard engaged a camera's zoom feature, and soon we were given to understand that a couple of bored shoppers were enjoying themselves by fornicating in the front seat of a parked car. An officer was dispatched to knock on their door and discreetly suggest that they move themselves along; the Mall of America was no place for this. "If they want to have sex they'll have to go elsewhere," a security officer told me. "We don't have anything against sex, per se, but we don't want it happening in our parking lots."

40 I left soon afterward for a tour of the mall's basement, a place of perpetual concrete corridors and home to a much-touted recyclery. Declaring itself "the most environmentally conscious shopping center in the industry," the Mall of America claims to recycle up to 80 percent of its considerable refuse and points to its "state-of-the-art" recycling system as a symbol of its dedication to Mother Earth. Yet Rick Doering of Browning-Ferris Industries—the company contracted to manage the mall's 700 tons of monthly garbage—described the on-site facility as primarily a public-relations gambit that actually recycles only a third of the mall's tenant waste and little of what is discarded by its thousands of visitors; furthermore, he admitted, the venture is unprofitable to Browning-Ferris, which would find it far cheaper to recycle the mall's refuse somewhere other than in its basement.

A third-floor "RecycleNOW Center," located next to Macy's and featuring educational exhibits, is designed to enhance the mall's self-styled image as a national recycling leader. Yet while the mall's developers gave Macy's $35 million to cover most of its "build-out" expenses (the cost of transforming the mall's basic structure into finished, customer-ready floor space), Browning-Ferris got nothing in build-out costs and operates the center at a total loss, paying rent equivalent to that paid by the mall's retailers. As a result, the company has had to look for ways to keep its costs to a minimum, and the mall's garbage is now sorted by developmentally disabled adults working a conveyor belt in the basement. Doering and I stood watching them as they picked at a stream of paper and plastic bottles; when I asked about their pay, he flinched and grimaced, then deflected me toward another supervisor, who said that wages were based on daily productivity. Did this mean that they made less than minimum wage? I inquired. The answer was yes.

Upstairs once again, I hoped for relief from the basement's oppressive, concrete gloom, but the mall felt densely crowded and with panicked urgency I made an effort to leave. I ended up instead at Knott's Camp Snoopy —the seven-acre theme park at the center of the complex—a place intended to alleviate claustrophobia by "bringing the outdoors indoors." Its interior land-scape, the press kit claims, "was inspired by Minnesota's natural habitat— forests, meadows, river banks, and marshes . . ." And "everything you see, feel, smell and hear adds to the illusion that it's summertime, seventy degrees and you're outside enjoying the awesome splendor of the Minnesota woods."

Creators of this illusion had much to contend with, including sixteen carnival-style midway rides, such as the Pepsi Ripsaw, the Screaming Yellow Eagle, Paul Bunyan's Log Chute by Brawny, Tumbler, Truckin', and Huff 'n' Puff; fifteen places for visitors to eat, such as Funnel Cakes, Stick Dogs and Campfire Burgers, Taters, Pizza Oven, and Wilderness Barbecue; seven shops with names like Snoopy's Boutique, Joe Cool's Hot Shop, and Camp Snoopy Toys; and such assorted attractions as Pan for Gold, Hunter's Paradise Shoot-ing Gallery, the Snoopy Fountain, and the video arcade that includes the game Mad Dog McCree.

As if all this were not enough to cast a serious pall over the Minnesota woods illusion, the theme park's designers had to contend with the fact that they could use few plants native to Minnesota. At a constant temperature of seventy degrees, the mall lends itself almost exclusively to tropical varieties— orange jasmine, black olive, oleander, hibiscus—and not at all to the conifers of Minnesota, which require a cold dormancy period. Deferring ineluctably to this troubling reality, Knott's Camp Snoopy brought in 526 tons of plants— tropical rhododendrons, willow figs, buddhist pines, azaleas—from such places as Florida, Georgia, and Mississippi.

Anne Pryor, a Camp Snoopy marketing representative, explained to me   45
that these plants were cared for via something called "integrated pest manage-ment," which meant the use of predators such as ladybugs instead of pesti-cides. Yet every member of the landscape staff I spoke to described a campaign of late-night pesticide spraying as a means of controlling the theme park's enemies—mealybugs, aphids, and spider mites. Two said they had argued for integrated pest management as a more environmentally sound method of con-trolling insects but that to date it had not been tried.

Even granting that Camp Snoopy is what it claims to be—an authentic version of Minnesota's north woods tended by environmentally correct means—the question remains whether it makes sense to place a forest in the middle of the country's largest shopping complex. Isn't it true that if people want woods, they are better off not going to a mall?

On Valentine's Day last February—cashing in on the promotional scheme of a local radio station—ninety-two couples were married en masse in a ceremony at the Mall of America. They rode the roller coaster and the Screaming Yellow Eagle and were photographed beside a frolicking Snoopy, who wore an immaculate tuxedo. "As we stand here together at the Mall of America," presiding district judge Richard Spicer declared, "we are reminded that there is a place for fun in your life and you have found it in each other." Six months earlier, the Reverend Leith Anderson of the Wooddale Church in Eden Prairie conducted services in the mall's rotunda. Six thousand people had congregated by 10:00 A.M., and Reverend Anderson delivered a sermon entitled "The Unknown God of the Mall." Characterizing the mall as a "direct descendant" of the ancient Greek agoras, the reverend pointed out that, like the Greeks before us, we Americans have many gods. Afterward, of course, the flock went shopping, much to the chagrin of Reverend Delton Krueger, president of the Mall Area Religious Council, who told the *Minneapolis Star Tribune* that as a site for church services, the mall may trivialize religion. "A good many people in the churches," said Krueger, "feel a lot of the trouble in the world is because of materialism."

But a good many people in the mall business today apparently think the trouble lies elsewhere. They are moving forward aggressively on the premise that the dawning era of electronic shopping does not preclude the building of shopping-and-pleasure palaces all around the globe. Japanese developers, in a joint venture with the Ghermezians known as International Malls Incorporated, are planning a $400 million Mall of Japan, with an ice rink, a water park, a fantasy-theme hotel, three breweries, waterfalls, and a sports center. We might shortly predict, too, a Mall of Europe, a Mall of New England, a Mall of California, and perhaps even a Mall of the World. The concept of shopping in a frivolous atmosphere, concocted to loosen consumers' wallets, is poised to proliferate globally. We will soon see monster malls everywhere, rooted in the soil of every nation and offering a preposterous, impossible variety of commodities and entertainments.

The new malls will be planets unto themselves, closed off from this world in the manner of space stations or of science fiction's underground cities. Like the Mall of America and West Edmonton Mall—prototypes for a new generation of shopping centers—they will project a separate and distinct reality in which an "outdoor café" is not outdoors, a "bubbling brook" is a concrete watercourse, and a "serpentine street" is a hallway. Safe, surreal, and outside of time and space, they will offer the mind a potent dreamscape from which there is no present waking. This carefully controlled fantasy—now operable in Minnesota—is so powerful as to inspire psychological addiction or to elicit in visitors a catatonic obsession with the mall's various hallucinations. The new malls will be theatrical, high-tech illusions capable of attracting enormous crowds from distant points and foreign ports. Their psychology has not yet been tried pervasively on the scale of the Mall of America, nor has it been perfected. But in time our marketplaces, all over the world, will be in essential ways interchangeable, so thoroughly divorced from the communities in which they sit that they will appear to rest like permanently docked spaceships against the landscape, windowless and turned in upon their own affairs. The affluent will travel as tourists to each, visiting the holy sites and taking photographs in the catacombs of far-flung temples.

Just as Victorian England is acutely revealed beneath the grandiose domes of its overwrought train stations, so is contemporary America well understood from the upper vistas of its shopping malls, places without either windows or clocks where the temperature is forever seventy degrees. It is facile to believe, from this vantage point, that the endless circumambulations of tens of thousands of strangers—all loaded down with the detritus of commerce—resemble anything akin to community. The shopping mall is not, as the architecture critic Witold Rybczynski has concluded, "poised to become a real urban place" with "a variety of commercial and noncommercial functions." On the contrary, it is poised to multiply around the world as an institution offering only a desolate substitute for the rich, communal lifeblood of the traditional marketplace, which will not survive its onslaught. 50

Standing on the Mall of America's roof, where I had ventured to inspect its massive ventilation units, I finally achieved a full sense of its vastness, of how it overwhelmed the surrounding terrain—the last sheep farm in sight, the Mississippi River incidental in the distance. Then I peered through the skylights down into Camp Snoopy, where throngs of my fellow citizens caroused happily in the vast entrails of the beast.

Questions

1. In this article, Guterson often uses lists. Why do you think he does so? What effect do the long lists have on readers?

2. At various points in the article, the Mall of America is compared to Mecca, heaven, or a church, and those who shop and seek entertainment there are referred to as "pilgrims." In other places, the mall is referred to as "an addiction" or a drug. Which metaphor do you find more persuasive? Why?

3. Guterson claims that "our architecture testifies to our view of ourselves and to the condition of our souls" (paragraph 4). Write an article about a building you frequently go to (for example, the building in which your classroom is housed; a church, mosque, or synagogue; your dorm; or your parents' home). What does the architecture of that building say about those who frequent it? How does the architecture influence behavior or beliefs?

Human Nature

Scott Russell Sanders *Looking at Women*

O N THAT SIZZLING July afternoon, the girl who crossed at the stoplight in front of our car looked, as my mother would say, as though she had been poured into her pink shorts. The girl's matching pink halter bared her stomach and clung to her nubbin breasts, leaving little to the imagination, as my mother would also say. Until that moment, it had never made any difference to me how much or little a girl's clothing revealed, for my imagination had been entirely devoted to other mysteries. I was eleven. The girl was about fourteen, the age of my buddy Norman who lounged in the back seat with me. Staring after her, Norman elbowed me in the ribs and murmured, "Check out that chassis."

His mother glared around from the driver's seat. "Hush your mouth."

"I was talking about that sweet Chevy," said Norman, pointing out a souped-up jalopy at the curb.

"I know what you were talking about," his mother snapped.

No doubt she did know, since mothers could read minds, but at first I did not have a clue. Chassis? I knew what it meant for a car, an airplane, a radio, or even a cannon to have a chassis. But could a girl have one as well? I glanced after the retreating figure, and suddenly noticed with a sympathetic twitching in my belly the way her long raven ponytail swayed in rhythm to her walk and the way her fanny jostled in those pink shorts. In July's dazzle of sun, her swinging legs and arms beamed at me a semaphore I could almost read.

As the light turned green and our car pulled away, Norman's mother cast one more scowl at her son in the rearview mirror, saying, "Just think how it makes her feel to have you two boys gawking at her."

How? I wondered.

"Makes her feel like hot stuff," said Norman, owner of a bold mouth.

"If you don't get your mind out of the gutter, you're going to wind up in the state reformatory," said his mother.

Norman gave a snort. I sank into the seat, and tried to figure out what power had sprung from that sashaying girl to zap me in the belly.

Only after much puzzling did it dawn on me that I must finally have drifted into the force-field of sex, as a space traveler who has lived all his years in free fall might rocket for the first time within gravitational reach of a star. Even as a bashful eleven-year-old I knew the word *sex*, of course, and I could

First published in the Georgia Review *(Spring 1989); later reprinted in Sanders's essay collection* Secrets of the Universe *(1991).*

paste that name across my image of the tantalizing girl. But a label for a mystery no more explains a mystery than the word *gravity* explains gravity. As I grew a beard and my taste shifted from girls to women, I acquired a more cagey language for speaking of desire, I picked up disarming theories. First by hearsay and then by experiment, I learned the delicious details of making babies. I came to appreciate the urgency for propagation that litters the road with maple seeds and drives salmon up waterfalls and yokes the newest crop of boys to the newest crop of girls. Books in their killjoy wisdom taught me that all the valentines and violins, the waltzes and glances, the long fever and ache of romance, were merely embellishments on biology's instructions that we multiply our kind. And yet, the fraction of desire that actually leads to procreation is so vanishingly small as to seem irrelevant. In his lifetime a man sways to a million longings, only a few of which, or perhaps none at all, ever lead to the fathering of children. Now, thirty years away from that July afternoon, firmly married, twice a father, I am still humming from the power unleashed by the girl in pink shorts, still wondering how it made her feel to have two boys gawk at her, still puzzling over how to dwell in the force-field of desire.

How should a man look at women? It is a peculiarly and perhaps neurotically human question. Billy goats do not fret over how they should look at nanny goats. They look or don't look, as seasons and hormones dictate, and feel what they feel without benefit of theory. There is more billy goat in most men than we care to admit. None of us, however, is pure goat. To live utterly as an animal would make the business of sex far tidier but also drearier. If we tried, like Rousseau,[1] to peel off the layers of civilization and imagine our way back to some pristine man and woman who have not yet been corrupted by hand-me-down notions of sexuality, my hunch is that we would find, in our speculative state of nature, that men regarded women with appalling simplicity. In any case, unlike goats, we dwell in history. What attracts our eyes and rouses our blood is only partly instinctual. Other forces contend in us as well: the voices of books and religions, the images of art and film and advertising, the entire chorus of culture. Norman's telling me to relish the sight of females and his mother's telling me to keep my eyes to myself are only two of the many voices quarreling in my head.

If there were a rule book for sex, it would be longer than the one for baseball (that byzantine sport), more intricate and obscure than tax instructions from the Internal Revenue Service. What I present here are a few images and reflections that cling, for me, to this one item in such a compendium of rules: How should a man look at women?

Well before I was to see any women naked in the flesh, I saw a bevy of them naked in photographs, hung in a gallery around the bed of my freshman room-

---

1. Jean-Jacques Rousseau (1712–1778), Swiss-born French philosopher, author, political theorist, and composer. His closeness to nature, individualism, rebellion against the established social and political order, and glorification of the emotions made him the father of French romanticism.

mate at college. A *Playboy* subscriber, he would pluck the centerfold from its staples each month and tape another airbrushed lovely to the wall. The gallery was in place when I moved in, and for an instant before I realized what I was looking at, all that expanse of skin reminded me of a meat locker back in Newton Falls, Ohio. I never quite shook that first impression, even after I had inspected the pinups at my leisure on subsequent days. Every curve of buttock and breast was news to me, an innocent kid from the Puritan back roads. Today you would be hard pressed to find a college freshman as ignorant as I was of female anatomy, if only because teenagers now routinely watch movies at home that would have been shown, during my teen years, exclusively on the fly-speckled screens of honky-tonk cinemas or in the basement of the Kinsey Institute.[2] I studied those alien shapes on the wall with a curiosity that was not wholly sexual, a curiosity tinged with the wonder that astronomers must have felt when they pored over the early photographs of the far side of the moon.

15   The paper women seemed to gaze back at me, enticing or mocking, yet even in my adolescent dither I was troubled by the phony stare, for I knew this was no true exchange of looks. Those mascaraed eyes were not fixed on me but on a camera. What the models felt as they posed I could only guess—perhaps the boredom of any numbskull job, perhaps the weight of dollar bills, perhaps the sweltering lights of fame, perhaps a tingle of the power that launched a thousand ships.

Whatever their motives, these women had chosen to put themselves on display. For the instant of the photograph, they had become their bodies, as a prizefighter does in the moment of landing a punch, as a weightlifter does in the moment of hoisting a barbell, as a ballerina does in the whirl of a pirouette, as we all do in the crisis of making love or dying. Men, ogling such photographs, are supposed to feel that where so much surface is revealed there can be no depths. Yet I never doubted that behind the makeup and the plump curves and the two dimensions of the image there was an inwardness, a feeling self as mysterious as my own. In fact, during moments when I should have been studying French or thermodynamics, I would glance at my roommate's wall and invent mythical lives for those goddesses. The lives I made up were adolescent ones, to be sure; but so was mine. Without that saving aura of inwardness, these women in the glossy photographs would have become merely another category of objects for sale, alongside the sports cars and stereo systems and liquors advertised in the same pages. If not extinguished, however, their humanity was severely reduced. And if by simplifying themselves they had lost some human essence, then by gaping at them I had shared in the theft.

What did that gaping take from me? How did it affect my way of seeing other women, those who would never dream of lying nude on a fake tiger rug before the million-faceted eye of a camera? The bodies in the photographs

2. Indiana University's Institute for Sex Research, directed, beginning in 1942, by American biologist Alfred Charles Kinsey (1894–1956).

were implausibly smooth and slick and inflated, like balloon caricatures that
might be floated overhead in a parade. Free of sweat and scars and imperfections, sensual without being fertile, tempting yet impregnable, they were Pla-
tonic ideals of the female form, divorced from time and the fluster of living,
excused from the perplexities of mind. No actual woman could rival their insipid perfection.

The swains who gathered to admire my roommate's gallery discussed the
pinups in the same tones and in much the same language as the farmers back
home in Ohio used for assessing cows. The relevant parts of male or female
bodies are quickly named—and, the *Kamasutra* and Marquis de Sade[3]
notwithstanding, the number of ways in which those parts can be stimulated
or conjoined is touchingly small—so these studly conversations were more tedious than chitchat about the weather. I would lie on my bunk pondering calculus or Aeschylus and unwillingly hear the same few nouns and fewer verbs
issuing from one mouth after another, and I would feel smugly superior. Here
I was, improving my mind, while theirs wallowed in the notorious gutter.
Eventually the swains would depart, leaving me in peace, and from the intellectual heights of my bunk I would glance across at those photographs—and
yield to the gravity of lust. Idiot flesh! How stupid that a counterfeit stare and
artful curves, printed in millions of copies on glossy paper, could arouse me.
But there it was, not the first proof of my body's automatism and not the last.

Nothing in men is more machinelike than the flipping of sexual switches.
I have never been able to read with a straight face the claims made by D. H.
Lawrence[4] and lesser pundits that the penis is a god, a lurking dragon. It more
nearly resembles a railroad crossing signal, which stirs into life at intervals to
announce, "Here comes a train." Or, if the penis must be likened to an animal,
let it be an ill-trained circus dog, sitting up and playing dead and heeling whenever it takes a notion, oblivious of the trainer's commands. Meanwhile, heart,
lungs, blood vessels, pupils, and eyelids all assert their independence like the
members of a rebellious troupe. Reason stands helpless at the center of the
ring, cracking its whip.

While he was president, Jimmy Carter raised a brouhaha by confessing in   20
a *Playboy* interview, of all shady places, that he occasionally felt lust in his
heart for women. What man hasn't, aside from those who feel lust in their
hearts for other men? The commentators flung their stones anyway. Naughty,
naughty, they chirped. Wicked Jimmy. Perhaps Mr. Carter could derive some
consolation from psychologist Allen Wheelis, who blames male appetite on biology: "We have been selected for desiring. Nothing could have convinced us by

3. The *Kamasutra*, detailed account (fourth-to-seventh centuries C.E.) of the art and
technique of Indian erotics by the sage Vātsyāyana; Marquis de Sade (1740–1814),
French author whose works, because of their pornographic and blasphemous subject
matter, led to his repeated imprisonment and have been suppressed by the French
courts as recently as 1957.

4. David Herbert Lawrence (1885–1930), English novelist and author of *Lady Chatter-
ley's Lover* (1928).

argument that it would be worthwhile to chase endlessly and insatiably after
women, but something has transformed us from within, a plasmid has invaded
our DNA, has twisted our nature so that now this is exactly what we *want* to
do." Certainly, by Darwinian logic, those males who were most avid in their
pursuit of females were also the most likely to pass on their genes. Consoling
it may be, yet it is finally no solution to blame biology. "I am extremely sexual
in my desires: I carry them everywhere and at all times," William Carlos
Williams[5] tells us on the opening page of his autobiography. "I think that from
that arises the drive which empowers us all. Given that drive, a man does with
it what his mind directs. In the manner in which he directs that power lies his
secret." Whatever the contents of my DNA, however potent the influence of
my ancestors, I still must direct that rebellious power. I still must live with the
consequences of my looking and my longing.

Aloof on their blankets like goddesses on clouds, the pinups did not belong to
my funky world. I was invisible to them, and they were immune to my gaze.
Not so the women who passed me on the street, sat near me in classes, shared
a table with me in the cafeteria: it was risky to stare at them. They could gaze
back, and sometimes did, with looks both puzzling and exciting. It only complicated matters for me to realize that so many of these strangers had taken
precautions that men should notice them. The girl in matching pink halter
and shorts who set me humming in my eleventh year might only have wanted
to keep cool in the sizzle of July. But these alluring college femmes had deeper
designs. Perfume, eye shadow, uplift bras (about which I learned in the Sears
catalog), curled hair, stockings, jewelry, lipstick, lace—what were these if not
hooks thrown out into male waters?

I recall being mystified in particular by spike heels. They looked painful to
me, and dangerous. Danger may have been the point, since the spikes would
have made good weapons—they were affectionately known, after all, as stilet-
tos. Or danger may have been the point in another sense, because a woman
teetering along on such heels is tipsy, vulnerable, broadcasting her need for
support. And who better than a man to prop her up, some guy who clomps
around in brogans wide enough for the cornerstones of flying buttresses? (For
years after college, I felt certain that spike heels had been forever banned, like
bustles and foot-binding, but lately they have come back in fashion, and once
more one encounters women teetering along on knife points.)

Back in those days of my awakening to women, I was also baffled by lin-
gerie. I do not mean underwear, the proletariat of clothing, and I do not mean
foundation garments, pale and sensible. I mean what the woman who lives in
the house behind ours—owner of a shop called "Bare Essentials"—refers to as
"intimate apparel." Those two words announce that her merchandise is both
sexy and expensive. These flimsy items cost more per ounce than truffles,
more than frankincense and myrrh. They are put-ons whose only purpose is in
being taken off. I have a friend who used to attend the men's-only nights at

5. American poet and physician (1883–1963).

Bare Essentials, during which he would invariably buy a slinky outfit or two, by way of proving his serious purpose, outfits that wound up in the attic because his wife would not be caught dead in them. Most of the customers at the shop are women, however, as the models are women, and the owner is a woman. What should one make of that? During my college days I knew about intimate apparel only by rumor, not being that intimate with anyone who would have tricked herself out in such finery, but I could see the spike heels and other female trappings everywhere I turned. Why, I wondered then and wonder still, do so many women decorate themselves like dolls? And does that mean they wish to be viewed as dolls?

On this question as on many others, Simone de Beauvoir has clarified matters for me, writing in *The Second Sex:*[6] "The 'feminine' woman in making herself prey tries to reduce man, also, to her carnal passivity; she occupies herself in catching him in her trap, in enchaining him by means of the desires she arouses in him in submissively making herself a thing." Those women who transform themselves into dolls, in other words, do so because that is the most potent identity available to them. "It must be admitted," Beauvoir concedes, "that the males find in woman more complicity than the oppressor usually finds in the oppressed. And in bad faith they take authorization from this to declare that she has *desired* the destiny they have imposed on her."

Complicity, oppressor, bad faith: such terms yank us into a moral realm unknown to goats. While I am saddled with enough male guilt to believe three-quarters of Beauvoir's claim, I still doubt that men are so entirely to blame for the turning of women into sexual dolls. I believe human history is more collaborative than her argument would suggest. It seems unlikely to me that one-half the species could have "imposed" a destiny on the other half, unless that other half were far more craven than the females I have known. Some women have expressed their own skepticism on this point. Thus Joan Didion: "That many women are victims of condescension and exploitation and sex-role stereotyping was scarcely news, but neither was it news that other women are not: nobody forces women to buy the package." Beauvoir herself recognized that many members of her sex refuse to buy the "feminine" package: "The emancipated woman, on the contrary, wants to be active, a taker, and refuses the passivity man means to impose on her."

Since my college years, back in the murky 1960s, emancipated women have been discouraging their unemancipated sisters from making spectacles of themselves. Don't paint your face like a clown's or drape your body like a mannequin's, they say. Don't bounce on the sidelines in skimpy outfits, screaming your fool head off, while men compete in the limelight for victories. Don't present yourself to the world as a fluff pastry, delicate and edible. Don't waddle across the stage in a bathing suit in hopes of being named Miss This or That.

25

6. De Beauvoir, French novelist and essayist (1908–1986) who served as one of the most articulate exponents of existentialism; *Le Deuxième Sexe* (1949; translated as *The Second Sex,* 1953), a thorough analysis of women's status in society, became a classic of feminist literature.

A great many women still ignore the exhortations. Wherever a crown for beauty is to be handed out, many still line up to stake their claims. Recently, Miss Indiana Persimmon Festival was quoted in our newspaper about the burdens of possessing the sort of looks that snag men's eyes. "Most of the time I enjoy having guys stare at me," she said, "but every once in a while it makes me feel like a piece of meat." The news photograph showed a cheerleader's perky face, heavily made-up, with starched hair teased into a blond cumulus. She put me in mind not of meat but of a plastic figurine, something you might buy from a booth outside a shrine. Nobody should ever be seen as meat, mere juicy stuff to satisfy an appetite. Better to appear as a plastic figurine, which is not meant for eating, and which is a gesture, however crude, toward art. Joyce[7] described the aesthetic response as a contemplation of form without the impulse to action. Perhaps that is what Miss Indiana Persimmon Festival wishes to inspire in those who look at her, perhaps that is what many women who paint and primp themselves desire: to withdraw from the touch of hands and dwell in the eye alone, to achieve the status of art.

By turning herself (or allowing herself to be turned into) a work of art, does a woman truly escape men's proprietary stare? Not often, says the British critic John Berger. Summarizing the treatment of women in Western painting, he concludes that—with a few notable exceptions, such as works by Rubens and Rembrandt—the woman on canvas is a passive object displayed for the pleasure of the male viewer, especially for the owner of the painting, who is, by extension, owner of the woman herself. Berger concludes: "Men look at women. Women watch themselves being looked at. This determines not only most relations between men and women but also the relation of women to themselves. The surveyor of woman in herself is male: the surveyed female. Thus she turns herself into an object—and most particularly an object of vision: a sight."

That sweeping claim, like the one quoted earlier from Beauvoir, also seems to me about three-quarters truth and one-quarter exaggeration. I know men who outdo the peacock for show, and I know women who are so fully possessed of themselves that they do not give a hang whether anybody notices them or not. The flamboyant gentlemen portrayed by Van Dyck are no less aware of being *seen* than are the languid ladies portrayed by Ingres.[8] With or without clothes, both gentlemen and ladies may conceive of themselves as objects of vision, targets of envy or admiration or desire. Where they differ is in their potential for action: the men are caught in the midst of a decisive gesture or on the verge of making one; the women wait like fuel for someone else to strike a match.

30   I am not sure the abstract nudes favored in modern art are much of an advance over the inert and voluptuous ones of the old school. Think of two famous examples: Duchamp's *Nude Descending a Staircase* (1912), where the

7. James Joyce (1882–1941), Irish novelist.
8. Anthony Van Dyck (1599–1641), Flemish painter who settled in England in 1632; Jean-Auguste-Dominique Ingres (1780–1867), French painter.

faceless woman has blurred into a waterfall of jagged shards, or Picasso's *Les Demoiselles d'Avignon* (1907), where the five angular damsels have been hammered as flat as cookie sheets and fitted with African masks. Neither painting invites us to behold a woman, but instead to behold what Picasso or Duchamp can make of one.

The naked women in Rubens, far from being passive, are gleefully active, exuberant, their sumptuous pink bodies like rainclouds or plump nebulae. "His nudes are the first ones that ever made me feel happy about my own body," a woman friend told me in one of the Rubens galleries of the Prado Museum. I do not imagine any pinup or store-window mannequin or bathing-suited Miss Whatsit could have made her feel that way. The naked women in Rembrandt, emerging from the bath or rising from bed, are so private, so cherished in the painter's gaze, that we as viewers see them not as sexual playthings but as loved persons. A man would do well to emulate that gaze.

I have never thought of myself as a sight. How much that has to do with being male and how much with having grown up on the back roads where money was scarce and eyes were few, I cannot say. As a boy, apart from combing my hair when I was compelled to and regretting the patches on my jeans (only the poor wore patches), I took no trouble over my appearance. It never occurred to me that anybody outside my family, least of all a girl, would look at me twice. As a young man, when young women did occasionally glance my way, without any prospect of appearing handsome I tried at least to avoid appearing odd. A standard haircut and the cheapest versions of the standard clothes were camouflage enough. Now as a middle-aged man I have achieved once more that boyhood condition of invisibility, with less hair to comb and fewer patches to humble me.

Many women clearly pass through the world aspiring to invisibility. Many others just as clearly aspire to be conspicuous. Women need not make spectacles of themselves in order to draw the attention of men. Indeed, for my taste, the less paint and fewer bangles the better. I am as helpless in the presence of subtle lures as a male moth catching a whiff of pheromones. I am a sucker for hair ribbons, a scarf at the throat, toes leaking from sandals, teeth bared in a smile. By contrast, I have always been more amused than attracted by the enameled exhibitionists whom our biblical mothers would identify as brazen hussies or painted Jezebels or, in the extreme cases, as whores of Babylon.

To encounter female exhibitionists in their full glory and variety, you need to go to a city. I never encountered ogling as a full-blown sport until I visited Rome, where bands of Italian men joined with gusto in appraising the charms of every passing female, and the passing females vied with one another in demonstrating their charms. In our own cities the most notorious bands of oglers tend to be construction gangs or street crews, men who spend much of their day leaning on the handles of shovels or pausing between bursts of riveting guns, their eyes tracing the curves of passersby. The first time my wife and kids and I drove into Boston we followed the signs to Chinatown, only to discover that Chinatown's miserably congested main street was undergoing repairs. That street also proved to be the city's home for X-rated cinemas and girlie shows and skin shops. LIVE SEX ACTS ON STAGE. PEEP SHOWS. PRIVATE BOOTHS. Caught in a traffic jam, we spent an hour listening to jackhammers and wolf whistles as we crept through the few blocks of pleasure palaces, my son and daughter with their noses hanging out the windows, my wife and I steaming. Lighted marquees peppered by burnt-out bulbs announced the titles of sleazy flicks; life-size posters of naked women flanked the doorways of clubs: leggy strippers in miniskirts, the originals for some of the posters, smoked on the curb between numbers.

35   After we had finally emerged from the zone of eros, eight-year-old Jesse inquired, "What was *that* place all about?"

"Sex for sale," my wife Ruth explained.

That might carry us some way toward a definition of pornography: making flesh into a commodity, flaunting it like any other merchandise, divorcing bodies from selves. By this reckoning, there is a pornographic dimension to much advertising, where a charge of sex is added to products ranging from cars to shaving cream. In fact, the calculated imagery of advertising may be more harmful than the blatant imagery of the pleasure palaces, that frank raunchiness which Kate Millett refers to as the "truthful explicitness of pornography." One can leave the X-rated zone of the city, but one cannot escape the sticky reach of commerce, which summons girls to the high calling of cosmetic glamor, fashion, and sexual display, while it summons boys to the panting chase.

You can recognize pornography, according to D. H. Lawrence, "by the insult it offers, invariably, to sex, and to the human spirit." He should know, Millett argues in *Sexual Politics,* for in her view Lawrence himself was a purveyor of patriarchal and often sadistic pornography. I think she is correct about the worst of Lawrence, and that she identifies a misogynist streak in his work; but she ignores his career-long struggle to achieve a more public, tolerant vision of sexuality as an exchange between equals. Besides, his novels and stories all bear within themselves their own critiques. George Steiner reminds us that "the list of writers who have had the genius to enlarge our actual compass of sexual awareness, who have given the erotic play of the mind a novel focus, an area of recognition previously unknown or fallow, is very small." Lawrence belongs on that brief list. The chief insult to the human spirit is to deny it, to claim that we are merely conglomerations of molecules, to pretend that we exist purely as bundles of appetites or as food for the appetites of others.

Men commit that insult toward women out of ignorance, but also out of dread. Allen Wheelis again: "Men gather in pornographic shows, not to stimulate desire, as they may think, but to diminish fear. It is the nature of the show to reduce the woman, discard her individuality, her soul, make her into an object, thereby enabling the man to handle her with greater safety, to use her as a toy. . . . As women move increasingly toward equality, the felt danger to men increases, leading to an increase in pornography and, since there are some men whose fears cannot even so be stilled, to an increase also in violence against women."

Make her into an object: all the hurtful ways for men to look at women are   40 variations on this betrayal. "Thus she turns herself into an object," writes Berger. A woman's ultimate degradation is in "submissively making herself a thing," writes Beauvoir. To be turned into an object—whether by the brush of a painter or the lens of a photographer or the eye of a voyeur, whether by hunger or poverty or enslavement, by mugging or rape, bullets or bombs, by hatred, racism, car crashes, fires, or falls—is for each of us the deepest dread; and to reduce another person to an object is the primal wrong.

Caught in the vortex of desire, we have to struggle to recall the wholeness of persons, including ourselves. Beauvoir speaks of the temptation we all occasionally feel to give up the struggle for a self and lapse into the inertia of an object: "Along with the ethical urge of each individual to affirm his subjective existence, there is also the temptation to forgo liberty and become a thing." A woman in particular, given so much encouragement to lapse into thinghood, "is often very well pleased with her role as the *Other.*"

Yet one need not forgo liberty and become a thing, without a center or a self, in order to become the Other. In our mutual strangeness, men and women can be doorways one for another, openings into the creative mystery that we share by virtue of our existence in the flesh. "To be sensual," James Baldwin writes, "is to respect and rejoice in the force of life, of life itself, and to be *present* in all that one does, from the effort of loving to the breaking of bread." The effort of loving is reciprocal, not only in act but in desire, an *I* addressing a *Thou,* a meeting in that vivid presence. The distance a man stares across at a woman, or a woman at a man, is a gulf in the soul, out of which a voice cries, *Leap, leap.* One day all men may cease to look on themselves as prototypically human and on women as lesser miracles; women may cease to feel themselves the targets for desire; men and women both may come to realize that we are all mere flickerings in the universal fire; and then none of us, male or female, need give up humanity in order to become the *Other.*

Ever since I gawked at the girl in pink shorts, I have dwelt knowingly in the force-field of sex. Knowingly or not, it is where we all dwell. Like the masses of planets and stars, our bodies curve the space around us. We radiate signals constantly, radio sources that never go off the air. We cannot help being centers of attraction and repulsion for one another. That is not all we are by a long shot, nor all we are capable of feeling, and yet, even after our much-needed revolution in sexual consciousness, the power of eros will still turn our heads and hearts. In a world without beauty pageants, there will still be beauty, however its definition may have changed. As long as men have eyes, they will gaze with yearning and confusion at women.

When I return to the street with the ancient legacy of longing coiled in my DNA, and the residues from a thousand generations of patriarchs silting my brain, I encounter women whose presence strikes me like a slap of wind in the face. I must prepare a gaze that is worthy of their splendor.

QUESTIONS

1. Several sections of this essay are grounded in specific episodes from Sanders's life. Identify the episodes and explain how he uses them.

2. The five sections of this essay are separated by typographical space rather than connected by prose transitions. Determine the content of each section and explain its relation to the content of the section that precedes it. Describe Sanders's strategies of organization and development.

3. In paragraph 12 Sanders asks: "How should a man look at women?" What is his answer? Where does he provide it?

4. Write an essay in which you answer, in your own terms, Sanders's question, "How should a man look at women?"

ANNA QUINDLEN   *Between the Sexes, a Great Divide*

PERHAPS WE ALL have the same memory of the first boy-girl party we attended. The floors were waxed, the music loud, the air thick with the smell of cologne. The boys stood on one side of the room and the girls on the other, each affecting a nonchalance belied by the shuffling male loafers and the occasional high birdlike sound of a female giggle.

Eventually, one of the taller, better-looking boys, perhaps dogged by two slightly shorter, squeakier acolytes, would make the big move across the chasm to ask the cutest girl to dance. Eventually, one of the girls would brave the divide to start a conversation on the other side. We would immediately develop a certain opinion of that girl, so that for the rest of our school years together, pajama parties would fairly crackle when she was not there.

None of us would consciously know it then, but what we were seeing, that great empty space in the center of the floor as fearful as a trapdoor, was the great division between the sexes. It was wonderful to think of the time when it would no longer be there, when the school gym would be a great meeting ground in which we would mingle freely, girl and boy, boy and girl, person to person, all alike. And maybe that's going to happen sometime in my lifetime, but I can't say I know when.

I've thought about this for some time, because I've written some loving things about men, and some nasty things too, and I meant them all. And I've always been a feminist, and I've been one of the boys as well, and I've given both sides a pretty good shot. I've spent a lot of time telling myself that men and women

Quindlen wrote a twice-weekly Op-Ed column for the New York Times *from 1981 to 1994. This essay appeared in the "Hers" column of the* Times *on March 24, 1988.*

are fundamentally alike, mainly in the service of arguing that women should not only be permitted but be welcomed into a variety of positions and roles that only men occupied.

And then something happens, a little thing usually, and all I can see is that great shiny space in the middle of the dance floor where no one ever meets. "I swear to God we are a different species," one of my friends said on the telephone recently. I can't remember whether the occasion was a fight with her husband, a scene at work or a contretemps with a mutual male friend of ours. No matter. She's said it before and she'll say it again, just like all my other friends have said it to me, and I to them. Men are the other.

We are the other, too, of course. That's why we want to believe so badly that there are no others at all, because over the course of human history being other has meant being symbols of divinity, evil, carnal degeneration, perfect love, fertility and death, to name a few. And anybody who has ever been a symbol knows that it's about as relaxing as sitting on a piece of Louis XV furniture. It is also true that over the course of history, we have been subordinate to others, symbols of weakness, dependency and emotions run amok.

Yet isn't it odd that I feel that the prejudice is somehow easier to deal with than the simple difference? Prejudice is evil and can be fought, while difference simply is. I live with three males, one husband and two sons, and occasionally I realize with great clarity that they are gazing across a divide at me, not because of big differences among us, but because of small ones.

The amaryllis bulb haunts me. "Why did you put an onion in a pot in the bathroom?" my elder son asked several months ago. I explained that it was not an onion but an amaryllis bulb and that soon it would grow into fabulous flowers. "What is that thing in the bathroom?" his father said later the same day. Impatiently I explained again. A look flashed between them, and then the littlest boy, too. Mom. Weird. Women.

Once I would have felt anger flame inside me at that. But I've done the same so many times now. On the telephone a friend and I will be commiserating about the failure of our husbands to listen when we talk, or their inexorable linear thinking, or their total blindness to the use and necessity of things like amaryllis bulbs. One of us will sigh, and the other will know what the sigh means. Husband. Strange. Men. Is it any wonder that our relationships are so often riddled with misunderstandings and disappointments?

In the children you can see the beginnings, even though we raise them in households in which mothers do things fathers once did, and vice versa. Children try to nail down the world, and themselves, early on and in a very primitive and real way. I remember a stage with my elder son in which, going through the supermarket or walking down the street, he would pin me down on each person walking by, and on such disparate cultural influences as Vanna White and Captain Kangaroo, by demanding that I tell him which genitalia category they fell in. Very soon, he got the idea: us and them, him and her. It was all very well to say that all people are the same inside (even if I had believed it) but he thought the outside was very important, too, and it helped him classify the world.

I must never forget, I suppose, that even in the gym, with all that space between us, we still managed to pick partners and dance. It's the dance that's important, not the difference. (I shouldn't leave out who leads and who
follows. But I speak to that from a strange perspective, since any man who
has ever danced with me can attest to the fact that I have never learned to
follow.)

I have just met the dance downstairs. My elder son has one of his best
friends over, and he does not care that she is a girl, and she does not care that
he is a boy. But she is complaining that he is chasing her with the plastic spider and making her scream, and he is grinning maniacally because that is just
exactly the response he is looking for, and they are both having a great time.
Two children, raised in egalitarian households in the 1980s. Between them
the floor already stretches, an ocean to cross before they can dance uneasily in
one another's arms.

QUESTIONS

1. Mark the places in this essay where Quindlen, after describing "the first boy-girl
party we attended" (paragraph 1), returns to it. How does she turn an event into a symbol of male–female differences?

2. Consider Quindlen's statement, "I've spent a lot of time telling myself that men and
women are fundamentally alike, mainly in the service of arguing that women should not
only be permitted but be welcomed into a variety of positions and roles that only men
occupied" (paragraph 4). Does her admission that they are not fundamentally alike
mean that women should not be welcomed into male positions and roles? Why?

3. As Quindlen, in this essay, casts men as the Other, so Scott Russell Sanders, in
"Looking at Women" (p. 118), casts women as the Other. How do they present and try
to decipher what they do not fully know or understand?

4. Write an essay in which you turn an event into a symbol.

LAUREN SLATER *Love*

M Y HUSBAND AND I got married at eight in the morning. It was winter, freezing, the trees encased in
ice and a few lone blackbirds balancing on telephone wires. We were in our early 30s, considered
ourselves hip and cynical, the types who decried
the institution of marriage even as we sought its
status. During our wedding brunch we put out a big suggestion box and asked
people to slip us advice on how to avoid divorce; we thought it was a funny,
clear-eyed, grounded sort of thing to do, although the suggestions were mostly
foolish: Screw the toothpaste cap on tight. After the guests left, the house got
quiet. There were flowers everywhere: puckered red roses and fragile ferns.
"What can we do that's really romantic?" I asked my newly wed one. Benjamin
suggested we take a bath. I didn't want a bath. He suggested a lunch of chilled
white wine and salmon. I was sick of salmon.

What can we do that's really romantic? The wedding was over, the silence
seemed suffocating, and I felt the familiar disappointment after a longed-for
event has come and gone. We were married. Hip, hip, hooray. I decided to take
a walk. I went into the center of town, pressed my nose against a bakery window, watched the man with flour on his hands, the dough as soft as skin,
pushed and pulled and shaped at last into stars. I milled about in an antique
store. At last I came to our town's tattoo parlor. Now I am not a tattoo type
person, but for some reason, on that cold silent Sunday, I decided to walk in.
"Can I help you?" a woman asked.

"Is there a kind of tattoo I can get that won't be permanent?" I asked.

"Henna[1] tattoos," she said.

She explained that they lasted for six weeks, were used at Indian wed   5
dings, were stark and beautiful and all brown. She showed me pictures of Indian women with jewels in their noses, their arms scrolled and laced with the
henna markings. Indeed they were beautiful, sharing none of the gaudy comic
strip quality of the tattoos we see in the United States. These henna tattoos
spoke of intricacy, of the webwork between two people, of ties that bind and
how difficult it is to find their beginnings and their ends. And because I had
just gotten married, and because I was feeling a post wedding letdown, and because I wanted something really romantic to sail me through the night, I decided to get one.

"Where?" she asked.

"Here," I said. I laid my hands over my breasts and belly.

Published in National Geographic *(February 2006), a magazine founded as a vehicle for
the "diffusion of geographical knowledge" and traditionally associated with travel and nature writing; recently the magazine has expanded to include articles of general human interest, while maintaining its commitment to issues of nature and the environment.*

1. A reddish dye derived from a shrub of the same name.

She raised her eyebrows. "Sure," she said.

I am a modest person. But I took off my shirt, lay on the table, heard her in the back room mixing powders and paints. She came to me carrying a small black-bellied pot inside of which was a rich red mush, slightly glittering. She adorned me. She gave me vines and flowers. She turned my body into a stake supporting whole new gardens of growth, and then, low around my hips, she painted a delicate chain-linked chastity belt. An hour later, the paint dry, I put my clothes back on, went home to find my newly wed one. This, I knew, was my gift to him, the kind of present you offer only once in your lifetime. I let him undress me.

10   "Wow," he said, standing back.

I blushed, and we began.

We are no longer beginning, my husband and I. This does not surprise me. Even back then, wearing the decor of desire, the serpentining tattoos, I knew they would fade, their red-clay color bleaching out until they were gone. On my wedding day I didn't care.

I do now. Eight years later, pale as a pillowcase, here I sit, with all the extra pounds and baggage time brings. And the questions have only grown more insistent. Does passion necessarily diminish over time? How reliable is romantic love, really, as a means of choosing one's mate? Can a marriage be good when Eros[2] is replaced with friendship, or even economic partnership, two people bound by bank accounts?

Let me be clear: I still love my husband. There is no man I desire more. But it's hard to sustain romance in the crumb-filled quotidian that has become our lives. The ties that bind have been frayed by money and mortgages and children, those little imps who somehow manage to tighten the knot while weakening its actual fibers. Benjamin and I have no time for chilled white wine and salmon. The baths in our house always include Big Bird.

15   If this all sounds miserable, it isn't. My marriage is like a piece of comfortable clothing; even the arguments have a feel of fuzziness to them, something so familiar it can only be called home. And yet . . .

In the Western world we have for centuries concocted poems and stories and plays about the cycles of love, the way it morphs and changes over time, the way passion grabs us by our flung-back throats and then leaves us for something saner. If *Dracula*—the frail woman, the sensuality of submission— reflects how we understand the passion of early romance, the *Flintstones* reflects our experiences of long-term love:[3] All is gravel and somewhat silly, the song so familiar you can't stop singing it, and when you do, the emptiness is almost unbearable.

2. Greek for romantic or sexual love.

3. *Dracula*: novel by Bram Stoker (1847–1912), published in 1897; it features a bloodsucking vampire by the same name and a beloved woman who wastes away. *Flintstones*: an animated television series dating from the 1960s, featuring the hi-jinks of a Stone Age family.

We have relied on stories to explain the complexities of love, tales of jealous gods and arrows. Now, however, these stories—so much a part of every civilization—may be changing as science steps in to explain what we have always felt to be myth, to be magic. For the first time, new research has begun to illuminate where love lies in the brain, the particulars of its chemical components.

Anthropologist Helen Fisher may be the closest we've ever come to having a doyenne of desire. At 60 she exudes a sexy confidence, with corn-colored hair, soft as floss, and a willowy build. A professor at Rutgers University, she lives in New York City, her book-lined apartment near Central Park, with its green trees fluffed out in the summer season, its paths crowded with couples holding hands.

Fisher has devoted much of her career to studying the biochemical pathways of love in all its manifestations: lust, romance, attachment, the way they wax and wane. One leg casually crossed over the other, ice clinking in her glass, she speaks with appealing frankness, discussing the ups and downs of love the way most people talk about real estate. "A woman unconsciously uses orgasms as a way of deciding whether or not a man is good for her. If he's impatient and rough, and she doesn't have the orgasm, she may instinctively feel he's less likely to be a good husband and father. Scientists think the fickle female orgasm may have evolved to help women distinguish Mr. Right from Mr. Wrong."

One of Fisher's central pursuits in the past decade has been looking at love, quite literally, with the aid of an MRI[4] machine. Fisher and her colleagues Arthur Aron and Lucy Brown recruited subjects who had been "madly in love" for an average of seven months. Once inside the MRI machine, subjects were shown two photographs, one neutral, the other of their loved one.

What Fisher saw fascinated her. When each subject looked at his or her loved one, the parts of the brain linked to reward and pleasure—the ventral tegmental area and the caudate nucleus—lit up. What excited Fisher most was not so much finding a location, an address, for love as tracing its specific chemical pathways. Love lights up the caudate nucleus because it is home to a dense spread of receptors for a neurotransmitter called dopamine, which Fisher came to think of as part of our own endogenous love potion. In the right proportions, dopamine creates intense energy, exhilaration, focused attention, and motivation to win rewards. It is why, when you are newly in love, you can stay up all night, watch the sun rise, run a race, ski fast down a slope ordinarily too steep for your skill. Love makes you bold, makes you bright, makes you run real risks, which you sometimes survive, and sometimes you don't.

I first fell in love when I was only 12, with a teacher. His name was Mr. McArthur, and he wore open-toed sandals and sported a beard. I had never had a male teacher before, and I thought it terribly exotic. Mr. McArthur did

20

---

4. Magnetic Resonance Imaging, a medical technique that reveals the insides of an organism.

things no other teacher dared to do. He explained to us the physics of farting. He demonstrated how to make an egg explode. He smoked cigarettes at recess, leaning languidly against the side of the school building, the ash growing longer and longer until he casually tapped it off with his finger.

What unique constellation of needs led me to love a man who made an egg explode is interesting, perhaps, but not as interesting, for me, as my memory of love's sheer physical facts. I had never felt anything like it before. I could not get Mr. McArthur out of my mind. I was anxious; I gnawed at the lining of my cheek until I tasted the tang of blood. School became at once terrifying and exhilarating. Would I see him in the hallway? In the cafeteria? I hoped. But when my wishes were granted, and I got a glimpse of my man, it satisfied nothing; it only inflamed me all the more. Had he looked at me? Why had he not looked at me? When would I see him again? At home I looked him up in the phone book; I rang him, this in a time before caller ID. He answered.

"Hello?" Pain in my heart, ripped down the middle. Hang up.

Call back. "Hello?" I never said a thing.

Once I called him at night, late, and from the way he answered the phone it was clear, even to a prepubescent like me, that he was with a woman. His voice fuzzy, the tinkle of her laughter in the background. I didn't get out of bed for a whole day.

Sound familiar? Maybe you were 30 when it happened to you, or 8 or 80 or 25. Maybe you lived in Kathmandu or Kentucky; age and geography are irrelevant. Donatella Marazziti is a professor of psychiatry at the University of Pisa in Italy who has studied the biochemistry of lovesickness. Having been in love twice herself and felt its awful power, Marazziti became interested in exploring the similarities between love and obsessive-compulsive disorder.

She and her colleagues measured serotonin levels in the blood of 24 subjects who had fallen in love within the past six months and obsessed about this love object for at least four hours every day. Serotonin is, perhaps, our star neurotransmitter,[5] altered by our star psychiatric medications: Prozac and Zoloft and Paxil, among others. Researchers have long hypothesized that people with obsessive-compulsive disorder (OCD) have a serotonin "imbalance." Drugs like Prozac seem to alleviate OCD by increasing the amount of this neurotransmitter available at the juncture between neurons.[6]

Marazziti compared the lovers' serotonin levels with those of a group of people suffering from OCD and another group who were free from both passion and mental illness. Levels of serotonin in both the obsessives' blood and the lovers' blood were 40 percent lower than those in her normal subjects. Translation: Love and obsessive-compulsive disorder could have a similar chemical profile. Translation: Love and mental illness may be difficult to tell apart. Translation: Don't be a fool. Stay away.

5. Chemicals that, when released into the juncture between nerve cells, enable the cells to communicate with each other.
6. A type of cell in the nervous system.

Of course that's a mandate none of us can follow. We do fall in love,   30
sometimes over and over again, subjecting ourselves, each time, to a very sick
state of mind. There is hope, however, for those caught in the grip of runaway
passion—Prozac. There's nothing like that bicolored bullet for damping down
the sex drive and making you feel "blah" about the buffet. Helen Fisher believes that the ingestion of drugs like Prozac jeopardizes one's ability to fall in
love—and stay in love. By dulling the keen edge of love and its associated li-
bido, relationships go stale. Says Fisher, "I know of one couple on the edge of
divorce. The wife was on an anti-depressant. Then she went off it, started having orgasms once more, felt the renewal of sexual attraction for her husband,
and they're now in love all over again."

Psychoanalysts have concocted countless theories about why we fall in
love with whom we do. Freud[7] would have said your choice is influenced by
the unrequited wish to bed your mother, if you're a boy, or your father, if
you're a girl. Jung[8] believed that passion is driven by some kind of collective
unconscious. Today psychiatrists such as Thomas Lewis from the University of
California at San Francisco's School of Medicine hypothesize that romantic
love is rooted in our earliest infantile experiences with intimacy, how we felt at
the breast, our mother's face, these things of pure unconflicted comfort that
get engraved in our brain and that we ceaselessly try to recapture as adults.
According to this theory we love whom we love not so much because of the future we hope to build but because of the past we hope to reclaim. Love is re-
active, not proactive, it arches us backward, which may be why a certain
person just "feels right." Or "feels familiar." He or she is familiar. He or she
has a certain look or smell or sound or touch that activates buried memories.

When I first met my husband, I believed this psychological theory was
more or less correct. My husband has red hair and a soft voice. A chemist, he
is whimsical and odd. One day before we married he dunked a rose in liquid
nitrogen so it froze, whereupon he flung it against the wall, spectacularly shattering it. That's when I fell in love with him. My father, too, has red hair, a soft
voice, and many eccentricities. He was prone to bursting into song, prompted
by something we never saw.

However, it turns out my theories about why I came to love my husband
may be just so much hogwash. Evolutionary psychology has said good riddance
to Freud and the Oedipal complex[9] and all that other transcendent stuff and
hello to simple survival skills. It hypothesizes that we tend to see as attractive,
and thereby choose as mates, people who look healthy. And health, say these
evolutionary psychologists, is manifested in a woman with a 70 percent waist-
to-hip ratio and men with rugged features that suggest a strong supply of

7. Sigmund Freud (1856–1939), Austrian neurologist and father of psychoanalysis.

8. Carl Jung (1865–1961), Swiss psychologist, father of "analytical psychology" and
originator of such concepts as the "collective unconscious," "archetype," and "extrovert–
introvert."

9. A concept developed by Sigmund Freud positing that boys unconsciously desire sexual relationships with their mothers and wish for their fathers' deaths.

testosterone in their blood. Waist-to-hip ratio is important for the successful birth of a baby, and studies have shown this precise ratio signifies higher fertility. As for the rugged look, well, a man with a good dose of testosterone probably also has a strong immune system and so is more likely to give his partner healthy children.

Perhaps our choice of mates is a simple matter of following our noses. Claus Wedekind of the University of Lausanne in Switzerland did an interesting experiment with sweaty T-shirts. He asked 49 women to smell T-shirts previously worn by unidentified men with a variety of the genotypes that influence both body odor and immune systems. He then asked the women to rate which T-shirts smelled the best, which the worst. What Wedekind found was that women preferred the scent of a T-shirt worn by a man whose genotype was most different from hers, a genotype that, perhaps, is linked to an immune system that possesses something hers does not. In this way she increases the chance that her offspring will be robust.

35   It all seems too good to be true, that we are so hardwired and yet unconscious of the wiring. Because no one to my knowledge has ever said, "I married him because of his B.O." No. We say, "I married him (or her) because he's intelligent, she's beautiful, he's witty, she's compassionate." But we may just be as deluded about love as we are when we're *in* love. If it all comes down to a sniff test, then dogs definitely have the edge when it comes to choosing mates.

Why doesn't passionate love last? How is it possible to see a person as beautiful on Monday, and 364 days later, on another Monday, to see that beauty as bland? Surely the object of your affection could not have changed that much. She still has the same shaped eyes. Her voice has always had that husky sound, but now it grates on you—she sounds like she needs an antibiotic. Or maybe you're the one who needs an antibiotic, because the partner you once loved and cherished and saw as though saturated with starlight now feels more like a low-level infection, tiring you, sapping all your strength.

Studies around the world confirm that, indeed, passion usually ends. Its conclusion is as common as its initial flare. No wonder some cultures think selecting a life-long mate based on something so fleeting is folly. Helen Fisher has suggested that relationships frequently break up after four years because that's about how long it takes to raise a child through infancy. Passion, that wild, prismatic insane feeling, turns out to be practical after all. We not only need to copulate; we also need enough passion to start breeding, and then feelings of attachment take over as the partners bond to raise a helpless human infant. Once a baby is no longer nursing, the child can be left with sister, aunts, friends. Each parent is now free to meet another mate and have more children.

Biologically speaking, the reasons romantic love fades may be found in the way our brains respond to the surge and pulse of dopamine that accompanies passion and makes us fly. Cocaine users describe the phenomenon of tolerance: The brain adapts to the excessive input of the drug. Perhaps the neurons become desensitized and need more and more to produce the high— to put out pixie dust, metaphorically speaking.

Maybe it's a good thing that romance fizzles. Would we have railroads, bridges, planes, faxes, vaccines, and television if we were all always besotted? In place of the ever evolving technology that has marked human culture from its earliest tool use, we would have instead only bonbons, bouquets, and birth control. More seriously, if the chemically altered state induced by romantic love is akin to a mental illness or a drug-induced euphoria, exposing yourself for too long could result in psychological damage. A good sex life can be as strong as Gorilla Glue,[10] but who wants that stuff on your skin?

Once upon a time, in India, a boy and a girl fell in love without their parents' permission. They were from different castes, their relationship radical and unsanctioned. Picture it: the sparkling sari, the boy in white linen, the clandestine meetings on tiled terraces with a fat, white moon floating overhead. Who could deny these lovers their pleasure, or condemn the force of their attraction?

Their parents could. In one recent incident a boy and girl from different castes were hanged at the hands of their parents as hundreds of villagers watched. A couple who eloped were stripped and beaten. Yet another couple committed suicide after their parents forbade them to marry.

Anthropologists used to think that romance was a Western construct, a bourgeois by-product of the Middle Ages. Romance was for the sophisticated, took place in cafés, with coffees and Cabernets, or on silk sheets, or in rooms with a flickering fire. It was assumed that non-Westerners, with their broad familial and social obligations, were spread too thin for particular passions. How could a collectivist culture celebrate or in any way sanction the obsession with one individual that defines new love? Could a lice-ridden peasant really feel passion?

Easily, as it turns out. Scientists now believe that romance is panhuman, embedded in our brains since Pleistocene times. In a study of 166 cultures, anthropologists William Jankowiak and Edward Fischer observed evidence of passionate love in 147 of them. In another study men and women from Europe, Japan, and the Philippines were asked to fill out a survey to measure their experiences of passionate love. All three groups professed feeling passion with the same searing intensity.

But though romantic love may be universal, its cultural expression is not. To the Fulbe tribe of northern Cameroon, poise matters more than passion. Men who spend too much time with their wives are taunted, and those who are weak-kneed are thought to have fallen under a dangerous spell. Love may be inevitable, but for the Fulbe its manifestations are shameful, equated with sickness and social impairment.

In India romantic love has traditionally been seen as dangerous, a threat to a well-crafted caste system in which marriages are arranged as a means of preserving lineage and bloodlines. Thus the gruesome tales, the warnings embedded in fables about what happens when one's wayward impulses take over.

10. An extremely strong household glue.

Today love marriages appear to be on the rise in India, often in defiance of parents' wishes. The triumph of romantic love is celebrated in Bollywood films. Yet most Indians still believe arranged marriages are more likely to succeed than love marriages. In one survey of Indian college students, 76 percent said they'd marry someone with all the right qualities even if they weren't in love with the person (compared with only 14 percent of Americans). Marriage is considered too important a step to leave to chance.

Renu Dinakaran is a striking 45-year-old woman who lives in Bangalore, India. When I meet her, she is dressed in Western-style clothes—black leggings and a T-shirt. Renu lives in a well-appointed apartment in this thronging city, where cows sleep on the highways as tiny cars whiz around them, plumes of black smoke rising from their sooty pipes.

Renu was born into a traditional Indian family where an arranged marriage was expected. She was not an arranged kind of person, though, emerging from her earliest days as a fierce tennis player, too sweaty for saris, and smarter than many of the men around her. Nevertheless at the age of 17 she was married off to a first cousin, a man she barely knew, a man she wanted to learn to love, but couldn't. Renu considers many arranged marriages to be acts of "state-sanctioned rape."

Renu hoped to fall in love with her husband, but the more years that passed, the less love she felt, until, at the end, she was shrunken, bitter, hiding behind the curtains of her in-laws' bungalow, looking with longing at the couple on the balcony across from theirs. "It was so obvious to me that couple had married for love, and I envied them. I really did. It hurt me so much to see how they stood together, how they went shopping for bread and eggs."

50   Exhausted from being forced into confinement, from being swaddled in saris that made it difficult to move, from resisting the pressure to eat off her husband's plate, Renu did what traditional Indian culture forbids one to do. She left. By this time she had had two children. She took them with her. In her mind was an old movie she'd seen on TV, a movie so strange and enticing to her, so utterly confounding and comforting at the same time, that she couldn't get it out of her head. It was 1986. The movie was *Love Story*.

"Before I saw movies like *Love Story*, I didn't realize the power that love can have," she says.

Renu was lucky in the end. In Mumbai she met a man named Anil, and it was then, for the first time, that she felt passion. "When I first met Anil, it was like nothing I'd ever experienced. He was the first man I ever had an orgasm with. I was high, just high, all the time. And I knew it wouldn't last, couldn't last, and so that infused it with a sweet sense of longing, almost as though we were watching the end approach while we were also discovering each other."

When Renu speaks of the end, she does not, to be sure, mean the end of her relationship with Anil; she means the end of a certain stage. The two are still happily married, companionable, loving if not "in love," with a playful black dachshund they bought together. Their relationship, once so full of fire, now seems to simmer along at an even temperature, enough to keep them well fed and warm. They are grateful.

"Would I want all that passion back?" Renu asks. "Sometimes, yes. But to tell you the truth, it was exhausting."

From a physiological point of view, this couple has moved from the dopamine-drenched state of romantic love to the relative quiet of an oxytocin-induced attachment. Oxytocin is a hormone that promotes a feeling of connection, bonding. It is released when we hug our long-term spouses, or our children. It is released when a mother nurses her infant. Prairie voles, animals with high levels of oxytocin, mate for life. When scientists block oxytocin receptors in these rodents, the animals don't form monogamous bonds and tend to roam. Some researchers speculate that autism, a disorder marked by a profound inability to forge and maintain social connections, is linked to an oxytocin deficiency. Scientists have been experimenting by treating autistic people with oxytocin, which in some cases has helped alleviate their symptoms.

In long-term relationships that work—like Renu and Anil's—oxytocin is believed to be abundant in both partners. In long-term relationships that never get off the ground, like Renu and her first husband's, or that crumble once the high is gone, chances are the couple has not found a way to stimulate or sustain oxytocin production.

"But there are things you can do to help it along," says Helen Fisher. "Massage. Make love. These things trigger oxytocin and thus make you feel much closer to your partner."

Well, I suppose that's good advice, but it's based on the assumption that you still want to have sex with that boring windbag of a husband. Should you fake-it-till-you-make-it?

"Yes," says Fisher. "Assuming a fairly healthy relationship, if you have enough orgasms with your partner, you may become attached to him or her. You will stimulate oxytocin."

This may be true. But it sounds unpleasant. It's exactly what your mother always said about vegetables: "Keep eating your peas. They are an acquired taste. Eventually, you will come to like them."

But I have never been a peas person.

It's 90 degrees on the day my husband and I depart, from Boston for New York City, to attend a kissing school. With two kids, two cats, two dogs, a lopsided house, and a questionable school system, we may know how to kiss, but in the rough and tumble of our harried lives we have indeed forgotten how to *kiss*.

The sky is paved with clouds, the air as sticky as jam in our hands and on our necks. The Kissing School, run by Cherie Byrd, a therapist from Seattle, is being held on the 12th floor of a run-down building in Manhattan. Inside, the room is whitewashed; a tiled table holds bottles of banana and apricot nectar, a pot of green tea, breath mints, and Chapstick. The other Kissing School students—sometimes they come from as far away as Vietnam and Nigeria—are sprawled happily on the bare floor, pillows and blankets beneath them. The class will be seven hours long.

Byrd starts us off with foot rubs. "In order to be a good kisser," she says, "you need to learn how to do the foreplay before the kissing." Foreplay involves rubbing my husband's smelly feet, but that is not as bad as when he has to rub mine. Right before we left the house, I accidentally stepped on a diaper the dog had gotten into, and although I washed, I now wonder how well.

65   "Inhale," Byrd says, and shows us how to draw in air.

"Exhale," she says, and then she jabs my husband in the back. "Don't focus on the toes so much," she says. "Move on to the calf."

Byrd tells us other things about the art of kissing. She describes the movement of energy through various chakras,[11] the manifestation of emotion in the lips; she describes the importance of embracing all your senses, how to make eye contact as a prelude, how to whisper just the right way. Many hours go by. My cell phone rings. It's our babysitter. Our one-year-old has a high fever. We must cut the long lesson short. We rush out. Later on, at home, I tell my friends what we learned at Kissing School: We don't have time to kiss.

A perfectly typical marriage. Love in the Western world.

Luckily I've learned of other options for restarting love. Arthur Aron, a psychologist at Stony Brook University in New York, conducted an experiment that illuminates some of the mechanisms by which people become and stay attracted. He recruited a group of men and women and put opposite sex pairs in rooms together, instructing each pair to perform a series of tasks, which included telling each other personal details about themselves. He then asked each couple to stare into each other's eyes for two minutes. After this encounter, Aron found most of the couples, previously strangers to each other, reported feelings of attraction. In fact, one couple went on to marry.

70   Fisher says this exercise works wonders for some couples. Aron and Fisher also suggest doing novel things together, because novelty triggers dopamine in the brain, which can stimulate feelings of attraction. In other words, if your heart flutters in his presence, you might decide it's not because you're anxious but because you love him. Carrying this a step further, Aron and others have found that even if you just jog in place and then meet someone, you're more likely to think they're attractive. So first dates that involve a nerve-racking activity, like riding a roller coaster, are more likely to lead to second and third dates. That's a strategy worthy of posting on Match.com. Play some squash. And in times of stress—natural disasters, blackouts, predators on the prowl— lock up tight and hold your partner.

In Somerville, Massachusetts, where I live with my husband, our predators are primarily mosquitoes. That needn't stop us from trying to enter the windows of each other's soul. When I propose this to Benjamin, he raises an eyebrow.

"Why don't we just go out for Cambodian food?" he says.

"Because that's not how the experiment happened."

As a scientist, my husband is always up for an experiment. But our lives are so busy that, in order to do this, we have to make a plan. We will meet next Wednesday at lunchtime and try the experiment in our car.

75   On the Tuesday night before our rendezvous, I have to make an un-

11. In several Asian cultures, the center of spiritual and/or physical energy residing in the body.

planned trip to New York. My husband is more than happy to forget our date. I, however, am not. That night, from my hotel room, I call him.

"We can do it on the phone," I say.

"What am I supposed to stare into?" he asks. "The keypad?"

"There's a picture of me hanging in the hall. Look at that for two minutes. I'll look at a picture I have of you in my wallet."

"Come on," he says.

"Be a sport," I say. "It's better than nothing."   80

Maybe not. Two minutes seems like a long time to stare at someone's picture with a receiver pressed to your ear. My husband sneezes, and I try to imagine his picture sneezing right along with him, and this makes me laugh.

Another 15 seconds pass, slowly, each second stretched to its limit so I can almost hear time, feel time, its taffy-like texture, the pop it makes when it's done. Pop pop pop. I stare and stare at my husband's picture. It doesn't produce any sense of startling intimacy, and I feel defeated.

Still, I keep on. I can hear him breathing on the other end. The photograph before me was taken a year or so ago, cut to fit my wallet, his strawberry blond hair pulled back in a ponytail. I have never really studied it before. And I realize that in this picture my husband is not looking straight back at me, but his pale blue eyes are cast sideways, off to the left, looking at something I can't see. I touch his eyes. I peer close, and then still closer, at his averted face. Is there something sad in his expression, something sad in the way he gazes off?

I look toward the side of the photo, to find what it is he's looking at, and then I see it: a tiny turtle coming toward him. Now I remember how he caught it after the camera snapped, how he held it gently in his hands, showed it to our kids, stroked its shell, his forefinger moving over the scaly dome, how he held the animal out toward me, a love offering. I took it, and together we sent it back to the sea.

QUESTIONS

1. "Love" might be called a "definition essay": it takes on a large concept and expands and enriches our understanding of it. What aspects of love that Slater describes did you recognize from experience? What new aspects or facts did you learn by reading this essay?

2. Slater draws on many experts in writing about love—on scientists, psychologists, historians, and so on. Find three or four places where she quotes these experts, and explain why she does so.

3. Even with Slater's frequent use of expert witnesses, we learn a lot about her own experiences in love. What does she reveal? What is the relationship between her personal experience and the information provided by experts?

4. Choose a concept that, like love, can become the title of a "definition essay": for example, human emotions (hate, anger, hope, doubt, happiness) or human states (friendship, childhood, marriage, divorce, death). As you think about the concept, look to the research and analysis of experts. Write an essay that interweaves your own experience with experts' testimony.

E. S. MADURO   *Excuse Me While I Explode:*
                              My Mother, Myself, My Anger

Y PARENTS MET and started dating on the same day, at the age of thirteen. Forty-five years later, my father still glows when he tells the story of seeing my mother on her first day at his school, and how he offered to walk her home that very afternoon. They dated throughout high school, went to the same college, and got married the day before their graduation, at age twenty-one—three years younger than I am today. After college my father went to graduate school and eventually became a history professor; my mother worked as a schoolteacher for a while; they bought a cheap house in the countryside and started a family. Presto, the American Dream.

When my older sister was born, my mother stopped working out of the house and became the mom I know her as. The mom who maintained a spotless house and a balanced checkbook and found the time to praise and nurture two growing children, all while having dinner ready and waiting, on the table, every night by 6:30. The mom who put off a career until her mid-forties so she would be available to her family—which she still is—though that is not to say she didn't work. My mother's job included, but was never limited to, pickling cucumbers, making jam, doing laundry for four people, changing diapers, teaching two children to read, doing all the grocery shopping for a family, cooking three meals a day (making sure a vegetable was included at dinner), cleaning the house, doing art projects, building snowmen, feeding a dog, driving to the doctor's office, picking kids up from piano lessons, going to parent-teacher conferences, sewing hems in school uniforms, ironing men's button-down shirts . . . and so on. I think there are few résumés out there that could top my mother's were she ever to think it worthy of writing—which she never would.

As a young child—naturally, I suppose—I don't really remember being aware that my mother existed between the time I left for school in the morning and the time she arrived at the bus stop to meet me coming home. Laundry and dusting and shopping were far outside my elementary-school-age mind, and if chores were done when I got home, it certainly didn't catch my attention. As I grew older, however, my awareness of our household began to change. My mother went back to school and, at age forty-five, became a special ed teacher. After that, she often came home exhausted at 5:30 and began making dinner. Saturdays and Sundays she woke up early to rush all over, cleaning, cooking, shopping, organizing the calendar. Monday mornings she'd be up at 4:30 to write a report that had been neglected over the weekend, then

Included in a collection titled The Bitch in the House: 26 Women Tell the Truth about Sex, Solitude, Work, Motherhood, and Marriage *(2002), edited by Cathi Hanauer. The collection was intended to explore the causes of the domestic anger experienced by women in contemporary society.*

she'd make me breakfast before school and zip off to work. Gradually, I began
to notice that she never seemed to have a moment to herself. Simultaneously,
I realized that my father, who took care of all the "manly" household chores—
chopping wood, killing mice—still had time for a well-respected career and a
whole slew of regular hobbies. The setup began to seem drastically unfair to
me. Free time, to my high school mind, was an absolute necessity, and I was
witness to the fact that my mother seemed to be getting none of it.

This is not to say that I suddenly dropped to my knees before my mother,
realized the saint that she was, and thanked her. Instead, I became disappointed in her and—to my current shame and regret—ridiculed her for being
so undemanding about her own needs and so willing to dedicate herself to
maintaining the house and serving us. I became angry at both of my parents:
at my father that his chores (take apart and reassemble the kitchen sink, work
in the garden, snow-blow the driveway) seemed interesting and challenging
and were always impressive to friends and relatives, while my mother's endless
chores seemed layered in routine and monotony. Both my parents had careers
now, but it still fell to my mother to do every trivial and mindless thing that
needed to be done, and I was frustrated with her for never seeming to mind
this or to demand more help from my father.

I spent hours as a teenager talking to her (rarely listening) about why she   5
was so accepting of her role in our family. I would recount the way my father
would stride into the house after work and she would politely have dinner
waiting for him; the way there was an unspoken sentiment in our house that
his career was more important than hers. "Why don't you divorce him and find
a husband who will offer to clean up the kitchen after dinner and let you sit
down for once?" I would yell; or, "How come his job takes precedence over
everything else while yours has to fit around all the other things you do and
have always done?" Somehow, my mother was always able to shrug me off—to
reply that she was fine, that someday I would understand. But I wasn't at all
sure that I would, or that she was. What's more, I believed myself to be a feminist, and I vowed never to fall into the same trap of domestic boredom and
servitude that I saw my mother as being fully entrenched in; never to settle for
a life that was, as I saw it, lacking independence, authority, and respect.

I met my own boyfriend, Paul, during my senior year of college. He was absolutely the furthest thing possible from my father, which was exactly what I
was looking for at the time. Though I love my father passionately, I was certain
that the man of my life would know how to cook dinner and clean the house,
would offer to do the dishes, would fold the laundry without being asked. My
goal was to avoid the domestic life that my mother had found for herself; the
first step was to have a liberal, open-minded boyfriend. I found one with
dreadlocks, a nose ring, and a passion for that most nonacademic of subjects,
music—just the opposite of my traditional and overly intellectual father.

On our first date, Paul offered to cook me dinner, and when it was over
he did all the dishes. When I'd stop by his house (which he shared with three
other male friends), I would marvel at the way he seemed to take care of

cleaning up the kitchen, the way he would look disapprovingly at his house-mates' dirty underwear on the bathroom floor. His books were neatly arranged on a shelf in his bedroom, his clothes were well folded in drawers, and he even had a laundry bag with his name on it. I was hooked. This man seemed to know how to do all the things my own father couldn't or wouldn't ever do. After a few months of dating, I called a friend from home one night and talked at length about how this guy seemed so perfect; how he was so responsible, so thoughtful; how I just couldn't imagine him ever expecting me to take care of all the housework, the child care, the dinners, were we ever to get married.

My mother and I had long conversations about how she had gone from her father to her husband without ever spending a segment of her life independently. She commented often about how lucky I was, and how glad she was for me, that I was part of a generation that got to make educated decisions about how their lives would go. "You have choices," she'd say. "Be thankful that you're so aware of the qualities that are important to you in a husband, before you run off to get married. When I was your age, girls didn't even realize what they were getting into when they got married. It was just the thing to do." Once, during one of these conversations, I asked her if she'd do it over again differently if she could. In one of her most open and honest moments with me, she said, "Yes. Definitely." Though I realize now that her answer had to do with more than just household responsibilities, at the time I felt so lucky knowing that I would never repeat her domestic lot, that I would not go from my father's home to my husband's. I felt proud that I would create a home with my husband based on shared responsibility and input; proud that I was, in fact, already on the road to doing it.

Then I visited Paul's family.

10   Paul and I were upstairs watching a movie when his mother called us down to dinner. The table was set, the food was ready, and we sat down. In a few moments Paul's father arrived and instantly complained that his favorite hot sauce was not on the table. His mother leapt up to get it. Dinner was over in about eight minutes, and almost as if by a feat of magic, everyone was gone from the kitchen before I had even put down my fork. Paul was on the piano, improvising a song to play for me; his father was upstairs reading the paper. Paul's mother and I spent the next twenty minutes cleaning up, loading the dishwasher, and putting the food away. A mother of two sons, she immediately loved me and has been fond of me ever since. She was delighted with Paul's choice.

I, on the other hand, suddenly felt my first twinge of anger and resentment toward Paul. *Surely he can't realize I'm still in the kitchen, washing his plate,* I thought. But I knew he did. And it was as if, in a matter of minutes, his personality had a whole new side I hadn't noticed before. This man, who had been so different from my father, was immediately just like him, all because of what he didn't do or even notice. And I believe, looking back on that evening, that had I not already been so filled with a kind of rage at the ease with which so many men seemed able to overlook the daily tasks that women did for them, I would not even have really minded doing dishes with Paul's mother. Certainly, I would not have suddenly decided to be on the lookout for this trend in him—would not have begun the awful, silent process of tallying up and storing away and keeping tabs on what he helped out with and what he did not.

Now it is almost three years later, and the same boyfriend is lying in our bed, in our apartment, trying to recover from a winter flu. I glance at him while writing these words, and seeing his peaceful breaths rise and fall under our soft down comforter, I feel total affection for him. He is delightful—considerate, attentive, and kind—and I feel lucky to share my life with him. I look the other way, however, into our kitchen, and upon seeing a pile of dirty dishes in the sink, I fall back into a silent conversation that has been going on in my head since we happily, if blindly, moved in together last fall.

It begins something like this: "Does it just not occur to him that I worked all day and might like to come home to a place where I don't immediately have to start cleaning in order to feel some sense of peace with where I am? Am I the only one who cares that our house is a mess?" And then the list of things he hasn't done, or has done wrong, comes flooding, pouring, rushing into my mind. I count the number of times I stopped at the grocery store on my way home this week and compare it with the number of times he has voluntarily done the same. I replay the scene from last weekend, when we were expecting friends to come for dinner, and he showed up at 5:30 after a full day of cross-country skiing with a friend and claimed to have "forgotten" that we were responsible for making a meal for four.

Or I think about the numerous times that I have come into the house, exhausted, at 7:00 after a full day of work and a meeting after school, and found him searching for music on the Internet instead of preparing a dinner for us both. On those days, I have silently walked into the kitchen and begun chopping vegetables or boiling water for spaghetti, and with every slice of my knife, every pot that I pulled from the cupboard, I grow angrier and angrier, until I could not even stand his presence in the same room. He might walk in and say something as innocent as "What can I do to help?" or even "Why don't you sit down and let me make dinner?" and I would absolutely explode with fury, shooting back at him, "Well, I'm starving and exhausted and I don't really feel like waiting around for you to finish your f***ing Internet search so that I can eat something before nine o'clock!"

On such occasions I will be angry for thirty minutes, or maybe until I have eaten something. I will ruminate on the place of the woman in today's "modern" society. I will cook and clean, and all the while think about how I am falling into the same trap of housework that my own mother fell into. As I scrub the kitchen sink, I will hear her voice saying, "You have choices," and I will scowl at the concept of a choice. I will decide that my modern, liberal, open-minded boyfriend, having been raised by a mother who did everything in the home (in addition to having a job), will never notice or care if his girlfriend or wife takes over those same domestic responsibilities. He is capable of doing

15

all of them, but if they get done for him, my thoughts go, he might never even realize that they needed doing in the first place.

But then slowly, as I finish picking up the dirty clothes from the floor, I will think about his day, will remember that he works long hours, too—and that he loves music, that finding new albums to record off our computer is a way for him to relax, to wind down. It will occur to me that maybe he was waiting for me to come home so that we could eat together; that he didn't know I would be arriving so late; that he was sincere, rather than just trying to avoid a fight, when he offered to cook for me. Perhaps I will remember that he had a meeting after school, too, and had probably arrived home only fifteen minutes before I did. Gradually, my anger will start to wane, and in its place will come guilt and confusion and sadness. I will imagine my own mother, coming in from a long day—or, worse, having never even left the work of the house—and wanting nothing more than to sit down and read the paper; and in a million years, her husband would never have offered to make her dinner, as my boyfriend has just done for me. The question in my mind then becomes, Why didn't I let him? Why, when he was standing right there, ready and willing, did I ignore the chance to pour myself a glass of wine and sit on the couch for twenty minutes while he prepared a meal for me? Why, instead, did I become so angry so fast?

The answer, sadly, surprisingly, self-defeatingly, is that I want to be angry. Or at least, I *choose* to be angry over the long list of alternate emotions waiting in line: guilt, sadness, the exhaustion of trying to change things, to figure it all out. I feel angry at the confusion of adoring my mother, of thinking she is a phenomenal woman who raised her children with grace and style, of thinking I would give anything to be like her . . . and at the same time, looking down on her for all the things she quietly accepted, and knowing that I want to be nothing like that. I feel angry at the confusion of wanting my own relationship to be balanced, to share all responsibilities equally, yet at the same time, wanting things done my way—with the tidiness and timeliness that I have inherited from my parents. I feel frustrated by the guilt that accompanies asking Paul to take the initiative to run the dishwasher, to do the laundry without shrinking my sweaters, to buy groceries that are healthy . . . to ask for what my mother never would have, to be what she would have considered a "nag." In wanting my home to be as well organized as my mother kept hers, I feel as though I must choose between doing everything myself and constantly asking Paul to do more.

I already know how to manage a household, not because I asked someone to teach me, but because I watched my mother and learned while I spent countless hours by her side (or on her hip) all those Saturdays when she worked from 7:00 A.M. to bedtime to keep our house running. I never asked for this knowledge. I never wanted the internal clock that tells me enough time has gone by that we really should change our sheets; never requested the awareness of how long it takes to make lasagna and thus the willingness to give up an afternoon so that dinner will be ready when the guests arrive. I never asked for anyone to teach me how to wash my silk shirts by hand. But, of course, as almost all girls do, I learned, and now I'm stuck with it. And no matter how much I sometimes wish I wasn't the one in my relationship who knows all this, I admit that I also sometimes feel proud of knowing it all, and proud that I do it all well.

Last weekend, Paul and I agreed to house-sit and baby-sit for neighbors of ours with four children. Almost immediately, I found myself taking over everything, rather than showing Paul how to do it. Though he asked me several times to show him how to run the fancy washing machine, I never did teach him. Instead, I did all the laundry myself, making the trip down the basement steps three or four times a day, furious that he was watching a movie with the kids while I was doing chores. When Keith, the six-year-old, needed breakfast, rather than mentioning it to Paul or asking him for help, I simply made pancakes for everyone, then fumed as we all ate them together. When Paul asked me what was the best way to clean a cast-iron skillet, I responded harshly to just leave it and I would take care of it myself. The weekend was a seemingly endless stream of moments when I angrily "did it myself" instead of showing him how. Every dish that he didn't notice I had picked up for him, every morsel of food he ate that I had cooked, every stair I descended that led to the clothes dryer, was another tick in my mental log of things to resent him for.

I returned home from the weekend of baby-sitting exhausted physically, mentally, and emotionally, commenting again and again how glad I was that we don't have kids or pets or even our own washing machine. But as my anger waned, I realized I was feeling something else, too: a sense of power and pride in knowing that I had been the supermom for the weekend. I was the one who had kept everything under control. It was I who'd made sure that the kids were picked up on time, took showers each night, ate a vegetable at dinner. I felt as though I could have done the whole thing myself. The package was complete: anger and pride.

So there it is. In trying to find a man as different as possible from my own father, in trying to avoid the life of an overworked housewife that I see my mother as having occupied for more than thirty years now, in choosing a boyfriend partly for his willingness and readiness to share the "woman's work," I am freely walking closer and closer to everything I had wanted to escape, enraged with every step I take. Somehow, some part of this cycle seems unavoidable, unchangeable. Paul will read what I've written here and ask me, so earnestly, "What can we do to solve this problem?" and already I know that I will shrug him off. "It's just me," I'll respond, "this is something I need to deal with."

Rather than trying to impart to him some of the domestic knowledge and sense of responsibility that I have, I will, I fear, go on being angry that he wasn't given it to begin with; angry that, unlike me, he was not closely observing, for his future, his own mother during the many hours she spent taking care of everyone in the family, and therefore now doesn't have the voice in his head telling him he *should* be constantly aware of tasks that need to be done, of meeting everyone else's needs before his own. And yet, side by side with this anger, will be the pride, the satisfaction of knowing that someday I could be an

20

excellent mother, always available to my children and maintaining a well-kept home, all with a kid by my side or on my hip—like my own mother. I will, I fear, go on doing as much as I can, caught between pride and anger, furious at my exhaustion and Paul's inadequacy. Almost as if to entitle my anger, to justify or even fuel a frustration that's already there, I will—for now, at least—refuse any help from anyone, then bask in the fury of having too much to do and no time for myself. Recently, I have been thinking back to the years I spent as a kid living at home with my parents. Only now, when I have an apartment of my own and am responsible for my own meals and dishes and laundry and everything else, am I beginning to gain a more complete understanding of what my mother was doing between five or six or seven in the morning and bedtime. Owning a home, raising a family, maintaining sanity in a house—these are not small jobs, and my mother accomplished them all expertly, even after she added a career to the list. Though I wish she could have been more relaxed, that she and my father could have shared the chores in the house more equally, I'm beginning to understand why she didn't leave him. I'm beginning to see that she didn't just lie down and accept everything from the start, but that her role, her tasks, her *dissatisfaction*, came gradually, over a period of years. And along with whatever anger she felt beneath her cool exterior, there must have been, too, a tremendous sense of pride that came with knowing she was such an integral part of our family.

Whether I will follow her steps and have a family of my own I don't yet know. I do know that as I write these words and glance at my still-sleeping companion, I feel an odd mixture of frustration and love. Together we have a wonderful, open, trusting relationship, but sometimes I wonder if the hostility already in me, and my need to be angry at someone or something, could eventually destroy our bond. I suppose only time will tell. Unlike my mother, I don't have to go from my father's house to my husband's. And perhaps it's simply this time and space to think about the future and to love and live with and learn from whomever I please—time and space and freedom my mother never had—that she referred to when she said I have choices. At twenty-four, living in this day and age, I still have years to figure things out; to try to learn how to feel pride and even power without running myself ragged; to be with a man without being angry for the rest of my life. I hope I can.

QUESTIONS

1. The roles of women in marriage—and the differences between mothers' and daughters' expectations—is a topic of great debate, a "hot button" issue. What critique of her mother's role in the family does Maduro offer? What differences does Maduro see (or wish to see) between herself and her mother? What does she suggest prevents her from being entirely different from her mother and achieving her own goals in a male-female relationship?

2. The title comes from a phrase used in ordinary conversation. What does that choice tell the reader about the approach that Maduro will take to family structure and gener-

ational differences? If you have read Lauren Slater's "Love," compare the authors' techniques and suggest the values of each.

3. The subtitle of Maduro's essay includes three parts: mother, myself, anger. What connection is there between anger and the first two?

4. How are you like your father or mother? How do you hope to be different? Write a personal essay that uses description, comparison, contrast, and analysis to present your views.

AMY CUNNINGHAM *Why Women Smile*

AFTER SMILING BRILLIANTLY for nearly four decades, I now find myself trying to quit. Or, at the very least, seeking to lower the wattage a bit.

Not everyone I know is keen on this. My smile has gleamed like a cheap plastic night-light so long and so reliably that certain friends and relatives worry that my mood will darken the moment my smile dims. "Gee," one says, "I associate you with your smile. It's the essence of you. I should think you'd want to smile more!" But the people who love me best agree that my smile—which springs forth no matter where I am or how I feel—hasn't been serving me well. Said my husband recently, "Your smiling face and unthreatening demeanor make people like you in a fuzzy way, but that doesn't seem to be what you're after these days."

Smiles are not the small and innocuous things they appear to be: Too many of us smile in lieu of showing what's really on our minds. Indeed, the success of the women's movement might be measured by the sincerity—and lack of it—in our smiles. Despite all the work we American women have done to get and maintain full legal control of our bodies, not to mention our destinies, we still don't seem to be fully in charge of a couple of small muscle groups in our faces.

We smile so often and so promiscuously—when we're angry, when we're tense, when we're with children, when we're being photographed, when we're interviewing for a job, when we're meeting candidates to employ—that the Smiling Woman has become a peculiarly American archetype. This isn't entirely a bad thing, of course. A smile lightens the load, diffuses unpleasantness, redistributes nervous tension. Women doctors smile more than their male counterparts, studies show, and are better liked by their patients.

Oscar Wilde's[1] old saw that "a woman's face is her work of fiction" is often quoted to remind us that what's on the surface may have little connection to

5

Many of Cunningham's writings have appeared in wide-circulation magazines aimed at women, like this 1993 essay from Lear's Magazine, *a periodical no longer published.*

1. Irish-born Victorian dramatist (1854–1900).

what we're feeling. What is it in our culture that keeps our smiles on automatic pilot? The behavior seems to be an equal blend of nature and nurture. Research has demonstrated that since females often mature earlier than males and are less irritable, girls smile more than boys from the very beginning. But by adolescence, the differences in the smiling rates of boys and girls are so robust that it's clear the culture has done more than its share of the dirty work. Just think of the mothers who painstakingly embroidered the words ENTER SMILING on little samplers, and then hung their handiwork on doors by golden chains. Translation: "Your real emotions aren't welcome here."

Clearly, our instincts are another factor. Our smiles have their roots in the greetings of monkeys, who pull their lips up and back to show their fear of attack, as well as their reluctance to vie for a position of dominance. And like the opossum caught in the light by the clattering garbage cans, we, too, flash toothy grimaces when we make major mistakes. By declaring ourselves nonthreatening, our smiles provide an extremely versatile means of protection.

Our earliest baby smiles are involuntary reflexes having only the vaguest connection to contentment or comfort. In short, we're genetically wired to pull on our parents' heartstrings. As Desmond Morris explains in *Babywatching*, this is our way of attaching ourselves to our caretakers, as truly as baby chimps clench their mothers' fur. Even as babies we're capable of projecting onto others (in this case, our parents) the feelings we know we need to get back in return.

Bona fide social smiles occur at two-and-a-half to three months of age, usually a few weeks after we first start gazing with intense interest into the faces of our parents. By the time we are six months old, we are smiling and laughing regularly in reaction to tickling, feedings, blown raspberries, hugs, and peekaboo games. Even babies who are born blind intuitively know how to react to pleasurable changes with a smile, though their first smiles start later than those of sighted children.

Psychologists and psychiatrists have noted that babies also smile and laugh with relief when they realize that something they thought might be dangerous is not dangerous after all. Kids begin to invite their parents to indulge them with "scary" approach-avoidance games; they love to be chased or tossed up into the air. (It's interesting to note that as adults, we go through the same gosh-that's-shocking-and-dangerous-but-it's-okay-to-laugh-and-smile cycles when we listen to raunchy stand-up comics.)

10   From the wilds of New Guinea to the sidewalks of New York, smiles are associated with joy, relief, and amusement. But smiles are by no means limited to the expression of positive emotions: People of many different cultures smile when they are frightened, embarrassed, angry, or miserable. In Japan, for instance, a smile is often used to hide pain or sorrow.

Psychologist Paul Ekman, the head of the University of California's Human Interaction Lab in San Francisco, has identified 18 distinct types of smiles, including those that show misery, compliance, fear, and contempt. The smile of true merriment, which Dr. Ekman calls the Duchenne Smile, after the 19th century French doctor who first studied it, is characterized by heightened circulation, a feeling of exhilaration, and the employment of two major facial muscles: the zygomaticus major of the lower face, and the orbicularis oculi, which crinkles the skin around the eyes. But since the average American woman's smile often has less to do with her actual state of happiness than it does with the social pressure to smile no matter what, her baseline social smile isn't apt to be a felt expression that engages the eyes like this. Ekman insists that if people learned to read smiles, they could see the sadness, misery, or pain lurking there, plain as day.

Evidently, a woman's happy, willing deference is something the world wants visibly demonstrated. Woe to the waitress, the personal assistant or receptionist, the flight attendant, or any other woman in the line of public service whose smile is not offered up to the boss or client as proof that there are no storm clouds—no kids to support, no sleep that's been missed—rolling into the sunny workplace landscape. Women are expected to smile no matter where they line up on the social, cultural, or economic ladder: College professors are criticized for not smiling, political spouses are pilloried for being too serious, and women's roles in films have historically been smiling ones. It's little wonder that men on the street still call out, "Hey, baby, smile! Life's not *that* bad, is it?" to women passing by, lost in thought.

A friend remembers being pulled aside by a teacher after class and asked, "What is wrong, dear? You sat there for the whole hour looking so sad!" "All I could figure," my friend says now, "is that I wasn't smiling. And the fact that *she* felt sorry for me for looking normal made me feel horrible."

Ironically, the social laws that govern our smiles have completely reversed themselves over the last 2,000 years. Women weren't always expected to seem animated and responsive; in fact, immoderate laughter was once considered one of the more conspicuous vices a woman could have, and mirth was downright sinful. Women were kept apart, in some cultures even veiled, so that they couldn't perpetuate Eve's seductive, evil work. The only smile deemed appropriate on a privileged woman's face was the serene, inward smile of the Virgin Mary at Christ's birth, and even that expression was best directed exclusively at young children. Cackling laughter and wicked glee were the kinds of sounds heard only in hell.

What we know of women's facial expressions in other centuries comes mostly from religious writings, codes of etiquette, and portrait paintings. In 15th century Italy, it was customary for artists to paint lovely, blank-faced women in profile. A viewer could stare endlessly at such a woman, but she could not gaze back. By the Renaissance, male artists were taking some pleasure in depicting women with a semblance of complexity, Leonardo da Vinci's Mona Lisa, with her veiled enigmatic smile, being the most famous example.

The Golden Age of the Dutch Republic marks a fascinating period for studying women's facial expressions. While we might expect the drunken young whores of Amsterdam to smile devilishly (unbridled sexuality and lasciviousness were *supposed* to addle the brain), it's the faces of the Dutch women from fine families that surprise us. Considered socially more free, these women demonstrate a fuller range of facial expressions than their European sisters. Frans Hals's 1622 portrait of Stephanus Geraerdt and Isabella Coymans, a married couple, is remarkable not just for the full, friendly smiles on each face, but for the frank and mutual pleasure the couple take in each other.

In the 1800s, sprightly, pretty women began appearing in advertisements for everything from beverages to those newfangled Kodak Land cameras. Women's faces were no longer impassive, and their willingness to bestow status, to offer, proffer, and yield, was most definitely promoted by their smiling images. The culture appeared to have turned the smile, originally a bond shared between intimates, into a socially required display that sold capitalist ideology as well as kitchen appliances. And female viewers soon began to emulate these highly idealized pictures. Many longed to be more like her, that perpetually smiling female. She seemed so beautiful. So content. So whole.

By the middle of the 19th century, the bulk of America's smile burden was falling primarily to women and African-American slaves, providing a very portable means of protection, a way of saying, "I'm harmless. I won't assert myself here." It reassured those in power to see signs of gratitude and contentment in the faces of subordinates. As long ago as 1963, adman David Ogilvy declared the image of a woman smiling approvingly at a product clichéd, but we've yet to get the message. Cheerful Americans still appear in ads today, smiling somewhat less disingenuously than they smiled during the middle of the century, but smiling broadly nonetheless.

Other countries have been somewhat reluctant to import our "Don't worry, be happy" American smiles. When McDonald's opened in Moscow not long ago and when EuroDisney debuted in France last year, the Americans involved in both business ventures complained that they couldn't get the natives they'd employed to smile worth a damn.

20   Europeans visiting the United States for the first time are often surprised at just how often Americans smile. But when you look at our history, the relentless good humor (or, at any rate, the pretense of it) falls into perspective. The American wilderness was developed on the assumption that this country had a shortage of people in relation to its possibilities. In countries with a more rigid class structure or caste system, fewer people are as captivated by the idea of quickly winning friends and influencing people. Here in the States, however, every stranger is a potential associate. Our smiles bring new people on board. The American smile is a democratic version of a curtsy or doffed hat, since, in this land of free equals, we're not especially formal about the ways we greet social superiors.

The civil rights movement never addressed the smile burden by name, but activists worked on their own to set new facial norms. African-American males stopped smiling on the streets in the 1960s, happily aware of the unsettling effect this action had on the white population. The image of the simpleminded, smiling, white-toothed black was rejected as blatantly racist, and it gradually retreated into the distance. However, like the women of Sparta and the wives of samurai, who were expected to look happy upon learning their sons or husbands had died in battle, contemporary American women have yet to unilaterally declare their faces their own property.

For instance, imagine a woman at a morning business meeting being asked if she could make a spontaneous and concise summation of a complicated project she's been struggling to get under control for months. She might draw the end of her mouth back and clench her teeth—*Eek!*—in a protective response, a polite, restrained expression of her surprise, not unlike the expression of a conscientious young schoolgirl being told to get out paper and pencil for a pop quiz. At the same time, the woman might be feeling resentful of the supervisor who sprang the request, but she fears taking that person on. So she holds back a comment. The whole performance resolves in a weird grin collapsing into a nervous smile that conveys discomfort and unpreparedness. A pointed remark by way of explanation or self-defense might've worked better for her—but her mouth was otherwise engaged.

We'd do well to realize just how much our smiles misrepresent us, and swear off for good the self-deprecating grins and ritual displays of deference. Real smiles have beneficial physiological effects, according to Paul Ekman. False ones do nothing for us at all.

"Smiles are as important as sound bites on television," insists producer and media coach Heidi Berenson, who has worked with many of Washington's most famous faces. "And women have always been better at understanding this than men. But the smile I'm talking about is not a cutesy smile. It's an authoritative smile. A genuine smile. Properly timed, it's tremendously powerful."

To limit a woman to one expression is like editing down an orchestra to 25 one instrument. And the search for more authentic means of expression isn't easy in a culture in which women are still expected to be magnanimous smilers, helpmates in crisis, and curators of everybody else's morale. But change is already floating in the high winds. We see a boon in assertive female comedians who are proving that women can *dish out* smiles, not just wear them. Actress Demi Moore has stated that she doesn't like to take smiling roles. Nike is running ads that show unsmiling women athletes sweating, reaching, pushing themselves. These women aren't overly concerned with issues of rapport; they're not being "nice" girls—they're working out.

If a woman's smile were truly her own, to be smiled or not, according to how the *woman* felt, rather than according to what someone else needed, she would smile more spontaneously, without ulterior, hidden motives. As Rainer Maria Rilke wrote in *The Journal of My Other Self*, "Her smile was not meant to be seen by anyone and served its whole purpose in being smiled."

That smile is my long-term aim. In the meantime, I hope to stabilize on the smile continuum somewhere between the eliciting grin of Farrah Fawcett and the haughty smirk of Jeane Kirkpatrick.[2]

2. Fawcett (b. 1947), television star and pinup girl of the 1970s, famous for her feathered hair; Kirkpatrick (1926–2006), American educator and diplomat and U.S. ambassador to the United Nations under Ronald Reagan, 1981–85.

QUESTIONS

1. Were you or some people you know urged to smile or to smile more? How was the advice given? What do you think was the motive?

2. Collect some observational data on the way men and women interact with strangers and see if you can confirm any part of Cunningham's essay.

3. Several years after Cunningham wrote "Why Women Smile," she discovered new research on smiling (see "All Smiles Now," below). This research has made her change her view on women's smiles. Write a brief account of what these changes are and what new evidence they reflect.

4. Do you think that Paul Ekman's research on Buddhist monks fully applies to American women and their smiles? What issues remain? Write about the issues in an essay that draws on your own experience and observation.

FRIDAY, DECEMBER 29, 2006[3]
ALL SMILES NOW

I once wrote an essay called "Why Women Smile" for the women's magazine *Lear's*. More than fifteen years later, I'm still receiving checks from academic presses planning to re-run the article because, apparently, it "teaches well" in first-year college writing classes. . . .

But here's the quandary: I now know that a whole chunk of my article is incorrect. . . . For my research at the time, I interviewed a noted psychologist and facial expression expert Paul Ekman. I remember that when the piece was published, Ekman didn't seem so thrilled with it. He didn't write me back. I now know that's because he had been trying to tell me that he was conceiving of the human smile in a new way and that the feminists who thought women should smile less weren't approaching smiles from the right perspective. But I couldn't hear him. Ekman then was just a short time from researching Tibetan monks and the Dalai Lama's smiling meditations. He was on his way to substantiating that smiles—even fake plastered-on smiles—can indeed lift our moods and keep us happier. So actually, smiling women have had the right idea all along.

But I was so attached to the notion that feminine niceness was some kind of pathology that I couldn't hear what Ekman was telling me. Indeed, I couldn't imagine that if you smiled while seated quietly in meditation, you would spread the energy of cheer throughout the world and rise up feeling better. I couldn't conceive of the topic spiritually.

Since then, Ekman has published his findings. And my melancholy little prose piece (which my mother always hated anyway) is out there like the Energizer Bunny banging its drum. So until I can make this wrong a right, do me a favor: Smile freely and broadly. Get happy.

3. Posted on Cunningham's blog (on Beliefnet.com) on this date.

ANDREW SULLIVAN   *What Is a Homosexual?*

GAY ADOLESCENTS are offered what every heterosexual teenager longs for: to be invisible in the girls' locker room. But you are invisible in the boys' locker room, your desire as unavoidable as its object. In that moment, you learn the first homosexual lesson: that your survival depends upon self-concealment. I remember specifically coming back to high school after a long summer when I was fifteen and getting changed in the locker room for the first time again with a guy I had long had a crush on. But since the vacation, he had developed enormously: suddenly he had hair on his chest, his body had grown and strengthened, he was—clearly—no longer a boy. In front of me, he took off his shirt, and unknowingly, slowly, erotically stripped. I became literally breathless, overcome by the proximity of my desire. The gay teenager learns in that kind of event a form of control and sublimation, of deception and self-contempt, that never leaves his consciousness. He learns that that which would most give him meaning is most likely to destroy him in the eyes of others; that the condition of his friendships is the subjugation of himself.

In the development of any human being, these are powerful emotions. They form a person. The homosexual learns to make distinctions between his sexual desire and his emotional longings—not because he is particularly prone to objectification of the flesh, but because he needs to survive as a social and sexual being. The society separates these two entities, and for a long time the homosexual has no option but to keep them separate. He learns certain rules; and, as with a child learning grammar, they are hard, later on in life, to unlearn.

It's possible, I think, that whatever society teaches or doesn't teach about homosexuality, this fact will always be the case. No homosexual child, surrounded overwhelmingly by heterosexuals, will feel at home in his sexual and emotional world, even in the most tolerant of cultures. And every homosexual child will learn the rituals of deceit, impersonation, and appearance. Anyone who believes political, social, or even cultural revolution will change this fundamentally is denying reality. This isolation will always hold. It is definitional of homosexual development. And children are particularly cruel. At the age of eleven, no one wants to be the odd one out; and in the arena of dating and hormones, the exclusion is inevitably a traumatic one.

It's also likely to be forlorn. Most people are liable to meet emotional rejection by sheer force of circumstance; but for a homosexual, the odds are simply far, far higher. My own experience suggests that somewhere between two and five percent of the population have involuntarily strong emotional and sexual attractions to the same sex. Which means that the pool of possible partners *starts* at one in twenty to one in fifty. It's no wonder, perhaps, that male homosexual culture has developed an ethic more of anonymous or promiscu-

From Sullivan's 1995 book, Virtually Normal: An Argument about Homosexuality.

ous sex than of committed relationships. It's as if the hard lessons of adolescence lower permanently—by the sheer dint of the odds—the aspiration for anything more.

5   Did I know what I was? Somewhere, maybe. But it was much easier to know what I wasn't. I wasn't going to be able to enter into the world of dating girls; I wasn't going to be able to feel fully comfortable among the heterosexual climate of the male teenager. So I decided, consciously or subconsciously, to construct a trajectory of my life that would remove me from their company; give me an excuse, provide a dignified way out. In Anglo-Saxon culture, the wonk has such an option: he's too nerdy or intellectual to be absorbed by girls. And there is something masculine and respected in the discipline of the arts and especially the sciences. You can gain respect and still be different.

So I threw myself into my schoolwork, into (more dubiously) plays, into creative writing, into science fiction. Other homosexuals I have subsequently met pursued other strategies: some paradoxically threw themselves into sports, outjocking the jocks, gaining ever greater proximity, seeking respect, while knowing all the time that they were doomed to rejection. Others withdrew into isolation and despair. Others still, sensing their difference, flaunted it. At my high school, an older boy insisted on wearing full makeup to class; and he was accepted in a patronizing kind of way, his brazen otherness putting others at ease. They knew where they were with him; and he felt at least comfortable with their stable contempt. The rest of us who lived in a netherworld of sexual insecurity were not so lucky.

Most by then had a far more acute sense of appearances than those who did not need to hide anything; and our sense of irony, and of aesthetics, assumed a precociously arch form, and drew us subtly together. Looking back, I realize that many of my best friends in my teen years were probably homosexual; and that somewhere in our coded, embarrassed dialogue we admitted it. Many of us also embraced those ideologies that seemed most alien to what we feared we might be: of the sports jock, of the altar boy, of the young conservative. They were the ultimate disguises. And our recognition of ourselves in the other only confirmed our desire to keep it quiet.

I should add that many young lesbians and homosexuals seem to have had a much easier time of it. For many, the question of sexual identity was not a critical factor in their life choices or vocation, or even a factor at all. Perhaps because of a less repressive upbringing or because of some natural ease in the world, they affected a simple comfort with their fate, and a desire to embrace it. These people alarmed me: their very ease was the sternest rebuke to my own anxiety, because it rendered it irrelevant. But later in life, I came to marvel at the naturalness of their self-confidence, in the face of such concerted communal pressure, and to envy it. I had the more common self-dramatizing urge of the tortured homosexual, trapped between feeling wicked and feeling ridiculous. It's shameful to admit it, but I was more traumatized by the latter than by the former: my pride was more formidable a force than my guilt.

When people ask the simple question, *What is a homosexual?* I can only answer with stories like these. I could go on, but too many stories have already been told. Ask any lesbian or homosexual, and they will often provide a similar account. I was once asked at a conservative think tank what evidence I had that homosexuality was far more of an orientation than a choice, and I was forced to reply quite simply: my life. It's true that I have met a handful of lesbians and gay men over the years who have honestly told me that they genuinely had a choice in the matter (and a few heterosexuals who claim they too chose their orientation). I believe them; but they are the exception and not the rule. As homosexual lives go, my own was somewhat banal and typical.

This is not, of course, the end of the matter. Human experience begins with such facts, it doesn't end with them. There's a lamentable tendency to try to find some definitive solution to permanent human predicaments—in a string of DNA, in a conclusive psychological survey, in an analysis of hypothalami, in a verse of the Bible—in order to cut the argument short. Or to insist on the emotional veracity of a certain experience and expect it to trump any other argument on the table. But none of these things can replace the political and moral argument about how a society should deal with the presence of homosexuals in its midst. I relate my experience here not to impress or to shock or to gain sympathy, but merely to convey what the homosexual experience is actually like. You cannot discuss something until you know roughly what it is. * * *

10

In a society more and more aware of its manifold cultures and subcultures, we have been educated to be familiar and comfortable with what has been called "diversity": the diversity of perspective, culture, meaning. And this diversity is usually associated with what are described as cultural constructs: race, gender, sexuality, and so on. But as the obsession with diversity intensifies, the possibility of real difference alarms and terrifies all the more. The notion of collective characteristics—of attributes more associated with blacks than with whites, with Asians than with Latinos, with gay men than with straight men, with men than with women—has become anathema. They are marginalized as "stereotypes." The acceptance of diversity has come to mean the acceptance of the essential sameness of all types of people, and the danger of generalizing among them at all. In fact, it has become virtually a definition of "racist" to make any substantive generalizations about a particular ethnicity, and a definition of "homophobic" to make any generalizations about homosexuals.

What follows, then, is likely to be understood as "homophobic." But I think it's true that certain necessary features of homosexual life lead to certain unavoidable features of homosexual character. This is not to say that they define any random homosexual: they do not. As with any group or way of life, there are many, many exceptions. Nor is it to say that they define the homosexual life: it should be clear by now that I believe that the needs and feelings of homosexual children and adolescents are largely interchangeable with those of their heterosexual peers. But there are certain generalizations that can be made about adult homosexuals and lesbians that have the ring of truth.

Of course, in a culture where homosexuals remain hidden and wrapped in self-contempt, in which their emotional development is often stunted and late, in which the closet protects all sorts of self-destructive behavior that a more open society would not, it is still very hard to tell what is inherent in a homosexual life that makes it different, and what is simply imposed upon it. Nevertheless, it seems to me that even in the most tolerant societies, some of the differences that I have just described would inhere.

The experience of growing up profoundly different in emotional and psychological makeup inevitably alters a person's self-perception, tends to make him or her more wary and distant, more attuned to appearance and its foibles, more self-conscious and perhaps more reflective. The presence of homosexuals in the arts, in literature, in architecture, in design, in fashion could be understood, as some have, as a simple response to oppression. Homosexuals have created safe professions within which to hide and protect each other. But why these professions? Maybe it's also that these are professions of appearance. Many homosexual children, feeling distant from their peers, become experts at trying to figure out how to disguise their inner feelings, to "pass." They notice the signs and signals of social interaction, because they do not come instinctively. They develop skills early on that help them notice the inflections of a voice, the quirks of a particular movement, and the ways in which meaning can be conveyed in code. They have an ear for irony and for double meanings. Sometimes, by virtue of having to suppress their natural emotions, they find formal outlets to express themselves: music, theater, art. And so their lives become set on a trajectory which reinforces these trends.

15   As a child, I remember, as I suppressed the natural emotions of an adolescent, how I naturally turned in on myself—writing, painting, and participating in amateur drama. Or I devised fantasies of future exploits—war leader, parliamentarian, famous actor—that could absorb those emotions that were being diverted from meeting other boys and developing natural emotional relationships with them. And I developed mannerisms, small ways in which I could express myself, tiny revolts of personal space—a speech affectation, a ridiculous piece of clothing—that were, in retrospect, attempts to communicate something in code which could not be communicated in language. In this homosexual archness there was, of course, much pain. And it came as no surprise that once I had become more open about my homosexuality, these mannerisms declined. Once I found the strength to be myself, I had no need to act myself. So my clothes became progressively more regular and slovenly; I lost interest in drama; my writing moved from fiction to journalism; my speech actually became less affected.

This, of course, is not a universal homosexual experience. Many homosexuals never become more open, and the skills required to survive the closet remain skills by which to earn a living. And many homosexuals, even once they no longer need those skills, retain them. My point is simply that the universal experience of self-conscious difference in childhood and adolescence—common, but not exclusive, to homosexuals—develops identifiable skills. They are the skills of mimesis; and one of the goods that homosexuals bring to society is undoubtedly a more highly developed sense of form, of style.

Even in the most open of societies, I think, this will continue to be the case. It is not something genetically homosexual; it is something environmentally homosexual. And it begins young.

QUESTIONS

1. Throughout this essay Sullivan distinguishes between the "human experience" of all adolescents and experiences particular to or common among "homosexuals." Make a list of each. Were there features that you would have listed in the opposite column? What features did you expect Sullivan to mention that he did not?

2. Sullivan notes that it is currently unfashionable to think in terms of "stereotypes" of any group, whether based on race, gender, sexuality, or some other classification (paragraph 11). Even so, he has set himself the task of answering the question "What is a homosexual?" How does he define this key term without resorting to stereotypes?

3. Although Sullivan does not advance a political agenda or a set of social reforms, his essay implies actions that would be beneficial to homosexuals and, more generally, to American society. What are these?

4. Write an essay that attempts to define the characteristics of a particular group, using a variation of Sullivan's title, "What Is a ——?"

ELISABETH KÜBLER-ROSS *On the Fear of Death*

> Let me not pray to be sheltered from
> dangers but to be fearless in facing them.
> Let me not beg for the stilling of
> my pain but for the heart to conquer it.
> Let me not look for allies in life's
> battlefield but to my own strength.
> Let me not crave in anxious fear to
> be saved but hope for the patience to
> win my freedom.
> Grant me that I may not be a
> coward, feeling your mercy in my
> success alone; but let me find the grasp
> of your hand in my failure.
>
> — RABINDRANATH TAGORE,
> *Fruit-Gathering*

EPIDEMICS HAVE TAKEN a great toll of lives in past generations. Death in infancy and early childhood was frequent and there were few families who didn't lose a member of the family at an early age. Medicine has changed greatly in the last decades. Widespread vaccinations have practically eradicated many illnesses, at least in western Europe and the United States. The use of chemotherapy, especially the antibiotics, has contributed to an ever decreasing number of fatalities in infectious diseases. Better child care and education has effected a low morbidity and mortality among children. The many diseases that have taken an impressive toll among the young and middle-aged have been conquered. The number of old people is on the rise, and with this fact come the number of people with malignancies and chronic diseases associated more with old age.

Pediatricians have less work with acute and life-threatening situations as they have an ever increasing number of patients with psychosomatic disturbances and adjustment and behavior problems. Physicians have more people in their waiting rooms with emotional problems than they have ever had before, but they also have more elderly patients who not only try to live with their decreased physical abilities and limitations but who also face loneliness and isolation with all its pains and anguish. The majority of these people are not seen by a psychiatrist. Their needs have to be elicited and gratified by other professional people, for instance, chaplains and social workers. It is for them that I am trying to outline the changes that have taken place in the last few decades, changes that are ultimately responsible for the in-

A chapter from Kübler-Ross's celebrated 1969 book, On Death and Dying, *which traces the "stages of grief"—denial, anger, bargaining, depression, and acceptance—through which a dying person passes when told of a terminal illness.*

creased fear of death, the rising number of emotional problems, and the greater need for understanding of and coping with the problems of death and dying.

When we look back in time and study old cultures and people, we are impressed that death has always been distasteful to man and will probably always be. From a psychiatrist's point of view this is very understandable and can perhaps best be explained by our basic knowledge that, in our unconscious, death is never possible in regard to ourselves. It is inconceivable for our unconscious to imagine an actual ending of our own life here on earth, and if this life of ours has to end, the ending is always attributed to a malicious intervention from the outside by someone else. In simple terms, in our unconscious mind we can only be killed; it is inconceivable to die of a natural cause or of old age. Therefore death in itself is associated with a bad act, a frightening happening, something that in itself calls for retribution and punishment.

One is wise to remember these fundamental facts as they are essential in understanding some of the most important, otherwise unintelligible communications of our patients.

The second fact that we have to comprehend is that in our unconscious mind we cannot distinguish between a wish and a deed. We are all aware of some of our illogical dreams in which two completely opposite statements can exist side by side—very acceptable in our dreams but unthinkable and illogical in our wakening state. Just as our unconscious mind cannot differentiate between the wish to kill somebody in anger and the act of having done so, the young child is unable to make this distinction. The child who angrily wishes his mother to drop dead for not having gratified his needs will be traumatized greatly by the actual death of his mother—even if this event is not linked closely in time with his destructive wishes. He will always take part or the whole blame for the loss of his mother. He will always say to himself—rarely to others—"I did it, I am responsible, I was bad, therefore Mommy left me." It is well to remember that the child will react in the same manner if he loses a parent by divorce, separation, or desertion. Death is often seen by a child as an impermanent thing and has therefore little distinction from a divorce in which he may have an opportunity to see a parent again.

Many a parent will remember remarks of their children such as, "I will bury my doggy now and next spring when the flowers come up again, he will get up." Maybe it was the same wish that motivated the ancient Egyptians to supply their dead with food and goods to keep them happy and the old American Indians to bury their relatives with their belongings.

When we grow older and begin to realize that our omnipotence is really not so omnipotent, that our strongest wishes are not powerful enough to make the impossible possible, the fear that we have contributed to the death of a loved one diminishes—and with it the guilt. The fear remains diminished, however, only so long as it is not challenged too strongly. Its vestiges can be seen daily in hospital corridors and in people associated with the bereaved.

A husband and wife may have been fighting for years, but when the partner dies, the survivor will pull his hair, whine and cry louder and beat his chest in regret, fear and anguish, and will hence fear his own death more than before, still believing in the law of talion—an eye for an eye, a tooth for a tooth— "I am responsible for her death, I will have to die a pitiful death in retribution."

Maybe this knowledge will help us understand many of the old customs and rituals which have lasted over the centuries and whose purpose is to diminish the anger of the gods or the people as the case may be, thus decreasing the anticipated punishment. I am thinking of the ashes, the torn clothes, the veil, the *Klage Weiber*[1] of the old days—they are all means to ask you to take pity on them, the mourners, and are expressions of sorrow, grief, and shame. If someone grieves, beats his chest, tears his hair, or refuses to eat, it is an attempt at self-punishment to avoid or reduce the anticipated punishment for the blame that he takes on the death of a loved one.

10   This grief, shame, and guilt are not very far removed from feelings of anger and rage. The process of grief always includes some qualities of anger. Since none of us likes to admit anger at a deceased person, these emotions are often disguised or repressed and prolong the period of grief or show up in other ways. It is well to remember that it is not up to us to judge such feelings as bad or shameful but to understand their true meaning and origin as something very human. In order to illustrate this I will again use the example of the child—and the child in us. The five-year-old who loses his mother is both blaming himself for her disappearance and being angry at her for having deserted him and for no longer gratifying his needs. The dead person then turns into something the child loves and wants very much but also hates with equal intensity for this severe deprivation.

The ancient Hebrews regarded the body of a dead person as something unclean and not to be touched. The early American Indians talked about the evil spirits and shot arrows in the air to drive the spirits away. Many other cultures have rituals to take care of the "bad" dead person, and they all originate in this feeling of anger which still exists in all of us, though we dislike admitting it. The tradition of the tombstone may originate in this wish to keep the bad spirits deep down in the ground, and the pebbles that many mourners put on the grave are left-over symbols of the same wish. Though we call the firing of guns at military funerals a last salute, it is the same symbolic ritual as the Indian used when he shot his spears and arrows into the skies.

I give these examples to emphasize that man has not basically changed. Death is still a fearful, frightening happening, and the fear of death is a universal fear even if we think we have mastered it on many levels.

What has changed is our way of coping and dealing with death and dying and our dying patients.

Having been raised in a country in Europe where science is not so advanced, where modern techniques have just started to find their way into medicine, and where people still live as they did in this country half a century ago,

---

1. Wailing wives.

I may have had an opportunity to study a part of the evolution of mankind in a shorter period.

I remember as a child the death of a farmer. He fell from a tree and was not expected to live. He asked simply to die at home, a wish that was granted without questioning. He called his daughters into the bedroom and spoke with each one of them alone for a few moments. He arranged his affairs quietly, though he was in great pain, and distributed his belongings and his land, none of which was to be split until his wife should follow him in death. He also asked each of his children to share in the work, duties, and tasks that he had carried on until the time of the accident. He asked his friends to visit him once more, to bid good-bye to them. Although I was a small child at the time, he did not exclude me or my siblings. We were allowed to share in the preparations of the family just as we were permitted to grieve with them until he died. When he did die, he was left at home, in his own beloved home which he had built, and among his friends and neighbors who went to take a last look at him where he lay in the midst of flowers in the place he had lived in and loved so much. In that country today there is still no make-believe slumber room, no embalming, no false makeup to pretend sleep. Only the signs of very disfiguring illnesses are covered up with bandages and only infectious cases are removed from the home prior to the burial.

Why do I describe such "old-fashioned" customs? I think they are an indication of our acceptance of a fatal outcome, and they help the dying patient as well as his family to accept the loss of a loved one. If a patient is allowed to terminate his life in the familiar and beloved environment, it requires less adjustment for him. His own family knows him well enough to replace a sedative with a glass of his favorite wine; or the smell of a home-cooked soup may give him the appetite to sip a few spoons of fluid which, I think, is still more enjoyable than an infusion. I will not minimize the need for sedatives and infusions and realize full well from my own experience as a country doctor that they are sometimes life-saving and often unavoidable. But I also know that patience and familiar people and foods could replace many a bottle of intravenous fluids given for the simple reason that it fulfills the physiological need without involving too many people and/or individual nursing care.

The fact that children are allowed to stay at home where a fatality has stricken and are included in the talk, discussions, and fears gives them the feeling that they are not alone in the grief and gives them the comfort of shared responsibility and shared mourning. It prepares them gradually and helps them view death as part of life, an experience which may help them grow and mature.

This is in great contrast to a society in which death is viewed as taboo, discussion of it is regarded as morbid, and children are excluded with the presumption and pretext that it would be "too much" for them. They are then sent off to relatives, often accompanied with some unconvincing lies of "Mother has gone on a long trip" or other unbelievable stories. The child senses that something is wrong, and his distrust in adults will only multiply if other relatives add new variations of the story, avoid his questions or suspicions, shower him with gifts as a meager substitute for a loss he is not permitted to deal with. Sooner or later the child will become aware of the changed family situation and, depending on the age and personality of the child, will have an unresolved grief and regard this incident as a frightening, mysterious, in any case very traumatic experience with untrustworthy grownups, which he has no way to cope with.

It is equally unwise to tell a little child who lost her brother that God loved little boys so much that he took little Johnny to heaven. When this little girl grew up to be a woman she never solved her anger at God, which resulted in a psychotic depression when she lost her own little son three decades later.

20   We would think that our great emancipation, our knowledge of science and of man, has given us better ways and means to prepare ourselves and our families for this inevitable happening. Instead the days are gone when a man was allowed to die in peace and dignity in his own home.

The more we are making advancements in science, the more we seem to fear and deny the reality of death. How is this possible?

We use euphemisms, we make the dead look as if they were asleep, we ship the children off to protect them from the anxiety and turmoil around the house if the patient is fortunate enough to die at home, we don't allow children to visit their dying parents in the hospitals, we have long and controversial discussions about whether patients should be told the truth—a question that rarely arises when the dying person is tended by the family physician who has known him from delivery to death and who knows the weaknesses and strengths of each member of the family.

I think there are many reasons for this flight away from facing death calmly. One of the most important facts is that dying nowadays is more gruesome in many ways, namely, more lonely, mechanical, and dehumanized; at times it is even difficult to determine technically when the time of death has occurred.

Dying becomes lonely and impersonal because the patient is often taken out of his familiar environment and rushed to an emergency room. Whoever has been very sick and has required rest and comfort especially may recall his experience of being put on a stretcher and enduring the noise of the ambulance siren and hectic rush until the hospital gates open. Only those who have lived through this may appreciate the discomfort and cold necessity of such transportation which is only the beginning of a long order—hard to endure when you are well, difficult to express in words when noise, light, pumps, and voices are all too much to put up with. It may well be that we might consider more the patient under the sheets and blankets and perhaps stop our well-meant efficiency and rush in order to hold the patient's hand, to smile, or to listen to a question. I include the trip to the hospital as the first episode in dying, as it is for many. I am putting it exaggeratedly in contrast to the sick man who is left at home—not to say that lives should not be saved if they can be saved by a hospitalization but to keep the focus on the patient's experience, his needs and his reactions.

25   When a patient is severely ill, he is often treated like a person with no

right to an opinion. It is often someone else who makes the decision if and when and where a patient should be hospitalized. It would take so little to remember that the sick person too has feelings, has wishes and opinions, and has—most important of all—the right to be heard.

Well, our presumed patient has now reached the emergency room. He will be surrounded by busy nurses, orderlies, interns, residents, a lab technician perhaps who will take some blood, an electrocardiogram technician who takes the cardiogram. He may be moved to X-ray and he will overhear opinions of his condition and discussions and questions to members of the family. He slowly but surely is beginning to be treated like a thing. He is no longer a person. Decisions are made often without his opinion. If he tries to rebel he will be sedated and after hours of waiting and wondering whether he has the strength, he will be wheeled into the operating room or intensive treatment unit and become an object of great concern and great financial investment.

He may cry for rest, peace, and dignity, but he will get infusions, transfusions, a heart machine, or tracheotomy if necessary. He may want one single person to stop for one single minute so that he can ask one single question—but he will get a dozen people around the clock, all busily preoccupied with his heart rate, pulse, electrocardiogram or pulmonary functions, his secretions or excretions but not with him as a human being. He may wish to fight it all but it is going to be a useless fight since all this is done in the fight for his life, and if they can save his life they can consider the person afterwards. Those who consider the person first may lose precious time to save his life! At least this seems to be the rationale or justification behind all this—or is it? Is the reason for this increasingly mechanical, depersonalized approach our own defensiveness? Is this approach our own way to cope with and repress the anxieties that a terminally or critically ill patient evokes in us? Is our concentration on equipment, on blood pressure our desperate attempt to deny the impending death which is so frightening and discomforting to us that we displace all our knowledge onto machines, since they are less close to us than the suffering face of another human being which would remind us once more of our lack of omnipotence, our own limits and failures, and last but not least perhaps our own mortality?

Maybe the question has to be raised: Are we becoming less human or more human? * * * [I]t is clear that whatever the answer may be, the patient is suffering more—not physically, perhaps, but emotionally. And his needs have not changed over the centuries, only our ability to gratify them.

QUESTIONS

1. In this essay Kübler-Ross incorporates various kinds of evidence: experience, observation, and reading. Mark the various kinds and describe how she integrates them into her text.

2. Kübler-Ross attends to the needs of the living and the rights of the dying. Describe

where and how she attends to each and how she presents the conflicts, actual and potential, between them.

3. In paragraphs 24–27 Kübler-Ross describes the experience of the trip by ambulance, the emergency room, and the hospital from a patient's point of view. What does this shift in point of view contribute to the essay?

4. Imagine a situation in which a child or children are not isolated from death. What might be the consequences? Using this situation and its possible consequences, write an essay in which you agree or disagree with Kübler-Ross's views.

MARY ROACH   *How to Know If You're Dead*

A PATIENT ON THE WAY to surgery travels at twice the speed of a patient on the way to the morgue. Gurneys that ferry the living through hospital corridors move forward in an aura of purpose and push, flanked by caregivers with long strides and set faces, steadying IVs, pumping ambu bags,[1] barreling into double doors. A gurney with a cadaver commands no urgency. It is wheeled by a single person, calmly and with little notice, like a shopping cart.

For this reason, I thought I would be able to tell when the dead woman was wheeled past. I have been standing around at the nurses' station on one of the surgery floors of the University of California at San Francisco Medical Center, watching gurneys go by and waiting for Von Peterson, public affairs manager of the California Transplant Donor Network, and a cadaver I will call H. "There's your patient," says the charge nurse. A commotion of turquoise legs passes with unexpected forward-leaning urgency.

H is unique in that she is both a dead person *and* a patient on the way to surgery. She is what's known as a "beating-heart cadaver," alive and well everywhere but her brain. Up until artificial respiration was developed, there was no such entity; without a functioning brain, a body will not breathe on its own. But hook it up to a respirator and its heart will beat, and the rest of its organs will, for a matter of days, continue to thrive.

H doesn't look or smell or feel dead. If you leaned in close over the gurney, you could see her pulse beating in the arteries of her neck. If you touched her arm, you would find it warm and resilient, like your own. This is perhaps why the nurses and doctors refer to H as a patient, and why she makes her entrance to the OR[2] at the customary presurgery clip.

A chapter from Stiff: The Curious Life of Human Cadavers *(2003). The book addresses the questions: What happens to our bodies when we die? When our bodies shut down, what comes next?*

1. A manual resuscitator that helps provide patients with artificial ventilation.
2. Operating room.

Since brain death is the legal definition of death in this country, H the   5
person is certifiably dead. But H the organs and tissues is very much alive.
These two seemingly contradictory facts afford her an opportunity most
corpses do not have: that of extending the lives of two or three dying strangers.
Over the next four hours, H will surrender her liver, kidneys, and heart. One at
a time, surgeons will come and go, taking an organ and returning in haste to
their stricken patients. Until recently, the process was known among transplant professionals as an "organ harvest," which had a joyous, celebratory ring
to it, perhaps a little too joyous, as it has been of late replaced by the more
businesslike "organ recovery."

In H's case, one surgeon will be traveling from Utah to recover her heart,
and another, the one recovering both the liver and the kidneys, will be taking
them two floors down. UCSF is a major transplant center, and organs removed
here often remain in house. More typically, a transplant patient's surgeon will
travel from UCSF to a small town somewhere to retrieve the organ—often
from an accident victim, someone young with strong, healthy organs, whose
brain took an unexpected hit. The doctor does this because typically there is
no doctor in that small town with experience in organ recovery. Contrary to rumors about surgically trained thugs cutting people open in hotel rooms and
stealing their kidneys, organ recovery is tricky work. If you want to be sure it's
done right, you get on a plane and go do it yourself.

Today's abdominal recovery surgeon is named Andy Posselt. He is holding
an electric cauterizing[3] wand, which looks like a cheap bank pen on a cord but
functions like a scalpel. The wand both cuts and burns, so that as the incision
is made, any vessels that are severed are simultaneously melted shut. The result is that there is a good deal less bleeding and a good deal more smoke and
smell. It's not a bad smell, but simply a seared-meat sort of smell. I want to ask
Dr. Posselt whether he likes it, but I can't bring myself to, so instead I ask
whether he thinks it's bad that I like the smell, which I don't really, or maybe
just a little. He replies that it is neither bad nor good, just morbid.

I have never before seen major surgery, only its scars. From the length of
them, I had imagined surgeons doing their business, taking things out and
putting them in, through an opening maybe eight or nine inches long, like a
woman poking around for her glasses at the bottom of her purse. Dr. Posselt
begins just above H's pubic hair and proceeds a good two feet north, to the
base of her neck. He's unzipping her like a parka. Her sternum is sawed
lengthwise so that her rib cage can be parted, and a large retractor is installed
to pull the two sides of the incision apart so that it is now as wide as it is long.
To see her this way, held open like a Gladstone bag,[4] forces a view of the human torso for what it basically is: a large, sturdy container for guts.

On the inside, H looks very much alive. You can see the pulse of her
heartbeat in her liver and all the way down her aorta. She bleeds where she is
cut and her organs are plump and slippery-looking. The electronic beat of the

3. Burning a part of the human body, with the goal of removing or sealing it.

4. A type of bag, named for British prime minister William Ewart Gladstone
(1809–1898), that has two hinged compartments.

heart monitor reinforces the impression that this is a living, breathing, thriving person. It is strange, almost impossible, really, to think of her as a corpse. When I tried to explain beating-heart cadavers to my step-daughter Phoebe yesterday, it didn't make sense to her. But if their heart is beating, aren't they still a person? she wanted to know. In the end she decided they were "a kind of person you could play tricks on but they wouldn't know." Which, I think, is a pretty good way of summing up most donated cadavers. The things that happen to the dead in labs and ORs are like gossip passed behind one's back. They are not felt or known and so they cause no pain.

10   The contradictions and counterintuitions of the beating-heart cadaver can exact an emotional toll on the intensive care unit (ICU) staff, who must, in the days preceding the harvest, not only think of patients like H as living beings, but treat and care for them that way as well. The cadaver must be monitored around the clock and "life-saving" interventions undertaken on its behalf. Since the brain can no longer regulate blood pressure or the levels of hormones and their release into the bloodstream, these things must be done by ICU staff, in order to keep the organs from degrading. Observed a group of Case Western Reserve University School of Medicine physicians in a *New England Journal of Medicine* article entitled "Psychosocial and Ethical Implications of Organ Retrieval": "Intensive care unit personnel may feel confused about having to perform cardiopulmonary resuscitation on a patient who has been declared dead, whereas a 'do not resuscitate' order has been written for a living patient in the next bed."

The confusion people feel over beating-heart cadavers reflects centuries of confusion over how, exactly, to define death, to pinpoint the precise moment when the spirit—the soul, the chi,[5] whatever you wish to call it—has ceased to exist and all that remains is a corpse. Before brain activity could be measured, the stopping of the heart had long been considered the defining moment. In point of fact, the brain survives for six to ten minutes after the heart has stopped pumping blood to it, but this is splitting hairs, and the definition works quite well for the most part. The problem, for centuries, was that doctors couldn't tell for sure whether the heart had ceased to beat or whether they were merely having trouble hearing it. The stethoscope wasn't invented until the mid-1800s, and the early models amounted to little more than a sort of medical ear trumpet. In cases where the heartbeat and pulse are especially faint—drownings, stroke, certain types of narcotic poisoning—even the most scrupulous physician had difficulty telling, and patients ran the risk of being dispatched to the undertaker before they'd actually expired.

To allay patients' considerable fears of live burial, as well as their own insecurities, eighteenth- and nineteenth-century physicians devised a diverting roster of methods for verifying death. Welsh physician and medical historian Jan Bondeson collected dozens of them for his witty and admirably researched book *Buried Alive*. The techniques seemed to fall into two categories: those that purported to rouse the unconscious patient with un-

5. A concept in Chinese culture that means, approximately, "life force."

speakable pain, and those that threw in a measure of humiliation. The soles of the feet were sliced with razors, and needles jammed beneath toenails. Ears were assaulted with bugle fanfares and "hideous Shrieks and excessive Noises." One French clergyman recommended thrusting a red-hot poker up what Bondeson genteelly refers to as "the rear passage." A French physician invented a set of nipple pincers specifically for the purpose of reanimation. Another invented a bagpipelike contraption for administering tobacco enemas, which he demonstrated enthusiastically on cadavers in the morgues of Paris. The seventeenth-century anatomist Jacob Winslow[6] entreated his colleagues to pour boiling Spanish wax on patients' foreheads and warm urine into their mouths. One Swedish tract on the matter suggested that a crawling insect be put into the corpse's ear. For simplicity and originality, though, nothing quite matches the thrusting of "a sharp pencil" up the presumed cadaver's nose.

In some cases, it is unclear who was the more humiliated, patient or doctor. French physician Jean Baptiste Vincent Laborde wrote at great length of his technique of rhythmic tongue-pulling, which was to be carried out for no less than three hours following the suspected death. (He later invented a hand-cranked tongue-pulling machine, which made the task less unpleasant though only marginally less tedious.) Another French physician instructed doctors to stick one of the patient's fingers in their ear, to listen for the buzzing sound produced by involuntary muscle movement.

Not all that surprisingly, none of these techniques gained wide acceptance, and most doctors felt that putrefaction was the only reliable way to verify that someone was dead. This meant that corpses had to sit around the house or the doctor's office for two or three days until the telltale signs and smells could be detected, a prospect perhaps even less appealing than giving them enemas. And so it was that special buildings, called waiting mortuaries, were built for the purpose of warehousing the moldering dead. These were huge, ornate halls, common in Germany in the 1800s. Some had separate halls for male and female cadavers, as though, even in death, men couldn't be trusted to comport themselves respectably in the presence of a lady. Others were segregated by class, with the well-to-do deceased paying extra to rot in luxury surroundings. Attendants were employed to keep watch for signs of life, which they did via a system of strings linking the fingers of corpses to a bell[7] or, in one case, the bellows of a large organ, so that any motion on the part of the deceased would alert the attendant, who was posted, owing to the considerable stench, in a separate room. As years passed and not a single resident was saved, the establishments began to close, and by 1940, the waiting mortuary had gone the way of the nipple pincer and the tongue puller.

---

6. Dutch anatomist (1669–1760).

7. I read on a Web site somewhere that this was the origin of the saying "Saved by the bell." In fact, by one reckoning, not a single corpse of the million-plus sent to waiting mortuaries over a twenty-year period awakened. If the bell alerted the attendant, which it often did, it was due to the corpse's shifting and collapsing as it decomposed. This was the origin of the saying "Driven to seek new employment by the bell," which you don't hear much anymore and probably never did, because I made it up [Roach's note].

* * *

15   With improvements in stethoscopes and gains in medical knowledge, physicians began to trust themselves to be able to tell when a heart had stopped,
and medical science came to agree that this was the best way to determine
whether a patient had checked out for good or was merely down the hall getting ice. Placing the heart center stage in our definition of death served to give
it, by proxy, a starring role in our definition of life and the soul, or spirit or self.
It has long had this anyway, as evidenced by a hundred thousand love songs
and sonnets and I ♥ bumper stickers. The concept of the beating-heart cadaver, grounded in a belief that the self resides in the brain and the brain
alone, delivered a philosophical curveball. The notion of the heart as fuel
pump took some getting used to.

The seat-of-the-soul debate has been ongoing some four thousand years.
It started out not as a heart-versus-brain debate, but as heart-versus-liver. The
ancient Egyptians were the original heart guys. They believed that the ka
resided in the heart. Ka was the essence of the person: spirit, intelligence,
feelings and passions, humor, grudges, annoying television theme songs, all
the things that make a person a person and not a nematode. The heart was the
only organ left inside a mummified corpse, for a man needed his ka in the afterlife. The brain he clearly did not need: cadaver brains were scrambled and
pulled out in globs, through the nostrils, by way of a hooked bronze needle.
Then they were thrown away. (The liver, stomach, intestines, and lungs were
taken out of the body, but kept: They were stored in earthen jars inside the
tomb, on the assumption, I guess, that it is better to overpack than to leave
something behind, particularly when packing for the afterlife.)

The Babylonians were the original liver guys, believing the organ to be the
source of human emotion and spirit. The Mesopotamians played both sides of
the argument, assigning emotion to the liver and intellect to the heart. These
guys clearly marched to the beat of a freethinking drummer, for they assigned
a further portion of the soul (cunning) to the stomach. Similar freethinkers
throughout history have included Descartes,[8] who wrote that the soul could be
found in the walnut-sized pineal gland, and the Alexandrian anatomist Strato,[9]
who decided it lived "behind the eyebrows."

With the rise of classical Greece, the soul debate evolved into the more
familiar heart-versus-brain, the liver having been demoted to an accessory
role.[10] Though Pythagoras and Aristotle[11] viewed the heart as the seat of the

---

8. René Descartes (1596–1650), French philosopher and mathematician.

9. Strato, short for Erasistratus (fl. 3rd century B.C.E.), placed the soul in the forefront
of the brain.

10. We are fortunate that this is so, for we would otherwise have been faced with Cé-
line Dion singing "My Liver Belongs to You" and movie houses playing *The Liver Is a
Lonely Hunter*. Every Spanish love song that contains the word *corazón*, which is all of
them, would contain the somewhat less lilting *higado*, and bumper stickers would proclaim, "I [liver symbol] my Pekingese" [Roach's note].

11. Pythagoras (582–507 B.C.E.) and Aristotle (384–322 B.C.E.), Greek philosophers.

soul—the source of "vital force" necessary to live and grow—they believed there to be a secondary, "rational" soul, or mind, located in the brain. Plato[12] agreed that both the heart and the brain were soul terrain, but assigned primacy to the brain. Hippocrates,[13] for his part, seemed confused (or perhaps it's me). He noted the effects of a crushed brain upon speech and intelligence, yet referred to it as a mucus-secreting gland, and wrote elsewhere that intelligence and "heat," which he said controlled the soul, were located in the heart.

The early anatomists weren't able to shed much light on the issue, as the soul wasn't something you could see or set your scalpel to. Lacking any scientific means of pinning down the soul, the first anatomists settled on generative primacy: What shows up first in the embryo must be most important and therefore most likely to hold the soul. The trouble with this particular avenue of learning, known as ensoulment, was that early first-trimester human embryos were difficult to come by. Classical scholars of ensoulment, Aristotle among them, attempted to get around the problem by examining the larger, more easily obtained poultry embryo. To quote Vivian Nutton, author of "The Anatomy of the Soul in Early Renaissance Medicine" in *The Human Embryo*, "Analogies drawn from the inspection of hen's eggs foundered on the objection that man was not a chicken."

According to Nutton, the man who came closest to actually examining a human embryo was an anatomist named Realdo Colombo,[14] who, at the behest of the Renaissance philosopher Girolamo Pontano,[15] dissected a one-month-old fetus. Colombo returned from his lab—which in all likelihood was not equipped with a microscope, as the device had barely been invented—bearing the fascinating if flat-out wrong news that the liver formed before the heart.

Living amid our culture's heart-centric rhetoric, the valentines and the pop song lyrics, it is hard to imagine assigning spiritual or emotional sovereignty to the liver. Part of the reason for its exalted status among the early anatomists was that they erroneously believed it to be the origin of all the body's blood vessels. (William Harvey's[16] discovery of the circulatory system dealt the liver-as-seat-of-the-soul theory a final fatal blow; Harvey, you will not be surprised to hear, believed that the soul was carried in the blood.) I think it was something else too. The human liver is a boss-looking organ. It's glossy, aerodynamic, Olympian. It looks like sculpture, not guts. I've been marveling at H's liver, currently being prepped for its upcoming journey. The organs around it are amorphous and unappealing. Stomachs are flappy, indistinct; intestines, chaotic and soupy. Kidneys skulk under bundles of fat. But the liver

12. Greek philosopher (428/7–347 B.C.E.).

13. Greek physician (460–377 B.C.E.), known today as the father of medicine.

14. Matteo Realdo Colombo (c. 1516–1559), professor of anatomy and surgeon at the University of Padua; Pontano (fl. 1597), Italian philosopher.

15. I'd never heard of him either [Roach's note].

16. British doctor (1578–1657).

gleams. It looks engineered and carefully wrought. Its flanks have a subtle curve, like the horizon seen from space. If I were an ancient Babylonian, I guess I might think God splashed down here too.

Dr. Posselt is isolating the vessels and connectors on the liver and kidneys, prepping them for the organs' removal. The heart will go first—hearts remain viable only four to six hours; kidneys, by contrast, can be held in cold storage eighteen or even twenty-four hours—but the heart recovery surgeon hasn't arrived. He's flying in from Utah.

Minutes later a nurse puts her head through the OR doors. "Utah's in the building." People who work in ORs talk to each other in the truncated, slang-heavy manner of pilots and flight control types. The schedule on the OR wall lists today's procedure—the removal of four vital organs in preparation for death-defying transplantation into three desperate human beings—as "Recovery abdm (liv/kid x2) ♥." A few minutes ago, someone made reference to "the panky," meaning "the pancreas."

"Utah's changing."

Utah is a gentle-looking man of perhaps fifty, with graying hair and a thin, tanned face. He has finished changing and a nurse is snapping on his gloves. He looks calm, competent, even a little bored. (This just slays me. The man is about to cut a beating heart out of a human chest.) The heart has been hidden until now behind the pericardium, a thick protective sac which Dr. Posselt now cuts away.

There is her heart. I've never seen one beating. I had no idea they moved so much. You put your hand on your heart and you picture something pulsing slightly but basically still, like a hand on a desktop tapping Morse code. This thing is going wild in there. It's a mixing-machine part, a stoat squirming in its burrow, an alien life form that's just won a Pontiac on *The Price Is Right*. If you were looking for the home of the human body's animating spirit, I could imagine believing it to be here, for the simple reason that it is the human body's most animated organ.

Utah places clamps on the arteries of H's heart, stanching the flow of blood in preparation for the cuts. You can tell by the vital signs monitor that something monumental is happening to her body. The ECG[17] has quit drawing barbed wire and begun to look like a toddler's Etch-a-Sketch scrawls. A quick geyser of blood splashes Utah's glasses, then subsides. If H weren't dead, she'd be dying now.

This is the moment, reported the Case Western Reserve group who interviewed transplant professionals, when OR staff have been known to report sensing a "presence" or "spirit" in the room. I try to raise the mental aerial and keep myself open to the vibes. Of course I have no idea how to do this. When I was six, I tried as hard as I could to will my brother's GI Joe to walk across the room to him. This is how these extrasensory deals go with me: Nothing comes of it, and then I feel stupid for trying.

Here is the deeply unnerving thing: The heart, cut from the chest, keeps

17. Short for electrocardiogram, an imaging of the electrical voltage of the heart.

beating on its own. Did Poe[18] know this when he wrote "The Tell-Tale Heart"? So animated are these freestanding hearts that surgeons have been known to drop them. "We wash them off and they do just fine," replied New York heart transplant surgeon Mehmet Oz when I asked him about it. I imagined the heart slipping across the linoleum, the looks exchanged, the rush to retrieve it and clean it off, like a bratwurst that's rolled off the plate in a restaurant kitchen. I ask about these things, I think, because of a need to make human what otherwise verges on the godlike: taking live organs from bodies and making them live in another body. I also asked whether the surgeons ever set aside the old, damaged hearts of transplant recipients for them to keep. Surprisingly (to me, anyway), only a few express an interest in seeing or keeping their hearts.

Oz told me that a human heart removed from its blood supply can continue beating for as long as a minute or two, until the cells begin to starve from lack of oxygen. It was phenomena like this that threw eighteenth-century medical philosophers into a tizzy: If the soul was in the brain and not the heart, as many believed at that time, how could the heart keep beating outside the body, cut off from the soul?

* * *

The modern medical community is on the whole quite unequivocal about the brain being the seat of the soul, the chief commander of life and death. It is similarly unequivocal about the fact that people like H are, despite the hoochy-koochy going on behind their sternums, dead. We now know that the heart keeps beating on its own not because the soul is in there, but because it contains its own bioelectric power source, independent of the brain. As soon as H's heart is installed in someone else's chest and that person's blood begins to run through it, it will start beating anew—with no signals from the recipient's brain.

The legal community took a little longer than the physicians to come around to the concept of brain death. It was 1968 when the *Journal of the American Medical Association* published a paper by the Ad Hoc Committee of the Harvard Medical School to Examine the Definition of Brain Death advocating that irreversible coma be the new criterion for death, and clearing the ethical footpath for organ transplantation. It wasn't until 1974 that the law began to catch up. What forced the issue was a bizarre murder trial in Oakland, California.

The killer, Andrew Lyons, shot a man in the head in September 1973 and left him brain-dead. When Lyons's attorneys found out that the victim's family had donated his heart for transplantation, they tried to use this in Lyons's defense: If the heart was still beating at the time of surgery, they maintained, then how could it be that Lyons had killed him the day before? They tried to convince the jury that, technically speaking, Andrew Lyons hadn't murdered the man, the organ recovery surgeon had. According to Stanford University heart transplant pioneer Norman Shumway, who testified in the case, the

18. Edgar Allan Poe (1809–1849), American poet and short story writer.

judge would have none of it. He informed the jury that the accepted criteria for death were those set forth by the Harvard committee, and that that should inform their decision. (Photographs of the victim's brains "oozing from his skull," to quote the *San Francisco Chronicle*, probably didn't help Lyons's case.) In the end, Lyons was convicted of murder. Based on the outcome of the case, California passed legislation making brain death the legal definition of death. Other states quickly followed suit.

Andrew Lyons's defense attorney wasn't the first person to cry murder when a transplant surgeon removed a heart from a brain-dead patient. In the earliest days of heart transplants, Shumway, the first U.S. surgeon to carry out the procedure, was continually harangued by the coroner in Santa Clara County, where he practiced. The coroner didn't accept the brain-death concept of death and threatened that if Shumway went ahead with his plans to remove a beating heart from a brain-dead person and use it to save another person's life, he would initiate murder charges. Though the coroner had no legal ground to stand on and Shumway went ahead anyway, the press gave it a vigorous chew. New York heart transplant surgeon Mehmet Oz recalls the Brooklyn district attorney around that time making the same threat. "He said he'd indict and arrest any heart transplant surgeon who went into his borough and harvested an organ."

35   The worry, explained Oz, was that someday someone who wasn't actually brain-dead was going to have his heart cut out. There exist certain rare medical conditions that can look, to the untrained or negligent eye, a lot like brain death, and the legal types didn't trust the medical types to get it right. To a very, very small degree, they had reason to worry. Take, for example, the condition known as "locked-in state." In one form of the disease, the nerves, from eyeballs to toes, suddenly and rather swiftly drop out of commission, with the result that the body is completely paralyzed, while the mind remains normal. The patient can hear what's being said but has no way of communicating that he's still in there, and that no, it's definitely not okay to give his organs away for transplant. In severe cases, even the muscles that contract to change the size of the pupils no longer function. This is bad news, for a common test of brain death is to shine a light in the patient's eyes to check for the reflexive contraction of the pupils. Typically, victims of locked-in state recover fully, provided no one has mistakenly wheeled them off to the OR to take out their heart.

Like the specter of live burial that plagued the French and German citizenry in the 1800s, the fear of live organ harvesting is almost completely without foundation. A simple EEG[19] will prevent misdiagnosis of the locked-in state and conditions like it.

On a rational level, most people are comfortable with the concept of brain death and organ donation. But on an emotional level, they may have a harder time accepting it, particularly when they are being asked to accept it by a

---

19. Short for electroencephalogram, an image representing the electric signals coursing through the brain.

transplant counselor who would like them to okay the removal of a family member's beating heart. Fifty-four percent of families asked refuse consent. "They can't deal with the fear, however irrational, that the true end of their loved one will come when the heart is removed," says Oz. That they, in effect, will have killed him.

Even heart transplant surgeons sometimes have trouble accepting the notion that the heart is nothing more than a pump. When I asked Oz where he thought the soul resided, he said, "I'll confide in you that I don't think it's all in the brain. I have to believe that in many ways the core of our existence *is* in our heart." Does that mean he thinks the brain-dead patient isn't dead? "There's no question that the heart without a brain is of no value. But life and death is not a binary system." It's a continuum. It makes sense, for many reasons, to draw the legal line at brain death, but that doesn't mean it's really a line. "In between life and death is a state of near-death, or pseudo-life. And most people don't want what's in between."

If the heart of a brain-dead heart donor does contain something loftier than tissue and blood, some vestige of the spirit, then one could imagine that this vestige might travel along with the heart and set up housekeeping in the person who receives it. Oz once got a letter from a transplant patient who, shortly after receiving his new heart, began to experience what he could only imagine was some sort of contact with the consciousness of its previous owner. The patient, Michael "Med-O" Whitson, gave permission to quote the letter:

> I write all this with respect for the possibility that rather than some kind of contact with the consciousness of my donor's heart, these are merely hallucinations from the medications or my own projections. I know this is a very slippery slope. . . .
>
> What came to me in the first contact . . . was the horror of dying. The utter suddenness, shock, and surprise of it all. . . . The feeling of being ripped off and the dread of dying before your time. . . . This and two other incidents are by far the most terrifying experiences I have ever had. . . .
>   What came to me on the second occasion was my donor's experience of having his heart being cut out of his chest and transplanted. There was a profound sense of violation by a mysterious, omnipotent outside force. . . .
>   . . . The third episode was quite different than the previous two. This time the consciousness of my donor's heart was in the present tense. . . . He was struggling to figure out where he was, even what he was. . . . It was as if none of your senses worked. . . . An extremely frightening awareness of total dislocation. . . . As if you are reaching with your hands to grasp something . . . but every time you reach forward your fingers end up only clutching thin air.

Of course, one man named Med-O does not a scientific inquiry make. A step in that direction is a study carried out in 1991 by a team of Viennese surgeons and psychiatrists. They interviewed forty-seven heart transplant patients about whether they had noticed any changes in their personality that they thought were due to the influence of the new heart and its former owner.

40

Forty-four of the forty-seven said no, although the authors, in the Viennese psychoanalytic tradition, took pains to point out that many of these people responded to the question with hostility or jokes, which, in Freudian theory, would indicate some level of denial about the issue.

The experiences of the three patients who answered yes were decidedly more prosaic than were Whitson's. The first was a forty-five-year-old man who had received the heart of a seventeen-year-old boy and told the researchers, "I love to put on earphones and play loud music, something I never did before. A different car, a good stereo—those are my dreams now." The other two were less specific. One said simply that the person who had owned his heart had been a calm person and that these feelings of calm had been "passed on" to him; another felt that he was living two people's lives, replying to questions with "we" instead of "I," but offered no details about the newly acquired personality or what sort of music he enjoyed.

For juicy details, we must turn to Paul Pearsall, the author of a book called *The Heart's Code* (and another called *Super Marital Sex* and one called *Superimmunity*). Pearsall interviewed 140 heart transplant patients and presented quotes from five of them as evidence for the heart's "cellular memory" and its influence on recipients of donated hearts. There was the woman who got the heart of a gay robber who was shot in the back, and suddenly began dressing in a more feminine manner and getting "shooting pains" in her back. There was another rendition of the middle-aged man with a teenage male heart who now feels compelled to "crank up the stereo and play loud rock-and-roll music"—which I had quickly come to see as the urban myth of heart transplantation. My out-and-out favorite was the woman who got a prostitute's heart and suddenly began renting X-rated videos, demanding sex with her husband every night, and performing strip teases for him. Of course, if the woman knew that her new heart had come from a prostitute, this might have caused the changes in her behavior. Pearsall doesn't mention whether the woman knew of her donor's occupation (or, for that matter, whether he'd sent her a copy of *Super Marital Sex* before the interview).

Pearsall is not a doctor, or not, at least, one of the medical variety. He is a doctor of the variety that gets a Ph.D. and attaches it to his name on self-help book covers. I found his testimonials iffy as evidence of any sort of "cellular" memory, based as they are on crude and sometimes absurd stereotypes: that women become prostitutes because they want to have sex all day long, that gay men—gay robbers, no less—like to dress in feminine clothing. But bear in mind that I am, to quote item 13 of Pearsall's Heart Energy Amplitude Test, "cynical and distrusting of others' motives."

Mehmet Oz, the transplant surgeon I spoke with, also got curious about the phenomenon of heart transplant patients' claiming to experience memories belonging to their donors. "There was this one fellow," he told me, "who said, 'I know who gave me this heart.' He gave me a detailed description of a young black woman who died in a car accident. 'I see myself in the mirror with blood on my face and I taste French fries in my mouth. I see that I'm black and I was in this accident.' It spooked me," says Oz, "and so I went back and checked.

The donor was an elderly white male." Did he have other patients who claimed to experience their donor's memories or to know something specific about their donor's life? He did. "They're all wrong."

After I spoke to Oz, I tracked down three more articles on the psycholog- 45 ical consequences of having someone else's heart stitched into your chest. Fully half of all transplant patients, I found out, develop postoperative psychological problems of some sort. Rausch and Kneen described a man utterly terrified by the prospect of the transplant surgery, fearing that in giving up his heart he would lose his soul. Another paper presented the case of a patient who became convinced that he had been given a hen's heart. No mention was made of why he might have come to believe this or whether he had been exposed to the writings of Robert Whytt,[20] which actually might have provided some solace, pointing out, as they do, that a chicken heart can be made to beat on for several hours in the event of decapitation—always a plus.

The worry that one will take on traits of the heart donor is quite common, particularly when patients have received, or think that they have, a heart from a donor of a different gender or sexual orientation. According to a paper by James Tabler and Robert Frierson, recipients often wonder whether the donor "was promiscuous or oversexed, homosexual or bisexual, excessively masculine or feminine or afflicted with some sort of sexual dysfunction." They spoke to a man who fantasized that his donor had had a sexual "reputation" and said he had no choice but to live up to it. Rausch and Kneen describe a forty-two-year-old firefighter who worried that his new heart, which had belonged to a woman, would make him less masculine and that his firehouse buddies would no longer accept him. (A male heart, Oz says, is in fact slightly different from a female heart. A heart surgeon can tell one from the other by looking at the ECG, because the intervals are slightly different. When you put a female heart into a man, it will continue to beat like a female heart. And vice versa.)

From reading a paper by Kraft, it would seem that when men believe their new hearts came from another man, they often believe this man to have been a stud and that some measure of this studliness has somehow been imparted to them. Nurses on transplant wards often remark that male transplant patients show a renewed interest in sex. One reported that a patient asked her to wear "something other than that shapeless scrub so he could see her breasts." A post-op who had been impotent for seven years before the operation was found holding his penis and demonstrating an erection. Another nurse spoke of a man who left the fly of his pajamas unfastened to show her his penis. Conclude Tabler and Frierson, "This irrational but common belief that the recipient will somehow develop characteristics of the donor is generally transitory but may alter sexual patterns . . . ." Let us hope that the man with the chicken heart was blessed with a patient and open-minded spouse.

The harvesting of H is winding down. The last organs to be taken, the kidneys, are being brought up and separated from the depths of her open torso. Her

---

20. British doctor and medical professor (1714–1766).

thorax and abdomen are filled with crushed ice, turned red from blood. "Cherry Sno-Kone," I write in my notepad. It's been almost four hours now, and H has begun to look more like a conventional cadaver, her skin dried and dulled at the edges of the incision.

The kidneys are placed in a blue plastic bowl with ice and perfusion fluid.[21] A relief surgeon arrives for the final step of the recovery, cutting off pieces of veins and arteries to be included, like spare sweater buttons, along with the organs, in case the ones attached to them are too short to work with. A half hour later, the relief surgeon steps aside and the resident comes over to sew H up.

50   As he talks to Dr. Posselt about the stitching, the resident strokes the bank of fat along H's incision with his gloved hand, then pats it twice, as though comforting her. When he turns back to his work, I ask him if it feels different to be working on a dead patient.

"Oh, yes," he answers. "I mean, I would never use this kind of stitch." He has begun stitching more widely spaced, comparatively crude loops, rather than the tight, hidden stitches used on the living.

I rephrase the question: Does it feel odd to perform surgery on someone who isn't alive?

His answer is surprising. "The patient *was* alive." I suppose surgeons are used to thinking about patients—particularly ones they've never met—as no more than what they see of them: open plots of organs. And as far as that goes, I guess you could say H *was* alive. Because of the cloths covering all but her opened torso, the young man never saw her face, didn't know if she was male or female.

While the resident sews, a nurse picks stray danglies of skin and fat off the operating table with a pair of tongs and drops them inside the body cavity, as though H were a handy waste basket. The nurse explains that this is done intentionally: "Anything not donated stays with her." The jigsaw puzzle put back in its box.

55   The incision is complete, and a nurse washes H off and covers her with a blanket for the trip to the morgue. Out of habit or respect, he chooses a fresh one. The transplant coordinator, Von, and the nurse lift H onto a gurney. Von wheels H into an elevator and down a hallway to the morgue. The workers are behind a set of swinging doors, in a back room. "Can we leave this here?" Von shouts. H has become a "this." We are instructed to wheel the gurney into the cooler, where it joins five others. H appears no different from the corpses already here.[22]

21. Liquid pumped into organs, usually by way of blood vessels.

22. Unless H's family is planning a naked open-casket service, no one at her funeral will be able to tell she's had organs removed. Only with tissue harvesting, which often includes leg and arm bones, does the body take on a slightly altered profile, and in this case PVC piping or dowels are inserted to normalize the form and make life easier for mortuary staff and others who need to move the otherwise somewhat noodle-ized body [Roach's note]. PVC: short for polyvinyl chloride, a material now commonly used in plumbing parts.

But H *is* different. She has made three sick people well. She has brought them extra time on earth. To be able, as a dead person, to make a gift of this magnitude is phenomenal. Most people don't manage this sort of thing while they're alive. Cadavers like H are the dead's heroes.

It is astounding to me, and achingly sad, that with eighty thousand people on the waiting list for donated hearts and livers and kidneys, with sixteen a day dying there on that list, that more than half of the people in the position H's family was in will say no, will choose to burn those organs or let them rot. We abide the surgeon's scalpel to save our own lives, our loved ones' lives, but not to save a stranger's life. H has no heart, but heartless is the last thing you'd call her.

QUESTIONS

1. The title of Roach's book—*Stiff*—and the title of this excerpt—"How to Know If You're Dead"—suggest that the author has a sense of humor. Where does Roach use humor? Why? How does humor allow Roach to raise questions about death that serious or solemn approaches might not allow?

2. In the second section of this essay, Roach introduces historical anecdotes that focus on the desire to define death and "pinpoint the precise moment when the spirit . . . has ceased to exist" (paragraph 11). What is at stake in this attempt? What role does belief in the "spirit" or "soul" play in understanding death? Why is the moment of "death" so difficult to know?

3. In addition to engaging in historical research, Roach interviews living scientists, doctors, and patients to explore her subject. Locate three or four of these interviews, and explain what they add to our understanding of human life and death.

4. Read either Elisabeth Kübler-Ross's "On the Fear of Death" (in "Human Nature," p. 160) or Jessica Mitford's "Behind the Formaldehyde Curtain" (in "Cultural Critique," p. 186), and compare Roach's treatment of the body and death with either of theirs. What concerns do they share? What different focuses and concerns emerge from your comparison?

CULTURAL CRITIQUE

ANTHONY BURGESS *Is America Falling Apart?*

I AM BACK IN BRACCIANO, a castellated town about 13 miles north of Rome, after a year in New Jersey. I find the Italian Government still unstable, gasoline more expensive than anywhere in the world, butchers and bank clerks and tobacconists (which also means saltsellers) ready to go on strike at the drop of a *cappello*,[1] neo-Fascists at their dirty work, the hammer and sickle painted on the rumps of public statues, a thousand-lire note (officially worth about $1.63) shrunk to the slightness of a dollar bill.

Nevertheless, it's delightful to be back. People are underpaid but they go through an act of liking their work, the open markets are luscious with esculent color, the community is more important than the state, the human condition is humorously accepted. The *tramontana*[2] blows viciously today, and there's no central heating to turn on, but it will be pleasant when the wind drops. The two television channels are inadequate, but next Wednesday's rerun of an old Western, with Gary Cooper coming into a saloon saying "*Ciao, ragazzi,*"[3] is something to look forward to. Manifold consumption isn't important here. The quality of life has nothing to do with the quantity of brand names. What matters is talk, family, cheap wine in the open air, the wresting of minimal sweetness out of the long-known bitterness of living. I was spoiled in New Jersey. The Italian for *spoiled* is *viziato,* cognate with *vitiated,* which has to do with vice.

Spoiled? Well, yes. I never had to shiver by a fire that wouldn't draw, or go without canned kraut juice or wild rice. America made me develop new appetites in order to make proper use of the supermarket. A character in Evelyn Waugh's *Put Out More Flags* said that the difference between prewar and postwar life[4] was that, prewar, if one thing went wrong the day was ruined; postwar,

Written during 1970–71, when Burgess, an English novelist then famous for A Clockwork Orange, *was a visiting professor at Princeton University; published in the* New York Times *(November 7, 1971).*

1. Hat.
2. North wind.
3. "Howdy, boys."
4. Waugh published *Put Out More Flags* in 1942. "Prewar" refers to conditions before World War II.

if one thing went right the day would be made. America is a prewar country, psychologically unprepared for one thing to go wrong. Now everything seems to be going wrong. Hence the neurosis, despair, the Kafka feeling that the whole marvelous fabric of American life is coming apart at the seams. Italy is used to everything going wrong. This is what the human condition is about.

Let me stay for a while on this subject of consumption. American individualism, on the face of it an admirable philosophy, wishes to manifest itself in independence of the community. You don't share things in common; you have your own things. A family's strength is signalized by its possessions. Herein lies a paradox. For the desire for possessions must eventually mean dependence on possessions. Freedom is slavery. Once let the acquisitive instinct burgeon (enough flour for the winter, not just for the week), and there are ruggedly individual forces only too ready to make it come to full and monstrous blossom. New appetites are invented; what to the European are bizarre luxuries become, to the American, plain necessities.

During my year's stay in New Jersey I let my appetites flower into full Americanism except for one thing. I did not possess an automobile. This self-elected deprivation was a way into the nastier side of the consumer society. Where private ownership prevails, public amenities decay or are prevented from coming into being. The wretched run-down rail services of America are something I try, vainly, to forget. The nightmare of filth, outside and in, that enfolds the trip from Springfield, Mass., to Grand Central Station would not be accepted in backward Europe. But far worse is the nightmare of travel in and around Los Angeles, where public transport does not exist and people are literally choking to death in their exhaust fumes. This is part of the price of the metaphysic of individual ownership.

But if the car owner can ignore the lack of public transport, he can hardly ignore the decay of services in general. His car needs mechanics, and mechanics grow more expensive and less efficient. The gadgets in the home are cheaper to replace than repair. The more efficiently self-contained the home, primary fortress of independence, seems to be, the more dependent it is on the great impersonal corporations, as well as a diminishing army of servitors. Skills at the lowest level have to be wooed slavishly and exorbitantly rewarded. Plumbers will not come. Nor, at the higher level, will doctors. And doctors and dentists, in a nation committed to maiming itself with sugar and cholesterol, know their scarcity value and behave accordingly.

Americans are at last realizing that the acquisition of goods is not the whole of life. Consumption, on one level, is turning insipid, especially as the quality of the artifacts themselves seems to be deteriorating. Planned obsolescence is not conducive to pride in workmanship. On another level, consumption is turning sour. There is a growing guilt about the masses of discarded junk—rusting automobiles and refrigerators and washing machines and dehumidifiers—that it is uneconomical to recycle. Indestructible plastic hasn't even the grace to undergo chemical change. America, the world's biggest consumer, is the world's biggest polluter. Awareness of this is a kind of redemptive

5

grace, but it doesn't appreciably lead to repentance and a revolution in consumer habits. Citizens of Los Angeles are horrified by that daily pall of golden smog, but they don't noticeably clamor for a decrease in the number of owner-vehicles. There is no worse neurosis than that which derives from a consciousness of guilt and an inability to reform.

America is anachronistic in so many ways, and not least in its clinging to a belief—now known to be unviable—in the capacity of the individual citizen to do everything for himself. Americans are admirable in their distrust of the corporate state—they have fought both Fascism and Communism—but they forget that there is a use for everything, even the loathesome bureaucratic machine. America needs a measure of socialization, as Britain needed it. Things—especially those we need most—don't always pay their way, and it is here that the state must enter, dismissing the profit element. Part of the present American neurosis, again, springs from awareness of this but inability to do anything about practical implementation. Perhaps only a country full of bombed cities feels capable of this kind of social revolution.

It would be supererogatory for me to list those areas in which thoughtful Americans feel that collapse is coming. It is enough for me to concentrate on what, during my New Jersey stay, impinged on my own life. Education, for instance, since I have a 6-year-old son to be brought up. America has always despised its teachers and, as a consequence, it has been granted the teachers it deserves. The quality of first-grade education that my son received, in a New Jersey town noted for the excellence of its public schools, could not, I suppose, be faulted on the level of dogged conscientiousness. The principal had read all the right pedagogic books, and was ready to quote these in the footnotes to his circular exhortations to parents. The teachers worked rigidly from the approved rigidly programed primers, ensuring that school textbook publication remains the big business it is.

10   But there seemed to be no spark; no daring, no madness, no readiness to engage the individual child's mind as anything other than raw material for statistical reductions. The fear of being unorthodox is rooted in the American teacher's soul: you can be fired for treading the path of experimental enterprise. In England, teachers cannot be fired, except for raping girl students and getting boy students drunk. In consequence, there is the kind of security that breeds eccentric genius, the capacity for firing mad enthusiasms.

I know that American technical genius, and most of all the moon landings, seems to give the lie to too summary a condemnation of the educational system, but there is more to education than the segmental equipping of the mind. There is that transmission of the value of the past as a force still miraculously fertile and moving—mostly absent from American education at all levels.

Of course, America was built on a rejection of the past. Even the basic Christianity which was brought to the continent in 1620 was of a novel and bizarre kind that would have nothing to do with the great rank river of belief that produced Dante and Michelangelo. America as a nation has never been able to settle to a common belief more sophisticated than the dangerous naiveté of the Declaration of Independence. "Life, liberty and the pursuit of happiness," indeed. And now America, filling in the vacuum left by the liquefied British Empire, has the task of telling the rest of the world that there's something better than Communism. The something better can only be money-making and consumption for its own sake. In the name of this ghastly creed the jungles must be defoliated.[5]

No wonder the guilt of the thoughtful Americans I met in Princeton and New York and, indeed, all over the Union tended to express itself as an extravagant masochism, a desire for flagellation. Americans want to take on all the blame they can find, gluttons for punishment. "What do Europeans really think of us?" is a common question at parties. The expected answer is: "They think you're a load of decadent, gross-lipped, potbellied, callous, overbearing neoimperialists." Then the head can be bowed and the chest smitten: "*Nostra culpa, nostra maxima culpa. . . .*"[6] But the fact is that such an answer, however much desired, would not be an honest one. Europeans think more highly of Americans now than they ever did. Let me try to explain why.

When Europe, after millennia of war, rapine, slavery, famine, intolerance, had sunk to the level of a sewer, America became the golden dream, the Eden where innocence could be recovered. Original sin was the monopoly of that dirty continent over there; in America man could glow in an aura of natural goodness, driven along his shining path by divine reason. The Declaration of Independence itself is a monument to reason. Progress was possible, and the wrongs committed against the Indians, the wildlife, the land itself, could be explained away in terms of the rational control of environment necessary for the building of a New Jerusalem.[7] Right and wrong made up the moral dichotomy; evil—that great eternal inextirpable entity—had no place in America.

At last, with the Vietnam war and especially the Mylai horror,[8] Americans are beginning to realize that they are subject to original sin as much as Europeans are. Some things—the massive crime figures, for instance—can now be explained only in terms of absolute evil. Europe, which has long known about evil and learned to live with it (*live* is *evil* spelled backwards), is now grimly pleased to find that America is becoming like Europe. America is no longer Europe's daughter nor her rich stepmother: she is Europe's sister. The agony that America is undergoing is not to be associated with breakdown so much as with the parturition of self-knowledge.

15

5. That is, in order to deny the enemy protective cover—a part of American strategy during the Vietnam War.

6. "Through our fault, through our most grievous fault," a modification of *Mea culpa, mea maxima culpa* ("Through my fault . . ."), part of the act of confession in the Roman Catholic Church.

7. The holy city described by John in Revelation 21, here a figurative expression for a perfected society.

8. A massacre by American troops of more than three hundred Vietnamese civilians in the village of My Lai.

It has been assumed by many that the youth of America has been in the vanguard of the discovery of both the disease and the cure. The various copping-out movements, however, from the Beats on, have committed the gross error of assuming that original sin rested with their elders, their rulers, and that they themselves could manifest their essential innocence by building little neo-Edens. The drug culture could confirm that the paradisal vision was available to all who sought it. But instant ecstasy has to be purchased, like any other commodity, and, in economic terms, that passive life of pure being involves parasitism. Practically all of the crime I encountered in New York—directly or through report—was a preying of the opium-eaters on the working community. There has to be a snake in paradise. You can't escape the heritage of human evil by building communes, usually on an agronomic ignorance that, intended to be a rejection of inherited knowledge, that suspect property of the elders, does violence to life. The American young are well-meaning but misguided, and must not themselves be taken as guides.

The guides, as always, lie among the writers and artists. And Americans ought to note that, however things may seem to be falling apart, arts and the humane scholarship are flourishing here, as they are not, for instance, in England. I'm not suggesting that Bellow, Mailer, Roth[9] and the rest have the task of finding a solution to the American mess, but they can at least clarify its nature and show how it relates to the human condition in general. Literature, that most directly human of the arts, often reacts magnificently to an ambience of unease or apparent breakdown. The Elizabethans,[10] to whose era we look back as to an irrecoverable Golden Age, were far more conscious than modern Americans of the chaos and corruption and incompetence of the state. Shakespeare's period was one of poverty, unemployment, ghastly inflation, violence in the streets. Twenty-six years after his death there was a bloody civil war, followed by a dictatorship of religious fanatics, followed by a calm respite in which the seeds of a revolution were sown. England survived. America will survive.

I'm not suggesting that Americans sit back and wait for a transient period of mistrust and despair to resolve itself, like a disease, through the unconscious healing forces which lie deep in organic nature. Man, as Thornton Wilder showed in The Skin of Our Teeth,[11] always comes through—though sometimes only just. Americans living here and now have a right to an improvement in the quality of their lives, and they themselves, not the remote governors, must do something about it. It is not right that men and women should fear to go on the streets at night, and that they should sometimes fear the police as much as the criminals, both of whom sometimes look like mirror images of each other. I have had too much evidence, in my year in New Jersey, of the police behaving like the "Fascist pigs" of the revolutionary press. There

9. Saul Bellow (1915–2005), Norman Mailer (b. 1923), and Philip Roth (b. 1933)—all American writers.

10. The British during the reign of Elizabeth I, 1558–1603.

11. Pulitzer Prize–winning comedy, written in 1942 by Thornton Wilder (1897–1975).

are too many guns about, and the disarming of the police should be a natural aspect of the disarming of the entire citizenry.

American politics, at both the state and the Federal levels, is too much concerned with the protection of large fortunes, America being the only example in history of a genuine timocracy.[12] The wealth qualification for the aspiring politician is taken for granted; a governmental system dedicated to the promotion of personal wealth in a few selected areas will never act for the public good. The time has come, nevertheless, for citizens to demand, from their government, a measure of socialization—the provision of amenities for the many, of which adequate state pensions and sickness benefits, as well as nationalized transport, should be priorities.

As for those remoter solutions to the American nightmare—only an aspect, after all, of the human nightmare—an Englishman must be diffident about suggesting that America made her biggest mistake in becoming America—meaning a revolutionary republic based on a romantic view of human nature. To reject a limited monarchy in favor of an absolute one (which is, after all, what the American Presidency is) argues a trust in the disinterestedness of an elected ruler which is, of course, no more than a reflection of belief in the innate goodness of man—so long as he happens to be American man. The American Constitution is out of date. Republics tend to corruption. Canada and Australia have their own problems, but they are happier countries than America.

This *Angst*[13] about America coming apart at the seams, which apparently is shared by nearly 50 per cent of the entire American population, is something to rejoice about. A sense of sin is always admirable, though it must not be allowed to become neurotic. If electric systems break down and gadgets disintegrate, it doesn't matter much. There is always wine to be drunk by candlelight, uniced. If America's position as a world power collapses, and the Union dissolves into independent states, there is still the life of the family or the individual to be lived. England has survived her own dissolution as an imperial power, and Englishmen seem to be happy enough. But I ask the reader to note that I, an Englishman, no longer live in England, and I can't spend more than six months at a stretch in Italy—or any other European country, for that matter. I come to America as to a country more stimulating than depressing. The future of mankind is being worked out there on a scale typically American— vast, dramatic, almost apocalyptical. I brave the brutality and the guilt in order to be in on the scene. I shall be back.

12. A state in which power depends on wealth.
13. Anxiety.

QUESTIONS

1. This essay appeared in 1971. What might Burgess leave out, add, or modify if he were to write it today?

2. Burgess says that in his son's school there was "no readiness to engage the individual child's mind as anything other than raw material for statistical reductions" (paragraph 10). Precisely what is he referring to? Does your own experience support or counter Burgess's claim?

3. Visitors like Burgess can sometimes see things natives miss; they can also overlook the obvious. Write a response to Burgess, pointing out where he is on target and what he has missed.

JESSICA MITFORD *Behind the Formaldehyde Curtain*

THE DRAMA BEGINS to unfold with the arrival of the corpse at the mortuary.

Alas, poor Yorick![1] How surprised he would be to see how his counterpart of today is whisked off to a funeral parlor and is in short order sprayed, sliced, pierced, pickled, trussed, trimmed, creamed, waxed, painted, rouged and neatly dressed—transformed from a common corpse into a Beautiful Memory Picture. This process is known in the trade as embalming and restorative art, and is so universally employed in the United States and Canada that the funeral director does it routinely, without consulting corpse or kin. He regards as eccentric those few who are hardy enough to suggest that it might be dispensed with. Yet no law requires embalming, no religious doctrine commends it, nor is it dictated by considerations of health, sanitation, or even of personal daintiness. In no part of the world but in Northern America is it widely used. The purpose of embalming is to make the corpse presentable for viewing in a suitably costly container; and here too the funeral director routinely, without first consulting the family, prepares the body for public display.

Is all this legal? The processes to which a dead body may be subjected are after all to some extent circumscribed by law. In most states, for instance, the signature of next of kin must be obtained before an autopsy may be performed, before the deceased may be cremated, before the body may be turned over to a medical school for research purposes; or such provision must be made in the decedent's will. In the case of embalming, no such permission is required nor is it ever sought. A textbook, *The Principles and Practices of Embalming*, comments on this: "There is some question regarding the legality of much that is done within the preparation room." The author points out that it would be

From The American Way of Death *(1963), an exposé of the funeral industry, which was revised and updated by Mitford just before her death in 1996 as* The American Way of Death Revisited *(1998).*

1. Hamlet says this (V.i.184) upon seeing the skull of the court clown he had known as a child.

most unusual for a responsible member of a bereaved family to instruct the mortician, in so many words, to "embalm" the body of a deceased relative. The very term "embalming" is so seldom used that the mortician must rely upon custom in the matter. The author concludes that unless the family specifies otherwise, the act of entrusting the body to the care of a funeral establishment carries with it an implied permission to go ahead and embalm.

Embalming is indeed a most extraordinary procedure, and one must wonder at the docility of Americans who each year pay hundreds of millions of dollars for its perpetuation, blissfully ignorant of what it is all about, what is done, how it is done. Not one in ten thousand has any idea of what actually takes place. Books on the subject are extremely hard to come by. They are not to be found in most libraries or bookshops.

In an era when huge television audiences watch surgical operations in the comfort of their living rooms, when, thanks to the animated cartoon, the geography of the digestive system has become familiar territory even to the nursery school set, in a land where the satisfaction of curiosity about almost all matters is a national pastime, the secrecy surrounding embalming can, surely, hardly be attributed to the inherent gruesomeness of the subject. Custom in this regard has within this century suffered a complete reversal. In the early days of American embalming, when it was performed in the home of the deceased, it was almost mandatory for some relative to stay by the embalmer's side and witness the procedure. Today, family members who might wish to be in attendance would certainly be dissuaded by the funeral director. All others, except apprentices, are excluded by law from the preparation room.

A close look at what does actually take place may explain in large measure the undertaker's intractable reticence concerning a procedure that has become his major *raison d'être*.[2] Is it possible he fears that public information about embalming might lead patrons to wonder if they really want this service? If the funeral men are loath to discuss the subject outside the trade, the reader may, understandably, be equally loath to go on reading at this point. For those who have the stomach for it, let us part the formaldehyde curtain. . . .

The body is first laid out in the undertaker's morgue—or rather, Mr. Jones is reposing in the preparation room—to be readied to bid the world farewell.

The preparation room in any of the better funeral establishments has the tiled and sterile look of a surgery, and indeed the embalmer-restorative artist who does his chores there is beginning to adopt the term "dermasurgeon" (appropriately corrupted by some mortician-writers as "demi-surgeon") to describe his calling. His equipment, consisting of scalpels, scissors, augers, forceps, clamps, needles, pumps, tubes, bowls and basins, is crudely imitative of the surgeon's, as is his technique, acquired in a nine- or twelve-month post-high-school course in an embalming school. He is supplied by an advanced chemical industry with a bewildering array of fluids, sprays, pastes, oils, powders, creams, to fix or soften tissue, shrink or distend it as needed, dry it here, restore the moisture there. There are cosmetics, waxes and paints to fill and

2. Reason for being.

cover features, even plaster of Paris to replace entire limbs. There are ingenious aids to prop and stabilize the cadaver: a Vari-Pose Head Rest, the Edwards Arm and Hand Positioner, the Repose Block (to support the shoulders
during the embalming), and the Throop Foot Positioner, which resembles an
old-fashioned stocks.

Mr. John H. Eckels, president of the Eckels College of Mortuary Science,
thus describes the first part of the embalming procedure: "In the hands of
a skilled practitioner, this work may be done in a comparatively short time and
without mutilating the body other than by slight incision—so slight that it
scarcely would cause serious inconvenience if made upon a living person. It is necessary to remove the blood, and doing this not only helps in
the disinfecting, but removes the principal cause of disfigurements due to
discoloration."

10   Another textbook discusses the all-important time element: "The earlier
this is done, the better, for every hour that elapses between death and embalming will add to the problems and complications encountered. . . ." Just
how soon should one get going on the embalming? The author tells us, "On
the basis of such scanty information made available to this profession through
its rudimentary and haphazard system of technical research, we must conclude that the best results are to be obtained if the subject is embalmed before
life is completely extinct—that is, before cellular death has occurred. In the
average case, this would mean within an hour after somatic death." For those
who feel that there is something a little rudimentary, not to say haphazard,
about this advice, a comforting thought is offered by another writer. Speaking
of fears entertained in early days of premature burial, he points out, "One of
the effects of embalming by chemical injection, however, has been to dispel
fears of live burial." How true; once the blood is removed, chances of live burial are indeed remote.

To return to Mr. Jones, the blood is drained out through the veins and replaced by embalming fluid pumped in through the arteries. As noted in *The
Principles and Practices of Embalming*, "every operator has a favorite injection
and drainage point—a fact which becomes a handicap only if he fails or refuses to forsake his favorites when conditions demand it." Typical favorites are
the carotid artery, femoral artery, jugular vein, subclavian vein. There are various choices of embalming fluid. If Flextone is used, it will produce a "mild,
flexible rigidity. The skin retains a velvety softness, the tissues are rubbery and
pliable. Ideal for women and children." It may be blended with B. and G.
Products Company's Lyf-Lyk tint, which is guaranteed to reproduce "nature's
own skin texture . . . the velvety appearance of living tissue." Suntone comes
in three separate tints: Suntan; Special Cosmetic Tint, a pink shade "especially indicated for young female subjects"; and Regular Cosmetic Tint, mod-
erately pink.

About three to six gallons of a dyed and perfumed solution of formaldehyde, glycerin, borax, phenol, alcohol and water is soon circulating through
Mr. Jones, whose mouth has been sewn together with a "needle directed upward between the upper lip and gum and brought out through the left nostril,"

with the corners raised slightly "for a more pleasant expression." If he should be bucktoothed, his teeth are cleaned with Bon Ami and coated with colorless nail polish. His eyes, meanwhile, are closed with flesh-tinted eye caps and eye cement.

The next step is to have at Mr. Jones with a thing called a trocar. This is a long, hollow needle attached to a tube. It is jabbed into the abdomen, poked around the entrails and chest cavity, the contents of which are pumped out and replaced with "cavity fluid." This done, and the hole in the abdomen sewn up, Mr. Jones's face is heavily creamed (to protect the skin from burns which may be caused by leakage of the chemicals), and he is covered with a sheet and left unmolested for a while. But not for long—there is more, much more, in store for him. He has been embalmed, but not yet restored, and the best time to start the restorative work is eight to ten hours after embalming, when the tissues have become firm and dry.

The object of all this attention to the corpse, it must be remembered, is to make it presentable for viewing in an attitude of healthy repose. "Our customs require the presentation of our dead in the semblance of normality . . . unmarred by the ravages of illness, disease or mutilation," says Mr. J. Sheridan Mayer in his *Restorative Art*. This is rather a large order since few people die in the full bloom of health, unravaged by illness and unmarked by some disfigurement. The funeral industry is equal to the challenge: "In some cases the gruesome appearance of a mutilated or disease-ridden subject may be quite discouraging. The task of restoration may seem impossible and shake the confidence of the embalmer. This is the time for intestinal fortitude and determination. Once the formative work is begun and affected tissues are cleaned or removed, all doubts of success vanish. It is surprising and gratifying to discover the results which may be obtained."

The embalmer, having allowed an appropriate interval to elapse, returns to the attack, but now he brings into play the skill and equipment of sculptor and cosmetician. Is a hand missing? Casting one in plaster of Paris is a simple matter. "For replacement purposes, only a cast of the back of the hand is necessary; this is within the ability of the average operator and is quite adequate." If a lip or two, a nose or an ear should be missing, the embalmer has at hand a variety of restorative waxes with which to model replacements. Pores and skin texture are simulated by stippling with a little brush, and over this cosmetics are laid on. Head off? Decapitation cases are rather routinely handled. Ragged edges are trimmed, and head joined to torso with a series of splints, wires and sutures. It is a good idea to have a little something at the neck—a scarf or a high collar—when time for viewing comes. Swollen mouth? Cut out tissue as needed from inside the lips. If too much is removed, the surface contour can easily be restored by padding with cotton. Swollen necks and cheeks are reduced by removing tissue through vertical incisions made down each side of the neck. "When the deceased is casketed, the pillow will hide the suture incisions . . . as an extra precaution against leakage, the suture may be painted with liquid sealer."

The opposite condition is more likely to present itself—that of emaciation. His hypodermic syringe now loaded with massage cream, the embalmer seeks out and fills the hollowed and sunken areas by injection. In this procedure the backs of the hands and fingers and the under-chin area should not be neglected.

Positioning the lips is a problem that recurrently challenges the ingenuity of the embalmer. Closed too tightly, they tend to give a stern, even disapproving expression. Ideally, embalmers feel, the lips should give the impression of being ever so slightly parted, the upper lip protruding slightly for a more youthful appearance. This takes some engineering, however, as the lips tend to drift apart. Lip drift can sometimes be remedied by pushing one or two straight pins through the inner margin of the lower lip and then inserting them between the two front upper teeth. If Mr. Jones happens to have no teeth, the pins can just as easily be anchored in his Armstrong Face Former and Denture Replacer. Another method to maintain lip closure is to dislocate the lower jaw, which is then held in its new position by a wire run through holes which have been drilled through the upper and lower jaws at the midline. As the French are fond of saying, *il faut souffrir pour être belle*.[3]

If Mr. Jones has died of jaundice, the embalming fluid will very likely turn him green. Does this deter the embalmer? Not if he has intestinal fortitude. Masking pastes and cosmetics are heavily laid on, burial garments and casket interiors are color-correlated with particular care, and Jones is displayed beneath rose-colored lights. Friends will say "How *well* he looks." Death by carbon monoxide, on the other hand, can be rather a good thing from the embalmer's viewpoint: "One advantage is the fact that this type of discoloration is an exaggerated form of a natural pink coloration." This is nice because the healthy glow is already present and needs but little attention.

The patching and filling completed, Mr. Jones is now shaved, washed and dressed. Cream-based cosmetic, available in pink, flesh, suntan, brunette and blond, is applied to his hands and face, his hair is shampooed and combed (and, in the case of Mrs. Jones, set), his hands manicured. For the horny-handed son of toil special care must be taken; cream should be applied to remove ingrained grime, and the nails cleaned. "If he were not in the habit of having them manicured in life, trimming and shaping is advised for better appearance—never questioned by kin."

20   Jones is now ready for casketing (this is the present participle of the verb "to casket"). In this operation his right shoulder should be depressed slightly "to turn the body a bit to the right and soften the appearance of lying flat on the back." Positioning the hands is a matter of importance, and special rubber positioning blocks may be used. The hands should be cupped slightly for a more lifelike, relaxed appearance. Proper placement of the body requires a delicate sense of balance. It should lie as high as possible in the casket, yet not so high that the lid, when lowered, will hit the nose. On the other hand, we are cautioned, placing the body too low "creates the impression that the body is in a box."

---

3. It is necessary to suffer to be beautiful.

Jones is next wheeled into the appointed slumber room where a few last touches may be added—his favorite pipe placed in his hand or, if he was a great reader, a book propped into position. (In the case of little Master Jones a Teddy bear may be clutched.) Here he will hold open house for a few days, visiting hours 10 A.M. to 9 P.M.

All now being in readiness, the funeral director calls a staff conference to make sure that each assistant knows his precise duties. Mr. Wilber Kriege writes: "This makes your staff feel that they are a part of the team, with a definite assignment that must be properly carried out if the whole plan is to succeed. You never heard of a football coach who failed to talk to his entire team before they go on the field. They have drilled on the plays they are to execute for hours and days, and yet the successful coach knows the importance of making even the bench-warming third-string substitute feel that he is important if the game is to be won." The winning of *this* game is predicated upon glass-smooth handling of the logistics. The funeral director has notified the pallbearers whose names were furnished by the family, has arranged for the presence of clergyman, organist, and soloist, has provided transportation for everybody, has organized and listed the flowers sent by friends. In *Psychology of Funeral Service* Mr. Edward A. Martin points out: "He may not always do as much as the family thinks he is doing, but it is his helpful guidance that they appreciate in knowing they are proceeding as they should. . . . The important thing is how well his services can be used to make the family believe they are giving unlimited expression to their own sentiment."

The religious service may be held in a church or in the chapel of the funeral home; the funeral director vastly prefers the latter arrangement, for not only is it more convenient for him but it affords him the opportunity to show off his beautiful facilities to the gathered mourners. After the clergyman has had his say, the mourners queue up to file past the casket for a last look at the deceased. The family is *never* asked whether they want an open-casket ceremony; in the absence of their instruction to the contrary, this is taken for granted. Consequently well over 90 per cent of all American funerals feature the open casket—a custom unknown in other parts of the world. Foreigners are astonished by it. An English woman living in San Francisco described her reaction in a letter to the writer:

> I myself have attended only one funeral here—that of an elderly fellow worker of mine. After the service I could not understand why everyone was walking towards the coffin (sorry, I mean casket), but thought I had better follow the crowd. It shook me rigid to get there and find the casket open and poor old Oscar lying there in his brown tweed suit, wearing a suntan makeup and just the wrong shade of lipstick. If I had not been extremely fond of the old boy, I have a horrible feeling that I might have giggled. Then and there I decided that I could never face another American funeral—even dead.

The casket (which has been resting throughout the service on a Classic Beauty Ultra Metal Casket Bier) is now transferred by a hydraulically operated device called Porto-Lift to a balloon-tired, Glide Easy casket carriage which will wheel it to yet another conveyance, the Cadillac Funeral Coach. This may be lavender, cream, light green—anything but black. Interiors, of course, are color-correlated, "for the man who cannot stop short of perfection."

25   At graveside, the casket is lowered into the earth. This office, once the prerogative of friends of the deceased, is now performed by a patented mechanical lowering device. A "Lifetime Green" artificial grass mat is at the ready to conceal the sere earth, and overhead, to conceal the sky, is a portable Steril Chapel Tent ("resists the intense heat and humidity of summer and the terrific storms of winter . . . available in Silver Grey, Rose or Evergreen"). Now is the time for the ritual scattering of earth over the coffin, as the solemn words "earth to earth, ashes to ashes, dust to dust" are pronounced by the officiating cleric. This can today be accomplished "with a mere flick of the wrist with the Gordon Leak-Proof Earth Dispenser. No grasping of a handful of dirt, no soiled fingers. Simple, dignified, beautiful, reverent! The modern way!" The Gordon Earth Dispenser (at $5) is of nickel-plated brass construction. It is not only "attractive to the eye and long wearing"; it is also "one of the 'tools' for building better public relations" if presented as "an appropriate non-commercial gift" to the clergyman. It is shaped something like a salt-shaker.

Untouched by human hand, the coffin and the earth are now united.

It is in the function of directing the participants through this maze of gadgetry that the funeral director has assigned to himself his relatively new role of "grief therapist." He has relieved the family of every detail, he has revamped the corpse to look like a living doll, he has arranged for it to nap for a few days in a slumber room, he has put on a well-oiled performance in which the concept of *death* has played no part whatsoever—unless it was inconsiderately mentioned by the clergyman who conducted the religious service. He has done everything in his power to make the funeral a real pleasure for everybody concerned. He and his team have given their all to score an upset victory over death.

QUESTIONS

1. Mitford's description might be called a "process essay"—that is, it describes the process by which a corpse becomes a "Beautiful Memory Picture." What are the stages of the process? Mark them in the margins of the essay, and think about how Mitford treats each one.

2. Mitford objects to the American funeral industry and its manipulation of death, yet she never directly says so. How do we as readers know her attitude? Cite words, phrases, or sentences that reveal her position.

3. Describe a process that you object to, letting your choice of words reveal your attitude.

JOHN MCMURTRY   *Kill 'Em! Crush 'Em! Eat 'Em Raw!*

A FEW MONTHS AGO my neck got a hard crick in it. I couldn't turn my head; to look left or right I'd have to turn my whole body. But I'd had cricks in my neck since I started playing grade-school football and hockey, so I just ignored it. Then I began to notice that when I reached for any sort of large book (which I do pretty often as a philosophy teacher at the University of Guelph) I had trouble lifting it with one hand. I was losing the strength in my left arm, and I had such a steady pain in my back I often had to stretch out on the floor of the room I was in to relieve the pressure.

A few weeks later I mentioned to my brother, an orthopedic surgeon, that I'd lost the power in my arm since my neck began to hurt. Twenty-four hours later I was in a Toronto hospital not sure whether I might end up with a wasted upper limb. Apparently the steady pounding I had received playing college and professional football in the late Fifties and early Sixties had driven my head into my backbone so that the discs had crumpled together at the neck—"acute herniation"—and had cut the nerves to my left arm like a pinched telephone wire (without nerve stimulation, of course, the muscles atrophy, leaving the arm crippled). So I spent my Christmas holidays in the hospital in heavy traction and much of the next three months with my neck in a brace. Today most of the pain has gone, and I've recovered most of the strength in my arm. But from time to time I still have to don the brace, and surgery remains a possibility.

Not much of this will surprise anyone who knows football. It is a sport in which body wreckage is one of the leading conventions. A few days after I went into hospital for that crick in my neck, another brother, an outstanding football player in college, was undergoing spinal surgery in the same hospital two floors above me. In his case it was a lower, more massive herniation, which every now and again buckled him so that he was unable to lift himself off his back for days at a time. By the time he entered the hospital for surgery he had already spent several months in bed. The operation was successful, but, as in all such cases, it will take him a year to recover fully.

These aren't isolated experiences. Just about anybody who has ever played football for any length of time, in high school, college or one of the professional leagues, has suffered for it later physically.

Indeed, it is arguable that body shattering is the very *point* of football, as killing and maiming are of war. (In the United States, for example, the game results in 15 to 20 deaths a year and about 50,000 major operations on knees alone.) To grasp some of the more conspicuous similarities between football and war, it is instructive to listen to the imperatives most frequently issued to the players by their coaches, teammates and fans. "Hurt 'em!" "Level 'em!"

5

Originally published in Maclean's *(October 1971), one of Canada's most prominent weekly magazines.*

"Kill 'em!" "Take 'em apart!" Or watch for the plays that are most enthusiastically applauded by the fans. Where someone is "smeared," "knocked silly,"
"creamed," "nailed," "broken in two," or even "crucified." (One of my coaches
when I played corner linebacker with the Calgary Stampeders in 1961 elaborated, often very inventively, on this language of destruction: admonishing us
to "unjoin" the opponent, "make 'im remember you" and "stomp 'im like a
bug.") Just as in hockey, where a fight will bring fans to their feet more often
than a skillful play, so in football the mouth waters most of all for the really
crippling block or tackle. For the kill. Thus the good teams are "hungry," the
best players are "mean," and "casualties" are as much a part of the game as
they are of a war.

The family resemblance between football and war is, indeed, striking.
Their languages are similar: "field general," "long bomb," "blitz," "take a shot,"
"front line," "pursuit," "good hit," "the draft" and so on. Their principles and
practices are alike: mass hysteria, the art of intimidation, absolute command
and total obedience, territorial aggression, censorship, inflated insignia and
propaganda, blackboard maneuvers and strategies, drills, uniforms, formations, marching bands and training camps. And the virtues they celebrate are
almost identical: hyper-aggressiveness, coolness under fire and suicidal brav-
ery. All this has been implicitly recognized by such jock-loving Americans as
media stars General Patton and President Nixon, who have talked about war
as a football game. Patton wanted to make his Second World War tank men
look like football players. And Nixon, as we know, was fond of comparing attacks on Vietnam to football plays and drawing coachly diagrams on a blackboard for TV war fans.

One difference between war and football, though, is that there is little or
no protest against football. Perhaps the most extraordinary thing about the
game is that the systematic infliction of injuries excites in people not concern,
as would be the case if they were sustained at, say, a rock festival, but a collective rejoicing and euphoria. Players and fans alike revel in the spectacle of a
combatant felled into semiconsciousness, "blindsided," "clotheslined" or "decapitated." I can remember, in fact, being chided by a coach in pro ball for not
"getting my hat" injuriously into a player who was already lying helpless on the
ground. (On another occasion, after the Stampeders had traded the celebrated
Joe Kapp to BC, we were playing the Lions in Vancouver and Kapp was forced
on one play to run with the ball. He was coming "down the chute," his bad
knee wobbling uncertainly, so I simply dropped on him like a blanket. After I
returned to the bench I was reproved for not exploiting the opportunity to un-
hinge his bad knee.)

After every game, of course, the papers are full of reports on the day's injuries, a sort of post-battle "body count," and the respective teams go to work
with doctors and trainers, tape, whirlpool baths, cortisone and morphine to
patch and deaden the wounds before the next game. Then the whole drama is
reenacted—injured athletes held together by adhesive, braces and drugs—and
the days following it are filled with even more feverish activity to put on the
show yet again at the end of the next week. (I remember being so taped up in

college that I earned the nickname "mummy.") The team that survives this
merry-go-round spectacle of skilled masochism with the fewest incapacitating
injuries usually wins. It is a sort of victory by ordeal: "We hurt them more than
they hurt us."

My own initiation into this brutal circus was typical. I loved the game
from the moment I could run with a ball. Played shoeless on a green open
field with no one keeping score and in a spirit of reckless abandon and laughter, it's a very different sport. Almost no one gets hurt and it's rugged, open and
exciting (it still is for me). But then, like everything else, it starts to be regu-
lated and institutionalized by adult authorities. And the fun is over.

So it was as I began the long march through organized football. Now   10
there was a coach and elders to make it clear by their behavior that beating
other people was the only thing to celebrate and that trying to shake someone
up every play was the only thing to be really proud of. Now there were severe
rule enforcers, audiences, formally recorded victors and losers, and heavy
equipment to permit crippling bodily moves and collisions (according to one
American survey, more than 80% of all football injuries occur to fully equipped
players). And now there was the official "given" that the only way to keep playing was to wear suffocating armor, to play to defeat, to follow orders silently
and to renounce spontaneity for joyless drill. The game had been, in short, ruined. But because I loved to play and play skillfully, I stayed. And progressively
and inexorably, as I moved through high school, college and pro leagues, my
body was dismantled. Piece by piece.

I started off with torn ligaments in my knee at 13. Then, as the organization and the competition increased, the injuries came faster and harder. Broken nose (three times), broken jaw (fractured in the first half and dismissed
as a "bad wisdom tooth," so I played with it for the rest of the game), ripped
knee ligaments again. Torn ligaments in one ankle and a fracture in the other
(which I remember feeling relieved about because it meant I could honorably
stop drill-blocking a 270-pound defensive end). Repeated rib fractures and
cartilage tears (usually carried, again, through the remainder of the game).
More dislocations of the left shoulder than I can remember (the last one I
played with because, as the Calgary Stampeder doctor said, it "couldn't be
damaged any more"). Occasional broken or dislocated fingers and toes.
Chronically hurt lower back (I still can't lift with it or change a tire without
worrying about folding). Separated right shoulder (as with many other injuries, like badly bruised hips and legs, needled with morphine for the
games). And so on. The last pro game I played—against Winnipeg Blue
Bombers in the Western finals in 1961—I had a recently dislocated left
shoulder, a more recently wrenched right shoulder and a chronic pain center
in one leg. I was so tied up with soreness I couldn't drive my car to the airport. But it never occurred to me or anyone else that I miss a play as a corner
linebacker.

By the end of my football career, I had learned that physical injury—
giving it and taking it—is the real currency of the sport. And that in the final
analysis the "winner" is the man who can hit to kill even if only half his limbs

are working. In brief, a warrior game with a warrior ethos into which (like almost everyone else I played with) my original boyish enthusiasm had been relentlessly taunted and conditioned.

In thinking back on how all this happened, though, I can pick out no villains. As with the social system as a whole, the game has a life of its own. Everyone grows up inside it, accepts it and fulfills its dictates as obediently as helots. Far from ever questioning the principles of the activity, people simply concentrate on executing these principles more aggressively than anybody around them. The result is a group of people who, as the leagues become of a higher and higher class, are progressively insensitive to the possibility that things could be otherwise. Thus, in football, anyone who might question the wisdom or enjoyment of putting on heavy equipment on a hot day and running full speed at someone else with the intention of knocking him senseless would be regarded simply as not really a devoted athlete and probably "chicken." The choice is made straightforward. Either you, too, do your very utmost to efficiently smash and be smashed, or you admit incompetence or cowardice and quit. Since neither of these admissions is very pleasant, people generally keep any doubts they have to themselves and carry on.

Of course, it would be a mistake to suppose that there is more blind acceptance of brutal practices in organized football than elsewhere. On the contrary, a recent Harvard study has approvingly argued that football's characteristics of "impersonal acceptance of inflicted injury," an overriding "organization goal," the "ability to turn oneself on and off" and being, above all, "out to win" are of "inestimable value" to big corporations. Clearly, our sort of football is no sicker than the rest of our society. Even its organized destruction of physical well-being is not anomalous. A very large part of our wealth, work and time is, after all, spent in systematically destroying and harming human life. Manufacturing, selling and using weapons that tear opponents to pieces. Making ever bigger and faster predator-named cars with which to kill and injure one another by the million every year. And devoting our very lives to outgunning one another for power in an ever more destructive rat race. Yet all these practices are accepted without question by most people, even zealously defended and honored. Competitive, organized injuring is integral to our way of life, and football is simply one of the more intelligible mirrors of the whole process: a sort of colorful morality play showing us how exciting and rewarding it is to Smash Thy Neighbor.

15   Now it is fashionable to rationalize our collaboration in all this by arguing that, well, man *likes* to fight and injure his fellows and such games as football should be encouraged to discharge this original-sin urge into less harmful channels than, say, war. Public-show football, this line goes, plays the same sort of cathartic role as Aristotle said stage tragedy does: without real blood (or not much), it releases players and audience from unhealthy feelings stored up inside them.

As an ex-player in the seasonal coast-to-coast drama, I see little to recommend such a view. What organized football did to me was make me *suppress* my natural urges and re-express them in an alienating, vicious form. Spontaneous desires for free bodily exuberance and fraternization with competitors were shamed and forced under ("If it ain't hurtin' it ain't helpin' ") and in their place were demanded armored mechanical moves and cool hatred of all opposition. Endless authoritarian drill and dressing-room harangues (ever wonder why competing teams can't prepare for a game in the same dressing room?) were the kinds of mechanisms employed to reconstruct joyful energies into mean and alien shapes. I am quite certain that everyone else around me was being similarly forced into this heavily equipped military precision and angry antagonism, because there was always a mutinous attitude about full-dress practices, and everybody (the pros included) had to concentrate incredibly hard for days to whip themselves into just one hour's hostility a week against another club. The players never speak of these things, of course, because everyone is so anxious to appear tough.

The claim that men like seriously to battle one another to some sort of finish is a myth. It only endures because it wears one of the oldest and most propagandized of masks—the romantic combatant. I sometimes wonder whether the violence all around us doesn't depend for its survival on the existence and preservation of this tough-guy disguise.

As for the effect of organized football on the spectator, the fan is not released from supposed feelings of violent aggression by watching his athletic heroes perform it so much as encouraged in the view that people-smashing is an admirable mode of self-expression. The most savage attackers, after all, are, by general agreement, the most efficient and worthy players of all (the biggest applause I ever received as a football player occurred when I ran over people or slammed them so hard they couldn't get up). Such circumstances can hardly be said to lessen the spectators' martial tendencies. Indeed it seems likely that the whole show just further develops and titillates the North American addiction for violent self-assertion. . . . Perhaps, as well, it helps explain why the greater the zeal of U.S. political leaders as football fans (Johnson, Nixon, Agnew), the more enthusiastic the commitment to hard-line politics. At any rate there seems to be a strong correlation between people who relish tough football and people who relish intimidating and beating the hell out of commies, hippies, protest marchers and other opposition groups.

Watching well-advertised strong men knock other people round, make them hurt, is in the end like other tastes. It does not weaken with feeding and variation in form. It grows.

I got out of football in 1962. I had asked to be traded after Calgary had offered me a $25-a-week-plus-commissions off-season job as a clothing-store salesman. ("Dear Mr. Finks:" I wrote. [Jim Finks was then the Stampeders' general manager.] "Somehow I do not think the dialectical subtleties of Hegel, Marx and Plato would be suitably oriented amidst the environmental stimuli of jockey shorts and herringbone suits. I hope you make a profitable sale or trade of my contract to the East.") So the Stampeders traded me to Montreal. In a preseason intersquad game with the Alouettes I ripped the cartilages in my ribs on the hardest block I'd ever thrown. I had trouble breathing and I had to shuffle-walk with my torso on a tilt. The doctor in the local hospital said three weeks rest, the coach said scrimmage in two days. Three days later I was back home reading philosophy.

QUESTIONS

1. What similarities does McMurtry see between football and war? How persuasive do you find the linkage?

2. Is McMurtry's essay mainly about his personal experiences in football, or is it about some larger point, with his experiences used as examples?

3. Draw connections between "real life" and some kind of game or play familiar to you. Does this illuminate any social arrangements or help you to see them in a new light? How far can one generalize?

MOLLY IVINS   *Get a Knife, Get a Dog,*
                 but Get Rid of Guns

G UNS. Everywhere guns.

Let me start this discussion by pointing out that I am not antigun. I'm proknife. Consider the merits of the knife.

In the first place, you have to catch up with someone in order to stab him. A general substitution of knives for guns would promote physical fitness. We'd turn into a whole nation of great runners. Plus, knives don't ricochet. And people are seldom killed while cleaning their knives.

As a civil libertarian, I, of course, support the Second Amendment. And I believe it means exactly what it says:

5   *A well-regulated militia being necessary to the security of a free state, the right of the people to keep and bear arms shall not be infringed.* Fourteen-year-old boys are not part of a well-regulated militia. Members of wacky religious cults are not part of a well-regulated militia. Permitting unregulated citizens to have guns is destroying the security of this free state.

I am intrigued by the arguments of those who claim to follow the judicial doctrine of original intent. How do they know it was the dearest wish of Thomas Jefferson's heart that teenage drug dealers should cruise the cities of this nation perforating their fellow citizens with assault rifles? Channeling?

There is more hooey spread about the Second Amendment. It says quite clearly that guns are for those who form part of a well-regulated militia, that is, the armed forces, including the National Guard. The reasons for keeping them away from everyone else get clearer by the day.

The comparison most often used is that of the automobile, another lethal object that is regularly used to wreak great carnage. Obviously, this society is

Written for Ivins's regular column in the Fort Worth Star-Telegram *and collected in* Nothin' but Good Times Ahead (1993). *Ivins (1944–2007) was famous for her outspoken style, as suggested in the title of her book* Molly Ivins Can't Say That, Can She? (1991).

full of people who haven't enough common sense to use an automobile properly. But we haven't outlawed cars yet.

We do, however, license them and their owners, restrict their use to presumably sane and sober adults, and keep track of who sells them to whom. At
a minimum, we should do the same with guns.

In truth, there is no rational argument for guns in this society. This is no   10
longer a frontier nation in which people hunt their own food. It is a crowded,
overwhelmingly urban country in which letting people have access to guns is a
continuing disaster. Those who want guns—whether for target shooting, hunting, or potting rattlesnakes (get a hoe)—should be subject to the same restrictions placed on gun owners in England, a nation in which liberty has survived
nicely without an armed populace.

The argument that "guns don't kill people" is patent nonsense. Anyone
who has ever worked in a cop shop knows how many family arguments end in
murder because there was a gun in the house. Did the gun kill someone? No.
But if there had been no gun, no one would have died. At least not without a
good foot race first. Guns do kill. Unlike cars, that is all they do.

Michael Crichton makes an interesting argument about technology in his
thriller *Jurassic Park*.[1] He points out that power without discipline is making
this society into a wreckage. By the time someone who studies the martial arts
becomes a master—literally able to kill with bare hands—that person has also
undergone years of training and discipline. But any fool can pick up a gun and
kill with it.

"A well-regulated militia" surely implies both long training and long discipline. That is the least, the very least, that should be required of those who are
permitted to have guns, because a gun is literally the power to kill. For years I
used to enjoy taunting my gun-nut friends about their psychosexual hang-ups—
always in a spirit of good cheer, you understand. But letting the noisy minority in
the NRA[2] force us to allow this carnage to continue is just plain insane.

I do think gun nuts have a power hang-up. I don't know what is missing in
their psyches that they need to feel they have the power to kill. But no sane society would allow this to continue.

Ban the damn things. Ban them all.   15

You want protection? Get a dog.

1. The 1990 novel *Jurassic Park*, made into a movie in 1994.
2. National Rifle Association.

QUESTIONS

1. What do you think of Ivins's examination of the Constitution? What kind of evidence
would convince you even more? Why doesn't Ivins provide more evidence?

2. Characterize Ivins's language. What words, phrases, or structures seem typical of her
style?

3. Examine the analogy between guns and cars. How does it hold up? Where does it
break down?

Nicholas D. Kristof *Saudis in Bikinis*

RIYADH, SAUDI ARABIA—On my first evening in Riyadh, I spotted a surreal scene: three giggly black ghosts, possibly young women enveloped in black cloaks called abayas, clustered around a display in a shopping mall, enthusiastically fingering a blouse so sheer and low-cut that my wife would never be caught dead in it. Afterward, I delicately asked a Saudi woman to explicate the scene.

"What do you think the 'black ghosts' wear underneath their abayas?" she replied archly.

Saudi women may be regarded in the West as antique doormats covered in black veils, but the women themselves vigorously reject that stereotype. "It hurts when you hear what people say about us, that we're repressed," Monira Abdulaziz, an assistant professor, said reproachfully.

"I cover up my body and my face, and I'm happy that I'm a religious girl obeying God's rules," a dietician named Lana scolded me after I wrote a typically snide reference to repressed Saudi women. "I can swim and do sports and go to restaurants and wear what I want, but not in front of men. Why should I show my legs and breasts to men? Is that really freedom?"

5   In Riyadh, several Saudi women offered the same scathing critique, effectively arguing that Saudi women are the free ones—free from sexual harassment, free from pornography, free from seeing their bodies used to market cars and colas. It is Western women, they say, who have been manipulated into becoming the toys of men.

Saudi Arabia is a bizarre place. It has McDonald's restaurants that look just like those at home except that there is one line for men and one for women. *Al Riyadh* newspaper has women journalists, but they're kept in their own room; when a male editor must edit a woman's copy, he does it by phone. Saudi women wear bikinis—but only in home swimming pools or in all-women pools. They claim all this reflects not repression but a culture they cherish.

"You can't go to an Indian woman and say, 'Why are you wearing a sari?'" fumed Hend al-Khuthaila, a university professor who was the first female university dean in Saudi Arabia. "You can't go up to a Western woman and say, 'Why are you wearing a short dress?' Well, this is our abaya. This is part of my culture. It's part of my tradition. It never bothered me."

Maha Muneef, a female pediatrician, emphasized that Saudi Arabia is progressing, albeit more slowly than many women would like. "My mother didn't go to any school at all, because then there were no girls' schools at all," she said. "My older sister, who is 20 years older than me, she went up to the sixth grade and then quit, because the feeling was that a girl only needs to

Published on October 25, 2002, in the New York Times, *where Kristof has written a twice-weekly Op-Ed column since 2001.*

learn to read and write. Then I went to college and medical school on scholarship to the States. My daughter, maybe she'll be president, or an astronaut."

Another doctor, Hanan Balkhy, seemed ambivalent. "I don't think women here have equal opportunities," she acknowledged. "There are meetings I can't go to. There are buildings I can't go into. But you have to look at the context of development. Discrimination will take time to overcome."

Dr. Balkhy emphasized that Saudi women want to solve their problems themselves. These days in particular, she said, even liberal Saudis feel on the defensive and are reluctant to discuss their concerns for fear that foreigners will seize upon the problems to discredit their country. 10

All this created an awkward series of interviews. I kept asking women how they felt about being repressed, and they kept answering indignantly that they aren't repressed.

So what should we make of this? Is it paternalistic of us in the West to try to liberate women who insist that they're happy as they are?

No, I think we're on firm ground.

If most Saudi women want to wear a tent, if they don't want to drive, then that's fine. But why not give them the choice? Why ban women drivers and why empower the religious police, the mutawwa, to scold those loose hussies who choose to show a patch of hair?

If Saudi Arabians choose to kill their economic development and sacrifice 15 international respect by clinging to the 15th century, if the women prefer to remain second-class citizens, then I suppose that's their choice. But if anyone chooses to behave so foolishly, is it any surprise that outsiders point and jeer?

QUESTIONS

1. Kristof believes that Saudi Arabia's strict rules for women—no driving, no public mixing of the sexes, no revealing clothing—are "foolish." What do you think? And what do you think of the Saudi Arabian women who defend such practices?

2. How should one country behave toward another that has starkly different standards of morality (e.g., capital punishment, polygamy, repression of women)? Think about the evidence you might give in support of your view.

3. Describe a time when you got into an argument or dispute over standards of behavior with someone you disagreed with. What triggered it? How did it get resolved? What happened?

FRED STREBEIGH *The Wheels of Freedom:*
Bicycles in China

"HELLO." She appeared at my right shoulder, her face inches from mine. We were cycling together, though I had never seen her before. We rode side by side through the city of Beijing, and around us streamed thousands of bicycles with red banners flying. Beijing was in revolt. And as we rode together we broke the law.

I had gone to China with an odd goal: to learn a bit about what the bicycle means to people who live in a country with only a few thousand privately owned cars but some 220 million cycles—vastly more than any other nation. And I had arrived at an odd time.

My first day in China was also the first day of what became known as the Beijing Spring of 1989. As I awoke, students and citizens by the hundreds of thousands were flowing from all over Beijing to Tiananmen Square, the vast plaza at the city's heart, creating the largest spontaneous demonstration in the history of China and perhaps the world. They came on foot and by bus and subway, of course, but mostly they came by bicycle, calling for freedom. (I could see why bicycles are forbidden in the capital of North Korea, China's more repressive neighbor. Its government reportedly fears that bikes give people too much independence.)

Within hours of my arrival in Beijing, bicycles became more crucial than ever. Buses stopped. Subways shut. Taxis struck. But on flowed the bikes of Beijing. Bicyclists carried messages from university to university. Tricyclists rushed round delivering food to demonstrators. Families and schoolmates and couples and commuters smiled and waved as they rode, in twos and threes and throngs.

5   On my own bicycle, hesitant at first and then lost in the cycling masses, I roamed freely. Daily I rode to Tiananmen Square, with its mood of carnival, its students from all regions, and its uncountable cycles. Bicycles and tricycles became flag holders and tent supporters. They became tea dispensers and cold-drink stands. They became photographers' perches, families' viewing platforms, old men's reading chairs, and children's racing toys.

On my bicycle I also strayed far from Tiananmen, to the quiet corners of the city. Everywhere the bicycle set the rhythm of life. Martial artists rode to practice with swords strapped to their bikes. Women in jet-black business suits pedalled their daughters to school. Boys fished beside parked bicycles at placid

Sent to China on a magazine assignment to analyze the cultural role of the bicycle, Strebeigh found himself immersed in a political uprising in Beijing, its capital. The essay was first published in Bicycling Magazine *(April 1991) and then adapted for* China Update *(Winter 1991), a magazine published by the Yale–China Association. The latter version is reprinted here.*

lakes. Bakers in white toques headed for work on transport tricycles. Pedalling beside them at their slow pace, I felt at ease and oddly at home. I felt as I had years ago in my small hometown, where automobiles never clogged the streets and where the bicycle offered a mix of peace and freedom.

Riding among the bicycles of Beijing, I began to recognize dozens of China's famous brands: Golden Lion and Mountain River, Plum Flower and Chrysanthemum, Red Flag and Red Cotton, Flying Arrival and Flying Pigeon, Pheasant and Phoenix and Forever. Long and stately bicycles, recalling decades past, they possessed the rake and sheer and grace that today I associ-

Afternoon rush hour in Chengdu.

ate less with cycling than with yachting. I felt as if I were cruising, on the
wake of clippers like *Red Jacket* or *Flying Cloud,* in a regatta of tall ships.

Then the Chinese government declared martial law. It forbade citizens to
attend the student demonstrations and forbade foreigners, like me, to visit
Tiananmen or talk to students. It sent its army in a first push into the city, but
citizens peacefully blocked its way. My Chinese hosts (I had been invited to
lecture at a couple of universities) warned me to obey the government, and I
said I would try.

In the second day under martial law, as I was riding down one of Beijing's
leafy boulevards, suddenly a young woman appeared at my shoulder. She said
"hello," and we were cycling together.

10   I had been rolling at Beijing speed, eight miles an hour—in synch with
commuters, demonstrators, and vegetable haulers. To catch me she had accel-
erated, maybe to eight-and-a-half miles an hour.

"What," she wanted to know, did I "think about the students?" She wore
tinted glasses, a shy smile in a radiant face, a lab coat—she was a science student, and by law we were forbidden to talk.

"I think what they are doing is very brave," I said, "and very scary." And so
we became two petty criminals, riding handlebar-to-handlebar.

We floated together and others floated past. But they travelled fractions of
a pedal-turn faster or fractions slower, and we were left alone in talk, our handlebars occasionally nudging each other, in the bizarre intimacy of Beijing
cycling. I worried aloud about the Chinese army—now half a mile to our west,
still blocked but still pressing towards us. She praised George Washington. We
would not have talked so freely in a restaurant or hotel, I realized; police could
have demanded our names. But here we were just two bicycles lost in the
mass—the most private place in Beijing.

Ahead of us appeared Tiananmen Square, where some of her classmates
had been starving themselves in protest and others had been singing "We Shall
Overcome." Within moments, she drifted south and I north. Soon I was at the
American embassy. They warned me against talking to students.

15   To stay in Beijing, I decided, was to endanger anyone I met. And so I resolved to travel out from the capital and return later, in order to talk about bicycles in a time of greater calm and, I hoped, greater freedom.

One of the people I most wanted to meet outside Beijing was a student in
Sichuan Province named Fang Hui. The year before, she had become the first
woman to ride a bicycle from Chengdu, the capital of Sichuan in central
China, to Lhasa, the capital of Tibet—bumping for thirteen hundred miles
over one of China's worst roads, a sawtooth of rock tracks and mountain
passes which reach altitudes above 15,000 feet. In recognition, China honored her as one of the nation's "Ten Brave Young People."

I didn't care much about Fang Hui's honors. I cared more about her motivations, her goals. I guess I expected her to be a hot but somewhat dull athlete, the sort who wins Chinese honors by excelling in volleyball. When we
met at her university in Chengdu, where she is a graduate student in English,
she surprised me.

As we pedalled through the streets of Chengdu, I asked Fang Hui if she had always been a cyclist. Not really, she said. Before her trip she had not owned a bicycle. The day before departing for Tibet she bought an old, single-speed Arched Eyebrow for 75 yuan ($15). She then taught herself to ride, over a thousand miles of mountains.

I asked how she chose Tibet. She said she had answered a poster advertisement. I was shocked. So, apparently, were the five men, mostly teachers from a local school, who had planned the trip and posted invitations for fellow travellers. Only Fang Hui accepted.

The men doubted she could reach Tibet, perhaps because she looked like   20
a pudgy schoolgirl. Uphill she always rode more slowly than they, falling miles behind. Downhill, because her old bike had wretched brakes, she squeezed its levers with all her strength as the Arched Eyebrow hurtled down pitted roads. "I went very fast," she said. "I felt as if I would become light." At the end of each day of clinging to her brake levers, her hands were so cramped she could not open them.

Eventually, the men admitted that her strength egged them on. "If even a girl can do this," they said, "how shameful for a man to give up."

Fang Hui had not really worried about giving up on the journey, she told me. But, earlier, she had worried about giving up on life. "Before," she said, "yesterday, today, tomorrow were all alike—so dull. What I most wanted was to meet something unexpected."

Not just the road's pain but also its loneliness changed Fang Hui. At remote outposts she would meet soldiers, mere isolated boys, who would write love letters that followed her up the Lhasa road, carried by lone truck drivers. In yet remoter terrain she would ride half a day, she recalled, and "not see a single man. So when I heard a dog bark, it would arouse a tender feeling—a reminder of the human world. When I came back, people all said I had changed. Now I can find something new in every day." And now at night, she added with glee, "sometimes I dream I am riding very fast downhill."

As I rode through Chengdu, sometimes talking with Fang Hui or with other university students and teachers, I began to see that the bicycle offered an escape not just *from* everyday life. It also offered escape within everyday life.

One day as Fang Hui and I rode through a crush of cyclists, a young cou-   25
ple passed us riding two bicycles side-by-side. They rode pedal-to-pedal and almost arm-in-arm. At first the girl rode with her left hand on the boy's right, controlling his hand and handlebar, steering them both. Then he moved his hand to round the small of her back. They reminded me of partners in a waltz.

The boy lowered his hand to the girl's bicycle seat and leaned to her, and as they rode they whispered. In the often-dehumanizing crush of urban China, two bicycles had made space for romance. Fang Hui said that young "lovers" often ride so utterly together, so alone in their world.

Providing such measures of human dignity, one professor told me, was one of the bicycle's gifts to China—and particularly to people like his parents, who were "peasants" (the term in China for all people who work the land).

Here in the center of China's richest farmlands, he said, I could watch the bicycle making life less hard. Flower farmers with hollyhocks and asters tied to their bicycles arrived in Chengdu at dawn, flicked down their kickstands on side streets, and began to sell. Farmers' sons strapped saws and other carpenters' tools to their bicycles, rode into the city, and waited at curbside for customers to hire them to build beds or bureaus. In Sichuan's booming "free markets" (free, that is, of government control), geese came to town on the backs of farmers' tricycles, were sold to families for domestic egg laying, and then departed with their wings still flapping, strapped to the buyers' handlebars. Everywhere, cycles kept life rolling.

The professor told me that peasants in his parents' remote village always refer to the bicycle, appreciatively, as the "foreign horse." The government opposes the name, he said, but it helps explain the history of the bicycle in China. The first bicycle arrived in 1886, carrying Thomas Stevens, a young San Franciscan who was completing the first cycling journey around the world. With its huge front wheel and small rear one, his penny-farthing[1] cycle must have looked very foreign but, unlike a good horse, not very practical.

The first practical bicycle to reach China came in 1891, again transporting a round-the-world cyclist. By the early twentieth century, the foreign horse had won the fascination of China's last emperor, the young Puyi, who rode one around his palace, Beijing's "Forbidden City."

Slowly cycling trickled down from the throne toward the masses. By the 1940s China's bicycle factories were producing a vehicle like today's most common model, a virtual twin of England's stately Raleigh Tourist.

In the years before the Chinese revolution of 1949, the professor told me, almost everyone called the bicycle "foreign horse," because "foreign" suggested both "modern" and "admirable." Since peasants carried most goods on their backs, they particularly admired the bicycle. Every peasant longed to shift his burden to the back of a foreign horse—a longing frustrated by high price and short supply.

Then came the revolution of 1949. Hoping to "raise the people's dignity," the professor continued, the young government made two decisions. Happily,

30

1. Referring to wheels of unequal size: pennies were big, farthings small.

in an effort to give wheels to an impoverished population, it encouraged bicycle production, which began doubling and redoubling. But sadly, because the old name suggested blind worship of foreign things, the government banned the lyrical phrase "foreign horse" (which, pronounced *yang ma* in Chinese, resounds like a ringing gong). The government imposed, instead, the unpoetic "self-running cart" (*zi xing che* in Chinese, which sounds like a dental problem).

Not surprisingly, the cycle's foreign resonance remains. Peasants in remote villages still pedal "foreign horses." And many Chinese factories, seeking a touch of class, still adorn their bicycles with prominent English names: "Forever" or "Light Roadster" or, on the most celebrated of foreign horses, "Flying Pigeon—The All-Steel Bicycle." (When George Bush[2] made his first presidential visit to China, his welcoming gift from the nation was a pair of Flying Pigeons.)

A regional branch of the Flying Pigeon Bicycle Factory lies an hour's ride from the center of Chengdu, and one day I was given a tour of its old-style assembly line by Jiang Guoji, the factory's present director—the first ever elected by its workers. He spoke with the ease of a manager whose workers trust his judgment and whose society trusts his product.

Since Jiang Guoji's factory sits in the middle of China's best farmland, he and his co-workers decided to specialize in what Jiang called the "ZA-62" or "Reinforced Flying Pigeon." This bike, which I came to think of as the "Peasant Pigeon," comes with massive tubing, a formidable rack, a second set of

35

2. George H. W. Bush (b. 1924), president of the United States from 1989 to 1993.

forks to hold the front wheels, and—probably unique among Chinese bicycles—a three-year warranty. It contains 68 pounds of steel which, together
with some leather and rubber, brings its total weight above 72 pounds—three
times that of my average American bike.

Jiang Guoji's factory has raised production steadily, along with all Chinese
cycle factories, creating an unprecedented problem. The year before my visit,
Chinese bicycle production reached 42 million cycles—dwarfing any other nation's output and, more significantly, overtaking Chinese demand for the first
time in history. For years, bicycles had been rationed, and families had longed
to own a good one. Now "if a person has money, he can buy," Jiang told me,
with a mix of pride and regret—because prices have begun dropping and "bicycle factories have real competition."

In response, Jiang said, he was trying to spur international demand for
Peasant Pigeons. Looking for good "propaganda," two years earlier he donated "Peasant Pigeons" to five local riders who wanted to go around the
world. Alas, one had been run down by a truck in Pakistan. But the other four
were riding on, circling the globe back towards his factory. He expected his
72-pound Pigeons home within a year, still under warranty. (He added that,
despite transport costs and import duties, he would gladly sell Peasant Pigeons wholesale in America for less than a dollar a pound.)

All Chinese bicycles—whether sturdy Flying Pigeons or sad Arched
Eyebrows—must survive long after their warranties have expired. To help them
along, repairmen have set up roadside stands in every city. Entering the business proves simple. A would-be repairman chooses a site, asks the city to license it to him, and lays down his tools. He then puts up his advertisement—a
circle of overlapping innertubes, colored black and deep pink, perhaps hung on
a tree limb.

Some Chinese portray repairmen in a style that outdoes American caricatures of car mechanics. Most of my Chinese acquaintances knew one repairman they relied on and dozens they distrusted. One university professor
insisted that underemployed repairmen scatter tacks to puncture passing tires
and inflate profits.

40   Another professor invited me to meet her revered neighborhood repairman. Since he worked incessantly and had little time for chatter, she devised a
ruse to buy time for asking questions: we would take him her Flying Arrival,
which had a useless rear brake.

We found him at the back gate of her university beneath a circle of innertubes. When my friend arrived, the repairman put aside a Phoenix he was polishing and greeted her as a long-term client. She presented the brake problem.
He took a quick look, produced two sets of pliers, loosened a nut, tightened a
cable, tensioned a spring and, after 30 seconds of work, handed the bike back
to her—fixed. He refused payment. The job was too small. He resumed polishing the Phoenix.

Though her ruse had failed, the professor pressed forward: How did he
become a repairman? Three years ago when he was twenty-seven, he told us,
he stopped working his family's farm because the land was small and the fam-

A bike repairman's job may be the freest in China. All that's needed is a street corner and a few tools.

ily had more than enough laborers—including his wife, their three children, his two sisters and two brothers, and their aging parents. He still lives on the farm but commutes three miles to the city on his Forever. He works seven days a week, from 9 A.M. to 8 P.M., except when it rains.

He likes bike repair because it "makes *money*," he said, emphasizing the word as if it were a novelty. Back on the farm, where he hopes never to work again, he "just produced *crops*," which sold for "not-so-much money."

When we asked him how much he made in a month, he told us 800 yuan ($216). The professor gasped. To me she said, quietly, "That's five university professors!" Still, she seemed to believe him. She pointed out to me that he had paid the government's penalty for having three children. The penalty in recent years has run as high as 2,000 yuan ($540), she said, too much for most professors—but not for an industrious bike fixer.

As I talked to more repairmen, I saw that their job may be the freest in China. A hard worker needed only a street corner and a few tools. Before his eyes bikes would inevitably break down and, if he was skilled, clients would multiply. Bicycle repair seemed to offer an extension of what the bike itself offered and what so many Chinese sought: modest dignity, new choices, ample freedom.

The farm country outside Chengdu, contrary to the complaints of one peasant-turned-repairman, generates much of the new agricultural wealth enjoyed by the Chinese people. In early June, by train and by bicycle, I travelled to the southern mountains that rim this rich agricultural bowl within Sichuan province. There I was the guest at another university, tucked in verdant hills.

During my stay, one teacher lent me an old "Peasant Pigeon"—one well past its warranty. I rode it daily over farm tracks of rut and rock that would

45

have jolted the nuts off my light American bike. The big Pigeon just bobbed along, high and easy.

One midday while I was exploring narrow paths through emerald-colored rice paddies, two girls whizzed past me, riding double on a black Forever. Both wore red uniforms and one carried an abacus—students dashing home for lunch.

With me was a professor who was fluent not only in English but also the quite-obscure local dialect. She suggested we follow the students so I could meet a "peasant family."

50   We travelled through flooded paddies, past water buffaloes, up to a newly built home that stretched around a cement courtyard, and found the older of the two girls talking with her mother next to their vegetable garden. The professor introduced us. Their mother, Mrs. Fang, invited us for tea and introduced her daughters: Liya, third-grader and bicycle passenger, and Jianmei, sixth-grader and bicyclist. Because Jianmei's Forever still had protective wrapping paper on its top bar, as if it had just come from the store, I asked if it was new.

Jianmei, who was gulping down rice in preparation for her afternoon at school, said proudly that she won it just last year. Her mother explained that the family offers their daughters prizes for each year that they sustain grades of 90% or better. In autumn each daughter names a prize she wants, and then for the rest of the school year she tries to win it. In third grade Jianmei won a set of nice clothes; in fourth grade, a golden wristwatch; in fifth grade, the Forever. (I said to the professor, in English, "Are you sure we're talking to *peasants*?")

Mrs. Fang then led us through her tiled kitchen to a room that held, along with awards won by Jianmei for track and basketball, another full-sized bicycle—a cherry-red "Cuckoo," also still wrapped to protect its paint. It was Jianmei's earlier bike. I was astonished; ten years ago here, the professor had told me, only one family in ten could afford even a single bicycle.

Jianmei explained that she wanted the Forever because it was strong and smooth enough to carry her little sister. With it, she rides not just to school but up to the university, off to a nearby temple, even to a town 22 miles away to see the world's largest carved Buddha.

As we walked away from the Fang household—so imbued with work and reward and independence—I said to the professor: "Don't you wish you grew up in a place like that?" A bit later I thought to myself: "I *did* grow up in a place like that." Riding off to school, studying hard, cycling ten and twenty miles on a whim—this was like being back in sixth grade in my small hometown.

55   On the same day I talked with the Fang family, stories of the Beijing massacre—of hundreds or perhaps thousands of citizens killed by army troops and tanks—were reaching our remote region. Soon travellers arrived with tales of killing in other provincial cities. Students began to flee our rural campus, fearing the army would next descend on them. I returned to Chengdu.

There, I tried to continue the work I had planned—looking for the city's used bicycle market, avoiding the army troops who had arrived to quell out-

These bicycles were more than crushed machines. They represented crushed dignity, humanity, and freedom.

bursts, gathering statistics on bicycle ownership. But I could not concentrate. My mind was on Beijing. Finally I decided to return, to what just days before had been the world's most exuberant city.

Again I rode its leafy boulevards, but no excited voice at my shoulder asked what I thought of the students. No banners waved. No people smiled. All faces seemed as if carved, years ago, in soft stone—at once fixed and badly weathered.

Each evening, Beijing television proudly showed the now-barren Tiananmen Square, cleared of all students and, for that matter, all life. Understandably, the TV cameras did not show what people in Beijing had seen: citizens trying to stop tanks by shoving bicycles at them, flatbed tricycles turned into ambulances for slaughtered children. Less understandably, the cameras often began their pan across the square with an image of a pile of crumpled bicycles.

That odd image haunted me for months, long after I had left China. Only slowly did I realize that the government had chosen that scene precisely. The government cameras wanted to show more than a few crushed machines. They wanted to show crushed dignity, crushed humanity, crushed freedom—so much that the bicycle means in China.

And finally I realized that of course the old men who cling to power in China would want to show off the crumpled bicycles of the young men and women who had called for freedom. How terrifying it must have been, to those old men, to see millions of young people cycling towards them—so independent, so alive, so free—all those wheels turning and turning beyond the control of fear or fiat. Of course those old men would want to crush the cycles of the young. For they would know too well that history itself runs in cycles—sometimes foreign horses, sometimes self-running carts, always wheels of change.

60

How sad: Four decades earlier these same old men, seeking to "raise the people's dignity," had set rolling the cycles of modern China. And then, in a few
days of a Beijing spring, they sought to crush, all at once, cycles and dignity
and change together. They might as easily have sought to stop the circling,
round the sun, of earth's revolution. For as each spring comes round, the old
fade and the young quicken. And every day throughout China, the wheels of
freedom roll.

QUESTIONS

1. Strebeigh's magazine assignment was to depict and analyze the role of bicycles in
modern-day China. What important roles does the bicycle play? Which do you think are
most important—to Strebeigh? to the Chinese people he interviewed?

2. The article is titled "The Wheels of Freedom." Why? What relationship between bicycles and freedom does the essay suggest?

3. Write about an important product or artifact in American culture, analyzing its significance to its users and, if relevant, to yourself.

BILL MCKIBBEN   *The Case for Single-Child Families*

THE BUILDING was nondescript; four stories of
modern concrete just down the street from Ottawa's Civic Hospital. The receptionist greeted me politely, told me the doctor was running a little late. And
so I sat on the couch next to the old and dog-eared
magazines and read one more time the list of ques-
tions Dr. Phil McGuire wanted his vasectomy patients to answer before he
performed The Procedure:

"What would you and your partner feel if you were told tomorrow that she
was pregnant? Joy? Despair? Resignation? What about in five years?

"Would you want the chance to have children with another partner if your
current relationship ended through separation or death?

5   "Would you want to have the chance to have more children if one or more
of your children died?

"Would more children be in your picture now if your financial circumstances improved significantly?"

These are tougher questions than you usually get asked in a doctor's of-

Published on May 13, 1998, in The Christian Century, *a Protestant magazine with a
stated mission to nurture faith and examine issues of politics, culture, and theology. This
essay was included in* Maybe One: A Personal and Environmental Argument for Single-
Child Families *(1998), a book that extends McKibben's work as a well-known environmental writer, most famous for* The End of the Earth *(1989).*

fice. If you have heart disease, you have to choose *what* to do; it's rare to have to choose, until the very end, whether you want to do *anything at all*. But I could have gotten up and left, no harm done. I have one child. I'd decided to have no more. But this seemed so final.

Then Dr. McGuire came in, wearing khakis, old Nikes, an earring, a plaid shirt. So far that day, he said, he'd done nine vasectomies, pruned branches of nine family trees. He was calm, gentle—sweet. "I had a couple this morning who'd had one child when they were in their 30s, spent the next ten years trying to have another, and failed. Now they were in their early 40s and just couldn't conceive of conceiving again, so they wanted some insurance." He'd had a police officer, and a guy who builds Web pages, and several couples in their early 30s, each with two kids.

And he'd talked with all of them. "I try to protect people if I don't think they're ready," he said. "I'm a general practitioner and I've seen so many women come in who are unexpectedly pregnant, and completely delighted about it." But when people have made up their minds, he's ready to help—he's done 1,100 vasectomies, more and more each year. "Someday I hope to have a clinic just devoted to vasectomies—a fish tank and all the hunting and fishing and outdoors magazines," he said.

I'd come to him because Ottawa is not far from my home, because I could afford him (he charged just over $200, less than most American operations), and because I could tell from his Web site (www.ottawa-vas.com) that he thought pretty deeply about the whole issue. He had a sense of humor (his toll-free number is 1-800-LASTKID), but he also had a sense of purpose. "Sometimes I turn people down," he said. "But it's so much safer than having a woman get a tubal ligation, which is a big operation inside a major body cavity with general anaesthesia."

So I sat on the table and pulled my pants down around my ankles. He   10
swabbed my scrotum with iodine ("The iodine needs to be a little warm—the last thing we want is any shrinkage before we start") and then injected a slug of anaesthetic into each side of my testicles. Yes, it was a needle down there, but no, it didn't hurt much—by chance I'd spent the previous afternoon in the dentist's chair, and this was much less painful. (And no flossing!) He cut a small hole in my scrotum, and with a forceps pulled out the vas deferens, the tube that carried sperm to my penis. Then he cauterized it and put it back inside, repeating the procedure on the other side. I could feel a little tugging, nothing more. The wound was so small it didn't require stitches, or even a Band-Aid. For a few days, he said, my groin would be a little sore. After that it would take 20 ejaculations or so to drain the last of the sperm already in my system. And that would be that. In evolutionary terms, I'd be out of business.

It's easy for me to explain why I was lying on the table at the Ottawa Vasectomy Clinic: all I need is a string of statistics. In one recent study, condoms broke 4.8 percent of the time that they were used. Sixty percent of all pregnancies in the U.S. are unintended—60 percent. That doesn't mean all those children are unwanted; half just come when their parents weren't planning on it. But half end in abortion. In fact, six in ten women having abortions did so because their contraceptives failed; among typical couples, 18 percent using diaphragms and 12 percent using condoms managed to get pregnant. And no one's doing much to improve the situation—a nation that spends $600 million developing new cosmetics and fragrances each year has exactly one pharmaceutical company still conducting research on improved methods of birth control. So if I was serious about stopping at one child, this was where I belonged. For my wife, Sue, getting sterilized would have meant a real operation, real risk; for me it meant a bag of ice on my lap as I drove home. It all added up.

Not that we'd come to our decision to have one child easily. Although my work on environmental issues keeps bringing population questions front and center, I have avoided the issue of population for years. I know that by 2050 there will be almost 50 percent more Americans (and nearly 100 percent more human beings) than there are now. I know that in the last ten or 20 or 30 years, our impact has grown so much that we're changing even those places we don't inhabit—changing the way the weather works, changing the plants and animals that live at the poles and deep in the jungle.

I am convinced, too, that simplifying lifestyles alone, although crucial, will not do enough to reduce our impact in the next 50 years. Americans' lifestyles are just so "big." During the next decade India and China will each add to the planet about ten times as many people as the U.S., but the stress on the natural world by those new Americans may exceed that from the new Indians and Chinese combined. My five-year-old daughter has already used more stuff and added more waste to the environment than many of the world's residents do in a lifetime.

When Sue and I faced the issue of how many children to have, these abstract issues of population became personal and practical. What about Sophie? Would being an only child damage her spirit and mind? I explored the myths surrounding "the only child," and the clichés about one child being spoiled and overly dependent. Although these questions are emotionally charged and complex, every bit of research in recent decades shows that only kids do just fine—that they achieve as much and are as well adjusted as children with siblings. So that wasn't the hitch.

15   Along with doing all the research, however, I had to confront the deeply ingrained sense in many of us that there's something inherently *selfish* about not being willing to have children. It's not as strong as the sense of selfishness that can attach itself to abortion, but it's there nonetheless, and particularly strong, I think, in people of faith. It's the relic of our long theological wrestle with the issue of birth control. And it is not easily dismissed. Condoms may not be sinful, but selfishness must be, if anything is. The children of small families are no more selfish than any other kids—but are the parents?

In a consumer society, where we've been drilled relentlessly in selfishness, it's a peril to take seriously. In her book *Beyond Motherhood*, Jeanne Safer interviews dozens of men and women who have decided against children. I have no wish to judge them, for it's often an honorable decision, and people should not bear children if they feel they can't cope with them. On the other hand, I have no wish to *become* them. They are selfish, and proudly; one New York literary agent describes herself as "an advocate of selfishness." Safer says she herself felt her biological clock ticking, but heard other clocks as well:

> My practice is just starting to take off—I'll lose all the momentum if I cut back to part-time. That summer I thought, it'll have to wait until after we get back from Bali and I'm no longer taking medication to prevent malaria. And what about the trip to Turkey we want to take next summer.

She was, she said, "particularly aware that children would change my marriage drastically. . . . Parenthood, I believed, would certainly spell the end of our nightly candlelit sandalwood-scented bubble baths complete with silly bath toys, where we played like children in a deliciously adult incarnation." Not only that, "I realized that having a child of my own would force me to spend a great deal of time doing things I'd disliked; I'd never been crazy about children's birthday parties when I'd attended them years earlier, and a trip to the circus is my idea of purgatory."

Safer found many like-minded folk. Sandra Singer, for instance, a photographer who moonlights as a belly dancer to "guarantee her allure" and who insists that "I've seen too many women who have children lose their sexuality as well as their identity. They let their bodies go, and they complain about their husband's sexual advances. I complain about the lack."

Safer reconciles herself to her decision not to have kids, and celebrates by giving her own belly-dancing performance. "Working through feelings about motherhood had unleashed hidden reserves of creativity and femininity, and I emerged liberated, energized and strong," she reports. In fact one night she dreams of a cantaloupe growing on a vine in her parents' garden in the middle of winter: "The cantaloupe was myself, the fruit of my parents' loins, which, though barren in the biological sense, was ripening out of season."

It's wrong to ridicule such attitudes, at least in a culture that still assigns the work of raising kids mostly to women and allows men to continue their careers at full tilt. Sometimes people have to rescue themselves; in Toni Morrisons novel *Sula*, the heroine won't marry or bear children in order to preserve her "Me-ness." When her grandmother wants her to have babies to "settle" her, Sula says, "I don't want to make somebody else. I want to make myself." Often it's women from very poor backgrounds who decide to remain childless, realizing that it's their best hope for upward mobility against strong odds; in a 1985 study of poor Southern high school students, the 16 percent who wanted no children were the ones with the loftiest ambitions, the ambitions that in other contexts we want such children to have.

But it's also possible to understand the concern of popes and rabbis and just ordinary folk that, for some people, the decision to have no children or a small family represents a decision to indulge yourself without a thought for anyone else, a decision to take sandalwood-scented candlelit baths without the danger that there might be stray Legos left in the tub to poke you in the backside.

Theologian Gilbert Meilaender quotes one young man who says, "When you have children, the focus changes from the couple to the kids. Suddenly everything is done for them. Well, I'm 27, I've used up a good portion of my life already. Why should I want to sacrifice for someone who's still got his whole life ahead of him?" Such an attitude is, among other things, environmentally problematic; even if this fellow has no kids, thereby sparing the planet some burden, he seems unlikely to do much else to ensure its future—he's the same guy who's going to be voting against gas taxes and demanding the right to drive his Suburban into the overheated sunset.

John Ryan, an American Catholic theologian of the first half of the 20th century, made this argument most powerfully. A man of impeccable progressive credentials, Ryan was known as "the Right Reverend New Dealer" for his unwavering support of the Roosevelt administration. But this same John Ryan also wanted everyone who married to have many children, not simply as proof that they weren't using birth control but because he thought that raising large families makes people better human beings.

Ryan argued that supporting large families demands "forms of discipline necessary for the successful life," a life "accomplished only at the cost of continuous and considerable sacrifice, of compelling ourselves to do without the immediate and pleasant goods for the sake of remote and permanent goods." One of eleven children himself, Ryan thought that most people practicing birth control would be doing it from a "decadent" frame of mind; that bachelors were not building the kind of character necessary to contribute to the common good of society. Not only that, those with few children might become too wealthy, which was as dangerous as being too poor. In the words of ethicist John Berkman, "He was appealing to hard work, and building character, and he thought that was best achieved for most people in the context of having a large family."

25   This pragmatic argument comes straight from the American sense of purpose. And it is by no means a negligible or stupid argument: successfully raising a large brood of well-adjusted children is a great accomplishment, one that cannot help but change and deepen the parents. You emerge different people when you spend your life focusing, as good parents must, on *someone else's* well-being. If maturity is the realization that you are not at the center of the world, then the most time-honored way to become mature is to be a parent many times over, and a good one. Not just because parenting is tough, but also because it's so *joyful*, because it shows you that real transcendent pleasure comes from putting someone else first. It teaches you how dull self-absorption can be.

Such lessons don't always take, of course. As essayist Katha Pollitt points out, the tendency to ascribe "particular virtues—compassion, patience, common sense, nonviolence—to mothers" is an overdone, and in some ways oppressive, cliché; telling yourself that toilet training a string of two-year-olds is good for your soul may keep you away from other worlds. And in a country where incredible numbers of fathers walk away from their kids, you could argue that fatherhood seems to barely dent the culture's pervasive selfishness. And yet when I think of my circle of friends and acquaintances, the single most common route to maturity has been through raising children, often lots of them.

The problem, of course, is that now we live in an era—maybe only a brief one, maybe only for a few generations—when parenting a bunch of kids clashes with the good of the planet. So is there a different way to achieve some of that maturity, with no children or only a single child to change your life? It's not that one kid won't alter most things in your life; he or she will. But Ryan was right—it's not the total commitment that comes with a large brood. Your career or a calling continues, however hobbled you may sometimes be. Alice Walker, in a pithy essay titled *"One* Child of One's Own," called her single daughter a "meaningful digression," and that's right in many ways; if she had borne five children, she probably wouldn't have been writing many books. But those books represent a serious attempt at maturity in another way, and perhaps that's a clue. We need to find ways to be adults, grownups, *people who focus on others,* without being parents of large families.

In the weeks leading up to the 1994 Cairo Conference on population, the pope led the fight against many of the provisions in the draft documents for that conclave. Though I disagreed with some of his stands, I found much of his language powerful and intriguing. The Catholic Church, he said, does not support "an ideology of fertility at all costs," but instead an ethic in which the decision "whether or not to have a child" is not "motivated by selfish or carelessness, but by a prudent, conscious generosity that weighs the possibilities and circumstances." True, he added that such an ethic "gives priority to the welfare of the unborn child," but several weeks later, arguing that radical individualism and "a sexuality apart from ethical references" was inhuman, he called for a "culture of responsible procreation."

In those words, and the words of many others, I think we can see the outline of an ethic that avoids self-indulgence yet does not deny the physical facts of a planet with 6 billion people who may soon nearly double their numbers— a planet that grows hotter, stormier and less stable by the day, a planet where huge swaths of God's creation are being wiped out by the one species told to tend this particular garden. I don't pretend it is an ethic that can be embraced by the Vatican, or the Hasidim; but I do think it is an ethic that might undergrid a more sustainable world.

The beginning of Genesis contains the fateful command, repeated elsewhere in the Hebrew Bible, to "be fruitful and multiply, and fill the earth." That this was the first commandment gave it special priority. And it was biological, too, a command that echoed what our genes already shouted.

30

But there is something else unique about it—it is the first commandment we have fulfilled. There's barely a habitable spot on the planet without a human being; in our lifetimes we've filled every inch of the planet with our presence. Everywhere the temperature climbs, the ultraviolet penetrates more deeply. In furthest Alaska, always our national metaphor for emptiness, the permafrost now melts at a rapid pace, trees move on to the tundra, insects infest forests in record numbers, and salmon turn back down streams because the water's gotten too warm to spawn. "There's been a permanent and significant climate regime shift," says an Alaskan scientist. "There has been nothing like this in the record." There's not a creature anywhere on earth whose blood doesn't show the presence of our chemicals, not an ocean that isn't higher because of us. For better and for worse, we are everywhere. We can check this commandment off the list.

And we can check it off for happier reasons as well. There's no denying that we've done great environmental damage, but it's also true that we've spread wondrous and diverse cultures, full of love and song, across the wide earth. We should add a holiday to the calendar of every church to celebrate this achievement.

But when you check something off a list, you don't just throw the list away. You look further down the list, see what comes next. And the list, of course, is long. The Gospels, the Torah, the Koran and a thousand other texts sacred and profane give us plenty of other goals toward which to divert some of the energy we've traditionally used in raising large families, goals on which we've barely begun. Feed the hungry, clothe the naked, comfort the oppressed; love your neighbor as yourself; heal the earth. We live on a planet where 3 billion people don't have clean water, where species die by the score each day, where kids grow up without fathers, where violence overwhelms us, where people judge each other by the color of their skin, where a hypersexualized culture poisons the adolescence of girls, where old people and young people need each other's support. And the energy freed by having smaller families may be some of the energy needed to take on these next challenges. To really take them on, not just to announce that they're important, or to send a check, or to read an article, but to make them central to our lives.

I have one child; she is the light of my life; she makes me care far more about the future than I used to. And I have one child; so even after my work I have some time, money and energy left to do other things. I get to work on Adirondack conservation issues and assist those who are fighting global warming; I've helped my wife start a new school in our town; I can teach Sunday school and help run a nationwide effort to decommercialize Christmas and sit on the board of the local college. (And I belly dance too, though in my case it's hiking, cross-country skiing, mountain biking.) If I had three kids, I would still do those things, but less of them; either that, or my work would come at their expense. As it is, once in a while I'm stretched too thin and don't see Sophie for a day, and that reminds me to slow down, to find the real center of my life. But I want to get further down that list.

35   So the pope strikes me as largely right in his reasoning if not his conclusions. Radical individualism is inhuman. Living as if you were the most important thing on earth is, literally, blasphemy; recreational sex may not bother me, but recreational life does. Our decisions should be motivated "not by selfishness or carelessness, but by a prudent conscious generosity." It's just that at the end of the twentieth century, on this planet, the signs of the times point me in the direction of the kinds of caring, the ways of maturing, that come with small, not large, families.

The church should not find that argument so foreign. Priests are celibate at least in part because it allows them to make Christ their bride, to devote all their energies to the other tasks set before us on this earth. And the wisdom of that argument is proved daily in a million places around the globe where committed priests and nuns take on the hardest and dirtiest challenges the earth has to offer. If we now have plenty of people to guarantee our survival as a race, and if lots more people may make that survival harder, then it's time to follow the lead of those clerics a little—not to embrace celibacy necessarily, but to love your child to pieces, and with whatever you have left to start working your way down the list.

And the same logic should make it clear, of course, that all sorts of other kinds of people—childless gay people, infertile people, people who do not feel called to parenthood—can become every bit as mature (or immature) as a parent of six, as long as they can find some substitute discipline for repeatedly placing someone or something else at the center of their lives.

Sometimes those disciplines are quiet and private, sometimes public. In Allan Gurganus's novel *Plays Well with Others*, his main character describes taking care of one friend after another as they succumbed to AIDS—describes the almost hydraulic outpouring of love it took to tend them. "My own loved ones were not brought into the world by me, but only, in my company, let out of it," he writes. His own obituary, he knows, will show that he left "no immediate survivors." "And yet I feel I've earned a family too." More so, of course, than many parents.

When she began studying the differences between pro-choice and pro-life advocates in the abortion dispute, Kristin Luker noticed something interesting. It was true that they differed over the morality of terminating pregnancy, but those differences were the product of other, more fundamental splits in their view of the world. They felt differently about God, about the role of women and, most interestingly, they felt very differently about the nature of planning.

Pro-choice activists, she observed, were almost obsessed with planning for their children, trying to give them "maximum parental guidance and every possible advantage," while parents active in the antiabortion movement "tend to be *laissez-faire* individualists in their attitude" toward child-rearing. "Pro-life people," she wrote, "believe that one becomes a parent by *being* a parent; parenthood is for them a 'natural' rather than a social role. The values implied by the in-vogue term 'parenting' (as in parenting classes) are alien to them." One woman she interviewed said, "I think people are foolish to worry about things in the future. The future takes care of itself." Too much planning, including too much family planning, means "playing God."

One of my favorite magazines comes from a small Ohio town. Called *Plain*, it is edited (and its type hand-set) by "conservative" Quakers, which is to say a group of men and women who live more or less in the fashion of Old Order Amish. The magazine recently reprinted a dinner conversation about the subject of family planning. The participants, each of them the parent of four children, were discussing their unease with contraception, and in terms very reminiscent of Luker's study:

Miriam: It breeds the mentality that "I want what I want, when I want."

Scott: It leads back to self-seeking, which eventually knows no bounds.

Marvin: Actually, it leads to a bottom-line refusal to accept God's will for our lives.

Scott: I think that one of the things Mary Ann and I have learned along the way, and which has further separated us from the mainstream culture, is the realization that we can always make room for one more. Because the room to be made is in our hearts.

That way of seeing the world attracts me—there is in its spontaneity and confidence something of real beauty. It offers a kind of freedom. Not the freedom of unlimited options that we've come to idolize, but a freedom from constant worrying and fretting. Sometimes I hate the calculator instinct in me, the part of me that constantly weighs benefits and risks, the part that keeps me safe and solvent at the expense of experience. There is something incredibly attractive about the mystery of the next child, and the next; I'd love to meet them. I'd love to leave it to God, or to chance, or to biology, or to destiny, or to the wind. Part of me thinks that those conservative Quakers, those pro-lifers, are unequivocally right.

The trouble is, there are now other ways to play God in this world, and *not* planning is one of them.

This was not always the case. In the Book of Job, God appears as a taunting voice from the whirlwind: "Where were you when I laid the foundations of the earth?" God asks Job. "Who shut up the sea with doors . . . and said here shall thy proud waves be stayed? . . . Who has cleft a channel for the torrents of rain, and a way for the thunderbolt?" Job has no way to reply, and no need; the earth is infinitely bigger than he; how absurd he would look standing at the edge of the sea and trying to whistle up the waves. God—the world—was huge, and we were tiny. Creation dwarfed us.

But now there are so many of us, and we have done such a poor job of planning for our numbers, that for the first time we can answer God back. We can say: we set the boundaries of the ocean. If we keep heating the planet at our current pace, the seas will rise two feet in the next century. Every one foot will bring the water 90 feet further inland across the typical American beach, drowning wetland and marsh. It's our lack of planning that changes the rainfall, that means more severe storms and worse flooding. It's not an "act of God." It's an act of us.

45   We no longer have the luxury of not planning; we're simply too big. We dominate the earth. When people first headed west across the plains, they didn't need a zoning board; now Californians try to channel and control growth lest they choke on it. In a crowded world, not planning has as many consequences as planning. This is a special time, and that turns everything on its head.

Questions

1. McKibben ends his essay by stating: "This is a special time, and that turns everything on its head." How does he demonstrate that this is "a special time"? Do you agree with him? In what sense does his argument depend on this being "a special time"?

2. McKibben tells of how his five-year-old daughter Sophie "has already used more stuff and added more waste to the environment than many of the world's residents do in a lifetime." Make an inventory of how much "stuff" you use in an average week, and then discuss whether your inventory proves McKibben's point.

3. Write an essay arguing that people who decide not to have children are or are not selfish.

BRENT STAPLES   *Black Men and Public Space*

M Y FIRST VICTIM was a woman—white, well dressed, probably in her early twenties. I came upon her late one evening on a deserted street in Hyde Park, a relatively affluent neighborhood in an otherwise mean, impoverished section of Chicago. As I swung onto the avenue behind her, there seemed to be a discreet, uninflammatory distance between us. Not so. She cast back a worried glance. To her, the youngish black man—a broad six feet two inches with a beard and billowing hair, both hands shoved into the pockets of a bulky military jacket—seemed menacingly close. After a few more quick glimpses, she picked up her pace and was soon running in earnest. Within seconds she disappeared into a cross street.

That was more than a decade ago, I was twenty-two years old, a graduate student newly arrived at the University of Chicago. It was in the echo of that terrified woman's footfalls that I first began to know the unwieldy inheritance I'd come into—the ability to alter public space in ugly ways. It was clear that she thought herself the quarry of a mugger, a rapist, or worse. Suffering a bout of insomnia, however, I was stalking sleep, not defenseless wayfarers. As a softy who is scarcely able to take a knife to a raw chicken—let alone hold one to a person's throat—I was surprised, embarrassed, and dismayed all at once. Her flight made me feel like an accomplice in tyranny. It also made it clear that I was indistinguishable from the muggers who occasionally seeped into the area from the surrounding ghetto. That first encounter, and those that followed, signified that a vast, unnerving gulf lay between nighttime pedestrians—particularly women—and me. And I soon gathered that being perceived as dangerous is a hazard in itself. I only needed to turn a corner into a dicey situation, or crowd some frightened, armed person in a foyer somewhere, or make an errant move after being pulled over by a policeman. Where fear and weapons meet—

Originally appeared in Harper's Magazine *(December 1986), an American monthly that continues its mission to "explore the issues and ideas in politics, science, and the arts that drive our national conversation." The essay was later incorporated into* Parallel Time: Growing Up in Black and White *(1994), an award-winning memoir of Staples's formative years in Chester, Pennsylvania, that chronicles his escape from poverty and crime and his brother's violent destruction.*

and they often do in urban America—there is always the possibility of death.

In that first year, my first away from my hometown, I was to become thoroughly familiar with the language of fear. At dark, shadowy intersections, I could cross in front of a car stopped at a traffic light and elicit the *thunk, thunk, thunk, thunk* of the driver—black, white, male, or female—hammering down the door locks. On less traveled streets after dark, I grew accustomed to but never comfortable with people crossing to the other side of the street rather than pass me. Then there were the standard unpleasantries with policemen, doormen, bouncers, cabdrivers, and others whose business it is to screen out troublesome individuals *before* there is any nastiness.

I moved to New York nearly two years ago and I have remained an avid night walker. In central Manhattan, the near-constant crowd cover minimizes tense one-on-one street encounters. Elsewhere—in SoHo, for example, where sidewalks are narrow and tightly spaced buildings shut out the sky—things can get very taut indeed.

5   After dark, on the warrenlike streets of Brooklyn where I live, I often see women who fear the worst from me. They seem to have set their faces on neutral, and with their purse straps strung across their chests bandolier-style, they forge ahead as though bracing themselves against being tackled. I understand, of course, that the danger they perceive is not a hallucination. Women are particularly vulnerable to street violence, and young black males are drastically overrepresented among the perpetrators of that violence. Yet these truths are no solace against the kind of alienation that comes of being ever the suspect, a fearsome entity with whom pedestrians avoid making eye contact.

It is not altogether clear to me how I reached the ripe old age of twenty-two without being conscious of the lethality nighttime pedestrians attributed to me. Perhaps it was because in Chester, Pennsylvania, the small, angry industrial town where I came of age in the 1960s, I was scarcely noticeable against a backdrop of gang warfare, street knifings, and murders. I grew up one of the good boys, had perhaps a half-dozen fistfights. In retrospect, my shyness of combat has clear sources.

As a boy, I saw countless tough guys locked away; I have since buried several, too. They were babies, really—a teenage cousin, a brother of twenty-two, a childhood friend in his mid-twenties—all gone down in episodes of bravado played out in the streets. I came to doubt the virtues of intimidation early on. I chose, perhaps unconsciously, to remain a shadow—timid, but a survivor.

The fearsomeness mistakenly attributed to me in public places often has a perilous flavor. The most frightening of these confusions occurred in the late 1970s and early 1980s, when I worked as a journalist in Chicago. One day, rushing into the office of a magazine I was writing for with a deadline story in hand, I was mistaken for a burglar. The office manager called security and, with an ad hoc[1] posse, pursued me through the labyrinthine halls, nearly to my editor's door. I had no way of proving who I was. I could only move briskly toward the company of someone who knew me.

---

1. For a particular purpose; improvised.

Another time I was on assignment for a local paper and killing time before an interview. I entered a jewelry store on the city's affluent Near North Side. The proprietor excused herself and returned with an enormous red Doberman pinscher straining at the end of a leash. She stood, the dog extended toward me, silent to my questions, her eyes bulging nearly out of her head. I took a cursory look around, nodded, and bade her good night.

Relatively speaking, however, I never fared as badly as another black male   10 journalist. He went to nearby Waukegan, Illinois, a couple of summers ago to work on a story about a murderer who was born there. Mistaking the reporter for the killer, police officers hauled him from his car at gunpoint and but for his press credentials would probably have tried to book him. Such episodes are not uncommon. Black men trade tales like this all the time.

Over the years, I learned to smother the rage I felt at so often being taken for a criminal. Not to do so would surely have led to madness. I now take precautions to make myself less threatening. I move about with care, particularly late in the evening. I give a wide berth to nervous people on subway platforms during the wee hours, particularly when I have exchanged business clothes for jeans. If I happen to be entering a building behind some people who appear skittish, I may walk by, letting them clear the lobby before I return, so as not to seem to be following them. I have been calm and extremely congenial on those rare occasions when I've been pulled over by the police.

And on late-evening constitutionals I employ what has proved to be an excellent tension-reducing measure: I whistle melodies from Beethoven and Vivaldi and the more popular classical composers. Even steely New Yorkers hunching toward nighttime destinations seem to relax, and occasionally they even join in the tune. Virtually everybody seems to sense that a mugger wouldn't be warbling bright, sunny selections from Vivaldi's *Four Seasons*.[2] It is my equivalent of the cowbell that hikers wear when they know they are in bear country.

2. Work by composer Antonio Vivaldi (1678–1741), celebrating the seasons.

QUESTIONS

1. Staples writes of situations rightly perceived as threatening and of situations misperceived as threatening. Give specific instances of each and tell how they are related.

2. Staples's essay contains a mixture of rage and humor. Does this mix distract from or contribute to the seriousness of the matter?

3. Write of a situation in which someone was wrongly perceived as threatening.

DEBRA DICKERSON *Who Shot Johnny?*

IVEN MY LEVEL of political awareness, it was inevitable that I would come to view the everyday events of my life through the prism of politics and the national discourse. I read *The Washington Post*, *The New Republic*, *The New Yorker*, *Harper's*, *The Atlantic Monthly*, *The Nation*, *National Review*, *Black Enterprise* and *Essence* and wrote a weekly column for the *Harvard Law School Record* during my three years just ended there. I do this because I know that those of us who are not well-fed white guys in suits must not yield the debate to them, however well-intentioned or well-informed they may be. Accordingly, I am unrepentant and vocal about having gained admittance to Harvard through affirmative action; I am a feminist, stoic about my marriage chances as a well-educated, 36-year-old black woman who won't pretend to need help taking care of herself. My strength flags, though, in the face of the latest role assigned to my family in the national drama. On July 27, 1995, my 16-year-old nephew was shot and paralyzed.

Talking with friends in front of his home, Johnny saw a car he thought he recognized. He waved boisterously—his trademark—throwing both arms in the air in a full-bodied, hip-hop Y. When he got no response, he and his friends sauntered down the walk to join a group loitering in front of an apartment building. The car followed. The driver got out, brandished a revolver and fired into the air. Everyone scattered. Then he took aim and shot my running nephew in the back.

Johnny never lost consciousness. He lay in the road, trying to understand what had happened to him, why he couldn't get up. Emotionlessly, he told the story again and again on demand, remaining apologetically firm against all demands to divulge the missing details that would make sense of the shooting but obviously cast him in a bad light. Being black, male and shot, he must, apparently, be gang- or drug-involved. Probably both. Witnesses corroborate his version of events.

Nearly six months have passed since that phone call in the night and my nightmarish, headlong drive from Boston to Charlotte. After twenty hours behind the wheel, I arrived haggard enough to reduce my mother to fresh tears and to find my nephew reassuring well-wishers with an eerie sangfroid.[1]

5   I take the day shift in his hospital room; his mother and grandmother, a clerk and cafeteria worker, respectively, alternate nights there on a cot. They don their uniforms the next day, gaunt after hours spent listening to Johnny moan in his sleep. How often must his subconscious replay those events

Published in the New Republic *(January 1, 1996), an American journal of politics and the arts. The essay was selected for* Best American Essays *(1997), a yearly series that reprints distinguished nonfiction from national and regional American magazines.*

1. Cold blood (French). Composure; self-assurance in the face of difficulty.

and curse its host for saying hello without permission, for being carefree and young while a would-be murderer hefted the weight of his uselessness and failure like Jacob Marley's chains?[2] How often must he watch himself lying stubbornly immobile on the pavement of his nightmares while the sound of running feet syncopate his attacker's taunts?

I spend these days beating him at gin rummy and Scrabble, holding a basin while he coughs up phlegm and crying in the corridor while he catheterizes himself. There are children here much worse off than he. I should be grateful. The doctors can't, or won't, say whether he'll walk again.

I am at once repulsed and fascinated by the bullet, which remains lodged in his spine (having done all the damage it can do, the doctors say). The wound is undramatic—small, neat and perfectly centered—an impossibly pink pit surrounded by an otherwise undisturbed expanse of mahogany. Johnny has asked me several times to describe it but politely declines to look in the mirror I hold for him.

Here on the pediatric rehab ward, Johnny speaks little, never cries, never complains, works diligently to become independent. He does whatever he is told; if two hours remain until the next pain pill, he waits quietly. Eyes bloodshot, hands gripping the bed rails. During the week of his intravenous feeding when he was tormented by the primal need to masticate, he never asked for food. He just listened while we counted down the days for him and planned his favorite meals. Now required to dress himself unassisted, he does so without demur, rolling himself back and forth valiantly on the bed and shivering afterwards, exhausted. He "ma'am"s and "sir"s everyone politely. Before his "accident," a simple request to take out the trash could provoke a firestorm of teenage attitude. We, the women who have raised him, have changed as well; we've finally come to appreciate those boxer-baring, oversized pants we used to hate—it would be much more difficult to fit properly sized pants over his diaper.

He spends a lot of time tethered to rap music still loud enough to break my concentration as I read my many magazines. I hear him try to soundlessly mouth the obligatory "mothafuckers" overlaying the funereal dirge of the music tracks. I do not normally tolerate disrespectful music in my or my mother's presence, but if it distracts him now . . .

"Johnny," I ask later, "do you still like gangster rap?" During the long pause I hear him think loudly, *I'm paralyzed Auntie, not stupid.* "I mostly just listen to hip hop," he says evasively into his *Sports Illustrated.* 10

Miserable though it is, time passes quickly here. We always seem to be jerking awake in our chairs just in time for the next pill, his every-other-night bowel program, the doctor's rounds. Harvard feels a galaxy away—the world revolves around Family Members Living With Spinal Cord Injury class, Johnny's urine output and strategizing with my sister to find affordable, accessible housing. There is always another long-distance uncle in need of an update, another

2. The ghost of Marley, in chains, visits Ebenezer Scrooge in Dickens's *A Christmas Carol.*

church member wanting to pray with us or Johnny's little brother in need of some attention.

We Dickerson women are so constant a presence the ward nurses and cleaning staff call us by name and join us for cafeteria meals and cigarette breaks. At Johnny's birthday pizza party, they crack jokes and make fun of each other's husbands (there are no men here). I pass slices around and try not to think, "17 with a bullet."

Oddly, we feel little curiosity or specific anger toward the man who shot him. We have to remind ourselves to check in with the police. Even so, it feels pro forma, like sending in those $2 rebate forms that come with new pantyhose: you know your request will fall into a deep, dark hole somewhere but, still, it's your duty to try. We push for an arrest because we owe it to Johnny and to ourselves as citizens. We don't think about it otherwise—our low expectations are too ingrained. A Harvard aunt notwithstanding, for people like Johnny, Marvin Gaye[3] was right that only three things are sure: taxes, death and trouble. At least it wasn't the second.

We rarely wonder about or discuss the brother who shot him because we already know everything about him. When the call came, my first thought was the same one I'd had when I'd heard about Rosa Parks's beating:[4] a brother did it. A non-job-having, middle-of-the-day malt-liquor-drinking, crotch-clutching, loud-talking brother with many neglected children born of many forgotten women. He lives in his mother's basement with furniture rented at an astronomical interest rate, the exact amount of which he does not know. He has a car phone, an $80 monthly cable bill and every possible phone feature but no savings. He steals Social Security numbers from unsuspecting relatives and assumes their identities to acquire large TV sets for which he will never pay. On the slim chance that he is brought to justice, he will have a colorful criminal history and no coherent explanation to offer for this act. His family will raucously defend him and cry cover-up. Some liberal lawyer just like me will help him plea bargain his way to yet another short stay in a prison pesthouse that will serve only to add another layer to the brother's sociopathology and formless, mindless nihilism. We know him. We've known and feared him all our lives.

15   As a teenager, he called, "Hey, baby, gimme somma that boodie!" at us from car windows. Indignant at our lack of response, he followed up with, "Fuck you, then, 'ho!" He called me a "white-boy lovin' nigger bitch oreo" for being in the gifted program and loving it. At 27, he got my 17-year-old sister pregnant with Johnny and lost interest without ever informing her that he was married. He snatched my widowed mother's purse as she waited in pre-dawn darkness for the bus to work and then broke into our house while she soldered on an assembly line. He chased all the small entrepreneurs from our neighbor-

3. African American soul singer (1939–1984) who was shot to death in an altercation with his father.
4. The elderly Rosa Parks, the 1950s civil rights pioneer, was the victim of a beating in the 1990s.

hood with his violent thievery, and put bars on our windows. He kept us from sitting on our own front porch after dark and laid the foundation for our periodic bouts of self-hating anger and racial embarrassment. He made our neighborhood a ghetto. He is the poster fool behind the maddening community knowledge that there are still some black mothers who raise their daughters but merely love their sons. He and his cancerous carbon copies eclipse the vast majority of us who are not sociopaths and render us invisible. He is the Siamese twin who has died but cannot be separated from his living, vibrant sibling; which of us must attract more notice? We despise and disown this anomalous loser but, for many, he *is* black America. We know him, we know that he is outside the fold, and we know that he will only get worse. What we didn't know is that, because of him, my little sister would one day be the latest hysterical black mother wailing over a fallen child on TV.

Alone, lying in the road bleeding and paralyzed but hideously conscious, Johnny had lain helpless as he watched his would-be murderer come to stand over him and offer this prophecy: "Betch'ou won't be doin' nomo' wavin', motha'fucker."

Fuck you, asshole. He's fine from the waist up. You just can't do anything right, can you?

QUESTIONS

1. Why did the *New Republic* include the first paragraph? Do you think the essay would be more or less effective if it began simply with the sentence "On July 27, 1995, my 16-year-old nephew was shot and paralyzed"?

2. Dickerson feels—and expresses—anger throughout this essay. How? Against what or whom?

3. Why does Dickerson use the term "brother" in the final paragraphs? How does this composite characterization work? How does it answer the question "Who shot Johnny?"

EDUCATION

FREDERICK DOUGLASS *Learning to Read*

I LIVED IN Master Hugh's family about seven years.[1] During this time, I succeeded in learning to read and write. In accomplishing this, I was compelled to resort to various stratagems. I had no regular teacher. My mistress, who had kindly commenced to instruct me, had, in compliance with the advice and direction of her husband, not only ceased to instruct, but had set her face against my being instructed by any one else. It is due, however, to my mistress to say of her, that she did not adopt this course of treatment immediately. She at first lacked the depravity indispensable to shutting me up in mental darkness. It was at least necessary for her to have some training in the exercise of irresponsible power, to make her equal to the task of treating me as though I were a brute.

My mistress was, as I have said, a kind and tender-hearted woman; and in the simplicity of her soul she commenced, when I first went to live with her, to treat me as she supposed one human being ought to treat another. In entering upon the duties of a slaveholder, she did not seem to perceive that I sustained to her the relation of a mere chattel, and that for her to treat me as a human being was not only wrong, but dangerously so. Slavery proved as injurious to her as it did to me. When I went there, she was a pious, warm, and tender-hearted woman. There was no sorrow or suffering for which she had not a tear. She had bread for the hungry, clothes for the naked, and comfort for every mourner that came within her reach. Slavery soon proved its ability to divest her of these heavenly qualities. Under its influence, the tender heart became stone, and the lamblike disposition gave way to one of tigerlike fierceness. The first step in her downward course was in her ceasing to instruct me. She now commenced to practise her husband's precepts. She finally became even more violent in her opposition than her husband himself. She was not satisfied with simply doing as well as he had commanded; she seemed anxious to do better. Nothing seemed to make her more angry than to see me with a newspaper. She seemed to think that here lay the danger. I have had her rush at me with a face made all up of fury, and snatch from me a newspaper, in a manner that fully revealed her apprehension. She was an apt woman; and a lit-

---

From Douglass's autobiography, Narrative of the Life of Frederick Douglass, An American Slave, Written by Himself *(1845), a landmark of African American literature.*

1. In Baltimore, Maryland.

tle experience soon demonstrated, to her satisfaction, that education and slavery were incompatible with each other.

From this time I was most narrowly watched. If I was in a separate room any considerable length of time, I was sure to be suspected of having a book, and was at once called to give an account of myself. All this, however, was too late. The first step had been taken. Mistress, in teaching me the alphabet, had given me the *inch*, and no precaution could prevent me from taking the *ell*.[2]

The plan which I adopted, and the one by which I was most successful, was that of making friends of all the little white boys whom I met in the street. As many of these as I could, I converted into teachers. With their kindly aid, obtained at different times and in different places, I finally succeeded in learning to read. When I was sent of errands, I always took my book with me, and by going one part of my errand quickly, I found time to get a lesson before my return. I used also to carry bread with me, enough of which was always in the house, and to which I was always welcome; for I was much better off in this regard than many of the poor white children in our neighborhood. This bread I used to bestow upon the hungry little urchins, who, in return, would give me that more valuable bread of knowledge. I am strongly tempted to give the names of two or three of those little boys, as a testimonial of the gratitude and affection I bear them; but prudence forbids;—not that it would injure me, but it might embarrass them; for it is almost an unpardonable offence to teach slaves to read in this Christian country. It is enough to say of the dear little fellows, that they lived on Philpot Street, very near Durgin and Bailey's ship-yard. I used to talk this matter of slavery over with them. I would sometimes say to them, I wished I could be as free as they would be when they got to be men. "You will be free as soon as you are twenty-one, *but I am a slave for life!* Have not I as good a right to be free as you have?" These words used to trouble them; they would express for me the liveliest sympathy, and console me with the hope that something would occur by which I might be free.

I was now about twelve years old, and the thought of being *a slave for life*   5
began to bear heavily upon my heart. Just about this time, I got hold of a book entitled "The Columbian Orator."[3] Every opportunity I got, I used to read this book. Among much of other interesting matter, I found in it a dialogue between a master and his slave. The slave was represented as having run away from his master three times. The dialogue represented the conversation which took place between them, when the slave was retaken the third time. In this dialogue, the whole argument in behalf of slavery was brought forward by the master, all of which was disposed of by the slave. The slave was made to say some very smart as well as impressive things in reply to his master—things which had the desired though unexpected effect; for the conversation resulted in the voluntary emancipation of the slave on the part of the master.

In the same book, I met with one of Sheridan's mighty speeches on and in

---

2. Once a unit of measurement equal to forty-five inches; the saying is proverbial.

3. A popular collection of poems, dialogues, plays, and speeches.

behalf of Catholic emancipation.[4] These were choice documents to me. I read them over and over again with unabated interest. They gave tongue to interesting thoughts of my own soul, which had frequently flashed through my mind, and died away for want of utterance. The moral which I gained from the dialogue was the power of truth over the conscience of even a slaveholder. What I got from Sheridan was a bold denunciation of slavery, and a powerful vindication of human rights. The reading of these documents enabled me to utter my thoughts, and to meet the arguments brought forward to sustain slavery; but while they relieved me of one difficulty, they brought on another even more painful than the one of which I was relieved. The more I read, the more I was led to abhor and detest my enslavers. I could regard them in no other light than a band of successful robbers, who had left their homes, and gone to Africa, and stolen us from our homes, and in a strange land reduced us to slavery. I loathed them as being the meanest as well as the most wicked of men. As I read and contemplated the subject, behold! that very discontentment which Master Hugh had predicted would follow my learning to read had already come, to torment and sting my soul to unutterable anguish. As I writhed under it, I would at times feel that learning to read had been a curse rather than a blessing. It had given me a view of my wretched condition, without the remedy. It opened my eyes to the horrible pit, but to no ladder upon which to get out. In moments of agony, I envied my fellow-slaves for their stupidity. I have often wished myself a beast. I preferred the condition of the meanest reptile to my own. Any thing, no matter what, to get rid of thinking! It was this everlasting thinking of my condition that tormented me. There was no getting rid of it. It was pressed upon me by every object within sight or hearing, animate or inanimate. The silver trump of freedom had roused my soul to eternal wakefulness. Freedom now appeared, to disappear no more forever. It was heard in every sound, and seen in every thing. It was ever present to torment me with a sense of my wretched condition. I saw nothing without seeing it, I heard nothing without hearing it, and felt nothing without feeling it. It looked from every star, it smiled in every calm, breathed in every wind, and moved in every storm.

I often found myself regretting my own existence, and wishing myself dead; and but for the hope of being free, I have no doubt but that I should have killed myself, or done something for which I should have been killed. While in this state of mind, I was eager to hear any one speak of slavery. I was a ready listener. Every little while, I could hear something about the abolitionists. It was some time before I found what the word meant. It was always used in such connections as to make it an interesting word to me. If a slave ran away and succeeded in getting clear, or if a slave killed his master, set fire to a barn, or did any thing very wrong in the mind of a slaveholder, it was spoken of as the fruit of *abolition*. Hearing the word in this connection very often, I

4. Richard Brinsley Sheridan (1751–1815), Irish dramatist and political leader. The speech, arguing for the abolition of laws denying Roman Catholics in Great Britain and Ireland civil and political liberties, was actually made by the Irish patriot Arthur O'Connor.

set about learning what it meant. The dictionary afforded me little or no help.
I found it was "the act of abolishing"; but then I did not know what was to be
abolished. Here I was perplexed. I did not dare to ask any one about its meaning, for I was satisfied that it was something they wanted me to know very little about. After a patient waiting, I got one of our city papers, containing an
account of the number of petitions from the north, praying for the abolition of
slavery in the District of Columbia, and of the slave trade between the States.
From this time I understood the words *abolition* and *abolitionist,* and always
drew near when that word was spoken, expecting to hear something of importance to myself and fellow-slaves. The light broke in upon me by degrees. I
went one day down on the wharf of Mr. Waters; and seeing two Irishmen un-
loading a scow of stone, I went, unasked, and helped them. When we had finished, one of them came to me and asked me if I were a slave. I told him I
was. He asked, "Are ye a slave for life?" I told him that I was. The good Irishman seemed to be deeply affected by the statement. He said to the other that
it was a pity so fine a little fellow as myself should be a slave for life. He said
it was a shame to hold me. They both advised me to run away to the north;
that I should find friends there, and that I should be free. I pretended not to
be interested in what they said, and treated them as if I did not understand
them; for I feared they might be treacherous. White men have been known to
encourage slaves to escape, and then, to get the reward, catch them and return them to their masters. I was afraid that these seemingly good men might
use me so; but I nevertheless remembered their advice, and from that time I
resolved to run away. I looked forward to a time at which it would be safe for
me to escape. I was too young to think of doing so immediately; besides, I
wished to learn how to write, as I might have occasion to write my own pass. I
consoled myself with the hope that I should one day find a good chance.
Meanwhile, I would learn to write.

The idea as to how I might learn to write was suggested to me by being in
Durgin and Bailey's ship-yard, and frequently seeing the ship carpenters, after
hewing, and getting a piece of timber ready for use, write on the timber the
name of that part of the ship for which it was intended. When a piece of timber
was intended for the larboard side, it would be marked thus—"L." When a
piece was for the starboard side, it would be marked thus—"S." A piece for the
larboard side forward, would be marked thus—"L. F." When a piece was for
starboard side forward, it would be marked thus—"S. F." For larboard aft, it
would be marked thus— "L. A." For starboard aft, it would be marked thus—
"S. A." I soon learned the names of these letters, and for what they were intended when placed upon a piece of timber in the shipyard. I immediately commenced copying them, and in a short time was able to make the four letters
named. After that, when I met with any boy who I knew could write, I would
tell him I could write as well as he. The next word would be, "I don't believe
you. Let me see you try it." I would then make the letters which I had been so
fortunate as to learn, and ask him to beat that. In this way I got a good many
lessons in writing, which it is quite possible I should never have gotten in any
other way. During this time, my copy-book was the board fence, brick wall, and

pavement; my pen and ink was a lump of chalk. With these, I learned mainly how to write. I then commenced and continued copying the Italics in Webster's Spelling Book,[5] until I could make them all without looking on the book. By this time, my little Master Thomas had gone to school, and learned how to write, and had written over a number of copy-books. These had been brought home, and shown to some of our near neighbors, and then laid aside. My mistress used to go to class meeting at the Wilk Street meetinghouse every Monday afternoon, and leave me to take care of the house. When left thus, I used to spend the time in writing in the spaces left in Master Thomas's copy-book, copying what he had written. I continued to do this until I could write a hand very similar to that of Master Thomas. Thus, after a long, tedious effort for years, I finally succeeded in learning how to write.

5. *The American Spelling Book* (1783) by Noah Webster (1758–1843), American lexicographer.

QUESTIONS

1. Douglass's story might today be called a "literacy narrative"—an account of how someone gains the skills of reading and writing. What are the key features of this narrative? What obstacles did Douglass face? How did he overcome them?

2. Many literacy narratives include an enabling figure, someone who helps the young learner along his or her way. Is there such a figure in Douglass's narrative? Why or why not?

3. At the end of this narrative Douglass mentions that he wrote "in the spaces left in Master Thomas's copy-book, copying what he had written" (paragraph 8). To what extent is imitation (copying) part of learning? To what extent does this narrative show originality?

4. Write your own literacy narrative—an account of how you learned to read and write.

Benjamin Franklin *Learning to Write*

ABOUT THIS TIME I met with an odd Volume of the *Specta-tor*.[1] I had never before seen any of them. I bought it, read it over and over, and was much delighted with it. I thought the Writing excellent, and wish'd if possible to imitate it. With that View, I took some of the Papers, and making short Hints of the Sentiment in each Sentence, laid them by a few Days, and then without looking at the Book, tried to complete the Papers again, by expressing each hinted Sentiment at length and as fully as it had been express'd before in any suitable Words that should come to hand.

Then I compar'd my *Spectator* with the Original, discover'd some of my Faults and corrected them. But I found I wanted a Stock of Words or a Readiness in recollecting and using them which I thought I should have acquir'd before that time, if I had gone on making Verses, since the continual Occasion for Words of the same Import but of different Length, to suit the Measure,[2] or of different Sound for the Rhyme, would have laid me under a constant Necessity of searching for Variety, and also have tended to fix that Variety in my Mind, and make me Master of it. Therefore I took some of the Tales and turn'd them into Verse: And after a time, when I had pretty well forgotten the Prose, turn'd them back again. I also sometimes jumbled my Collections of Hints into Confusion, and after some Weeks, endeavor'd to reduce them into the best Order, before I began to form the full Sentences, and complete the Paper. This was to teach me Method in the Arrangement of Thoughts. By comparing my Work afterwards with the original, I discover'd many faults and amended them; but I sometimes had the Pleasure of Fancying that in certain Particulars of small Import, I had been lucky enough to improve the Method or the Language and this encourag'd me to think I might possibly in time come to be a tolerable English Writer, of which I was extremely ambitious.

My Time for these Exercises and for Reading, was at Night after Work, or before Work began in the Morning; or on Sundays, when I contrived to be in the Printing-House alone, evading as much as I could the common Attendance on public Worship, which my Father used to exact of me when I was under his Care: And which indeed I still thought a Duty; tho' I could not, as it seemed to me, afford the Time to practice it.

When about 16 Years of Age, I happen'd to meet with a Book written by one Tryon,[3] recommending a Vegetable Diet. I determined to go into it. My

Drawn from Franklin's Autobiography, *his classic account of his life, first published in 1791.*

1. Daily English periodical noted for its excellence in prose.
2. Meter.
3. Thomas Tryon (1634–1703), author of *Way to Health and Happiness* (1682).

Brother being yet unmarried, did not keep House, but boarded himself and his Apprentices in another Family. My refusing to eat Flesh occasioned an Inconveniency, and I was frequently chid for my singularity. I made myself acquainted with Tryon's Manner of preparing some of his Dishes, such as Boiling Potatoes or Rice, making Hasty Pudding,[4] and a few others, and then propos'd to my Brother, that if he would give me Weekly half the Money he paid for my Board, I would board myself. He instantly agreed to it, and I presently found that I could save half what he paid me. This was an additional Fund for buying Books: But I had another Advantage in it. My Brother and the rest going from the Printing-House to their Meals, I remain'd there alone, and dispatching presently my light Repast, (which often was no more than a Biscuit or a Slice of Bread, a Handful of Raisins or a Tart from the Pastry Cook's, and a Glass of Water) had the rest of the Time till their Return, for Study, in which I made the greater Progress from that greater Clearness of Head and quicker Apprehension which usually attend Temperance in Eating and Drinking. And now it was that being on some Occasion made asham'd of my Ignorance in Figures; which I had twice fail'd in learning when at School, I took Cocker's Book of Arithmetic,[5] and went thro' the whole by myself with great Ease. I also read Seller's[6] and Sturmy's[7] Books of Navigation, and became acquainted with the little Geometry they contain, but never proceeded far in that Science. And I read about this Time Locke on Human Understanding and the Art of Thinking by Messrs. du Port Royal.[8]

5   While I was intent on improving my Language, I met with an English Grammar (I think it was Greenwood's[9]) at the End of which there were two little Sketches of the Arts of Rhetoric and Logic, the latter finishing with a Specimen of a Dispute in the Socratic Method. And soon after I procur'd Xenophon's Memorable Things of Socrates,[10] wherein there are many Instances of the same Method. I was charm'd with it, adopted it, dropped my abrupt Contradiction and positive Argumentation, and put on the humble Enquirer and Doubter. And being then, from reading Shaftesbury[11] and Collins,[12]

---

4. Cornmeal mush.

5. Well-known textbook, first published in 1677.

6. John Seller (c. 1658–1698), author of *Practical Navigation* (1694).

7. Samuel Sturmy (1633–1669), author of *The Mariner's Magazine* (1699).

8. John Locke (1632–1704), British philosopher and author of *An Essay Concerning Human Understanding* (1690); Pierre Nicole (1625–1695) of Port Royal published his book in 1662; it was translated into English as *Logic: Or the Art of Thinking* in 1687.

9. James Greenwood (d. 1737), author of *An Essay towards a Practical English Grammar* (1711).

10. Xenophon's (c. 430–355 B.C.E.) *The Memorable Things of Socrates* was published in English translation by Edward Bysshe in 1712.

11. Anthony Ashley Cooper, earl of Shaftesbury (1671–1713), famous for his *Characteristics of Men, Manners, Opinions, Times* (1711).

12. Anthony Collins (1676–1729), a friend of Locke; author of *A Discourse of Free Thinking* (1713).

became a real Doubter in many Points of our Religious Doctrine. I found this Method safest for myself and very embarrassing to those against whom I used it, therefore I took a Delight in it, practic'd it continually and grew very artful and expert in drawing People even of superior Knowledge into Concessions the Consequences of which they did not foresee, entangling them in Difficulties out of which they could not extricate themselves, and so obtaining Victories that neither myself nor my Cause always deserved. I continu'd this Method some few Years, but gradually left it, retaining only the Habit of expressing myself in Terms of modest Diffidence, never using when I advance any thing that may possibly be disputed, the Words, *Certainly, undoubtedly*, or any others that give the Air of Positiveness to an Opinion; but rather say, *I conceive*, or *I apprehend* a Thing to be so or so. *It appears to me*, or *I should think it so or so for such and such Reasons*, or *I imagine* it to be so, or *it is so if I am not mistaken*. This Habit I believe has been of great Advantage to me, when I have had occasion to inculcate my Opinions and persuade Men into Measures that I have been from time to time engag'd in promoting. And as the chief Ends of Conversation are to *inform*, or to be *informed*, to *please* or to *persuade*, I wish well-meaning sensible Men would not lessen their Power of doing Good by a Positive assuming Manner that seldom fails to disgust, tends to create Opposition, and to defeat every one of those Purposes for which Speech was given us, to wit, giving or receiving Information, or Pleasure: For if you would *inform*, a positive dogmatical Manner in advancing your Sentiments, may provoke Contradiction and prevent a candid Attention. If you wish Information and Improvement from the Knowledge of others and yet at the same time express yourself as firmly fix'd in your present Opinions, modest sensible Men, who do not love Disputation, will probably leave you undisturb'd in the Possession of your Error; and by such a Manner you can seldom hope to recommend yourself in *pleasing* your Hearers, or to persuade those whose Concurrence you desire. Pope says, judiciously,

> Men should be taught as if you taught them not,
> And things unknown propos'd as things forgot,

farther recommending it to us,

> To speak tho' sure, with seeming Diffidence.[13]

And he might have coupled with this Line that which he has coupled with another, I think less properly,

> For want of Modesty is want of Sense.

---

13. Adapted from Alexander Pope's (1688–1744) *An Essay on Criticism* (1711).

If you ask why *less properly*, I must repeat the Lines;

> "Immodest Words admit of *no* Defence;
> For Want of Modesty is Want of Sense."[14]

Now is not *Want of Sense*, (where a Man is so unfortunate as to want it) some Apology for his *Want of Modesty*? and would not the Lines stand more justly thus?

> Immodest Words admit *but this* Defence.
> That Want of Modesty is Want of Sense.

This however I should submit to better Judgments.

14. Franklin wrongly attributes these two lines to Pope. They are by Wentworth Dillon (1633?–1685), from his *Essay on Translated Verse* (1684). The second line should read "For want of Decency is want of Sense."

QUESTIONS

1. Franklin describes his youthful practice of imitating successful writers' sentences. Have you ever done this? What do you think of the practice? What are writers likely to learn from such a practice?

2. When he was sixteen, Franklin read a book about vegetarian diets and immediately was converted. Write about how you or someone you know was converted to following a distinct path, either religious, ethical, or physical (examples you might choose: a religious sect, a strict diet, exercise). Did the conversion happen suddenly, as it did with Franklin, or did it take place slowly, over time? How long did the conversion last?

3. Franklin is a classic auto-didact, a self-teacher. Recount what Franklin learned in this manner, and note what he failed to teach himself. What kinds of knowledge did Franklin seek to acquire? Was his learning broad or narrow? What kinds of endeavors was this knowledge most suited for?

JOHN HOLT   *How Teachers Make Children Hate Reading*

W HEN I WAS TEACHING English at the Colorado Rocky Mountain School, I used to ask my students the kinds of questions that English teachers usually ask about reading assignments—questions designed to bring out the points that *I* had decided *they* should know. They, on their part, would try to get me to give them hints and clues as to what I wanted. It was a game of wits. I never gave my students an opportunity to say what they really thought about a book.

I gave vocabulary drills and quizzes too. I told my students that every time they came upon a word in their book they did not understand, they were to look it up in the dictionary. I even devised special kinds of vocabulary tests, allowing them to use their books to see how the words were used. But looking back, I realize that these tests, along with many of my methods, were foolish.

My sister was the first person who made me question my conventional ideas about teaching English. She had a son in the seventh grade in a fairly good public school. His teacher had asked the class to read Cooper's *The Deerslayer.*[1] The choice was bad enough in itself; whether looking at man or nature, Cooper was superficial, inaccurate and sentimental, and his writing is ponderous and ornate. But to make matters worse, this teacher had decided to give the book the microscope and x-ray treatment. He made the students look up and memorize not only the definitions but the derivations of every big word that came along—and there were plenty. Every chapter was followed by close questioning and testing to make sure the students "understood" everything.

Being then, as I said, conventional, I began to defend the teacher, who was a good friend of mine, against my sister's criticisms. The argument soon grew hot. What was wrong with making sure that children understood everything they read? My sister answered that until this year her boy had always loved reading, and had read a lot on his own; now he had stopped. (He was not really to start again for many years.)

Still I persisted. If children didn't look up the words they didn't know, how   5
would they ever learn them? My sister said, "Don't be silly! When you were little you had a huge vocabulary, and were always reading very grown-up books. When did you ever look up a word in a dictionary?"

She had me. I don't know that we had a dictionary at home; if we did, I didn't use it. I don't use one today. In my life I doubt that I have looked up as many as fifty words, perhaps not even half that.

Since then I have talked about this with a number of teachers. More than

From The Under-Achieving School *(1967), Holt's third book-length critique of American education.*

1. James Fenimore Cooper (1789–1851), American novelist; *The Deerslayer* was published in 1841.

once I have said, "According to tests, educated and literate people like you have a vocabulary of about twenty-five thousand words. How many of these did you learn by looking them up in a dictionary?" They usually are startled. Few claim to have looked up even as many as a thousand. How did they learn the rest?

They learned them just as they learned to talk—by meeting words over and over again, in different contexts, until they saw how they fitted.

Unfortunately, we English teachers are easily hung up on this matter of understanding. Why should children understand everything they read? Why should anyone? Does anyone? I don't, and I never did. I was always reading books that teachers would have said were "too hard" for me, books full of words I didn't know. That's how I got to be a good reader. When about ten, I read all the D'Artagnan stories[2] and loved them. It didn't trouble me in the least that I didn't know why France was at war with England or who was quarreling with whom in the French court or why the Musketeers should always be at odds with Cardinal Richelieu's men. I didn't even know who the Cardinal was, except that he was a dangerous and powerful man that my friends had to watch out for. This was all I needed to know.

10   Having said this, I will now say that I think a big, unabridged dictionary is a fine thing to have in any home or classroom. No book is more fun to browse around in—*if* you're not made to. Children, depending on their age, will find many pleasant and interesting things to do with a big dictionary. They can look up funny-sounding words, which they like, or words that nobody else in the class has ever heard of, which they like, or long words, which they like, or forbidden words, which they like best of all. At a certain age, and particularly with a little encouragement from parents or teachers, they may become very interested in where words came from and when they came into the language and how their meanings have changed over the years. But exploring for the fun of it is very different from looking up words out of your reading because you're going to get into trouble with your teacher if you don't.

While teaching fifth grade two years or so after the argument with my sister, I began to think again about reading. The children in my class were supposed to fill out a card—just the title and author and a one-sentence summary—for every book they read. I was not running a competition to see which child could read the most books, a competition that almost always leads to cheating. I just wanted to know what the children were reading. After a while it became clear that many of these very bright kids, from highly literate and even literary backgrounds, read very few books and deeply disliked reading. Why should this be?

At this time I was coming to realize, as I described in my book *How Chil-*

---

2. Alexandre Dumas (1802–1870), called Dumas *père* to distinguish him from his son Alexandre, called Dumas *fils*, wrote *The Three Musketeers* (1844), a historical novel set in seventeenth-century France. D'Artagnan, the hero of the novel, meets three friends, already musketeers (soldiers who carry muskets), and joins them in fighting cardinals, dodging assassins, and seeking romance.

dren Fail, that for most children school was a place of danger, and their main business in school was staying out of danger as much as possible. I now began to see also that books were among the most dangerous things in school.

From the very beginning of school we make books and reading a constant source of possible failure and public humiliation. When children are little we make them read aloud, before the teacher and other children, so that we can be sure they "know" all the words they are reading. This means that when they don't know a word, they are going to make a mistake, right in front of everyone. Instantly they are made to realize that they have done something wrong. Perhaps some of the other children will begin to wave their hands and say, "Ooooh! O-o-o-oh!" Perhaps they will just giggle, or nudge each other, or make a face. Perhaps the teacher will say, "Are you sure?" or ask someone else what he thinks. Or perhaps, if the teacher is kindly, she will just smile a sweet, sad smile—often one of the most painful punishments a child can suffer in school. In any case, the child who has made the mistake knows he has made it, and feels foolish, stupid, and ashamed, just as any of us would in his shoes.

Before long many children associate books and reading with mistakes, real or feared, and penalties and humiliation. This may not seem sensible, but it is natural. Mark Twain once said that a cat that sat on a hot stove lid would never sit on one again—but it would never sit on a cold one either. As true of children as of cats. If they, so to speak, sit on a hot book a few times, if books cause them humiliation and pain, they are likely to decide that the safest thing to do is to leave all books alone.

After having taught fifth-grade classes for four years I felt quite sure of this theory. In my next class were many children who had had great trouble with schoolwork, particularly reading. I decided to try at all costs to rid them of their fear and dislike of books, and to get them to read oftener and more adventurously.

One day soon after school had started, I said to them, "Now I'm going to say something about reading that you have probably never heard a teacher say before. I would like you to read a lot of books this year, but I want you to read them only for pleasure. I am not going to ask you questions to find out whether you understand the books or not. If you understand enough of a book to enjoy it and want to go on reading it, that's enough for me. Also I'm not going to ask you what words mean.

"Finally," I said, "I don't want you to feel that just because you start a book, you have to finish it. Give an author thirty or forty pages or so to get his story going. Then if you don't like the characters and don't care what happens to them, close the book, put it away, and get another. I don't care whether the books are easy or hard, short or long, as long as you enjoy them. Furthermore I'm putting all this in a letter to your parents, so they won't feel they have to quiz and heckle you about books at home."

The children sat stunned and silent. Was this a teacher talking? One girl, who had just come to us from a school where she had had a very hard time, and who proved to be one of the most interesting, lively, and intelligent children I have ever known, looked at me steadily for a long time after I had fin-

15

ished. Then, still looking at me, she said slowly and solemnly, "Mr. Holt, do you really mean that?" I said just as solemnly, "I mean every word of it."

Apparently she decided to believe me. The first book she read was Dr. Seuss's *How the Grinch Stole Christmas,* not a hard book even for most third graders. For a while she read a number of books on this level. Perhaps she was clearing up some confusion about reading that her teachers, in their hurry to get her up to "grade level," had never given her enough time to clear up. After she had been in the class six weeks or so and we had become good friends, I very tentatively suggested that, since she was a skillful rider and loved horses, she might like to read *National Velvet.*[3] I made my sell as soft as possible, saying only that it was about a girl who loved and rode horses, and that if she didn't like it, she could put it back. She tried it, and though she must have found it quite a bit harder than what she had been reading, finished it and liked it very much.

20   During the spring she really astonished me, however. One day, in one of our many free periods, she was reading at her desk. From a glimpse of the illustrations I thought I knew what the book was. I said to myself, "It can't be," and went to take a closer look. Sure enough, she was reading *Moby Dick,* in the edition with woodcuts by Rockwell Kent. When I came close to her desk she looked up. I said, "Are you really reading that?" She said she was. I said, "Do you like it?" She said, "Oh, yes, it's neat!" I said, "Don't you find parts of it rather heavy going?" She answered, "Oh, sure, but I just skip over those parts and go on to the next good part."

This is exactly what reading should be and in school so seldom is—an exciting, joyous adventure. Find something, dive into it, take the good parts, skip the bad parts, get what you can out of it, go on to something else. How different is our mean-spirited, picky insistence that every child get every last little scrap of "understanding" that can be dug out of a book.

For teachers who really enjoy doing it, and will do it with gusto, reading aloud is a very good idea. I have found that not just fifth graders but even ninth and eleventh graders enjoy it. Jack London's "To Build a Fire" is a good read-aloud story. So are ghost stories, and "August Heat," by W. F. Harvey, and "The Monkey's Paw," by W. W. Jacobs, are among the best. Shirley Jackson's "The Lottery" is sure-fire, and will raise all kinds of questions for discussion and argument.[4] Because of a TV program they had seen and that excited them, I once started reading my fifth graders William Golding's *Lord of the Flies,*[5] thinking to read only a few chapters, but they made me read it to the end.

In my early fifth-grade classes the children usually were of high IQ, came from literate backgrounds and were generally felt to be succeeding in school. Yet it was astonishingly hard for most of those children to express themselves in speech or in writing. I have known a number of five-year-olds who were

3. Enid Bagnold (1889–1981), British author, published *National Velvet* in 1935.

4. London (1876–1916) and Jackson (1919–1965) are American novelists; Harvey (1885–1937) and Jacobs (1863–1943) are British novelists.

5. British novelist (1911–1993), published *Lord of the Flies* in 1954.

considerably more articulate than most of the fifth graders I have known in school. Asked to speak, my fifth graders were covered with embarrassment; many refused altogether. Asked to write, they would sit for minutes on end, staring at the paper. It was hard for most of them to get down a half page of writing, even on what seemed to be interesting topics or topics they chose themselves.

In desperation I hit on a device that I named the Composition Derby. I divided the class into teams, and told them that when I said, "Go," they were to start writing something. It could be about anything they wanted, but it had to be about something—they couldn't just write "dog dog dog dog" on the paper. It could be true stories, descriptions of people or places or events, wishes, made-up stories, dreams—anything they liked. Spelling didn't count, so they didn't have to worry about it. When I said, "Stop," they were to stop and count up the words they had written. The team that wrote the most words would win the derby.

It was a success in many ways and for many reasons. The first surprise was that the two children who consistently wrote the most words were two of the least successful students in the class. They were bright, but they had always had a very hard time in school. Both were very bad spellers, and worrying about this had slowed down their writing without improving their spelling. When they were free of this worry and could let themselves go, they found hidden and unsuspected talents.

One of the two, a very driven and anxious little boy, used to write long adventures, or misadventures, in which I was the central character—"The Day Mr. Holt Went to Jail," "The Day Mr. Holt Fell Into the Hole," "The Day Mr. Holt Got Run Over," and so on. These were very funny, and the class enjoyed hearing me read them aloud. One day I asked the class to write a derby on a topic I would give them. They groaned; they liked picking their own. "Wait till you hear it," I said. "It's 'The Day the School Burned Down.' "

With a shout of approval and joy they went to work, and wrote furiously for 20 minutes or more, laughing and chuckling as they wrote. The papers were all much alike; in them the children danced around the burning building, throwing in books and driving me and the other teachers back in when we tried to escape.

In our first derby the class wrote an average of about ten words a minute; after a few months their average was over 20. Some of the slower writers tripled their output. Even the slowest, one of whom was the best student in the class, were writing 15 words a minute. More important, almost all the children enjoyed the derbies and wrote interesting things.

Some time later I learned that Professor S. I. Hayakawa, teaching freshman English, had invented a better technique. Every day in class he asked his students to write without stopping for about half an hour. They could write on whatever topic or topics they chose, but the important thing was not to stop. If they ran dry, they were to copy their last sentence over and over again until new ideas came. Usually they came before the sentence had been copied once. I use this idea in my own classes, and call this kind of paper a Non-Stop.

Sometimes I ask students to write a Non-Stop on an assigned topic, more often on anything they choose. Once in a while I ask them to count up how many words they have written, though I rarely ask them to tell me; it is for their own information. Sometimes these papers are to be handed in; often they are what I call private papers, for the students' eyes alone.

30   The private paper has proved very useful. In the first place, in any English class—certainly any large English class—if the amount the students write is limited by what the teacher can find time to correct, or even to read, the students will not write nearly enough. The only remedy is to have them write a great deal that the teacher does not read. In the second place, students writing for themselves will write about many things that they would never write on a paper to be handed in, once they have learned (sometimes it takes a while) that the teacher means what he says about the papers' being private. This is important, not just because it enables them to get things off their chest, but also because they are most likely to write well, and to pay attention to how they write, when they are writing about something important to them.

Some English teachers, when they first hear about private papers, object that students do not benefit from writing papers unless the papers are corrected. I disagree for several reasons. First, most students, particularly poor students, do not read the corrections on their papers; it is boring, even painful. Second, even when they do read these corrections, they do not get much help from them, do not build the teacher's suggestions into their writing. This is true even when they really believe the teacher knows what he is talking about.

Third, and most important, we learn to write by writing, not by reading other people's ideas about writing. What most students need above all else is practice in writing, and particularly in writing about things that matter to them, so that they will begin to feel the satisfaction that comes from getting important thoughts down in words and will care about stating these thoughts forcefully and clearly.

Teachers of English—or, as some schools say (ugh!), Language Arts—spend a lot of time and effort on spelling. Most of it is wasted; it does little good, and often more harm than good. We should ask ourselves, "How do good spellers spell? What do they do when they are not sure which spelling of a word is right?" I have asked this of a number of good spellers. Their answer never varies. They do not rush for a dictionary or rack their brains trying to remember some rules. They write down the word both ways, or several ways, look at them and pick the one that looks best. Usually they are right.

Good spellers know what words look like and even, in their writing muscles, feel like. They have a good set of word images in their minds, and are willing to trust these images. The things we do to "teach" spelling to children do little to develop these skills or talents, and much to destroy them or prevent them from developing.

35   The first and worst thing we do is to make children anxious about spelling. We treat a misspelled word like a crime and penalize the misspeller severely; many teachers talk of making children develop a "spelling conscience," and fail otherwise excellent papers because of a few spelling mis-

takes. This is self-defeating. When we are anxious, we don't perceive clearly or remember what we once perceived. Everyone knows how hard it is to recall even simple things when under emotional pressure; the harder we rack our brains, the less easy it is to find what we are looking for. If we are anxious enough, we will not trust the messages that memory sends us. Many children spell badly because although their first hunches about how to spell a word may be correct, they are afraid to trust them. I have often seen on children's papers a word correctly spelled, then crossed out and misspelled.

There are some tricks that might help children get sharper word images. Some teachers may be using them. One is the trick of air writing; that is, of "writing" a word in the air with a finger and "seeing" the image so formed. I did this quite a bit with fifth graders, using either the air or the top of a desk, on which their fingers left no mark. Many of them were tremendously excited by this. I can still hear them saying, "There's nothing there, but I can see it!" It seemed like black magic. I remember that when I was little I loved to write in the air. It was effortless, voluptuous, satisfying, and it was fun to see the word appear in the air. I used to write "Money Money Money," not so much because I didn't have any as because I liked the way it felt, particularly that *y* at the end, with its swooping tail.

Another thing to help sharpen children's image-making machinery is taking very quick looks at words—or other things. The conventional machine for doing this is the tachistoscope. But these are expensive, so expensive that most children can have few chances to use them, if any at all. With some three-by-five and four-by-eight file cards you can get the same effect. On the little cards you put the words or the pictures that the child is going to look at. You hold the larger card over the card to be read, uncover it for a split second with a quick wrist motion, then cover it up again. Thus you have a tachistoscope that costs one cent and that any child can work by himself.

Once when substituting in a first-grade class, I thought that the children, who were just beginning to read and write, might enjoy some of the kind of free, nonstop writing that my fifth graders had. One day about 40 minutes before lunch, I asked them all to take pencil and paper and start writing about anything they wanted to. They seemed to like the idea, but right away one child said anxiously, "Suppose we can't spell a word."

"Don't worry about it," I said. "Just spell it the best way you can."

A heavy silence settled on the room. All I could see were still pencils and anxious faces. This was clearly not the right approach. So I said, "All right, I'll tell you what we'll do. Any time you want to know how to spell a word, tell me and I'll write it on the board."

40

They breathed a sigh of relief and went to work. Soon requests for words were coming fast; as soon as I wrote one, someone asked me another. By lunchtime, when most of the children were still busily writing, the board was full. What was interesting was that most of the words they had asked for were much longer and more complicated than anything in their reading books or workbooks. Freed from worry about spelling, they were willing to use the most difficult and interesting words that they knew.

The words were still on the board when we began school next day. Before I began to erase them, I said to the children, "Listen, everyone. I have to erase these words, but before I do, just out of curiosity, I'd like to see if you remember some of them."

The result was surprising. I had expected that the child who had asked for and used a word might remember it, but I did not think many others would. But many of the children still knew many of the words. How had they learned them? I suppose each time I wrote a word on the board a number of children had looked up, relaxed yet curious, just to see what the word looked like, and these images and the sound of my voice saying the word had stuck in their minds until the next day. This, it seems to me, is how children may best learn to write and spell.

What can a parent do if a school, or a teacher, is spoiling the language for a child by teaching it in some tired way? First, try to get them to change, or at least let them know that you are eager for change. Talk to other parents; push some of these ideas in the PTA; talk to the English department at the school; talk to the child's own teacher. Many teachers and schools want to know what the parents want.

45   If the school or teacher cannot be persuaded, then what? Perhaps all you can do is try not to let your child become too bored or discouraged or worried by what is happening in school. Help him meet the school's demands, foolish though they may seem, and try to provide more interesting alternatives at home—plenty of books and conversation, and a serious and respectful audience when a child wants to talk. Nothing that ever happened to me in English classes at school was as helpful to me as the long conversations I used to have every summer with my uncle, who made me feel that the difference in our ages was not important and that he was really interested in what I had to say.

At the end of her freshman year in college a girl I know wrote home to her mother, "Hooray! Hooray! Just think—I never have to take English any more!" But this girl had always been an excellent English student, had always loved books, writing, ideas. It seems unnecessary and foolish and wrong that English teachers should so often take what should be the most flexible, exciting, and creative of all school courses and make it into something that most children can hardly wait to see the last of. Let's hope that we can and soon will begin to do much better.

QUESTIONS

1. Mark the anecdotes that Holt uses and describe how he orders them in time and by theme. Consider the advantages and disadvantages of his organizing this essay to reflect his own learning.

2. "[F]or most children," Holt observes, "school was a place of danger, and their main business in school was staying out of danger as much as possible" (paragraph 12). Locate instances in which he makes this point explicit and instances in which he implies it.

3. Holt's "Composition Derby" and Hayakawa's "Non-Stop" are now usually called free-writing. Have your teachers used freewriting? In what grades? From your own experience, how much has the teaching of writing changed since 1967, when Holt wrote this essay?

4. Holt begins this essay by describing the "game of wits" played by teachers and students alike: teachers ask students what teachers want students to know and students ask teachers for clues about what teachers want (paragraph 1). Do you recognize this game? Do you remember learning to play it? Do you think you play it well? Do you like playing it? Write an essay that answers these questions. Be sure to include anecdotes from your own experience.

WILLIAM ZINSSER *College Pressures*

> Dear Carlos: I desperately need a dean's excuse for my chem midterm which will begin in about 1 hour. All I can say is that I totally blew it this week. I've fallen incredibly, inconceivably behind.
>
> Carlos: Help! I'm anxious to hear from you. I'll be in my room and won't leave it until I hear from you. Tomorrow is the last day for . . .
>
> Carlos: I left town because I started bugging out again. I stayed up all night to finish a take-home make-up exam & am typing it to hand in on the 10th. It was due on the 5th. P.S. I'm going to the dentist. Pain is pretty bad.
>
> Carlos: Probably by Friday I'll be able to get back to my studies. Right now I'm going to take a long walk. This whole thing has taken a lot out of me.
>
> Carlos: I'm really up the proverbial creek. The problem is I really *bombed* the history final. Since I need that course for my major I . . .
>
> Carlos: Here follows a tale of woe. I went home this weekend, had to help my Mom, & caught a fever so didn't have much time to study. My professor . . .
>
> Carlos: Aargh! Trouble. Nothing original but everything's piling up at once. To be brief, my job interview . . .
>
> Hey Carlos, good news! I've got mononucleosis.

Who are these wretched supplicants, scribbling notes so laden with anxiety, seeking such miracles of postponement and balm? They are men and women who belong to Branford College, one of the twelve residential colleges at Yale University, and the messages are just a few of the hundreds that they left for their dean, Carlos Hortas—often slipped under his door at 4 A.M.—last year.

But students like the ones who wrote those notes can also be found on

Written when Zinsser was Master (head) of a Yale residential college and published in a small circulation bimonthly magazine about rural life, Blair and Ketchum's Country Journal *(April 1979), which has since ceased publication.*

campuses from coast to coast—especially in New England and at many other private colleges across the country that have high academic standards and highly motivated students. Nobody could doubt that the notes are real. In their urgency and their gallows humor they are authentic voices of a generation that is panicky to succeed.

My own connection with the message writers is that I am master of Branford College. I live in its Gothic quadrangle and know the students well. (We have 485 of them.) I am privy to their hopes and fears—and also to their stereo music and their piercing cries in the dead of night ("Does anybody ca-a-are?"). If they went to Carlos to ask how to get through tomorrow, they come to me to ask how to get through the rest of their lives.

Mainly I try to remind them that the road ahead is a long one and that it will have more unexpected turns than they think. There will be plenty of time to change jobs, change careers, change whole attitudes and approaches. They don't want to hear such liberating news. They want a map—right now—that they can follow unswervingly to career security, financial security, Social Security and, presumably, a prepaid grave.

5   What I wish for all students is some release from the clammy grip of the future. I wish them a chance to savor each segment of their education as an experience in itself and not as a grim preparation for the next step. I wish them the right to experiment, to trip and fall, to learn that defeat is as instructive as victory and is not the end of the world.

My wish, of course, is naive. One of the few rights that America does not proclaim is the right to fail. Achievement is the national god, venerated in our media—the million-dollar athlete, the wealthy executive—and glorified in our praise of possessions. In the presence of such a potent state religion, the young are growing up old.

I see four kinds of pressure working on college students today: economic pressure, parental pressure, peer pressure, and self-induced pressure. It is easy to look around for villains—to blame the colleges for charging too much money, the professors for assigning too much work, the parents for pushing their children too far, the students for driving themselves too hard. But there are no villains; only victims.

"In the late 1960s," one dean told me, "the typical question that I got from students was 'Why is there so much suffering in the world?' or 'How can I make a contribution?' Today it's 'Do you think it would look better for getting into law school if I did a double major in history and political science, or just majored in one of them?' " Many other deans confirmed this pattern. One said: "They're trying to find an edge—the intangible something that will look better on paper if two students are about equal."

Note the emphasis on looking better. The transcript has become a sacred document, the passport to security. How one appears on paper is more important than how one appears in person. *A* is for Admirable and *B* is for Borderline, even though, in Yale's official system of grading, *A* means "excellent" and *B* means "very good." Today, looking very good is no longer good enough, especially for students who hope to go on to law school or medical school. They know that entrance into the better schools will be an entrance into the better law firms and better medical practices where they will make a lot of money. They also know that the odds are harsh. Yale Law School, for instance, matriculates 170 students from an applicant pool of 3,700; Harvard enrolls 550 from a pool of 7,000.

It's all very well for those of us who write letters of recommendation for   10
our students to stress the qualities of humanity that will make them good lawyers or doctors. And it's nice to think that admission officers are really reading our letters and looking for the extra dimension of commitment or concern. Still, it would be hard for a student not to visualize these officers shuffling so many transcripts studded with As that they regard a B as positively shameful.

The pressure is almost as heavy on students who just want to graduate and get a job. Long gone are the days of the "gentleman's C," when students journeyed through college with a certain relaxation, sampling a wide variety of courses—music, art, philosophy, classics, anthropology, poetry, religion—that would send them out as liberally educated men and women. If I were an employer I would rather employ graduates who have this range and curiosity than those who narrowly pursued safe subjects and high grades. I know countless students whose inquiring minds exhilarate me. I like to hear the play of their ideas. I don't know if they are getting As or Cs, and I don't care. I also like them as people. The country needs them, and they will find satisfying jobs. I tell them to relax. They can't.

Nor can I blame them. They live in a brutal economy. Tuition, room, and board at most private colleges now comes to at least $7,000, not counting books and fees. This might seem to suggest that the colleges are getting rich. But they are equally battered by inflation. Tuition covers only 60 percent of what it costs to educate a student, and ordinarily the remainder comes from what colleges receive in endowments, grants, and gifts. Now the remainder keeps being swallowed by the cruel costs—higher every year—of just opening the doors. Heating oil is up. Insurance is up. Postage is up. Health-premium costs are up. Everything is up. Deficits are up. We are witnessing in America the creation of a brotherhood of paupers—colleges, parents, and students, joined by the common bond of debt.

Today it is not unusual for a student, even if he works part time at college and full time during the summer, to accrue $5,000 in loans after four years— loans that he must start to repay within one year after graduation. Exhorted at commencement to go forth into the world, he is already behind as he goes forth. How could he not feel under pressure throughout college to prepare for this day of reckoning? I have used "he," incidentally, only for brevity. Women at Yale are under no less pressure to justify their expensive education to themselves, their parents, and society. In fact, they are probably under more pressure. For although they leave college superbly equipped to bring fresh leadership to traditionally male jobs, society hasn't yet caught up with this fact.

Along with economic pressure goes parental pressure. Inevitably, the two are deeply intertwined.

15   I see many students taking pre-medical courses with joyless tenacity. They go off to their labs as if they were going to the dentist. It saddens me because I know them in other corners of their life as cheerful people.

"Do you want to go to medical school?" I ask them.

"I guess so," they say, without conviction, or "Not really."

"Then why are you going?"

"Well, my parents want me to be a doctor. They're paying all this money and . . ."

20   Poor students, poor parents. They are caught in one of the oldest webs of love and duty and guilt. The parents mean well; they are trying to steer their sons and daughters toward a secure future. But the sons and daughters want to major in history or classics or philosophy—subjects with no "practical" value. Where's the payoff on the humanities? It's not easy to persuade such loving parents that the humanities do indeed pay off. The intellectual faculties developed by studying subjects like history and classics—an ability to synthesize and relate, to weigh cause and effect, to see events in perspective—are just the faculties that make creative leaders in business or almost any general field. Still, many fathers would rather put their money on courses that point toward a specific profession—courses that are pre-law, pre-medical, pre-business, or, as I sometimes heard it put, "pre-rich."

But the pressure on students is severe. They are truly torn. One part of them feels obligated to fulfill their parents' expectations; after all, their parents are older and presumably wiser. Another part tells them that the expectations that are right for their parents are not right for them.

I know a student who wants to be an artist. She is very obviously an artist and will be a good one—she has already had several modest local exhibits. Meanwhile she is growing as a well-rounded person and taking humanistic subjects that will enrich the inner resources out of which her art will grow. But her father is strongly opposed. He thinks that an artist is a "dumb" thing to be. The student vacillates and tries to please everybody. She keeps up with her art somewhat furtively and takes some of the "dumb" courses her father wants her to take—at least they are dumb courses for her. She is a free spirit on a campus of tense students—no small achievement in itself—and she deserves to follow her muse.

Peer pressure and self-induced pressure are also intertwined, and they begin almost at the beginning of freshman year.

"I had a freshman student I'll call Linda," one dean told me, "who came in and said she was under terrible pressure because her roommate, Barbara, was much brighter and studied all the time. I couldn't tell her that Barbara had come in two hours earlier to say the same thing about Linda."

25   The story is almost funny—except that it's not. It's symptomatic of all the pressures put together. When every student thinks every other student is working harder and doing better, the only solution is to study harder still. I see stu-

dents going off to the library every night after dinner and coming back when it closes at midnight. I wish they would sometimes forget about their peers and go to a movie. I hear the clacking of typewriters in the hours before dawn. I see the tension in their eyes when exams are approaching and papers are due: *"Will I get everything done?"*

Probably they won't. They will get sick. They will get "blocked." They will sleep. They will oversleep. They will bug out. *Hey Carlos, help!*

Part of the problem is that they do more than they are expected to do. A professor will assign five-page papers. Several students will start writing ten-page papers to impress him. Then more students will write ten-page papers, and a few will raise the ante to fifteen. Pity the poor student who is still just doing the assignment.

"Once you have twenty or thirty percent of the student population deliberately overexerting," one dean points out, "it's bad for everybody. When a teacher gets more and more effort from his class, the student who is doing normal work can be perceived as not doing well. The tactic works, psychologically."

Why can't the professor just cut back and not accept longer papers? He can, and he probably will. But by then the term will be half over and the damage done. Grade fever is highly contagious and not easily reversed. Besides, the professor's main concern is with his course. He knows his students only in relation to the course and doesn't know that they are also overexerting in their other courses. Nor is it really his business. He didn't sign up for dealing with the student as a whole person and with all the emotional baggage the student brought along from home. That's what deans, masters, chaplains, and psychiatrists are for.

To some extent this is nothing new: a certain number of professors have 30 always been self-contained islands of scholarship and shyness, more comfortable with books than with people. But the new pauperism has widened the gap still further, for professors who actually like to spend time with students don't have as much time to spend. They also are overexerting. If they are young, they are busy trying to publish in order not to perish, hanging by their finger nails onto a shrinking profession. If they are old and tenured, they are buried under the duties of administering departments—as departmental chairmen or members of committees—that have been thinned out by the budgetary axe.

Ultimately it will be the students' own business to break the circles in which they are trapped. They are too young to be prisoners of their parents' dreams and their classmates' fears. They must be jolted into believing in themselves as unique men and women who have the power to shape their own future.

"Violence is being done to the undergraduate experience," says Carlos Hortas. "College should be open-ended: at the end it should open many, many roads. Instead, students are choosing their goal in advance, and their choices narrow as they go along. It's almost as if they think that the country has been codified in the type of jobs that exist—that they've got to fit into certain slots. Therefore, fit into the best-paying slot."

"They ought to take chances. Not taking chances will lead to a life of colorless mediocrity. They'll be comfortable. But something in the spirit will be missing."

I have painted too drab a portrait of today's students, making them seem a solemn lot. That is only half of their story; if they were so dreary I wouldn't so thoroughly enjoy their company. The other half is that they are easy to like. They are quick to laugh and to offer friendship. They are not introverts. They are unusually kind and are more considerate of one another than any student generation I have known.

35   Nor are they so obsessed with their studies that they avoid sports and extracurricular activities. On the contrary, they juggle their crowded hours to play on a variety of teams, perform with musical and dramatic groups, and write for campus publications. But this in turn is one more cause of anxiety. There are too many choices. Academically, they have 1,300 courses to select from; outside class they have to decide how much spare time they can spare and how to spend it.

This means that they engage in fewer extracurricular pursuits than their predecessors did. If they want to row on the crew and play in the symphony they will eliminate one; in the '60s they would have done both. They also tend to choose activities that are self-limiting. Drama, for instance, is flourishing in all twelve of Yale's residential colleges as it never has before. Students hurl themselves into these productions—as actors, directors, carpenters, and technicians—with a dedication to create the best possible play, knowing that the day will come when the run will end and they can get back to their studies.

They also can't afford to be the willing slave of organizations like the *Yale Daily News*. Last spring at the one-hundredth anniversary banquet of that paper—whose past chairmen include such once and future kings as Potter Stewart, Kingman Brewster, and William F. Buckley, Jr.—much was made of the fact that the editorial staff used to be small and totally committed and that "newsies" routinely worked fifty hours a week. In effect they belonged to a club; Newsies is how they defined themselves at Yale. Today's student will write one or two articles a week, when he can, and he defines himself as a student. I've never heard the word Newsie except at the banquet.

If I have described the modern undergraduate primarily as a driven creature who is largely ignoring the blithe spirit inside who keeps trying to come out and play, it's because that's where the crunch is, not only at Yale but throughout American education. It's why I think we should all be worried about the values that are nurturing a generation so fearful of risk and so goal-obsessed at such an early age.

I tell students that there is no one "right" way to get ahead—that each of them is a different person, starting from a different point and bound for a different destination. I tell them that change is a tonic and that all the slots are not codified nor the frontiers closed. One of my ways of telling them is to invite men and women who have achieved success outside the academic world to come and talk informally with my students during the year. They are heads of companies or ad agencies, editors of magazines, politicians, public officials, television magnates, labor leaders, business executives, Broadway producers, artists, writers, economists, photographers, scientists, historians—a mixed bag of achievers.

I ask them to say a few words about how they got started. The students as- 40
sume that they started in their present profession and knew all along that it was what they wanted to do. Luckily for me, most of them got into their field by a circuitous route, to their surprise, after many detours. The students are startled. They can hardly conceive of a career that was not pre-planned. They can hardly imagine allowing the hand of God or chance to nudge them down some unforeseen trail.

QUESTIONS

1. What are the four kinds of pressure Zinsser describes for the 1970s? Are they the same kinds of pressure that trouble students today? Or have new ones taken their place?

2. Some people believe that students perform best when subjected to pressure, others that they perform best when relatively free of pressure. How do you respond to pressure? How much pressure is enough? How much is too much?

3. Write an essay in which you compare your expectations of college pressures with the reality as you have experienced it to date.

CAROLINE BIRD   *College Is a Waste of Time and Money*

A GREAT MAJORITY of our nine million college students are not in school because they want to be or because they want to learn. They are there because it has become the thing to do or because college is a pleasant place to be; because it's the only way they can get parents or taxpayers to support them without working at a job they don't like; because Mother wanted them to go, or some other reason entirely irrelevant to the course of studies for which college is supposedly organized.

As I crisscross the United States lecturing on college campuses, I am dismayed to find that professors and administrators, when pressed for a candid opinion, estimate that no more than 25 percent of their students are turned on by classwork. For the rest, college is at best a social center or aging vat, and at worst a young folks' home or even a prison that keeps them out of the mainstream of economic life for a few more years.

From Bird's book The Case Against College *(1975).*

The premise—which I no longer accept—that college is the best place for all high-school graduates grew out of a noble American ideal. Just as the United States was the first nation to aspire to teach every small child to read and write, so, during the 1950s, we became the first and only great nation to aspire to higher education for all. During the '60s we damned the expense and built great state university systems as fast as we could. And adults—parents, employers, high-school counselors—began to push, shove and cajole youngsters to "get an education."

It became a mammoth industry, with taxpayers footing more than half the bill. By 1970, colleges and universities were spending more than 30 billion dollars annually. But still only half our high-school graduates were going on. According to estimates made by the economist Fritz Machlup, if we had been educating every young person until age 22 in that year of 1970, the bill for higher education would have reached 47.5 billion dollars, 12.5 billion more than the total corporate profits for the year.

5   Figures such as these have begun to make higher education for all look financially prohibitive, particularly now when colleges are squeezed by the pressures of inflation and a drop-off in the growth of their traditional market.

Predictable demography has caught up with the university empire builders. Now that the record crop of postwar babies has graduated from college, the rate of growth of the student population has begun to decline. To keep their mammoth plants financially solvent, many institutions have begun to use hard-sell, Madison-Avenue techniques to attract students. They sell college like soap, promoting features they think students want: innovative programs, an environment conducive to meaningful personal relationships, and a curriculum so free that it doesn't sound like college at all.

Pleasing the customers is something new for college administrators. Colleges have always known that most students don't like to study, and that at least part of the time they are ambivalent about college, but before the student riots of the 1960s educators never thought it either right or necessary to pay any attention to student feelings. But when students rebelling against the Vietnam war and the draft discovered they could disrupt a campus completely, administrators had to act on some student complaints. Few understood that the protests had tapped the basic discontent with college itself, a discontent that did not go away when the riots subsided.

Today students protest individually rather than in concert. They turn inward and withdraw from active participation. They drop out to travel to India or to feed themselves on subsistence farms. Some refuse to go to college at all. Most, of course, have neither the funds nor the self-confidence for constructive articulation of their discontent. They simply hang around college unhappily and reluctantly.

All across the country, I have been overwhelmed by the prevailing sadness on American campuses. Too many young people speak little, and then only in drowned voices. Sometimes the mood surfaces as diffidence, wariness, or coolness, but whatever its form, it looks like a defense mechanism, and that rings a bell. This is the way it used to be with women, and just as society had systematically damaged women by insisting that their proper place was in the home, so we may be systematically damaging 18-year-olds by insisting that their proper place is in college.

Campus watchers everywhere know what I mean when I say students are sad, but they don't agree on the reason for it. During the Vietnam war some ascribed the sadness to the draft; now others blame affluence, or say it has something to do with permissive upbringing.

Not satisfied with any of these explanations, I looked for some answers with the journalistic tools of my trade—scholarly studies, economic analyses, the historical record, the opinions of the especially knowledgeable, conversations with parents, professors, college administrators, and employers, all of whom spoke as alumni too. Mostly I learned from my interviews with hundreds of young people on and off campuses all over the country.

My unnerving conclusion is that students are sad because they are not needed. Somewhere between the nursery and the employment office, they become unwanted adults. No one has anything in particular against them. But no one knows what to do with them either. We already have too many people in the world of the 1970s, and there is no room for so many newly minted 18-year-olds. So we temporarily get them out of the way by sending them to college where in fact only a few belong.

To make it more palatable, we fool ourselves into believing that we are sending them there for their own best interests, and that it's good for them, like spinach. Some, of course, learn to like it, but most wind up preferring green peas.

Educators admit as much. Nevitt Sanford, distinguished student of higher education, says students feel they are "capitulating to a kind of voluntary servitude." Some of them talk about their time in college as if it were a sentence to be served. I listened to a 1970 Mount Holyoke graduate: "For two years I was really interested in science, but in my junior and senior years I just kept saying, 'I've done two years; I'm going to finish.' When I got out I made up my mind that I wasn't going to school anymore because so many of my courses had been bullshit."

But bad as it is, college is often preferable to a far worse fate. It is better than the drudgery of an uninspiring nine-to-five job, and better than doing nothing when no jobs are available. For some young people, it is a graceful way to get away from home and become independent without losing the financial support of their parents. And sometimes it is the only alternative to an intolerable home situation.

It is difficult to assess how many students are in college reluctantly. The conservative Carnegie Commission estimates from 5 to 30 percent. Sol Linowitz, who was once chairman of a special committee on campus tension of the American Council on Education, found that "a significant number were not happy with their college experience because they felt they were there only in order to get the 'ticket to the big show' rather than to spend the years as productively as they otherwise could."

Older alumni will identify with Richard Baloga, a policeman's son, who

10

15

stayed in school even though he "hated it" because he thought it would do him some good. But fewer students each year feel this way. Daniel Yankelovich has surveyed undergraduate attitudes for a number of years, and reported in 1971 that 74 percent thought education was "very important." But just two years earlier, 80 percent thought so.

The doubters don't mind speaking up. Leon Lefkowitz, chairman of the department of social studies at Central High School in Valley Stream, New York, interviewed 300 college students at random, and reports that 200 of them didn't think that the education they were getting was worth the effort. "In two years I'll pick up a diploma," said one student, "and I can honestly say it was a waste of my father's bread."

Nowadays, says one sociologist, you don't have to have a reason for going to college; it's an institution. His definition of an institution is an arrangement everyone accepts without question; the burden of proof is not on why you go, but why anyone thinks there might be a reason for not going. The implication is that an 18-year-old is too young and confused to know what he wants to do, and that he should listen to those who know best and go to college.

20   I don't agree. I believe that college has to be judged not on what other people think is good for students, but on how good it feels to the students themselves.

I believe that people have an inside view of what's good for them. If a child doesn't want to go to school some morning, better let him stay at home, at least until you find out why. Maybe he knows something you don't. It's the same with college. If high-school graduates don't want to go, or if they don't want to go right away, they may perceive more clearly than their elders that college is not for them. It is no longer obvious that adolescents are best off studying a core curriculum that was constructed when all educated men could agree on what made them educated, or that professors, advisors, or parents can be of any particular help to young people in choosing a major or a career. High-school graduates see college graduates driving cabs, and decide it's not worth going. College students find no intellectual stimulation in their studies and drop out.

If students believe that college isn't necessarily good for them, you can't expect them to stay on for the general good of mankind. They don't go to school to beat the Russians to Jupiter, improve the national defense, increase the GNP, or create a new market for the arts—to mention some of the benefits taxpayers are supposed to get for supporting higher education.

Nor should we expect to bring about social equality by putting all young people through four years of academic rigor. At best, it's a roundabout and expensive way to narrow the gap between the highest and lowest in our society anyway. At worst, it is unconsciously elitist. Equalizing opportunity through universal higher education subjects the whole population to the intellectual mode natural only to a few. It violates the fundamental egalitarian principle of respect for the differences between people.

Of course, most parents aren't thinking of the "higher" good at all. They

send their children to college because they are convinced young people benefit financially from those four years of higher education. But if money is the
only goal, college is the dumbest investment you can make. I say this because
a young banker in Poughkeepsie, New York, Stephen G. Necel, used a computer to compare college as an investment with other investments available in
1974 and college did not come out on top.

For the sake of argument, the two of us invented a young man whose rich   25
uncle gave him, in cold cash, the cost of a four-year education at any college
he chose, but the young man didn't have to spend the money on college. After
bales of computer paper, we had our mythical student write to his uncle:
"Since you said I could spend the money foolishly if I wished, I am going to
blow it all on Princeton."

The much respected financial columnist Sylvia Porter echoed the common assumption when she said last year, "A college education is among the
very best investments you can make in your entire life." But the truth is not
quite so rosy, even if we assume that the Census Bureau is correct when it
says that as of 1972, a man who completed four years of college would expect
to earn $199,000 more between the ages of 22 and 64 than a man who had
only a high-school diploma.

If a 1972 Princeton-bound high-school graduate had put the $34,181 that
his four years of college would have cost him into a savings bank at 7.5 per
cent interest compounded daily, he would have had at age 64 a total of
$1,129,200, or $528,200 more than the earnings of a male college graduate,
and more than five times as much as the $199,000 extra the more educated
man could expect to earn between 22 and 64.

The big advantage of getting your college money in cash now is that you
can invest it in something that has a higher return than a diploma. For instance, a Princeton-bound high-school graduate of 1972 who liked fooling
around with cars could have banked his $34,181, and gone to work at the
local garage at close to $1,000 more per year than the average high-school
graduate. Meanwhile, as he was learning to be an expert auto mechanic, his
money would be ticking away in the bank. When he became 28, he would
have earned $7,199 less on his job from age 22 to 28 than his college-
educated friend, but he would have had $73,113 in his passbook—enough to
buy out his boss, go into the used-car business, or acquire his own new-car
dealership. If successful in business, he could expect to make more than the
average college graduate. And if he had the brains to get into Princeton, he
would be just as likely to make money without the four years spent on campus.
Unfortunately, few college-bound high-school graduates get the opportunity
to bank such a large sum of money, and then wait for it to make them rich.
And few parents are sophisticated enough to understand that in financial returns alone, their children would be better off with the money than with the
education.

Rates of return and dollar signs on education are fascinating brain
teasers, but obviously there is a certain unreality to the game. Quite aside
from the noneconomic benefits of college, and these should loom larger once

the dollars are cleared away, there are grave difficulties in assigning a dollar value to college at all.

30   In fact there is no real evidence that the higher income of college graduates is due to college. College may simply attract people who are slated to earn more money anyway; those with higher IQs, better family backgrounds, a more enterprising temperament. No one who has wrestled with the problem is prepared to attribute all of the higher income to the impact of college itself.

Christopher Jencks, author of *Inequality,* a book that assesses the effect of family and schooling in America, believes that education in general accounts for less than half of the difference in income in the American population. "The biggest single source of income differences," writes Jencks, "seems to be the fact that men from high-status families have higher incomes than men from low-status families even when they enter the same occupations, have the same amount of education, and have the same test scores."

Jacob Mincer of the National Bureau of Economic Research and Columbia University states flatly that of "20 to 30 percent of students at any level, the additional schooling has been a waste, at least in terms of earnings." College fails to work its income-raising magic for almost a third of those who go. More than half of those people in 1972 who earned $15,000 or more reached that comfortable bracket without the benefit of a college diploma. Jencks says that financial success in the U.S. depends a good deal on luck, and the most sophisticated regression analyses have yet to demonstrate otherwise.

But most of today's students don't go to college to earn more money anyway. In 1968, when jobs were easy to get, Daniel Yankelovich made his first nationwide survey of students. Sixty-five percent of them said they "would welcome less emphasis on money." By 1973, when jobs were scarce, that figure jumped to 80 percent.

The young are not alone. Americans today are all looking less to the pay of a job than to the work itself. They want "interesting" work that permits them "to make a contribution," "express themselves" and "use their special abilities," and they think college will help them find it.

35   Jerry Darring of Indianapolis knows what it is to make a dollar. He worked with his father in the family plumbing business, on the line at Chevrolet, and in the Chrysler foundry. He quit these jobs to enter Wright State University in Dayton, Ohio, because "in a job like that a person only has time to work, and after that he's so tired that he can't do anything else but come home and go to sleep."

Jerry came to college to find work "helping people." And he is perfectly willing to spend the dollars he earns at dull, well-paid work to prepare for lower-paid work that offers the reward of service to others.

Jerry's case is not unusual. No one works for money alone. In order to deal with the nonmonetary rewards of work, economists have coined the concept of "psychic income," which according to one economic dictionary means "income that is reckoned in terms of pleasure, satisfaction, or general feelings of euphoria."

Psychic income is primarily what college students mean when they talk about getting a good job. During the most affluent years of the late 1960s and early 1970s college students told their placement officers that they wanted to be researchers, college professors, artists, city planners, social workers, poets, book publishers, archeologists, ballet dancers, or authors.

The psychic income of these and other occupations popular with students is so high that these jobs can be filled without offering high salaries. According to one study, 93 percent of urban university professors would choose the same vocation again if they had the chance, compared with only 16 per cent of unskilled auto workers. Even though the monetary gap between college professor and auto worker is now surprisingly small, the difference in psychic income is enormous.

But colleges fail to warn students that jobs of these kinds are hard to come   40
by, even for qualified applicants, and they rarely accept the responsibility of helping students choose a career that will lead to a job. When a young person says he is interested in helping people, his counselor tells him to become a psychologist. But jobs in psychology are scarce. The Department of Labor, for instance, estimates there will be 4,300 new jobs for psychologists in 1975 while colleges are expected to turn out 58,430 B.A.s in psychology that year.

Of 30 psych majors who reported back to Vassar what they were doing a year after graduation in 1972, only five had jobs in which they could possibly use their courses in psychology, and two of these were working for Vassar.

The outlook isn't much better for students majoring in other psychic-pay disciplines: sociology, English, journalism, anthropology, forestry, education. Whatever college graduates want to do, most of them are going to wind up doing what there is to do.

John Shingleton, director of placement at Michigan State University, accuses the academic community of outright hypocrisy. "Educators have never said, 'Go to college and get a good job,' but this has been implied, and now students expect it. . . . If we care what happens to students after college, then let's get involved with what should be one of the basic purposes of education: career preparation."

In the 1970s, some of the more practical professors began to see that jobs for graduates meant jobs for professors too. Meanwhile, students themselves reacted to the shrinking job market, and a "new vocationalism" exploded on campus. The press welcomed the change as a return to the ethic of achievement and service. Students were still idealistic, the reporters wrote, but they now saw that they could best make the world better by healing the sick as physicians or righting individual wrongs as lawyers.

But there are no guarantees in these professions either. The American En-   45
terprise Institute estimated in 1971 that there would be more than the target ratio of 100 doctors for every 100,000 people in the population by 1980. And the odds are little better for would-be lawyers. Law schools are already graduating twice as many new lawyers every year as the Department of Labor thinks will be needed, and the oversupply is growing every year.

And it's not at all apparent that what is actually learned in a "professional" education is necessary for success. Teachers, engineers and others I talked to said they find that on the job they rarely use what they learned in school. In order to see how well college prepared engineers and scientists for actual paid work in their fields, The Carnegie Commission queried all the employees with degrees in these fields in two large firms. Only one in five said the work they were doing bore a "very close relationship" to their college studies, while almost a third saw "very little relationship at all." An overwhelming majority could think of many people who were doing their same work, but had majored in different fields.

Majors in nontechnical fields report even less relationship between their studies and their jobs. Charles Lawrence, a communications major in college and now the producer of "Kennedy & Co.," the Chicago morning television show, says, "You have to learn all that stuff and you never use it again. I learned my job doing it." Others employed as architects, nurses, teachers and other members of the so-called learned professions report the same thing.

Most college administrators admit that they don't prepare their graduates for the job market. "I just wish I had the guts to tell parents that when you get out of this place you aren't prepared to do anything," the academic head of a famous liberal-arts college told us. Fortunately, for him, most people believe that you don't have to defend a liberal-arts education on those grounds. A liberal-arts education is supposed to provide you with a value system, a standard, a set of ideas, not a job. "Like Christianity, the liberal arts are seldom practiced and would probably be hated by the majority of the populace if they were," said one defender.

The analogy is apt. The fact is, of course, that the liberal arts are a religion in every sense of that term. When people talk about them, their language becomes elevated, metaphorical, extravagant, theoretical and reverent. And faith in personal salvation by the liberal arts is professed in a creed intoned on ceremonial occasions such as commencements.

50   If the liberal arts are a religious faith, the professors are its priests. But disseminating ideas in a four-year college curriculum is slow and most expensive. If you want to learn about Milton, Camus, or even Margaret Mead you can find them in paperback books, the public library, and even on television.

And when most people talk about the value of a college education, they are not talking about great books. When at Harvard commencement, the president welcomes the new graduates into "the fellowship of educated men and women," what he could be saying is, "Here is a piece of paper that is a passport to jobs, power and instant prestige." As Glenn Bassett, a personnel specialist at G.E. says, "In some parts of G.E., a college degree appears completely irrelevant to selection to, say, a manager's job. In most, however, it is a ticket of admission."

But now that we have doubled the number of young people attending college, a diploma cannot guarantee even that. The most charitable conclusion we can reach is that college probably has very little, if any, effect on people and things at all. Today, the false premises are easy to see:

First, college doesn't make people intelligent, ambitious, happy, or liberal. It's the other way around. Intelligent, ambitious, happy, liberal people are attracted to higher education in the first place.

Second, college can't claim much credit for the learning experiences that really change students while they are there. Jobs, friends, history, and most of all the sheer passage of time have as big an impact as anything even indirectly related to the campus.

Third, colleges have changed so radically that a freshman entering in the   55
fall of 1974 can't be sure to gain even the limited value research studies assigned to colleges in the '60s. The sheer size of undergraduate campuses of the 1970s makes college even less stimulating now than it was 10 years ago. Today even motivated students are disappointed with their college courses and professors.

Finally, a college diploma no longer opens as many vocational doors. Employers are beginning to realize that when they pay extra for someone with a diploma, they are paying only for an empty credential. The fact is that most of the work for which employers now expect college training is now or has been capably done in the past by people without higher educations.

College, then, may be a good place for those few young people who are really drawn to academic work, who would rather read than eat, but it has become too expensive, in money, time, and intellectual effort to serve as a holding pen for large numbers of our young. We ought to make it possible for those reluctant, unhappy students to find alternative ways of growing up, and more realistic preparation for the years ahead.

QUESTIONS

1. Much of Bird's article focuses on the economic value (or lack thereof) of a college education. Are there other reasons, beyond (or in addition to) economics, why you or your classmates are attending college? To what extent does Bird consider or ignore these other reasons for attending college?

2. In paragraphs 48–50, Bird compares liberal arts education to religion. Why does she make this comparison? What do you think her attitude is toward the liberal arts? Is it similar to or different from yours?

3. In paragraphs 5–6, Bird discusses the hard-sell advertising techniques of many academic institutions. Look into your own school's "advertising techniques" (view books, pamphlets, information sent to homes and high schools, Web site, etc.). How do these sources present the school to parents and potential students? Write an analysis of one of these sources.

BRENT STAPLES *Why Colleges Shower Their Students with A's*

THE ECONOMIST Milton Friedman taught that superior products flourished and shabby ones died out when consumers voted emphatically with their dollars. But the truth of the marketplace is that shabby products can do just fine if they sustain the veneer of quality while slipping downhill, as has much of higher education. Faced with demanding consumers and stiff competition, colleges have simply issued more and more A's, stoking grade inflation and devaluing degrees.

Grade inflation is in full gallop at every level, from struggling community institutions to the elites of the Ivy League. In some cases, campuswide averages have crept up from a C just 10 years ago to B-plus today.

Some departments shower students with A's to fill poorly attended courses that might otherwise be canceled. Individual professors inflate grades after consumer-conscious administrators hound them into it. Professors at every level inflate to escape negative evaluations by students, whose opinions now figure in tenure and promotion decisions.

The most vulnerable teachers are the part-timers who have no job security and who now teach more than half of all college courses. Writing in the last issue of the journal *Academe,* two part-timers suggest that students routinely corner adjuncts, threatening to complain if they do not turn C's into A's. An Ivy League professor said recently that if tenure disappeared, universities would be "free to sell diplomas outright."

5   The consumer appetite for less rigorous education is nowhere more evident than in the University of Phoenix, a profit-making school that shuns traditional scholarship and offers a curriculum so superficial that critics compare it to a drive-through restaurant. Two hundred colleges have closed since a businessman dreamed up Phoenix 20 years ago. Meanwhile, the university has expanded to 60 sites spread around the country, and more than 40,000 students, making it the country's largest private university.

Phoenix competes directly with the big state universities and lesser-known small colleges, all of which fear a student drain. But the elite schools fear each other and their customers, the students, who are becoming increasingly restive about the cost of a first-tier diploma, which now exceeds $120,000. Faced with the prospect of crushing debt, students are treating grades as a matter of life and death—occasionally even suing to have grades revised upward.

Twenty years ago students grumbled, then lived with the grades they were given. Today, colleges of every stature permit them to appeal low grades through deans or permanent boards of inquiry. In *The Chronicle of Higher Ed-*

Published on the Op-Ed page of the New York Times *(March 8, 1998).*

ucation, Prof. Paul Korshin of the University of Pennsylvania recently described his grievance panel as the "rhinoplasty committee," because it does "cosmetic surgery" on up to 500 transcripts a year.

The argument that grades are rising because students are better prepared is simply not convincing. The evidence suggests that students and parents are demanding—and getting—what they think of as their money's worth.

One way to stanch inflation is to change the way the grade point average is calculated. Under most formulas, all courses are given equal weight, so math, science and less-challenging courses have equal impact on the averages. This arrangement rewards students who gravitate to courses where high marks are generously given and punishes those who seek out math and science courses, where far fewer students get the top grade.

Valen Johnson, a Duke University statistics professor, came under heavy 10 fire from both students and faculty when he proposed recalculating the grade point average to give rigorously graded courses greater weight. The student government beat back the plan with the help of teachers in the humanities, who worried that students might abandon them for other courses that they currently avoided. Other universities have expressed interest in adopting the Johnson plan, but want their names kept secret to avoid a backlash.

Addicted to counterfeit excellence, colleges, parents and students are unlikely to give it up. As a consequence, diplomas will become weaker and more ornamental as the years go by.

QUESTIONS

1. What is the grade situation on your campus? Have you been showered with A's recently? Have you noticed professors inflating grades?

2. Staples writes, "An Ivy League professor said recently that if tenure disappeared, universities would be 'free to sell diplomas outright'" (paragraph 4). Analyze this statement. What are its implications? Why does the professor think tenured faculty serve as protection against the "selling" of diplomas? What level of confidence does this professor have in the administration?

3. A Duke University statistics professor proposed "recalculating the grade point average to give rigorously graded courses greater weight" (paragraph 10). He was opposed by humanities professors. What might have been the source of their opposition? What do you think is meant by "rigorously graded"? What is the situation on your campus: do math profs grade more "rigorously" than English profs? Who are the hardest graders?

4. How broad is Staples's range of examples? Would he need to adjust his position if he considered other colleges? Write an analysis of the situation at your college either to confirm or to contest Staples's argument.

DAVID BROOKS   *The Gender Gap at School*

THERE ARE THREE gender-segregated sections in any airport: the restrooms, the security pat-down area and the bookstore. In the men's sections of the bookstore, there are books describing masterly men conquering evil. In the women's sections there are novels about well, I guess feelings and stuff.

The same separation occurs in the home. Researchers in Britain asked 400 accomplished women and 500 accomplished men to name their favorite novels. The men preferred novels written by men, often revolving around loneliness and alienation. Camus's *The Stranger*, Salinger's *Catcher in the Rye* and Vonnegut's *Slaughterhouse-Five* topped the male list.

The women leaned toward books written by women. The women's books described relationships and are a lot better than the books the men chose. The top six women's books were *Jane Eyre*, *Wuthering Heights*, *The Handmaid's Tale*, *Middlemarch*, *Pride and Prejudice* and *Beloved*.

There are a couple of reasons why the two lists might diverge so starkly. It could be men are insensitive dolts who don't appreciate subtle human connections and good literature. Or, it could be that the part of the brain where men experience negative emotion, the amygdala[1], is not well connected to the part of the brain where verbal processing happens, whereas the part of the brain where women experience negative emotion, the cerebral cortex,[2] is well connected. It could be that women are better at processing emotion through words.

5   Over the past two decades, there has been a steady accumulation of evidence that male and female brains work differently. Women use both sides of their brain more symmetrically than men. Men and women hear and smell differently (women are much more sensitive). Boys and girls process colors differently (young girls enjoy an array of red, green and orange crayons whereas young boys generally stick to black, gray and blue). Men and women experience risk differently (men enjoy it more).

It could be, in short, that biological factors influence reading tastes, even after accounting for culture. Women who have congenital adrenal hyperplasia[3], which leads to high male hormone secretions, are more likely to choose violent stories than other women.

This wouldn't be a problem if we all understood these biological factors and if teachers devised different curriculums to instill an equal love of reading in both boys and girls.

Published on June 11, 2006, in the New York Times, *where Brooks writes a regular Op-Ed column.*

1. The portion of the brain that controls emotions and memory.

2. The part of the brain that controls awareness, language, and consciousness.

3. A genetic defect of the adrenal glands. A person with adrenal hyperplasia cannot produce several vital hormones known as corticosteroids, which are significant in sex identification.

The problem is that even after the recent flurry of attention about why boys are falling behind, there is still intense social pressure not to talk about biological differences between boys and girls (ask Larry Summers)[4]. There is still resistance, especially in the educational world, to the findings of brain researchers. Despite some innovations here and there, in most classrooms boys and girls are taught the same books in the same ways.

Young boys are compelled to sit still in schools that have sacrificed recess for test prep. Many are told in a thousand subtle ways they are not really good students. They are sent home with these new-wave young adult problem novels, which all seem to be about introspectively morose young women whose parents are either suicidal drug addicts or fatally ill manic depressives.

It shouldn't be any surprise that according to a National Endowment for the Arts study, the percentage of young men who read has plummeted over the past 14 years. Reading rates are falling three times as fast among young men as among young women. Nor should it be a surprise that men are drifting away from occupations that involve reading and school. Men now make up a smaller share of teachers than at any time in the past 40 years.

Dr. Leonard Sax,[5] whose book *Why Gender Matters* is a lucid guide to male and female brain differences, emphasizes that men and women can excel at any subject. They just have to be taught in different ways. Sax is a big believer in single-sex schools, which he says allow kids to open up and break free from gender stereotypes. But for most kids it would be a start if they were assigned books they might actually care about. For boys, that probably means more Hemingway, Tolstoy, Homer and Twain.

During the 1970's, it was believed that gender is a social construct and that gender differences could be eliminated via consciousness-raising. But it turns out gender is not a social construct. Consciousness-raising doesn't turn boys into sensitively poetic pacifists. It just turns many of them into high school and college dropouts who hate reading.

4. President of Harvard, 2001–06, who resigned after making controversial remarks about women's biological fitness to pursue careers in science.
5. A Maryland family physician and psychologist who wrote *Why Gender Matters* and *Boys Adrift: What's Really Behind the Growing Epidemic of Unmotivated Boys?*

QUESTIONS

1. Does your experience bear out Brooks's claim that boys and girls read differently? Use some examples from people you know.

2. Examine the evidence that Brooks marshals for his claim that girls' and boys' brains are different. Do you think Brooks produces enough evidence to support his claim? Do you know of evidence that he omits?

3. Do a brief survey of favorite books of males and females, and see if it bears out Brooks's claim. Write up your findings in a brief report or counterargument.

JENNIFER BRITZ   *The Dean's Daughter Gets Thin Envelope*

A FEW DAYS AGO I watched my daughter Madalyn open a thin envelope from one of the five colleges to which she had applied. "Why?" was what she was obviously asking herself as she handed me the letter saying she was waitlisted.

Why, indeed? She had taken the toughest courses in her high school and had done well, sat through several Saturday mornings taking SAT's and the like, participated in the requisite number of extracurricular activities, written a heartfelt and well-phrased essay and even taken the extra step of touring the campus.

She had not, however, been named a National Merit finalist, dug a well for a village in Africa or climbed to the top of Mount Ranier. She is a smart, well-meaning, hard-working teenage girl, but in this day and age of swollen applicant pools that are decidedly female, that wasn't enough. The fat acceptance envelope is simply more elusive for today's accomplished young women.

I know this well. At my own college these days, we have three applicants for every one we can admit. Just three years ago, it was two to one. Though Kenyon was a men's college until 1969, more than 55 percent of our applicants are female, a proportion that is steadily increasing. My staff and I carefully read these young women's essays about their passion for poetry, their desire to discover vaccines and their conviction that they can make the world a better place.

5   I was once one of those girls applying to college, but that was 30 years ago, when applying to college was only a tad more difficult than signing up for a membership at the Y. Today, it's a complicated and prolonged dance that begins early, and for young women, there is little margin for error: A grade of C in Algebra II/Trig? Off to the waitlist you go.

Rest assured that admissions officers are not cavalier in making their decisions. Last week, the 10 officers at my college sat around a table, 12 hours every day, deliberating the applications of hundreds of talented young men and women. While gulping down coffee and poring over statistics, we heard about a young woman from Kentucky we were not yet ready to admit outright. She was the leader/president/editor/captain/lead actress in every activity in her school. She had taken six advanced placement courses and had been selected for a prestigious state leadership program. In her free time, this whirlwind of achievement had accumulated more than 300 hours of community service in four different organizations.

Written by an admissions officer at Kenyon College, and originally published with the title "To All the Girls I've Rejected" in the New York Times *(March 23, 2006); this Op-Ed was reprinted under different titles in many other U.S. newspapers during the college admissions season.*

Few of us sitting around the table were as talented and as directed at age 17 as this young woman. Unfortunately, her test scores and grade point average placed her in the middle of our pool. We had to have a debate before we decided to swallow the middling scores and write "admit" next to her name.

Had she been a male applicant, there would have been little, if any, hesitation to admit. The reality is that because young men are rarer, they're more valued applicants. Today, two-thirds of colleges and universities report that they get more female than male applicants, and more than 56 percent of undergraduates nationwide are women. Demographers predict that by 2009, only 42 percent of all baccalaureate degrees awarded in the United States will be given to men.

We have told today's young women that the world is their oyster; the problem is, so many of them believed us that the standards for admission to today's most selective colleges are stiffer for women than men.

How's that for an unintended consequence of the women's liberation movement?   10

The elephant that looms large in the middle of the room is the importance of gender balance. Should it trump the qualifications of talented young female applicants? At those colleges that have reached what the experts call a "tipping point," where 60 percent or more of their enrolled students are female, you'll hear a hint of desperation in the voices of admissions officers.

Beyond the availability of dance partners for the winter formal, gender balance matters in ways both large and small on a residential college campus. Once you become decidedly female in enrollment, fewer males and, as it turns out, fewer females find your campus attractive.

What are the consequences of young men discovering that even if they do less, they have more options? And what messages are we sending young women that they must, nearly 25 years after the defeat of the Equal Rights Amendment, be even more accomplished than men to gain admission to the nation's top colleges? These are questions that admissions officers like me grapple with.

In the meantime, I'm sending out wait list and rejection letters for nearly 3,000 students. Unfortunately, a majority of them will be female, young women just like my daughter. I will linger over letters, remembering individual students I've met, essays I loved, accomplishments I've admired. I know all too well that parents will ache when their talented daughters read the letters and will feel a bolt of anger at the college admissions officers who didn't recognize how special their daughters are.

Yes, of course, these talented young women will all find fine places to attend college—Maddie has four acceptance letters in hand—but it doesn't dilute the disappointment they will feel when they receive a rejection or waitlist offer.   15

I admire the brilliant successes of our daughters. To parents and the students getting thin envelopes, I apologize for the demographic realities.

QUESTIONS

1. Britz wrote this Op-Ed while serving as an admissions officer and while her own daughter was applying to college. Does the fact that Britz's daughter received four acceptances from colleges change your attitude toward the author's case?

2. In the course of her commentary Britz marshals statistics. What function do they serve? How does she balance—or reflect on—statistics with anecdotes, memories, and probing questions?

3. Compare Britz's essay with Brooks's "The Gender Gap at School" (p. 262) and decide whether colleges should have different standards for judging male and female candidates.

4. In paragraph 11, Britz poses a question: "Should it [gender balance] trump the qualifications of talented young female applicants?" Write an opinion piece in which you address this question, using facts and statistics as well as personal experience and anecdotes.

WILLIAM GOLDING *Thinking as a Hobby*

WHILE I WAS STILL A BOY, I came to the conclusion that there were three grades of thinking; and since I was later to claim thinking as my hobby, I came to an even stranger conclusion—namely, that I myself could not think at all.

I must have been an unsatisfactory child for grownups to deal with. I remember how incomprehensible they appeared to me at first, but not, of course, how I appeared to them. It was the headmaster of my grammar school who first brought the subject of thinking before me—though neither in the way, nor with the result he intended. He had some statuettes in his study. They stood on a high cupboard behind his desk. One was a lady wearing nothing but a bath towel. She seemed frozen in an eternal panic lest the bath towel slip down any farther; and since she had no arms, she was in an unfortunate position to pull the towel up again. Next to her, crouched the statuette of a leopard, ready to spring down at the top drawer of a filing cabinet labeled A-AH. My innocence interpreted this as the victim's last, despairing cry. Beyond the leopard was a naked, muscular gentleman, who sat, looking down, with his chin on his fist and his elbow on his knee. He seemed utterly miserable.

Some time later, I learned about these statuettes. The headmaster had placed them where they would face delinquent children, because they symbolized to him the whole of life. The naked lady was the Venus of Milo. She was Love. She was not worried about the towel. She was just busy being beautiful.

First published in Holiday *(August 1961), a popular monthly travel magazine.*

The leopard was Nature, and he was being natural. The naked, muscular gentleman was not miserable. He was Rodin's Thinker, an image of pure thought.[1] It is easy to buy small plaster models of what you think life is like.

I had better explain that I was a frequent visitor to the headmaster's study, because of the latest thing I had done or left undone. As we now say, I was not integrated. I was, if anything, disintegrated; and I was puzzled. Grownups never made sense. Whenever I found myself in a penal position before the headmaster's desk, with the statuettes glimmering whitely above him, I would sink my head, clasp my hands behind my back and writhe one shoe over the other.

The headmaster would look opaquely at me through flashing spectacles.   5

"What are we going to do with you?"

Well, what *were* they going to do with me? I would writhe my shoe some more and stare down at the worn rug.

"Look up, boy! Can't you look up?"

Then I would look up at the cupboard, where the naked lady was frozen in her panic and the muscular gentleman contemplated the hindquarters of the leopard in endless gloom. I had nothing to say to the headmaster. His spectacles caught the light so that you could see nothing human behind them. There was no possibility of communication.

"Don't you ever think at all?"   10

No, I didn't think, wasn't thinking, couldn't think—I was simply waiting in anguish for the interview to stop.

"Then you'd better learn—hadn't you?"

On one occasion the headmaster leaped to his feet, reached up and plonked Rodin's masterpiece on the desk before me.

"That's what a man looks like when he's really thinking."

I surveyed the gentleman without interest or comprehension.   15

"Go back to your class."

Clearly there was something missing in me. Nature had endowed the rest of the human race with a sixth sense and left me out. This must be so, I mused, on my way back to the class, since whether I had broken a window, or failed to remember Boyle's Law, or been late for school, my teachers produced me one, adult answer: "Why can't you think?"

As I saw the case, I had broken the window because I had tried to hit Jack Arney with a cricket ball and missed him; I could not remember Boyle's Law because I had never bothered to learn it; and I was late for school because I preferred looking over the bridge into the river. In fact, I was wicked. Were my teachers, perhaps, so good that they could not understand the depths of my depravity? Were they clear, untormented people who could direct their every action by this mysterious business of thinking? The whole thing was incom-

---

1. François-Auguste-René Rodin (1840–1917), French sculptor whose famous *The Thinker* was originally created as part of a larger bronze piece, *The Gates of Hell* (1880). The sculpture was meant to represent Dante in front of the Gates of Hell pondering his great poem *Inferno*, but is now generally interpreted, as Golding suggests, as "an image of pure thought."

prehensible. In my earlier years, I found even the statuette of the Thinker confusing. I did not believe any of my teachers were naked, ever. Like someone born deaf, but bitterly determined to find out about sound, I watched my teachers to find out about thought.

There was Mr. Houghton. He was always telling me to think. With a modest satisfaction, he would tell me that he had thought a bit himself. Then why did he spend so much time drinking? Or was there more sense in drinking than there appeared to be? But if not, and if drinking were in fact ruinous to health—and Mr. Houghton was ruined, there was no doubt about that—why was he always talking about the clean life and the virtues of fresh air? He would spread his arms wide with the action of a man who habitually spent his time striding along mountain ridges.

20   "Open air does me good, boys—I know it!"

Sometimes, exalted by his own oratory, he would leap from his desk and hustle us outside into a hideous wind.

"Now, boys! Deep breaths! Feel it right down inside you—huge draughts of God's good air!"

He would stand before us, rejoicing in his perfect health, an open-air man. He would put his hands on his waist and take a tremendous breath. You could hear the wind, trapped in the cavern of his chest and struggling with all the unnatural impediments. His body would reel with shock and his ruined face go white at the unaccustomed visitation. He would stagger back to his desk and collapse there, useless for the rest of the morning.

Mr. Houghton was given to high-minded monologues about the good life, sexless and full of duty. Yet in the middle of one of these monologues, if a girl passed the window, tapping along on her neat little feet, he would interrupt his discourse, his neck would turn of itself and he would watch her out of sight. In this instance, he seemed to me ruled not by thought but by an invisible and irresistible spring in his nape.

25   His neck was an object of great interest to me. Normally it bulged a bit over his collar. But Mr. Houghton had fought in the First World War alongside both Americans and French, and had come—by who knows what illogic?—to a settled detestation of both countries. If either country happened to be prominent in current affairs, no argument could make Mr. Houghton think well of it. He would bang the desk, his neck would bulge still further and go red. "You can say what you like," he would cry, "but I've thought about this—and I know what I think!"

Mr. Houghton thought with his neck.

There was Miss Parsons. She assured us that her dearest wish was our welfare, but I knew even then, with the mysterious clairvoyance of childhood, that what she wanted most was the husband she never got. There was Mr. Hands—and so on.

I have dealt at length with my teachers because this was my introduction to the nature of what is commonly called thought. Through them I discovered that thought is often full of unconscious prejudice, ignorance and hypocrisy. It will lecture on disinterested purity while its neck is being remorselessly twisted toward a skirt. Technically, it is about as proficient as most businessmen's golf, as honest as most politicians' intentions, or—to come near my own preoccupation—as coherent as most books that get written. It is what I came to call grade-three thinking, though more properly, it is feeling, rather than thought.

True, often there is a kind of innocence in prejudices, but in those days I viewed grade-three thinking with an intolerant contempt and an incautious mockery. I delighted to confront a pious lady who hated the Germans with the proposition that we should love our enemies. She taught me a great truth in dealing with grade-three thinkers; because of her, I no longer dismiss lightly a mental process which for nine-tenths of the population is the nearest they will ever get to thought. They have immense solidarity. We had better respect them, for we are outnumbered and surrounded. A crowd of grade-three thinkers, all shouting the same thing, all warming their hands at the fire of their own prejudices, will not thank you for pointing out the contradictions in their beliefs. Man is a gregarious animal, and enjoys agreement as cows will graze all the same way on the side of a hill.

Grade-two thinking is the detection of contradictions. I reached grade two   30
when I trapped the poor, pious lady. Grade-two thinkers do not stampede easily, though often they fall into the other fault and lap behind. Grade-two thinking is a withdrawal, with eyes and ears open. It became my hobby and brought satisfaction and loneliness in either hand. For grade-two thinking destroys without having the power to create. It set me watching the crowds cheering His Majesty and King and asking myself what all the fuss was about, without giving me anything positive to put in the place of that heady patriotism. But there were compensations. To hear people justify their habit of hunting foxes and tearing them to pieces by claiming that the foxes liked it. To hear our Prime Minister talk about the great benefit we conferred on India by jailing people like Pandit Nehru and Gandhi. To hear American politicians talk about peace in one sentence and refuse to join the League of Nations in the next. Yes, there were moments of delight.

But I was growing toward adolescence and had to admit that Mr. Houghton was not the only one with an irresistible spring in his neck. I, too, felt the compulsive hand of nature and began to find that pointing out contradiction could be costly as well as fun. There was Ruth, for example, a serious and attractive girl. I was an atheist at the time. Grade-two thinking is a menace to religion and knocks down sects like skittles. I put myself in a position to be converted by her with an hypocrisy worthy of grade three. She was a Methodist—or at least, her parents were, and Ruth had to follow suit. But, alas, instead of relying on the Holy Spirit to convert me, Ruth was foolish enough to open her pretty mouth in argument. She claimed that the Bible (King James Version) was literally inspired. I countered by saying that the Catholics believed in the literal inspiration of Saint Jerome's *Vulgate*,[2] and the two books were different. Argument flagged.

2. The King James Bible (1611) is the authorized text for English-speaking Protestants, so-called because King James I of England (1566–1625) commissioned its translation; the Vulgate is the Latin Bible revised in the fourth century C.E. by Jerome and used thereafter as the authoritative text for Roman Catholics.

At last she remarked that there were an awful lot of Methodists, and they couldn't be wrong, could they—not all those millions? That was too easy, said I restively (for the nearer you were to Ruth, the nicer she was to be near to) since there were more Roman Catholics than Methodists anyway; and they couldn't be wrong, could they—not all those hundreds of millions? An awful flicker of doubt appeared in her eyes. I slid my arm around her waist and murmured breathlessly that if we were counting heads, the Buddhists were the boys for my money. But Ruth had *really* wanted to do me good, because I was so nice. She fled. The combination of my arm and those countless Buddhists was too much for her.

That night her father visited my father and left, red-cheeked and indignant. I was given the third degree to find out what had happened. It was lucky we were both of us only fourteen. I lost Ruth and gained an undeserved reputation as a potential libertine.

So grade-two thinking could be dangerous. It was in this knowledge, at the age of fifteen, that I remember making a comment from the heights of grade two, on the limitations of grade three. One evening I found myself alone in the school hall, preparing it for a party. The door of the headmaster's study was open. I went in. The headmaster had ceased to thump Rodin's Thinker down on the desk as an example to the young. Perhaps he had not found any more candidates, but the statuettes were still there, glimmering and gathering dust on top of the cupboard. I stood on a chair and rearranged them. I stood Venus in her bath towel on the filing cabinet, so that now the top drawer caught its breath in a gasp of sexy excitement. "A-ah!" The portentous Thinker I placed on the edge of the cupboard so that he looked down at the bath towel and waited for it to slip.

35   Grade-two thinking, though it filled life with fun and excitement, did not make for content. To find out the deficiencies of our elders bolsters the young ego but does not make for personal security. I found that grade two was not only the power to point out contradictions. It took the swimmer some distance from the shore and left him there, out of his depth. I decided that Pontius Pilate[3] was a typical grade-two thinker. "What is truth?" he said, a very common grade-two thought, but one that is used always as the end of an argument instead of the beginning. There is still a higher grade of thought which says, "What is truth?" and sets out to find it.

But these grade-one thinkers were few and far between. They did not visit my grammar school in the flesh though they were there in books. I aspired to them, partly because I was ambitious and partly because I now saw my hobby as an unsatisfactory thing if it went no further. If you set out to climb a mountain, however high you climb, you have failed if you cannot reach the top.

I *did* meet an undeniably grade-one thinker in my first year at Oxford. I was looking over a small bridge in Magdalen Deer Park, and a tiny mustached and hatted figure came and stood by my side. He was a German who had just fled from the Nazis to Oxford as a temporary refuge. His name was Einstein.

3. The Roman procurator who ruled Judaea from 26 to 36 C.E. and oversaw the trial of Jesus.

But Professor Einstein knew no English at that time and I knew only two words of German. I beamed at him, trying wordlessly to convey by my bearing all the affection and respect that the English felt for him. It is possible—and I have to make the admission—that I felt here were two grade-one thinkers standing side by side; yet I doubt if my face conveyed more than a formless awe. I would have given my Greek and Latin and French and a good slice of my English for enough German to communicate. But we were divided; he was as inscrutable as my headmaster. For perhaps five minutes we stood together on the bridge, undeniable grade-one thinker and breathless aspirant. With true greatness, Professor Einstein realized that any contact was better than none. He pointed to a trout wavering in midstream.

He spoke: *"Fisch."*

My brain reeled. Here I was, mingling with the great, and yet helpless as   40
the veriest grade-three thinker. Desperately I sought for some sign by which I might convey that I, too, revered pure reason. I nodded vehemently. In a brilliant flash I used up half of my German vocabulary.

"Fisch. Ja Ja."

For perhaps another five minutes we stood side by side. Then Professor Einstein, his whole figure still conveying good will and amiability, drifted away out of sight.

I, too, would be a grade-one thinker. I was irreverent at the best of times. Political and religious systems, social customs, loyalties and traditions, they all came tumbling down like so many rotten apples off a tree. This was a fine hobby and a sensible substitute for cricket, since you could play it all the year round. I came up in the end with what must always remain the justification for grade-one thinking, its sign, seal and charter. I devised a coherent system for living. It was a moral system, which was wholly logical. Of course, as I readily admitted, conversion of the world to my way of thinking might be difficult, since my system did away with a number of trifles, such as big business, centralized government, armies, marriage. . . .

It was Ruth all over again. I had some very good friends who stood by me, and still do. But my acquaintances vanished, taking the girls with them. Young women seemed oddly contented with the world as it was. They valued the meaningless ceremony with a ring. Young men, while willing to concede the chaining sordidness of marriage, were hesitant about abandoning the organizations which they hoped would give them a career. A young man on the first rung of the Royal Navy, while perfectly agreeable to doing away with big business and marriage, got as rednecked as Mr. Houghton when I proposed a world without any battleships in it.

Had the game gone too far? Was it a game any longer? In those prewar   45
days, I stood to lose a great deal, for the sake of a hobby.

Now you are expecting me to describe how I saw the folly of my ways and came back to the warm nest, where prejudices are so often called loyalties, where pointless actions are hallowed into custom by repetition, where we are content to say we think when all we do is feel.

But you would be wrong. I dropped my hobby and turned professional.

If I were to go back to the headmaster's study and find the dusty statuettes still there, I would arrange them differently. I would dust Venus and put her aside, for I have come to love her and know her for the fair thing she is. But I would put the Thinker, sunk in his desperate thought, where there were shadows before him—and at his back, I would put the leopard, crouched and ready to spring.

QUESTIONS

1. Trace Golding's reflections on the statues in his headmaster's office throughout the essay. In what ways do these reflections reflect Golding's changing understanding of "thought"?

2. Define Golding's three grades of thinking. Which grade is most clear to you? Which could use further explanation?

3. Write a personal essay in which you, like Golding, use personal experience to illustrate your developing understanding of "thought" or some other abstraction (such as "love," "faith," "independence," or "growth").

ADRIENNE RICH   *Taking Women Students Seriously*

I SEE MY FUNCTION here today as one of trying to create a context, delineate a background, against which we might talk about women as students and students as women. I would like to speak for a while about this background, and then I hope that we can have, not so much a question period, as a raising of concerns, a sharing of questions for which we as yet may have no answers, an opening of conversations which will go on and on.

When I went to teach at Douglass, a women's college,[1] it was with a particular background which I would like briefly to describe to you. I had graduated from an all-girls' school in the 1940s, where the head and the majority of the faculty were independent, unmarried women. One or two held doctorates, but had been forced by the Depression (and by the fact that they were women) to take secondary school teaching jobs. These women cared a great deal about the life of the mind, and they gave a great deal of time and energy—beyond any limit of teaching hours—to those of us who showed special intellectual interest or ability. We were taken to libraries, art museums, lectures at neighboring colleges, set to work on extra research projects, given extra French or Latin

The talk that follows was addressed to teachers of women. . . . It was given for the New Jersey College and University Coalition on Women's Education, May 9, 1978 [Rich's note]. Reprinted in On Lies, Secrets, and Silence: Selected Prose, 1966–1978 (1979).

1. Part of Rutgers University in New Jersey.

reading. Although we sometimes felt "pushed" by them, we held those women in a kind of respect which even then we dimly perceived was not generally accorded to women in the world at large. They were vital individuals, defined not by their relationships but by their personalities; and although under the pressure of the culture we were all certain we wanted to get married, their lives did not appear empty or dreary to us. In a kind of cognitive dissonance, we knew they were "old maids" and therefore supposed to be bitter and lonely; yet we saw them vigorously involved with life. But despite their existence as alternate models of women, the *content* of the education they gave us in no way prepared us to survive as women in a world organized by and for men.

From that school, I went on to Radcliffe, congratulating myself that now I would have great men as my teachers. From 1947 to 1951, when I graduated, I never saw a single woman on a lecture platform, or in front of a class, except when a woman graduate student gave a paper on a special topic. The "great men" talked of other "great men," of the nature of Man, the history of Mankind, the future of Man; and never again was I to experience, from a teacher, the kind of prodding, the insistence that my best could be even better, that I had known in high school. Women students were simply not taken very seriously. Harvard's message to women was an elite mystification: we were, of course, part of Mankind; we were special, achieving women, or we would not have been there; but of course our real goal was to marry—if possible, a Harvard graduate.

In the late sixties, I began teaching at the City College of New York—a crowded, public, urban, multiracial institution as far removed from Harvard as possible. I went there to teach writing in the SEEK Program,[2] which predated Open Admissions and which was then a kind of model for programs designed to open up higher education to poor, black, and Third World students. Although during the next few years we were to see the original concept of SEEK diluted, then violently attacked and betrayed, it was for a short time an extraordinary and intense teaching and learning environment. The characteristics of this environment were a deep commitment on the part of teachers to the minds of their students; a constant, active effort to create or discover the conditions for learning, and to educate ourselves to meet the needs of the new college population; a philosophical attitude based on open discussion of racism, oppression, and the politics of literature and language; and a belief that learning in the classroom could not be isolated from the student's experience as a member of an urban minority group in white America. Here are some of the kinds of questions we, as teachers of writing, found ourselves asking:

(1) What has been the student's experience of education in the inadequate, often abusively racist public school system, which rewards passivity and treats a questioning attitude or independent mind as a behavior

---

2. SEEK is an acronym for "Search for Education, Elevation, and Knowledge"; the instructors in the program included not only college teachers but also creative artists and writers.

problem? What has been her or his experience in a society that consistently undermines the selfhood of the poor and the nonwhite? How can such a student gain that sense of self which is necessary for active participation in education? What does all this mean for us as teachers?

(2) How do we go about teaching a canon of literature which has consistently excluded or depreciated nonwhite experience?

(3) How can we connect the process of learning to write well with the student's own reality, and not simply teach her/him how to write acceptable lies in standard English?

5   When I went to teach at Douglass College in 1976, and in teaching women's writing workshops elsewhere, I came to perceive stunning parallels to the questions I had first encountered in teaching the so-called disadvantaged students at City. But in this instance, and against the specific background of the women's movement, the questions framed themselves like this:

(1) What has been the student's experience of education in schools which reward female passivity, indoctrinate girls and boys in stereotypic sex roles, and do not take the female mind seriously? How does a woman gain a sense of her *self* in a system—in this case, patriarchal capitalism—which devalues work done by women, denies the importance and uniqueness of female experience, and is physically violent toward women? What does this mean for a woman teacher?

(2) How do we, as women, teach women students a canon of literature which has consistently excluded or depreciated female experience, and which often expresses hostility to women and validates violence against us?

(3) How can we teach women to move beyond the desire for male approval and getting "good grades" and seek and write their own truths that the culture has distorted or made taboo? (For women, of course, language itself is exclusive: I want to say more about this further on.)

In teaching women, we have two choices: to lend our weight to the forces that indoctrinate women to passivity, self-depreciation, and a sense of powerlessness, in which case the issue of "taking women students seriously" is a moot one; or to consider what we have to work against, as well as with, in ourselves, in our students, in the content of the curriculum, in the structure of the institution, in the society at large. And this means, first of all, taking ourselves seriously: Recognizing that central responsibility of a woman to herself, without which we remain always the Other, the defined, the object, the victim; believing that there is a unique quality of validation, affirmation, challenge, support, that one woman can offer another. Believing in the value and significance of women's experience, traditions, perceptions. Thinking of ourselves seriously, not as one of the boys, not as neuters, or androgynes, but *as women*.
Suppose we were to ask ourselves, simply: What does a woman need to

know? Does she not, as a self-conscious, self-defining human being, need a knowledge of her own history, her much-politicized biology, an awareness of the creative work of women of the past, the skills and crafts and techniques and powers exercised by women in different times and cultures, a knowledge of women's rebellions and organized movements against our oppression and how they have been routed or diminished? Without such knowledge women live and have lived without context, vulnerable to the projections of male fantasy, male prescriptions for us, estranged from our own experience because our education has not reflected or echoed it. I would suggest that not biology, but ignorance of our selves, has been the key to our powerlessness.

But the university curriculum, the high-school curriculum, do not provide this kind of knowledge for women, the knowledge of Womankind, whose experience has been so profoundly different from that of Mankind. Only in the precariously budgeted, much-condescended-to area of women's studies is such knowledge available to women students. Only there can they learn about the lives and work of women other than the few select women who are included in the "mainstream" texts, usually misrepresented even when they do appear. Some students, at some institutions, manage to take a majority of courses in women's studies, but the message from on high is that this is self-indulgence, soft-core education: the "real" learning is the study of Mankind.

If there is any misleading concept, it is that of "coeducation": that because women and men are sitting in the same classrooms, hearing the same lectures, reading the same books, performing the same laboratory experiments, they are receiving an equal education. They are not, first because the content of education itself validates men even as it invalidates women. Its very message is that men have been the shapers and thinkers of the world, and that this is only natural. The bias of higher education, including the so-called sciences, is white and male, racist and sexist; and this bias is expressed in both subtle and blatant ways. I have mentioned already the exclusiveness of grammar itself: "The student should test himself on the above questions"; "The poet is representative. He stands among partial men for the complete man." Despite a few half-hearted departures from custom, what the linguist Wendy Martyna has named "He-Man" grammar prevails throughout the culture. The efforts of feminists to reveal the profound ontological implications of sexist grammar are routinely ridiculed by academicians and journalists, including the professedly liberal *Times* columnist, Tom Wicker, and the professed humanist, Jacques Barzun. Sexist grammar burns into the brains of little girls and young women a message that the male is the norm, the standard, the central figure beside which we are the deviants, the marginal, the dependent variables. It lays the foundation for androcentric thinking, and leaves men safe in their solipsistic tunnel-vision.

Women and men do not receive an equal education because outside the classroom women are perceived not as sovereign beings but as prey. The growing incidence of rape on and off the campus may or may not be fed by the proliferations of pornographic magazines and X-rated films available to young

10

males in fraternities and student unions; but it is certainly occurring in a context of widespread images of sexual violence against women, on billboards and in so-called high art. More subtle, more daily than rape is the verbal abuse experienced by the woman student on many campuses—Rutgers for example—where, traversing a street lined with fraternity houses, she must run a gauntlet of male commentary and verbal assault. The undermining of self, of a woman's sense of her right to occupy space and walk freely in the world, is deeply relevant to education. The capacity to think independently, to take intellectual risks, to assert ourselves mentally, is inseparable from our physical way of being in the world, our feelings of personal integrity. If it is dangerous for me to walk home late of an evening from the library, *because I am a woman and can be raped,* how self-possessed, how exuberant can I feel as I sit working in that library? how much of my working energy is drained by the subliminal knowledge that, as a woman, I test my physical right to exist each time I go out alone? Of this knowledge, Susan Griffin has written:

> . . . more than rape itself, the fear of rape permeates our lives. And what does one do from day to day, with *this* experience, which says, without words and directly to the heart, *your existence, your experience, may end at any moment.* Your experience may end, and the best defense against this is not to be, to deny being in the body, as a self, to . . . avert your gaze, make yourself, as a presence in the world, less felt.[3]

Finally, rape of the mind. Women students are more and more often now reporting sexual overtures by male professors—one part of our overall growing consciousness of sexual harassment in the workplace. At Yale a legal suit has been brought against the university by a group of women demanding an explicit policy against sexual advances toward female students by male professors. Most young women experience a profound mixture of humiliation and intellectual self-doubt over seductive gestures by men who have the power to award grades, open doors to grants and graduate school, or extend special knowledge and training. Even if turned aside, such gestures constitute mental rape, destructive to a woman's ego. They are acts of domination, as despicable as the molestation of the daughter by the father.

But long before entering college the woman student has experienced her alien identity in a world which misnames her, turns her to its own uses, denying her the resources she needs to become self-affirming, self-defined. The nuclear family teaches her that relationships are more important than selfhood or work; that "whether the phone rings for you, and how often," having the right clothes, doing the dishes, take precedence over study or solitude; that too much intelligence or intensity may make her unmarriageable; that marriage and children—service to others—are, finally, the points on which her life will be judged a success or a failure. In high school, the polarization between feminine attractiveness and independent intelligence comes to an absolute. Meanwhile, the

---

3. Rich is quoting from the manuscript of Griffin's *Rape: The Power of Consciousness* (New York, 1979).

culture resounds with messages. During Solar Energy Week in New York I saw young women wearing "ecology" T-shirts with the legend: CLEAN, CHEAP AND AVAILABLE; a reminder of the 1960s antiwar button which read: CHICKS SAY YES TO MEN WHO SAY NO. Department store windows feature female mannequins in chains, pinned to the wall with legs spread, smiling in positions of torture. Feminists are depicted in the media as "shrill," "strident," "puritanical," or "humorless," and the lesbian choice—the choice of the woman-identified woman—as pathological or sinister. The young woman sitting in the philosophy classroom, the political science lecture, is already gripped by tensions between her nascent sense of self-worth, and the battering force of messages like these.

Look at a classroom: look at the many kinds of women's faces, postures, expressions. Listen to the women's voices. Listen to the silences, the unasked questions, the blanks. Listen to the small, soft voices, often courageously trying to speak up, voices of women taught early that tones of confidence, challenge, anger, or assertiveness, are strident and unfeminine. Listen to the voices of the women and the voices of the men; observe the space men allow themselves, physically and verbally, the male assumption that people will listen, even when the majority of the group is female. Look at the faces of the silent, and of those who speak. Listen to a woman groping for language in which to express what is on her mind, sensing that the terms of academic discourse are not her language, trying to cut down her thought to the dimensions of a discourse not intended for her (*for it is not fitting that a woman speak in public*); or reading her paper aloud at breakneck speed, throwing her words away, deprecating her own work by a reflex prejudgment: *I do not deserve to take up time and space.*

As women teachers, we can either deny the importance of this context in which women students think, write, read, study, project their own futures; or try to work with it. We can either teach passively, accepting these conditions, or actively, helping our students identify and resist them.

One important thing we can do is *discuss* the context. And this need not happen only in a women's studies course; it can happen anywhere. We can refuse to accept passive, obedient learning and insist upon critical thinking. We can become harder on our women students, giving them the kinds of "cultural prodding" that men receive, but on different terms and in a different style. Most young women need to have their intellectual lives, their work, legitimized against the claims of family, relationships, the old message that a woman is always available for service to others. We need to keep our standards very high, not to accept a woman's preconceived sense of her limitations; we need to be hard to please, while supportive of risk-taking, because self-respect often comes only when exacting standards have been met. At a time when adult literacy is generally low, we need to demand more, not less, of women, both for the sake of their futures as thinking beings, and because historically women have always had to be better than men to do half as well. A romantic sloppiness, an inspired lack of rigor, a self-indulgent incoherence, are symptoms of female self-depreciation. We should help our women students to look very critically at such symptoms, and to understand where they are rooted.

15

Nor does this mean we should be training women students to "think like men." Men in general think badly: in disjuncture from their personal lives, claiming objectivity where the most irrational passions seethe, losing, as Virginia Woolf[4] observed, their senses in the pursuit of professionalism. It is not easy to think like a woman in a man's world, in the world of the professions; yet the capacity to do that is a strength which we can try to help our students develop. To think like a woman in a man's world means thinking critically, refusing to accept the givens, making connections between facts and ideas which men have left unconnected. It means remembering that every mind resides in a body; remaining accountable to the female bodies in which we live; constantly retesting given hypotheses against lived experience. It means a constant critique of language, for as Wittgenstein[5] (no feminist) observed, "The limits of my language are the limits of my world." And it means that most difficult thing of all: listening and watching in art and literature, in the social sciences, in all the descriptions we are given of the world, for the silences, the absences, the nameless, the unspoken, the encoded—for there we will find the true knowledge of women. And in breaking those silences, naming our selves, uncovering the hidden, making ourselves present, we begin to define a reality which resonates to *us*, which affirms *our* being, which allows the woman teacher and the woman student alike to take ourselves, and each other, seriously: meaning, to begin taking charge of our lives.

4. British novelist, essayist, and feminist (1882–1941).
5. Ludwig Wittgenstein (1889–1951), Austrian-born British philosopher.

QUESTIONS

1. Rich discusses the importance of listening to silences and of paying attention to absences. In one of your classes, listen and observe; take note of who speaks and who doesn't; and watch for responses from the instructor. What sense can you make of these silences and absences? Do your conclusions correspond to Rich's, or do they differ?

2. Rich and David Brooks (in "The Gender Gap at School" in this section) come to very different conclusions. What do you think accounts for their differences?

3. In paragraph 10, Rich discusses the relationship between intellectual independence and physical safety. Do some research on the public safety policies on your own campus (escorts, lighting, etc.) and also consider your own experiences. Do you feel safe walking alone on campus? To what extent does your sense of physical safety affect your intellectual work? Write a journal entry or article for your school's newspaper on these issues.

LANGUAGE AND
COMMUNICATION

GLORIA NAYLOR *"Mommy, What Does 'Nigger' Mean?"*

LANGUAGE IS THE SUBJECT. It is the written form with which I've managed to keep the wolf away from the door and, in diaries, to keep my sanity. In spite of this, I consider the written word inferior to the spoken, and much of the frustration experienced by novelists is the awareness that whatever we manage to capture in even the most transcendent passages falls far short of the richness of life. Dialogue achieves its power in the dynamics of a fleeting moment of sight, sound, smell and touch.

I'm not going to enter the debate here about whether it is language that shapes reality or vice versa. That battle is doomed to be waged whenever we seek intermittent reprieve from the chicken and egg dispute. I will simply take the position that the spoken word, like the written word, amounts to a nonsensical arrangement of sounds or letters without a consensus that assigns "meaning." And building from the meanings of what we hear, we order reality. Words themselves are innocuous; it is the consensus that gives them true power.

I remember the first time I heard the word nigger. In my third-grade class, our math tests were being passed down the rows, and as I handed the papers to a little boy in back of me, I remarked that once again he had received a much lower mark than I did. He snatched his test from me and spit out that word. Had he called me a nymphomaniac or a necrophiliac, I couldn't have been more puzzled. I didn't know what a nigger was, but I knew that whatever it meant, it was something he shouldn't have called me. This was verified when I raised my hand, and in a loud voice repeated what he had said and watched the teacher scold him for using a "bad" word. I was later to go home and ask the inevitable question that every black parent must face—"Mommy, what does 'nigger' mean?"

And what exactly did it mean? Thinking back, I realize that this could not have been the first time the word was used in my presence. I was part of a large extended family that had migrated from the rural South after World War II and formed a close-knit network that gravitated around my maternal grandparents. Their ground-floor apartment in one of the buildings they

Originally published in the "Hers" column of the New York Times *(February 20, 1986), which featured essays and commentary by women writers.*

owned in Harlem was a weekend mecca for my immediate family, along with countless aunts, uncles and cousins who brought along assorted friends. It was a bustling and open house with assorted neighbors and tenants popping in and out to exchange bits of gossip, pick up an old quarrel or referee the ongoing checkers game in which my grandmother cheated shamelessly. They were all there to let down their hair and put up their feet after a week of labor in the factories, laundries and shipyards of New York.

5   Amid the clamor, which could reach deafening proportions—two or three conversations going on simultaneously, punctuated by the sound of a baby's crying somewhere in the back rooms or out on the street—there was still a rigid set of rules about what was said and how. Older children were sent out of the living room when it was time to get into the juicy details about "you-know-who" up on the third floor who had gone and gotten herself "p-r-e-g-n-a-n-t!" But my parents, knowing that I could spell well beyond my years, always demanded that I follow the others out to play. Beyond sexual misconduct and death, everything else was considered harmless for our young ears. And so among the anecdotes of the triumphs and disappointments in the various workings of their lives, the word nigger was used in my presence, but it was set within contexts and inflections that caused it to register in my mind as something else.

In the singular, the word was always applied to a man who had distinguished himself in some situation that brought their approval for his strength, intelligence or drive:

"Did Johnny really do that?"

"I'm telling you, that nigger pulled in $6,000 of overtime last year. Said he got enough for a down payment on a house."

When used with a possessive adjective by a woman—"my nigger"—it became a term of endearment for husband or boyfriend. But it could be more than just a term applied to a man. In their mouths it became the pure essence of manhood—a disembodied force that channeled their past history of struggle and present survival against the odds into a victorious statement of being: "Yeah, that old foreman found out quick enough—you don't mess with a nigger."

10   In the plural, it became a description of some group within the community that had overstepped the bounds of decency as my family defined it: Parents who neglected their children, a drunken couple who fought in public, people who simply refused to look for work, those with excessively dirty mouths or unkempt households were all "trifling niggers." This particular circle could forgive hard times, unemployment, the occasional bout of depression—they had gone through all of that themselves—but the unforgivable sin was lack of self-respect.

A woman could never be a "nigger" in the singular, with its connotation of confirming worth. The noun girl was its closest equivalent in that sense, but only when used in direct address and regardless of the gender doing the addressing. "Girl" was a token of respect for a woman. The one-syllable word was drawn out to sound like three in recognition of the extra ounce of wit, nerve or daring that the woman had shown in the situation under discussion.

"G-i-r-l, stop. You mean you said that to his face?"

But if the word was used in a third-person reference or shortened so that it almost snapped out of the mouth, it always involved some element of communal disapproval. And age became an important factor in these exchanges. It was only between individuals of the same generation, or from an older person to a younger (but never the other way around), that "girl" would be considered a compliment.

I don't agree with the argument that use of the word nigger at this social stratum of the black community was an internalization of racism. The dynamics were the exact opposite: the people in my grandmother's living room took a word that whites used to signify worthlessness or degradation and rendered it impotent. Gathering there together, they transformed "nigger" to signify the varied and complex human beings they knew themselves to be. If the word was to disappear totally from the mouths of even the most liberal of white society, no one in that room was naïve enough to believe it would disappear from white minds. Meeting the word head-on, they proved it had absolutely nothing to do with the way they were determined to live their lives.

So there must have been dozens of times that the word "nigger" was spo- 15
ken in front of me before I reached the third grade. But I didn't "hear" it until it was said by a small pair of lips that had already learned it could be a way to humiliate me. That was the word I went home and asked my mother about. And since she knew that I had to grow up in America, she took me in her lap and explained.

QUESTIONS

1. In her opening paragraph, Naylor writes that she considers "the written word inferior to the spoken." In what ways does she demonstrate the superiority of the spoken word in this essay?

2. Naylor claims that "[w]ords themselves are innocuous; it is consensus that gives them true power" (paragraph 2). As a class, brainstorm a list of words that can have different meanings and connotations, depending on who uses the words.

3. Think of a word that has several different meanings in your own family or community. Write a personal essay in which you detail those meanings. Like Naylor, use grammatical terms (as well as age- and gender-specifics, if applicable) to categorize the different meanings.

MAXINE HONG KINGSTON *Tongue-Tied*

L ONG AGO IN CHINA, knot-makers tied string into buttons and frogs, and rope into bell pulls. There was one knot so complicated that it blinded the knot-maker. Finally an emperor outlawed this cruel knot, and the nobles could not order it anymore. If I had lived in China, I would have been an outlaw knot-maker.

Maybe that's why my mother cut my tongue. She pushed my tongue up and sliced the frenum.[1] Or maybe she snipped it with a pair of nail scissors. I don't remember her doing it, only her telling me about it, but all during childhood I felt sorry for the baby whose mother waited with scissors or knife in hand for it to cry—and then, when its mouth was wide open like a baby bird's, cut. The Chinese say "a ready tongue is an evil."

I used to curl up my tongue in front of the mirror and tauten my frenum into a white line, itself as thin as a razor blade. I saw no scars in my mouth. I thought perhaps I had had two frena, and she had cut one. I made other children open their mouths so I could compare theirs to mine. I saw perfect pink membranes stretching into precise edges that looked easy enough to cut. Sometimes I felt very proud that my mother committed such a powerful act upon me. At other times I was terrified—the first thing my mother did when she saw me was to cut my tongue.

"Why did you do that to me, Mother?"

5 "I told you."

"Tell me again."

"I cut it so that you would not be tongue-tied. Your tongue would be able to move in any language. You'll be able to speak languages that are completely different from one another. You'll be able to pronounce anything. Your frenum looked too tight to do those things, so I cut it."

"But isn't 'a ready tongue an evil'?"

"Things are different in this ghost country."[2]

10 "Did it hurt me? Did I cry and bleed?"

"I don't remember. Probably."

She didn't cut the other children's. When I asked cousins and other Chinese children whether their mothers had cut their tongues loose, they said, "What?"

"Why didn't you cut my brothers' and sisters' tongues?"

"They didn't need it."

Published as the first chapter of The Woman Warrior: Memoirs of a Girlhood among Ghosts (1976), *Kingston's highly acclaimed account of her Asian American girlhood and her family history.*

1. The connecting fold of membrane on the underside of the tongue.
2. In Kingston's story, the Chinese immigrants see white Americans as "ghosts," whose language and values they must adopt to become American.

"Why not? Were theirs longer than mine?"   15

"Why don't you quit blabbering and get to work?"

If my mother was not lying she should have cut more, scraped away the rest of the frenum skin, because I have a terrible time talking. Or she should not have cut at all, tampering with my speech. When I went to kindergarten and had to speak English for the first time, I became silent. A dumbness—a shame—still cracks my voice in two, even when I want to say "hello" casually, or ask an easy question in front of the check-out counter, or ask directions of a bus driver. I stand frozen, or I hold up the line with the complete, grammatical sentence that comes squeaking out at impossible length. "What did you say?" says the cab driver, or "Speak up," so I have to perform again, only weaker the second time. A telephone call makes my throat bleed and takes up that day's courage. It spoils my day with self-disgust when I hear my broken voice come skittering out into the open. It makes people wince to hear it. I'm getting better, though. Recently I asked the postman for special-issue stamps; I've waited since childhood for postmen to give me some of their own accord. I am making progress, a little every day.

My silence was thickest—total—during the three years that I covered my school paintings with black paint. I painted layers of black over houses and flowers and suns, and when I drew on the blackboard, I put a layer of chalk on top. I was making a stage curtain, and it was the moment before the curtain parted or rose. The teachers called my parents to school, and I saw they had been saving my pictures, curling and cracking, all alike and black. The teachers pointed to the pictures and looked serious, talked seriously too, but my parents did not understand English. ("The parents and teachers of criminals were executed," said my father.) My parents took the pictures home. I spread them out (so black and full of possibilities) and pretended the curtains were swinging open, flying up, one after another, sunlight underneath, mighty operas.

During the first silent year I spoke to no one at school, did not ask before going to the lavatory, and flunked kindergarten. My sister also said nothing for three years, silent in the playground and silent at lunch. There were other quiet Chinese girls not of our family, but most of them got over it sooner than we did. I enjoyed the silence. At first it did not occur to me I was supposed to talk or to pass kindergarten. I talked at home and to one or two of the Chinese kids in class. I made motions and even made some jokes. I drank out of a toy saucer when the water spilled out of the cup, and everybody laughed, pointing at me, so I did it some more. I didn't know that Americans don't drink out of saucers.

I liked the Negro students (Black Ghosts) best because they laughed the   20
loudest and talked to me as if I were a daring talker too. One of the Negro girls had her mother coil braids over her ears Shanghai-style like mine; we were Shanghai twins except that she was covered with black like my paintings. Two Negro kids enrolled in Chinese school, and the teachers gave them Chinese names. Some Negro kids walked me to school and home, protecting me from the Japanese kids, who hit me and chased me and stuck gum in my ears. The

Japanese kids were noisy and tough. They appeared one day in kindergarten, released from concentration camp,[3] which was a tic-tac-toe mark, like barbed wire, on the map.

It was when I found out I had to talk that school became a misery, that the silence became a misery. I did not speak and felt bad each time that I did not speak. I read aloud in first grade, though, and heard the barest whisper with little squeaks come out of my throat. "Louder," said the teacher, who scared the voice away again. The other Chinese girls did not talk either, so I knew the silence had to do with being a Chinese girl.

Reading out loud was easier than speaking because we did not have to make up what to say, but I stopped often, and the teacher would think I'd gone quiet again. I could not understand "I." The Chinese "I" had seven strokes, intricacies. How could the American "I," assuredly wearing a hat like the Chinese, have only three strokes, the middle so straight? Was it out of politeness that this writer left off strokes the way a Chinese has to write her own name small and crooked? No, it was not politeness; "I" is a capital and "you" is a lower-case. I stared at that middle line and waited so long for its black center to resolve into tight strokes and dots that I forgot to pronounce it. The other troublesome word was "here," no strong consonant to hang on to, and so flat, when "here" is two mountainous ideographs. The teacher, who had already told me every day how to read "I" and "here," put me in the low corner under the stairs again, where the noisy boys usually sat.

When my second grade class did a play, the whole class went to the auditorium except the Chinese girls. The teacher, lovely and Hawaiian, should have understood about us, but instead left us behind in the classroom. Our voices were too soft or nonexistent, and our parents never signed the permission slips anyway. They never signed anything unnecessary. We opened the door a crack and peeked out, but closed it again quickly. One of us (not me) won every spelling bee, though.

I remember telling the Hawaiian teacher, "We Chinese can't sing 'land where our fathers died.'" She argued with me about politics, while I meant because of curses. But how can I have that memory when I couldn't talk? My mother says that we, like the ghosts, have no memories.

25   After American school, we picked up our cigar boxes, in which we had arranged books, brushes, and an inkbox neatly, and went to Chinese school, from 5:00 to 7:30 P.M. There we chanted together, voices rising and falling, loud and soft, some boys shouting, everybody reading together, reciting together and not alone with one voice. When we had a memorization test, the teacher let each of us come to his desk and say the lesson to him privately, while the rest of the class practiced copying or tracing. Most of the teachers were men. The boys who were so well behaved in the American school played tricks on them and talked back to them. The girls were not mute. They screamed and yelled during recess, when there were no rules; they had fist-

3. During World War II, more than 100,000 Japanese Americans were imprisoned in "War Relocation Camps" in the United States.

fights. Nobody was afraid of children hurting themselves or of children hurting school property. The glass doors to the red and green balconies with the gold joy symbols were left wide open so that we could run out and climb the fire escapes. We played capture-the-flag in the auditorium, where Sun Yat-sen and Chiang Kai-shek's[4] pictures hung at the back of the stage, the Chinese flag on their left and the American flag on their right. We climbed the teak ceremonial chairs and made flying leaps off the stage. One flag headquarters was behind the glass door and the other on stage right. Our feet drummed on the hollow stage. During recess the teachers locked themselves up in their office with the shelves of books, copybooks, inks from China. They drank tea and warmed their hands at a stove. There was no play supervision. At recess we had the school to ourselves, and also we could roam as far as we could go—downtown, Chinatown stores, home—as long as we returned before the bell rang.

At exactly 7:30 the teacher again picked up the brass bell that sat on his desk and swung it over our heads, while we charged down the stairs, our cheering magnified in the stairwell. Nobody had to line up.

Not all of the children who were silent at American school found voice at Chinese school. One new teacher said each of us had to get up and recite in front of the class, who was to listen. My sister and I had memorized the lesson perfectly. We said it to each other at home, one chanting, one listening. The teacher called on my sister to recite first. It was the first time a teacher had called on the second-born to go first. My sister was scared. She glanced at me and looked away; I looked down at my desk. I hoped that she could do it because if she could, then I wouldn't have to. She opened her mouth and a voice came out that wasn't a whisper, but it wasn't a proper voice either. I hoped that she would not cry, fear breaking up her voice like twigs underfoot. She sounded as if she were trying to sing through weeping and strangling. She did not pause or stop to end the embarrassment. She kept going until she said the last word, and then she sat down. When it was my turn, the same voice came out, a crippled animal running on broken legs. You could hear splinters in my voice, bones rubbing jagged against one another. I was loud, though. I was glad I didn't whisper. There was one little girl who whispered.

4. Sun Yat-sen (1866–1925) and his successor, Chiang Kai-shek (1888–1975), led the Guomindang (or Nationalist party) campaign to unify China in the 1920s and 1930s.

Questions

1. Like Gloria Anzaldúa in "How to Tame a Wild Tongue" (p. 294), Kingston uses the tongue as both a physical body part and a metaphor for speech. Locate examples of these uses of "tongue" and explain them.

2. Why does Kingston call non-Asians "ghosts"? Are these the only ghosts Kingston confronts? Discuss her usage of this term in the essay and in the subtitle of her autobiography, *Memoirs of a Girlhood among Ghosts*.

3. If you have had difficulty speaking up or if you have faced a language problem in your past, write about it in an essay that explains your experience in terms of a family or social context.

RICHARD RODRIGUEZ *Aria*

SUPPORTERS OF bilingual education today imply that students like me miss a great deal by not being taught in their family's language. What they seem not to recognize is that, as a socially disadvantaged child, I considered Spanish to be a private language. What I needed to learn in school was that I had the right—and the obligation—to speak the public language of *los gringos*. The odd truth is that my first-grade classmates could have become bilingual, in the conventional sense of that word, more easily than I. Had they been taught (as upper-middle-class children are often taught early) a second language like Spanish or French, they could have regarded it simply as that: another public language. In my case such bilingualism could not have been so quickly achieved. What I did not believe was that I could speak a single public language.

Without question, it would have pleased me to hear my teachers address me in Spanish when I entered the classroom. I would have felt much less afraid. I would have trusted them and responded with ease. But I would have delayed—for how long postponed?—having to learn the language of public society. I would have evaded—and for how long could I have afforded to delay?—learning the great lesson of school, that I had a public identity.

Fortunately, my teachers were unsentimental about their responsibility. What they understood was that I needed to speak a public language. So their voices would search me out, asking me questions. Each time I'd hear them, I'd look up in surprise to see a nun's face frowning at me. I'd mumble, not really meaning to answer. The nun would persist, "Richard, stand up. Don't look at the floor. Speak up. Speak to the entire class, not just to me!" But I couldn't believe that the English language was mine to use. (In part, I did not want to believe it.) I continued to mumble. I resisted the teacher's demands. (Did I somehow suspect that once I learned public language my pleasing family life would be changed?) Silent, waiting for the bell to sound, I remained dazed, diffident, afraid.

Because I wrongly imagined that English was intrinsically a public language and Spanish an intrinsically private one, I easily noted the difference between classroom language and the language of home. At school, words were directed to a general audience of listeners. ("Boys and girls.") Words were

From Hunger of Memory: The Education of Richard Rodriguez *(1982), an autobiography of Rodriguez's experiences as a student, including his controversial argument against bilingual education.*

meaningfully ordered. And the point was not self-expression alone but to make oneself understood by many others. The teacher quizzed: "Boys and girls, why do we use that word in this sentence? Could we think of a better word to use there? Would the sentence change its meaning if the words were differently arranged? And wasn't there a better way of saying much the same thing?" (I couldn't say. I wouldn't try to say.)

Three months. Five. Half a year passed. Unsmiling, ever watchful, my   5
teachers noted my silence. They began to connect my behavior with the difficult progress my older sister and brother were making. Until one Saturday morning three nuns arrived at the house to talk to our parents. Stiffly, they sat on the blue living room sofa. From the doorway of another room, spying the visitors, I noted the incongruity—the clash of two worlds, the faces and voices of school intruding upon the familiar setting of home. I overheard one voice gently wondering, "Do your children speak only Spanish at home, Mrs. Rodriguez?" While another voice added, "That Richard especially seems so timid and shy."

That Rich-heard!

With great tact the visitors continued, "Is it possible for you and your husband to encourage your children to practice their English when they are home?" Of course, my parents complied. What would they not do for their children's well-being? And how could they have questioned the Church's authority which those women represented? In an instant, they agreed to give up the language (the sounds) that had revealed and accentuated our family's closeness. The moment after the visitors left, the change was observed. "*Ahora,* speak to us *en inglés,*"[1] my father and mother united to tell us.

At first, it seemed a kind of game. After dinner each night, the family gathered to practice "our" English. (It was still then *inglés,* a language foreign to us, so we felt drawn as strangers to it.) Laughing, we would try to define words we could not pronounce. We played with strange English sounds, often overanglicizing our pronunciations. And we filled the smiling gaps of our sentences with familiar Spanish sounds. But that was cheating, somebody shouted. Everyone laughed. In school, meanwhile, like my brother and sister, I was required to attend a daily tutoring session. I needed a full year of special attention. I also needed my teachers to keep my attention from straying in class by calling out, *Rich-heard*—their English voices slowly prying loose my ties to my other name, its three notes, *Ri-car-do.* Most of all I needed to hear my mother and father speak to me in a moment of seriousness in broken—suddenly heartbreaking—English. The scene was inevitable: One Saturday morning I entered the kitchen where my parents were talking in Spanish. I did not realize that they were talking in Spanish however until, at the moment they saw me, I heard their voices change to speak English. Those *gringo* sounds they uttered startled me. Pushed me away. In that moment of trivial misunderstanding and profound insight, I felt my throat twisted by unsounded grief. I turned quickly and left the room. But I had no place to escape to with

---

1. "*Now,* speak to us *in English.*"

Spanish. (The spell was broken.) My brother and sisters were speaking English in another part of the house.

Again and again in the days following, increasingly angry, I was obliged to hear my mother and father: "Speak to us *en inglés.*" (*Speak.*) Only then did I determine to learn classroom English. Weeks after, it happened: One day in school I raised my hand to volunteer an answer. I spoke out in a loud voice. And I did not think it remarkable when the entire class understood. That day, I moved very far from the disadvantaged child I had been only days earlier. The belief, that calming assurance that I belonged in public, had at last taken hold.

10   Shortly after, I stopped hearing the high and loud sounds of *los gringos.* A more and more confident speaker of English, I didn't trouble to listen to *how* strangers sounded, speaking to me. And there simply were too many English-speaking people in my day for me to hear American accents anymore. Conversations quickened. Listening to persons who sounded eccentrically pitched voices, I usually noted their sounds for an initial few seconds before I concentrated on *what* they were saying. Conversations became content-full. Transparent. Hearing someone's *tone* of voice—angry or questioning or sarcastic or happy or sad—I didn't distinguish it from the words it expressed. Sound and word were thus tightly wedded. At the end of a day, I was often bemused, always relieved, to realize how "silent," though crowded with words, my day in public had been. (This public silence measured and quickened the change in my life.)

At last, seven years old, I came to believe what had been technically true since my birth: I was an American citizen.

But the special feeling of closeness at home was diminished by then. Gone was the desperate, urgent, intense feeling of being at home; rare was the experience of feeling myself individualized by family intimates. We remained a loving family, but one greatly changed. No longer so close; no longer bound tight by the pleasing and troubling knowledge of our public separateness. Neither my older brother nor sister rushed home after school anymore. Nor did I. When I arrived home there would often be neighborhood kids in the house. Or the house would be empty of sounds.

Following the dramatic Americanization of their children, even my parents grew more publicly confident. Especially my mother. She learned the names of all the people on our block. And she decided we needed to have a telephone installed in the house. My father continued to use the word *gringo.* But it was no longer charged with the old bitterness or distrust. (Stripped of any emotional content, the word simply became a name for those Americans not of Hispanic descent.) Hearing him, sometimes, I wasn't sure if he was pronouncing the Spanish word *gringo* or saying gringo in English.

Matching the silence I started hearing in public was a new quiet at home. The family's quiet was partly due to the fact that, as we children learned more and more English, we shared fewer and fewer words with our parents. Sentences needed to be spoken slowly when a child addressed his mother or father. (Often the parent wouldn't understand.) The child would need to repeat himself. (Still the parent misunderstood.) The young voice, frustrated, would end up saying, "Never mind"—the subject was closed. Dinners would be noisy with the clinking of knives and forks against dishes. My mother would smile softly between her remarks; my father at the other end of the table would chew and chew at his food, while he stared over the heads of his children.

My *mother*! My *father*! After English became my primary language, I no longer knew what words to use in addressing my parents. The old Spanish words (those tender accents of sound) I had used earlier—*mamá* and *papá*—I couldn't use anymore. They would have been too painful reminders of how much had changed in my life. On the other hand, the words I heard neighborhood kids call *their* parents seemed equally unsatisfactory. *Mother* and *Father*; *Ma, Papa, Pa, Dad, Pop* (how I hated the all American sound of that last word especially)—all these terms I felt were unsuitable, not really terms of address for *my* parents. As a result, I never used them at home. Whenever I'd speak to my parents, I would try to get their attention with eye contact alone. In public conversations, I'd refer to "my parents" or "my mother and father."

My mother and father, for their part, responded differently, as their children spoke to them less. She grew restless, seemed troubled and anxious at the scarcity of words exchanged in the house. It was she who would question me about my day when I came home from school. She smiled at small talk. She pried at the edges of my sentences to get me to say something more. (What?) She'd join conversations she overheard, but her intrusions often stopped her children's talking. By contrast, my father seemed reconciled to the new quiet. Though his English improved somewhat, he retired into silence. At dinner he spoke very little. One night his children and even his wife helplessly giggled at his garbled English pronunciation of the Catholic Grace before Meals. Thereafter he made his wife recite the prayer at the start of each meal, even on formal occasions, when there were guests in the house. Hers became the public voice of the family. On official business, it was she, not my father, one would usually hear on the phone or in stores, talking to strangers. His children grew so accustomed to his silence that, years later, they would speak routinely of his shyness. (My mother would often try to explain: Both his parents died when he was eight. He was raised by an uncle who treated him like little more than a menial servant. He was never encouraged to speak. He grew up alone. A man of few words.) But my father was not shy, I realized, when I'd watch him speaking Spanish with relatives. Using Spanish, he was quickly effusive. Especially when talking with other men, his voice would spark, flicker, flare alive with sounds. In Spanish, he expressed ideas and feelings he rarely revealed in English. With firm Spanish sounds, he conveyed confidence and authority English would never allow him.

The silence at home, however, was finally more than a literal silence. Fewer words passed between parent and child, but more profound was the silence that resulted from my inattention to sounds. At about the time I no longer bothered to listen with care to the sounds of English in public, I grew careless about listening to the sounds family members made when they spoke. Most of the time I heard someone speaking at home and didn't distinguish his

15

sounds from the words people uttered in public. I didn't even pay much attention to my parents' accented and ungrammatical speech. At least not at home. Only when I was with them in public would I grow alert to their accents. Though, even then, their sounds caused me less and less concern. For I was increasingly confident of my own public identity.

I would have been happier about my public success had I not sometimes recalled what it had been like earlier, when my family had conveyed its intimacy through a set of conveniently private sounds. Sometimes in public, hearing a stranger, I'd hark back to my past. A Mexican farmworker approached me downtown to ask directions to somewhere, *"¡Hijito . . . ? "*[2] he said. And his voice summoned deep longing. Another time, standing beside my mother in the visiting room of a Carmelite convent,[3] before the dense screen which rendered the nuns shadowy figures, I heard several Spanish-speaking nuns—their busy, singsong overlapping voices—assure us that yes, yes, we were remembered, all our family was remembered in their prayers. (Their voices echoed faraway family sounds.) Another day, a dark-faced old woman—her hand light on my shoulder—steadied herself against me as she boarded a bus. She murmured something I couldn't quite comprehend. Her Spanish voice came near, like the face of a never-before-seen relative in the instant before I was kissed. Her voice, like so many of the Spanish voices I'd hear in public, recalled the golden age of my youth. Hearing Spanish then, I continued to be a careful, if sad, listener to sounds. Hearing a Spanish-speaking family walking behind me, I turned to look. I smiled for an instant, before my glance found the Hispanic-looking faces of strangers in the crowd going by.

Today I hear bilingual educators say that children lose a degree of "individuality" by becoming assimilated into public society. (Bilingual schooling was popularized in the seventies, that decade when middle-class ethnics began to resist the process of assimilation—the American melting pot.) But the bilingualists simplistically scorn the value and necessity of assimilation. They do not seem to realize that there are *two* ways a person is individualized. So they do not realize that while one suffers a diminished sense of *private* individuality by becoming assimilated into public society, such assimilation makes possible the achievement of *public* individuality.

20   The bilingualists insist that a student should be reminded of his difference from others in mass society, his heritage. But they equate mere separateness with individuality. The fact is that only in private—with intimates—is separateness from the crowd a prerequisite for individuality. (An intimate draws me apart, tells me that I am unique, unlike all others.) In public, by contrast, full individuality is achieved, paradoxically, by those who are able to consider themselves members of the crowd. Thus it happened for me: Only when I was able to think of myself as an American, no longer an alien in *gringo* society, could I seek the rights and opportunities necessary for full public indi-

2. "Little boy . . . ?"
3. Of the Catholic Order of Our Lady of Mount Carmel.

viduality. The social and political advantages I enjoy as a man result from the day that I came to believe that my name, indeed, is *Rich-heard Road-ree-guess*. It is true that my public society today is often impersonal. (My public society is usually mass society). Yet despite the anonymity of the crowd and despite the fact that the individuality I achieve in public is often tenuous—because it depends on my being one in a crowd—I celebrate the day I acquired my new name. Those middle-class ethnics who scorn assimilation seem to me filled with decadent self-pity, obsessed by the burden of public life. Dangerously, they romanticize public separateness and they trivialize the dilemma of the socially disadvantaged.

My awkward childhood does not prove the necessity of bilingual education. My story discloses instead an essential myth of childhood—inevitable pain. If I rehearse here the changes in my private life after my Americanization, it is finally to emphasize the public gain. The loss implies the gain: The house I returned to each afternoon was quiet. Intimate sounds no longer rushed to the door to greet me. There were other noises inside. The telephone rang. Neighborhood kids ran past the door of the bedroom where I was reading my schoolbooks—covered with shopping-bag paper. Once I learned public language, it would never again be easy for me to hear intimate family voices. More and more of my day was spent hearing words. But that may only be a way of saying that the day I raised my hand in class and spoke loudly to an entire roomful of faces, my childhood started to end.

QUESTIONS

1. What, according to Rodriguez, did he lose because he attended an English-speaking (Catholic) school without a bilingual program? What did he gain?

2. Rodriguez frames this section of his autobiography with an argument against bilingual education. How convincing is his evidence? Does he claim that all nonnative speakers of English educated in English would have the same losses and gains as he did?

3. According to Rodriguez, what are the differences between private and public languages, private and public individuality? Can both exist when the family language and the school language are English? How might a native speaker of English describe the differences?

4. Make a case, in writing, for or against bilingual education using material from Gloria Naylor's "Mommy, What Does 'Nigger' Mean?" (p. 279), Maxine Hong Kingston's "Tongue-Tied" (p. 282), Gloria Anzaldúa's "How to Tame a Wild Tongue" (p. 294), and Majorie Agosín's "Always Living in Spanish" (p. 292), as well as your own experience, observation, and reading.

MARJORIE AGOSÍN *Always Living in Spanish*

I N THE EVENINGS in the northern hemisphere, I repeat the ancient ritual that I observed as a child in the southern hemisphere: going out while the night is still warm and trying to recognize the stars as it begins to grow dark silently. In the sky of my country, Chile, that long and wide stretch of land that the poets blessed and dictators abused, I could easily name the stars: the three Marias, the Southern Cross, and the three Lilies, names of beloved and courageous women.

But here in the United States, where I have lived since I was a young girl, the solitude of exile makes me feel that so little is mine, that not even the sky has the same constellations, the trees and the fauna the same names or sounds, or the rubbish the same smell. How does one recover the familiar? How does one name the unfamiliar? How can one be another or live in a foreign language? These are the dilemmas of one who writes in Spanish and lives in translation.

Since my earliest childhood in Chile I lived with the tempos and the melodies of a multiplicity of tongues: German, Yiddish,[1] Russian, Turkish, and many Latin songs. Because everyone was from somewhere else, my relatives laughed, sang, and fought in a Babylon of languages. Spanish was reserved for matters of extreme seriousness, for commercial transactions, or for illnesses, but everyone's mother tongue was always associated with the memory of spaces inhabited in the past: the shtetl,[2] the flowering and vast Vienna avenues, the minarets of Turkey, and the Ladino[3] whispers of Toledo. When my paternal grandmother sang old songs in Turkish, her voice and body assumed the passion of one who was there in the city of Istanbul, gazing by turns toward the west and the east.

Destiny and the always ambiguous nature of history continued my family's enforced migration, and because of it I, too, became one who had to live and speak in translation. The disappearances, torture, and clandestine deaths in my country in the early seventies drove us to the United States, that other America that looked with suspicion at those who did not speak English and especially those who came from the supposedly uncivilized regions of Latin America. I had left a dangerous place that was my home, only to arrive in a dangerous place that was not: a high school in the small town of Athens, Geor-

Published in Poets & Writers *(March–April 1999), by a professor of Spanish at Wellesley College in Massachusetts. The magazine is the publication of Poets & Writers, Inc., an organization that provides "information, support and guidance for creative writers."*

1. A Germanic language with a Hebrew alphabet, spoken by the Ashkenazi Jews who once populated Eastern Europe.

2. Yiddish word meaning "small town."

3. A nearly extinct language, based on Spanish and spoken by Sephardic Jews who fled Spain and settled in North Africa and the Balkans.

gia, where my poor English and my accent were the cause of ridicule and insult. The only way I could recover my usurped country and my Chilean childhood was by continuing to write in Spanish, the same way my grandparents had sung in their own tongues in diasporic[4] sites.

The new and learned English language did not fit with the visceral emotions and themes that my poetry contained, but by writing in Spanish I could recover fragrances, spoken rhythms, and the passion of my own identity. Daily I felt the need to translate myself for the strangers living all around me, to tell them why we were in Georgia, why we ate differently, why we had fled, why my accent was so thick, and why I did not look Hispanic. Only at night, writing poems in Spanish, could I return to my senses, and soothe my own sorrow over what I had left behind.

This is how I became a Chilean poet who wrote in Spanish and lived in the southern United States. And then, one day, a poem of mine was translated and published in the English language. Finally, for the first time since I had left Chile, I felt I didn't have to explain myself. My poem, expressed in another language, spoke for itself . . . and for me.

Sometimes the austere sounds of English help me bear the solitude of knowing that I am foreign and so far away from those about whom I write. I must admit I would like more opportunities to read in Spanish to people whose language and culture is also mine, to join in our common heritage and in the feast of our sound. I would also like readers of English to understand the beauty of the spoken word in Spanish, that constant flow of oxytonic and paraoxytonic[5] syllables (*Verde que te quiero verde*),[6] the joy of writing—of dancing—in another language. I believe that many exiles share the unresolvable torment of not being able to live in the language of their childhood.

I miss that undulating and sensual language of mine, those baroque descriptions, the sense of being and feeling that Spanish gives me. It is perhaps for this reason that I have chosen and will always choose to write in Spanish. Nothing else from my childhood world remains. My country seems to be frozen in gestures of silence and oblivion. My relatives have died, and I have grown up not knowing a young generation of cousins and nieces and nephews. Many of my friends were disappeared, others were tortured, and the most fortunate, like me, became guardians of memory. For us, to write in Spanish is to always be in active pursuit of memory. I seek to recapture a world lost to me on that sorrowful afternoon when the blue electric sky and the Andean cordillera[7] bade me farewell. On that, my last Chilean day, I carried under my arm my innocence recorded in a little blue notebook I kept even then. Gradu-

---

4. Relating to a diaspora, or the spread of a people out from a single geographic area

5. Oxytonic: term for the stress falling on the last syllable of a word; paraoxytonic: term for the stress falling on the next-to-last syllable of a word.

6. Spanish: "Green, how I want you green." This opening line of a poem by Frederico Garcia Lorca illustrates oxytonic and paraoxytonic stress.

7. Spanish: a mountain range with a string of summits..

ally that diary filled with memoranda, poems written in free verse, descriptions of dreams and of the thresholds of my house surrounded by cherry trees and gardenias. To write in Spanish is for me a gesture of survival. And because of translation, my memory has now become a part of the memory of many others.

Translators are not traitors, as the proverb says, but rather splendid friends in this great human community of language.

QUESTIONS

1. Agosín obviously knows English, but she continues to write in Spanish. What is her reason for doing so? What do you think of such a practice?

2. Compare Agosín's attitude toward the Spanish of her youth to Anzaldúa's (below) or Rodriguez's (p. 286). What do they have in common? What are their differences? Which attitude attracts you more? Why?

3. Agosín writes of a Babylon of language, a concept that has negative connotations. What is wrong with so many languages being used? Can you see how some could find it distasteful, while others would celebrate diversity? Write about where you stand on this question.

GLORIA ANZALDÚA *How to Tame a Wild Tongue*

"WE'RE GOING TO have to control your tongue," the dentist says, pulling out all the metal from my mouth. Silver bits plop and tinkle into the basin. My mouth is a motherlode.

The dentist is cleaning out my roots. I get a whiff of the stench when I gasp. "I can't cap that tooth yet, you're still draining," he says.

"We're going to have to do something about your tongue," I hear the anger rising in his voice. My tongue keeps pushing out the wads of cotton, pushing back the drills, the long thin needles. "I've never seen anything as strong or as stubborn," he says. And I think, how do you tame a wild tongue, train it to be quiet, how do you bridle and saddle it? How do you make it lie down?

> "Who is to say that robbing a people of
> its language is less violent than war?"
>
> —RAY GWYN SMITH[1]

From Borderlands/La Frontera (1987), *a collection of experimental essays and memoirs that combine English, Spanish, and Chicano Spanish. All notes are the author's. The author has asked that no translations of Spanish or Chicano Spanish be included.*

1. Ray Gwyn Smith, Moorland Is Cold Country, unpublished book.

I remember being caught speaking Spanish at recess—that was good for three licks on the knuckles with a sharp ruler. I remember being sent to the corner of the classroom for "talking back" to the Anglo teacher when all I was trying to do was tell her how to pronounce my name. "If you want to be American, speak 'American.' If you don't like it, go back to Mexico where you belong."

"I want you to speak English. *Pa'hallar buen trabajo tienes que saber hablar el inglés bien. Qué vale toda tu educación si todavía hablas inglés con un* 'accent,'" my mother would say, mortified that I spoke English like a Mexican. At Pan American University, I, and all Chicano students were required to take two speech classes. Their purpose: to get rid of our accents.

Attacks on one's form of expression with the intent to censor are a violation of the First Amendment. *El Anglo con cara de inocente nos arrancó la lengua.* Wild tongues can't be tamed, they can only be cut out.

Overcoming the Tradition of Silence

> *Ahogadas, escupimos el oscuro.*
> *Peleando con nuestra propia sombra*
> *el silencio nos sepulta.*

En boca cerrada no entran moscas. "Flies don't enter a closed mouth" is a saying I kept hearing when I was a child. *Ser habladora* was to be a gossip and a liar, to talk too much. *Muchachitas bien criadas,* well-bred girls don't answer back. *Es una falta de respeto* to talk back to one's mother or father. I remember one of the sins I'd recite to the priest in the confession box the few times I went to confession: talking back to my mother, *hablar pa' 'trás, repelar. Hocicona, repelona, chismosa,* having a big mouth, questioning, carrying tales are all signs of being *mal criada.* In my culture they are all words that are derogatory if applied to women—I've never heard them applied to men.

The first time I heard two women, a Puerto Rican and a Cuban, say the word "*nosotras,*" I was shocked. I had not known the word existed. Chicanas use *nosotros* whether we're male or female. We are robbed of our female being by the masculine plural. Language is a male discourse.

> And our tongues have become
> dry   the wilderness has
> dried out our tongues   and
> we have forgotten speech.
>
> —Irena Klepfisz[2]

Even our own people, other Spanish speakers *nos quieren poner candados en la boca.* They would hold us back with their bag of *reglas de academia.*

---

2. Irena Klepfisz, "*Di rayze aheym*/The Journey Home," in <u>The Tribe of Dina: A Jewish Women's Anthology</u>, Melanie Kaye/Kantrowitz and Irena Klepfisz, eds. (Montpelier, VT: Sinister Wisdom Books, 1986), 49.

Oyé como ladra: el lenguaje de la frontera

Quien tiene boca se equivoca.

—MEXICAN SAYING

10   "*Pocho*, cultural traitor, you're speaking the oppressor's language by speaking English, you're ruining the Spanish language," I have been accused by various Latinos and Latinas. Chicano Spanish is considered by the purist and by most Latinos deficient, a mutilation of Spanish.

But Chicano Spanish is a border tongue which developed naturally. Change, *evolución, enriquecimiento de palabras nuevas por invención o adopción* have created variants of Chicano Spanish, *un nuevo lenguaje. Un lenguaje que corresponde a un modo de vivir.* Chicano Spanish is not incorrect, it is a living language.

For a people who are neither Spanish nor live in a country in which Spanish is the first language; for a people who live in a country in which English is the reigning tongue but who are not Anglo; for a people who cannot entirely identify with either standard (formal, Castillian) Spanish nor standard English, what recourse is left to them but to create their own language? A language which they can connect their identity to, one capable of communicating the realities and values true to themselves—a language with terms that are neither *español ni inglés,* but both. We speak a patois, a forked tongue, a variation of two languages.

Chicano Spanish sprang out of the Chicanos' need to identify ourselves as a distinct people. We needed a language with which we could communicate with ourselves, a secret language. For some of us, language is a homeland closer than the Southwest—for many Chicanos today live in the Midwest and the East. And because we are a complex, heterogeneous people, we speak many languages. Some of the languages we speak are:

1. Standard English

2. Working class and slang English

3. Standard Spanish

4. Standard Mexican Spanish

5. North Mexican Spanish dialect

6. Chicano Spanish (Texas, New Mexico, Arizona and California have regional variations)

7. Tex-Mex

8. *Pachuco* (called *caló*)

My "home" tongues are the languages I speak with my sister and brothers, with my friends. They are the last five listed, with 6 and 7 being closest to my heart. From school, the media and job situations, I've picked up standard and working class English. From Mamagrande Locha and from reading Spanish and Mexican literature, I've picked up Standard Spanish and Standard Mexican Spanish. From *los recién llegados,* Mexican immigrants, and *braceros,* I learned the North Mexican dialect. With Mexicans I'll try to speak either Standard Mexican Spanish or the North Mexican dialect. From my parents and Chicanos living in the Valley, I picked up Chicano Texas Spanish, and I speak it with my mom, younger brother (who married a Mexican and who rarely mixes Spanish with English), aunts and older relatives.

With Chicanas from *Nuevo México* or *Arizona* I will speak Chicano Spanish a little, but often they don't understand what I'm saying. With most California Chicanas I speak entirely in English (unless I forget). When I first moved to San Francisco, I'd rattle off something in Spanish, unintentionally embarrassing them. Often it is only with another Chicana *tejana* that I can talk freely.

15

Words distorted by English are known as anglicisms or *pochismos.* The *pocho* is an anglicized Mexican or American of Mexican origin who speaks Spanish with an accent characteristic of North Americans and who distorts and reconstructs the language according to the influence of English.[3] Tex-Mex, or Spanglish, comes most naturally to me. I may switch back and forth from English to Spanish in the same sentence or in the same word. With my sister and my brother Nune and with Chicano *tejano* contemporaries I speak in Tex-Mex.

From kids and people my own age I picked up *Pachuco.* Pachuco (the language of the zoot suiters) is a language of rebellion, both against Standard Spanish and Standard English. It is a secret language. Adults of the culture and outsiders cannot understand it. It is made up of slang words from both English and Spanish. *Ruca* means girl or woman, *vato* means guy or dude, *chale* means no, *simón* means yes, *churo* is sure, talk is *periquiar, pigionear* means petting, *que gacho* means how nerdy, *ponte águila* means watch out, death is called *la pelona.* Through lack of practice and not having others who can speak it, I've lost most of the *Pachuco* tongue.

Chicano Spanish

Chicanos, after 250 years of Spanish/Anglo colonization have developed significant differences in the Spanish we speak. We collapse two adjacent vowels into a single syllable and sometimes shift the stress in certain words such as *maíz/maiz, cohete/cuete.* We leave out certain consonants when they appear between vowels: *lado/lao, mojado/mojao.* Chicanos from South Texas pronounced *f* as *j* as in *jue (fue).* Chicanos use "archaisms," words that are no longer in the Spanish language, words that have been evolved out. We say *semos, truje, haiga, ansina,* and *naiden.* We retain the "archaic" *j,* as in *jalar,* that derives from an earlier *h* (the French *halar* or the Germanic *halon* which was lost to standard Spanish in the 16th century), but which is still found in several regional dialects such as the one spoken in South Texas. (Due to geography, Chicanos from the Valley of South Texas were cut off linguistically from

3. R. C. Ortega, *Dialectología Del Barrio,* trans. Hortencia S. Alwan (Los Angeles, CA: R. C. Ortega Publisher & Bookseller, 1977), 132.

other Spanish speakers. We tend to use words that the Spaniards brought over from Medieval Spain. The majority of the Spanish colonizers in Mexico and the Southwest came from Extremadura—Hernán Cortés was one of them—and Andalucía. Andalucians pronounce *ll* like a *y*, and their *d*'s tend to be absorbed by adjacent vowels: *tirado* becomes *tirao*. They brought *el lenguaje popular, dialectos y regionalismos.*[4])

Chicanos and other Spanish speakers also shift *ll* to *y* and *z* to *s*.[5] We leave out initial syllables, saying *tar* for *estar, toy* for *estoy, hora* for *ahora* (*cubanos* and *puertorriqueños* also leave out initial letters of some words.) We also leave out the final syllable such as *pa* for *para*. The intervocalic *y*, the *ll* as in *tortilla, ella, botella*, gets replaced by *tortia* or *tortiya, ea, botea*. We add an additional syllable at the beginning of certain words: *atocar* for *tocar, agastar* for *gastar*. Sometimes we'll say *lavaste las vacijas*, other times *lavates* (substituting the *ates* verb endings for the *aste*).

20   We use anglicisms, words borrowed from English: *bola* from ball, *carpeta* from carpet, *máchina de lavar* (instead of *lavadora*) from washing machine. Tex-Mex argot, created by adding a Spanish sound at the beginning or end of an English word such as *cookiar* for cook, *watchar* for watch, *parkiar* for park, and *rapiar* for rape, is the result of the pressures on Spanish speakers to adapt to English.

We don't use the word *vosotros/as* or its accompanying verb form. We don't say *claro* (to mean yes), *imagínate*, or *me emociona*, unless we picked up Spanish from Latinas, out of a book, or in a classroom. Other Spanish-speaking groups are going through the same, or similar, development in their Spanish.

Linguistic Terrorism

> *Deslenguadas. Somos los del español deficiente.* We are your linguistic nightmare, your linguistic aberration, your linguistic *mestizaje*, the subject of your *burla*. Because we speak with tongues of fire we are culturally crucified. Racially, culturally and linguistically *somos huérfanos*—we speak an orphan tongue.

Chicanas who grew up speaking Chicano Spanish have internalized the belief that we speak poor Spanish. It is illegitimate, a bastard language. And because we internalize how our language has been used against us by the dominant culture, we use our language differences against each other.

Chicana feminists often skirt around each other with suspicion and hesitation. For the longest time I couldn't figure it out. Then it dawned on me. To be close to another Chicana is like looking into the mirror. We are afraid of what we'll see there. *Pena*. Shame. Low estimation of self. In childhood we are told that our language is wrong. Repeated attacks on our native tongue diminish our sense of self. The attacks continue throughout our lives.

---

4. Eduardo Hernandéz-Chávez, Andrew D. Cohen, and Anthony F. Beltramo, <u>El Lenguaje de los Chicanos: Regional and Social Characteristics of Language Used By Mexican Americans</u> (Arlington, VA: Center for Applied Linguistics, 1975), 39.

5. Hernandéz-Chávez, xvii.

Chicanas feel uncomfortable talking in Spanish to Latinas, afraid of their censure. Their language was not outlawed in their countries. They had a whole lifetime of being immersed in their native tongue; generations, centuries in which Spanish was a first language, taught in school, heard on radio and TV, and read in the newspaper.

If a person, Chicana or Latina, has a low estimation of my native tongue,   25
she also has a low estimation of me. Often with *mexicanas y latinas* we'll speak English as a neutral language. Even among Chicanas we tend to speak English at parties or conferences. Yet, at the same time, we're afraid the other will think we're *agringadas* because we don't speak Chicano Spanish. We oppress each other trying to out-Chicano each other, vying to be the "real" Chicanas, to speak like Chicanos. There is no one Chicano language just as there is no one Chicano experience. A monolingual Chicana whose first language is English or Spanish is just as much a Chicana as one who speaks several variants of Spanish. A Chicana from Michigan or Chicago or Detroit is just as much a Chicana as one from the Southwest. Chicano Spanish is as diverse linguistically as it is regionally.

By the end of this century, Spanish speakers will comprise the biggest minority group in the U.S., a country where students in high schools and colleges are encouraged to take French classes because French is considered more "cultured." But for a language to remain alive it must be used.[6] By the end of this century English, and not Spanish, will be the mother tongue of most Chicanos and Latinos.

So, if you want to really hurt me, talk badly about my language. Ethnic identity is twin skin to linguistic identity—I am my language. Until I can take pride in my language, I cannot take pride in myself. Until I can accept as legitimate Chicano Texas Spanish, Tex-Mex and all the other languages I speak, I cannot accept the legitimacy of myself. Until I am free to write bilingually and to switch codes without having always to translate, while I still have to speak English or Spanish when I would rather speak Spanglish, and as long as I have to accommodate the English speakers rather than having them accommodate me, my tongue will be illegitimate.

I will no longer be made to feel ashamed of existing. I will have my voice: Indian, Spanish, white. I will have my serpent's tongue—my woman's voice, my sexual voice, my poet's voice. I will overcome the tradition of silence.

> My fingers
> move sly against your palm
> Like women everywhere, we speak in code . . . .
> —Melanie Kaye/Kantrowitz[7]

6. Irena Klepfisz, "Secular Jewish Identity: Yidishkayt in America," in <u>The Tribe of Dina</u>, Kaye/Kantrowitz and Klepfisz, eds., 43.
7. Melanie Kaye/Kantrowitz, "Sign," in <u>We Speak in Code: Poems and Other Writings</u> (Pittsburgh, PA: Motheroot Publications, Inc., 1980), 85.

"Vistas," corridos, y comida: My Native Tongue

In the 1960s, I read my first Chicano novel. It was *City of Night* by John Rechy, a gay Texan, son of a Scottish father and a Mexican mother. For days I walked around in stunned amazement that a Chicano could write and could get published. When I read *I Am Joaquín*[8] I was surprised to see a bilingual book by a Chicano in print. When I saw poetry written in Tex-Mex for the first time, a feeling of pure joy flashed through me. I felt like we really existed as a people. In 1971, when I started teaching High School English to Chicano students, I tried to supplement the required texts with works by Chicanos, only to be reprimanded and forbidden to do so by the principal. He claimed that I was supposed to teach "American" and English literature. At the risk of being fired, I swore my students to secrecy and slipped in Chicano short stories, poems, a play. In graduate school, while working toward a Ph.D., I had to "argue" with one advisor after the other, semester after semester, before I was allowed to make Chicano literature an area of focus.

30   Even before I read books by Chicanos or Mexicans, it was the Mexican movies I saw at the drive-in—the Thursday night special of $1.00 a carload— that gave me a sense of belonging. *"Vámonos a las vistas,"* my mother would call out and we'd all—grandmother, brothers, sister and cousins—squeeze into the car. We'd wolf down cheese and bologna white bread sandwiches while watching Pedro Infante in melodramatic tear-jerkers like *Nosotros los pobres,* the first "real" Mexican movie (that was not an imitation of European movies). I remember seeing *Cuando los hijos se van* and surmising that all Mexican movies played up the love a mother has for her children and what ungrateful sons and daughters suffer when they are not devoted to their mothers. I remember the singing-type "westerns" of Jorge Negrete and Miguel Aceves Mejía. When watching Mexican movies, I felt a sense of homecoming as well as alienation. People who were to amount to something didn't go to Mexican movies, or *bailes* or tune their radios to *bolero, rancherita,* and *corrido* music.

The whole time I was growing up, there was *norteño* music sometimes called North Mexican border music, or Tex-Mex music, or Chicano music, or *cantina* (bar) music. I grew up listening to *conjuntos,* three- or four-piece bands made up of folk musicians playing guitar, *bajo sexto,* drums and button accordion, which Chicanos had borrowed from the German immigrants who had come to Central Texas and Mexico to farm and build breweries. In the Rio Grande Valley, Steve Jordan and Little Joe Hernández were popular, and Flaco Jiménez was the accordion king. The rhythms of Tex-Mex music are those of the polka, also adapted from the Germans, who in turn had borrowed the polka from the Czechs and Bohemians.

I remember the hot, sultry evenings when *corridos*—songs of love and death on the Texas-Mexican borderlands—reverberated out of cheap amplifiers from the local *cantinas* and wafted in through my bedroom window.

8. Rodolfo Gonzales, I Am Joaquín / Yo Soy Joaquín (New York, NY: Bantam Books, 1972). It was first published in 1967.

Corridos first became widely used along the South Texas/Mexican border during the early conflict between Chicanos and Anglos. The *corridos* are usually about Mexican heroes who do valiant deeds against the Anglo oppressors. Pancho Villa's song, "*La cucaracha*," is the most famous one. *Corridos* of John F. Kennedy and his death are still very popular in the Valley. Older Chicanos remember Lydia Mendoza, one of the great border *corrido* singers who was called *la Gloria de Tejas*. Her "*El tango negro*," sung during the Great Depression, made her a singer of the people. The everpresent *corridos* narrated one hundred years of border history, bringing news of events as well as entertaining. These folk musicians and folk songs are our chief cultural mythmakers, and they made our hard lives seem bearable.

I grew up feeling ambivalent about our music. Country-western and rock-and-roll had more status. In the 50s and 60s, for the slightly educated and *agringado* Chicanos, there existed a sense of shame at being caught listening to our music. Yet I couldn't stop my feet from thumping to the music, could not stop humming the words, nor hide from myself the exhilaration I felt when I heard it.

There are more subtle ways that we internalize identification, especially in the   35
forms of images and emotions. For me food and certain smells are tied to my identity, to my homeland. Woodsmoke curling up to an immense blue sky; woodsmoke perfuming my grandmother's clothes, her skin. The stench of cow manure and the yellow patches on the ground; the crack of a .22 rifle and the reek of cordite. Homemade white cheese sizzling in a pan, melting inside a folded *tortilla*. My sister Hilda's hot, spicy *menudo*, *chile colorado* making it deep red, pieces of *panza* and hominy floating on top. My brother Carito barbecuing *fajitas* in the backyard. Even now and 3,000 miles away, I can see my mother spicing the ground beef, pork and venison with *chile*. My mouth salivates at the thought of the hot steaming *tamales* I would be eating if I were home.

Si le preguntas a mi mamá, "*¿Qué eres?*"

> "Identity is the essential core of who
> we are as individuals, the conscious
> experience of the self inside."
>
> —Kaufman[9]

Nosotros los Chicanos straddle the borderlands. On one side of us, we are constantly exposed to the Spanish of the Mexicans, on the other side we hear the Anglos' incessant clamoring so that we forget our language. Among ourselves we don't say *nosotros los americanos, o nosotros los españoles, o nosotros los hispanos*. We say *nosotros los mexicanos* (by *mexicanos* we do not mean citizens of Mexico; we do not mean a national identity, but a racial one). We distinguish between *mexicanos del otro lado* and *mexicanos de este lado*. Deep in

9. Kaufman, 68.

our hearts we believe that being Mexican has nothing to do with which country one lives in. Being Mexican is a state of soul—not one of mind, not one of citizenship. Neither eagle nor serpent, but both. And like the ocean, neither animal respects borders.

> *Dime con quien andas y te diré quien eres.*
> (Tell me who your friends are and I'll tell you who you are.)
> — MEXICAN SAYING

Si le preguntas a mi mamá, "¿Qué eres?" te dirá, "Soy mexicana." My brothers and sister say the same. I sometimes will answer *"soy mexicana"* and at others will say *"soy Chicana" o "soy tejana."* But I identified as *"Raza"* before I ever identified as *"mexicana"* or "Chicana."

As a culture, we call ourselves Spanish when referring to ourselves as a linguistic group and when copping out. It is then that we forget our predominant Indian genes. We are 70 to 80% Indian.[10] We call ourselves Hispanic[11] or Spanish-American or Latin American or Latin when linking ourselves to other Spanish-speaking peoples of the Western hemisphere and when copping out. We call ourselves Mexican-American[12] to signify we are neither Mexican nor American, but more the noun "American" than the adjective "Mexican" (and when copping out).

Chicanos and other people of color suffer economically for not acculturating. This voluntary (yet forced) alienation makes for psychological conflict, a kind of dual identity—we don't identify with the Anglo-American cultural values and we don't totally identify with the Mexican cultural values. We are a synergy of two cultures with various degrees of Mexicanness or Angloness. I have so internalized the borderland conflict that sometimes I feel like one cancels out the other and we are zero, nothing, no one. *A veces no soy nada ni nadie. Pero hasta cuando no lo soy, lo soy.*

40   When not copping out, when we know we are more than nothing, we call ourselves Mexican, referring to race and ancestry; *mestizo* when affirming both our Indian and Spanish (but we hardly ever own our Black ancestry); Chicano when referring to a politically aware people born and/or raised in the U.S.; *Raza* when referring to Chicanos; *tejanos* when we are Chicanos from Texas.

Chicanos did not know we were a people until 1965 when Cesar Chavez and the farmworkers united and *I Am Joaquín* was published and *la Raza Unida* party was formed in Texas. With that recognition, we became a distinct people. Something momentous happened to the Chicano soul—we became aware of our reality and acquired a name and a language (Chicano

---

10. Chávez, 88–90.

11. "Hispanic" is derived from *Hispanis* (*España*, a name given to the Iberian Peninsula in ancient times when it was a part of the Roman Empire) and is a term designated by the U.S. government to make it easier to handle us on paper.

12. The Treaty of Guadalupe Hidalgo created the Mexican-American in 1848.

Spanish) that reflected that reality. Now that we had a name, some of the fragmented pieces began to fall together—who we were, what we were, how we had evolved. We began to get glimpses of what we might eventually become.

Yet the struggle of identities continues, the struggle of borders is our reality still. One day the inner struggle will cease and a true integration take place. In the meantime, *tenemos que hacerla lucha. ¿Quién está protegiendo los ranchos de mi gente? ¿Quién está tratando de cerrar la fisura entre la india y el blanco en nuestra sangre? El Chicano, sí, el Chicano que anda como un ladrón en su propia casa.*

Los Chicanos, how patient we seem, how very patient. There is the quiet of the Indian about us.[13] We know how to survive. When other races have given up their tongue, we've kept ours. We know what it is to live under the hammer blow of the dominant *norteamericano* culture. But more than we count the blows, we count the days the weeks the years the centuries the eons until the white laws and commerce and customs will rot in the deserts they've created, lie bleached. *Humildes* yet proud, *quietos* yet wild, *nosotros los mexicanos*-Chicanos will walk by the crumbling ashes as we go about our business. Stubborn, persevering, impenetrable as stone, yet possessing a malleability that renders us unbreakable, we, the *mestizas* and *mestizos*, will remain.

13. Anglos, in order to alleviate their guilt for dispossessing the Chicano, stressed the Spanish part of us and perpetrated the myth of the Spanish Southwest. We have accepted the fiction that we are Hispanic, that is Spanish, in order to accommodate ourselves to the dominant culture and its abhorrence of Indians. Chávez, 88–91.

QUESTIONS

1. Anzaldúa includes many Spanish words and phrases, some of which she explains, others which she leaves untranslated. Why? What different responses might bilingual versus English-only readers have to her writing?

2. The essay begins with an example of Anzaldúa's "untamed tongue." What meanings, many metaphoric, does Anzaldúa give for "tongue" or "wild tongue"? How does the essay develop these meanings?

3. Anzaldúa speaks of Chicano Spanish as a "living language" (paragraph 11). What does she mean? What is her evidence for this point? What other languages do you know that are living, and how do you know they are living?

4. If you speak or write more than one language, or if you come from a linguistic community that has expressions specific to itself, write an essay in which you incorporate that language and/or alternate it with English. Think about the ways that Anzaldúa uses both English and Spanish.

GARRISON KEILLOR *How to Write a Letter*

WE SHY PERSONS need to write a letter now and then, or else we'll dry up and blow away. It's true. And I speak as one who loves to reach for the phone, dial the number, and talk. I say, "Big Bopper[1] here— what's shakin', babes?" The telephone is to shyness what Hawaii is to February, it's a way out of the woods, *and yet*: a letter is better.

Such a sweet gift—a piece of handmade writing, in an envelope that is not a bill, sitting in our friend's path when she trudges home from a long day spent among wahoos and savages, a day our words will help repair. They don't need to be immortal, just sincere. She can read them twice and again tomorrow: *You're someone I care about, Corinne, and think of often and every time I do you make me smile.*

We need to write, otherwise nobody will know who we are. They will have only a vague impression of us as A Nice Person, because, frankly, we don't shine at conversation, we lack the confidence to thrust our faces forward and say, "Hi, I'm Heather Hooten; let me tell you about my week." Mostly we say "Uh-huh" and "Oh, really." People smile and look over our shoulder, looking for someone else to meet.

So a shy person sits down and writes a letter. To be known by another person—to meet and talk freely on the page—to be close despite distance. To escape from anonymity and be our own sweet selves and express the music of our souls.

5   Same thing that moves a giant rock star to sing his heart out in front of 123,000 people moves us to take ballpoint in hand and write a few lines to our dear Aunt Eleanor. *We want to be known.* We want her to know that we have fallen in love, that we quit our job, that we're moving to New York, and we want to say a few things that might not get said in casual conversation: *Thank you for what you've meant to me, I am very happy right now.*

The first step in writing letters is to get over the guilt of *not* writing. You don't "owe" anybody a letter. Letters are a gift. The burning shame you feel when you see unanswered mail makes it harder to pick up a pen and makes for a cheerless letter when you finally do. *I feel bad about not writing, but I've been so busy*, etc. Skip this. Few letters are obligatory, and they are *Thanks for the wonderful gift* and *I am terribly sorry to hear about George's death* and *Yes, you're welcome to stay with us next month*, and not many more than that. Write those promptly if you want to keep your friends. Don't worry about the others, except love letters, of course. When your true love writes, *Dear Light of My*

From We Are Still Married *(1989), a collection of Keillor's stories, letters, and skits. Many of Keillor's humorous pieces are aired on his popular radio program,* A Prairie Home Companion.

1. American disc-jockey turned rock star (1930–1959), popular in the late 1950s.

Life, Joy of My Heart, O Lovely Pulsating Core of My Sensate Life, some response is called for.

Some of the best letters are tossed off in a burst of inspiration, so keep your writing stuff in one place where you can sit down for a few minutes and (*Dear Roy, I am in the middle of a book entitled* We Are Still Married *but thought I'd drop you a line. Hi to your sweetie, too*) dash off a note to a pal. Envelopes, stamps, address book, everything in a drawer so you can write fast when the pen is hot.

A blank white eight-by-eleven sheet can look as big as Montana if the pen's not so hot—try a smaller page and write boldly. Or use a note card with a piece of fine art on the front; if your letter ain't good, at least they get the Matisse.[2] Get a pen that makes a sensuous line, get a comfortable typewriter, a friendly word processor—which feels easy to the hand.

Sit for a few minutes with the blank sheet in front of you, and meditate on the person you will write to, let your friend come to mind until you can almost see her or him in the room with you. Remember the last time you saw each other and how your friend looked and what you said and what perhaps was unsaid between you, and when your friend becomes real to you, start to write.

Write the salutation—*Dear* You—and take a deep breath and plunge in. A simple declarative sentence will do, followed by another and another and another. Tell us what you're doing and tell it like you were talking to us. Don't think about grammar, don't think about lit'ry style, don't try to write dramatically, just give us your news. Where did you go, who did you see, what did they say, what do you think?

If you don't know where to begin, start with the present moment: *I'm sitting at the kitchen table on a rainy Saturday morning. Everyone is gone and the house is quiet.* Let your simple description of the present moment lead to something else, let the letter drift gently along.

The toughest letter to crank out is one that is meant to impress, as we all know from writing job applications; if it's hard work to slip off a letter to a friend, maybe you're trying too hard to be terrific. A letter is only a report to someone who already likes you for reasons other than your brilliance. Take it easy.

Don't worry about form. It's not a term paper. When you come to the end of one episode, just start a new paragraph. You can go from a few lines about the sad state of pro football to the fight with your mother to your fond memories of Mexico to your cat's urinary-tract infection to a few thoughts on personal indebtedness and on to the kitchen sink and what's in it. The more you write, the easier it gets, and when you have a True True Friend to write to, a *compadre*, a soul sibling, then it's like driving a car down a country road, you just get behind the keyboard and press on the gas.

Don't tear up the page and start over when you write a bad line—try to write your way out of it. Make mistakes and plunge on. Let the letter cook along and let yourself be bold. Outrage, confusion, love—whatever is in your mind, let it find a way to the page. Writing is a means of discovery, always, and

10

2. French painter (1869–1954).

when you come to the end and write *Yours ever* or *Hugs and kisses*, you'll know something you didn't when you wrote *Dear Pal*.

15   Probably your friend will put your letter away, and it'll be read again a few years from now—and it will improve with age. And forty years from now, your friend's grandkids will dig it out of the attic and read it, a sweet and precious relic of the ancient eighties that gives them a sudden clear glimpse of you and her and the world we old-timers knew. You will then have created an object of art. Your simple lines about where you went, who you saw, what they said, will speak to those children and they will feel in their hearts the humanity of our times.

You can't pick up a phone and call the future and tell them about our times. You have to pick up a piece of paper.

Postcards

A postcard takes about fifty words gracefully, which is how to write one. A few sweet strokes in a flowing hand—pink roses, black-face sheep in a wet meadow, the sea, the Swedish coast—your friend in Washington gets the idea. She doesn't need your itinerary to know that you remember her.

Fifty words is a strict form but if you write tiny and sneak over into the address side to squeeze in a hundred, the grace is gone and the result is not a poem but notes for a letter you don't have time to write, which will make her feel cheated.

So many persons traveling to a strange land are inclined to see its life so clearly, its essential national character, they could write a book about it as other foreign correspondents have done ("highly humorous . . . definitely a must"), but fifty words is a better length for what you really know.

Fifty words and a picture. Say you are in Scotland, the picture is of your hotel, a stone pile looking across the woods of Druimindarroch to Loch Nan Uamh near the village of Arisaig. You've never seen this country. For the past year you've worked like a prisoner in the mines. Write.

---

5   Scotland is the most beautiful country in the world and I am drinking coffee in the library of what once was the manor of people who inherited everything and eventually lost it. Thus it became a hotel. I'm with English people whose correctness is overpowering. What wild good luck to be here. And to be an American! I'm so happy, bubba.

In the Highlands, many one-lane roads which widen at curves and hills—a driving thrill, especially when following a native who drives like hell—you stick close to him, like the second car of the roller-coaster, but lose your nerve. Sixty mph down a one-lane winding road. I prefer a career.

The arrogance of Americans who, without so much as a *"mi scusi"* or *"bitte"* or *"s'il vous plaît,"* words that a child could learn easily, walk up to a stranger and say, "Say, where's the museum?" as if English and rudeness rule the world, never ceases to amaze. You hear the accent and sink under the table.

Woke up at six, dark. Switzerland. Alps. Raining. Lights of villages high in the sky. Too dark to see much so snoozed awhile. Woke up in sunny Italy. Field after field of corn, like Iowa in August. Mamas, papas, grammas, grampas, little babies. Skinny trees above the whitewashed houses.

Arrived in Venice. A pipe had burst at the hotel and we were sent to another not as good. Should you spend time arguing for a refund? Went to San Marco,[1] on which the doges overspent. A cash register in the sanctuary: five hundred lire to see the gold altar. Now we understand the Reformation.

On the train to Vienna, she, having composed the sentences carefully from old memory of intermediate German, asked the old couple if the train went to Vienna. *"Ja, ja!"* Did we need to change trains? *"Nein."* Later she successfully ordered dinner and registered at the hotel. *Mein wundercompanion.*

People take me for an American tourist and stare at me, maybe because I walk slow and stare at them, so today I walked like a bat out of hell along the Ringstrasse, past the Hofburg Palace to Stephans Platz and back, and if anyone stared, I didn't notice. Didn't see much of Vienna but felt much better.

One week in a steady drizzle of German and now I am starting to lose my grip on English, I think. Don't know what to write. How are you? Are the Twins going to be in the World Series?

You get to Mozart's apartment[2] through the back door of a restaurant. Kitchen smells, yelling, like at Burger King. The room where he wrote *Figaro* is bare, as if he moved out this morning. It's a nice apartment. His grave at the cemetery is now marked, its whereabouts being unknown. Mozart our brother.

Copenhagen is raining and all the Danes seem unperturbed. A calm humorous people. Kids are the same as anywhere, wild, and nobody hits them. Men wear pastels, especially turquoise. Narrow streets, no cars, little shops, and in the old square a fruit stand and an old woman with flowers yelling, "WŌSA FOR TEW-VA!"

1. The Basilica di San Marco of Venice, a magnificent hodgepodge of Byzantine domes, mosaics, and plundered treasure from the Near East and Asia, is one of the largest and most famous cathedrals in the world.
2. Mozart's "Figarohaus," where he lived from October 1784 to April 1787, is behind St. Stephen's Cathedral in Vienna.

15   Sunbathing yesterday. A fine woman took off her shirt, jeans, pants, nearby, and lay on her belly, then turned over. Often she sat up to apply oil. Today my back is burned bright red (as St. Paul warns) from my lying and looking at her so long but who could ignore such beauty and *so generous*.

QUESTION

1. In "How to Write a Letter," Keillor offers several suggestions. Make a list of the suggestions that seem most helpful. Why might Keillor have included the other, less practical suggestions?

2. Keillor addresses "How to Write a Letter" to shy people (a group in which he includes himself—"We shy persons . . ."). Does his advice also apply to those who are not shy? Why or why not?

3. Analyze the progression of "Postcards." How is the piece organized? Why do you think Keillor chose this organization?

4. Keillor wrote these pieces in the 1980s before people communicated by email. Does any of his advice fit email correspondence? Write a how-to piece entitled "How to Write an Email." Email it to the class.

5. Pick up several postcards from your college bookstore. Write fifty-word messages on each and send them to family and friends—or, if assigned—to your classmates and teacher.

LEWIS THOMAS   *Notes on Punctuation*

THERE ARE NO precise rules about punctuation (Fowler[1] lays out some general advice (as best he can under the complex circumstances of English prose (he points out, for example, that we possess only four stops (the comma, the semicolon, the colon and the period (the question mark and exclamation point are not, strictly speaking, stops; they are indicators of tone (oddly enough, the Greeks employed the semicolon for their question mark (it produces a strange sensation to read a Greek sentence which is a straightforward question: Why weepest thou; (instead of Why weepest thou? (and, of course, there are parentheses (which are surely a kind of punctuation making this whole much more complicated by having to count up the left-handed parentheses in order to be

From The Medusa and the Snail: More Notes of a Biology Watcher *(1979), a collection of science writing.*

1. H. W. Fowler, author of *Modern English Usage* (1926).

sure of closing with the right number (but if the parentheses were left out, with nothing to work with but the stops, we would have considerably more flexibility in the deploying of layers of meaning than if we tried to separate all the clauses by physical barriers (and in the latter case, while we might have more precision and exactitude for our meaning, we would lose the essential flavor of language, which is its wonderful ambiguity)))))))))))).

The commas are the most useful and usable of all the stops. It is highly important to put them in place as you go along. If you try to come back after doing a paragraph and stick them in the various spots that tempt you you will discover that they tend to swarm like minnows into all sorts of crevices whose existence you hadn't realized and before you know it the whole long sentence becomes immobilized and lashed up squirming in commas. Better to use them sparingly, and with affection, precisely when the need for each one arises, nicely, by itself.

I have grown fond of semicolons in recent years. The semicolon tells you that there is still some question about the preceding full sentence; something needs to be added; it reminds you sometimes of the Greek usage. It is almost always a greater pleasure to come across a semicolon than a period. The period tells you that that is that; if you didn't get all the meaning you wanted or expected, anyway you got all the writer intended to parcel out and now you have to move along. But with a semicolon there you get a pleasant little feeling of expectancy; there is more to come; read on; it will get clearer.

Colons are a lot less attractive, for several reasons: firstly, they give you the feeling of being rather ordered around, or at least having your nose pointed in a direction you might not be inclined to take if left to yourself, and, secondly, you suspect you're in for one of those sentences that will be labeling the points to be made: firstly, secondly and so forth, with the implication that you haven't sense enough to keep track of a sequence of notions without having them numbered. Also, many writers use this system loosely and incompletely, starting out with number one and number two as though counting off on their fingers but then going on and on without the succession of labels you've been led to expect, leaving you floundering about searching for the ninthly or seventeenthly that ought to be there but isn't.

Exclamation points are the most irritating of all. Look! they say, look at what I just said! How amazing is my thought! It is like being forced to watch someone else's small child jumping up and down crazily in the center of the living room shouting to attract attention. If a sentence really has something of importance to say, something quite remarkable, it doesn't need a mark to point it out. And if it is really, after all, a banal sentence needing more zing, the exclamation point simply emphasizes its banality!

Quotation marks should be used honestly and sparingly, when there is a genuine quotation at hand, and it is necessary to be very rigorous about the words enclosed by the marks. If something is to be quoted, the *exact* words must be used. If part of it must be left out because of space limitations, it is good manners to insert three dots to indicate the omission, but it is unethical to do this if it means connecting two thoughts which the original author did

5

not intend to have tied together. Above all, quotation marks should not be used for ideas that you'd like to disown, things in the air so to speak. Nor should they be put in place around clichés; if you want to use a cliché you must take full responsibility for it yourself and not try to job it off on anon., or on society. The most objectionable misuse of quotation marks, but one which illustrates the dangers of misuse in ordinary prose, is seen in advertising, especially in advertisements for small restaurants, for example "just around the corner," or "a good place to eat." No single, identifiable, citable person ever really said, for the record, "just around the corner," much less "a good place to eat," least likely of all for restaurants of the type that use this type of prose.

The dash is a handy device, informal and essentially playful, telling you that you're about to take off on a different tack but still in some way connected with the present course—only you have to remember that the dash is there, and either put a second dash at the end of the notion to let the reader know that he's back on course, or else end the sentence, as here, with a period.

The greatest danger in punctuation is for poetry. Here it is necessary to be as economical and parsimonious with commas and periods as with the words themselves, and any marks that seem to carry their own subtle meanings, like dashes and little rows of periods, even semicolons and question marks, should be left out altogether rather than inserted to clog up the thing with ambiguity. A single exclamation point in a poem, no matter what else the poem has to say, is enough to destroy the whole work.

The things I like best in T. S. Eliot's poetry, especially in the *Four Quartets,* are the semicolons. You cannot hear them, but they are there, laying out the connections between the images and the ideas. Sometimes you get a glimpse of a semicolon coming, a few lines farther on, and it is like climbing a steep path through woods and seeing a wooden bench just at a bend in the road ahead, a place where you can expect to sit for a moment, catching your breath.

10   Commas can't do this sort of thing; they can only tell you how the different parts of a complicated thought are to be fitted together, but you can't sit, not even take a breath, just because of a comma,

QUESTIONS

1. The title of this piece begins with the word "notes." Is that the right word? Is this a series of notes or something else?

2. How long did it take you to realize that Thomas is playing a kind of game with his readers? (For instance, paragraph 1 is a single sentence.) Is punctuation the kind of thing people usually play games with?

3. Choose one or two writers from the next section, "An Album of Styles," and describe how they employ commas, colons, and semicolons. Do any of the semicolons serve as "a wooden bench just at a bend in the road ahead" (paragraph 9)?

4. Compare Thomas's technique of illustrating his points as he explains them with Garrison Keillor's similar technique in "Postcards" (p. 306). What other forms of writing might be treated this way? Find other examples that, like Thomas's "Notes" or Keillor's "Postcards," merge form and content.

PATRICIA WILLIAMS *The Death of the Profane:*
The Rhetoric of Race and Rights

BUZZERS ARE BIG IN NEW YORK CITY. Favored particularly by smaller stores and boutiques, merchants throughout the city have installed them as screening devices to reduce the incidence of robbery: if the face at the door looks desirable, the buzzer is pressed and the door is unlocked. If the face is that of an undesirable, the door stays locked. Predictably, the issue of undesirability has revealed itself to be a racial determination. While controversial enough at first, even civil-rights organizations backed down eventually in the face of arguments that the buzzer system is a "necessary evil," that it is a "mere inconvenience" in comparison to the risks of being murdered, that suffering discrimination is not as bad as being assaulted, and that in any event it is not all blacks who are barred, just "17-year-old black males wearing running shoes and hooded sweatshirts."[1]

The installation of these buzzers happened swiftly in New York; stores that had always had their doors wide open suddenly became exclusive or received people by appointment only. I discovered them and their meaning one Saturday in 1986. I was shopping in Soho and saw in a store window a sweater that I wanted to buy for my mother. I pressed my round brown face to the window and my finger to the buzzer, seeking admittance. A narrow-eyed, white teenager wearing running shoes and feasting on bubble gum glared out, evaluating me for signs that would pit me against the limits of his social understanding. After about five seconds, he mouthed "We're closed," and blew pink rubber at me. It was two Saturdays before Christmas, at one o'clock in the afternoon; there were several white people in the store who appeared to be shopping for things for *their* mothers.

I was enraged. At that moment I literally wanted to break all the windows of the store and *take* lots of sweaters for my mother. In the flicker of his judg-

A chapter in Williams's book The Alchemy of Race and Rights *(1991), which probes the roots of racism through anecdote and personal witness, as well as scholarly analysis of the law's inadequacies. All notes in the essay are the author's.*

1. "When 'By Appointment' Means Keep Out," *New York Times*, December 17, 1986, p. B1. Letter to the Editor from Michael Levin and Marguerita Levin, *New York Times*, January 11, 1987, p. E32.

mental gray eyes, that saleschild had transformed my brightly sentimental, joy-to-the-world, pre-Christmas spree to a shambles. He snuffed my sense of humanitarian catholicity, and there was nothing I could do to snuff his, without making a spectacle of myself.

I am still struck by the structure of power that drove me into such a blizzard of rage. There was almost nothing I could do, short of physically intruding upon him, that would humiliate him the way he humiliated me. No words, no gestures, no prejudices of my own would make a bit of difference to him; his refusal to let me into the store—it was Benetton's, whose colorfully punnish ad campaign is premised on wrapping every one of the world's peoples in its cottons and woolens—was an outward manifestation of his never having let someone like me into the realm of his reality. He had no compassion, no remorse, no reference to me; and no desire to acknowledge me even at the estranged level of arm's-length transactor. He saw me only as one who would take his money and therefore could not conceive that I was there to give him money.

5   In this weird ontological imbalance, I realized that buying something in that store was like bestowing a gift, the gift of my commerce, the lucre of my patronage. In the wake of my outrage, I wanted to take back the gift of appreciation that my peering in the window must have appeared to be. I wanted to take it back in the form of unappreciation, disrespect, defilement. I wanted to work so hard at wishing he could feel what I felt that he would never again mistake my hatred for some sort of plaintive wish to be included. I was quite willing to disenfranchise myself, in the heat of my need to revoke the flattery of my purchasing power. I was willing to boycott Benetton's, random white-owned businesses, and anyone who ever blew bubble gum in my face again.

My rage was admittedly diffuse, even self-destructive, but it was symmetrical. The perhaps loose-ended but utter propriety of that rage is no doubt lost not just to the young man who actually barred me, but to those who would appreciate my being barred only as an abstract precaution, who approve of those who would bar even as they deny that they would bar *me*.

The violence of my desire to burst into Benetton's is probably quite apparent. I often wonder if the violence, the exclusionary hatred, is equally apparent in the repeated public urgings that blacks understand the buzzer system by putting themselves in the shoes of white storeowners—that, in effect, blacks look into the mirror of frightened white faces for the reality of their undesirability; and that then blacks would "just as surely conclude that [they] would not let [themselves] in under similar circumstances."[2] (That some blacks might agree merely shows that some of us have learned too well the lessons of privatized intimacies of self-hatred and rationalized away the fullness of our public, participatory selves.)

On the same day I was barred from Benetton's, I went home and wrote the above impassioned account in my journal. On the day after that, I found I was still brooding, so I turned to a form of catharsis I have always found healing. I typed up as much of the story as I have just told, made a big poster of it,

2. *New York Times*, January 11, 1987, p. E32.

put a nice colorful border around it, and, after Benetton's was truly closed, stuck it to their big sweater-filled window. I exercised my first-amendment right to place my business with them right out in the street.

So that was the first telling of this story. The second telling came a few months later, for a symposium on Excluded Voices sponsored by a law review. I wrote an essay summing up my feelings about being excluded from Benetton's and analyzing "how the rhetoric of increased privatization, in response to racial issues, functions as the rationalizing agent of public unaccountability and, ultimately, irresponsibility." Weeks later, I received the first edit. From the first page to the last, my fury had been carefully cut out. My rushing, run-on-rage had been reduced to simple declarative sentences. The active personal had been inverted in favor of the passive impersonal. My words were different; they spoke to me upsidedown. I was afraid to read too much of it at a time— meanings rose up at me oddly, stolen and strange.

A week and a half later, I received the second edit. All reference to Benetton's had been deleted because, according to the editors and the faculty adviser, it was defamatory; they feared harassment and liability; they said printing it would be irresponsible. I called them and offered to supply a footnote attesting to this as my personal experience at one particular location and of a buzzer system not limited to Benetton's; the editors told me that they were not in the habit of publishing things that were unverifiable. I could not but wonder, in this refusal even to let me file an affadavit, what it would take to make my experience verifiable. The testimony of an independent white bystander? (a requirement in fact imposed in U.S. Supreme Court holdings through the first part of the century[3]).

Two days *after* the piece was sent to press, I received copies of the final page proofs. All reference to my race had been eliminated because it was against "editorial policy" to permit descriptions of physiognomy. "I realize," wrote one editor, "that this was a very personal experience, but any reader will know what you must have looked like when standing at that window." In a telephone conversation to them, I ranted wildly about the significance of such an omission. "It's irrelevant," another editor explained in a voice gummy with soothing and patience; "It's nice and poetic," but it doesn't "advance the discussion of any principle . . . This is a law review, after all." Frustrated, I accused him of censorship; calmly he assured me it was not. "This is just a matter of style," he said with firmness and finality.

Ultimately I did convince the editors that mention of my race was central to the whole sense of the subsequent text; that my story became one of extreme paranoia without the information that I am black; or that it became one in which the reader had to fill in the gap by assumption, presumption, prejudgment, or prejudice. What was most interesting to me in this experience was how the blind application of principles of neutrality, through the device of omission, acted either to make me look crazy or to make the reader participate in old habits of cultural bias.

3. See generally *Blyew v. U.S.*, 80 U.S. 581 (1871), upholding a state's right to forbid blacks to testify against whites.

That was the second telling of my story. The third telling came last April, when I was invited to participate in a law-school conference on Equality and Difference. I retold my sad tale of exclusion from Soho's most glitzy boutique, focusing in this version on the law-review editing process as a consequence of an ideology of style rooted in a social text of neutrality. I opined:

Law and legal writing aspire to formalized, color-blind, liberal ideals. Neutrality is the standard for assuring these ideals; yet the adherence to it is often determined by reference to an aesthetic of uniformity, in which difference is simply omitted. For example, when segregation was eradicated from the American lexicon, its omission led many to actually believe that racism therefore no longer existed. Race-neutrality in law has become the presumed antidote for race bias in real life. With the entrenchment of the notion of race-neutrality came attacks on the concept of affirmative action and the rise of reverse discrimination suits. Blacks, for so many generations deprived of jobs based on the color of our skin, are now told that we ought to find it demeaning to be hired, based on the color of our skin. Such is the silliness of simplistic either-or inversions as remedies to complex problems.

What is truly demeaning in this era of double-speak-no-evil is going on interviews and not getting hired because someone doesn't think we'll be comfortable. It is demeaning not to get promoted because we're judged "too weak," then putting in a lot of energy the next time and getting fired because we're "too strong." It is demeaning to be told what we find demeaning. It is very demeaning to stand on street corners unemployed and begging. It is downright demeaning to have to explain why we haven't been employed for months and then watch the job go to someone who is "more experienced." It is outrageously demeaning that none of this can be called racism, even if it happens only to, or to large numbers of, black people; as long as it's done with a smile, a handshake and a shrug; as long as the phantom-word "race" is never used.

The image of race as a phantom-word came to me after I moved into my late godmother's home. In an attempt to make it my own, I cleared the bedroom for painting. The following morning the room asserted itself, came rushing and raging at me through the emptiness, exactly as it had been for twenty-five years. One day filled with profuse and overwhelming complexity, the next day filled with persistently recurring memories. The shape of the past came to haunt me, the shape of the emptiness confronted me each time I was about to enter the room. The force of its spirit still drifts like an odor throughout the house.

The power of that room, I have thought since, is very like the power of racism as status quo: it is deep, angry, eradicated from view, but strong enough to make everyone who enters the room walk around the bed that isn't there, avoiding the phantom as they did the substance, for fear of bodily harm. They do not even know they are avoiding; they defer to the unseen shapes of things with subtle responsiveness, guided by an impulsive awareness of nothingness, and the deep knowledge and denial of witchcraft at work.

The phantom room is to me symbolic of the emptiness of formal equal opportunity, particularly as propounded by President Reagan, the Reagan Civil Rights Commission and the Reagan Supreme Court. Blindly formalized constructions of equal opportunity are the creation of a space that is filled in by a meandering stream of unguided hopes, dreams, fantasies, fears, recollections. They are the presence of the past in imaginary, imagistic form—the phantom-roomed exile of our longing.

It is thus that I strongly believe in the efficacy of programs and paradigms like affirmative action. Blacks are the objects of a constitutional omission which has been incorporated into a theory of neutrality. It is thus that omission is really a form of expression, as oxymoronic as that sounds: racial omission is a literal part of original intent; it is the fixed, reiterated prophecy of the Founding Fathers. It is thus that affirmative action is an affirmation; the affirmative act of hiring—or hearing—blacks is a recognition of individuality that re-places blacks as a social statistic, that is profoundly interconnective to the fate of blacks and whites either as sub-groups or as one group. In this sense, affirmative action is as mystical and beyond-the-self as an initiation ceremony. It is an act of verification and of vision. It is an act of social as well as professional responsibility.

The following morning I opened the local newspaper, to find that the event of my speech had commanded two columns on the front page of the Metro section. I quote only the opening lines: "Affirmative action promotes prejudice by denying the status of women and blacks, instead of affirming them as its name suggests. So said New York City attorney Patricia Williams to an audience Wednesday."[4]

I clipped out the article and put it in my journal. In the margin there is a note to myself: eventually, it says, I should try to pull all these threads together into yet another law-review article. The problem, of course, will be that in the hierarchy of law-review citation, the article in the newspaper will have more authoritative weight about me, as a so-called "primary resource," than I will have; it will take precedence over my own citation of the unverifiable testimony of my speech.

I have used the Benetton's story a lot, in speaking engagements at various schools. I tell it whenever I am too tired to whip up an original speech from scratch. Here are some of the questions I have been asked in the wake of its telling:

Am I not privileging a racial perspective, by considering only the black point of view? Don't I have an obligation to include the "salesman's side" of the story?

Am I not putting the salesman on trial and finding him guilty of racism without giving him a chance to respond to or cross-examine me?

Am I not using the store window as a "metaphorical fence" against the potential of his explanation in order to represent my side as "authentic"?

How can I be sure I'm right?

What makes my experience the real black one anyway?

Isn't it possible that another black person would disagree with my experience? If so, doesn't that render my story too unempirical and subjective to pay any attention to?

15

20

4. "Attorney Says Affirmative Action Denies Racism, Sexism," *Dominion Post* (Morgantown, West Virginia), April 8, 1988, p. B1.

Always a major objection is to my having put the poster on Benetton's window. As one law professor put it: "It's one thing to publish this in a law review, where no one can take it personally, but it's another thing altogether to put your own interpretation right out there, just like that, uncontested, I mean, with nothing to counter it."*

QUESTIONS

1. Williams's essay is about how the "objective," "neutral" forms writing often takes can drain away the significance of a particular person's story. Can you find examples of this phenomenon in other writing you read? Or can you find examples of it on TV or radio talk shows, for instance?

2. How does Williams move from the Benetton story to her larger point?

3. How would you characterize the tone of Williams's essay? Does any of her original rage remain?

4. What do you think of Williams's posting her reaction on the Benetton window? Write your opinion of the function and effectiveness of this action.

*At the end of her essay, Williams added these observations. "These questions put me on trial—an imaginary trial where it is I who have the burden of proof—and proof being nothing less than the testimony of the salesman actually confessing yes yes I am a racist. These questions question my own ability to know, to assess, to be objective. And of course, since anything that happens to me is inherently subjective, they take away my power to know what happens to me in the world. Others, by this standard, will always know better than I. And my insistence on recounting stories from my own perspective will be treated as presumption, slander, paranoid hallucination, or just plain lies.

"Recently I got an urgent call from Thomas Grey of Stanford Law School. He had used this piece in his jurisprudence class, and a rumor got started that the Benetton's story wasn't true, that I had made it up, that it was a fantasy, a lie that was probably the product of a diseased mind trying to make all white people feel guilty. At this point I realized it almost didn't make any difference whether I was telling the truth or not—that the greater issue I had to face was the overwhelming weight of a disbelief that goes beyond mere disinclination to believe and becomes active suppression of anything I might have to say. The greater problem is a powerfully oppressive mechanism for denial of black self-knowledge and expression. And this denial cannot be separated from the simultaneously pathological willingness to believe certain things about blacks—not to believe them, but things about them.

"When students in Grey's class believed and then claimed that I had made it all up, they put me in a position like that of Tawana Brawley [a black woman who falsely claimed she was abducted and raped by white men (eds.)]. I mean that specifically: the social consequence of concluding that we are liars operates as a kind of public absolution of racism—the conclusion is not merely that we are troubled or that I am eccentric, but that we, as liars, are the norm. Therefore, the nonbelievers can believe, things of this sort really don't happen (even in the face of statistics to the contrary). Racism or rape is all a big fantasy concocted by troublesome minorities and women. It is interesting to recall the outcry in every national medium, from the *New York Post* to the *Times* to the major networks, in the wake of the Brawley case: who will ever again believe a black woman who cries rape by a white man? Now shift the frame a bit, and imagine a

GEORGE ORWELL *Politics and the English Language*

OST PEOPLE who bother with the matter at all would admit that the English language is in a bad way, but it is generally assumed that we cannot by conscious action do anything about it. Our civilization is decadent and our language—so the argument runs—must inevitably share in the general collapse. It follows that any struggle against the abuse of language is a sentimental archaism, like preferring candles to electric light or hansom cabs to aeroplanes. Underneath this lies the half-conscious belief that language is a natural growth and not an instrument which we shape for our own purposes.

Now, it is clear that the decline of a language must ultimately have political and economic causes: it is not due simply to the bad influence of this or that individual writer. But an effect can become a cause, reinforcing the original cause and producing the same effect in an intensified form, and so on indefinitely. A man may take to drink because he feels himself to be a failure, and then fail all the more completely because he drinks. It is rather the same thing that is happening to the English language. It becomes ugly and inaccurate because our thoughts are foolish, but the slovenliness of our language makes it easier for us to have foolish thoughts. The point is that the process is reversible. Modern English, especially written English, is full of bad habits which spread by imitation and which can be avoided if one is willing to take the necessary trouble. If one gets rid of these habits one can think more clearly, and to think clearly is a necessary first step towards political regeneration: so that the fight against bad English is not frivolous and is not the exclusive concern of professional writers. I will come back to this presently, and I hope that by that time the meaning of what I have said here will have become clearer. Meanwhile, here are five specimens of the English language as it is now habitually written.

These five passages have not been picked out because they are especially bad—I could have quoted far worse if I had chosen—but because they illus-

From Shooting an Elephant, and Other Essays (1950), *a collection of Orwell's best-known essays. "Politics and the English Language" is the most famous modern argument for a clear, unadorned writing style—not only as a matter of good sense, but as a political virtue.*

white male facing a consensus that he lied. Would there be a difference? Consider Charles Stuart, for example, the white Bostonian who accused a black man of murdering his pregnant wife and whose brother later alleged that in fact the brothers had conspired to murder her. Most people and the media not only did not claim but actively resisted believing that Stuart represented any kind of "white male" norm. Instead he was written off as a troubled weirdo, a deviant—again even in the face of spousal-abuse statistics to the contrary. There was not a story I could find that carried on about "who will ever believe" the next white man who cries murder."

trate various of the mental vices from which we now suffer. They are a little below the average, but are fairly representative samples. I number them so that I can refer back to them when necessary:

"(1) I am not, indeed, sure whether it is not true to say that the Milton who once seemed not unlike a seventeenth-century Shelley had not become, out of an experience ever more bitter in each year, more alien [sic] to the founder of that Jesuit sect which nothing could induce him to tolerate."

PROFESSOR HAROLD LASKI (ESSAY IN *FREEDOM OF EXPRESSION*).

"(2) Above all, we cannot play ducks and drakes with a native battery of idioms which prescribes such egregious collocations of vocables as the Basic *put up with* for *tolerate* or *put at a loss* for *bewilder*."

PROFESSOR LANCELOT HOGBEN (*INTERGLOSSA*).

"(3) On the one side we have the free personality: by definition it is not neurotic, for it has neither conflict nor dream. Its desires, such as they are, are transparent, for they are just what institutional approval keeps in the forefront of consciousness; another institutional pattern would alter their number and intensity; there is little in them that is natural, irreducible, or culturally dangerous. But *on the other side,* the social bond itself is nothing but the mutual reflection of these self-secure integrities. Recall the definition of love. Is not this the very picture of a small academic? Where is there a place in this hall of mirrors for either personality or fraternity?"

ESSAY ON PSYCHOLOGY IN *POLITICS* (NEW YORK).

"(4) All the 'best people' from the gentlemen's clubs, and all the frantic fascist captains, united in common hatred of Socialism and bestial horror of the rising tide of the mass revolutionary movement, have turned to acts of provocation, to foul incendiarism, to medieval legends of poisoned wells, to legalize their own destruction of proletarian organizations, and rouse the agitated petty-bourgeoisie to chauvinistic fervour on behalf of the fight against the revolutionary way out of the crisis."

COMMUNIST PAMPHLET.

"(5) If a new spirit *is* to be infused into this old country, there is one thorny and contentious reform which must be tackled, and that is the humanization and galvanization of the B.B.C. Timidity here will bespeak cancer and atrophy of the soul. The heart of Britain may be sound and of strong beat, for instance, but the British lion's roar at present is like that of Bottom in Shakespeare's *Midsummer Night's Dream*—as gentle as any sucking dove. A virile new Britain cannot continue indefinitely to be traduced in the eyes or rather ears, of the world by the effete languors of Langham Place, brazenly masquerading as 'standard English'. When the Voice of Britain is heard at nine o'clock, better far and infinitely less ludicrous to hear aitches honestly dropped than the present priggish, inflated, inhibited, school-ma'amish arch braying of blameless bashful mewing maidens!"

LETTER IN *TRIBUNE*.

Each of these passages has faults of its own, but, quite apart from avoidable ugliness, two qualities are common to all of them. The first is staleness of imagery; the other is lack of precision. The writer either has a meaning and cannot express it, or he inadvertently says something else, or he is almost indifferent as to whether his words mean anything or not. This mixture of vagueness and sheer incompetence is the most marked characteristic of modern English prose, and especially of any kind of political writing. As soon as certain topics are raised, the concrete melts into the abstract and no one seems able to think of turns of speech that are not hackneyed: prose consists less and less of *words* chosen for the sake of their meaning, and more and more of *phrases* tacked together like the sections of a prefabricated henhouse. I list below, with notes and examples, various of the tricks by means of which the work of prose-construction is habitually dodged:

Dying Metaphors

A newly invented metaphor assists thought by evoking a visual image, while on the other hand a metaphor which is technically "dead" (e.g. *iron resolution*) has in effect reverted to being an ordinary word and can generally be used without loss of vividness. But in between these two classes there is a huge dump of worn-out metaphors which have lost all evocative power and are merely used because they save people the trouble of inventing phrases for themselves. Examples are: *Ring the changes on, take up the cudgels for, toe the line, ride roughshod over, stand shoulder to shoulder with, play into the hands of, no axe to grind, grist to the mill, fishing in troubled waters, on the order of the day, Achilles' heel, swan song, hotbed.* Many of these are used without knowledge of their meaning (what is a "rift," for instance?), and incompatible metaphors are frequently mixed, a sure sign that the writer is not interested in what he is saying. Some metaphors now current have been twisted out of their original meaning without those who use them even being aware of the fact. For example, *toe the line* is sometimes written *tow the line*. Another example is *the hammer and the anvil*, now always used with the implication that the anvil gets the worst of it. In real life it is always the anvil that breaks the hammer, never the other way about: a writer who stopped to think what he was saying would be aware of this, and would avoid perverting the original phrase.

5

Operators or Verbal False Limbs

These save the trouble of picking out appropriate verbs and nouns, and at the same time pad each sentence with extra syllables which give it an appearance of symmetry. Characteristic phrases are: *render inoperative, militate against, make contact with, be subjected to, give rise to, give grounds for, have the effect of, play a leading part (role) in, make itself felt, take effect, exhibit a tendency to, serve the purpose of, etc., etc.* The keynote is the elimination of simple verbs. Instead of being a single word, such as *break, stop, spoil, mend, kill*, a verb becomes a *phrase*, made up of a noun or adjective tacked on to some general-purposes verb such as *prove, serve, form, play, render*. In addition, the passive voice is wherever possible used in preference to the active, and noun constructions are used instead of gerunds (*by examination of* instead of *by examining*). The range of verbs is further cut down by means of the *-ize* and *de-* formation, and the banal statements are given an appearance of profundity by means of the *not un-* formation. Simple conjunctions and prepositions are replaced by such phrases as *with respect to, having regard to, the fact that, by dint of, in view of, in the interests of, on the hypothesis that;* and the ends of sentences are saved from anticlimax by such resounding commonplaces as *greatly to be desired, cannot be left out of account, a development to be expected in the near future, deserving of serious consideration, brought to a satisfactory conclusion,* and so on and so forth.

PRETENTIOUS DICTION

Words like *phenomenon, element, individual* (as noun), *objective, categorical, effective, virtual, basic, primary, promote, constitute, exhibit, exploit, utilize, eliminate, liquidate,* are used to dress up simple statements and give an air of scientific impartiality to biased judgments. Adjectives like *epoch-making, epic, historic, unforgettable, triumphant, age-old, inevitable, inexorable, veritable,* are used to dignify the sordid processes of international politics, while writing that aims at glorifying war usually takes on an archaic colour, its characteristic words being: *realm, throne, chariot, mailed fist, trident, sword, shield, buckler, banner, jackboot, clarion.* Foreign words and expressions such as *cul de sac, ancien régime, deus ex machina, mutatis mutandis, status quo, gleichschaltung, weltanschauung,* are used to give an air of culture and elegance. Except for the useful abbreviations *i.e., e.g.,* and *etc.,* there is no real need for any of the hundreds of foreign phrases now current in English. Bad writers, and especially scientific, political and sociological writers, are nearly aways haunted by the notion that Latin or Greek words are grander than Saxon ones, and unnecessary words like *expedite, ameliorate, predict, extraneous, deracinated, clandestine, subaqueous* and hundreds of others constantly gain ground from their Anglo-Saxon opposite numbers.[1] The jargon peculiar to Marxist writing (*hyena, hangman, cannibal, petty bourgeois, these gentry, lackey, flunkey, mad dog, White Guard,* etc.) consists largely of words and phrases translated from Russian, German or French; but the normal way of coining a new word is to use a Latin or Greek root with the appropriate affix and, where necessary, the *-ize* formation. It is often easier to make up words of this kind (*deregionalize, impermissible, extramarital, nonfragmentatory* and so forth) than to think up the English words that will cover one's meaning. The result, in general, is an increase in slovenliness and vagueness.

---

1. An interesting illustration of this is the way in which the English flower names which were in use till very recently are being ousted by Greek ones, *snapdragon* becoming *antirrhinum, forget-me-not* becoming *myosotis,* etc. It is hard to see any practical reason for this change of fashion: it is probably due to an instinctive turning-away from the more homely word and a vague feeling that the Greek word is scientific [Orwell's note].

Meaningless Words

In certain kinds of writing, particularly in art criticism and literary criticism, it is normal to come across long passages which are almost completely lacking in meaning.[2] Words like *romantic, plastic, values, human, dead, sentimental, natural, vitality,* as used in art criticism, are strictly meaningless in the sense that they not only do not point to any discoverable object, but are hardly ever expected to do so by the reader. When one critic writes, "The outstanding feature of Mr. X's work is its living quality," while another writes, "The immediately striking thing about Mr. X's work is its peculiar deadness," the reader accepts this as a simple difference of opinion. If words like *black* and *white* were involved, instead of the jargon words *dead* and *living,* he would see at once that language was being used in an improper way. Many political words are similarly abused. The word *Fascism* has now no meaning except in so far as it signifies "something not desirable." The words *democracy, socialism, freedom, patriotic, realistic, justice,* have each of them several different meanings which cannot be reconciled with one another. In the case of a word like *democracy,* not only is there no agreed definition, but the attempt to make one is resisted from all sides. It is almost universally felt that when we call a country democratic we are praising it: consequently the defenders of every kind of régime claim that it is a democracy, and fear that they might have to stop using the word if it were tied down to any one meaning. Words of this kind are often used in a consciously dishonest way. That is, the person who uses them has his own private definition, but allows his hearer to think he means something quite different. Statements like *Marshal Pétain was a true patriot, The Soviet Press is the freest in the world, The Catholic Church is opposed to persecution,* are almost always made with intent to deceive. Other words used in variable meanings, in most cases more or less dishonestly, are: *class, totalitarian, science, progressive, reactionary, bourgeois, equality.*

Now that I have made this catalogue of swindles and perversions, let me give another example of the kind of writing that they lead to. This time it must of its nature be an imaginary one. I am going to translate a passage of good English into modern English of the worst sort. Here is a well-known verse from *Ecclesiastes:*

> "I returned and saw under the sun, that the race is not to the swift, nor the battle to the strong, neither yet bread to the wise, nor yet riches to men of understanding, nor yet favour to men of skill; but time and chance happeneth to them all."

Here it is in modern English:

> "Objective consideration of contemporary phenomena compels the conclusion that success or failure in competitive activities exhibits no ten-

10

2. Example: "Comfort's catholicity of perception and image, strangely Whitmanesque in range, almost the exact opposite in aesthetic compulsion, continues to evoke that trembling atmospheric accumulative hinting at a cruel, an inexorably serene timelessness. . . . Wrey Gardiner scores by aiming at simple bull's-eyes with precision. Only they are not so simple, and through this contented sadness runs more than the surface bittersweet of resignation" (*Poetry Quarterly*) [Orwell's note].

dency to be commensurate with innate capacity, but that a considerable element of the unpredictable must invariably be taken into account."

This is a parody, but not a very gross one. Exhibit (3), above, for instance, contains several patches of the same kind of English. It will be seen that I have not made a full translation. The beginning and ending of the sentence follow the original meaning fairly closely, but in the middle the concrete illustrations—race, battle, bread—dissolve into the vague phrase "success or failure in competitive activities." This had to be so, because no modern writer of the kind I am discussing—no one capable of using phrases like "objective consideration of contemporary phenomena"—would ever tabulate his thoughts in that precise and detailed way. The whole tendency of modern prose is away from concreteness. Now analyse these two sentences a little more closely. The first contains forty-nine words but only sixty syllables, and all its words are those of everyday life. The second contains thirty-eight words of ninety syllables: eighteen of its words are from Latin roots, and one from Greek. The first sentence contains six vivid images, and only one phrase ("time and chance") that could be called vague. The second contains not a single fresh, arresting phrase, and in spite of its ninety syllables it gives only a shortened version of the meaning contained in the first. Yet without a doubt it is the second kind of sentence that is gaining ground in modern English. I do not want to exaggerate. This kind of writing is not yet universal, and outcrops of simplicity will occur here and there in the worst-written page. Still, if you or I were told to write a few lines on the uncertainty of human fortunes, we should probably come much nearer to my imaginary sentence than to the one from *Ecclesiastes*.

As I have tried to show, modern writing at its worst does not consist in picking out words for the sake of their meaning and inventing images in order to make the meaning clearer. It consists in gumming together long strips of words which have already been set in order by someone else, and making the results presentable by sheer humbug. The attraction of this way of writing is that it is easy. It is easier—even quicker, once you have the habit—to say *In my opinion it is a not unjustifiable assumption that* than to say *I think*. If you use ready-made phrases, you not only don't have to hunt about for words; you also don't have to bother with the rhythms of your sentences, since these phrases are generally so arranged as to be more or less euphonious. When you are composing in a hurry—when you are dictating to a stenographer, for instance, or making a public speech—it is natural to fall into a pretentious, Latinized style. Tags like *a consideration which we should do well to bear in mind* or *a conclusion to which all of us would readily assent* will save many a sentence from coming down with a bump. By using stale metaphors, similes and idioms, you save much mental effort, at the cost of leaving your meaning vague, not only for your reader but for yourself. This is the significance of mixed metaphors. The sole aim of a metaphor is to call up a visual image. When these images clash—as in *The Fascist octopus has sung its swan song, the jackboot is thrown into the melting pot*—it can be taken as certain that the writer is not seeing a mental image of the objects he is naming; in other words he is not really thinking. Look again at the examples I gave at the beginning of this essay. Professor Laski (1) uses five negatives in fifty-three words. One of these is superfluous, making nonsense of the whole passage, and in addition there is the slip *alien* for akin, making further nonsense, and several avoidable pieces of clumsiness which increase the general vagueness. Professor Hogben (2) plays ducks and drakes with a battery which is able to write prescriptions, and, while disapproving of the everyday phrase *put up with,* is unwilling to look *egregious* up in the dictionary and see what it means. (3), if one takes an uncharitable attitude towards it, is simply meaningless: probably one could work out its intended meaning by reading the whole of the article in which it occurs. In (4), the writer knows more or less what he wants to say, but an accumulation of stale phrases chokes him like tea leaves blocking a sink. In (5), words and meaning have almost parted company. People who write in this manner usually have a general emotional meaning—they dislike one thing and want to express solidarity with another—but they are not interested in the detail of what they are saying. A scrupulous writer, in every sentence that he writes, will ask himself at least four questions, thus: What am I trying to say? What words will express it? What image or idiom will make it clearer? Is this image fresh enough to have an effect? And he will probably ask himself two more: Could I put it more shortly? Have I said anything that is avoidably ugly? But you are not obliged to go to all this trouble. You can shirk it by simply throwing your mind open and letting the ready-made phrases come crowding in. They will construct your sentences for you—even think your thoughts for you, to a certain extent—and at need they will perform the important service of partially concealing your meaning even from yourself. It is at this point that the special connection between politics and the debasement of language becomes clear.

In our time it is broadly true that political writing is bad writing. Where it is not true, it will generally be found that the writer is some kind of rebel, expressing his private opinions and not a "party line." Orthodoxy, of whatever colour, seems to demand a lifeless, imitative style. The political dialects to be found in pamphlets, leading articles, manifestos, White Papers and the speeches of under-secretaries do, of course, vary from party to party, but they are all alike in that one almost never finds in them a fresh, vivid, homemade turn of speech. When one watches some tired hack on the platform mechanically repeating the familiar phrases—*bestial atrocities, iron heel, blood-stained tyranny, free peoples of the world, stand shoulder to shoulder*—one often has a curious feeling that one is not watching a live human being but some kind of dummy: a feeling which suddenly becomes stronger at moments when the light catches the speaker's spectacles and turns them into blank discs which seem to have no eyes behind them. And this is not altogether fanciful. A speaker who uses that kind of phraseology has gone some distance towards turning himself into a machine. The appropriate noises are coming out of his larynx, but his brain is not involved as it would be if he were choosing his words for himself. If the speech he is making is one that he is accustomed to make over and over again, he may be almost unconscious of what he is saying, as one is when one utters the responses in church. And this reduced state of consciousness, if not indispensable, is at any rate favourable to political conformity.

In our time, political speech and writing are largely the defence of the indefensible. Things like the continuance of British rule in India, the Russian purges and deportations, the dropping of the atom bombs on Japan, can indeed be defended, but only by arguments which are too brutal for most people to face, and which do not square with the professed aims of political parties. Thus political language has to consist largely of euphemism, question-begging and sheer cloudy vagueness. Defenceless villages are bombarded from the air, the inhabitants driven out into the countryside, the cattle machine-gunned, the huts set on fire with incendiary bullets: this is called *pacification*. Millions of peasants are robbed of their farms and sent trudging along the roads with no more than they can carry: this is called *transfer of population* or *rectification of frontiers*. People are imprisoned for years without trial, or shot in the back of the neck or sent to die of scurvy in Arctic lumber camps: this is called *elimination of unreliable elements*. Such phraseology is needed if one wants to name things without calling up mental pictures of them. Consider for instance some comfortable English professor defending Russian totalitarianism. He cannot say outright, "I believe in killing off your opponents when you can get good results by doing so." Probably, therefore, he will say something like this:

15   "While freely conceding that the Soviet régime exhibits certain features which the humanitarian may be inclined to deplore, we must, I think, agree that a certain curtailment of the right to political opposition is an unavoidable concomitant of transitional periods, and that the rigors which the Russian people have been called upon to undergo have been amply justified in the sphere of concrete achievement."

The inflated style is itself a kind of euphemism. A mass of Latin words falls upon the facts like soft snow, blurring the outlines and covering up all the details. The great enemy of clear language is insincerity. When there is a gap between one's real and one's declared aims, one turns as it were instinctively to long words and exhausted idioms, like a cuttlefish squirting out ink. In our age there is no such thing as "keeping out of politics." All issues are political issues, and politics itself is a mass of lies, evasions, folly, hatred and schizophrenia. When the general atmosphere is bad, language must suffer. I should expect to find—this is a guess which I have not sufficient knowledge to verify—that the German, Russian and Italian languages have all deteriorated in the last ten or fifteen years, as a result of dictatorship.

But if thought corrupts language, language can also corrupt thought. A bad usage can spread by tradition and imitation, even among people who should and do know better. The debased language that I have been discussing is in some ways very convenient. Phrases like *a not unjustifiable assumption, leaves much to be desired, would serve no good purpose, a consideration which we should do well to bear in mind,* are a continuous temptation, a packet of aspirins always at one's elbow. Look back through this essay, and for certain you will find that I have again and again committed the very faults I am protesting against. By this morning's post I have received a pamphlet dealing with conditions in Germany. The author tells me that he "felt impelled" to write it. I open it at random, and here is almost the first sentence that I see: "(The Allies) have an opportunity not only of achieving a radical transformation of Germany's social and political structure in such a way as to avoid a nationalistic reaction in Germany itself, but at the same time of laying the foundations of a co-operative and unified Europe." You see, he "feels impelled" to write—feels, presumably, that he has something new to say—and yet his words, like cavalry horses answering the bugle, group themselves automatically into the familiar dreary pattern. This invasion of one's mind by ready-made phrases (*lay the foundations, achieve a radical transformation*) can only be prevented if one is constantly on guard against them, and every such phrase anaesthetizes a portion of one's brain.

I said earlier that the decadence of our language is probably curable. Those who deny this would argue, if they produced an argument at all, that language merely reflects existing social conditions, and that we cannot influence its development by any direct tinkering with words and constructions. So far as the general tone or spirit of a language goes, this may be true, but it is not true in detail. Silly words and expressions have often disappeared, not through any evolutionary process but owing to the conscious action of a minority. Two recent examples were *explore every avenue* and *leave no stone unturned*, which were killed by the jeers of a few journalists. There is a long list of fly-blown metaphors which could similarly be got rid of if enough people would interest themselves in the job; and it should also be possible to laugh the *not un-* formation out of existence,[3] to reduce the amount of Latin and Greek in the average sentence, to drive out foreign phrases and strayed scientific words, and, in general, to make pretentiousness unfashionable. But all these are minor points. The defence of the English language implies more than this, and perhaps it is best to start by saying what it does *not* imply.

To begin with it has nothing to do with archaism, with the salvaging of obsolete words and turns of speech, or with the setting up of a "standard English" which must never be departed from. On the contrary, it is especially concerned with the scrapping of every word or idiom which has outworn its usefulness. It has nothing to do with correct grammar and syntax, which are of no importance so long as one makes one's meaning clear, or with the avoidance of Americanisms, or with having what is called a "good prose style." On the other hand it is not concerned with fake simplicity and the attempt to make written English colloquial. Nor does it even imply in every case preferring the Saxon word to the Latin one, though it does imply using the fewest and shortest words that will cover one's meaning. What is above all needed is to let the meaning choose the word, and not the other way about. In prose, the worst thing one can do with words is to surrender to them. When you think of

---

3. One can cure oneself of the *not un-* formation by memorizing this sentence: *A not unblack dog was chasing a not unsmall rabbit across a not ungreen field* [Orwell's note].

a concrete object, you think wordlessly, and then, if you want to describe the thing you have been visualizing you probably hunt about till you find the exact words that seem to fit. When you think of something abstract you are more inclined to use words from the start, and unless you make a conscious effort to prevent it, the existing dialect will come rushing in and do the job for you, at the expense of blurring or even changing your meaning. Probably it is better to put off using words as long as possible and get one's meaning as clear as one can through pictures or sensations. Afterwards one can choose—not simply *accept*—the phrases that will best cover the meaning, and then switch round and decide what impression one's words are likely to make on another person. This last effort of the mind cuts out all stale or mixed images, all prefabricated phrases, needless repetitions, and humbug and vagueness generally. But one can often be in doubt about the effect of a word or a phrase, and one needs rules that one can rely on when instinct fails. I think the following rules will cover most cases:

(i)   Never use a metaphor, simile or other figure of speech which you are used to seeing in print.

(ii) Never use a long word where a short one will do.

(iii) If it is possible to cut a word out, always cut it out.

(iv) Never use the passive where you can use the active.

(v)   Never use a foreign phrase, a scientific word or a jargon word if you can think of an everyday English equivalent.

(vi) Break any of these rules sooner than say anything outright barbarous.

These rules sound elementary, and so they are, but they demand a deep change of attitude in anyone who has grown used to writing in the style now fashionable. One could keep all of them and still write bad English, but one could not write the kind of stuff that I quoted in those five specimens at the beginning of this article.

20   I have not here been considering the literary use of language, but merely language as an instrument for expressing and not for concealing or preventing thought. Stuart Chase[4] and others have come near to claiming that all abstract words are meaningless, and have used this as a pretext for advocating a kind of political quietism. Since you don't know what Fascism is, how can you struggle against Fascism? One need not swallow such absurdities as this, but one ought to recognize that the present political chaos is connected with the decay of language, and that one can probably bring about some improvement by starting at the verbal end. If you simplify your English, you are freed from the worst follies of orthodoxy. You cannot speak any of the necessary dialects, and

4. Chase (in *The Tyranny of Words* [1938] and *The Power of Words* [1954]) and S. I. Hayakawa (in *Language in Action* [1939]) popularized the semantic theories of Alfred Korzybski.

when you make a stupid remark its stupidity will be obvious, even to yourself. Political language—and with variations this is true of all political parties, from Conservatives to Anarchists—is designed to make lies sound truthful and murder respectable, and to give an appearance of solidity to pure wind. One cannot change this all in a moment, but one can at least change one's own habits, and from time to time one can even, if one jeers loudly enough, send some worn-out and useless phrase—some *jackboot, Achilles' heel, hotbed, melting pot, acid test, veritable inferno* or other lump of verbal refuse—into the dustbin where it belongs.

QUESTIONS

1. State Orwell's main point as precisely as possible.

2. What kinds of prose does Orwell analyze in this essay? Look, in particular, at the passages he quotes in paragraph 3. Where would you find their contemporary equivalents?

3. Apply Orwell's rule iv, "Never use the passive where you can use the active" (paragraph 19), to paragraph 14 of his essay. What happens when you change his passive constructions to active? Has Orwell forgotten rule iv or is he covered by rule vi, "Break any of these rules sooner than say anything outright barbarous"?

4. Orwell wrote this essay in 1946. Choose at least two examples of political discourse from current media and discuss, in an essay, whether Orwell's analysis of the language of politics is still valid. If it is, which features that he singles out for criticism appear most frequently in your examples?

An Album of Styles

What is style? The question eludes easy answers. "Le style est l'homme même," the Count de Buffon observed in 1753, in an address on his admission to the French Academy. His words, translated into English, have become proverbial: "The style is the man." (To avoid the false generic man, we might translate his statement as "The style is the person.")

Buffon's words suggest that we can gain insight into a person's character by considering the mode of self-presentation, whether in action or in words. A writer's style is a recognizable expression of self that permeates a text, the clear, distinct, and individual voice that readers "hear" when they read an essay. We can work toward an understanding of a writer's style by examining the elements that create it—words, metaphors, syntax, rhetorical techniques and maneuvers.

Although a writer's style reflects an individual personality and a personal set of preferences, it is also influenced by the historical context in which the writer lives. Different historical periods privileged different prose styles. For example, the "Metaphysical" writers of the early seventeenth century used elaborate metaphors, or "conceits." This stylistic preference appears in the selection from John Donne's meditation "No Man Is an Island," where Donne reflects on the interconnectedness of all humankind by positing that each of us is part of a continent or mainland, no one an "island, entire of itself." The "Augustan" writers of the eighteenth century preferred periodic sentences—sentences that used frequent parallel construction; introductory, dependent clauses before the main, independent clause; and balanced correlatives such as neither and nor, not only with but also, or both and and. Examples of the periodic style appear in the excerpts from Samuel Johnson and Mary Wollstonecraft—as in Johnson's final sentence, which balances the verbs "imagine" and "dream" in the opening dependent clause and the verbs "survey" and "confess" in the main clause: "Whoever thou art, that, not content with a moderate condition, imaginest happiness in royal magnificence, and dreamest that command or riches can feed the appetite of novelty with perpetual gratifications, survey the pyramids, and confess thy folly!" When Wollstonecraft uses the periodic sentence in A Vindication of the Rights of Woman (1792), she is not only expressing her feminist sentiments but also demonstrating her mastery of the dominant literary style of the day.

Modern American writers tend to appear—at least to our contemporary eyes—more simple, direct, and concise than their literary predecessors. No doubt Ernest Hemingway's crisp, precise style—dominated by strong nouns and verbs, virtually free of adjectives—has influenced recent generations of American writers. But before concluding that modern styles are less elaborate, more straightforword than older ones, we should study carefully the prose patterns of Terry

328

Tempest Williams, who sometimes uses short, simple observations ("I love sitting by the river") but also creates longer, more intricate sentences that mimic the movement of flowing water: "Around and around, a cottonwood leaf spins; a breeze gives it a nudge, and it glides downriver, this river braided with light."

Reading the prose and studying the style of authors, both old and new, can help aspiring writers develop their own styles. Ben Franklin tells us in his Auto-biography that, as a young man, he would read the essays of Joseph Addison and Richard Steele, then close his book and try to write out the essays in his (and their) best style. Ben Jonson advises us, in his book Timber, or Discoveries, *"For a man to write well, there are required three necessaries: to read the best authors, observe the best speakers, and much exercise of his own style." As usual, Samuel Johnson's reflection on writing speaks volumes: "What is written without effort is in general read without pleasure."*

FRANCIS BACON: *Of Youth and Age*

A man that is young in years may be old in hours, if he have lost no time. But that happeneth rarely. Generally, youth is like the first cogitations, not so wise as the second. For there is a youth in thoughts as well as in ages. And yet the invention of young men is more lively than that of old, and imaginations stream into their minds better, and as it were more divinely. Natures that have much heat, and great and violent desires and perturbations, are not ripe for action till they have passed the meridian of their years: as it was with Julius Caesar,[1] and Septimius Severus. Of the latter of whom it is said, *Juventutem egit erroribus, imo furoribus, plenam:*[2] and yet he was the ablest emperor, almost, of all the list. But reposed natures may do well in youth. As it is seen in Augustus Caesar, Cosmus, Duke of Florence, Gaston de Foix,[3] and others. On the other side, heat and vivacity in age is an excellent composition for business. Young men are fitter to invent than to judge, fitter for execution than for counsel, and fitter for new projects than for settled business. For the experience of age, in things that fall within the compass of it, directeth them, but in new things abuseth them. The errors of young men are the ruin of business; but the errors of aged men amount but to this, that more might have been done, or sooner. Young men, in the conduct and manage of actions, embrace more than they can hold; stir more than they can quiet; fly to the end, without consideration of the means and degrees; pursue some few principles which they have chanced upon

From Bacon's Essays, *the first edition of which appeared in 1597, with augmented and revised editions in 1612 and 1625. Bacon's essays are known for their objective, judicial style.*

1. Julius Caesar (100–44 B.C.E.) became dictator of Rome in 49 B.C.E.

2. Severus (145/6–211 C.E.) became emperor of Rome in 193 C.E. "He passed a youth full of folly, or rather of madness," according to Spartianus (*Life of Severus*).

3. Augustus Caesar (63 B.C.E.–14 C.E.) became ruler of Rome in 27 B.C.E.; Cosimo de' Medici (1519–1574) became ruler of Florence in 1537; Gaston de Foix, duke of Nemours and nephew of Louis XII of France, died in battle in 1512, at twenty-two.

absurdly; care not to innovate,[4] which draws unknown inconveniences; use extreme remedies at first; and, that which doubleth all errors, will not acknowledge or retract them; like an unready horse that will neither stop nor turn. Men of age object too much, consult too long, adventure too little, repent too soon, and seldom drive business home to the full period, but content themselves with a mediocrity of success. Certainly it is good to compound employments of both; for that will be good for the present, because the virtues of either age may correct the defects of both; and good for succession, that young men may be learners while men in age are actors; and, lastly, good for extern accidents, because authority followeth old men, and favour and popularity youth. But for the moral part, perhaps youth will have the pre-eminence, as age hath for the politic. A certain rabbin, upon the text, *Your young men shall see visions, and your old men shall dream dreams,*[5] inferreth that young men are admitted nearer to God than old, because vision is a clearer revelation than a dream. And certainly, the more a man drinketh of the world, the more it intoxicateth; and age doth profit rather in the powers of understanding than in the virtues of the will and affections. There be some have an over-early ripeness in their years, which fadeth betimes. These are, first, such as have brittle wits, the edge whereof is soon turned; such as was Hermogenes the rhetorician, whose books are exceeding subtle, who afterwards waxed stupid.[6] A second sort is of those that have some natural dispositions which have better grace in youth than in age, such as is a fluent and luxuriant speech, which becomes youth well, but not age: so Tully saith of Hortensius, *Idem manebat, neque idem docebat.*[7] The third is of such as take too high a strain at the first, and are magnanimous more than tract of years can uphold. As was Scipio Africanus, of whom Livy saith in effect, *Ultima primis cedebant.*[8]

4. Are not careful about innovating.

5. Joel 2.28. "Rabbin" means "rabbi."

6. Hermogenes, Greek rhetorician of the 2nd century C.E., is said to have lost his memory when young.

7. "He remained the same when the same style no longer became him" (Cicero, *Brutus*); said by Cicero (or Tully) of a rival orator.

8. "His last actions were not the equal of his first" (*Heroides* 9); Bacon quotes from the poet Ovid (43 B.C.E.–17 C.E.) to express the gist of what the historian Livy (59 B.C.E.–17 C.E.) said of Africanus (236–183 or 184 B.C.E.), Roman conqueror of Africa.

John Donne: *No Man Is an Island*

No man is an island, entire of itself; every man is a piece of the continent, a part of the main.[1] If a clod be washed away by the sea, Europe is the less, as well as if a promontory were, as well as if a manor of thy friend's or of thine own were. Any man's death diminishes me, because I am involved in mankind; and therefore never send to know for whom the bell tolls; it tolls for thee.[2]

Originally given as a sermon; later published as Meditation 17 *of Donne's* Devotions upon Emergent Occasions *(1623).*

1. Mainland.
2. Church bells were rung to mark the death of parishoners.

Samuel Johnson: *The Pyramids*

Of the wall [of China] it is very easy to assign the motives. It secured a wealthy and timorous nation from the incursions of Barbarians, whose unskillfulness in arts made it easier for them to supply their wants by rapine than by industry, and who from time to time poured in upon the habitations of peaceful commerce, as vultures descend upon domestic fowl. Their celerity and fierceness made the wall necessary, and their ignorance made it efficacious.

But for the pyramids no reason has ever been given adequate to the cost and labor of the work. The narrowness of the chambers proves that it could afford no retreat from enemies, and treasures might have been reposited at far less expense with equal security. It seems to have been erected only in compliance with that hunger of imagination which preys incessantly upon life, and must be always appeased by some employment. Those who have already all that they can enjoy, must enlarge their desires. He that has built for use, till use is supplied, must begin to build for vanity, and extend his plan to the utmost power of human performance, that he may not be soon reduced to form another wish.

I consider this mighty structure as a monument of the insufficiency of human enjoyments. A king, whose power is unlimited, and whose treasures surmount all real and imaginary wants, is compelled to solace, by the erection of a pyramid, the satiety of dominion and tastelessness of pleasures, and to amuse the tediousness of declining life, by seeing thousands laboring without end, and one stone, for no purpose, laid upon another. Whoever thou art, that, not content with a moderate condition, imaginest happiness in royal

From Rasselas *(1759), a didactic tale about an emperor's son who grows weary of life in the "happy valley" where he was born and who sets out to study the conditions of other men's lives.*

magnificence, and dreamest that command or riches can feed the appetite of novelty with perpetual gratifications, survey the pyramids, and confess thy folly!

MARY WOLLSTONECRAFT: from *A Vindication of the Rights of Woman*

The education of women has, of late, been more attended to than formerly; yet they are still reckoned a frivolous sex, and ridiculed or pitied by the writers who endeavour by satire or instruction to improve them. It is acknowledged that they spend many of the first years of their lives in acquiring a smattering of accomplishments; meanwhile strength of body and mind are sacrificed to libertine notions of beauty, to the desire of establishing themselves,—the only way women can rise in the world,—by marriage. And this desire making mere animals of them, when they marry they act as such children may be expected to act:—they dress; they paint, and nickname God's creatures.[1]—Surely these weak beings are only fit for a seraglio!—Can they be expected to govern a family with judgment, or take care of the poor babes whom they bring into the world?

If then it can be fairly deduced from the present conduct of the sex, from the prevalent fondness for pleasure which takes place of ambition and those nobler passions that open and enlarge the soul; that the instruction which women have hitherto received has only tended, with the constitution of civil society, to render them insignificant objects of desire—mere propagators of fools!—if it can be proved that in aiming to accomplish them, without cultivating their understandings, they are taken out of their sphere of duties, and made ridiculous and useless when the short-lived bloom of beauty is over,[2] I presume that *rational* men will excuse me for endeavouring to persuade them to become more masculine and respectable.

Indeed the word masculine is only a bugbear: there is little reason to fear that women will acquire too much courage or fortitude; for their apparent inferiority with respect to bodily strength, must render them, in some degree, dependent on men in the various relations of life, but why should it be increased by prejudices that give a sex to virtue, and confound simple truths with sensual reveries?

Women are, in fact, so much degraded by mistaken notions of female ex-

---

From A Vindication of the Rights of Woman *(1792), written after the publication of* Thomas Paine's A Vindication of the Rights of Man *(1790) as an argument for the extension of political, legal, and educational rights to women.*

1. In Shakespeare's *Hamlet* (III.i.143–45), the hero accuses Ophelia: "You jig, you amble, and you lisp, and nickname God's creatures, and make your wantonness your ignorance"—a sequence of feminine faults that Wollstonecraft echoes.

2. "A lively writer, I cannot recollect his name, asks what business women turned of forty have to do in the world?" [Wollstonecraft's note].

cellence, that I do not mean to add a paradox when I assert, that this artificial weakness produces a propensity to tyrannize, and gives birth to cunning, the natural opponent of strength, which leads them to play off those contemptible infantine airs that undermine esteem even whilst they excite desire. Let men become more chaste and modest, and if women do not grow wiser in the same ratio, it will be clear that they have weaker understandings. It seems scarcely necessary to say, that I now speak of the sex in general. Many individuals have more sense than their male relatives; and, as nothing preponderates where there is a constant struggle or an equilibrium, without it has[3] naturally more gravity, some women govern their husbands without degrading themselves, because intellect will always govern.

3. Unless it has.

JOHN HENRY NEWMAN: *Knowledge and Virtue*

Knowledge is one thing, virtue is another; good sense is not conscience, refinement is not humility, nor is largeness and justness of view faith. Philosophy, however enlightened, however profound, gives no command over the passions, no influential motives, no vivifying principles. Liberal Education makes not the Christian, not the Catholic, but the gentleman. It is well to be a gentleman, it is well to have a cultivated intellect, a delicate taste, a candid, equitable, dispassionate mind, a noble and courteous bearing in the conduct of life—these are the connatural qualities of a large knowledge; they are the objects of a University; I am advocating, I shall illustrate and insist upon them; but still, I repeat, they are no guarantee for sanctity or even for conscientiousness, they may attach to the man of the world, to the profligate, to the heartless, pleasant, alas, and attractive as he shows when decked out in them. Taken by themselves, they do but seem to be what they are not; they look like virtue at a distance, but they are detected by close observers, and on the long run; and hence it is that they are popularly accused of pretense and hypocrisy, not, I repeat, from their own fault, but because their professors and their admirers persist in taking them for what they are not, and are officious in arrogating for them a praise to which they have no claim. Quarry the granite rock with razors, or moor the vessel with a thread of silk; then may you hope with such keen and delicate instruments as human knowledge and human reason to contend against those giants, the passion and the pride of man.

From The Idea of a University Defined and Illustrated (1852), *Newman's classic statement on the role and value of education. The book emerged from Newman's work as rector of a new Catholic University in Dublin and his various lectures and articles on university education.*

Abraham Lincoln: *The Gettysburg Address*

Four score and seven years ago our fathers brought forth on this continent, a new nation, conceived in Liberty, and dedicated to the proposition that all men are created equal.

Now we are engaged in a great civil war, testing whether that nation, or any nation so conceived and so dedicated, can long endure. We are met on a great battlefield of that war. We have come to dedicate a portion of that field, as a final resting place for those who here gave their lives that that nation might live. It is altogether fitting and proper that we should do this.

But, in a larger sense, we can not dedicate—we can not consecrate—we can not hallow—this ground. The brave men, living and dead, who struggled here, have consecrated it, far above our poor power to add or detract. The world will little note, nor long remember what we say here, but it can never forget what they did here. It is for us the living, rather, to be dedicated here to the unfinished work which they who fought here have thus far so nobly advanced. It is rather for us to be here dedicated to the great task remaining before us—that from these honored dead we take increased devotion to that cause for which they gave the last full measure of devotion—that we here highly resolve that these dead shall not have died in vain—that this nation, under God, shall have a new birth of freedom—and that government of the people, by the people, for the people, shall not perish from the earth.

A presidential address delivered on November 19, 1863, during the height of the American Civil War, on the battlefield at Gettysburg, Pennsylvania.

Ernest Hemingway: from *A Farewell to Arms*

I was always embarrassed by the words sacred, glorious, and sacrifice and the expression in vain. We had heard them, sometimes standing in the rain almost out of earshot, so that only the shouted words came through, and had read them, on proclamations that were slapped up by billposters over other proclamations, now for a long time, and I had seen nothing sacred, and the things that were glorious had no glory and the sacrifices were like the stockyards at Chicago if nothing was done with the meat except to bury it. There were many words that you could not stand to hear and finally only the names of places had dignity. Certain numbers were the same way and certain dates and these with the names of places were all you could say and have them mean anything. Abstract words such as glory, honor, courage, or hallow were obscene beside the concrete names of villages, the numbers of roads, the names of rivers, the numbers of regiments and the dates.

From A Farewell to Arms (1929), a novel depicting the tragedy and destructiveness, personal and cultural, of World War I.

WILLIAM FAULKNER: *Nobel Prize Award Speech*

I feel that this award was not made to me as a man but to my work—a life's work in the agony and sweat of the human spirit, not for glory and least of all for profit, but to create out of the materials of the human spirit something which did not exist before. So this award is only mine in trust. It will not be difficult to find a dedication for the money part of it commensurate with the purpose and significance of its origin. But I would like to do the same with the acclaim too, by using this moment as a pinnacle from which I might be listened to by the young men and women already dedicated to the same anguish and travail, among whom is already that one who will some day stand here where I am standing.

Our tragedy today is a general and universal physical fear so long sustained by now that we can even bear it. There are no longer problems of the spirit. There is only the question: When will I be blown up? Because of this, the young man or woman writing today has forgotten the problems of the human heart in conflict with itself which alone can make good writing because only that is worth writing about, worth the agony and the sweat.

He must learn them again. He must teach himself that the basest of all things is to be afraid; and, teaching himself that, forget it forever, leaving no room in his workshop for anything but the old verities and truths of the heart, the old universal truths lacking which any story is ephemeral and doomed— love and honor and pity and pride and compassion and sacrifice. Until he does so, he labors under a curse. He writes not of love but of lust, of defeats in which nobody loses anything of value, of victories without hope and, worst of all, without pity or compassion. His griefs grieve on no universal bones leaving no scars. He writes not of the heart but of the glands.

Until he relearns these things, he will write as though he stood alone and watched the end of man. I decline to accept the end of man. It is easy enough to say that man is immortal simply because he will endure; that when the last ding-dong of doom has clanged and faded from the last worthless rock hanging tideless in the last red and dying evening, that even then there will still be one more sound: that of his puny inexhaustible voice, still talking. I refuse to accept this. I believe that man will not merely endure; he will prevail. He is immortal, not because he alone among creatures has an inexhaustible voice but because he has a soul, a spirit capable of compassion and sacrifice and endurance. The poet's, the writer's, duty is to write about these things. It is his privilege to help man endure by lifting his heart, by reminding him of the courage and honor and hope and pride and compassion and pity and sacrifice which have been the glory of his past. The poet's voice need not merely be the record of man, it can be one of the props, the pillars to help him endure and prevail.

On acceptance of the Nobel Prize in Literature for 1949, Faulkner gave this speech at a banquet in City Hall, Stockholm, Sweden, on December 10, 1850 (the anniversary of the death of Alfred Nobel, founder of the prize). The Nobel Prizes are presented by the king of Sweden, then King Gustaf VI Adolf (1882–1973).

JOHN UPDIKE: *Beer Can*

This seems to be an era of gratuitous inventions and negative improvements. Consider the beer can. It was beautiful—as beautiful as the
clothespin, as inevitable as the wine bottle, as dignified and reassuring as the
fire hydrant. A tranquil cylinder of delightfully resonant metal, it could be
opened in an instant, requiring only the application of a handy gadget freely
dispensed by every grocer. Who can forget the small, symmetrical thrill of
those two triangular punctures, the dainty *pffff*, the little crest of suds that
foamed eagerly in the exultation of release? Now we are given, instead, a top
beetling with an ugly, shmoo-shaped "tab,"[1] which, after fiercely resisting the
tugging, bleeding fingers of the thirsty man, threatens his lips with a dangerous and hideous hole. However, we have discovered a way to thwart Progress,
usually so unthwartable. *Turn the beer can upside down and open the bottom.*
The bottom is still the way the top used to be. True, this operation gives the
beer an unsettling jolt, and the sight of a consistently inverted beer can might
make people edgy, not to say queasy. But the latter difficulty could be eliminated if manufacturers would design cans that looked the same whichever end
was up, like playing cards. What we need is Progress with an escape hatch.

Originally published in the New Yorker *(January 18, 1964), an American magazine of literature, politics, the arts, and culture.*

1. The first tabs, made of plastic, reminded Updike of shmoos, bloblike creatures invented by Al Capp in the comic strip *Li'l Abner.*

TERRY TEMPEST WILLIAMS: *River Music*

River. The river is brown is red is green is turquoise. On any given day, the
river is light, liquid light, a traveling mirror in the desert.

> Love this river, stay by it, learn from it. . . . It seemed to him that whoever
> understood this river and its secrets, would understand much more, many
> secrets, all secrets.   —SIDDHARTHA

I love sitting by the river. A deep calm washes over me in the face of this
fluid continuity where it always appears the same, yet I know each moment of
the Rio Colorado is new.

"*Have you learned that secret from the river; that there is no such thing as
time?*"

May 28, 2000—a relatively uneventful day. A few herons fly by, a few mer-
gansers. Two rafts float through the redrock corridor. I wave. They wave back.
One man is playing a harmonica, the oars resting on his lap as he coasts
through flat water.

5   Sweet echoes continue to reach me.

From the author's 2001 book Red: Passion and Patience in the Desert.

I sit on the fine pink sand, still damp from high water days, and watch the river flow, the clouds shift, and the colors of the cliffs deepen from orange to red to maroon.

Present. Completely present. My eyes focus on one current in particular, a small eddy that keeps circling back on itself. Around and around, a cottonwood leaf spins; a breeze gives it a nudge, and it glides downriver, this river braided with light.

The eddy continues to coil the currents.

Boredom could catch up with me. But it never does, only the music, river music, the continual improvisation of water. Perhaps the difference between repetition and boredom lies in our willingness to believe in surprise, the subtle shifts of form that loom large in a trained and patient eye.

I think about a night of lovemaking with the man I live with, how it is that a body so known and familiar can still take my breath all the way down, then rise and fall, the river that flows through me, through him, this river, the Colorado River keeps moving, beckoning us to do the same, nothing stagnant, not today, not ever, as my mind moves as the river moves. 10

"To find one's own equilibrium" he tells me this morning by the river. "That is what I want to learn."

He finds rocks that stand on their own and bear the weight of others. An exercise in balance and form. Down river, I watch him place a thin slab of sandstone on a rock pedestal, perfectly poised. He continues placing pebbles on top, testing the balance. In another sculpture, he leans two flat rocks against each other like hands about to pray.

The stillness of stones, their silence, is a rest note against the music of the river.

Our shadows on the moving water are no different than those cast by the boulders on the bank. Composition. What is the composition of the river, these boulders, these birds, our own flesh? What is the composition of a poem except a series of musical lines?

River. River music. Day and night. Shadow and light. The roar and roll of 15 cobbles being churned by the current is strong. This river has muscle when flexed against stone carved stone, stones that appear as waves of rock, secret knowledge known only through engagement. I am no longer content to sit, but stand and walk, walk to the river, enter the river, surrender my body to water now red, red is the Colorado, blood of my veins.

QUESTIONS ON AN ALBUM OF STYLES

1. For any selection: What kinds of words does the writer use? From what sources (Anglo-Saxon, Latin, Greek, French, and so on)? (Most good collegiate dictionaries list word origins.) What effects are created by the writer's choice of words?

2. For any selection: What types of sentences does the writer prefer? Long or short? Loose or carefully balanced? What effects does the writer achieve with sentence form and length?

3. For any selection: What metaphors or similes does the writer use? Are they funda-mental to the argument or primarily ornamental?

4. For any selection: What is the writer's characteristic voice or tone? What kind of per-son do you imagine this writer to be?

5. Which selection do you like best? Why? Identify and analyze those aspects of style that create this positive impression.

NATURE AND THE ENVIRONMENT

RACHEL CARSON   *Tides*

> In every country the moon keeps ever the rule of
> alliance with the sea which it once for all has agreed
> upon.   —THE VENERABLE BEDE[1]

THERE IS NO drop of water in the ocean, not even in the deepest parts of the abyss, that does not know and respond to the mysterious forces that create the tide. No other force that affects the sea is so strong. Compared with the tide the wind-created waves are surface movements felt, at most, no more than a hundred fathoms below the surface. So, despite their impressive sweep, are the planetary currents, which seldom involve more than the upper several hundred fathoms. The masses of water affected by the tidal movement are enormous, as will be clear from one example. Into one small bay on the east coast of North America—Passamaquoddy—2 billion tons of water are carried by the tidal currents twice each day; into the whole Bay of Fundy, 100 billion tons.

Here and there we find dramatic illustration of the fact that the tides affect the whole ocean, from its surface to its floor. The meeting of opposing tidal currents in the Strait of Messina creates whirlpools (one of them is Charybdis of classical fame)[2] which so deeply stir the waters of the strait that fish bearing all the marks of abyssal existence, their eyes atrophied or abnormally large, their bodies studded with phosphorescent organs, frequently are cast up on the lighthouse beach, and the whole area yields a rich collection of deep-sea fauna for the Institute of Marine Biology at Messina.

The tides are a response of the mobile waters of the ocean to the pull of the moon and the more distant sun. In theory, there is a gravitational attraction between every drop of sea water and even the outermost star of the universe. In practice, however, the pull of the remote stars is so slight as to be

A chapter from Carson's best-selling book The Sea Around Us *(1951), which won the National Book Award and the John Burroughs Medal, the latter awarded annually to a distinguished book of natural history.*

1. British Benedictine monk and scholar (673–735), canonized in 1899.
2. The Strait of Messina lies between Sicily and the Italian mainland; thought to be the original of Scylla and Charybdis, i.e., the rocks and the whirlpool in Homer's *Odyssey.*

obliterated in the vaster movements by which the ocean yields to the moon and the sun. Anyone who has lived near tidewater knows that the moon, far more than the sun, controls the tides. He has noticed that, just as the moon rises later each day by fifty minutes, on the average, than the day before, so, in most places, the time of high tide is correspondingly later each day. And as the moon waxes and wanes in its monthly cycle, so the height of the tide varies. Twice each month, when the moon is a mere thread of silver in the sky, and again when it is full, we have the highest of the high tides, called the springs. At these times sun, moon, and earth are directly in line and the pull of the two heavenly bodies is added together to bring the water high on the beaches, and send its surf leaping upward against the sea cliffs, and draw a brimming tide into the harbors so that the boats float high beside their wharfs. And twice each month, at the quarters of the moon, when sun, moon, and earth lie at the apexes of a triangle, and the pull of sun and moon are opposed, we have the least tides of the lunar month, called the neaps.

That the sun, with a mass 27 million times that of the moon, should have less influence over the tides than a small satellite of the earth is at first surprising. But in the mechanics of the universe, nearness counts for more than distant mass, and when all the mathematical calculations have been made we find that the moon's power over the tides is more than twice that of the sun.

5   The tides are enormously more complicated than all this would suggest. The influence of sun and moon is constantly changing, varying with the phases of the moon, with the distance of moon and sun from the earth, and with the position of each to north or south of the equator. They are complicated further by the fact that every body of water, whether natural or artificial, has its own period of oscillation. Disturb its waters and they will move with a seesaw or rocking motion, with the most pronounced movement at the ends of the container, the least motion at the center. Tidal scientists now believe that the ocean contains a number of "basins," each with its own period of oscillation determined by its length and depth. The disturbance that sets the water in motion is the attracting force of the moon and sun. But the kind of motion, that is, the period of the swing of the water, depends upon the physical dimensions of the basin. What this means in terms of actual tides we shall presently see.

The tides present a striking paradox, and the essence of it is this: the force that sets them in motion is cosmic, lying wholly outside the earth and presumably acting impartially on all parts of the globe, but the nature of the tide at any particular place is a local matter, with astonishing differences occurring within a very short geographic distance. When we spend a long summer holiday at the seashore we may become aware that the tide in our cove behaves very differently from that at a friend's place twenty miles up the coast, and is strikingly different from what we may have known in some other locality. If we are summering on Nantucket Island our boating and swimming will be little disturbed by the tides, for the range between high water and low is only about a foot or two. But if we choose to vacation near the upper part of the Bay of Fundy, we must accommodate ourselves to a rise and fall of 40 to 50 feet, although both places are included within the same body of water—the Gulf of

Maine. Or if we spend our holiday on Chesapeake Bay we may find that the time of high water each day varies by as much as 12 hours in different places on the shores of the same bay.

The truth of the matter is that local topography is all-important in determining the features that to our minds make "the tide." The attractive force of the heavenly bodies sets the water in motion, but how, and how far, and how strongly it will rise depend on such things as the slope of the bottom, the depth of a channel, or the width of a bay's entrance.

If the history of the earth's tides should one day be written by some observer of the universe, it would no doubt be said that they reached their greatest grandeur and power in the younger days of Earth, and that they slowly grew feebler and less imposing until one day they ceased to be. For the tides were not always as they are today, and as with all that is earthly, their days are numbered.

In the days when the earth was young, the coming in of the tide must have been a stupendous event. If the moon was * * * formed by the tearing away of a part of the outer crust of the earth, it must have remained for a time very close to its parent. Its present position is the consequence of being pushed farther and farther away from the earth for some 2 billion years. When it was half its present distance from the earth, its power over the ocean tides was eight times as great as now, and the tidal range may even then have been several hundred feet on certain shores. But when the earth was only a few million years old, assuming that the deep ocean basins were then formed, the sweep of the tides must have been beyond all comprehension. Twice each day, the fury of the incoming waters would inundate all the margins of the continents. The range of the surf must have been enormously extended by the reach of the tides, so that the waves would batter the crests of high cliffs and sweep inland to erode the continents. The fury of such tides would contribute not a little to the general bleakness and grimness and uninhabitability of the young earth.

Under such conditions, no living thing could exist on the shores or pass   10
beyond them, and, had conditions not changed, it is reasonable to suppose that life would have evolved no further than the fishes. But over the millions of years the moon has receded, driven away by the friction of the tides it creates. The very movement of the water over the bed of the ocean, over the shallow edges of the continents, and over the inland seas carries within itself the power that is slowly destroying the tides, for tidal friction is gradually slowing down the rotation of the earth. In those early days we have spoken of, it took the earth a much shorter time—perhaps only about 4 hours—to make a complete rotation on its axis. Since then, the spinning of the globe has been so greatly slowed that a rotation now requires, as everyone knows, about 24 hours. This retarding will continue, according to mathematicians, until the day is about 50 times as long as it is now.

And all the while the tidal friction will be exerting a second effect, pushing the moon farther away, just as it has already pushed it out more than 200,000 miles. As the moon recedes, it will, of course, have less power over the tides and they will grow weaker. It will also take the moon longer to complete its orbit around the earth. When finally the length of the day and of the month coincide, the moon will no longer rotate relatively to the earth, and there will be no lunar tides.

All this, of course, will require time on a scale the mind finds it difficult to conceive, and before it happens it is quite probable that the human race will have vanished from the earth. This may seem, then, like a Wellsian fantasy[3] of a world so remote that we may dismiss it from our thoughts. But already, even in our allotted fraction of earthly time, we can see some of the effects of these cosmic processes. Our day is believed to be several seconds longer than that of Babylonian times. Britain's Astronomer Royal recently called the attention of the American Philosophical Society to the fact that the world will soon have to choose between two kinds of time. The tide-induced lengthening of the day has already complicated the problems of human systems of keeping time. Conventional clocks, geared to the earth's rotation, do not show the effect of the lengthening days. New atomic clocks now being constructed will show actual time and will differ from other clocks.

Although the tides have become tamer, and their range is now measured in tens instead of hundreds of feet, mariners are nevertheless greatly concerned not only with the stages of the tide and the set of the tidal currents, but with the many violent movements and disturbances of the sea that are indirectly related to the tides. Nothing the human mind has invented can tame a tide rip or control the rhythm of the water's ebb and flow, and the most modern instruments cannot carry a vessel over a shoal until the tide has brought a sufficient depth of water over it. Even the *Queen Mary* waits for slack water to come to her pier in New York; otherwise the set of the tidal current might swing her against the pier with enough force to crush it. On the Bay of Fundy, because of the great range of tide, harbor activities follow a pattern as rhythmic as the tides themselves, for vessels can come to the docks to take on or discharge cargo during only a few hours on each tide, leaving promptly to avoid being stranded in mud at low water.

In the confinement of narrow passages or when opposed by contrary winds and swells, the tidal currents often move with uncontrollable violence, creating some of the most dangerous waterways of the world. It is only necessary to read the Coast Pilots and Sailing Directions for various parts of the world to understand the menace of such tidal currents to navigation.

15   "Vessels around the Aleutians are in more danger from tidal currents than from any other cause, save the lack of surveys," says the postwar edition of the *Alaska Pilot*. Through Unalga and Akutan Passes, which are among the most-used routes for vessels entering the Bering Sea from the Pacific, strong tidal currents pour, making their force felt well offshore and setting vessels unexpectedly against the rocks. Through Akun Strait the flood tide has the velocity of a mountain torrent, with dangerous swirls and over-falls. In each of these passes the tide will raise heavy, choppy seas if opposed by wind or swells.

3. H. G. Wells (1866–1946), British author whose works include science fiction.

"Vessels must be prepared to take seas aboard," warns the *Pilot,* for a 15-foot wave of a tide rip may suddenly rise and sweep across a vessel, and more than one man has been carried off to his death in this way.

On the opposite side of the world, the tide setting eastward from the open Atlantic presses between the islands of the Shetlands and Orkneys into the North Sea, and on the ebb returns through the same narrow passages. At certain stages of the tide these waters are dotted with dangerous eddies, with strange upward domings, or with sinister pits or depressions. Even in calm weather boats are warned to avoid the eddies of Pentland Firth, which are known as the Swilkie; and with an ebb tide and a northwest wind the heavy breaking seas of the Swilkie are a menace to vessels "which few, having once experienced, would be rash enough to encounter a second time."

* * *

The influence of the tide over the affairs of sea creatures as well as men may be seen all over the world. The billions upon billions of sessile animals, like oysters, mussels, and barnacles, owe their very existence to the sweep of the tides, which brings them the food which they are unable to go in search of. By marvelous adaptations of form and structure, the inhabitants of the world between the tide lines are enabled to live in a zone where the danger of being dried up is matched against the danger of being washed away, where for every enemy that comes by sea there is another that comes by land, and where the most delicate of living tissues must somehow withstand the assault of storm waves that have the power to shift tons of rock or to crack the hardest granite.

The most curious and incredibly delicate adaptations, however, are the ones by which the breeding rhythm of certain marine animals is timed to coincide with the phases of the moon and the stages of the tide. In Europe it has been well established that the spawning activities of oysters reach their peak on the spring tides, which are about two days after the full or the new moon. In the waters of northern Africa there is a sea urchin that, on the nights when the moon is full and apparently only then, releases its reproductive cells into the sea. And in tropical waters in many parts of the world there are small marine worms whose spawning behavior is so precisely adjusted to the tidal calendar that, merely from observing them, one could tell the month, the day, and often the time of day as well.

Near Samoa in the Pacific, the palolo worm lives out its life on the bottom of the shallow sea, in holes in the rocks and among the masses of corals. Twice each year, during the neap tides of the moon's last quarter in October and November, the worms forsake their burrows and rise to the surface in swarms that cover the water. For this purpose, each worm has literally broken its body in two, half to remain in its rocky tunnel, half to carry the reproductive products to the surface and there to liberate the cells. This happens at dawn on the day before the moon reaches its last quarter, and again on the following day; on the second day of the spawning the quantity of eggs liberated is so great that the sea is discolored.

The Fijians, whose waters have a similar worm, call them "Mbalolo" and have designated the periods of their spawning "Mbalolo lailai" (little) for Octo-   20 ber and "Mbalolo levu" (large) for November. Similar forms near the Gilbert Islands respond to certain phases of the moon in June and July; in the Malay Archipelago a related worm swarms at the surface on the second and third nights after the full moon of March and April, when the tides are running highest. A Japanese palolo swarms after the new moon and again after the full moon in October and November.

Concerning each of these, the question recurs but remains unanswered: is it the state of the tides that in some unknown way supplies the impulse from which springs this behavior, or is it, even more mysteriously, some other influence of the moon? It is easier to imagine that it is the press and the rhythmic movement of the water that in some way brings about this response. But why is it only certain tides of the year, and why for some species is it the fullest tides of the month and for others the least movements of the waters that are related to the perpetuation of the race? At present, no one can answer.

No other creature displays so exquisite an adaptation to the tidal rhythm as the grunion—a small, shimmering fish about as long as a man's hand. Through no one can say what processes of adaptation, extending over no one knows how many millennia, the grunion has come to know not only the daily rhythm of the tides, but the monthly cycle by which certain tides sweep higher on the beaches than others. It has so adapted its spawning habits to the tidal cycle that the very existence of the race depends on the precision of this adjustment.

Shortly after the full moon of the months from March to August, the grunion appear in the surf on the beaches of California. The tide reaches flood stage, slackens, hesitates, and begins to ebb. Now on these waves of the ebbing tide the fish begin to come in. Their bodies shimmer in the light of the moon as they are borne up the beach on the crest of a wave, they lie glittering on the wet sand for a perceptible moment of time, then fling themselves into the wash of the next wave and are carried back to sea. For about an hour after the turn of the tide this continues, thousands upon thousands of grunion coming up onto the beach, leaving the water, returning to it. This is the spawning act of the species.

During the brief interval between successive waves, the male and female have come together in the wet sand, the one to shed her eggs, the other to fertilize them. When the parent fish return to the water, they have left behind a mass of eggs buried in the sand. Succeeding waves on that night do not wash out the eggs because the tide is already ebbing. The waves of the next high tide will not reach them, because for a time after the full of the moon each tide will halt its advance a little lower on the beach than the preceding one. The eggs, then, will be undisturbed for at least a fortnight. In the warm, damp, incubating sand they undergo their development. Within two weeks the magic change from fertilized egg to larval fishlet is completed, the perfectly formed little grunion still confined within the membranes of the egg, still buried in the sand, waiting for release. With the tides of the new moon it comes. Their waves wash over the places where the little masses of the grunion eggs were buried, the swirl and rush of the surf stirring the sand deeply. As the sand is washed away, and the eggs feel the touch of the cool sea water, the membranes rupture, the fishlets hatch, and the waves that released them bear them away to the sea.

But the link between tide and living creature I like best to remember is that of a very small worm, flat of body, with no distinction of appearance, but with one unforgettable quality. The name of this worm is *Convoluta roscoffensis,* and it lives on the sandy beaches of northern Brittany and the Channel Islands. Convoluta has entered into a remarkable partnership with a green alga, whose cells inhabit the body of the worm and lend to its tissues their own green color. The worm lives entirely on the starchy products manufactured by its plant guest, having become so completely dependent upon this means of nutrition that its digestive organs have degenerated. In order that the algal cells may carry on their function of photosynthesis (which is dependent upon sunlight) Convoluta rises from the damp sands of the intertidal zone as soon as the tide has ebbed, the sand becoming spotted with large green patches composed of thousands of the worms. For the several hours while the tide is out, the worms lie thus in the sun, and the plants manufacture their starches and sugars; but when the tide returns, the worms must again sink into the sand to avoid being washed away, out into deep water. So the whole lifetime of the worm is a succession of movements conditioned by the stages of the tide—upward into sunshine on the ebb, downward on the flood.

What I find most unforgettable about Convoluta is this: sometimes it happens that a marine biologist, wishing to study some related problem, will transfer a whole colony of the worms into the laboratory, there to establish them in an aquarium, where there are no tides. But twice each day Convoluta rises out of the sand on the bottom of the aquarium, into the light of the sun. And twice each day it sinks again into the sand. Without a brain, or what we would call a memory, or even any very clear perception, Convoluta continues to live out its life in this alien place, remembering, in every fiber of its small green body, the tidal rhythm of the distant sea.

QUESTIONS

1. No one would call Carson's prose style lively. (Look closely, for example, at her verbs.) How, then, does this piece work? What accounts for its overall impact?

2. *The Sea Around Us* was translated into over thirty languages. Do you think it was easy or difficult to translate? On what characteristics of Carson's writing do you base your opinion?

3. Write about a common natural phenomenon like tides, using research or personal knowledge or both.

JOHN MUIR　　　　*A Wind-Storm in the Forests*

T
HE MOUNTAIN WINDS, like the dew and rain, sunshine and snow, are measured and bestowed with love on the forests to develop their strength and beauty. However restricted the scope of other forest influences, that of the winds is universal. The snow bends and trims the upper forests every winter, the lightning strikes a single tree here and there, while avalanches mow down thousands at a swoop as a gardener trims out a bed of flowers. But the winds go to every tree, fingering every leaf and branch and furrowed bole; not one is forgotten; the Mountain Pine towering with outstretched arms on the rugged buttresses of the icy peaks, the lowliest and most retiring tenant of the dells; they seek and find them all, caressing them tenderly, bending them in lusty exercise, stimulating their growth, plucking off a leaf or limb as required, or removing an entire tree or grove, now whispering and cooing through the branches like a sleepy child, now roaring like the ocean; the winds blessing the forests, the forests the winds, with ineffable beauty and harmony as the sure result.

After one has seen pines six feet in diameter bending like grasses before a mountain gale, and ever and anon some giant falling with a crash that shakes the hills, it seems astonishing that any, save the lowest thickset trees, could ever have found a period sufficiently stormless to establish themselves; or, once established, that they should not, sooner or later, have been blown down. But when the storm is over, and we behold the same forests tranquil again, towering fresh and unscathed in erect majesty, and consider what centuries of storms have fallen upon them since they were first planted,—hail, to break the tender seedlings; lightning, to scorch and shatter; snow, winds, and avalanches, to crush and overwhelm,—while the manifest result of all this wild storm-culture is the glorious perfection we behold; then faith in Nature's forestry is established, and we cease to deplore the violence of her most destructive gales, or of any other storm-implement whatsoever.

There are two trees in the Sierra forests that are never blown down, so long as they continue in sound health. These are the Juniper and the Dwarf Pine of the summit peaks. Their stiff, crooked roots grip the storm-beaten ledges like eagles' claws, while their lithe, cord-like branches bend round compliantly, offering but slight holds for winds, however violent. The other alpine conifers—the Needle Pine, Mountain Pine, Two-leaved Pine, and Hemlock Spruce—are never thinned out by this agent to any destructive extent, on account of their admirable toughness and the closeness of their growth. In general the same is true of the giants of the lower zones. The kingly Sugar Pine, towering aloft to a height of more than 200 feet, offers a fine mark to storm-

From Muir's classic account The Mountains of California *(1894), a book of scientific observation and personal memoir.*

346

A wind-storm in the California forests (after a sketch by the author)

winds: but it is not densely foliaged, and its long, horizontal arms swing round compliantly in the blast, like tresses of green, fluent algæ in a brook; while the Silver Firs in most places keep their ranks well together in united strength. The Yellow or Silver Pine is more frequently overturned than any other tree on the Sierra, because its leaves and branches form a larger mass in proportion to its height, while in many places it is planted sparsely, leaving open lanes through which storms may enter with full force. Furthermore, because it is distributed along the lower portion of the range, which was the first to be left bare on the breaking up of the ice-sheet at the close of the glacial winter, the soil it is growing upon has been longer exposed to post-glacial weathering, and consequently is in a more crumbling, decayed condition than the fresher soils farther up the range, and therefore offers a less secure anchorage for the roots.

While exploring the forest zones of Mount Shasta, I discovered the path of a hurricane strewn with thousands of pines of this species. Great and small had been uprooted or wrenched off by sheer force, making a clean gap, like that made by a snow avalanche. But hurricanes capable of doing this class of work are rare in the Sierra, and when we have explored the forests from one extremity of the range to the other, we are compelled to believe that they are the most beautiful on the face of the earth, however we may regard the agents that have made them so.

There is always something deeply exciting, not only in the sounds of winds in the woods, which exert more or less influence over every mind, but in their varied waterlike flow as manifested by the movements of the trees, especially those of the conifers. By no other trees are they rendered so extensively and impressively visible, not even by the lordly tropic palms or tree-ferns responsive to the gentlest breeze. The waving of a forest of the giant Sequoias is indescribably impressive and sublime, but the pines seem to me the best interpreters of winds. They are mighty waving goldenrods, ever in tune, singing and writing wind-music all their long century lives. Little, however, of this noble tree-waving and tree-music will you see or hear in the strictly alpine portion of the forests. The burly Juniper, whose girth sometimes more than equals its

5

height, is about as rigid as the rocks on which it grows. The slender lash-like sprays of the Dwarf Pine stream out in wavering ripples, but the tallest and slenderest are far too unyielding to wave even in the heaviest gales. They only shake in quick, short vibrations. The Hemlock Spruce, however, and the Mountain Pine, and some of the tallest thickets of the Two-leaved species bow in storms with considerable scope and gracefulness. But it is only in the lower and middle zones that the meeting of winds and woods is to be seen in all its grandeur.

One of the most beautiful and exhilarating storms I ever enjoyed in the Sierra occurred in December, 1874, when I happened to be exploring one of the tributary valleys of the Yuba River. The sky and the ground and the trees had been thoroughly rain-washed and were dry again. The day was intensely pure, one of those incomparable bits of California winter, warm and balmy and full of white sparkling sunshine, redolent of all the purest influences of the spring, and at the same time enlivened with one of the most bracing wind-storms conceivable. Instead of camping out, as I usually do, I then chanced to be stopping at the house of a friend. But when the storm began to sound, I lost no time in pushing out into the woods to enjoy it. For on such occasions Nature has always something rare to show us, and the danger to life and limb is hardly greater than one would experience crouching deprecatingly beneath a roof.

It was still early morning when I found myself fairly adrift. Delicious sunshine came pouring over the hills, lighting the tops of the pines, and setting free a stream of summery fragrance that contrasted strangely with the wild tones of the storm. The air was mottled with pine-tassels and bright green plumes, that went flashing past in the sunlight like birds pursued. But there was not the slightest dustiness, nothing less pure than leaves, and ripe pollen, and flecks of withered bracken and moss. I heard trees falling for hours at the rate of one every two or three minutes; some uprooted, partly on account of the loose, water-soaked condition of the ground; others broken straight across, where some weakness caused by fire had determined the spot. The gestures of the various trees made a delightful study. Young Sugar Pines, light and feathery as squirrel-tails, were bowing almost to the ground; while the grand old patriarchs, whose massive boles had been tried in a hundred storms, waved solemnly above them, their long, arching branches streaming fluently on the gale, and every needle thrilling and ringing and shedding off keen lances of light like a diamond. The Douglas Spruces,[1] with long sprays drawn out in level tresses, and needles massed in a gray, shimmering glow, presented a most striking appearance as they stood in bold relief along the hilltops. The madroños[2] in the dells, with their red bark and large glossy leaves tilted every way, reflected the sunshine in throbbing spangles like those one so often sees on the rippled surface of a glacier lake. But the Silver Pines were now the most impressively beautiful of all. Colossal spires 200 feet in height waved like supple goldenrods chanting and bowing low as if in worship, while the whole mass

1. Another name for Douglas fir.
2. A type of evergreen tree.

of their long, tremulous foliage was kindled into one continuous blaze of white sun-fire. The force of the gale was such that the most steadfast monarch of them all rocked down to its roots with a motion plainly perceptible when one leaned against it. Nature was holding high festival, and every fiber of the most rigid giants thrilled with glad excitement.

I drifted on through the midst of this passionate music and motion, across many a glen, from ridge to ridge; often halting in the lee of a rock for shelter, or to gaze and listen. Even when the grand anthem had swelled to its highest pitch, I could distinctly hear the varying tones of individual trees,—Spruce, and Fir, and Pine, and leafless Oak—and even the infinitely gentle rustle of the withered grasses at my feet. Each was expressing itself in its own way,— singing its own song, and making its own peculiar gestures,—manifesting a richness of variety to be found in no other forest I have yet seen. The coniferous woods of Canada, and the Carolinas, and Florida, are made up of trees that resemble one another about as nearly as blades of grass, and grow close together in much the same way. Coniferous trees, in general, seldom possess individual character, such as is manifest among Oaks and Elms. But the California forests are made up of a greater number of distinct species than any other in the world. And in them we find, not only a marked differentiation into special groups, but also a marked individuality in almost every tree, giving rise to storm effects indescribably glorious.

Toward midday, after a long, tingling scramble through copses of hazel and ceanothus,[3] I gained the summit of the highest ridge in the neighborhood; and then it occurred to me that it would be a fine thing to climb one of the trees to obtain a wider outlook and get my ear close to the Æolian music[4] of its topmost needles. But under the circumstances the choice of a tree was a serious matter. One whose instep was not very strong seemed in danger of being blown down, or of being struck by others in case they should fall; another was branchless to a considerable height above the ground, and at the same time too large to be grasped with arms and legs in climbing; while others were not favorably situated for clear views. After cautiously casting about, I made choice of the tallest of a group of Douglas Spruces that were growing close together like a tuft of grass, no one of which seemed likely to fall unless all the rest fell with it. Though comparatively young, they were about 100 feet high, and their lithe, brushy tops were rocking and swirling in wild ecstasy. Being accustomed to climb trees in making botanical studies, I experienced no difficulty in reaching the top of this one, and never before did I enjoy so noble an exhilaration of motion. The slender tops fairly flapped and swished in the passionate torrent, bending and swirling backward and forward, round and round, tracing indescribable combinations of vertical and horizontal curves, while I clung with muscles firm braced, like a bobolink on a reed.

3. A type of evergreen shrub.
4. Music made by the wind, from Aeolus, the Greek god of the winds, the strings of whose harp were sounded by the wind.

10   In its widest sweeps my tree-top described an arc of from twenty to thirty degrees, but I felt sure of its elastic temper, having seen others of the same species still more severely tried—bent almost to the ground indeed, in heavy snows—without breaking a fiber. I was therefore safe, and free to take the wind into my pulses and enjoy the excited forest from my superb outlook. The view from here must be extremely beautiful in any weather. Now my eye roved over the piny hills and dales as over fields of waving grain, and felt the light running in ripples and broad swelling undulations across the valleys from ridge to ridge, as the shining foliage was stirred by corresponding waves of air. Oftentimes these waves of reflected light would break up suddenly into a kind of beaten foam, and again, after chasing one another in regular order, they would seem to bend forward in concentric curves, and disappear on some hillside, like sea-waves on a shelving shore. The quantity of light reflected from the bent needles was so great as to make whole groves appear as if covered with snow, while the black shadows beneath the trees greatly enhanced the effect of the silvery splendor.

Excepting only the shadows there was nothing somber in all this wild sea of pines. On the contrary, notwithstanding this was the winter season, the colors were remarkably beautiful. The shafts of the pine and libocedrus[5] were brown and purple, and most of the foliage was well tinged with yellow; the laurel groves, with the pale undersides of their leaves turned upward, made masses of gray; and then there was many a dash of chocolate color from clumps of manzanita,[6] and jet of vivid crimson from the bark of the madroños, while the ground on the hillsides, appearing here and there through openings between the groves, displayed masses of pale purple and brown.

The sounds of the storm corresponded gloriously with this wild exuberance of light and motion. The profound bass of the naked branches and boles booming like waterfalls; the quick, tense vibrations of the pine-needles, now rising to a shrill, whistling hiss, now falling to a silky murmur; the rustling of laurel groves in the dells, and the keen metallic click of leaf on leaf—all this was heard in easy analysis when the attention was calmly bent.

The varied gestures of the multitude were seen to fine advantage, so that one could recognize the different species at a distance of several miles by this means alone, as well as by their forms and colors, and the way they reflected the light. All seemed strong and comfortable, as if really enjoying the storm, while responding to its most enthusiastic greetings. We hear much nowadays concerning the universal struggle for existence, but no struggle in the common meaning of the word was manifest here; no recognition of danger by any tree; no deprecation; but rather an invincible gladness as remote from exultation as from fear.

I kept my lofty perch for hours, frequently closing my eyes to enjoy the music by itself, or to feast quietly on the delicious fragrance that was stream-

---

5. A genus of cedar trees. In the Sierra Nevada, *Libocedrus decurans* often reaches a height of 150 feet.

6. A type of evergreen shrub.

ing past. The fragrance of the woods was less marked than that produced during warm rain, when so many balsamic buds and leaves are steeped like tea; but, from the chafing of resiny branches against each other, and the incessant attrition of myriads of needles, the gale was spiced to a very tonic degree. And besides the fragrance from these local sources there were traces of scents brought from afar. For this wind came first from the sea, rubbing against its fresh, briny waves, then distilled through the redwoods, threading rich ferny gulches, and spreading itself in broad undulating currents over many a flower-enameled ridge of the coast mountains, then across the golden plains, up the purple foot-hills, and into these piny woods with the varied incense gathered by the way.

Winds are advertisements of all they touch, however much or little we may be able to read them; telling their wanderings even by their scents alone. Mariners detect the flowery perfume of land-winds far at sea, and sea-winds carry the fragrance of dulse and tangle far inland, where it is quickly recognized, though mingled with the scents of a thousand land-flowers. As an illustration of this, I may tell here that I breathed sea-air on the Firth of Forth, in Scotland, while a boy; then was taken to Wisconsin, where I remained nineteen years; then, without in all this time having breathed one breath of the sea, I walked quietly, alone, from the middle of the Mississippi Valley to the Gulf of Mexico, on a botanical excursion, and while in Florida, far from the coast, my attention wholly bent on the splendid tropical vegetation about me, I suddenly recognized a sea-breeze, as it came sifting through the palmettos and blooming vine-tangles, which at once awakened and set free a thousand dormant associations, and made me a boy again in Scotland, as if all the intervening years had been annihilated.

Most people like to look at mountain rivers, and bear them in mind; but few care to look at the winds, though far more beautiful and sublime, and though they become at times about as visible as flowing water. When the north winds in winter are making upward sweeps over the curving summits of the High Sierra, the fact is sometimes published with flying snow-banners a mile long. Those portions of the winds thus embodied can scarce be wholly invisible, even to the darkest imagination. And when we look around over an agitated forest, we may see something of the wind that stirs it, by its effects upon the trees. Yonder it descends in a rush of water-like ripples, and sweeps over the bending pines from hill to hill. Nearer, we see detached plumes and leaves, now speeding by on level currents, now whirling in eddies, or, escaping over the edges of the whirls, soaring aloft on grand, upswelling domes of air, or tossing on flame-like crests. Smooth, deep currents, cascades, falls, and swirling eddies, sing around every tree and leaf, and over all the varied topography of the region with telling changes of form, like mountain rivers conforming to the features of their channels.

After tracing the Sierra streams from their fountains to the plains, marking where they bloom white in falls, glide in crystal plumes, surge gray and foam-filled in boulder-choked gorges, and slip through the woods in long, tranquil reaches—after thus learning their language and forms in detail, we may at

15

length hear them chanting all together in one grand anthem, and comprehend them all in clear inner vision, covering the range like lace. But even this spectacle is far less sublime and not a whit more substantial than what we may behold of these storm-streams of air in the mountain woods.

We all travel the milky way together, trees and men; but it never occurred to me until this stormday, while swinging in the wind, that trees are travelers, in the ordinary sense. They make many journeys, not extensive ones, it is true; but our own little journeys, away and back again, are only little more than tree-wavings—many of them not so much.

When the storm began to abate, I dismounted and sauntered down through the calming woods. The storm-tones died away, and, turning toward the east, I beheld the countless hosts of the forests hushed and tranquil, towering above one another on the slopes of the hills like a devout audience. The setting sun filled them with amber light, and seemed to say, while they listened, "My peace I give unto you."

20   As I gazed on the impressive scene, all the so-called ruin of the storm was forgotten, and never before did these noble woods appear so fresh, so joyous, so immortal.

QUESTIONS

1. What preconceptions did you bring to Muir's title, "A Wind-Storm in the Forests"? How does the opening sentence—indeed, the entire opening paragraph—suggest a different perspective?

2. The central adventure in this essay occurs when Muir climbs a Douglas Spruce (paragraph 9). Why does Muir undertake this climb? What does he wish to experience?

3. Write about an experience you have had in nature, whether dramatic (as in Muir's essay) or more quiet (as in Aldo Leopold's, also in this section).

EDWARD ABBEY   *The Serpents of Paradise*

THE APRIL MORNINGS are bright, clear and calm. Not until the afternoon does the wind begin to blow, raising dust and sand in funnel-shaped twisters that spin across the desert briefly, like dancers, and then collapse—whirlwinds from which issue no voice or word except the forlorn moan of the elements under stress. After the reconnoitering dust devils comes the real, the serious wind, the voice of the desert rising to a demented howl and blotting out sky

From Abbey's classic book Desert Solitaire: A Season in the Wilderness *(1968). Drawings by Peter Parnall were added in the 1990 edition and are included here.*

and sun behind yellow clouds of dust, sand, confusion, embattled birds, last year's scrub-oak leaves, pollen, the husks of locusts, bark of juniper. . . .

Time of the red eye, the sore and bloody nostril, the sand-pitted windshield, if one is foolish enough to drive his car into such a storm. Time to sit indoors and continue that letter which is never finished—while the fine dust forms neat little windrows under the edge of the door and on the windowsills. Yet the springtime winds are as much a part of the canyon country as the silence and the glamorous distances; you learn, after a number of years, to love them also.

The mornings therefore, as I started to say and meant to say, are all the sweeter in the knowledge of what the afternoon is likely to bring. Before beginning the morning chores I like to sit on the sill of my doorway, bare feet planted on the bare ground and a mug of hot coffee in hand, facing the sunrise. The air is gelid, not far above freezing, but the butane heater inside the trailer keeps my back warm, the rising sun warms the front, and the coffee warms the interior.

Perhaps this is the loveliest hour of the day, though it's hard to choose. Much depends on the season. In midsummer the sweetest hour begins at sundown, after the awful heat of the afternoon. But now, in April, we'll take the opposite, that hour beginning with the sunrise. The birds, returning from wherever they go in winter, seem inclined to agree. The pinyon jays are whirling in garrulous, gregarious flocks from one stunted tree to the next and back again, erratic exuberant games without any apparent practical function. A few big ravens hang around and croak harsh clanking statements of smug satisfaction from the rimrock, lifting their greasy wings now and then to probe for lice. I can hear but seldom see the canyon wrens singing their distinctive song from somewhere up on the cliffs: a flutelike descent—never ascent—of the whole tone scale. Staking out new nesting claims, I understand. Also invisible but invariably present at some indefinable distance are the mourning doves whose plaintive call suggests irresistibly a kind of seeking out, the attempt by separated souls to restore a lost communion:

Hello . . . they seem to cry, *who . . . are . . . you?*

5

And the reply from a different quarter. *Hello . . .* (pause) *where . . . are . . . you?*

No doubt this line of analogy must be rejected. It's foolish and unfair to impute to the doves, with serious concerns of their own, an interest in questions more appropriate to their human kin. Yet their song, if not a mating call or a warning, must be what it sounds like, a brooding meditation on space, on solitude. The game.

Other birds, silent, which I have not yet learned to identify, are also lurking in the vicinity, watching me. What the ornithologist terms l.g.b.'s— little gray birds—they flit about from point to point on noiseless wings, their origins obscure.

* * * I share the housetrailer with a number of mice. I don't know how many but apparently only a few, perhaps a single family. They don't disturb me and are welcome to my crumbs and leavings. Where they came from, how they got into the trailer, how they survived before my arrival (for the trailer had been locked up for six months), these are puzzling matters I am not prepared to resolve. My only reservation concerning the mice is that they do attract rattlesnakes.

10   I'm sitting on my doorstep early one morning, facing the sun as usual, drinking coffee, when I happen to look down and see almost between my bare feet, only a couple of inches to the rear of my heels, the very thing I had in mind. No mistaking that wedgelike head, that tip of horny segmented tail peeping out of the coils. He's under the doorstep and in the shade where the ground and air remain very cold. In his sluggish condition he's not likely to strike unless I rouse him by some careless move of my own.

There's a revolver inside the trailer, a huge British Webley .45, loaded, but it's out of reach. Even if I had it in my hands I'd hesitate to blast a fellow creature at such close range, shooting between my own legs at a living target flat on solid rock thirty inches away. It would be like murder; and where would I set my coffee? My cherrywood walking stick leans against the trailerhouse wall only a few feet away, but I'm afraid that in leaning over for it I might stir up the rattler or spill some hot coffee on his scales.

Other considerations come to mind. Arches National Monument[1] is meant

---

1. Near Moab, Utah, in the spectacular Canyonlands region, where Abbey lived at the time.

to be among other things a sanctuary for wildlife—for all forms of wildlife. It is my duty as a park ranger to protect, preserve and defend all living things within the park boundaries, making no exceptions. Even if this were not the case I have personal convictions to uphold. Ideals, you might say. I prefer not to kill animals. I'm a humanist; I'd rather kill a *man* than a snake.

What to do. I drink some more coffee and study the dormant reptile at my heels. It is not after all the mighty diamondback, *Crotalus atrox*, I'm confronted with but a smaller species known locally as the horny rattler or more precisely as the Faded Midget. An insulting name for a rattlesnake, which may explain the Faded Midget's alleged bad temper. But the name is apt: he is small and dusty-looking, with a little knob above each eye—the horns. His bite though temporarily disabling would not likely kill a full-grown man in normal health. Even so I don't really want him around. Am I to be compelled to put on boots or shoes every time I wish to step outside? The scorpions, tarantulas, centipedes, and black widows are nuisance enough.

I finish my coffee, lean back and swing my feet up and inside the doorway of the trailer. At once there is a buzzing sound from below and the rattler lifts his head from his coils, eyes brightening, and extends his narrow black tongue to test the air.

After thawing out my boots over the gas flame I pull them on and come back to the doorway. My visitor is still waiting beneath the doorstep, basking in the sun, fully alert. The trailerhouse has two doors. I leave by the other and get a long-handled spade out of the bed of the government pickup. With this tool I scoop the snake into the open. He strikes, I can hear the click of the fangs against steel, see the stain of venom. He wants to stand and fight, but I am patient; I insist on herding him well away from the trailer. On guard, head aloft—that evil slit-eyed weaving head shaped like the ace of spades—tail whirring, the rattler slithers sideways, retreating slowly before me until he reaches the shelter of a sandstone slab. He backs under it.

You better stay there, cousin, I warn him; if I catch you around the trailer again I'll chop your head off.

A week later he comes back. If not him his twin brother. I spot him one morning under the trailer near the kitchen drain, waiting for a mouse. I have to keep my promise.

This won't do. If there are midget rattlers in the area there may be diamondbacks too—five, six or seven feet long, thick as a man's wrist, dangerous.

15

I don't want them camping under my home. It looks as though I'll have to trap
the mice.

However, before being forced to take that step I am lucky enough to capture
a gopher snake. Burning garbage one morning at the park dump, I see a long
slender yellow-brown snake emerge from a mound of old tin cans and plastic
picnic plates and take off down the sandy bed of a gulch. There is a burlap sack
in the cab of the truck which I carry when plucking Kleenex flowers from the
brush and cactus along the road; I grab that and my stick, run after the snake
and corner it beneath the exposed roots of a bush. Making sure it's a gopher
snake and not something less useful, I open the neck of the sack and with a
great deal of coaxing and prodding get the snake into it. The gopher snake, *Drymarchon corais couperi,* or bull snake, has a reputation as the enemy of rattlesnakes, destroying or driving them away whenever encountered.

20   Hoping to domesticate this sleek, handsome and docile reptile, I release
him inside the trailerhouse and keep him there for several days. Should I attempt to feed him? I decide against it—let him eat mice. What little water he
may need can also be extracted from the flesh of his prey.

The gopher snake and I get along nicely. During the day he curls up like a
cat in the warm corner behind the heater and at night he goes about his business. The mice, singularly quiet for a change, make themselves scarce. The
snake is passive, apparently contented, and makes no resistance when I pick
him up with my hands and drape him over an arm or around my neck. When
I take him outside into the wind and sunshine his favorite place seems to be
inside my shirt, where he wraps himself around my waist and rests on my belt.
In this position he sometimes sticks his head out between shirt buttons for a
survey of the weather, astonishing and delighting any tourists who may happen
to be with me at the time. The scales of a snake are dry and smooth, quite
pleasant to the touch. Being a cold blooded creature, of course, he takes his
temperature from that of the immediate environment—in this case my body.

We are compatible. From my point of view, friends. After a week of close
association I turn him loose on the warm sandstone at my doorstep and leave
for a patrol of the park. At noon when I return he is gone. I search everywhere
beneath, nearby and inside the trailerhouse, but my companion has disappeared. Has he left the area entirely or is he hiding somewhere close by? At
any rate I am troubled no more by rattlesnakes under the door.

The snake story is not yet ended.

In the middle of May, about a month after the gopher snake's disappearance, in the evening of a very hot day, with all the rosy desert cooling like a
griddle with the fire turned off, he reappears. This time with a mate.

25   I'm in the stifling heat of the trailer opening a can of beer, barefooted,
about to go outside and relax after a hard day watching cloud formations. I
happen to glance out the little window near the refrigerator and see two gopher snakes on my verandah engaged in what seems to be a kind of ritual
dance. Like a living caduceus they wind and unwind about each other in un-
dulant, graceful, perpetual motion, moving slowly across a dome of sandstone.
Invisible but tangible as music is the passion which joins them—sexual? com-

bative? both? A shameless *voyeur,* I stare at the lovers, and then to get a closer view run outside and around the trailer to the back. There I get down on hands and knees and creep toward the dancing snakes, not wanting to frighten or disturb them. I crawl to within six feet of them and stop, flat on my belly, watching from the snake's eye level. Obsessed with their ballet, the serpents seem unaware of my presence.

The two gopher snakes are nearly identical in length and coloring; I cannot be certain that either is actually my former household pet. I cannot even be sure that they are male and female, though their performance resembles so strongly a *pas de deux*[2] by formal lovers. They intertwine and separate, glide side by side in perfect congruence, turn like mirror images of each other and glide back again, wind and unwind again. This is the basic pattern but there is a variation: at regular intervals the snakes elevate their heads, facing one another, as high as they can go, as if each is trying to outreach or overawe the other. Their heads and bodies rise, higher and higher, then topple together and the rite goes on.

I crawl after them, determined to see the whole thing. Suddenly and simultaneously they discover me, prone on my belly a few feet away. The dance stops. After a moment's pause the two snakes come straight toward me, still in flawless unison, straight toward my face, the forked tongues flickering, their intense wild yellow eyes staring directly into my eyes. For an instant I am paralyzed by wonder; then, stung by a fear too ancient and powerful to overcome I scramble back, rising, to my knees. The snakes veer and turn and race away from me in parallel motion, their lean elegant bodies making a soft hissing noise as they slide over the sand and stone. I follow them for a short distance, still plagued by curiosity, before remembering my place and the requirements of common courtesy. For godsake let them go in peace, I tell myself. Wish them luck and (if lovers) innumerable offspring, a life of happily ever after. Not for their sake alone but for your own.

In the long hot days and cool evenings to come I will not see the gopher snakes again. Nevertheless I will feel their presence watching over me like totemic deities, keeping the rattlesnakes far back in the brush where I like them best, cropping off the surplus mouse population, maintaining useful connections with the primeval. Sympathy, mutual aid, symbiosis, continuity.

How can I descend to such anthropomorphism? Easily—but is it, in this case, entirely false? Perhaps not. I am not attributing human motives to my snake and bird acquaintances. I recognize that when and where they serve purposes of mine they do so for beautifully selfish reasons of their own. Which is exactly the way it should be. I suggest, however, that it's a foolish, simpleminded rationalism which denies any form of emotion to all animals but man and his dog. This is no more justified than the Moslems are in denying souls to women. It seems to me possible, even probable, that many of the nonhuman undomesticated animals experience emotions unknown to us. What do the

2. Literally, step for two (French), a dance for two dancers.

coyotes mean when they yodel at the moon? What are the dolphins trying so patiently to tell us? Precisely what did those two enraptured gopher snakes have in mind when they came gliding toward my eyes over the naked sandstone? If I had been as capable of trust as I am susceptible to fear I might have learned something new or some truth so very old we have all forgotten it.

> They do not sweat and whine about their condition.
> They do not lie awake in the dark and weep for their sins.[3]

30   All men are brothers, we like to say, half-wishing sometimes in secret it were not true. But perhaps it is true. And is the evolutionary hue from protozoan to Spinoza[4] any less certain? That also may be true. We are obliged, therefore, to spread the news, painful and bitter though it may be for some to hear, that all living things on hand are kindred. . . .

3. From Walt Whitman's *Song of Myself*, sec. 32.
4. Baruch Spinoza (1632–1677), Dutch philosopher known today for his writings on the doctrine of pantheism.

QUESTIONS

1. Why is the word "paradise" included in the title? What does it reveal about Abbey's attitude toward the desert in which he lives?

2. "I'd rather kill a *man* than a snake," writes Abbey in paragraph 12; yet several paragraphs later he threatens, "if I catch you around the trailer again I'll chop your head off" (paragraph 16). What are the rhetorical purposes of these statements? How do they articulate the thematic concerns of the essay?

3. Write an essay in which you use your own experience in nature to defend an ecological or environmental cause.

4. Write about your own encounter with an animal, whether domesticated or wild.

ALEXANDER PETRUNKEVITCH *The Spider and the Wasp*

IN THE FEEDING and safeguarding of their progeny insects and spiders exhibit some interesting analogies to reasoning and some crass examples of blind instinct. The case I propose to describe here is that of the tarantula spiders and their archenemy, the digger wasps of the genus Pepsis. It is a classic example of what looks like intelligence pitted against instinct—a strange situa-

Published as an article in Scientific American *(August 1952), America's leading scientific monthly for nonspecialist readers. The illustrations appeared with the original article.*

tion in which the victim, though fully able to defend itself, submits unwittingly
to its destruction.

Most tarantulas live in the tropics, but several species occur in the temperate zone and a few are common in the southern U.S. Some varieties are
large and have powerful fangs with which they can inflict a deep wound.
These formidable looking spiders do not, however, attack man; you can hold
one in your hand, if you are gentle, without being bitten. Their bite is dangerous only to insects and small mammals such as mice; for man it is no worse
than a hornet's sting.

Tarantulas customarily live in deep cylindrical burrows, from which they
emerge at dusk and into which they retire at dawn. Mature males wander
about after dark in search of females and occasionally stray into houses. After
mating, the male dies in a few weeks, but a female lives much longer and can
mate several years in succession. In a Paris museum is a tropical specimen
which is said to have been living in captivity for 25 years.

A fertilized female tarantula lays from 200 to 400 eggs at a time; thus it is
possible for a single tarantula to produce several thousand young. She takes
no care of them beyond weaving a cocoon of silk to enclose the eggs. After
they hatch, the young walk away, find convenient places in which to dig their
burrows and spend the rest of their lives in solitude. The eyesight of tarantulas

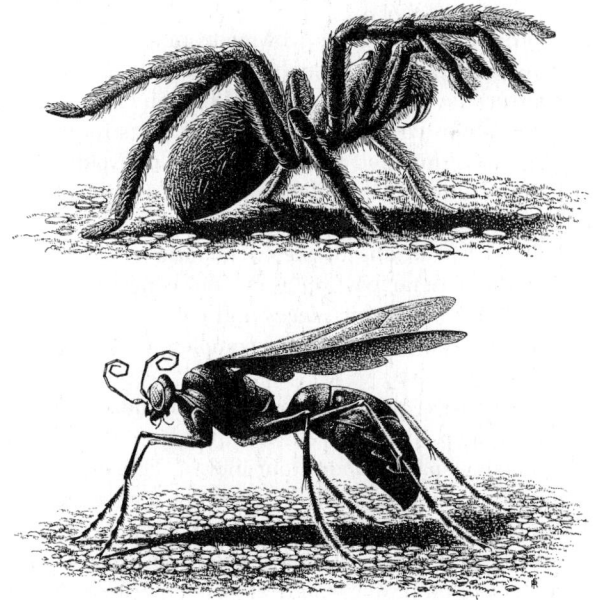

SPIDER AND WASP are the tarantula *Cyrtopholis portoricae* (*top*) and the
digger wasp *Pepsis marginata* (*bottom*). The tarantula is shown in an attitude of defense. The wasps of the genus Pepsis are either a deep blue or
blue with rust-colored wings. The largest species of the genus have a wing-
spread of about four inches.

is poor, being limited to a sensing of change in the intensity of light and to the perception of moving objects. They apparently have little or no sense of hearing, for a hungry tarantula will pay no attention to a loudly chirping cricket placed in its cage unless the insect happens to touch one of its legs.

5   But all spiders, and especially hairy ones, have an extremely delicate sense of touch. Laboratory experiments prove that tarantulas can distinguish three types of touch: pressure against the body wall, stroking of the body hair, and riffling of certain very fine hairs on the legs called trichobothria. Pressure against the body, by the finger or the end of a pencil, causes the tarantula to move off slowly for a short distance. The touch excites no defensive response unless the approach is from above where the spider can see the motion, in which case it rises on its hind legs, lifts its front legs, opens its fangs and holds this threatening posture as long as the object continues to move.

The entire body of a tarantula, especially its legs, is thickly clothed with hair. Some of it is short and wooly, some long and stiff. Touching this body hair produces one of two distinct reactions. When the spider is hungry, it responds with an immediate and swift attack. At the touch of a cricket's antennae the tarantula seizes the insect so swiftly that a motion picture taken at the rate of 64 frames per second shows only the result and not the process of capture. But when the spider is not hungry, the stimulation of its hairs merely causes it to shake the touched limb. An insect can walk under its hairy belly unharmed.

The trichobothria, very fine hairs growing from dislike[1] membranes on the legs, are sensitive only to air movement. A light breeze makes them vibrate slowly, without disturbing the common hair. When one blows gently on the trichobothria, the tarantula reacts with a quick jerk of its four front legs. If the front and hind legs are stimulated at the same time, the spider makes a sudden jump. This reaction is quite independent of the state of its appetite.

These three tactile responses—to pressure on the body wall, to moving of the common hair, and to flexing of the trichobothria—are so different from one another that there is no possibility of confusing them. They serve the tarantula adequately for most of its needs and enable it to avoid most annoyances and dangers. But they fail the spider completely when it meets its deadly enemy, the digger wasp Pepsis.

These solitary wasps are beautiful and formidable creatures. Most species are either a deep shiny blue all over, or deep blue with rusty wings. The largest have a wing span of about four inches. They live on nectar. When excited, they give off a pungent odor—a warning that they are ready to attack. The sting is much worse than that of a bee or common wasp, and the pain and swelling last longer. In the adult stage the wasp lives only a few months. The female produces but a few eggs, one at a time at intervals of two or three days. For each egg the mother must provide one adult tarantula, alive but paralyzed. The mother wasp attaches the egg to the paralyzed spider's abdomen. Upon hatching from the egg, the larva is many hundreds of times

1. Unlike or dissimilar.

smaller than its living but helpless victim. It eats no other food and drinks no water. By the time it has finished its single Gargantuan meal and become ready for wasphood, nothing remains of the tarantula but its indigestible chitinous skeleton.

The mother wasp goes tarantula-hunting when the egg in her ovary is al-   10
most ready to be laid. Flying low over the ground late on a sunny afternoon, the wasp looks for its victim or for the mouth of a tarantula burrow, a round hole edged by a bit of silk. The sex of the spider makes no difference, but the mother is highly discriminating as to species. Each species of Pepsis requires a certain species of tarantula, and the wasp will not attack the wrong species. In a cage with a tarantula which is not its normal prey, the wasp avoids the spider and is usually killed by it in the night.

Yet when a wasp finds the correct species, it is the other way about. To identify the species the wasp apparently must explore the spider with her an-tennae. The tarantula shows an amazing tolerance to this exploration. The wasp crawls under it and walks over it without evoking any hostile response. The molestation is so great and so persistent that the tarantula often rises on all eight legs, as if it were on stilts. It may stand this way for several minutes. Meanwhile the wasp, having satisfied itself that the victim is of the right species, moves off a few inches to dig the spider's grave. Working vigorously with legs and jaws, it excavates a hole 8 to 10 inches deep with a diameter slightly larger than the spider's girth. Now and again the wasp pops out of the hole to make sure that the spider is still there.

When the grave is finished, the wasp returns to the tarantula to complete her ghastly enterprise. First she feels it all over once more with her antennae. Then her behavior becomes more aggressive. She bends her abdomen, pro-truding her sting, and searches for the soft membrane at the point where the spider's legs join its body—the only spot where she can penetrate the horny skeleton. From time to time, as the exasperated spider slowly shifts ground, the wasp turns on her back and slides along with the aid of her wings, trying to get under the tarantula for a shot at the vital spot. During all this maneu-vering, which can last for several minutes, the tarantula makes no move to save itself. Finally the wasp corners it against some obstruction and grasps one of its legs in her powerful jaws. Now at last the harassed spider tries a desperate but vain defense. The two contestants roll over and over on the ground. It is a terrifying sight and the outcome is always the same. The wasp finally manages to thrust her sting into the soft spot and holds it there for a few seconds while she pumps in the poison. Almost immediately the tarantula falls paralyzed on its back. Its legs stop twitching; its heart stops beating. Yet it is not dead, as is shown by the fact that if taken from the wasp it can be re-stored to some sensitivity by being kept in a moist chamber for several months.

After paralyzing the tarantula, the wasp cleans herself by dragging her body along the ground and rubbing her feet, sucks the drop of blood oozing from the wound in the spider's abdomen, then grabs a leg of the flabby, help-less animal in her jaws and drags it down to the bottom of the grave. She stays

DEATH OF THE SPIDER is shown in
these drawings. In the first drawing
the wasp digs a grave, occasionally
looking out.

there for many minutes, sometimes for several hours, and what she does all
that time in the dark we do not know. Eventually she lays her egg and attaches
it to the side of the spider's abdomen with a sticky secretion. Then she
emerges, fills the grave with soil carried bit by bit in her jaws, and finally tramples the ground all around to hide any trace of the grave from prowlers. Then
she flies away, leaving her descendant safely started in life.

In all this the behavior of the wasp evidently is qualitatively different from
that of the spider. The wasp acts like an intelligent animal. This is not to say
that instinct plays no part or that she reasons as man does. But her actions are
to the point; they are not automatic and can be modified to fit the situation.
We do not know for certain how she identifies the tarantula—probably it is by
some olfactory or chemo-tactile sense—but she does it purposefully and does
not blindly tackle a wrong species.

15   On the other hand, the tarantula's behavior shows only confusion. Evidently the wasp's pawing gives it no pleasure, for it tries to move away. That
the wasp is not simulating sexual stimulation is certain because male and female tarantulas react in the same way to its advances. That the spider is not
anesthetized by some odorless secretion is easily shown by blowing lightly at
the tarantula and making it jump suddenly. What, then, makes the tarantula
behave as stupidly as it does?

No clear, simple answer is available. Possibly the stimulation by the wasp's
antennae is masked by a heavier pressure on the spider's body, so that it reacts
as when prodded by a pencil. But the explanation may be much more complex.
Initiative in attack is not in the nature of tarantulas; most species fight only
when cornered so that escape is impossible. Their inherited patterns of behavior apparently prompt them to avoid problems rather than attack them. For
example, spiders always weave their webs in three dimensions, and when a spider finds that there is insufficient space to attach certain threads in the third
dimension, it leaves the place and seeks another, instead of finishing the web
in a single plane. This urge to escape seems to arise under all circumstances,
in all phases of life, and to take the place of reasoning. For a spider to change

The spider stands with its legs extended after raising its body so the wasp
could pass under it. In the second drawing the wasp stings the spider,
which falls on its back. In the third the wasp licks a drop of blood from the
wound. In the final drawing the spider lies in its grave with the egg of the
wasp on its abdomen.

the pattern of its web is as impossible as for an inexperienced man to build a
bridge across a chasm obstructing his way.

In a way the instinctive urge to escape is not only easier but often more
efficient than reasoning. The tarantula does exactly what is most efficient in
all cases except in an encounter with a ruthless and determined attacker
dependent for the existence of her own species on killing as many tarantulas
as she can lay eggs. Perhaps in this case the spider follows its usual pattern of
trying to escape, instead of seizing and killing the wasp, because it is not
aware of its danger. In any case, the survival of the tarantula species as a
whole is protected by the fact that the spider is much more fertile than the
wasp.

QUESTIONS

1. Why is Petrunkevitch's initial description of the tarantula longer than his initial description of the wasp?

2. What are the major points of contrast between the spider and the wasp? Why does
Petrunkevitch emphasize these particular points rather than others?

3. Petrunkevitch suggests more than one hypothesis for the behavior of the tarantula;
indeed, he says that "no clear, simple answer is available" (paragraph 16). How does he
test the possible explanations? Which one do you think he prefers?

4. What evidence is there that Petrunkevitch sees the tarantula and the wasp at least
partly in human terms? In a brief essay explain why you think this is or is not a legitimate perspective for a scientist.

WE KNOW THAT the white man does not understand our ways. One portion of the land is the same to him as the next, for he is a stranger who comes in the night and takes from the land whatever he needs. The earth is not his brother, but his enemy, and when he has conquered it, he moves on. He leaves his fathers' graves, and his children's birthright is forgotten. The sight of your cities pains the eyes of the red man. But perhaps it is because the red man is a savage and does not understand.

There is no quiet place in the white man's cities. No place to hear the leaves of spring or the rustle of insects' wings. But perhaps because I am a savage and do not understand, the clatter only seems to insult the ears. The Indian prefers the soft sound of the wind darting over the face of the pond, the smell of the wind itself cleansed by a mid-day rain, or scented with the piñon pine. The air is precious to the red man. For all things share the same breath—the beasts, the trees, the man. Like a man dying for many days, he is numb to the stench.

What is man without the beasts? If all the beasts were gone, men would die from great loneliness of spirit, for whatever happens to the beasts also happens to man. All things are connected. Whatever befalls the earth befalls the sons of the earth.

It matters little where we pass the rest of our days; they are not many. A few more hours, a few more winters, and none of the children of the great tribes that once lived on this earth, or that roamed in small bands in the woods, will be left to mourn the graves of a people once as powerful and hopeful as yours.

5   The whites, too, shall pass—perhaps sooner than other tribes. Continue to contaminate your bed, and you will one night suffocate in your own waste. When the buffalo are all slaughtered, the wild horses all tamed, the secret corners of the forest heavy with the scent of many men, and the view of the ripe hills blotted by talking wires,[1] where is the thicket? Gone. Where is the eagle? Gone. And what is it to say goodby to the swift and the hunt, the end of living and the beginning of survival? We might understand if we knew what it was that the white man dreams, what he describes to his children on the long winter nights, what visions he burns into their minds, so they will wish for tomorrow. But we are savages. The white man's dreams are hidden from us.

Because of its origin as an oration given in Salish, there are many different versions of Chief Seattle's speech; this one comes from Native American Testimony: An Anthology of Indian and White Relations, *edited by Peter Nabokov (1977).*

1. I.e., the telegraph.

QUESTIONS

1. Chief Seattle repeatedly refers to the red man as "a savage" who "does not under-stand," yet in the course of this letter he gives evidence of a great deal of understanding. What is the purpose of such ironic comments and apparently self-disparaging remarks?

2. Scholars have recently suggested that Chief Seattle's "Letter" is in fact the creation of a white man, based on Seattle's public oratory. If so, what rhetorical techniques does the white editor associate with Indian speech? Why might he have done so?

3. A surprisingly modern note of ecological awareness resounds in the statement "[W]hatever happens to the beasts also happens to man. All things are connected" (paragraph 3). Locate two or three similar observations, and explain their effectiveness.

4. Chief Seattle says that the red man might understand the white man better "if we knew what it was that the white man dreams, what he describes to his children on the long winter nights, what visions he burns into their minds, so they will wish for tomorrow" (paragraph 5). Write a short essay explaining, either straightforwardly or ironically, how "the white man" might reply. If you prefer, write the reply itself.

AL GORE   *The Climate Emergency*

April 13, 2004

I'M AL GORE. I used to be the next president of the United States.[1] This has been an interesting period of my life. I wanted to start by inviting you to put yourselves in my shoes for a minute. It hasn't been easy, you know. For eight years I flew on Air Force II,[2] and now I have to take off my shoes to get on an airplane.

Not long after Tipper[3] and I left the White House, we were driving from our home in Nashville to a small farm we have fifty miles east of Nashville. We were driving ourselves. I looked in the rear view mirror and all of a sudden it

Al Gore gave this speech during the 2004 presidential campaign; it became the basis of his documentary film and book, An Inconvenient Truth *(2006). This version was given with extensive illustrations, charts, and graphs on April 13, 2004, at the Yale School of Forestry and Environmental Science, and was included in a collection of speeches,* Red, White, Blue and Green: Politics and the Environment in the 2004 Election *(2004), edited by members of YSFES, James R. Lyons, Heather S. Kaplan, Fred Strebeigh, and Kathleen E. Campbell.*

1. Gore ran for president in 2000 and won more popular votes than George W. Bush, who was nonetheless elected because of his majority in the electoral college.

2. Part of the presidential fleet of airplanes.

3. Al Gore's wife, Tipper Gore (b. 1948).

just hit me that there was no motorcade. Some of you may have heard of phantom limb pain.[4]

It was mealtime, so we looked for a place to eat. We pulled off the interstate highway and finally found a Shoney's Restaurant, a low-cost, family restaurant chain. We walked in and sat down. The waitress came over and made a big commotion over Tipper. She took our order and then went to the couple in the booth next to us, and lowered her voice so much I had to really strain to hear what she was saying: "Yes, that's former Vice President Al Gore and his wife Tipper." And the man said, "He's come down a long way, hasn't he?"

The very next day, continuing a true story, I got on a plane and flew to Africa, to Nigeria, to the city of Lagos, to make a speech about energy. I began my speech by telling that story, that had just happened the day before back in Tennessee, and I told it pretty much the same way I just told it here. They laughed. Then I went on and gave my speech and went back to the airport and flew back toward the U.S. I fell asleep on the plane, and was awakened in the middle of the night when we were landing on the Azores Islands out in the middle of the Atlantic. They opened the door of the plane to let some fresh air in, and I looked out, and here came a man running across the runway waving a piece of paper saying "Call Washington, call Washington."

5   I thought—what in the world, in the middle of the night, in the middle of the Atlantic, what in the world could be wrong in Washington? And then I remembered it could be a bunch of things. But what it turned out to be was that my staff back in Washington was very, very upset. A wire service reporter in Lagos had written a story about my speech, and it had already been transmitted to the U.S. and printed all over the country. The story began: "Former Vice President Al Gore announced in Nigeria yesterday 'My wife Tipper and I opened a low-cost family restaurant named Shoney's and we are running it ourselves.' " Before I could get back to U.S. soil, the late-night comics Leno and Letterman[5] had already started in on me. They had me in a big white chef's hat and Tipper was taking orders—"One more with fries!" Three days later I got a nice long handwritten letter from my friend Bill Clinton[6] that said "Congratulations on the new restaurant, Al!" We like to celebrate each other's successes in life.

Anyway, it really is an honor to be here and to share some words about the climate issue. The title I chose for this speech is not a misprint. The phrase "climate emergency" is intended to convey what it conveys—that this is a crisis with an unusual sense of urgency attached to it, and we should see it as an emergency. The fact that we don't, or that most people don't, is part of what I want to cover here.

4. The sensation of pain in a missing limb.

5. Jay Leno (b. 1950) and David Letterman (b. 1947), contemporary American comedians.

6. Bill Clinton (b. 1946), forty-second American president (1993–2001); Gore was his vice president.

CLIMATE CHANGE: IMPACTS AND EVIDENCE

There is a very famous picture called Earth Rise. A young astronaut named William Anders took it on December 24, 1968.[7] This mission, Apollo 7, was the first one to go around the moon. It went on Christmas Eve, and they had just been on the dark side of the moon, coming back around, seeing the earth for the first time. Anders—the rookie astronaut, without a big fancy camera—took this snapshot and it instantly became an icon. Many people believe that this one picture, Earth Rise, in many ways was responsible for the birth of the modern environmental movement. Less than two years after this picture was printed, the first Earth Day[8] was organized. This picture became a powerful force in changing the way people thought about the earth and about the environment.

The environment is often felt to be relatively invulnerable because the earth is so big. People tend to assume that the earth is so big that we as human beings can't possibly have any impact on it. That is a mistake. The most vulnerable part of earth's environment is the atmosphere. It's astonishingly thin, as any image from space shows. The space is so small that we are able to fill it up with greenhouse gases, such as CO_2,[9] which form a thick blanket of gas surrounding the earth, trapping some of the sun's radiation. This process, called the "greenhouse effect," is what leads to increased global temperatures or what most refer to as climate change.

In Europe during the summer of 2003, we experienced an extreme heat wave that killed an estimated 20,000 people, and many predict such events will be much more commonplace as a result of increasing temperatures. The anomaly was extreme, particularly in France, with consequences that were well reported in the press. Year-to-year, decade-to-decade there's variation, but the overall upward trend worldwide since the American Civil War is really clear and really obvious, at least to me.

If you look at the glaciers around the world, you see that many are melting away. A friend of mine named Lonnie Thompson of Ohio State studies glaciers, and he reports that 15 to 20 years from now there will be no more snows of Kilimanjaro. This shrinking of glaciers is happening all around the world, including Latin America, China, and the U.S. In our own Glacier National Park, all of the glaciers are predicted to be gone within 15 to 20 years.

One of the remarkable things about glaciers is that they really could care less about politics. They either melt or freeze. Rhetoric has no impact on them whatsoever. A few years ago some hikers in the Alps between Austria and Italy were walking along and they ran across what looked like a 5,000-year-old man.

10

7. William Anders (b. 1933), United States Air Force officer and astronaut on the Apollo 8 (not 7) mission, took this famous photograph depicting the moon, partially in light, off the edge of the earth.

8. An annual celebration of the environment, intended to increase awareness and activism, and held at different points around the world.

9. Carbon dioxide.

Tomorrow's CO₂ Concentration

Projected Concentration
After 50 More Years of
Unrestricted Fossil Fuel Burning

Today's CO₂
Concentration

CO₂ Concentration

Temperature in C°

| 400,000 | 300,000 | 200,000 | 100,000 | 0 |

Years Before Present   Next to Last Ice Age   Most Recent Ice Age

Actually he was from 3,000 B.C., and you don't see that every day. The reason you don't is that the ice there hasn't melted for 5,000 years. Every mountain glacier in the entire world, with the exception of a few in Scandinavia that are affected by the Gulf Stream patterns, is melting rapidly.

Lonnie Thompson and his team of researchers don't just watch glaciers melt. They drill down into the glaciers and pull up columns of ice. Then they study the bubbles of air trapped in the ice, and they can do that year by year because every year there's a new layer. In Antarctica the layers are paper-thin and they stack up 400,000 years back. Ninety-five percent of all the fresh water in the world is locked up as ice in Antarctica. It's two miles high.

When Lonnie and his team drill down through Antarctica, they're able to get 400,000 years worth of ice. They can then look at the little bubbles of atmosphere and measure the CO_2 content, and they can also measure temperature by comparing the ratio of different oxygen isotopes.[10] However that works, it's extremely accurate and not controversial. And here's what that record shows where carbon dioxide is concerned:

Now, there are two points here. The first is: Do those lines—the line for level of temperature and the line for concentration of CO_2—look like they go together to you? They do to me. The second point is: Here in New Haven,[11] on the temperature line, the difference of approximately 15°C of average temperature is the difference between a nice day and having one mile of ice

10. Different forms of chemical elements.
11. City in Connecticut where this speech was given.

over your head. What has been happening lately is that the concentration of CO_2 is approaching 380 parts per million. So that's way, way above anything that has been seen for as far back as we can measure—400,000 years. And within fifty years it's going to approach 600 parts per million. So if a difference of approximately 200 parts per million of CO_2 on the cold side is a mile of ice over your head, what does that much difference represent on the warm side?

Or to state the question another way, is it perfectly sane and rational and reasonable to go ahead and do this? Or is it in fact crazy? It is crazy, but that is what the world is doing right now. And fifty years is not a long time. Unless we make decisions very soon, we will reach much higher levels. So, when I use the phrase *climate emergency*, I have partly in mind the fact that this is happening right now. And it carries with it, unless we do something, catastrophic consequences for all civilization.

In Antarctica you've heard about ice shelves the size of Rhode Island[12] coming off and calving. There are actually a bunch of them in the Antarctic, and also in Greenland. Incidentally, there was a flurry of publicity on April 9th about a new study showing that if greenhouse gas emissions continue to rise at current rates the disappearance of Greenland's ice sheet is inevitable, unless we act fairly soon.

When ice melts in mountains and in Antarctica and Greenland—when land-based ice melts—it raises sea level. When you have rivers that are close to the ocean like the Thames River in London, the water level goes up, and it threatens the lower lying areas. London, in 1983, built barriers to protect the city against flooding from higher sea level and thus higher storm surges. These barriers had to be closed only once in 1983. Twenty years later, in 2003, they were closed 19 times. Again, the same pattern shows up wherever you look.

An area of Bangladesh is due to be flooded where ten million people live. A large area of Florida is due to be flooded. The Florida Keys are very much at risk. The Everglades are at risk.

Now the Arctic is very different from the Antarctic because, while the Antarctic is land surrounded by ocean, the Arctic is ocean surrounded by land. And the ice in the Arctic is floating on top of the ocean, so it doesn't get nearly as thick. Instead of two miles thick, it's only ten feet thick—that is, it used to be ten feet. Just in the last few decades it has melted quite a bit. I went up there twice in a submarine. They have these specially designed submarines where the wings rotate vertically so that they can cut through the ice. Ice in water, or thinner ice, melts more rapidly and leads to temperature increases because, as soon as a little bit of ice melts, the water absorbs a lot more temperature. This effect is now happening to the entire Arctic Ocean. The Arctic ice cap has thinned by 40 percent in the last 40 years. Let me repeat that. Listen to that number. The Arctic ice cap has thinned 40 percent in 40 years. Within 50 years it may be entirely gone.

That's a big problem because when the sun hits the ice cap, 95 percent of

12. Rhode Island is about 37 miles wide by 48 miles long.

Effect of global warming on Arctic ice cap.

the energy bounces off like a big mirror. But when it hits the open ocean more than 90 percent is absorbed. So it's a phase change, it's not a gradual change. Ice is that way—the difference between 33F° and 31F° is not just two degrees. That puts more energy into the system and it changes the amount of evaporation off the oceans, so you get more rain and snow but it comes at different times and you get more soil erosion as well. You get simultaneously more flooding and more droughts, which is really a bad thing. You get more precipitation in one-time storm events. More of it comes at one time in big storms.

The trend is very clear. What's behind it all? I've come to believe that global warming, the disappearance of the ocean fisheries, the destruction of the rain forests, the stratospheric ozone depletion problem, the extinction crisis, all of these are really symptoms of an underlying cause. The underlying cause is a collision between our civilization and the earth. The relationship between the human species and our planet has been completely changed. All of our culture, all of our literature, all of our history, everything we've learned, was premised on one relationship between the earth and us, and now we have a different one.

THREE LEADING CAUSES: POPULATION GROWTH, TECHNOLOGY, AND OUR WAY OF THINKING

The new relationship between humankind and the earth has been caused by a confluence of three factors.

The first is population, which has been growing rapidly. The population crisis has actually been a success story in some ways. We've slowed it down, but the momentum of the population increases is really incredible. Say the scientists are right and we emerged as a species 160,000 years ago. It took from that time, almost 160,000 years until the end of World War II, before we got to a population of 2 billion. Since I've been alive, as part of the baby boom generation, it has gone from 2 billion to 6.3 billion. So if it takes more than 10,000 generations to reach 2 billion and one human lifetime to go from 2 to 6, and if I live to the demographic average of the baby boom generation, it'll go close to 9 billion. That is one of the reasons why the relationship between our species and the earth is different now than ever before.

Some of the other global patterns, species loss for example, match the human population pattern. Most importantly, however, the increase in the population of developing nations is driving food demand, water demand, and energy demand, creating intense pressures on human resources. We are seeing a pattern of devastation and destruction that is simply driven by those factors. And it really is a political issue. We in the U.S. are responsible for more greenhouse gas emissions than Africa, South America, Central America, India, and China combined. The world average is way below where we are. Just to recap—this is 1,000 years of carbon emissions, CO_2 concentrations, and temperature. This is not rocket science. Those lines match up.

The second factor that changes the relationship between humans and the earth is technology. In many ways, it is more powerful and significant than the population explosion because new technologies have increased our power beyond imagination. That's a good thing often in areas like medicine or communications—you can fill in the blanks. There are all kinds of great things that represent progress. Even cleaning up the environment with new technology. There are a lot of great things that have come out of this, but when we don't examine habits that have persisted for a long time, and then use the same habits with new technology and don't take into account the new power that we have, then the consequences can get away from us. One quick example: warfare was one thing with swords and bows and arrows and even muskets, but when nuclear weapons were created, the consequences of war were utterly

25

transformed. So we had to think differently about war. And what happened? The cold war emerged and unfortunately the other kind didn't completely go away, but we're in the midst of rethinking that age-old habit of warfare. We just have to, because the new technologies make it unthinkable to continue as we were doing in the past.

Now think about that pattern: old habits, new technologies. Think about the subsistence that we have always drawn from the earth. The plow was a great advance, as was irrigation. But then we began to get more powerful with these tools. At the Aral Sea[13] in Russia, something as simple as irrigation on a large scale led to the virtual disappearance of the fourth largest inland body of water in the world. We're changing the surface of the earth, and technology sometimes seems to dwarf our human scale. We now have to try to change this pattern.

First modern humans

160,000 BC   100,000 BC   10,000 BC   7000 BC   6000 BC   5000 BC   4000 BC

Population Growth Throughout History

13. A landlocked Central Asian sea.

The third factor is our way of thinking. We have to change our way of thinking. One illustration comes from the fact that, as I said earlier, we have these big assumptions that we don't question. I had a classmate in the sixth grade. Every time our geography teacher put a map of the world up he would mutter. One time, he got up his courage and pointed to the outline of South America and the outline of Africa and said, "Did they ever fit together?" And the teacher said "Of course not. That's the most ridiculous thing I've ever heard." In fact, until about the 1960s, the guy who talked about continental drift was thought to be a kook because he said that Africa and South America fit together. It turns out that they did, but the teacher in this story had an assumption in his mind. Continents are so big they obviously don't move, thereby illustrating the old philosopher's saying that "What gets us into trouble

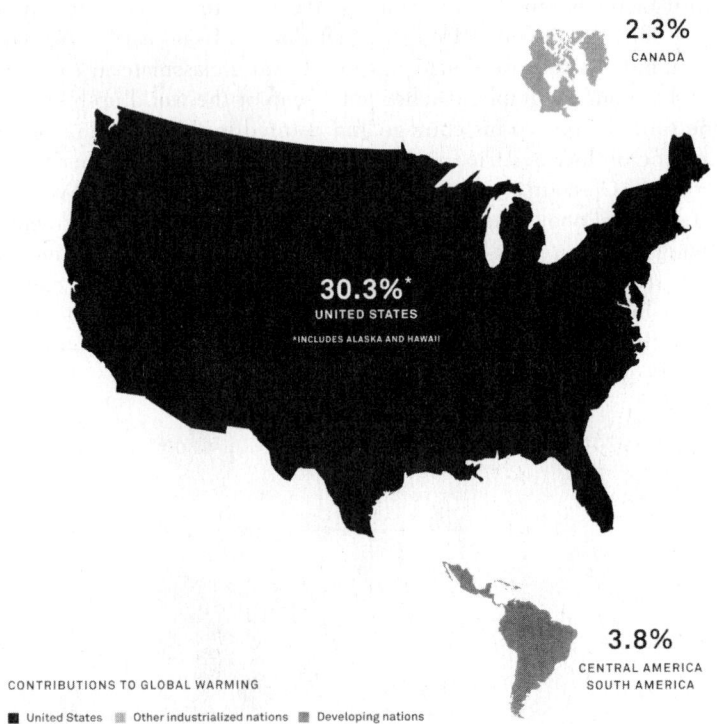

2.3%
CANADA

30.3%*
UNITED STATES
*INCLUDES ALASKA AND HAWAII

3.8%
CENTRAL AMERICA
SOUTH AMERICA

CONTRIBUTIONS TO GLOBAL WARMING

■ United States ▨ Other industrialized nations ■ Developing nations

is not what we don't know. It's what we know for sure that just ain't so" (Yogi Berra).[14] We know for sure that the earth is so big we can't have a big impact on it, but that's just not so.

You know this cliché, I'm sure: That a frog's nervous system is such that if it's dropped into a pot of boiling water it will jump right out because it perceives the contrast, but if it's put in a pot of tepid water which is slowly heated, it doesn't jump out unless it's rescued. Here's the deeper meaning of that cliché: the frog did perceive the sudden boiling water, but did not perceive the slow process.

Global warming seems to be gradual in the context of a human life, but it is actually fairly sudden. Another problem with our thinking is that there are people who are paid money by some coal companies and oil companies to go out and pretend that the science says something that it doesn't say. These are scientific camp followers who are willing to do things for money. And some of the very same individuals who are doing this now (i.e., trying to persuade people that global warming is not a problem) were some of the same people who took money from the tobacco companies after the Surgeon General's report came out warning of the dangers of smoking. The tobacco companies hired these scientific

14. Berra (b. 1925), famous New York Yankee and wordsmith.

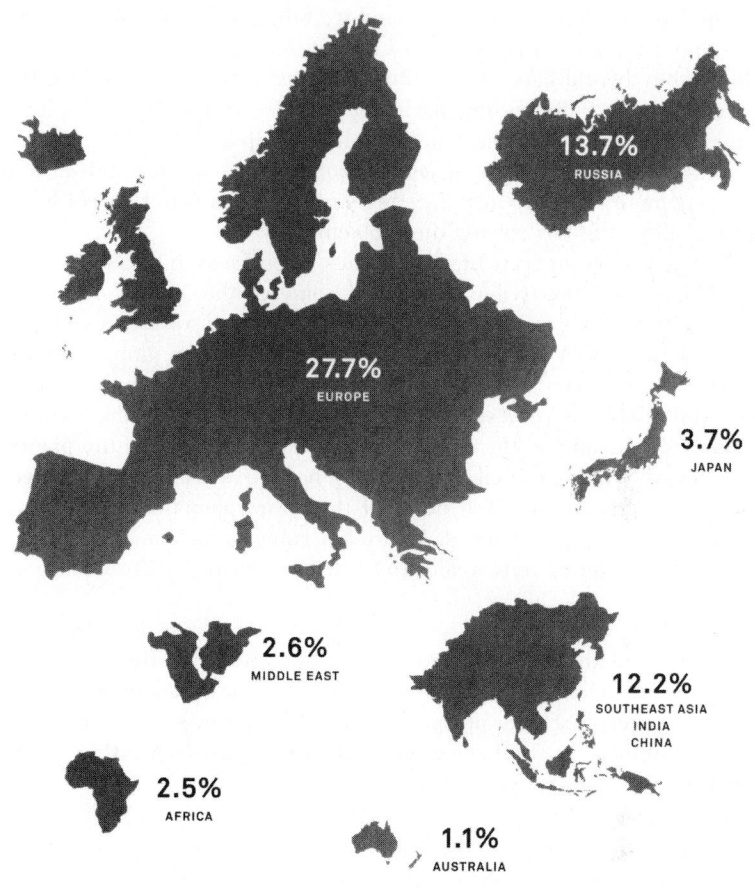

13.7%
RUSSIA

27.7%
EUROPE

3.7%
JAPAN

2.6%
MIDDLE EAST

12.2%
SOUTHEAST ASIA
INDIA
CHINA

2.5%
AFRICA

1.1%
AUSTRALIA

SOURCE: U.S. DEPARTMENT OF ENERGY, ENERGY INFORMATION ADMINISTRATION, CARBON DIOXIDE INFORMATION ANALYSIS CENTER

camp followers to go out and try to confuse the public into thinking that the science wasn't clear. They produced marketing campaigns like "More doctors smoke Camels." On a similar note, the Republican pollster Frank Luntz advised the White House that the issue of the environment is important, but the way to deal with it is to make the lack of scientific certainly a primary issue by finding people who are willing to say that it's confusing when it's really not.

There's another assumption that needs to be questioned. In contrast to the idea that the earth is so big that we can't have any impact on it, there are others who assume that the climate change problem is so big we can't solve it. I, however, believe that we can if we put our minds to it. We had a problem with the ozone hole, a big global problem that seemed too big to solve. In response, we had political leadership and the world passed a treaty outlawing chlorofluorocarbons, the chemicals that caused this problem.

30

The United States led the way, and we brought about a dramatic drop in CFCs and are now in the process of solving that problem. We now have the ability to buy hybrid cars like the Toyota Prius and the marketplace for new sources of energy is increasing dramatically. We're also seeing new efficiencies with energy savings. If we have political leadership and the collective political will to say it is important to solve this problem, we can not only solve it, we can create more jobs, we can create higher incomes, a better way of life, and a higher quality of life by solving the problem.

And finally, it's an issue of values. Back when I was in the Senate, the first President Bush[15] was trying to fend off some of the attacks by myself and many others in Congress who were saying we have to solve this global warming problem. So they had a White House conference on global stewardship. One of their view graphs caught my attention. Their view of the global environmental crisis was represented by a scale with money, in the form of gold bars on one side, and on the other side of the scales was the entire planet. The point they were trying to make was that we have to find a balance between our monetary wealth and the well being of the entire planet. Boy, that's a tough one! It's a false choice—because you're not going to have much wealth if you lose the planet and there is wealth to be made in saving it. We have to get our perspective right.

Everything we have ever known—and Carl Sagan[16] made a beautiful long statement about this—all the wars, all the heartbreak, all the romance, every triumph, every mistake, everything we've ever known is contained in this small planet. If we keep the right perspective and keep our eyes on the prize, we *can* solve this problem, we *will* solve this problem, we *must* solve this problem. It really is up to you.

15. George H. W. Bush (b. 1924), forty-first American president; his son, George W. Bush (b. 1946), followed in his footsteps as forty-third president.
16. American astronomer (1934–1996).

Questions

1. This speech begins with a self-introduction. Why does Al Gore, a well-known public figure, introduce himself to the audience? How do his humorous tactics aid in his presentation of the serious part of his speech?

2. Gore's serious presentation of the climate emergency begins with the section "Climate Change: Impacts and Evidence." (The section headings were added by the editors of *Red, White, Blue and Green*.) Where does he define "climate emergency"? What examples does he give as evidence?

3. Gore introduces and interprets a graph to make a point about temperature change (paragraphs 12–14)—a technique used in scientific writing. Yet Gore's interpretation is not "scientific" in style. How does he make clear to the audience the meaning of this graph?

4. Gore gives three leading causes of the climate emergency: population growth, technology, and our way of thinking. List the kinds of evidence and examples he uses in this

part of his speech, and suggest how the diversity of evidence and examples helps him communicate with his audience.

5. Write a speech about a current crisis, drawing on a variety of examples and, if possible, using illustrations, charts, and graphs.

ALDO LEOPOLD   *Marshland Elegy*

A DAWN WIND STIRS on the great marsh. With almost imperceptible slowness it rolls a bank of fog across the wide morass. Like the white ghost of a glacier the mists advance, riding over phalanxes of tamarack, sliding across bog-meadows heavy with dew. A single silence hangs from horizon to horizon.

Out of some far recess of the sky a tinkling of little bells falls soft upon the listening land. Then again silence. Now comes a baying of some sweet-throated hound, soon the clamor of a responding pack. Then a far clear blast of hunting horns, out of the sky into the fog.

High horns, low horns, silence, and finally a pandemonium of trumpets, rattles, croaks, and cries that almost shakes the bog with its nearness, but without yet disclosing whence it comes. At last a glint of sun reveals the approach of a great echelon of birds. On motionless wing they emerge from the lifting mists, sweep a final arc of sky, and settle in clangorous descending spirals to their feeding grounds. A new day has begun on the crane marsh.

A sense of time lies thick and heavy on such a place. Yearly since the ice age it has awakened each spring to the clangor of cranes. The peat layers that comprise the bog are laid down in the basin of an ancient lake. The cranes stand, as it were, upon the sodden pages of their own history. These peats are the compressed remains of the mosses that clogged the pools, of the tamaracks that spread over the moss, of the cranes that bugled over the tamaracks since the retreat of the ice sheet. An endless caravan of generations has built of its own bones this bridge into the future, this habitat where the oncoming host again may live and breed and die.

To what end? Out on the bog a crane, gulping some luckless frog, springs his ungainly hulk into the air and flails the morning sun with mighty wings. The tamaracks re-echo with his bugled certitude. He seems to know.   5

Our ability to perceive quality in nature begins, as in art, with the pretty. It expands through successive stages of the beautiful to values as yet uncaptured by language. The quality of cranes lies, I think, in this higher gamut, as yet beyond the reach of words.

First appeared in American Forests *(October 1937), a century-old journal that calls itself "the quarterly magazine of trees and forests"; later reprinted in Leopold's classic book of nature writing* A Sand County Almanac *(1949).*

This much, though, can be said: our appreciation of the crane grows with the slow unraveling of earthly history. His tribe, we now know, stems out of the remote Eocene.[1] The other members of the fauna in which he originated are long since entombed within the hills. When we hear his call we hear no mere bird. We hear the trumpet in the orchestra of evolution. He is the symbol of our untamable past, of that incredible sweep of millennia which underlies and conditions the daily affairs of birds and men.

And so they live and have their being—these cranes—not in the constricted present, but in the wider reaches of evolutionary time. Their annual return is the ticking of the geologic clock. Upon the place of their return they confer a peculiar distinction. Amid the endless mediocrity of the commonplace, a crane marsh holds a palentological patent of nobility, won in the march of aeons, and revocable only by shotgun. The sadness discernible in some marshes arises, perhaps, from their once having harbored cranes. Now they stand humbled, adrift in history.

Some sense of this quality in cranes seems to have been felt by sportsmen and ornithologists of all ages. Upon such quarry as this the Holy Roman Emperor Frederick loosed his gyrfalcons.[2] Upon such quarry as this once swooped the hawks of Kublai Khan. Marco Polo tells us: "He derives the highest amusement from sporting with gyrfalcons and hawks. At Changanor the Khan has a great Palace surrounded by a fine plain where are found cranes in great numbers. He causes millet and other grains to be sown in order that the birds may not want."[3]

10   The ornithologist Bengt Berg,[4] seeing cranes as a boy upon the Swedish heaths, forthwith made them his life work. He followed them to Africa and discovered their winter retreat on the White Nile. He says of his first encounter: "It was a spectacle which eclipsed the flight of the roc in the Thousand and One Nights."[5]

When the glacier came down out of the north, crunching hills and gouging valleys, some adventuring rampart of the ice climbed the Baraboo Hills[6] and fell back into the outlet gorge of the Wisconsin River. The swollen waters backed up and formed a lake half as long as the state, bordered on the east by cliffs of ice, and fed by the torrents that fell from melting mountains. The

1. The epoch forty to fifty-five million years ago, when mammals first appeared.
2. Frederick (c. 1123–1190), Holy Roman Emperor (1152–90), known as Frederick Barbarossa; gyrfalcon, a large white falcon used for hunting.
3. Kublai Khan (1215–1294), Chinese emperor, founder of the Mongol dynasty; Marco Polo (c. 1254–1324), Italian traveler to China during Kublai Khan's reign; chapter 56 of Marco Polo's *Travels* describes the Khan's palace at Changanor, where he maintained a marsh for cranes so that he could hunt them.
4. Swedish ornithologist and nature photographer (1885–1967).
5. Roc is the giant Arabian bird who carries off Sinbad in *The Thousand and One Nights*, the famous Middle Eastern collection of tales.
6. A range in south-central Wisconsin.

shorelines of this old lake are still visible; its bottom is the bottom of the great marsh.

The lake rose through the centuries, finally spilling over east of the Baraboo range. There it cut a new channel for the river, and thus drained itself. To the residual lagoons came the cranes, bugling the defeat of the retreating winter, summoning the on-creeping host of living things to their collective task of marsh-building. Floating bogs of sphagnum moss clogged the lowered waters, filled them. Sedge and leatherleaf, tamarack and spruce successively advanced over the bog, anchoring it by their root fabric, sucking out its water, making peat. The lagoons disappeared, but not the cranes. To the moss-meadows that replaced the ancient waterways they returned each spring to dance and bugle and rear their gangling sorrel-colored young. These, albeit birds, are not properly called chicks, but *colts*. I cannot explain why. On some dewy June morning watch them gambol over their ancestral pastures at the heels of the roan mare, and you will see for yourself.

One year not long ago a French trapper in buckskins pushed his canoe up one of the moss-clogged creeks that thread the great marsh. At this attempt to invade their miry stronghold the cranes gave vent to loud and ribald laughter. A century or two later Englishmen came in covered wagons. They chopped clearings in the timbered moraines that border the marsh, and in them planted corn and buckwheat. They did not intend, like the Great Khan at Changanor, to feed the cranes. But the cranes do not question the intent of glaciers, emperors, or pioneers. They ate the grain, and when some irate farmer failed to concede their usufruct in his corn, they trumpeted a warning and sailed across the marsh to another farm.

There was no alfalfa in those days, and the hill-farms made poor hay land, especially in dry years. One dry year someone set a fire in the tamaracks. The burn grew up quickly to bluejoint grass,[7] which, when cleared of dead trees, made a dependable hay meadow. After that, each August, men appeared to cut hay. In winter, after the cranes had gone South, they drove wagons over the frozen bogs and hauled the hay to their farms in the hills. Yearly they plied the marsh with fire and axe, and in two short decades hay meadows dotted the whole expanse.

Each August when the haymakers came to pitch their camps, singing   15
and drinking and lashing their teams with whip and tongue, the cranes whinnied to their colts and retreated to the far fastnesses. "Red shitepokes" the haymakers called them, from the rusty hue which at that season often stains the battleship-gray of crane plumage. After the hay was stacked and the marsh again their own, the cranes returned, to call down out of October skies the migrant flocks from Canada. Together they wheeled over the new-cut stubbles and raided the corn until frosts gave the signal for the winter exodus.

These haymeadow days were the Arcadian age[8] for marsh dwellers. Man

7. A reed grass that grows rapidly on soil that has been burned.
8. An era of innocent peace and contentment.

and beast, plant and soil lived on and with each other in mutual toleration, to the mutual benefit of all. The marsh might have kept on producing hay and prairie chickens, deer and muskrat, crane-music and cranberries forever.

The new overlords did not understand this. They did not include soil, plants, or birds in their ideas of mutuality. The dividends of such a balanced economy were too modest. They envisaged farms not only around, but *in* the marsh. An epidemic of ditch-digging and land-booming set in. The marsh was gridironed with drainage canals, speckled with new fields and farmsteads.

But crops were poor and beset by frosts, to which the expensive ditches added an aftermath of debt. Farmers moved out. Peat beds dried, shrank, caught fire. Sun-energy out of the Pleistocene[9] shrouded the countryside in acrid smoke. No man raised his voice against the waste, only his nose against the smell. After a dry summer not even the winter snows could extinguish the smoldering marsh. Great pockmarks were burned into field and meadow, the scars reaching down to the sands of the old lake, peat-covered these hundred centuries. Rank weeds sprang out of the ashes, to be followed after a year or two by aspen scrub. The cranes were hard put, their numbers shrinking with the remnants of unburned meadow. For them, the song of the power shovel came near being an elegy. The high priests of progress knew nothing of cranes, and cared less. What is a species more or less among engineers? What good is an undrained marsh anyhow?

For a decade or two crops grew poorer, fires deeper, wood-fields larger, and cranes scarcer, year by year. Only reflooding, it appeared, could keep the peat from burning. Meanwhile cranberry growers had, by plugging drainage ditches, reflooded a few spots and obtained good yields. Distant politicians bugled about marginal land, over-production, unemployment relief, conservation. Economists and planners came to look at the marsh. Surveyors, technicians, CCC's,[10] buzzed about. A counter-epidemic of reflooding set in. Government bought land, resettled farmers, plugged ditches wholesale. Slowly the bogs are re-wetting. The fire-pocks become ponds. Grass fires still burn, but they can no longer burn the wetted soil.

20   All this, once the CCC camps were gone, was good for cranes, but not so the thickets of scrub popple that spread inexorably over the old burns, and still less the maze of new roads that inevitably follow governmental conservation. To build a road is so much simpler than to think of what the country really needs. A roadless marsh is seemingly as worthless to the alphabetical conservationist as an undrained one was to the empire-builders. Solitude, the one natural resource still undowered of alphabets, is so far recognized as valuable only by ornithologists and cranes.

Thus always does history, whether of marsh or market place, end in para-

9. The epoch beginning two million years ago and ending about ten thousand years ago; this era saw the last Ice Age and the first appearance of modern humans.

10. Civilian Conservation Corps, a Depression-era agency that sent the unemployed to work in forests and wild areas.

dox. The ultimate value in these marshes is wildness, and the crane is wildness incarnate. But all conservation of wildness is self-defeating, for to cherish we must see and fondle, and when enough have seen and fondled, there is no wilderness left to cherish.

Some day, perhaps in the very process of our benefactions, perhaps in the fullness of geologic time, the last crane will trumpet his farewell and spiral skyward from the great marsh. High out of the clouds will fall the sound of hunting horns, the baying of the phantom pack, the tinkle of little bells, and then a silence never to be broken, unless perchance in some far pasture of the Milky Way.

QUESTIONS

1. Why does Leopold connect cranes with significant historical figures and epochs?

2. Leopold employs white spaces in addition to normal paragraph divisions. Can you explain how these white spaces work in his essay?

3. Is the last paragraph a kind of warning about increased hunting? Fifty years after Leopold's essay, have other dangers to marshlands become more worrisome?

4. Write your own account of a natural phenomenon that has disappeared in your lifetime—or that is in the process of disappearing.

TERRY TEMPEST WILLIAMS *The Clan of One-Breasted Women*

I BELONG TO a Clan of One-breasted Women. My mother, my grandmothers, and six aunts have all had mastectomies. Seven are dead. The two who survive have just completed rounds of chemotherapy and radiation.

I've had my own problems: two biopsies for breast cancer and a small tumor between my ribs diagnosed as "a border-line malignancy."

This is my family history.

Most statistics tell us breast cancer is genetic, hereditary, with rising percentages attached to fatty diets, childlessness, or becoming pregnant after thirty. What they don't say is living in Utah may be the greatest hazard of all.

From the winter 1989 issue of the Witness, *a small circulation journal that calls itself "a feisty, independent, provocative, intelligent, feminist voice of Christian social conscience"; later included in* Refuge: An Unnatural History of Family and Place *(1991).*

5   We are a Mormon family with roots in Utah since 1847. The word-of-wisdom, a religious doctrine of health, kept the women in my family aligned with good foods: no coffee, no tea, tobacco, or alcohol. For the most part, these women were finished having their babies by the time they were thirty. And only one faced breast cancer prior to 1960. Traditionally, as a group of people, Mormons have a low rate of cancer.

Is our family a cultural anomaly? The truth is we didn't think about it. Those who did, usually the men, simply said, "bad genes." The women's attitude was stoic. Cancer was part of life. On February 16, 1971, the eve before my mother's surgery, I accidently picked up the telephone and overheard her ask my grandmother what she could expect.

"Diane, it is one of the most spiritual experiences you will ever encounter."

I quietly put down the receiver.

Two days later, my father took my three brothers and me to the hospital to visit her. She met us in the lobby in a wheelchair. No bandages were visible. I'll never forget her radiance, the way she held herself in a purple velour robe and how she gathered us around her.

10   "Children, I am fine. I want you to know I felt the arms of God around me."

We believed her. My father cried. Our mother, his wife, was thirty-eight years old.

Two years ago, after my mother's death from cancer, my father and I were having dinner together. He had just returned from St. George where his construction company was putting in natural gas lines for towns in southern Utah. He spoke of his love for the country: the sandstoned landscape, bareboned and beautiful. He had just finished hiking the Kolob trail in Zion National Park. We got caught up in reminiscing, recalling with fondness our walk up Angel's Landing on his fiftieth birthday and the years our family had vacationed there. This was a remembered landscape where we had been raised.

Over dessert, I shared a recurring dream of mine. I told my father that for years, as long as I could remember, I saw this flash of light in the night in the desert. That this image had so permeated my being, I could not venture south without seeing it again, on the horizon, illuminating buttes and mesas.

"You did see it," he said.

15   "Saw what?" I asked, a bit tentative.

"The bomb. The cloud. We were driving home from Riverside, California. You were sitting on your mother's lap. She was pregnant. In fact, I remember the date, September 7, 1957. We had just gotten out of the Service. We were driving north, past Las Vegas. It was an hour or so before dawn, when this explosion went off. We not only heard it, but felt it. I thought the oil tanker in front of us had blown up. We pulled over and suddenly, rising from the desert floor, we saw it, clearly, this golden-stemmed cloud, the mushroom. The sky seemed to vibrate with an eerie pink glow. Within a few minutes, a light ash was raining on the car."

I stared at my father. This was new information to me.

"I thought you knew that," my father said. "It was a common occurrence in the fifties."

It was at this moment I realized the deceit I had been living under. Children growing up in the American Southwest, drinking contaminated milk from contaminated cows, even from the contaminated breasts of their mother, my mother—members, years later, of the Clan of One-breasted Women.

It is a well-known story in the Desert West, "The Day We Bombed Utah," or perhaps, "The Years We Bombed Utah."[1] Above ground atomic testing in Nevada took place from January 27, 1951, through July 11, 1962. Not only were the winds blowing north, covering "low use segments of the population" with fallout and leaving sheep dead in their tracks, but the climate was right.[2] The United States of the 1950s was red, white, and blue. The Korean War was raging. McCarthyism was rampant. Ike was it and the Cold War was hot.[3] If you were against nuclear testing, you were for a Communist regime.

Much has been written about this "American nuclear tragedy." Public health was secondary to national security. The Atomic Energy Commissioner, Thomas Murray said, "Gentlemen, we must not let anything interfere with this series of tests, nothing."[4]

Again and again, the American public was told by its government, in spite of burns, blisters, and nausea, "It has been found that the tests may be conducted with adequate assurance of safety under conditions prevailing at the bombing reservations."[5] Assuaging public fears was simply a matter of public relations. "Your best action," an Atomic Energy Commission booklet read, "is not to be worried about fallout." A news release typical of the times stated, "We find no basis for concluding that harm to any individual has resulted from radioactive fallout."[6]

On August 30, 1979, during Jimmy Carter's presidency, a suit was filed

1. Fuller, John G., *The Day We Bombed Utah* (New York: New American Library, 1984) [Williams's note].

2. Discussion on March 14, 1988, with Carole Gallagher, photographer and author, *American Ground Zero: The Secret Nuclear War*, published by Random House, 1994 [Williams's note].

3. Events and figures of the 1950s: the Korean War (1950–53) pitted the combined forces of the Republic of Korea and the United Nations (primarily the United States) against the invading armies of Communist North Korea; McCarthyism, after Republican senator Joseph S. McCarthy, refers to the Communist "witch-hunt" led by the senator; Ike is the nickname of Dwight D. Eisenhower, president from 1953 to 1961; the Cold War refers to the power struggle between the Western powers and the Communist bloc that began at the end of World War II.

4. Szasz, Ferenc M., "Downwind From the Bomb," *Nevada Historical Society Quarterly,* Fall 1987, Vol. XXX, No. 3, p. 185 [Williams's note].

5. Fradkin, Philip L., *Fallout* (Tucson: University of Arizona Press, 1989), 98 [Williams's note].

6. Ibid., 109 [Williams's note].

entitled "Irene Allen vs. the United States of America." Mrs. Allen was the first
to be alphabetically listed with twenty-four test cases, representative of nearly
1200 plaintiffs seeking compensation from the United States government for
cancers caused from nuclear testing in Nevada.

Irene Allen lived in Hurricane, Utah. She was the mother of five children
and had been widowed twice. Her first husband with their two oldest boys had
watched the tests from the roof of the local high school. He died of leukemia
in 1956. Her second husband died of pancreatic cancer in 1978.

25   In a town meeting conducted by Utah Senator Orrin Hatch, shortly before the suit was filed, Mrs. Allen said, "I am not blaming the government, I
want you to know that, Senator Hatch. But I thought if my testimony could
help in any way so this wouldn't happen again to any of the generations coming up after us . . . I am really happy to be here this day to bear testimony of
this."[7]

God-fearing people. This is just one story in an anthology of thousands.

On May 10, 1984, Judge Bruce S. Jenkins handed down his opinion. Ten
of the plaintiffs were awarded damages. It was the first time a federal court
had determined that nuclear tests had been the cause of cancers. For the remaining fourteen test cases, the proof of causation was not sufficient. In spite
of the split decision, it was considered a landmark ruling.[8] It was not to remain
so for long.

In April, 1987, the 10th Circuit Court of Appeals overturned Judge Jenkins' ruling on the basis that the United States was protected from suit by the
legal doctrine of sovereign immunity, the centuries-old idea from England in
the days of absolute monarchs.[9]

In January, 1988, the Supreme Court refused to review the Appeals Court
decision. To our court system, it does not matter whether the United States
Government was irresponsible, whether it lied to its citizens or even that citizens died from the fallout of nuclear testing. What matters is that our government is immune. "The King can do no wrong."

30   In Mormon culture, authority is respected, obedience is revered, and independent thinking is not. I was taught as a young girl not to "make waves" or
"rock the boat."

"Just let it go—" my mother would say. "You know how you feel, that's
what counts."

For many years, I did just that—listened, observed, and quietly formed my
own opinions within a culture that rarely asked questions because they had all
the answers. But one by one, I watched the women in my family die common,
heroic deaths. We sat in waiting rooms hoping for good news, always receiving

7. Town meeting held by Senator Orrin Hatch in St. George, Utah, April 17, 1979,
transcript, 26–28 [Williams's note].

8. Fradkin, Op. cit., 228 [Williams's note].

9. U.S. vs. Allen, 816 Federal Reporter, 2d/1417 (10th Circuit Court 1987), cert. denied, 108 S. CT. 694 (1988) [Williams's note].

the bad. I cared for them, bathed their scarred bodies and kept their secrets. I watched beautiful women become bald as cytoxan, cisplatin and adriamycin were injected into their veins. I held their foreheads as they vomited green-black bile and I shot them with morphine when the pain became inhuman. In the end, I witnessed their last peaceful breaths, becoming a midwife to the re-birth of their souls. But the price of obedience became too high.

The fear and inability to question authority that ultimately killed rural communities in Utah during atmospheric testing of atomic weapons was the same fear I saw being held in my mother's body. Sheep. Dead sheep. The evidence is buried.

I cannot prove that my mother, Diane Dixon Tempest, or my grandmothers, Lettie Romney Dixon and Kathryn Blackett Tempest, along with my aunts contracted cancer from nuclear fallout in Utah. But I can't prove they didn't.

My father's memory was correct, the September blast we drove through in 1957 was part of Operation Plumbbob, one of the most intensive series of bomb tests to be initiated. The flash of light in the night in the desert I had al-ways thought was a dream developed into a family nightmare. It took fourteen years, from 1957 to 1971, for cancer to show up in my mother—the same time, Howard L. Andrews, an authority on radioactive fallout at the National Institutes of Health, says radiation cancer requires to become evident.[10] The more I learn about what it means to be a "downwinder," the more questions I drown in.

What I do know, however, is that as a Mormon woman of the fifth gener-ation of "Latter-Day-Saints," I must question everything, even if it means los-ing my faith, even if it means becoming a member of a border tribe among my own people. Tolerating blind obedience in the name of patriotism or religion ultimately takes our lives.

When the Atomic Energy Commission described the country north of the Nevada Test Site as "virtually uninhabited desert terrain," my family members were some of the "virtual uninhabitants."

One night, I dreamed women from all over the world circling a blazing fire in the desert. They spoke of change, of how they hold the moon in their bellies and wax and wane with its phases. They mocked at the presumption of even-tempered beings and made promises that they would never fear the witch in-side themselves. The women danced wildly as sparks broke away from the flames and entered the night sky as stars.

And they sang a song given to them by Shoshoni grandmothers:

> *Ah ne nah, nah*
> *nin nah nah—*
> *Ah ne nah, nah*
> *nin nah nah—*
> *Nyaga mutzi*

10. Fradkin, Op. cit., 116 [Williams's note].

oh ne nay—
Nyaga mutzi
oh ne nay—[11]

40   The women danced and drummed and sang for weeks, preparing themselves for what was to come. They would reclaim the desert for the sake of
their children, for the sake of the land.

A few miles downwind from the fire circle, bombs were being tested. Rabbits felt the tremors. Their soft leather pads on paws and feet recognized the
shaking sands while the roots of mesquite and sage were smoldering. Rocks
were hot from the inside out and dust devils hummed unnaturally. And each
time there was another nuclear test, ravens watched the desert heave. Stretch
marks appeared. The land was losing its muscle.

The women couldn't bear it any longer. They were mothers. They had suffered labor pains but always under the promise of birth. The red hot pains beneath the desert promised death only as each bomb became a stillborn. A
contract had been broken between human beings and the land. A new contract was being drawn by the women who understood the fate of the earth as
their own.

Under the cover of darkness, ten women slipped under the barbed wire
fence and entered the contaminated country. They were trespassing. They
walked toward the town of Mercury in moonlight, taking their cues from coy-
ote, kit fox, antelope squirrel, and quail. They moved quietly and deliberately
through the maze of Joshua trees. When a hint of daylight appeared they
rested, drinking tea and sharing their rations of food. The women closed their
eyes. The time had come to protest with the heart, that to deny one's genealogy with the earth was to commit treason against one's soul.

At dawn, the women draped themselves in mylar, wrapping long streamers
of silver plastic around their arms to blow in the breeze. They wore clear
masks that became the faces of humanity. And when they arrived on the edge
of Mercury, they carried all the butterflies of a summer day in their wombs.
They paused to allow their courage to settle.

45   The town which forbids pregnant women and children to enter because of
radiation risks to their health was asleep. The women moved through the
streets as winged messengers, twirling around each other in slow motion,
peeking inside homes and watching the easy sleep of men and women. They
were astonished by such stillness and periodically would utter a shrill note or
low cry just to verify life.

The residents finally awoke to what appeared as strange apparitions. Some
simply stared. Others called authorities, and in time, the women were appre-
hended by wary soldiers dressed in desert fatigues. They were taken to a white,

11. This song was sung by the Western Shoshone women as they crossed the line at
the Nevada Test Site on March 18, 1988, as part of their "Reclaim the Land" action.
The translation they gave was: "Consider the rabbits how gently they walk on the earth.
Consider the rabbits how gently they walk on the earth. We remember them. We can
walk gently also. We remember them. We can walk gently also" [Williams's note].

square building on the other edge of Mercury. When asked who they were and why they were there, the women replied, "We are mothers and we have come to reclaim the desert for our children."

The soldiers arrested them. As the ten women were blindfolded and handcuffed, they began singing:

> *You can't forbid us everything*
> *You can't forbid us to think—*
> *You can't forbid our tears to flow*
> *And you can't stop the songs that we sing.*

The women continued to sing louder and louder, until they heard the voices of their sisters moving across the mesa.

> *Ah ne nah, nah*
> *nin nah nah—*
> *Ah ne nah, nah*
> *nin nah nah—*
> *Nyaga mutzi*
> *oh ne nay—*
> *Nyaga mutzi*
> *oh ne nay—*

"Call for re-enforcement," one soldier said.

"We have," interrupted one woman. "We have—and you have no idea of our numbers." 50

On March 18, 1988, I crossed the line at the Nevada Test Site and was arrested with nine other Utahns for trespassing on military lands. They are still conducting nuclear tests in the desert. Ours was an act of civil disobedience. But as I walked toward the town of Mercury, it was more than a gesture of peace. It was a gesture on behalf of the Clan of One-Breasted Women.

As one officer cinched the handcuffs around my wrists, another frisked my body. She found a pen and a pad of paper tucked inside my left boot.

"And these?" she asked sternly.

"Weapons," I replied.

Our eyes met. I smiled. She pulled the leg of my trousers back over my 55 boot.

"Step forward, please," she said as she took my arm.

We were booked under an afternoon sun and bussed to Tonapah, Nevada. It was a two-hour ride. This was familiar country to me. The Joshua trees standing their ground had been named by my ancestors who believed they looked like prophets pointing west to the promised land. These were the same trees that bloomed each spring, flowers appearing like white flames in the Mojave. And I recalled a full moon in May when my mother and I had walked among them, flushing out mourning doves and owls.

The bus stopped short of town. We were released. The officials thought it was a cruel joke to leave us stranded in the desert with no way to get home. What they didn't realize is that we were home, soul-centered and strong, women who recognized the sweet smell of sage as fuel for our spirits.

QUESTIONS

1. Williams uses a variety of evidence in this essay, including personal memory, family history, government documents, and other sources. List the evidence and the order in which she uses it. Why does Williams present her material in this order?

2. The essay begins with a description of what Williams later calls a "family nightmare" and ends with a dream vision. What is the rhetorical effect of this interactive opening and closing?

3. What does Williams mean by the statement "I must question everything" (paragraph 36)?

4. Do some research on an environmental issue that affects you or your family, and, using Williams as a model, write an essay that combines your personal experience and your research.

ETHICS

MARK TWAIN *Advice to Youth*

B EING TOLD I WOULD be expected to talk here, I inquired what sort of a talk I ought to make. They said it should be something suitable to youth—something didactic, instructive, or something in the nature of good advice. Very well. I have a few things in my mind which I have often longed to say for the instruction of the young; for it is in one's tender early years that such things will best take root and be most enduring and most valuable. First, then, I will say to you, my young friends—and I say it beseechingly, urgingly—

Always obey your parents, when they are present. This is the best policy in the long run, because if you don't they will make you. Most parents think they know better than you do, and you can generally make more by humoring that superstition than you can by acting on your own better judgment.

Be respectful to your superiors, if you have any, also to strangers, and sometimes to others. If a person offend you, and you are in doubt as to whether it was intentional or not, do not resort to extreme measures; simply watch your chance and hit him with a brick. That will be sufficient. If you shall find that he had not intended any offense, come out frankly and confess yourself in the wrong when you struck him; acknowledge it like a man and say you didn't mean to. Yes, always avoid violence; in this age of charity and kindliness, the time has gone by for such things. Leave dynamite to the low and unrefined.

Go to bed early, get up early—this is wise. Some authorities say get up with the sun; some others say get up with one thing, some with another. But a lark is really the best thing to get up with. It gives you a splendid reputation with everybody to know that you get up with the lark; and if you get the right kind of a lark, and work at him right, you can easily train him to get up at half past nine, every time—it is no trick at all.

Now as to the matter of lying. You want to be very careful about lying; otherwise you are nearly sure to get caught. Once caught, you can never again be, in the eyes of the good and the pure, what you were before. Many a young person has injured himself permanently through a single clumsy and illfinished lie, the result of carelessness born of incomplete training. Some authorities hold that the young ought not to lie at all. That, of course, is putting it rather stronger than necessary; still, while I cannot go quite so far as that, I do maintain, and I believe I am right, that the young ought to be temperate in the use

5

Text of a lecture given by Twain (a.k.a. Samuel Clemens) in 1882. The original audience and occasion for this lecture remain unknown.

of this great art until practice and experience shall give them that confidence, elegance, and precision which alone can make the accomplishment graceful and profitable. Patience, diligence, painstaking attention to detail—these are the requirements; these, in time, will make the student perfect; upon these, and upon these only, may he rely as the sure foundation for future eminence. Think what tedious years of study, thought, practice, experience, went to the equipment of that peerless old master who was able to impose upon the whole world the lofty and sounding maxim that "truth is mighty and will prevail"—the most majestic compound fracture of fact which any of woman born has yet achieved. For the history of our race, and each individual's experience, are sown thick with evidence that a truth is not hard to kill and that a lie told well is immortal. There is in Boston a monument of the man who discovered anaesthesia; many people are aware, in these latter days, that that man didn't discover it at all, but stole the discovery from another man. Is this truth mighty, and will it prevail? Ah no, my hearers, the monument is made of hardy material, but the lie it tells will outlast it a million years. An awkward, feeble, leaky lie is a thing which you ought to make it your unceasing study to avoid; such a lie as that has no more real permanence than an average truth. Why, you might as well tell the truth at once and be done with it. A feeble, stupid, preposterous lie will not live two years—except it be a slander upon somebody. It is indestructible, then, of course, but that is no merit of yours. A final word: begin your practice of this gracious and beautiful art early—begin now. If I had begun earlier, I could have learned how.

Never handle firearms carelessly. The sorrow and suffering that have been caused through the innocent but heedless handling of firearms by the young! Only four days ago, right in the next farmhouse to the one where I am spending the summer, a grandmother, old and gray and sweet, one of the loveliest spirits in the land, was sitting at her work, when her young grandson crept in and got down an old, battered, rusty gun which had not been touched for many years and was supposed not to be loaded, and pointed it at her, laughing and threatening to shoot. In her fright she ran screaming and pleading toward the door on the other side of the room; but as she passed him he placed the gun almost against her very breast and pulled the trigger! He had supposed it was not loaded. And he was right—it wasn't. So there wasn't any harm done. It is the only case of that kind I ever heard of. Therefore, just the same, don't you meddle with old unloaded firearms; they are the most deadly and unerring things that have ever been created by man. You don't have to take any pains at all with them; you don't have to have a rest, you don't have to have any sights on the gun, you don't have to take aim, even. No, you just pick out a relative and bang away, and you are sure to get him. A youth who can't hit a cathedral at thirty yards with a Gatling gun in three-quarters of an hour, can take up an old empty musket and bag his grandmother every time, at a hundred. Think what Waterloo[1] would have been if one of the armies had been boys armed with old muskets

---

1. The bloody battle (1815) in which Napoleon suffered his final defeat at the hands of English and German troops under the Duke of Wellington.

supposed not to be loaded, and the other army had been composed of their female relations. The very thought of it makes one shudder.

There are many sorts of books; but good ones are the sort for the young to
read. Remember that. They are a great, an inestimable, an unspeakable means
of improvement. Therefore be careful in your selection, my young friends; be
very careful; confine yourselves exclusively to Robertson's Sermons, Baxter's
Saint's Rest, The Innocents Abroad, and works of that kind.[2]

But I have said enough. I hope you will treasure up the instructions which
I have given you, and make them a guide to your feet and a light to your understanding. Build your character thoughtfully and painstakingly upon these
precepts, and by and by, when you have got it built, you will be surprised and
gratified to see how nicely and sharply it resembles everybody else's.

2. The five volumes of sermons by Frederick William Robertson (1816–1853), an English clergyman, and Richard Baxter's *Saints' Everlasting Rest* (1650) were well-known
religious works; *The Innocents Abroad* is Twain's own collection of humorous travel
sketches.

QUESTIONS

1. Underline the various pieces of "serious" advice that Twain offers and notice where
and how he begins to turn each one upside down.

2. Mark Twain was already known as a comic author when he delivered "Advice to
Youth" as a lecture in 1882; it was not published until 1923. We do not know the circumstances under which he delivered it or to whom. Using evidence from the text,
imagine both the circumstances and the audience.

3. Rewrite "Advice to Youth" for a modern audience, perhaps as a lecture for a school
assembly or a commencement address.

JONATHAN RAUCH   *In Defense of Prejudice*

THE WAR ON PREJUDICE is now, in all likelihood, the
most uncontroversial social movement in America. Opposition to "hate speech," formerly identified
with the liberal left, has become a bipartisan piety. In
the past year, groups and factions that agree on
nothing else have agreed that the public expression
of any and all prejudices must be forbidden. On the left, protesters and edito-

Originally published in Harper's Magazine *(May 1995) with the subtitle "Why Incendiary
Speech Must Be Protected." Articles in* Harper's *focus on current issues in politics, science,
and the arts.*

rialists have insisted that Francis L. Lawrence resign as president of Rutgers University for describing blacks as "a disadvantaged population that doesn't have that genetic, hereditary background to have a higher average." On the other side of the ideological divide, Ralph Reed, the executive director of the Christian Coalition, responded to criticism of the religious right by calling a press conference to denounce a supposed outbreak of "name-calling, scapegoating, and religious bigotry." Craig Rogers, an evangelical Christian student at California State University, recently filed a $2.5 million sexual-harassment suit against a lesbian professor of psychology, claiming that anti-male bias in one of her lectures violated campus rules and left him feeling "raped and trapped."

In universities and on Capitol Hill, in workplaces and newsrooms, authorities are declaring that there is no place for racism, sexism, homophobia, Christian-bashing, and other forms of prejudice in public debate or even in private thought. "Only when racism and other forms of prejudice are expunged," say the crusaders for sweetness and light, "can minorities be safe and society be fair." So sweet, this dream of a world without prejudice. But the very last thing society should do is seek to utterly eradicate racism and other forms of prejudice.

I suppose I should say, in the customary I-hope-I-don't-sound-too-defensive tone, that I am not a racist and that this is not an article favoring racism or any other particular prejudice. It is an article favoring intellectual pluralism, which permits the expression of various forms of bigotry and always will. Although we like to hope that a time will come when no one will believe that people come in types and that each type belongs with its own kind, I doubt such a day will ever arrive. By all indications, *Homo sapiens* is a tribal species for whom "us versus them" comes naturally and must be continually pushed back. Where there is genuine freedom of expression, there will be racist expression. There will also be people who believe that homosexuals are sick or threaten children or—especially among teenagers—are rightful targets of manly savagery. Homosexuality will always be incomprehensible to most people, and what is incomprehensible is feared. As for anti-Semitism, it appears to be a hardier virus than influenza. If you want pluralism, then you get racism and sexism and homophobia, and communism and fascism and xenophobia and tribalism, and that is just for a start. If you want to believe in intellectual freedom and the progress of knowledge and the advancement of science and all those other good things, then you must swallow hard and accept this: for as thickheaded and wayward an animal as us, the realistic question is how to make the best of prejudice, not how to eradicate it.

Indeed, "eradicating prejudice" is so vague a proposition as to be meaningless. Distinguishing prejudice reliably and nonpolitically from nonprejudice, or even defining it crisply, is quite hopeless. We all feel we know prejudice when we see it. But do we? At the University of Michigan, a student said in a classroom discussion that he considered homosexuality a disease treatable with therapy. He was summoned to a formal disciplinary hearing for violating the school's policy against speech that "victimizes" people based on "sexual orientation." Now, the evidence is abundant that this particular hypothesis is wrong, and any American homosexual can attest to the harm that the student's hypothesis has inflicted on many real people. But was it a statement of prejudice or of misguided belief? Hate speech or hypothesis? Many Americans who do not regard themselves as bigots or haters believe that homosexuality is a treatable disease. They may be wrong, but are they all bigots? I am unwilling to say so, and if you are willing, beware. The line between a prejudiced belief and a merely controversial one is elusive, and the harder you look the more elusive it becomes. "God hates homosexuals" is a statement of fact, not of bias, to those who believe it; "American criminals are disproportionately black" is a statement of bias, not of fact, to those who disbelieve it.

Who is right? You may decide, and so may others, and there is no need to agree. That is the great innovation of intellectual pluralism (which is to say, of post-Enlightenment science, broadly defined). We cannot know in advance or for sure which belief is prejudice and which is truth, but to advance knowledge we don't need to know. The genius of intellectual pluralism lies not in doing away with prejudices and dogmas but in channeling them—making them socially productive by pitting prejudice against prejudice and dogma against dogma, exposing all to withering public criticism. What survives at the end of the day is our base of knowledge.

5

What they told us in high school about this process is very largely a lie. The Enlightenment tradition taught us that science is orderly, antiseptic, rational, the province of detached experimenters and high-minded logicians. In the popular view, science stands for reason against prejudice, openmindedness against dogma, calm consideration against passionate attachment—all personified by pop-science icons like the magisterially deductive Sherlock Holmes, the coolly analytic Mr. Spock, the genially authoritative Mr. Science (from our junior-high science films). Yet one of science's dirty secrets is that although science as a whole is as unbiased as anything human can be, scientists are just as biased as anyone else, sometimes more so. "One of the strengths of science," writes the philosopher of science David L. Hull, "is that it does not require that scientists be unbiased, only that different scientists have different biases." Another dirty secret is that, no less than the rest of us, scientists can be dogmatic and pigheaded. "Although this pigheadedness often damages the careers of individual scientists," says Hull, "it is beneficial for the manifest goal of science," which relies on people to invest years in their ideas and defend them passionately. And the dirtiest secret of all, if you believe in the antiseptic popular view of science, is that this most ostensibly rational of enterprises depends on the most irrational of motives—ambition, narcissism, animus, even revenge. "Scientists acknowledge that among their motivations are natural curiosity, the love of truth, and the desire to help humanity, but other inducements exist as well, and one of them is to 'get that son of a bitch,'" says Hull. "Time and again, scientists whom I interviewed described the powerful spur that 'showing that son of a bitch' supplied to their own research."

Many people, I think, are bewildered by this unvarnished and all too human view of science. They believe that for a system to be unprejudiced, the people in it must also be unprejudiced. In fact, the opposite is true. Far from eradicating ugly or stupid ideas and coarse or unpleasant motives, intellectual pluralism relies upon them to excite intellectual passion and redouble scientific effort. I know of no modern idea more ugly and stupid than that the Holocaust never happened, nor any idea more viciously motivated. Yet the deniers' claims that the Auschwitz gas chambers could not have worked led to closer study and, in 1993, research showing, at last, how they actually did work. Thanks to prejudice and stupidity, another opening for doubt has been shut.

An enlightened and efficient intellectual regime lets a million prejudices bloom, including many that you or I may regard as hateful or grotesque. It avoids any attempt to stamp out prejudice, because stamping out prejudice really means forcing everyone to share the same prejudice, namely that of whoever is in authority. The great American philosopher Charles Sanders Peirce wrote in 1877: "When complete agreement could not otherwise be reached, a general massacre of all who have not thought in a certain way has proved a very effective means of settling opinion in a country." In speaking of "settling opinion," Peirce was writing about one of the two or three most fundamental problems that any human society must confront and solve. For most societies down through the centuries, this problem was dealt with in the manner he described: errors were identified by the authorities—priests, politburos, dictators—or by mass opinion, and then the error-makers were eliminated along with their putative mistakes. "Let all men who reject the established belief be terrified into silence," wrote Peirce, describing this system. "This method has, from the earliest times, been one of the chief means of upholding correct theological and political doctrines."

Intellectual pluralism substitutes a radically different doctrine: we kill our mistakes rather than each other. Here I draw on another great philosopher, the late Karl Popper, who pointed out that the critical method of science "consists in letting our hypotheses die in our stead." Those who are in error are not (or are not supposed to be) banished or excommunicated or forced to sign a renunciation or required to submit to "rehabilitation" or sent for psychological counseling. It is the error we punish, not the errant. By letting people make errors—even mischievous, spiteful errors (as, for instance, Galileo's insistence on Copernicanism was taken to be in 1633)—pluralism creates room to challenge orthodoxy, think imaginatively, experiment boldly. Brilliance and bigotry are empowered in the same stroke.

10   Pluralism is the principle that protects and makes a place in human company for that loneliest and most vulnerable of all minorities, the minority who is hounded and despised among blacks and whites, gays and straights, who is suspect or criminal among every tribe and in every nation of the world, and yet on whom progress depends: the dissident. I am not saying that dissent is always or even usually enlightened. Most of the time it is foolish and self-serving. No dissident has the right to be taken seriously, and the fact that Aryan Nation[1] racists or Nation of Islam[2] anti-Semites are unorthodox does

1. A white separatist religious group in the United States.
2. An African American religious organization in the United States that combines some of the practices and beliefs of Islam with a philosophy of black separatism.

not entitle them to respect. But what goes around comes around. As a supporter of gay marriage, for example, I reject the majority's view of family, and
as a Jew I reject its view of God. I try to be civil, but the fact is that most
Americans regard my views on marriage as a reckless assault on the most fundamental of all institutions, and many people are more than a little discom-
fited by the statement, "Jesus Christ was no more divine than anybody else"
(which is why so few people ever say it). Trap the racists and anti-Semites, and
you lay a trap for me too. Hunt for them with eradication in your mind, and
you have brought dissent itself within your sights.

The new crusade against prejudice waves aside such warnings. Like earlier crusades against antisocial ideas, the mission is fueled by good (if cock-
sure) intentions and a genuine sense of urgency. Some kinds of error are held
to be intolerable, like pollutants that even in small traces poison the water for
a whole town. Some errors are so pernicious as to damage real people's lives,
so wrongheaded that no person of right mind or goodwill could support them.
Like their forebears of other stripe—the Church in its campaigns against
heretics, the McCarthyites in their campaigns against Communists[3]—the
modern anti-racist and anti-sexist and anti-homophobic campaigners are totalists, demanding not that misguided ideas and ugly expressions be corrected or
criticized but that they be eradicated. They make war not on errors but on error, and like other totalists they act in the name of public safety—the safety,
especially, of minorities.

The sweeping implications of this challenge to pluralism are not, I think, well
enough understood by the public at large. Indeed, the new brand of totalism
has yet even to be properly named. "Multiculturalism," for instance, is much
too broad. "Political correctness" comes closer but is too trendy and snide. For
lack of anything else, I will call the new anti-pluralism "purism," since its major tenet is that society cannot be just until the last traces of invidious prejudice have been scrubbed away. Whatever you call it, the purists' way of seeing
things has spread through American intellectual life with remarkable speed, so
much so that many people will blink at you uncomprehendingly or even call
you a racist (or sexist or homophobe, etc.) if you suggest that expressions of
racism should be tolerated or that prejudice has its part to play.

The new purism sets out, to begin with, on a campaign against words, for
words are the currency of prejudice, and if prejudice is hurtful then so must
be prejudiced words. "We are not safe when these violent words are among
us," wrote Mari Matsuda, then a UCLA law professor. Here one imagines
gangs of racist words swinging chains and smashing heads in back alleys. To
suppress bigoted language seems, at first blush, reasonable, but it quickly
leads to a curious result. A peculiar kind of verbal shamanism takes root, as

---

3. In the early 1950s, Senator Joseph McCarthy pursued suspected Communists in the
government and throughout the nation. Although his "Fight for America" did not result
in a single conviction, he and his followers ruined the lives and careers of many they investigated. McCarthy was later condemned for "conduct contrary to Senatorial traditions."

though certain expressions, like curses or magical incantations, carry in themselves the power to hurt or heal—as though words were bigoted rather than people. "Context is everything," people have always said. The use of the word "nigger" in *Huckleberry Finn*[4] does not make the book an "act" of hate speech—or does it? In the new view, this is no longer so clear. The very utterance of the word "nigger" (at least by a non-black) is a racist act. When a *Sacramento Bee* cartoonist put the word "nigger" mockingly in the mouth of a white supremacist, there were howls of protest and 1,400 canceled subscriptions and an editorial apology, even though the word was plainly being invoked against racists, not against blacks.

Faced with escalating demands of verbal absolutism, newspapers issue lists of forbidden words. The expressions "gyp" (derived from "Gypsy") and "Dutch treat" were among the dozens of terms stricken as "offensive" in a much-ridiculed (and later withdrawn) *Los Angeles Times* speech code. The University of Missouri journalism school issued a *Dictionary of Cautionary Words and Phrases*, which included "*Buxom*: Offensive reference to a woman's chest. Do not use. See 'Woman.' *Codger*: Offensive reference to a senior citizen."

15   As was bound to happen, purists soon discovered that chasing around after words like "gyp" or "buxom" hardly goes to the roots of the problem. As long as they remain bigoted, bigots will simply find other words. If they can't call you a kike then they will say Jewboy, Judas, or Hebe, and when all those are banned they will press words like "oven" and "lampshade" into their service. The vocabulary of hate is potentially as rich as your dictionary, and all you do by banning language used by cretins is to let them decide what the rest of us may say. The problem, some purists have concluded, must therefore go much deeper than laws: it must go to the deeper level of ideas. Racism, sexism, homophobia, and the rest must be built into the very structure of American society and American patterns of thought, so pervasive yet so insidious that, like water to a fish, they are both omnipresent and unseen. The mere existence of prejudice constructs a society whose very nature is prejudiced.

This line of thinking was pioneered by feminists, who argued that pornography, more than just being expressive, is an act by which men construct an oppressive society. Racial activists quickly picked up the argument. Racist expressions are themselves acts of oppression, they said. "All racist speech constructs the social reality that constrains the liberty of nonwhites because of their race," wrote Charles R. Lawrence III, then a law professor at Stanford. From the purist point of view, a society with even one racist is a racist society, because the idea itself threatens and demeans its targets. They cannot feel wholly safe or wholly welcome as long as racism is present. Pluralism says: There will always be some racists. Marginalize them, ignore them, exploit them, ridicule them, take pains to make their policies illegal, but otherwise leave them alone. Purists say: That's not enough. Society cannot be just until these pervasive and oppressive ideas are searched out and eradicated.

And so what is now under way is a growing drive to eliminate prejudice

---

4. Mark Twain's 1889 novel includes coarse language, some of it now called racist.

from every corner of society. I doubt that many people have noticed how far-reaching this anti-pluralist movement is becoming.

In universities: Dozens of universities have adopted codes proscribing speech or other expression that (this is from Stanford's policy, which is more or less representative) "is intended to insult or stigmatize an individual or a small number of individuals on the basis of their sex, race, color, handicap, religion, sexual orientation or national and ethnic origin." Some codes punish only persistent harassment of a targeted individual, but many, following the purist doctrine that even one racist is too many, go much further. At Penn, an administrator declared: "We at the University of Pennsylvania have guaranteed students and the community that they can live in a community free of sexism, racism, and homophobia." Here is the purism that gives "political correctness" its distinctive combination of puffy high-mindedness and authoritarian zeal.

In school curricula: "More fundamental than eliminating racial segregation has to be the removal of racist thinking, assumptions, symbols, and materials in the curriculum," writes theorist Molefi Kete Asante. In practice, the effort to "remove racist thinking" goes well beyond striking egregious references from textbooks. In many cases it becomes a kind of mental engineering in which students are encouraged to see prejudice.

Ah, but the task of scouring minds clean is Augean.[5] "Nobody escapes," said a Rutgers University report on campus prejudice. Bias and prejudice, it found, cross every conceivable line, from sex to race to politics: "No matter who you are, no matter what the color of your skin, no matter what your gender or sexual orientation, no matter what you believe, no matter how you behave, there is somebody out there who doesn't like people of your kind." Charles Lawrence writes: "Racism is ubiquitous. We are all racists." If he means that most of us think racist thoughts of some sort at one time or another, he is right. If we are going to "eliminate prejudices and biases from our society," then the work of the prejudice police is unending. They are doomed to hunt and hunt, scour and scour and scour.

20

What is especially dismaying is that the purists pursue prejudice in the name of protecting minorities. In order to protect people like me (homosexual), they must pursue people like me (dissident). In order to bolster minority self-esteem, they suppress minority opinion. There are, of course, all kinds of practical and legal problems with the purists' campaign: the incursions against the First Amendment; the inevitable abuses by prosecutors and activists who define as "hateful" or "violent" whatever speech they dislike or can score points off of; the lack of any evidence that repressing prejudice eliminates rather than inflames it. But minorities, of all people, ought to remember that by definition we cannot prevail by numbers, and we generally cannot

5. In Greek mythology, Heracles was assigned twelve difficult and dangerous tasks, referred to as the Labors of Heracles. One task required cleaning the enormous stables of Augeas, king of Elis, which Heracles did by diverting the rivers Alpheus and Peneus so that they flowed through the stables and swept them clean.

prevail by force. Against the power of ignorant mass opinion and group prejudice and superstition, we have only our voices. If you doubt that minorities'
voices are powerful weapons, think of the lengths to which Southern officials
went to silence the Reverend Martin Luther King Jr. (recall that the city commissioner of Montgomery, Alabama, won a $500,000 libel suit, later over-
turned in *New York Times v. Sullivan* [1964], regarding an advertisement in
the *Times* placed by civil-rights leaders who denounced the Montgomery police). Think of how much gay people have improved their lot over twenty-five
years simply by refusing to remain silent. Recall the Michigan student who
was prosecuted for saying that homosexuality is a treatable disease, and notice that he was black. Under that Michigan speech code, more than twenty
blacks were charged with racist speech, while no instance of racist speech by
whites was punished. In Florida, the hate-speech law was invoked against a
black man who called a policeman a "white cracker"; not so surprisingly, in
the first hate-crimes case to reach the Supreme Court, the victim was white
and the defendant black.

In the escalating war against "prejudice," the right is already learning to
play by the rules that were pioneered by the purist activists of the left. Last
year leading Democrats, including the President, criticized the Republican
Party for being increasingly in the thrall of the Christian right. Some of the
rhetoric was harsh ("fire-breathing Christian radical right"), but it wasn't vicious or even clearly wrong. Never mind: when Democratic Representative
Vic Fazio said Republicans were "being forced to the fringes by the aggressive
political tactics of the religious right," the chairman of the Republican National Committee, Haley Barbour, said, "Christian-bashing" was "the left's
preferred form of religious bigotry." Bigotry! Prejudice! "Christians active in
politics are now on the receiving end of an extraordinary campaign of bias
and prejudice," said the conservative leader William J. Bennett. One discerns,
here, where the new purism leads. Eventually, any criticism of any group will
be "prejudice."

Here is the ultimate irony of the new purism: words, which pluralists
hope can be substituted for violence, are redefined by purists *as* violence. "The
experience of being called 'nigger,' 'spic,' 'Jap,' or 'kike' is like receiving a slap in
the face," Charles Lawrence wrote in 1990. "Psychic injury is no less an injury
than being struck in the face, and it often is far more severe." This kind of talk
is commonplace today. Epithets, insults, often even polite expressions of
what's taken to be prejudice are called by purists "assaultive speech," "words
that wound," "verbal violence." "To me, racial epithets are not speech," one
University of Michigan law professor said. "They are bullets." In her speech
accepting the 1993 Nobel Prize for Literature in Stockholm, Sweden, the author Toni Morrison[6] said this: "Oppressive language does more than represent
violence; it is violence."

It is not violence. I am thinking back to a moment on the subway in
Washington, a little thing. I was riding home late one night and a squad of

6. African American author (b. 1931).

noisy kids, maybe seventeen or eighteen years old, noisily piled into the car. They yelled across the car and a girl said, "Where do we get off?"

A boy said, "Farragut North."   25

The girl: "*Faggot* North!"

The boy: "Yeah! Faggot North!"

General hilarity.

First, before the intellect resumes control, there is a moment of fear, an animal moment. Who are they? How many of them? How dangerous! Where is the way out? All of these things are noted preverbally and assessed by the gut. Then the brain begins an assessment: they are sober, this is probably too public a place for them to do it, there are more girls than boys, they were just talking, it is probably nothing.

They didn't notice me and there was no incident. The teenage babble   30
flowed on, leaving me to think. I became interested in my own reaction: the jump of fear out of nowhere like an alert animal, the sense for a brief time that one is naked and alone and should hide or run away. For a time, one ceases to be a human being and becomes instead a faggot.

The fear engendered by these words is real. The remedy is as clear and as imperfect as ever: protect citizens against violence. This, I grant, is something that American society has never done very well and now does quite poorly. It is no solution to define words as violence or prejudice as oppression, and then by cracking down on words or thoughts pretend that we are doing something about violence and oppression. No doubt it is easier to pass a speech code or hate-crimes law and proclaim the streets safer than actually to make the streets safer, but the one must never be confused with the other. Every cop or prosecutor chasing words is one fewer chasing criminals. In a world rife with real violence and oppression, full of Rwandas and Bosnias and eleven-year-olds spraying bullets at children in Chicago and in turn being executed by gang lords, it is odious of Toni Morrison to say that words are violence.

Indeed, equating "verbal violence" with physical violence is a treacherous, mischievous business. Not long ago a writer was charged with viciously and gratuitously wounding the feelings and dignity of millions of people. He was charged, in effect, with exhibiting flagrant prejudice against Muslims and outrageously slandering their beliefs. "What is freedom of expression?" mused Salman Rushdie[7] a year after the ayatollahs sentenced him to death and put a price on his head. "Without the freedom to offend, it ceases to exist." I can think of nothing sadder than that minority activists, in their haste to make the world better, should be the ones to forget the lesson of Rushdie's plight: for minorities, pluralism, not purism, is the answer. The campaigns to eradicate prejudice—all of them, the speech codes and workplace restrictions and

7. British novelist of Indian descent (b. 1947). Muslims condemned Rushdie's novel *The Satanic Verses* (1988) as an attack on the Islamic faith; in 1989, Iran's Ayatollah Khomeini declared that Rushdie and everyone involved in the book's publication should be put to death; the death sentence was lifted in 1998.

mandatory therapy for accused bigots and all the rest—should stop, now. The whole objective of eradicating prejudice, as opposed to correcting and criticizing it, should be repudiated as a fool's errand. Salman Rushdie is right, Toni Morrison wrong, and minorities belong at his side, not hers.

Questions

1. Rauch advances a controversial argument: that we should allow prejudice to be expressed rather than seek to repress or eradicate it. How, in the opening paragraphs, does he establish himself as a reasonable, even likable person whose views should be heard? Where else in the essay does he create this persona? Why is persona (or *ethos*) important in ethical argument?

2. What does Rauch mean by "intellectual pluralism" (paragraph 3)? Where does he come closest to giving a definition? How does he use examples to imply a definition?

3. In the third section of the essay (paragraphs 12–20), Rauch defines the position antithetical to his own as "purism." Why does he choose this term rather than another? What does it mean?

4. What are some counterarguments to Rauch's position? How many of these arguments does Rauch himself raise and refute? How effective is he at refuting them?

5. Rauch ends with quotations from Toni Morrison and Salman Rushdie. Why? What do their experiences as writers add to his argument?

Michael Levin   *The Case for Torture*

I T IS GENERALLY assumed that torture is impermissible, a throwback to a more brutal age. Enlightened societies reject it outright, and regimes suspected of using it risk the wrath of the United States.

I believe this attitude is unwise. There are situations in which torture is not merely permissible but morally mandatory. Moreover, these situations are moving from the realm of imagination to fact.

Death: Suppose a terrorist has hidden an atomic bomb on Manhattan Island which will detonate at noon on July 4 unless . . . (here follow the usual demands for money and release of his friends from jail). Suppose, further, that he is caught at 10 a.m. of the fateful day, but—preferring death to failure—won't disclose where the bomb is. What do we do? If we follow due process—wait for his lawyer, arraign him—millions of people will die. If the only way to

Originally published in Newsweek *in the "My Turn" column on June 7, 1982. The magazine introduced the column in 1972 to encourage members of the general public, as well as professional writers, to voice their views on current events and issues.*

save those lives is to subject the terrorist to the most excruciating possible pain, what grounds can there be for not doing so? I suggest there are none. In any case, I ask you to face the question with an open mind.

Torturing the terrorist is unconstitutional? Probably. But millions of lives surely outweigh constitutionality. Torture is barbaric? Mass murder is far more barbaric. Indeed, letting millions of innocents die in deference to one who flaunts his guilt is moral cowardice, an unwillingness to dirty one's hands. If *you* caught the terrorist, could you sleep nights knowing that millions died because you couldn't bring yourself to apply the electrodes?

Once you concede that torture is justified in extreme cases, you have admitted that the decision to use torture is a matter of balancing innocent lives against the means needed to save them. You must now face more realistic cases involving more modest numbers. Someone plants a bomb on a jumbo jet. He alone can disarm it, and his demands cannot be met (or if they can, we refuse to set a precedent by yielding to his threats). Surely we can, we must, do anything to the extortionist to save the passengers. How can we tell 300, or 100, or 10 people who never asked to be put in danger, "I'm sorry, you'll have to die in agony, we just couldn't bring ourselves to . . ."

Here are the results of an informal poll about a third, hypothetical, case. Suppose a terrorist group kidnapped a newborn baby from a hospital. I asked four mothers if they would approve of torturing kidnappers if that were necessary to get their own newborns back. All said yes, the most "liberal" adding that she would like to administer it herself.

I am not advocating torture as punishment. Punishment is addressed to deeds irrevocably past. Rather, I am advocating torture as an acceptable measure for preventing future evils. So understood, it is far less objectionable than many extant punishments. Opponents of the death penalty, for example, are forever insisting that executing a murderer will not bring back his victim (as if the purpose of capital punishment were supposed to be resurrection, not deterrence or retribution). But torture, in the cases described, is intended not to bring anyone back but to keep innocents from being dispatched. The most powerful argument against using torture as a punishment or to secure confessions is that such practices disregard the rights of the individual. Well, if the individual is all that important—and he is—it is correspondingly important to protect the rights of individuals threatened by terrorists. If life is so valuable that it must never be taken, the lives of the innocents must be saved even at the price of hurting the one who endangers them.

Better precedents for torture are assassination and pre-emptive attack. No Allied leader would have flinched at assassinating Hitler, had that been possible. (The Allies did assassinate Heydrich.)[1] Americans would be angered to learn that Roosevelt could have had Hitler killed in 1943—thereby shortening the war and saving millions of lives—but refused on moral grounds. Similarly, if nation A learns that nation B is about to launch an unprovoked attack, A has

1. Reinhard Heydrich (1904–1942), German head of the Nazi SS who was shot by Czech resistance fighters.

a right to save itself by destroying B's military capability first. In the same way, if the police can by torture save those who would otherwise die at the hands of kidnappers or terrorists, they must.

Idealism: There is an important difference between terrorists and their victims that should mute talk of the terrorists' "rights." The terrorist's victims are at risk unintentionally, not having asked to be endangered. But the terrorist knowingly initiated his actions. Unlike his victims, he volunteered for the risks of his deed. By threatening to kill for profit or idealism, he renounces civilized standards, and he can have no complaint if civilization tries to thwart him by whatever means necessary.

10   Just as torture is justified only to save lives (not extort confessions or recantations), it is justifiably administered only to those *known* to hold innocent lives in their hands. Ah, but how can the authorities ever be sure they have the right malefactor? Isn't there a danger of error and abuse? Won't We turn into Them?

Questions like these are disingenuous in a world in which terrorists proclaim themselves and perform for television. The name of their game is public recognition. After all, you can't very well intimidate a government into releasing your freedom fighters unless you announce that it is your group that has seized its embassy. "Clear guilt" is difficult to define, but when 40 million people see a group of masked gunmen seize an airplane on the evening news, there is not much question about who the perpetrators are. There will be hard cases where the situation is murkier. Nonetheless, a line demarcating the legitimate use of torture can be drawn. Torture only the obviously guilty, and only for the sake of saving innocents, and the line between Us and Them will remain clear.

There is little danger that the Western democracies will lose their way if they choose to inflict pain as one way of preserving order. Paralysis in the face of evil is the greater danger. Some day soon a terrorist will threaten tens of thousands of lives, and torture will be the only way to save them. We had better start thinking about this.

QUESTIONS

1. On what assumptions about torture (and its efficacy) does Levin's argument rest? Do you agree with his assumptions? Why or why not?

2. What support does Levin provide for his position? List the key evidence that Levin gives, and analyze how it is or is not compelling.

3. Write your own argument for or against the use of torture. Be sure to consider how you will support your position and how you will answer readers who hold a different view.

Tom Regan   *The Case for Animal Rights*

I REGARD MYSELF as an advocate of animal rights—as a part of the animal rights movement. That movement, as I conceive it, is committed to a number of goals, including:

- the total abolition of the use of animals in science;
- the total dissolution of commercial animal agriculture;
- the total elimination of commercial and sport hunting and trapping.

There are, I know, people who profess to believe in animal rights but do not avow these goals. Factory farming, they say, is wrong—it violates animals' rights—but traditional animal agriculture is all right. Toxicity tests of cosmetics on animals violates their rights, but important medical research—cancer research, for example—does not. The clubbing of baby seals is abhorrent, but not the harvesting of adult seals. I used to think I understood this reasoning. Not any more. You don't change unjust institutions by tidying them up.

What's wrong—fundamentally wrong—with the way animals are treated isn't the details that vary from case to case. It's the whole system. The forlornness of the veal calf is pathetic, heart-wrenching; the pulsing pain of the chimp with electrodes planted deep in her brain is repulsive; the slow, tortuous death of the racoon caught in the leg-hold trap is agonizing. But what is wrong isn't the pain, isn't the suffering, isn't the deprivation. These compound what's wrong. Sometimes—often—they make it much, much worse. But they are not the fundamental wrong.

The fundamental wrong is the system that allows us to view animals as *our resources,* here for *us*—to be eaten, or surgically manipulated, or exploited for sport or money. Once we accept this view of animals—as our resources—the rest is as predictable as it is regrettable. Why worry about their loneliness, their pain, their death? Since animals exist for us, to benefit us in one way or another, what harms them really doesn't matter—or matters only if it starts to bother us, makes us feel a trifle uneasy when we eat our veal escalope, for example. So, yes, let us get veal calves out of solitary confinement, give them more space, a little straw, a few companions. But let us keep our veal escalope.

But a little straw, more space and a few companions won't eliminate—won't even touch—the basic wrong that attaches to our viewing and treating these animals as our resources. A veal calf killed to be eaten after living in close confinement is viewed and treated in this way: but so, too, is another who is raised (as they say) "more humanely." To right the wrong of our treat-

From In Defense of Animals (1985), *one of several books Regan has published on this ethical issue. Others include* The Case for Animal Rights (1983) *and* Defending Animal Rights (2001).

ment of farm animals requires more than making rearing methods "more humane"; it requires the total dissolution of commercial animal agriculture.

5   How we do this, whether we do it or, as in the case of animals in science,
whether and how we abolish their use—these are to a large extent political
questions. People must change their beliefs before they change their habits.
Enough people, especially those elected to public office, must believe in
change—must want it—before we will have laws that protect the rights of animals. This process of change is very complicated, very demanding, very exhausting, calling for the efforts of many hands in education, publicity, political
organization and activity, down to the licking of envelopes and stamps. As a
trained and practicing philosopher, the sort of contribution I can make is limited but, I like to think, important. The currency of philosophy is ideas—their
meaning and rational foundation—not the nuts and bolts of the legislative
process, say, or the mechanics of community organization. That's what I have
been exploring over the past ten years or so in my essays and talks and, most
recently, in my book, *The Case for Animal Rights*. I believe the major conclusions I reach in the book are true because they are supported by the weight of
the best arguments. I believe the idea of animal rights has reason, not just
emotion, on its side.

In the space I have at my disposal here I can only sketch, in the barest
outline, some of the main features of the book. Its main themes—and we
should not be surprised by this—involve asking and answering deep, founda-
tional moral questions about what morality is, how it should be understood
and what is the best moral theory, all considered. I hope I can convey something of the shape I think this theory takes. The attempt to do this will be (to
use a word a friendly critic once used to describe my work) cerebral, perhaps
too cerebral. But this is misleading. My feelings about how animals are sometimes treated run just as deep and just as strong as those of my more volatile
compatriots. Philosophers do—to use the jargon of the day—have a right side
to their brains. If it's the left side we contribute (or mainly should), that's because what talents we have reside there.

How to proceed? We begin by asking how the moral status of animals has
been understood by thinkers who deny that animals have rights. Then we test
the mettle of their ideas by seeing how well they stand up under the heat of
fair criticism. If we start our thinking in this way, we soon find that some people believe that we have no duties directly to animals, that we owe nothing to
them, that we can do nothing that wrongs them. Rather, we can do wrong
acts that involve animals, and so we have duties regarding them, though none
to them. Such views may be called indirect duty views. By way of illustration:
suppose your neighbor kicks your dog. Then your neighbor has done something wrong. But not to your dog. The wrong that has been done is a wrong
to you. After all, it is wrong to upset people, and your neighbor's kicking your
dog upsets you. So you are the one who is wronged, not your dog. Or again:
by kicking your dog your neighbor damages your property. And since it is
wrong to damage another person's property, your neighbor has done something wrong—to you, of course, not to your dog. Your neighbor no more

wrongs your dog than your car would be wronged if the wind-shield were smashed. Your neighbor's duties involving your dog are indirect duties to you. More generally, all of our duties regarding animals are indirect duties to one another—to humanity.

How could someone try to justify such a view? Someone might say that your dog doesn't feel anything and so isn't hurt by your neighbor's kick, doesn't care about the pain since none is felt, is as unaware of anything as is your windshield. Someone might say this, but no rational person will, since, among other considerations, such a view will commit anyone who holds it to the position that no human being feels pain either—that human beings also don't care about what happens to them. A second possibility is that though both humans and your dog are hurt when kicked, it is only human pain that matters. But, again, no rational person can believe this. Pain is pain wherever it occurs. If your neighbor's causing you pain is wrong because of the pain that is caused, we cannot rationally ignore or dismiss the moral relevance of the pain that your dog feels.

Philosophers who hold indirect duty views—and many still do—have come to understand that they must avoid the two defects just noted: that is, both the view that animals don't feel anything as well as the idea that only human pain can be morally relevant. Among such thinkers the sort of view now favored is one or other form of what is called *contractarianism*.

Here, very crudely, is the root idea: morality consists of a set of rules that individuals voluntarily agree to abide by, as we do when we sign a contract (hence the name contractarianism). Those who understand and accept the terms of the contract are covered directly; they have rights created and recognized by, and protected in, the contract and these contractors can also have protection spelled out for others who, though they lack the ability to understand morality and so cannot sign the contract themselves, are loved or cherished by those who can. Thus young children, for example, are unable to sign contracts and lack rights. But they are protected by the contract none the less because of the sentimental interests of others, most notably their parents. So we have, then, duties involving these children, duties regarding them, but no duties to them. Our duties in their case are indirect duties to other human beings, usually their parents.

As for animals, since they cannot understand contracts, they obviously cannot sign; and since they cannot sign, they have no rights. Like children, however, some animals are the objects of the sentimental interest of others. You, for example, love your dog or cat. So those animals that enough people care about (companion animals, whales, baby seals, the American bald eagle), though they lack rights themselves, will be protected because of the sentimental interests of people. I have, then, according to contractarianism, no duty directly to your dog or any other animal, not even the duty not to cause them pain or suffering; my duty not to hurt them is a duty I have to those people who care about what happens to them. As for other animals, where no or little sentimental interest is present—in the case of farm animals, for example, or laboratory rats—what duties we have grow weaker and weaker, perhaps to van-

10

ishing point. The pain and death they endure, though real, are not wrong if no one cares about them.

When it comes to the moral status of animals, contractarianism could be a hard view to refute if it were an adequate theoretical approach to the moral status of human beings. It is not adequate in this latter respect, however, which makes the question of its adequacy in the former case, regarding animals, utterly moot. For consider: morality, according to the (crude) contractarian position before us, consists of rules that people agree to abide by. What people? Well, enough to make a difference—enough, that is, *collectively* to have the power to enforce the rules that are drawn up in the contract. This is very well and good for the signatories but not so good for anyone who is not asked to sign. And there is nothing in contractarianism of the sort we are discussing that guarantees or requires that everyone will have a chance to participate equally in framing the rules of morality. The result is that this approach to ethics could sanction the most blatant forms of social, economic, moral and political injustice, ranging from a repressive caste system to systematic racial or sexual discrimination. Might, according to this theory, does make right. Let those who are the victims of injustice suffer as they will. It matters not so long as no one else—no contractor, or too few of them—cares about it. Such a theory takes one's moral breath away . . . as if, for example, there would be nothing wrong with apartheid in South Africa if few white South Africans were upset by it. A theory with so little to recommend it at the level of the ethics of our treatment of our fellow humans cannot have anything more to recommend it when it comes to the ethics of how we treat our fellow animals.

The version of contractarianism just examined is, as I have noted, a crude variety, and in fairness to those of a contractarian persuasion it must be noted that much more refined, subtle and ingenious varieties are possible. For example, John Rawls,[1] in his *A Theory of Justice,* sets forth a version of contractarianism that forces contractors to ignore the accidental features of being a human being—for example, whether one is white or black, male or female, a genius or of modest intellect. Only by ignoring such features, Rawls believes, can we ensure that the principles of justice that contractors would agree upon are not based on bias or prejudice. Despite the improvement a view such as Rawls's represents over the cruder forms of contractarianism, it remains deficient: it systematically denies that we have direct duties to those human beings who do not have a sense of justice—young children, for instance, and many mentally retarded humans. And yet it seems reasonably certain that, were we to torture a young child or a retarded elder, we would be doing something that wronged him or her, not something that would be wrong if (and only if) other humans with a sense of justice were upset. And since this is true in the case of these humans, we cannot rationally deny the same in the case of animals.

Indirect duty views, then, including the best among them, fail to command our rational assent. Whatever ethical theory we should accept rationally,

1. American philosopher (1921–2002).

therefore, it must at least recognize that we have some duties directly to animals, just as we have some duties directly to each other. The next two theories I'll sketch attempt to meet this requirement.

The first I call the cruelty-kindness view. Simply stated, this says that we   15
have a direct duty to be kind to animals and a direct duty not to be cruel to them. Despite the familiar, reassuring ring of these ideas, I do not believe that this view offers an adequate theory. To make this clearer, consider kindness. A kind person acts from a certain kind of motive—compassion or concern, for example. And that is a virtue. But there is no guarantee that a kind act is a right act. If I am a generous racist, for example, I will be inclined to act kindly towards members of my own race, favoring their interests above those of others. My kindness would be real and, so far as it goes, good. But I trust it is too obvious to require argument that my kind acts may not be above moral reproach—may, in fact, be positively wrong because rooted in injustice. So kindness, notwithstanding its status as a virtue to be encouraged, simply will not carry the weight of a theory of right action.

Cruelty fares no better. People or their acts are cruel if they display either a lack of sympathy for or, worse, the presence of enjoyment in another's suffering. Cruelty in all its guises is a bad thing, a tragic human failing. But just as a person's being motivated by kindness does not guarantee that he or she does what is right, so the absence of cruelty does not ensure that he or she avoids doing what is wrong. Many people who perform abortions, for example, are not cruel, sadistic people. But that fact alone does not settle the terribly difficult question of the morality of abortion. The case is no different when we examine the ethics of our treatment of animals. So, yes, let us be for kindness and against cruelty. But let us not suppose that being for the one and against the other answers questions about moral right and wrong.

Some people think that the theory we are looking for is utilitarianism. A utilitarian accepts two moral principles. The first is that of equality: everyone's interests count, and similar interests must be counted as having similar weight or importance. White or black, American or Iranian, human or animal—everyone's pain or frustration matter, and matter just as much as the equivalent pain or frustration of anyone else. The second principle a utilitarian accepts is that of utility: do the act that will bring about the best balance between satisfaction and frustration for everyone affected by the outcome.

As a utilitarian, then, here is how I am to approach the task of deciding what I morally ought to do: I must ask who will be affected if I choose to do one thing rather than another, how much each individual will be affected, and where the best results are most likely to lie—which option, in other words, is most likely to bring about the best results, the best balance between satisfaction and frustration. That option, whatever it may be, is the one I ought to choose. That is where my moral duty lies.

The great appeal of utilitarianism rests with its uncompromising *egalitarianism*: everyone's interests count and count as much as the like interests of everyone else. The kind of odious discrimination that some forms of contractarianism can justify—discrimination based on race or sex, for example—

seems disallowed in principle by utilitarianism, as is speciesism, systematic discrimination based on species membership.

20   The equality we find in utilitarianism, however, is not the sort an advocate of animal or human rights should have in mind. Utilitarianism has no room for the equal moral rights of different individuals because it has no room for their equal inherent value or worth. What has value for the utilitarian is the satisfaction of an individual's interests, not the individual whose interests they are. A universe in which you satisfy your desire for water, food and warmth is, other things being equal, better than a universe in which these desires are frustrated. And the same is true in the case of an animal with similar desires. But neither you nor the animal have any value in your own right. Only your feelings do.

Here is an analogy to help make the philosophical point clearer: a cup contains different liquids, sometimes sweet, sometimes bitter, sometimes a mix of the two. What has value are the liquids: the sweeter the better, the bitterer the worse. The cup, the container, has no value. It is what goes into it, not what they go into, that has value. For the utilitarian you and I are like the cup; we have no value as individuals and thus no equal value. What has value is what goes into us, what we serve as receptacles for; our feelings of satisfaction have positive value, our feelings of frustration negative value.

Serious problems arise for utilitarianism when we remind ourselves that it enjoins us to bring about the best consequences. What does this mean? It doesn't mean the best consequences for me alone, or for my family or friends, or any other person taken individually. No, what we must do is, roughly, as follows: we must add up (somehow!) the separate satisfactions and frustrations of everyone likely to be affected by our choice, the satisfactions in one column, the frustrations in the other. We must total each column for each of the options before us. That is what it means to say the theory is aggregative. And then we must choose that option which is most likely to bring about the best balance of totaled satisfactions over totaled frustrations. Whatever act would lead to this outcome is the one we ought morally to perform—it is where our moral duty lies. And that act quite clearly might not be the same one that would bring about the best results for me personally, or for my family or friends, or for a lab animal. The best aggregated consequences for everyone concerned are not necessarily the best for each individual.

That utilitarianism is an aggregative theory—different individuals' satisfactions or frustrations are added, or summed, or totaled—is the key objection to this theory. My Aunt Bea is old, inactive, a cranky, sour person, though not physically ill. She prefers to go on living. She is also rather rich. I could make a fortune if I could get my hands on her money, money she intends to give me in any event, after she dies, but which she refuses to give me now. In order to avoid a huge tax bite, I plan to donate a handsome sum of my profits to a local children's hospital. Many, many children will benefit from my generosity, and much joy will be brought to their parents, relatives and friends. If I don't get the money rather soon, all these ambitions will come to naught. The once-in-a-lifetime opportunity to make a real killing will be gone. Why, then, not kill my Aunt Bea? Oh, of course I *might* get caught. But I'm no fool and, besides, her doctor can be counted on to cooperate (he has an eye for the same investment and I happen to know a good deal about his shady past). The deed can be done . . . professionally, shall we say. There is *very* little chance of getting caught. And as for my conscience being guilt-ridden, I am a resourceful sort of fellow and will take more than sufficient comfort—as I lie on the beach at Acapulco—in contemplating the joy and health I have brought to so many others.

Suppose Aunt Bea is killed and the rest of the story comes out as told. Would I have done anything wrong? Anything immoral? One would have thought that I had. Not according to utilitarianism. Since what I have done has brought about the best balance between totaled satisfaction and frustration for all those affected by the outcome, my action is not wrong. Indeed, in killing Aunt Bea the physician and I did what duty required.

This same kind of argument can be repeated in all sorts of cases, illustrating, time after time, how the utilitarian's position leads to results that impartial people find morally callous. It *is* wrong to kill my Aunt Bea in the name of bringing about the best results for others. A good end does not justify an evil means. Any adequate moral theory will have to explain why this is so. Utilitarianism fails in this respect and so cannot be the theory we seek.

What to do? Where to begin anew? The place to begin, I think, is with the utilitarian's view of the value of the individual—or, rather, lack of value. In its place, suppose we consider that you and I, for example, do have value as individuals—what we'll call *inherent value*. To say we have such value is to say that we are something more than, something different from, mere receptacles. Moreover, to ensure that we do not pave the way for such injustices as slavery or sexual discrimination, we must believe that all who have inherent value have it equally, regardless of their sex, race, religion, birthplace and so on. Similarly to be discarded as irrelevant are one's talents or skills, intelligence and wealth, personality or pathology, whether one is loved and admired or despised and loathed. The genius and the retarded child, the prince and the pauper, the brain surgeon and the fruit vendor, Mother Teresa[2] and the most unscrupulous used-car salesman—all have inherent value, all possess it equally, and all have an equal right to be treated with respect, to be treated in ways that do not reduce them to the status of things, as if they existed as resources for others. My value as an individual is independent of my usefulness to you. Yours is not dependent on your usefulness to me. For either of us to treat the other in ways that fail to show respect for the other's independent value is to act immorally, to violate the individual's rights.

Some of the rational virtues of this view—what I call the rights view— should be evident. Unlike (crude) contractarianism, for example, the rights view *in principle* denies the moral tolerability of any and all forms of racial, sexual or social discrimination; and unlike utilitarianism, this view *in principle*

25

---

2. Nun (1910–1998) who founded the Missionaries of Charity in Calcutta, India, and is now proverbially known as the ultimate good person.

denies that we can justify good results by using evil means that violate an individual's rights—denies, for example, that it could be moral to kill my Aunt Bea to harvest beneficial consequences for others. That would be to sanction the disrespectful treatment of the individual in the name of the social good, something the rights view will not—categorically will not—ever allow.

The rights view, I believe, is rationally the most satisfactory moral theory. It surpasses all other theories in the degree to which it illuminates and explains the foundation of our duties to one another—the domain of human morality. On this score it has the best reasons, the best arguments, on its side. Of course, if it were possible to show that only human beings are included within its scope, then a person like myself, who believes in animal rights, would be obliged to look elsewhere.

But attempts to limit its scope to humans only can be shown to be rationally defective. Animals, it is true, lack many of the abilities humans possess. They can't read, do higher mathematics, build a bookcase or make *baba ghanoush*.[3] Neither can many human beings, however, and yet we don't (and shouldn't) say that they (these humans) therefore have less inherent value, less of a right to be treated with respect, than do others. It is the *similarities* between those human beings who most clearly, most noncontroversially have such value (the people reading this, for example), not our differences, that matter most. And the really crucial, the basic similarity is simply this: we are each of us the experiencing subject of a life, a conscious creature having an individual welfare that has importance to us whatever our usefulness to others. We want and prefer things, believe and feel things, recall and expect things. And all these dimensions of our life, including our pleasure and pain, our enjoyment and suffering, our satisfaction and frustration, our continued existence or our untimely death—all make a difference to the quality of our life as lived, as experienced, by us as individuals. As the same is true of those animals that concern us (the ones that are eaten and trapped, for example), they too must be viewed as the experiencing subjects of a life, with inherent value of their own.

30   Some there are who resist the idea that animals have inherent value. "Only humans have such value," they profess. How might this narrow view be defended? Shall we say that only humans have the requisite intelligence, or autonomy, or reason? But there are many, many humans who fail to meet these standards and yet are reasonably viewed as having value above and beyond their usefulness to others. Shall we claim that only humans belong to the right species, the species *Homo sapiens*?[4] But this is blatant speciesism. Will it be said, then, that all—and only—humans have immortal souls? Then our opponents have their work cut out for them. I am myself not ill-disposed to the proposition that there are immortal souls. Personally, I profoundly hope I have one. But I would not want to rest my position on a controversial ethical issue

3. An eggplant-sesame spread or dip popular in the Middle East.
4. Latin for "man with intellect," the taxonomic designation for the modern human species.

on the even more controversial question about who or what has an immortal soul. That is to dig one's hole deeper, not to climb out. Rationally, it is better to resolve moral issues without making more controversial assumptions than are needed. The question of who has inherent value is such a question, one that is resolved more rationally without the introduction of the idea of immortal souls than by its use.

Well, perhaps some will say that animals have some inherent value, only less than we have. Once again, however, attempts to defend this view can be shown to lack rational justification. What could be the basis of our having more inherent value than animals? Their lack of reason, or autonomy, or intellect? Only if we are willing to make the same judgment in the case of humans who are similarly deficient. But it is not true that such humans—the retarded child, for example, or the mentally deranged—have less inherent value than you or I. Neither, then, can we rationally sustain the view that animals like them in being the experiencing subjects of a life have less inherent value. *All* who have inherent value have it *equally*, whether they be human animals or not.

Inherent value, then, belongs equally to those who are the experiencing subjects of a life. Whether it belongs to others—to rocks and rivers, trees and glaciers, for example—we do not know and may never know. But neither do we need to know, if we are to make the case for animal rights. We do not need to know, for example, how many people are eligible to vote in the next presidential election before we can know whether I am. Similarly, we do not need to know how many individuals have inherent value before we can know that some do. When it comes to the case for animal rights, then, what we need to know is whether the animals that, in our culture, are routinely eaten, hunted and used in our laboratories, for example, are like us in being subjects of a life. And we do know this. We do know that many—literally, billions and billions— of these animals are the subjects of a life in the sense explained and so have inherent value if we do. And since, in order to arrive at the best theory of our duties to one another, we must recognize our equal inherent value as individuals, reason—not sentiment, not emotion—reason compels us to recognize the equal inherent value of these animals and, with this, their equal right to be treated with respect.

That, *very* roughly, is the shape and feel of the case for animal rights. Most of the details of the supporting argument are missing. They are to be found in the book to which I alluded earlier. Here, the details go begging, and I must, in closing, limit myself to four final points.

The first is how the theory that underlies the case for animal rights shows that the animal rights movement is a part of, not antagonistic to, the human rights movement. The theory that rationally grounds the rights of animals also grounds the rights of humans. Thus those involved in the animal rights movement are partners in the struggle to secure respect for human rights—the rights of women, for example, or minorities, or workers. The animal rights movement is cut from the same moral cloth as these.

Second, having set out the broad outlines of the rights view, I can now say   35 why its implications for farming and science, among other fields, are both clear and uncompromising. In the case of the use of animals in science, the rights view is categorically abolitionist. Lab animals are not our tasters; we are not their kings. Because these animals are treated routinely, systematically as if their value were reducible to their usefulness to others, they are routinely, systematically treated with a lack of respect, and thus are their rights routinely, systematically violated. This is just as true when they are used in trivial, duplicative, unnecessary or unwise research as it is when they are used in studies that hold out real promise of human benefits. We can't justify harming or killing a human being (my Aunt Bea, for example) just for these sorts of reason. Neither can we do so even in the case of so lowly a creature as a laboratory rat. It is not just refinement or reduction that is called for, not just larger, cleaner cages, not just more generous use of anaesthetic or the elimination of multiple surgery, not just tidying up the system. It is complete replacement. The best we can do when it comes to using animals in science is—not to use them. That is where our duty lies, according to the rights view.

As for commercial animal agriculture, the rights view takes a similar abolitionist position. The fundamental moral wrong here is not that animals are kept in stressful close confinement or in isolation, or that their pain and suffering, their needs and preferences are ignored or discounted. All these *are* wrong, of course, but they are not the fundamental wrong. They are symptoms and effects of the deeper, systematic wrong that allows these animals to be viewed and treated as lacking independent value, as resources for us—as, indeed, a renewable resource. Giving farm animals more space, more natural environments, more companions does not right the fundamental wrong, any more than giving lab animals more anaesthesia or bigger, cleaner cages would right the fundamental wrong in their case. Nothing less than the total dissolution of commercial animal agriculture will do this, just as, for similar reasons I won't develop at length here, morality requires nothing less than the total elimination of hunting and trapping for commercial and sporting ends. The rights view's implications, then, as I have said, are clear and uncompromising.

My last two points are about philosophy, my profession. It is, most obviously, no substitute for political action. The words I have written here and in other places by themselves don't change a thing. It is what we do with the thoughts that the words express—our acts, our deeds—that changes things. All that philosophy can do, and all I have attempted, is to offer a vision of what our deeds should aim at. And the why. But not the how.

Finally, I am reminded of my thoughtful critic, the one I mentioned earlier, who chastised me for being too cerebral. Well, cerebral I have been: indirect duty views, utilitarianism, contractarianism—hardly the stuff deep passions are made of. I am also reminded, however, of the image another friend once set before me—the image of the ballerina as expressive of disciplined passion. Long hours of sweat and toil, of loneliness and practice, of doubt and fatigue: those are the discipline of her craft. But the passion is there too, the fierce drive to excel, to speak through her body, to do it right, to pierce our minds. That is the image of philosophy I would leave with you, not "too cerebral" but *disciplined passion.* Of the discipline enough has been seen. As for the passion: there are times, and these not infrequent, when tears come to my eyes when I see, or read, or hear of the wretched plight of animals in the hands of humans. Their pain, their suffering, their loneliness, their innocence, their death. Anger. Rage. Pity. Sorrow. Disgust. The whole creation groans under the weight of the evil we humans visit upon these mute, powerless creatures. It *is* our hearts, not just our heads, that call for an end to it all, that demand of us that we overcome, for them, the habits and forces behind their systematic oppression. All great movements, it is written, go through three stages: ridicule, discussion, adoption. It is the realization of this third stage, adoption, that requires both our passion and our discipline, our hearts and our heads. The fate of animals is in our hands. God grant we are equal to the task.

QUESTIONS

1. Regan argues against four views that deny rights to animals: indirect duty, contractarianism, cruelty-kindness, and utilitarianism. Locate his account of each and explain his objections to it.

2. Regan then argues for what he calls a "rights view," which is, he claims, "rationally the most satisfactory moral theory" (paragraph 28). Explain both his view and his claim.

3. What are the advantages of arguing for views that conflict with one's own before arguing for one's own? What are the disadvantages?

4. Regan includes among his goals "the total dissolution of commercial animal agriculture" and "the total elimination of commercial and sport hunting and trapping" (paragraph 1). Do these goals include vegetarianism? If so, why does he not use the word "vegetarian"?

5. Write an essay in which you take a position on an issue about which you have strong feelings. Following Regan's example, focus on argument while both acknowledging and excluding your feelings.

MICHAEL POLLAN *An Animal's Place*

T HE FIRST TIME I opened Peter Singer's *Animal Lib-eration*, I was dining alone at the Palm,[1] trying to enjoy a rib-eye steak cooked medium-rare. If this sounds like a good recipe for cognitive dissonance (if not indigestion), that was sort of the idea. Preposterous as it might seem, to supporters of animal rights, what I was doing was tantamount to reading *Uncle Tom's Cabin* on a plantation in the Deep South in 1852.

Singer and the swelling ranks of his followers ask us to imagine a future in which people will look back on my meal, and this steakhouse, as relics of an equally backward age. Eating animals, wearing animals, experimenting on animals, killing animals for sport: all these practices, so resolutely normal to us, will be seen as the barbarities they are, and we will come to view "speciesism"—a neologism I had encountered before only in jokes—as a form of discrimination as indefensible as racism or anti-Semitism.

Even in 1975, when *Animal Liberation* was first published, Singer, an Australian philosopher now teaching at Princeton, was confident that he had the wind of history at his back. The recent civil rights past was prologue, as one liberation movement followed on the heels of another. Slowly but surely, the white man's circle of moral consideration was expanded to admit first blacks, then women, then homosexuals. In each case, a group once thought to be so different from the prevailing "we" as to be undeserving of civil rights was, after a struggle, admitted to the club. Now it was animals' turn.

That animal liberation is the logical next step in the forward march of moral progress as no longer the fringe idea it was back in 1975. A growing and increasingly influential group of philosophers, ethicists, law professors and activists are convinced that the great moral struggle of our time will be for the rights of animals.

5   So far the movement has scored some of its biggest victories in Europe. Earlier this year, Germany became the first nation to grant animals a constitutional right: the words "and animals" were added to a provision obliging the state to respect and protect the dignity of human beings. The farming of animals for fur was recently banned in England. In several European nations, sows may no longer be confined to crates nor laying hens to "battery cages"—stacked wired cages so small the birds cannot stretch their wings. The Swiss are amending their laws to change the status of animals from "things" to "beings."

Though animals are still very much "things" in the eyes of American law, change is in the air. Thirty-seven states have recently passed laws making

Published on November 10, 2002, in the New York Times Magazine, *a supplement to the Sunday newspaper.*

1. Famous New York City steakhouse.

some forms of animal cruelty a crime, twenty-one of them by ballot initiative. Following protests by activists, McDonald's and Burger King forced significant improvements in the way the U.S. meat industry slaughters animals. Agribusiness and the cosmetics and apparel industries are all struggling to defuse mounting public concerns over animal welfare.

Once thought of as a left-wing concern, the movement now cuts across ideological lines. Perhaps the most eloquent recent plea on behalf of animals, a new book called *Dominion*, was written by a former speechwriter for President Bush. And once outlandish ideas are finding their way into mainstream opinion. A recent Zogby poll found that fifty-one percent of Americans believe that *primates* are entitled to the same rights as human children.

What is going on here? A certain amount of cultural confusion, for one thing. For at the same time many people seem eager to extend the circle of our moral consideration to animals, in our factory farms and laboratories we are inflicting more suffering on more animals than at any time in history. One by one, science is dismantling our claims to uniqueness as a species, discovering that such things as culture, toolmaking, language and even possibly self-consciousness are not the exclusive domain of *Homo sapiens*. Yet most of the animals we kill lead lives organized very much in the spirit of Descartes,[2] who famously claimed that animals were mere machines, incapable of thought or feeling. There's a schizoid quality to our relationship with animals, in which sentiment and brutality exist side by side. Half the dogs in America will receive Christmas presents this year, yet few of us pause to consider the miserable life of the pig—an animal easily as intelligent as a dog—that becomes the Christmas ham.

We tolerate this disconnect because the life of the pig has moved out of view. When's the last time you saw a pig? (Babe doesn't count.) Except for our pets, real animals—animals living and dying—no longer figure in our everyday lives. Meat comes from the grocery store, where it is cut and packaged to look as little like parts of animals as possible. The disappearance of animals from our lives has opened a space in which there's no reality check, either on the sentiment or the brutality. This is pretty much where we live now, with respect to animals, and it is a space in which the Peter Singers and Frank Perdues of the world can evidently thrive equally well.

Several years ago, the English critic John Berger wrote an essay, "Why 10 Look at Animals?," in which he suggested that the loss of everyday contact between ourselves and animals—and specifically the loss of eye contact—has left us deeply confused about the terms of our relationship to other species. That eye contact, always slightly uncanny, had provided a vivid daily reminder that animals were at once crucially like and unlike us; in their eyes we glimpsed something unmistakably familiar (pain, fear, tenderness) and something irretrievably alien. Upon this paradox people built a relationship in which they felt they could both honor and eat animals without looking away. But that accommodation has pretty much broken down; nowadays, it seems, we either look

2. René Descartes (1596–1650), French philosopher.

away or become vegetarians. For my own part, neither option seemed especially appetizing. Which might explain how I found myself reading *Animal Liberation* in a steakhouse.

This is not something I'd recommend if you're determined to continue eating meat. Combining rigorous philosophical argument with journalistic description, *Animal Liberation* is one of those rare books that demand that you either defend the way you live or change it. Because Singer is so skilled in argument, for many readers it is easier to change. His book has converted countless thousands to vegetarianism, and it didn't take long for me to see why: within a few pages, he had succeeded in throwing me on the defensive.

Singer's argument is disarmingly simple and, if you accept its premises, difficult to refute. Take the premise of equality, which most people readily accept. Yet what do we really mean by it? People are not, as a matter of fact, equal at all—some are smarter than others, better looking, more gifted. "Equality is a moral idea," Singer points out, "not an assertion of fact." The moral idea is that everyone's interests ought to receive equal consideration, regardless of "what abilities they may possess." Fair enough; many philosophers have gone this far. But fewer have taken the next logical step. "If possessing a higher degree of intelligence does not entitle one human to use another for his or her own ends, how can it entitle humans to exploit nonhumans for the same purpose?"

This is the nub of Singer's argument, and right around here I began scribbling objections in the margin. *But humans differ from animals in morally significant ways.* Yes they do, Singer acknowledges, which is why we shouldn't treat pigs and children alike. Equal consideration of interests is not the same as equal treatment, he points out: children have an interest in being educated; pigs, in rooting around in the dirt. But where their interests are the same, the principle of equality demands they receive the same consideration. And the one all-important interest that we share with pigs, as with all sentient creatures, is an interest in avoiding pain.

Here Singer quotes a famous passage from Jeremy Bentham, the eighteenth-century utilitarian philosopher, that is the wellspring of the animal rights movement. Bentham was writing in 1789, soon after the French colonies freed black slaves, granting them fundamental rights. "The day *may* come," he speculates, "when the rest of the animal creation may acquire those rights." Bentham then asks what characteristic entitles any being to moral consideration. "Is it the faculty of reason or perhaps the faculty of discourse?" Obviously not, since "a full-grown horse or dog is beyond comparison a more rational, as well as a more conversable animal, than an infant." He concludes: "The question is not, Can they *reason?* nor, Can they *talk?* but, Can they *suffer?*"

15   Bentham here is playing a powerful card philosophers call the "argument from marginal cases," or AMC for short. It goes like this: There are humans—infants, the severely retarded, the demented—whose mental function cannot match that of a chimpanzee. Even though these people cannot reciprocate our

moral attentions, we nevertheless include them in the circle of our moral consideration. So on what basis do we exclude the chimpanzee?

Because he's a chimp, I furiously scribbled in the margin, *and they're human!* For Singer that's not good enough. To exclude the chimp from moral consideration simply because he's not human is no different from excluding the slave simply because he's not white. In the same way we'd call that exclusion racist, the animal rightist contends that it is speciesist to discriminate against the chimpanzee solely because he's not human.

But the differences between blacks and whites are trivial compared with the differences between my son and a chimp. Singer counters by asking us to imagine a hypothetical society that discriminates against people on the basis of something nontrivial—say, intelligence. If that scheme offends our sense of equality, then why is the fact that animals lack certain human characteristics any more just as a basis for discrimination? Either we do not owe any justice to the severely retarded, he concludes, or we do owe it to animals with higher capabilities.

This is where I put down my fork. If I believe in equality, and equality is based on interests rather than characteristics, then I have to either take the interests of the steer I'm eating into account or concede that I am a speciesist. For the time being, I decided to plead guilty as charged. I finished my steak.

But Singer had planted a troubling notion, and in the days afterward, it grew and grew, watered by the other animal rights thinkers I began reading: the philosophers Tom Regan and James Rachels; the legal theorist Steven M. Wise; the writers Joy Williams and Matthew Scully. I didn't *think* I minded being a speciesist, but could it be, as several of these writers suggest, that we will someday come to regard speciesism as an evil comparable to racism? Will history someday judge us as harshly as it judges the Germans who went about their ordinary lives in the shadow of Treblinka? Precisely that question was recently posed by J. M. Coetzee, the South African novelist, in a lecture delivered at Princeton; he answered it in the affirmative. If animal rightists are right, "a crime of stupefying proportions" (in Coetzee's words) is going on all around us every day, just beneath our notice.

It's an idea almost impossible to entertain seriously, much less to accept, and in the weeks following my restaurant face-off between Singer and the steak, I found myself marshaling whatever mental power I could muster to try to refute it. Yet Singer and his allies managed to trump almost all my objections.   20

My first line of defense was obvious. *Animals kill one another all the time. Why treat animals more ethically than they treat one another?* (Ben Franklin tried this one long before me: during a fishing trip, he wondered, "If you eat one another, I don't see why we may not eat you." He admits, however, that the rationale didn't occur to him until the fish were in the frying pan, smelling "admirably well." The advantage of being a "reasonable creature," Franklin remarks, is that you can find a reason for whatever you want to do.) To the "they do it too" defense, the animal rightist has a devastating reply: Do you really want to base your morality on the natural order? Murder and rape are natural too. Besides, humans don't need to kill other creatures in order to survive; animals do. (Though if my cat, Otis, is any guide, animals sometimes kill for sheer pleasure.)

This suggests another defense. *Wouldn't life in the wild be worse for these farm animals?* "Defenders of slavery imposed on black Africans often made a similar point," Singer retorts. "The life of freedom is to be preferred."

But domesticated animals can't survive in the wild; in fact, without us they wouldn't exist at all. Or as one nineteenth-century political philosopher put it, "The pig has a stronger interest than anyone in the demand for bacon. If all the world were Jewish, there would be no pigs at all." But it turns out that this would be fine by the animal rightists: for if pigs don't exist, they can't be wronged.

Animals on factory farms have never known any other life. Singer replies that "animals feel a need to exercise, stretch their limbs or wings, groom themselves and turn around, whether or not they have ever lived in conditions that permit this." The measure of their suffering is not their prior experiences but the unremitting daily frustration of their instincts.

25   *OK, the suffering of animals is a legitimate problem, but the world is full of problems, and surely human problems must come first!* Sounds good, and yet all the animal people are asking me to do is to stop eating meat and wearing animal furs and hides. There's no reason I can't devote myself to solving humankind's problems while being a vegetarian who wears synthetics.

But doesn't the fact that we could choose to forgo meat for moral reasons point to a crucial moral difference between animals and humans? As Kant pointed out, the human being is the only moral animal, the only one even capable of entertaining a concept of "rights." What's wrong with reserving moral consideration for those able to reciprocate it? Right here is where you run smack into the AMC: the moral status of the retarded, the insane, the infant and the Alzheimer's patient. Such "marginal cases," in the detestable argot of modern moral philosophy, cannot participate in moral decision-making any more than a monkey can, yet we nevertheless grant them rights.

That's right, I respond, for the simple reason that they're one of us. And all of us have been, and will probably once again be, marginal cases ourselves. What's more, these people have fathers and mothers, daughters and sons, which makes our interest in their welfare deeper than our interest in the welfare of even the most brilliant ape.

Alas, none of these arguments evade the charge of speciesism; the racist, too, claims that it's natural to give special consideration to one's own kind. A utilitarian like Singer would agree, however, that the feelings of relatives do count for something. Yet the principle of equal consideration of interests demands that, given the choice between performing a painful medical experiment on a severely retarded orphan and on a normal ape, we must sacrifice the child. Why? Because the ape has a greater capacity for pain.

Here in a nutshell is the problem with the AMC: it can be used to help the animals, but just as often it winds up hurting the marginal cases. Giving up our speciesism will bring us to a moral cliff from which we may not be prepared to jump, even when logic is pushing us.

And yet this isn't the moral choice I am being asked to make. (Too bad; it would be so much easier!) In everyday life, the choice is not between babies and chimps but between the pork and the tofu. Even if we reject the "hard utilitarianism" of a Peter Singer, there remains the question of whether we owe animals that can feel pain *any* moral consideration, and this seems impossible to deny. And if we do owe them moral consideration, how can we justify eating them?

This is why killing animals for meat (and clothing) poses the most difficult animal rights challenge. In the case of animal testing, all but the most radical animal rightists are willing to balance the human benefit against the cost to the animals. That's because the unique qualities of human consciousness carry weight in the utilitarian calculus: human pain counts for more than that of a mouse, since our pain is amplified by emotions like dread; similarly, our deaths are worse than an animal's because we understand what death is in a way they don't. So the argument over animal testing is really in the details: Is this particular procedure or test *really* necessary to save human lives? (Very often it's not, in which case we probably shouldn't do it:) But if humans no longer need to eat meat or wear skins, then what exactly are we putting on the human side of the scale to outweigh the interests of the animal?

I suspect that this is finally why the animal people managed to throw me on the defensive. It's one thing to choose between the chimp and the retarded child or to accept the sacrifice of all those pigs surgeons practiced on to develop heart-bypass surgery. But what happens when the choice is between "a lifetime of suffering for a nonhuman animal and the gastronomic preference of a human being?" You look away—or you stop eating animals. And if you don't want to do either? Then you have to try to determine if the animals you're eating have really endured "a lifetime of suffering."

Whether our interest in eating animals outweighs their interest in not being eaten (assuming for the moment that is their interest) turns on the vexed question of animal suffering. Vexed, because it is impossible to know what really goes on in the mind of a cow or a pig or even an ape. Strictly speaking, this is true of other humans, too, but since humans are all basically wired the same way, we have excellent reason to assume that other people's experience of pain feels much like our own. Can we say that about animals? Yes and no.

I have yet to find anyone who still subscribes to Descartes's belief that animals cannot feel pain because they lack a soul. The general consensus among scientists and philosophers is that when it comes to pain, the higher animals are wired much the way we are for the same evolutionary reasons, so we should take the writhings of the kicked dog at face value. Indeed, the very premise of a great deal of animal testing—the reason it has value—is that animals' experience of physical and even some psychological pain closely resembles our own. Otherwise, why would cosmetics testers drip chemicals into the eyes of rabbits to see if they sting? Why would researchers study head trauma

by traumatizing chimpanzee heads? Why would psychologists attempt to induce depression and "learned helplessness" in dogs by exposing them to ceaseless random patterns of electrical shock?

35   That said, it can be argued that human pain differs from animal pain by
an order of magnitude. This qualitative difference is largely the result of our
possession of language and, by virtue of language, an ability to have thoughts
about thoughts and to imagine alternatives to our current reality. The philosopher Daniel C. Dennett suggests that we would do well to draw a distinction
between pain, which a great many animals experience, and suffering, which
depends on a degree of self-consciousness only a few animals appear to command. Suffering, in this view, is not just lots of pain but pain intensified by human emotions like loss, sadness, worry, regret, self-pity, shame, humiliation
and dread.

Consider castration. No one would deny the procedure is painful to animals, yet animals appear to get over it in a way humans do not. (Some rhesus
monkeys competing for mates will bite off a rival's testicle; the very next day
the victim may be observed mating, seemingly little the worse for wear.) Surely
the suffering of a man able to comprehend the full implications of castration,
to anticipate the event and contemplate its aftermath, represents an agony of
another order.

By the same token, however, language and all that comes with it can also
make certain kinds of pain *more* bearable. A trip to the dentist would be a torment for an ape that couldn't be made to understand the purpose and duration
of the procedure.

As humans contemplating the pain and suffering of animals, we do need
to guard against projecting onto them what the same experience would feel
like to us. Watching a steer force-marched up the ramp to the kill-floor door,
as I have done, I need to remind myself that this is not Sean Penn in *Dead
Man Walking*, that in a bovine brain the concept of nonexistence is blissfully
absent. "If we fail to find suffering in the [animal] lives we can see," Dennett
writes in *Kinds of Minds*, "we can rest assured there is no invisible suffering
somewhere in their brains. If we find suffering, we will recognize it without
difficulty."

Which brings us—reluctantly, necessarily—to the American factory farm, the
place where all such distinctions turn to dust. It's not easy to draw lines between pain and suffering in a modern egg or confinement hog operation.
These are places where the subtleties of moral philosophy and animal cogni-
tion mean less than nothing, where everything we've learned about animals at
least since Darwin has been simply . . . set aside. To visit a modern CAFO
(Confined Animal Feeding Operation) is to enter a world that, for all its technological sophistication, is still designed according to Cartesian principles: animals are machines incapable of feeling pain. Since no thinking person can
possibly believe this anymore, industrial animal agriculture depends on a suspension of disbelief on the part of the people who operate it and a willingness
to avert your eyes on the part of everyone else.

From everything I've read, egg and hog operations are the worst. Beef cat-   40
tle in America at least still live outdoors, albeit standing ankle deep in their
own waste, eating a diet that makes them sick. And broiler chickens, although
they do get their beaks snipped off with a hot knife to keep them from cannibalizing one another under the stress of their confinement, at least don't spend
their eight-week lives in cages too small to ever stretch a wing. That fate is reserved for the American laying hen, who passes her brief span piled together
with a half-dozen other hens in a wire cage whose floor a single page of this
magazine could carpet. Every natural instinct of this animal is thwarted, leading to a range of behavioral "vices" that can include cannibalizing her cage-
mates and rubbing her body against the wire mesh until it is featherless and
bleeding. Pain? Suffering? Madness? The operative suspension of disbelief depends on more neutral descriptors, like "vices" and "stress." Whatever you
want to call what's going on in those cages, the ten percent or so of hens that
can't bear it and simply die is built into the cost of production. And when the
output of the others begins to ebb, the hens will be "force-molted"—starved of
food and water and light for several days in order to stimulate a final bout of
egg-laying before their life's work is done.

Simply reciting these facts, most of which are drawn from poultry-trade
magazines, makes me sound like one of those animal people, doesn't it? I don't
mean to, but this is what can happen when . . . you look. It certainly wasn't my
intention to ruin anyone's breakfast. But now that I probably have spoiled the
eggs, I do want to say one thing about the bacon, mention a single practice (by
no means the worst) in modern hog production that points to the compound
madness of an impeccable industrial logic.

Piglets in confinement operations are weaned from their mothers ten days
after birth (compared with thirteen weeks in nature) because they gain weight
faster on their hormone- and antibiotic-fortified feed. This premature weaning
leaves the pigs with a life-long craving to suck and chew, a desire they gratify
in confinement by biting the tail of the animal in front of them. A normal pig
would fight off his molester, but a demoralized pig has stopped caring.
"Learned helplessness" is the psychological term, and it's not uncommon in
confinement operations, where tens of thousands of hogs spend their entire
lives ignorant of sunshine or earth or straw, crowded together beneath a metal
roof upon metal slats suspended over a manure pit. So it's not surprising that
an animal as sensitive and intelligent as a pig would get depressed, and a depressed pig will allow his tail to be chewed on to the point of infection. Sick
pigs, being underperforming "production units," are clubbed to death on the
spot. The USDA's recommended solution to the problem is called "tail docking." Using a pair of pliers (and no anesthetic), most but not all of the tail is
snipped off. Why the little stump? Because the whole point of the exercise is
not to remove the object of tail-biting so much as to render it *more* sensitive.
Now, a bite on the tail is so painful that even the most demoralized pig will
mount a struggle to avoid it.

Much of this description is drawn from *Dominion*, Matthew Scully's recent book in which he offers a harrowing description of a North Carolina hog

operation. Scully, a Christian conservative, has no patience for lefty rights talk, arguing instead that while God did give man "dominion" over animals ("Every moving thing that liveth shall be meat for you"), he also admonished us to show them mercy. "We are called to treat them with kindness, not because they have rights or power or some claim to equality but . . . because they stand unequal and powerless before us."

Scully calls the contemporary factory farm "our own worst nightmare" and, to his credit, doesn't shrink from naming the root cause of this evil: unfettered capitalism. (Perhaps this explains why he resigned from the Bush administration just before his book's publication.) A tension has always existed between the capitalist imperative to maximize efficiency and the moral imperatives of religion or community which have historically served as a counterweight to the moral blindness of the market. This is one of "the cultural contradictions of capitalism"—the tendency of the economic impulse to erode the moral underpinnings of society. Mercy toward animals is one such casualty.

45   More than any other institution, the American industrial animal farm offers a nightmarish glimpse of what capitalism can look like in the absence of moral or regulatory constraint. In these places life itself is redefined—as protein production—and with it suffering. *That* venerable word becomes "stress," an economic problem in search of a cost-effective solution, like tail-docking or beak-clipping or, in the industry's latest plan, by simply engineering the "stress gene" out of pigs and chickens. "Our own worst nightmare" such a place may well be; it is also real life for the billions of animals unlucky enough to have been born beneath these grim steel roofs, into the brief, pitiless life of a "production unit" in the days before the suffering gene was found.

Vegetarianism doesn't seem an unreasonable response to such an evil. Who would want to be made complicit in the agony of these animals by eating them? You want to throw *something* against the walls of those infernal sheds, whether it's the Bible, a new constitutional right or a whole platoon of animal rightists bent on breaking in and liberating the inmates. In the shadow of these factory farms, Coetzee's notion of a "stupefying crime" doesn't seem far-fetched at all.

But before you swear off meat entirely, let me describe a very different sort of animal farm. It is typical of nothing, and yet its very existence puts the whole moral question of animal agriculture in a different light. Polyface Farm occupies 550 acres of rolling grassland and forest in the Shenandoah Valley of Virginia. Here, Joel Salatin and his family raise six different food animals—cattle, pigs, chickens, rabbits, turkeys and sheep—in an intricate dance of symbiosis designed to allow each species, in Salatin's words, "to fully express its physiological distinctiveness."

What this means in practice is that Salatin's chickens live like chickens; his cows, like cows; pigs, pigs. As in nature, where birds tend to follow herbivores, once Salatin's cows have finished grazing a pasture, he moves them out and tows in his "eggmobile," a portable chicken coop that houses several hundred laying hens—roughly the natural size of a flock. The hens fan out over the pasture, eating the short grass and picking insect larvae out of the cow-pats—all the while spreading the cow manure and eliminating the farm's parasite problem. A diet of grubs and grass makes for exceptionally tasty eggs and contented chickens, and their nitrogenous manure feeds the pasture. A few weeks later, the chickens move out and the sheep come in, dining on the lush new growth as well as on the weed species (nettles, nightshade) that the cattle and chickens won't touch.

Meanwhile, the pigs are in the barn turning the compost. All winter long, while the cattle were indoors, Salatin layered their manure with straw, wood chips—and corn. By March, this steaming compost layer cake stands three feet high, and the pigs, whose powerful snouts can sniff out and retrieve the fermented corn at the bottom, get to spend a few happy weeks rooting through the pile, aerating it as they work. All you can see of these pigs, intently nosing out the tasty alcoholic morsels, are their upturned pink hams and corkscrew tails churning the air. The finished compost will go to feed the grass; the grass, the cattle; the cattle, the chickens; and eventually all of these animals will feed us.

I thought a lot about vegetarianism and animal rights during the day I spent on Joel Salatin's extraordinary farm. So much of what I'd read, so much of what I'd accepted, looked very different from here. To many animal rightists, even Polyface Farm is a death camp. But to look at these animals is to see this for the sentimental conceit it is. In the same way that we can probably recognize animal suffering when we see it, animal happiness is unmistakable, too, and here I was seeing it in abundance. 50

For any animal, happiness seems to consist in the opportunity to express its creaturely character—its essential pigness or wolfness or chickenness. Aristotle speaks of each creature's "characteristic form of life." For domesticated species, the good life, if we can call it that, cannot be achieved apart from humans—apart from our farms and, therefore, our meat-eating. This, it seems to me, is where animal rightists betray a profound ignorance about the workings of nature. To think of domestication as a form of enslavement or even exploitation is to misconstrue the whole relationship, to project a human idea of power onto what is, in fact, an instance of mutualism between species. Domestication is an evolutionary, rather than a political, development. It is certainly not a regime humans imposed on animals some ten thousand years ago.

Rather, domestication happened when a small handful of especially opportunistic species discovered through Darwinian trial and error that they were more likely to survive and prosper in an alliance with humans than on their own. Humans provided the animals with food and protection, in exchange for which the animals provided the humans their milk and eggs and—yes—their flesh. Both parties were transformed by the relationship: animals grew tame and lost their ability to fend for themselves (evolution tends to edit out unneeded traits), and humans gave up their hunter-gatherer ways for the settled life of agriculturists. (Humans changed biologically too, evolving such new traits as a tolerance for lactose as adults.)

From the animals' point of view, the bargain with humanity has been a great success, at least until our own time. Cows, pigs, dogs, cats and chickens have thrived, while their wild ancestors have languished. (There are ten thousand wolves in North America, fifty million dogs.) Nor does their loss of autonomy seem to trouble these creatures. It is wrong, the rightists say, to treat animals as "means" rather than "ends," yet the happiness of a working animal like the dog consists precisely in serving as a "means." Liberation is the last thing such a creature wants. To say of one of Joel Salatin's caged chickens that "the life of freedom is to be preferred" betrays an ignorance about chicken preferences—which on this farm are heavily focused on not getting their heads bitten off by weasels.

But haven't these chickens simply traded one predator for another—weasels for humans? True enough, and for the chickens this is probably not a bad deal. For brief as it is, the life expectancy of a farm animal would be considerably briefer in the world beyond the pasture fence or chicken coop. A sheep farmer told me that a bear will eat a lactating ewe alive, starting with her udders. "As a rule," he explained, "animals don't get 'good deaths' surrounded by their loved ones."

55   The very existence of predation—animals eating animals—is the cause of much anguished hand-wringing in animal rights circles. "It must be admitted," Singer writes, "that the existence of carnivorous animals does pose one problem for the ethics of Animal Liberation, and that is whether we should do anything about it." Some animal rightists train their dogs and cats to become vegetarians. (Note: cats will require nutritional supplements to stay healthy.) Matthew Scully calls predation "the intrinsic evil in nature's design . . . among the hardest of all things to fathom." *Really?* A deep Puritan streak pervades animal rights activists, an abiding discomfort not only with our animality but with the animals' animality too.

However it may appear to us, predation is not a matter of morality or politics; it, also, is a matter of symbiosis. Hard as the wolf may be on the deer he eats, the herd depends on him for its well-being; without predators to cull the herd, deer overrun their habitat and starve. In many places, human hunters have taken over the predator's ecological role. Chickens also depend for their continued well-being on their human predators—not individual chickens, but chickens as a species. The surest way to achieve the extinction of the chicken would be to grant chickens a "right to life."

Yet here's the rub: the animal rightist is not concerned with species, only individuals. Tom Regan, author of *The Case for Animal Rights*, bluntly asserts that because "species are not individuals . . . the rights view does not recognize the moral rights of species to anything, including survival." Singer concurs, insisting that only sentient individuals have interests. But surely a species can have interests—in its survival, say—just as a nation or community or a corporation can. The animal rights movement's exclusive concern with individual animals makes perfect sense given its roots in a culture of liberal individualism, but does it make any sense in nature?

Consider this hypothetical episode: In 1611 Juan da Goma (a.k.a. Juan the Disoriented) made accidental landfall on Wrightson Island, a six-square-mile rock in the Indian Ocean. The island's sole distinction is as the only known home of the Arcania tree and the bird that nests in it, the Wrightson giant sea sparrow. Da Goma and his crew stayed a week, much of that time spent in a failed bid to recapture the ship's escaped goat—who happened to be pregnant. Nearly four centuries later, Wrightson Island is home to 380 goats that have consumed virtually every scrap of vegetation in their reach. The youngest Arcania tree on the island is more than three hundred years old, and only fifty-two sea sparrows remain. In the animal rights view, any one of those goats have at least as much right to life as the last Wrightson sparrow on earth, and the trees, because they are not sentient, warrant no moral consideration whatsoever. (In the mid-1980s a British environmental group set out to shoot the goats, but was forced to cancel the expedition after the Mammal Liberation Front bombed its offices.)

The story of Wrightson Island (invented by the biologist David Ehrenfeld in *Beginning Again*) suggests at the very least that a human morality based on individual rights makes for an awkward fit when applied to the natural world. This should come as no surprise: morality is an artifact of human culture, devised to help us negotiate social relations. It's very good for that. But just as we recognize that nature doesn't provide an adequate guide for human social conduct, isn't it anthropocentric to assume that our moral system offers an adequate guide for nature? We may require a different set of ethics to guide our dealings with the natural world, one as well suited to the particular needs of plants and animals and habitats (where sentience counts for little) as rights suit us humans today.

To contemplate such questions from the vantage of a farm is to appreciate just how parochial and urban an ideology animal rights really is. It could thrive only in a world where people have lost contact with the natural world, where animals no longer pose a threat to us and human mastery of nature seems absolute. "In our normal life," Singer writes, "there is no serious clash of interests between human and nonhuman animals." Such a statement assumes a decidedly urbanized "normal life," one that certainly no farmer would recognize.   60

The farmer would point out that even vegans have a "serious clash of interests" with other animals. The grain that the vegan eats is harvested with a combine that shreds field mice, while the farmer's tractor crushes woodchucks in their burrows, and his pesticides drop songbirds from the sky. Steve Davis, an animal scientist at Oregon State University, has estimated that if America were to adopt a strictly vegetarian diet, the total number of animals killed every year would actually *increase*, as animal pasture gave way to row crops. Davis contends that if our goal is to kill as few animals as possible, then people should eat the largest possible animal that can live on the least intensively cultivated land: grass-fed beef for everybody. It would appear that killing animals is unavoidable no matter what we choose to eat.

When I talked to Joel Salatin about the vegetarian utopia, he pointed out that it would also condemn him and his neighbors to importing their food from distant places, since the Shenandoah Valley receives too little rainfall to grow many row crops. Much the same would hold true where I live, in New England. We get plenty of rain, but the hilliness of the land has dictated an agriculture based on animals since the time of the Pilgrims. The world is full of places where the best, if not the only, way to obtain food from the land is by grazing animals on it—especially ruminants, which alone can transform grass into protein and whose presence can actually improve the health of the land.

The vegetarian utopia would make us even more dependent than we already are on an industrialized national food chain. That food chain would in turn be even more dependent than it already is on fossil fuels and chemical fertilizer, since food would need to travel farther and manure would be in short supply. Indeed, it is doubtful that you can build a more sustainable agriculture without animals to cycle nutrients and support local food production. If our concern is for the health of nature—rather than, say, the internal consistency of our moral code or the condition of our souls—then eating animals may sometimes be the most ethical thing to do.

There is, too, the fact that we humans have been eating animals as long as we have lived on this earth. Humans may not need to eat meat in order to survive, yet doing so is part of our evolutionary heritage, reflected in the design of our teeth and the structure of our digestion. Eating meat helped make us what we are, in a social and biological sense. Under the pressure of the hunt, the human brain grew in size and complexity, and around the fire where the meat was cooked, human culture first flourished. Granting rights to animals may lift us up from the brutal world of predation, but it will entail the sacrifice of part of our identity—our own animality.

65   Surely this is one of the odder paradoxes of animal rights doctrine. It asks us to recognize all that we share with animals and then demands that we act toward them in a most unanimalistic way. Whether or not this is a good idea, we should at least acknowledge that our desire to eat meat is not a trivial matter, no mere "gastronomic preference." We might as well call sex—also now technically unnecessary—a mere "recreational preference." Whatever else it is, our meat-eating is something very deep indeed.

Are any of these good enough reasons to eat animals? I'm mindful of Ben Franklin's definition of the reasonable creature as one who can come up with reasons for whatever he wants to do. So I decided I would track down Peter Singer and ask him what he thought. In an e-mail message, I described Polyface and asked him about the implications for his position of the Good Farm—one where animals got to live according to their nature and to all appearances did not suffer.

"I agree with you that it is better for these animals to have lived and died than not to have lived at all," Singer wrote back. Since the utilitarian is concerned exclusively with the sum of happiness and suffering and the slaughter of an animal that doesn't comprehend that death need not involve suffering, the Good Farm adds to the total of animal happiness, provided you replace the slaughtered animal with a new one. However, he added, this line of thinking doesn't obviate the wrongness of killing an animal that "has a sense of its own existence over time and can have preferences for its own future." In other words, it's OK to eat the chicken, but he's not so sure about the pig. Yet, he wrote, "I would not be sufficiently confident of my arguments to condemn someone who purchased meat from one of these farms."

Singer went on to express serious doubts that such farms could be practical on a large scale, since the pressures of the marketplace will lead their owners to cut costs and corners at the expense of the animals. He suggested, too, that killing animals is not conducive to treating them with respect. Also, since humanely raised food will be more expensive, only the well-to-do can afford morally defensible animal protein. These are important considerations, but they don't alter my essential point: what's wrong with animal agriculture— with eating animals—is the practice, not the principle.

What this suggests to me is that people who care should be working not for animal rights but animal welfare—to ensure that farm animals don't suffer and that their deaths are swift and painless. In fact, the decent-life-merciful-death line is how Jeremy Bentham justified his own meat-eating. Yes, the philosophical father of animal rights was himself a carnivore. In a passage rather less frequently quoted by animal rightists, Bentham defended eating animals on the grounds that "we are the better for it, and they are never the worse . . . The death they suffer in our hands commonly is, and always may be, a speedier and, by that means, a less painful one than that which would await them in the inevitable course of nature."

My guess is that Bentham never looked too closely at what happens in a [70] slaughterhouse, but the argument suggests that, in theory at least, a utilitarian can justify the killing of humanely treated animals—for meat or, presumably, for clothing. (Though leather and fur pose distinct moral problems. Leather is a byproduct of raising domestic animals for food, which can be done humanely. However, furs are usually made from wild animals that die brutal deaths—usually in leg-hold traps—and since most fur species aren't domesticated, raising them on farms isn't necessarily more humane.) But whether the issue is food or fur or hunting, what should concern us is the suffering, not the killing. All of which I was feeling pretty good about—until I remembered that utilitarians can also justify killing retarded orphans. Killing just isn't the problem for them that it is for other people, including me.

During my visit to Polyface Farm, I asked Salatin where his animals were slaughtered. He does the chickens and rabbits right on the farm, and would do the cattle, pigs and sheep there too if only the USDA would let him. Salatin showed me the open-air abattoir he built behind the farmhouse—a sort of outdoor kitchen on a concrete slab, with stainless-steel sinks, scalding tanks, a feather-plucking machine and metal cones to hold the birds upside down while they're being bled. Processing chickens is not a pleasant job, but Salatin insists on doing it himself because he's convinced he can do it more humanely and cleanly than any processing plant. He slaughters every other Saturday through the summer. Anyone's welcome to watch.

I asked Salatin how he could bring himself to kill a chicken.

"People have a soul; animals don't," he said. "It's a bedrock belief of mine." Salatin is a devout Christian. "Unlike us, animals are not created in God's image, so when they die, they just die."

The notion that only in modern times have people grown uneasy about killing animals is a flattering conceit. Taking a life is momentous, and people have been working to justify the slaughter of animals for thousands of years. Religion and especially ritual has played a crucial part in helping us reckon the moral costs. Native Americans and other hunter-gatherers would give thanks to their prey for giving up its life so the eater might live (sort of like saying grace). Many cultures have offered sacrificial animals to the gods, perhaps as a way to convince themselves that it was the gods' desires that demanded the slaughter, not their own. In ancient Greece, the priests responsible for the slaughter (priests!—now we entrust the job to minimum-wage workers) would sprinkle holy water on the sacrificial animal's brow. The beast would promptly shake its head, and this was taken as a sign of assent. Slaughter doesn't necessarily preclude respect. For all these people, it was the ceremony that allowed them to look, then to eat.

75   Apart from a few surviving religious practices, we no longer have any rituals governing the slaughter or eating of animals, which perhaps helps to explain why we find ourselves where we do, feeling that our only choice is to either look away or give up meat. Frank Perdue is happy to serve the first customer; Peter Singer, the second.

Until my visit to Polyface Farm, I had assumed these were the only two options. But on Salatin's farm, the eye contact between people and animals whose loss John Berger mourned is still a fact of life—and of death, for neither the lives nor the deaths of these animals have been secreted behind steel walls. "Food with a face," Salatin likes to call what he's selling, a slogan that probably scares off some customers. People see very different things when they look into the eyes of a pig or a chicken or a steer—a being without a soul, a "subject of a life" entitled to rights, a link in a food chain, a vessel for pain and pleasure, a tasty lunch. But figuring out what we do think, and what we can eat, might begin with the looking.

We certainly won't philosophize our way to an answer. Salatin told me the story of a man who showed up at the farm one Saturday morning. When Salatin noticed a PETA bumper sticker on the man's car, he figured he was in for it. But the man had a different agenda. He explained that after sixteen years as a vegetarian, he had decided that the only way he could ever eat meat again was if he killed the animal himself. He had come to *look*.

"Ten minutes later we were in the processing shed with a chicken," Salatin recalled. "He slit the bird's throat and watched it die. He saw that the animal did not look at him accusingly, didn't do a Disney double take. The animal had been treated with respect when it was alive, and he saw that it could also have a respectful death—that it wasn't being treated as a pile of protoplasm."

Salatin's open-air abattoir is a morally powerful idea. Someone slaughtering a chicken in a place where he can be watched is apt to do it scrupulously, with consideration for the animal as well as for the eater. This is going to sound quixotic, but maybe all we need to do to redeem industrial animal agriculture in this country is to pass a law requiring that the steel and concrete walls of the CAFOs and slaughterhouses be replaced with . . . glass. If there's any new "right" we need to establish, maybe it's this one: the right to look.

No doubt the sight of some of these places would turn many people into   80
vegetarians. Many others would look elsewhere for their meat, to farmers like Salatin. There are more of them than I would have imagined. Despite the relentless consolidation of the American meat industry, there has been a revival of small farms where animals still live their "characteristic form of life." I'm thinking of the ranches where cattle still spend their lives on grass, the poultry farms where chickens still go outside and the hog farms where pigs live as they did fifty years ago—in contact with the sun, the earth and the gaze of a farmer.

For my own part, I've discovered that if you're willing to make the effort, it's entirely possible to limit the meat you eat to nonindustrial animals. I'm tempted to think that we need a new dietary category, to go with the vegan and lactovegetarian and piscatorian. I don't have a catchy name for it yet (humanocarnivore?), but this is the only sort of meat-eating I feel comfortable with these days. I've become the sort of shopper who looks for labels indicating that his meat and eggs have been humanely grown (the American Humane Association's new "Free Farmed" label seems to be catching on), who visits the farms where his chicken and pork come from and who asks kinky-sounding questions about touring slaughterhouses. I've actually found a couple of small processing plants willing to let a customer onto the kill floor, including one, in Cannon Falls, Minnesota, with a glass abattoir.

The industrialization—and dehumanization—of American animal farming is a relatively new, evitable and local phenomenon: no other country raises and slaughters its food animals quite as intensively or as brutally as we do. Were the walls of our meat industry to become transparent, literally or even figuratively, we would not long continue to do it this way. Tail-docking and sow crates and beak-clipping would disappear overnight, and the days of slaughtering four hundred head of cattle an hour would come to an end. For who could stand the sight? Yes, meat would get more expensive. We'd probably eat less of it, too, but maybe when we did eat animals, we'd eat them with the consciousness, ceremony and respect they deserve.

QUESTIONS

1. Precisely how much of the Animal Liberation approach has Pollan accepted? How can you tell?

2. Things change when Pollan visits Polyface farm, the humane operation run by Joel Salatin. What about the farm convinces Pollan that it represents an alternative to Peter Singer's approach?

3. Describe the structure of Pollan's essay. How does he introduce Animal Liberation and how does he argue against it?

ALDO LEOPOLD   *The Land Ethic*

WHEN GOD-LIKE ODYSSEUS returned from the wars in Troy, he hanged all on one rope a dozen slave-girls of his household whom he suspected of misbehavior during his absence.

This hanging involved no question of propriety. The girls were property. The disposal of property was then, as now, a matter of expediency, not of right and wrong.

Concepts of right and wrong were not lacking from Odysseus' Greece: witness the fidelity of his wife through the long years before at last his black-prowed galleys clove the wine-dark seas for home. The ethical structure of that day covered wives, but had not yet been extended to human chattels. During the three thousand years which have since elapsed, ethical criteria have been extended to many fields of conduct, with corresponding shrinkages in those judged by expediency only.

THE ETHICAL SEQUENCE

This extension of ethics, so far studied only by philosophers, is actually a process in ecological evolution. Its sequences may be described in ecological as well as in philosophical terms. An ethic, ecologically, is a limitation on freedom of action in the struggle for existence. An ethic, philosophically, is a differentiation of social from anti-social conduct. These are two definitions of one thing. The thing has its origin in the tendency of interdependent individuals or groups to evolve modes of co-operation. The ecologist calls these symbioses. Politics and economics are advanced symbioses in which the original free-for-all competition has been replaced, in part, by co-operative mechanisms with an ethical content.

5   The complexity of co-operative mechanisms has increased with population density, and with the efficiency of tools. It was simpler, for example, to define the anti-social uses of sticks and stones in the days of the mastodons than of bullets and billboards in the age of motors.

The first ethics dealt with the relation between individuals; the Mosaic Decalogue[1] is an example. Later accretions dealt with the relation between the individual and society. The Golden Rule tries to integrate social organization to the individual.

There is as yet no ethic dealing with man's relation to land and to the animals and plants which grow upon it. Land, like Odysseus' slave-girls, is still property. The land-relation is still strictly economic, entailing privileges but not obligations.

The final essay in Leopold's A Sand County Almanac *(1949), which combines journal entries and essays on his home in Wisconsin to reflect on nature and environmental issues.*

1. The Ten Commandments.

The extension of ethics to this third element in human environment is, if I read the evidence correctly, an evolutionary possibility and an ecological necessity. It is the third step in a sequence. The first two have already been taken. Individual thinkers since the days of Ezekiel and Isaiah[2] have asserted that the despoliation of land is not only inexpedient but wrong. Society, however, has not yet affirmed their belief. I regard the present conservation movement as the embryo of such an affirmation.

An ethic may be regarded as a mode of guidance for meeting ecological situations so new or intricate, or involving such deferred reactions, that the path of social expediency is not discernible to the average individual. Animal instincts are modes of guidance for the individual in meeting such situations. Ethics are possibly a kind of community instinct in-the-making.

THE COMMUNITY CONCEPT

All ethics so far evolved rest upon a single premise: that the individual is a   10
member of a community of interdependent parts. His instincts prompt him to compete for his place in that community, but his ethics prompt him also to cooperate (perhaps in order that there may be a place to compete for).

The land ethic simply enlarges the boundaries of the community to include soils, waters, plants, and animals, or collectively: the land.

This sounds simple: do we not already sing our love for and obligation to the land of the free and the home of the brave? Yes, but just what and whom do we love? Certainly not the soil, which we are sending helter-skelter downriver. Certainly not the waters, which we assume have no function except to turn turbines, float barges, and carry off sewage. Certainly not the plants, of which we exterminate whole communities without batting an eye. Certainly not the animals, of which we have already extirpated many of the largest and most beautiful species. A land ethic of course cannot prevent the alteration, management, and use of these "resources," but it does affirm their right to continued existence, and, at least in spots, their continued existence in a natural state.

In short, a land ethic changes the role of *Homo sapiens* from conqueror of the land-community to plain member and citizen of it. It implies respect for his fellow-members, and also respect for the community as such.

In human history, we have learned (I hope) that the conqueror role is eventually self-defeating. Why? Because it is implicit in such a role that the conqueror knows, *ex cathedra*,[3] just what makes the community clock tick, and just what and who is valuable, and what and who is worthless, in community life. It always turns out that he knows neither, and this is why his conquests eventually defeat themselves.

In the biotic community, a parallel situation exists. Abraham knew exactly   15
what the land was for: it was to drip milk and honey into Abraham's mouth. At

2. Ezekiel (sixth century B.C.E.) and Isaiah (eighth century B.C.E.) were prophets of ancient Israel; the biblical books Ezekiel and Isaiah were named after them.

3. From the official throne of the bishop; hence, with authority.

the present moment, the assurance with which we regard this assumption is inverse to the degree of our education.

The ordinary citizen today assumes that science knows what makes the community clock tick; the scientist is equally sure that he does not. He knows that the biotic mechanism is so complex that its workings may never be fully understood.

That man is, in fact, only a member of a biotic team is shown by an ecological interpretation of history. Many historical events, hitherto explained solely in terms of human enterprise, were actually biotic interactions between people and land. The characteristics of the land determined the facts quite as potently as the characteristics of the men who lived on it.

Consider, for example, the settlement of the Mississippi valley. In the years following the Revolution, three groups were contending for its control: the native Indian, the French and English traders, and the American settlers. Historians wonder what would have happened if the English at Detroit had thrown a little more weight into the Indian side of those tipsy scales which decided the outcome of the colonial migration into the cane-lands of Kentucky. It is time now to ponder the fact that the cane-lands, when subjected to the particular mixture of forces represented by the cow, plow, fire, and axe of the pioneer, became bluegrass. What if the plant succession inherent in this dark and bloody ground had, under the impact of these forces, given us some worthless sedge, shrub, or weed? Would Boone and Kenton[4] have held out? Would there have been any overflow into Ohio, Indiana, Illinois, and Missouri? Any Louisiana Purchase? Any transcontinental union of new states? Any Civil War?

Kentucky was one sentence in the drama of history. We are commonly told what the human actors in this drama tried to do, but we are seldom told that their success, or the lack of it, hung in large degree on the reaction of particular soils to the impact of the particular forces exerted by their occupancy. In the case of Kentucky, we do not even know where the bluegrass came from—whether it is a native species, or a stowaway from Europe.

20   Contrast the cane-lands with what hindsight tells us about the Southwest, where the pioneers were equally brave, resourceful, and persevering. The impact of occupancy here brought no bluegrass, or other plant fitted to withstand the bumps and buffetings of hard use. This region, when grazed by livestock, reverted through a series of more and more worthless grasses, shrubs, and weeds to a condition of unstable equilibrium. Each recession of plant types bred erosion; each increment to erosion bred a further recession of plants. The result today is a progressive and mutual deterioration, not only of plants and soils, but of the animal community subsisting thereon. The early settlers did not expect this: on the ciénegas[5] of New Mexico some even cut

4. Daniel Boone (1734–1820), American frontiersman who explored and helped settle the West; Simon Kenton (1755–1836), frontiersman and friend of Daniel Boone, famous for his miraculous escape from the Shawnee Indians.

5. Marshes, swamps (Spanish).

ditches to hasten it. So subtle has been its progress that few residents of the region are aware of it. It is quite invisible to the tourist who finds this wrecked landscape colorful and charming (as indeed it is, but it bears scant resemblance to what it was in 1848).

This same landscape was "developed" once before, but with quite different results. The Pueblo Indians settled the Southwest in pre-Columbian times,[6] but they happened *not* to be equipped with range livestock. Their civilization expired, but not because their land expired.

In India, regions devoid of any sod-forming grass have been settled, apparently without wrecking the land, by the simple expedient of carrying the grass to the cow, rather than vice versa. (Was this the result of some deep wisdom, or was it just good luck? I do not know.)

In short, the plant succession steered the course of history; the pioneer simply demonstrated, for good or ill, what successions inhered in the land. Is history taught in this spirit? It will be, once the concept of land as a community really penetrates our intellectual life.

THE ECOLOGICAL CONSCIENCE

Conservation is a state of harmony between men and land. Despite nearly a century of propaganda, conservation still proceeds at a snail's pace; progress still consists largely of letterhead pieties and convention oratory. On the back forty[7] we still slip two steps backward for each forward stride.

The usual answer to this dilemma is "more conservation education." No one will debate this, but is it certain that only the *volume* of education needs stepping up? Is something lacking in the *content* as well? 25

It is difficult to give a fair summary of its content in brief form, but, as I understand it, the content is substantially this: obey the law, vote right, join some organizations, and practice what conservation is profitable on your own land; the government will do the rest.

Is not this formula too easy to accomplish anything worth-while? It defines no right or wrong, assigns no obligation, calls for no sacrifice, implies no change in the current philosophy of values. In respect of land-use, it urges only enlightened self-interest. Just how far will such education take us? An example will perhaps yield a partial answer.

By 1930 it had become clear to all except the ecologically blind that southwestern Wisconsin's topsoil was slipping seaward. In 1933 the farmers were told that if they would adopt certain remedial practices for five years, the public would donate CCC[8] labor to install them, plus the necessary machinery and materials. The offer was widely accepted, but the practices were widely forgotten when the five-year contract period was up. The farmers continued

6. Before the arrival of Christopher Columbus in the New World.

7. Acres of a farm.

8. Civilian Conservation Corps, established in 1933 during the Great Depression to employ thousands of unemployed young men and send them into battle against the destruction of America's natural resources.

only those practices that yielded an immediate and visible economic gain for themselves.

This led to the idea that maybe farmers would learn more quickly if they themselves wrote the rules. Accordingly the Wisconsin Legislature in 1937 passed the Soil Conservation District Law. This said to farmers, in effect: *We, the public, will furnish you free technical service and loan you specialized machinery, if you will write your own rules for land-use. Each county may write its own rules, and these will have the force of law.* Nearly all the counties promptly organized to accept the proffered help, but after a decade of operation, *no county has yet written a single rule.* There has been visible progress in such practices as strip-cropping, pasture renovation, and soil liming, but none in fencing woodlots against grazing, and none in excluding plow and cow from steep slopes. The farmers, in short, have selected those remedial practices which were profitable anyhow, and ignored those which were profitable to the community, but not clearly profitable to themselves.

30   When one asks why no rules have been written, one is told that the community is not yet ready to support them; education must precede rules. But the education actually in progress makes no mention of obligations to land over and above those dictated by self-interest. The net result is that we have more education but less soil, fewer healthy woods, and as many floods as in 1937.

The puzzling aspect of such situations is that the existence of obligations over and above self-interest is taken for granted in such rural community enterprises as the betterment of roads, schools, churches, and baseball teams. Their existence is not taken for granted, nor as yet seriously discussed, in bettering the behavior of the water that falls on the land, or in the preserving of the beauty or diversity of the farm landscape. Land-use ethics are still governed wholly by economic self-interest, just as social ethics were a century ago.

To sum up: we asked the farmer to do what he conveniently could to save his soil, and he has done just that, and only that. The farmer who clears the woods off a 75 per cent slope, turns his cows into the clearing, and dumps its rainfall, rocks, and soil into the community creek, is still (if otherwise decent) a respected member of society. If he puts lime on his fields and plants his crops on contour, he is still entitled to all the privileges and emoluments of his Soil Conservation District. The District is a beautiful piece of social machinery, but it is coughing along on two cylinders because we have been too timid, and too anxious for quick success, to tell the farmer the true magnitude of his obligations. Obligations have no meaning without conscience, and the problem we face is the extension of the social conscience from people to land.

No important change in ethics was ever accomplished without an internal change in our intellectual emphasis, loyalties, affections, and convictions. The proof that conservation has not yet touched these foundations of conduct lies in the fact that philosophy and religion have not yet heard of it. In our attempt to make conservation easy, we have made it trivial.

THE OUTLOOK

It is inconceivable to me that an ethical relation to land can exist without love, respect, and admiration for land, and a high regard for its value. By value, I of course mean something far broader than mere economic value; I mean value in the philosophical sense.

Perhaps the most serious obstacle impeding the evolution of a land ethic is the fact that our educational and economic system is headed away from, rather than toward, an intense consciousness of land. Your true modern is separated from the land by many middlemen, and by innumerable physical gadgets. He has no vital relation to it; to him it is the space between cities on which crops grow. Turn him loose for a day on the land, and if the spot does not happen to be a golf links or a "scenic" area, he is bored stiff. If crops could be raised by hydroponics instead of farming, it would suit him very well. Synthetic substitutes for wood, leather, wool, and other natural land products suit him better than the originals. In short, land is something he has "outgrown." 35

Almost equally serious as an obstacle to a land ethic is the attitude of the farmer for whom the land is still an adversary, or a taskmaster that keeps him in slavery. Theoretically, the mechanization of farming ought to cut the farmer's chains, but whether it really does is debatable.

One of the requisites for an ecological comprehension of land is an understanding of ecology, and this is by no means co-extensive with "education"; in fact, much higher education seems deliberately to avoid ecological concepts. An understanding of ecology does not necessarily originate in courses bearing ecological labels; it is quite as likely to be labeled geography, botany, agronomy, history, or economics. This is as it should be, but whatever the label, ecological training is scarce.

The case for a land ethic would appear hopeless but for the minority which is in obvious revolt against these "modern" trends.

The "key-log" which must be moved to release the evolutionary process for an ethic is simply this: quit thinking about decent land-use as solely an economic problem. Examine each question in terms of what is ethically and esthetically right, as well as what is economically expedient. A thing is right when it tends to preserve the integrity, stability, and beauty of the biotic community. It is wrong when it tends otherwise.

It of course goes without saying that economic feasibility limits the tether of what can or cannot be done for land. It always has and it always will. The fallacy the economic determinists have tied around our collective neck, and which we now need to cast off, is the belief that economics determines *all* land-use. This is simply not true. An innumerable host of actions and attitudes, comprising perhaps the bulk of all land relations, is determined by the land-users' tastes and predilections, rather than by his purse. The bulk of all land relations hinges on investments of time, forethought, skill, and faith rather than on investments of cash. As a land-user thinketh, so is he. 40

I have purposely presented the land ethic as a product of social evolution because nothing so important as an ethic is ever "written." Only the most superficial student of history supposes that Moses "wrote" the Decalogue; it evolved in the minds of a thinking community, and Moses wrote a tentative summary of it for a "seminar." I say tentative because evolution never stops.

The evolution of a land ethic is an intellectual as well as emotional process. Conservation is paved with good intentions which prove to be futile, or even dangerous, because they are devoid of critical understanding either of the land, or of economic land-use. I think it is a truism that as the ethical frontier advances from the individual to the community, its intellectual content increases.

The mechanism of operation is the same for any ethic: social approbation for right actions: social disapproval for wrong actions.

By and large, our present problem is one of attitudes and implements. We are remodeling the Alhambra[9] with a steam-shovel, and we are proud of our yardage. We shall hardly relinquish the shovel, which after all has many good points, but we are in need of gentler and more objective criteria for its successful use.

9. Moorish palace in Grenada, Spain, built between 1338 and 1390.

QUESTIONS

1. Leopold begins with a story of the Greek hero Odysseus returning from the Trojan War and executing "a dozen slave-girls of his household." What relevance does this story have to his argument about progress in human ethics?

2. What is the "ethical sequence"? What three aspects or stages of ethical development does Leopold include?

3. How does the concept of a biotic community alter the relationship of humans to the land? Why does Leopold use the Latin designation *Homo sapiens* in paragraph 13 as he redefines this relationship?

4. What problems does Leopold anticipate in putting a land ethic into effect? Do environmentalists face the same or different problems today?

5. How far have Americans come since 1949, when Leopold's essay was published? If your course includes a research paper, consider writing on contemporary responses to problems that Leopold enumerated in his day.

MARY GORDON   *A Moral Choice*

I AM HAVING LUNCH with six women. What is unusual is that four of them are in their seventies, two of them widowed, the other two living with husbands beside whom they've lived for decades. All of them have had children. Had they been men, they would have published books and hung their paintings on the walls of important galleries. But they are women of a certain generation, and their lives were shaped around their families and personal relations. They are women you go to for help and support. We begin talking about the latest legislative act that makes abortion more difficult for poor women to obtain. An extraordinary thing happens. Each of them talks about the illegal abortions she had during her young womanhood. Not one of them was spared the experience. Any of them could have died on the table of whatever person (not a doctor in any case) she was forced to approach, in secrecy and in terror, to end a pregnancy that she felt would blight her life.

I mention this incident for two reasons: first as a reminder that all kinds of women have always had abortions; second because it is essential that we remember that an abortion is performed on a living woman who has a life in which a terminated pregnancy is only a small part. Morally speaking, the decision to have an abortion doesn't take place in a vacuum. It is connected to other choices that a woman makes in the course of an adult life.

Anti-choice propagandists paint pictures of women who choose to have abortions as types of moral callousness, selfishness, or irresponsibility. The woman choosing to abort is the dressed-for-success yuppie who gets rid of her baby so that she won't miss her Caribbean vacation or her chance for promotion. Or she is the feckless, promiscuous ghetto teenager who couldn't bring herself to just say no to sex. A third, purportedly kinder, gentler picture has recently begun to be drawn. The woman in the abortion clinic is there because she is misinformed about the nature of the world. She is having an abortion because society does not provide for mothers and their children, and she mistakenly thinks that another mouth to feed will be the ruin of her family, not understanding that the temporary truth of family unhappiness doesn't stack up beside the eternal verity that abortion is murder. Or she is the dupe of her husband or boyfriend, who talks her into having an abortion because a child will be a drag on his life-style. None of these pictures created by the anti-choice movement assumes that the decision to have an abortion is made responsibly, in the context of a morally lived life, by a free and responsible moral agent.

Published in the Atlantic Monthly *(April 1990), one of America's oldest and most prestigious magazines of literature, culture, and politics.*

THE ONTOLOGY OF THE FETUS

How would a woman who habitually makes choices in moral terms come to the decision to have an abortion? The moral discussion of abortion centers on the issue of whether or not abortion is an act of murder. At first glance it would seem that the answer should follow directly upon two questions: Is the fetus human? and Is it alive? It would be absurd to deny that a fetus is alive or that it is human. What would our other options be—to say that it is inanimate or belongs to another species? But we habitually use the terms "human" and "live" to refer to parts of our body—"human hair," for example, or "live red-blood cells"—and we are clear in our understanding that the nature of these objects does not rank equally with an entire personal existence. It then seems important to consider whether the fetus, this alive human thing, is a *person*, to whom the term "murder" could sensibly be applied. How would anyone come to a decision about something so impalpable as personhood? Philosophers have struggled with the issue of personhood, but in language that is so abstract that it is unhelpful to ordinary people making decisions in the course of their lives. It might be more productive to begin thinking about the status of the fetus by examining the language and customs that surround it. This approach will encourage us to focus on the choosing, acting woman, rather than the act of abortion—as if the act were performed by abstract forces without bodies, histories, attachments.

5   This focus on the acting woman is useful because a pregnant woman has an identifiable, consistent ontology,[1] and a fetus takes on different ontological identities over time. But common sense, experience, and linguistic usage point clearly to the fact that we habitually consider, for example, a seven-week-old fetus to be different from a seven-month-old one. We can tell this by the way we respond to the involuntary loss of one as against the other. We have different language for the experience of the involuntary expulsion of the fetus from the womb depending upon the point of gestation at which the experience occurs. If it occurs early in the pregnancy, we call it a miscarriage; if late, we call it a stillbirth.

We would have an extreme reaction to the reversal of those terms. If a woman referred to a miscarriage at seven weeks as a stillbirth, we would be alarmed. It would shock our sense of propriety; it would make us uneasy; we would find it disturbing, misplaced—as we do when a bag lady sits down in a restaurant and starts shouting, or an octogenarian arrives at our door in a sailor suit. In short, we would suspect that the speaker was mad. Similarly, if a doctor or a nurse referred to the loss of a seven-month-old fetus as a miscarriage, we would be shocked by that person's insensitivity: could she or he not understand that a fetus that age is not what it was months before?

Our ritual and religious practices underscore the fact that we make distinctions among fetuses. If a woman took the bloody matter—indistinguishable from a heavy period—of an early miscarriage and insisted upon putting it in a tiny coffin and marking its grave, we would have serious concerns about

1. Concerned with existence or being.

her mental health. By the same token, we would feel squeamish about flushing a seven-month-old fetus down the toilet—something we would quite normally do with an early miscarriage. There are no prayers for the matter of a miscarriage, nor do we feel there should be. Even a Catholic priest would not baptize the issue of an early miscarriage.

The difficulties stem, of course, from the odd situation of a fetus's ontology: a complicated, differentiated, and nuanced response is required when we are dealing with an entity that changes over time. Yet we are in the habit of making distinctions like this. At one point we know that a child is no longer a child but an adult. That this question is vexed and problematic is clear from our difficulty in determining who is a juvenile offender and who is an adult criminal and at what age sexual intercourse ceases to be known as statutory rape. So at what point, if any, do we on the pro-choice side say that the developing fetus is a person, with rights equal to its mother's?

The anti-choice people have one advantage over us; their monolithic position gives them unity on this question. For myself, I am made uneasy by third-trimester abortions, which take place when the fetus could live outside the mother's body, but I also know that these are extremely rare and often performed on very young girls who have had difficulty comprehending the realities of pregnancy. It seems to me that the question of late abortions should be decided case by case, and that fixation on this issue is a deflection from what is most important: keeping early abortions, which are in the majority by far, safe and legal. I am also politically realistic enough to suspect that bills restricting late abortions are not good-faith attempts to make distinctions about the nature of fetal life. They are, rather, the cynical embodiments of the hope among anti-choice partisans that technology will be on their side and that medical science's ability to create situations in which younger fetuses are viable outside their mothers' bodies will increase dramatically in the next few years. Ironically, medical science will probably make the issue of abortion a minor one in the near future. The RU-486 pill, which can induce abortion early on, exists, and whether or not it is legally available (it is not on the market here, because of pressure from anti-choice groups), women will begin to obtain it. If abortion can occur through chemical rather than physical means, in the privacy of one's home, most people not directly involved will lose interest in it. As abortion is transformed from a public into a private issue, it will cease to be perceived as political; it will be called personal instead.

An Equivocal Good

But because abortion will always deal with what it is to create and sustain life, it will always be a moral issue. And whether we like it or not, our moral thinking about abortion is rooted in the shifting soil of perception. In an age in which much of our perception is manipulated by media that specialize in the sound bite and the photo op, the anti-choice partisans have a twofold advantage over us on the pro-choice side. The pro-choice moral position is more complex, and the experience we defend is physically repellent to contemplate.

None of us in the pro-choice movement would suggest that abortion is not a regrettable occurrence. Anti-choice proponents can offer pastel photographs of babies in buntings, their eyes peaceful in the camera's gaze. In answer, we can't offer the material of an early abortion, bloody, amorphous in a paper cup, to prove that what has just been removed from the woman's body is not a child, not in the same category of being as the adorable bundle in an adoptive mother's arms. It is not a pleasure to look at the physical evidence of abortion, and most of us don't get the opportunity to do so.

The theologian Daniel Maguire, uncomfortable with the fact that most theological arguments about the nature of abortion are made by men who have never been anywhere near an actual abortion, decided to visit a clinic and observe abortions being performed. He didn't find the experience easy, but he knew that before he could in good conscience make a moral judgment on abortion, he needed to experience through his senses what an aborted fetus is like: he needed to look at and touch the controversial entity. He held in his hand the bloody fetal stuff; the eight-week-old fetus fit in the palm of his hand, and it certainly bore no resemblance to either of his two children when he had held them moments after their birth. He knew at that point what women who have experienced early abortions and miscarriages know: that some event occurred, possibly even a dramatic one, but it was not the death of a child.

Because issues of pregnancy and birth are both physical and metaphorical, we must constantly step back and forth between ways of perceiving the world. When we speak of gestation, we are often talking in terms of potential, about events and objects to which we attach our hopes, fears, dreams, and ideals. A mother can speak to the fetus in her uterus and name it; she and her mate may decorate a nursery according to their vision of the good life; they may choose for an embryo a college, a profession, a dwelling. But those of us who are trying to think morally about pregnancy and birth must remember that these feelings are our own projections onto what is in reality an inappropriate object. However charmed we may be by an expectant father's buying a little football for something inside his wife's belly, we shouldn't make public policy based on such actions, nor should we force others to live their lives conforming to our fantasies.

As a society, we are making decisions that pit the complicated future of a complex adult against the fate of a mass of cells lacking cortical development. The moral pressure should be on distinguishing the true from the false, the real suffering of living persons from our individual and often idiosyncratic dreams and fears. We must make decisions on abortion based on an understanding of how people really do live. We must be able to say that poverty is worse than not being poor, that having dignified and meaningful work is better than working in conditions of degradation, that raising a child one loves and has desired is better than raising a child in resentment and rage, that it is better for a twelve-year-old not to endure the trauma of having a child when she is herself a child.

When we put these ideas against the ideas of "child" or "baby," we seem to be making a horrifying choice of life-style over life. But in fact we are telling the truth of what it means to bear a child, and what the experience of abortion really is. This is extremely difficult, for the object of the discussion is hidden, changing, potential. We make our decisions on the basis of approximate and inadequate language, often on the basis of fantasies and fears. It will always be crucial to try to separate genuine moral concern from phobia, punitiveness, superstition, anxiety, a desperate search for certainty in an uncertain world.

One of the certainties that is removed if we accept the consequences of the pro-choice position is the belief that the birth of a child is an unequivocal good. In real life we act knowing that the birth of a child is not always a good thing: people are sometimes depressed, angry, rejecting, at the birth of a child. But this is a difficult truth to tell; we don't like to say it, and one of the fears preyed on by anti-choice proponents is that if we cannot look at the birth of a child as an unequivocal good, then there is nothing to look toward. The desire for security of the imagination, for typological fixity, particularly in the area of "the good," is an understandable desire. It must seem to some anti-choice people that we on the pro-choice side are not only murdering innocent children but also murdering hope. Those of us who have experienced the birth of a desired child and felt the joy of that moment can be tempted into believing that it was the physical experience of the birth itself that was the joy. But it is crucial to remember that the birth of a child itself is a neutral occurrence emotionally: the charge it takes on is invested in it by the people experiencing or observing it.

THE FEAR OF SEXUAL AUTONOMY

These uncertainties can lead to another set of fears, not only about abortion but about its implications. Many anti-choice people fear that to support abortion is to cast one's lot with the cold and technological rather than with the warm and natural, to head down the slippery slope toward a brave new world where handicapped children are left on mountains to starve and the old are put out in the snow. But if we look at the history of abortion, we don't see the embodiment of what the anti-choice proponents fear. On the contrary, excepting the grotesque counterexample of the People's Republic of China (which practices forced abortion), there seems to be a real link between repressive anti-abortion stances and repressive governments. Abortion was banned in Fascist Italy and Nazi Germany; it is illegal in South Africa and in Chile. It is paid for by the governments of Denmark, England, and the Netherlands, which have national health and welfare systems that foster the health and well-being of mothers, children, the old, and the handicapped.

Advocates of outlawing abortion often refer to women seeking abortion as self-indulgent and materialistic. In fact these accusations mask a discomfort with female sexuality, sexual pleasure, and sexual autonomy. It is possible for a woman to have a sexual life unriddled by fear only if she can be confident that she need not pay for a failure of technology or judgment (and who among us has never once been swept away in the heat of a sexual moment?) by taking upon herself the crushing burden of unchosen motherhood.

It is no accident, therefore, that the increased appeal of measures to restrict maternal conduct during pregnancy—and a new focus on the physical autonomy of the pregnant woman—have come into public discourse at precisely the time when women are achieving unprecedented levels of economic and political autonomy. What has surprised me is that some of this new anti-autonomy talk comes to us from the left. An example of this new discourse is an article by Christopher Hitchens that appeared in *The Nation* last April, in which the author asserts his discomfort with abortion. Hitchens's tone is impeccably British: arch, light, we're men of the left.

> Anyone who has ever seen a sonogram or has spent even an hour with a textbook on embryology knows that the emotions are not the deciding factor. In order to terminate a pregnancy, you have to still a heartbeat, switch off a developing brain, and whatever the method, break some bones and rupture some organs. As to whether this involves pain on the "Silent Scream" scale, I have no idea. The "right to life" leadership, again, has cheapened everything it touches.

"It is a pity," Hitchens goes on to say, "that . . . the majority of feminists and their allies have stuck to the dead ground of 'Me Decade' possessive individualism, an ideology that has more in common than it admits with the prehistoric right, which it claims to oppose but has in fact encouraged." Hitchens proposes, as an alternative, a program of social reform that would make contraception free and support a national adoption service. In his opinion, it would seem, women have abortions for only two reasons: because they are selfish or because they are poor. If the state will take care of the economic problems and the bureaucratic messiness around adoption, it remains only for the possessive individualists to get their act together and walk with their babies into the communal utopia of the future. Hitchens would allow victims of rape or incest to have free abortions, on the grounds that since they didn't choose to have sex, the women should not be forced to have the babies. This would seem to put the issue of volition in a wrong and telling place. To Hitchens's mind, it would appear, if a woman chooses to have sex, she can't choose whether or not to have a baby. The implications of this are clear. If a woman is consciously and volitionally sexual, she should be prepared to take her medicine. And what medicine must the consciously sexual male take? Does Hitchens really believe, or want us to believe, that every male who has unintentionally impregnated a woman will be involved in the lifelong responsibility for the upbringing of the engendered child? Can he honestly say that he has observed this behavior—or, indeed, would want to see it observed—in the world in which he lives?

REAL CHOICES

20   It is essential for a moral decision about abortion to be made in an atmosphere of open, critical thinking. We on the pro-choice side must accept that there are indeed anti-choice activists who take their position in good faith. I believe, however, that they are people for whom childbirth is an emotionally overladen

topic, people who are susceptible to unclear thinking because of their unrealistic hopes and fears. It is important for us in the pro-choice movement to be open in discussing those areas involving abortion which are nebulous and unclear. But we must not forget that there are some things that we know to be undeniably true. There are some undeniable bad consequences of a woman's being forced to bear a child against her will. First is the trauma of going through a pregnancy and giving birth to a child who is not desired, a trauma more long-lasting than that experienced by some (only some) women who experience an early abortion: The grief of giving up a child at its birth—and at nine months it is a child whom one has felt move inside one's body—is underestimated both by anti-choice partisans and by those for whom access to adoptable children is important. This grief should not be forced on any woman—or, indeed, encouraged by public policy.

We must be realistic about the impact on society of millions of unwanted children in an overpopulated world. Most of the time, human beings have sex not because they want to make babies. Yet throughout history sex has resulted in unwanted pregnancies. And women have always aborted. One thing that is not hidden, mysterious, or debatable is that making abortion illegal will result in the deaths of women, as it has always done. Is our historical memory so short that none of us remember aunts, sisters, friends, or mothers who were killed or rendered sterile by septic abortions?[2] Does no one in the anti-choice movement remember stories or actual experiences of midnight drives to filthy rooms from which aborted women were sent out, bleeding, to their fate? Can anyone genuinely say that it would be a moral good for us as a society to return to those conditions?

Thinking about abortion, then, forces us to take moral positions as adults who understand the complexities of the world and the realities of human suffering, to make decisions based on how people actually live and choose, and not on our fears, prejudices, and anxieties about sex and society, life and death.

2. Leading to bacterial infection.

QUESTIONS

1. How would you characterize Gordon's tone throughout the essay, keeping in mind that she is dealing with a hotly debated topic?

2. Gordon takes on only some of the arguments against abortion. Why do you think she leaves many arguments out?

3. Make an outline of Gordon's arguments. Which strikes you as the most important? Why?

4. Write an essay in which you compare Gordon's position on abortion with that of Sallie Tisdale in the next essay, "We Do Abortions Here: A Nurse's Story."

We Do Abortions Here:
A Nurse's Story

W E DO ABORTIONS here; that is all we do. There are weary, grim moments when I think I cannot bear another basin of bloody remains, utter another kind phrase of reassurance. So I leave the procedure room in the back and reach for a new chart. Soon I am talking to an eighteen-year-old woman pregnant for the fourth time. I push up her sleeve to check her blood pressure and find row upon row of needle marks, neat and parallel and discolored. She has been so hungry for her drug for so long that she has taken to using the loose skin of her upper arms; her elbows are already a permanent ruin of bruises. She is surprised to find herself nearly four months pregnant. I suspect she is often surprised, in a mild way, by the blows she is dealt. I prepare myself for another basin, another brief and chafing loss.

"How can you stand it?" Even the clients ask. They see the machine, the strange instruments, the blood, the final stroke that wipes away the promise of pregnancy. Sometimes I see that too: I watch a woman's swollen abdomen sink to softness in a few stuttering moments and my own belly flip-flops with sorrow. But all it takes for me to catch my breath is another interview, one more story that sounds so much like the last one. There is a numbing sameness lurking in this job: the same questions, the same answers, even the same trembling tone in the voices. The worst is the sameness of human failure, of inadequacy in the face of each day's dull demands.

In describing this work, I find it difficult to explain how much I enjoy it most of the time. We laugh a lot here, as friends and as professional peers. It's nice to be with women all day. I like the sudden, transient bonds I forge with some clients: moments when I am in my strength, remembering weakness, and a woman in weakness reaches out for my strength. What I offer is not power, but solidness, offered almost eagerly. Certain clients waken in me every tender urge I have—others make me wince and bite my tongue. Both challenge me to find a balance. It is a sweet brutality we practice here, a stark and loving dispassion.

I look at abortion as if I am standing on a cliff with a telescope, gazing at some great vista. I can sweep the horizon with both eyes, survey the scene in all its distance and size. Or I can put my eye to the lens and focus on the small details, suddenly so close. In abortion the absolute must always be tempered by the contextual, because both are real, both valid, both hard. How can we do this? How can we refuse? Each abortion is a measure of our failure to protect, to nourish our own. Each basin I empty is a promise—but a promise broken a long time ago.

From Harper's Magazine (*October 1990*), *a monthly that includes fiction, essays, reviews, and commentary on American politics and culture.*

I grew up on the great promise of birth control. Like many women my age,   5
I took the pill as soon as I was sexually active. To risk pregnancy when it was
so easy to avoid seemed stupid, and my contraceptive success, as it were, was
part of the promise of social enlightenment. But birth control fails, far more
frequently than laboratory trials predict. Many of our clients take the pill; its
failure to protect them is a shocking realization. We have clients who have
been sterilized, whose husbands have had vasectomies; each one is a statistical
misfit, fine print come to life. The anger and shame of these women I hold in
one hand, and the basin in the other. The distance between the two, the
length I pace and try to measure, is the size of an abortion.

The procedure is disarmingly simple. Women are surprised, as though the
mystery of conception, a dark and hidden genesis, requires an elaborate finale.
In the first trimester of pregnancy, it's a mere few minutes of vacuuming, a
neat tidying up. I give a woman a small yellow Valium, and when it has begun
to relax her, I lead her into the back, into bareness, the stirrups. The doctor
reaches in her, opening the narrow tunnel to the uterus with a succession of
slim, smooth bars of steel. He inserts a plastic tube and hooks it to a hose on
the machine. The woman is framed against white paper that crackles as she
moves, the light bright in her eyes. Then the machine rumbles low and loud in
the small windowless room; the doctor moves the tube back and forth with an
efficient rhythm, and the long tail of it fills with blood that spurts and stumbles along into a jar. He is usually finished in a few minutes. They are long
minutes for the woman; her uterus frequently reacts to its abrupt emptying
with a powerful, unceasing cramp, which cuts off the blood vessels and enfolds the irritated, bleeding tissue.

I am learning to recognize the shadows that cross the faces of the women
I hold. While the doctor works between her spread legs, the paper drape hiding his intent expression, I stand beside the table. I hold the woman's hands in
mine, resting them just below her ribs. I watch her eyes, finger her necklace,
stroke her hair. I ask about her job, her family; in a haze she answers me; we
chatter, faces close, eyes meeting and sliding apart.

I watch the shadows that creep up unnoticed and suddenly darken her
face as she screws up her features and pushes a tear out each side to slide
down her cheeks. I have learned to anticipate the quiver of chin, the rapid in-
take of breath and the surprising sobs that rise soon after the machine starts to
drum. I know this is when the cramp deepens, and the tears are partly the
tears that follow pain—the sharp, childish crying when one bumps one's head
on a cabinet door. But a well of woe seems to open beneath many women
when they hear that thumping sound. The anticipation of the moment has finally come to fruit; the moment has arrived when the loss is no longer an
imagined one. It has come true.

I am struck by the sameness and I am struck every day by the variety
here—how this commonplace dilemma can so display the differences of
women. A twenty-one-year-old woman, unemployed, uneducated, without
family, in the fifth month of her fifth pregnancy. A forty-two-year-old mother of
teenagers, shocked by her condition, refusing to tell her husband. A twenty-

three-year-old mother of two having her seventh abortion, and many women in their thirties having their first. Some are stoic, some hysterical, a few giggle uncontrollably, many cry.

10   I talk to a sixteen-year-old uneducated girl who was raped. She has gonorrhea. She describes blinding headaches, attacks of breathlessness, nausea. "Sometimes I feel like two different people," she tells me with a calm smile, "and I talk to myself."

I pull out my plastic models. She listens patiently for a time, and then holds her hands wide in front of her stomach.

"When's the baby going to go up into my stomach?" she asks.

I blink. "What do you mean?"

"Well," she says, still smiling, "when women get so big, isn't the baby in your stomach? Doesn't it hatch out of an egg there?"

15   My first question in an interview is always the same. As I walk down the hall with the woman, as we get settled in chairs and I glance through her files, I am trying to gauge her, to get a sense of the words, and the tone, I should use. With some I joke, with others I chat, sometimes I fall into a brisk, business-like patter. But I ask every woman, "Are you sure you want to have an abortion?" Most nod with grim knowing smiles. "Oh, yes," they sigh. Some seek forgiveness, offer excuses. Occasionally a woman will flinch and say, "Please don't use that word."

Later I describe the procedure to come, using care with my language. I don't say "pain" any more than I would say "baby." So many are afraid to ask how much it will hurt. "My sister told me—" I hear. "A friend of mine said—" and the dire expectations unravel. I prick the index finger of a woman for a drop of blood to test, and as the tiny lancet approaches the skin she averts her eyes, holding her trembling hand out to me and jumping at my touch.

It is when I am holding a plastic uterus in one hand, a suction tube in the other, moving them together in imitation of the scrubbing to come, that women ask the most secret question. I am speaking in a matter-of-fact voice about "the tissue" and "the contents" when the woman suddenly catches my eye and asks, "How big is the baby now?" These words suggest a quiet need for a definition of the boundaries being drawn. It isn't so odd, after all, that she feels relief when I describe the growing bud's bulbous shape, its miniature nature. Again I gauge, and sometimes lie a little, weaseling around its infantile features until its clinging power slackens.

But when I look in the basin, among the curdlike blood clots, I see an elfin thorax, attenuated, its pencilline ribs all in parallel rows with tiny knobs of spine rounding upwards. A translucent arm and hand swim beside.

A sleepy-eyed girl, just fourteen, watched me with a slight and goofy smile all through her abortion. "Does it have little feet and little fingers and all?" she'd asked earlier. When the suction was over she sat up woozily at the end of the table and murmured, "Can I see it?" I shook my head firmly.

20   "It's not allowed," I told her sternly, because I knew she didn't really want to see what was left. She accepted this statement of authority, and a shadow of confused relief crossed her plain, pale face.

Privately, even grudgingly, my colleagues might admit the power of abortion to provoke emotion. But they seem to prefer the broad view and disdain the telescope. Abortion is a matter of choice, privacy, control. Its uncertainty lies in specific cases: retarded women and girls too young to give consent for surgery, women who are ill or hostile or psychotic. Such common dilemmas are met with both compassion and impatience: they slow things down. We are too busy to chew over ethics. One person might discuss certain concerns, behind closed doors, or describe a particularly disturbing dream. But generally there is to be no ambivalence.

Every day I take calls from women who are annoyed that we cannot see them, cannot do their abortion today, this morning, now. They argue the price, demand that we stay after hours to accommodate their job or class schedule. Abortion is so routine that one expects it to be like a manicure: quick, cheap, and painless.

Still, I've cultivated a certain disregard. It isn't negligence, but I don't always pay attention. I couldn't be here if I tried to judge each case on its merits; after all, we do over a hundred abortions a week. At some point each individual in this line of work draws a boundary and adheres to it. For one physician the boundary is a particular week of gestation; for another, it is a certain number of repeated abortions. But these boundaries can be fluid too: one physician overruled his own limit to abort a mature but severely malformed fetus. For me, the limit is allowing my clients to carry their own burden, shoulder the responsibility themselves. I shoulder the burden of trying not to judge them.

This city has several "crisis pregnancy centers" advertised in the Yellow Pages. They are small offices staffed by volunteers, and they offer free pregnancy testing, glossy photos of dead fetuses, and movies. I had a client recently whose mother is active in the anti-abortion movement. The young woman went to the local crisis center and was told that the doctor would make her touch her dismembered baby, that the pain would be the most horrible she could imagine, and that she might, after an abortion, never be able to have children. All lies. They called her at home and at work, over and over and over, but she had been wise enough to give a false name. She came to us a fugitive. We who do abortions are marked, by some, as impure. It's dirty work.

When a deliveryman comes to the sliding glass window by the reception   25
desk and tilts a box toward me, I hesitate. I read the packing slip, assess the shape and weight of the box in light of its supposed contents. We request familiar faces. The doors are carefully locked; I have learned to half glance around at bags and boxes, looking for a telltale sign. I register with security when I arrive, and I am careful not to bang a door. We are all a little on edge here.

Concern about size and shape seem to be natural, and so is the relief that follows. We make the powerful assumption that the fetus is different from us, and even when we admit the similarities, it is too simplistic to be seduced by form alone. But the form is enormously potent—humanoid, powerless, palm-sized, and pure, it evokes an almost fierce tenderness when viewed simply as what it appears to be. But appearance, and even potential, aren't enough. The fetus, in becoming itself, can ruin others; its utter dependence has a sinister side. When I am struck in the moment by the contents in the basin, I am careful to remember the context, to note the tearful teenager and the woman sighing with something more than relief. One kind of question, though, I find considerably trickier.

"Can you tell what it is?" I am asked, and this means gender. This question is asked by couples, not women alone. Always couples would abort a girl and keep a boy. I have been asked about twins, and even if I could tell what race the father was.

An eighteen-year-old woman with three daughters brought her husband to the interview. He glared first at me, then at his wife, as he sank lower and lower in the chair, picking his teeth with a toothpick. He interrupted a conversation with his wife to ask if I could tell whether the baby would be a boy or a girl. I told him I could not.

"Good," he replied in a slow and strangely malevolent voice, " 'cause if it was a boy I'd wring her neck."

30   In a literal sense, abortion exists because we are able to ask such questions, able to assign a value to the fetus which can shift with changing circumstances. If the human bond to a child were as primitive and unflinchingly narrow as that of other animals, there would be no abortion. There would be no abortion because there would be nothing more important than caring for the young and perpetuating the species, no reason for sex but to make babies. I sense this sometimes, this wordless organic duty, when I do ultrasounds.

We do ultrasound, a sound-wave test that paints a faint, gray picture of the fetus, whenever we're uncertain of gestation. Age is measured by the width of the skull and confirmed by the length of the femur or thighbone; we speak of a pregnancy as being a certain "femur length" in weeks. The usual concern is whether a pregnancy is within the legal limit for an abortion. Women this far along have bellies which swell out round and tight like trim muscles. When they lie flat, the mound rises softly above the hips, pressing the umbilicus upward.

It takes practice to read an ultrasound picture, which is grainy and etched as though in strokes of charcoal. But suddenly a rapid rhythmic motion appears—the beating heart. Nearby is a soft oval, scratched with lines—the skull. The leg is harder to find, and then suddenly the fetus moves, bobbing in the surf. The skull turns away, an arm slides across the screen, the torso rolls. I know the weight of a baby's head on my shoulder, the whisper of lips on ears, the delicate curve of a fragile spine in my hand. I know how heavy and correct a newborn cradled feels. The creature I watch in secret requires nothing from me but to be left alone, and that is precisely what won't be done.

These inadvertently made beings are caught in a twisting web of motive and desire. They are at least inconvenient, sometimes quite literally dangerous in the womb, but most often they fall somewhere in between—consequences never quite believed in come to roost. Their virtue rises and falls outside their own nature: they become only what we make them. A fetus created by accident is the most absolute kind of surprise. Whether the blame lies in a failed IUD, a slipped condom, or a false impression of safety, that fetus is a thing whose creation has been actively worked against. Its existence is an error. I think this is why so few women, even late in a pregnancy, will consider giving a baby up for adoption. To do so means making the fetus real—imagining it as something whole and outside oneself. The decision to terminate a pregnancy is sometimes so difficult and confounding that it creates an enormous demand for immediate action. The decision is a rejection; the pregnancy has become something to be rid of, a condition to be ended. It is a burden, a weight, a thing separate.

Women have abortions because they are too old, and too young, too poor, and too rich, too stupid, and too smart. I see women who berate themselves with violent emotions for their first and only abortion, and others who return three times, five times, hauling two or three children, who cannot remember to take a pill or where they put the diaphragm. We talk glibly about choice. But the choice for what? I see all the broken promises in lives lived like a series of impromptu obstacles. There are the sweet, light promises of love and intimacy, the glittering promise of education and progress, the warm promise of safe families, long years of innocence and community. And there is the promise of freedom: freedom from failure, from faithlessness. Freedom from biology. The early feminist defense of abortion asked many questions, but the one I remember is this: Is biology destiny? And the answer is yes, sometimes it is. Women who have the fewest choices of all exercise their right to abortion the most.

Oh, the ignorance. I take a woman to the back room and ask her to undress; a few minutes later I return and find her positioned discreetly behind a drape, still wearing underpants. "Do I have to take these off too?" she asks, a little shocked. Some swear they have not had sex, many do not know what a uterus is, how sperm and egg meet, how sex makes babies. Some late seekers do not believe themselves pregnant; they believe themselves *impregnable*. I was chastised when I began this job for referring to some clients as girls: it is a feminist heresy. They come so young, snapping gum, sockless and sneakered, and their shakily applied eyeliner smears when they cry. I call them girls with maternal benignity. I cannot imagine them as mothers.

35

The doctor seats himself between the woman's thighs and reaches into the dilated opening of a five-month pregnant uterus. Quickly he grabs and crushes the fetus in several places, and the room is filled with a low clatter and snap of forceps, the click of the tanaculum, and a pulling, sucking sound. The paper crinkles as the drugged and sleepy woman shifts, the nurse's low, honey-brown voice explains each step in delicate words.

I have fetus dreams, we all do here: dreams of abortions one after the other; of buckets of blood splashed on the walls; trees full of crawling fetuses. I dreamed that two men grabbed me and began to drag me away. "Let's do an abortion," they said with a sickening leer, and I began to scream, plunged into a vision of sucking, scraping pain, of being spread and torn by impartial instruments that do only what they are bidden. I woke from this dream barely able to breathe and thought of kitchen tables and coat hangers, knitting needles striped with blood, and women all alone clutching a pillow in their teeth to keep the screams from piercing the apartment-house walls. Abortion is the narrowest edge between kindness and cruelty. Done as well as it can be, it is still violence—merciful violence, like putting a suffering animal to death.

Maggie, one of the nurses, received a call at midnight not long ago. It was a woman in her twentieth week of pregnancy; the necessarily gradual process of cervical dilation begun the day before had stimulated labor, as it sometimes does. Maggie and one of the doctors met the woman at the office in the night. Maggie helped her onto the table, and as she lay down the fetus was delivered into Maggie's hands. When Maggie told me about it the next day, she cupped her hands into a small bowl—"It was just like a little kitten," she said softly, wonderingly. "Everything was still attached."

At the end of the day I clean out the suction jars, pouring blood into the sink, splashing the sides with flecks of tissue. From the sink rises a rich and humid smell, hot, earthy, and moldering; it is the smell of something recently alive beginning to decay. I take care of the plastic tub on the floor, filled with pieces too big to be trusted to the trash. The law defines the contents of the bucket I hold protectively against my chest as "tissue." Some would say my complicity in filling that bucket gives me no right to call it anything else. I slip the tissue gently into a bag and place it in the freezer, to be burned at another time. Abortion requires of me an entirely new set of assumptions. It requires a willingness to live with conflict, fearlessness, and grief. As I close the freezer door, I imagine a world where this won't be necessary, and then return to the world where it is.

QUESTIONS

1. Tisdale speaks of taking both broad views—"as if I am standing on a cliff with a telescope"—and narrow views—"I can put my eye to the lens and focus on the small details" (paragraph 4). Choose one section of this essay (such as the second, third, or fourth) and mark the passages you would describe as taking broad views and the passages you would describe as taking narrow views. What is the effect of Tisdale's going back and forth between them? How does she manage transitions?

2. "We are too busy to chew over ethics" (paragraph 21), Tisdale observes. What does she mean by ethics? Does she engage with what you consider ethical issues in this essay? Explain.

3. Although Tisdale takes a pro-choice position, a pro-lifer could use parts of her essay against her. What parts? What are the advantages and disadvantages of including material that could be used in support of the opposition?

4. Write a pro-choice or pro-life essay of your own. Include material that could be used in support of the opposition. You may use Tisdale's essay (with proper credit), but you need not.

PAUL FUSSELL *Thank God for the Atom Bomb*

MANY YEARS AGO in New York I saw on the side of a bus a whiskey ad I've remembered all this time. It's been for me a model of the short poem, and indeed I've come upon few short poems subsequently that exhibited more poetic talent. The ad consisted of two eleven-syllable lines of "verse," thus:

In life, experience is the great teacher.
In Scotch, Teacher's is the great experience.

For present purposes we must jettison the second line (licking our lips, to be sure, as it disappears), leaving the first to register a principle whose banality suggests that it enshrines a most useful truth. I bring up the matter because, writing on the forty-second anniversary of the atom-bombing of Hiroshima and Nagasaki, I want to consider something suggested by the long debate about the ethics, if any, of that ghastly affair. Namely, the importance of experience, sheer, vulgar experience, in influencing, if not determining, one's views about that use of the atom bomb.

The experience I'm talking about is having to come to grips, face to face, with an enemy who designs your death. The experience is common to those in the marines and the infantry and even the line navy, to those, in short, who fought the Second World War mindful always that their mission was, as they were repeatedly assured, "to close with the enemy and destroy him." *Destroy*, notice: not hurt, frighten, drive away, or capture. I think there's something to be learned about that war, as well as about the tendency of historical memory unwittingly to resolve ambiguity and generally clean up the premises, by considering the way testimonies emanating from real war experience tend to complicate attitudes about the most cruel ending of that most cruel war.

"What did you do in the Great War, Daddy?" The recruiting poster deserves ridicule and contempt, of course, but here its question is embarrassingly relevant, and the problem is one that touches on the dirty little secret of social class in America. Arthur T. Hadley said recently that those for whom the use of the A-bomb was "wrong" seem to be implying "that it would have been better to allow thousands on thousands of American and Japanese infantrymen to die in honest hand-to-hand combat on the beaches than to drop those two bombs." People holding such views, he notes, "do not come from the ranks of society that produce infantrymen or pilots." And there's an eloquence problem: most of those with firsthand experience of the war at its worst were not elaborately educated people. Relatively inarticulate, most have remained silent about what they know. That is, few of those destined to be blown to pieces if the main Japanese islands had been invaded went on to become our

Originally published as an article in the New Republic *(August 22, 1981); later included in Fussell's* Thank God for the Atom Bomb, and Other Essays *(1988).*

451

most effective men of letters or impressive ethical theorists or professors of contemporary history or of international law. The testimony of experience has tended to come from rough diamonds—James Jones[1] is an example—who went through the war as enlisted men in the infantry or the Marine Corps.

Anticipating objections from those without such experience, in his book *WWII* Jones carefully prepares for his chapter on the A-bombs by detailing the plans already in motion for the infantry assaults on the home islands of Kyushu (thirteen divisions scheduled to land in November 1945) and ultimately Honshu (sixteen divisions scheduled for March 1946). Planners of the invasion assumed that it would require a full year, to November 1946, for the Japanese to be sufficiently worn down by land-combat attrition to surrender. By that time, one million American casualties was the expected price. Jones observes that the forthcoming invasion of Kyushu "was well into its collecting and stockpiling stages before the war ended." (The island of Saipan was designated a main ammunition and supply base for the invasion, and if you go there today you can see some of the assembled stuff still sitting there.) "The assault troops were chosen and already in training," Jones reminds his readers, and he illuminates by the light of experience what this meant:

> What it must have been like to some old-timer buck sergeant or staff sergeant who had been through Guadalcanal or Bougainville or the Philippines, to stand on some beach and watch this huge war machine beginning to stir and move all around him and know that he very likely had survived this far only to fall dead on the dirt of Japan's home islands, hardly bears thinking about.

5   Another bright enlisted man, this one an experienced marine destined for the assault on Honshu, adds his testimony. Former Pfc. E. B. Sledge, author of the splendid memoir *With the Old Breed at Peleliu and Okinawa*, noticed at the time that the fighting grew "more vicious the closer we got to Japan," with the carnage of Iwo Jima and Okinawa worse than what had gone before. He points out that

> what we had *experienced* [my emphasis] in fighting the Japs (pardon the expression) on Peleliu and Okinawa caused us to formulate some very definite opinions that the invasion . . . would be a ghastly bloodletting. . . . It would shock the American public and the world. [Every Japanese] soldier, civilian, woman, and child would fight to the death with whatever weapons they had, rifle, grenade, or bamboo spear.

The Japanese pre-invasion patriotic song, "One Hundred Million Souls for the Emperor," says Sledge, "meant just that." Universal national kamikaze was the point. One kamikaze pilot, discouraged by his unit's failure to impede the Americans very much despite the bizarre casualties it caused, wrote before diving his plane onto an American ship, "I see the war situation becoming more desperate. All Japanese must become soldiers and die for the Emperor."

1. American novelist (1921–1977), author of *From Here to Eternity* (1951), the first volume in a trilogy about World War II.

Sledge's First Marine Division was to land close to the Yokosuka Naval Base, "one of the most heavily defended sectors of the island." The marines were told, he recalls, that

> due to the strong beach defenses, caves, tunnels, and numerous Jap suicide torpedo boats and manned mines, few Marines in the first five assault waves would get ashore alive—my company was scheduled to be in the first and second waves. The veterans in the outfit felt we had already run out of luck anyway. . . . We viewed the invasion with complete resignation that we would be killed—either on the beach or inland.

And the invasion was going to take place: there's no question about that. It was not theoretical or merely rumored in order to scare the Japanese. By July 10, 1945, the prelanding naval and aerial bombardment of the coast had begun, and the battleships *Iowa*, *Missouri*, *Wisconsin*, and *King George V* were steaming up and down the coast, softening it up with their sixteen-inch shells.

On the other hand, John Kenneth Galbraith[2] is persuaded that the Japanese would have surrendered surely by November without an invasion. He thinks the A-bombs were unnecessary and unjustified because the war was ending anyway. The A-bombs meant, he says, "a difference, at most, of two or three weeks." But at the time, with no indication that surrender was on the way, the kamikazes were sinking American vessels, the *Indianapolis* was sunk (880 men killed), and Allied casualties were running to over 7,000 per week. "Two or three weeks," says Galbraith. Two weeks more means 14,000 more killed and wounded, three weeks more, 21,000. Those weeks mean the world if you're one of those thousands or related to one of them. During the time between the dropping of the Nagasaki bomb on August 9 and the actual surrender on the fifteenth, the war pursued its accustomed course: on the twelfth of August eight captured American fliers were executed (heads chopped off); the fifty-first United States submarine, *Bonefish*, was sunk (all aboard drowned); the destroyer *Callaghan* went down, the seventieth to be sunk, and the Destroyer Escort *Underhill* was lost. That's a bit of what happened in six days of the two or three weeks posited by Galbraith. What did he do in the war? He worked in the Office of Price Administration in Washington. I don't demand that he experience having his ass shot off. I merely note that he didn't.

Likewise, the historian Michael Sherry, author of a recent book on the rise of the American bombing mystique, *The Creation of Armageddon*, argues that we didn't delay long enough between the test explosion in New Mexico and the mortal explosions in Japan. More delay would have made possible deeper moral considerations and perhaps laudable second thoughts and restraint. "The risks of delaying the bomb's use," he says, "would have been small—not the thousands of casualties expected of invasion but only a few days or weeks of relatively routine operations." While the mass murders represented by these

---

2. American economist and professor of economics at Harvard University (1908–2006). During World War II he was in charge of wartime price control, and after the war he went to Japan with other economists to study the economic and social conditions.

"relatively routine operations" were enacting, Michael Sherry was safe at home. Indeed, when the bombs were dropped he was going on eight months old, in danger only of falling out of his pram. In speaking thus of Galbraith and Sherry, I'm aware of the offensive implications *ad hominem*.[3] But what's at stake in an infantry assault is so entirely unthinkable to those without the experience of one, or several, or many, even if they possess very wide-ranging imaginations and warm sympathies, that experience is crucial in this case.

10   In general, the principle is, the farther from the scene of horror, the easier the talk. One young combat naval officer close to the action wrote home in the fall of 1943, just before the marines underwent the agony of Tarawa: "When I read that we will fight the Japs for years if necessary and will sacrifice hundreds of thousands if we must, I always like to check from where he's talking: it's seldom out here." That was Lieutenant (j.g.) John F. Kennedy. And Winston Churchill, with an irony perhaps too broad and easy, noted in Parliament that the people who preferred invasion to A-bombing seemed to have "no intention of proceeding to the Japanese front themselves."

A remoteness from experience like Galbraith's and Sherry's, and a similar rationalistic abstraction from actuality, seem to motivate the reaction of an anonymous reviewer of William Manchester's *Goodbye Darkness: A Memoir of the Pacific War* for *The New York Review of Books.* The reviewer naturally dislikes Manchester's still terming the enemy Nips or Japs, but what really shakes him (her?) is this passage of Manchester's:

> After Biak the enemy withdrew to deep caverns. Rooting them out became a bloody business which reached its ultimate horrors in the last months of the war. You think of the lives which would have been lost in an invasion of Japan's home islands—a staggering number of Americans but millions more of Japanese—and you thank God for the atomic bomb.

Thank God for the atom bomb. From this, "one recoils," says the reviewer. One does, doesn't one?

And not just a staggering number of Americans would have been killed in the invasion. Thousands of British assault troops would have been destroyed too, the anticipated casualties from the almost 200,000 men in the six divisions (the same number used to invade Normandy) assigned to invade the Malay Peninsula on September 9. Aimed at the reconquest of Singapore, this operation was expected to last until about March 1946—that is, seven more months of infantry fighting. "But for the atomic bombs," a British observer intimate with the Japanese defenses notes, "I don't think we would have stood a cat in hell's chance. We would have been murdered in the biggest massacre of the war. They would have annihilated the lot of us."

The Dutchman Laurens van der Post had been a prisoner of the Japanese for three and a half years. He and thousands of his fellows, enfeebled by beriberi and pellagra, were being systematically starved to death, the Japanese rationalizing this treatment not just because the prisoners were white men but

---

3. Marked by an attack on an opponent's character; literally, to the man (Latin).

because they had allowed themselves to be captured at all and were therefore moral garbage. In the summer of 1945 Field Marshal Terauchi issued a significant order: at the moment the Allies invaded the main islands, all prisoners were to be killed by the prison-camp commanders. But thank God that did not happen. When the A-bombs were dropped, van der Post recalls, "This cataclysm I was certain would make the Japanese feel that they could withdraw from the war without dishonor, because it would strike them, as it had us in the silence of our prison night, as something supernatural."

In an exchange of views not long ago in *The New York Review of Books*, Joseph Alsop and David Joravsky set forth the by now familiar argument on both sides of the debate about the "ethics" of the bomb. It's not hard to guess which side each chose once you know that Alsop experienced capture by the Japanese at Hong Kong early in 1942, while Joravsky came into no deadly contact with the Japanese: a young, combat-innocent soldier, he was on his way to the Pacific when the war ended. The editors of *The New York Review* gave the debate the tendentious title "Was the Hiroshima Bomb Necessary?" surely an unanswerable question (unlike "Was It Effective?") and one precisely indicating the intellectual difficulties involved in imposing *ex post facto*[4] a rational and even a genteel ethics on this event. In arguing the acceptability of the bomb, Alsop focuses on the power and fanaticism of War Minister Anami, who insisted that Japan fight to the bitter end, defending the main islands with the same techniques and tenacity employed at Iwo and Okinawa. Alsop concludes: "Japanese surrender could never have been obtained, at any rate without the honor-satisfying bloodbath envisioned by . . . Anami, if the hideous destruction of Hiroshima and Nagasaki had not finally galvanized the peace advocates into tearing up the entire Japanese book of rules." The Japanese plan to deploy the undefeated bulk of their ground forces, over two million men, plus 10,000 kamikaze planes, plus the elderly and all the women and children with sharpened spears they could muster in a suicidal defense makes it absurd, says Alsop, to "hold the common view, by now hardly challenged by anyone, that the decision to drop the two bombs on Japan was wicked in itself, and that President Truman and all others who joined in making or who [like Robert Oppenheimer][5] assented to this decision shared in the wickedness." And in explanation of "the two bombs," Alsop adds: "The true, climactic, and successful effort of the Japanese peace advocates . . . did not begin in deadly earnest until *after* the second bomb had destroyed Nagasaki. The Nagasaki bomb was thus the trigger to all the developments that led to peace." At this time the army was so unready for surrender that most looked forward to the

4. After the fact (Latin).

5. J. Robert Oppenheimer (1904–1967), American physicist and organizer of the research station at Los Alamos, New Mexico, that developed the atomic bomb, and after World War II, chair of the U.S. Atomic Energy Commission. As chair of the AEC, he opposed developing even more powerful hydrogen bombs but conceded when President Truman approved the legislation to do so.

forthcoming invasion as an indispensable opportunity to show their mettle, enthusiastically agreeing with the army spokesman who reasoned early in 1945, "Since the retreat from Guadalcanal, the Army has had little opportunity to engage the enemy in land battles. But when we meet in Japan proper, our Army will demonstrate its invincible superiority." This possibility foreclosed by the Emperor's post-A-bomb surrender broadcast, the shocked, disappointed officers of one infantry battalion, anticipating a professionally impressive defense of the beaches, killed themselves in the following numbers: one major, three captains, ten first lieutenants, and twelve second lieutenants.

15   David Joravsky, now a professor of history at Northwestern, argued on the other hand that those who decided to use the A-bombs on cities betray defects of "reason and self-restraint." It all needn't have happened, he says, "if the U.S. government had been willing to take a few more days and to be a bit more thoughtful in opening up the age of nuclear warfare." I've already noted what "a few more days" would mean to the luckless troops and sailors on the spot, and as to being thoughtful when "opening up the age of nuclear warfare," of course no one was focusing on anything as portentous as that, which reflects a historian's tidy hind-sight. The U.S. government was engaged not in that sort of momentous thing but in ending the war conclusively, as well as irrationally Remembering Pearl Harbor with a vengeance. It didn't know then what everyone knows now about leukemia and various kinds of carcinoma and birth defects. Truman was not being sly or coy when he insisted that the bomb was "only another weapon." History, as Eliot's "Gerontion" notes,

> . . . has many cunning passages, contrived corridors
> And issues, deceives with whispering ambitions,
> Guides us by vanities. . . .
>
> > Think
>
> Neither fear nor courage saves us.
>   Unnatural vices
> Are fathered by our heroism. Virtues
> Are forced upon us by our impudent crimes.

Understanding the past requires pretending that you don't know the present. It requires feeling its own pressure on your pulses without any *ex post facto* illumination. That's a harder thing to do than Joravsky seems to think.

        The Alsop-Joravsky debate, reduced to a collision between experience and theory, was conducted with a certain civilized respect for evidence. Not so the way the scurrilous, agitprop *New Statesman* conceives those justifying the dropping of the bomb and those opposing. They are, on the one hand, says Bruce Page, "the imperialist class-forces acting through Harry Truman" and, on the other, those representing "the humane, democratic virtues"—in short, "fascists" as opposed to "populists." But ironically the bomb saved the lives not of any imperialists but only of the low and humble, the quintessentially demo-

cratic huddled masses—the conscripted enlisted men manning the fated invasion divisions and the sailors crouching at their gun-mounts in terror of the
Kamikazes. When the war ended, Bruce Page was nine years old. For someone
of his experience, phrases like "imperialist class forces" come easily, and the issues look perfectly clear.

He's not the only one to have forgotten, if he ever knew, the unspeakable
savagery of the Pacific war. The dramatic postwar Japanese success at hustling
and merchandising and tourism has (happily, in many ways) effaced for most
people the vicious assault context in which the Hiroshima horror should be
viewed. It is easy to forget, or not to know, what Japan was like before it was
first destroyed, and then humiliated, tamed, and constitutionalized by the
West. "Implacable, treacherous, barbaric"—those were Admiral Halsey's char-
acterizations of the enemy, and at the time few facing the Japanese would deny
that they fit to a T. One remembers the captured American airmen—the lucky
ones who escaped decapitation—locked for years in packing crates. One remembers the gleeful use of bayonets on civilians, on nurses and the wounded,
in Hong Kong and Singapore. Anyone who actually fought in the Pacific recalls the Japanese routinely firing on medics, killing the wounded (torturing
them first, if possible), and cutting off the penises of the dead to stick in the
corpses' mouths. The degree to which Americans register shock and extraordinary shame about the Hiroshima bomb correlates closely with lack of information about the Pacific war.

And of course the brutality was not just on one side. There was much
sadism and cruelty, undeniably racist, on ours. (It's worth noting in passing
how few hopes blacks could entertain of desegregation and decent treatment
when the U.S. Army itself slandered the enemy as "the little brown Jap.")
Marines and soldiers could augment their view of their own invincibility by
possessing a well-washed Japanese skull, and very soon after Guadalcanal it
was common to treat surrendering Japanese as handy rifle targets. Plenty of
Japanese gold teeth were extracted—some from still living mouths—with Marine Corps Ka-Bar Knives,[6] and one of E. B. Sledge's fellow marines went
around with a cut-off Japanese hand. When its smell grew too offensive and
Sledge urged him to get rid of it, he defended his possession of this trophy
thus: "How many Marines you reckon that hand pulled the trigger on?" (It's
hardly necessary to observe that a soldier in the ETO would probably not have
dealt that way with a German or Italian—that is, a "white person's"—hand.) In
the Pacific the situation grew so public and scandalous that in September
1942, the Commander in Chief of the Pacific Fleet issued this order: "No part
of the enemy's body may be used as a souvenir. Unit Commanders will take
stern disciplinary action. . . ."

Among Americans it was widely held that the Japanese were really subhu-
man, little yellow beasts, and popular imagery depicted them as lice, rats, bats,
vipers, dogs, and monkeys. What was required, said the Marine Corps journal

---

6. High-carbon steel knives carried by Marines (officers and gunners) who did not
carry bayonet-bearing rifles.

The Leatherneck in May 1945, was "a gigantic task of extermination." The Japanese constituted a "pestilence," and the only appropriate treatment was "annihilation." Some of the marines landing on Iwo Jima had "Rodent Exterminator" written on their helmet covers, and on one American flagship the naval commander had erected a large sign enjoining all to "KILL JAPS! KILL JAPS! KILL MORE JAPS!" Herman Wouk remembers the Pacific war scene correctly while analyzing Ensign Keith in *The Caine Mutiny*: "Like most of the naval executioners of Kwajalein, he seemed to regard the enemy as a species of animal pest." And the feeling was entirely reciprocal: "From the grim and desperate taciturnity with which the Japanese died, they seemed on their side to believe that they were contending with an invasion of large armed ants." Hiroshima seems to follow in natural sequence: "This obliviousness of both sides to the fact that the opponents were human beings may perhaps be cited as the key to the many massacres of the Pacific war." Since the Jap vermin resist so madly and have killed so many of us, let's pour gasoline into their bunkers and light it and then shoot those afire who try to get out. Why not? Why not blow them all up, with satchel charges or with something stronger? Why not, indeed, drop a new kind of bomb on them, and on the un-uniformed ones too, since the Japanese government has announced that women from ages of seventeen to forty are being called up to repel the invasion? The intelligence officer of the U.S. Fifth Air Force declared on July 21, 1945, that "the entire population of Japan is a proper military target," and he added emphatically, "*There are no civilians in Japan*." Why delay and allow one more American high school kid to see his own intestines blown out of his body and spread before him in the dirt while he screams and screams when with the new bomb we can end the whole thing just like that?

20   On Okinawa, only weeks before Hiroshima, 123,000 Japanese and Americans *killed* each other. (About 140,000 Japanese died at Hiroshima.) "Just awful" was the comment on the Okinawa slaughter not of some pacifist but of General MacArthur. On July 14, 1945, General Marshall sadly informed the Combined Chiefs of Staff—he was not trying to scare the Japanese—that it's "now clear . . . that in order to finish with the Japanese quickly, it will be necessary to invade the industrial heart of Japan." The invasion was definitely on, as I know because I was to be in it.

When the atom bomb ended the war, I was in the Forty-fifth Infantry Division, which had been through the European war so thoroughly that it had needed to be reconstituted two or three times. We were in a staging area near Rheims, ready to be shipped back across the United States for refresher training at Fort Lewis, Washington, and then sent on for final preparation in the Philippines. My division, like most of the ones transferred from Europe, was to take part in the invasion of Honshu. (The earlier landing on Kyushu was to be carried out by the 700,000 infantry already in the Pacific, those with whom James Jones has sympathized.) I was a twenty-one-year-old second lieutenant of infantry leading a rifle platoon. Although still officially fit for combat, in the German war I had already been wounded in the back and the leg badly enough to be adjudged, after the war, 40 percent disabled. But even if my leg buckled and I fell to the ground whenever I jumped out of the back of a truck, and even if the very idea of more combat made me breathe in gasps and shake all over, my condition was held to be adequate for the next act. When the atom bombs were dropped and news began to circulate that "Operation Olympic" would not, after all, be necessary, when we learned to our astonishment that we would not be obliged in a few months to rush up the beaches near Tokyo assault-firing while being machine-gunned, mortared, and shelled, for all the practiced phlegm of our tough façades we broke down and cried with relief and joy. We were going to live. We were going to grow to adulthood after all. The killing was all going to be over, and peace was actually going to be the state of things. When the *Enola Gay* dropped its package, "There were cheers," says John Toland, "over the intercom; it meant the end of the war." Down on the ground the reaction of Sledge's marine buddies when they heard the news was more solemn and complicated. They heard about the end of the war

> with quiet disbelief coupled with an indescribable sense of relief. We thought the Japanese would never surrender. Many refused to believe it. . . . Sitting in stunned silence, we remembered our dead. So many dead. So many maimed. So many bright futures consigned to the ashes of the past. So many dreams lost in the madness that had engulfed us. Except for a few widely scattered shouts of joy, the survivors of the abyss sat hollow-eyed and silent, trying to comprehend a world without war.

These troops who cried and cheered with relief or who sat stunned by the weight of their experience are very different from the high-minded, guilt-ridden GIs we're told about by J. Glenn Gray in his sensitive book *The Warriors*. During the war in Europe Gray was an interrogator in the Army Counterintelligence Corps, and in that capacity he experienced the war at Division level. There's no denying that Gray's outlook on everything was admirably noble, elevated, and responsible. After the war he became a much-admired professor of philosophy at Colorado College and an esteemed editor of Heidegger.[7] But *The Warriors*, his meditation on the moral and psychological dimensions of modern soldiering, gives every sign of error occasioned by remoteness from experience. Division headquarters is miles—*miles*—behind the line where soldiers experience terror and madness and relieve those pressures by crazy brutality and sadism. Indeed, unless they actually encountered the enemy during the war, most "soldiers" have very little idea what "combat" was like. As William Manchester says, "All who wore uniforms are called veterans, but more than 90 percent of them are as uninformed about the killing zones as those on the home front." Manchester's fellow marine E. B. Sledge thoughtfully and responsibly invokes the terms *drastically* and *totally* to underline the differences in experience between front and rear, and not even the far rear, but the close rear. "Our code of conduct toward the enemy," he notes, "differed drastically from that prevailing back at the division CP." (He's de-

---

7. Martin Heidegger (1889–1976), German existentialist philosopher.

scribing gold-tooth extraction from still-living Japanese.) Again he writes: "We existed in an environment totally incomprehensible to men behind the lines . . . ," even, he would insist, to men as intelligent and sensitive as Glenn Gray, who missed seeing with his own eyes Sledge's marine friends sliding under fire down a shell-pocked ridge slimy with mud and liquid dysentery shit into the maggoty Japanese and USMC corpses at the bottom, vomiting as the maggots burrowed into their own foul clothing. "We didn't talk about such things," says Sledge. "They were too horrible and obscene even for hardened veterans. . . . Nor do authors normally write about such vileness; unless they have seen it with their own eyes, it is too preposterous to think that men could actually live and fight for days and nights on end under such terrible conditions and not be driven insane." And Sledge has added a comment on such experience and the insulation provided by even a short distance: "Often people just behind our rifle companies couldn't understand what we knew." Glenn Gray was not in a rifle company, or even just behind one. "When the news of the atomic bombing of Hiroshima and Nagasaki came," he asks us to believe, "many an American soldier felt shocked and ashamed." Shocked, OK, but why ashamed? Because we'd destroyed civilians? We'd been doing that for years, in raids on Hamburg and Berlin and Cologne and Frankfurt and Mannheim and Dresden, and Tokyo, and besides, the two A-bombs wiped out 10,000 Japanese troops, not often thought of now, John Hersey's[8] kindly physicians and Jesuit priests being more touching. If around division headquarters some of the people Gray talked to felt ashamed, down in the rifle companies no one did, despite Gray's assertions. "The combat soldier," he says,

> knew better than did Americans at home what those bombs meant in suffering and injustice. The man of conscience realized intuitively that the vast majority of Japanese in both cities were no more, if no less, guilty of the war than were his own parents, sisters, or brothers.

I find this canting nonsense. The purpose of the bombs was not to "punish" people but to stop the war. To intensify the shame Gray insists we feel, he seems willing to fiddle the facts. The Hiroshima bomb, he says, was dropped "without any warning." But actually, two days before, 720,000 leaflets were dropped on the city urging everyone to get out and indicating that the place was going to be (as the Potsdam Declaration[9] had promised) obliterated. Of course few left.

Experience whispers that the pity is not that we used the bomb to end the Japanese war but that it wasn't ready in time to end the German one. If only it could have been rushed into production faster and dropped at the right mo-

8. American fiction and nonfiction writer (1914–1993), author of *Hiroshima* (1946), a moving account of the devastation and human suffering caused by the atomic bomb.

9. An agreement signed on July 26, 1945, by the president of the United States and the prime minister of Great Britain, with the concurrence of Generalissimo Chiang Kaishek of Nationalist China, that mandated Japanese surrender, offering them a choice between unconditional surrender and total destruction, and that set forth the principles under which the defeated Axis territories would be governed and rebuilt.

ment on the Reich Chancellery or Berchtesgaden or Hitler's military head-quarters in East Prussia (where Colonel Stauffenberg's July 20 bomb didn't do the job because it wasn't big enough), much of the Nazi hierarchy could have been pulverized immediately, saving not just the embarrassment of the Nuremberg trials but the lives of around four million Jews, Poles, Slavs, and gypsies, not to mention the lives and limbs of millions of Allied and German soldiers. If the bomb had only been ready in time, the young men of my infantry platoon would not have been so cruelly killed and wounded.

All this is not to deny that like the Russian Revolution, the atom-bombing of Japan was a vast historical tragedy, and every passing year magnifies the dilemma into which it has lodged the contemporary world. As with the Russian Revolution, there are two sides—that's why it's a tragedy instead of a disaster—and unless we are, like Bruce Page, simple-mindedly unimaginative and cruel, we will be painfully aware of both sides at once. To observe that from the viewpoint of the war's victims-to-be the bomb seemed precisely the right thing to drop is to purchase no immunity from horror. To experience both sides, one might study the book *Unforgettable Fire: Pictures Drawn by Atomic Bomb Survivors,* which presents a number of amateur drawings and watercolors of the Hiroshima scene made by middle-aged and elderly survivors for a peace exhibition in 1975. In addition to the almost unbearable pictures, the book offers brief moments of memoir not for the weak-stomached:

> While taking my severely wounded wife out to the river bank . . . , I was horrified indeed at the sight of a stark naked man standing in the rain with his eyeball in his palm. He looked to be in great pain but there was nothing that I could do for him. I wonder what became of him. Even today, I vividly remember the sight. I was simply miserable.

These childlike drawings and paintings are of skin hanging down, breasts torn off, people bleeding and burning, dying mothers nursing dead babies. A bloody woman holds a bloody child in the ruins of a house, and the artist remembers her calling, "Please help this child! Someone, please help this child. Please help! Someone, please." As Samuel Johnson said of the smothering of Desdemona, the innocent in another tragedy, "It is not to be endured." Nor, it should be noticed, is an infantryman's account of having his arm blown off in the Arno Valley in Italy in 1944:

> I wanted to die and die fast. I wanted to forget this miserable world. I cursed the war, I cursed the people who were responsible for it, I cursed God for putting me here . . . to suffer for something I never did or knew anything about.

(A good place to interrupt and remember Glenn Gray's noble but hope-lessly one-sided remarks about "injustice," as well as "suffering.")
"For this was hell," the soldier goes on,

> and I never imagined anything or anyone could suffer so bitterly. I screamed and cursed. Why? What had I done to deserve this? But no answer came. I yelled for medics, because subconsciously I wanted to live. I

25

tried to apply my right hand over my bleeding stump, but I didn't have the strength to hold it. I looked to the left of me and saw the bloody mess that was once my left arm; its fingers and palm were turned upward, like a flower looking to the sun for its strength.

The future scholar-critic who writes *The History of Canting in the Twentieth Century* will find much to study and interpret in the utterances of those who dilate on the special wickedness of the A-bomb-droppers. He will realize that such utterance can perform for the speaker a valuable double function. First, it can display the fineness of his moral weave. And second, by implication it can also inform the audience that during the war he was not socially so unfortunate as to find himself down there with the ground forces, where he might have had to compromise the purity and clarity of his moral system by the experience of weighing his own life against someone else's. Down there, which is where the other people were, is the place where coarse self-interest is the rule. When the young soldier with the wild eyes comes at you, firing, do you shoot him in the foot, hoping he'll be hurt badly enough to drop or mis-aim the gun with which he's going to kill you, or do you shoot him in the chest (or, if you're a prime shot, in the head) and make certain that you and not he will be the survivor of that mortal moment?

30   It would be not just stupid but would betray a lamentable want of human experience to expect soldiers to be very sensitive humanitarians. The Glenn Grays of this world need to have their attention directed to the testimony of those who know, like, say, Admiral of the Fleet Lord Fisher, who said, "Moderation in war is imbecility," or Sir Arthur Harris, director of the admittedly wicked aerial-bombing campaign designed, as Churchill put it, to "dehouse" the German civilian population, who observed that "War is immoral," or our own General W. T. Sherman: "War is cruelty, and you cannot refine it." Lord Louis Mountbatten, trying to say something sensible about the dropping of the A-bomb, came up only with "War is crazy." Or rather, it requires choices among crazinesses. "It would seem even more crazy," he went on, "if we were to have more casualties on our side to save the Japanese." One of the unpleasant facts for anyone in the ground armies during the war was that you had to become pro tem[10] a subordinate of the very uncivilian George S. Patton[11] and respond somehow to his unremitting insistence that you embrace his view of things. But in one of his effusions he was right, and his observation tends to suggest the experimental dubiousness of the concept of "just wars." "War is not a contest with gloves," he perceived. "It is resorted to only when laws, which are rules, have failed." Soldiers being like that, only the barest decencies should be expected of them. They did not start the war, except in the terrible sense hinted at in Frederic Manning's observation based on his front-line experience in the Great War: "War is waged by men; not by beasts, or by gods.

10. Short for *pro tempore*: temporarily; literally, for the time being (Latin).
11. American general who served in North Africa and Sicily in World War II before becoming commander of the Third Army, which drove the Nazis from France and back into Germany (1885–1945).

It is a peculiarly human activity. To call it a crime against mankind is to miss at least half its significance; it is also the punishment of a crime." Knowing that unflattering truth by experience, soldiers have every motive for wanting a war stopped, by any means.

The stupidity, parochialism, and greed in the international mismanagement of the whole nuclear challenge should not tempt us to misimagine the circumstances of the bomb's first "use." Nor should our well-justified fears and suspicions occasioned by the capture of the nuclear-power trade by the inept and the mendacious (who have fucked up the works at Three Mile Island, Chernobyl, etc.)[12] tempt us to infer retrospectively extraordinary corruption, imbecility, or motiveless malignity in those who decided, all things considered, to drop the bomb. Times change. Harry Truman * * * knew war, and he knew better than some of his critics then and now what he was doing and why he was doing it. "Having found the bomb," he said, "we have used it. . . . We have used it to shorten the agony of young Americans."

The past, which as always did not know the future, acted in ways that ask to be imagined before they are condemned. Or even simplified.

12. Two disasters at nuclear power plants: the first, near Harrisburg, Pennsylvania, occurred in the spring of 1979; the second, in the Soviet Union, occurred in the spring of 1986.

Questions

1. Note the places where Fussell includes personal experience in this essay. How much is his own, how much belongs to others? Why does he include both kinds?

2. Fussell dismisses with contempt those who disagree with him. Locate some examples. How do you respond to them? Would you use Fussell's strategies to dismiss those who disagree with you? Explain.

3. Mark some instances of Fussell's "voice." What kind of voice does he adopt? What kind of person does he present himself as?

4. Write a similarly argumentative essay in which you take a strong position. Include your own experience and the experience of others if appropriate.

HISTORY

Henry David Thoreau *The Battle of the Ants*

O NE DAY WHEN I went out to my wood-pile, or rather my pile of stumps, I observed two large ants, the one red, the other much larger, nearly half an inch long, and black, fiercely contending with one another. Having once got hold they never let go, but struggled and wrestled and rolled on the chips incessantly. Looking farther, I was surprised to find that the chips were covered with such combatants, that it was not a *duellum*, but a *bellum*, a war between two races of ants, the red always pitted against the black, and frequently two red ones to one black. The legions of these Myrmidons[1] covered all the hills and vales in my wood-yard, and the ground was already strewn with the dead and dying, both red and black. It was the only battle which I have ever witnessed, the only battle-field I ever trod while the battle was raging; internecine war; the red republicans on the one hand, and the black imperialists on the other. On every side they were engaged in deadly combat, yet without any noise that I could hear, and human soldiers never fought so resolutely. I watched a couple that were fast locked in each other's embraces, in a little sunny valley amid the chips, now at noonday prepared to fight till the sun went down, or life went out. The smaller red champion had fastened himself like a vice to his adversary's front, and through all the tumblings on that field never for an instant ceased to gnaw at one of his feelers near the root, having already caused the other to go by the board; while the stronger black one dashed him from side to side, and, as I saw on looking nearer, had already divested him of several of his members. They fought with more pertinacity than bulldogs. Neither manifested the least disposition to retreat. It was evident that their battle-cry was "Conquer or die." In the meanwhile there came along a single red ant on the hillside of this valley, evidently full of excitement, who either had despatched his foe, or had not yet taken part in the battle; probably the latter, for he had lost none of his limbs; whose mother had charged him to return with his shield or upon it. Or perchance he was some Achilles, who had nourished his wrath apart, and had now come to avenge or rescue his Patroclus.[2] He saw

---

From Thoreau's most famous book, Walden (1854), *an account of his life in a small cabin on Walden Pond, outside the village of Concord, Massachusetts.*

1. The reference is to the powerful soldiers of Achilles in Homer's *Iliad*.
2. In the *Iliad*, the Greek warrior and friend whose death Achilles avenges. Achilles had previously refused to fight after a falling-out with Agamemnon, the leader of the Greek army.

this unequal combat from afar—for the blacks were nearly twice the size of the red—he drew near with rapid pace till he stood on his guard within half an inch of the combatants; then, watching his opportunity, he sprang upon the black warrior, and commenced his operations near the root of his right fore leg, leaving the foe to select among his own members; and so there were three united for life, as if a new kind of attraction had been invented which put all other locks and cements to shame. I should not have wondered by this time to find that they had their respective musical bands stationed on some eminent chip, and playing their national airs the while, to excite the slow and cheer the dying combatants. I was myself excited somewhat even as if they had been men. The more you think of it, the less the difference. And certainly there is not the fight recorded in Concord history, at least, if in the history of America, that will bear a moment's comparison with this, whether for the numbers engaged in it, or for the patriotism and heroism displayed. For numbers and for carnage it was an Austerlitz or Dresden.[3] Concord Fight! Two killed on the patriots' side, and Luther Blanchard wounded! Why here every ant was a Buttrick—"Fire! for God's sake fire!"—and thousands shared the fate of Davis and Hosmer. There was not one hireling there. I have no doubt that it was a principle they fought for, as much as our ancestors, and not to avoid a three-penny tax on their tea; and the results of this battle will be as important and memorable to those whom it concerns as those of the battle of Bunker Hill, at least.

I took up the chip on which the three I have particularly described were struggling, carried into my house, and placed it under a tumbler on my windowsill, in order to see the issue. Holding a microscope to the first-mentioned red ant, I saw that, though he was assiduously gnawing at the near fore leg of his enemy, having severed his remaining feeler, his own breast was all torn away, exposing what vitals he had there to the jaws of the black warrior, whose breastplate was apparently too thick for him to pierce; and the dark carbuncles of the sufferer's eyes shone with ferocity such as war only could excite. They struggled half an hour longer under the tumbler, and when I looked again the black soldier had severed the heads of his foes from their bodies, and the still living heads were hanging on either side of him like ghastly trophies at his saddle-bow, still apparently as firmly fastened as ever, and he was endeavoring with feeble struggles, being without feelers, and with only the remnant of a leg, and I know not how many other wounds, to divest himself of them; which at length, after half an hour more, he accomplished. I raised the glass, and he went off over the window-sill in that crippled state. Whether he finally survived that combat, and spent the remainder of his days in some Hôtel des Invalides,[4] I do not know; but I thought that his industry would not be worth much thereafter. I never learned which party was victorious, nor the cause of the war, but I felt for the rest of that day as if I had my feelings excited and

3. Austerlitz and Dresden were bloody Napoleonic victories. The battles at Lexington and Concord, opening the American Revolution, took place on April 19, 1775; the names that follow are those of men who took part, and the words "Fire! for God's sake fire!" were those that, by popular account, started the war.

4. A French hospital for wounded soldiers and sailors.

harrowed by witnessing the struggle, the ferocity and carnage, of a human battle before my door.

Kirby and Spence tell us that the battles of ants have long been celebrated
and the date of them recorded, though they say that Huber[5] is the only modern author who appears to have witnessed them. "Aeneas Sylvius," say they,
"after giving a very circumstantial account of one contested with great obsti-
nacy by a great and small species on the trunk of a pear tree," adds that " 'this
action was fought in the pontificate of Eugenius the Fourth, in the presence of
Nicholas Pistoriensis, an eminent lawyer, who related the whole history of the
battle with the greatest fidelity.' A similar engagement between great and small
ants is recorded by Olaus Magnus, in which the small ones, being victorious,
are said to have buried the bodies of their own soldiers, but left those of their
giant enemies a prey to the birds. This event happened previous to the expulsion of the tyrant Christiern the Second from Sweden." The battle which I
witnessed took place in the Presidency of Polk, five years before the passage of
Webster's Fugitive-Slave Bill.[6]

5. Kirby and Spence were nineteenth-century American entomologists; François Huber
(1750–1831) was a great Swiss entomologist.
6. Passed in 1851.

QUESTIONS

1. Thoreau uses the Latin word *bellum* to describe the battle of the ants and follows it
with a reference to the Myrmidons, the soldiers of Achilles in Homer's *Iliad*. Locate additional examples of this kind of allusion. How does it work? Why does Thoreau compare the ants to Greek soldiers?

2. Ordinarily we speak of accounts of natural events as "natural history" and accounts
of human events as "history." How does Thoreau, in this selection, blur the distinction?
To what effect?

3. Look up a description of the behavior of ants in a book by one of the entomologists
Thoreau refers to or in another scientific text. Compare the scientist's style with
Thoreau's. Take another event in nature and describe it twice, once in scientific and
once in allusive language. Or write an essay in which you describe and analyze the differences between the scientist's style and Thoreau's.

Barbara Tuchman "This Is the End of the World": The Black Death

I N OCTOBER 1347, two months after the fall of Calais,[1] Genoese trading ships put into the harbor of Messina in Sicily with dead and dying men at the oars. The ships had come from the Black Sea port of Caffa (now Feodosiya) in the Crimea, where the Genoese maintained a trading post. The diseased sailors showed strange black swellings about the size of an egg or an apple in the armpits and groin. The swellings oozed blood and pus and were followed by spreading boils and black blotches on the skin from internal bleeding. The sick suffered severe pain and died quickly within five days of the first symptoms. As the disease spread, other symptoms of continuous fever and spitting of blood appeared instead of the swellings or buboes. These victims coughed and sweated heavily and died even more quickly, within three days or less, sometimes in 24 hours. In both types everything that issued from the body—breath, sweat, blood from the buboes and lungs, bloody urine, and blood-blackened excrement—smelled foul. Depression and despair accompanied the physical symptoms, and before the end "death is seen seated on the face."

The disease was bubonic plague, present in two forms: one that infected the bloodstream, causing the buboes and internal bleeding, and was spread by contact; and a second, more virulent pneumonic type that infected the lungs and was spread by respiratory infection. The presence of both at once caused the high mortality and speed of contagion. So lethal was the disease that cases were known of persons going to bed well and dying before they woke, of doctors catching the illness at a bedside and dying before the patient. So rapidly did it spread from one to another that to a French physician, Simon de Covino, it seemed as if one sick person "could infect the whole world." The malignity of the pestilence appeared more terrible because its victims knew no prevention and no remedy.

The physical suffering of the disease and its aspect of evil mystery were expressed in a strange Welsh lament which saw "death coming into our midst like black smoke, a plague which cuts off the young, a rootless phantom which has no mercy for fair countenance. Woe is me of the shilling in the armpit! It is seething, terrible . . . a head that gives pain and causes a loud cry . . . a painful angry knob . . . Great is its seething like a burning cinder . . . a grievous thing of ashy color." Its eruption is ugly like the "seeds of black peas, broken fragments of brittle sea-coal . . . the early ornaments of black death,

From A Distant Mirror: The Calamitous Fourteenth Century *(1978), in which Tuchman presents a vivid picture of life in medieval France and draws parallels between the disasters of that time and those in our own.*

1. After a year-long siege, the French citizens of Calais surrendered to Edward III, king of England and self-declared king of France.

The Triumph of Death. A detail from a fresco by Francesco Traini in the Camposanto, Pisa, c. 1350.

cinders of the peelings of the cockle weed, a mixed multitude, a black plague like halfpence, like berries. . . ."

Rumors of a terrible plague supposedly arising in China and spreading through Tartary (Central Asia) to India and Persia, Mesopotamia, Syria, Egypt, and all of Asia Minor had reached Europe in 1346. They told of a death toll so devastating that all of India was said to be depopulated, whole territories covered by dead bodies, other areas with no one left alive. As added up by Pope Clement VI at Avignon, the total of reported dead reached 23,840,000. In the absence of a concept of contagion, no serious alarm was felt in Europe until the trading ships brought their black burden of pestilence into Messina while other infected ships from the Levant carried it to Genoa and Venice.

5   By January 1348 it penetrated France via Marseille, and North Africa via Tunis. Shipborne along coasts and navigable rivers, it spread westward from Marseille through the ports of Languedoc to Spain and northward up the Rhône to Avignon, where it arrived in March. It reached Narbonne, Montpellier, Carcassonne, and Toulouse between February and May, and at the same time in Italy spread to Rome and Florence and their hinterlands. Between June and August it reached Bordeaux, Lyon, and Paris, spread to Burgundy and Normandy, and crossed the Channel from Normandy into southern England. From Italy during the same summer it crossed the Alps into Switzerland and reached eastward to Hungary.

In a given area the plague accomplished its kill within four to six months and then faded, except in the larger cities, where, rooting into the close-

Burial of the plague victim. From *Annales de Gilles li Muisis.*

quartered population, it abated during the winter, only to reappear in spring and rage for another six months.

In 1349 it resumed in Paris, spread to Picardy, Flanders, and the Low Countries, and from England to Scotland and Ireland as well as to Norway, where a ghost ship with a cargo of wool and a dead crew drifted offshore until it ran aground near Bergen. From there the plague passed into Sweden, Denmark, Prussia, Iceland, and as far as Greenland. Leaving a strange pocket of immunity in Bohemia, and Russia unattacked until 1351, it had passed from most of Europe by mid-1350. Although the mortality rate was erratic, ranging from one fifth in some places to nine tenths or almost total elimination in others, the overall estimate of modern demographers has settled—for the area extending from India to Iceland—around the same figure expressed in Froissart's casual words: "a third of the world died." His estimate, the common one at the time, was not an inspired guess but a borrowing of St. John's figure for mortality from plague in Revelation, the favorite guide to human affairs of the Middle Ages.

A third of Europe would have meant about 20 million deaths. No one knows in truth how many died. Contemporary reports were an awed impression, not an accurate count. In crowded Avignon, it was said, 400 died daily; 7,000 houses emptied by death were shut up; a single graveyard received 11,000 corpses in six weeks; half the city's inhabitants reportedly died, including 9 cardinals or one third of the total, and 70 lesser prelates. Watching the endlessly passing death carts, chroniclers let normal exaggeration take wings and put the Avignon death toll at 62,000 and even at 120,000, although the city's total population was probably less than 50,000.

When graveyards filled up, bodies at Avignon were thrown into the Rhône until mass burial pits were dug for dumping the corpses. In London in such pits corpses piled up in layers until they overflowed. Everywhere reports speak of the sick dying too fast for the living to bury. Corpses were dragged out of homes and left in front of doorways. Morning light revealed new piles of bodies. In Florence the dead were gathered up by the Compagnia della Misericordia—founded in 1244 to care for the sick—whose members wore red robes and hoods masking the face except for the eyes. When their efforts failed, the dead lay putrid in the streets for days at a time. When no coffins were to be had, the bodies were laid on boards, two or three at once, to be carried to graveyards or common pits. Families dumped their own relatives into the pits, or buried them so hastily and thinly "that dogs dragged them forth and devoured their bodies."

10   Amid accumulating death and fear of contagion, people died without last rites and were buried without prayers, a prospect that terrified the last hours of the stricken. A bishop in England gave permission to laymen to make confession to each other as was done by the Apostles, "or if no man is present then even to a woman," and if no priest could be found to administer extreme unction, "then faith must suffice." Clement VI found it necessary to grant remissions of sin to all who died of the plague because so many were unattended by priests. "And no bells tolled," wrote a chronicler of Siena, "and nobody wept no matter what his loss because almost everyone expected death. . . . And people said and believed, 'This is the end of the world.' "

In Paris, where the plague lasted through 1349, the reported death rate was 800 a day, in Pisa 500, in Vienna 500 to 600. The total dead in Paris numbered 50,000 or half the population. Florence, weakened by the famine of 1347, lost three to four fifths of its citizens, Venice two thirds, Hamburg and Bremen, though smaller in size, about the same proportion. Cities, as centers of transportation, were more likely to be affected than villages, although once a village was infected, its death rate was equally high. At Givry, a prosperous village in Burgundy of 1,200 to 1,500 people, the parish register records 615 deaths in the space of fourteen weeks, compared to an average of thirty deaths a year in the previous decade. In three villages of Cambridgeshire, manorial records show a death rate of 47 percent, 57 percent, and in one case 70 percent. When the last survivors, too few to carry on, moved away, a deserted village sank back into the wilderness and disappeared from the map altogether, leaving only a grass-covered ghostly outline to show where mortals once had lived.

In enclosed places such as monasteries and prisons, the infection of one person usually meant that of all, as happened in the Franciscan convents of Carcassonne and Marseille, where every inmate without exception died. Of the 140 Dominicans at Montpellier only seven survived. Petrarch's[2] brother Gherardo, member of a Carthusian monastery, buried the prior and 34 fellow monks one by one, sometimes three a day, until he was left alone with his dog and fled to look for a place that would take him in. Watching every comrade

---

2. Francesco Petrarch (1304–1374), Italian writer whose sonnets to "my lady Laura" influenced a tradition of European love poetry for centuries.

die, men in such places could not but wonder whether the strange peril that filled the air had not been sent to exterminate the human race. In Kilkenny, Ireland, Brother John Clyn of the Friars Minor, another monk left alone among dead men, kept a record of what had happened lest "things which should be remembered perish with time and vanish from the memory of those who come after us." Sensing "the whole world, as it were, placed within the grasp of the Evil One," and waiting for death to visit him too, he wrote, "I leave parchment to continue this work, if perchance any man survive and any of the race of Adam escape this pestilence and carry on the work which I have begun." Brother John, as noted by another hand, died of the pestilence, but he foiled oblivion.

The largest cities of Europe, with populations of about 100,000, were Paris and Florence, Venice and Genoa. At the next level, with more than 50,000, were Ghent and Bruges in Flanders, Milan, Bologna, Rome, Naples, and Palermo, and Cologne. London hovered below 50,000, the only city in England except York with more than 10,000. At the level of 20,000 to 50,000 were Bordeaux, Toulouse, Montpellier, Marseille, and Lyon in France, Barcelona, Seville, and Toledo in Spain, Siena, Pisa, and other secondary cities in Italy, and the Hanseatic trading cities of the Empire. The plague raged through them all, killing anywhere from one third to two thirds of their inhabitants. Italy, with a total population of 10 to 11 million, probably suffered the heaviest toll. Following the Florentine bankruptcies, the crop failures and workers' riots of 1346–47, the revolt of Cola di Rienzi that plunged Rome into anarchy, the plague came as the peak of successive calamities. As if the world were indeed in the grasp of the Evil One, its first appearance on the European mainland in January 1348 coincided with a fearsome earthquake that carved a path of wreckage from Naples up to Venice. Houses collapsed, church towers toppled, villages were crushed, and the destruction reached as far as Germany and Greece. Emotional response, dulled by horrors, underwent a kind of atrophy epitomized by the chronicler who wrote, "And in these days was burying without sorrowe and wedding without friendschippe."

In Siena, where more than half the inhabitants died of the plague, work was abandoned on the great cathedral, planned to be the largest in the world, and never resumed, owing to loss of workers and master masons and "the melancholy and grief" of the survivors. The cathedral's truncated transept still stands in permanent witness to the sweep of death's scythe. Agnolo di Tura, a chronicler of Siena, recorded the fear of contagion that froze every other instinct. "Father abandoned child, wife husband, one brother another," he wrote, "for this plague seemed to strike through the breath and sight. And so they died. And no one could be found to bury the dead for money or friendship. . . . And I, Agnolo di Tura, called the Fat, buried my five children with my own hands, and so did many others likewise."

There were many to echo his account of inhumanity and few to balance it, for the plague was not the kind of calamity that inspired mutual help. Its loathsomeness and deadliness did not herd people together in mutual distress, but only prompted their desire to escape each other. "Magistrates and notaries

15

refused to come and make the wills of the dying," reported a Franciscan friar of Piazza in Sicily; what was worse, "even the priests did not come to hear their confessions." A clerk of the Archbishop of Canterbury reported the same of English priests who "turned away from the care of their benefices from fear of death." Cases of parents deserting children and children their parents were reported across Europe from Scotland to Russia. The calamity chilled the hearts of men, wrote Boccaccio[3] in his famous account of the plague in Florence that serves as introduction to the *Decameron.* "One man shunned another . . . kinsfolk held aloof, brother was forsaken by brother, oftentimes husband by wife; nay, what is more, and scarcely to be believed, fathers and mothers were found to abandon their own children to their fate, untended, unvisited as if they had been strangers." Exaggeration and literary pessimism were common in the 14th century, but the Pope's physician, Guy de Chauliac, was a sober, careful observer who reported the same phenomenon: "A father did not visit his son, nor the son his father. Charity was dead."

Yet not entirely. In Paris, according to the chronicler Jean de Venette, the nuns of the Hôtel Dieu or municipal hospital, "having no fear of death, tended the sick with all sweetness and humility." New nuns repeatedly took the places of those who died, until the majority "many times renewed by death now rest in peace with Christ as we may piously believe."

When the plague entered northern France in July 1348, it settled first in Normandy and, checked by winter, gave Picardy a deceptive interim until the next summer. Either in mourning or warning, black flags were flown from church towers of the worst-stricken villages of Normandy. "And in that time," wrote a monk of the abbey of Fourcarment, "the mortality was so great among the people of Normandy that those of Picardy mocked them." The same unneighborly reaction was reported of the Scots, separated by a winter's immunity from the English. Delighted to hear of the disease that was scourging the "southrons," they gathered forces for an invasion, "laughing at their enemies." Before they could move, the savage mortality fell upon them too, scattering some in death and the rest in panic to spread the infection as they fled.

In Picardy in the summer of 1349 the pestilence penetrated the castle of Coucy to kill Enguerrand's[4] mother, Catherine, and her new husband. Whether her nine-year-old son escaped by chance or was perhaps living elsewhere with one of his guardians is unrecorded. In nearby Amiens, tannery workers, responding quickly to losses in the labor force, combined to bargain for higher wages. In another place villagers were seen dancing to drums and trumpets, and on being asked the reason, answered that, seeing their neighbors die day by day while their village remained immune, they believed they could keep the plague from entering "by the jollity that is in us. That is why we

3. Giovanni Boccaccio (1313–1375), Italian writer best known for his collection of stories, *The Decameron,* in which seven young ladies and three young men flee from Florence to escape the Black Death and tell stories to while away the time.

4. Enguerrand de Coucy, a French nobleman, is the historical figure around whom Tuchman constructs her account of the fourteenth century.

dance." Further north in Tournai on the border of Flanders, Gilles li Muisis, Abbot of St. Martin's, kept one of the epidemic's most vivid accounts. The passing bells rang all day and all night, he recorded, because sextons were anxious to obtain their fees while they could. Filled with the sound of mourning, the city became oppressed by fear, so that the authorities forbade the tolling of bells and the wearing of black and restricted funeral services to two mourners. The silencing of funeral bells and of criers' announcements of deaths was ordained by most cities. Siena imposed a fine on the wearing of mourning clothes by all except widows.

Flight was the chief recourse of those who could afford it or arrange it. The rich fled to their country places like Boccaccio's young patricians of Florence, who settled in a pastoral palace "removed on every side from the roads" with "wells of cool water and vaults of rare wines." The urban poor died in their burrows, "and only the stench of their bodies informed neighbors of their death." That the poor were more heavily afflicted than the rich was clearly remarked at the time, in the north as in the south. A Scottish chronicler, John of Fordun, stated flatly that the pest "attacked especially the meaner sort and common people—seldom the magnates." Simon de Covino of Montpellier made the same observation. He ascribed it to the misery and want and hard lives that made the poor more susceptible, which was half the truth. Close contact and lack of sanitation was the unrecognized other half. It was noticed too that the young died in greater proportion than the old; Simon de Covino compared the disappearance of youth to the withering of flowers in the fields.

In the countryside peasants dropped dead on the roads, in the fields, in 20
their houses. Survivors in growing helplessness fell into apathy, leaving ripe wheat uncut and livestock untended. Oxen and asses, sheep and goats, pigs and chickens ran wild and they too, according to local reports, succumbed to the pest. English sheep, bearers of the precious wool, died throughout the country. The chronicler Henry Knighton, canon of Leicester Abbey, reported 5,000 dead in one field alone, "their bodies so corrupted by the plague that neither beast nor bird would touch them," and spreading an appalling stench. In the Austrian Alps wolves came down to prey upon sheep and then, "as if alarmed by some invisible warning, turned and fled back into the wilderness." In remote Dalmatia bolder wolves descended upon a plague-stricken city and attacked human survivors. For want of herdsmen, cattle strayed from place to place and died in hedgerows and ditches. Dogs and cats fell like the rest.

The dearth of labor held a fearful prospect because the 14th century lived close to the annual harvest both for food and for next year's seed. "So few servants and laborers were left," wrote Knighton, "that no one knew where to turn for help." The sense of a vanishing future created a kind of dementia of despair. A Bavarian chronicler of Neuberg on the Danube recorded that "Men and women . . . wandered around as if mad" and let their cattle stray "because no one had any inclination to concern themselves about the future." Fields went uncultivated, spring seed unsown. Second growth with nature's awful energy crept back over cleared land, dikes crumbled, salt water reinvaded and soured the lowlands. With so few hands remaining to restore the work of centuries, people felt, in Walsingham's words, that "the world could never again regain its former prosperity."

Though the death rate was higher among the anonymous poor, the known and the great died too. King Alfonso XI of Castile was the only reigning monarch killed by the pest, but his neighbor King Pedro of Aragon lost his wife, Queen Leonora, his daughter Marie, and a niece in the space of six months. John Cantacuzene, Emperor of Byzantium, lost his son. In France the lame Queen Jeanne and her daughter-in-law Bonne de Luxemburg, wife of the Dauphin, both died in 1349 in the same phase that took the life of Enguerrand's mother. Jeanne, Queen of Navarre, daughter of Louis X, was another victim. Edward III's second daughter, Joanna, who was on her way to marry Pedro, the heir of Castile, died in Bordeaux. Women appear to have been more vulnerable than men, perhaps because, being more housebound, they were more exposed to fleas. Boccaccio's mistress Fiammetta, illegitimate daughter of the King of Naples, died, as did Laura, the beloved—whether real or fictional—of Petrarch. Reaching out to us in the future, Petrarch cried, "Oh happy posterity who will not experience such abysmal woe and will look upon our testimony as a fable."

In Florence Giovanni Villani, the great historian of his time, died at 68 in the midst of an unfinished sentence: ". . . e dure questo pistolenza fino a . . . (in the midst of this pestilence there came to an end . . .)." Siena's master painters, the brothers Ambrogio and Pietro Lorenzetti, whose names never appear after 1348, presumably perished in the plague, as did Andrea Pisano, architect and sculptor of Florence. William of Ockham and the English mystic Richard Rolle of Hampole both disappear from mention after 1349. Francisco Datini, merchant of Prato, lost both his parents and two siblings. Curious sweeps of mortality afflicted certain bodies of merchants in London. All eight wardens of the Company of Cutters, all six wardens of the Hatters, and four wardens of the Goldsmiths died before July 1350. Sir John Pulteney, master draper and four times Mayor of London, was a victim, likewise Sir John Montgomery, Governor of Calais.

Among the clergy and doctors the mortality was naturally high because of the nature of their professions. Out of 24 physicians in Venice, 20 were said to have lost their lives in the plague, although, according to another account, some were believed to have fled or to have shut themselves up in their houses. At Montpellier, site of the leading medieval medical school, the physician Simon de Covino reported that, despite the great number of doctors, "hardly one of them escaped." In Avignon, Guy de Chauliac confessed that he performed his medical visits only because he dared not stay away for fear of infamy, but "I was in continual fear." He claimed to have contracted the disease but to have cured himself by his own treatment; if so, he was one of the few who recovered.

25   Clerical mortality varied with rank. Although the one-third toll of cardinals reflects the same proportion as the whole, this was probably due to their concentration in Avignon. In England, in strange and almost sinister procession, the Archbishop of Canterbury, John Stratford, died in August 1348, his appointed successor died in May 1349, and the next appointee three months

later, all three within a year. Despite such weird vagaries, prelates in general managed to sustain a higher survival rate than the lesser clergy. Among bishops the deaths have been estimated at about one in twenty. The loss of priests, even if many avoided their fearful duty of attending the dying, was about the same as among the population as a whole.

Government officials, whose loss contributed to the general chaos, found, on the whole, no special shelter. In Siena four of the nine members of the governing oligarchy died, in France one third of the royal notaries, in Bristol 15 out of the 52 members of the Town Council or almost one third. Tax-collecting obviously suffered, with the result that Philip VI was unable to collect more than a fraction of the subsidy granted him by the Estates in the winter of 1347–48.

Lawlessness and debauchery accompanied the plague as they had during the great plague of Athens of 430 B.C., when according to Thucydides, men grew bold in the indulgence of pleasure: "For seeing how the rich died in a moment and those who had nothing immediately inherited their property, they reflected that life and riches were alike transitory and they resolved to enjoy themselves while they could." Human behavior is timeless. When St. John had his vision of plague in Revelation, he knew from some experience or race memory that those who survived "repented not of the work of their hands. . . . Neither repented they of their murders, nor of their sorceries, nor of their fornication, nor of their thefts."

Ignorance of the cause augmented the sense of horror. Of the real carriers, rats and fleas, the 14th century had no suspicion, perhaps because they were so familiar. Fleas, though a common household nuisance, are not once mentioned in contemporary plague writings, and rats only incidentally, although folklore commonly associated them with pestilence. The legend of the Pied Piper arose from an outbreak of 1284. The actual plague bacillus, *Pasturella pestis,* remained undiscovered for another 500 years. Living alternately in the stomach of the flea and the bloodstream of the rat who was the flea's host, the bacillus in its bubonic form was transferred to humans and animals by the bite of either rat or flea. It traveled by virtue of *Rattus rattus,* the small medieval black rat that lived on ships, as well as by the heavier brown or sewer rat. What precipitated the turn of the bacillus from innocuous to virulent form is unknown, but the occurrence is now believed to have taken place not in China but somewhere in central Asia and to have spread along the caravan routes. Chinese origin was a mistaken notion of the 14th century based on real but belated reports of huge death tolls in China from drought, famine, and pestilence which have since been traced to the 1330s, too soon to be responsible for the plague that appeared in India in 1346.

The phantom enemy had no name. Called the Black Death only in later recurrences, it was known during the first epidemic simply as the Pestilence or Great Mortality. Reports from the East, swollen by fearful imaginings, told of strange tempests and "sheets of fire" mingled with huge hailstones that "slew almost all," or a "vast rain of fire" that burned up men, beasts, stones, trees, villages, and cities. In another version, "foul blasts of wind" from the fires carried the infection to Europe "and now as some suspect it cometh round the seacoast." Accurate observation in this case could not make the mental jump to ships and rats because no idea of animal- or insect-borne contagion existed.

The earthquake was blamed for releasing sulfurous and foul fumes from the earth's interior, or as evidence of a titanic struggle of planets and oceans causing waters to rise and vaporize until fish died in masses and corrupted the air. All these explanations had in common a factor of poisoned air, of miasmas and thick, stinking mists traced to every kind of natural or imagined agency from stagnant lakes to malign conjunction of the planets, from the hand of the Evil One to the wrath of God. Medical thinking, trapped in the theory of astral influences, stressed air as the communicator of disease, ignoring sanitation or visible carriers. The existence of two carriers confused the trail, the more so because the flea could live and travel independently of the rat for as long as a month and, if infected by the particularly virulent septicemic form of the bacillus, could infect humans without reinfecting itself from the rat. The simultaneous presence of the pneumonic form of the disease, which was indeed communicated through the air, blurred the problem further.

The mystery of the contagion was "the most terrible of all the terrors," as an anonymous Flemish cleric in Avignon wrote to a correspondent in Bruges. Plagues had been known before, from the plague of Athens (believed to have been typhus) to the prolonged epidemic of the 6th century A.D., to the recurrence of sporadic outbreaks in the 12th and 13th centuries, but they had left no accumulated store of understanding. That the infection came from contact with the sick or with their houses, clothes, or corpses was quickly observed but not comprehended. Gentile da Foligno, renowned physician of Perugia and doctor of medicine at the universities of Bologna and Padua, came close to respiratory infection when he surmised that poisonous material was "communicated by means of air breathed out and in." Having no idea of microscopic carriers, he had to assume that the air was corrupted by planetary influences. Planets, however, could not explain the ongoing contagion. The agonized search for an answer gave rise to such theories as transference by sight. People fell ill, wrote Guy de Chauliac, not only by remaining with the sick but "even by looking at them." Three hundred years later Joshua Barnes, the 17th century biographer of Edward III, could write that the power of infection had entered into beams of light and "darted death from the eyes."

Doctors struggling with the evidence could not break away from the terms of astrology, to which they believed all human physiology was subject. Medicine was the one aspect of medieval life, perhaps because of its links with the Arabs, not shaped by Christian doctrine. Clerics detested astrology, but could not dislodge its influence. Guy de Chauliac, physician to three popes in succession, practiced in obedience to the zodiac. While his *Cirurgia* was the major treatise on surgery of its time, while he understood the use of anesthesia made from the juice of opium, mandrake, or hemlock, he nevertheless prescribed bleeding and purgatives by the planets and divided chronic from acute diseases on the basis of one being under the rule of the sun and the other of the moon.

In October 1348 Philip VI asked the medical faculty of the University of

Paris for a report on the affliction that seemed to threaten human survival. With careful thesis, antithesis, and proofs, the doctors ascribed it to a triple conjunction of Saturn, Jupiter, and Mars in the 40th degree of Aquarius said to have occurred on March 20, 1345. They acknowledged, however, effects "whose cause is hidden from even the most highly trained intellects." The verdict of the masters of Paris became the official version. Borrowed, copied by scribes, carried abroad, translated from Latin into various vernaculars, it was everywhere accepted, even by the Arab physicians of Cordova and Granada, as the scientific if not the popular answer. Because of the terrible interest of the subject, the translations of the plague tracts stimulated use of national languages. In that one respect, life came from death.

To the people at large there could be but one explanation—the wrath of God. Planets might satisfy the learned doctors, but God was closer to the average man. A scourge so sweeping and unsparing without any visible cause could only be seen as Divine punishment upon mankind for its sins. It might even be God's terminal disappointment in his creature. Matteo Villani compared the plague to the Flood in ultimate purpose and believed he was recording "the extermination of mankind." Efforts to appease Divine wrath took many forms, as when the city of Rouen ordered that everything that could anger God, such as gambling, cursing, and drinking, must be stopped. More general were the penitent processions authorized at first by the Pope, some lasting as long as three days, some attended by as many as 2,000, which everywhere accompanied the plague and helped to spread it.

Barefoot in sackcloth, sprinkled with ashes, weeping, praying, tearing their hair, carrying candles and relics, sometimes with ropes around their necks or beating themselves with whips, the penitents wound through the streets, imploring the mercy of the Virgin and saints at their shrines. In a vivid illustration for the *Très Riches Heures* of the Duc de Berry, the Pope is shown in a penitent procession attended by four cardinals in scarlet from hat to hem. He raises both arms in supplication to the angel on top of the Castel Sant' Angelo, while white-robed priests bearing banners and relics in golden cases turn to look as one of their number, stricken by the plague, falls to the ground, his face contorted with anxiety. In the rear, a gray-clad monk falls beside another victim already on the ground as the townspeople gaze in horror. (Nominally the illustration represents a 6th century plague in the time of Pope Gregory the Great, but as medieval artists made no distinction between past and present, the scene is shown as the artist would have seen it in the 14th century.) When it became evident that these processions were sources of infection, Clement VI had to prohibit them.

In Messina, where the plague first appeared, the people begged the Archbishop of neighboring Catania to lend them the relics of St. Agatha. When the Catanians refused to let the relics go, the Archbishop dipped them in holy water and took the water himself to Messina, where he carried it in a procession with prayers and litanies through the streets. The demonic, which shared the medieval cosmos with God, appeared as "demons in the shape of dogs" to ter-

Penitential procession led by the Pope during the plague (pictured in 14th century Rome although it purports to illustrate the 6th century plague under Gregory the Great). By Pol de Limbourg for the *Très Riches Heures* of the Duc de Berry, c. 1410.

rify the people. "A black dog with a drawn sword in his paws appeared among them, gnashing his teeth and rushing upon them and breaking all the silver vessels and lamps and candlesticks on the altars and casting them hither and thither. . . . So the people of Messina, terrified by this prodigious vision, were all strangely overcome by fear."

The apparent absence of earthly cause gave the plague a supernatural and sinister quality. Scandinavians believed that a Pest Maiden emerged from the mouth of the dead in the form of a blue flame and flew through the air to infect the next house. In Lithuania the Maiden was said to wave a red scarf through the door or window to let in the pest. One brave man, according to legend, deliberately waited at his open window with drawn sword and, at the fluttering of the scarf, chopped off the hand. He died of his deed, but his village was spared and the scarf long preserved as a relic in the local church.

Beyond demons and superstition the final hand was God's. The Pope acknowledged it in a Bull of September 1348, speaking of the "pestilence with which God is afflicting the Christian people." To the Emperor John Cantacuzene it was manifest that a malady of such horrors, stenches, and agonies, and especially one bringing the dismal despair that settled upon its victims before they died, was not a plague "natural" to mankind but "a chastisement from Heaven." To Piers Plowman[5] "these pestilences were for pure sin."

The general acceptance of this view created an expanded sense of guilt, for if the plague were punishment there had to be terrible sin to have occasioned it. What sins were on the 14th century conscience? Primarily greed, the sin of avarice, followed by usury, worldliness, adultery, blasphemy, falsehood, luxury, irreligion. Giovanni Villani, attempting to account for the cascade of calamity that had fallen upon Florence, concluded that it was retribution for the sins of avarice and usury that oppressed the poor. Pity and anger about the condition of the poor, especially victimization of the peasantry in war, was often expressed by writers of the time and was certainly on the conscience of the century. Beneath it all was the daily condition of medieval life, in which hardly an act or thought, sexual, mercantile, or military, did not contravene the dictates of the Church. Mere failure to fast or attend mass was sin. The result was an underground lake of guilt in the soul that the plague now tapped.

That the mortality was accepted as God's punishment may explain in part   40
the vacuum of comment that followed the Black Death. An investigator has noticed that in the archives of Périgord references to the war are innumerable, to the plague few. Froissart mentions the great death but once, Chaucer gives it barely a glance. Divine anger so great that it contemplated the extermination of man did not bear close examination.

5. The main character (and title) of a fourteenth-century poem by the English poet William Langland (c. 1330–c. 1386).

Questions

1. Why does Tuchman begin with the account of the Genoese trading ships?

2. What ways does Tuchman find to group related facts together—in other words, what categories does she develop? Suggest other categories that Tuchman might have used in arranging her facts. What would she have gained or lost by using such categories?

3. Can you determine a basis for Tuchman's decision sometimes to quote a source, sometimes to recount it in her own words?

4. Write a brief account of a modern disaster, based on research from several sources.

PHILIP ALCABES   *The Bioterrorism Scare:*
A Historical Perspective

SINCE THE FALL OF 2001, when America embarked on a "war on terrorism" and federal officials started warning us about the next plague, here are some events that have not happened: a U.S. epidemic of sudden acute respiratory syndrome (SARS),[1] a widespread anthrax outbreak, any smallpox attack, the discovery of hard evidence of a biological weapons program in Iraq. Yet the talk about "biopreparedness" continues. Some people in Washington want the Centers for Disease Control and Prevention to be transferred from the Department of Health and Human Services to Homeland Security. There is even a professional journal, *Biosecurity and Bioterrorism*, devoted to learned discussions of the topic. Is it sound public policy to rush to protect the country against the threat of attack with germs that could cause an epidemic? Does the bio in biosecurity mean that we should turn our public health into a matter of civil defense? Or have we Americans been sold a bill of goods?

Throughout history, the responses to both actual communicable disease and the threat of it have been guided by the metaphor of the stranger as the spreader of contagion. Allegations that epidemic disease was caused by foreigners are ancient. Thucydides[2] reported that his contemporaries, in the fifth century B.C., attributed the Plague of Athens[3] to Ethiopians. Later on, such thinking was refined to impute causation specifically to enemy foreigners. Many European and American authors still believe that the Black Death[4] entered western Europe after the Mongols, besieging the city of Kefe (or Kaffa, now Feodosiya in Ukraine) in 1346, catapulted into the European-held city the corpses of comrades who had died of plague. When the siege was lifted, the theory goes, the disease reached Genoa aboard ships. Although Kefe clearly experienced plague in 1346, the story of its source is almost certainly apocryphal: Xenopsylla cheopis, the flea that usually carries the plague bacillus, has affinity only for warm bodies and will desert a corpse within hours of death. But the myth's persistence attests to the readiness of some, even centuries later, to believe that epidemics were caused by enemies.

Published in the American Scholar, *the magazine of the Phi Beta Kappa Society (Spring 2004).*

1. Severe Acute Respiratory Syndrome, a pneumonia-like condition that broke out in Singapore and China in 2002.

2. Greek historian (c. 460–400 B.C.E.).

3. An epidemic that struck Athens in 430 B.C.E. during the second year of the Peloponnesian War against Sparta.

4. An epidemic of bubonic plague that struck Europe in the fourteenth century, killing approximately one-third of the population.

Similarly, Londoners believed that the Great Plague of 1665[5] was brought by the Dutch, with whom England was then at war (echoes of that belief appear in both Defoe's *Journal of the Plague Year* and Samuel Pepys's *Diary*),[6] although there is no evidence that plague in fact came to England from Holland. The great influenza pandemic of 1918–19, which killed more than 20 million people—possibly as many as 40 million—in a world at war, was attributed to various enemies. In fact, the name by which we remember this epidemic, "Spanish Flu," seems to have been a compromise acceptable to the warring parties (Spain was neutral in the war). And in a telling instance, very shortly after Germany broke its pact with the Soviet Union and invaded its former ally, Hitler[7] used the term Pestherd—"plague focus"—to refer to Russia, accusing the Soviets of infecting Europe with Jewish "bacilli." It was the metaphor of foreign culpability for disease turned inside out, Hitler imputing pathogenic properties to Jews and creating a new enemy by alleging that it was Russia that had spawned them. More recently, Tanzanians attributed the high death rate from AIDS in their Kagera province to HIV infections brought by Idi Amin's[8] Ugandan troops, who crossed the border into Tanzania in the late 1970s. "It made sense, then," Laurie Garrett[9] writes in *The Coming Plague*, "to assume that the new disease came from old enemies." When West Nile encephalitis made its Western hemisphere debut in New York in 1999, epidemiologists received calls from the FBI; they (and the CIA, too) were concerned that it might be the work of foreign bioterrorists.

The Stranger Spreading Germs shows up often in literature and film. Alessandro Manzoni's[10] 1821 novel, *I Promessi Sposi*, attributes the advance of plague in 1629 to the German army, then campaigning through the valleys of northern Italy in the Thirty Years' War. In the novel, foreigners, particularly the French, come under suspicion in plague-ridden Milan, where they are accused of "daubing" plague-inducing substances on walls or sprinkling plague powders on the streets; those found guilty of such felonious behavior are tortured to death. In F. W. Murnau's[11] classic silent film *Nosferatu*, plague arrives in Bremen by sea, brought from the East by the odious Other, the undead Nos-

5. An epidemic of bubonic plague that hit London in the seventeenth century, killing up to a fifth of the population.

6. Daniel Defoe (1660–1731), British writer best known for his novel *Robinson Crusoe* (1719); Pepys (1633–1703), British naval administrator and politician known for his diary written in code.

7. Adolf Hitler (1889–1945), Austrian-born Chancellor of Germany, leader of the Nazi party, and perpetrator of World War II.

8. Dictatorial Ugandan president (1924–2003) who ruled during the 1970s.

9. Pulitzer Prize–winning science writer and author of *The Coming Plague* (1994) and *Betrayal of Trust: The Collapse of Global Public Health* (2000).

10. Italian writer (1775–1883) whose novel *I Promessi Sposi* (translated into English as "The Betrothed") includes a detailed description of the plague that Milan suffered in 1630.

11. German film director (1888–1931) who based his film *Nosferatu* (1922) on Bram Stoker's novel *Dracula* (1897).

feratu. In 1922, just after the carnage of World War I and the far greater mortality of the Spanish Flu pandemic, Murnau depicted Evil as the man who was beyond death, the inscrutable and indomitable being who brings pestilence from the benighted Ausland.[12]

5   Sometimes, of course, epidemics have come from the enemy foreigner. Clearly, Cortes[13] was able to conquer Mexico because of smallpox. The disease appeared among the Taino[14] on Hispaniola in 1518, brought by Spaniards who had colonized the island; later, it would contribute to the Taino's extinction. By 1519 smallpox was in Cuba. Cortes, who was secretary to the governor of Cuba, left to take Tenochtitlan from the Aztec chief Montezuma;[15] either Cortes's Spanish troops or those of Narvaez,[16] who led a relief expedition against the Aztecs after they repulsed Cortes's initial sallies, brought smallpox to the Aztecs. The disease, to which the Aztecs were immunologically naive, so diminished their numbers that Cortes had only to finish them off. Smallpox thence spread southward, killing the Incan emperor Huayna Capac[17] and then his son in 1524–25, and plunging their people into civil war. Francisco Pizarro had little more to do to vanquish the Incas than march into Cuzco.[18]

It is unlikely that the Spaniards infected the American natives deliberately—and the Aztecs, at least, seemed to interpret the devastation as evidence of divine disfavor, not treachery on the part of Spain. But in the French and Indian War, in the early 1760s, smallpox does seem to have been spread deliberately. During the conflict known as Pontiac's Rebellion, Sir Jeffrey Amherst, the British commanding general, approved a plan to distribute smallpox-contaminated blankets "to innoculate the Indians" besieging Fort Pitt, at the fork of the Ohio River. That epidemic smallpox occurred in the Ohio Valley at the time is an established fact.

Around the same time, the Polish army considered producing cannon shells filled with the saliva of rabid dogs, in an attempt to poison the air the enemy breathed. Later, during World War I, the German biological warfare program sought to create animal epidemics—epizootics, in the lingo of epidemiology—that would diminish their enemies' ability to fight. German agents deliberately infected their neutral trading partners' livestock and animal feed with the agents of glanders (principally an equine disease) and anthrax. Ro-

12. German for "foreign country."

13. Hernando Cortes (1485–1547), Spanish conquistador who brought about the demise of the Aztec Empire in present-day Mexico.

14. Natives of Cuba, Haiti, the Dominican Republic, Puerto Rico, and Jamaica, whom Columbus encountered upon his arrival in the Americas.

15. Tenochtitlan: capital of the Aztec Empire, which was destroyed by conquering Spaniards and became the site of present-day Mexico City; Montezuma (c. 1466–1520), emperor of the Aztecs at the beginning of the Spanish conquest.

16. Panfilo de Narvaez (1470–1528), Spanish conquistador.

17. Chief of the Incas (1493–1527), a people native to South America.

18. Pizarro (1475–1541), Spanish conquistador who helped bring about the demise of the Inca Empire; Cuzco was its capital.

manian sheep were infected with both microbes in 1916 before export to Russia; more than two hundred Argentine mules intended as dray animals[19] for Allied forces died after being inoculated with both bacteria; French cavalry horses were infected with glanders; and attempts were made to contaminate animal feed in the United States. During World War II, the Third Reich avowedly eschewed use of biological warfare, but one report holds that Colorado beetles were dropped by German airplanes on potato crops in southern England. The U.S. Army claims that the retreating Wehrmacht[20] contaminated a reservoir in Bohemia with sewage, presumably to produce disease in the advancing Soviet army.

The best documented, and most successful, deliberately caused human epidemic was set by the infamous Unit 731 of the Japanese Imperial Army, stationed in conquered China during World War II. In addition to numerous heinous medical "experiments"—tortures, really—the unit dropped plague-carrying fleas on eleven Chinese towns. The number of Chinese who died of plague was probably about seven hundred. Unit 731 also produced cholera. In fact, Japanese soldiers, whom the unit had failed to warn or prepare, died in large numbers after entering Chinese areas seeded with Vibrio cholerae.[21] Some historians put the total number of deaths attributable to the unit's intentional contaminations, including others involving anthrax and typhoid, in the thousands.

In connection with humans deliberately causing epidemics, the smallpox germ, variola virus, is the one we hear most about. It enjoyed a five-hundred-year career as a natural epidemic pathogen, from roughly the late fifteenth century until the late twentieth. Then smallpox was eradicated from the earth. Variola killed several hundred million people in the first half of the twentieth century alone—a public-health menace to be reckoned with. No doubt because of its fearsome reputation, it is the subject of a great number of speculative scenarios about how it might be resurrected as an epidemic scourge.

In fact, though, none of those scenarios is even remotely likely. First, not   10
many people have access to viable smallpox stocks. Second, the disease that variola virus produces is fairly easy to diagnose. Third, vaccination will prevent disease even in already-infected contacts of smallpox cases, and vaccine stocks are reasonably large nowadays. The hubbub about smallpox has had the effect of sharpening physicians' diagnostic skills (indeed, so much so that instances of overdiagnosis produce false alarms) and expanding the supply of available vaccine. At this point, standard public-health procedures, including case diagnosis, contact investigation, and immunization of possibly infected individuals, would be adequate to prevent an outbreak in the unlikely event that some individuals were deliberately infected.

Anthrax is the second most popular topic of bioterrorism conversation. We have seen intentional anthrax infection—the much-ballyhooed postal an-

---

19. Animals used to move wagons, such as horses, oxen, and mules.
20. German for "defense force," the name of the German army under Adolf Hitler.
21. The bacterium that causes cholera.

thrax events that took place in the fall of 2001. Three characteristics of that outbreak are of note: very few people became ill; very, very few died; and it was almost certainly not produced by a stranger. Environmental studies in mailrooms indicated that many hundreds of people were probably exposed to anthrax spores that fall, yet only twenty-two people got sick. And of those twenty-two, half had cutaneous anthrax, the rarely-life-threatening skin form of the disease. Only five died. In the jargon of epidemiology, anthrax turned out to be neither very infectious nor very pathogenic. That experience should tell us that spraying anthrax spores from crop dusters or releasing them from aerosol cans into the subway is highly unlikely to make many people ill. Speculation about subway attacks stems from a real event in March 1995, when the Japanese religious cult Aum Shinrikyo released the nerve toxin sarin in the Tokyo subway system. Twelve people died. Two subsequent attempts to release toxins in the Tokyo subways were foiled. Note that Aum was using a gas, which does not have to be sprayed; it diffuses by itself. This is not how germs are disseminated, and it is a distinction worth bearing in mind. And even that ignores the more central question of likelihood. Large-scale poisonings are not easy to carry out well. The light death toll from mailed anthrax was a result of the low pathogenicity of the bacteria—half the cases were not pulmonary and were therefore unlikely to be fatal—and the comparative treatability of anthrax disease once detected. Do five deaths constitute a public-health crisis? Along with his colleagues, Victor Sidel, Distinguished Professor of Social Medicine at Albert Einstein College of Medicine in New York, has noted that a fraction of our nation's expenditure on biopreparedness would pay for effective treatment of tuberculosis for all of the two million people who get TB each year in India, thereby preventing close to half a million deaths a year. Half a million deaths because commonly available antibiotics are not affordable—now there's a public-health problem.

The other microbe that is on the lists of virtually all the bioterrorism watchers is the plague bacillus. It is true that Unit 731 produced plague outbreaks in China by dropping infected fleas on towns. But at that time plague was a recurring problem in Asia: a ferocious epidemic struck Manchuria in 1910, and another occurred in 1921. (It still is a problem: a large outbreak caused many deaths in India as recently as 1994.) By contrast, despite the presence of Yersinia pestis, the plague bacterium, in wild rodents in the Western Hemisphere, there has never been an extensive epidemic of human plague in this country. Even when plague epidemics moved out of Asia through much of South America, circa 1900, the U.S. saw only a small outbreak in San Francisco's Chinatown. The reason is not that Americans are immune to plague; it is that the urban arrangements that we have been accustomed to for the past two hundred years are inhospitable to the rat-flea-bacillus ecosystem. Such reforms as garbage removal, pest control, and better housing explain why plague disappeared from eastern Europe in the early 1700s and has never troubled us seriously here. Since epidemics of plague are unlikely, should we then worry that terrorists will produce isolated cases? Perhaps, but garden-variety antibiotics are very effective at treating the disease and interrupting transmission. There is no potential for the next catastrophe there.

Other pathogens have been mentioned as possible bioweapons—for example, the agents of tularemia, botulism, and Q fever.[22] These organisms are not generally transmitted from person to person, so they carry little or no outbreak potential. Hemorrhagic fever viruses are sometimes transmitted by mosquitoes or by the bite of infected animals. It has never been shown that they can be manipulated into transportable weapons and then elude standard mosquito- and animal-control programs.

All in all, there is little evidence that terrorists are more likely, or better able, to use microbes as part of their armamentarium than ever before. If there were evidence, would editorialists in the nation's most prestigious medical journal need to argue, as they did in the context of the purported smallpox threat, that public-health decisions should rely on "theoretical data"? Consider the ratio of known success to attempts at bioterrorism. Jessica Stern reports in *The Ultimate Terrorists* that the Aura Shinrikyo cult drove three trucks set up to spray botulinum toxin through Tokyo in 1990, but no cases of botulism resulted. Judith Miller, William Broad, and Stephen Engelberg report in their book, *Germs*, that Aura sprayed anthrax spores from the roof of its building in Tokyo in 1993. This apparently killed some birds, but no humans got sick. Aum members also reportedly tried to procure Ebola virus in the 1990s from what was then Zaire, but if they were able to get the virus, they were unable to produce any cases of Ebola.

In the 1960s, a Japanese researcher purposely contaminated food with Salmonella typhi,[23] producing outbreaks of typhoid fever and dysentery, but no deaths. In 1970, four Canadian students got sick after eating food that had been deliberately contaminated with pig ringworm ova. A neo-Nazi group in the U.S. stockpiled the typhoid bacterium in 1972, with the intent of contaminating the water supplies of midwestern cities. They failed. In 1984, members of the Rajneeshee cult[24] contaminated ten Oregon salad bars with Salmonella typhimurium, which causes diarrhea. Federal investigators located 751 cases of salmonellosis, but no deaths occurred. In 1996, twelve people in Texas developed dysentery after eating doughnuts or muffins purposely contaminated with shigella bacteria[25] by a disgruntled lab worker. Again, no deaths.

Presumably, these initiatives represent only a small subset—the known ones—of all attempts to cause mayhem by deliberately introducing germs into a population. Indeed, one systematic study uncovered twenty-nine such attempts to use germs to harm others, although a large proportion seemed to have been perpetrated by single individuals whose aims were against other in-

---

22. Tularemia: highly infectious disease with flulike symptoms; botulism: an often food-borne illness that can cause paralysis; Q fever: short for "Query Fever," an extremely infectious illness that can be contracted through inhalation of bacteria, so called because its discoverer could not recognize it.

23. The bacterium responsible for typhoid fever and salmonellosis.

24. Followers of the controversial cult leader Rajneesh Chandra Mohan Jain.

25. A family of bacteria, named for the Japanese scientist Shiga who discovered it, that causes diarrhea, fever, and stomach cramps.

dividuals rather than the population. No doubt there are still more instances, unknown because they were unsuccessful. And yet we can enumerate on the fingers of one hand the deadly epidemics that have in fact been caused deliberately. In the creation of epidemics, the gap between intention and the deed itself is a wide one.

Americans began looking at new infectious diseases as a grave social menace in the early 1990s, and that anxiety resonated loudly after the publication of Laurie Garrett's *Coming Plague* in 1994. In a sense, the relatively recent worry about bioterrorism is a spin-off of the past decade's concern about the "coming plague." In reality, the intensity of even naturally occurring new epidemics never matches that anticipation.

Our most recent experience with so-called emerging infections has been SARS. It appeared suddenly in southern China in late 2002, the causative virus probably having entered the human population through people who had substantial contact with domestic animals. Although SARS affected more than 8,000 people worldwide and killed more than 700, it was a negligible problem in the U.S. (eight cases, no deaths) and produced no more than a mild epidemic in most other countries: despite the high case-fatality ratio (people diagnosed with SARS had about one chance in ten of dying from the disease), only in China, Hong Kong, Singapore, and Canada were there more than five SARS deaths. Only nineteen countries saw more than a single SARS case. In all the affected areas, the outbreak was brought under control within about six months of its onset.

Two aspects of the SARS experience are important. First, though it is easy to acquire the virus by inhaling respiratory secretions from a SARS sufferer, it also turns out to be easy to prevent or control an outbreak. The key is to use standard infectious-disease-control measures, including case finding and reporting, active surveillance at points of entry to the country, isolation of possible cases, and recommendations against travel to heavily affected regions. None of these measures requires cutting-edge technology; all have been used in controlling communicable disease for well over a century.

20   Second, SARS made news partly because it was not the expected epidemic. For six months before the advent of SARS, Americans had been worrying very publicly about smallpox. Urged toward apprehension by the federal government, we had alarmed ourselves about the possibility that the long-defunct disease would be reborn in the hands of bioterrorists. The administration made ready, in mid-2002, to vaccinate half a million armed-services personnel and half a million health-care workers. The former plan it came close to accomplishing; the latter was abandoned because so many health-care workers refused to show up for vaccination. All of it repeatedly made the headlines and the evening news reports. Yet what happened in the end was not smallpox, or smallpox prevention; it was SARS. Had our faces not already been turned toward epidemic disease and our anxieties about infection elevated, had the news hours not been hungry for new news after a month of relentless coverage of the Iraq war, SARS might not have made such big headlines.

The lesson we should learn from our experience with SARS is that if we are vigilant about spotting new disease outbreaks and equally vigilant about applying public-health programs to curtail their spread, we can limit them, although we cannot ward them off completely. We cannot make life risk-free. Had we dealt with AIDS and West Nile encephalitis the way we dealt with SARS (which, of course, may return in the future and therefore requires continued vigilance), their course might have been different. West Nile, ending only its fifth season in the U.S. as I write, is already virtually a national epidemic; AIDS went national within six or seven years of its appearance. But in its initial season, 1999, in New York City, West Nile virus caused forty-six cases of encephalitis and seven deaths: not negligible, but a public-health problem more minor than Lyme disease (and far less extensive, in New York, than asthma or lead poisoning). AIDS began with a handful of cases—there were only a few hundred in 1981, the first year it was recognized—and the U.S. might have kept the toll fairly small had we had the political nerve to do something about it at the time. The point is that, at the outset, none of these "plagues" were cataclysmic. Epidemics do not work that way. Errant microbes do not find their way into the human ecosystem and wipe out most of the population unannounced. The Andromeda Strain[26] is fantasy.

The crystal ball with which we divine epidemic mayhem is no clearer now than it used to be, and no clearer than the vision with which we try to foresee the coming plague. No one can dispute, after the events of September 11, 2001, that some people wish us harm. However, that harm is not likely to come from bioterrorism. To worry that the Middle Easterner, the Arab, or any Muslim—however the Stranger is configured—will use germs to attack us would be to pretend that we can indeed foresee great epidemics. For two reasons, that is certainly not the case. First, humans, even ill-tempered and badly behaved humans, have never been able to use germs or weapons to the terrible degree of mortal effect that nature always has been able to use germs. Just four communicable diseases—malaria, smallpox, AIDS, and tuberculosis—killed well over half a billion people in the twentieth century, or about ten times the combined tolls of World Wars I and II, history's bloodiest conflicts. Even today, with good vaccines and effective antibiotics to stop them, infectious diseases kill about 10 million people each year.

The worst catastrophes the world has seen have been not the genocides, however gruesome, but the cataclysmic disease outbreaks. When a few million people are killed by design with Zyklon B,[27] the machete, or the machine gun, it is a horror and an outrage; it shakes our moral faith. But the Black Death killed a third of Europe's population in just four years in the mid-1300s. Smallpox wiped out entire tribes of American natives after Europeans arrived in the 1500s. Plague killed over 50,000 in Moscow alone in just a few months in 1771. The Spanish Flu killed between 20 and 40 million in sixteen months in 1918–19.

26. A contagious illness of extraterrestrial origin and boundless danger, invented by novelist Michael Crichton in his book of the same title.

27. A cyanide-based insecticide with which the Nazis killed millions in gas chambers.

And that suddenness is the second point. Prevision is of little help against epidemic disasters. Each of the disasters I just mentioned, and every other great epidemic of history, was unimaginable until the moment it began. But neither is prescience necessary: each epidemic, even the ones that turned out to be most terrible, began slowly, percolated a while, and could have been stopped with conventional public-health responses had anyone acted in time. SARS reminded us of that.

25   Whether or not the Stranger is an enemy avowedly bent on terror, casting him in the role of microbial evildoer has the perilous effect of distracting us from realizing two truths: the disheartening one that the epidemic crystal ball is always cloudy, and the uncomfortable one that it is usually social circumstances that make epidemics possible and public-health funding that stops them.

Worrying about the germ-bearing Stranger, we forgo the upkeep of a workaday public-health apparatus in favor of fabricating modern wonders. The CDC now operates what it calls a "war room." From there, it can coordinate activities around SARS, West Nile virus, and other infections, as well as bioterrorism—if it can be found—using high-tech communications equipment. The war room is in an "undisclosed location." Once, CDC[28] officials knew they were running a public-health agency. Now, apparently, they must act as if they are in charge of national defense. After the U.S. Department of Health and Human Services scotched the 2002 plan to vaccinate health-care workers, the CDC announced it would continue its effort to vaccinate police officers and firefighters, despite numerous reasons to stop: several deaths directly attributable to the vaccine; several more possibly attributable; evidence that people who might be predisposed to heart disease (something like 10 or 15 percent of the middle-aged population) can be harmed by the vaccination; certainty that people with HIV infection (a sizable percentage of the adult population in some big-city neighborhoods) must not be vaccinated; and of course the complete absence of natural smallpox infection anywhere in the world for the past twenty-five years.

Federal grant money, under President Bush's multimillion-dollar Project BioShield program, has been allocated to technologic innovation for bioterrorism prevention. By 2003, according to *The Chronicle of Higher Education*, the National Institutes of Health were supporting almost seventy extramural research projects on anthrax alone. The NIH has funded two new National Biocontainment Laboratories and new facilities at Regional Biocontainment Laboratories, most at major universities, to the tune of $360 million in start-up costs. The University of Pittsburgh just lured the top staff of the Center for Civilian Biodefense Strategies away from Johns Hopkins by offering to set up a Center for Biosecurity with a $12 million endowment. The University of South Florida recently received $5 million in federal grant money for its Center for Biological Defense, which has projects like "Photocatalytic Air Disinfection" and "Aquatic Real-time Monitoring System (ARMS) for Bioterrorism Events." And Auburn University received a million-dollar federal bioprepared-

28. Centers for Disease Control and Prevention.

ness grant for something called a Canine Detection Center. When Harvard received a $1.2 million federal grant in 2002 to set up a program for detecting "events possibly related to bioterrorism" by electronically linking 20 million patient-care records from around the country (an endeavor called syndromic surveillance), the grant was a mere drop in the bucket: Congress soon allotted $420 million to Homeland Security for a larger linked health-monitoring network. A consortium led by the New York Academy of Medicine then developed software for syndromic surveillance. The new software allows public health officials to monitor what are called "aberrant clusters health events"—translation: more than the expected number of cases of some symptom that might be related to a disease that might be produced by an organism that might be in the possession of terrorists. Syndromic surveillance works fine if someone knows what to look for. But it is of no help at all with the unexpected. When there really was bioterrorism in the U.S.—the anthrax attacks in fall 2001—linked databases were useless; it took a smart clinician to figure out that anthrax was around, and old-fashioned shoe-leather epidemiology quickly worked out which people had been affected. West Nile virus, ditto. A friend who is an official of a local health department tells me that the syndromic surveillance experts find it works well for predicting the first influenza outbreak each year. But anyone's grandmother can predict the first influenza outbreak where I live, in the New York City area, since the symptoms are always the same and flu always starts here in the two weeks preceding Thanksgiving. For all its meager productivity, the syndromic surveillance software also throws out plenty of false-positive "clusters" that waste investigators' time. It is our new and expensive white elephant, justified by the fear of evildoers and germs.

It all sounds a little phantasmagoric.

In "The Expose of 1935," Walter Benjamin[29] identified certain phantasmagorias of modern life as Wunschbilder, "wish symbols," that seek to "transfigure the . . . inadequacies in the social organization." Benjamin was concerned with phantasmagorias as magical images, as he put it in his Passagen-Werk, "residues of a dream world," revelations of unfulfilled wishes. In this sense we might ask whether the many projects of the Bioshield—the electronic anthrax detectors, the hyperdatabanks, the supersecure biohazard-level-4 labs, the men and women in full-body protective suits, the urban-evacuation exercises, whatever it is they are doing with dogs at Auburn University, and so on—are emblems of some shared desire to feel that all the effort America expends on technology development protects us from something. We might ask whether the something is the Stranger Spreading Germs. And we must ask what the cost is.

The core issue here is that the Stranger Spreading Germs is a metaphor, and largely an empty one. Bioterrorism is not a public-health problem, and will not become one. The next plague, whatever it is, will not decimate us unheralded. In signing the contract on biopreparedness, we have bought a confection, a defense against the chimeric stranger with the metaphorical germs.

30

29. German literary critic and philosopher (1892–1940).

And the costs of buy-in? When our public-health "leaders" corroborate government rhetoric about bioterrorists by reassuring us that our state or municipal health department is ready for any smallpox, anthrax, or plague attack, they legitimate both their own efforts and the standing of their offices. The planned result is that we will not question spending tax dollars so those officials can continue to defend us, even when it means closing down municipal clinics or shortchanging programs for the poor, and even if such biodefense is not what we most need or want.

The biopreparedness campaign goes to work. It discredits the simple logic of public health. Lose the distinction between the minuscule risk of dying in an intentional outbreak and the millionfold-higher chance of dying in a natural pandemic, it says. Ignore the hundredfold-higher-still chance of dying of cancer or heart disease. Defund the prenatal-care clinics, the chest clinics, the exercise and cancer screening and lead abatement programs. Ignore the lessons of history: forget that human attempts to create epidemics have almost always failed, and dismiss the repeated ability of a well-funded public-health apparatus to control epidemic disease with time-tested measures. Just think about germs, and tremble.

The lesson of history that we ignore at our peril is this: nobody can tell us how the next epidemic will happen. New germs come and go, epidemics wax and wane, but national catastrophes happen rarely. And when they do, it is never because of a stranger spreading germs. Anyone who promises certain protection from the next plague is selling us a bill of goods.

QUESTIONS

1. Philip Alcabes argues that, historically, most plagues and epidemics have been wrongly interpreted in terms of "the stranger as the spreader of contagion" (paragraph 2). What historical evidence does he supply to support this claim in the opening paragraphs (1–9)? Why does he wish to refute the belief that strangers are the source of disease, plagues, epidemics, and other such biological invasions?

2. What role have books, films, and other fictional media played in past and current "bioterrorism scares"? Locate Alcabes's examples of fictional scare tactics, and analyze his treatment of these media.

3. Instead of buying into the current "bioterrorism scare," what does Alcabes suggest Americans do? What does he, as a professor of urban public health, advance as an appropriate set of actions?

4. Test Alcabes's claim that a "core issue [in the current bioterrorism scare] is that the Stranger Spreading Germs is a metaphor, and largely an empty one" (paragraph 30) by examining newspaper and magazine articles about SARS, anthrax, or other scares. Write up what you find about the use of this metaphor and/or other metaphors in these articles.

WALT WHITMAN   *Death of Abraham Lincoln*

I SHALL NOT easily forget the first time I ever saw Abraham Lincoln. It must have been about the 18th or 19th of February, 1861. It was rather a pleasant afternoon, in New York City, as he arrived there from the West, to remain a few hours, and then pass on to Washington, to prepare for his inauguration. I saw him in Broadway, near the site of the present Post-office. He came down, I think from Canal street, to stop at the Astor House. The broad spaces, sidewalks, and streets in the neighborhood, and for some distance, were crowded with solid masses of people, many thousands. The omnibuses and other vehicles had all been turn'd off, leaving an unusual hush in that busy part of the city. Presently two or three shabby hack barouches made their way with some difficulty through the crowd, and drew up at the Astor House entrance. A tall figure stepp'd out of the centre of these barouches, paus'd leisurely on the sidewalk, look'd up at the granite walls and looming architecture of the grand old hotel—then, after a relieving stretch of arms and legs, turn'd round for over a minute to slowly and good-humoredly scan the appearance of the vast and silent crowds. There were no speeches—no compliments—no welcome—as far as I could hear, not a word said. Still much anxiety was conceal'd in the quiet. Cautious persons had fear'd some mark'd insult or indignity to the President-elect—for he possess'd no personal popularity at all in New York City, and very little political. But it was evidently tacitly agreed that if the few political supporters of Mr. Lincoln present would entirely abstain from any demonstration on their side, the immense majority, who were anything but supporters, would abstain on their sides also. The result was a sulky, unbroken silence, such as certainly never before characterized so great a New York crowd.

Almost in the same neighborhood I distinctly remember'd seeing Lafayette on his visit to America in 1825. I had also personally seen and heard, various years afterward, how Andrew Jackson, Clay, Webster, Hungarian Kossuth, Filibuster Walker, the Prince of Wales[1] on his visit, and other *célèbres*, native and foreign, had been welcom'd there—all that indescribable human roar and magnetism, unlike any other sound in the universe—the glad exulting thunder-shouts of countless unloos'd throats of men! But on this oc-

From Whitman's collection of prose writings, Speciman Days *(1882).*

1. Marquis de Lafayette (1757–1834), French statesman and general who fought for the United States in the War of Independence; Jackson (1767–1845), seventh president of the United States, 1829–37; Henry Clay (1777–1852), American statesman and orator; Daniel Webster (1782–1852), American statesman and orator; Lajos Kossuth (1802–1894), Hungarian patriot and statesman; William Walker (1824–1860), an American who filibustered (i.e., undertook unsanctioned revolutionary activities) in Central America; the future Edward VII (1841–1910), Queen Victoria's son.

casion, not a voice—not a sound. From the top of an omnibus, (driven up one side, close by, and block'd by the curbstone and the crowds), I had, I say, a capital view of it all, and especially of Mr. Lincoln, his look and gait—his perfect composure and coolness—his unusual and uncouth height, his dress of complete black, stovepipe hat push'd back on the head, dark-brown complexion, seam'd and wrinkled yet canny-looking face, black, bushy head of hair, disproportionately long neck, and his hands held behind as he stood observing the people. He look'd with curiosity upon that immense sea of faces, and the sea of faces return'd the look with similar curiosity. In both there was a dash of comedy, almost farce, such as Shakspere puts in his blackest tragedies. The crowd that hemm'd around consisted I should think of thirty to forty thousand men, not a single one his personal friend—while I have no doubt, (so frenzied were the ferments of the time,) many an assassin's knife and pistol lurk'd in hip or breast-pocket there, ready, soon as break and riot came.

But no break or riot came. The tall figure gave another relieving stretch or two of arms and legs; then with moderate pace, and accompanied by a few unknown-looking persons, ascended the portico-steps of the Astor House, disappear'd through its broad entrance—and the dumb-show ended.

I saw Abraham Lincoln often the four years following that date. He changed rapidly and much during his Presidency—but this scene, and him in it, are indelibly stamp'd upon my recollection. As I sat on the top of my omnibus, and had a good view of him, the thought, dim and inchoate then, has since come out clear enough, that four sorts of genius, four mighty and primal hands, will be needed to the complete limning of this man's future portrait—the eyes and brains and finger-touch of Plutarch and Eschylus and Michel Angelo, assisted now by Rabelais.[2]

5   And now—(Mr. Lincoln passing on from this scene to Washington, where he was inaugurated, amid armed cavalry, and sharpshooters at every point—the first instance of the kind in our history—and I hope it will be the last)—now the rapid succession of well-known events, (too well-known—I believe, these days, we almost hate to hear them mention'd)—the national flag fired on at Sumter—the uprising of the North, in paroxysms of astonishment and rage—the chaos of divided councils—the call for troops—the first Bull Run—the stunning cast-down, shock, and dismay of the North—and so in full flood the Secession war. Four years of lurid, bleeding, murky, murderous war. Who paint those years, with all their scenes?—the hard-fought engagements—the defeats, plans, failures—the gloomy hours, days, when our Nationality seem'd hung in pall of doubt, perhaps death—the Mephistophelean sneers of foreign lands and attachés—the dreaded Scylla of European interference, and the Charybdis of the tremendously dangerous latent strata of secession sympathiz-

2. Plutarch (46?–120 C.E.), Greek author who wrote the histories of famous Greeks and Romans; Aeschylus (525–456 B.C.E.), Greek tragic dramatist; Michelangelo Buonarroti (1475–1574), Italian architect, painter, sculptor, and poet; François Rabelais (1493–1553), French author who created the giants Gargantua and Pantagruel.

ers throughout the free States,[3] (far more numerous than is supposed)—the long marches in summer—the hot sweat, and many a sunstroke, as on the rush to Gettysburg in '63—the night battles in the woods, as under Hooker at Chancellorsville—the camps in winter—the military prisons—the hospitals— (alas! alas! the hospitals.)

The Secession war? Nay, let me call it the Union war. Though whatever call'd, it is even yet too near us—too vast and too closely overshadowing—its branches unform'd yet, (but certain,) shooting too far into the future—and the most indicative and mightiest of them yet ungrown. A great literature will yet arise out of the era of those four years, those scenes—era compressing centuries of native passion, first-class pictures, tempests of life and death— an inexhaustible mine for the histories, drama, romance, and even philosophy, of peoples to come—indeed the verteber[4] of poetry and art, (of personal character too,) for all future America—far more grand, in my opinion, to the hands capable of it, than Homer's siege of Troy, or the French wars to Shakspere.[5]

But I must leave these speculations, and come to the theme I have assign'd and limited myself to. Of the actual murder of President Lincoln, though so much has been written, probably the facts are yet very indefinite in most persons' minds. I read from my memoranda, written at the time, and revised frequently and finally since.

The day, April 14, 1865, seems to have been a pleasant one throughout the whole land—the moral atmosphere pleasant too—the long storm, so dark, so fratricidal, full of blood and doubt and gloom, over and ended at last by the sunrise of such an absolute National victory, and utter break-down of Secessionism—we almost doubted our own senses! Lee had capitulated beneath the apple-tree of Appomattox. The other armies, the flanges of the revolt, swiftly follow'd. And could it really be, then? Out of all the affairs of this world of woe and failure and disorder, was there really come the confirm'd, unerring sign of plan, like a shaft of pure light—of rightful rule—of God? So the day, as I say, was propitious. Early herbage, early flowers, were out. (I remember where I was stopping at the time, the season being advanced, there were many lilacs in full bloom. By one of those caprices that enter and give tinge to events without being at all a part of them, I find myself always reminded of the great tragedy of that day by the sight and odor of these blossoms.[6] It never fails.)

But I must not dwell on accessories. The deed hastens. The popular after-

---

3. Mephistopheles is the name of an evil spirit to whom men legendarily sell their souls in exchange for something they desire; the character appears in European literature most frequently in tales and drama about Faust, a German conjurer who lived from about 1488 to 1541. In Homer's *Odyssey*, Scylla and Charybdis are the rocks and the whirlpool between which Odysseus must navigate.

4. Vertebra.

5. In the *Iliad* and in Shakespeare's history plays.

6. Cf. Whitman's elegy on Lincoln, "When Lilacs Last in the Dooryard Bloom'd" (1865–66).

noon paper of Washington, the little *Evening Star,* has spatter'd all over its
third page, divided among the advertisements in a sensational manner, in a
hundred different places, *"The President and his Lady will be at the Theatre
this evening. . . ."* (Lincoln was fond of the theatre. I have myself seen him
there several times. I remember thinking how funny it was that he, in some respects the leading actor in the stormiest drama known to real history's stage
through centuries, should sit there and be so completely interested and absorb'd in those human jackstraws, moving about with their silly little gestures,
foreign spirit, and flatulent text.)

10   On this occasion the theatre was crowded, many ladies in rich and gay
costumes, officers in their uniforms, many well-known citizens, young folks,
the usual clusters of gas-lights, the usual magnetism of so many people, cheerful, with perfumes, music of violins and flutes—(and over all, and saturating
all, that vast, vague wonder, *Victory,* the nation's victory, the triumph of the
Union, filling the air, the thought, the sense, with exhilaration more than all
music and perfumes.)

The President came betimes, and, with his wife, witness'd the play from
the large stage-boxes of the second tier, two thrown into one, and profusely
drap'd with the national flag. The acts and scenes of the piece—one of those
singularly written compositions which have at least the merit of giving entire
relief to an audience engaged in mental action or business excitements and
cares during the day, as it makes not the slightest call on either the moral,
emotional, esthetic, or spiritual nature—a piece, (*Our American Cousin,*)[7] in
which, among other characters so call'd, a Yankee, certainly such a one as was
never seen, or the least like it ever seen, in North America, is introduced in
England, with a varied fol-de-rol of talk, plot, scenery, and such phantasmago-
ria as goes to make up a modern popular drama—had progress'd through perhaps a couple of its acts, when in the midst of this comedy, or non-such, or
whatever it is to be call'd, and to offset it, or finish it out, as if in Nature's and
the great Muse's mockery of those poor mimes, came interpolated that scene,
not really or exactly to be described at all, (for on the many hundreds who
were there it seems to this hour to have left a passing blur, a dream, a
blotch)—and yet partially to be described as I now proceed to give it. There is
a scene in the play representing a modern parlor, in which two unprecedented
English ladies are inform'd by the impossible Yankee that he is not a man
of fortune, and therefore undesirable for marriage-catching purposes; after
which, the comments being finish'd, the dramatic trio make exit, leaving the
stage clear for a moment. At this period came the murder of Abraham Lincoln.
Great as all its manifold train, circling round it, and stretching into the future
for many a century, in the politics, history, art &c., of the New World, in point
of fact the main thing, the actual murder, transpired with the quiet and simplicity of any commonest occurrence—the bursting of a bud or pod in the
growth of vegetation, for instance. Through the general hum following the
stage pause, with the change of positions, came the muffled sound of a pistol-

7. By the British playwright Tom Taylor (1817–1880).

shot, which not one-hundredth part of the audience heard at the time—and yet a moment's hush—somehow, surely, a vague startled thrill—and then, through the ornamented, draperied, starr'd and striped space-way of the President's box, a sudden figure, a man, raises himself with hands and feet, stands a moment on the railing, leaps below to the stage, (a distance of perhaps fourteen or fifteen feet), falls out of position, catching his boot-heel in the copious drapery, (the American flag,) falls on one knee, quickly recovers himself, rises as if nothing had happen'd, (he really sprains his ankle, but unfelt then)—and so the figure, Booth,[8] the murderer, dress'd in plain black broadcloth, bareheaded, with full, glossy, raven hair, and his eyes like some mad animal's flashing with light and resolution, yet with a certain strange calmness, holds aloft in one hand a large knife—walks along not much back from the footlights—turns fully toward the audience his face of statuesque beauty, lit by those basilisk eyes, flashing with desperation, perhaps insanity—launches out in a firm and steady voice the words *Sic semper tyrannis*[9]—and then walks with neither slow nor very rapid pace diagonally across to the back of the stage, and disappears. (Had not all this terrible scene—making the mimic ones preposterous—had it not all been rehears'd, in blank, by Booth, beforehand?)

A moment's hush—a scream—the cry of *"murder"*—Mrs. Lincoln leaning out of the box, with ashy cheeks and lips, with involuntary cry, pointing to the retreating figure, *"He has kill'd the President."* And still a moment's strange, incredulous suspense—and then the deluge! then that mixture of horror, noises, uncertainty—(the sound, somewhere back, of a horse's hoofs clattering with speed)—the people burst through chairs and railings, and break them up—there is inextricable confusion and terror—women faint—quite feeble persons fall, and are trampl'd on—many cries of agony are heard—the broad stage suddenly fills to suffocation with a dense and motley crowd, like some horrible carnival—the audience rush generally upon it, at least the strong men do—the actors and actresses are all there in their playcostumes and painted faces, with mortal fright showing through the rouge—the screams and calls, confused talk—redoubled, trebled—two or three manage to pass up water from the stage to the President's box—others try to clamber up—&c., &c.

In the midst of all this, the soldiers of the President's guard, with others, suddenly drawn to the scene, burst in—(some two hundred altogether)—they storm the house, through all the tiers, especially the upper ones, inflam'd with fury, literally charging the audience with fix'd bayonets, muskets, and pistols, shouting *"Clear out! clear out! you sons of* ——". . . . Such a wild scene, or a suggestion of it rather, inside the play-house that night.

Outside, too, in the atmosphere of shock and craze, crowds of people, fill'd with frenzy, ready to seize any outlet for it, come near committing murder several times on innocent individuals. One such case was especially exciting. The infuriated crowd, through some chance, got started against one man, either for words he utter'd, or perhaps without any cause at all, and were pro-

8. John Wilkes Booth (1835–1865).
9. "Thus always to tyrants," the motto of the state of Virginia.

ceeding at once to actually hang him on a neighboring lamp-post, when he was rescued by a few heroic policemen, who placed him in their midst, and fought their way slowly and amid great peril toward the station-house. It was a fitting episode of the whole affair. The crowd rushing and eddying to and fro—the night, the yells, the pale faces, many frighten'd people trying in vain to extricate themselves—the attack'd man, not yet freed from the jaws of death, looking like a corpse—the silent, resolute, half-dozen policemen, with no weapons but their little clubs, yet stern and steady through all those eddying swarms—made a fitting side-scene to the grand tragedy of the murder. They gain'd the station house with the protected man, whom they placed in security for the night, and discharged him in the morning.

15   And in the midst of that pandemonium, infuriated soldiers, the audience and the crowd, the stage, and all its actors and actresses, its paint-pots, spangles, and gas-lights—the life blood from those veins, the best and sweetest of the land, drips slowly down, and death's ooze already begins its little bubbles on the lips.

Thus the visible incidents and surroundings of Abraham Lincoln's murder, as they really occur'd. Thus ended the attempted secession of these States: thus the four years' war. But the main things come subtly and invisibly afterward, perhaps long afterward—neither military, political, nor (great as those are,) historical. I say, certain secondary and indirect results, out of the tragedy of this death, are, in my opinion, greatest. Not the event of the murder itself. Not that Mr. Lincoln strings the principal points and personages of the period, like beads, upon the single string of his career. Not that his idiosyncrasy, in its sudden appearance and disappearance, stamps this Republic with a stamp more mark'd and enduring than any yet given by any one man—(more even than Washington's;)—but, join'd with these, the immeasurable value and meaning of that whole tragedy lies, to me, in senses finally dearest to a nation, (and here all our own)—the imaginative and artistic senses—the literary and dramatic ones. Not in any common or low meaning of those terms, but a meaning precious to the race, and to every age. A long and varied series of contradictory events arrives at last at its highest poetic, single, central, pictorial *dénouement*. The whole involved, baffling, multiform whirl of the secession period comes to a head, and is gather'd in one brief flash of lightning-illumination—one simple, fierce deed. Its sharp culmination, and as it were solution, of so many bloody and angry problems, illustrates those climax-moments on the stage of universal Time, where the historic Muse at one entrance, and the tragic Muse at the other, suddenly ringing down the curtain, close an immense act in the long drama of creative thought, and give it radiation, tableau, stranger than fiction. Fit radiation—fit close! How the imagination—how the student loves these things! America, too, is to have them. For not in all great deaths, not far or near—not Caesar in the Roman senate-house, or Napoleon passing away in the wild night-storm at St. Helena—not Paleologus,[10] falling, desperately fighting, piled over dozens deep with Grecian

10. Emperor Constantine XI, who yielded Constantinople to the Turks in 1453.

corpses—not calm old Socrates, drinking the hemlock—outvies that terminus of the secession war, in one man's life, here in our midst, in our time—that seal of the emancipation of three million slaves—that parturition and delivery of our at last really free Republic, born again, henceforth to commence its career of genuine homogeneous Union, compact, consistent with itself.

Nor will ever future American Patriots and Unionists, indifferently over the whole land, or North or South, find a better moral to their lesson. The final use of the greatest men of a Nation is, after all, not with reference to their deeds in themselves, or their direct bearing on their times or lands. The final use of a heroic-eminent life—especially of a heroic-eminent death—is its indirect filtering into the nation and the race, and to give, often at many removes, but unerringly, age after age, color and fibre to the personalism of the youth and maturity of that age, and of mankind. Then, there is a cement to the whole people, subtler, more underlying, than any thing in written constitution, or courts or armies—namely, the cement of a death identified thoroughly with that people, at its head, and for its sake. Strange, (is it not?) that battles, martyrs, agonies, blood, even assassination, should so condense—perhaps only really, lastingly condense—a Nationality.

I repeat it—the grand deaths of the race—the dramatic deaths of every nationality—are its most important inheritance-value—in some respects beyond its literature and art—(as the hero is beyond his finest portrait, and the battle itself beyond its choicest song or epic.) Is not here indeed the point underlying all tragedy? the famous pieces of the Grecian masters—and all masters? Why, if the old Greeks had had this man, what trilogies of plays—what epics—would have been made out of him! How the rhapsodes would have recited him! How quickly that quaint tall form would have enter'd into the region where men vitalize gods, and gods divinify men! But Lincoln, his times, his death—great as any, any age—belong altogether to our own, and are autochthonic.[11] (Sometimes indeed I think our American days, our own stage—the actors we know and have shaken hands, or talk'd with—more fateful than any thing in Eschylus—more heroic than the fighters around Troy—afford kings of men for our Democracy prouder than Agamemnon—models of character cute and hardy as Ulysses—deaths more pitiful than Priam's.)[12]

When centuries hence, (as it must, in my opinion, be centuries hence before the life of these States, or of Democracy, can be really written and illustrated,) the leading historians and dramatists seek for some personage, some special event, incisive enough to mark with deepest cut, and mnemonize, this turbulent nineteenth century of ours, (not only these States, but all over the political and social world)—something, perhaps, to close that gorgeous procession of European feudalism, with all its pomp and caste-prejudices, (of whose

11. Native, indigenous.

12. Eschylus (i.e., Aeschylus), Greek tragic dramatist (525–456 B.C.E.) whose plays, like Homer's epics, deal with such figures of the Trojan War as Agamemnon, leader of the Greek forces; Ulysses (Odysseus), whose return to Ithaca after the war took ten years; and Priam, slaughtered king of Troy. "Cute" here means "acute."

long train we in America are yet so inextricably the heirs)—something to identify with terrible identification, by far the greatest revolutionary step in the history of the United States, (perhaps the greatest of the world, our century)—the absolute extirpation and erasure of slavery from the States—those historians will seek in vain for any point to serve more thoroughly their purpose, than Abraham Lincoln's death.

20   Dear to the Muse—thrice dear to Nationality—to the whole human race—precious to this Union—precious to Democracy—unspeakably and forever precious—their first great Martyr Chief.

QUESTIONS

1. Whitman delivered this piece as a lecture. What features suggest a lecture? How might it have differed if he had composed it as an essay to be read rather than a lecture to be heard?

2. The events of the assassination lead Whitman to mention his perception of Lincoln's fondness for the theater. How does he make this observation serve a larger purpose?

3. At the end of this speech, Whitman speaks grandly of Lincoln's significance for far more than the citizens of the United States. As he sees it, what do all these people have in common that allows for Lincoln's more-than-national significance?

4. How does Whitman convey the sense of horror and confusion in the scene when Lincoln is shot? Using some of Whitman's techniques, write an account of a similar scene that produces a strong emotional effect.

HANNAH ARENDT   *Deportations from Western Europe*

A T THE WANNSEE CONFERENCE,[1] Martin Luther, of the Foreign Office, warned of great difficulties in the Scandinavian countries, notably in Norway and Denmark. (Sweden was never occupied, and Finland, though in the war on the side of the Axis, was one country the Nazis never even approached on the Jewish question. This surprising exception of Finland, with some two thousand Jews, may have been due to Hitler's great esteem for the Finns, whom perhaps he did not

Originally published in the "Reporter at Large" section of the New Yorker *(February–March 1963), Arendt's articles covered the trial of Adolf Eichmann, the Nazi lieutenant colonel responsible for transporting countless Jews to concentration camps. This selection comes from the book version of her account,* Eichmann in Jerusalem: A Report on the Banality of Evil *(1963), which, beyond reportage, raises larger questions about the crime of genocide and the nature of totalitarianism.*

1. A meeting of German officials on "the Jewish question."

want to subject to threats and humiliating blackmail.) Luther proposed postponing evacuations from Scandinavia for the time being, and as far as Denmark was concerned, this really went without saying, since the country retained its independent government, and was respected as a neutral state, until the fall of 1943, although it, along with Norway, had been invaded by the German Army in April, 1940. There existed no Fascist or Nazi movement in Denmark worth mentioning, and therefore no collaborators. In Norway, however, the Germans had been able to find enthusiastic supporters; indeed, Vidkun Quisling, leader of the pro-Nazi and anti-Semitic Norwegian party, gave his name to what later became known as a "quisling government." The bulk of Norway's seventeen hundred Jews were stateless, refugees from Germany; they were seized and interned in a few lightning operations in October and November, 1942. When Eichmann's[2] office ordered their deportation to Auschwitz, some of Quisling's own men resigned their government posts. This may not have come as a surprise to Mr. Luther and the Foreign Office, but what was much more serious, and certainly totally unexpected, was that Sweden immediately offered asylum, and even Swedish nationality, to all who were persecuted. Dr. Ernst von Weizsäcker, Undersecretary of State of the Foreign Office, who received the proposal, refused to discuss it, but the offer helped nevertheless. It is always relatively easy to get out of a country illegally, whereas it is nearly impossible to enter the place of refuge without permission and to dodge the immigration authorities. Hence, about nine hundred people, slightly more than half of the small Norwegian community, could be smuggled into Sweden.

It was in Denmark, however, that the Germans found out how fully justified the Foreign Office's apprehensions had been. The story of the Danish Jews is *sui generis*,[3] and the behavior of the Danish people and their government was unique among all the countries in Europe—whether occupied, or a partner of the Axis, or neutral and truly independent. One is tempted to recommend the story as required reading in political science for all students who wish to learn something about the enormous power potential inherent in nonviolent action and in resistance to an opponent possessing vastly superior means of violence. To be sure, a few other countries in Europe lacked proper "understanding of the Jewish question," and actually a majority of them were opposed to "radical" and "final" solutions. Like Denmark, Sweden, Italy, and Bulgaria proved to be nearly immune to anti-Semitism, but of the three that were in the German sphere of influence, only the Danes dared speak out on the subject to their German masters. Italy and Bulgaria sabotaged German orders and indulged in a complicated game of double-dealing and double-crossing, saving their Jews by a tour de force of sheer ingenuity, but they never contested the policy as such. That was totally different from what the Danes did. When the Germans approached them rather cautiously about introducing

2. Adolf Eichmann (1906–1962), German Nazi in charge of the execution of Jews (1942–45).

3. Unique; literally, of its own kind (Latin).

the yellow badge, they were simply told that the King would be the first to wear it, and the Danish government officials were careful to point out that anti-Jewish measures of any sort would cause their own immediate resignation. It was decisive in this whole matter that the Germans did not even succeed in introducing the vitally important distinction between native Danes of Jewish origin, of whom there were about sixty-four hundred, and the fourteen hundred German Jewish refugees who had found asylum in the country prior to the war and who now had been declared stateless by the German government. This refusal must have surprised the Germans no end, since it appeared so "illogical" for a government to protect people to whom it had categorically denied naturalization and even permission to work. (Legally, the prewar situation of refugees in Denmark was not unlike that in France, except that the general corruption in the Third Republic's civil services enabled a few of them to obtain naturalization papers, through bribes or "connections," and most refugees in France could work illegally, without a permit. But Denmark, like Switzerland, was no country *pour se débrouiller*.)[4] The Danes, however, explained to the German officials that because the stateless refugees were no longer German citizens, the Nazis could not claim them without Danish assent. This was one of the few cases in which statelessness turned out to be an asset, although it was of course not statelessness per se that saved the Jews but, on the contrary, the fact that the Danish government had decided to protect them. Thus, none of the preparatory moves, so important for the bureaucracy of murder, could be carried out, and operations were postponed until the fall of 1943.

What happened then was truly amazing; compared with what took place in other European countries, everything went topsy-turvy. In August, 1943— after the German offensive in Russia had failed, the Afrika Korps had surrendered in Tunisia, and the Allies had invaded Italy—the Swedish government canceled its 1940 agreement with Germany which had permitted German troops the right to pass through the country. Thereupon, the Danish workers decided that they could help a bit in hurrying things up; riots broke out in Danish shipyards, where the dock workers refused to repair German ships and then went on strike. The German military commander proclaimed a state of emergency and imposed martial law, and Himmler[5] thought this was the right moment to tackle the Jewish question, whose "solution" was long overdue. What he did not reckon with was that—quite apart from Danish resistance— the German officials who had been living in the country for years were no longer the same. Not only did General von Hannecken, the military commander, refuse to put troops at the disposal of the Reich plenipotentiary, Dr. Werner Best; the special S.S. units (*Einsatzkommandos*) employed in Denmark very frequently objected to "the measures they were ordered to carry out by the central agencies"—according to Best's testimony of Nuremberg. And Best

---

4. For wangling—using bribery to circumvent bureaucratic regulations.

5. Heinrich Himmler (1900–1945), high-ranking official in Nazi Germany who organized the SS (*Schutzstaffel*, Elite Guard) in 1929 and the Gestapo in 1933.

himself, an old Gestapo man and former legal adviser to Heydrich, author of a then famous book on the police, who had worked for the military government in Paris to the entire satisfaction of his superiors, could no longer be trusted, although it is doubtful that Berlin ever learned the extent of his unreliability. Still, it was clear from the beginning that things were not going well, and Eichmann's office sent one of its best men to Denmark—Rolf Günther, whom no one had ever accused of not possessing the required "ruthless toughness." Günther made no impression on his colleagues in Copenhagen, and now von Hannecken refused even to issue a decree requiring all Jews to report for work.

Best went to Berlin and obtained a promise that all Jews from Denmark would be sent to Theresienstadt[6] regardless of their category—a very important concession, from the Nazis' point of view. The night of October 1 was set for their seizure and immediate departure—ships were ready in the harbor— and since neither the Danes nor the Jews nor the German troops stationed in Denmark could be relied on to help, police units arrived from Germany for a door-to-door search. At the last moment, Best told them that they were not permitted to break into apartments, because the Danish police might then interfere, and they were not supposed to fight it out with the Danes. Hence they could seize only those Jews who voluntarily opened their doors. They found exactly 477 people, out of a total of more than 7,800, at home and willing to let them in. A few days before the date of doom, a German shipping agent, Georg F. Duckwitz, having probably been tipped off by Best himself, had revealed the whole plan to Danish government officials, who, in turn, had hurriedly informed the heads of the Jewish community. They, in marked contrast to Jewish leaders in other countries, had then communicated the news openly in the synagogues on the occasion of the New Year services. The Jews had just time enough to leave their apartments and go into hiding, which was very easy in Denmark, because, in the words of the judgment, "all sections of the Danish people, from the King down to simple citizens," stood ready to receive them.

They might have remained in hiding until the end of the war if the Danes   5
had not been blessed with Sweden as a neighbor. It seemed reasonable to ship the Jews to Sweden, and this was done with the help of the Danish fishing fleet. The cost of transportation for people without means—about a hundred dollars per person—was paid largely by wealthy Danish citizens, and that was perhaps the most astounding feat of all, since this was a time when Jews were paying for their own deportation, when the rich among them were paying fortunes for exit permits (in Holland, Slovakia, and, later, in Hungary) either by bribing the local authorities or by negotiating "legally" with the S.S., who accepted only hard currency and sold exit permits, in Holland, to the tune of five or ten thousand dollars per person. Even in places where Jews met with genuine sympathy and a sincere willingness to help, they had to pay for it, and the chances poor people had of escaping were nil.

6. A camp for certain classes of prisoners who were supposed to receive special treatment.

It took the better part of October to ferry all the Jews across the five to fifteen miles of water that separates Denmark from Sweden. The Swedes received 5,919 refugees, of whom at least 1,000 were of German origin, 1,310 were half-Jews, and 686 were non-Jews married to Jews. (Almost half the Danish Jews seem to have remained in the country and survived the war in hiding.) The non-Danish Jews were better off than ever before; they all received permission to work. The few hundred Jews whom the German police had been able to arrest were shipped to Theresienstadt. They were old or poor people, who either had not received the news in time or had not been able to comprehend its meaning. In the ghetto, they enjoyed greater privileges than any other group because of the never-ending "fuss" made about them by Danish institutions and private persons. Forty-eight persons died, a figure that was not particularly high, in view of the average age of the group. When everything was over, it was the considered opinion of Eichmann that "for various reasons the action against the Jews in Denmark has been a failure," whereas the curious Dr. Best declared that "the objective of the operation was not to seize a great number of Jews but to clean Denmark of Jews, and this objective has now been achieved."

Politically and psychologically, the most interesting aspect of this incident is perhaps the role played by the German authorities in Denmark, their obvious sabotage of orders from Berlin. It is the only case we know of in which the Nazis met with *open* native resistance, and the result seems to have been that those exposed to it changed their minds. They themselves apparently no longer looked upon the extermination of a whole people as a matter of course. They had met resistance based on principle, and their "toughness" had melted like butter in the sun; they had even been able to show a few timid beginnings of genuine courage. That the ideal of "toughness," except, perhaps, for a few half-demented brutes, was nothing but a myth of self-deception, concealing a ruthless desire for conformity at any price, was clearly revealed at the Nuremberg Trials, where the defendants accused and betrayed each other and assured the world that they "had always been against it" or claimed, as Eichmann was to do, that their best qualities had been "abused" by their superiors. (In Jerusalem, he accused "those in power" of having abused his "obedience." "The subject of a good government is lucky, the subject of a bad government is unlucky. I had no luck.") The atmosphere had changed, and although most of them must have known that they were doomed, not a single one of them had the guts to defend the Nazi ideology. Werner Best claimed at Nuremberg that he had played a complicated double role and that it was thanks to him that the Danish officials had been warned of the impending catastrophe; documentary evidence showed, on the contrary, that he himself had proposed the Danish operation in Berlin, but he explained that this was all part of the game. He was extradited to Denmark and there condemned to death, but he appealed the sentence, with surprising results; because of "new evidence," his sentence was commuted to five years in prison, from which he was released soon afterward. He must have been able to prove to the satisfaction of the Danish court that he really had done his best.

QUESTIONS

1. Why do you think the Danes spoke out against anti-Semitism when other countries under German influence chose different methods of response or resistance? What details or hints does Arendt provide?

2. In paragraph 7, Arendt writes about Nazis who, when "met with open native resistance," changed their minds. What possible reasons does Arendt offer for this change? Are there other reasons you can think of for such change?

3. In paragraph 2, Arendt writes about "the enormous power potential inherent in nonviolent action and in resistance to an opponent possessing vastly superior means of violence." Research a more recent political situation in which you think a government or group of people could productively respond in a nonviolent manner, and write about it.

World War II: Victims, Villains, Heroes

MATT BAI   *He Said No to Internment*

In February 1942, a little more than two months after the attack on Pearl Harbor,[1] Franklin Roosevelt signed Executive Order 9066, which effectively decreed that West Coast residents of Japanese ancestry—whether American citizens or not—were now "enemy aliens." More than 100,000 Japanese-Americans reported to government staging areas, where they were processed and taken off to 10 internment camps. Fred Korematsu, the son of Japanese immigrants, was at the time a 23-year-old welder at Bay Area shipyards. His parents left their home and reported to a racetrack south of San Francisco, but Korematsu chose not to follow them. He stayed behind in Oakland with his Italian-American girlfriend and then fled, even having plastic surgery on his eyes to avoid recognition. In May 1942, he was arrested and branded a spy in the newspapers.

In search of a test case, Ernest Besig, then the executive director of the American Civil Liberties Union for Northern California, went to see Korematsu in jail and asked if he would be willing to challenge the internment policy in court. Korematsu said he would. Besig posted $5,000 bail, but instead of freeing him, federal authorities sent him to the internment camp at Topaz, Utah. He and Besig sued the government, appealing their case all the way to the Supreme Court, which in a 6-to-3 decision that stands as one of the most

The New York Times Magazine *published these three short biographies of World War II survivors in a special issue (December 25, 2005) on known and unknown heroes who had died during the year.*

1. The Japanese attacked this American military base in Honolulu, on the island of Oahu, on December 7, 1941, prompting America to enter World War II. Franklin Roosevelt (1882–1945) was then president of the United States.

Fred Korematsu, b. 1919.

ignoble in its history, rejected his argument and upheld the government's right to intern its citizens.

After the war, Korematsu married, returned to the Bay Area and found work as a draftsman. He might have been celebrated in his community, the Rosa Parks[2] of Japanese-American life; in fact, he was shunned. Even during his time in Topaz, other prisoners refused to talk to him. "All of them turned their backs on me at that time because they thought I was a troublemaker," he later recalled. His ostracism didn't end with the war. The overwhelming majority of Japanese-Americans had reacted to the internment by acquiescing to the government's order, hoping to prove their loyalty as Americans. To them, Korematsu's opposition was treacherous to both his country and his community.

In the years after the war, details of the internment were lost behind a wall of repression. It was common for Japanese-American families not to talk about the experience, or to talk about it only obliquely. Korematsu, too, remained silent, but for different reasons. "He felt responsible for the internment in a sort of backhanded way, because his case had been lost in the Supreme Court," Peter Irons, a legal historian, recalled in a PBS documentary. Korematsu's own daughter has said she didn't learn of his wartime role until she was a junior in high school.

5   Korematsu might have faded into obscurity had it not been for Irons, who in 1981 asked the Justice Department for the original documents in the Korematsu case. Irons found a memo in which a government lawyer had accused the solicitor general of lying to the Supreme Court about the danger posed by Japanese-Americans. Irons tracked down Korematsu and asked if he would be willing, once again, to go to court.

Perhaps Korematsu had been waiting all those years for a chance to clear his name. Or maybe he saw, in Irons's entreaty, an opportunity to vindicate

2. Parks (1913–2005), African-American civil rights activist whose refusal to give up her bus seat for a white passenger became an iconic moment in the U.S. history of civil rights.

himself with other Japanese-Americans. Whatever his thinking, not only did Korematsu agree to return to court but he also became an ardent public critic of the internment. When government lawyers offered Korematsu a pardon, he refused. "As long as my record stands in federal court," Korematsu, then 64, said in an emotional courtroom oration, "any American citizen can be held in prison or concentration camps without a trial or a hearing." The judged agreed, ruling from the bench that Korematsu had been innocent. Just like that, the legality of the internment was struck down forever.

In the last decade of his life, Korematsu became, for some Americans, a symbol of principled resistance. President Clinton[3] awarded Korematsu the Presidential Medal of Freedom in 1998. Six years later, outraged by the prolonged detention of prisoners at Guantánamo Bay,[4] Korematsu filed an amicus brief with the Supreme Court, warning that the mistakes of the internment were being repeated. Still, Korematsu's place among contemporaries in his own community remained obscured by lingering resentments and a reluctance to revisit the past. When he died from a respiratory illness in March [2005], not a single public building or landmark bore his name. It wasn't until last month [November 2005] that officials in Davis, Calif., dedicated the Fred Korematsu Elementary School. It was an especially fitting tribute for Korematsu, whose legacy rested with a generation of Japanese-Americans who were beginning to remember, at long last, what their parents had labored to forget.

3. William Jefferson Clinton (b. 1946), president of the United States from 1993 to 2001.

4. Site of a U.S.-owned prison in Cuba where militants from Iraq and Afghanistan are currently being detained.

Questions

1. Many Americans do not know the history of the government's internment of its own citizens during World War II. Where does Matt Bai provide the necessary background so that the reader understands this history? Where does he supply the after-events of the history?

2. Was Fred Korematsu a hero? What responses to this question does Bai provide in his biography? What is his opinion as biographer? How do you know?

3. Interview someone—a family member, a neighbor, an older person on your campus—who has lived through an important era of American history. Write a short biography in which you interweave his or her experience with facts and background information about that era.

He was prodded to his feet by rifle barrels. This was northern Tunisia, Nov. 29, 1942. Just after midnight, following faulty intelligence, he had led his men into enemy territory. Now he stood surrounded, trembling, sickened by the gravity of his mistake. A German sergeant jammed a pistol into Joe Frelinghuysen's gut and joked that he'd been easier to catch than a rabbit.

This indignity stayed with him. He was flown to Italy and put in a series of Fascist-run prison camps in a mountainous area northeast of Rome. There he studied the walls, filled with self-recrimination.

He had been easier to catch than a rabbit. It wouldn't happen again. He nourished himself with potato peels sneaked from the cook's garbage. He did push-ups, paced the fence line of the camp. A guard gave him an Italian grammar book, which he studied feverishly, memorizing 30 words a day.

He had been imprisoned nearly 10 months—had lost 70 pounds and was tormented by nightmares—when Dick Rossbach showed up. Rossbach didn't give a damn. He had tried to escape twice already, once by flinging himself out the window of a moving train near the Austrian border. Fear, Rossbach liked to say, was better than a martini.

5   Nine days later, they left together, wriggling in the twilight under one barbed-wire fence, then another, then under two more and finally scaled a wall. They climbed a dark mountain and did not look back. Life from here on out boiled down to one thing: not getting caught.

With his grasp of Italian, Frelinghuysen was in charge of begging for food. In a small, silent village, he encountered an old woman who, upon seeing him, gathered her skirts and fled. The Germans had posted signs: anyone caught helping a prisoner would be shot. So they slept in caves and in clearings in the woods. The only warm night came when a sympathetic shepherd allowed them to sleep pressed up against his pregnant sow. They ate what was handed to them: apples, cheese, a sheep's lung wrapped in newspaper.

What felt perverse was how beautiful the setting was. Frelinghuysen would later describe in his memoir the stunning beech and oak forests of those valleys in the region called Abruzzi—the flaming colors of autumn and the toylike villages stacked into the hills.

After three weeks, it felt like the end. Rossbach had damaged his knee and could barely walk. Their skin was filthy; their bodies were malnourished. If this was freedom, they were ready to trade it for something that less approximated a slow, limping death.

But then, high in the Apennine mountains, more than an hour's walk from the nearest road, they came upon a stooped man with a black mustache, working his fields with a hoe. He wore a sweat-stained hat and smiled easily. When they asked for food, he directed them toward a stone farmhouse.

10   Being hunted by soldiers with dogs can kill a person's faith, but there are simple things that revive it. Inside the farmhouse, Rosa DiGiacomantonio—the wife of the man with the hoe—served them sausage with steaming polenta, scooped from an iron caldron on the hearth, flavored with garlic and

pepper, drizzled with rich olive oil. She poured two glasses of red wine.

Already, she had fed dozens of these filthy, starved men. She'd chopped, simmered and ladled up just about everything her family had harvested that summer. But the prisoners kept coming. The farmhouse sat on a grassy saddle between mountain ranges, a natural stopping point for P.O.W.'s picking their way south toward the Allies. The only things she wouldn't share were the chickens' eggs, which she fed to Letizia, her hugely pregnant daughter-in-law. That night, when the two fugitives asked for a barn to sleep in, Antonio, Rosa's husband, led them instead to a candlelit room with a double bed and spotless white sheets and a pink blanket. He all but tucked them in.

Back home, Joe Frelinghuy-

Letizia and Berardino DiGiacomantonio, at home in Raritan, N.J., risked their lives to save Frelinghuysen from the Nazis in Italy. He gave them their start in America.

sen had a wife named Emily and two small children who wouldn't recognize him. To think of them was painful, so he avoided it. But for more than two weeks in October 1943, he and Rossbach had the DiGiacomantonios, who fed and helped shelter them and who jubilantly shared a bottle of tawny wine with them on the night when Letizia, cloistered upstairs, gave birth to a son. Letizia's husband, Berardino, became a friend—traveling to town to gather news of the war, arranging for a doctor to look at Rossbach's knee. The doctor wrapped his knee, but there was no time for it to mend. Nazi patrols were now searching houses in the valleys below.

One day when the two Americans were out doing reconnaissance, they were surrounded by three German soldiers on a hillside. Rossbach grabbed the barrel of the corporal's gun and pointed it to his chest, announcing that he was injured and demanding that they shoot him right there. It was grand the-ater—Frelinghuysen knew this—a diversion so that he, the only one able, could run. When the soldiers marched them inside a nearby hut, Rossbach of-fered food to their bewildered captors. When the Germans set down their ri-fles to eat, Rossbach looked impatiently at Frelinghuysen, then at the door.

He ran like hell. Leaving his friend to an uncertain fate, he hurled himself outside and down a slick embankment. He ran for miles, soaked by a hard, cold rain. For a while, they chased him. Their bullets ricocheted off the trees.

He ran, then walked, then finally dragged himself toward safety. He crossed into British territory 12 days later on Nov. 15, 1943.

15   He returned to his house in New Jersey—to Emily and the kids, to his 1937 Dodge and his job in insurance. He was snappish, disoriented. This time he had made it—and still he was full of self-recrimination.

Some soldiers put war behind them, and others live it forever. Joe Frelinghuysen wanted only to make amends. He tracked down Dick Rossbach, who had been badly beaten by the three soldiers and then trucked to German prisons, eventually landing in a Russian camp. Undaunted, Rossbach escaped again, talking his way to the American Embassy in Moscow. When Frelinghuysen unloaded his guilt over having abandoned him, Rossbach dismissed it. "Oh, for God's sake, Joe," he said. For many years they met regularly in Manhattan for lunch.

The DiGiacomantonios survived the war, though German soldiers lined up 26 people against a stone wall in a nearby village and shot them for helping prisoners. In 1956, Frelinghuysen returned to the farmhouse, carrying a gift of gold rosary beads for Rosa. While his parents were content to stay on the farm, Berardino expressed a desire to emigrate. Frelinghuysen found a way, creating a position in his family's dairy business for an Italian cheesemaker. He settled Berardino, Letizia and their children into a home near his own, and over time, let go of his guilt.

They live there still, Berardino and his wife. During 1943 and 1944, they say, their family harbored more than 100 escaped American and British soldiers. They can recall the desperation and hunger and nervous gratitude these men showed at the time. But only one found them again after the war. No one else even sent a letter.

QUESTIONS

1. Who are the heroes in this historical vignette: Joe Frelinghuysen and Dick Rossbach? Rosa and Antonio DiGiacomantonio? Are there any anti-heroes? Find the evidence that Corbett includes to support your answer.

2. Corbett's essay ponders the question: What turns an ordinary person into a hero? What answers does she provide, either directly or indirectly?

3. Write a mini-biography or short narrative of someone you think is an ordinary hero. Use Sara Corbett's piece or one of the others in this section as a model.

DANIEL BERGNER *Chasing Evil*

Peter Malkin wore a pair of fur-lined leather gloves when he seized Adolf Eichmann[1] on a street in suburban Buenos Aires. It was 1960. For 15 years, one of the chief engineers of Hitler's Final Solution[2] had escaped capture. Now Malkin, the point man of a small team of clandestine Israeli agents, helped to wrestle him into the back of a waiting car and, Malkin would recount in his memoir, "Eichmann in My Hands," written with Harry Stein, pressed his hand over Eichmann's mouth so he could not scream. Malkin wore the gloves, he wrote, because "the thought of placing my bare hand over the mouth that had ordered the death of millions, of feeling the hot breath and saliva on my skin, filled me with an overwhelming sense of revulsion." But the leather and fur weren't enough. They were quickly "soaked through with his spittle."

It was the beginning of strange intimacy. Malkin—whose sister had been killed along with her children in Poland during the Holocaust, after Malkin, his two brothers and his parents managed to flee to Palestine—had already prepared a bedroom for Eichmann in the safe house where the agents would keep him hidden until, against international law, they could spirit him out of Argentina to stand trial in Israel. Malkin had made the bed with fresh sheets and laid out a towel and toiletries and a pair of striped pajamas. The room, where Malkin would spend much of the next 10 days in solo shifts watching over one of the 20th century's greatest murderers, was spare and tiny; captor and captive, alone, were never more than two or three steps apart. A blanket covered the only window.

Malkin would wash and shave Eichmann's face, tracing, over and over, the contours of his cheeks and jaw. Malkin fed him, lifting a spoon to his lips, and dressed and undressed him. (The memoir implies that Eichmann's hands were kept loosely bound, yet the leader of the Israeli team, Rafi Eitan, told me recently that, after the first day, Eichmann's hands were not bound during the daytime.) Malkin held Eichmann's hands, aiding him as he did deep knee bends for exercise.

And when Eichmann said that he adored fine red wine, Malkin stole an expensive bottle that another agent had been saving for the Sabbath. He served him wine and played him music—a flamenco, a tango—on an old wind-up record player.

Partly, Malkin wrote, his ministering to Eichmann was an attempt to preserve him for public justice. In captivity, Eichmann became passive and seemed utterly incapable of caring for himself (Malkin had to bark orders at him to get him to move his bowels), and Malkin worried that his body and mind would deteriorate irreparably before he could be put on trial. Partly, too, Malkin's caring was calculated seduction: he hoped that Eichmann would reveal the whereabouts of the fugitive Nazi doctor Josef Mengele, and that Eichmann would sign

5

---

1. Eichmann (1906–1962), the German Nazi who organized the deportation of thousands of Jews to Nazi death camps.

2. The "final solution to the Jewish question," engineered by German leader Adolf Hitler (1889–1945), was genocide against Jews in German-occupied territories.

THE PROVINCIAL TERRITORIAL DIVISION OF
ARGENTINA

Malkin's drawing of Eichmann after
he was caught by Israeli agents in
Argentina.

a document stating that he was traveling to Israel to stand trial of his own free will. But meanwhile, in a way, the killer became Malkin's muse.

Malkin—an explosives specialist in the fight for Israeli statehood before he was recruited into the Israeli intelligence services—was an expert in disguises and an amateur painter, avid and skilled. Within the room's close walls, with oil-based pencils from his disguise kit, he began to evoke Eichmann on the pages of a guidebook to South America, which he'd brought along on the mission. The first portrait (above) was done in black and gray on a map of Argentina. Eichmann might simply be a tired clerk, an accountant worn down by numbers, with just a tentative suggestion of emotional depth, of self-reflection, of conscience, in the blurred black irises of the eyes.

"Then I flipped the page and did him in his SS regalia,"[3] Malkin wrote. "I continued drawing in a kind of frenzy. Now I had him watching a railroad train, counting the cars; now in abstract, lying prone atop a flatcar, bearing a machine gun; now, on facing pages, appeared Hitler and Mussolini;[4] now my parents and, in muted pastels, her eyes immense and brooding, my sister, Fruma."

As days and nights went by, Malkin told none of the other agents about his portraits of their prisoner; Eichmann was the only one who knew, remarking, when Malkin turned the guidebook and showed him a work in progress, an image of himself, "Nice. Very nice." Nor, at first, did Malkin tell anyone about their conversations: dialogues spurred by Malkin's questions about the killer's motives; talks driven by the prisoner's fear for his family; chats about music or the pair's "shared love of nature and the wild." Malkin wasn't supposed to converse with Eichmann at all; talk was to be left to sessions with the

3. Short for *Schutzstaffel*, German for "protective echelon," SS refers to the military and security organization that worked for Hitler's Nazi government.
4. Benito Mussolini (1883–1945), fascist Italian dictator from 1922 until 1945.

team's official, harsh-tongued interrogator. And except as Eichmann ate or went to the bathroom, he was supposed to be kept blindfolded. Malkin broke this rule as well. "We found ourselves co-conspirators of a sort," he wrote. "He knew as well as I did to fall silent at the sound of approaching footsteps."

The touching of the face; the portraiture; the talks of Eichmann's beloved young son and of all the children, like Fruma's, he had sent to death (discussions during which Malkin barely controlled his voice and his rage, as he strained to coax words from Eichmann that would somehow offer explanation of his deeds); the removal of the blindfold—Malkin wanted desperately to see into him. By the end of the 10 days, the memoir relates, another of the agents, the team's only woman, would accuse Malkin: "You act like you're in love with him." But the object of desire was elusive. In words, Eichmann gave up little beyond versions of what he would ultimately claim in court in Jerusalem, that in orchestrating the killing of millions he had merely followed orders. And in art, Malkin could create of Eichmann only unyielding surfaces.

During the years to come, Malkin would rise to be chief of operations in   10
the Mossad, Israel's famed intelligence agency. Later, in retirement, he devoted himself to his art. He collected and painted on maps from all over the world. Israel Perry, the owner of the Manhattan gallery that represents Malkin's work, told me that Malkin used the maps for inspiration, to pull himself back into the past, back toward people and scenes that had floated by in his widely traveled, covert life. In this way, he found other subjects, other faces besides Eichmann's; in this way, perhaps, he found other, easier paths to the human soul.

Questions

1. Bergner's mini-biography of Peter Malkin is based on a memoir, *Eichmann in My Hands*, written by Malkin himself. Where does Bergner draw on that memoir for his mini-biography? Where does he provide other information or offer his own interpretation?

2. In paragraph 9, Bergner quotes a female Israeli agent, who accuses Malkin: "You act like you're in love with him." What evidence does Bergner supply that might support this accusation? Does he agree with it, or does the final paragraph offer another interpretation of Malkin's actions?

3. Read Peter Malkin's memoir, *Eichmann in My Hands*, and/or other accounts of the capture and trial of Adolf Eichmann. Write your own explanation of why Malkin and other members of the Israeli team found it essential to capture and bring Eichmann to trial.

POLITICS AND GOVERNMENT

GEORGE ORWELL *Shooting an Elephant*

I N MOULMEIN, in Lower Burma, I was hated by large numbers of people—the only time in my life that I have been important enough for this to happen to me. I was sub-divisional police officer of the town, and in an aimless, petty kind of way anti-European feeling was very bitter. No one had the guts to raise a riot, but if a European woman went through the bazaars alone somebody would probably spit betel juice over her dress. As a police officer I was an obvious target and was baited whenever it seemed safe to do so. When a nimble Burman tripped me up on the football field and the referee (another Burman) looked the other way, the crowd yelled with hideous laughter. This happened more than once. In the end the sneering yellow faces of young men that met me everywhere, the insults hooted after me when I was at a safe distance, got badly on my nerves. The young Buddhist priests were the worst of all. There were several thousands of them in the town and none of them seemed to have anything to do except stand on street corners and jeer at Europeans.

All this was perplexing and upsetting. For at that time I had already made up my mind that imperialism was an evil thing and the sooner I chucked up my job and got out of it the better. Theoretically—and secretly, of course—I was all for the Burmese and all against their oppressors, the British. As for the job I was doing, I hated it more bitterly than I can perhaps make clear. In a job like that you see the dirty work of Empire at close quarters. The wretched prisoners huddling in the stinking cages of the lock-ups, the grey, cowed faces of the long-term convicts, the scarred buttocks of the men who had been flogged with bamboos—all these oppressed me with an intolerable sense of guilt. But I could get nothing into perspective. I was young and ill-educated and I had had to think out my problems in the utter silence that is imposed on every Englishman in the East. I did not even know that the British Empire is dying, still less did I know that it is a great deal better than the younger empires that are going to supplant it. All I knew was that I was stuck between my hatred of the empire I served and my rage against the evil-spirited little beasts who tried

First published in the periodical New Writing *(Fall 1936), at the beginning of Orwell's writing career and soon after his novel* Burmese Days *(1934) appeared. The essay later became the title piece in a collection,* Shooting an Elephant, and Other Essays *(1950).*

to make my job impossible. With one part of my mind I thought of the British Raj[1] as an unbreakable tyranny, as something clamped down, in *saecula saeculorum*,[2] upon the will of prostrate peoples; with another part I thought that the greatest joy in the world would be to drive a bayonet into a Buddhist priest's guts. Feelings like these are the normal by-products of imperialism; ask any Anglo-Indian official, if you can catch him off duty.

One day something happened which in a roundabout way was enlightening. It was a tiny incident in itself, but it gave me a better glimpse than I had had before of the real nature of imperialism—the real motives for which despotic governments act. Early one morning the sub-inspector at a police station the other end of the town rang me up on the 'phone and said that an elephant was ravaging the bazaar. Would I please come and do something about it? I did not know what I could do, but I wanted to see what was happening and I got on to a pony and started out. I took my rifle, an old .44 Winchester and much too small to kill an elephant, but I thought the noise might be useful *in terrorem*. Various Burmans stopped me on the way and told me about the elephant's doings. It was not, of course, a wild elephant, but a tame one which had gone "must."[3] It had been chained up, as tame elephants always are when their attack of "must" is due, but on the previous night it had broken its chain and escaped. Its mahout, the only person who could manage it when it was in that state, had set out in pursuit, but had taken the wrong direction and was now twelve hours' journey away, and in the morning the elephant had suddenly reappeared in the town. The Burmese population had no weapons and were quite helpless against it. It had already destroyed somebody's bamboo hut, killed a cow and raided some fruit-stalls and devoured the stock; also it had met the municipal rubbish van and, when the driver jumped out and took to his heels, had turned the van over and inflicted violences upon it.

The Burmese sub-inspector and some Indian constables were waiting for me in the quarter where the elephant had been seen. It was a very poor quarter, a labyrinth of squalid bamboo huts, thatched with palm-leaf, winding all over a steep hillside. I remember that it was a cloudy, stuffy morning at the beginning of the rains. We began questioning the people as to where the elephant had gone and, as usual, failed to get any definite information. That is invariably the case in the East; a story always sounds clear enough at a distance, but the nearer you get to the scene of events the vaguer it becomes. Some of the people said that the elephant had gone in one direction, some said that he had gone in another, some professed not even to have heard of any elephant. I had almost made up my mind that the whole story was a pack of lies, when we heard yells a little distance away. There was a loud, scandalized cry of "Go away, child! Go away this instant!" and an old woman with a switch in her hand came round the corner of a hut, violently shooing away a crowd of naked children. Some more women followed, clicking their tongues

1. The imperial government of British India and Burma.
2. Forever and ever.
3. Gone into sexual heat.

and exclaiming; evidently there was something that the children ought not to have seen. I rounded the hut and saw a man's dead body sprawling in the mud. He was an Indian, a black Dravidian coolie,[4] almost naked, and he could not have been dead many minutes. The people said that the elephant had come suddenly upon him round the corner of the hut, caught him with its trunk, put its foot on his back and ground him into the earth. This was the rainy season and the ground was soft, and his face had scored a trench a foot deep and a couple of yards long. He was lying on his belly with arms crucified and head sharply twisted to one side. His face was coated with mud, the eyes wide open, the teeth bared and grinning with an expression of unendurable agony. (Never tell me, by the way, that the dead look peaceful. Most of the corpses I have seen looked devilish.) The friction of the great beast's foot had stripped the skin from his back as neatly as one skins a rabbit. As soon as I saw the dead man I sent an orderly to a friend's house nearby to borrow an elephant rifle. I had already sent back the pony, not wanting it to go mad with fright and throw me if it smelt the elephant.

5   The orderly came back in a few minutes with a rifle and five cartridges, and meanwhile some Burmans had arrived and told us that the elephant was in the paddy fields below, only a few hundred yards away. As I started forward practically the whole population of the quarter flocked out of the houses and followed me. They had seen the rifle and were all shouting excitedly that I was going to shoot the elephant. They had not shown much interest in the elephant when he was merely ravaging their homes, but it was different now that he was going to be shot. It was a bit of fun to them, as it would be to an English crowd; besides they wanted the meat. It made me vaguely uneasy. I had no intention of shooting the elephant—I had merely sent for the rifle to defend myself if necessary—and it is always unnerving to have a crowd following you. I marched down the hill, looking and feeling a fool, with the rifle over my shoulder and an ever-growing army of people jostling at my heels. At the bottom, when you got away from the huts, there was a metalled road and beyond that a miry waste of paddy fields a thousand yards across, not yet ploughed but soggy from the first rains and dotted with coarse grass. The elephant was standing eight yards from the road, his left side towards us. He took not the slightest notice of the crowd's approach. He was tearing up bunches of grass, beating them against his knees to clean them and stuffing them into his mouth.

I had halted on the road. As soon as I saw the elephant I knew with perfect certainty that I ought not to shoot him. It is a serious matter to shoot a working elephant—it is comparable to destroying a huge and costly piece of machinery—and obviously one ought not to do it if it can possibly be avoided. And at that distance, peacefully eating, the elephant looked no more dangerous than a cow. I thought then and I think now that his attack of "must" was already passing off; in which case he would merely wander harmlessly about until the mahout came back and caught him. Moreover, I did not in the least

4. A hired worker from southern India, one speaking a Dravidian language. The word "coolie" comes from Koli, or Kuli, the name of an aboriginal race of western India.

want to shoot him. I decided that I would watch him for a little while to make sure that he did not turn savage again, and then go home.

But at that moment I glanced round at the crowd that had followed me. It was an immense crowd, two thousand at the least and growing every minute. It blocked the road for a long distance on either side. I looked at the sea of yellow faces above the garish clothes—faces all happy and excited over this bit of fun, all certain that the elephant was going to be shot. They were watching me as they would watch a conjurer about to perform a trick. They did not like me, but with the magical rifle in my hands I was momentarily worth watching. And suddenly I realized that I should have to shoot the elephant after all. The people expected it of me and I had got to do it; I could feel their two thousand wills pressing me forward, irresistibly. And it was at this moment, as I stood there with the rifle in my hands, that I first grasped the hollowness, the futility of the white man's dominion in the East. Here was I, the white man with his gun, standing in front of the unarmed native crowd—seemingly the leading actor of the piece; but in reality I was only an absurd puppet pushed to and fro by the will of those yellow faces behind. I perceived in this moment that when the white man turns tyrant it is his own freedom that he destroys. He becomes a sort of hollow, posing dummy, the conventionalized figure of a sahib. For it is the condition of his rule that he shall spend his life in trying to impress the "natives," and so in every crisis he has got to do what the "natives" expect of him. He wears a mask, and his face grows to fit it. I had got to shoot the elephant. I had committed myself to doing it when I sent for the rifle. A sahib has got to act like a sahib; he has got to appear resolute, to know his own mind and do definite things. To come all that way, rifle in hand, with two thousand people marching at my heels, and then to trail feebly away, having done nothing—no, that was impossible. The crowd would laugh at me. And my whole life, every white man's life in the East, was one long struggle not to be laughed at.

But I did not want to shoot the elephant. I watched him beating his bunch of grass against his knees, with that preoccupied grandmotherly air that elephants have. It seemed to me that it would be murder to shoot him. At that age I was not squeamish about killing animals, but I had never shot an elephant and never wanted to. (Somehow it always seems worse to kill a *large* animal.) Besides, there was the beast's owner to be considered. Alive, the elephant was worth at least a hundred pounds; dead, he would only be worth the value of his tusks, five pounds, possibly. But I had got to act quickly. I turned to some experienced-looking Burmans who had been there when we arrived, and asked them how the elephant had been behaving. They all said the same thing: he took no notice of you if you left him alone, but he might charge if you went too close to him.

It was perfectly clear to me what I ought to do. I ought to walk up to within, say, twenty-five yards of the elephant and test his behavior. If he charged, I could shoot; if he took no notice of me, it would be safe to leave him until the mahout came back. But also I knew that I was going to do no such thing. I was a poor shot with a rifle and the ground was soft mud into which one would sink at every step. If the elephant charged and I missed him,

I should have about as much chance as a toad under a steam-roller. But even then I was not thinking particularly of my own skin, only of the watchful yellow faces behind. For at that moment, with the crowd watching me, I was not afraid in the ordinary sense, as I would have been if I had been alone. A white man mustn't be frightened in front of "natives"; and so, in general, he isn't frightened. The sole thought in my mind was that if anything went wrong those two thousand Burmans would see me pursued, caught, trampled on and reduced to a grinning corpse like that Indian up the hill. And if that happened it was quite probable that some of them would laugh. That would never do. There was only one alternative. I shoved the cartridges into the magazine and lay down on the road to get a better aim.

10   The crowd grew very still, and a deep, low, happy sigh, as of people who see the theatre curtain go up at last, breathed from innumerable throats. They were going to have their bit of fun after all. The rifle was a beautiful German thing with cross-hair sights. I did not then know that in shooting an elephant one would shoot to cut an imaginary bar running from ear-hole to ear-hole. I ought, therefore, as the elephant was sideways on, to have aimed straight at his ear-hole; actually I aimed several inches in front of this, thinking the brain would be further forward.

When I pulled the trigger I did not hear the bang or feel the kick—one never does when a shot goes home—but I heard the devilish roar of glee that went up from the crowd. In that instant, in too short a time, one would have thought, even for the bullet to get there, a mysterious, terrible change had come over the elephant. He neither stirred nor fell, but every line of his body had altered. He looked suddenly stricken, shrunken, immensely old, as though the frightful impact of the bullet had paralysed him without knocking him down. At last, after what seemed a long time—it might have been five seconds, I dare say—he sagged flabbily to his knees. His mouth slobbered. An enormous senility seemed to have settled upon him. One could have imagined him thousands of years old. I fired again into the same spot. At the second shot he did not collapse but climbed with desperate slowness to his feet and stood weakly upright, with legs sagging and head drooping. I fired a third time. That was the shot that did for him. You could see the agony of it jolt his whole body and knock the last remnant of strength from his legs. But in falling he seemed for a moment to rise, for as his hind legs collapsed beneath him he seemed to tower upward like a huge rock toppling, his trunk reaching skywards like a tree. He trumpeted, for the first and only time. And then down he came, his belly towards me, with a crash that seemed to shake the ground even where I lay.

I got up. The Burmans were already racing past me across the mud. It was obvious that the elephant would never rise again, but he was not dead. He was breathing very rhythmically with long rattling gasps, his great mound of a side painfully rising and falling. His mouth was wide open—I could see far down into caverns of pale pink throat. I waited a long time for him to die, but his breathing did not weaken. Finally I fired my two remaining shots into the spot where I thought his heart must be. The thick blood welled out of him like red velvet, but still he did not die. His body did not even jerk when the shots hit him, the tortured breathing continued without a pause. He was dying, very slowly and in great agony, but in some world remote from me where not even a bullet could damage him further. I felt that I had got to put an end to that dreadful noise. It seemed dreadful to see the great beast lying there, powerless to move and yet powerless to die, and not even to be able to finish him. I sent back for my small rifle and poured shot after shot into his heart and down his throat. They seemed to make no impression. The tortured gasps continued as steadily as the ticking of a clock.

In the end I could not stand it any longer and went away. I heard later that it took him half an hour to die. Burmans were bringing dahs[5] and baskets even before I left, and I was told they had stripped his body almost to the bones by the afternoon.

Afterwards, of course, there were endless discussions about the shooting of the elephant. The owner was furious, but he was only an Indian and could do nothing. Besides, legally I had done the right thing, for a mad elephant has to be killed, like a mad dog, if its owner fails to control it. Among the Europeans opinion was divided. The older men said I was right, the younger men said it was a damn shame to shoot an elephant for killing a coolie, because an elephant was worth more than any damn Coringhee coolie.[6] And afterwards I was very glad that the coolie had been killed; it put me legally in the right and it gave me a sufficient pretext for shooting the elephant. I often wondered whether any of the others grasped that I had done it solely to avoid looking a fool.

5. Butcher knives.
6. A hired worker from the seaport of Coringa, in Madras, India.

QUESTIONS

1. Why did Orwell shoot the elephant? Account for the motives that led him to shoot. Then categorize them as personal motives, circumstantial motives, social motives, or political motives. Is it easy to assign his motives to categories? Why or why not?

2. In this essay the proportion of narrative to analysis is high. Mark each paragraph as narrative or analytic, and note, in particular, how much analysis Orwell places in the middle of the essay. What are the advantages and disadvantages of having it there rather than at the beginning or the end of the essay?

3. Facts ordinarily do not speak for themselves. How does Orwell present his facts to make them speak in support of his analytic points? Look, for example, at the death of the elephant (paragraphs 11 to 13).

4. Write an essay in which you present a personal experience that illuminates a larger issue: schooling, or affirmative action, or homelessness, or law enforcement, or taxes, or some other local or national issue.

Jonathan Swift *A Modest Proposal*

For Preventing the Children of Poor People in Ireland from Being a Burden to Their Parents or Country, and for Making Them Beneficial to the Public

I T IS A MELANCHOLY object to those who walk through this great town[1] or travel in the country, when they see the streets, the roads, and cabin doors, crowded with beggars of the female-sex, followed by three, four, or six children, all in rags and importuning every passenger for an alms. These mothers, instead of being able to work for their honest livelihood, are forced to employ all their time in strolling to beg sustenance for their helpless infants, who, as they grow up, either turn thieves for want of work, or leave their dear native country to fight for the Pretender in Spain, or sell themselves to the Barbadoes.[2]

I think it is agreed by all parties that this prodigious number of children in the arms, or on the backs, or at the heels of their mothers, and frequently of their fathers, is in the present deplorable state of the kingdom a very great additional grievance; and therefore whoever could find out a fair, cheap, and easy method of making these children sound, useful members of the commonwealth would deserve so well of the public as to have his statue set up for a preserver of the nation.

But my intention is very far from being confined to provide only for the children of professed beggars; it is of a much greater extent, and shall take in the whole number of infants at a certain age who are born of parents in effect as little able to support them as those who demand our charity in the streets.

As to my own part, having turned my thoughts for many years upon this important subject, and maturely weighed the several schemes of other projectors,[3] I have always found them grossly mistaken in their computation. It is true, a child just dropped from its dam may be supported by her milk for a solar year, with little other nourishment; at most not above the value of two shillings,[4] which the mother may certainly get, or the value in scraps, by her

Printed in 1729 as a pamphlet, a form commonly used for political debate in the eighteenth century.

1. Dublin.
2. Many poor Irish sought to escape poverty by emigrating to the Barbadoes and other western English colonies, paying for transport by binding themselves to work for a landowner there for a period of years. The Pretender, claimant to the English throne, was barred from succession after his father, King James II, was deposed in a Protestant revolution; thereafter, many Irish Catholics joined the Pretender in his exile in France and Spain and in his unsuccessful attempts at counterrevolution.
3. People with projects; schemers.
4. A shilling used to be worth about twenty-five cents.

lawful occupation of begging; and it is exactly at one year old that I propose to provide for them in such a manner as instead of being a charge upon their parents or the parish, or wanting food and raiment for the rest of their lives, they shall on the contrary contribute to the feeding, and partly to the clothing, of many thousands.

There is likewise another great advantage in my scheme, that it will prevent those voluntary abortions, and that horrid practice of women murdering their bastard children, alas, too frequent among us, sacrificing the poor innocent babes, I doubt, more to avoid the expense than the shame, which would move tears and pity in the most savage and inhuman breast.

The number of souls in this kingdom being usually reckoned one million and a half, of these I calculate there may be about two hundred thousand couple whose wives are breeders; from which number I subtract thirty thousand couples who are able to maintain their own children, although I apprehend there cannot be so many under the present distresses of the kingdom; but this being granted, there will remain an hundred and seventy thousand breeders. I again subtract fifty thousand for those women who miscarry, or whose children die by accident or disease within the year. There only remain an hundred and twenty thousand children of poor parents annually born. The question therefore is, how this number shall be reared and provided for, which, as I have already said, under the present situation of affairs, is utterly impossible by all the methods hitherto proposed. For we can neither employ them in handicraft or agriculture; we neither build houses (I mean in the country) nor cultivate land. They can very seldom pick up a livelihood by stealing till they arrive at six years old, except where they are of towardly parts;[5] although I confess they learn the rudiments much earlier, during which time they can however be looked upon only as probationers, as I have been informed by a principal gentleman in the county of Cavan, who protested to me that he never knew above one or two instances under the age of six, even in a part of the kingdom so renowned for the quickest proficiency in that art.

I am assured by our merchants that a boy or a girl before twelve years old is no salable commodity; and even when they come to this age they will not yield above three pounds, or three pounds and half a crown[6] at most on the Exchange; which cannot turn to account either to the parents or the kingdom, the charge of nutriment and rags having been at least four times that value.

I shall now therefore humbly propose my own thoughts, which I hope will not be liable to the least objection.

I have been assured by a very knowing American of my acquaintance in London, that a young healthy child well nursed is at a year old a most delicious, nourishing, and wholesome food, whether stewed, roasted, baked, or boiled; and I make no doubt that it will equally serve in a fricassee or a ragout.

I do therefore humbly offer it to public consideration that of the hundred and twenty thousand children, already computed, twenty thousand may be re-

5. Promising abilities.
6. A crown was one quarter of a pound.

served for breed, whereof only one fourth part to be males, which is more than we allow to sheep, black cattle, or swine; and my reason is that these children are seldom the fruits of marriage, a circumstance not much regarded by our savages, therefore one male will be sufficient to serve four females. That the remaining hundred thousand may at a year old be offered in sale to the persons of quality and fortune through the kingdom, always advising the mother to let them suck plentifully in the last month, so as to render them plump and fat for a good table. A child will make two dishes at an entertainment for friends; and when the family dines alone, the fore or hind quarter will make a reasonable dish, and seasoned with a little pepper or salt will be very good boiled on the fourth day, especially in winter.

I have reckoned upon a medium that a child just born will weigh twelve pounds, and in a solar year if tolerably nursed increaseth to twenty-eight pounds.

I grant this food will be somewhat dear, and therefore very proper for landlords, who, as they have already devoured most of the parents, seem to have the best title to the children.

Infant's flesh will be in season throughout the year, but more plentiful in March, and a little before and after. For we are told by a grave author, an eminent French physician,[7] that fish being a prolific diet, there are more children born in Roman Catholic countries about nine months after Lent than at any other season; therefore, reckoning a year after Lent, the markets will be more glutted than usual, because the number of popish infants is at least three to one in this kingdom; and therefore it will have one other collateral advantage, by lessening the number of Papists among us.[8]

I have already computed the charge of nursing a beggar's child (in which list I reckon all cottagers, laborers, and four fifths of the farmers) to be about two shillings per annum, rags included; and I believe no gentleman would repine to give ten shillings for the carcass of a good fat child, which, as I have said, will make four dishes of excellent nutritive meat, when he hath only some particular friend or his own family to dine with him. Thus the squire will learn to be a good landlord, and grow popular among the tenants; the mother will have eight shillings net profit, and be fit for work till she produces another child.

15   Those who are more thrifty (as I must confess the times require) may flay the carcass; the skin of which artificially[9] dressed will make admirable gloves for ladies, and summer boots for fine gentlemen.

As to our city of Dublin, shambles[10] may be appointed for this purpose in the most convenient parts of it, and butchers we may be assured will not be wanting; although I rather recommend buying the children alive, and dressing them hot from the knife as we do roasting pigs.

7. The comic writer François Rabelais (1483–1553).

8. The speaker is addressing Protestant Anglo-Irish, who were the chief landowners and administrators, and his views of Catholicism in Ireland and abroad echo theirs.

9. Skillfully.

10. Slaughterhouses.

A very worthy person, a true lover of his country, and whose virtues I highly esteem, was lately pleased in discoursing on this matter to offer a refinement upon my scheme. He said that many gentlemen of this kingdom, having of late destroyed their deer, he conceived that the want of venison might be well supplied by the bodies of young lads and maidens, not exceeding fourteen years of age nor under twelve, so great a number of both sexes in every county being now ready to starve for want of work and service; and these to be disposed of by their parents, if alive, or otherwise by their nearest relations. But with due deference to so excellent a friend and so deserving a patriot, I cannot be altogether in his sentiments; for as to the males, my American acquaintance assured me from frequent experience that their flesh was generally tough and lean, like that of our schoolboys, by continual exercise, and their taste disagreeable; and to fatten them would not answer the charge. Then as to the females, it would, I think with humble submission, be a loss to the public, because they soon would become breeders themselves: and besides, it is not improbable that some scrupulous people might be apt to censure such a practice (although indeed very unjustly) as a little bordering upon cruelty; which, I confess, hath always been with me the strongest objection against any project, how well soever intended.

But in order to justify my friend, he confessed that this expedient was put into his head by the famous Psalmanazar, a native of the island Formosa,[11] who came from thence to London above twenty years ago, and in conversation told my friend that in his country when any young person happened to be put to death, the executioner sold the carcass to persons of quality as a prime dainty; and that in his time the body of a plump girl of fifteen, who was crucified for an attempt to poison the emperor, was sold to his Imperial Majesty's prime minister of state, and other great mandarins of the court, in joints from the gibbet, at four hundred crowns. Neither indeed can I deny that if the same use were made of several plump young girls in this town, who without one single groat[12] to their fortunes cannot stir abroad without a chair,[13] and appear at the playhouse and assemblies in foreign fineries which they never will pay for, the kingdom would not be the worse.

Some persons of a desponding spirit are in great concern about that vast number of poor people who are aged, diseased, or maimed, and I have been desired to employ my thoughts what course may be taken to ease the nation of so grievous an encumbrance. But I am not in the least pain upon that matter, because it is very well known that they are every day dying and rotting by cold and famine, and filth and vermin, as fast as can be reasonably expected. And as to the younger laborers, they are now in almost as hopeful a condition. They cannot get work, and consequently pine away for want of nourishment to

---

11. Actually a Frenchman, George Psalmanazar had passed himself off as from Formosa (now Taiwan) and had written a fictitious book about his "homeland," with descriptions of human sacrifice and cannibalism.

12. A coin worth about four English pennies.

13. A sedan chair.

a degree that if at any time they are accidentally hired to common labor, they have not strength to perform it; and thus the country and themselves are happily delivered from the evils to come.

20   I have too long digressed, and therefore shall return to my subject. I think the advantages by the proposal which I have made are obvious and many, as well as of the highest importance.

For first, as I have already observed, it would greatly lessen the number of Papists, with whom we are yearly overrun, being the principal breeders of the nation as well as our most dangerous enemies; and who stay at home on purpose to deliver the kingdom to the Pretender, hoping to take their advantage by the absence of so many good Protestants, who have chosen rather to leave their country than to stay at home and pay tithes against their conscience to an Episcopal curate.

Secondly, the poorer tenants will have something valuable of their own, which by law may be made liable to distress,[14] and help to pay their landlord's rent, their corn and cattle being already seized and money a thing unknown.

Thirdly, whereas the maintenance of an hundred thousand children, from two years old and upwards, cannot be computed at less than ten shillings a piece per annum, the nation's stock will be thereby increased fifty thousand pounds per annum, besides the profit of a new dish introduced to the tables of all gentlemen of fortune in the kingdom who have any refinement in taste. And the money will circulate among ourselves, the goods being entirely of our own growth and manufacture.

Fourthly, the constant breeders, besides the gain of eight shillings sterling per annum by the sale of their children, will be rid of the charge of maintaining them after the first year.

25   Fifthly, this food would likewise bring great custom to taverns, where the vintners will certainly be so prudent as to procure the best receipts for dressing it to perfection, and consequently have their houses frequented by all the fine gentlemen, who justly value themselves upon their knowledge in good eating; and a skillful cook, who understands how to oblige his guests, will contrive to make it as expensive as they please.

Sixthly, this would be a great inducement to marriage, which all wise nations have either encouraged by rewards or enforced by laws and penalties. It would increase the care and tenderness of mothers toward their children, when they were sure of a settlement for life to the poor babes, provided in some sort by the public, to their annual profit instead of expense. We should see an honest emulation among the married women, which of them could bring the fattest child to the market. Men would become as fond of their wives during the time of their pregnancy as they are now of their mares in foal, their cows in calf, or sows when they are ready to farrow; nor offer to beat or kick them (as is too frequent a practice) for fear of a miscarriage.

Many other advantages might be enumerated. For instance, the addition of some thousand carcasses in our exportation of barreled beef, the propaga-

14. Seizure for the payment of debts.

tion of swine's flesh, and improvement in the art of making good bacon, so much wanted among us by the great destruction of pigs, too frequent at our tables, which are no way comparable in taste or magnificence to a well-grown, fat, yearling child, which roasted whole will make a considerable figure at a lord mayor's feast or any other public entertainment. But this and many others I omit, being studious of brevity.

Supposing that one thousand families in this city would be constant customers for infants' flesh, besides others who might have it at merry meetings, particularly weddings and christenings, I compute that Dublin would take off annually about twenty thousand carcasses, and the rest of the kingdom (where probably they will be sold somewhat cheaper) the remaining eighty thousand.

I can think of no one objection that will possibly be raised against this proposal, unless it should be urged that the number of people will be thereby much lessened in the kingdom. This I freely own, and it was indeed one principal design in offering it to the world. I desire the reader will observe, that I calculate my remedy for this one individual kingdom of Ireland and for no other that ever was, is, or I think ever can be upon earth. Therefore let no man talk to me of other expedients: of taxing our absentees at five shillings a pound: of using neither clothes nor household furniture except what is of our own growth and manufacture: of utterly rejecting the materials and instruments that promote foreign luxury: of curing the expensiveness of pride, vanity, idleness, and gaming in our women: of introducing a vein of parsimony, prudence, and temperance: of learning to love our country, in the want of which we differ even from Laplanders and the inhabitants of Topinamboo:[15] of quitting our animosities and factions, nor acting any longer like the Jews, who were murdering one another at the very moment their city was taken: of being a little cautious not to sell our country and conscience for nothing: of teaching landlords to have at least one degree of mercy toward their tenants: lastly, of putting a spirit of honesty, industry, and skill into our shopkeepers; who, if a resolution could now be taken to buy only our native goods, would immediately unite to cheat and exact upon us in the price, the measure, and the goodness, nor could ever yet be brought to make one fair proposal of just dealing, though often and earnestly invited to it.[16]

Therefore I repeat, let no man talk to me of these and the like expedients, till he hath at least some glimpse of hope that there will ever be some hearty and sincere attempt to put them in practice. 30

But as to myself, having been wearied out for many years with offering vain, idle, visionary thoughts, and at length utterly despairing of success, I fortunately fell upon this proposal, which, as it is wholly new, so it hath something solid and real, of no expense and little trouble, full in our own power, and whereby we can incur no danger in disobliging England. For this kind of commodity will not bear exportation, the flesh being of too tender a consis-

15. A district in Brazil.

16. Swift himself had made these proposals seriously in various previous works, but to no avail.

tence to admit a long continuance in salt, although perhaps I could name a country[17] which would be glad to eat up our whole nation without it.

After all, I am not so violently bent upon my own opinion as to reject any offer proposed by wise men, which shall be found equally innocent, cheap, easy, and effectual. But before something of that kind shall be advanced in contradiction to my scheme, and offering a better, I desire the author or authors will be pleased maturely to consider two points. First, as things now stand, how they will be able to find food and raiment for an hundred thousand useless mouths and backs. And secondly, there being a round million of creatures in human figure throughout this kingdom, whose sole subsistence put into a common stock would leave them in debt two millions of pounds sterling, adding those who are beggars by profession to the bulk of farmers, cottagers, and laborers, with their wives and children who are beggars in effect; I desire those politicians who dislike my overture, and may perhaps be so bold to attempt an answer, that they will first ask the parents of these mortals whether they would not at this day think it a great happiness to have been sold for food at a year old in the manner I prescribe, and thereby have avoided such a perpetual scene of misfortunes as they have since gone through by the oppression of landlords, the impossibility of paying rent without money or trade, the want of common sustenance, with neither house nor clothes to cover them from the inclemencies of the weather, and the most inevitable prospect of entailing the like or greater miseries upon their breed forever.

I profess, in the sincerity of my heart, that I have not the least personal interest in endeavoring to promote this necessary work, having no other motive than the public good of my country, by advancing our trade, providing for infants, relieving the poor, and giving some pleasure to the rich. I have no children by which I can propose to get a single penny; the youngest being nine years old, and my wife past childbearing.

17. England.

QUESTIONS

1. Identify examples of the reasonable voice of Swift's authorial persona, such as the title of the essay itself.

2. Look, in particular, at instances in which Swift's authorial persona proposes shocking things. How does the style of the "Modest Proposal" affect its content?

3. Verbal irony consists of saying one thing and meaning another. At what point in this essay do you begin to suspect that Swift is using irony? What additional evidence of irony can you find?

4. Write a modest proposal of your own in the manner of Swift to remedy a real problem; that is, propose an outrageous remedy in a reasonable voice.

The Morals of the Prince

On the Reasons Why Men Are Praised or Blamed— Especially Princes

I T REMAINS now to be seen what style and principles a prince ought to adopt in dealing with his subjects and friends. I know the subject has been treated frequently before, and I'm afraid people will think me rash for trying to do so again, especially since I intend to differ in this discussion from what others have said. But since I intend to write something useful to an understanding reader, it seemed better to go after the real truth of the matter than to repeat what people have imagined. A great many men have imagined states and princedoms such as nobody ever saw or knew in the real world, for there's such a difference between the way we really live and the way we ought to live that the man who neglects the real to study the ideal will learn how to accomplish his ruin, not his salvation. Any man who tries to be good all the time is bound to come to ruin among the great number who are not good. Hence a prince who wants to keep his post must learn how not to be good, and use that knowledge, or refrain from using it, as necessity requires.

Putting aside, then, all the imaginary things that are said about princes, and getting down to the truth, let me say that whenever men are discussed (and especially princes because they are prominent), there are certain qualities that bring them either praise or blame. Thus some are considered generous, others stingy (I use a Tuscan term, since "greedy" in our speech means a man who wants to take other people's goods. We call a man "stingy" who clings to his own); some are givers, others grabbers; some cruel, others merciful; one man is treacherous, another faithful; one is feeble and effeminate, another fierce and spirited; one humane, another proud; one lustful, another chaste; one straightforward, another sly; one harsh, another gentle; one serious, another playful; one religious, another skeptical, and so on. I know everyone will agree that among these many qualities a prince certainly ought to have all those that are considered good. But since it is impossible to have and exercise them all, because the conditions of human life simply do not allow it, a prince must be shrewd enough to avoid the public disgrace of those vices that would lose him his state. If he possibly can, he should also guard against vices that will not lose him his state; but if he cannot prevent them, he should not be too worried about indulging them. And furthermore, he should not be too worried about incurring blame for any vice without which he would find it hard to save his state. For if you look at matters carefully, you will see that something resembling virtue, if you follow it, may be your ruin, while some-

From The Prince *(1513), a book on statecraft written for Giuliano de' Medici (1479–1516), a member of one of the most famous and powerful families of Renaissance Italy. Excerpted from an edition translated and edited by Robert M. Adams (1977).*

thing else resembling vice will lead, if you follow it, to your security and well-being.

ON LIBERALITY AND STINGINESS

Let me begin, then, with the first of the qualities mentioned above, by saying that a reputation for liberality is doubtless very fine; but the generosity that earns you that reputation can do you great harm. For if you exercise your generosity in a really virtuous way, as you should, nobody will know of it, and you cannot escape the odium of the opposite vice. Hence if you wish to be widely known as a generous man, you must seize every opportunity to make a big display of your giving. A prince of this character is bound to use up his entire revenue in works of ostentation. Thus, in the end, if he wants to keep a name for generosity, he will have to load his people with exorbitant taxes and squeeze money out of them in every way he can. This is the first step in making him odious to his subjects; for when he is poor, nobody will respect him. Then, when his generosity has angered many and brought rewards to a few, the slightest difficulty will trouble him, and at the first approach of danger, down he goes. If by chance he foresees this, and tries to change his ways, he will immediately be labeled a miser.

Since a prince cannot use this virtue of liberality in such a way as to become known for it unless he harms his own security, he won't mind, if he judges prudently of things, being known as a miser. In due course he will be thought the more liberal man, when people see that his parsimony enables him to live on his income, to defend himself against his enemies, and to undertake major projects without burdening his people with taxes. Thus he will be acting liberally toward all those people from whom he takes nothing (and there are an immense number of them), and in a stingy way toward those people on whom he bestows nothing (and they are very few). In our times, we have seen great things being accomplished only by men who have had the name of misers; all the others have gone under. Pope Julius II, though he used his reputation as a generous man to gain the papacy, sacrificed it in order to be able to make war; the present king of France has waged many wars without levying a single extra tax on his people, simply because he could take care of the extra expenses out of the savings from his long parsimony. If the present king of Spain had a reputation for generosity, he would never have been able to undertake so many campaigns, or win so many of them.

5   Hence a prince who prefers not to rob his subjects, who wants to be able to defend himself, who wants to avoid poverty and contempt, and who doesn't want to become a plunderer, should not mind in the least if people consider him a miser; this is simply one of the vices that enable him to reign. Someone may object that Caesar used a reputation for generosity to become emperor, and many other people have also risen in the world, because they were generous or were supposed to be so. Well, I answer, either you are a prince already, or you are in the process of becoming one; in the first case, this reputation for generosity is harmful to you, in the second case it is very necessary. Caesar

was one of those who wanted to become ruler in Rome; but after he had reached his goal, if he had lived, and had not cut down on his expenses, he would have ruined the empire itself. Someone may say: there have been plenty of princes, very successful in warfare, who have had a reputation for generosity. But I answer: either the prince is spending his own money and that of his subjects, or he is spending someone else's. In the first case, he ought to be sparing; in the second case, he ought to spend money like water. Any prince at the head of his army, which lives on loot, extortion, and plunder, disposes of other people's property, and is bound to be very generous; otherwise, his soldiers would desert him. You can always be a more generous giver when what you give is not yours or your subjects'; Cyrus, Caesar, and Alexander[1] were generous in this way. Spending what belongs to other people does no harm to your reputation, rather it enhances it; only spending your own substance harms you. And there is nothing that wears out faster than generosity; even as you practice it, you lose the means of practicing it, and you become either poor and contemptible or (in the course of escaping poverty) rapacious and hateful. The thing above all against which a prince must protect himself is being contemptible and hateful; generosity leads to both. Thus, it's much wiser to put up with the reputation of being a miser, which brings you shame without hate, than to be forced—just because you want to appear generous—into a reputation for rapacity, which brings shame on you and hate along with it.

On Cruelty and Clemency: Whether It Is Better to Be Loved or Feared

Continuing now with our list of qualities, let me say that every prince should prefer to be considered merciful rather than cruel, yet he should be careful not to mismanage this clemency of his. People thought Cesare Borgia[2] was cruel, but that cruelty of his reorganized the Romagna, united it, and established it in peace and loyalty. Anyone who views the matter realistically will see that this prince was much more merciful than the people of Florence, who, to avoid the reputation of cruelty, allowed Pistoia to be destroyed.[3] Thus, no prince should mind being called cruel for what he does to keep his subjects united and loyal; he may make examples of a very few, but he will be more merciful in reality than those who, in their tenderheartedness, allow disorders to occur, with their attendant murders and lootings. Such turbulence brings harm to an entire community, while the executions ordered by a prince affect only one individual at a time. A new prince, above all others, cannot possibly avoid a name for cruelty, since new states are always in danger. And Virgil, speaking through the mouth of Dido,[4] says:

1. Persian, Roman, and Macedonian conquerors and rulers in ancient times.
2. The son of Pope Alexander VI; he was duke of Romagna, which he subjugated in 1499–1502.
3. By unchecked rioting between opposing factions in 1502.
4. Queen of Carthage and tragic heroine of Virgil's epic, the *Aeneid*.

> My cruel fate
> And doubts attending an unsettled state
> Force me to guard my coast from foreign foes.

Yet a prince should be slow to believe rumors and to commit himself to action on the basis of them. He should not be afraid of his own thoughts; he ought to proceed cautiously, moderating his conduct with prudence and humanity, allowing neither overconfidence to make him careless, nor overtimidity to make him intolerable.

Here the question arises: is it better to be loved than feared, or vice versa? I don't doubt that every prince would like to be both; but since it is hard to accommodate these qualities, if you have to make a choice, to be feared is much safer than to be loved. For it is a good general rule about men, that they are ungrateful, fickle, liars and deceivers, fearful of danger and greedy for gain. While you serve their welfare, they are all yours, offering their blood, their belongings, their lives, and their children's lives, as we noted above—so long as the danger is remote. But when the danger is close at hand, they turn against you. Then, any prince who has relied on their words and has made no other preparations will come to grief; because friendships that are bought at a price, and not with greatness and nobility of soul, may be paid for but they are not acquired, and they cannot be used in time of need. People are less concerned with offending a man who makes himself loved than one who makes himself feared: the reason is that love is a link of obligation which men, because they are rotten, will break any time they think doing so serves their advantage; but fear involves dread of punishment, from which they can never escape.

Still, a prince should make himself feared in such a way that, even if he gets no love, he gets no hate either; because it is perfectly possible to be feared and not hated, and this will be the result if only the prince will keep his hands off the property of his subjects or citizens, and off their women. When he does have to shed blood, he should be sure to have a strong justification and manifest cause; but above all, he should not confiscate people's property, because men are quicker to forget the death of a father than the loss of a patrimony. Besides, pretexts for confiscation are always plentiful, it never fails that a prince who starts living by plunder can find reasons to rob someone else. Excuses for proceeding against someone's life are much rarer and more quickly exhausted.

But a prince at the head of his armies and commanding a multitude of soldiers should not care a bit if he is considered cruel; without such a reputation, he could never hold his army together and ready for action. Among the marvelous deeds of Hannibal,[5] this was prime: that, having an immense army, which included men of many different races and nations, and which he led to battle in distant countries, he never allowed them to fight among themselves

---

5. Carthaginian general who led a massive but unsuccessful invasion of Rome in 218–203 B.C.E.

or to rise against him, whether his fortune was good or bad. The reason for this could only be his inhuman cruelty, which, along with his countless other talents, made him an object of awe and terror to his soldiers; and without the cruelty, his other qualities would never have sufficed. The historians who pass snap judgments on these matters admire his accomplishments and at the same time condemn the cruelty which was their main cause.

When I say, "His other qualities would never have sufficed," we can see   10
that this is true from the example of Scipio,[6] an outstanding man not only among those of his own time, but in all recorded history; yet his armies revolted in Spain, for no other reason than his excessive leniency in allowing his soldiers more freedom than military discipline permits. Fabius Maximus rebuked him in the senate for this failing, calling him the corrupter of the Roman armies. When a lieutenant of Scipio's plundered the Locrians,[7] he took no action in behalf of the people, and did nothing to discipline that insolent lieutenant; again, this was the result of his easygoing nature. Indeed, when someone in the senate wanted to excuse him on this occasion, he said there are many men who knew better how to avoid error themselves than how to correct error in others. Such a soft temper would in time have tarnished the fame and glory of Scipio, had he brought it to the office of emperor; but as he lived under the control of the senate, this harmful quality of his not only remained hidden but was considered creditable.

Returning to the question of being feared or loved, I conclude that since men love at their own inclination but can be made to fear at the inclination of the prince, a shrewd prince will lay his foundations on what is under his own control, not on what is controlled by others. He should simply take pains not to be hated, as I said.

THE WAY PRINCES SHOULD KEEP THEIR WORD

How praiseworthy it is for a prince to keep his word and live with integrity rather than by craftiness, everyone understands; yet we see from recent experience that those princes have accomplished most who paid little heed to keeping their promises, but who knew how craftily to manipulate the minds of men. In the end, they won out over those who tried to act honestly.

You should consider then, that there are two ways of fighting, one with laws and the other with force. The first is properly a human method, the second belongs to beasts. But as the first method does not always suffice, you sometimes have to turn to the second. Thus a prince must know how to make good use of both the beast and the man. Ancient writers made subtle note of this fact when they wrote that Achilles and many other princes of antiquity were sent to be reared by Chiron the centaur, who trained them in his disci-

6. The Roman general whose successful invasion of Carthage in 203 B.C.E. caused Hannibal's army to be recalled from Rome. The episode described here occurred in 206 B.C.E.
7. Fabius Maximus, not only a senator but also a high public official and general who had fought against Hannibal in Italy; Locrians, people of Sicily defeated by Scipio in 205 B.C.E. and placed under Q. Pleminius.

pline.[8] Having a teacher who is half man and half beast can only mean that a prince must know how to use both these two natures, and that one without the other has no lasting effect.

Since a prince must know how to use the character of beasts, he should pick for imitation the fox and the lion. As the lion cannot protect himself from traps, and the fox cannot defend himself from wolves, you have to be a fox in order to be wary of traps, and a lion to overawe the wolves. Those who try to live by the lion alone are badly mistaken. Thus a prudent prince cannot and should not keep his word when to do so would go against his interest, or when the reasons that made him pledge it no longer apply. Doubtless if all men were good, this rule would be bad; but since they are a sad lot, and keep no faith with you, you in your turn are under no obligation to keep it with them.

15   Besides, a prince will never lack for legitimate excuses to explain away his breaches of faith. Modern history will furnish innumerable examples of this behavior, showing how many treaties and promises have been made null and void by the faithlessness of princes, and how the man succeeded best who knew best how to play the fox. But it is a necessary part of this nature that you must conceal it carefully; you must be a great liar and hypocrite. Men are so simple of mind, and so much dominated by their immediate needs, that a deceitful man will always find plenty who are ready to be deceived. One of many recent examples calls for mention. Alexander VI[9] never did anything else, never had another thought, except to deceive men, and he always found fresh material to work on. Never was there a man more convincing in his assertions, who sealed his promises with more solemn oaths, and who observed them less. Yet his deceptions were always successful, because he knew exactly how to manage this sort of business.

In actual fact, a prince may not have all the admirable qualities we listed, but it is very necessary that he should seem to have them. Indeed, I will venture to say that when you have them and exercise them all the time, they are harmful to you; when you just seem to have them, they are useful. It is good to appear merciful, truthful, humane, sincere, and religious; it is good to be so in reality. But you must keep your mind so disposed that, in case of need, you can turn to the exact contrary. This has to be understood: a prince, and especially a new prince, cannot possibly exercise all those virtues for which men are called "good." To preserve the state, he often has to do things against his word, against charity, against humanity, against religion. Thus he has to have a mind ready to shift as the winds of fortune and the varying circumstances of life may dictate. And as I said above, he should not depart from the good if he can hold to it, but he should be ready to enter on evil if he has to.

Hence a prince should take great care never to drop a word that does not seem imbued with the five good qualities noted above; to anyone who sees or

8. Achilles was foremost among the Greek heroes in the Trojan War. Half man and half horse, the mythical Chiron was said to have taught the arts of war and peace, including hunting, medicine, music, and prophecy.
9. Pope from 1492 to 1503.

hears him, he should appear all compassion, all honor, all humanity, all integrity, all religion. Nothing is more necessary than to seem to have this last virtue. Men in general judge more by the sense of sight than by the sense of touch, because everyone can see but only a few can test by feeling. Everyone sees what you seem to be, few know what you really are; and those few do not dare take a stand against the general opinion, supported by the majesty of the government. In the actions of all men, and especially of princes who are not subject to a court of appeal, we must always look to the end. Let a prince, therefore, win victories and uphold his state; his methods will always be considered worthy, and everyone will praise them, because the masses are always impressed by the superficial appearance of things, and by the outcome of an enterprise. And the world consists of nothing but the masses; the few who have no influence when the many feel secure. A certain prince of our own time, whom it's just as well not to name,[10] preaches nothing but peace and mutual trust, yet he is the determined enemy of both; and if on several different occasions he had observed either, he would have lost both his reputation and his throne.

10. Probably Ferdinand of Spain, then allied with the house of Medici.

QUESTIONS

1. This selection contains four sections of *The Prince*: "On the Reasons Why Men Are Praised or Blamed—Especially Princes"; "On Liberality and Stinginess"; "On Cruelty and Clemency: Whether It Is Better to Be Loved or Feared"; and "The Way Princes Should Keep Their Word." How, in each section, does Machiavelli contrast the ideal and the real, what he calls "the way we really live and the way we ought to live" (paragraph 1)? Mark some of the sentences in which he expresses these contrasts.

2. Rewrite some of Machiavelli's advice to princes less forcibly and shockingly, and more palatably. For example, "Any man who tries to be good all the time is bound to come to ruin among the great number who are not good" (paragraph 1) might be rewritten as "Good men are often taken advantage of and harmed by men who are not good."

3. Describe Machiavelli's view of human nature. How do his views of government follow from it?

4. Machiavelli might be described as a sixteenth-century spin doctor teaching a ruler how to package himself. Adapt his advice to a current figure in national, state, or local politics and write about that figure in a brief essay.

THOMAS JEFFERSON AND OTHERS *The Declaration of Independence*

IN CONGRESS, JULY 4, 1776
THE UNANIMOUS DECLARATION OF THE
THIRTEEN UNITED STATES OF AMERICA

WHEN IN THE Course of human events it becomes necessary for one people to dissolve the political bands which have connected them with another, and to assume among the powers of the earth, the separate and equal station to which the Laws of Nature and of Nature's God entitle them, a decent respect to the opinions of mankind requires that they should declare the causes which impel them to the separation.

We hold these truths to be self-evident, that all men are created equal, that they are endowed by their Creator with certain unalienable Rights, that among these are Life, Liberty and the pursuit of Happiness. That to secure these rights, Governments are instituted among Men, deriving their just powers from the consent of the governed. That whenever any Form of Government becomes destructive of these ends, it is the Right of the People to alter or to abolish it, and to institute new Government, laying its foundation on such principles and organizing its powers in such form, as to them shall seem most likely to effect their Safety and Happiness. Prudence, indeed, will dictate that Governments long established should not be changed for light and transient causes; and accordingly all experience hath shewn that mankind are more disposed to suffer, while evils are sufferable, than to right themselves by abolishing the forms to which they are accustomed. But when a long train of abuses and usurpations, pursuing invariably the same Object evinces a design to reduce them under absolute Despotism, it is their right, it is their duty, to throw off such Government, and to provide new Guards for their future security. Such has been the patient sufferance of these Colonies; and such is now the necessity which constrains them to alter their former Systems of Government. The history of the present King of Great Britain is a history of repeated injuries and usurpations, all having in direct object the establishment of an absolute Tyranny over these States. To prove this, let Facts be submitted to a candid world.

He has refused his Assent to Laws, the most wholesome and necessary for the public good.

He has forbidden his Government to pass laws of immediate and pressing importance, unless suspended in their operation till his Assent should be obtained; and when so suspended, he has utterly neglected to attend to them.

This final version of the Declaration of Independence resulted from revisions made to Jefferson's original draft by members of the committee to draft the declaration, including John Adams and Benjamin Franklin, and by members of the Continental Congress.

He has refused to pass other Laws for the accommodation of large districts   5
of people, unless those people would relinquish the right of Representation in
the Legislature, a right inestimable to them and formidable to tyrants only.

He has called together legislative bodies at places unusual, uncomfortable, and distant from the depository of their Public Records, for the sole purpose of fatiguing them into compliance with his measures.

He has dissolved Representative Houses repeatedly, for opposing with
manly firmness his invasions on the rights of the people.

He has refused for a long time, after such dissolutions, to cause others to
be elected; whereby the Legislative Powers, incapable of Annihilation, have returned to the People at large for their exercise; the State remaining in the
mean time exposed to all the dangers of invasion from without, and convul-
sions within.

He has endeavored to prevent the population of these States; for that purpose obstructing the Laws for Naturalization of Foreigners; refusing to pass
others to encourage their migration hither, and raising the conditions of new
Appropriations of Lands.

He has obstructed the Administration of Justice, by refusing his Assent to   10
Laws for establishing Judiciary Powers.

He has made Judges dependent on his Will alone, for the tenure of their
offices, and the amount and payment of their salaries.

He has erected a multitude of New Offices, and sent hither swarms of Officers to harass our people, and eat out their substance.

He has kept among us, in times of peace, Standing Armies without the
Consent of our legislatures.

He has affected to render the Military independent of and superior to the
Civil Power.

He has combined with others to subject us to a jurisdiction foreign to our   15
constitution, and unacknowledged by our laws; giving his Assent to their Acts
of pretended Legislation: For quartering large bodies of armed troops among
us: For protecting them, by a mock Trial, from punishment for any Murders
which they should commit on the Inhabitants of these States: For cutting off
our Trade with all parts of the world: For imposing Taxes on us without our
Consent: For depriving us in many cases, of the benefits of Trial by Jury: For
transporting us beyond Seas to be tried for pretended offenses: For abolishing
the free System of English Laws in a neighboring Province, establishing
therein an Arbitrary government, and enlarging its Boundaries so as to render
it at once an example and fit instrument for introducing the same absolute
rule into these Colonies: For taking away our Charters, abolishing our most
valuable Laws, and altering fundamentally the Forms of our Governments: For
suspending our own Legislatures, and declaring themselves invested with
power to legislate for us in all cases whatsoever.

He has abdicated Government here, by declaring us out of his Protection
and waging War against us.

He has plundered our seas, ravaged our Coasts, burnt our towns, and destroyed the lives of our people.

He is at this time transporting large Armies of foreign Mercenaries to complete the works of death, desolation and tyranny, already begun with circumstances of Cruelty & Perfidy scarcely paralleled in the most barbarous ages, and totally unworthy the Head of a civilized nation.

He has constrained our fellow Citizens taken Captive on the high Seas to bear Arms against their Country, to become the executioners of their friends and Brethren, or to fall themselves by their Hands.

20   He has excited domestic insurrections amongst us, and has endeavored to bring on the inhabitants of our frontiers, the merciless Indian Savages, whose known rule of warfare, is an undistinguished destruction of all ages, sexes, and conditions.

In every stage of these Oppressions We have Petitioned for Redress in the most humble terms: Our repeated Petitions have been answered only by repeated injury. A Prince, whose character is thus marked by every act which may define a Tyrant, is unfit to be the ruler of a free people.

Nor have We been wanting in attention to our British brethren. We have warned them from time to time of attempts by their legislature to extend an unwarrantable jurisdiction over us. We have reminded them of the circumstances of our emigration and settlement here. We have appealed to their native justice and magnanimity, and we have conjured them by the ties of our common kindred to disavow these usurpations, which would inevitably interrupt our connections and correspondence. They too have been deaf to the voice of justice and of consanguinity. We must, therefore, acquiesce in the necessity, which denounces our Separation, and hold them, as we hold the rest of mankind, Enemies in War, in Peace Friends.

We, THEREFORE the Representatives of the UNITED STATES OF AMERICA, in General Congress, Assembled, appealing to the Supreme Judge of the world for the rectitude of our intentions, do, in the Name, and by Authority of the good People of these Colonies, solemnly publish and declare, That these United Colonies are, and of Right ought to be FREE AND INDEPENDENT STATES; that they are Absolved from all Allegiance to the British Crown, and that all political connection between them and the State of Great Britain, is and ought to be totally dissolved; and that as Free and Independent States, they have full Power to levy War, conclude Peace, contract Alliances, establish Commerce, and to do all other Acts and Things which Independent States may of right do. And for the support of this Declaration, with a firm reliance on the protection of Divine Providence, we mutually pledge to each other our Lives, our Fortunes, and our sacred Honor.

QUESTIONS

1. The Declaration of Independence is an example of deductive argument: Jefferson sets up general principles, details particular instances, and then draws conclusions. In both the original and the final drafts, locate the three sections of the declaration that use deduction. Explain how they work as argument.

2. Locate the general principles (or "truths") that Jefferson sets up in the first section of both the original and the final drafts. Mark the language he uses to describe them: for example, he calls them "sacred & undeniable" in the original draft, "self-evident" in the final draft. What kinds of authority does his language appeal to? Why might he or others have revised the language?

3. Write an essay explaining Jefferson's views on the nature of humankind, the function of government, and the relationship between morality and political life, as expressed in the Declaration of Independence. What assumptions are necessary to make these views, as he says in the final draft, "self-evident"?

ELIZABETH CADY STANTON *Declaration of Sentiments and Resolutions*

WHEN, IN THE course of human events, it becomes necessary for one portion of the family of man to assume among the people of the earth a position different from that which they have hitherto occupied, but one to which the laws of nature and of nature's God entitle them, a decent respect to the opinions of mankind requires that they should declare the causes that impel them to such a course.

We hold these truths to be self-evident: that all men and women are created equal; that they are endowed by their Creator with certain inalienable rights; that among these are life, liberty, and the pursuit of happiness; that to secure these rights governments are instituted, deriving their just powers from the consent of the governed. Whenever any form of government becomes destructive of these ends, it is the right of those who suffer from it to refuse allegiance to it, and to insist upon the institution of a new government, laying its foundation on such principles, and organizing its powers in such form, as to them shall seem most likely to effect their safety and happiness. Prudence indeed, will dictate that governments long established should not be changed for light and transient causes; and accordingly all experience hath shown that mankind are more disposed to suffer, while evils are sufferable, than to right themselves by abolishing the forms to which they were accustomed. But when a long train of abuses and usurpations, pursuing invariably the same object evinces a design to reduce them under absolute despotism, it is their duty to throw off such government, and to provide new guards for their future security. Such has been the patient sufferance of the women under this government, and such is now the necessity which constrains them to demand the equal station to which they are entitled.

Written and presented at the first U.S. women's rights convention, in Seneca Falls, New York, in 1848. Stanton published this version in A History of Woman Suffrage (1881), edited by herself, Susan B. Anthony, and Matilda Joslyn Gage, all prominent leaders of the American women's movement.

The history of mankind is a history of repeated injuries and usurpations on the part of man toward woman, having in direct object the establishment of an absolute tyranny over her. To prove this, let facts be submitted to a candid world.

He has never permitted her to exercise her inalienable right to the elective franchise.

5 He has compelled her to submit to laws, in the formation of which she had no voice.

He has withheld from her rights which are given to the most ignorant and degraded men—both natives and foreigners.

Having deprived her of this first right of a citizen, the elective franchise, thereby leaving her without representation in the halls of legislation, he has oppressed her on all sides.

He has made her, if married, in the eye of the law, civilly dead.

He has taken from her all right in property, even to the wages she earns.

10 He has made her, morally, an irresponsible being, as she can commit many crimes with impunity, provided they be done in the presence of her husband. In the covenant of marriage, she is compelled to promise obedience to her husband, he becoming, to all intents and purposes, her master—the law giving him power to deprive her of her liberty, and to administer chastisement.

He has so framed the laws of divorce, as to what shall be the proper causes, and in case of separation, to whom the guardianship of the children shall be given, as to be wholly regardless of the happiness of women—the law, in all cases, going upon a false supposition of the supremacy of man, and giving all power into his hands.

After depriving her of all rights as a married woman, if single, and the owner of property, he has taxed her to support a government which recognizes her only when her property can be made profitable to it.

He has monopolized nearly all the profitable employments, and from those she is permitted to follow, she receives but a scanty remuneration. He closes against her all the avenues to wealth and distinction which he considers most honorable to himself. As a teacher of theology, medicine, or law, she is not known.

He has denied her the facilities for obtaining a thorough education, all colleges being closed against her.

15 He allows her in Church, as well as State, but a subordinate position, claiming Apostolic authority for her exclusion from the ministry, and, with some exceptions, from any public participation in the affairs of the Church.

He has created a false public sentiment by giving to the world a different code of morals for men and women, by which moral delinquencies which exclude women from society, are not only tolerated, but deemed of little account in man.

He has usurped the prerogative of Jehovah himself, claiming it as his right to assign for her a sphere of action, when that belongs to her conscience and to her God.

He has endeavored, in every way that he could, to destroy her confidence in her own powers, to lessen her self-respect, and to make her willing to lead a dependent and abject life.

Now, in view of this entire disfranchisement of one-half the people of this country, their social and religious degradation—in view of the unjust laws above mentioned, and because women do feel themselves aggrieved, oppressed, and fraudulently deprived of their most sacred rights, we insist that they have immediate admission to all the rights and privileges which belong to them as citizens of the United States.

In entering upon the great work before us, we anticipate no small amount of misconception, misrepresentation, and ridicule; but we shall use every instrumentality within our power to effect our object. We shall employ agents, circulate tracts, petition the State and National legislatures, and endeavor to enlist the pulpit and the press in our behalf. We hope this Convention will be followed by a series of Conventions embracing every part of the country.

20

QUESTIONS

1. Stanton imitates both the argument and the style of the Declaration of Independence. Where does her declaration diverge from Jefferson's? For what purpose?

2. Stanton's declaration was presented at the first conference on women's rights, in Seneca Falls, New York, in 1848. Using books or Web resources, do research on this conference; then use your research to explain the political aims of one of the resolutions.

3. Write your own "declaration" of political, educational, or social rights, using the declarations of Jefferson and Stanton as models.

ABRAHAM LINCOLN *Second Inaugural Address*

A T THIS SECOND appearing to take the oath of the presidential office, there is less occasion for an extended address than there was at the first. Then a statement, somewhat in detail, of a course to be pursued, seemed fitting and proper. Now, at the expiration of four years, during which public declarations have been constantly called forth on every point and phase of the great contest which still absorbs the attention, and engrosses the energies of the nation, little that is new could be presented. The progress of our arms, upon which all else chiefly depends, is as well known to the public as to myself; and it is, I

Delivered on March 4, 1865, as Lincoln took office for a second term as America's sixteenth president. In the nineteenth century U.S. presidents took office in March, not in January as they do today.

trust, reasonably satisfactory and encouraging to all. With high hope for the future, no prediction in regard to it is ventured.

On the occasion corresponding to this four years ago, all thoughts were anxiously directed to an impending civil war. All dreaded it—all sought to avert it. While the inaugural address was being delivered from this place, devoted altogether to *saving* the Union without war, insurgent agents were in the city seeking to *destroy* it without war—seeking to dissolve the Union, and divide effects, by negotiation. Both parties deprecated war; but one of them would *make* war rather than let the nation survive; and the other would *accept* war rather than let it perish. And the war came.

One-eighth of the whole population were colored slaves, not distributed generally over the Union, but localized in the Southern part of it. These slaves constituted a peculiar and powerful interest. All knew that this interest was, somehow, the cause of the war. To strengthen, perpetuate, and extend this interest was the object for which the insurgents would rend the Union, even by war; while the government claimed no right to do more than to restrict the territorial enlargement of it. Neither party expected for the war, the magnitude, or the duration, which it has already attained. Neither anticipated that the *cause* of the conflict might cease with, or even before, the conflict itself should cease. Each looked for an easier triumph, and a result less fundamental and astounding. Both read the same Bible, and pray to the same God; and each invokes His aid against the other. It may seem strange that any men should dare to ask a just God's assistance in wringing their bread from the sweat of other men's faces; but let us judge not that we be not judged.[1] The prayers of both could not be answered; that of neither has been answered fully. The Almighty has His own purposes. "Woe unto the world because of offenses! for it must needs be that offenses come; but woe to that man by whom the offense cometh!"[2] If we shall suppose that American slavery is one of those offenses which, in the providence of God, must needs come, but which, having continued through His appointed time, He now wills to remove, and that He gives to both North and South, this terrible war, as the woe due to those by whom the offense came, shall we discern therein any departure from those divine attributes which the believers in a Living God always ascribe to Him? Fondly do we hope—fervently do we pray—that this mighty scourge of war may speedily pass away. Yet, if God wills that it continue, until all the wealth piled by the bondman's two hundred and fifty years of unrequited toil shall be sunk, and until every drop of blood drawn with the lash, shall be paid by another drawn with the sword, as was said three thousand years ago, so still it must be said "the judgments of the Lord are true and righteous altogether."[3]

With malice toward none; with charity for all; with firmness in the right,

---

1. Lincoln alludes to Jesus' statement in the Sermon on the Mount—"Judge not, that ye be not judged" (Matthew 7.1)—and to God's curse on Adam—"In the sweat of thy face shalt thou eat bread, till thou return unto the ground" (Genesis 3.19).

2. From Jesus' speech to his disciples (Matthew 18.7).

3. Psalms 19.9.

as God gives us to see the right, let us strive on to finish the work we are in; to bind up the nation's wounds; to care for him who shall have borne the battle, and for his widow, and his orphan—to do all which may achieve and cherish a just, and a lasting peace, among ourselves, and with all nations.

QUESTIONS

1. Lincoln's speech includes both allusions to and direct quotations from the Bible. What argument does he use these references to support? Why are biblical references important as a persuasive technique?

2. In paragraphs 1–2, Lincoln reflects on his first inaugural speech in order to set the stage for his present speech. Find a copy of the first inaugural speech online or in the library. In what ways does that thirty-five-paragraph speech help inform this four-paragraph speech? What aspects of the Second Inaugural Address does it clarify?

3. Read the text of a more recent presidential address and compare or contrast it to Lincoln's address. (John F. Kennedy's inaugural address is included in this section; others can be found online.) Does the more recent address use a similar style, language, or set of allusions? How does it differ?

JOHN F. KENNEDY   *Inaugural Address*

WE OBSERVE TODAY not a victory of a party but a celebration of freedom—symbolizing an end as well as a beginning—signifying renewal as well as change. For I have sworn before you and Almighty God the same solemn oath our forebears prescribed nearly a century and three quarters ago.

The world is very different now. For man holds in his mortal hands the power to abolish all forms of human poverty and all forms of human life. And yet the same revolutionary beliefs for which our forebears fought are still at issue around the globe—the belief that the rights of man come not from the generosity of the state but from the hand of God.

We dare not forget today that we are the heirs of that first revolution. Let the word go forth from this time and place, to friend and foe alike, that the torch has been passed to a new generation of Americans—born in this century, tempered by war, disciplined by a hard and bitter peace, proud of our ancient heritage—and unwilling to witness or permit the slow undoing of those human rights to which this nation has always been committed, and to which we are committed today at home and around the world.

The inaugural address of John F. Kennedy (1917–1963), America's thirty-fifth president, delivered on January 21, 1961.

Let every nation know, whether it wishes us well or ill, that we shall pay any price, bear any burden, meet any hardship, support any friend, oppose any foe to assure the survival and success of liberty.

5   This much we pledge—and more.

To those old allies whose cultural and spiritual origins we share, we pledge the loyalty of faithful friends. United, there is little we cannot do in a host of cooperative ventures. Divided, there is little we can do—for we dare not meet a powerful challenge at odds and split asunder.

To those new states whom we welcome to the ranks of the free, we pledge our word that one form of colonial control shall not have passed away merely to be replaced by a far more iron tyranny. We shall not always expect to find them supporting our view. But we shall always hope to find them strongly supporting their own freedom—and to remember that, in the past, those who foolishly sought power by riding the back of the tiger ended up inside.

To those peoples in the huts and villages of half the globe struggling to break the bonds of mass misery, we pledge our best efforts to help them help themselves, for whatever period is required—not because the Communists may be doing it, not because we seek their votes, but because it is right. If a free society cannot help the many who are poor, it cannot save the few who are rich.

To our sister republics south of our border,[1] we offer a special pledge— to convert our good words into good deeds—in a new alliance for progress—to assist free men and free governments in casting off the chains of poverty. But this peaceful revolution of hope cannot become the prey of hostile powers. Let all our neighbors know that we shall join with them to oppose aggression or subversion anywhere in the Americas. And let every other power know that this hemisphere intends to remain the master of its own house.

10   To that world assembly of sovereign states, the United Nations, our last best hope in an age where the instruments of war have far outpaced the instruments of peace, we renew our pledge of support—to prevent it from becoming merely a forum for invective—to strengthen its shield of the new and the weak—and to enlarge the area in which its writ may run.

Finally, to those nations who would make themselves our adversary, we offer not a pledge but a request: that both sides begin anew the quest for peace, before the dark powers of destruction unleashed by science[2] engulf all humanity in planned or accidental self-destruction.

We dare not tempt them with weakness. For only when our arms are sufficient beyond doubt can we be certain beyond doubt that they will never be employed.

But neither can two great and powerful groups of nations take comfort from our present course—both sides overburdened by the cost of modern weapons, both rightly alarmed by the steady spread of the deadly atom, yet both racing to alter that uncertain balance of terror that stays the hand of mankind's final war.

1. This paragraph is laced with references to Cuba, which by 1961 had turned to socialism under Fidel Castro and had allied itself with the Soviet Union.

2. A reference to atomic weapons.

So let us begin anew—remembering on both sides that civility is not a sign of weakness, and sincerity is always subject to proof. Let us never negotiate out of fear. But let us never fear to negotiate.

Let both sides explore what problems unite us instead of belaboring those problems which divide us. Let both sides, for the first time, formulate serious and precise proposals for the inspection and control of arms—and bring the absolute power to destroy other nations under the absolute control of all nations.

Let both sides seek to invoke the wonders of science instead of its terrors. Together let us explore the stars, conquer the deserts, eradicate disease, tap the ocean depths, and encourage the arts and commerce.

Let both sides unite to heed in all corners of the earth the command of Isaiah—to "undo the heavy burdens and to let the oppressed go free."[3]

And if a beachhead of cooperation may push back the jungle of suspicion, let both sides join in creating a new endeavor—not a new balance of power but a new world of law, where the strong are just and the weak secure and the peace preserved.

All this will not be finished in the first one hundred days. Nor will it be finished in the first one thousand days, nor in the life of this administration, nor even perhaps in our lifetime on this planet. But let us begin.

In your hands, my fellow citizens, more than mine, will rest the final success or failure of our course. Since this country was founded, each generation of Americans has been summoned to give testimony to its national loyalty. The graves of young Americans who answered the call to service surround the globe.

Now the trumpet summons us again—not as a call to bear arms, though arms we need—not as a call to battle, though embattled we are—but a call to bear the burden of a long twilight struggle, year in and year out, "rejoicing in hope, patient in tribulation"[4]—a struggle against the common enemies of man: tyranny, poverty, disease, and war itself.

Can we forge against these enemies a grand and global alliance, North and South, East and West, that can assure a more fruitful life for all mankind? Will you join in that historic effort?

In the long history of the world, only a few generations have been granted the role of defending freedom in its hour of maximum danger. I do not shrink from this responsibility—I welcome it. I do not believe that any of us would exchange places with any other people or any other generation. The energy, the faith, the devotion which we bring to this endeavor will light our country and all who serve it—and the glow from that fire can truly light the world.

And so, my fellow Americans, ask not what your country can do for you—ask what you can do for your country.

My fellow citizens of the world, ask not what America will do for you, but what together we can do for the freedom of man.

3. Isaiah 58.6.
4. Romans 12.12.

Finally, whether you are citizens of America or citizens of the world, ask of us here the same high standards of strength and sacrifice which we ask of you. With a good conscience our only sure reward, with history the final judge of our deeds, let us go forth to lead the land we love, asking His blessing and His help, but knowing that here on earth God's work must truly be our own.

QUESTIONS

1. Choose three rhetorical devices from this speech and show how they are constructed. What are their common elements? Their differences?

2. On what level of generality is Kennedy operating? When does he get specific?

3. Kennedy was the youngest man to be elected president. Speculate on how that fact might be reflected in this speech.

E. B. WHITE   *Democracy*

WE RECEIVED a letter from the Writers' War Board the other day asking for a statement on "The Meaning of Democracy." It presumably is our duty to comply with such a request, and it is certainly our pleasure.

Surely the Board knows what democracy is. It is the line that forms on the right. It is the don't in don't shove. It is the hole in the stuffed shirt through which the sawdust slowly trickles; it is the dent in the high hat. Democracy is the recurrent suspicion that more than half of the people are right more than half of the time. It is the feeling of privacy in the voting booths, the feeling of communion in the libraries, the feeling of vitality everywhere. Democracy is a letter to the editor. Democracy is the score at the beginning of the ninth. It is an idea which hasn't been disproved yet, a song the words of which have not gone bad. It's the mustard on the hot dog and the cream in the rationed coffee. Democracy is a request from a War Board, in the middle of a morning in the middle of a war, wanting to know what democracy is.

First appeared in the New Yorker *during World War II (July 3, 1943); later reprinted in* The Wild Flag (1946).

QUESTIONS

1. Consult a standard desk dictionary for the definition of "democracy." Of the several meanings given, which one best encompasses White's definitions? What other meanings do his definitions engage?

2. Translate White's examples into nonmetaphoric language. For example, "It is the line that forms on the right" might be translated as "It has no special privileges." Can "It is the don't in don't shove" also be translated as "It has no special privileges"? Consider what is lost in translation or, more important, what is gained by metaphor.

3. Using White's technique, write a definition for an abstract term; you might consider such terms as "generosity," "love," "sophistication," "tolerance," "virtue."

LANI GUINIER   *The Tyranny of the Majority*

I HAVE ALWAYS WANTED to be a civil rights lawyer. This lifelong ambition is based on a deep-seated commitment to democratic fair play—to playing by the rules as long as the rules are fair. When the rules seem unfair, I have worked to change them, not subvert them. When I was eight years old, I was a Brownie. I was especially proud of my uniform, which represented a commitment to good citizenship and good deeds. But one day, when my Brownie group staged a hatmaking contest, I realized that uniforms are only as honorable as the people who wear them. The contest was rigged. The winner was assisted by her milliner mother, who actually made the winning entry in full view of all the participants. At the time, I was too young to be able to change the rules, but I was old enough to resign, which I promptly did.

To me, fair play means that the rules encourage everyone to play. They should reward those who win, but they must be acceptable to those who lose. The central theme of my academic writing is that not all rules lead to elemental fair play. Some even commonplace rules work against it.

The professional milliner competing with amateur Brownies stands as an example of rules that are patently rigged or patently subverted. Yet, sometimes, even when rules are perfectly fair in form, they serve in practice to exclude particular groups from meaningful participation. When they do not encourage everyone to play, or when, over the long haul, they do not make the losers feel as good about the outcomes as the winners, they can seem as unfair as the milliner who makes the winning hat for her daughter.

Sometimes, too, we construct rules that force us to be divided into winners and losers when we might have otherwise joined together. This idea was cogently expressed by my son, Nikolas, when he was four years old, far exceeding the thoughtfulness of his mother when she was an eight-year-old Brownie. While I was writing one of my law journal articles, Nikolas and I had a conversation about voting prompted by a *Sesame Street Magazine* exercise. The maga-

From The Tyranny of the Majority *(1994), a collection of essays on affirmative action published after Guinier's unsuccessful nomination for assistant attorney general for civil rights in 1993. In it she clarifies her views on democracy, political equality, and majority rule.*

zine pictured six children: four children had raised their hands because they wanted to play tag; two had their hands down because they wanted to play hide-and-seek. The magazine asked its readers to count the number of children whose hands were raised and then decide what game the children would play.

5   Nikolas quite realistically replied, "They will play both. First they will play tag. Then they will play hide-and-seek." Despite the magazine's "rules," he was right. To children, it is natural to take turns. The winner may get to play first or more often, but even the "loser" gets something. His was a positive-sum solution that many adult rule-makers ignore.

The traditional answer to the magazine's problem would have been a zero-sum solution: "The children—all the children—will play tag, and only tag." As a zero-sum solution, everything is seen in terms of "I win; you lose." The conventional answer relies on winner-take-all majority rule, in which the tag players, as the majority, win the right to decide for all the children what game to play. The hide-and-seek preference becomes irrelevant. The numerically more powerful majority choice simply subsumes minority preferences.

In the conventional case, the majority that rules gains all the power and the minority that loses gets none. For example, two years ago Brother Rice High School in Chicago held two senior proms. It was not planned that way. The prom committee at Brother Rice, a boys' Catholic high school, expected just one prom when it hired a disc jockey, picked a rock band, and selected music for the prom by consulting student preferences. Each senior was asked to list his three favorite songs, and the band would play the songs that appeared most frequently on the lists.

Seems attractively democratic. But Brother Rice is predominantly white, and the prom committee was all white. That's how they got two proms. The black seniors at Brother Rice felt so shut out by the "democratic process" that they organized their own prom. As one black student put it: "For every vote we had, there were eight votes for what they wanted. . . . [W]ith us being in the minority we're always outvoted. It's as if we don't count."

Some embittered white seniors saw things differently. They complained that the black students should have gone along with the majority: "The majority makes a decision. That's the way it works."

10   In a way, both groups were right. From the white students' perspective, this was ordinary decisionmaking. To the black students, majority rule sent the message: "we don't count" is the "way it works" for minorities. In a racially divided society, majority rule may be perceived as majority tyranny.

That is a large claim, and I do not rest my case for it solely on the actions of the prom committee in one Chicago high school. To expand the range of the argument, I first consider the ideal of majority rule itself, particularly as reflected in the writings of James Madison[1] and other founding members of our Republic. These early democrats explored the relationship between majority rule and democracy. James Madison warned, "If a majority be united by a

1. Founding Father (1751–1836) and fourth president of the United States, from 1809 to 1817.

common interest, the rights of the minority will be insecure." The tyranny of the majority, according to Madison, requires safeguards to protect "one part of the society against the injustice of the other part."

For Madison, majority tyranny represented the great danger to our early constitutional democracy. Although the American revolution was fought against the tyranny of the British monarch, it soon became clear that there was another tyranny to be avoided. The accumulations of all powers in the same hands, Madison warned, "whether of one, a few, or many, and whether hereditary, self-appointed, or elective, may justly be pronounced the very definition of tyranny."

As another colonist suggested in papers published in Philadelphia, "We have been so long habituated to a jealousy of tyranny from monarchy and aristocracy, that we have yet to learn the dangers of it from democracy." Despotism had to be opposed "whether it came from Kings, Lords or the people."

The debate about majority tyranny reflected Madison's concern that the majority may not represent the whole. In a homogeneous society, the interest of the majority would likely be that of the minority also. But in a heterogeneous community, the majority may not represent all competing interests. The majority is likely to be self-interested and ignorant or indifferent to the concerns of the minority. In such case, Madison observed, the assumption that the majority represents the minority is "altogether fictitious."

Yet even a self-interested majority can govern fairly if it cooperates with the minority. One reason for such cooperation is that the self-interested majority values the principle of reciprocity. The self-interested majority worries that the minority may attract defectors from the majority and become the next governing majority. The Golden Rule principle of reciprocity functions to check the tendency of a self-interested majority to act tyrannically.

15

So the argument for the majority principle connects it with the value of reciprocity: You cooperate when you lose in part because members of the current majority will cooperate when they lose. The conventional case for the fairness of majority rule is that it is not really the rule of a fixed group—The Majority—on all issues; instead it is the rule of shifting majorities, as the losers at one time or on one issue join with others and become part of the governing coalition at another time or on another issue. The result will be a fair system of mutually beneficial cooperation. I call a majority that rules but does not dominate a Madisonian Majority.

The problem of majority tyranny arises, however, when the self-interested majority does not need to worry about defections. When the majority is fixed and permanent, there are no checks on its ability to be overbearing. A majority that does not worry about defectors is a majority with total power.

In such a case, Madison's concern about majority tyranny arises. In a heterogeneous community, any faction with total power might subject "the minority to the caprice and arbitrary decisions of the majority, who instead of consulting the interest of the whole community collectively, attend sometimes to partial and local advantages."

"What remedy can be found in a republican Government, where the majority must ultimately decide," argued Madison, but to ensure "that no one common interest or passion will be likely to unite a majority of the whole number in an unjust pursuit." The answer was to disaggregate the majority to ensure checks and balances or fluid, rotating interests. The minority needed protection against an overbearing majority, so that "a common sentiment is less likely to be felt, and the requisite concert less likely to be formed, by a majority of the whole."

20   Political struggles would not be simply a contest between rulers and people; the political struggles would be among the people themselves. The work of government was not to transcend different interests but to reconcile them. In an ideal democracy, the people would rule, but the minorities would also be protected against the power of majorities. Again, where the rules of decision-making protect the minority, the Madisonian Majority rules without dominating.

But if a group is unfairly treated, for example, when it forms a racial minority, *and* if the problems of unfairness are not cured by conventional assumptions about majority rule, then what is to be done? The answer is that we may need an *alternative* to winner-take-all majoritarianism. In this book, a collection of my law review articles, I describe the alternative, which, with Nikolas's help, I now call the "principle of taking turns." In a racially divided society, this principle does better than simple majority rule if it accommodates the values of self-government, fairness, deliberation, compromise, and consensus that lie at the heart of the democratic ideal.

In my legal writing, I follow the caveat of James Madison and other early American democrats. I explore decisionmaking rules that might work in a multi-racial society to ensure that majority rule does not become majority tyranny. I pursue voting systems that might disaggregate The Majority so that it does not exercise power unfairly or tyrannically. I aspire to a more cooperative political style of decisionmaking to enable all of the students at Brother Rice to feel comfortable attending the same prom. In looking to create Madisonian Majorities, I pursue a positive-sum, taking-turns solution.

Structuring decisionmaking to allow the minority "a turn" may be necessary to restore the reciprocity ideal when a fixed majority refuses to cooperate with the minority. If the fixed majority loses its incentive to follow the Golden Rule principle of shifting majorities, the minority never gets to take a turn. Giving the minority a turn does not mean the minority gets to rule; what it does mean is that the minority gets to influence decisionmaking and the majority rules more legitimately.

Instead of automatically rewarding the preferences of the monolithic majority, a taking-turns approach anticipates that the majority rules, but is not overbearing. Because those with 51 percent of the votes are not assured 100 percent of the power, the majority cooperates with, or at least does not tyrannize, the minority.

The sports analogy of "I win; you lose" competition within a political hierarchy makes sense when only one team can win; Nikolas's intuition that it is often possible to take turns suggests an alternative approach. Take family decisionmaking, for example. It utilizes a taking-turns approach. When parents sit around the kitchen table deciding on a vacation destination or activities for a rainy day, often they do not simply rely on a show of hands, especially if that means that the older children always prevail or if affinity groups among the children (those who prefer movies to video games, or those who prefer baseball to playing cards) never get to play their activity of choice. Instead of allowing the majority simply to rule, the parents may propose that everyone take turns, going to the movies one night and playing video games the next. Or as Nikolas proposes, they might do both on a given night.

Taking turns attempts to build consensus while recognizing political or social differences, and it encourages everyone to play. The taking-turns approach gives those with the most support more turns, but it also legitimates the outcome from each individual's perspective, including those whose views are shared only by a minority.

In the end, I do not believe that democracy should encourage rule by the powerful—even a powerful majority. Instead, the idea of democracy promises a fair discussion among self-defined equals about how to achieve our common aspirations. To redeem that promise, we need to put the idea of taking turns and disaggregating the majority at the center of our conception of representation. Particularly as we move into the twenty-first century as a more highly diversified citizenry, it is essential that we consider the ways in which voting and representational systems succeed or fail at encouraging Madisonian Majorities.

To use Nikolas's terminology, "it is no fair" if a fixed, tyrannical majority excludes or alienates the minority. It is no fair if a fixed, tyrannical majority monopolizes all the power all the time. It is no fair if we engage in the periodic ritual of elections, but only the permanent majority gets to choose who is elected. Where we have tyranny by The Majority, we do not have genuine democracy.

QUESTIONS

1. Throughout her essay, Guinier uses personal anecdotes to support and illustrate her argument. Which one do you think best supports her points? Why?

2. In her final paragraph Guinier repeats the phrase "it is no fair" three times in three successive sentences. Why does Guinier deliberately repeat this phrase? What is the effect?

3. Think of a time when you—in either a majority or a minority position—used cooperation or "turn-taking" to build consensus. Write an essay about that experience.

Martin Luther King Jr. *Letter from Birmingham Jail*[1]

Y Dear Fellow Clergymen:

While confined here in the Birmingham city jail, I came across your recent statement calling my present activities "unwise and untimely." Seldom do I pause to answer criticism of my work and ideas. If I sought to answer all the criticisms that cross my desk, my secretaries would have little time for anything other than such correspondence in the course of the day, and I would have no time for constructive work. But since I feel that you are men of genuine good will and that your criticisms are sincerely set forth, I want to try to answer your statement in what I hope will be patient and reasonable terms.

I think I should indicate why I am here in Birmingham, since you have been influenced by the view which argues against "outsiders coming in." I have the honor of serving as president of the Southern Christian Leadership Conference, an organization operating in every southern state, with headquarters in Atlanta, Georgia. We have some eighty-five affiliated organizations across the South, and one of them is the Alabama Christian Movement for Human Rights. Frequently we share staff, educational, and financial resources with our affiliates. Several months ago the affiliate here in Birmingham asked us to be on call to engage in a nonviolent direct-action program if such were deemed necessary. We readily consented, and when the hour came we lived up to our promise. So I, along with several members of my staff, am here because I was invited here. I am here because I have organizational ties here.

But more basically, I am in Birmingham because injustice is here. Just as the prophets of the eighth century B.C. left their villages and carried their "thus saith the Lord" far beyond the boundaries of their home towns, and just as the Apostle Paul left his village of Tarsus and carried the gospel of Jesus Christ to the far corners of the Greco-Roman world, so am I compelled to carry the gospel of freedom beyond my own home town. Like Paul, I must constantly respond to the Macedonian call for aid.

Moreover, I am cognizant of the interrelatedness of all communities and states. I cannot sit idly by in Atlanta and not be concerned about what hap-

Written on April 16, 1963, while King was jailed for civil disobedience; subsequently published in Why We Can't Wait *(1964).*

1. This response to a published statement by eight fellow clergymen from Alabama (Bishop C. C. J. Carpenter, Bishop Joseph A. Durick, Rabbi Milton L. Grafman, Bishop Paul Hardin, Bishop Holan B. Harmon, the Reverend George M. Murray, the Reverend Edward V. Ramage and the Reverend Earl Stallings) was composed under somewhat constricting circumstances. Begun on the margins of the newspaper in which the statement appeared while I was in jail, the letter was continued on scraps of writing paper supplied by a friendly Negro trusty, and concluded on a pad my attorneys were eventually permitted to leave me. Although the text remains in substance unaltered, I have indulged in the author's prerogative of polishing it for publication [King's note].

pens in Birmingham. Injustice anywhere is a threat to justice everywhere. We are caught in an inescapable network of mutuality, tied in a single garment of destiny. Whatever affects one directly, affects all indirectly. Never again can we afford to live with the narrow, provincial "outside agitator" idea. Anyone who lives inside the United States can never be considered an outsider anywhere within its bounds.

You deplore the demonstrations taking place in Birmingham. But your statement, I am sorry to say, fails to express a similar concern for the conditions that brought about the demonstrations. I am sure that none of you would want to rest content with the superficial kind of social analysis that deals merely with effects and does not grapple with underlying causes. It is unfortunate that demonstrations are taking place in Birmingham, but it is even more unfortunate that the city's white power structure left the Negro community with no alternative. 5

In any nonviolent campaign there are four basic steps: collection of the facts to determine whether injustices exist; negotiation; self-purification; and direct action. We have gone through all these steps in Birmingham. There can be no gainsaying the fact that racial injustice engulfs this community. Birmingham is probably the most thoroughly segregated city in the United States. Its ugly record of brutality is widely known. Negroes have experienced grossly unjust treatment in the courts. There have been more unsolved bombings of Negro homes and churches in Birmingham than in any other city in the nation. These are the hard, brutal facts of the case. On the basis of these conditions, Negro leaders sought to negotiate with the city fathers. But the latter consistently refused to engage in good-faith negotiation.

Then, last September, came the opportunity to talk with leaders of Birmingham's economic community. In the course of the negotiations, certain promises were made by the merchants—for example, to remove the stores' humiliating racial signs. On the basis of these promises, the Reverend Fred Shuttlesworth and the leaders of the Alabama Christian Movement for Human Rights agreed to a moratorium on all demonstrations. As the weeks and months went by, we realized that we were the victims of a broken promise. A few signs, briefly removed, returned; the others remained.

As in so many past experiences, our hopes had been blasted, and the shadow of deep disappointment settled upon us. We had no alternative except to prepare for direct action, whereby we would present our very bodies as a means of laying our case before the conscience of the local and the national community. Mindful of the difficulties involved, we decided to undertake a process of self-purification. We began a series of workshops on nonviolence, and we repeatedly asked ourselves: "Are you able to accept blows without retaliating?" "Are you able to endure the ordeal of jail?" We decided to schedule our direct-action program for the Easter season, realizing that except for Christmas, this is the main shopping period of the year. Knowing that a strong economic-withdrawal program would be the by-product of direct action, we felt that this would be the best time to bring pressure to bear on the merchants for the needed change.

Then it occurred to us that Birmingham's mayoral election was coming up in March, and we speedily decided to postpone action until after election day. When we discovered that the Commissioner of Public Safety, Eugene "Bull" Connor, had piled up enough votes to be in the run-off, we decided again to postpone action until the day after the run-off so that the demonstrations could not be used to cloud the issues. Like many others, we wanted to see Mr. Connor defeated, and to this end we endured postponement after postponement. Having aided in this community need, we felt that our direct-action program could be delayed no longer.

10   You may well ask, "Why direct action? Why sit-ins, marches, and so forth? Isn't negotiation a better path?" You are quite right in calling for negotiation. Indeed, this is the very purpose of direct action. Nonviolent direct action seeks to create such a crisis and foster such a tension that a community which has constantly refused to negotiate is forced to confront the issue. It seeks so to dramatize the issue that it can no longer be ignored. My citing the creation of tension as part of the work of the nonviolent-resister may sound rather shocking. But I must confess that I am not afraid of the word "tension." I have earnestly opposed violent tension, but there is a type of constructive, nonviolent tension which is necessary for growth. Just as Socrates felt that it was necessary to create a tension in the mind so that individuals could rise from the bondage of myths and half-truths to the unfettered realm of creative analysis and objective appraisal, so must we see the need for nonviolent gadflies to create the kind of tension in society that will help men rise from the dark depths of prejudice and racism to the majestic heights of understanding and brotherhood.

The purpose of our direct-action program is to create a situation so crisis-packed that it will inevitably open the door to negotiation. I therefore concur with you in your call for negotiation. Too long has our beloved Southland been bogged down in a tragic effort to live in monologue rather than dialogue.

One of the basic points in your statement is that the action that I and my associates have taken in Birmingham is untimely. Some have asked: "Why didn't you give the new city administration time to act?" The only answer that I can give to this query is that the new Birmingham administration must be prodded about as much as the outgoing one, before it will act. We are sadly mistaken if we feel that the election of Albert Boutwell as mayor will bring the millennium to Birmingham. While Mr. Boutwell is a much more gentle person than Mr. Connor, they are both segregationists, dedicated to maintenance of the status quo. I have hoped that Mr. Boutwell will be reasonable enough to see the futility of massive resistance to desegregation. But he will not see this without pressure from devotees of civil rights. My friends, I must say to you that we have not made a single gain in civil rights without determined legal and nonviolent pressure. Lamentably, it is an historical fact that privileged groups seldom give up their privileges voluntarily. Individuals may see the moral light and voluntarily give up their unjust posture; but, as Reinhold Niebuhr[2] has reminded us, groups tend to be more immoral than individuals.

2. American Protestant theologian (1892–1971).

We know through painful experience that freedom is never voluntarily given by the oppressor; it must be demanded by the oppressed. Frankly, I have yet to engage in a direct-action campaign that was "well timed" in the view of those who have not suffered unduly from the disease of segregation. For years now I have heard the word "Wait!" It rings in the ear of every Negro with piercing familiarity. This "Wait" has almost always meant "Never." We must come to see, with one of our distinguished jurists, that "justice too long delayed is justice denied."

We have waited for more than 340 years for our constitutional and God-given rights. The nations of Asia and Africa are moving with jetlike speed toward gaining political independence, but we still creep at horse-and-buggy pace toward gaining a cup of coffee at a lunch counter. Perhaps it is easy for those who have never felt the stinging darts of segregation to say, "Wait." But when you have seen vicious mobs lynch your mothers and fathers at will and drown your sisters and brothers at whim; when you have seen hate-filled policemen curse, kick, and even kill your black brothers and sisters; when you see the vast majority of your twenty million Negro brothers smothering in an airtight cage of poverty in the midst of an affluent society; when you suddenly find your tongue twisted and your speech stammering as you seek to explain to your six-year-old daughter why she can't go to the public amusement park that has just been advertised on television, and see tears welling up in her eyes when she is told that Funtown is closed to colored children, and see ominous clouds of inferiority beginning to form in her little mental sky, and see her beginning to distort her personality by developing an unconscious bitterness toward white people; when you have to concoct an answer for a five-year-old son who is asking, "Daddy, why do white people treat colored people so mean?"; when you take a cross-country drive and find it necessary to sleep night after night in the uncomfortable corners of your automobile because no motel will accept you; when you are humiliated day in and day out by nagging signs reading "white" and "colored"; when your first name becomes "nigger," your middle name becomes "boy" (however old you are) and your last name becomes "John," and your wife and mother are never given the respected title "Mrs."; when you are harried by day and haunted by night by the fact that you are a Negro, living constantly at tiptoe stance, never quite knowing what to expect next, and are plagued with inner fears and outer resentments; when you are forever fighting a degenerating sense of "nobodiness"—then you will understand why we find it difficult to wait. There comes a time when the cup of endurance runs over, and men are no longer willing to be plunged into the abyss of despair. I hope, sirs, you can understand our legitimate and unavoidable impatience.

You express a great deal of anxiety over our willingness to break laws. This   15
is certainly a legitimate concern. Since we so diligently urge people to obey the Supreme Court's decision of 1954 outlawing segregation in the public schools, at first glance it may seem rather paradoxical for us consciously to break laws. One may well ask: "How can you advocate breaking some laws and obeying others?" The answer lies in the fact that there are two types of laws: just and unjust. I would be the first to advocate obeying just laws. One has not only a

legal but a moral responsibility to obey just laws. Conversely, one has a moral responsibility to disobey unjust laws. I would agree with St. Augustine[3] that "an unjust law is no law at all."

Now, what is the difference between the two? How does one determine whether a law is just or unjust? A just law is a man-made code that squares with the moral law or the law of God. An unjust law is a code that is out of harmony with the moral law. To put it in the terms of St. Thomas Aquinas:[4] An unjust law is a human law that is not rooted in eternal law and natural law. Any law that uplifts human personality is just. Any law that degrades human personality is unjust. All segregation statutes are unjust because segregation distorts the soul and damages the personality. It gives the segregator a false sense of superiority and the segregated a false sense of inferiority. Segregation, to use the terminology of the Jewish philosopher Martin Buber,[5] substitutes an "I-it" relationship for an "I-thou" relationship and ends up relegating persons to the status of things. Hence segregation is not only politically, economically, and sociologically unsound, it is morally wrong and sinful. Paul Tillich[6] has said that sin is separation. Is not segregation an existential expression of man's tragic separation, his awful estrangement, his terrible sinfulness? Thus it is that I can urge men to obey the 1954 decision of the Supreme Court, for it is morally right; and I can urge them to disobey segregation ordinances, for they are morally wrong.

Let us consider a more concrete example of just and unjust laws. An unjust law is a code that a numerical or power majority group compels a minority group to obey but does not make binding on itself. This is *difference* made legal. By the same token, a just law is a code that a majority compels a minority to follow and that it is willing to follow itself. This is *sameness* made legal.

Let me give another explanation. A law is unjust if it is inflicted on a minority that, as a result of being denied the right to vote, had no part in enacting or devising the law. Who can say that the legislature of Alabama which set up that state's segregation laws was democratically elected? Throughout Alabama all sorts of devious methods are used to prevent Negroes from becoming registered voters, and there are some counties in which, even though Negroes constitute a majority of the population, not a single Negro is registered. Can any law enacted under such circumstances be considered democratically structured?

Sometimes a law is just on its face and unjust in its application. For instance, I have been arrested on a charge of parading without a permit. Now, there is nothing wrong in having an ordinance which requires a permit for a parade. But such an ordinance becomes unjust when it is used to maintain segregation and to deny citizens the First-Amendment privilege of peaceful assembly and protest.

3. Early Christian church father (354–430).
4. Christian philosopher and theologian (1225–1274).
5. German-born Israeli philosopher (1878–1965).
6. German-born American Protestant theologian (1886–1965).

I hope you are able to see the distinction I am trying to point out. In no 20 sense do I advocate evading or defying the law, as would the rabid segregationist. That would lead to anarchy. One who breaks an unjust law must do so openly, lovingly, and with a willingness to accept the penalty. I submit that an individual who breaks a law that conscience tells him is unjust, and who willingly accepts the penalty of imprisonment in order to arouse the conscience of the community over its injustice, is in reality expressing the highest respect for law.

Of course, there is nothing new about this kind of civil disobedience. It was evidenced sublimely in the refusal of Shadrach, Meshach, and Abednego to obey the laws of Nebuchadnezzar,[7] on the ground that a higher moral law was at stake. It was practiced superbly by the early Christians, who were willing to face hungry lions and the excruciating pain of chopping blocks rather than submit to certain unjust laws of the Roman Empire. To a degree, academic freedom is a reality today because Socrates practiced civil disobedience.[8] In our own nation, the Boston Tea Party represented a massive act of civil disobedience.

We should never forget that everything Adolf Hitler did in Germany was "legal" and everything the Hungarian freedom fighters[9] did in Hungary was "illegal." It was "illegal" to aid and comfort a Jew in Hitler's Germany. Even so, I am sure that, had I lived in Germany at the time, I would have aided and comforted my Jewish brothers. If today I lived in a Communist country where certain principles dear to the Christian faith are suppressed, I would openly advocate disobeying that country's anti-religious laws.

I must make two honest confessions to you, my Christian and Jewish brothers. First, I must confess that over the past few years I have been gravely disappointed with the white moderate. I have almost reached the regrettable conclusion that the Negro's great stumbling block in his stride toward freedom is not the White Citizen's Counciler or the Ku Klux Klanner, but the white moderate, who is more devoted to "order" than to justice; who prefers a negative peace which is the absence of tension to a positive peace which is the presence of justice; who constantly says, "I agree with you in the goal you seek, but I cannot agree with your methods of direct action"; who paternalistically believes he can set the timetable for another man's freedom; who lives by a mythical concept of time and who constantly advises the Negro to wait for a "more convenient season." Shallow understanding from people of good will is more frustrating than absolute misunderstanding from people of ill will. Lukewarm acceptance is much more bewildering than outright rejection.

I had hoped that the white moderate would understand that law and order exist for the purpose of establishing justice and that when they fail in this pur-

7. Their story is told in Daniel 3.

8. The ancient Greek philosopher Socrates was tried by the Athenians for corrupting their youth through his skeptical, questioning manner of teaching. He refused to change his ways and was condemned to death.

9. In the anti-Communist revolution of 1956, which was quickly put down by the Soviet army.

pose they become the dangerously structured dams that block the flow of social progress. I had hoped that the white moderate would understand that the
present tension in the South is a necessary phase of the transition from an ob-
noxious negative peace, in which the Negro passively accepted his unjust
plight, to a substantive and positive peace, in which all men will respect the
dignity and worth of human personality. Actually, we who engage in nonviolent
direct action are not the creators of tension. We merely bring to the surface
the hidden tension that is already alive. We bring it out in the open, where it
can be seen and dealt with. Like a boil that can never be cured so long as it is
covered up but must be opened with all its ugliness to the natural medicines
of air and light, injustice must be exposed, with all the tension its exposure
creates, to the light of human conscience and the air of national opinion, before it can be cured.

25   In your statement you assert that our actions, even though peaceful, must
be condemned because they precipitate violence. But is this a logical assertion? Isn't this like condemning a robbed man because his possession of
money precipitated the evil act of robbery? Isn't this like condemning Socrates because his unswerving commitment to truth and his philosophical in-
quiries precipitated the act by the misguided populace in which they made
him drink hemlock? Isn't this like condemning Jesus because his unique God-
consciousness and never-ceasing devotion to God's will precipitated the evil
act of crucifixion? We must come to see that, as the federal courts have consistently affirmed, it is wrong to urge an individual to cease his efforts to gain
his basic constitutional rights because the quest may precipitate violence. Society must protect the robbed and punish the robber.

I had also hoped that the white moderate would reject the myth concerning time in relation to the struggle for freedom. I have just received a letter
from a white brother in Texas. He writes: "All Christians know that the colored
people will receive equal rights eventually, but it is possible that you are in too
great a religious hurry. It has taken Christianity almost two thousand years to
accomplish what it has. The teachings of Christ take time to come to earth."
Such an attitude stems from a tragic misconception of time, from the
strangely irrational notion that there is something in the very flow of time that
will inevitably cure all ills. Actually, time itself is neutral; it can be used either
destructively or constructively. More and more I feel that the people of ill will
have used time much more effectively than have the people of good will. We
will have to repent in this generation not merely for the hateful words and actions of the bad people, but for the appalling silence of the good people. Human progress never rolls in on wheels of inevitability; it comes through the
tireless efforts of men willing to be co-workers with God, and without this
hard work, time itself becomes an ally of the forces of social stagnation. We
must use time creatively, in the knowledge that the time is always ripe to do
right. Now is the time to make real the promise of democracy and transform
our pending national elegy into a creative psalm of brotherhood. Now is the
time to lift our national policy from the quicksand of racial injustice to the
solid rock of human dignity.

You speak of our activity in Birmingham as extreme. At first I was rather disappointed that fellow clergymen would see my nonviolent efforts as those of an extremist. I began thinking about the fact that I stand in the middle of two opposing forces in the Negro community. One is a force of complacency, made up in part of Negroes who, as a result of long years of oppression, are so drained of self-respect and a sense of "somebodiness" that they have adjusted to segregation; and in part of a few middle-class Negroes who, because of a degree of academic and economic security and because in some ways they profit by segregation, have become insensitive to the problems of the masses. The other force is one of bitterness and hatred, and it comes perilously close to advocating violence. It is expressed in the various black nationalist groups that are springing up across the nation, the largest and best-known being Elijah Muhammad's Muslim movement.[10] Nourished by the Negro's frustration over the continued existence of racial discrimination, this movement is made up of people who have lost faith in America, who have absolutely repudiated Christianity, and who have concluded that the white man is an incorrigible "devil."

I have tried to stand between these two forces, saying that we need emulate neither the "do-nothingism" of the complacent nor the hatred and despair of the black nationalist. For there is the more excellent way of love and nonviolent protest. I am grateful to God that, through the influence of the Negro church, the way of nonviolence became an integral part of our struggle.

If this philosophy had not emerged, by now many streets of the South would, I am convinced, be flowing with blood. And I am further convinced that if our white brothers dismiss as "rabblerousers" and "outside agitators" those of us who employ nonviolent direct action, and if they refuse to support our nonviolent efforts, millions of Negroes will, out of frustration and despair, seek solace and security in black-nationalist ideologies—a development that would inevitably lead to a frightening racial nightmare.

Oppressed people cannot remain oppressed forever. The yearning for freedom eventually manifests itself, and that is what has happened to the American Negro. Something within has reminded him of his birthright of freedom, and something without has reminded him that it can be gained. Consciously or unconsciously, he has been caught up by the *Zeitgeist*,[11] and with his black brothers of Africa and his brown and yellow brothers of Asia, South America, and the Caribbean, the United States Negro is moving with a sense of great urgency toward the promised land of racial justice. If one recognizes this vital urge that has engulfed the Negro community, one should readily understand why public demonstrations are taking place. The Negro has many pent-up resentments and latent frustrations, and he must release them. So let him march; let him make prayer pilgrimages to the city hall; let him go on freedom rides—and try to understand why he must do so. If his repressed emotions are not released in nonviolent ways, they will seek expression through violence;

10. Elijah Muhammed (1897–1975) succeeded to the leadership of the Nation of Islam in 1934.
11. The spirit of the times.

this is not a threat but a fact of history. So I have not said to my people, "Get rid of your discontent." Rather, I have tried to say that this normal and healthy discontent can be channeled into the creative outlet of nonviolent direct action. And now this approach is being termed extremist.

But though I was initially disappointed at being categorized as an extremist, as I continued to think about the matter I gradually gained a measure of satisfaction from the label. Was not Jesus an extremist for love: "Love your enemies, bless them that curse you, do good to them that hate you, and pray for them which despitefully use you, and persecute you." Was not Amos an extremist for justice: "Let justice roll down like waters and righteousness like an ever-flowing stream." Was not Paul an extremist for the Christian gospel: "I bear in my body the marks of the Lord Jesus." Was not Martin Luther an extremist: "Here I stand; I cannot do otherwise, so help me God." And John Bunyan:[12] "I will stay in jail to the end of my days before I make a butchery of my conscience." And Abraham Lincoln: "This nation cannot survive half slave and half free." And Thomas Jefferson: "We hold these truths to be self-evident, that all men are created equal. . . ." So the question is not whether we will be extremists, but what kind of extremists we will be. Will we be extremists for hate or for love? Will we be extremists for the preservation of injustice or for the extension of justice? In that dramatic scene on Calvary's hill three men were crucified. We must never forget that all three were crucified for the same crime—the crime of extremism. Two were extremists for immorality, and thus fell below their environment. The other, Jesus Christ, was an extremist for love, truth, and goodness, and thereby rose above his environment. Perhaps the South, the nation, and the world are in dire need of creative extremists.

I had hoped that the white moderate would see this need. Perhaps I was too optimistic; perhaps I expected too much. I suppose I should have realized that few members of the oppressor race can understand the deep groans and passionate yearnings of the oppressed race, and still fewer have the vision to see that injustice must be rooted out by strong, persistent, and determined action. I am thankful, however, that some of our white brothers in the South have grasped the meaning of this social revolution and committed themselves to it. They are still all too few in quantity, but they are big in quality. Some—such as Ralph McGill, Lillian Smith, Harry Golden, James McBridge Dabbs, Ann Braden, and Sarah Patton Boyle—have written about our struggle in eloquent and prophetic terms. Others have marched with us down nameless streets of the South. They have languished in filthy, roach-infested jails, suffering the abuse and brutality of policemen who view them as "dirty nigger-lovers." Unlike so many of their moderate brothers and sisters, they have recognized the urgency of the moment and sensed the need for powerful "action" antidotes to combat the disease of segregation.

Let me take note of my other major disappointment. I have been so

---

12. Amos was an Old Testament prophet; Paul a New Testament apostle; Luther (1483–1546), German Protestant reformer; Bunyan, English preacher and author (1628–1688).

greatly disappointed with the white church and its leadership. Of course, there are some notable exceptions. I am not unmindful of the fact that each of you has taken some significant stands on this issue. I commend you, Reverend Stallings, for your Christian stand on this past Sunday, in welcoming Negroes to your worship service on a nonsegregated basis. I commend the Catholic leaders of this state for integrating Spring Hill College several years ago.

But despite these notable exceptions, I must honestly reiterate that I have been disappointed with the church. I do not say this as one of those negative critics who can always find something wrong with the church. I say this as a minister of the gospel, who loves the church; who was nurtured in its bosom; who has been sustained by its spiritual blessings and who will remain true to it as long as the cord of life shall lengthen.

When I was suddenly catapulted into the leadership of the bus protest in Montgomery, Alabama, a few years ago,[13] I felt we would be supported by the white church. I felt that the white ministers, priests, and rabbis of the South would be among our strongest allies. Instead, some have been outright opponents, refusing to understand the freedom movement and misrepresenting its leaders; all too many others have been more cautious than courageous and have remained silent behind the anesthetizing security of stained-glass windows. 35

In spite of my shattered dreams, I came to Birmingham with the hope that the white religious leadership of this community would see the justice of our cause and, with deep moral concern, would serve as the channel through which our just grievances could reach the power structure. I had hoped that each of you would understand. But again I have been disappointed.

I have heard numerous southern religious leaders admonish their worshipers to comply with a desegregation decision because it is the law, but I have longed to hear white ministers declare: "Follow this decree because integration is morally right and because the Negro is your brother." In the midst of blatant injustices inflicted upon the Negro, I have watched white churchmen stand on the sideline and mouth pious irrelevancies and sanctimonious trivialities. In the midst of a mighty struggle to rid our nation of racial and economic injustice, I have heard many ministers say: "Those are social issues, with which the gospel has no real concern." And I have watched many churches commit themselves to a completely otherworldly religion which makes a strange, un-Biblical distinction between body and soul, between the sacred and the secular.

I have traveled the length and breadth of Alabama, Mississippi, and all the other southern states. On sweltering summer days and crisp autumn mornings I have looked at the South's beautiful churches with their lofty spires pointing heavenward. I have beheld the impressive outlines of her massive religious-education buildings. Over and over I have found myself asking: "What kind of people worship here? Who is their God? Where were their voices when the lips of Governor Barnett dripped with words of interposition and nullification?

13. In December 1955, when Rosa Parks refused to move to the back of a bus.

Where were they when Governor Wallace gave a clarion call for defiance and hatred?[14] Where were their voices of support when bruised and weary Negro men and women decided to rise from the dark dungeons of complacency to the bright hills of creative protest?"

Yes, these questions are still in my mind. In deep disappointment I have wept over the laxity of the church. But be assured that my tears have been tears of love. There can be no deep disappointment where there is not deep love. Yes, I love the church. How could I do otherwise? I am in the rather unique position of being the son, the grandson, and the great-grandson of preachers. Yes, I see the church as the body of Christ. But, oh! How we have blemished and scarred that body through social neglect and through fear of being nonconformists.

40   There was a time when the church was very powerful—in the time when the early Christians rejoiced at being deemed worthy to suffer for what they believed. In those days the church was not merely a thermometer that recorded the ideas and principles of popular opinion; it was a thermostat that transformed the mores of society. Whenever the early Christians entered a town, the people in power became disturbed and immediately sought to convict the Christians for being "disturbers of the peace" and "outside agitators." But the Christians pressed on, in the conviction that they were "a colony of heaven," called to obey God rather than man. Small in number, they were big in commitment. They were too God-intoxicated to be "astronomically intimidated." By their effort and example they brought an end to such ancient evils as infanticide and gladiatorial contests.

Things are different now. So often the contemporary church is a weak, ineffectual voice with an uncertain sound. So often it is an archdefender of the status quo. Far from being disturbed by the presence of the church, the power structure of the average community is consoled by the church's silent—and often even vocal—sanction of things as they are.

But the judgment of God is upon the church as never before. If today's church does not recapture the sacrificial spirit of the early church, it will lose its authenticity, forfeit the loyalty of millions, and be dismissed as an irrelevant social club with no meaning for the twentieth century. Every day I meet young people whose disappointment with the church has turned into outright disgust.

Perhaps I have once again been too optimistic. Is organized religion too inextricably bound to the status quo to save our nation and the world? Perhaps I must turn my faith to the inner spiritual church, the church within the church, as the true *ekklesia*[15] and the hope of the world. But again I am thankful to God that some noble souls from the ranks of organized religion have broken loose from the paralyzing chains of conformity and joined us as active partners in the struggle for freedom. They have left their secure congregations

14. Ross Barnett (1898–1988), governor of Mississippi, opposed James Meredith's admission to the University of Mississippi; George Wallace (1919–1998), governor of Alabama, opposed admission of several black students to the University of Alabama.

15. The Greek New Testament word for the early Christian church.

and walked the streets of Albany, Georgia, with us. They have gone down the highways of the South on tortuous rides for freedom. Yes, they have gone to jail with us. Some have been dismissed from their churches, have lost the support of their bishops and fellow ministers. But they have acted in the faith that right defeated is stronger than evil triumphant. Their witness has been the spiritual salt that has preserved the true meaning of the gospel in these troubled times. They have carved a tunnel of hope through the dark mountain of disappointment.

I hope the church as a whole will meet the challenge of this decisive hour. But even if the church does not come to the aid of justice, I have no despair about the future. I have no fear about the outcome of our struggle in Birmingham, even if our motives are at present misunderstood. We will reach the goal of freedom in Birmingham and all over the nation, because the goal of America is freedom. Abused and scorned though we may be, our destiny is tied up with America's destiny. Before the pilgrims landed at Plymouth, we were here. Before the pen of Jefferson etched the majestic words of the Declaration of Independence across the pages of history, we were here. For more than two centuries our forebears labored in this country without wages; they made cotton king; they built the homes of their masters while suffering gross injustice and shameful humiliation—and yet out of a bottomless vitality they continued to thrive and develop. If the inexpressible cruelties of slavery could not stop us, the opposition we now face will surely fail. We will win our freedom because the sacred heritage of our nation and the eternal will of God are embodied in our echoing demands.

Before closing I feel impelled to mention one other point in your statement that has troubled me profoundly. You warmly commended the Birmingham police force for keeping "order" and "preventing violence." I doubt that you would have so warmly commended the police force if you had seen its dogs sinking their teeth into unarmed, nonviolent Negroes. I doubt that you would so quickly commend the policemen if you were to observe their ugly and inhumane treatment of Negroes here in the city jail; if you were to watch them push and curse old Negro women and young Negro girls; if you were to see them slap and kick old Negro men and young boys; if you were to observe them, as they did on two occasions, refuse to give us food because we wanted to sing our grace together. I cannot join you in your praise of the Birmingham police department.

It is true that the police have exercised a degree of discipline in handling the demonstrators. In this sense they have conducted themselves rather "nonviolently" in public. But for what purpose? To preserve the evil system of segregation. Over the past few years I have consistently preached that nonviolence demands that the means we use must be as pure as the ends we seek. I have tried to make clear that it is wrong to use immoral means to attain moral ends. But now I must affirm that it is just as wrong, or perhaps even more so, to use moral means to preserve immoral ends. Perhaps Mr. Connor and his policemen have been rather nonviolent in public, as was Chief Pritchett in Albany, Georgia, but they have used the moral means of nonviolence to maintain the im-

45

moral end of racial injustice. As T. S. Eliot has said, "The last temptation is the greatest treason: To do the right deed for the wrong reason."[16]

I wish you had commended the Negro sit-inners and demonstrators of Birmingham for their sublime courage, their willingness to suffer, and their amazing discipline in the midst of great provocation. One day the South will recognize its real heroes. They will be the James Merediths,[17] with the noble sense of purpose that enables them to face jeering and hostile mobs, and with the agonizing loneliness that characterizes the life of the pioneer. They will be old, oppressed, battered Negro women, symbolized in a seventy-two-year-old woman in Montgomery, Alabama, who rose up with a sense of dignity and with her people decided not to ride segregated buses, and who responded with un-grammatical profundity to one who inquired about her weariness: "My feets is tired, but my soul is at rest." They will be the young high school and college students, the young ministers of the gospel and a host of their elders, coura-geously and nonviolently sitting in at lunch counters and willingly going to jail for conscience' sake. One day the South will know that when these disinher-ited children of God sat down at lunch counters, they were in reality standing up for what is best in the American dream and for the most sacred values in our Judaeo-Christian heritage, thereby bringing our nation back to those great wells of democracy which were dug deep by the founding fathers in their for-mulation of the Constitution and the Declaration of Independence.

Never before have I written so long a letter. I'm afraid it is much too long to take your precious time. I can assure you that it would have been much shorter if I had been writing from a comfortable desk, but what else can one do when he is alone in a narrow jail cell, other than write long letters, think long thoughts, and pray long prayers?

If I have said anything in this letter that overstates the truth and indicates an unreasonable impatience, I beg you to forgive me. If I have said anything that understates the truth and indicates my having a patience that allows me to settle for anything less than brotherhood, I beg God to forgive me.

50   I hope this letter finds you strong in the faith. I also hope that circum-stances will soon make it possible for me to meet each of you, not as an inte-grationist or a civil-rights leader but as a fellow clergyman and a Christian brother. Let us all hope that the dark clouds of racial prejudice will soon pass away and the deep fog of misunderstanding will be lifted from our fear-drenched communities, and in some not too distant tomorrow the radiant stars of love and brotherhood will shine over our great nation with all their scintillating beauty.

Yours for the cause of Peace and Brotherhood,
MARTIN LUTHER KING, JR.

---

16. American-born English poet (1888–1965); the lines are from his play *Murder in the Cathedral*.

17. Meredith was the first black to enroll at the University of Mississippi.

QUESTIONS

1. King addressed the "Letter from Birmingham Jail" to eight fellow clergymen who had written a statement criticizing his activities (see note 1). Where and how, in the course of the "Letter," does he attempt to make common cause with them?

2. King was trained in oral composition, that is, in composing and delivering sermons. One device he uses as an aid to oral comprehension is prediction: he announces, in advance, the organization of what he is about to say. Locate examples of prediction in the "Letter."

3. Describe King's theory of nonviolent resistance.

4. Imagine an unjust law that, to you, would justify civil disobedience. Describe the law, the form your resistance would take, and the penalties you would expect to incur.

SCIENCE AND TECHNOLOGY

JACOB BRONOWSKI *The Nature of Scientific Reasoning*

W‌HAT IS THE INSIGHT in which the scientist tries to see into nature? Can it indeed be called either imaginative or creative? To the literary man the question may seem merely silly. He has been taught that science is a large collection of facts; and if this is true, then the only seeing which scientists need to do is, he supposes, seeing the facts. He pictures them, the colorless professionals of science, going off to work in the morning into the universe in a neutral, unexposed state. They then expose themselves like a photographic plate. And then in the darkroom or laboratory they develop the image, so that suddenly and startlingly it appears, printed in capital letters, as a new formula for atomic energy.

Men who have read Balzac and Zola[1] are not deceived by the claims of these writers that they do no more than record the facts. The readers of Christopher Isherwood[2] do not take him literally when he writes "I am a camera." Yet the same readers solemnly carry with them from their school-days this foolish picture of the scientist fixing by some mechanical process the facts of nature. I have had of all people a historian tell me that science is a collection of facts, and his voice had not even the ironic rasp of one filing cabinet reproving another.

It seems impossible that this historian had ever studied the beginnings of a scientific discovery. The Scientific Revolution can be held to begin in the year 1543 when there was brought to Copernicus, perhaps on his deathbed, the first printed copy of the book he had finished about a dozen years earlier. The thesis of this book is that the earth moves around the sun. When did Copernicus go out and record this fact with his camera? What appearance in nature prompted his outrageous guess? And in what odd sense is this guess to be called a neutral record of fact?

First delivered as a lecture at the Massachusetts Institute of Technology and then reprinted as part of Bronowski's book Science and Human Values *(1956).*

1. Honoré de Balzac (1799–1850) and Émile Zola (1840–1902), nineteenth-century French novelists.
2. English novelist and playwright (1904–1986) whose writing was the basis for the musical *Cabaret*.

Less than a hundred years after Copernicus, Kepler published (between 1609 and 1619) the three laws which describe the paths of the planets. The work of Newton and with it most of our mechanics spring from these laws.[3] They have a solid, matter-of-fact sound. For example, Kepler says that if one squares the year of a planet, one gets a number which is proportional to the cube of its average distance from the sun. Does anyone think that such a law is found by taking enough readings and then squaring and cubing everything in sight? If he does, then, as a scientist, he is doomed to a wasted life; he has as little prospect of making a scientific discovery as an electronic brain has.

It was not this way that Copernicus and Kepler thought, or that scientists think today. Copernicus found that the orbits of the planets would look simpler if they were looked at from the sun and not from the earth. But he did not in the first place find this by routine calculation. His first step was a leap of imagination—to lift himself from the earth, and put himself wildly, speculatively into the sun. "The earth conceives from the sun," he wrote; and "the sun rules the family of stars." We catch in his mind an image, the gesture of the virile man standing in the sun, with arms outstretched, overlooking the planets. Perhaps Copernicus took the picture from the drawings of the youth with outstretched arms which the Renaissance teachers put into their books on the proportions of the body. Perhaps he had seen Leonardo's[4] drawings of his loved pupil Salai. I do not know. To me, the gesture of Copernicus, the shining youth looking outward from the sun, is still vivid in a drawing which William Blake[5] in 1780 based on all these: the drawing which is usually called *Glad Day.*

Kepler's mind, we know, was filled with just such fanciful analogies; and we know what they were. Kepler wanted to relate the speeds of the planets to the musical intervals. He tried to fit the five regular solids into their orbits. None of these likenesses worked, and they have been forgotten; yet they have been and they remain the stepping stones of every creative mind. Kepler felt for his laws by way of metaphors, he searched mystically for likenesses with what he knew in every strange corner of nature. And when among these guesses he hit upon his laws, he did not think of their numbers as the balancing of a cosmic bank account, but as a revelation of the unity in all nature. To us, the analogies by which Kepler listened for the movement of the planets in the music of the spheres are farfetched. Yet are they more so than the wild leap by which Rutherford and Bohr[6] in our own century found a model for the atom in, of all places, the planetary system?

5

3. Nicolaus Copernicus (1473–1543), Polish astronomer; Johannes Kepler (1571–1630), German astronomer; Isaac Newton (1642–1727), English physicist and mathematician.

4. Leonardo da Vinci (1452–1519), Italian artist, inventor, and designer.

5. English poet, artist, and engraver (1757–1827).

6. Ernest Rutherford (1871–1937), British physicist; Niels Bohr (1885–1962), Danish physicist.

No scientific theory is a collection of facts. It will not even do to call a theory true or false in the simple sense in which every fact is either so or not so. The Epicureans held that matter is made of atoms two thousand years ago and we are now tempted to say that their theory was true. But if we do so we confuse their notion of matter with our own. John Dalton[7] in 1808 first saw the structure of matter as we do today, and what he took from the ancients was not their theory but something richer, their image: the atom. Much of what was in Dalton's mind was as vague as the Greek notion, and quite as mistaken. But he suddenly gave life to the new facts of chemistry and the ancient theory together, by fusing them to give what neither had: a coherent picture of how matter is linked and built up from different kinds of atoms. The act of fusion is the creative act.

All science is the search for unity in hidden likenesses. The search may be on a grand scale, as in the modern theories which try to link the fields of gravitation and electromagnetism. But we do not need to be browbeaten by the scale of science. There are discoveries to be made by snatching a small likeness from the air too, if it is bold enough. In 1935 the Japanese physicist Hideki Yukawa wrote a paper which can still give heart to a young scientist. He took as his starting point the known fact that waves of light can sometimes behave as if they were separate pellets. From this he reasoned that the forces which hold the nucleus of an atom together might sometimes also be observed as if they were solid pellets. A schoolboy can see how thin Yukawa's analogy is, and his teacher would be severe with it. Yet Yukawa without a blush calculated the mass of the pellet he expected to see, and waited. He was right; his meson was found, and a range of other mesons, neither the existence nor the nature of which had been suspected before. The likeness had borne fruit.

The scientist looks for order in the appearances of nature by exploring such likenesses. For order does not display itself of itself; if it can be said to be there at all, it is not there for the mere looking. There is no way of pointing a finger or camera at it; order must be discovered and, in a deep sense, it must be created. What we see, as we see it, is mere disorder.

This point has been put trenchantly in a fable by Karl Popper.[8] Suppose that someone wished to give his whole life to science. Suppose that he therefore sat down, pencil in hand, and for the next twenty, thirty, forty years recorded in notebook after notebook everything that he could observe. He may be supposed to leave out nothing: today's humidity, the racing results, the level of cosmic radiation and the stockmarket prices and the look of Mars, all would be there. He would have compiled the most careful record of nature that has ever been made; and, dying in the calm certainty of a life well spent, he would of course leave his notebooks to the Royal Society. Would the Royal Society thank him for the treasure of a lifetime of observation? It would not. The

7. British chemist and physicist (1766–1844) who developed the atomic theory of matter and thus is considered a father of modern physical science.
8. Austrian-born British philosopher (1902–1994).

Royal Society would treat his notebooks exactly as the English bishops have treated Joanna Southcott's box.[9] It would refuse to open them at all, because it would know without looking that the notebooks contain only a jumble of disorderly and meaningless items.

Science finds order and meaning in our experience, and sets about this in quite a different way. It sets about it as Newton did in the story which he himself told in his old age, and of which the schoolbooks give only a caricature. In the year 1665, when Newton was twenty-two, the plague broke out in southern England, and the University of Cambridge was closed. Newton therefore spent the next eighteen months at home, removed from traditional learning, at a time when he was impatient for knowledge and, in his own phrase, "I was in the prime of my age for invention." In this eager, boyish mood, sitting one day in the garden of his widowed mother, he saw an apple fall. So far the books have the story right; we think we even know the kind of apple; tradition has it that it was a Flower of Kent. But now they miss the crux of the story. For what struck the young Newton at the sight was not the thought that the apple must be drawn to the earth by gravity; that conception was older than Newton. What struck him was the conjecture that the same force of gravity, which reaches to the top of the tree, might go on reaching out beyond the earth and its air, endlessly into space. Gravity might reach the moon: this was Newton's new thought; and it might be gravity which holds the moon in her orbit. There and then he calculated what force from the earth (falling off as the square of the distance) would hold the moon, and compared it with the known force of gravity at tree height. The forces agreed; Newton says laconically, "I found them answer pretty nearly." Yet they agreed only nearly: the likeness and the approximation go together, for no likeness is exact. In Newton's science modern science is full grown.

It grows from a comparison. It has seized a likeness between two unlike appearances; for the apple in the summer garden and the grave moon overhead are surely as unlike in their movements as two things can be. Newton traced in them two expressions of a single concept, gravitation: and the concept (and the unity) are in that sense his free creation. The progress of science is the discovery at each step of a new order which gives unity to what had long seemed unlike.

* * *

9. Southcott was a nineteenth-century English farm servant who claimed to be a prophet. She left behind a box that was to be opened in a time of national emergency in the presence of all the English bishops. In 1927, a bishop agreed to officiate; when the box was opened, it was found to contain only some odds and ends.

QUESTIONS

1. Mark the generalizations Bronowski makes in the course of "The Nature of Scientific Reasoning"; for example, "No scientific theory is a collection of facts" (paragraph 7). Where is the information that supports them?

2. Bronowski tells the well-known story of Newton and the apple (paragraphs 11–12). How many of his generalizations does it exemplify, and how?

3. "The scientist," Bronowski observes, "looks for order in the appearances of nature" (paragraph 9). Is this operation unique to scientists? Consider the operations of "knowers" in humanities and social science disciplines such as history, literature, psychology, and sociology.

4. Bronowski sets up an adversary, a literary person who believes that scientists observe, collect, and record facts, and writes his essay as a refutation. Adapt his rhetorical strategy in an essay of your own: explain your beliefs about something by refuting the beliefs of someone who disagrees with them.

ISAAC ASIMOV   *The Eureka Phenomenon*

I N THE OLD DAYS, when I was writing a great deal of fiction, there would come, once in a while, moments when I was stymied. Suddenly, I would find I had written myself into a hole and could see no way out. To take care of that, I developed a technique which invariably worked.

It was simply this—I went to the movies. Not just any movie. I had to pick a movie which was loaded with action but which made no demands on the intellect. As I watched, I did my best to avoid any conscious thinking concerning my problem, and when I came out of the movie I knew exactly what I would have to do to put the story back on the track.

It never failed.

In fact, when I was working on my doctoral dissertation, too many years ago, I suddenly came across a flaw in my logic that I had not noticed before and that knocked out everything I had done. In utter panic, I made my way to a Bob Hope movie—and came out with the necessary change in point of view.

5   It is my belief, you see, that thinking is a double phenomenon like breathing.

You can control breathing by deliberate voluntary action: you can breathe deeply and quickly, or you can hold your breath altogether, regardless of the body's needs at the time. This, however, doesn't work well for very long. Your chest muscles grow tired, your body clamors for more oxygen, or less, and you relax. The automatic involuntary control of breathing takes over, adjusts it to the body's needs and unless you have some respiratory disorder, you can forget about the whole thing.

Well, you can think by deliberate voluntary action, too, and I don't think it is much more efficient on the whole than voluntary breath control is. You can deliberately force your mind through channels of deductions and associations in search of a solution to some problem and before long you have dug mental

From The Left Hand of the Electron, *Asimov's 1971 collection of popular scientific essays.*

furrows for yourself and find yourself circling round and round the same limited pathways. If those pathways yield no solution, no amount of further conscious thought will help.

On the other hand, if you let go, then the thinking process comes under automatic involuntary control and is more apt to take new pathways and make erratic associations you would not think of consciously. The solution will then come while you *think* you are *not* thinking.

The trouble is, though, that conscious thought involves no muscular action and so there is no sensation of physical weariness that would force you to quit. What's more, the panic of necessity tends to force you to go on uselessly, with each added bit of useless effort adding to the panic in a vicious cycle.

It is my feeling that it helps to relax, deliberately, by subjecting your mind to material complicated enough to occupy the voluntary faculty of thought, but superficial enough not to engage the deeper involuntary one. In my case, it is an action movie; in your case, it might be something else.

I suspect it is the involuntary faculty of thought that gives rise to what we call "a flash of intuition," something that I imagine must be merely the result of unnoticed thinking.

Perhaps the most famous flash of intuition in the history of science took place in the city of Syracuse in third-century B.C. Sicily. Bear with me and I will tell you the story—

About 250 B.C., the city of Syracuse was experiencing a kind of Golden Age. It was under the protection of the rising power of Rome, but it retained a king of its own and considerable self-government; it was prosperous; and it had a flourishing intellectual life.

The king was Hieron II, and he had commissioned a new golden crown from a goldsmith, to whom he had given an ingot of gold as raw material. Hieron, being a practical man, had carefully weighed the ingot and then weighed the crown he received back. The two weights were precisely equal. Good deal!

But then he sat and thought for a while. Suppose the goldsmith had subtracted a little bit of the gold, not too much, and had substituted an equal weight of the considerably less valuable copper. The resulting alloy would still have the appearance of pure gold, but the goldsmith would be plus a quantity of gold over and above his fee. He would be buying gold with copper, so to speak, and Hieron would be neatly cheated.

Hieron didn't like the thought of being cheated any more than you or I would, but he didn't know how to find out for sure if he had been. He could scarcely punish the goldsmith on mere suspicion. What to do?

Fortunately, Hieron had an advantage few rulers in the history of the world could boast. He had a relative of considerable talent. The relative was named Archimedes and he probably had the greatest intellect the world was to see prior to the birth of Newton.

Archimedes was called in and was posed the problem. He had to determine whether the crown Hieron showed him was pure gold, or was gold to which a small but significant quantity of copper had been added.

If we were to reconstruct Archimedes' reasoning, it might go as follows. Gold was the densest known substance (at that time). Its density in modern terms is 19.3 grams per cubic centimeter. This means that a given weight of gold takes up less volume than the same weight of anything else! In fact, a given weight of pure gold takes up less volume than the same weight of *any* kind of impure gold.

20   The density of copper is 8.92 grams per cubic centimeter, just about half that of gold. If we consider 100 grams of pure gold, for instance, it is easy to calculate it to have a volume of 5.18 cubic centimeters. But suppose that 100 grams of what looked like pure gold was really only 90 grams of gold and 10 grams of copper. The 90 grams of gold would have a volume of 4.66 cubic centimeters, while the 10 grams of copper would have a volume of 1.12 cubic centimeters; for a total value of 5.78 cubic centimeters.

The difference between 5.18 cubic centimeters and 5.78 cubic centimeters is quite a noticeable one, and would instantly tell if the crown were of pure gold, or if it contained 10 per cent copper (with the missing 10 per cent of gold tucked neatly in the goldsmith's strongbox).

All one had to do, then, was measure the volume of the crown and compare it with the volume of the same weight of pure gold.

The mathematics of the time made it easy to measure the volume of many simple shapes: a cube, a sphere, a cone, a cylinder, any flattened object of simple regular shape and known thickness, and so on.

We can imagine Archimedes saying, "All that is necessary, sire, is to pound that crown flat, shape it into a square of uniform thickness, and then I can have the answer for you in a moment."

25   Whereupon Hieron must certainly have snatched the crown away and said, "No such thing. I can do that much without you; I've studied the principles of mathematics, too. This crown is a highly satisfactory work of art and I won't have it damaged. Just calculate its volume without in any way altering it."

But Greek mathematics had no way of determining the volume of anything with a shape as irregular as the crown, since integral calculus had not yet been invented (and wouldn't be for two thousand years, almost). Archimedes would have had to say, "There is no known way, sire, to carry through a nondestructive determination of volume."

"Then think of one," said Hieron testily.

And Archimedes must have set about thinking of one, and gotten nowhere. Nobody knows how long he thought, or how hard, or what hypotheses he considered and discarded, or any of the details.

What we do know is that, worn out with thinking, Archimedes decided to visit the public baths and relax. I think we are quite safe in saying that Archimedes had no intention of taking his problem to the baths with him. It would be ridiculous to imagine he would, for the public baths of a Greek metropolis weren't intended for that sort of thing.

30   The Greek baths were a place for relaxation. Half the social aristocracy of the town would be there and there was a great deal more to do than wash. One steamed one's self, got a massage, exercised, and engaged in general socializing. We can be sure that Archimedes intended to forget the stupid crown for a while.

One can envisage him engaging in light talk, discussing the latest news from Alexandria and Carthage, the latest scandals in town, the latest funny jokes at the expense of the country-squire Romans—and then he lowered himself into a nice hot bath which some bumbling attendant had filled too full.

The water in the bath slopped over as Archimedes got in. Did Archimedes notice that at once, or did he sigh, sink back, and paddle his feet awhile before noting the water-slop. I guess the latter. But, whether soon or late, he noticed, and that one fact, added to all the chains of reasoning his brain had been working on during the period of relaxation when it was unhampered by the comparative stupidities (even in Archimedes) of voluntary thought, gave Archimedes his answer in one blinding flash of insight.

Jumping out of the bath, he proceeded to run home at top speed through the streets of Syracuse. He did *not* bother to put on his clothes. The thought of Archimedes running naked through Syracuse has titillated dozens of generations of youngsters who have heard this story, but I must explain that the ancient Greeks were quite lighthearted in their attitude toward nudity. They thought no more of seeing a naked man on the streets of Syracuse, than we would on the Broadway stage.

And as he ran, Archimedes shouted over and over, "I've got it! I've got it!" Of course, knowing no English, he was compelled to shout it in Greek, so it came out, *"Eureka! Eureka!"*

Archimedes' solution was so simple that anyone could understand it— once Archimedes explained it. 35

If an object that is not affected by water in any way, is immersed in water, it is bound to displace an amount of water equal to its own volume, since two objects cannot occupy the same space at the same time.

Suppose, then, you had a vessel large enough to hold the crown and suppose it had a small overflow spout set into the middle of its side. And suppose further that the vessel was filled with water exactly to the spout, so that if the water level were raised a bit higher, however slightly, some would overflow.

Next, suppose that you carefully lower the crown into the water. The water level would rise by an amount equal to the volume of the crown, and that volume of water would pour out the overflow and be caught in a small vessel. Next, a lump of gold, known to be pure and exactly equal in weight to the crown, is also immersed in the water and again the level rises and the overflow is caught in a second vessel.

If the crown were pure gold, the overflow would be exactly the same in each case, and the volume of water caught in the two small vessels would be equal. If, however, the crown were of alloy, it would produce a larger overflow than the pure gold would and this would be easily noticeable.

What's more, the crown would in no way be harmed, defaced, or even as much as scratched. More important, Archimedes had discovered the "principle of buoyancy." 40

And was the crown pure gold? I've heard that it turned out to be alloy and that the goldsmith was executed, but I wouldn't swear to it.

How often does this "Eureka phenomenon" happen? How often is there this flash of deep insight during a moment of relaxation, this triumphant cry of

"I've got it! I've got it!" which must surely be a moment of the purest ecstasy this sorry world can afford?

I wish there were some way we could tell. I suspect that in the history of science it happens *often*; I suspect that very few significant discoveries are made by the pure technique of voluntary thought; I suspect that voluntary thought may possibly prepare the ground (if even that), but that the final touch, the real inspiration, comes when thinking is under involuntary control.

But the world is in a conspiracy to hide the fact. Scientists are wedded to reason, to the meticulous working out of consequences from assumptions to the careful organization of experiments designed to check those consequences. If a certain line of experiments ends nowhere, it is omitted from the final report. If an inspired guess turns out to be correct, it is *not* reported as an inspired guess. Instead, a solid line of voluntary thought is invented after the fact to lead up to the thought, and that is what is inserted in the final report.

45   The result is that anyone reading scientific papers would swear that *nothing* took place but voluntary thought maintaining a steady clumping stride from origin to destination, and that just can't be true.

It's such a shame. Not only does it deprive science of much of its glamour (how much of the dramatic story in Watson's *Double Helix* do you suppose got into the final reports announcing the great discovery of the structure of DNA?),[1] but it hands over the important process of "insight," "inspiration," "revelation" to the mystic.

The scientist actually becomes ashamed of having what we might call a revelation, as though to have one is to betray reason—when actually what we call revelation in a man who has devoted his life to reasoned thought, is after all merely reasoned thought that is not under voluntary control.

Only once in a while in modern times do we ever get a glimpse into the workings of involuntary reasoning, and when we do, it is always fascinating. Consider, for instance, the case of Friedrich August Kekule von Stradonitz.

In Kekule's time, a century and a quarter ago, a subject of great interest to chemists was the structure of organic molecules (those associated with living tissue). Inorganic molecules were generally simple in the sense that they were made up of few atoms. Water molecules, for instance, are made up of two atoms of hydrogen and one of oxygen (H_2O). Molecules of ordinary salt are made up of one atom of sodium and one of chlorine ($NaCl$), and so on.

50   Organic molecules, on the other hand, often contained a large number of atoms. Ethyl alcohol molecules have two carbon atoms, six hydrogen atoms, and an oxygen atom (C_2H_6O); the molecule of ordinary cane sugar is $C_{12}H_{22}O_{11}$, and other molecules are even more complex.

Then, too, it is sufficient, in the case of inorganic molecules generally, merely to know the kinds and numbers of atoms in the molecule; in organic molecules, more is necessary. Thus, dimethyl ether has the formula C_2H_6O, just as ethyl alcohol does, and yet the two are quite different in properties. Ap-

1. I'll tell you, in case you're curious. None! [Asimov's note]. How Francis Crick and James Watson discovered the molecular structure of this vital substance is told in Watson's autobiographical book, *The Double Helix*.

parently, the atoms are arranged differently within the molecules—but how to determine the arrangements?

In 1852, an English chemist, Edward Frankland, had noticed that the atoms of a particular element tended to combine with a fixed number of other atoms. This combining number was called "valence." Kekule in 1858 reduced this notion to a system. The carbon atom, he decided (on the basis of plenty of chemical evidence) had a valence of four; the hydrogen atom, a valence of one; and the oxygen atom, a valence of two (and so on).

Why not represent the atoms as their symbols plus a number of attached dashes, that number being equal to the valence. Such atoms could then be put together as though they were so many Tinker Toy units and "structural formulas" could be built up.

It was possible to reason out that the structural formula of ethyl alcohol was

$$
\begin{array}{ccc}
H & H & \\
| & | & \\
H-C-C-O-H, \\
| & | & \\
H & H &
\end{array}
$$

while that of dimethyl ether was

$$
\begin{array}{ccc}
H & & H \\
| & & | \\
H-C-O-C-H. \\
| & & | \\
H & & H
\end{array}
$$

In each case, there were two carbon atoms, each with four dashes attached; six hydrogen atoms, each with one dash attached; and an oxygen atom with two dashes attached. The molecules were built up of the same components, but in different arrangements.

Kekule's theory worked beautifully. It has been immensely deepened and elaborated since his day, but you can still find structures very much like Kekule's Tinker Toy formulas in any modern chemical textbook. They represent oversimplifications of the true situation, but they remain extremely useful in practice even so.

The Kekule structures were applied to many organic molecules in the years after 1858 and the similarities and contrasts in the structures neatly matched similarities and contrasts in properties. The key to the rationalization of organic chemistry had, it seemed, been found.

Yet there was one disturbing fact. The well-known chemical benzene wouldn't fit. It was known to have a molecule made up of equal numbers of carbon and hydrogen atoms. Its molecular weight was known to be 78 and a single carbon-hydrogen combination had a weight of 13. Therefore, the benzene molecule had to contain six carbon-hydrogen combinations and its formula had to be C_6H_6.

But that meant trouble. By the Kekule formulas, the hydrocarbons (molecules made up of carbon and hydrogen atoms only) could easily be envisioned as chains of carbon atoms with hydrogen atoms attached. If all the valences of the carbon atoms were filled with hydrogen atoms, as in "hexane," whose molecule looks like this—

$$
\begin{array}{ccccccc}
\text{H} & \text{H} & \text{H} & \text{H} & \text{H} & \text{H} \\
| & | & | & | & | & | \\
\text{H}-\text{C}-\text{C}-\text{C}-\text{C}-\text{C}-\text{C}-\text{H} \\
| & | & | & | & | & | \\
\text{H} & \text{H} & \text{H} & \text{H} & \text{H} & \text{H}
\end{array}
$$

the compound is said to be saturated. Such saturated hydrocarbons were found to have very little tendency to react with other substances.

If some of the valences were not filled, unused bonds were added to those connecting the carbon atoms. Double bonds were formed as in "hexene"—

$$
\begin{array}{ccccccc}
\text{H} & \text{H} & \text{H} & \text{H} & \text{H} & \text{H} \\
| & | & | & | & | & | \\
\text{H}-\text{C}-\text{C}-\text{C}=\text{C}-\text{C}-\text{C}-\text{H} \\
| & | & & & | & | \\
\text{H} & \text{H} & & & \text{H} & \text{H}
\end{array}
$$

Hexene is unsaturated, for that double bond has a tendency to open up and add other atoms. Hexene is chemically active.

When six carbons are present in a molecule, it takes fourteen hydrogen atoms to occupy all the valence bonds and make it inert—as in hexane. In hexene, on the other hand, there are only twelve hydrogens. If there were still fewer hydrogen atoms, there would be more than one double bond; there might even be triple bonds, and the compound would be still more active than hexene.

Yet benzene, which is C_6H_6 and has eight fewer hydrogen atoms than hexane, is *less* active than hexene, which has only two fewer hydrogen atoms than hexane. In fact, benzene is even less active than hexane itself. The six hydrogen atoms in the benzene molecule seem to satisfy the six carbon atoms to a greater extent than do the fourteen hydrogen atoms in hexane.

For heaven's sake, why?

This might seem unimportant. The Kekule formulas were so beautifully suitable in the case of so many compounds that one might simply dismiss benzene as an exception to the general rule.

Science, however, is not English grammar. You can't just categorize something as an exception. If the exception doesn't fit into the general system, then the general system must be wrong.

Or, take the more positive approach. An exception can often be made to fit into a general system, provided the general system is broadened. Such broadening generally represents a great advance and for this reason, exceptions ought to be paid great attention.

For some seven years, Kekule faced the problem of benzene and tried to puzzle out how a chain of six carbon atoms could be completely satisfied with as few as six hydrogen atoms in benzene and yet be left unsatisfied with twelve hydrogen atoms in hexene.

Nothing came to him!

And then one day in 1865 (he tells the story himself) he was in Ghent, Belgium, and in order to get to some destination, he boarded a public bus. He was tired and, undoubtedly, the droning beat of the horses' hooves on the cobblestones, lulled him. He fell into a comatose half-sleep.

In that sleep, he seemed to see a vision of atoms attaching themselves to each other in chains that moved about. (Why not? It was the sort of thing that constantly occupied his waking thoughts.) But then one chain twisted in such a way that head and tail joined, forming a ring—and Kekule woke with a start.

To himself, he must surely have shouted "Eureka," for indeed he had it. The six carbon atoms of benzene formed a ring and not a chain, so that the structural formula looked like this:

To be sure, there were still three double bonds, so you might think the molecule had to be very active—but now there was a difference. Atoms in a ring might be expected to have different properties from those in a chain and double bonds in one case might not have the properties of those in the other. At least, chemists could work on that assumption and see if it involved them in contradictions.

It didn't. The assumption worked excellently well. It turned out that organic molecules could be divided into two groups: aromatic and aliphatic. The former had the benzene ring (or certain other similar rings) as part of the structure and the latter did not. Allowing for different properties within each group, the Kekule structures worked very well.

For nearly seventy years, Kekule's vision held good in the hard field of actual chemical techniques, guiding the chemist through the jungle of reactions that led to the synthesis of more and more molecules. Then, in 1932, Linus Pauling applied quantum mechanics to chemical structure with sufficient subtlety to explain just why the benzene ring was so special and what had proven correct in practice proved correct in theory as well.

75   Other cases? Certainly.

In 1764, the Scottish engineer James Watt was working as an instrument maker for the University of Glasgow. The university gave him a model of a Newcomen steam engine, which didn't work well, and asked him to fix it. Watt fixed it without trouble, but even when it worked perfectly, it didn't work well. It was far too inefficient and consumed incredible quantities of fuel. Was there a way to improve that?

Thought didn't help; but a peaceful, relaxed walk on a Sunday afternoon did. Watt returned with the key notion in mind of using two separate chambers, one for steam only and one for cold water only, so that the same chamber did not have to be constantly cooled and reheated to the infinite waste of fuel.

The Irish mathematician William Rowan Hamilton worked up a theory of "quaternions" in 1843 but couldn't complete that theory until he grasped the fact that there were conditions under which $p \times q$ was *not* equal to $q \times p$. The necessary thought came to him in a flash one time when he was walking to town with his wife.

The German physiologist Otto Loewi was working on the mechanism of nerve action, in particular, on the chemicals produced by nerve endings. He awoke at 3 A.M. one night in 1921 with a perfectly clear notion of the type of experiment he would have to run to settle a key point that was puzzling him. He wrote it down and went back to sleep. When he woke in the morning, he found he couldn't remember what his inspiration had been. He remembered he had written it down, but he couldn't read his writing.

80   The next night, he woke again at 3 A.M. with the clear thought once more in mind. This time, he didn't fool around. He got up, dressed himself, went straight to the laboratory and began work. By 5 A.M. he had proved his point and the consequences of his findings became important enough in later years so that in 1936 he received a share in the Nobel prize in medicine and physiology.

How very often this sort of thing must happen, and what a shame that scientists are so devoted to their belief in conscious thought that they so consistently obscure the actual methods by which they obtain their results.

QUESTIONS

1. Consider Asimov's narrative of Archimedes' and Kekule's discoveries. What elements does he heighten and how? How does he include the scientific information necessary to understand them? How does he make (or attempt to make) this information accessible to nonscientists?

2. Scientists, Asimov concludes, "are so devoted to their belief in conscious thought that they . . . consistently obscure the actual methods by which they obtain their results" (paragraph 81). Consider your own experiments in science courses and the way you have been taught to report them. Do you agree or disagree with Asimov? Why?

3. Have you ever had a "Eureka" experience? Does Asimov's account of the "Eureka phenomenon" help you to understand it? Write about your experience with reference to Asimov's essay.

HENRY WECHSLER, ANDREA DAVENPORT,
GEORGE DOWDALL, BARBARA MOEYKENS,
AND SONIA CASTILLO

Health and Behavioral Consequences of Binge Drinking in College: A National Survey of Students at 140 Campuses

Objective.—To examine the extent of binge drinking by college students and the ensuing health and behavioral problems that binge drinkers create for themselves and others on their campus.

Design.—Self-administered survey mailed to a national representative sample of US 4-year college students.

Setting.—One hundred forty US 4-year colleges in 1993.

Participants.—A total of 17,592 college students.

Main Outcome Measures.—Self-reports of drinking behavior, alcohol-related health problems, and other problems.

Results.—Almost half (44%) of college students responding to the survey were binge drinkers, including almost one fifth (19%) of the students who were frequent binge drinkers. Frequent binge drinkers are more likely to experience serious health and other consequences of their drinking behavior than other students. Almost half (47%) of the frequent binge drinkers experienced five or more different drinking-related problems, including injuries and engaging in unplanned sex, since the beginning of the school year. Most binge drinkers do not consider themselves to be problem drinkers and have not sought treatment for an alcohol problem. Binge drinkers create problems for classmates who are not binge drinkers. Students who are not binge drinkers at schools with higher binge rates were more likely than students at schools with lower binge rates to experience

Originally published as "Health and Behavioral Consequences of Binge Drinking in College," Journal of the American Medical Association (December 7, 1994). The authors' notes are collected at the end as "References," in the style of JAMA.

problems such as being pushed, hit, or assaulted or experiencing an unwanted sexual advance.

Conclusions.—Binge drinking is widespread on college campuses. Programs aimed at reducing this problem should focus on frequent binge drinkers, refer them to treatment or educational programs, and emphasize the harm they cause for students who are not binge drinkers (*JAMA*, 1994; 272:1672–1677).

Heavy episodic or binge drinking poses a danger of serious health and other consequences for alcohol abusers and for others in the immediate environment. Alcohol contributes to the leading causes of accidental death in the United States, such as motor vehicle crashes and falls.[1] Alcohol abuse is seen as contributing to almost half of motor vehicle fatalities, the most important cause of death among young Americans.[2] Unsafe sex—a growing threat with the spread of acquired immunodeficiency syndrome (AIDS) and other sexually transmitted diseases—and unintentional injuries have been associated with alcohol intoxication.[3–5] These findings support the view of college presidents who believe that alcohol abuse is the No. 1 problem on campus.[6]

Despite the fact that alcohol is illegal for most undergraduates, alcohol continues to be widely used on most college campuses today. Since the national study by Straus and Bacon in 1949,[7] numerous subsequent surveys have documented the overwhelming use of alcohol by college students and have pointed to problem drinking among this group.[8–10] Most previous studies of drinking by college students have been conducted on single college campuses and have not used random sampling of students.[9–12] While these studies are in general agreement about the prevalence and consequences of binge drinking, they do not provide a national representative sample of college drinking.

A few large-scale, multicollege surveys have been conducted in recent years. However, these have not selected a representative national sample of colleges, but have used colleges in one state[3] or those participating in a federal program,[5] or have followed a sample of high school seniors through college.[1,3]

In general, studies of college alcohol use have consistently found higher rates of binge drinking among men than women. However, these studies used the same definition of binge drinking for men and women, without taking into account sex differences in metabolism of ethanol or in body mass.[3,5,9–12,14–17]

5   The consequences of binge drinking often pose serious risks for drinkers and for others in the college environment. Binge drinking has been associated with unplanned and unsafe sexual activity, physical and sexual assault, unintentional injuries, other criminal violations, interpersonal problems, physical or cognitive impairment, and poor academic performance.[3–5]

This study examines the nature and extent of binge drinking among a representative national sample of students at 140 US 4-year colleges and details the problems such drinking causes for drinkers themselves and for others on their college campus. Binge drinking is defined through a sex-specific mea-sure to take into account sex differences in the dosage effects of ethanol.

Methods

The Colleges

A national sample of 179 colleges was selected from the American Council on Education's list of 4-year colleges and universities accredited by one of the six regional bodies covering the United States. The sample was selected using probability proportionate to enrollment size sampling. All full-time undergraduate students at a university were eligible to be chosen for this study, regardless of the college in which they were enrolled. This sample contained few women-only colleges and few colleges with less than 1000 students. To correct for this problem, an oversample of 15 additional colleges with enrollments of less than 1000 students and 10 all-women's colleges were added to the sample. Nine colleges were subsequently dropped because they were considered inappropriate. These included seminary schools, military schools, and allied health schools.

One hundred forty (72%) of the final sample of 195 colleges agreed to participate. The primary reason stated for nonparticipation by college administrators was inability to provide a random sample of students and their addresses within the time requirements of the study. The 140 participating colleges are located in 40 states and the District of Columbia. They represent a cross-section of US higher education. Two thirds of the colleges sampled are public and one third are private. Approximately two thirds are located in a suburban or urban setting and one third in a small town/rural setting. Four percent are women-only, and 4% are predominantly black institutions.

When the 55 nonparticipating schools were compared with the 140 in the study, the only statistically significant difference found was in terms of enrollment size. Proportionately fewer small colleges (fewer than 1000 students) participated in the study. Since these were oversampled, sufficient numbers are present for statistical analysis.

Sampling Procedures

Colleges were sent a set of specific guidelines for drawing a random sample of students based on the total enrollment of full-time undergraduates. Depending on enrollment size, every xth student was selected from the student registry using a random starting point. A sample of undergraduate students was provided by each of the 140 participating colleges: 215 students at each of 127 colleges, and 108 at each of 13 colleges (12 of which were in the oversample). The final student sample included 28,709 students.

10

The Questionnaire

The 20-page survey instrument asked students a number of questions about their drinking behavior as well as other health issues. Whenever possible, the survey instrument included questions that had been used previously in other national or large-scale epidemiological studies.[13,14] A drink was defined as a 12-oz (360-mL) can (or bottle) of beer, a 4-oz (120-mL) glass of wine, a 12-oz (360-mL) bottle (or can) of wine cooler, or a shot (1.25 oz [37-mL]) of liquor straight or in a mixed drink. The following four questions were used to assess binge drinking: (1) sex; (2) recency of last drink ("never," "not in past year," "within last year but more than 30 days ago," "within 30 days but more than 1 week ago," or "within week"); (3) "Think back over the last two weeks. How many times have you had five or more drinks in a row?" (The use of this question, without specification of time elapsed in a drinking episode, is consistent with standard practice in recent research on alcohol use among this population.[3,5,13,18]); and (4) "During the last two weeks, how many times have you had four drinks in a row (but no more than that) (for women)?" Missing responses to any of these four questions excluded the student from the binging analyses.

Students were also asked the extent to which they had experienced any of the following 12 problems as a consequence of their drinking since the beginning of the school year: have a hangover; miss a class; get behind in schoolwork; do something you later regretted; forget where you were or what you did; argue with friends; engage in unplanned sexual activity; not use protection when you had sex; damage property; get into trouble with campus or local police; get hurt or injured; or require medical treatment for an alcohol overdose. They were also asked if, since the beginning of the school year, they had experienced any of the following eight problems caused by other students' drinking: been insulted or humiliated; had a serious argument or quarrel; been pushed, hit, or assaulted; had your property damaged; had to "babysit" or take care of another student who drank too much; had your studying or sleep interrupted; experienced an unwanted sexual advance; or had been a victim of sexual assault or date rape.

The Mailing

The initial mailing of questionnaires to students began on February 5, 1993. By the end of March, 87% of the final group of questionnaires had been received, with another 10% in April and 2% in May and June. There are no discernible differences in binging rates among questionnaires received in each of the 5 months of the survey. Mailings were modified to take into account spring break, so that students would be responding about their binge drinking behavior during a 2-week time on campus. Responses were voluntary and anonymous. Four separate mailings, usually 10 days apart, were sent at each college: a questionnaire, a reminder postcard, a second questionnaire, and a second reminder postcard. To encourage students to respond, the following cash awards were offered: one $1000 award to a student whose name was drawn from among students responding within 1 week, and one $500 award and ten $100 awards to students selected from all those who responded.

The Response Rate

The questionnaires were mailed to 28,709 students. Overall, 3,082 students were eliminated from the sample because of school reports of incorrect addresses, withdrawal from school, or leaves of absence, reducing the sample size to 25,627. A total of 17,592 students returned questionnaires, yielding an overall student response rate of approximately 69%. The response rate is likely to be underestimated since it does not take into account all of the students who may not have received questionnaires. At 104 of the colleges, response rates were between 60% and 80%, and only six colleges had response rates less than 50%. Response rate was not associated with the binging rate (i.e., the Pearson correlation coefficient between the binge drinking rate at the college and the response rate was 0.06 with a P value of .46).

When responses of early and late responders to the survey were com-   15
pared, there were no significant differences in the percent of nondrinkers, nonbinge drinkers, and binge drinkers. In the case of 11,557 students who could be classified as early or late responders, there was no significant differences in terms of binge drinking (43% for the early responders vs 42% for the late responders). An additional short form of the questionnaire was mailed to a segment of students who had failed to return the questionnaire. The rate of binge drinking of these nonresponders did not differ from that of responders to the original student survey.

Data Analysis

All statistical analyses were carried out using the current version of SAS.[19]* Comparisons of unweighted and weighted sample results suggested little difference between them, so unweighted results are reported here. Chi-square analyses among students who had a drink in the past year were used to compare nonbinge drinkers, infrequent binge drinkers, and binge drinkers. Binge drinking was defined as the consumption of five or more drinks in a row for men and four or more drinks in a row for women during the 2 weeks prior to the survey. An extensive analysis showed that this sex-specific measure accurately indicates an equivalent likelihood of alcohol-related problems. In this article, the term "binge drinker" is used to refer to students who binged at least once in the previous 2 weeks. Frequent binge drinkers were defined as those who binged three or more times in the past 2 weeks and infrequent binge drinkers as those who binged one or two times in the past 2 weeks. Nonbinge drinkers were those who had consumed alcohol in the past year, but had not binged.

Logistic regression analyses were used to examine how much more likely frequent binge drinkers were to experience an alcohol-related problem or driving behavior compared with nonbinge drinkers, and to compare infrequent binge drinkers with nonbinge drinkers. Odds ratios were adjusted for age, sex, race, marital status, and parents' college education.

In examining secondary binge effects, schools were divided into three groups on the basis of the percentage of students who were binge drinkers at each school. The responses of students who had not binged in the past 2 weeks (including those who had never had a drink) and who resided in dormitories, fraternities, or sororities were compared through χ^2† analyses across the three school types. High-level binge schools (where 51% or more students were binge drinkers) included 44 schools with 6,084 students; middle-

* A standard social science statistical program.
† Chi-square.

level binge schools (36% to 50% of students were binge drinkers) included 53 schools with 6,455 students; and low-level binge schools (35% or less of students were binge drinkers) included 43 schools with 5,043 students (for 10 students, information regarding school of attendance was missing). For two of the problems that occurred primarily or almost exclusively to women (sexual assault and experiencing an unwanted sexual advance), only women were included in the analyses.

RESULTS

Characteristics of the Student Sample

This analysis is based on data from 17,592 undergraduate students at 140 US 4-year colleges. The student sample includes more women (58%) than men (42%), due in part to the inclusion of six all-women's institutions. This compares with national 1991 data that report 51% of undergraduates at 4-year institutions are women.[20] The sample is predominantly white (81%). This coincides exactly with national 1991 data that report 81% of undergraduates at 4-year institutions are white.[20] Minority groups included Asian/Pacific Islander (7%), Spanish/Hispanic (7%), black/African American (6%), and Native American (1%). The age of the students was distributed as follows: 45% younger than 21 years, 38% aged 21 to 23 years, and 17% aged 24 years or more. There were slightly more juniors (25%) and seniors (26%) in the sample than freshmen (20%) and sophomores (19%), probably because 30% of the students were transfers from other institutions. Ten percent of the students were in their fifth undergraduate year of school or beyond. Religious affiliation was discerned by asking students in which of the following religions they were raised: Protestant (44%), Catholic (36%), Jewish (3%), Muslim (1%), other (4%), and none (12%). Religion was cited as an important to very important activity among 36% of the students. Approximately three of five students (59%) worked for pay. Approximately half (49%) of the students had a grade-point average of A, A–, or B+.

Extent of Binge Drinking

20   Because of missing responses, there were 496 students excluded from binging analyses (i.e., 17,096 were included). Most students drank alcohol during the past year. Only about one of six (16%) were nondrinkers (15% of the men and 16% of the women). About two of five students (41%) drank but were non-binge drinkers (35% of the men and 45% of the women). Slightly fewer than half (44%) of the students were binge drinkers (50% of the men and 39% of the women). About half of this group of binge drinkers, or about one in five students (19%) overall, were frequent binge drinkers (overall, 23% of the men and 17% of the women).

Binge Drinking Rates at Colleges

The Figure shows that binge drinking rates vary extensively among the 140 colleges in the study. While 1% of the students were binge drinkers at the school with the lowest rate of binge drinkers, 70% of students were binge drinkers at

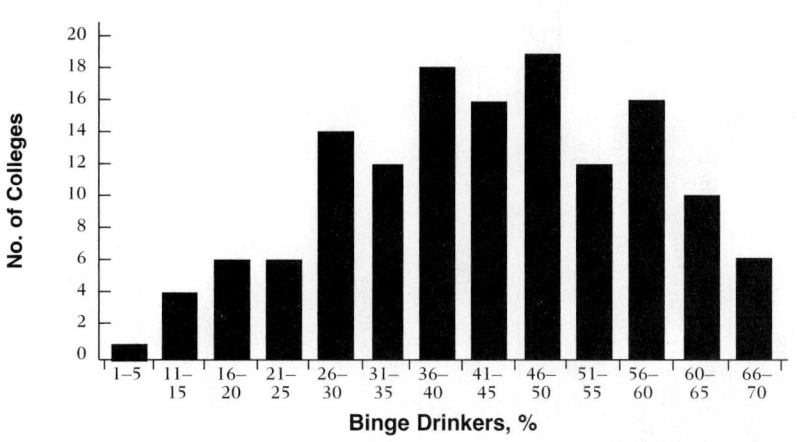

Distribution of colleges by percentage of binge drinkers.

the school with the highest rate. At 44 schools, more than half of the responding students were binge drinkers.

When the 140 colleges were divided into levels of binging rate, χ^2 analyses showed that several college characteristics were individually associated (at $P <$ .05) with binging rate. Colleges located in the Northeast or North Central regions of the United States (compared with those in the West or South) or those that were residential (compared with commuter schools, where 90% or more of the students lived off campus)[21] tended to have higher rates of binging. In addition, traditionally black institutions and women's colleges had lower binge rates than schools that were not traditionally black or were coeducational colleges. Other characteristics, such as whether the college was public or private and its enrollment size, were not related to binge drinker rates.

Examination of whether college alcohol programs and policies have any association with binge drinking will be presented in a separate publication. There is little evidence to conclude that current policies have had strong impacts on overall drinking levels. Preliminary analyses suggest that individual binge drinking is less likely if the institution does not have any alcohol outlets within 1 mile of campus, or if it prohibits alcohol use for all persons (even those older than 21 years) on campus.

Drinking Patterns of Binge Drinkers

Table 1 indicates that our designations of binge drinker and frequent binge drinker are strongly indicative of a drinking style that involves more frequent and heavier drinking. Furthermore, intoxication (often intentional) is associated with binge drinking in men and women.

Binge drinking is related to age. Students who are in the predominant college age group (between 17 and 23 years) have much higher binging rates than older students. However, within the predominant college age group, students who are younger than the legal drinking age of 21 years do not differ in

25

TABLE 1
Drinking Styles of Students Who Were Nonbinge Drinkers,
Infrequent Binge Drinkers, or Frequent Binge Drinkers*

Drinking Styles	Nonbinge Drinkers, %†		Infrequent Binge Drinkers, %‡		Frequent Binge Drinkers, %§	
	Men (n=2,539)	Women (n=4,400)	Men (n=1,968)	Women (n=2,130)	Men (n=1,630)	Women (n=1,684)
Drank on 10 or more occasions in the past 30 days‖	3	1	11	6	61	39
Usually binges when drinks	4	4	43	45	83	82
Was drunk three or more times in past month	2	1	17	13	70	55
Drinks to get drunk¶	22	18	49	44	73	68

*Chi-square comparisons of students who were nonbinge drinkers, infrequent binge drinkers, and frequent binge drinkers and each of the four drinking styles were significant for men and women separately at $P<.001$. Sample sizes vary slightly for each question because of missing values. Binging is defined as four or more drinks for women and five or more drinks for men.
†Students who consumed alcohol in the past year, but did not binge.
‡Students who binged one or two times in a 2-week period.
§Students who binged three or more times in a 2-week period.
‖Question asked, "On how many occasions have you had a drink of alcohol in the past 30 days?" Response categories were 1 to 2 occasions, 3 to 5 occasions, 6 to 9 occasions, 10 to 19 occasions, 20 to 39 occasions, and 40 or more occasions.
¶Says that to get drunk is an important reason for drinking.

TABLE 2

RISK OF ALCOHOL-RELATED PROBLEMS COMPARING STUDENTS WHO WERE INFREQUENT BINGE DRINKERS OR FREQUENT BINGE DRINKERS WITH STUDENTS WHO WERE NONBINGE DRINKERS AMONG COLLEGE STUDENTS WHO HAD A DRINK IN THE PAST YEAR*

Reporting Problem	Nonbinge Drinkers, % (n=6,894)	Infrequent Binge Drinkers		Frequent Binge Drinkers	
		% (n=4,090)	Adjusted OR (95% CI)†	% (n=3,291)	Adjusted OR (95% CI)‡
Have a hangover	30	75	6.28 (5.73–6.87)	90	17.62 (15.20–20.04)
Do something you regret	14	37	3.31 (3.00–3.64)	63	8.98 (8.11–9.95)
Miss a class	8	30	4.66 (4.15–5.24)	61	16.58 (14.73–18.65)
Forget where you were or what you did	8	26	3.62 (3.22–4.06)	54	11.23 (10.05–12.65)
Get behind in school work	6	21	3.70 (3.26–4.20)	46	11.43 (10.09–12.94)
Argue with friends	8	22	3.06 (2.72–3.46)	42	7.77 (6.90–8.74)
Engage in unplanned sexual activity	8	20	2.78 (2.46–3.13)	41	7.17 (6.37–8.06)
Get hurt or injured	2	9	3.65 (3.01–4.13)	23	10.43 (8.70–12.52)
Damage property	2	8	3.09 (2.53–3.77)	22	9.49 (7.86–11.43)
Not use protection when having sex	4	10	2.90 (2.45–3.42)	22	7.11 (6.07–8.34)
Get into trouble with campus or local police	1	4	2.50 (1.92–3.26)	11	6.92 (5.44–8.81)
Require medical treatment of alcohol overdose	<1	<1	NS	1	2.81 (1.39–5.68)
Have five or more alcohol-related problems since the beginning of the school year§	3	14	4.95 (4.17–5.89)	47	25.10 (21.30–29.58)

*Problem occurred not at all or one or more times. Chi-square comparisons of nonbinge drinkers, infrequent binge drinkers, and frequent binge drinkers and each of the problems are significant at P<.001, except for alcohol overdose (P=.002). Sample sizes vary slightly for each problem of missing values. OR indicates odds ratio; CI, confidence interval. See Table 1 for explanation of drinking classification.

†Adjusted ORs of infrequent binge drinkers vs. nonbinge drinkers are significant at P<.001.

‡Adjusted ORs of frequent binge drinkers vs. nonbinge drinkers are significant at P<.001, except for alcohol overdose, P<.01.

§Excludes hangover and includes driving after drinking as one of the problems.

TABLE 3

ALCOHOL-RELATED DRIVING BEHAVIOR FOR A 30-DAY PERIOD COMPARING STUDENTS WHO WERE INFREQUENT BINGE DRINKERS OR FREQUENT BINGE DRINKERS WITH STUDENTS WHO WERE NONBINGE DRINKERS*

Drinking Behavior	Nonbinge Drinkers		Infrequent Binge Drinkers			Frequent Binge Drinkers		
	Men, % (n=2,531)	Women, % (n=4,393)	Men, % (n=1,975)	Women, % (n=2,132)	Adjusted OR 95% CI)†	Men, % (n=1,630)	Women, % (n=1,684)	Adjusted OR (95% CI)‡
Drove after drinking alcohol	20	13	47	33	5.13 (4.67–5.64)	62	49	10.33 (9.34–11.42)
Drove after having five or more drinks	2	1	18	7	22.23 (16.89–29.26)	40	21	74.30 (56.56–97.58)
Rode with a driver who was high or drunk	7	7	23	22	4.73 (4.20–5.32)	t53	48	15.97 (14.22–17.95)

*Chi-square comparisons of nonbinge drinkers, infrequent binge drinkers, and frequent binge drinkers and each of the three driving behaviors were all significant for men and women separately at $P<.001$. Sample sizes vary slightly for each question because of missing values. OR indicates odds ratio; CI, confidence interval. See Table 1 for explanation of drinking classification.

†Adjusted OR of infrequent binge drinkers vs nonbinge drinkers (sex combined) are significant at $P<.001$.

‡Adjusted OR of frequent binge drinkers vs nonbinge drinkers (sex combined) are significant at $P<.001$.

binging rates from students aged 21 to 23 years. In contrast to the modest effects of age, there is no relationship between year in school and binging, with rates of binge drinking virtually identical among students across the years of college attendance.

Alcohol-Related Health and Other Problems

There is a strong, positive relationship between the frequency of binge drinking and alcohol-related health and other problems reported by the students (Table 2). Among the more serious alcohol-related problems, the frequent binge drinkers were seven to 10 times more likely than the nonbinge drinkers to not use protection when having sex, to engage in unplanned sexual activity, to get into trouble with campus police, to damage property, or to get hurt or injured. A similar comparison between the infrequent binge drinkers and nonbinge drinkers also shows a strong relationship.

Men and women reported similar frequencies for most of the problems, except for damaging property or getting into trouble with the campus police. Among the frequent binge drinkers, 35% of the men and 9% of the women reported damaging property, and 16% of the men and 6% of the women reported getting into trouble with the campus police.

Drinking and Driving

There is also a positive relationship between binge drinking and driving under the influence of alcohol (Table 3). A large proportion of the student population reported driving after drinking alcohol. Binge drinkers, particularly frequent binge drinkers, reported significantly ($P<.001$) higher frequencies of dangerous driving behaviors than nonbinge drinkers.

Number of Problems

Nearly half (47%) of the frequent binge drinkers reported having experienced five or more of the 12 problems listed in Table 2 (omitting hangover and including driving after drinking) since the beginning of the school year, compared with 14% of infrequent binge drinkers and 3% of nonbinge drinkers. The adjusted odds ratios indicate that frequent binge drinkers were 25 times more likely than nonbinge drinkers to experience five or more of these problems, while the infrequent binge drinkers were five times more likely than nonbinge drinkers to experience five or more problems.

Self-assessment of Drinking Problem

Few students describe themselves as having a drinking problem. When asked to classify themselves in terms of their current alcohol use, less than 1% of the total sample (0.2%), including only 0.6% of the frequent binge drinkers, designated themselves as problem drinkers. In addition, few students have ever sought treatment for a problem with alcohol.

A somewhat larger proportion of students indicated that they had ever had a drinking problem. Slightly more than one fifth (22%) of the frequent binge drinkers thought that they ever had a drinking problem, compared with 12% of the infrequent binge drinkers and 7% of the nonbinge drinkers.

30

Secondary Binge Effects

Table 4 reports on the percentage of nonbinging students who experienced "secondary binge effects," each of eight types of problems due to other students' drinking at each of the three different school types (i.e., schools with high, middle, and low binge levels). For seven of the eight problems studied, students at schools with high and middle binge levels were more likely than students at schools with low binge levels to experience problems as a result of the drinking behaviors of others. Odds ratios (adjusted for age, sex, race, marital status, and parents' college education) indicated that nonbinging students at schools with the high binge levels were more likely than nonbinging students at schools with low binge levels to experience secondary binge effects.

The odds of experiencing at least one of the eight problems was roughly 4:1 when students at schools with high binge levels were compared with students at schools with low binge levels.

Table 4

Students Experiencing Secondary Binge Effects
(Based on Students Who Were Not Binge Drinkers and Living
in Dormitories, Fraternities, or Sororities)*

| | | School's Binging Level | | | |
| | | Middle | | High | |
Secondary Binge Effect	Low, % (n=801)	% (n=1,115)	Adjusted OR (95% CI)†	% (n=1,064)	Adjusted OR (95% CI)‡
Been insulted or humiliated	21	30	1.6 (1.3–2.1)	34	1.9 (1.5–2.3)
Had a serious argument or quarrel	13	18	1.3 (1.0–1.7)	20	1.5 (1.1–2.0)
Been pushed, hit, or assaulted	7	10	1.4 (1.0–2.1)	13	2.0 (1.4–2.8)
Had your property damaged	6	13	2.0 (1.4–2.8)	15	2.3 (1.6–3.2)
Had to take care of drunken student	31	47	1.9 (1.6–2.3)	54	2.5 (2.0–3.0)
Had your study/sleep interrupted	42	64	2.3 (1.9–2.8)	68	2.6 (2.2–3.2)
Experienced an unwanted sexual advance§	15	21	1.7 (1.2–2.3)	26	2.1 (1.5–2.8)
Been a victim of sexual assault or date rape§	2	1	NS	2	NS
Experienced at least one of the above problems	62	82	2.8 (2.3–3.5)	87	4.1 (3.2–5.2)

*OR indicates odds ratio; CI, confidence interval.

†Adjusted OR of students at schools with middle levels of binging vs. students at schools with low levels are significant at P<.05.

‡Adjusted OR of students at schools with high levels of binging vs. students at schools with low levels are significant at P<.05.

§Based on women only.

Binge Drinking in High School

Most students reported the same drinking behavior in high school as in college. Almost half (47%) had not been binge drinkers in high school and did not binge in college, while one fifth (22%) binged in high school and in college. One fifth (22%) of the students were binge drinkers in college but not in high school, while 10% were not binge drinkers at the time of the survey in college, but reported having been binge drinkers in high school.

COMMENT

To our knowledge, this is the first study that has used a representative national sample, and the first large-scale study to measure binge drinking under a sex-specific definition. Forty-four percent of the college students in this study were classified as binge drinkers. This finding is consistent with the findings of other national studies such as the University of Michigan's Monitoring the Future Project, which found that 41% of college students were binge drinkers,[1,3] and the Core Alcohol and Drug Survey, which found that 42% of college students were binge drinkers.[5] All three studies used a definition of binging over a 2-week period, but the other studies used the same five-drink measure for both sexes. Binge drinking was defined in terms of the number of drinks consumed in a single episode. No attempt was made to specify the duration of time for each episode. Future research might examine whether subgroup differences exist in duration and whether such differences are linked to outcomes.

A possible limitation of surveys using self-reports of drinking behavior pertains to the validity of responses; however, a number of studies have confirmed the validity of self-reported of alcohol and substance use.[22–24] Findings indicate that if a self-report bias exists, it is largely limited to the heaviest use group[2,5] and should not affect such a conservative estimate of heavy volume as five drinks.

The results confirm that binge drinking is widespread on college campuses. Overall, almost half of all students were binge drinkers. One fifth of all students were frequent binge drinkers (had three or more binge drinking occasions in the past 2 weeks) and were deeply involved in a lifestyle characterized by frequent and deliberate intoxication. Frequent binge drinkers are much more likely to experience serious health and other consequences of their drinking behavior than other students. Almost half of them have experienced five or more alcohol-related problems since the beginning of the school year, one of three report they were hurt or injured, and two in five engaged in unplanned sexual activity. Frequent binge drinkers also report drinking and driving. Three of five male frequent binge drinkers drove after drinking some alcohol in the 30 days prior to the survey, and two of five drove after having five or more drinks. A recent national report that reviewed published studies concluded that alcohol was involved in two thirds of college student suicides, in 90% of campus rapes, and in 95% of violent crime on campus.[2,6]

Almost a third of the colleges in the study have a majority of students who binge. Not only do these binge drinkers put themselves at risk, they also create problems for their fellow students who are not binge drinking. Students who did not binge and who reside at schools with high levels of binge drinkers were up to three times as likely to report being bothered by the drinking-related behaviors of other students than students who did not binge and who reside at schools with lower levels of binge drinkers. These problems included being pushed, hit, or assaulted and experiencing an unwanted sexual advance.

Effective interventions face a number of challenges. Drinking is not typically a behavior learned in college and often continues patterns established earlier. In fact, one of three students in the present study was already a binge drinker in the year before college.

40   The prominence of drinking on college campuses reflects its importance in the wider society, but drinking has traditionally occupied a unique place in campus life. Despite the overall decline in drinking in US society, recent time-trend studies have failed to show a corresponding decrease in binge drinking on college campuses.[3,13] The variation in binge drinking rates among the colleges in this study suggests that colleges may create and unwittingly perpetuate their own drinking cultures through selection, tradition, policy, and other strategies. On many campuses, drinking behavior that would elsewhere be classified as alcohol abuse may be socially acceptable, or even socially attractive, despite its documented implication in automobile crashes, other injury, violence, suicide, and high-risk sexual behavior.

The scope of the problem makes immediate results of any interventions highly unlikely. Colleges need to be committed to large-scale and long-term behavior change strategies, including referral of alcohol abusers to appropriate treatment. Frequent binge drinkers on college campuses are similar to other alcohol abusers elsewhere in their tendency to deny that they have a problem. Indeed, their youth, the visibility of others who drink the same way, and the shelter of the college community may make them less likely to recognize the problem. In addition to addressing the health problems of alcohol abusers, a major effort should address the large group of students who are not binge drinkers on campus who are adversely affected by the alcohol-related behavior of binge drinkers.

This study was supported by the Robert Wood Johnson Foundation. We wish to thank the following persons who assisted with the project: Lloyd Johnston, PhD, Thomas J. Mangione, PhD, Anthony M. Roman, MD, Nan Laird, PhD, Jeffrey Hansen, Avtar Khalsa, MSW, and Marianne Lee, MPA.

REFERENCES

1. US Dept of Health and Human Services, *Alcohol and Health.* Rockville, Md: National Institute on Alcohol Abuse and Alcoholism: 1990.

2. Robert Wood Johnson Foundation. *Substance Abuse: The Nation's Number One Health Problem. Key Indicators for Policy.* Princeton, NJ: Robert Wood Johnson Foundation; October 1993.

3. Wechsler H, Isaac N. 'Binge' drinkers at Massachusetts colleges: prevalence, drinking styles, time trends, and associated problems. *JAMA.* 1992;267:2929–2931.

4. Hanson DJ, Engs RC. College students' drinking problems: a national study, 1982–1991. *Psychol Rep.* 1992;71:39–42.

5. Presley CA, Meilman PW, Lyerla R. *Alcohol and Drugs on American College Campuses: Use, Consequence, and Perceptions of the Campus Environment, Volume I: 1989–1991.* Carbondale, Ill: The Core Institute: 1993.

6. The Carnegie Foundation for the Advancement of Teaching. *Campus Life: In Search of Community.* Princeton, NJ: Princeton University Press: 1990.

7. Straus R, Bacon SD. *Drinking in College.* New Haven, Conn: Yale University Press: 1953.

8. Berkowitz AD, Perkins HW. Problem drinking among college students: a review of recent research. *J Am Coll Health.* 1986;35:21–28.

9. Saltz R, Elandt D. College student drinking studies: 1976–1986. *Contemp Drug Probl.* 1986;13:117–157.

10. Haworth-Hoeppner S, Globetti G, Stem J, Morasco F. The quantity and frequency of drinking among undergraduates at a southern university. *Int J Addict.* 1989; 24:829–857.

11. Liljestrand P. Quality in college student drinking research: conceptual and methodological issues. *J Alcohol Drug Educ.* 1993;38:1–36.

12. Hughes S, Dodder R. Alcohol consumption patterns among college populations. *J Coll Student Personnel.* 1983;20:257–264.

13. Johnston LD, O'Malley PM, Bachman JG. *Drug Use Among American High School Seniors, College Students, and Young Adults,* 1975–1990, Volume 2. Washington, DC: Government Printing Office; 1991. US Dept of Health and Human Services publication ADM 91-1835.

14. Wechsler H, McFadden M. Drinking among college students in New England. *J Stud Alcohol.* 1979;40:969–996.

15. O'Hare TM. Drinking in college: consumption patterns, problems, sex differences, and legal drinking age. *J Stud Alcohol.* 1990;51:536–541.

16. Engs RC, Hanson DJ. The drinking patterns and problems of college students: 1983. *J Alcohol Drug Educ.* 1985;31:65–83.

17. Brennan AF, Walfish S, AuBuchon P. Alcohol use and abuse in college students, I: a review of individual and personality correlates. *Int J Addict.* 1986;21:449–474.

18. Room R. Measuring alcohol consumption in the US: methods and rationales. In: Clark WB, Hilton ME, eds. *Alcohol in America: Drinking Practices and Problems.* Albany: State University of New York Press, 1991:26–50.

19. SAS Institute Inc. *SAS/STAT User's Guide, Release 6.03 ed.* Cary, NC: SAS Institute Inc; 1988.

20. US Dept of Education. *Digest of Educational Statistics.* Washington, DC: National Center of Educational Statistics: 1993:180,205.

21. *Barron's Profiles of American Colleges.* Hauppauge, NY: Barron's Educational Series Inc: 1992.

22. Midanik L. Validity of self-reported alcohol use: a literature review and assessment. *Br J Addict.* 1988;83:1019–1030.

23. Cooper AM, Sobell MB, Sobell LC, Maisto SA. Validity of alcoholics' self-reports: duration data. *Int J Addict.* 1981;16:401–406.

24. Reinisch OJ, Bell RM, Ellickson PL. *How Accurate Are Adolescent Reports of Drug Use?* Santa Monica, Calif: RAND; 1991. RAND publication N-3189-CHF.

25. Room R. Survey vs sales data for the US. *Drink Drug Pract Surv.* 1971;3:15–16.

26. CASA Commission on Substance Abuse at Colleges and Universities. *Rethinking Rites of Passage: Substance Abuse on America's Campuses.* New York, NY: Columbia University; June 1994.

QUESTIONS

1. This article's conclusions depend on the wording of the questions asked. A central question is "Think back over the last two weeks. How many times have you had five or more drinks in a row?" What do you think "in a row" means? Do you think the question is precise or fuzzy? Why was it asked this way?

2. How do you and people you know define "binge drinking"? How close is your definition to the definition used by Wechsler et al.?

3. At 44 of the 140 colleges surveyed, more than 50 percent of the students were binge drinkers. Does that sound alarming? Accurate? What might some of those colleges be?

EDWARD O. WILSON *Intelligent Evolution*

> We must acknowledge, as it seems to me, that man with all his noble qualities, with sympathy which feels for the most debased, with benevolence which extends not only to other men but to the humblest living creature, with his god-like intellect which has penetrated into the movements and constitution of the solar system—with all these exalted powers—Man still bears in his bodily frame the indelible stamp of his lowly origin.
>
> —CHARLES DARWIN[1]
> *The Descent of Man, and Selection*
> *in Relation to Sex* (1871)

GREAT SCIENTIFIC DISCOVERIES are like sunrises. They illuminate first the steeples of the unknown, then its dark hollows. Such expansive influence has been enjoyed by the scientific writings of Charles Darwin. For over 150 years his books * * * have spread light on the living world and the human condition. They have not lost their freshness: more than any other work in history's scientific canon, they are both timeless and persistently inspirational.

The four classics, flowing along one to the next like a well-wrought narrative, trace the development of Darwin's thought across almost all of his adult

First published in Harvard Magazine *(November/December 2005); a slightly different version appeared as a general introduction to* From So Simple a Beginning: The Four Great Books of Charles Darwin *(2005). The drawings come from the American edition of Charles Darwin's* The Descent of Man, and Selection in Relation to Sex *(1871).*

1. English naturalist (1809–1882) who theorized that living beings evolve through natural selection.

life. The first, *Voyage of the Beagle* (1845), one
of literature's great travel books, is richly
stocked with observations in natural history
of the kind that were to guide the young Darwin toward his evolutionary worldview. Next
comes the "one long argument," as he later
put it, of *On the Origin of Species* (1859), ar-
guably history's most influential book. In it the
now middle-aged Darwin massively documents the evidences of organic evolution and
introduces the theory of natural selection. *The
Descent of Man* (1871) then addresses the
burning topic foretold in *On the Origin of
Species*: "Light will be thrown on the origin of
man and his history." Finally, *The Expression
of the Emotions in Man and Animals* (1872)
draws close to the heart of the matter that
concerns us all: the origin and nature of

Crabo cribrarius.

mind, the "citadel" that Darwin could see but knew that science at the time
could not conquer.

The adventure that Darwin launched on all our behalf, and which continues into the twenty-first century, is driven by a deceptively simple idea, of which
Darwin's friend and staunch supporter Thomas Henry Huxley[2] said, and spoke
for many to follow, "How extremely stupid of me not to have thought of that!"
Evolution by natural selection is perhaps the only one true law unique to biological systems, as opposed to nonliving physical systems, and in recent decades
it has taken on the solidity of a mathematical theorem. It states simply that if a
population of organisms contains multiple hereditary variants in some trait (say,
red versus blue eyes in a bird population), and if one of these variants succeeds
in contributing more offspring to the next generation than the other variants,
the overall composition of the population changes, and *evolution has occurred*.
Further, if new genetic variants appear regularly in the population (by mutation
or immigration), *evolution never ends*. Think of red-eyed and blue-eyed birds in
a breeding population, and let the red-eyed birds be better adapted to the environment. The population will in time come to consist mostly or entirely of red-
eyed birds. Now let green-eyed mutants appear that are even better adapted to
the environment that the red-eyed form. As a consequence the species eventually becomes green-eyed. Evolution has thus taken two more small steps.

The full importance of Darwin's theory can be better understood by realizing that modern biology is guided by two overwhelmingly powerful and creative ideas. The first is that all biological processes are ultimately obedient to
even though far from fully explained by, the laws of physics and chemistry. The
second is that all biological processes arose through evolution of these physico-

---

2. English scientist (1825–1895) who defended and popularized Darwin's theory of
evolution.

chemical systems through natural selection. The first principle is concerned with the *how* of biology. The second is concerned with the ways the systems adapted to the environment over periods of time long enough for evolution to occur—in other words the *why* of biology.

5   Knowledge addressing the first principle is called functional biology; that addressing the second is called evolutionary biology. If a moving automobile were an organism, functional biology would explain how it is constructed and operates, while evolutionary biology would reconstruct its origin and history—how it came to be made and its journey thus far.

The impact of the theory of evolution by natural selection, nowadays grown very sophisticated (and often referred to as the Modern Synthesis), has been profound. To the extent it can be upheld, and the evidence to date has done so compellingly, we must conclude that life has diversified on Earth autonomously without any kind of external guidance. Evolution in a pure Darwinian world has no goal or purpose: the exclusive driving force is random mutations sorted out by natural selection from one generation to the next.

What then are we to make of the purposes and goals obviously chosen by human bings? They are, in Darwinian interpretation, processes evolved as adaptive devices by an otherwise purposeless natural selection. Evolution by natural selection means, finally, that the essential qualities of the human mind also

Top: *Tragelaphus strepsiceros.* Bottom: *Sitana minor* (male with the gular pouch expanded).

evolved autonomously. Humanity was thus born of Earth. However elevated in power over the rest of life, however exalted in self-image, we were descended from animals by the same blind force that created those animals, and we remain a member species of this planet's biosphere.

The revolution in astronomy begun by Nicolaus Copernicus[3] in 1543 proved that Earth is not the center of the universe, nor even the center of the solar system. The revolution begun by Darwin was even more humbling: it showed that humanity is not the center of creation, and not its purpose either.

3. Polish astronomer (1473–1543) who posited that the solar system is heliocentric, with the sun rather than the earth at its center.

But in freeing our minds from our imagined demigod bondage, even at the price of humility, Darwin turned our attention to the astounding power of the natural creative process and the magnificence of its products:

> There is grandeur in this view of life, with its several powers, having been originally breathed into a few forms or into one; and that, whilst this planet has gone cycling on according to the fixed law of gravity, from so simple a beginning endless forms most beautiful and most wonderful have been, and are being, evolved.
>
>   Darwin, *On the Origin of Species* (first edition, 1859)

> If I lived twenty more years and was able to work, how I should have to modify the *Origin*, and how much the views on all points will have to be modified! Well, it is a beginning, and that is something.
>   —CHARLES DARWIN
>   Letter to J. D. Hooker,[4] 1869

Darwin lived thirteen more years after writing this letter to Joseph Hooker, and he did manage to modify the theory of evolution by natural selection, expanding it in *The Descent of Man* (1871) to include human origins and in *The Expression of the Emotions in Man and Animals* (1872) to address the evolution of instinct. The ensuing 130 years have seen an enormous growth of the Darwinian heritage. Joined with molecular and cellular biology, that accumulated knowledge is today a large part of modern biology. Its centrality justifies the famous remark made by the evolutionary geneticist Theodosius Dobzhansky[5] in 1973 that "nothing in biology makes sense except in the light of evolution." In fact, nothing in science as a whole has been more firmly established by interwoven factual documentation, or more illuminating, than the universal occurrence of biological evolution. Further, few natural processes have been more convincingly explained than evolution by the theory of natural selection or, as it is popularly called, Darwinism.

Thus it is surpassingly strange that half of Americans recently polled (2004) not only do not believe in evolution by natural selection but do not believe in evolution at all. Americans are certainly capable of belief, and with rocklike conviction if it originates in religious dogma. In evidence is the 60 percent that accept the prophecies of the Book of Revelation[6] as truth, and yet in more evidence is the weight that faith-based positions hold in political life. Most of the religious Right opposes the teaching of evolution in public schools, either by an outright ban on the subject or, at the least, by insisting that it be treated as "only a theory" rather than a "fact."

10

Yet biologists, particularly those statured by the peer review and publication of substantial personal research on the subject in leading journals of

4. English botanist (1817–1911) and champion of Darwin's evolutionary theory.
5. Ukrainian evolutionary biologist and geneticist (1900–1975).
6. The final book of the New Testament, which contains visions of apocalypse.

Top: *Cercopithecus petaurista.*
Bottom, from left to right: *Semnopithecus comatus, Cebus capucinus, Ateles marginatus,* and *Cebus vellerosus.*

Callionymus lyra (upper figure, male; lower figure, female).

science, are unanimous in concluding that evolution is a *fact*. The evidence they and thousands of others have adduced over 150 years falls together in intricate and interlocking detail. The multitudinous examples range from the small changes in DNA[7] sequences observed as they occur in real time to finely graded sequences within larger evolutionary changes in the fossil record. Further, on the basis of comparably firm evidence, natural selection grows ever stronger as the prevailing explanation of evolution.

Many who accept the fact of evolution cannot, however, on religious grounds, accept the operation of blind chance and the absence of divine purpose implicit in natural selection. They support the alternative explanation of intelligent design. The reasoning they offer is not based on evidence but on the lack of it. The formulation of intelligent design is a default argument advanced in support of a non sequitur. It is in essence the following: There are some phenomena that have not yet been explained and that (and most importantly) the critics personally cannot imagine being explained; therefore there must be a supernatural designer at work. The designer is seldom specified, but in the canon of intelligent design it is most certainly not Satan and his angels, nor any god or gods conspicuously different from those accepted in the believer's faith.

Flipping the scientific argument upside down, the intelligent designers join the strict creationists (who insist that no evolution ever occurred in the first

7. Deoxyribonucleic acid, which contains and encodes genetic information in living organisms.

Dog "in a humble and affectionate frame of mind."

place) by arguing that scientists resist the supernatural theory because it is counter to their own personal secular beliefs. This may have a kernel of truth; everybody suffers from some amount of bias. But in this case bias is easily overcome. The critics forget how the reward system in science works. Any researcher who can prove the existence of intelligent design within the accepted framework of science will make history and achieve eternal fame. He will prove at last that *science and religious dogma are compatible!* Even a combined Nobel Prize and Templeton Prize (the latter designed to encourage search for just such harmony) would fall short as proper recognition. Every scientist would like to accomplish such an epoch-making advance. But no one has even come close, because unfortunately there is no evidence, no theory, and no criteria for proof that even marginally might pass for science. There is only the residue of hoped for default, which steadily shrinks as the science of biology expands.

In all of the history of science only one other disparity of comparable magnitude to evolution has occurred between a scientific event and the impact it has had on the public mind. This was the discovery by Copernicus that Earth and therefore humanity are not the center of the universe, and the universe is not a closed spherical bubble. Copernicus delayed publication of his masterwork *On the Revolution of the Heavenly Spheres* until the year of his death (1543). For his extension of the idea subsequently, Bruno was burned at the stake, and for its documentation Galileo was shown the instruments of torture at Rome and remained under house arrest for the remainder of his life.[8]

8. Giordano Bruno (1548–1600), Italian astronomer, priest, and philosopher burned at the stake for his unconventional beliefs, including in the existence of planets outside our solar system; Galileo Galilei (1564–1642), Italian astronomer whose research supported Copernicus's heliocentric view of the universe.

Today we live in a less barbaric age, but an otherwise comparable disjunction between science and religion, the one born of Darwinism, still roils the public mind. Why does such intense and pervasive resistance to evolution continue 150 years after the publication of *The Origin of Species*, and in the teeth of the overwhelming accumulated evidence favoring it? The answer is simply that the Darwinian revolution, even more than the Copernican revolution, challenges the prehistoric and still-regnant self-image of humanity. Evolution by natural selection, to be as concise as possible, has changed everything.

In the more than slightly schizophrenic circumstances of the present era, global culture is divided into three opposing images of the human condition, each logically consistent within its own, independent premises. The dominant of these hypotheses, exemplified by the creation myths of the Abrahamic monotheistic religions[9] (Judaism, Christianity, and Islam), sees humanity as a creation of God. He brought us into being and He guides us still as father, judge, and friend. We interpret his will from sacred scriptures and the wisdom of ecclesiastical authorities.

Pneumora.

The second worldview is that of political behaviorism. Still beloved by the now rapidly fading Marxist-Leninist[10] states, it says that the brain is largely a blank state devoid of any inborn inscription beyond reflexes and primitive bodily urges. As a consequence the mind originates almost wholly as a result of learning, and it is the product of a culture that itself evolves by historical contingency. Because there is no biologically based "human nature," people can be molded to the best possible political and economic system, namely, as urged upon the world through most of the twentieth century, communism.[11] In practical politics, this belief has been repeatedly tested and, after economic collapses and tens of millions of deaths in a dozen dysfunctional states, is generally deemed a failure.

Both of these worldviews, God-centered religion and atheistic communism, are opposed by a third and in some ways more radical worldview, scientific humanism. Still held by only a tiny minority of the world's population, it

9. Jewish, Christian, and Muslim faiths that trace their lineage to the ancient Hebrew Abraham (ca. 2000 B.C.E.–1500 B.C.E.).

10. Socialist thinking in the style or tradition of German thinker Karl Marx (1818–1883) and Russian politician Vladimir Lenin (1870–1924).

11. A social philosophy that seeks to eliminate class structure and private property in favor of common ownership.

Rhynchaea capensis.

considers humanity to be a biological species that evolved over millions of years in a biological world, acquiring unprecedented intelligence yet still guided by complex inherited emotions and biased channels of learning. Human nature exists, and it was self-assembled. It is the commonality of the hereditary responses and propensities that define our species. Having arisen by evolution during the far simpler conditions in which humanity lived during more than 99 percent of its existence, it forms the behavioral part of what, in *The Descent of Man*, Darwin called the indelible stamp of our lowly origin.

To understand biological human nature in depth is to drain the fever swamps of religious and blank-slate dogma.[12] But it also imposes the heavy burden of individual choice that goes with intellectual freedom.

20   Such was the long journey for Darwin, the architect of the naturalistic worldview. He began his voyage on the *Beagle* as a devout Christian who trained for the ministry. "Whilst on board the *Beagle* I was quite orthodox," he

12. The idea that humans are born without personality or knowledge and that their experience is entirely responsible for forming them.

wrote much later in his autobiography, "and I remember being heartily laughed at by several of the officers (though themselves orthodox) for quoting the Bible as an unanswerable authority on some point of morality." His later drift from the religion of his birth was stepwise and slow. Still on H.M.S. *Beagle* during its circumnavigation of the globe (1831–1836) he came to believe that the "false history" and reports of God's vengeful feelings made the Old Testament "no more to be trusted than the sacred books of the Hindoos,[13] or the beliefs of any barbarian." The miracles of Jesus seemed to him to suggest that people living at the time of the Gospels were "ignorant and credulous to a degree almost incomprehensible by us." The growth of disbelief was so slow that Darwin felt no distress. In a striking passage of his autobiography he expressed his final and complete rejection of Christian dogma based solely on blind faith:

> I can indeed hardly see how anyone ought to wish Christianity to be true; for if so the plain language of the text seems to show that the men who do not believe, and this would include my Father, Brother and almost all my best friends, will be everlastingly punished. And that is a damnable doctrine.

Did Charles Darwin recant in his last days, as some religious critics have hopefully suggested? There is not a shred of evidence that he did or that he was presented with any reason to do so. Further, it would have been wholly contrary to the deliberate, careful manner with which he approached every subject.

The great naturalist did not abandon Abrahamic and other religious dogmas because of his discovery of evolution by natural selection, as one might reasonably suppose. The reverse occurred. The shedding of blind faith gave him the intellectual fearlessness to explore human evolution wherever logic and evidence took him. And so he set forth boldly, in *The Descent of Man* to track the origin of humanity, and in *The Expression of the Emotions in Man and Animals* to address the evolution of instinct. Thus was born scientific humanism, the only worldview compatible with science's growing knowledge of the real world and the laws of nature.

So, will science and religion find common ground, or at least agree to divide the fundamentals into mutually exclusive domains? A great many well-meaning scholars believe that such rapprochement is both possible and desirable. A few disagree, and I am one of them. I think Darwin would have held to the same position. The battle line is, as it has ever been, in biology. The inexorable growth of this science continues to widen, not to close, the tectonic gap between science and faith-based religion.

Rapprochement may be neither possible nor desirable. There is something deep in religious belief that divides people and amplifies societal conflict. In the early part of this century, the toxic mix of religion and tribalism has become so dangerous as to justify taking seriously the alternative view, that hu-

13. Hindus.

manism based on science is the effective antidote, the light and the way at last placed before us.

25   In any case, the dilemma to be solved is truly profound. On the one side the input of religion on human history has been beneficent in many ways. It has generated much of which is best in culture, including the ideals of altruism and public service. From the beginning of history it has inspired the arts. Creation myths were in a sense the beginning of science itself. Fabricating them was the best the early scribes could do to explain the universe and human existence.

Yet the high risk is the ease with which alliances between religions and tribalism are made. Then comes bigotry and the dehumanization of infidels. Our gods, the true believer asserts, stand against your false idols, our spiritual purity against your corruption, our divinely sanctioned knowledge against your errancy. In past ages the posture provided an advantage. It united each tribe during life-and-death struggles with other tribes. It buoyed the devotees with a sense of superiority. It sacralized tribal laws and mores, and encouraged altruistic behaviors. Through sacred rites it lent solemnity to the passages of life. And it comforted the anxious and afflicted. For all this and more it gave people an identity and purpose, and vouchsafed tribal fitness—yet, unfortunately, at the expense of less united or otherwise less fortunate tribes.

Religions continue both to render their special services and to exact their heavy costs. Can scientific humanism do as well or better, at a lower cost? Surely that ranks as one of the great unanswered questions of philosophy. It is the noble yet troubling legacy that Charles Darwin left us.

QUESTIONS

1. As the contextual note explains, Edward Wilson wrote this essay to introduce a new edition of the scientific works of Charles Darwin. What parts of the essay provide information about Darwin and his work? What parts extend Darwin's theories to present-day debates about evolution and intelligent design? Why does Wilson arrange these parts in the order they appear?

2. Wilson uses similes (comparisons with *like* or *as*) and metaphors (comparisons without connectives) to explain key concepts. Analyze the similes in paragraphs 1 (sunrises), 5 (automobile), and 13 (designers), and explain their function in the argument.

3. In the last section of the essay Wilson defines three worldviews: religious, Marxist-Leninist, and scientific. How does he define each? How do his classifications and definitions help advance his argument in this essay?

4. Choose one of Darwin's four books or one of the scientists Wilson mentions. Do research about your choice, and write a brief account of its importance in the history of science.

DAVID BALTIMORE *Limiting Science: A Biologist's Perspective*

ONTEMPORARY RESEARCH in molecular biology has grown up in an era of almost complete permissiveness. Its practitioners have been allowed to decide their own priorities and have met with virtually no restraints on the types of work they can do. Viewed as a whole, the field has not even met with fiscal restraints because, relative to "big science," molecular biology has been a relatively cheap enterprise.

Some of the funds that fueled the initial, seminal investigations in molecular biology were granted because of the medical implications of work in basic biology. Most continue to come from agencies concerned with health. Although basic research in biology has yet to have a major impact on the prevention and treatment of human disease, a backlash already seems to be developing in which various groups in our society question whether the freedom that has characteristically been granted to research biologists by a permissive public requires modification. Among the numerous elements prompting this questioning are impatience with the lack of practical results, and fears that direct hazards might result from the experimentation, that basic research may not be an appropriate investment of significant funds, and that dangerous new technologies may flow from discoveries in basic biology. Lay critics as well as a few members of the profession have argued that molecular biologists should concentrate their efforts in certain areas of research, like fertility mechanisms, while other areas, like genetics or aging, are possibly dangerous and certainly not worthy of financial support from the public. These critics believe that they can channel contemporary biology to fit their own conception of appropriate research.

I wish to argue that the traditional pact between society and its scientists, in which the scientist is given the responsibility for determining the direction of his work, is a necessary relationship if basic science is to be an effective endeavor. This does not mean that society is at the mercy of science, but rather that society, while it must determine the pace of basic scientific innovation, should not attempt to prescribe its directions.

What we call molecular biology today had its origins in individual decisions of a small number of scientists during the period from the late 1930s through the early 1950s. These people were trained in diverse fields, among them physics, medicine, microbiology, and crystallography.[1] They created mo-

Written by a Nobel Prize–winning scientist and originally published in Dædalus *(Spring 1978), the professional journal of the American Academy of Arts and Sciences; the Academy re-published the essay in* Dædalus *(Fall 2005).*

1. The science of the formation and structure of crystals.

lecular biology out of the realization that the problems posed by genetics were central to understanding the structures of living systems. No one channeled them towards this line of thinking, no one cajoled them to tackle these problems; rather, their own curiosity and sense of timing led them to try to elucidate these mysteries. This history provides a model of how the most effective science is done.

It is partly the successes of molecular biology that have brought on the questioning of whether scientists should be allowed their freedom of decision. It is therefore worthwhile tracing the development of concerns about whether certain areas of science should be closed to investigation. Molecular biology is the science that has revealed to us the nature of one of the most fundamental of all substances of life, the gene. There is a very simple underlying reality to the transmission of characteristics from parents to children: a code based on four different chemicals, denoted by the letters A, T, G, and C,[2] is used to store the information of heredity. The order in which these four chemicals appear in a virtually endless polymer, called DNA,[3] is the language of life.

Knowing that DNA was the physical storehouse of the genes, Watson and Crick in 1953 first solved the problem of how the DNA is organized to assure that information is transferred with almost perfect reliability from parent cells to progeny cells.[4] They showed that DNA is made of two strands intertwined together into a helix and also that the four sub-units in DNA are physically related so that only A and T form a specific pair as do G and C. The two strands are held together by this specific pairing so that the two strands carry redundant information. Each gene is thus really a gene and a mirror-gene; this self-complementarity allows DNA to repair itself—and therefore maintain the fidelity of its information—and also to duplicate itself, sending identical copies into the two daughter cells resulting from a round of cell division.

Following the monumental discovery of the structure of DNA, many scientists have contributed to learning how to make DNA, how to read DNA, how to cut DNA, how to rejoin DNA, and in general, how to manipulate at will the genes of very simple organisms.

What good has all of this new knowledge brought to the average person? First and of great importance is the contribution that scientific advances make to human culture. The continued accumulation of knowledge about ourselves and our environment is a crucial cultural aspect of contemporary life. Science as well as art illuminates man's view of himself and his relation to others. Our knowledge of how we work, how one person differs from and is similar to another, what is health and what disease, what we need to support health, and so

2. Short for adenine, thymine, guanine, cytosine, the main four substances that make up DNA and RNA.

3. Polymer: a molecule that comprises many repeating units; DNA: Deoxyribonucleic acid, which contains genetic information that determines the characteristics of living organisms.

4. James Watson (b. 1928) and Francis Crick (1916–2004), discoverers of DNA's double-helix structure. Parent cells are the units of life that, in cell division, create progeny cells.

on, helps to set the ground rules for the debates of politics and the productions of art.

The more practical benefits of biology can be expected to come in the future in the form of medical advances, or increases in food production, or in other manipulations of life processes that will be able to provide positive contributions to civilization. But molecular biology, for all of its power as a basic science, has not been easily translated into tangible benefits. This is a situation that could change very soon. New discoveries are rapidly bringing molecular biology closer to an ability to affect the lives of the general public.

Of the advances that have occurred, a critical one has been the development of a process called recombinant DNA research. This is a technique whereby different pieces of DNA are sewn together using enzymes;[5] the chimeric DNA is then inserted into a bacterium where it can be multiplied indefinitely. Because the method allows genes from any species in the world to be put into a common type of bacterium, there is a theoretical possibility of hazard in this research. The potential for unforeseen occurrences led a number of scientists, including me, to issue in 1974 a call for restraint in the application of these new methods. We were addressing a limited problem, whether there could be a recognizable hazard in the performance of certain experiments. That limited question opened a floodgate; other questions came pouring out and are still coming. They have led to front-cover stories in weekly magazines, to serious attempts at federal legislation, to a demoralization of some of the community of basic research biologists, and, most significantly, to a deep questioning of whether further advances in biology are likely to be beneficial or harmful to our society.

10

Much of the discussion about recombinant DNA research has centered on whether the work is likely to create hazardous organisms. The mayor of Cambridge, Massachusetts, raised the specter of Frankenstein monsters emerging from MIT and Harvard laboratories, and speculations about the possibility of inadvertent development of a destructive organism like the fictitious Andromeda Strain have been much in the news.[6] I am personally satisfied that most of such talk is simply science fiction and that the research can be made as safe as any other research. The people who understand infectious diseases best make the arguments most strongly that recombinant DNA research is not going to create monsters. But rather than defend my judgment that the safety issue has been blown out of proportion, I want to consider some of the more general issues that have been raised by the controversy.

If safety were the most important consideration behind the debate about recombinant DNA, then we might expect the debate to focus on the hazards of

---

5. Proteins that facilitate chemical reactions.

6. In Mary Shelley's 1818 novel, *Frankenstein*, Dr. Frankenstein creates a terrifying, not-quite-human monster through scientific manipulation; in *The Andromeda Strain*, Michael Crichton's 1969 science fiction novel, an extraterrestrial disease causes fatal blood clots.

doing recombinant DNA experiments. Instead, many of the discussions that start considering such questions soon turn to a consideration of genetic engineering.

Two techniques labeled genetic engineering exist. Both originated because not everybody's genes are perfectly designed for the job of being a functioning human being, so that many instances of blood disorders, mental problems, and a host of other disabilities are traceable to a malfunctioning gene. It would be a triumph of medicine if the effects of such genes could be countered, and two approaches for countering them have been considered, both of which are called genetic engineering. One approach involves altering some cells of the body so that they can carry out the needed function. A patient could, for instance, be treated in this way for a blood disease caused by an abnormal protein made by a mutant gene. A normal gene would be inserted into the precursor cells—immature bone marrow cells that ultimately develop into functioning blood cells. In this way, a normal protein could be made in place of, or along with, the aberrant protein. The genetically altered blood cell precursor could then cure the patient's disease. But the malfunctioning gene would still be transmitted to the patient's offspring. Because this form of genetic engineering would not change the gene pool of the species and because it may prove an effective medical treatment of disease, it does not present the same moral problem as the other form. It is likely to be the first type of genetic engineering tried on human beings, and might be tried within the next five years.

The second type of genetic engineering presents more of a dilemma because it could change the human gene pool. This would involve replacement of genes in the germ cells, cells that transmit their genes to our offspring. Such a change would represent a permanent alteration of the types of the genetic information that constitutes our species. Replacement of germ cell genes would be very difficult and is, I suspect, at least twenty years away. It presents no theoretical problems, only formidable logistic problems.

15   Both forms of genetic engineering, but especially the engineering of germ cells, present two very deep and perplexing problems: who is to decide, and how shall they decide what genes are malfunctional? Decisions about which genes are good and which bad truly represent decisions of morality and are therefore highly subjective. Fear that dictators will decide which genes should be suppressed and which promoted, and that their criteria for decision will be how best to maintain their own power, has made the phrase "genetic engineering" symbolic of the moral problems that can be created by modern biology.

Genetic engineering of human beings is not the same as recombinant DNA research. Genetic engineering is a process carried out on human beings; recombinant DNA methods are ways to purify genes. Such genes might be used in genetic engineering procedures but are much more likely to be used as tools in studies of biological organization or as elements in a biological manufacturing process. Although genetic engineering is not the same as recombinant DNA research, the two are rightly linked because recombinant DNA work is hastening the day when genetic engineering will be a feasible process for use on certain human diseases. Since recombinant DNA work is also bringing closer the discovery of many other possible new medical treatments, and is likely to bring other new capabilities, why is there so much focus on genetic engineering? I believe that genetic engineering, because of its tabloid appeal, has become a symbol to many people of the frightening potential of modern-day technology. Rather than seeing in molecular biology the same complex mixtures of appropriate and inappropriate applications that characterize all powerful sciences, many people have allowed the single negative catch phrase "genetic engineering" to dominate discussions. People worry that if the possibility of curing a genetic defect by gene therapy should ever become a reality, the inevitable result would be "people made to order." It is argued that unless we block recombinant DNA research now, we will never have another chance to control our fate.

To see the form of the argument against recombinant DNA research most clearly and to highlight its danger to intellectual freedom and creativity, we should realize that similar arguments have been put forward relative to other areas of basic biology. One of the most respected critics of recombinant DNA research, Robert Sinsheimer, has for instance, made comparable analyses of two other research topics, research on aging and attempts to contact extraterrestrial beings.[7] He argues that if research on aging were to be successful, people could live to much older ages and the changed age structure of the population would bring serious stresses to society. His fear about searching for extraterrestrial beings is, again, that we could be successful, and he considers that the discovery of civilizations much more advanced than ours would have effects on us like those the Europeans had on native Americans after the discovery of the New World. In the case of recombinant DNA research as well as the other topics, Dr. Sinsheimer says we should avoid studying these areas of science. Rather, he believes, we should put our resources into investigating areas of proven need, such as fertility control.

These examples—and I could choose many others, especially outside of biology—have the same general form: certain people believe that there are areas of research that should be taboo because their outcome might be, or in some scenarios will be, detrimental to the stable relationships that characterize contemporary society. I have heard the argument in a different and more pernicious form from members of a Boston area group called Science for the People. They argue that some research in genetics should not go on because its findings might be detrimental to the relationships they believe should characterize a just society. Such arguments are reminiscent of those surrounding the eugenics[8] movements that developed in Germany and Russia in the 1920s.

7. R. L. Sinsheimer, "Inquiry to Inquiry: Two Opposing Views," *The Hastings Center Report* 6 (4) (1976): 18 [Baltimore's note].

8. A philosophy (or program) advocating the adjustment or improvement of inherited human traits through genetic manipulation.

After a period of intense debate, these countries with opposing ideologies settled on opposing analyses of the role of genetics in determining human diversity.[9] German scientists and politicians espoused a theory of racial purification by selective breeding, while Russia accepted the Lamarckian principle of transmission of acquired characteristics.[10] In both cases, science was forced into a mold created by political and social ideology, and in both cases the results were disastrous.

As I see it, we are being faced today with the following question: should limits be placed on biological research because of the danger that new knowledge can present to the established or desired order of our society? Having thus posed the question, I believe that there are two simple, and almost universally applicable, answers. First, the criteria determining what areas to restrain inevitably express certain sociopolitical attitudes that reflect a dominant ideology. Such criteria cannot be allowed to guide scientific choices. Second, attempts to restrain directions of scientific inquiry are more likely to be generally disruptive of science than to provide the desired specific restraints. These answers to the question of whether limits should be imposed can be stated in two arguments. One is that science should not be the servant of ideology, because ideology assumes answers, but science asks questions. The other is that attempts to make science serve ideology will merely make science impotent without assuring that only desired questions are investigated. I am stating simply that we should not control the direction of science and, moreover, that we cannot do so with any precision.

20   Before trying to substantiate these arguments I must make a crucial distinction. The arguments pertain to basic scientific research, not to the technological applications of science. As we go from the fundamental to the applied, my arguments fall away. There is every reason why technology should and must serve specific needs. Conversely, there are many technological possibilities that ought to be restrained.

To return to basic research, let me first consider the danger of restricting types of investigation because their outcome could be disruptive to society. There are three aspects of danger. One is the fallacy that you can predict what society will be like even in the near future. To say, for instance, that it would be bad for Americans to live longer assumes that the birth rate will stay near where it is. But what happens if the birth rate falls even lower than it is now in the United States and also stabilizes elsewhere in the world? We might welcome a readjustment of the life span. In any case, we have built a world around a given human life span; we could certainly adjust to a longer span, and it would be hard to predict whether in the long run the results would be better or worse.

9. L. R. Graham, "Political Ideology and Genetic Theory: Russia and Germany in the 1920's," *The Hastings Center Report* 7 (5) (1977): 30–39 [Baltimore's note].

10. Based on the philosophy of Jean-Baptiste Pierre Antoine de Monet, Chevalier de Lamarck (1744–1829), who believed that living creatures could inherit acquired traits.

In a general form, I would call this argument for restricting research the Error of Futurism. The futurist believes that the present holds enough readable clues about the future to provide a good basis for prediction. I doubt this assumption; to think that the data of today can be analyzed well enough to predict the future with any accuracy seems nonsensical to me.

The second danger in restricting areas of scientific investigation is more crucial: although we often worry most about keeping society stable, in fact societies need certain kinds of upheaval and renewal to stay vital. The new ideas and insights of science, much as we may fight against them, provide an important part of the renewal process that maintains the fascination of life. Freedom is the range of opportunities available to an individual—the more he has to choose from, the freer his choice. Science creates freedom by widening our range of understanding and therefore the possibilities from which we can choose.

Finally, attempts to dictate scientific limits on political or social considerations have another disastrous implication. Scientific orthodoxy is usually dictated by the state when its leaders fear that truths could undermine their power. Their repressive dicta are interpreted by the citizens as an admission of the leaders' insecurity and may thus lead to unrest requiring further repression. A social system that leaves science free to explore, and encourages scientific discoveries rather than trying to make science serve it by producing the truths necessary for its stability, transmits to the members of that society strength, not fear, and can endure.

The other argument I mentioned in opposing imposition of orthodoxy on science is the practical impossibility of stopping selected areas of research. Take aging as a prime example. It is one of the mystery areas of modern biology. The questions are clear. Why do we get older? Why do organ systems slowly fail? Why does one species of animal live three years and another live for one hundred? These seemingly straightforward questions are unapproachably difficult for modern biology. Not only can we not understand events that occur over years, but we even have difficulty understanding questions about events that require minutes to transpire. In fact, molecular biologists are really only experts in the millisecond range of time. Such times are those of chemical reactions; to understand events in longer time frames probably requires knowing how individual reactions are integrated to produce clocks that measure time in seconds to years. Clues to the great mysteries of biology—memory, aging, and differentiation—lie in understanding how biological systems tell time.

There are a few hints about where answers to the puzzle of aging might be found, but they are only the vaguest suggestions. In such an area of science, history tells us that successes are likely to come from unpredictable directions. A scientist working on vitamins or viruses or even plants is just as likely to find a clue to the problem of aging as is a scientist working on the problem directly. In fact, someone outside the field is more likely to make a revolutionary discovery than someone inside the field.

Another example will help to show the generality of this contention. Imag-

25

ine that we were living at the turn of the last century and had wanted to help medical diagnosis by devising a method of seeing into the insides of people. We would probably have decided to fund medical scientists to learn how to use bright lights to see through patients' skin. Little would we have guessed that the solution would be revolutionary and would come, not from a medical research scientist, but from a physicist who would discover a new form of radiation, X-rays.[11]

Major breakthroughs cannot be programmed. They come from people and areas of research that are not predictable. So if you wanted to cut off an area of fundamental research, how would you be able to devise the controls? I contend that it would be impossible. You could close the National Institute of Aging Research, but I doubt that any major advance in that field *could* be prevented. Only the shutdown of all scientific research can guarantee such an outcome.

Although they would fail to produce their desired result, attempts explicitly to control the directions of basic research would hardly be benign. Instead, disruption and demoralization would follow from attempts to determine when a scientist was doing work in approved directions and when he was not. Creative people would shun whole areas of science if they knew that in those areas their creativity would be channeled, judged, and limited. The net effect of constraining biologists to approved lines of investigation would be to degrade the effectiveness of the whole science of biology.

30   Put this way, the penalty for trying to control lines of investigation seems to me greater than any conceivable benefit. I conclude that society can choose to have either more science or less science, but choosing *which* science to have is not a feasible alternative.

I must repeat a qualification of this broad generalization: the less basic the research area in which controls are imposed, the less general disruption will be caused by the controls. The development of a specific sweetener, pesticide, or weapon could be prevented with little generalized effect.

While it seems necessary that scientific research be free of overt restraints, it would be naive to think that science is not directed at all. Many crucial decisions are made about general directions of science, usually by the control of available resources. Again, the formula I used before is applicable: the less basic the area of research, the easier it is to target the problems. A fallacy behind some of the hopes for the "War on Cancer" was the assumption that the problems to be solved were sufficiently well defined to allow a targeted, applied approach to the disease. Some problems could be defined and those were appropriate targets for a war on the disease, but the deeper mysteries of cancer are so close to the frontiers of biology that targets are hard to discern.

I have painted a picture of inexorable, uncontrollable development of basic scientific knowledge. The response of many people to such a vision might well

11. Dr. Mahlon Hoagland first suggested to me this example [Baltimore's note].

be "If we can't put any controls on research, maybe we shouldn't have any research." I see the rationale in this criticism because it is conceivable that the rate of accretion of knowledge could become so high that a brake might be needed. A way exists to produce a slowdown, that is, by controlling the overall availability of resources. A nonselective brake on fundamental biology would decrease productivity without the disruptive and dangerous effects of trying to halt one area and advance another.

Because such a brake was applied in the late 1960s, today we have less basic research, measured in constant dollars spent on it, than we had then. As a result of the slowdown, the danger seen by many is not that we have too much basic research, but rather that we are living on our intellectual capital and that an infusion of funds into basic areas of research is needed before these scientific resources are exhausted. It must also be realized that our commitment to the solution of problems like cancer requires that we develop much more basic knowledge.

I may seem to have strayed from my topic of recombinant DNA research, but I think not. In 1977, there was a draft bill in the U.S. Senate to set up a National Commission on Recombinant DNA Research. The charge to this commission discussed mainly questions of safety, but at the end of the bill questions of ethics and morality entered. The bill was a clear invitation to begin the process of deciding what research shall be allowed and what research prevented. The battle to stop the creation of this commission was waged by scientists, university presidents, and other concerned individuals across the country. I believe that the long-term success or failure of these efforts will determine whether America continues to have a tradition of free inquiry into matters of science or falls under the fist of orthodoxy.

35

To finish this discussion, let me quote from the most eloquent analyst of contemporary biology, Lewis Thomas,[12] the president of the Memorial Sloan-Kettering Cancer Center in New York. Writing in the *New England Journal of Medicine* about the recombinant DNA issue, Dr. Thomas ended with this analysis of the role of scientific research in the life of the mind:

> Is there something fundamentally unnatural, or intrinsically wrong, or hazardous for the species, in the ambition that drives us all to reach a comprehensive understanding of nature, including ourselves? I cannot believe it. It would seem to me a more unnatural thing, and more of an offense against nature, for us to come on the same scene endowed as we are with curiosity, filled to overbrimming as we are with questions, and naturally talented as we are for the asking of clear questions, and then for us to do nothing about it, or worse, to try to suppress the questions. This is the greater danger for our species, to try to pretend that we are another kind of animal, that we do not need to satisfy our curiosity, exploration, and experimentation, and that the human mind can rise above its ignorance by simply asserting that there are things it has no need to know.[13]

12. American physician, educator, and science writer (1913–1993).

13. Lewis Thomas in the *New England Journal of Medicine* 296 (1977): 328 [Baltimore's note].

QUESTIONS

1. David Baltimore argues that scientists must have the freedom to pursue their research without governmental or societal interference. Where does he state this argument? What function does the paragraph preceding it have?

2. Why does Baltimore give a history of the discovery of DNA? What evidence does that history supply in support of his argument?

3. Midway through his argument, Baltimore acknowledges the difficulties that genetic engineering raises. Why does he describe two different forms of genetic engineering? What careful distinctions does he make between them—and why?

4. Write an essay in which you support or disagree with Baltimore's argument, in terms of contemporary issues in biological research. Incorporate, as Baltimore does, definitions and careful distinctions as you support your position.

NEIL POSTMAN   *Virtual Students, Digital Classroom*

I F ONE HAS a trusting relationship with one's students (let us say, graduate students), it is not altogether gauche to ask them if they believe in God (with a capital G). I have done this three or four times and most students say they do. Their answer is preliminary to the next question: If someone you love were desperately ill, and you had to choose between praying to God for his or her recovery or administering an antibiotic (as prescribed by a competent physician), which would you choose?

Most say the question is silly since the alternatives are not mutually exclusive. Of course. But suppose they were—which would you choose? God helps those who help themselves, some say in choosing the antibiotic, therefore getting the best of two possible belief systems. But if pushed to the wall (e.g., God does not always help those who help themselves; God helps those who pray and who believe), most choose the antibiotic, after noting that the question is asinine and proves nothing. Of course, the question was not asked, in the first place, to prove anything but to begin a discussion of the nature of belief. And I do not fail to inform the students, by the way, that there has recently emerged evidence of a "scientific" nature that when sick people are prayed for they do better than those who aren't.

As the discussion proceeds, important distinctions are made among the different meanings of "belief," but at some point it becomes far from asinine to speak of the god of Technology—in the sense that people believe technology

Originally published in the liberal weekly The Nation *(October 9, 1995), this article reflects Postman's lifelong interest in the impact of technology on modern culture, as also reflected in his book* Technopoly: The Surrender of Culture to Technology *(1992).*

works, that they rely on it, that it makes promises, that they are bereft when denied access to it, that they are delighted when they are in its presence, that for most people it works in mysterious ways, that they condemn people who speak against it, that they stand in awe of it and that, in the "born again" mode, they will alter their life-styles, their schedules, their habits, and their relationships to accommodate it. If this be not a form of religious belief, what is?

In all strands of American cultural life, you can find so many examples of technological adoration that it is possible to write a book about it. And I would if it had not already been done so well. But nowhere do you find more enthusiasm for the god of Technology than among educators. In fact, there are those, like Lewis Perelman, who argue (for example, in his book, *School's Out*) that modern information technologies have rendered schools entirely irrelevant since there is now much more information available outside the classroom than inside it. This is by no means considered an outlandish idea. Dr. Diane Ravitch, former Assistant Secretary of Education, envisions, with considerable relish, the challenge that technology presents to the tradition that "children (and adults) should be educated in a specific place, for a certain number of hours, and a certain number of days during the week and year." In other words, that children should be educated in school. Imagining the possibilities of an information superhighway offering perhaps a thousand channels, Dr. Ravitch assures us that:

> In this new world of pedagogical plenty, children and adults will be able to dial up a program on their home television to learn whatever they want to know, at their own convenience. If Little Eva cannot sleep, she can learn algebra instead. At her home-learning station, she will tune in to a series of interesting problems that are presented in an interactive medium, much like video games. . . .
>
> Young John may decide that he wants to learn the history of modern Japan, which he can do by dialing up the greatest authorities and teachers on the subject, who will not only use dazzling graphs and illustrations, but will narrate a historical video that excites his curiosity and imagination.

In this vision there is, it seems to me, a confident and typical sense of unreality. Little Eva can't sleep, so she decides to learn a little algebra? Where does Little Eva come from? Mars? If not, it is more likely she will tune in to a good movie. Young John decides that he wants to learn the history of modern Japan? How did young John come to this point? How is it that he never visited a library up to now? Or is it that he, too, couldn't sleep and decided that a little modern Japanese history was just what he needed?

What Ravitch is talking about here is not a new technology but a new species of child, one who, in any case, no one has seen up to now. Of course, new technologies do make new kinds of people, which leads to a second objection to Ravitch's conception of the future. There is a kind of forthright determinism about the imagined world described in it. The technology is here or will be; we must use it because it is there; we will become the kind of people the technology requires us to be, and whether we like it or not, we will remake our institutions to accommodate technology. All of this must happen because

5

it is good for us, but in any case, we have no choice. This point of view is present in very nearly every statement about the future relationship of learning to technology. And, as in Ravitch's scenario, there is always a cheery, gee-whiz tone to the prophecies. Here is one produced by the National Academy of Sciences, written by Hugh McIntosh.

> School for children of the Information Age will be vastly different than it was for Mom and Dad.
>
> Interested in biology? Design your own life forms with computer simulation.
>
> Having trouble with a science project? Teleconference about it with a research scientist.
>
> Bored with the real world? Go into a virtual physics lab and rewrite the laws of gravity.
>
> These are the kinds of hands-on learning experiences schools could be providing right now. The technologies that make them possible are already here, and today's youngsters, regardless of economic status, know how to use them. They spend hours with them every week—not in the classroom, but in their own homes and in video game centers at every shopping mall.

It is always interesting to attend to the examples of learning, and the motivations that ignite them, in the songs of love that technophiles perform for us. It is, for example, not easy to imagine research scientists all over the world teleconferencing with thousands of students who are having difficulty with their science projects. I can't help thinking that most research scientists would put a stop to this rather quickly. But I find it especially revealing that in the scenario above we have an example of a technological solution to a psychological problem that would seem to be exceedingly serious. We are presented with a student who is "bored with the real world." What does it mean to say someone is bored with the real world, especially one so young? Can a journey into virtual reality cure such a problem? And if it can, will our troubled youngster want to return to the real world? Confronted with a student who is bored with the real world, I don't think we can solve the problem so easily by making available a virtual reality physics lab.

The role that new technology should play in schools or anywhere else is something that needs to be discussed without the hyperactive fantasies of cheerleaders. In particular, the computer and its associated technologies are awesome additions to a culture, and are quite capable of altering the psychic, not to mention the sleeping, habits of our young. But like all important technologies of the past, they are Faustian bargains,[1] giving and taking away, sometimes in equal measure, sometimes more in one way than the other. It is strange—indeed, shocking—that with the twenty-first century so close, we can still talk of new technologies as if they were unmixed blessings—gifts, as it were, from the gods. Don't we all know what the combustion engine has done for us and against us? What television is doing for us and against us? At the

---

1. The legendary Doctor Faustus exchanged his soul for infinite knowledge in a pact with the Devil.

very least, what we need to discuss about Little Eva, Young John, and McIntosh's trio is what they will lose, and what we will lose, if they enter a world in which computer technology is their chief source of motivation, authority, and, apparently, psychological sustenance. Will they become, as Joseph Weizenbaum warns,[2] more impressed by calculation than human judgment? Will speed of response become, more than ever, a defining quality of intelligence? If, indeed, the idea of a school will be dramatically altered, what kinds of learning will be neglected, perhaps made impossible? Is virtual reality a new form of therapy? If it is, what are its dangers?

These are serious matters, and they need to be discussed by those who know something about children from the planet Earth, and whose vision of children's needs, and the needs of society, go beyond thinking of school mainly as a place for the convenient distribution of information. Schools are not now and have never been largely about getting information to children. That has been on the schools' agenda, of course, but has always been way down on the list. For technological utopians, the computer vaults information access to the top. This reshuffling of priorities comes at a most inopportune time. The goal of giving people greater access to more information faster, more conveniently, and in more diverse forms was the main technological thrust of the nineteenth century. Some folks haven't noticed it but that problem was largely solved, so that for almost a hundred years there has been more information available to the young outside the school than inside. That fact did not make the schools obsolete, nor does it now make them obsolete. Yes, it is true that Little Eva, the insomniac from Mars, could turn on an algebra lesson, thanks to the computer, in the wee hours of the morning. She could also, if she wished, read a book or magazine, watch television, turn on the radio or listen to music. All of this she could have done before the computer. The computer does not solve any problem she has but does exacerbate one. For Little Eva's problem is not how to get access to a well-structured algebra lesson but what to do with all the information available to her during the day, as well as during sleepless nights. Perhaps this is why she couldn't sleep in the first place. Little Eva, like the rest of us, is overwhelmed by information. She lives in a culture that has 260,000 billboards, 17,000 newspapers, 12,000 periodicals, 27,000 video outlets for renting tapes, 400 million television sets, and well over 500 million radios, not including those in automobiles. There are 40,000 new book titles published every year, and each day 41 million photographs are taken. And thanks to the computer, more than 60 billion pieces of advertising junk come into our mailboxes every year. Everything from telegraphy and photography in the nineteenth century to the silicon chip in the twentieth has amplified the din of information intruding on Little Eva's consciousness. From millions of sources all over the globe, through every possible channel and medium—light waves, air waves, ticker tape,

2. Weizenbaum's 1976 book, *Computer Power and Human Reason: From Judgment to Calculation,* raises these questions.

computer banks, telephone wires, television cables, satellites, and printing presses—information pours in. Behind it in every imaginable form of storage—on paper, on video, on audiotape, on disks, film, and silicon chips—is an even greater volume of information waiting to be retrieved. In the face of this we might ask. What can schools do for Little Eva besides making still more information available? If there is nothing, then new technologies will indeed make schools obsolete. But in fact, there is plenty.

10   One thing that comes to mind is that schools can provide her with a serious form of technology education. Something quite different from instruction in using computers to process information, which, it strikes me, is a trivial thing to do, for two reasons. In the first place, approximately 35 million people have already learned how to use computers without the benefit of school instruction. If the schools do nothing, most of the population will know how to use computers in the next ten years, just as most of the population learns how to drive a car without school instruction. In the second place, what we needed to know about cars—as we need to know about computers, television, and other important technologies—is not how to use them but how they use *us*. In the case of cars, what we needed to think about in the early twentieth century was not how to drive them but what they would do to our air, our landscape, our social relations, our family life, and our cities. Suppose in 1946 we had started to address similar questions about television: What will be its effects on our political institutions, our psychic habits, our children, our religious conceptions, our economy? Would we be better positioned today to control TV's massive assault on American culture? I am talking here about making technology itself an object of inquiry so that Little Eva and Young John are more interested in asking questions about the computer than getting answers from it.

        I am not arguing against using computers in school. I am arguing against our sleepwalking attitudes toward it, against allowing it to distract us from important things, against making a god of it. This is what Theodore Roszak warned against in *The Cult of Information*: "Like all cults," he wrote, "this one also has the intention of enlisting mindless allegiance and acquiescence. People who have no clear idea of what they mean by information or why they should want so much of it are nonetheless prepared to believe that we live in an Information Age, which makes every computer around us what the relics of the True Cross were in the Age of Faith: emblems of salvation." To this, I would add the sage observation of Alan Kay of Apple Computer. Kay is widely associated with the invention of the personal computer, and certainly has an interest in schools using them. Nonetheless, he has repeatedly said that any problems the schools cannot solve without computers, they cannot solve with them. What are some of those problems? There is, for example, the traditional task of teaching children how to behave in groups. One might even say that schools have never been essentially about individualized learning. It is true, of course, that groups do not learn, individuals do. But the idea of a school is that individuals must learn in a setting in which individual needs are subordinated to group interests. Unlike other media of mass communication, which celebrate individual response and are experienced in private, the classroom is intended to tame the ego, to connect the individual with others, to demonstrate the value and necessity of group cohesion. At present, most scenarios describing the uses of computers have children solving problems alone; Little Eva, Young John, and the others are doing just that. The presence of other children may, indeed, be an annoyance.

Like the printing press before it, the computer has a powerful bias toward amplifying personal autonomy and individual problem-solving. That is why educators must guard against computer technology's undermining some of the important reasons for having the young assemble (to quote Ravitch) "in a specific place, for a certain number of hours, and a certain number of days during the week and year."

Although Ravitch is not exactly against what she calls "state schools," she imagines them as something of a relic of a pretechnological age. She believes that the new technologies will offer all children equal access to information. Conjuring up a hypothetical Little Mary who is presumably from a poorer home than Little Eva, Ravitch imagines that Mary will have the same opportunities as Eva "to learn any subject, and to learn it from the same master teachers as children in the richest neighborhood." For all of its liberalizing spirit, this scenario makes some important omissions. One is that though new technologies may be a solution to the learning of "subjects," they work against the learning of what are called "social values," including an understanding of democratic processes. If one reads the first chapter of Robert Fulghum's *All I Really Need to Know I Learned in Kindergarten,* one will find an elegant summary of a few things Ravitch's scenario has left out. They include learning the following lessons: Share everything, play fair, don't hit people, put things back where you found them, clean up your own mess, wash your hands before you eat, and, of course, flush. The only thing wrong with Fulghum's book is that no one has learned all these things at kindergarten's end. We have ample evidence that it takes many years of teaching these values in school before they have been accepted and internalized. That is why it won't do for children to learn in "settings of their own choosing." That is also why schools require children to be in a certain place at a certain time and to follow certain rules, like raising their hands when they wish to speak, not talking when others are talking, not chewing gum, not leaving until the bell rings, exhibiting patience toward slower learners, etc. This process is called making civilized people. The god of Technology does not appear interested in this function of schools. At least, it does not come up much when technology's virtues are enumerated.

The god of Technology may also have a trick or two up its sleeve about something else. It is often asserted that new technologies will equalize learning opportunities for the rich and poor. It is devoutly to be wished for, but I doubt it will happen. In the first place, it is generally understood by those who have studied the history of technology that technological change always produces winners and losers. There are many reasons for this, among them economic differences. Even in the case of the automobile, which is a commodity most people can buy (although not all), there are wide differences between the rich and poor in the quality of what is available to them. It would be quite astonishing if computer technology equalized all learning opportunities, irrespective of economic differences. One may be delighted that Little Eva's parents could afford the technology and software to make it possible for her to learn algebra at midnight. But Little Mary's parents may not be able to, may not even know such things are available. And if we say that the school could make the technology available to Little Mary (at least during the day), there may be something else Little Mary is lacking.

15   It turns out, for example, that Little Mary may be having sleepless nights as frequently as Little Eva but not because she wants to get a leg up on her algebra. Maybe because she doesn't know who her father is, or, if she does, where he is. Maybe we can understand why McIntosh's kid is bored with the real world. Or is the child confused about it? Or terrified? Are there educators who seriously believe that these problems can be addressed by new technologies?

I do not say, of course, that schools can solve the problems of poverty, alienation, and family disintegration, but schools can *respond* to them. And they can do this because there are people in them, because these people are concerned with more than algebra lessons or modern Japanese history, and because these people can identify not only one's level of competence in math but one's level of rage and confusion and depression. I am talking here about children as they really come to us, not children who are invented to show us how computers may enrich their lives. Of course, I suppose it is possible that there are children who, waking at night, want to study algebra or who are so interested in their world that they yearn to know about Japan. If there be such children, and one hopes there are, they do not require expensive computers to satisfy their hunger for learning. They are on their way, with or without computers. Unless, of course, they do not care about others or have no friends, or little respect for democracy or are filled with suspicion about those who are not like them. When we have machines that know how to do something about these problems, that is the time to rid ourselves of the expensive burden of schools or to reduce the function of teachers to "coaches" in the uses of machines (as Ravitch envisions). Until then, we must be more modest about this god of Technology and certainly not pin our hopes on it.

We must also, I suppose, be empathetic toward those who search with good intentions for technological panaceas. I am a teacher myself and know how hard it is to contribute to the making of a civilized person. Can we blame those who want to find an easy way, through the agency of technology? Perhaps not. After all, it is an old quest. As early as 1918, H. L. Mencken[3] (although completely devoid of empathy) wrote, "There is no sure-cure so idiotic that some superintendent of schools will not swallow it. The aim seems to be reduce the whole teaching process to a sort of automatic reaction, to discover some master formula that will not only take the place of competence and resourcefulness in the teacher but that will also create an artificial receptivity in the child."

3. American journalist (1880–1956).

Mencken was not necessarily speaking of technological panaceas but he may well have been. In the early 1920s a teacher wrote the following poem:

> Mr. Edison says
> That the radio will supplant the teacher.
> Already one may learn languages by means of Victrola records.
> The moving picture will visualize
> What the radio fails to get across.
> Teachers will be relegated to the backwoods,
> With fire-horses,
> And long-haired women;
> Or, perhaps shown in museums.
> Education will become a matter
> Of pressing the button.
> Perhaps I can get a position at the switchboard.

I do not go as far back as the radio and Victrola, but I am old enough to remember when 16-millimeter film was to be the sure-cure. Then closed-circuit television. Then 8-millimeter film. Then teacher-proof textbooks. Now computers.

I know a false god when I see one. 20

QUESTIONS

1. In paragraph 10 Postman says that "schools can provide . . . a serious form of technology education" and argues for "making technology itself an object of inquiry." Since this is exactly what Postman does as a writer and professor, is this argument an instance of self-interested special pleading? Why or why not?

2. Consult Postman's biography in the "Authors" section at the back of this book; then look through his essay for evidence of his professional expertise. What kinds of sources does he refer to? What is the range of his reading? Is he writing for a specific community of readers?

3. Write about computers in your own formal education, arguing from your own experiences whether Postman makes a good case or not.

STEPHEN JAY GOULD *Darwin's Middle Road*

"WE BEGAN TO SAIL up the narrow strait lamenting," narrates Odysseus. "For on the one hand lay Scylla, with twelve feet all dangling down; and six necks exceeding long, and on each a hideous head, and therein three rows of teeth set thick and close, full of black death. And on the other mighty Charybdis sucked down the salt sea water.[1] As often as she belched it forth, like a cauldron on a great fire she would seethe up through all her troubled deeps." Odysseus managed to swerve around Charybdis, but Scylla grabbed six of his finest men and devoured them in his sight—"the most pitiful thing mine eyes have seen of all my travail in searching out the paths of the sea."

False lures and dangers often come in pairs in our legends and metaphors—consider the frying pan and the fire, or the devil and the deep blue sea. Prescriptions for avoidance either emphasize a dogged steadiness—the straight and narrow of Christian evangelists—or an averaging between unpleasant alternatives—the golden mean of Aristotle. The idea of steering a course between undesirable extremes emerges as a central prescription for a sensible life.

The nature of scientific creativity is both a perennial topic of discussion and a prime candidate for seeking a golden mean. The two extreme positions have not been directly competing for allegiance of the unwary. They have, rather, replaced each other sequentially, with one now in the ascendency, the other eclipsed.

The first—inductivism—held that great scientists are primarily great observers and patient accumulators of information. For new and significant theory, the inductivists claimed, can only arise from a firm foundation of facts. In this architectural view, each fact is a brick in a structure built without blueprints. Any talk or thought about theory (the completed building) is fatuous and premature before the bricks are set. Inductivism once commanded great prestige within science, and even represented an "official" position of sorts, for it touted, however falsely, the utter honesty, complete objectivity, and almost automatic nature of scientific progress towards final and incontrovertible truth.

5   Yet, as its critics so rightly claimed, inductivism also depicted science as a heartless, almost inhuman discipline offering no legitimate place to quirkiness, intuition, and all the other subjective attributes adhering to our vernacular notion of genius. Great scientists, the critics claimed, are distinguished more by their powers of hunch and synthesis, than their skill in experiment or

For many years Gould wrote a monthly column for the magazine Natural History. *This essay appeared there in December 1979 and was reprinted in Gould's collection* The Panda's Thumb *(1980).*

1. Scylla was a female monster who lived in a cave and threatened Odysseus and his sailors in the *Odyssey*. Located opposite it was Charybdis, a whirlpool in the narrow channel of the Strait of Messina, between Sicily and mainland Italy.

observation. The criticisms of inductivism are certainly valid and I welcome its dethroning during the past thirty years as a necessary prelude to better understanding. Yet, in attacking it so strongly, some critics have tried to substitute an alternative equally extreme and unproductive in its emphasis on the essential subjectivity of creative thought. In this "eureka" view, creativity is an ineffable something, accessible only to persons of genius. It arises like a bolt of lightning, unanticipated, unpredictable and unanalyzable—but the bolts strike only a few special people. We ordinary mortals must stand in awe and thanks. (The name refers, of course, to the legendary story of Archimedes running naked through the streets of Syracuse shouting eureka [I have discovered it] when water displaced by his bathing body washed the scales abruptly from his eyes and suggested a method for measuring volumes.)

I am equally disenchanted by both these opposing extremes. Inductivism reduces genius to dull, rote operations; eurekaism grants it an inaccessible status more in the domain of intrinsic mystery than in a realm where we might understand and learn from it. Might we not marry the good features of each view, and abandon both the elitism of eurekaism and the pedestrian qualities of inductivism? May we not acknowledge the personal and subjective character of creativity, but still comprehend it as a mode of thinking that emphasizes or exaggerates capacities sufficiently common to all of us that we may at least understand if not hope to imitate?

In the hagiography of science, a few men hold such high positions that all arguments must apply to them if they are to have any validity. Charles Darwin, as the principal saint of evolutionary biology, has therefore been presented both as an inductivist and as a primary example of eurekaism. I will attempt to show that these interpretations are equally inadequate, and that recent scholarship on Darwin's own odyssey towards the theory of natural selection supports an intermediate position.

So great was the prestige of inductivism in his own day, that Darwin himself fell under its sway and, as an old man, falsely depicted his youthful accomplishments in its light. In an autobiography, written as a lesson in morality for his children and not intended for publication, he penned some famous lines that misled historians for nearly a hundred years. Describing his path to the theory of natural selection, he claimed: "I worked on true Baconian principles, and without any theory collected facts on a wholesale scale."[2]

The inductivist interpretation focuses on Darwin's five years aboard the *Beagle* and explains his transition from a student for the ministry to the nemesis of preachers as the result of his keen powers of observation applied to the whole world. Thus, the traditional story goes, Darwin's eyes opened wider and wider as he saw, in sequence, the bones of giant South American fossil mammals, the turtles and finches of the Galapagos, and the marsupial fauna of Australia. The truth of evolution and its mechanism of natural selection crept up gradually upon him as he sifted facts in a sieve of utter objectivity.

2. Francis Bacon (1561–1626), English philosopher, statesman, and essayist, and the first apostle of inductivism.

10   The inadequacies of this tale are best illustrated by the falsity of its conventional premier example—the so-called Darwin's finches of the Galapagos. We now know that although these birds share a recent and common ancestry on the South American mainland, they have radiated into an impressive array of species on the outlying Galapagos. Few terrestrial species manage to cross the wide oceanic barrier between South America and the Galapagos. But the fortunate migrants often find a sparsely inhabited world devoid of the competitors that limit their opportunities on the crowded mainland. Hence, the finches evolved into roles normally occupied by other birds and developed their famous set of adaptations for feeding—seed crushing, insect eating, even grasping and manipulating a cactus needle to dislodge insects from plants. Isolation—both of the islands from the mainland and among the islands themselves—provided an opportunity for separation, independent adaptation, and speciation.

        According to the traditional view, Darwin discovered these finches, correctly inferred their history, and wrote the famous lines in his notebook: "If there is the slightest foundation for these remarks the zoology of Archipelagoes will be worth examining; for such facts would undermine the stability of Species." But, as with so many heroic tales from Washington's cherry tree to the piety of Crusaders, hope rather than truth motivates the common reading. Darwin found the finches to be sure. But he didn't recognize them as variants of a common stock. In fact, he didn't even record the island of discovery for many of them—some of his labels just read "Galapagos Islands." So much for his immediate recognition of the role of isolation in the formation of new species. He reconstructed the evolutionary tale only after his return to London, when a British Museum ornithologist correctly identified all the birds as finches.

        The famous quotation from his notebook refers to Galapagos tortoises and to the claim of native inhabitants that they can "at once pronounce from which Island any Tortoise may have been brought" from subtle differences in size and shape of body and scales. This is a statement of different, and much reduced, order from the traditional tale of finches. For the finches are true and separate species—a living example of evolution. The subtle differences among tortoises represent minor geographic variation within a species. It is a jump in reasoning, albeit a valid one as we now know, to argue that such small differences can be amplified to produce a new species. All creationists, after all, acknowledged geographic variation (consider human races), but argued that it could not proceed beyond the rigid limits of a created archetype.

        I don't wish to downplay the pivotal influence of the *Beagle* voyage on Darwin's career. It gave him space, freedom and endless time to think in his favored mode of independent self-stimulation. (His ambivalence towards university life, and his middling performance there by conventional standards, reflected his unhappiness with a curriculum of received wisdom.) He writes from South America in 1834: "I have not one clear idea about cleavage, stratification, lines of upheaval. I have no books, which tell me much and what they do I cannot apply to what I see. In consequence I draw my own conclusions, and most gloriously ridiculous ones they are." The rocks and plants and animals that he saw did provoke him to the crucial attitude of doubt—midwife of all creativity. Sydney, Australia—1836. Darwin wonders why a rational God would create so many marsupials on Australia since nothing about its climate or geography suggests any superiority for pouches: "I had been lying on a sunny bank and was reflecting on the strange character of the animals of this country as compared to the rest of the World. An unbeliever in everything beyond his own reason might exclaim, 'Surely two distinct Creators must have been at work.'"

Nonetheless, Darwin returned to London without an evolutionary theory. He suspected the truth of evolution, but had no mechanism to explain it. Natural selection did not arise from any direct reading of the *Beagle*'s facts, but from two subsequent years of thought and struggle as reflected in a series of remarkable notebooks that have been unearthed and published during the past twenty years. In these notebooks, we see Darwin testing and abandoning a number of theories and pursuing a multitude of false leads—so much for his later claim about recording facts with an empty mind. He read philosophers, poets, and economists, always searching for meaning and insight—so much for the notion that natural selection arose inductively from the *Beagle*'s facts. Later, he labelled one notebook as "full of metaphysics on morals."

Yet if this tortuous path belies the Scylla of inductivism, it has engendered an equally simplistic myth—the Charybdis of eurekaism. In his maddeningly misleading autobiography, Darwin does record a eureka and suggests that natural selection struck him as a sudden, serendipitous flash after more than a year of groping frustration:

> In October 1838, that is, fifteen months after I had begun my systematic inquiry, I happened to read for amusement Malthus on Population,[3] and being well prepared to appreciate the struggle for existence which everywhere goes on from long-continued observation of the habits of animals and plants, it at once struck me that under these circumstances favorable variations would tend to be preserved, and unfavorable ones to be destroyed. The result of this would be the formation of new species. Here, then, I had at last got a theory by which to work.

Yet, again, the notebooks belie Darwin's later recollections—in this case by their utter failure to record, at the time it happened, any special exultation over his Malthusian insight. He inscribes it as a fairly short and sober entry without a single exclamation point, though he habitually used two or three in moments of excitement. He did not drop everything and reinterpret a confusing world in its light. On the very next day, he wrote an even longer passage on the sexual curiosity of primates.

The theory of natural selection arose neither as a workmanlike induction from nature's facts, nor as a mysterious bolt from Darwin's subconscious, triggered by an accidental reading of Malthus. It emerged instead as the result of a conscious and productive search, proceeding in a ramifying but ordered

3. Thomas Malthus (1766–1834), whose book *An Essay on the Principle of Population* was published under several titles between 1798 and 1817.

manner, and utilizing both the facts of natural history and an astonishingly broad range of insights from disparate disciplines far from his own. Darwin trod the middle path between inductivism and eurekaism. His genius is neither pedestrian nor inaccessible.

Darwinian scholarship has exploded since the centennial of the *Origin*[4] in 1959. The publication of Darwin's notebooks and the attention devoted by several scholars to the two crucial years between the *Beagle*'s docking and the demoted Malthusian insight has clinched the argument for a "middle path" theory of Darwin's creativity. Two particularly important works focus on the broadest and narrowest scales. Howard E. Gruber's masterful intellectual and psychological biography of this phase in Darwin's life, *Darwin on Man*, traces all the false leads and turning points in Darwin's search. Gruber shows that Darwin was continually proposing, testing, and abandoning hypotheses, and that he never simply collected facts in a blind way. He began with a fanciful theory involving the idea that new species arise with a prefixed life span, and worked his way gradually, if fitfully, towards an idea of extinction by competition in a world of struggle. He recorded no exultation upon reading Malthus, because the jigsaw puzzle was only missing a piece or two at the time.

Silvan S. Schweber has reconstructed, in detail as minute as the record will allow, Darwin's activities during the few weeks before Malthus (The Origin of the *Origin* Revisited, *Journal of the History of Biology,* 1977). He argues that the final pieces arose not from new facts in natural history, but from Darwin's intellectual wanderings in distant fields. In particular, he read a long review of social scientist and philosopher Auguste Comte's most famous work, the *Cours de philosophie positive.* He was particularly struck by Comte's insistence that a proper theory be predictive and at least potentially quantitative. He then turned to Dugald Stewart's *On the Life and Writing of Adam Smith*,[5] and imbibed the basic belief of the Scottish economists that theories of overall social structure must begin by analyzing the unconstrained actions of individuals. (Natural selection is, above all, a theory about the struggle of individual organisms for success in reproduction.) Then, searching for quantification, he read a lengthy analysis of work by the most famous statistician of his time—the Belgian Adolphe Quetelet. In the review of Quetelet, he found, among other things, a forceful statement of Malthus's quantitative claim—that population would grow geometrically and food supplies only arithmetically, thus guaranteeing an intense struggle for existence. In fact, Darwin had read the Malthusian statement several times before; but only now was he prepared to appreciate its significance. Thus, he did not turn to Malthus by accident, and he already knew what it contained. His "amusement," we must assume, consisted only in a desire to read in its original formulation the familiar statement that had so impressed him in Quetelet's secondary account.

---

4. *The Origin of Species* (1859).

5. *Cours de philosophie positive* (Course in positivist philosophy) (1830–42). Dugald Stewart (1753–1828) wrote a brief biography of Adam Smith in 1811, which was frequently included in editions of Smith's *The Wealth of Nations* (1776).

In reading Schweber's detailed account of the moments preceding Darwin's formulation of natural selection, I was particularly struck by the absence of deciding influence from his own field of biology. The immediate precipitators were a social scientist, an economist, and a statistician. If genius has any common denominator, I would propose breadth of interest and the ability to construct fruitful analogies between fields.

In fact, I believe that the theory of natural selection should be viewed as an extended analogy—whether conscious or unconscious on Darwin's part I do not know—to the laissez faire economics of Adam Smith. The essence of Smith's argument is a paradox of sorts: if you want an ordered economy providing maximal benefits to all, then let individuals compete and struggle for their own advantages. The result, after appropriate sorting and elimination of the inefficient, will be a stable and harmonious polity. Apparent order arises naturally from the struggle among individuals, not from predestined principles or higher control. Dugald Stewart epitomized Smith's system in the book Darwin read:

> The most effective plan for advancing a people . . . is by allowing every man, as long as he observes the rules of justice, to pursue his own interest in his own way, and to bring both his industry and his capital into the freest competition with those of his fellow citizens. Every system of policy which endeavors . . . to draw towards a particular species of industry a greater share of the capital of the society than would naturally go to it . . . is, in reality, subversive of the great purpose which it means to promote.

As Schweber states: "The Scottish analysis of society contends that the combined effect of individual actions results in the institutions upon which society is based, and that such a society is a stable and evolving one and functions without a designing and directing mind."

We know that Darwin's uniqueness does not reside in his support for the idea of evolution—scores of scientists had preceded him in this. His special contribution rests upon his documentation and upon the novel character of his theory about how evolution operates. Previous evolutionists had proposed unworkable schemes based on internal perfecting tendencies and inherent directions. Darwin advocated a natural and testable theory based on immediate interaction among individuals (his opponents considered it heartlessly mechanistic). The theory of natural selection is a creative transfer to biology of Adam Smith's basic argument for a rational economy: the balance and order of nature does not arise from a higher, external (divine) control, or from the existence of laws operating directly upon the whole, but from struggle among individuals for their own benefits (in modern terms, for the transmission of their genes to future generations through differential success in reproduction).

Many people are distressed to hear such an argument. Does it not compromise the integrity of science if some of its primary conclusions originate by analogy from contemporary politics and culture rather than from data of the discipline itself? In a famous letter to Engels, Karl Marx identified the similarities between natural selection and the English social scene:

> It is remarkable how Darwin recognizes among beasts and plants his English society with its division of labor, competition, opening up of new markets, 'invention,' and the Malthusian 'struggle for existence.' It is Hobbes' *bellum omnium contra omnes* (the war of all against all).[6]

Yet Marx was a great admirer of Darwin—and in this apparent paradox lies resolution. For reasons involving all the themes I have emphasized here—that inductivism is inadequate, that creativity demands breadth, and that analogy is a profound source of insight—great thinkers cannot be divorced from their social background. But the source of an idea is one thing; its truth or fruitfulness is another. The psychology and utility of discovery are very different subjects indeed. Darwin may have cribbed the idea of natural selection from economics, but it may still be right. As the German socialist Karl Kautsky wrote in 1902: "The fact that an idea emanates from a particular class, or accords with their interests, of course proves nothing as to its truth or falsity." In this case, it is ironic that Adam Smith's system of laissez faire does not work in his own domain of economics, for it leads to oligopoly and revolution, rather than to order and harmony. Struggle among individuals does, however, seem to be the law of nature.

Many people use such arguments about social context to ascribe great insights primarily to the indefinable phenomenon of good luck. Thus, Darwin was lucky to be born rich, lucky to be on the *Beagle,* lucky to live amidst the ideas of his age, lucky to trip over Parson Malthus—essentially little more than a man in the right place at the right time. Yet, when we read of his personal struggle to understand, the breadth of his concerns and study, and the directedness of his search for a mechanism of evolution, we understand why Pasteur made his famous quip that fortune favors the prepared mind.[7]

6. From *Leviathan* (1651), by the English philosopher Thomas Hobbes.
7. Louis Pasteur (1822–1895), French chemist and microbiologist.

QUESTIONS

1. What, according to Gould, constituted Darwin's scientific research? How and why did he depict it falsely in his autobiography (paragraph 8)?

2. Rather than isolating scientific research from social and political experience, Darwin, Gould explains, was influenced by a social scientist, an economist, and a statistician (paragraph 20). Identify each one and explain what he contributed to Darwin's theory of natural selection.

3. Consider a recent experience of writing an essay. Did you, thinking and writing, shuttle between inductivism and prediction as Gould claims Darwin did? Describe your experience using Gould's analytic vocabulary.

LITERATURE, THE ARTS, AND MEDIA

EUDORA WELTY   *One Writer's Beginnings*

I LEARNED FROM the age of two or three that any room in our house, at any time of day, was there to read in, or to be read to. My mother read to me. She'd read to me in the big bedroom in the mornings, when we were in her rocker together, which ticked in rhythm as we rocked, as though we had a cricket accompanying the story. She'd read to me in the diningroom on winter afternoons in front of the coal fire, with our cuckoo clock ending the story with "Cuckoo," and at night when I'd got in my own bed. I must have given her no peace. Sometimes she read to me in the kitchen while she sat churning, and the churning sobbed along with *any* story. It was my ambition to have her read to me while *I* churned; once she granted my wish, but she read off my story before I brought her butter. She was an expressive reader. When she was reading "Puss in Boots,"[1] for instance, it was impossible not to know that she distrusted *all* cats.

It had been startling and disappointing to me to find out that story books had been written by *people,* that books were not natural wonders, coming up of themselves like grass. Yet regardless of where they came from, I cannot remember a time when I was not in love with them—with the books themselves, cover and binding and the paper they were printed on, with their smell and their weight and with their possession in my arms, captured and carried off to myself. Still illiterate, I was ready for them, committed to all the reading I could give them.

Neither of my parents had come from homes that could afford to buy many books, but though it must have been something of a strain on his salary, as the youngest officer in a young insurance company, my father was all the while carefully selecting and ordering away for what he and Mother thought we children should grow up with. They bought first for the future.

Besides the bookcase in the livingroom, which was always called "the li-

From a set of three lectures delivered at Harvard University in April 1983, to inaugurate the William E. Massey lecture series, and later published in One Writer's Beginnings *(1984).*

1. A fairy tale.

brary," there were the encyclopedia tables and dictionary stand under windows in our diningroom. Here to help us grow up arguing around the diningroom table were the Unabridged Webster, the Columbia Encyclopedia, Compton's Pictured Encyclopedia, the Lincoln Library of Information, and later the Book of Knowledge. And the year we moved into our new house, there was room to celebrate it with the new 1925 edition of the Britannica, which my father, his face always deliberately turned toward the future, was of course disposed to think better than any previous edition.

5   In "the library," inside the mission-style bookcase with its three diamond-latticed glass doors, with my father's Morris chair and the glass-shaded lamp on its table beside it, were books I could soon begin on—and I did, reading them all alike and as they came, straight down their rows, top shelf to bottom. There was the set of Stoddard's Lectures, in all its late nineteenth-century vocabulary and vignettes of peasant life and quaint beliefs and customs, with matching halftone illustrations: Vesuvius erupting, Venice by moonlight, gypsies glimpsed by their campfires. I didn't know then the clue they were to my father's longing to see the rest of the world. I read straight through his other love-from-afar: the Victrola Book of the Opera, with opera after opera in synopsis, with portraits in costume of Melba, Caruso, Galli-Curci, and Geraldine Farrar,[2] some of whose voices we could listen to on our Red Seal records.

My mother read secondarily for information; she sank as a hedonist into novels. She read Dickens in the spirit in which she would have eloped with him. The novels of her girlhood that had stayed on in her imagination, besides those of Dickens and Scott and Robert Louis Stevenson,[3] were *Jane Eyre, Trilby, The Woman in White, Green Mansions, King Solomon's Mines*.[4] Marie Corelli's[5] name would crop up but I understood she had gone out of favor with my mother, who had only kept *Ardath* out of loyalty. In time she absorbed herself in Galsworthy, Edith Wharton, above all in Thomas Mann of the *Joseph* volumes.[6]

St. Elmo[7] was not in our house; I saw it often in other houses. This wildly popular Southern novel is where all the Edna Earles in our population started coming from. They're all named for the heroine, who succeeded in bringing a dissolute, sinning roué and atheist of a lover (St. Elmo) to his knees. My mother was

2. Nellie Melba (1861–1931), Enrico Caruso (1837–1921), Amelita Galli-Curci (1889–1964), Geraldine Farrar (1882–1967), all opera stars.

3. Charles Dickens (1812–1870), Sir Walter Scott (1771–1832), Robert Louis Stevenson (1850–1894). The first was English, the others Scottish.

4. Respectively by Charlotte Brontë (1816–1855), George Du Maurier (1834–1896), Wilkie Collins (1824–1889), William Henry Hudson (1841–1922), Sir H. Rider Haggard (1856–1925). All were British.

5. The pen name of Mary Mills Mackay (1855–1924), a popular and prolific British novelist.

6. John Galsworthy (1867–1933), British; Edith Wharton (1862–1937), American; Thomas Mann (1875–1955), German, whose *Joseph* novels appeared in four parts, from 1933 to 1943.

7. By Augusta Jane Evans (1835–1909).

able to forgo it. But she remembered the classic advice given to rose growers on how to water their bushes long enough: "Take a chair and *St. Elmo.*"

To both my parents I owe my early acquaintance with a beloved Mark Twain. There was a full set of Mark Twain and a short set of Ring Lardner in our bookcase,[8] and those were the volumes that in time united us all, parents and children.

Reading everything that stood before me was how I came upon a worn old book without a back that had belonged to my father as a child. It was called *Sanford and Merton.* Is there anyone left who recognizes it, I wonder? It is the famous moral tale written by Thomas Day in the 1780s, but of him no mention is made on the title page of *this* book; here it is *Sanford and Merton in Words of One Syllable* by Mary Godolphin. Here are the rich boy and the poor boy and Mr. Barlow, their teacher and interlocutor, in long discourses alternating with dramatic scenes—danger and rescue allotted to the rich and the poor respectively. It may have only words of one syllable, but one of them is "quoth." It ends with not one but two morals, both engraved on rings: "Do what you ought, come what may," and "If we would be great, we must first learn to be good."

This book was lacking its front cover, the back held on by strips of pasted paper, now turned golden, in several layers, and the pages stained, flecked, and tattered around the edges; its garish illustrations had come unattached but were preserved, laid in. I had the feeling even in my heedless childhood that this was the only book my father as a little boy had had of his own. He had held onto it, and might have gone to sleep on its coverless face: he had lost his mother when he was seven. My father had never made any mention to his own children of the book, but he had brought it along with him from Ohio to our house and shelved it in our bookcase.

My mother had brought from West Virginia that set of Dickens; those books looked sad, too—they had been through fire and water before I was born, she told me, and there they were, lined up—as I later realized, waiting for *me.*

I was presented, from as early as I can remember, with books of my own, which appeared on my birthday and Christmas morning. Indeed, my parents could not give me books enough. They must have sacrificed to give me on my sixth or seventh birthday—it was after I became a reader for myself—the ten-volume set of Our Wonder World. These were beautifully made, heavy books I would lie down with on the floor in front of the diningroom hearth, and more often than the rest volume 5, *Every Child's Story Book,* was under my eyes. There were the fairy tales—Grimm, Andersen, the English, the French, "Ali Baba and the Forty Thieves"; and there was Aesop and Reynard the Fox; there were the myths and legends, Robin Hood, King Arthur, and St. George and the Dragon, even the history of Joan of Arc; a whack of *Pilgrim's Progress* and a long piece of *Gulliver.*[9] They all carried their classic illustrations. I located my-

10

8. Mark Twain, the pen name of Samuel Langhorne Clemens (1835–1910); Ring (Ringgold Wilmer) Lardner (1885–1933). Both were American.
9. *The Pilgrim's Progress* by John Bunyan (1628–1688) and *Gulliver's Travels* by Jonathan Swift (1667–1745).

self in these pages and could go straight to the stories and pictures I loved; very often "The Yellow Dwarf" was first choice, with Walter Crane's Yellow Dwarf in full color making his terrifying appearance flanked by turkeys.[10] Now that volume is as worn and backless and hanging apart as my father's poor *Sanford and Merton*. The precious page with Edward Lear's "Jumblies"[11] on it has been in danger of slipping out for all these years. One measure of my love for Our Wonder World was that for a long time I wondered if I would go through fire and water for it as my mother had done for Charles Dickens; and the only comfort was to think I could ask my mother to do it for me.

I believe I'm the only child I know of who grew up with this treasure in the house. I used to ask others, "Did you have Our Wonder World?" I'd have to tell them The Book of Knowledge could not hold a candle to it.

I live in gratitude to my parents for initiating me—and as early as I begged for it, without keeping me waiting—into knowledge of the word, into reading and spelling, by way of the alphabet. They taught it to me at home in time for me to begin to read before starting to school. I believe the alphabet is no longer considered an essential piece of equipment for traveling through life. In my day it was the keystone to knowledge. You learned the alphabet as you learned to count to ten, as you learned "Now I lay me" and the Lord's Prayer and your father's and mother's name and address and telephone number, all in case you were lost.

15   My love for the alphabet, which endures, grew out of reciting it but, before that, out of seeing the letters on the page. In my own story books, before I could read them for myself, I fell in love with various winding, enchanting-looking initials drawn by Walter Crane at the heads of fairy tales. In "Once upon a time," an "O" had a rabbit running it as a treadmill, his feet upon flowers. When the day came, years later, for me to see the Book of Kells,[12] all the wizardry of letter, initial, and word swept over me a thousand times over, and the illumination, the gold, seemed a part of the word's beauty and holiness that had been there from the start.

Learning stamps you with its moments. Childhood's learning is made up of moments. It isn't steady. It's a pulse.

In a children's art class, we sat in a ring on kindergarten chairs and drew three daffodils that had just been picked out of the yard; and while I was drawing, my sharpened pencil and the cup of the yellow daffodil gave off whiffs just alike. That the pencil doing the drawing should give off the same smell as the flower it drew seemed a part of the art lesson—as shouldn't it be? Children, like animals, use all their senses to discover the world. Then artists come

---

10. A fairy tale illustrated by Walter Crane (1845–1915), popular illustrator of children's books.

11. A narrative poem about creatures called Jumblies who went to sea in a sieve. Edward Lear (1812–1888), British, wrote nonsense poems for children.

12. An illustrated Irish manuscript of the four Gospels from the eighth or ninth century.

along and discover it the same way, all over again. Here and there, it's the same world. Or now and then we'll hear from an artist who's never lost it.

In my sensory education I include my physical awareness of the *word*. Of a certain word, that is; the connection it has with what it stands for. At around age six, perhaps, I was standing by myself in our front yard waiting for supper, just at that hour in a late summer day when the sun is already below the horizon and the risen full moon in the visible sky stops being chalky and begins to take on light. There comes the moment, and I saw it then, when the moon goes from flat to round. For the first time it met my eyes as a globe. The word "moon" came into my mouth as though fed to me out of a silver spoon. Held in my mouth the moon became a word. It had the roundness of a Concord grape Grandpa took off his vine and gave me to suck out of its skin and swallow whole, in Ohio.

This love did not prevent me from living for years in foolish error about the moon. The new moon just appearing in the west was the rising moon to me. The new should be rising. And in early childhood the sun and moon, those opposite reigning powers, I just as easily assumed rose in east and west respectively in their opposite sides of the sky, and like partners in a reel they advanced, sun from the east, moon from the west, crossed over (when I wasn't looking) and went down on the other side. My father couldn't have known I believed that when, bending behind me and guiding my shoulder, he positioned me at our telescope in the front yard and, with careful adjustment of the focus, brought the moon close to me.

The night sky over my childhood Jackson[13] was velvety black. I could see   20
the full constellations in it and call their names; when I could read, I knew their myths. Though I was always waked for eclipses, and indeed carried to the window as an infant in arms and shown Halley's Comet[14] in my sleep, and though I'd been taught at our diningroom table about the solar system and knew the earth revolved around the sun, and our moon around us, I never found out the moon didn't come up in the west until I was a writer and Herschel Brickell, the literary critic, told me after I misplaced it in a story. He said valuable words to me about my new profession: "Always be sure you get your moon in the right part of the sky."

My mother always sang to her children. Her voice came out just a little bit in the minor key. "Wee Willie Winkie's" song was wonderfully sad when she sang the lullabies.

"Oh, but now there's a record. She could have her own record to listen to," my father would have said. For there came a Victrola record of "Bobby Shafftoe" and "Rock-a-Bye Baby,"[15] all of Mother's lullabies, which could be

13. Jackson, Mississippi, where Welty grew up.
14. A comet named after Edmund Halley (1656–1742), English astronomer.
15. "Wee Willie Winkie," a nursery rhyme of 1841 in which sleep is personified; "Bobby Shafftoe," a traditional sea chantey dating from about 1750; "Rock-a-Bye Baby," words from *Mother Goose's Melodies* (1765), set to music in 1884.

played to take her place. Soon I was able to play her my own lullabies all day long.

Our Victrola stood in the diningroom. I was allowed to climb onto the seat of a diningroom chair to wind it, start the record turning, and set the needle playing. In a second I'd jumped to the floor, to spin or march around the table as the music called for—now there were all the other records I could play too. I skinned back onto the chair just in time to lift the needle at the end, stop the record and turn it over, then change the needle. That brass receptacle with a hole in the lid gave off a metallic smell like human sweat, from all the hot needles that were fed it. Winding up, dancing, being cocked to start and stop the record, was of course all in one the act of *listening*—to "Overture to *Daughter of the Regiment*," "Selections from *The Fortune Teller*," "Kiss Me Again," "Gypsy Dance from *Carmen*," "Stars and Stripes Forever," "When the Midnight Choo-Choo Leaves for Alabam," or whatever came next.[16] Movement must be at the very heart of listening.

Ever since I was first read to, then started reading to myself, there has never been a line read that I didn't *hear*. As my eyes followed the sentence, a voice was saying it silently to me. It isn't my mother's voice, or the voice of any person I can identify, certainly not my own. It is human, but inward, and it is inwardly that I listen to it. It is to me the voice of the story or the poem itself. The cadence, whatever it is that asks you to believe, the feeling that resides in the printed word, reaches me through the reader-voice. I have supposed, but never found out, that this is the case with all readers—to read as listeners— and with all writers, to write as listeners. It may be part of the desire to write. The sound of what falls on the page begins the process of testing it for truth, for me. Whether I am right to trust so far I don't know. By now I don't know whether I could do either one, reading or writing, without the other.

25   My own words, when I am at work on a story, I hear too as they go, in the same voice that I hear when I read in books. When I write and the sound of it comes back to my ears, then I act to make my changes. I have always trusted this voice.

16. *Daughter of the Regiment*, an opera (1840) by the Italian composer Gaetano Donizetti; *The Fortune Teller*, an operetta (1898) by the American Victor Herbert; "Kiss Me Again," a song from Herbert's *Mlle. Modiste* (1905); *Carmen*, an opera (1875) by the French composer Georges Bizet; "Stars and Stripes Forever," a march (1897) by the American John Philip Sousa; "When the Midnight Choo-Choo Leaves for Alabam," a popular song (1912) by the American Irving Berlin.

QUESTIONS

1. In the opening paragraphs Welty speaks of what she later calls her "sensory education." What does she mean? What examples does she give?

2. Throughout her essay Welty lists the titles of books that she and her mother read. What is the effect of these lists? Have you read any of the books? Or books like them? How important were they to you?

3. Welty concludes her essay by talking of the writer's voice—of "testing it for truth" and "trust[ing] this voice" (paragraphs 24 and 25). What meanings does she give the key words "truth" and "trust"?

4. Read John Holt's essay "How Teachers Make Children Hate Reading" (p. 237). Write an essay of your own, entitled "How Children Learn to Love Reading," drawing your evidence from Welty's "One Writer's Beginnings" and your experience, observation, and reading.

5. Welty grew up before the advent of television. How does television affect a child's "sensory education"? Write an essay comparing a modern child's sensory education with Welty's.

VLADIMIR NABOKOV *Good Readers and Good Writers*

"How to be a Good Reader" or "Kindness to Authors"—something of that sort might serve to provide a subtitle for these various discussions of various authors, for my plan is to deal lovingly, in loving and lingering detail, with several European masterpieces. A hundred years ago, Flaubert[1] in a letter to his mistress made the following remark: *Comme l'on serait savant si l'on connaissait bien seulement cinq à six livres:* "What a scholar one might be if one knew well only some half a dozen books."

In reading, one should notice and fondle details. There is nothing wrong about the moonshine of generalization when it comes *after* the sunny trifles of the book have been lovingly collected. If one begins with a ready-made generalization, one begins at the wrong end and travels away from the book before one has started to understand it. Nothing is more boring or more unfair to the author than starting to read, say, *Madame Bovary,* with the preconceived notion that it is a denunciation of the bourgeoisie. We should always remember that the work of art is invariably the creation of a new world, so that the first thing we should do is to study that new world as closely as possible, approaching it as something brand new, having no obvious connection with the worlds we already know. When this new world has been closely studied, then and only then let us examine its links with other worlds, other branches of knowledge.

Another question: Can we expect to glean information about places and times from a novel? Can anybody be so naive as to think he or she can learn anything about the past from those buxom best-sellers that are hawked around by book clubs under the heading of historical novels? But what about the mas-

A lecture delivered to Nabokov's undergraduate class at Cornell University, where he taught from 1948 to 1959; published in Lectures on Literature *in 1980.*

1. Gustave Flaubert (1821–1880), French novelist, author of *Madame Bovary.*

terpieces? Can we rely on Jane Austen's[2] picture of landowning England with baronets and landscaped grounds when all she knew was a clergyman's parlor? And *Bleak House,*[3] that fantastic romance within a fantastic London, can we call it a study of London a hundred years ago? Certainly not. And the same holds for other such novels in this series. The truth is that great novels are great fairy tales—and the novels in this series are supreme fairy tales.

Time and space, the colors of the seasons, the movements of muscles and minds, all these are for writers of genius (as far as we can guess and I trust we guess right) not traditional notions which may be borrowed from the circulating library of public truths but a series of unique surprises which master artists have learned to express in their own unique way. To minor authors is left the ornamentation of the commonplace: these do not bother about any reinventing of the world; they merely try to squeeze the best they can out of a given order of things, out of traditional patterns of fiction. The various combinations these minor authors are able to produce within these set limits may be quite amusing in a mild ephemeral way because minor readers like to recognize their own ideas in a pleasing disguise. But the real writer, the fellow who sends planets spinning and models a man asleep and eagerly tampers with the sleeper's rib, that kind of author has no given values at his disposal: he must create them himself. The art of writing is a very futile business if it does not imply first of all the art of seeing the world as the potentiality of fiction. The material of this world may be real enough (as far as reality goes) but does not exist at all as an accepted entirety: it is chaos, and to this chaos the author says "go!" allowing the world to flicker and to fuse. It is now recombined in its very atoms, not merely in its visible and superficial parts. The writer is the first man to map it and to name the natural objects it contains. Those berries there are edible. That speckled creature that bolted across my path might be tamed. That lake between those trees will be called Lake Opal or, more artistically, Dishwater Lake. That mist is a mountain—and that mountain must be conquered. Up a trackless slope climbs the master artist, and at the top, on a windy ridge, whom do you think he meets? The panting and happy reader, and there they spontaneously embrace and are linked forever if the book lasts forever.

5   One evening at a remote provincial college through which I happened to be jogging on a protracted lecture tour, I suggested a little quiz—ten definitions of a reader, and from these ten the students had to choose four definitions that would combine to make a good reader. I have mislaid the list, but as far as I remember the definitions went something like this. Select four answers to the question what should a reader be to be a good reader:

1. The reader should belong to a book club.

2. The reader should identify himself or herself with the hero or heroine.

---

2. British novelist (1775–1817).

3. Novel by Charles Dickens (1812–1870) that alternates scenes in London and the country and includes a satire on the British judicial system.

3. The reader should concentrate on the social-economic angle.

4. The reader should prefer a story with action and dialogue to one with none.

5. The reader should have seen the book in a movie.

6. The reader should be a budding author.

7. The reader should have imagination.

8. The reader should have memory.

9. The reader should have a dictionary.

10. The reader should have some artistic sense.

The students leaned heavily on emotional identification, action, and the social-economic or historical angle. Of course, as you have guessed, the good reader is one who has imagination, memory, a dictionary, and some artistic sense—which sense I propose to develop in myself and in others whenever I have the chance.

Incidentally, I use the word *reader* very loosely. Curiously enough, one cannot *read* a book: one can only reread it. A good reader, a major reader, an active and creative reader is a rereader. And I shall tell you why. When we read a book for the first time the very process of laboriously moving our eyes from left to right, line after line, page after page, this complicated physical work upon the book, the very process of learning in terms of space and time what the book is about, this stands between us and artistic appreciation. When we look at a painting we do not have to move our eyes in a special way even if, as in a book, the picture contains elements of depth and development. The element of time does not really enter in a first contact with a painting. In reading a book, we must have time to acquaint ourselves with it. We have no physical organ (as we have the eye in regard to a painting) that takes in the whole picture and then can enjoy its details. But at a second, or third, or fourth reading we do, in a sense, behave towards a book as we do towards a painting. However, let us not confuse the physical eye, that monstrous masterpiece of evolution, with the mind, an even more monstrous achievement. A book, no matter what it is—a work of fiction or a work of science (the boundary line between the two is not as clear as is generally believed)—a book of fiction appeals first of all to the mind. The mind, the brain, the top of the tingling spine, is, or should be, the only instrument used upon a book.

Now, this being so, we should ponder the question how does the mind work when the sullen reader is confronted by the sunny book. First, the sullen mood melts away, and for better or worse the reader enters into the spirit of the game. The effort to begin a book, especially if it is praised by people whom the young reader secretly deems to be too old-fashioned or too serious, this effort is often difficult to make; but once it is made, rewards are various and abundant. Since the master artist used his imagination in creating his book, it is natural and fair that the consumer of a book should use his imagination too.

There are, however, at least two varieties of imagination in the reader's case. So let us see which one of the two is the right one to use in reading a book. First, there is the comparatively lowly kind which turns for support to the simple emotions and is of a definitely personal nature. (There are various subvarieties here, in this first section of emotional reading.) A situation in a book is intensely felt because it reminds us of something that happened to us or to someone we know or knew. Or, again, a reader treasures a book mainly because it evokes a country, a landscape, a mode of living which he nostalgically recalls as part of his own past. Or, and this is the worst thing a reader can do, he identifies himself with a character in the book. This lowly variety is not the kind of imagination I would like readers to use.

So what is the authentic instrument to be used by the reader? It is impersonal imagination and artistic delight. What should be established, I think, is an artistic harmonious balance between the reader's mind and the author's mind. We ought to remain a little aloof and take pleasure in this aloofness while at the same time we keenly enjoy—passionately enjoy, enjoy with tears and shivers—the inner weave of a given masterpiece. To be quite objective in these matters is of course impossible. Everything that is worthwhile is to some extent subjective. For instance, you sitting there may be merely my dream, and I may be your nightmare. But what I mean is that the reader must know when and where to curb his imagination and this he does by trying to get clear the specific world the author places at his disposal. We must see things and hear things, we must visualize the rooms, the clothes, the manners of an author's people. The color of Fanny Price's eyes in *Mansfield Park*[4] and the furnishing of her cold little room are important.

10   We all have different temperaments, and I can tell you right now that the best temperament for a reader to have, or to develop, is a combination of the artistic and the scientific one. The enthusiastic artist alone is apt to be too subjective in his attitude towards a book, and so a scientific coolness of judgment will temper the intuitive heat. If, however, a would-be reader is utterly devoid of passion and patience—of an artist's passion and a scientist's patience—he will hardly enjoy great literature.

Literature was born not the day when a boy crying wolf, wolf came running out of the Neanderthal valley with a big gray wolf at his heels: literature was born on the day when a boy came crying wolf, wolf and there was no wolf behind him. That the poor little fellow because he lied too often was finally eaten up by a real beast is quite incidental. But here is what is important. Between the wolf in the tall grass and the wolf in the tall story there is a shimmering go-between. That go-between, that prism, is the art of literature.

Literature is invention. Fiction is fiction. To call a story a true story is an insult to both art and truth. Every great writer is a great deceiver, but so is that arch-cheat Nature. Nature always deceives. From the simple deception of propagation to the prodigiously sophisticated illusion of protective colors in butterflies or birds, there is in Nature a marvelous system of spells and wiles. The writer of fiction only follows Nature's lead.

4. Novel by Jane Austen published in 1814.

Going back for a moment to our wolf-crying woodland little woolly fellow, we may put it this way: the magic of art was in the shadow of the wolf that he deliberately invented, his dream of the wolf; then the story of his tricks made a good story. When he perished at last, the story told about him acquired a good lesson in the dark around the camp fire. But he was the little magician. He was the inventor.

There are three points of view from which a writer can be considered: he may be considered as a storyteller, as a teacher, and as an enchanter. A major writer combines these three—storyteller, teacher, enchanter—but it is the enchanter in him that predominates and makes him a major writer.

To the storyteller we turn for entertainment, for mental excitement of the 15 simplest kind, for emotional participation, for the pleasure of traveling in some remote region in space or time. A slightly different though not necessarily higher mind looks for the teacher in the writer. Propagandist, moralist, prophet—this is the rising sequence. We may go to the teacher not only for moral education but also for direct knowledge, for simple facts. Alas, I have known people whose purpose in reading the French and Russian novelists was to learn something about life in gay Paree or in sad Russia. Finally, and above all, a great writer is always a great enchanter, and it is here that we come to the really exciting part when we try to grasp the individual magic of his genius and to study the style, the imagery, the pattern of his novels or poems.

The three facets of the great writer—magic, story, lesson—are prone to blend in one impression of unified and unique radiance, since the magic of art may be present in the very bones of the story, in the very marrow of thought. There are masterpieces of dry, limpid, organized thought which provoke in us an artistic quiver quite as strongly as a novel like *Mansfield Park* does or as any rich flow of Dickensian sensual imagery. It seems to me that a good formula to test the quality of a novel is, in the long run, a merging of the precision of poetry and the intuition of science. In order to bask in that magic a wise reader reads the book of genius not with his heart, not so much with his brain, but with his spine. It is there that occurs the telltale tingle even though we must keep a little aloof, a little detached when reading. Then with a pleasure which is both sensual and intellectual we shall watch the artist build his castle of cards and watch the castle of cards become a castle of beautiful steel and glass.

QUESTIONS

1. Make a list of the qualities that Nabokov believes "good readers" should have; then make a list of the qualities he believes "good writers" should have. Do they correspond? Why or why not?

2. Nabokov, as he points out in the conclusion to his essay (paragraphs 14–16), considers the writer from three points of view: as storyteller, as teacher, and as enchanter. He has not, however, organized his essay by these points of view. Where and how does he discuss each one? Why does he consider the last the most important?

3. Take Nabokov's quiz (paragraph 5). Write an essay in which you explain your "right" answers (as Nabokov sees "good readers") and defend your "wrong" ones.

4. How would Eudora Welty (see "One Writer's Beginnings," p. 625) and Katha Pollitt (see "Does a Literary Canon Matter?," below) do on Nabokov's quiz? Give what you think would be their answers and explain, using information from their essays, what you think their reasons would be.

KATHA POLLITT

Does a Literary Canon Matter?

OR THE PAST couple of years we've all been witness to a furious debate about the literary canon. What books should be assigned to students? What books should critics discuss? What books should the rest of us read, and who are "we" anyway? Like everyone else, I've given these questions some thought, and when an invitation came my way, I leaped to produce my own manifesto. But to my surprise, when I sat down to write—in order to discover, as E. M. Forster[1] once said, what I really think—I found that I agreed with all sides in the debate at once.

Take the conservatives. Now, this rather dour collection of scholars and diatribists—Allan Bloom, Hilton Kramer, John Silber[2] and so on—are not a particularly appealing group of people. They are arrogant, they are rude, they are gloomy, they do not suffer fools gladly, and everywhere they look, fools are what they see. All good reasons not to elect them to public office, as the voters of Massachusetts recently decided. But what is so terrible, really, about what they are saying? I too believe that some books are more profound, more complex, more essential to an understanding of our culture than others; I too am appalled to think of students graduating from college not having read Homer, Plato, Virgil, Milton, Tolstoy[3]—all writers, dead white Western men though they be, whose works have meant a great deal to me. As a teacher of literature and of writing, I too have seen at first hand

Pollitt writes a regular column in the Nation, *a liberal weekly magazine. This selection was her contribution for September 23, 1991.*

1. British novelist (1879–1970) and member of the Bloomsbury group.

2. Bloom (1930–1992), professor of political philosophy at the University of Chicago and author of *The Closing of the American Mind* (1987); Kramer, art critic, editor of the *New Criterion*, and author of *The Revenge of the Philistines: Art and Culture, 1972–84* (1985); Silber (b. 1926), president, then chancellor, of Boston University, author of *Straight Shooting: What's Wrong with America and How to Fix It* (1989), ran for governor of Massachusetts.

3. Homer (eighth century B.C.E.), Greek epic poet, author of the *Iliad* and the *Odyssey*; Plato (427–347 B.C.E.), Greek philosopher; Virgil (Publius Vergilius Maro, 70–19 B.C.E.), Roman poet, author of the *Aeneid*; John Milton (1608–1674), British poet, author of *Paradise Lost* (1667); Leo (Count Lev Nikolayevich) Tolstoy (1828–1910), Russian novelist and essayist.

how ill-educated many students are, and how little aware they are of this important fact about themselves. Last year I taught a graduate seminar in the writing of poetry. None of my students had read more than a smattering of poems by anyone, male or female, published more than ten years ago. Robert Lowell was as far outside their frame of reference as Alexander Pope.[4] When I gently suggested to one student that it might benefit her to read some poetry if she planned to spend her life writing it, she told me that yes, she knew she should read more but when she encountered a really good poem it only made her depressed. That contemporary writing has a history which it profits us to know in some depth, that we ourselves were not born yesterday, seems too obvious even to argue.

But ah, say the liberals, the canon exalted by the conservatives is itself an artifact of history. Sure, some books are more rewarding than others, but why can't we change our minds about which books those are? The canon itself was not always as we know it today: Until the 1920s, Moby-Dick[5] was shelved with the boys' adventure stories. If T. S. Eliot could single-handedly dethrone the Romantic poets in favor of the neglected Metaphysicals and place John Webster alongside Shakespeare, why can't we dip into the sea of stories and fish out Edith Wharton or Virginia Woolf?[6] And this position too makes a great deal of sense to me. After all, alongside the many good reasons for a book to end up on the required-reading shelf are some rather suspect reasons for its exclusion: because it was written by a woman and therefore presumed to be too slight; because it was written by a black person and therefore presumed to be too unsophisticated or to reflect too special a case. By all means, say the liberals, let's have great books and a shared culture. But let's make sure that all the different kinds of greatness are represented and that the culture we share reflects the true range of human experience.

If we leave the broadening of the canon up to the conservatives, this will never happen, because to them change only means defeat. Look at the recent fuss over the latest edition of the Great Books series published by Encyclopaedia Britannica, headed by that old snake-oil salesman Mortimer Adler. Four women have now been added to the series: Virginia Woolf, Willa Cather, Jane Austen and George Eliot.[7] That's nice, I suppose, but really! Jane Austen has been a certified Great Writer for a hundred years! Lionel Trilling[8] said so!

4. Lowell (1917–1977), American poet; Pope (1688–1744), British poet.

5. Novel by Herman Melville (1819–1891) published in 1851.

6. Eliot (1888–1965), American-born British poet and literary critic; Webster (c. 1578–c. 1632), English playwright; William Shakespeare (1564–1616), English playwright; Wharton (1862–1937), American novelist; Woolf (1882–1941), British novelist and essayist.

7. Cather (1876–1947), American novelist; Austen (1775–1817), British novelist; George Eliot, pseudonym of Mary Ann Evans (1819–1890), British novelist and literary critic.

8. American literary critic (1905–1975) whose important studies The Opposing Self (1955) and Beyond Culture (1966) include discussions of Jane Austen's novels.

There's something truly absurd about the conservatives earnestly sitting in judgment on the illustrious dead, as though up in Writers' Heaven Jane and George and Willa and Virginia were breathlessly waiting to hear if they'd finally made it into the club, while Henry Fielding, newly dropped from the list, howls in outer darkness and the Brontës,[9] presumably, stamp their feet in frustration and hope for better luck in twenty years, when *Jane Eyre* and *Wuthering Heights* will suddenly turn out to have qualities of greatness never before detected in their pages. It's like Poets' Corner at Manhattan's Cathedral of St. John the Divine, where mortal men—and a woman or two—of letters actually vote on which immortals to honor with a plaque, a process no doubt complete with electoral campaigns, compromise candidates and all the rest of the underside of the literary life. "No, I'm sorry, I just can't vote for Whitman. I'm a Washington Irving[10] man myself."

5   A liberal is not a very exciting thing to be, and so we have the radicals, who attack the concepts of "greatness," "shared," "culture" and "lists." (I'm overlooking here the ultraradicals, who attack the "privileging" of "texts," as they insist on calling books, and think one might as well spend one's college years deconstructing *Leave It to Beaver*.)[11] Who is to say, ask the radicals, what is a great book? What's so terrific about complexity, ambiguity, historical centrality and high seriousness? If *The Color Purple*,[12] say, gets students thinking about their own experience, maybe they ought to read it and forget about— and here you can fill in the name of whatever classic work you yourself found dry and tedious and never got around to finishing. For the radicals the notion of a shared culture is a lie, because it means presenting as universally meaningful and politically neutral books that reflect the interests and experiences and values of privileged white men at the expense of those of others—women, blacks, Latinos, Asians, the working class, whoever. Why not scrap the one-list-for-everyone idea and let people connect with books that are written by people like themselves about people like themselves? It will be a more accurate reflection of a multifaceted and conflict-ridden society, and will do wonders for everyone's self-esteem, except, of course, living white men—but they have too much self-esteem already.

Now, I have to say that I dislike the radicals' vision intensely. How foolish to argue that Chekhov[13] has nothing to say to a black woman—or, for that matter, myself—merely because he is Russian, long dead, a man. The notion that one reads to increase one's self-esteem sounds to me like more snake oil.

9. Fielding (1707–1754), British novelist; Charlotte (1816–1855), Emily (1818–1848), and Anne (1820–1849) Brontë, authors of *Jane Eyre*, *Wuthering Heights*, and *Agnes Grey*, respectively.

10. Walt Whitman (1819–1892), American poet; Irving (1783–1859), American essayist and fiction writer.

11. Television sitcom popular in the 1950s and 1960s.

12. Novel by Alice Walker (b. 1944), African American fiction writer and essayist, published in 1982.

13. Anton Chekhov (1860–1904), Russian dramatist and fiction writer.

Literature is not an aerobics class or a session at the therapist's. But then I think of myself as a child, leafing through anthologies of poetry for the names of women. I never would have admitted that I needed a role model, even if that awful term had existed back in the prehistory of which I speak, but why was I so excited to find a female name, even when, as was often the case, it was attached to a poem of no interest to me whatsoever? Anna Laetitia Barbauld, author of "Life! I know not what thou art / but know that thou and I must part!"; Lady Anne Lindsay,[14] writer of languid ballads in incomprehensible Scots dialect; and the other minor female poets included by chivalrous Sir Arthur Quiller-Couch in the old *Oxford Book of English Verse*: I have to admit it, just by their presence in that august volume they did something for me. And although it had nothing to do with reading or writing, it was an important thing they did.

What are we to make of this spluttering debate, in which charges of imperialism are met by equally passionate accusations of vandalism, in which each side hates the others, and yet each one seems to have its share of reason? Perhaps what we have here is one of those debates in which the opposing sides, unbeknownst to themselves, share a myopia that will turn out to be the most telling feature of the whole discussion: a debate, for instance, like that of our Founding Fathers over the nature of the franchise. Think of all the energy and passion spent pondering the question of property qualifications or direct versus legislative elections while all along, unmentioned and unimagined, was the fact—to us so central—that women and slaves were never considered for any kind of vote.

Something is being overlooked: the state of reading, and books, and literature in our country at this time. Why, ask yourself, is everyone so hot under the collar about what to put on the required-reading shelf? It is because while we have been arguing so fiercely about which books make the best medicine, the patient has been slipping deeper and deeper into a coma.

Let us imagine a country in which reading is a popular voluntary activity. There, parents read books for their own edification and pleasure, and are seen by their children at this silent and mysterious pastime. These parents also read to their children, give them books for presents, talk to them about books and underwrite, with their taxes, a public library system that is open all day, every day. In school—where an attractive library is invariably to be found—the children study certain books together but also have an active reading life of their own. Years later it may even be hard for them to remember if they read *Jane Eyre* at home and Judy Blume[15] in class, or the other way around. In college young people continue to be assigned certain books, but far more important are the books they discover for themselves—browsing in the library, in bookstores, on the shelves of friends, one book leading to another, back and forth in history and across languages and cultures. After graduation they continue to

14. Barbauld (1743–1825), British poet; Lady Anne Lindsay Barnard (1750–1825), Scottish poet.
15. American writer (b. 1938) of young adult fiction.

read, and in the fullness of time produce a new generation of readers. Oh happy land! I wish we all lived there.

10   In that other country of real readers—voluntary, active, self-determined readers—a debate like the current one over the canon would not be taking place. Or if it did, it would be as a kind of parlor game: What books would you take to a desert island? Everyone would know that the top-ten list was merely a tiny fraction of the books one would read in a life-time. It would not seem racist or sexist or hopelessly hidebound to put Hawthorne on the syllabus and not Toni Morrison.[16] It would be more like putting oatmeal and not noodles on the breakfast menu—a choice part arbitrary, part a nod to the national past, part, dare one say it, a kind of reverse affirmative action: School might frankly be the place where one read the books that are a little off-putting, that have gone a little cold, that you might pass over because they do not address, in reader-friendly contemporary fashion, the issues most immediately at stake in modern life, but that, with a little study, turn out to have a great deal to say. Being on the list wouldn't mean so much. It might even add to a writer's cachet not to be on the list, to be in one way or another too heady, too daring, too exciting to be ground up into institutional fodder for teenagers. Generations of high school kids have been turned off to George Eliot by being forced to read *Silas Marner* at a tender age. One can imagine a whole new readership for her if grown-ups were left to approach *Middlemarch* and *Daniel Deronda*[17] with open minds, at their leisure.

Of course, they rarely do. In America today the assumption underlying the canon debate is that the books on the list are the only books that are going to be read, and if the list is dropped no books are going to be read. Becoming a textbook is a book's only chance; all sides take that for granted. And so all agree not to mention certain things that they themselves, as highly educated people and, one assumes, devoted readers, know perfectly well. For example, that if you read only twenty-five, or fifty, or a hundred books, you can't understand them, however well chosen they are. And that if you don't have an independent reading life—and very few students do—you won't like reading the books on the list and will forget them the minute you finish them. And that books have, or should have, lives beyond the syllabus—thus, the totally misguided attempt to put current literature in the classroom. How strange to think that people need professorial help to read John Updike[18] or Alice Walker, writers people actually do read for fun. But all sides agree, if it isn't taught, it doesn't count.

Let's look at the canon question from another angle. Instead of asking what books we want others to read, let's ask why we read books ourselves. I think the canon debaters are being a little disingenuous here, are suppressing, in the interest of their own agendas, their personal experience of reading.

16. Nathaniel Hawthorne (1804–1864), American novelist; Toni Morrison (b. 1931), African American novelist.

17. Novels by George Eliot written in 1861, 1871–72, and 1874–76, respectively.

18. Updike (b. 1932), American fiction writer and literary critic.

Sure, we read to understand our American culture and history, and we also read to recover neglected masterpieces, and to learn more about the accomplishments of our subgroup and thereby, as I've admitted about myself, increase our self-esteem. But what about reading for the aesthetic pleasures of language, form, image? What about reading to learn something new, to have a vicarious adventure, to follow the workings of an interesting, if possibly skewed, narrow and ill-tempered mind? What about reading for the story? For an expanded sense of sheer human variety? There are a thousand reasons why a book might have a claim on our time and attention other than its canonization. I once infuriated an acquaintance by asserting that Trollope, although in many ways a lesser writer than Dickens,[19] possessed some wonderful qualities Dickens lacked: a more realistic view of women, a more skeptical view of good intentions, a subtler sense of humor, a drier vision of life which I myself found congenial. You'd think I'd advocated throwing Dickens out and replacing him with a toaster. Because Dickens is a certified Great Writer, and Trollope is not.

Am I saying anything different from what Randall Jarrell[20] said in his great 1953 essay "The Age of Criticism"? Not really, so I'll quote him. Speaking of the literary gatherings of the era, Jarrell wrote:

> If at such parties, you wanted to talk about *Ulysses* or *The Castle* or *The Brothers Karamazov* or *The Great Gatsby* or Graham Greene's last novel—Important books—you were at the right place. (Though you weren't so well off if you wanted to talk about *Remembrance of Things Past*. Important, but too long.) But if you wanted to talk about Turgenev's novelettes, or *The House of the Dead*, or *Lavengro*, or *Life on the Mississippi*, or *The Old Wives' Tale*, or *The Golovlyov Family*, or Cunningham-Grahame's stories, or Saint-Simon's memoirs, or *Lost Illusions*, or *The Beggar's Opera*, or *Eugene Onegin*, or *Little Dorrit*, or the Burnt Njál Saga, or *Persuasion*, or *The Inspector-General*, or *Oblomov*, or *Peer Gynt*, or *Far from the Madding Crowd*, or *Out of Africa*, or the *Parallel Lives*, or *A Dreary Story*, or *Debits and Credits*, or *Arabia Deserta*, or *Elective Affinities*, or *Schweik*, or—any of a thousand good or interesting but Unimportant books, you couldn't expect a very ready knowledge or sympathy from most of the readers there. They had looked at the big sights, the current sights, hard, with guides and glasses; and those walks in the country, over unfrequented or thrice-familiar territory, all alone—those walks from which most of the joy and good of reading come—were walks that they hadn't gone on very often.

I suspect that most canon debaters have taken those solitary rambles, if only out of boredom—how many times, after all, can you reread the *Aeneid*, or *Mrs. Dalloway*, or *Cotton Comes to Harlem*[21] (to pick one book from each column)? But those walks don't count, because of another assumption all sides

19. Anthony Trollope (1815–1882), British novelist; Charles Dickens (1812–1870), British novelist.

20. American poet and literary critic (1914–1965).

21. The *Aeneid* (composed 29–19 B.C.E.), Latin epic poem by Virgil; *Mrs. Dalloway* (1925), novel by Virginia Woolf; *Cotton Comes to Harlem* (1965), detective novel by Chester Himes (1909–1984).

hold in common, which is that the purpose of reading is none of the many varied and delicious satisfactions I've mentioned; it's medicinal. The chief end of reading is to produce a desirable kind of person and a desirable kind of society. A respectful, high-minded citizen of a unified society for the conservatives, an up-to-date and flexible sort for the liberals, a subgroup-identified, robustly confident one for the radicals. How pragmatic, how moralistic, how American! The culture debaters turn out to share a secret suspicion of culture itself, as well as the antipornographer's belief that there is a simple, one-to-one correlation between books and behavior. Read the conservatives' list and produce a nation of sexists and racists—or a nation of philosopher kings. Read the liberals' list and produce a nation of spineless relativists—or a nation of open-minded world citizens. Read the radicals' list and produce a nation of psychobabblers and ancestor-worshipers—or a nation of stalwart proud-to-be-me pluralists.

15   But is there any list of a few dozen books that can have such a magical effect, for good or for ill? Of course not. It's like arguing that a perfectly nutritional breakfast cereal is enough food for the whole day. And so the canon debate is really an argument about what books to cram down the resistant throats of a resentful captive populace of students; and the trick is never to mention the fact that, in such circumstances, one book is as good, or as bad, as another. Because, as the debaters know from their own experience as readers, books are not pills that produce health when ingested in measured doses. Books do not shape character in any simple way—if, indeed, they do so at all—or the most literate would be the most virtuous instead of just the ordinary run of humanity with larger vocabularies. Books cannot mold a common national purpose when, in fact, people are honestly divided about what kind of country they want—and are divided, moreover, for very good and practical reasons, as they always have been.

For these burly and energetic purposes, books are all but useless. The way books affect us is an altogether more subtle, delicate, wayward and individual, not to say private, affair. And that reading is being made to bear such an inappropriate and simplistic burden speaks to the poverty both of culture and of frank political discussion in our time.

On his deathbed, Dr. Johnson[22]—once canonical, now more admired than read—is supposed to have said to a friend who was energetically rearranging his bedclothes, "Thank you, this will do all that a pillow can do." One might say that the canon debaters are all asking of their handful of chosen books that they do a great deal more than any handful of books can do.

22. Samuel Johnson (1709–1784), British author and compiler of the *Dictionary of the English Language* (1755).

QUESTIONS

1. Pollitt's strategy of argument is classification; she enunciates three positions on the literary canon. How many times does this three-part classification appear in her essay? Mark them.

2. What are the points of difference among the three positions? More important to Pollitt's own argument, what are their points of similarity?

3. What are the strengths and weaknesses of Pollitt's finding herself in partial agreement with all three positions? You may want to contrast her style of argument with Michael Levin's in "The Case for Torture" (p. 400). Levin, like a debater, argues only his own position and puts down, entirely, the counterarguments of those who disagree with him. Is Pollitt's or Levin's approach more congenial to you?

4. Write a two- or three-part essay in which you argue the strengths and weaknesses of all three positions outlined by Pollitt.

VIRGINIA WOOLF   *In Search of a Room of One's Own*

IT WAS DISAPPOINTING not to have brought back in the evening some important statement, some authentic fact. Women are poorer than men because—this or that. Perhaps now it would be better to give up seeking for the truth, and receiving on one's head an avalanche of opinion hot as lava, discolored as dish-water. It would be better to draw the curtains; to shut out distractions; to light the lamp; to narrow the enquiry and to ask the historian, who records not opinions but facts, to describe under what conditions women lived, not throughout the ages, but in England, say in the time of Elizabeth.

For it is a perennial puzzle why no woman wrote a word of that extraordinary literature when every other man, it seemed, was capable of song or sonnet. What were the conditions in which women lived, I asked myself; for fiction, imaginative work that is, is not dropped like a pebble upon the ground, as science may be; fiction is like a spider's web, attached ever so lightly perhaps, but still attached to life at all four corners. Often the attachment is scarcely perceptible; Shakespeare's plays, for instance, seem to hang there complete by themselves. But when the web is pulled askew, hooked up at the edge, torn in the middle, one remembers that these webs are not spun in midair by incorporeal creatures, but are the work of suffering human beings, and are attached to grossly material things, like health and money and the houses we live in.

I went, therefore, to the shelf where the histories stand and took down one of the latest, Professor Trevelyan's *History of England*. Once more I looked

From chapter 3 of Woolf's A Room of One's Own (1929), a long essay that began as lectures given at Newnham College and Girton College, women's colleges at Cambridge University, in 1928. In chapter 1, Woolf advances the proposition that "a woman must have money and a room of her own if she is to write fiction." In chapter 2, she describes a day spent at the British Museum (now the British Library) looking for information about the lives of women.

up Women, found "position of," and turned to the pages indicated. "Wife-beating," I read, "was a recognised right of man, and was practised without shame by high as well as low. . . . Similarly," the historian goes on, "the daughter who refused to marry the gentleman of her parents' choice was liable to be locked up, beaten and flung about the room, without any shock being inflicted on public opinion. Marriage was not an affair of personal affection, but of family avarice, particularly in the 'chivalrous' upper classes. . . . Betrothal often took place while one or both of the parties was in the cradle, and marriage when they were scarcely out of the nurses' charge." That was about 1470, soon after Chaucer's time. The next reference to the position of women is some two hundred years later, in the time of the Stuarts. "It was still the exception for women of the upper and middle class to choose their own husbands, and when the husband had been assigned, he was lord and master, so far at least as law and custom could make him. Yet even so," Professor Trevelyan concludes, "neither Shakespeare's women nor those of authentic seventeenth-century memoirs, like the Verneys and the Hutchinsons, seem wanting in personality and character." Certainly, if we consider it, Cleopatra must have had a way with her; Lady Macbeth, one would suppose, had a will of her own; Rosalind, one might conclude, was an attractive girl. Professor Trevelyan is speaking no more than the truth when he remarks that Shakespeare's women do not seem wanting in personality and character. Not being a historian, one might go even further and say that women have burnt like beacons in all the works of all the poets from the beginning of time—Clytemnestra, Antigone, Cleopatra, Lady Macbeth, Phèdre, Cressida, Rosalind, Desdemona, the Duchess of Malfi, among the dramatists; then among the prose writers: Millamant, Clarissa, Becky Sharp, Anna Karenina, Emma Bovary, Madame de Guermantes—the names flock to mind, nor do they recall women "lacking in personality and character." Indeed, if woman had no existence save in the fiction written by men, one would imagine her a person of the utmost importance; very various; heroic and mean; splendid and sordid; infinitely beautiful and hideous in the extreme; as great as a man, some think even greater.[1] But this is woman in fiction. In fact, as Professor Trevelyan points out, she was locked up, beaten and flung about the room.

---

1. "It remains a strange and almost inexplicable fact that in Athena's city, where women were kept in almost Oriental suppression as odalisques or drudges, the stage should yet have produced figures like Clytemnestra and Cassandra, Atossa and Antigone, Phèdre and Medea, and all the other heroines who dominate play after play of the 'misogynist' Euripides. But the paradox of this world where in real life a respectable woman could hardly show her face alone in the street, and yet on the stage woman equals or surpasses man, has never been satisfactorily explained. In modern tragedy the same predominance exists. At all events, a very cursory survey of Shakespeare's work (similarly with Webster, though not with Marlowe or Jonson) suffices to reveal how this dominance, this initiative of women, persists from Rosalind to Lady Macbeth. So too in Racine; six of his tragedies bear their heroines' names; and what male characters of his shall we set against Hermione and Andromaque, Bérénice and Roxane, Phèdre and Athalie? So again with Ibsen; what men shall we match with Solveig and Nora, Hedda and Hilda Wangel and Rebecca West?"—F. L. LUCAS, Tragedy, pp. 114–15 [Woolf's note].

A very queer, composite being thus emerges. Imaginatively she is of the highest importance; practically she is completely insignificant. She pervades poetry from cover to cover; she is all but absent from history. She dominates the lives of kings and conquerors in fiction; in fact she was the slave of any boy whose parents forced a ring upon her finger. Some of the most inspired words, some of the most profound thoughts in literature fall from her lips; in real life she could hardly read, could scarcely spell, and was the property of her husband.

It was certainly an odd monster that one made up by reading the histori-   5
ans first and the poets afterwards—a worm winged like an eagle; the spirit of life and beauty in a kitchen chopping up suet. But these monsters, however amusing to the imagination, have no existence in fact. What one must do to bring her to life was to think poetically and prosaically at one and the same moment, thus keeping in touch with fact—that she is Mrs. Martin, aged thirty-six, dressed in blue, wearing a black hat and brown shoes; but not losing sight of fiction either—that she is a vessel in which all sorts of spirits and forces are coursing and flashing perpetually. The moment, however, that one tries this method with the Elizabethan woman, one branch of illumination fails; one is held up by the scarcity of facts. One knows nothing detailed, nothing perfectly true and substantial about her. History scarcely mentions her. And I turned to Professor Trevelyan again to see what history meant to him. I found by looking at his chapter headings that it meant—

"The Manor Court and the Methods of Open-field Agriculture . . . The Cistercians and Sheep-farming . . . The Crusades . . . The University . . . The House of Commons . . . The Hundred Years' War . . . The Wars of the Roses . . . The Renaissance Scholars . . . The Dissolution of the Monasteries . . . Agrarian and Religious Strife . . . The Origin of English Seapower . . . The Armada . . ." and so on. Occasionally an individual woman is mentioned, an Elizabeth, or a Mary; a queen or a great lady. But by no possible means could middle-class women with nothing but brains and character at their command have taken part in any one of the great movements which, brought together, constitute the historian's view of the past. Nor shall we find her in any collection of anecdotes. Aubrey[2] hardly mentions her. She never writes her own life and scarcely keeps a diary; there are only a handful of her letters in existence. She left no plays or poems by which we can judge her. What one wants, I thought—and why does not some brilliant student at Newnham or Girton supply it?—is a mass of information; at what age did she marry; how many children had she as a rule; what was her house like; had she a room to herself; did she do the cooking; would she be likely to have a servant? All these facts lie somewhere, presumably, in parish registers and account books; the life of the average Elizabethan woman must be scattered about somewhere, could one collect it and make a book of it. It would be ambitious beyond my daring, I thought, looking about the shelves for books that were not there, to suggest to the students of those famous colleges that they should re-write history, though I own that it often seems a little queer as it is, unreal, lop-sided; but why

2. John Aubrey (1626–1697), whose biographical writings were published posthumously as *Brief Lives*.

should they not add a supplement to history? calling it, of course, by some in-
conspicuous name so that women might figure there without impropriety? For
one often catches a glimpse of them in the lives of the great, whisking away
into the background, concealing, I sometimes think, a wink, a laugh, perhaps
a tear. And, after all, we have lives enough of Jane Austen; it scarcely seems
necessary to consider again the influence of the tragedies of Joanna Baillie
upon the poetry of Edgar Allan Poe; as for myself, I should not mind if the
homes and haunts of Mary Russell Mitford[3] were closed to the public for a
century at least. But what I find deplorable, I continued, looking about the
bookshelves again, is that nothing is known about women before the eighteenth century. I have no model in my mind to turn about this way and that.
Here am I asking why women did not write poetry in the Elizabethan age, and
I am not sure how they were educated; whether they were taught to write;
whether they had sitting-rooms to themselves; how many women had children
before they were twenty-one; what, in short, they did from eight in the morning till eight at night. They had no money evidently; according to Professor
Trevelyan they were married whether they liked it or not before they were out
of the nursery, at fifteen or sixteen very likely. It would have been extremely
odd, even upon this showing, had one of them suddenly written the plays of
Shakespeare, I concluded, and I thought of that old gentleman, who is dead
now, but was a bishop, I think, who declared that it was impossible for any
woman, past, present, or to come, to have the genius of Shakespeare. He
wrote to the papers about it. He also told a lady who applied to him for information that cats do not as a matter of fact go to heaven, though they have, he
added, souls of a sort. How much thinking those old gentlemen used to save
one! How the borders of ignorance shrank back at their approach! Cats do not
go to heaven. Women cannot write the plays of Shakespeare.

　　Be that as it may, I could not help thinking, as I looked at the works of
Shakespeare on the shelf, that the bishop was right at least in this; it would
have been impossible, completely and entirely, for any woman to have written
the plays of Shakespeare in the age of Shakespeare. Let me imagine, since
facts are so hard to come by, what would have happened had Shakespeare had
a wonderfully gifted sister, called Judith, let us say. Shakespeare himself went,
very probably—his mother was an heiress—to the grammar school, where he
may have learnt Latin—Ovid, Virgil and Horace—and the elements of grammar and logic. He was, it is well known, a wild boy who poached rabbits, perhaps shot a deer, and had, rather sooner than he should have done, to marry a
woman in the neighborhood, who bore him a child rather quicker than was
right. That escapade sent him to seek his fortune in London. He had, it
seemed, a taste for the theatre; he began by holding horses at the stage door.
Very soon he got work in the theatre, became a successful actor, and lived at
the hub of the universe, meeting everybody, knowing everybody, practicing his

3. Austen (1775–1817), English novelist; Baillie (1762–1851), Scottish dramatist and
poet; Poe (1809–1849), American poet; Mitford (1787–1855), English novelist and
essayist.

art on the boards, exercising his wits in the streets, and even getting access to the palace of the queen. Meanwhile his extraordinarily gifted sister, let us suppose, remained at home. She was as adventurous, as imaginative, as agog to see the world as he was. But she was not sent to school. She had no chance of learning grammar and logic, let alone of reading Horace and Virgil. She picked up a book now and then, one of her brother's perhaps, and read a few pages. But then her parents came in and told her to mend the stockings or mind the stew and not moon about with books and papers. They would have spoken sharply but kindly, for they were substantial people who knew the conditions of life for a woman and loved their daughter—indeed, more likely than not she was the apple of her father's eye. Perhaps she scribbled some pages up in an apple loft on the sly, but was careful to hide them or set fire to them. Soon, however, before she was out of her teens, she was to be betrothed to the son of a neighboring wool-stapler. She cried out that marriage was hateful to her, and for that she was severely beaten by her father. Then he ceased to scold her. He begged her instead not to hurt him, not to shame him in this matter of her marriage. He would give her a chain of beads or a fine petticoat, he said; and there were tears in his eyes. How could she disobey him? How could she break his heart? The force of her own gift alone drove her to it. She made up a small parcel of her belongings, let herself down by a rope one summer's night and took the road to London. She was not seventeen. The birds that sang in the hedge were not more musical than she was. She had the quickest fancy, a gift like her brother's, for the tune of words. Like him, she had a taste for the theatre. She stood at the stage door; she wanted to act, she said. Men laughed in her face. The manager—a fat, loose-lipped man—guffawed. He bellowed something about poodles dancing and women acting—no woman, he said, could possibly be an actress.[4] He hinted—you can imagine what. She could get no training in her craft. Could she even seek her dinner in a tavern or roam the streets at midnight? Yet her genius was for fiction and lusted to feed abundantly upon the lives of men and women and the study of their ways. At last—for she was very young, oddly like Shakespeare the poet in her face, with the same grey eyes and rounded brows—at last Nick Greene the actor-manager took pity on her; she found herself with child by that gentleman and so—who shall measure the heat and violence of the poet's heart when caught and tangled in a woman's body?—killed herself one winter's night and lies buried at some cross-roads where the omnibuses now stop outside the Elephant and Castle.[5]

That, more or less, is how the story would run, I think, if a woman in Shakespeare's day had had Shakespeare's genius. But for my part, I agree with the deceased bishop, if such he was—it is unthinkable that any woman in Shakespeare's day should have had Shakespeare's genius. For genius like Shakespeare's is not born among laboring, uneducated, servile people. It was not born in England among the Saxons and the Britons. It is not born today

4. In the Elizabethan theater boys played women's parts.
5. A prominent landmark in London, south of the Thames.

among the working classes. How, then, could it have been born among women whose work began, according to Professor Trevelyan, almost before they were out of the nursery, who were forced to it by their parents and held to it by all the power of law and custom? Yet genius of a sort must have existed among women as it must have existed among the working classes. Now and again an Emily Brontë or a Robert Burns blazes out and proves its presence.[6] But certainly it never got itself on to paper. When, however, one reads of a witch being ducked, of a woman possessed by devils, of a wise woman selling herbs, or even of a very remarkable man who had a mother, then I think we are on the track of a lost novelist, a suppressed poet, of some mute and inglorious Jane Austen,[7] some Emily Brontë who dashed her brains out on the moor or mopped and mowed about the highways crazed with the torture that her gift had put her to. Indeed, I would venture to guess that Anon, who wrote so many poems without signing them, was often a woman. It was a woman Edward Fitzgerald,[8] I think, suggested who made the ballads and the folk-songs, crooning them to her children, beguiling her spinning with them, or the length of the winter's night.

This may be true or it may be false—who can say?—but what is true in it, so it seemed to me, reviewing the story of Shakespeare's sister as I had made it, is that any woman born with a great gift in the sixteenth century would certainly have gone crazed, shot herself, or ended her days in some lonely cottage outside the village, half witch, half wizard, feared and mocked at. For it needs little skill in psychology to be sure that a highly gifted girl who had tried to use her gift for poetry would have been so thwarted and hindered by other people, so tortured and pulled asunder by her own contrary instincts, that she must have lost her health and sanity to a certainty. No girl could have walked to London and stood at a stage door and forced her way into the presence of actor-managers without doing herself a violence and suffering an anguish which may have been irrational—for chastity may be a fetish invented by certain societies for unknown reasons—but were none the less inevitable. Chastity had then, it has even now, a religious importance in a woman's life, and has so wrapped itself round with nerves and instincts that to cut it free and bring it to the light of day demands courage of the rarest. To have lived a free life in London in the sixteenth century would have meant for a woman who was poet and playwright a nervous stress and dilemma which might well have killed her. Had she survived, whatever she had written would have been twisted and deformed, issuing from a strained and morbid imagination. And undoubtedly, I thought, looking at the shelf where there are no plays by women, her work would have gone unsigned. That refuge she would have sought certainly. It was the relic of the sense of chastity that dictated

---

6. Woolf's examples are Emily Brontë (1818–1848), the English novelist, and Robert Burns (1759–1796), the Scottish poet.

7. Woolf alludes to Thomas Gray's "Elegy Written in a Country Churchyard": "Some mute inglorious Milton here may rest."

8. Edward Fitzgerald (1809–1883), poet and translator of the *Rubáiyát of Omar Khayyám*.

anonymity to women even so late as the nineteenth century. Currer Bell, George Eliot, George Sand,[9] all the victims of inner strife as their writings prove, sought ineffectively to veil themselves by using the name of a man. Thus they did homage to the convention, which if not implanted by the other sex was liberally encouraged by them (the chief glory of a woman is not to be talked of, said Pericles,[10] himself a much-talked-of man), that publicity in women is detestable. Anonymity runs in their blood. The desire to be veiled still possesses them. They are not even now as concerned about the health of their fame as men are, and, speaking generally, will pass a tombstone or a signpost without feeling an irresistible desire to cut their names on it, as Alf, Bert or Chas. must do in obedience to their instinct, which murmurs if it sees a fine woman go by, or even a dog, Ce chien est à moi.[11] And, of course, it may not be a dog, I thought, remembering Parliament Square, the Sieges Allee and other avenues; it may be a piece of land or a man with curly black hair. It is one of the great advantages of being a woman that one can pass even a very fine negress without wishing to make an Englishwoman of her.

That woman, then, who was born with a gift of poetry in the sixteenth   10
century, was an unhappy woman, a woman at strife against herself. All the conditions of her life, all her own instincts, were hostile to the state of mind which is needed to set free whatever is in the brain. But what is the state of mind that is most propitious to the act of creation, I asked. Can one come by any notion of the state that furthers and makes possible that strange activity? Here I opened the volume containing the Tragedies of Shakespeare. What was Shakespeare's state of mind, for instance, when he wrote *Lear* and *Antony and Cleopatra*? It was certainly the state of mind most favorable to poetry that there has ever existed. But Shakespeare himself said nothing about it. We only know casually and by chance that he "never blotted a line."[12] Nothing indeed was ever said by the artist himself about his state of mind until the eighteenth century perhaps. Rousseau perhaps began it.[13] At any rate, by the nineteenth century self-consciousness had developed so far that it was the habit for men of letters to describe their minds in confessions and autobiographies. Their lives also were written, and their letters were printed after their deaths. Thus, though we do not know what Shakespeare went through when he wrote *Lear,* we do know what Carlyle went through when he wrote the *French Revolution;* what Flaubert went through when he wrote *Madame Bovary;* what Keats was going through when he tried to write poetry against the coming of death and the indifference of the world.

9. The pseudonyms of Charlotte Brontë (1816–1855), English novelist; Mary Ann Evans (1819–1880), English novelist; and Amandine Aurore Lucie Dupin, Baronne Dudevant (1804–1876), French novelist.

10. Pericles (d. 429 B.C.E.), Athenian statesman.

11. That dog is mine (French).

12. As recorded by his contemporary Ben Jonson in *Timber, or Discoveries Made upon Men and Matter.*

13. Jean-Jacques Rousseau (1712–1778), whose *Confessions* were published posthumously.

And one gathers from this enormous modern literature of confession and self-analysis that to write a work of genius is almost always a feat of prodigious difficulty. Everything is against the likelihood that it will come from the writer's mind whole and entire. Generally material circumstances are against it. Dogs will bark; people will interrupt; money must be made; health will break down. Further, accentuating all these difficulties and making them harder to bear is the world's notorious indifference. It does not ask people to write poems and novels and histories; it does not need them. It does not care whether Flaubert finds the right word or whether Carlyle scrupulously verifies this or that fact. Naturally, it will not pay for what it does not want. And so the writer, Keats, Flaubert, Carlyle, suffers, especially in the creative years of youth, every form of distraction and discouragement. A curse, a cry of agony, rises from those books of analysis and confession. "Mighty poets in their misery dead"[14]—that is the burden of their song. If anything comes through in spite of all this, it is a miracle, and probably no book is born entire and uncrippled as it was conceived.

But for women, I thought, looking at the empty shelves, these difficulties were infinitely more formidable. In the first place, to have a room of her own, let alone a quiet room or a sound-proof room, was out of the question, unless her parents were exceptionally rich or very noble, even up to the beginning of the nineteenth century. Since her pin money, which depended on the good will of her father, was only enough to keep her clothed, she was debarred from such alleviations as came even to Keats or Tennyson or Carlyle,[15] all poor men, from a walking tour, a little journey to France, from the separate lodging which, even if it were miserable enough, sheltered them from the claims and tyrannies of their families. Such material difficulties were formidable; but much worse were the immaterial. The indifference of the world which Keats and Flaubert and other men of genius have found so hard to bear was in her case not indifference but hostility. The world did not say to her as it said to them, Write if you choose; it makes no difference to me. The world said with a guffaw, Write? What's the good of your writing? Here the psychologists of Newnham and Girton might come to our help, I thought, looking again at the blank spaces on the shelves. For surely it is time that the effect of discouragement upon the mind of the artist should be measured, as I have seen a dairy company measure the effect of ordinary milk and Grade A milk upon the body of the rat. They set two rats in cages side by side, and of the two one was furtive, timid and small, and the other was glossy, bold and big. Now what food do we feed women as artists upon? I asked, remembering, I suppose, that dinner of prunes and custard.[16] To answer that question I had only to open the

14. From William Wordsworth's poem "Resolution and Independence."
15. John Keats (1795–1821) and Alfred, Lord Tennyson (1809–1892) were English poets; Thomas Carlyle (1795–1881) was a Scottish essayist.
16. In chapter 1, Woolf contrasts the lavish dinner—partridge and wine—she ate as a guest at a men's college at Cambridge University with the plain fare—prunes and custard—served at a women's college.

evening paper and to read that Lord Birkenhead is of opinion—but really I am not going to trouble to copy out Lord Birkenhead's opinion upon the writing of women. What Dean Inge says I will leave in peace. The Harley Street specialist may be allowed to rouse the echoes of Harley Street with his vociferations without raising a hair on my head. I will quote, however, Mr. Oscar Browning,[17] because Mr. Oscar Browning was a great figure in Cambridge at one time, and used to examine the students at Girton and Newnham. Mr. Oscar Browning was wont to declare "that the impression left on his mind, after looking over any set of examination papers, was that, irrespective of the marks he might give, the best woman was intellectually the inferior of the worst man." After saying that Mr. Browning went back to his rooms—and it is this sequel that endears him and makes him a human figure of some bulk and majesty—he went back to his rooms and found a stable-boy lying on the sofa—"a mere skeleton, his cheeks were cavernous and sallow, his teeth were black, and he did not appear to have the full use of his limbs. . . . 'That's Arthur' [said Mr. Browning]. 'He's a dear boy really and most high-minded.' " The two pictures always seem to me to complete each other. And happily in this age of biography the two pictures often do complete each other, so that we are able to interpret the opinions of great men not only by what they say, but by what they do.

But though this is possible now, such opinions coming from the lips of important people must have been formidable enough even fifty years ago. Let us suppose that a father from the highest motives did not wish his daughter to leave home and become writer, painter or scholar. "See what Mr. Oscar Browning says," he would say; and there was not only Mr. Oscar Browning; there was the *Saturday Review*; there was Mr. Greg[18]—the "essentials of a woman's being," said Mr. Greg emphatically, "are that *they are supported by, and they minister to, men*"—there was an enormous body of masculine opinion to the effect that nothing could be expected of women intellectually. Even if her father did not read out loud these opinions, any girl could read them for herself; and the reading, even in the nineteenth century, must have lowered her vitality, and told profoundly upon her work. There would always have been that assertion—you cannot do this, you are incapable of doing that—to protest against, to overcome. Probably for a novelist this germ is no longer of much effect; for there have been women novelists of merit. But for painters it must still have some sting in it; and for musicians, I imagine, is even now active and poisonous in the extreme. The women composer stands where the actress stood in the time of Shakespeare. Nick Greene, I thought, remembering the story I had made about Shakespeare's sister, said that a woman acting put him in mind of a dog dancing. Johnson repeated the phrase two hundred years

17. In chapter 2, Woolf lists the fruits of her day's research on the lives of women, which include Lord Birkenhead's, Dean Inge's, and Mr. Oscar Browning's opinions of women; she does not, however, quote them. Harley Street is where fashionable medical doctors in London have their offices.

18. Mr. Greg does not appear on Woolf's list (see preceding note).

later of women preaching.[19] And here, I said, opening a book about music, we have the very words used again in this year of grace, 1928, of women who try to write music. "Of Mlle. Germaine Tailleferre one can only repeat Dr. Johnson's dictum concerning a woman preacher, transposed into terms of music. 'Sir, a woman's composing is like a dog's walking on his hind legs. It is not done well, but you are surprised to find it done at all.' "[20] So accurately does history repeat itself.

Thus, I concluded, shutting Mr. Oscar Browning's life and pushing away the rest, it is fairly evident that even in the nineteenth century a woman was not encouraged to be an artist. On the contrary, she was snubbed, slapped, lectured and exhorted. Her mind must have been strained and her vitality lowered by the need of opposing this, of disproving that. For here again we come within range of that very interesting and obscure masculine complex which has had so much influence upon the woman's movement; that deep-seated desire, not so much that *she* shall be inferior as that *he* shall be superior, which plants him wherever one looks, not only in front of the arts, but barring the way to politics too, even when the risk to himself seems infinitesimal and the suppliant humble and devoted. Even Lady Bessborough, I remembered, with all her passion for politics, must humbly bow herself and write to Lord Granville Leveson-Gower[21]: " . . . notwithstanding all my violence in politics and talking so much on that subject, I perfectly agree with you that no woman has any business to meddle with that or any other serious business, farther than giving her opinion (if she is ask'd)." And so she goes on to spend her enthusiasm where it meets with no obstacle whatsoever upon that immensely important subject, Lord Granville's maiden speech in the House of Commons. The spectacle is certainly a strange one, I thought. The history of men's opposition to women's emancipation is more interesting perhaps than the story of that emancipation itself. An amusing book might be made of it if some young student at Girton or Newnham would collect examples and deduce a theory—but she would need thick gloves on her hands, and bars to protect her of solid gold.

15   But what is amusing now, I recollected, shutting Lady Bessborough, had to be taken in desperate earnest once. Opinions that one now pastes in a book labelled cock-a-doodle-dum and keeps for reading to select audiences on summer nights once drew tears, I can assure you. Among your grandmothers and great-grandmothers there were many that wept their eyes out. Florence Nightingale shrieked aloud in her agony.[22] Moreover, it is all very well for you, who have got yourselves to college and enjoy sitting-rooms—or is it only bed-

---

19. Johnson's opinion is recorded in James Boswell's *The Life of Samuel Johnson, L.L.D.* Woolf, in her tale of Judith Shakespeare, imagines the manager bellowing "something about poodles dancing and women acting."

20. *A Survey of Contemporary Music,* Cecil Gray, p. 246 [Woolf's note].

21. Henrietta, countess of Bessborough (1761–1821), and Lord Granville Leveson Gower, first Earl Granville (1773–1846). Their correspondence, edited by Castalia Countess Granville, was published as his *Private Correspondence, 1781 to 1821,* in 1916.

22. See *Cassandra,* by Florence Nightingale, printed in *The Cause,* by R. Strachey [Woolf's note]. Florence Nightingale (1820–1910), English nurse and philanthropist.

sitting-rooms?—of your own to say that genius should disregard such opinions; that genius should be above caring what is said of it. Unfortunately, it is precisely the men or women of genius who mind most what is said of them. Remember Keats. Remember the words he had cut on his tombstone. Think of Tennyson;[23] think—but I need hardly multiply instances of the undeniable, if very unfortunate, fact that it is the nature of the artist to mind excessively what is said about him. Literature is strewn with the wreckage of men who have minded beyond reason the opinions of others.

And this susceptibility of theirs is doubly unfortunate, I thought, returning again to my original enquiry into what state of mind is most propitious for creative work, because the mind of an artist, in order to achieve the prodigious effort of freeing whole and entire the work that is in him, must be incandescent, like Shakespeare's mind, I conjectured, looking at the book which lay open at *Antony and Cleopatra*. There must be no obstacle in it, no foreign matter unconsumed.

For though we say that we know nothing about Shakespeare's state of mind, even as we say that, we are saying something about Shakespeare's state of mind. The reason perhaps why we know so little of Shakespeare—compared with Donne or Ben Jonson or Milton[24]—is that his grudges and spites and antipathies are hidden from us. We are not held up by some "revelation" which reminds us of the writer. All desire to protest, to preach, to proclaim an injury, to pay off a score, to make the world the witness of some hardship or grievance was fired out of him and consumed. Therefore his poetry flows from him free and unimpeded. If ever a human being got his work expressed completely, it was Shakespeare. If ever a mind was incandescent, unimpeded, I thought, turning again to the bookcase, it was Shakespeare's mind.

23. Keats's epitaph reads "Here lies one whose name was writ in water." Tennyson was notably sensitive to reviews of his poetry.
24. John Donne (1572–1631), Jonson (1572–1637), and John Milton (1608–1674) were English poets and, in contrast to Shakespeare, all learned men.

Questions

1. At the beginning of her essay Woolf wonders about the conditions in which women lived that made it difficult, if not impossible, for them to produce literature (paragraph 2). What does she reveal about those conditions in the course of her essay?

2. Throughout her essay Woolf supplies many examples of the obstacles faced by women writers. Choose two or three that you found particularly effective and explain why they are effective.

3. How does the phrase "A Room of One's Own" suggest a solution to the problems Woolf has enumerated for women writers?

4. Has the woman writer of the twenty-first century overcome the obstacles Woolf describes as inhibiting the work of nineteenth-century women writers? Write an essay, based on research and/or interviews, in which you argue yes or no.

Susan Sontag   *A Century of Cinema*

INEMA'S HUNDRED YEARS appear to have the shape of a life cycle: an inevitable birth, the steady accumulation of glories, and the onset in the last decade of an ignominious, irreversible decline. This doesn't mean that there won't be any more new films one can admire. But such films will not simply be exceptions; that's true of great achievement in any art. They will have to be heroic violations of the norms and practices which now govern moviemaking everywhere in the capitalist and would-be capitalist world—which is to say, everywhere. And ordinary films, films made purely for entertainment (that is, commercial) purposes, will continue to be astonishingly witless; already the vast majority fail resoundingly to appeal to their cynically targeted audiences. While the point of a great film is now, more than ever, to be a one-of-a-kind achievement, the commercial cinema has settled for a policy of bloated, derivative filmmaking, a brazen combinatory or re-combinatory

"The Arrival of a Train at La Ciotat Station," 1895.

art, in the hope of reproducing past successes. Every film that hopes to reach the largest possible audience is designed as some kind of remake. Cinema, once heralded as *the* art of the twentieth century, seems now, as the century closes numerically, to be a decadent art.

Perhaps it is not cinema which has ended but only cinephilia—the name of the distinctive kind of love that cinema inspired. Each art breeds its fanatics. The love movies aroused was more imperial. It was born of the conviction that cinema was an art unlike any other: quintessentially modern; distinctively accessible; poetic and mysterious and erotic and moral—all at the same time. Cinema had apostles (it was like religion). Cinema was a crusade. Cinema was a world view. Lovers of poetry or opera or dance don't think there is *only* poetry or opera or dance. But lovers of cinema could think there was only cinema. That the movies encapsulated everything—and they did. It was both the book of art and the book of life.

Written in 1995 for the German newspaper Frankfurter Rundschau and published in shortened form in the New York Times Magazine (February 25, 1996); later reprinted in a small circulation American journal Parnassus (1997) and, with editorial changes, in Sontag's collection of essays Where the Stress Falls (2001).

"The 400 Blows," 1959.

most of what was to follow. With the coming of sound, the image-making lost much of its brilliance and poetry, and commercial standards tightened. This way of making movies—the Hollywood system—dominated filmmaking for about twenty-five years (roughly from 1930 to 1955). The most original directors, like Erich von Stroheim and Orson Welles,[4] were defeated by the system and eventually went into artistic exile in Europe—where more or less the same quality-defeating system was in place with lower budgets; only in France were a large number of superb films produced throughout this period. Then, in the mid-1950s, vanguard ideas took hold again, rooted in the idea of cinema as a craft pioneered by the Italian films of the early postwar era. A dazzling number of original, passionate films of the highest seriousness got made with new actors and tiny crews, went to film festivals (of which there were more and more), and from there, garlanded with festival prizes, into movie theatres

Kaufman, 1896–1954), Soviet film director who developed the "film-eye" theory, which made the camera operate as an instrument much like the human eye; Georg Wilhelm Pabst (1885–1967), German film director who developed "montage" in such works as *The Joyless Street* (1925) and *The Threepenny Opera* (1931); Friedrich Wilhelm Murnau (1889–1931), German film director whose works include *Nosferatu* (1922), *The Last Laugh* (1924), and *Sunrise* (1927); King Vidor (1894–1982), American film director who created *The Crowd* (1928) and later *The Citadel* (1938), the black-and-white scenes of *The Wizard of Oz* (1939), *The Fountainhead* (1949), and *War and Peace* (1956).

4. Erich von Stroheim (1885–1957), German filmmaker, most famous for *Greed* (1925); Orson Welles (1915–1985), American film director, most famous for *Citizen Kane* (1941).

"Persona," 1967.

around the world. This golden age actually lasted as long as twenty years.

It was at this specific moment in the hundred-year history of cinema that going to movies, thinking about movies, talking about movies became a passion among university students and other young people. You fell in love not just with actors but with cinema itself. Cinephilia had first become visible in the 1950s in France: its forum was the legendary film magazine *Cahiers du Cinéma* (followed by similarly fervent magazines in Germany, Italy, Great Britain, Sweden, the United States, Canada). Its temples, as it spread throughout Europe and the Americas, were the cinematheques and film clubs specializing in films from the past and directors' retrospectives. The 1960s and early 1970s were the age of feverish moviegoing, with the full-time cinephile always hoping to find a seat as close as possible to the big screen, ideally the third row center. "One can't live without Rossellini," declares a character in Bertolucci's *Before the Revolution* (1964)—and means it.

Cinephilia—a source of exultation in the films of Godard and Truffaut and the early Bertolucci and Syberberg;[5] a morose lament in the recent films of Nanni Moretti[6]—was mostly a Western European affair. The great directors of "the other Europe" (Zanussi in Poland, Angelopoulos in Greece, Tarkovsky and Sokurov in Russia, Jancsó and Tarr in Hungary) and the great Japanese directors (Ozu, Mizoguchi, Kurosawa, Naruse, Oshima, Imamura) have tended not to be cinephiles, perhaps because in Budapest or Moscow or Tokyo or Warsaw or Athens there wasn't a chance to get a cinematheque education. The distinctive thing about cinephile taste was that it embraced both "art" films and popular films. Thus, European cinephilia had a romantic rela-

5. Jean-Luc Godard (b. 1930), French film director known for *Breathless* (1959), among others; François Truffaut (1932–1984), French director whose films include *The 400 Blows* (1959), *Day for Night* (1973), and *The Last Métro* (1980); Bernardo Bertolucci (b. 1940), Italian filmmaker whose work includes *Last Tango in Paris* (1973) and *The Last Emperor* (1987); Hans-Jurgen Syberberg (b. 1935), German director and critic, known for his *Parsifal* (1988) and his book *Hitler: A Film from Germany* (1982), for which Sontag wrote the English preface.

6. Italian filmmaker, best known for *Caro Diario* (Dear diary, 1993).

"Breathless," 1959.

tion to the films of certain directors in Hollywood at the apogee of the studio
system: Godard for Howard Hawks, Fassbinder for Douglas Sirk. Of course,
this moment—when cinephilia emerged—was also the moment when the Hollywood studio system was breaking up. It seemed that moviemaking had re-
won the right to experiment; cinephiles could *afford* to be passionate (or
sentimental) about the old Hollywood genre films. A host of new people came
into cinema, including a generation of young film critics from *Cahiers du
Cinéma*; the towering figure of that generation, indeed of several decades of
filmmaking anywhere, was Jean-Luc Godard. A few writers turned out to be
wildly talented filmmakers: Alexander Kluge in Germany, Pier Paolo Pasolini in
Italy. (The model for the writer who turns to filmmaking actually emerged earlier, in France, with Pagnol in the 1930s and Cocteau in the 1940s; but it was
not until the 1960s that this seemed, at least in Europe, normal.) Cinema appeared to be reborn.

For some fifteen years there was a profusion of masterpieces, and one al-   10
lowed oneself to imagine that this would go on forever. To be sure, there was
always a conflict between cinema as an industry and cinema as an art, cinema
as routine and cinema as experiment. But the conflict was not such as to make
impossible the making of wonderful films, sometimes within and sometimes
outside of mainstream cinema. Now the balance has tipped decisively in favor
of cinema as an industry. The great cinema of the 1960s and 1970s has been
thoroughly repudiated. Already in the 1970s Hollywood was plagiarizing and
banalizing the innovations in narrative method and editing of successful new
European and ever-marginal independent American films. Then came the catastrophic rise in production costs in the 1980s, which secured the worldwide

reimposition of industry standards of making and distributing films on a far more coercive, this time truly global, scale. The result can be seen in the melancholy fate of some of the greatest directors of the last decades. What place is there today for a maverick like Hans Jurgen Syberberg, who has stopped making films altogether, or for the great Godard, who now makes films about the history of film on video? Consider some other cases. The internationalizing of financing and therefore of casts was a disaster for Andrei Tarkovsky[7] in the last two films of his stupendous, tragically abbreviated career. And these conditions for making films have proved to be as much an artistic disaster for two of the most valuable directors still working: Krzysztof Zanussi (*The Structure of Crystals, Illumination, Spiral, Contract*) and Theo Angelopoulos (*Reconstruction, Days of '36, The Travelling Players*). And what will happen now to Béla Tarr (*Damnation, Satantango*)? And how will Aleksandr Sokurov (*Save and Protect, Days of Eclipse, The Second Circle, Stone, Whispering Pages*) find the money to go on making films, his sublime films, under the rude conditions of Russian capitalism?[8]

Predictably, the love of cinema has waned. People still like going to the movies, and some people still care about and expect something special, necessary from a film. And wonderful films are still being made: Mike Leigh's *Naked*, Gianni Amelio's *Lamerica*, Hou Hsiao-hsien's *Goodbye South, Goodbye*, and Abbas Kiarostami's *Close-Up* and Koker trilogy. But one hardly finds anymore, at least among the young, the distinctive cinephilic love of movies, which is not simply love of but a certain *taste* in films (grounded in a vast appetite for seeing and re-seeing as much as possible of cinema's glorious past). Cinephilia itself has come under attack, as something quaint, outmoded, snobbish. For cinephilia implies that films are unique, unrepeatable, magic experiences. Cinephilia tells us that the Hollywood remake of Godard's *Breathless* cannot be as good as the original. Cinephilia has no role in the era of hyperindustrial films. For by the very range and eclecticism of its passions, cinephilia cannot help but sponsor the idea of the film as, first of all, a poetic object; and cannot help but incite those outside the movie industry, like painters and writers, to want to make films, too. It is precisely this that must be defeated. That has been defeated.

If cinephilia is dead, then movies are dead . . . no matter how many movies, even very good ones, go on being made. If cinema can be resurrected, it will only be through the birth of a new kind of cine-love.

---

7. Soviet film director (1932–1986), whose work was censored at home but won acclaim in the West. His *Katok i skripka* (The steamroller and the violin, 1960) won a prize at the New York Film Festival, and his first full-length feature film, *Ivanovo detstvo* (Ivan's childhood, 1962), established his international reputation.

8. Zanussi (b. 1939), Polish film director; Angelopolous (b. 1935), Greek film director; Tarr (b. 1955), Hungarian filmmaker; Sokurov (b. 1951), Russian filmmaker who in 1997 produced the award-winning *Mat i syn* (Mother and son).

QUESTIONS

1. In her essay Sontag summarizes one hundred years of film history, from 1895 to 1995. Diagram her periodization of this history. Locate her moviegoing period (she was born in 1933) and yours on it. Which of the older films Sontag mentions have you seen? If you have seen other films made before you began going to the movies, name some of them. How did you see them—in a film-studies course, for example, or on your own?

2. What is Sontag's definition of a "cinephile"? Are you one?

3. Sontag has harsh things to say about contemporary films: they are "astonishingly wit-less," "bloated, derivative," "a brazen combinatory or re-combinatory art" (paragraph 1), reduced to "assaultive images, and the unprincipled manipulation of images (faster and faster cutting) to be more attention-grabbing" and, at the same time, "disincarnated, lightweight," and they don't "demand anyone's full attention" (paragraph 6). Using at least three contemporary films that you have seen, write an essay in which you agree with, disagree with, or modify her charges.

From Understanding Comics, *a graphic book published in 1994.*

WORDS AND PICTURES IN COMBINATION MAY NOT BE MY *DEFINITION* OF COMICS, BUT THE COMBINATION HAS HAD *TREMENDOUS INFLUENCE* ON ITS *GROWTH.*

com·ics (kom'iks)**n.** pl. ... form, used with a singular... Juxtaposed pictori... ...her images in deliberate... ...ence, — intended to conve... ...on and/or to prod... response in the... **2.** Superheroes... costumes, fight... ...villains who want... ...the world, in violent s... ...use.

A HUGE RANGE OF HUMAN EXPERIENCES CAN BE *PORTRAYED* IN COMICS THROUGH EITHER WORDS OR PICTURES.

AS A RESULT--AND DESPITE ITS MANY *OTHER* POTENTIAL USES -- COMICS HAVE BECOME *FIRMLY IDENTIFIED* WITH THE ART OF *STORYTELLING.*

AND *INDEED,* WORDS AND PICTURES HAVE *GREAT* POWERS TO TELL STORIES WHEN CREATORS FULLY EXPLOIT THEM *BOTH.*

DADA
BIOGRAPHY HORROR
ROMANCE SURREALISM
BLANK VERSE HISTORICAL FICTION
EPIC POETRY FOLK TALES
SOCIAL ALLEGORY EROTICA
SEQUENTIAL ART MYSTERY
ADAPTATIONS RELIGIOUS TOPICS
STREAM OF CONSCIOUSNESS
SATIRE

AND SO FAR, WE'VE ONLY SEEN THE *TIP OF THE ICEBERG!*

AS CHILDREN, WE "SHOW AND TELL" *INTERCHANGEABLY,* WORDS AND IMAGES COMBINING TO TRANSMIT A *CONNECTED SERIES OF IDEAS.*

IT'S GOT ONE OF *THESE* THINGS.

THE DIFFERENT WAYS IN WHICH WORDS AND PICTURES CAN *COMBINE* IN COMICS IS VIRTUALLY *UNLIMITED.*

BUT LET'S TRY TO BREAK IT DOWN INTO SOME DISTINCT *CATEGORIES.*

PERHAPS THE MOST *COMMON* TYPE OF WORD/PICTURE COMBINATION IS THE ***INTER-DEPENDENT***, WHERE WORDS AND PICTURES GO *HAND IN HAND* TO CONVEY AN IDEA THAT NEITHER COULD CONVEY *ALONE*.

MEANWHILE...

DID ANYONE *SEE* YOU?

THIS IS ALL I NEED TO *STOP* HIM!

I ASK YOU, DOES THIS GUY LOOK LIKE A *C.E.O.* TO *YOU*??

"AND JUST *GUESS* WHO DROVE UP IN BOB'S TRUCK AN HOUR LATER!"

HEY, MARGE!

OH, MY GOD!

"AFTER COLLEGE, I PURSUED A CAREER IN *HIGH FINANCE*."

HURRY UP, WILLYA?!

HE'S LYING.

UH-HUH.

INTERDEPENDENT COMBINATIONS AREN'T ALWAYS AN *EQUAL BALANCE* THOUGH AND MAY FALL *ANYWHERE* ON A SCALE BETWEEN TYPES ONE AND TWO.

GENERALLY SPEAKING, THE MORE IS SAID WITH *WORDS*, THE MORE THE PICTURES CAN BE FREED TO GO EXPLORING AND *VICE VERSA*.

$$\frac{P}{W}$$

$$\frac{W}{P}$$

QUESTIONS

1. Scott McCloud announces in his title that he wants to help the reader "understand comics." What features of comics does McCloud explain? How do the features of the comic strip form itself aid in that explanation?

2. Choose a frame in which you think word and image work well together, and analyze why they do so. Use one or more of McCloud's categories of analysis.

3. Using the categories that McCloud introduces in the second half of this selection, analyze how a comic strip in your local newspaper works. If relevant, suggest how it might work even better.

JOHN UPDIKE   *Moving Along*

IN DREAMS, one is frequently travelling, and the more hallucinatory moments of our waking life, many of them, are spent in cars, trains, and airplanes. For millennia, Man has walked or run to where he wanted to go; the first naked ape who had the mad idea of mounting a horse (or was it a *Camelops*?)[1] launched a series of subtle internal dislocations of which jet lag is a vivid modern form. When men come to fly through space at near the speed of light, they will return to earth a century later but only a few years older. Now, driving (say) from Boston to Pittsburgh in a day, we arrive feeling greatly aged by the engine's innumerable explosive heartbeats, by the monotony of the highway surface and the constant windy press of unnatural speed. Beside the highway, a clamorous parasitic life signals for attention and halt; localities where generations have lived, bred, labored, and died are flung through the windshield and out through the rearview mirror. Men on the move brutalize themselves and render the world they arrow through phantasmal.

Our two artists, separated by two centuries, capture well the eeriness of travel. In the Punjab Hills painting, Baz Bahadur, prince of Malwa, has eloped with the lovely Rupmati;[2] in order to keep him faithful to her, the legend goes, she takes him riding by moonlight. The moon appears to exist not only in the sky but behind a grove of trees. Deer almost blend into the mauve-gray hills. A little citadel basks in starlight on a hilltop. In this soft night, nothing is brighter than the scarlet pasterns of the horses. Baz Bahadur's steed bears on his hide a paler version of the starry sky, and in his violet genitals carries a hint

"Moving Along" was originally written for the English version of the glossy French monthly Réalités; *they were reprinted in Updike's* Just Looking *(1981), a collection of essays on art.*

1. Extinct genus of camel.
2. Baz Bahadur and his beautiful wife Rani Rupmati ruled Malwa in India during the sixteenth century.

ARTIST UNKNOWN
Baz Bahadur and Rupmati Riding by Moonlight, c. 1780
Pahari miniature in Kangra style, $8\frac{3}{4} \times 6\frac{1}{4}$ ″
The British Museum, Department of Oriental Antiquities, London

ROY DE FOREST
Canoe of Fate, 1974
Polymer on canvas, 66 ¾ × 90¼ ˝
Philadelphia Museum of Art
The Adele Haas Turner and Beatrice Pastorius Turner Fund

of this nocturnal ride's sexual undercurrent. To judge from the delicacy of their gestures and glances, the riders are being borne along as smoothly as on a merry-go-round. Though these lovers and their panoply are formalized to static perfection, if we cover them, a surprising depth appears in the top third of the painting, and carries the eye away.

The riders in Roy de Forest's[3] contemporary painting move through a forest as crowded, garish, and menacing as the neon-lit main drag of a city. A throng of sinister bystanders, one built of brick and another with eyes that are paste gems, witness the passage of this *Canoe of Fate*, which with the coarseness of its stitching and the bulk of its passengers would make slow headway even on a less crowded canvas. Beyond the mountains, heavenly medallions and balloons of stippled color pre-empt space. Only the gesture of the black brave, echoing that of George Washington in another fabulous American crossing,[4] gives a sense of direction and promises to open a path. Two exotic birds, a slavering wolf, and what may be a fair captive (gazing backward toward

3. American artist (b. 1930).
4. A reference to Emanuel Leutze's famous 1851 painting, "Washington Crossing the Delaware." In Leutze's painting Washington is standing but not pointing; Updike may have misremembered the "gesture."

settlements where other red-haired bluefaces mourn her) freight the canoe with a suggestion of allegory, of myths to which we have lost the key. The personnel of the aboriginal New World, at any rate, are here deep-dyed but not extinguished by the glitter and jazz of an urban-feeling wilderness.

In both representations, the movement is from right to left, like that of writing in the Semitic languages, like the motion of a mother when she instinctively shifts her baby to her left arm, to hold it closer to her heart. It feels natural, this direction, and slightly uphill. We gaze at these dreamlike tapestries of travel confident that no progress will be made—we will awaken in our beds.

QUESTIONS

1. One reviewer of *Just Looking*, the book from which this short essay is taken, called Updike a dilettante about art; another said these pieces produced not criticism of art but "an enhanced understanding of the writer and his . . . preoccupations." Using this essay as an example, show how these critiques of Updike are or are not true.

2. On the basis of this essay, what seem to be Updike's major interests when it comes to viewing pictures?

3. Compare the painting by Leutze (see www.metmuseum.org/explore/gw/el_gw.htm) to that of de Forest. What kinds of echoes does Updike seem most interested in bringing to our attention? Do you see any other connections?

ANTHONY LANE   *The Sound of Music*

Let's start at the very beginning. (It's a very good place to start.) Maria Augusta Kutschera was born in 1905. As a young woman, she became a postulant at the Nonnberg Abbey, in Salzburg, Austria, but suffered from ill health. It was deemed beneficial that she should venture outside and adopt the post of governess in the home of a naval captain. She married him in 1927, which put an end to any postulating. The captain already had seven children; Maria bore him three more and formed a family musical group, whose success was cut short when Hitler invaded his native land. Even now, no historian has been able to ascertain if this was a genuine bid for power or the only possible means whereby the Führer could eradicate the threat of close-harmony singing.

Maria and her family fled to Italy, England, and, finally, the United States. The captain died in 1947; two years later, Maria published *The Story of the Trapp Family Singers*. In 1956, the book was turned into a hit German movie;

Originally appeared in The New Yorker *(February 14, 2000), a magazine of literature, music, drama, and art; later included in a collection of Lane's reviews,* Nobody's Perfect *(2002).*

theatrical producers began to sniff around, and in November 1959, *The Sound of Music*, with original songs by Rodgers and Hammerstein, opened on Broadway. Twentieth Century Fox soon acquired the movie rights, but the film proved hard to bring to birth. After nearly five years of wrangles and pangs, *The Sound of Music*, directed by Robert Wise and starring Julie Andrews, had its New York premiere, on March 2, 1965. To date, the picture has earned 160 million dollars. It remains the most popular musical film in history. One woman in Wales has seen it almost a thousand times. In Hong Kong, it is entitled *Fairy Music Blow Fragrant Place, Place Hear*.

All of which is how I came to be standing on a sidewalk on a dark December evening, waving a foam nun.

The Prince Charles Cinema sits in central London, a hundred yards east of Piccadilly, between the Notre Dame dance hall and a row of Chinese restaurants. When it opened, in 1991, the idea was that you could catch new and recent pictures for less than two dollars—a fraction of what they cost around the corner, in the plush movie theatres of Leicester Square. Even now, the Prince Charles has nobly resisted the urge to smarten up; the furnishings are a touching tribute to wartime brown, and the stalls, flouting a rule of theatrical design which has obtained since the fifth century B.C., appear to slope downward toward the back, so that customers in the rear seats can enjoy an uncluttered view of their own knees. The cinema shows three or four films a day; come the weekend, everything explodes. Since August, every Friday evening and Sunday afternoon the program has been the same: "Singalong-a-Sound-of-Music."

5   The idea is simple. You watch the film—uncut, as nature intended, in a scuzzy print, with alarming color shifts as the reels change. The only difference is the added subtitles, which come alive, like the hills, during every song. These enable viewers to join in, which they do with undisguised lustiness. The titling of *The Sound of Music* was prepared by Martin Wagner, for London's National Film Theatre, and it struck me as the one work of unquestionable genius that I encountered last year. I tend to be embarrassed by subtitles; their audacious efforts to snatch at foreign vernaculars end up stressing, rather than allaying, the alien qualities of the setting. With *The Sound of Music*, however, they bring home just how tightly, even soothingly, we are wrapped in this unignorable film. In a sense, Wagner had a head start; what was required was not translation from another tongue but the simple transcription, for karaoke purposes, of words that most of us know pretty well. (I was appalled to discover that, after a thirty-year break, I was close to word-perfect.) This, however, is where Wagner shows his hand; who else would have thought to include the *Latin chant* that rises from the abbey as we pan down from Julie Andrews on a hillside and get ready for "(How Do You Solve a Problem Like) Maria?" I had never noticed it before—no audience is meant to notice filler, the blah that keeps a soundtrack ticking along—but suddenly there it was at the bottom of the screen (*"In saecula saeculorum"*). Things get even better halfway through the picture, as the children gather at the foot of the stairs to bid the party guests good night. Friedrich sings, and the titles follow him closely.

So long, farewell, auf Wiedersehen, adieu,
Adieu, adieu, to yieu and yieu and yieu.

That was it for me. For thirty years, I have wondered about this torturing little rhyme. It should have been easy to avoid; if you want "Adieu" to chime with "you," don't pronounce it in French—simply opt for the Anglicized version, "Adyoo," and take it from there. But no: *The Sound of Music* made a tragic move to sound classy, and it paid the price. As for the yodelling in the puppet scene, it inspires Wagner to his finest work—a cluster bomb of meaningless vowels. For anyone who believes that *The Sound of Music* shows Hollywood at its most hopelessly square, what could be more bracing than to see it reborn as a Dadaist art happening?

All nonsense is a pleasure, of course, from Lewis Carroll down to Alexander Haig, but what lends particular spice to *The Sound of Music* is that it is known nonsense, remembered and revered. And that is why the Prince Charles has become a place of pilgrimage. It occasionally screens *The Rocky Horror Picture Show*, too, to a gathering of addicts. But that film is already armored by a sense of camp; nothing you can throw at it will dent its knowingness, whereas *The Sound of Music*, the most unwitting of cults, is blissfully up for grabs.

When I arrived on a Friday night, an hour before the start, the area around the cinema was packed. To be specific, it was packed with nuns. Many of them bore guitars. I was one of the few pathetic creatures who had not made the effort to come in costume. There were Nazis, naturally, as in every major city, plus a load of people who looked like giant parcels. I didn't get it. "Who are they?" I said to a nun who was having a quick cigarette before the film. She looked at me with celestial pity and blew smoke. "Brown Paper Packages Tied Up with Strings," she replied. I am relieved, on the whole, that I missed the rugby team who piled into one screening as Girls in White Dresses with Blue Satin Sashes; on the other hand, it is a source of infinite sadness to me that I wasn't at the Prince Charles when a guy turned up in a skintight, all-over body costume in bright yellow; asked which character he was intended to represent, he explained that he was Ray, a Drop of Golden Sun. I have hung around the entrance a couple of times as showtime approached, just in case this heroic gentleman returns as Warm Woollen Mittens—or, more challenging still, as Tea, a Drink with Jam and Bread—but no luck so far.

The impressive thing about all this is the apostolic level of dedication. I sat in a whole row of nuns—nurses from a private hospital, as it happened, having a cheap night out. (One had lovingly constructed her wimple from black cloth and a rolled-up pair of white knickers.) During the screening, they drank beer in almost Austrian quantities; one of them kept jumping up and hurrying to the exit; "What's the matter with that nun?" I asked the beefy sister beside me. "Pregnant," she said.

Nominally a reserved people, the British like to bottle up their exhibitionist tendencies and then, at opportune moments, let them flood out in a rush; this is the basis of pantomime, for instance, with its flagrant worship of cross- 10 dressing. Even now, there is almost certainly a quiet soul who is preparing to attend *The Sound of Music* as Schnitzel with Noodles. To brush yourself with egg and roll around in bread crumbs for a while requires a nerveless ingenuity; but to walk to the nearest tube trailing ribbons of buttered pasta, and to sit on the train with a dignified expression, in the thick of the Friday rush hour, argues a fortitude bordering on the superhuman. I couldn't do it, but somebody will, and I think I know who that somebody will be. "Singalong-a-Sound-of-Music" is currently starting a British national tour, and then, in April, it will hit America, where bottling is less of an issue. Twentieth Century Fox will not yet name the lucky cinemas where it will screen, but I can safely reveal that New York and San Francisco, among others, should be girding their loins for Schnitzel Time.

It goes without saying that "Singalong-a-Sound-of-Music" is now a compulsory fixture on the gay calendar; it began life, indeed, as a one-off special for the London Lesbian and Gay Film Festival. Every screening gets its own emcee, who oversees a Best Costume competition during the intermission. (One week, just to confuse the issue, the winner was a *real nun*. What did she think the other nuns were?) At my screening, there was Rhona Cameron, a cheery Scottish lesbian who hosts a gay show on British TV. Rhona checked that there were no children in the audience, and then issued instructions: "Don't worry if you can't sing; the gay men in the audience will carry you." Fragrant music blow fairy place, place go wild.

I usually loathe any hint of live entertainment at the movies, preferring to hibernate in peace and quiet; but "Singalong-a-Sound-of-Music" launches so frontal an assault on reticence that everyone caves in. It is a stout rebuke to the couch culture of "home cinema"—a contradiction in terms, if ever I heard one. The bloodless interaction promised by DVD technology, for instance, in which the lone viewer can pause *The Matrix* to command a reverse view of Keanu Reeves's butt, cannot hold a candle to the sight of two hundred people whistling at Christopher Plummer when he enters with a riding crop, and waving their lighters above their heads, like a rock crowd, during his rendition of "Edelweiss." For an extra five dollars, ticket-holders at the Prince Charles can buy a helpful gift pack that includes a fake edelweiss, a packet of cough drops for sore throats, a head scarf, and, yes, a small foam-rubber nun, in which you are urged to "stick your fingers" and "sway along."

The repartee at "Singalong-a-Sound-of-Music" is of the very highest order. "Free the nuns!" was the cry as the sisters clustered behind an iron grille during Maria's wedding. Some of the backchat involves a dexterous cross-reference to other works; when Maria, having been ticked off by the Baroness (Eleanor Parker), packs her bag to leave, someone shouted, "Don't forget the hat stand!"—reminding us of a similar scene in *Mary Poppins*. And, as the Mother Abbess lingered in the shadows in preparation for "Climb Ev'ry Mountain," she was told in no uncertain terms, "Do not go into the light!"—the tag line from *Poltergeist*, if you please. The instructions issued to Rolf as he danced with Liesl in the gazebo came from somewhere behind my shoulder; they were explicit, and they were repeated with such urgency that, after a

while, they acquired the pathos of a plea—as if it were in some way unsports-
manlike, even unromantic, for a seventeen-year-old Nazi not to deflower a
motherless sixteen-year-old while he had the chance. "You need someone older
and wiser telling you what to do," crooned Rolf, and we sniggered at his nerve.

The joke is, of course, that Charmian Carr, who plays Liesl, was already
twenty-one when the film was made (she kept quiet at the audition), and thus
in no need of tutelage from a mere boy; the deeper joke is that, in the history
of blockbusting movies, nothing can touch *The Sound of Music* for sheer,
blank indifference to the reproductive act. No wonder Heather Menzies, who
played Louisa, answered the call to strip for *Playboy* in the 1970s; the pressure
of untouchability must have felt like prison. Captain Von Trapp has seven children, but the enigma of his fertility remains as unplumbed as his willingness,
as a serving naval officer, to play the guitar in public. The baroness, with her
glinting coiffure and cinched suits, could be taken, in a certain light, for a
woman of the world; yet the captain throws her over for the sake of a certifi-
able virgin with a boy's haircut. "For here you are, standing there, loving me,"
he and Maria sing to one another; love, in so immaculate a world, is pure abstraction, unruffled by the physical. In the intermission at the Prince Charles,
Rhona Cameron asked one nun what she liked best about the film. Without
hesitation, the nun replied, "The sex."

The Sound of Music is not a good film. It is blithe, efficient, and constructed   15
with care; the songs are carolled con brio; but it is not a good film. Famously,
it received some of the most noxious notices of its era. Steeped in the flow of
the counterculture, American critics should have been ready for the sight of
small children dressed in flowery curtains, but somehow the psychedelic properties of the film eluded them. In the *Herald Tribune*, Judith Crist called it
"icky sticky," as if she'd needed to rinse her hands afterward. In *McCall's*,
Pauline Kael continued the candy motif, trashing the movie as a "sugar-coated
lie that people seem to want to eat"; her review so affronted readers that she
was fired from her post and landed shortly afterward at this magazine. Here
she reigned supreme for the next quarter of a century, thus proving that *The
Sound of Music* is so saintly that it confers a happy ending on all who touch its
hem, even those of little faith. The film did more than any other, perhaps, to
widen the split between critics and public from crack to chasm; it encouraged
producers, like political hopefuls, to reach out over the heads of professional
carpers and appeal directly to popular taste. (That it collared the Academy
Award for Best Picture in 1966 merely sealed the deal.) The way to solve a
problem like Maria is to love her for what she is, with or without wimple, and
the movie begs the same indulgence; by ignoring the mean of spirit, it wishes
them away.

All of which serves only to confirm the Kael line, and to demonstrate that
you can fool all of the people all of the time. The lies perpetuated by Wise's
film range from the personal—the real Maria Von Trapp, for instance, looked
nothing like Julie Andrews and an awful not like Nice Guy Eddie from *Reservoir Dogs*—to the broadly historical. If the Nazis' worst crime had indeed been

to hang swastikas over people's doorways, the twentieth century would have been somewhat easier to bear. I was a sucker for such untruths; my family even travelled to Salzburg in order to haunt the byways where Julie Andrews had made so ringingly clear what the first three notes just happened to be. Being below critical age, I did not yet grasp the criteria by which a film could be adjudged good or bad, much less the procedures by which it arrived onscreen. If you had explained that the screenplay for *The Sound of Music* came from the pen of one Ernest Lehman, who had written *North by Northwest* and *Sweet Smell of Success*, this bewildering detail would have been lost on me.

To be fair, even some of his friends had trouble taking it in. When Burt Lancaster ran into Lehman at the Fox commissary and learned what he was working on, he said, "Jesus, you must need the money." That story comes from Julia Antopol Hirsch's *The Sound of Music: The Making of America's Favorite Movie*, a loving compendium of arcana. Here we learn, for instance, that both Walter Matthau and Sean "Edelweish" Connery were considered for the role of the captain. A more damning fact is that some of the Osmond boys turned up to audition, thus demonstrating that, however much *The Sound of Music* makes your flesh crawl, it could have been so much worse.

You could argue that the triumphal saga of the Von Trapp family was so sweetly outlandish that any dramatic representation of it was doomed to rot the teeth. But consider another family, the Smiths of Missouri—equally close, no less pure of heart, and, like the Von Trapps, given to bursting into song at the slightest provocation. So why does *Meet Me in St. Louis* maintain the status of a nimble masterpiece, while *The Sound of Music* limps along behind? Then again, how come Vincente Minnelli's picture of 1944 was reckoned merely a success, while Robert Wise's picture, made twenty years later, is a gold-plated phenomenon? The answer to both questions is the same: because Minnelli showed happiness to be the most fragile of possessions, whereas Wise backed it as a sure thing. For all the highs and lows of its melodrama, *The Sound of Music* never dreams that there is any way but up, whether you are ascending a scale or an alp; and that, today and forever, is what moviegoers want to hear. "From now on, our troubles will be out of sight," Judy Garland sings near the end of *Meet Me in St. Louis*, but the throb and catch in her voice give the lie to such game hope, and, by the penultimate line of the number, the message is decidedly mixed: "We'll have to muddle through somehow." Julie Andrews, by comparison, is a muddle-free zone: "I have confidence in confidence alone; Besides which, you see, I have confidence in me!"

Garland was singing during the Second World War, of course, when a certain lyrical worry was inevitable. Andrews hit her stride in the midst of the cold war; the whole of *The Sound of Music* can perhaps be read as the artistic equivalent of antifreeze. It offered one of the last breaths of innocence in American cinema—after all, the same year saw female nudity in *The Pawnbroker*, and *Bonnie and Clyde* was only two years away. That is why we go back to Wise's film; we all know better now, but most of us secretly wish that we didn't. The atmosphere at the Prince Charles, during "Singalong-a-Sound-of-Music," was strangely unmocking, even in its coarsest moments. We assume that deconstruction is a heartless business, in which the vengeful ironist strips the decorous past to its underclothes; but the hoarse crowd that streamed out into Leicester Square seemed to have drawn strength from a communal act of fond consolidation. When they cried at "Edelweiss," it was not because the song is, in itself, anything more than slush; it was because they had cried at it in 1965.

Film, in other words, has revivified the Proustian principle that memory is not ours to command; that, for all our searchings and suppressings, the past comes unbidden or not at all. If, for millions of people, that past consists of a lonely goatherd on strings, so be it. Proust himself was more fortunate; for him, a typical throwback consisted of tripping over a paving stone and suddenly recalling a similar stumble in Venice. Few of us can rely on such tasteful apparitions. It is generally agreed, for example, that the last Golden Age of cinema occurred in the mid-seventies—the epoch of *The Godfather, Chinatown,* and *McCabe and Mrs. Miller.* I feel privileged to have been there; unfortunately, I spent my pocket money on tickets for *Zeppelin, Earthquake,* and *Rollercoaster* (in Sensurround). I now realize that *Chinatown* is a great picture and that *The Towering Inferno* is dreck; but the sight of a weary, begrimed Steve McQueen emerging from the tower is burned into my mind with a fierceness that Jack Nicholson, with his nicked nostril, can never match. I missed the Golden Age; catching up later was an education, but nothing I can do will bring it back.

What we feel about a movie—or, indeed, about any work of art, high or low—matters less than the rise and fall of our feelings over time. The *King Lear* that we see as sons and daughters (of Cordelia's age, say) can never be the same play that we attend as parents; the sound of paternal fury, and of the mortal fears that echo beyond it, will knock ever more insistently at our hearts. Weekly critics cannot do justice to that process; when we are asked to nominate favorite films, all we can say is "Well, just now I quite like *Citizen Kane* or *Police Academy 4,* but ask me again next year." By then we will have grown, by a small but significant slippage, into someone else, and we have yet to know who that person will be, or what friable convictions he or she will hold. The revellers at the Prince Charles Cinema were all in their thirties and forties; no one younger than us would have had the remotest clue what we were doing there, or why we were having such fun. Even our younger selves, of ten years ago, would probably have been mystified, if not humiliated, by the air of semi-delirium that prevailed; how could consenting adults join forces to declare their love for a bad film? Time, as ever, has played its comic trick, and all I can do is adapt the words of Captain Von Trapp and his lovely governess: somewhere in our youth or childhood, we must have seen something good.

Questions

1. Anthony Lane describes his experience of seeing *The Sound of Music* in London at the Prince Charles Cinema, where it was playing as a cult film. What innovative features had been added to the film? What innovations did the audience bring to it? Why does Lane devote half of the essay (paragraphs 3–14) to this popular cult experience?

2. After describing an example of popular culture, Lane turns to an aesthetic judgment of *The Sound of Music*. What evidence does he give to support his assertion, "*The Sound of Music* is not a good film"? Is aesthetic judgment the primary goal of this essay?

3. In the final two paragraphs, Lane speculates about why some films grip our emotions, while others do not. What explanations does he suggest? What does he mean by "the Proustian principle"? What other explanations can you offer?

4. Analyze a film that has had an impact on you, trying to understand what in the film causes its effect but also what in your experience contributes to the experience.

AARON COPLAND   *How We Listen*

WE ALL LISTEN to music according to our separate capacities. But, for the sake of analysis, the whole listening process may become clearer if we break it up into its component parts, so to speak. In a certain sense we all listen to music on three separate planes. For lack of a better terminology, one might name these: (1) the sensuous plane, (2) the expressive plane, (3) the sheerly musical plane. The only advantage to be gained from mechanically splitting up the listening process into these hypothetical planes is the clearer view to be had of the way in which we listen.

The simplest way of listening to music is to listen for the sheer pleasure of the musical sound itself. That is the sensuous plane. It is the plane on which we hear music without thinking, without considering it in any way. One turns on the radio while doing something else and absentmindedly bathes in the sound. A kind of brainless but attractive state of mind is engendered by the mere sound appeal of the music.

You may be sitting in a room reading this book. Imagine one note struck on the piano. Immediately that one note is enough to change the atmosphere of the room—proving that the sound element in music is a powerful and mysterious agent, which it would be foolish to deride or belittle.

The surprising thing is that many people who consider themselves qualified music lovers abuse that plane in listening. They go to concerts in order to lose themselves. They use music as a consolation or an escape. They enter an ideal world where one doesn't have to think of the realities of everyday life. Of course they aren't thinking about the music either. Music allows them to leave it, and they go off to a place to dream, dreaming because of and apropos of the music yet never quite listening to it.

5   Yes, the sound appeal of music is a potent and primitive force, but you must not allow it to usurp a disproportionate share of your interest. The sen-

From Copland's classic guide, What to Listen for in Music *(1957).*

suous plane is an important one in music, a very important one, but it does not constitute the whole story.

There is no need to digress further on the sensuous plane. Its appeal to every normal human being is self-evident. There is, however, such a thing as becoming more sensitive to the different kinds of sound stuff as used by various composers. For all composers do not use that sound stuff in the same way. Don't get the idea that the value of music is commensurate with its sensuous appeal or that the loveliest sounding music is made by the greatest composer. If that were so, Ravel would be a greater creator than Beethoven.[1] The point is that the sound element varies with each composer, that his usage of sound forms an integral part of his style and must be taken into account when listening. The reader can see, therefore, that a more conscious approach is valuable even on this primary plane of music listening.

The second plane on which music exists is what I have called the expressive one. Here, immediately, we tread on controversial ground. Composers have a way of shying away from any discussion of music's expressive side. Did not Stravinsky[2] himself proclaim that his music was an "object," a "thing," with a life of its own, and with no other meaning than its own purely musical existence? This intransigent attitude of Stravinsky's may be due to the fact that so many people have tried to read different meanings into so many pieces. Heaven knows it is difficult enough to say precisely what it is that a piece of music means, to say it definitely, to say it finally so that everyone is satisfied with your explanation. But that should not lead one to the other extreme of denying to music the right to be "expressive."

My own belief is that all music has an expressive power, some more and some less, but that all music has a certain meaning behind the notes and that that meaning behind the note constitutes, after all, what the piece is saying, what the piece is about. This whole problem can be stated quite simply by asking, "Is there a meaning to music?" My answer to that would be, "Yes." And "Can you state in so many words what the meaning is?" My answer to that would be, "No." Therein lies the difficulty.

Simple-minded souls will never be satisfied with the answer to the second of these questions. They always want music to have a meaning, and the more concrete it is the better they like it. The more the music reminds them of a train, a storm, a funeral, or any other familiar conception the more expressive it appears to be to them. This popular idea of music's meaning—stimulated and abetted by the usual run of musical commentator—should be discouraged wherever and whenever it is met. One timid lady once confessed to me that she suspected something seriously lacking in her appreciation of music because of her inability to connect it with anything definite. That is getting the whole thing backward, of course.

Still, the question remains, How close should the intelligent music lover   10

---

1. Maurice Ravel (1875–1937), French composer; Ludwig van Beethoven (1770–1827), German composer.

2. Igor Stravinsky (1882–1971), Russian-born American composer.

wish to come to pinning a definite meaning to any particular work? No closer than a general concept, I should say. Music expresses, at different moments, serenity or exuberance, regret or triumph, fury or delight. It expresses each of these moods, and many others, in a numberless variety of subtle shadings and differences. It may even express a state of meaning for which there exists no adequate word in any language. In that case, musicians often like to say that it has only a purely musical meaning. They sometimes go farther and say that *all* music has only a purely musical meaning. What they really mean is that no appropriate word can be found to express the music's meaning and that, even if it could, they do not feel the need of finding it.

But whatever the professional musician may hold, most musical novices still search for specific words with which to pin down their musical reactions. That is why they always find Tchaikovsky[3] easier to "understand" than Beethoven. In the first place, it is easier to pin a meaning-word on a Tchaikovsky piece than on a Beethoven one. Much easier. Moreover, with the Russian composer, every time you come back to a piece of his it almost always says the same thing to you, whereas with Beethoven it is often quite difficult to put your finger right on what he is saying. And any musician will tell you that that is why Beethoven is the greater composer. Because music which always says the same thing to you will necessarily soon become dull music, but music whose meaning is slightly different with each hearing has a greater chance of remaining alive.

Listen, if you can, to the forty-eight fugue themes of Bach's *Well Tempered Clavichord*.[4] Listen to each theme, one after another. You will soon realize that each theme mirrors a different world of feeling. You will also soon realize that the more beautiful a theme seems to you the harder it is to find any word that will describe it to your complete satisfaction. Yes, you will certainly know whether it is a gay theme or a sad one. You will be able, in other words, in your own mind, to draw a frame of emotional feeling around your theme. Now study the sad one a little closer. Try to pin down the exact quality of its sadness. Is it pessimistically sad or resignedly sad; is it fatefully sad or smilingly sad?

Let us suppose that you are fortunate and can describe to your own satisfaction in so many words the exact meaning of your chosen theme. There is still no guarantee that anyone else will be satisfied. Nor need they be. The important thing is that each one feel for himself the specific expressive quality of a theme or, similarly, an entire piece of music. And if it is a great work of art, don't expect it to mean exactly the same thing to you each time you return to it.

Themes or pieces need not express only one emotion, of course. Take such a theme as the first main one of the *Ninth Symphony*,[5] for example. It is clearly made up of different elements. It does not say only one thing. Yet

3. Peter Ilich Tchaikovsky (1840–1893), Russian composer.
4. A work composed by Johann Sebastian Bach (1685–1750) in which forty-eight themes are presented by themselves and then elaborated in three voices.
5. Composed by Beethoven.

anyone hearing it immediately gets a feeling of strength, a feeling of power. It isn't a power that comes simply because the theme is played loudly. It is a power inherent in the theme itself. The extraordinary strength and vigor of the theme results in the listener's receiving an impression that a forceful statement has been made. But one should never try to boil it down to "the fateful hammer of life," etc. That is where the trouble begins. The musician, in his exasperation, says it means nothing but the notes themselves, whereas the nonprofessional is only too anxious to hang on to any explanation that gives him the illusion of getting closer to the music's meaning.

Now, perhaps, the reader will know better what I mean when I say that   15
music does have an expressive meaning but that we cannot say in so many words what that meaning is.

The third plane on which music exists is the sheerly musical plane. Besides the pleasurable sound of music and the expressive feeling that it gives off, music does exist in terms of the notes themselves and of their manipulation. Most listeners are not sufficiently conscious of this third plane. * * *

Professional musicians, on the other hand, are, if anything, too conscious of the mere notes themselves. They often fall into the error of becoming so engrossed with their arpeggios and staccatos that they forget the deeper aspects of the music they are performing. But from the layman's standpoint, it is not so much a matter of getting over bad habits on the sheerly musical plane as of increasing one's awareness of what is going on, in so far as the notes are concerned.

When the man in the street listens to the "notes themselves" with any degree of concentration, he is most likely to make some mention of the melody. Either he hears a pretty melody or he does not, and he generally lets it go at that. Rhythm is likely to gain his attention next, particularly if it seems exciting. But harmony and tone color are generally taken for granted, if they are thought of consciously at all. As for music's having a definite form of some kind, that idea seems never to have occurred to him.

It is very important for all of us to become more alive to music on its sheerly musical plane. After all, an actual musical material is being used. The intelligent listener must be prepared to increase his awareness of the musical material and what happens to it. He must hear the melodies, the rhythms, the harmonies, the tone colors in a more conscious fashion. But above all he must, in order to follow the line of the composer's thought, know something of the principles of musical form. Listening to all of these elements is listening on the sheerly musical plane.

Let me repeat that I have split up mechanically the three separate planes   20
on which we listen merely for the sake of greater clarity. Actually, we never listen on one or the other of these planes. What we do is to correlate them—listening in all three ways at the same time. It takes no mental effort, for we do it instinctively.

Perhaps an analogy with what happens to us when we visit the theater will make this instinctive correlation clearer. In the theater, you are aware of the actors and actresses, costumes and sets, sounds and movements. All these give one the sense that the theater is a pleasant place to be in. They constitute the sensuous plane in our theatrical reactions.

The expressive plane in the theater would be derived from the feeling that you get from what is happening on the stage. You are moved to pity, excitement, or gayety. It is this general feeling, generated aside from the particular words being spoken, a certain emotional something which exists on the stage, that is analogous to the expressive quality in music.

The plot and plot development is equivalent to our sheerly musical plane. The playwright creates and develops a character in just the same way that a composer creates and develops a theme. According to the degree of your awareness of the way in which the artist in either field handles his material will you become a more intelligent listener.

It is easy enough to see that the theatergoer never is conscious of any of these elements separately. He is aware of them all at the same time. The same is true of music listening. We simultaneously and without thinking listen on all three planes.

25 In a sense, the ideal listener is both inside and outside the music at the same moment, judging it and enjoying it, wishing it would go one way and watching it go another—almost like the composer at the moment he composes it; because in order to write his music, the composer must also be inside and outside his music, carried away by it and yet coldly critical of it. A subjective and objective attitude is implied in both creating and listening to music.

What the reader should strive for, then, is a more *active* kind of listening. Whether you listen to Mozart or Duke Ellington,[6] you can deepen your understanding of music only by being a more conscious and aware listener—not someone who is just listening, but someone who is listening *for* something.

6. Wolfgang Amadeus Mozart (1756–1791), Austrian composer; Edward Kennedy ("Duke") Ellington (1899–1974), American jazz composer and band leader.

QUESTIONS

1. List Copland's "three planes" of listening to music and explain what each entails. Are these three planes comprehensive? Is there another you would add?

2. In paragraphs 21–24, Copland uses the experience of going to the theater to illustrate his three planes of listening. Can you think of other artistic experiences that can be divided up into different "planes"? To what extent would the planes be the same as Copland's?

3. Copland uses classical music as examples in his explanation of the way humans listen to music. Write an essay about the ways you listen to another kind of music: folk, rap, jazz, hip-hop, pop, or rock.

Philosophy and Religion

Langston Hughes *Salvation*

Iwas saved from sin when I was going on thirteen. But not really saved. It happened like this. There was a big revival at my Auntie Reed's church. Every night for weeks there had been much preaching, singing, praying, and shouting, and some very hardened sinners had been brought to Christ, and the membership of the church had grown by leaps and bounds. Then just before the revival ended, they held a special meeting for children, "to bring the young lambs to the fold." My aunt spoke of it for days ahead. That night I was escorted to the front row and placed on the mourners' bench[1] with all the other young sinners, who had not yet been brought to Jesus.

My aunt told me that when you were saved you saw a light, and something happened to you inside! And Jesus came into your life! And God was with you from then on! She said you could see and hear and feel Jesus in your soul. I believed her. I had heard a great many old people say the same thing and it seemed to me they ought to know. So I sat there calmly in the hot, crowded church, waiting for Jesus to come to me.

The preacher preached a wonderful rhythmical sermon, all moans and shouts and lonely cries and dire pictures of hell, and then he sang a song about the ninety and nine safe in the fold, but one little lamb was left out in the cold.[2] Then he said: "Won't you come? Won't you come to Jesus? Young lambs, won't you come?" And he held out his arms to all us young sinners there on the mourners' bench. And the little girls cried. And some of them jumped up and went to Jesus right away. But most of us just sat there.

A great many old people came and knelt around us and prayed, old women with jet-black faces and braided hair, old men with work-gnarled hands. And the church sang a song about the lower lights are burning, some poor sinners to be saved. And the whole building rocked with prayer and song.

From The Big Sea *(1940), Hughes's autobiography of his early life.*

1. A place in the front where potential converts sat during an evangelical service.
2. "The Ninety and Nine" and "Let the Lower Lights Be Burning," mentioned in the next paragraph, are the titles of famous evangelical hymns collected by Ira Sankey (1840–1908).

5   Still I kept waiting to *see* Jesus.

Finally all the young people had gone to the altar and were saved, but one boy and me. He was a rounder's[3] son named Westley. Westley and I were surrounded by sisters and deacons praying. It was very hot in the church, and getting late now. Finally Westley said to me in a whisper: "God damn! I'm tired o' sitting here. Let's get up and be saved." So he got up and was saved.

Then I was left all alone on the mourners' bench. My aunt came and knelt at my knees and cried, while prayers and songs swirled all around me in the little church. The whole congregation prayed for me alone, in a mightly wail of moans and voices. And I kept waiting serenely for Jesus, waiting, waiting—but he didn't come. I wanted to see him, but nothing happened to me. Nothing! I wanted something to happen to me, but nothing happened.

I heard the songs and the minister saying: "Why don't you come? My dear child, why don't you come to Jesus? Jesus is waiting for you. He wants you. Why don't you come? Sister Reed, what is this child's name?"

"Langston," my aunt sobbed.

10   "Langston, why don't you come? Why don't you come and be saved? Oh, Lamb of God! Why don't you come?"

Now it was really getting late. I began to be ashamed of myself, holding everything up so long. I began to wonder what God thought about Westley, who certainly hadn't seen Jesus either, but who was now sitting proudly on the platform, swinging his knickerbockered legs and grinning down at me, surrounded by deacons and old women on their knees praying. God had not struck Westley dead for taking his name in vain or for lying in the temple. So I decided that maybe to save further trouble, I'd better lie, too, and say that Jesus had come, and get up and be saved.

So I got up.

Suddenly the whole room broke into a sea of shouting, as they saw me rise. Waves of rejoicing swept the place. Women leaped in the air. My aunt threw her arms around me. The minister took me by the hand and led me to the platform.

When things quieted down, in a hushed silence, punctuated by a few ecstatic "Amens," all the new young lambs were blessed in the name of God. Then joyous singing filled the room.

15   That night, for the last time in my life but one—for I was a big boy twelve years old—I cried. I cried, in bed alone, and couldn't stop. I buried my head under the quilts, but my aunt heard me. She woke up and told my uncle I was crying because the Holy Ghost had come into my life, and because I had seen Jesus. But I was really crying because I couldn't bear to tell her that I had lied, that I had deceived everybody in the church, and I hadn't seen Jesus, and that now I didn't believe there was a Jesus any more, since he didn't come to help me.

---

3. A rounder was a loafer or wastrel.

QUESTIONS

1. Hughes describes how he lost his faith in Jesus at the age of twelve. How did the grown-ups in his life contribute to the experience?

2. Hughes expected to "see" Jesus. How did he understand the word "see"? How did he need to understand it?

3. Hughes was twelve ("going on thirteen") when the event he describes in first-person narration took place. How careful is he to restrict himself to the point of view of a twelve-year-old child? How does he insure that we, as readers, understand things that the narrator does not?

4. Write a first-person narrative in which you describe a failure—yours or someone else's—to live up to the expectations of parents or other authority figures.

ANDRÉ ACIMAN   *In a Double Exile*

THERE COMES the time at every Passover Seder when someone opens a door to let in the prophet Elijah. At that moment, something like a spell invariably descends over the celebrants, and everyone stares into the doorway, trying to make out the quiet movements of the prophet as he glides his way in and takes the empty seat among us.

But by then my mind has already drifted many, many times, and like all disbelievers who find themselves wondering why they are attending a Seder after last year's resolution, I begin to think of how little this ritual means to me—recalling the ten plagues, the crossing of the Red Sea, manna from heaven. All of it keenly arranged to let every kind of Jew find something to celebrate.

For the religious, Passover is the grateful remembrance of a homeward journey after years of suffering.

For those who believe in the spirit more than in the letter of the occasion, the holiday celebrates survival and deliverance from all forms of tyranny—survival after Auschwitz, freedom from anti-Semitism in Russia, Ethiopia, and Syria.

For yet others, Passover is an occasion to gather around a table and link arms with Jews from everywhere and all times.   5

I don't know Hebrew. Nor do I know any of the songs or prayers. I can't even tell when the Seder is officially over. Often I suspect the whole ceremony has petered out or has been cut short for my benefit—or been drawn out to

Included in Aciman's collection False Papers *(2000), a book of fourteen essays that explore the writer's experience of loss, from his forced departure from Alexandria as a teenager, through a period in Europe, to his making a home in New York City.*

prove a point. I always attend with misgivings, which I communicate to others at the table, and try to atone for by reading aloud when my turn comes, only to resent having been asked to read.

And as I sit and stew, feeling ever more trapped among the observant, I too begin to think of Egypt, of this Egypt everyone will invoke at sundown tomorrow night and which symbolizes suffering, exile, and captivity, and suddenly appears in our dining room like a mummy whose sleep has been disturbed: unreal, mythic, faraway Egypt, which everyone calls by its Hebrew name, *Mizrayim*; in Arabic, it is *Misr*. The same words, but eons apart.

Then, as happens every year, I begin to think of another Egypt, the one I was born in and knew and got to love and would never have left had a modern pharaoh by the name of President Nasser not forced me out for being Jewish. This was an Egypt many of us would have stayed in, even as the last Jews of the land, which we nearly were, even if we had had to beg to stay, which indeed we did.

Often in those years in Alexandria, when I was growing up, Passover coincided with Easter and Ramadan. During Ramadan, we would be let out of school at about noon every day, because Muslims, who fasted all day, needed to rest in the afternoon before breaking their fast at sunset.

10   To those of us who did not have to nap, these were the most magical hours of the year. The city was always quiet then, there was hardly any homework, and summer was only a few weeks away.

At the Seder, the men in my family would spar, my father begging my uncle to speed it up, my uncle deferring to tradition instead; everyone more or less giggling, including the one or two Christians visiting that evening who were hauled in to a dinner that reminded them so much of the Last Supper, they said, everyone garbling everything in a blithe chorus of "*Next year in Jerusalem*," until we heard the cannon of Ramadan announce it was time for devout Muslims to eat.

It never occurred to us that a Seder in Egypt was a contradiction in terms.

Now, when everyone speaks of Pharaoh at Passover, I think back to my very last Seder in Egypt, on the eve of our departure for Italy in 1965—a long, mirthless, desultory affair, celebrated with weak lights and all the shutters drawn so that no one in the street might suspect what we were up to that night.

After almost three centuries of religious tolerance, we found ourselves celebrating Passover the way our Marrano ancestors had done under the Spanish Inquisition: in secret, verging on shame, without conviction, in great haste, and certainly without a clear notion of what we were celebrating. Was it the first exodus from Egypt? Or maybe the second from Spain? Or the third from Turkey? Or the fourth, when my family members fled Italy just before the Nazis took over? Or were we celebrating the many exoduses that went unrecorded but that every Jew knows he can remember if he tries hard enough, for each one of us is a dislodged citizen of a country that was never really his but that he has learned to long for and cannot forget. The fault lines of exile and diaspora always run deep, and we are always from elsewhere, and from elsewhere before that.

Everything in history happens twice, wrote Marx, the first time as tragedy,   15
the second as farce. He forgot to add that Jewish history is repetition, the history of repetition.

Caught in these loops and coils, my family forgot to remember the obvious—that Egypt was never our home, that we should never have come back after Moses, that we didn't even know where our home was, much less which
language was ours. We had borrowed everyone else's. Some of us forgot we
were Jews. Alexandria was our mirage—in the desert, we dreamed awhile
longer.

In the end, Egyptian nationalism drove us all away. Today, religious intolerance wants to finish the job for everyone who remains, not just Jews.
Copts—Christians who are thought to be among the most direct descendants
of the ancient Egyptians—and Westernized Egyptians are watching the clouds
darken around the country. Will Egypt drown again? In 1981, the assassination of President Anwar al-Sadat, in recent years the killings of tourists and
Egyptian intellectuals, and in October 1995 the stabbing of the writer and Nobel laureate Naguib Mahfouz—are these the new plagues? Must I worry and
remember for Egypt as well now?

Passover is the night for it. For on that night all Jews remember the night
when Jewish memory began. That night each one of us thinks back to that private Egypt we each carry with us wherever we are. We may not always know
what to remember, but we know we must remember.

In my case, I remember a city called Alexandria, a city as remote to me
now as Egypt is to my American friends who will celebrate Passover, a city that
was never mine, that no longer exists as I knew it, but that rushes into the
room each time they open the door for Elijah to remind me that I will never
say, Next year in Jerusalem, in Alexandria again.

QUESTIONS

1. Aciman writes of himself as an unbeliever participating in a religious ceremony.
What are his motivations for participating? What do you think of his participation?

2. How does Aciman structure his essay? What devices or themes hold it together,
since it's not a narrative with chronological order to give it shape?

3. Write of someone's ambivalence about a recurring ceremony that family members
regard as important, for example, a religious ceremony, a birthday, a graduation, or some
similar ceremony with cultural or family significance. What motivates the person who is
ambivalent? How is his or her ambivalence dealt with by other family members?

Henry David Thoreau *Where I Lived, and What I Lived For*

WHEN I FIRST took up my abode in the woods, that is, began to spend my nights as well as days there, which, by accident, was on Independence day, or the fourth of July, 1845, my house was not finished for winter, but was merely a defence against the rain, without plastering or chimney, the walls being of rough weather-stained boards, with wide chinks, which made it cool at night. The upright white hewn studs and freshly planed door and window casings gave it a clean and airy look, especially in the morning, when its timbers were saturated with dew, so that I fancied that by noon some sweet gum would exude from them. To my imagination it retained throughout the day more or less of this auroral character, reminding me of a certain house on a mountain which I had visited the year before. This was an airy and unplastered cabin, fit to entertain a travelling god, and where a goddess might trail her garments. The winds which passed over my dwelling were such as sweep over the ridges of mountains, bearing the broken strains, or celestial parts only, of terrestrial music. The morning wind forever blows, the poem of creation is uninterrupted; but few are the ears that hear it. Olympus[1] is but the outside of the earth every where.

The only house I had been the owner of before, if I except a boat, was a tent, which I used occasionally when making excursions in the summer, and this is still rolled up in my garret; but the boat, after passing from hand to hand, has gone down the stream of time. With this more substantial shelter about me, I had made some progress toward settling in the world. This frame, so slightly clad, was a sort of crystallization around me, and reacted on the builder. It was suggestive somewhat as a picture in outlines. I did not need to go out doors to take the air, for the atmosphere within had lost none of its freshness. It was not so much within doors as behind a door where I sat, even in the rainiest weather. The Harivansa[2] says, "An abode without birds is like a meat without seasoning." Such was not my abode, for I found myself suddenly neighbor to the birds; not by having imprisoned one, but having caged myself near them. I was not only nearer to some of those which commonly frequent the garden and the orchard, but to those wilder and more thrilling songsters of the forest which never, or rarely, serenade a villager,—the wood-thrush, the veery, the scarlet tanager, the field-sparrow, the whippoorwill, and many others.

I was seated by the shore of a small pond, about a mile and a half south of

From Thoreau's most famous book, Walden (1854), *an account of his life in a small cabin on* Walden Pond, *outside the village of Concord, Massachusetts; in* Walden *Thoreau not only describes his life in the woods but also develops a philosophy for living.*

1. The mountain where the Greek gods dwell.
2. Fifth-century epic poem about the Hindu god Krishna.

the village of Concord and somewhat higher than it, in the midst of an extensive wood between that town and Lincoln, and about two miles south of that
our only field known to fame, Concord Battle Ground;[3] but I was so low in the
woods that the opposite shore, half a mile off, like the rest, covered with wood,
was my most distant horizon. For the first week, whenever I looked out on the
pond it impressed me like a tarn high up on the side of a mountain, its bottom
far above the surface of other lakes, and, as the sun arose, I saw it throwing off
its nightly clothing of mist, and here and there, by degrees, its soft ripples or
its smooth reflecting surface was revealed, while the mists, like ghosts, were
stealthily withdrawing in every direction into the woods, as at the breaking up
of some nocturnal conventicle. The very dew seemed to hang upon the trees
later into the day than usual, as on the sides of mountains.

This small lake was of most value as a neighbor in the intervals of a gentle rain storm in August, when, both air and water being perfectly still, but the
sky overcast, mid-afternoon had all the serenity of evening, and the wood-
thrush sang around, and was heard from shore to shore. A lake like this is
never smoother than at such a time; and the clear portion of the air above it
being shallow and darkened by clouds, the water, full of light and reflections,
becomes a lower heaven itself so much the more important. From a hill top
near by, where the wood had been recently cut off, there was a pleasing vista
southward across the pond, through a wide indentation in the hills which form
the shore there, where their opposite sides sloping toward each other suggested a stream flowing out in that direction through a wooded valley, but
stream there was none. That way I looked between and over the near green
hills to some distant and higher ones in the horizon, tinged with blue. Indeed,
by standing on tiptoe I could catch a glimpse of some of the peaks of the still
bluer and more distant mountain ranges in the north-west, those true-blue
coins from heaven's own mint, and also of some portion of the village. But in
other directions, even from this point, I could not see over or beyond the
woods which surrounded me. It is well to have some water in your neighborhood, to give buoyancy to and float the earth. One value even of the smallest
well is, that when you look into it you see that earth is not continent but insu-
lar. This is as important as that it keeps butter cool. When I looked across the
pond from this peak toward the Sudbury meadows, which in time of flood I
distinguished elevated perhaps by a mirage in their seething valley, like a coin
in a basin, all the earth beyond the pond appeared like a thin crust insulated
and floated even by this small sheet of intervening water, and I was reminded
that this on which I dwelt was but *dry land.*

Though the view from my door was still more contracted, I did not feel   5
crowded or confined in the least. There was pasture enough for my imagination. The low shrub-oak plateau to which the opposite shore arose, stretched
away toward the prairies of the West and the steppes of Tartary,[4] affording am-

3. Site of the famous Battle of Concord, April 19, 1775, considered the start of the
American Revolution.
4. A region that includes what is today northern Pakistan.

ple room for all the roving families of men. "There are none happy in the world but beings who enjoy freely a vast horizon,"—said Damodara,[5] when his herds required new and larger pastures.

Both place and time were changed, and I dwelt nearer to those parts of the universe and to those eras in history which had most attracted me. Where I lived was as far off as many a region viewed nightly by astronomers. We are wont to imagine rare and delectable places in some remote and more celestial corner of the system, behind the constellation of Cassiopeia's Chair, far from noise and disturbance. I discovered that my house actually had its site in such a withdrawn, but forever new and unprofaned, part of the universe. If it were worth the while to settle in those parts near to the Pleiades or the Hyades, to Aldebaran or Altair,[6] then I was really there, or at an equal remoteness from the life which I had left behind, dwindled and twinkling with as fine a ray to my nearest neighbor, and to be seen only in moonless nights by him. Such was that part of creation where I had squatted;—

> "There was a shepherd that did live,
>   And held his thoughts as high
> As were the mounts whereon his flocks
>   Did hourly feed him by."[7]

What should we think of the shepherd's life if his flocks always wandered to higher pastures than his thoughts?

Every morning was a cheerful invitation to make my life of equal simplicity, and I may say innocence, with Nature herself. I have been as sincere a worshipper of Aurora[8] as the Greeks. I got up early and bathed in the pond; that was a religious exercise, and one of the best things which I did. They say that characters were engraven on the bathing tub of king Tching-thang[9] to this effect: "Renew thyself completely each day; do it again, and again, and forever again." I can understand that. Morning brings back the heroic ages. I was as much affected by the faint hum of a mosquito making its invisible and unimaginable tour through my apartment at earliest dawn, when I was sitting with door and windows open, as I could be by any trumpet that ever sang of fame. It was Homer's[10] requiem; itself an Iliad and Odyssey in the air, singing its own wrath and wanderings. There was something cosmical about it; a standing advertisement, till forbidden, of the everlasting vigor and fertility of the world. The morning, which is the most memorable season of the day, is the

---

5. One of the many names of Krishna, the Hindu god.

6. Cassiopeia's Chair, the Pleiades, and the Hyades are constellations; Aldebaran and Altair are stars.

7. Lines from "The Shepherd's Love for Philladay," from Thomas Evan's *Old Ballads* (1810).

8. Goddess of the dawn.

9. Confucius (551–479 B.C.E.), Chinese philosopher.

10. Greek epic poet (eighth century B.C.E.), author of the *Odyssey* and the *Iliad*.

awakening hour. Then there is least somnolence in us; and for an hour, at least, some part of us awakes which slumbers all the rest of the day and night. Little is to be expected of that day, if it can be called a day, to which we are not awakened by our Genius, but by the mechanical nudgings of some servitor, are not awakened by our own newly-acquired force and aspirations from within, accompanied by the undulations of celestial music, instead of factory bells, and a fragrance filling the air—to a higher life than we fell asleep from; and thus the darkness bear its fruit, and prove itself to be good, no less than the light. That man who does not believe that each day contains an earlier, more sacred, and auroral hour than he has yet profaned, has despaired of life, and is pursuing a descending and darkening way. After a partial cessation of his sensuous life, the soul of man, or its organs rather, are reinvigorated each day, and his Genius tries again what noble life it can make. All memorable events, I should say, transpire in morning time and in a morning atmosphere. The Vedas[11] say, "All intelligences awake with the morning." Poetry and art, and the fairest and most memorable of the actions of men, date from such an hour. All poets and heroes, like Memnon,[12] are the children of Aurora, and emit their music at sunrise. To him whose elastic and vigorous thought keeps pace with the sun, the day is a perpetual morning. It matters not what the clocks say or the attitudes and labors of men. Morning is when I am awake and there is a dawn in me. Moral reform is the effort to throw off sleep. Why is it that men give so poor an account of their day if they have not been slumbering? They are not such poor calculators. If they had not been overcome with drowsiness they would have performed something. The millions are awake enough for physical labor; but only one in a million is awake enough for effective intellectual exertion, only one in a hundred millions to a poetic or divine life. To be awake is to be alive. I have never yet met a man who was quite awake. How could I have looked him in the face?

We must learn to reawaken and keep ourselves awake, not by mechanical aids, but by an infinite expectation of the dawn, which does not forsake us in our soundest sleep. I know of no more encouraging fact than the unquestionable ability of man to elevate his life by a conscious endeavor. It is something to be able to paint a particular picture, or to carve a statue, and so to make a few objects beautiful; but it is far more glorious to carve and paint the very atmosphere and medium through which we look, which morally we can do. To affect the quality of the day, that is the highest of arts. Every man is tasked to make his life, even in its details, worthy of the contemplation of his most elevated and critical hour. If we refused, or rather used up, such paltry information as we get, the oracles would distinctly inform us how this might be done.

I went to the woods because I wished to live deliberately, to front only the essential facts of life, and see if I could not learn what it had to teach, and not,

11. Sacred texts that contain hymns, incantations, and rituals from ancient India.

12. Son of Aurora, the goddess of dawn, and a mortal, Memnon was king of the Ethiopians; he was slain by Achilles while fighting the Greeks in Troy. When he died, his sad mother's tears formed the morning dew.

when I came to die, discover that I had not lived. I did not wish to live what was not life, living is so dear, nor did I wish to practise resignation, unless it was quite necessary. I wanted to live deep and suck out all the marrow of life, to live so sturdily and Spartan-like as to put to rout all that was not life, to cut a broad swath and shave close, to drive life into a corner, and reduce it to its lowest terms, and, if it proved to be mean, why then to get the whole and genuine meanness of it, and publish its meanness to the world; or if it were sublime, to know it by experience, and be able to give a true account of it in my next excursion. For most men, it appears to me, are in a strange uncertainty about it, whether it is of the devil or of God, and have *somewhat hastily* concluded that it is the chief end of man here to "glorify God and enjoy him forever."

10   Still we live meanly, like ants; though the fable tells us that we were long ago changed into men;[13] like pygmies we fight with cranes;[14] it is error upon error, and clout upon clout, and our best virtue has for its occasion a superfluous and evitable wretchedness. Our life is frittered away by detail. An honest man has hardly need to count more than his ten fingers, or in extreme cases he may add his ten toes, and lump the rest. Simplicity, simplicity, simplicity! I say, let your affairs be as two or three, and not a hundred or a thousand; instead of a million count half a dozen, and keep your accounts on your thumb nail. In the midst of this chopping sea of civilized life, such are the clouds and storms and quicksands and thousand-and-one items to be allowed for, that a man has to live, if he would not founder and go to the bottom and not make his port at all, by dead reckoning, and he must be a great calculator indeed who succeeds. Simplify, simplify. Instead of three meals a day, if it be necessary eat but one; instead of a hundred dishes, five; and reduce other things in proportion. Our life is like a German Confederacy, made up of petty states, with its boundary forever fluctuating, so that even a German cannot tell you how it is bounded at any moment. The nation itself, with all its so called internal improvements, which, by the way, are all external and superficial, is just such an unwieldy and overgrown establishment, cluttered with furniture and tripped up by its own traps, ruined by luxury and heedless expense, by want of calculation and a worthy aim, as the million households in the land; and the only cure for it as for them is in a rigid economy, a stern and more than Spartan simplicity of life and elevation of purpose. It lives too fast. Men think that it is essential that the *Nation* have commerce, and export ice, and talk through a telegraph, and ride thirty miles an hour, without a doubt, whether *they* do or not; but whether we should live like baboons or like men, is a little uncertain. If we do not get our sleepers, and forge rails, and devote days and nights to the work, but go to tinkering upon our *lives* to improve *them*, who will build railroads? And if railroads are not built, how shall we get to heaven in season? But

13. In a Greek fable Aeacus asks Zeus to increase a scanty population by turning ants into men.
14. From the *Iliad*, Book III, lines 2–6, in which the Trojans are represented as the cranes.

if we stay at home and mind our business, who will want railroads? We do not ride on the railroad; it rides upon us. Did you ever think what those sleepers are that underlie the railroad? Each one is a man, an Irishman, or a Yankee man. The rails are laid on them, and they are covered with sand, and the cars run smoothly over them. They are sound sleepers, I assure you. And every few years a new lot is laid down and run over; so that, if some have the pleasure of riding on a rail, others have the misfortune to be ridden upon. And when they run over a man that is walking in his sleep, a supernumerary sleeper in the wrong position, and wake him up, they suddenly stop the cars, and make a hue and cry about it, as if this were an exception. I am glad to know that it takes a gang of men for every five miles to keep the sleepers down and level in their beds as it is, for this is a sign that they may sometime get up again.

Why should we live with such hurry and waste of life? We are determined to be starved before we are hungry. Men say that a stitch in time saves nine, and so they take a thousand stitches to-day to save nine to-morrow. As for *work*, we haven't any of any consequence. We have the Saint Vitus' dance,[15] and cannot possibly keep our heads still. If I should only give a few pulls at the parish bell-rope, as for a fire, that is, without setting the bell, there is hardly a man on his farm in the outskirts of Concord, notwithstanding that press of engagements which was his excuse so many times this morning, nor a boy, nor a woman, I might almost say, but would forsake all and follow that sound, not mainly to save property from the flames, but, if we will confess the truth, much more to see it burn, since burn it must, and we, be it known, did not set it on fire,—or to see it put out, and have a hand in it, if that is done as handsomely; yes, even if it were the parish church itself. Hardly a man takes a half hour's nap after dinner, but when he wakes he holds up his head and asks, "What's the news?" as if the rest of mankind had stood his sentinels. Some give directions to be waked every half hour, doubtless for no other purpose; and then, to pay for it, they tell what they have dreamed. After a night's sleep the news is as indispensable as the breakfast. "Pray tell me any thing new that has happened to a man any where on this globe,"—and he reads it over his coffee and rolls, that a man has had his eyes gouged out this morning on the Wachito River;[16] never dreaming the while that he lives in the dark unfathomed mammoth cave of this world, and has but the rudiment of an eye himself.

For my part, I could easily do without the post-office. I think that there are very few important communications made through it. To speak critically, I never received more than one or two letters in my life—I wrote this some years ago—that were worth the postage. The penny-post is, commonly, an institution through which you seriously offer a man that penny for his thoughts which is so often safely offered in jest. And I am sure that I never read any memorable news in a newspaper. If we read of one man robbed, or murdered, or killed by accident, or one house burned, or one vessel wrecked, or one

15. A nervous disorder marked by jerky, spasmodic movements that occurs in cases of rheumatic fever involving the connective tissue of the brain.

16. In southern Arkansas.

steamboat blown up, or one cow run over on the Western Railroad, or one mad dog killed, or one lot of grasshoppers in the winter,—we never need read of another. One is enough. If you are acquainted with the principle, what do you care for a myriad instances and applications? To a philosopher all *news*, as it is called, is gossip, and they who edit and read it are old women over their tea. Yet not a few are greedy after this gossip. There was such a rush, as I hear, the other day at one of the offices to learn the foreign news by the last arrival, that several large squares of plate glass belonging to the establishment were broken by the pressure,—news which I seriously think a ready wit might write a twelvemonth or twelve years beforehand with sufficient accuracy. As for Spain, for instance, if you know how to throw in Don Carlos and the Infanta, and Don Pedro and Seville and Granada, from time to time in the right pro-portions,—they may have changed the names a little since I saw the papers,— and serve up a bull-fight when other entertainments fail, it will be true to the letter, and give us as good an idea of the exact state of ruin of things in Spain as the most succinct and lucid reports under this head in the newspapers: and as for England, almost the last significant scrap of news from that quarter was the revolution of 1649;[17] and if you have learned the history of her crops for an average year, you never need attend to that thing again, unless your specu-lations are of a merely pecuniary character. If one may judge who rarely looks into the newspapers, nothing new does ever happen in foreign parts, a French revolution not excepted.

What news! how much more important to know what that is which was never old! "Kieou-he-yu (great dignitary of the state of Wei) sent a man to Khoung-tseu to know his news. Khoung-tseu caused the messenger to be seated near him, and questioned him in these terms: What is your master do-ing? The messenger answered with respect: My master desires to diminish the number of his faults, but he cannot come to the end of them. The messenger being gone, the philosopher remarked: What a worthy messenger! What a wor-thy messenger!" The preacher, instead of vexing the ears of drowsy farmers on their day of rest at the end of the week,—for Sunday is the fit conclusion of an ill-spent week, and not the fresh and brave beginning of a new one,—with this one other draggle-tail of a sermon, should shout with thundering voice,— "Pause! Avast! Why so seeming fast, but deadly slow?"

Shams and delusions are esteemed for soundest truths, while reality is fabulous. If men would steadily observe realities only, and not allow them-selves to be deluded, life, to compare it with such things as we know, would be like a fairy tale and the Arabian Nights' Entertainments. If we respected only what is inevitable and has a right to be, music and poetry would resound along the streets. When we are unhurried and wise, we perceive that only great and worthy things have any permanent and absolute existence,—that petty fears and petty pleasures are but the shadow of the reality. This is always exhilarat-ing and sublime. By closing the eyes and slumbering, and consenting to be de-

17. Sometimes called the Cromwellian Interlude, the period in British history between 1649 and 1660 in which the monarchy was replaced by the Commonwealth and Oliver Cromwell became Lord Protector.

ceived by shows, men establish and confirm their daily life of routine and habit every where, which still is built on purely illusory foundations. Children, who play life, discern its true law and relations more clearly than men, who fail to live it worthily, but who think that they are wiser by experience, that is, by failure. I have read in a Hindoo book, that "There was a king's son, who, being expelled in infancy from his native city, was brought up by a forester, and, growing up to maturity in that state, imagined himself to belong to the barbarous race with which he lived. One of his father's ministers having discovered him, revealed to him what he was, and the misconception of his character was removed, and he knew himself to be a prince. So soul," continues the Hindoo philosopher, "from the circumstances in which it is placed, mistakes its own character, until the truth is revealed to it by some holy teacher, and then it knows itself to be *Brahme*."[18] I perceive that we inhabitants of New England live this mean life that we do because our vision does not penetrate the surface of things. We think that that *is* which *appears* to be. If a man should walk through this town and see only the reality, where, think you, would the "Mill-dam"[19] go to? If he should give us an account of the realities he beheld there, we should not recognize the place in his description. Look at a meeting-house, or a court-house, or a jail, or a shop, or a dwelling-house, and say what that thing really is before a true gaze, and they would all go to pieces in your account of them. Men esteem truth remote, in the outskirts of the system, behind the farthest star, before Adam and after the last man. In eternity there is indeed something true and sublime. But all these times and places and occasions are now and here. God himself culminates in the present moment, and will never be more divine in the lapse of all the ages. And we are enabled to apprehend at all what is sublime and noble only by the perpetual instilling and drenching of the reality that surrounds us. The universe constantly and obediently answers to our conceptions; whether we travel fast or slow, the track is laid for us. Let us spend our lives in conceiving then. The poet or the artist never yet had so fair and noble a design but some of his posterity at least could accomplish it.

Let us spend one day as deliberately as Nature, and not be thrown off the   15
track by every nutshell and mosquito's wing that falls on the rails. Let us rise early and fast, or break fast, gently and without perturbation; let company come and let company go, let the bells ring and the children cry,—determined to make a day of it. Why should we knock under and go with the stream? Let us not be upset and overwhelmed in that terrible rapid and whirlpool called a dinner, situated in the meridian shallows. Weather this danger and you are safe, for the rest of the way is down hill. With unrelaxed nerves, with morning vigor, sail by it, looking another way, tied to the mast like Ulysses. If the engine whistles, let it whistle till it is hoarse for its pains. If the bell rings, why should we run? We will consider what kind of music they are like. Let us settle ourselves, and work and wedge our feet downward through the mud and slush of

18. The supreme soul, the essence of all being, in Hinduism.
19. A dam built in 1635 in the town of Concord on the site of an Indian fishing weir. The places listed after are near it.

opinion, and prejudice, and tradition, and delusion, and appearance, that allu-
vion which covers the globe, through Paris and London, through New York
and Boston and Concord, through church and state, through poetry and philosophy and religion, till we come to a hard bottom and rocks in place, which
we can call *reality*, and say, This is, and no mistake; and then begin, having a
point d'appui,[20] below freshet and frost and fire, a place where you might
found a wall or a state, or set a lamp-post safely, or perhaps a gauge, not a
Nilometer,[21] but a Realometer, that future ages might know how deep a
freshet of shams and appearances had gathered from time to time. If you
stand right fronting and face to face to a fact, you will see the sun glimmer on
both its surfaces, as if it were a cimeter,[22] and feel its sweet edge dividing you
through the heart and marrow, and so you will happily conclude your mortal
career. Be it life or death, we crave only reality. If we are really dying, let us
hear the rattle in our throats and feel cold in the extremities; if we are alive, let
us go about our business.

Time is but the stream I go a-fishing in. I drink at it; but while I drink I
see the sandy bottom and detect how shallow it is. Its thin current slides away,
but eternity remains. I would drink deeper; fish in the sky, whose bottom is
pebbly with stars. I cannot count one. I know not the first letter of the alphabet. I have always been regretting that I was not as wise as the day I was born.
The intellect is a cleaver; it discerns and rifts its way into the secret of things.
I do not wish to be any more busy with my hands than is necessary. My head
is hands and feet. I feel all my best faculties concentrated in it. My instinct
tells me that my head is an organ for burrowing, as some creatures use their
snout and forepaws, and with it I would mine and burrow my way through
these hills. I think that the richest vein is somewhere hereabouts; so by the di-
vining rod and thin rising vapors I judge; and here I will begin to mine.

20. Reference point.
21. A gauge placed in the Nile River in ancient times to measure the rise of the water.
22. A saber with a curved blade, usually spelled "scimitar."

QUESTIONS

1. Thoreau's title might be rephrased as two questions: "Where did I live?" and "What
did I live for?" What answers does Thoreau give to each?

2. Throughout this essay Thoreau poses questions—for example, "Why is it that men
give so poor an account of their day if they have not been slumbering?" (paragraph 7) or
"Why should we live with such hurry and waste of life?" (paragraph 11). To what extent
does he answer them? Why might he leave some unanswered or only partially answered?

3. Thoreau is known for his aphorisms (short, witty nuggets of wisdom). Find one you
like and explain what it means.

4. If you have ever chosen to live unconventionally at some period of your life, even if
only briefly, write about your decision, including the reasons and the consequences.

VIRGINIA WOOLF   *The Death of the Moth*

Moths that fly by day are not properly to be called moths; they do not excite that pleasant sense of dark autumn nights and ivy-blossom which the commonest yellow-underwing asleep in the shadow of the curtain never fails to rouse in us. They are hybrid creatures, neither gay like butterflies nor sombre like their own species. Nevertheless the present specimen, with his narrow hay-colored wings, fringed with a tassel of the same color, seemed to be content with life. It was a pleasant morning, mid-September, mild, benignant, yet with a keener breath than that of the summer months. The plough was already scoring the field opposite the window, and where the share had been, the earth was pressed flat and gleamed with moisture. Such vigor came rolling in from the fields and the down beyond that it was difficult to keep the eyes strictly turned upon the book. The rooks too were keeping one of their annual festivities; soaring round the tree tops until it looked as if a vast net with thousands of black knots in it had been cast up into the air; which, after a few moments sank slowly down upon the trees until every twig seemed to have a knot at the end of it. Then, suddenly, the net would be thrown into the air again in a wider circle this time, with the utmost clamor and vociferation, as though to be thrown into the air and settle slowly down upon the tree tops were a tremendously exciting experience.

The same energy which inspired the rooks, the ploughmen, the horses, and even, it seemed, the lean bare-backed downs, sent the moth fluttering from side to side of his square of the window-pane. One could not help watching him. One was, indeed, conscious of a queer feeling of pity for him. The possibilities of pleasure seemed that morning so enormous and so various that to have only a moth's part in life, and a day moth's at that, appeared a hard fate, and his zest in enjoying his meagre opportunities to the full, pathetic. He flew vigorously to one corner of his compartment, and, after waiting there a second, flew across to the other. What remained for him but to fly to a third corner and then to a fourth? That was all he could do, in spite of the size of the downs, the width of the sky, the far-off smoke of houses, and the romantic voice, now and then, of a steamer out at sea. What he could do he did. Watching him, it seemed as if a fiber, very thin but pure, of the enormous energy of the world had been thrust into his frail and diminutive body. As often as he crossed the pane, I could fancy that a thread of vital light became visible. He was little or nothing but life.

Yet, because he was so small, and so simple a form of the energy that was rolling in at the open window and driving its way through so many narrow and intricate corridors in my own brain and in those of other human beings, there was something marvellous as well as pathetic about him. It was as if someone

The title essay of Woolf's collection The Death of the Moth, and Other Essays *(1942), compiled after her death in 1941.*

697

had taken a tiny bead of pure life and decking it as lightly as possible with down and feathers, had set it dancing and zig-zagging to show us the true nature of life. Thus displayed one could not get over the strangeness of it. One is apt to forget all about life, seeing it humped and bossed and garnished and cumbered so that it has to move with the greatest circumspection and dignity. Again, the thought of all that life might have been had he been born in any other shape caused one to view his simple activities with a kind of pity.

After a time, tired by his dancing apparently, he settled on the window ledge in the sun, and, the queer spectacle being at an end, I forgot about him. Then, looking up, my eye was caught by him. He was trying to resume his dancing, but seemed either so stiff or so awkward that he could only flutter to the bottom of the window-pane; and when he tried to fly across it he failed. Being intent on other matters I watched these futile attempts for a time without thinking, unconsciously waiting for him to resume his flight, as one waits for a machine, that has stopped momentarily, to start again without considering the reason of its failure. After perhaps a seventh attempt he slipped from the wooden ledge and fell, fluttering his wings, on to his back on the window sill. The helplessness of his attitude roused me. It flashed upon me that he was in difficulties; he could no longer raise himself; his legs struggled vainly. But, as I stretched out a pencil, meaning to help him to right himself, it came over me that the failure and awkwardness were the approach of death. I laid the pencil down again.

5   The legs agitated themselves once more. I looked as if for the enemy against which he struggled. I looked out of doors. What had happened there? Presumably it was midday, and work in the fields had stopped. Stillness and quiet had replaced the previous animation. The birds had taken themselves off to feed in the brooks. The horses stood still. Yet the power was there all the same, massed outside indifferent, impersonal, not attending to anything in particular. Somehow it was opposed to the little hay-colored moth. It was useless to try to do anything. One could only watch the extraordinary efforts made by those tiny legs against an oncoming doom which could, had it chosen, have submerged an entire city, not merely a city, but masses of human beings; nothing, I knew, had any chance against death. Nevertheless after a pause of exhaustion the legs fluttered again. It was superb this last protest, and so frantic that he succeeded at last in righting himself. One's sympathies, of course, were all on the side of life. Also, when there was nobody to care or to know, this gigantic effort on the part of an insignificant little moth, against a power of such magnitude, to retain what no one else valued or desired to keep, moved one strangely. Again, somehow, one saw life, a pure bead. I lifted the pencil again, useless though I knew it to be. But even as I did so, the unmistakable tokens of death showed themselves. The body relaxed, and instantly grew stiff. The struggle was over. The insignificant little creature now knew death. As I looked at the dead moth, this minute wayside triumph of so great a force over so mean an antagonist filled me with wonder. Just as life had been strange a few minutes before, so death was now as strange. The moth having righted himself now lay most decently and uncomplainingly composed. O yes, he seemed to say, death is stronger than I am.

QUESTIONS

1. Trace the sequence in which Woolf comes to identify with the moth. How does she make her identification explicit? How is it implicit in the language she uses to describe the moth?

2. Choose one of the descriptions of a small living creature or creatures in Annie Dillard's "Sight into Insight" below and compare it with Woolf's description of the moth. Does a similar identification take place in Dillard's essay? If so, how; if not, why not?

3. Henry David Thoreau, in "The Battle of the Ants" (p. 464), also humanizes small living creatures. How do his strategies differ from Woolf's?

4. Write two descriptions of the same living creature, one using Woolf's strategies, the other using Thoreau's. Or, alternatively, write an essay in which you analyze the differences between them.

ANNIE DILLARD   *Sight into Insight*

WHEN I WAS SIX or seven years old, growing up in Pittsburgh, I used to take a penny of my own and hide it for someone else to find. It was a curious compulsion; sadly, I've never been seized by it since. For some reason I always "hid" the penny along the same stretch of sidewalk up the street. I'd cradle it at the roots of a maple, say, or in a hole left by a chipped-off piece of sidewalk. Then I'd take a piece of chalk and, starting at either end of the block, draw huge arrows leading up to the penny from both directions. After I learned to write I labeled the arrows "SURPRISE AHEAD" or "MONEY THIS WAY." I was greatly excited, during all this arrowdrawing, at the thought of the first lucky passerby who would receive in this way, regardless of merit, a free gift from the universe. But I never lurked about. I'd go straight home and not give the matter another thought, until, some months later, I would be gripped by the impulse to hide another penny.

There are lots of things to see, unwrapped gifts and free surprises. The world is fairly studded and strewn with pennies cast broadside from a generous hand. But—and this is the point—who gets excited by a mere penny? If you follow one arrow, if you crouch motionless on a bank to watch a tremulous ripple thrill on the water, and are rewarded by the sight of a muskrat kit paddling from its den, will you count that sight a chip of copper only, and go your rueful way? It is very dire poverty indeed for a man to be so malnourished and fatigued that he won't stoop to pick up a penny. But if you cultivate a healthy

Originally published in Harper's Magazine *(February 1974), an American monthly that explores "the issues and ideas in politics, science, and the arts that drive our national conversation"; included in Dillard's Pulitzer Prize–winning book,* Pilgrim at Tinker Creek *(1974).*

poverty and simplicity, so that finding a penny will make your day, then, since the world is in fact planted in pennies, you have with your poverty bought a lifetime of days. What you see is what you get.

Unfortunately, nature is very much a now-you-see-it, now-you-don't affair. A fish flashes, then dissolves in the water before my eyes like so much salt. Deer apparently ascend bodily into heaven; the brightest oriole fades into leaves. These disappearances stun me into stillness and concentration; they say of nature that it conceals with a grand nonchalance, and they say of vision that it is a deliberate gift, the revelation of a dancer who for my eyes only flings away her seven veils.

For nature does reveal as well as conceal: now-you-don't-see-it, now-you-do. For a week this September migrating red-winged blackbirds were feeding heavily down by Tinker Creek at the back of the house. One day I went out to investigate the racket; I walked up to a tree, an Osage orange, and a hundred birds flew away. They simply materialized out of the tree. I saw a tree, then a whisk of color, then a tree again. I walked closer and another hundred black-birds took flight. Not a branch, not a twig budged: the birds were apparently weightless as well as invisible. Or, it was as if the leaves of the Osage orange had been freed from a spell in the form of redwinged blackbirds; they flew from the tree, caught my eye in the sky, and vanished. When I looked again at the tree, the leaves had reassembled as if nothing had happened. Finally I walked directly to the trunk of the tree and a final hundred, the real diehards, appeared, spread, and vanished. How could so many hide in the tree without my seeing them? The Osage orange, unruffled, looked just as it had looked from the house, when three hundred red-winged blackbirds cried from its crown. I looked upstream where they flew, and they were gone. Searching, I couldn't spot one. I wandered upstream to force them to play their hand, but they'd crossed the creek and scattered. One show to a customer. These appearances catch at my throat; they are the free gifts, the bright coppers at the roots of trees.

5   It's all a matter of keeping my eyes open. Nature is like one of those line drawings that are puzzles for children: Can you find hidden in the tree a duck, a house, a boy, a bucket, a giraffe, and a boot? Specialists can find the most incredibly hidden things. A book I read when I was young recommended an easy way to find caterpillars: you simply find some fresh caterpillar droppings, look up, and there's your caterpillar. More recently an author advised me to set my mind at ease about those piles of cut stems on the ground in grassy fields. Field mice make them; they cut the grass down by degrees to reach the seeds at the head. It seems that when the grass is tightly packed, as in a field of ripe grain, the blade won't topple at a single cut through the stem; instead, the cut stem simply drops vertically, held in the crush of grain. The mouse severs the bottom again and again, the stem keeps dropping an inch at a time, and finally the head is low enough for the mouse to reach the seeds. Meanwhile the mouse is positively littering the field with its little piles of cut stems into which, presumably, the author is constantly stumbling.

If I can't see these minutiae, I still try to keep my eyes open. I'm always on the lookout for ant lion traps in sandy soil, monarch pupae near milkweed, skipper larvae in locust leaves. These things are utterly common, and I've not seen one. I bang on hollow trees near water, but so far no flying squirrels have appeared. In flat country I watch every sunset in hopes of seeing the green ray. The green ray is a seldom-seen streak of light that rises from the sun like a spurting fountain at the moment of sunset; it throbs into the sky for two seconds and disappears. One more reason to keep my eyes open. A photography professor at the University of Florida just happened to see a bird die in mid-flight; it jerked, died, dropped, and smashed on the ground.

I squint at the wind because I read Stewart Edward White: "I have always maintained that if you looked closely enough you could *see* the wind—the dim, hardly-made-out, fine débris fleeing high in the air." White was an excellent observer, and devoted an entire chapter of *The Mountains* to the subject of seeing deer: "As soon as you can forget the naturally obvious and construct an artificial obvious, then you too will see deer."

But the artificial obvious is hard to see. My eyes account for less than 1 percent of the weight of my head; I'm bony and dense; I see what I expect. I once spent a full three minutes looking at a bullfrog that was so unexpectedly large I couldn't see it even though a dozen enthusiastic campers were shouting directions. Finally I asked, "What color am I looking for?" and a fellow said, "Green." When at last I picked out the frog, I saw what painters are up against: the thing wasn't green at all, but the color of wet hickory bark.

The lover can see, and the knowledgeable. I visited an aunt and uncle at a quarter-horse ranch in Cody, Wyoming. I couldn't do much of anything useful, but I could, I thought, draw. So, as we all sat around the kitchen table after supper, I produced a sheet of paper and drew a horse. "That's one lame horse," my aunt volunteered. The rest of the family joined in: "Only place to saddle that one is his neck"; "Looks like we better shoot the poor thing, on account of those terrible growths." Meekly, I slid the pencil and paper down the table. Everyone in that family, including my three young cousins, could draw a horse. Beautifully. When the paper came back it looked as though five shining, real quarter horses had been corraled by mistake with a papier-mâché moose; the real horses seemed to gaze at the monster with a steady, puzzled air. I stay away from horses now, but I can do a creditable goldfish. The point is that I just don't know what the lover knows; I just can't see the artificial obvious that those in the know construct. The herpetologist asks the native, "Are there snakes in that ravine?" "Nosir." And the herpetologist comes home with, yessir, three bags full. Are there butterflies on that mountain? Are the bluets in bloom, are there arrowheads here, or fossil shells in the shale?

Peeping through my keyhole I see within the range of only about 30 percent of the light that comes from the sun; the rest is infrared and some little ultraviolet, perfectly apparent to many animals, but invisible to me. A nightmare network of ganglia, charged and firing without my knowledge, cuts and splices what I do see, editing it for my brain. Donald E. Carr points out that the sense impressions of one-celled animals are *not* edited for the brain: "This

10

is philosophically interesting in a rather mournful way, since it means that only the simplest animals perceive the universe as it is."

A fog that won't burn away drifts and flows across my field of vision. When you see fog move against a backdrop of deep pines, you don't see the fog itself, but streaks of clearness floating across the air in dark shreds. So I see only tatters of clearness through a pervading obscurity. I can't distinguish the fog from the overcast sky; I can't be sure if the light is direct or reflected. Everywhere darkness and the presence of the unseen appalls. We estimate now that only one atom dances alone in every cubic meter of intergalactic space. I blink and squint. What planet or power yanks Halley's Comet out of orbit? We haven't seen it yet; it's a question of distance, density, and the pallor of reflected light. We rock, cradled in the swaddling band of darkness. Even the simple darkness of night whispers suggestions to the mind. This summer, in August, I stayed at the creek too late.

Where Tinker Creek flows under the sycamore log bridge to the tear-shaped island, it is slow and shallow, fringed thinly in cattail marsh. At this spot an astonishing bloom of life supports vast breeding populations of insects, fish, reptiles, birds, and mammals. On windless summer evenings I stalk along the creek bank or straddle the sycamore log in absolute stillness, watching for muskrats. The night I stayed too late I was hunched on the log staring spellbound at spreading, reflected stains of lilac on the water. A cloud in the sky suddenly lighted as if turned on by a switch; its reflection just as suddenly materialized on the water upstream, flat and floating, so that I couldn't see the creek bottom, or life in the water under the cloud. Downstream, away from the cloud on the water, water turtles smooth as beans were gliding down with the current in a series of easy, weightless push-offs, as men bound on the moon. I didn't know whether to trace the progress of one turtle I was sure of, risking sticking my face in one of the bridge's spider webs made invisible by the gathering dark, or take a chance on seeing the carp, or scan the mudbank in hope of seeing a muskrat, or follow the last of the swallows who caught at my heart and trailed it after them like streamers as they appeared from directly below, under the log, flying upstream with their tails forked, so fast.

But shadows spread and deepened and stayed. After thousands of years we're still strangers to darkness, fearful aliens in an enemy camp with our arms crossed over our chests. I stirred. A land turtle on the bank, startled, hissed the air from its lungs and withdrew to its shell. An uneasy pink here, an unfathomable blue there, gave great suggestion of lurking beings. Things were going on. I couldn't see whether that rustle I heard was a distant rattlesnake, slit-eyed, or a nearby sparrow kicking in the dry flood debris slung at the foot of a willow. Tremendous action roiled the water everywhere I looked, big action, inexplicable. A tremor welled up beside a gaping muskrat burrow in the bank and I caught my breath, but no muskrat appeared. The ripples continued to fan upstream with a steady, powerful thrust. Night was knitting an eyeless mask over my face, and I still sat transfixed. A distant airplane, a delta wing out of nightmare, made a gliding shadow on the creek's bottom that looked like a stingray cruising upstream. At once a black fin slit the pink cloud on the water, shearing it in two. The two halves merged together and seemed to dissolve before my eyes. Darkness pooled in the cleft of the creek and rose, as water collects in a well. Untamed, dreaming lights flickered over the sky. I saw hints of hulking underwater shadows, two pale splashes out of the water, and round ripples rolling close together from a blackened center.

At last I stared upstream where only the deepest violet remained of the cloud, a cloud so high its underbelly still glowed, its feeble color reflected from a hidden sky lighted in turn by a sun halfway to China. And out of that violet, a sudden enormous black body arced over the water. Head and tail, if there was a head and tail, were both submerged in cloud. I saw only one ebony fling, a headlong dive to darkness; then the waters closed, and the lights went out.

I walked home in a shivering daze, up hill and down. Later I lay open-mouthed in bed, my arms flung wide at my sides to steady the whirling darkness. At this latitude I'm spinning 836 miles an hour round the earth's axis; I feel my sweeping fall as a breakneck arc like the dive of dolphins, and the hollow rushing of wind raises the hairs on my neck and the side of my face. In orbit around the sun I'm moving 64,800 miles an hour. The solar system as a whole, like a merry-go-round unhinged, spins, bobs, and blinks at the speed of 43,200 miles an hour along a course set east of Hercules. Someone has piped, and we are dancing a tarantella until the sweat pours. I open my eyes and I see dark, muscled forms curl out of water, with flapping gills and flattened eyes. I close my eyes and I see stars, deep stars giving way to deeper stars, deeper stars bowing to deepest stars at the crown of an infinite cone.

"Still," wrote Van Gogh[1] in a letter, "a great deal of light falls on everything." If we are blinded by darkness, we are also blinded by light. Sometimes here in Virginia at sunset low clouds on the southern or northern horizon are completely invisible in the lighted sky. I only know one is there because I can see its reflection in still water. The first time I discovered this mystery I looked from cloud to no-cloud in bewilderment, checking my bearings over and over, thinking maybe the ark of the covenant[2] was just passing by south of Dead Man Mountain. Only much later did I learn the explanation: polarized light from the sky is very much weakened by reflection, but the light in clouds isn't polarized. So invisible clouds pass among visible clouds, till all slide over the mountains; so a greater light extinguishes a lesser as though it didn't exist.

In the great meteor shower of August, the Perseid, I wail all day for the shooting stars I miss. They're out there showering down committing hara-kiri in a flame of fatal attraction, and hissing perhaps at last into the ocean. But at dawn what looks like a blue dome clamps down over me like a lid on a pot.

1. Vincent van Gogh (1853–1890), Dutch Postimpressionist painter.
2. Repository for the stone tablets of the Ten Commandments, carried by the ancient Israelites during their desert wanderings.

The stars and planets could smash and I'd never know. Only a piece of ashen moon occasionally climbs up or down the inside of the dome, and our local star without surcease explodes on our heads. We have really only that one light, one source for all power, and yet we must turn away from it by universal decree. Nobody here on the planet seems aware of this strange, powerful taboo, that we all walk about carefully averting our faces, this way and that, lest our eyes be blasted forever.

Darkness appalls and light dazzles; the scrap of visible light that doesn't hurt my eyes hurts my brain. What I see sets me swaying. Size and distance and the sudden swelling of meanings confuse me, bowl me over. I straddle the sycamore log bridge over Tinker Creek in the summer. I look at the lighted creek bottom: snail tracks tunnel the mud in quavering curves. A crayfish jerks, but by the time I absorb what has happened, he's gone in a billowing smoke screen of silt. I look at the water; minnows and shiners. If I'm thinking minnows, a carp will fill my brain till I scream. I look at the water's surface: skaters, bubbles, and leaves sliding down. Suddenly, my own face, reflected, startles me witless. Those snails have been tracking my face! Finally, with a shuddering wrench of the will, I see clouds, cirrus clouds. I'm dizzy, I fall in.

This looking business is risky. Once I stood on a humped rock on nearby Purgatory Mountain, watching through binoculars the great autumn hawk migration below, until I discovered that I was in danger of joining the hawks on a vertical migration of my own. I was used to binoculars, but not, apparently, to balancing on humped rocks while looking through them. I reeled. Everything advanced and receded by turns; the world was full of unexplained foreshortenings and depths. A distant huge object, a hawk the size of an elephant, turned out to be the browned bough of a nearby loblolly pine. I followed a sharp-shinned hawk against a featureless sky, rotating my head unawares as it flew, and when I lowered the glass a glimpse of my own looming shoulder sent me staggering. What prevents the men at Palomar[3] from falling, voiceless and blinded, from their tiny, vaulted chairs?

20   I reel in confusion: I don't understand what I see. With the naked eye I can see two million light-years to the Andromeda galaxy. Often I slop some creek water in a jar, and when I get home I dump it in a white china bowl. After the silt settles I return and see tracings of minute snails on the bottom, a planarian or two winding round the rim of water, roundworms shimmying, frantically, and finally, when my eyes have adjusted to these dimensions, amoebae. At first the amoebae look like *muscae volitantes,* those curled moving spots you seem to see in your eyes when you stare at a distant wall. Then I see the amoebae as drops of water congealed, bluish, translucent, like chips of sky in the bowl. At length I choose one individual and give myself over to its idea of an evening. I see it dribble a grainy foot before it on its wet, unfathomable way. Do its unedited sense impressions include the fierce focus of my eyes? Shall I take it outside and show it Andromeda, and blow its little en-

3. An astronomical observatory in California.

doplasm? I stir the water with a finger, in case it's running out of oxygen. Maybe I should get a tropical aquarium with motorized bubblers and lights, and keep this one for a pet. Yes, it would tell its fissioned descendants, the universe is two feet by five, and if you listen closely you can hear the buzzing music of the spheres.

Oh, it's mysterious, lamplit evenings here in the galaxy, one after the other. It's one of those nights when I wander from window to window, looking for a sign. But I can't see. Terror and a beauty insoluble are a riband of blue woven into the fringe of garments of things both great and small. No culture explains, no bivouac offers real haven or rest. But it could be that we are not seeing something. Galileo[4] thought comets were an optical illusion. This is fertile ground: since we are certain that they're not, we can look at what our scientists have been saying with fresh hope. What if there are *really* gleaming, castellated cities hung up-side-down over the desert sand? What limpid lakes and cool date palms have our caravans always passed untried? Until, one by one, by the blindest of leaps, we light on the road to these places, we must stumble in darkness and hunger. I turn from the window. I'm blind as a bat, sensing only from every direction the echo of my own thin cries.

I chanced on a wonderful book called *Space and Sight,* by Marius Von Senden. When Western surgeons discovered how to perform safe cataract operations, they ranged across Europe and America operating on dozens of men and women of all ages who had been blinded by cataracts since birth. Von Senden collected accounts of such cases; the histories are fascinating. Many doctors had tested their patients' sense perceptions and ideas of space both before and after the operations. The vast majority of patients, of both sexes and all ages, had, in Von Senden's opinion, no idea of space whatsoever. Form, distance, and size were so many meaningless syllables. A patient "had no idea of depth, confusing it with roundness." Before the operation a doctor would give a blind patient a cube and a sphere; the patient would tongue it or feel it with his hands, and name it correctly. After the operation the doctor would show the same objects to the patient without letting him touch them; now he had no clue whatsoever to what he was seeing. One patient called lemonade "square" because it pricked on his tongue as a square shape pricked on the touch of his hands. Of another post-operative patient the doctor writes, "I have found in her no notion of size, for example, not even within the narrow limits which she might have encompassed with the aid of touch. Thus when I asked her to show me how big her mother was, she did not stretch out her hands, but set her two index fingers a few inches apart."

For the newly sighted, vision is pure sensation unencumbered by meaning. When a newly sighted girl saw photographs and paintings, she asked, " 'Why do they put those dark marks all over them?' 'Those aren't dark marks,' her mother explained, 'those are shadows. That is one of the ways the eye

4. Italian astronomer (1564–1642).

knows that things have shape. If it were not for shadows, many things would look flat.' 'Well, that's how things do look,' Joan answered. 'Everything looks flat with dark patches.' "

In general the newly sighted see the world as a dazzle of "colorpatches." They are pleased by the sensation of color, and learn quickly to name the colors, but the rest of seeing is tormentingly difficult. Soon after his operation a patient "generally bumps into one of these color-patches and observes them to be substantial, since they resist him as tactual objects do. In walking about it also strikes him—or can if he pays attention—that he is continually passing in between the colors he sees, that he can go past a visual object, that a part of it then steadily disappears from view; and that in spite of this, however he twists and turns—whether entering the room from the door, for example, or returning back to it—he always has a visual space in front of him. Thus he gradually comes to realize that there is also a space behind him, which he does not see."

25   The mental effort involved in these reasonings proves overwhelming for many patients. It oppresses them to realize that they have been visible to people all along, perhaps unattractively so, without their knowledge or consent. A disheartening number of them refuse to use their new vision, continuing to go over objects with their tongues, and lapsing into apathy and despair.

On the other hand, many newly sighted people speak well of the world, and teach us how dull our own vision is. To one patient, a human hand, unrecognized, is "something bright and then holes." Shown a bunch of grapes, a boy calls out, "It is dark, blue and shiny. . . . It isn't smooth, it has bumps and hollows." A little girl visits a garden. "She is greatly astonished, and can scarcely be persuaded to answer, stands speechless in front of the tree, which she only names on taking hold of it, and then as 'the tree with the lights in it.' " Another patient, a twenty-two-year-old girl, was dazzled by the world's brightness and kept her eyes shut for two weeks. When at the end of that time she opened her eyes again, she did not recognize any objects, but "the more she now directed her gaze upon everything about her, the more it could be seen how an expression of gratification and astonishment overspread her features; she repeatedly exclaimed: 'Oh God! How beautiful!' "

I saw color-patches for weeks after I read this wonderful book. It was summer; the peaches were ripe in the valley orchards. When I woke in the morning, color-patches wrapped round my eyes, intricately, leaving not one unfilled spot. All day long I walked among shifting color-patches that parted before me like the Red Sea and closed again in silence,[5] transfigured, wherever I looked back. Some patches swelled and loomed, while others vanished utterly, and dark marks flitted at random over the whole dazzling sweep. But I couldn't sustain the illusion of flatness. I've been around for too long. Form is condemned to an eternal danse macabre with meaning: I couldn't unpeach the peaches. Nor can I remember ever having seen without understanding; the color-patches of infancy are lost. My brain then must have been smooth as any

---

5. According to the Bible, the Red Sea parted for the Israelites and closed over the Egyptians pursuing them (Exodus 15).

balloon. I'm told I reached for the moon; many babies do. But the color-patches of infancy swelled as meaning filled them; they arrayed themselves in solemn ranks down distance which unrolled and stretched before me like a plain. The moon rocketed away. I live now in a world of shadows that shape and distance color, a world where space makes a kind of terrible sense. What Gnosticism[6] is this, and what physics? The fluttering patch I saw in my nursery window—silver and green and shape-shifting blue—is gone; a row of Lombardy poplars takes its place, mute, across the distant lawn. That humming oblong creature pale as light that stole along the walls of my room at night, stretching exhilaratingly around the corners, is gone, too, gone the night I ate of the bittersweet fruit, put two and two together and puckered forever my brain. Martin Buber[7] tells this tale: "Rabbi Mendel once boasted to his teacher Rabbi Elimelekh that evenings he saw the angel who rolls away the light before the darkness, and mornings the angel who rolls away the darkness before the light. 'Yes,' said Rabbi Elimelekh, 'in my youth I saw that too. Later on you don't see these things anymore.'"

Why didn't someone hand those newly sighted people paints and brushes from the start, when they still didn't know what anything was? Then maybe we all could see color-patches too, the world unraveled from reason, Eden before Adam gave names. The scales would drop from my eyes; I'd see trees like men walking; I'd run down the road against all orders, hallooing and leaping.

Seeing is of course very much a matter of verbalization. Unless I call my attention to what passes before my eyes, I simply won't see it. If Tinker Mountain erupted, I'd be likely to notice. But if I want to notice the lesser cataclysms of valley life, I have to maintain in my head a running description of the present. It's not that I'm observant; it's just that I talk too much. Otherwise, especially in a strange place, I'll never know what's happening. Like a blind man at the ball game, I need a radio.

When I see this way I analyze and pry. I hurl over logs and roll away stones; I study the bank a square foot at a time, probing and tilting my head. Some days when a mist covers the mountains, when the muskrats won't show and the microscope's mirror shatters, I want to climb up the blank blue dome as a man would storm the inside of a circus tent, wildly, dangling, and with a steel knife claw a rent in the top, peep, and, if I must, fall.

But there is another kind of seeing that involves a letting go. When I see this way I sway transfixed and emptied. The difference between the two ways of seeing is the difference between walking with and without a camera. When I walk with a camera I walk from shot to shot, reading the light on a calibrated meter. When I walk without a camera, my own shutter opens, and the moment's light prints on my own silver gut. When I see this second way I am above all an unscrupulous observer.

It was sunny one evening last summer at Tinker Creek; the sun was low in

30

6. Promise of secret knowledge of the divine.
7. Jewish religious philosopher (1878–1965).

the sky, upstream. I was sitting on the sycamore log bridge with the sunset at my back, watching the shiners the size of minnows who were feeding over the muddy sand in skittery schools. Again and again, one fish, then another, turned for a split second across the current and flash! the sun shot out from its silver side. I couldn't watch for it. It was always just happening somewhere else, and it drew my vision just as it disappeared: flash! like a sudden dazzle of the thinnest blade, a sparking over a dun and olive ground at chance intervals from every direction. Then I noticed white specks, some sort of pale petals, small, floating from under my feet on the creek's surface, very slow and steady. So I blurred my eyes and gazed toward the brim of my hat and saw a new world. I saw the pale white circles roll up, roll up, like the world's turning, mute and perfect, and I saw the linear flashes, gleaming silver, like stars being born at random down a rolling scroll of time. Something broke and something opened. I filled up like a new wineskin. I breathed an air like light; I saw a light like water. I was the lip of a fountain the creek filled forever; I was ether, the leaf in the zephyr; I was flesh-flake, feather, bone.

When I see this way I see truly. As Thoreau[8] says, I return to my senses. I am the man who watches the baseball game in silence in an empty stadium. I see the game purely; I'm abstracted and dazed. When it's all over and the white-suited players lope off the green field to their shadowed dugouts, I leap to my feet, I cheer and cheer.

But I can't go out and try to see this way. I'll fail, I'll go mad. All I can do is try to gag the commentator, to hush the noise of useless interior babble that keeps me from seeing just as surely as a newspaper dangled before my eyes. The effort is really a discipline requiring a lifetime of dedicated struggle; it marks the literature of saints and monks of every order east and west, under every rule and no rule, discalced[9] and shod. The world's spiritual geniuses seem to discover universally that the mind's muddy river, this ceaseless flow of trivia and trash, cannot be dammed, and that trying to dam it is a waste of effort that might lead to madness. Instead you must allow the muddy river to flow unheeded in the dim channels of consciousness; you raise your sights; you look along it, mildly, acknowledging its presence without interest and gazing beyond it into the realm of the real where subjects and objects act and rest purely, without utterance. "Launch into the deep," says Jacques Ellul,[10] "and you shall see."

35   The secret of seeing, then, is the pearl of great price. If I thought he could teach me to find it and keep it forever I would stagger barefoot across a hundred deserts after any lunatic at all. But although the pearl may be found, it may not be sought. The literature of illumination reveals this above all: although it comes to those who wait for it, it is always, even to the most practiced and adept, a gift and a total surprise. I return from one walk knowing

8. Henry David Thoreau (1817–1862), American writer; see "Where I Lived, and What I Lived For" (p. 688).
9. Shoeless, as the order of the Discalced Carmelites.
10. French Protestant theologian and critic of technology (1912–1994).

where the killdeer nests in the field by the creek and the hour the laurel blooms. I return from the same walk a day later scarcely knowing my own name. Litanies hum in my ears; my tongue flaps in my mouth, *Alim non,* alleluia![11] I cannot cause light; the most I can do is try to put myself in the path of its beam. It is possible, in deep space, to sail on solar wind. Light, be it particle or wave, has force: you rig a giant sail and go. The secret of seeing is to sail on solar wind. Hone and spread your spirit till you yourself are a sail, whetted, translucent, broadside to the merest puff.

When her doctor took her bandages off and led her into the garden, the girl who was no longer blind saw "the tree with the lights in it." It was for this tree I searched through the peach orchards of summer, in the forests of fall and down winter and spring for years. Then one day I was walking along Tinker Creek thinking of nothing at all and I saw the tree with the lights in it. I saw the backyard cedar where the mourning doves roost charged and transfigured, each cell buzzing with flame. I stood on the grass with the lights in it, grass that was wholly fire, utterly focused and utterly dreamed. It was less like seeing than like being for the first time seen, knocked breathless by a powerful glance. The flood of fire abated, but I'm still spending the power. Gradually the lights went out in the cedar, the colors died, the cells unflamed and disappeared. I was still ringing. I had been my whole life a bell, and never knew it until at that moment I was lifted and struck. I have since only very rarely seen the tree with the lights in it. The vision comes and goes, mostly goes, but I live for it, for the moment when the mountains open and a new light roars in spate through the crack, and the mountains slam.

11. To paraphrase, "A Muslim learned man no, praise ye Jehovah!"

QUESTIONS

1. Dillard works by accumulation: she heaps up examples. Sometimes, not always, they are accompanied by a terse, apothegmatic general statement, such as "nature is very much a now-you-see-it, now-you-don't affair" (paragraph 3). Locate other examples of these accumulations; mark the general statements that accompany them. What uses do these accumulations serve? In what kinds of writing are they appropriate, in what kinds inappropriate?

2. How does the kind of seeing Dillard describes at the end of her essay differ from the kind of seeing she describes at the beginning? How does the material that appears in the sections on sight help her describe insight?

3. Take one of Dillard's terse, apothegmatic general statements and write your own accumulation of examples for it.

4. Dillard says, "I see what I expect" (paragraph 8). Write a description of something familiar, paying attention to how you "edit" your seeing. Then write a parallel description of it as if you were seeing it "unedited," as Dillard tries to see "color-patches" like the newly sighted do (paragraph 27).

The Allegory of the Cave

ND NOW, I said, let me show in a figure how far our nature is enlightened or unenlightened: Behold! human beings living in an underground den, which has a mouth open toward the light and reaching all along the den; here they have been from their childhood, and have their legs and necks chained so that they cannot move, and can only see before them, being prevented by the chains from turning round their heads. Above and behind them a fire is blazing at a distance, and between the fire and the prisoners there is a raised way; and you will see, if you look, a low wall built along the way, like the screen which marionette players have in front of them, over which they show the puppets.

I see.

And do you see, I said, men passing along the wall carrying all sorts of vessels, and statues and figures of animals made of wood and stone and various materials, which appear over the wall? Some of them are talking, others silent.

You have shown me a strange image, and they are strange prisoners.

Like ourselves, I replied; and they see only their own shadows, or the shadows of one another, which the fire throws on the opposite wall of the cave?

True, he said; how could they see anything but the shadows if they were never allowed to move their heads?

And of the objects which are being carried in like manner they would only see the shadows?

Yes, he said.

And if they were able to converse with one another, would they not suppose that they were naming what was actually before them?

Very true.

And suppose further that the prison had an echo which came from the other side, would they not be sure to fancy when one of the passers-by spoke that the voice which they heard came from the passing shadow?

No question, he replied.

To them, I said, the truth would be literally nothing but the shadows of the images.

That is certain.

And now look again, and see what will naturally follow if the prisoners are released and disabused of their error. At first, when any of them is liberated and compelled suddenly to stand up and turn his neck round and walk and look toward the light, he will suffer sharp pains; the glare will distress him and he will be unable to see the realities of which in his former state he had seen the shadows; and then conceive some one saying to him, that what he saw be-

From the Republic, *a dialogue in ten books written by Plato in the early years of his Academy, a school he founded (c. 380 B.C.E.) to give a philosophical education to men embarking on political careers. In this section Socrates questions Glaucon, a student.*

fore was an illusion, but that now, when he is approaching nearer to being and his eye is turned toward more real existence, he has a clearer vision—what will be his reply? And you may further imagine that his instructor is pointing to the objects as they pass and requiring him to name them—will he not be perplexed? Will he not fancy that the shadows which he formerly saw are truer than the objects which are now shown to him?

Far truer.

And if he is compelled to look straight at the light, will he not have a pain in his eyes which will make him turn away to take refuge in the objects of vision which he can see, and which he will conceive to be in reality clearer than the things which are now being shown to him?

True, he said.

And suppose once more, that he is reluctantly dragged up a steep and rugged ascent, and held fast until he is forced into the presence of the sun himself, is he not likely to be pained and irritated? When he approaches the light his eyes will be dazzled and he will not be able to see anything at all of what are now called realities.

Not all in a moment, he said. 20

He will require to grow accustomed to the sight of the upper world. And first he will see the shadows best, next the reflections of men and other objects in the water, and then the objects themselves; then he will gaze upon the light of the moon and the stars and the spangled heaven; and he will see the sky and the stars by night better than the sun or the light of the sun by day?

Certainly.

Last of all he will be able to see the sun, and not mere reflections of him in the water, but he will see him in his own proper place, and not in another; and he will contemplate him as he is.

Certainly.

He will then proceed to argue that this is he who gives the season and the 25 years, and is the guardian of all that is in the visible world, and in a certain way the cause of all things which he and his fellows have been accustomed to behold?

Clearly, he said, he would first see the sun and then reason about him.

And when he remembered his old habitation, and the wisdom of the den and his fellow-prisoners, do you not suppose that he would felicitate himself on the change, and pity them?

Certainly, he would.

And if they were in the habit of conferring honors among themselves on those who were quickest to observe the passing shadows and to remark which of them went before, and which followed after, and which were together; and who were therefore best able to draw conclusions as to the future, do you think that he would care for such honors and glories, or envy the possessors of them? Would he not say with Homer,

Better to be the poor servant of a poor master,

and to endure anything, rather than think as they do and live after their manner?

30   Yes, he said, I think that he would rather suffer anything than entertain these false notions and live in this miserable manner.

Imagine once more, I said, such an one coming suddenly out of the sun to be replaced in his old situation; would he not be certain to have his eyes full of darkness?

To be sure, he said.

And if there were a contest, and he had to compete in measuring the shadows with the prisoners who had never moved out of the den, while his sight was still weak, and before his eyes had become steady (and the time which would be needed to acquire this new habit of sight might be very considerable) would he not be ridiculous? Men would say of him that up he went and down he came without his eyes; and that it was better not even to think of ascending; and if any one tried to loose another and lead him up to the light, let them only catch the offender, and they would put him to death.

No question, he said.

35   This entire allegory, I said, you may now append, dear Glaucon, to the previous argument; the prison-house is the world of sight, the light of the fire is the sun, and you will not misapprehend me if you interpret the journey upwards to be the ascent of the soul into the intellectual world according to my poor belief, which, at your desire, I have expressed—whether rightly or wrongly God knows. But, whether true or false, my opinion is that in the world of knowledge the idea of good appears last of all, and is seen only with an effort; and, when seen, is also inferred to be the universal author of all things beautiful and right, parent of light and of the lord of light in this visible world, and the immediate source of reason and truth in the intellectual; and that this is the power upon which he who would act rationally either in public or private life must have his eye fixed.

I agree, he said, as far as I am able to understand you.

Moreover, I said, you must not wonder that those who attain to this beatific vision are unwilling to descend to human affairs; for their souls are ever hastening into the upper world where they desire to dwell; which desire of theirs is very natural, if our allegory may be trusted.

Yes, very natural.

And is there anything surprising in one who passes from divine contemplations to the evil state of man, misbehaving himself in a ridiculous manner; if, while his eyes are blinking and before he has become accustomed to the surrounding darkness, he is compelled to fight in courts of law, or in other places, about the images or the shadows of images of justice, and is endeavoring to meet the conceptions of those who have never yet seen absolute justice?

40   Anything but surprising, he replied.

Any one who has common sense will remember that the bewilderments of the eyes are of two kinds, and arise from two causes, either from coming out of the light or from going into the light, which is true of the mind's eye, quite as much as of the bodily eye; and he who remembers this when he sees any one whose vision is perplexed and weak, will not be too ready to laugh; he will first ask whether that soul of man has come out of the brighter life, and is unable to see because unaccustomed to the dark, or having turned from darkness to the day is dazzled by excess of light. And he will count the one happy in his condition and state of being, and he will pity the other; or, if he have a mind to laugh at the soul which comes from below into the light, there will be more reason in this than in the laugh which greets him who returns from above out of the light into the den.

That, he said, is a very just distinction.

QUESTIONS

1. Socrates's dialogue with Glaucon uses an allegory—a form of narrative in which persons, objects, ad actions are equated with meanings outside the narrative itself. How do you interpret the key elements of the allegory—the underground den, the fire, the shadows?

2. Write your own version of a moral that might be deduced from Plato's narrative. Is it possible to deduce more than one? Why? What about Plato's allegory makes it difficult to sum up in a single sentence?

3. Write a personal essay in which you use your personal experience to demonstrate the truth of Plato's "Allegory of the Cave."

JESUS *Parables of the Kingdom*

THE TEN VIRGINS

THEN SHALL the kingdom of heaven be likened unto ten virgins, which took their lamps, and went forth to meet the bridegroom.

And five of them were wise, and five were foolish.

They that were foolish took their lamps, and took no oil with them:

But the wise took oil in their vessels with their lamps.

While the bridegroom tarried, they all slumbered and slept.

And at midnight there was a cry made, Behold, the bridegroom cometh; go ye out to meet him.

Then all those virgins arose, and trimmed their lamps.

And the foolish said unto the wise, Give us of your oil; for our lamps are gone out.

5

From Jesus' teachings, as written in Matthew 25 and Luke 15, King James Bible (1611).

But the wise answered, saying Not so; lest there be not enough for us and you: but go ye rather to them that sell, and buy for yourselves.

10   And while they went to buy, the bridegroom came; and they that were ready went in with him to the marriage: and the door was shut.

Afterward came also the other virgins, saying, Lord, Lord, open to us.

But he answered and said, Verily I say unto you, I know you not.

Watch therefore, for ye know neither the day nor the hour wherein the Son of man cometh.

THE TEN TALENTS

For the kingdom of heaven is as a man travelling into a far country, who called his own servants, and delivered unto them his goods.

And unto one he gave five talents,[1] to another two, and to another one; to every man according to his several ability; and straightway took his journey.

Then he that had received the five talents went and traded with the same, and made them other five talents.

And likewise he that had received two, he also gained other two.

5   But he that had received one went and digged in the earth, and hid his lord's money.

After a long time the lord of those servants cometh, and reckoneth with them.

And so he that had received five talents came and brought other five talents, saying, Lord, thou deliveredst unto me five talents: behold, I have gained beside them five talents more.

His lord said unto him, Well done, thou good and faithful servant: thou hast been faithful over a few things, I will make thee ruler over many things: enter thou into the joy of thy lord.

He also that had received two talents came and said, Lord, thou deliverdst unto me two talents: behold, I have gained two other talents beside them.

10   His lord said unto him, Well done, good and faithful servant; thou hast been faithful over a few things, I will make thee ruler over many things: enter thou into the joy of thy lord.

Then he which had received the one talent came and said, Lord, I knew thee that thou art an hard man, reaping where thou hast not sown, and gathering where thou hast not strawed:

And I was afraid, and went and hid thy talent in the earth: lo, there thou hast that is thine.

His lord answered and said unto him, Thou wicked and slothful servant, thou knewest that I reap where I sowed not, and gather where I have not strawed:

Thou oughtest therefore to have put my money to the exchanges, and then at my coming I should have received mine own with usury.

15   Take therefore the talent from him, and give it unto him which hath ten talents.

1. A talent was a Middle Eastern coin.

For unto every one that hath shall be given, and he shall have abundance: but from him that hath not shall be taken away even that which he hath.

And cast ye the unprofitable servant into outer darkness: there shall be weeping and gnashing of teeth.

When the Son of man shall come in his glory, and all the holy angels with him, then shall he sit upon the throne of his glory:

And before him shall be gathered all nations: and he shall separate them one from another, as a shepherd divideth his sheep from the goats:

And he shall set the sheep on his right hand, but the goats on the left.   20

Then shall the King say unto them on his right hand, Come, ye blessed of my Father, inherit the kingdom prepared for you from the foundation of the world:

For I was an hungred, and ye gave me meat: I was thirsty, and ye gave me drink: I was a stranger, and ye took me in:

Naked, and ye clothed me: I was sick, and ye visited me: I was in prison, and ye came unto me.

Then shall the righteous answer him, saying, Lord, when saw we thee an hungred, and fed thee? or thirsty, and gave thee drink?

When saw we thee a stranger, and took thee in? or naked, and clothed thee?   25

Or when saw we thee sick, or in prison, and came unto thee?

And the King shall answer and say unto them, Verily I say unto you, Inasmuch as ye have done it unto one of the least of these my brethren, ye have done it unto me.

Then shall he say also unto them on the left hand, Depart from me, ye cursed, into everlasting fire, prepared for the devil and his angels:

For I was an hungred, and ye gave me no meat: I was thirsty, and ye gave me no drink.

I was a stranger, and ye took me not in: naked, and ye clothed me not: 30
sick, and in prison, and ye visited me not.

Then shall they also answer him, saying, Lord, when saw we thee an hungred, or athirst, or a stranger, or naked, or sick, or in prison, and did not minister unto thee?

Then shall he answer them, saying, Verily I say unto you, Inasmuch as ye did it not to one of the least of these, ye did it not to me.

And these shall go away into everlasting punishment: but the righteous into life eternal.

THE PRODIGAL SON

And he said, A certain man had two sons;

And the younger of them said to his father, Father, give me the portion of goods that falleth to me. And he divided unto them his living.

And not many days after that, the younger son gathered all together, and took his journey into a far country, and there wasted his substance with riotous living.

And when he had spent all, there arose a mighty famine in that land; and he began to be in want.

5   And he went and joined himself to a citizen of that country; and he sent him into his fields to feed swine.

    And he would fain have filled his belly with the husks that the swine did eat; and no man gave unto him.

    And when he came to himself, he said, How many of my father's hired servants have bread enough and to spare, and I perish with hunger!

    I will arise and go to my father, and will say unto him, Father, I have sinned against heaven, and before thee,

    And am no more worthy to be called thy son; make me as one of thy hired servants.

10   And he arose, and came to his father. But when he was yet a great way off, his father saw him, and had compassion, and ran, and fell on his neck, and kissed him.

    And the son said unto him, Father, I have sinned against heaven, and in thy sight, and am no more worthy to be called thy son.

    But the father said to his servants, Bring forth the best robe, and put it on him; and put a ring on his hand, and shoes on his feet.

    And bring the fatted calf, and kill it; and let us eat, and be merry.

    For this, my son, was dead, and is alive again; he was lost, and is found. And they began to be merry.

15   Now his elder son was in the field; and as he came and drew nigh to the house, he heard music and dancing.

    And he called one of the servants, and asked what these things meant.

    And he said unto him, Thy brother is come; and thy father hath killed the fatted calf, because he hath received him safe and sound.

    And he was angry, and would not go in; therefore came his father out, and entreated him.

    And he, answering, said to his father, Lo, these many years do I serve thee, neither transgressed I at any time thy commandment; and yet thou never gavest me a kid, that I might make merry with my friends.

20   But as soon as this, thy son, was come, who hath devoured thy living with harlots, thou hast killed for him the fatted calf.

    And he said unto him, Son, thou art ever with me, and all that I have is thine.

    It was meet that we should make merry, and be glad; for this, thy brother, was dead, and is alive again; and was lost, and is found.

QUESTIONS

1. Parables are allegorical stories meant to teach a principle or moral lesson. What is the lesson of each of these parables? In a small group or as a class, discuss your interpretation of one of these parables and see whether it differs from your classmates' interpretations.

2. After you determine the meaning of individual parables, consider whether the lesson in one parable might conflict with the lesson in another. Also determine whether the

lessons in different parables reinforce each other. What is the relationship between these parables?

3. Consider the formal qualities of the "Parables of the Kingdom" (the narrative structure, the use of repetition, the ordinary characters, and so on). Using a similar form, write a parable that illustrates a principle important to you.

Zen Parables

MUDDY ROAD

TANZAN AND EKIDO were once traveling together down a muddy road. A heavy rain was still falling.

Coming around a bend, they met a lovely girl in a silk kimono and sash, unable to cross the intersection.

"Come on, girl," said Tanzan at once. Lifting her in his arms, he carried her over the mud.

Ekido did not speak again until that night when they reached a lodging temple. Then he no longer could restrain himself. "We monks don't go near females," he told Tanzan, "especially not young and lovely ones. It is dangerous. Why did you do that?"

"I left the girl there," said Tanzan. "Are you still carrying her?"   5

A PARABLE

Buddha told a parable in a sutra:

A man traveling across a field encountered a tiger. He fled, the tiger after him. Coming to a precipice, he caught hold of the root of a wild vine and swung himself down over the edge. The tiger sniffed at him from above. Trembling, the man looked down to where, far below, another tiger was waiting to eat him. Only the vine sustained him.

Two mice, one white and one black, little by little started to gnaw away the vine. The man saw a luscious strawberry near him. Grasping the vine with one hand, he plucked the strawberry with the other. How sweet it tasted!

LEARNING TO BE SILENT

The pupils of the Tendai school used to study meditation before Zen entered Japan. Four of them who were intimate friends promised one another to observe seven days of silence.

On the first day all were silent. Their meditation had begun auspiciously, but when night came and the oil lamps were growing dim one of the pupils could not help exclaiming to a servant: "Fix those lamps."

Zen Buddhists use parables, called koans, *as a means to enlightenment. These translations come from* Zen Flesh, Zen Bones *(1957).*

The second pupil was surprised to hear the first one talk. "We are not supposed to say a word," he remarked.

"You two are stupid. Why did you talk?" asked the third.

5   "I am the only one who has not talked," concluded the fourth pupil.

QUESTIONS

1. Do some research on basic philosophical and ethical tenets of Zen Buddhism.
Which of those tenets are illustrated by these parables?

2. The Zen parables included here are very short. How does length influence message?
What are the benefits and potential problems of short pieces meant to teach a lesson?

3. With which principle illustrated by these Zen parables do you most agree or disagree? Write a position paper in which you explain why you agree or disagree with the
principle illustrated. Be sure to provide specific reasons to support your position.

GILBERT HIGHET   *The Mystery of Zen*

HE MIND NEED never stop growing. Indeed, one of
the few experiences which never pall is the experience of watching one's own mind, and observing how
it produces new interests, responds to new stimuli, and
develops new thoughts, apparently without effort
and almost independently of one's own conscious
control. I have seen this happen to myself a hundred times; and every time it
happens again, I am equally fascinated and astonished.

Some years ago a publisher sent me a little book for review. I read it, and
decided it was too remote from my main interests and too highly specialized. It
was a brief account of how a young German philosopher living in Japan had
learned how to shoot with a bow and arrow, and how this training had made it
possible for him to understand the esoteric doctrines of the Zen sect of Buddhism. Really, what could be more alien to my own life, and to that of everyone I knew, than Zen Buddhism and Japanese archery? So I thought, and put
the book away.

Yet I did not forget it. It was well written, and translated into good English. It was delightfully short, and implied much more than it said. Although
its theme was extremely odd, it was at least highly individual; I had never read
anything like it before or since. It remained in my mind. Its name was *Zen in
the Art of Archery*, its author Eugen Herrigel, its publisher Pantheon of New

From Talents and Geniuses: The Pleasures of Appreciation (1975), *a collection of essays
on literature, philosophy, and the arts. Many of the essays originated in Tuesday evening
broadcasts that Highet gave on the radio station WQXR in New York City, often about
books that he was reading or writing.*

York. One day I took it off the shelf and read it again; this time it seemed even stranger than before and even more unforgettable. Now it began to cohere with other interests of mine. Something I had read of the Japanese art of flower arrangement seemed to connect with it; and then, when I wrote an essay on the peculiar Japanese poems called *haiku,* other links began to grow. Finally I had to read the book once more with care, and to go through some other works which illuminated the same subject. I am still grappling with the theme; I have not got anywhere near understanding it fully; but I have learned a good deal, and I am grateful to the little book which refused to be forgotten.

The author, a German philosopher, got a job teaching philosophy at the University of Tokyo (apparently between the wars), and he did what Germans in foreign countries do not usually do: he determined to adapt himself and to learn from his hosts. In particular, he had always been interested in mysticism— which, for every earnest philosopher, poses a problem that is all the more inescapable because it is virtually insoluble. Zen Buddhism is not the only mystical doctrine to be found in the East, but it is one of the most highly developed and certainly one of the most difficult to approach. Herrigel knew that there were scarcely any books which did more than skirt the edge of the subject, and that the best of all books on Zen (those by the philosopher D. T. Suzuki) constantly emphasize that Zen can never be learned from books, can never be studied as we can study other disciplines such as logic or mathematics. Therefore he began to look for a Japanese thinker who could teach him directly.

At once he met with embarrassed refusals. His Japanese friends explained   5
that he would gain nothing from trying to discuss Zen as a philosopher, that its theories could not be spread out for analysis by a detached mind, and in fact that the normal relationship of teacher and pupil simply did not exist within the sect, because the Zen masters felt it useless to explain things stage by stage and to argue about the various possible interpretations of their doctrine. Herrigel had read enough to be prepared for this. He replied that he did not want to dissect the teachings of the school, because he knew that would be useless. He wanted to become a Zen mystic himself. (This was highly intelligent of him. No one could really penetrate into Christian mysticism without being a devout Christian; no one could appreciate Hindu mystical doctrine without accepting the Hindu view of the universe.) At this, Herrigel's Japanese friends were more forthcoming. They told him that the best way, indeed the only way, for a European to approach Zen mysticism was to learn one of the arts which exemplified it. He was a fairly good rifle shot, so he determined to learn archery; and his wife co-operated with him by taking lessons in painting and flower arrangement. How any philosopher could investigate a mystical doctrine by learning to shoot with a bow and arrow and watching his wife arrange flowers, Herrigel did not ask. He had good sense.

A Zen master who was a teacher of archery agreed to take him as a pupil. The lessons lasted six years, during which he practiced every single day. There are many difficult courses of instruction in the world: the Jesuits, violin virtuosi, Talmudic scholars, all have long and hard training, which in one sense never comes to an end; but Herrigel's training in archery equaled them all in intensity. If I were trying to learn archery, I should expect to begin by looking at a target and shooting arrows at it. He was not even allowed to aim at a target for the first four years. He had to begin by learning how to hold the bow and arrow, and then how to release the arrow; this took ages. The Japanese bow is not like our sporting bow, and the stance of the archer in Japan is different from ours. We hold the bow at shoulder level, stretch our left arm out ahead, pull the string and the nocked arrow to a point either below the chin or sometimes past the right ear, and then shoot. The Japanese hold the bow above the head, and then pull the hands apart to left and right until the left hand comes down to eye level and the right hand comes to rest above the right shoulder; then there is a pause, during which the bow is held at full stretch, with the tip of the three-foot arrow projecting only a few inches beyond the bow; after that, the arrow is loosed. When Herrigel tried this, even without aiming, he found it was almost impossible. His hands trembled. His legs stiffened and grew cramped. His breathing became labored. And of course he could not possibly aim. Week after week he practiced this, with the Master watching him carefully and correcting his strained attitude; week after week he made no progress whatever. Finally he gave up and told his teacher that he could not learn: it was absolutely impossible for him to draw the bow and loose the arrow.

To his astonishment, the Master agreed. He said, "Certainly you cannot. It is because you are not breathing correctly. You must learn to breathe in a steady rhythm, keeping your lungs full most of the time, and drawing in one rapid inspiration with each stage of the process, as you grasp the bow, fit the arrow, raise the bow, draw, pause, and loose the shot. If you do, you will both grow stronger and be able to relax." To prove this, he himself drew his massive bow and told his pupil to feel the muscles of his arms: they were perfectly relaxed, as though he were doing no work whatever.

Herrigel now started breathing exercises; after some time he combined the new rhythm of breathing with the actions of drawing and shooting; and, much to his astonishment, he found that the whole thing, after this complicated process, had become much easier. Or rather, not easier, but different. At times it became quite unconscious. He says himself that he felt he was not breathing, but being breathed; and in time he felt that the occasional shot was not being dispatched by him, but shooting itself. The bow and arrow were in charge; he had become merely a part of them.

All this time, of course, Herrigel did not even attempt to discuss Zen doctrine with his Master. No doubt he knew that he was approaching it, but he concentrated solely on learning how to shoot. Every stage which he surmounted appeared to lead to another stage even more difficult. It took him months to learn how to loosen the bowstring. The problem was this. If he gripped the string and arrowhead tightly, either he froze, so that his hands were slowly pulled together and the shot was wasted, or else he jerked, so that the arrow flew up into the air or down into the ground; and if he was relaxed, then the bowstring and arrow simply *leaked* out of his grasp before he could reach full stretch, and the arrow went nowhere. He explained this problem to the Master. The Master understood perfectly well. He replied, "You must hold the drawn bowstring like a child holding a grownup's finger. You know how firmly a child grips; and yet when it lets go, there is not the slightest jerk—because the child does not think of itself, it is not self-conscious, it does not say, 'I will now let go and do something else,' it merely acts instinctively. That is what you must learn to do. Practice, practice, and practice, and then the string will loose itself at the right moment. The shot will come as effortlessly as snow slipping from a leaf." Day after day, week after week, month after month, Herrigel practiced this; and then, after one shot, the Master suddenly bowed and broke off the lesson. He said "Just then it shot. Not you, but *it.*" And gradually thereafter more and more right shots achieved themselves; the young philosopher forgot himself, forgot that he was learning archery for some other purpose, forgot even that he was practicing archery, and became part of that unconsciously active complex, the bow, the string, the arrow, and the man.

Next came the target. After four years, Herrigel was allowed to shoot at   10
the target. But he was strictly forbidden to aim at it. The Master explained that even he himself did not aim; and indeed, when he shot, he was so absorbed in the act, so selfless and unanxious, that his eyes were almost closed. It was difficult, almost impossible, for Herrigel to believe that such shooting could ever be effective; and he risked insulting the Master by suggesting that he ought to be able to hit the target blindfolded. But the Master accepted the challenge. That night, after a cup of tea and long meditation, he went into the archery hall, put on the lights at one end and left the target perfectly dark, with only a thin taper burning in front of it. Then, with habitual grace and precision, and with that strange, almost sleepwalking, selfless confidence that is the heart of Zen, he shot two arrows into the darkness. Herrigel went out to collect them. He found that the first had gone to the heart of the bull's eye, and that the second had actually hit the first arrow and splintered it. The Master showed no pride. He said, "Perhaps, with unconscious memory of the position of the target, *I* shot the first arrow; but the second arrow? *It* shot the second arrow, and *it* brought it to the center of the target."

At last Herrigel began to understand. His progress became faster and faster; easier, too. Perfect shots (perfect because perfectly unconscious) occurred at almost every lesson; and finally, after six years of incessant training, in a public display he was awarded the diploma. He needed no further instruction: he had himself become a Master. His wife meanwhile had become expert both in painting and in the arrangement of flowers—two of the finest of Japanese arts. (I wish she could be persuaded to write a companion volume, called *Zen in the Art of Flower Arrangement;* it would have a wider general appeal than her husband's work.) I gather also from a hint or two in his book that she had taken part in the archery lessons. During one of the most difficult periods in Herrigel's training, when his Master had practically refused to continue teaching him—because Herrigel had tried to cheat by *consciously* opening his hand at the moment of loosing the arrow—his wife had advised him against that solution, and sympathized with him when it was rejected. She in her own way had learned more quickly than he, and reached the final point together with him. All their effort had not been in vain: Herrigel and his wife had really acquired a new and valuable kind of wisdom. Only at this point, when he was about to abandon his lessons forever, did his

Master treat him almost as an equal and hint at the innermost doctrines of Zen Buddhism. Only hints he gave; and yet, for the young philosopher who had now become a mystic, they were enough. Herrigel understood the doctrine, not with his logical mind, but with his entire being. He at any rate had solved the mystery of Zen.

Without going through a course of training as absorbing and as complete as Herrigel's, we can probably never penetrate the mystery. The doctrine of Zen cannot be analyzed from without: it must be lived.

But although it cannot be analyzed, it can be hinted at. All the hints that the adherents of this creed give us are interesting. Many are fantastic; some are practically incomprehensible, and yet unforgettable. Put together, they take us toward a way of life which is utterly impossible for westerners living in a western world, and nevertheless has a deep fascination and contains some values which we must respect.

The word Zen means "meditation." (It is the Japanese word, correspond-ing to the Chinese Ch'an and the Hindu Dhyana.) It is the central idea of a special sect of Buddhism which flourished in China during the Sung period (between A.D. 1000 and 1300) and entered Japan in the twelfth century. Without knowing much about it, we might be certain that the Zen sect was a worthy and noble one, because it produced a quantity of highly distinguished art, specifically painting. And if we knew anything about Buddhism itself, we might say that Zen goes closer than other sects to the heart of Buddha's teaching: because Buddha was trying to found, not a religion with temples and rituals, but a way of life based on meditation. However, there is something eccentric about the Zen life which is hard to trace in Buddha's teaching; there is an active energy which he did not admire, there is a rough grasp on reality which he himself eschewed, there is something like a sense of humor, which he rarely displayed. The gravity and serenity of the Indian preacher are transformed, in Zen, to the earthy liveliness of Chinese and Japanese sages. The lotus brooding calmly on the water has turned into a knotted tree covered with spring blossoms.

15   In this sense, "meditation" does not mean what we usually think of when we say a philosopher meditates: analysis of reality, a long-sustained effort to solve problems of religion and ethics, the logical dissection of the universe. It means something not divisive, but whole; not schematic, but organic; not long-drawn-out, but immediate. It means something more like our words "intuition" and "realization." It means a way of life in which there is no division between thought and action; none of the painful gulf, so well known to all of us, between the unconscious and the conscious mind; and no absolute distinction between the self and the external world, even between the various parts of the external world and the whole.

When the German philosopher took six years of lessons in archery in order to approach the mystical significance of Zen, he was not given direct philosophical instruction. He was merely shown how to breathe, how to hold and loose the bowstring, and finally how to shoot in such a way that the bow and arrow used him as an instrument. There are many such stories about Zen teachers. The strangest I know is one about a fencing master who undertook to train a young man in the art of the sword. The relationship of teacher and pupil is very important, almost sacred, in the Far East; and the pupil hardly ever thinks of leaving a master or objecting to his methods, however extraordinary they may seem. Therefore this young fellow did not at first object when he was made to act as a servant, drawing water, sweeping floors, gathering wood for the fire, and cooking. But after some time he asked for more direct instruction. The master agreed to give it, but produced no swords. The routine went on just as before, except that every now and then the master would strike the young man with a stick. No matter what he was doing, sweeping the floor or weeding in the garden, a blow would descend on him apparently out of nowhere; he had always to be on the alert, and yet he was constantly receiving unexpected cracks on the head or shoulders. After some months of this, he saw his master stooping over a boiling pot full of vegetables; and he thought he would have his revenge. Silently he lifted a stick and brought it down; but without any effort, without even a glance in his direction, his master parried the blow with the lid of the cooking pot. At last, the pupil began to understand the instinctive alertness, the effortless perception and avoidance of danger, in which his master had been training him. As soon as he had achieved it, it was child's play for him to learn the management of the sword: he could parry every cut and turn every slash without anxiety, until his opponent, exhausted, left an opening for his counterattack. (The same principle was used by the elderly samurai for selecting his comrades in the Japanese motion picture *The Magnificent Seven*.[1])

These stories show that Zen meditation does not mean sitting and thinking. On the contrary, it means acting with as little thought as possible. The fencing master trained his pupil to guard against every attack with the same immediate, instinctive rapidity with which our eyelid closes over our eye when something threatens it. His work was aimed at breaking down the wall between thought and act, at completely fusing body and senses and mind so that they might all work together rapidly and effortlessly. When a Zen artist draws a picture, he does it in a rhythm almost the exact reverse of that which is followed by a Western artist. We begin by blocking out the design and then filling in the details, usually working more and more slowly as we approach the completion of the picture. The Zen artist sits down very calmly; examines his brush carefully; prepares his own ink; smooths out the paper on which he will work; falls into a profound silent ecstasy of contemplation—during which he does not think anxiously of various details, composition, brushwork, shades of tone, but rather attempts to become the vehicle through which the subject can express itself in painting; and then, very quickly and almost unconsciously, with sure effortless strokes, draws a picture containing the fewest and most effective lines. Most of the paper is left blank; only the essential is depicted, and that not completely. One long curving line will be enough to show a mountainside; seven streaks will become a group of bamboos bending in the wind; and yet, though technically incomplete, such pictures are unforgettably clear. They show the heart of reality.

All this we can sympathize with, because we can see the results. The

---

1. *The Seven Samurai* (1956), directed by Akira Kurosawa (1910–1998), is the Japanese film; *The Magnificent Seven* (1960) is an American remake of it as a Western.

young swordsman learns how to fence. The intuitional painter produces a fine picture. But the hardest thing for us to appreciate is that the Zen masters refuse to teach philosophy or religion directly, and deny logic. In fact, they despise logic as an artificial distortion of reality. Many philosophical teachers are difficult to understand because they analyze profound problems with subtle intricacy: such is Aristotle in his *Metaphysics*.[2] Many mystical writers are difficult to understand because, as they themselves admit, they are attempting to use words to describe experiences which are too abstruse for words, so that they have to fall back on imagery and analogy, which they themselves recognize to be poor media, far coarser than the realities with which they have been in contact. But the Zen teachers seem to deny the power of language and thought altogether. For example, if you ask a Zen master what is the ultimate reality, he will answer, without the slightest hesitation, "The bamboo grove at the foot of the hill" or "A branch of plum blossom." Apparently he means that these things, which we can see instantly without effort, or imagine in the flash of a second, are real with the ultimate reality; that nothing is more real than these; and that we ought to grasp ultimates as we grasp simple immediates. A Chinese master was once asked the central question, "What is the Buddha?" He said nothing whatever, but held out his index finger. What did he mean? It is hard to explain; but apparently he meant "Here. Now. Look and realize with the effortlessness of seeing. Do not try to use words. Do not think. Make no efforts toward withdrawal from the world. Expect no sublime ecstasies. Live. All *that* is the ultimate reality, and it can be understood from the motion of a finger as well as from the execution of any complex ritual, from any subtle argument, or from the circling of the starry universe."

In making that gesture, the master was copying the Buddha himself, who once delivered a sermon which is famous, but was hardly understood by his pupils at the time. Without saying a word, he held up a flower and showed it to the gathering. One man, one alone, knew what he meant. The gesture became renowned as the Flower Sermon.

20   In the annals of Zen there are many cryptic answers to the final question, "What is the Buddha?"—which in our terms means "What is the meaning of life? What is truly real?" For example, one master, when asked "What is the Buddha?" replied, "Your name is Yecho." Another said, "Even the finest artist cannot paint him." Another said, "No nonsense here." And another answered, "The mouth is the gate of woe." My favorite story is about the monk who said to a Master, "Has a dog Buddha-nature too?" The Master replied, "Wu"— which is what the dog himself would have said.

Now, some critics might attack Zen by saying that this is the creed of a savage or an animal. The adherents of Zen would deny that—or more probably they would ignore the criticism, or make some cryptic remark which meant that it was pointless. Their position—if they could ever be persuaded to put in into

---

2. The *Metaphysics* of Aristotle (384–322 B.C.E.) is a compilation of Aristotle's philosophical treatises and lecture notes put together by Andronicus of Rhodes and called by him *Metaphysica* because in his edition they came "after the physics."

words—would be this. An animal is instinctively in touch with reality, and so far is living rightly, but it has never had a mind and so cannot perceive the Whole, only that part with which it is in touch. The philosopher sees both the Whole and the parts, and enjoys them all. As for the savage, he exists only through the group; he feels himself as part of a war party or a ceremonial dance team or a ploughing-and-sowing group or the Snake clan; he is not truly an individual at all, and therefore is less than fully human. Zen has at its heart an inner solitude; its aim is to teach us to live, as in the last resort we do all have to live, alone.

A more dangerous criticism of Zen would be that it is nihilism, that its purpose is to abolish thought altogether. (This criticism is handled, but not fully met, by the great Zen authority Suzuki in his *Introduction to Zen Buddhism*.) It can hardly be completely confuted, for after all the central doctrine of Buddhism is—Nothingness. And many of the sayings of Zen masters are truly nihilistic. The first patriarch of the sect in China was asked by the emperor what was the ultimate and holiest principle of Buddhism. He replied, "Vast emptiness, and nothing holy in it." Another who was asked the searching question "Where is the abiding-place for the mind?" answered, "Not in this dualism of good and evil, being and non-being, thought and matter." In fact, thought is an activity which divides. It analyzes, it makes distinctions, it criticizes, it judges, it breaks reality into groups and classes and individuals. The aim of Zen is to abolish that kind of thinking, and to substitute—not unconsciousness, which would be death, but a consciousness that does not analyze but experiences life directly. Although it has no prescribed prayers, no sacred scriptures, no ceremonial rites, no personal god, and no interest in the soul's future destination, Zen is a religion rather than a philosophy. Jung[3] points out that its aim is to produce a religious conversion, a "transformation": and he adds, "The transformation process is incommensurable with intellect." Thought is always interesting, but often painful; Zen is calm and painless. Thought is incomplete; Zen enlightenment brings a sense of completeness. Thought is a process; Zen illumination is a state. But it is a state which cannot be defined. In the Buddhist scriptures there is a dialogue between a master and a pupil in which the pupil tries to discover the exact meaning of such a state. The master says to him, "If a fire were blazing in front of you, would you know that it was blazing?"

"Yes, master."

"And would you know the reason for its blazing?"

"Yes, because it had a supply of grass and sticks."

"And would you know if it were to go out?"

"Yes, master."

"And on its going out, would you know where the fire had gone? To the east, to the west, to the north, or to the south?"

"The question does not apply, master. For the fire blazed because it had a supply of grass and sticks. When it had consumed this and had no other fuel, then it went out."

25

---

3. Carl Gustav Jung (1875–1961), Swiss psychologist, one of Freud's early followers, who explored symbolism and the unconscious.

30   "In the same way," replies the master, "no question will apply to the meaning of Nirvana, and no statement will explain it."

        Such, then, neither happy nor unhappy but beyond all divisive descrip-
tion, is the condition which students of Zen strive to attain. Small wonder that
they can scarcely explain it to us, the unilluminated.

QUESTIONS

1. In his essay Highet depends heavily on Eugen Herrigel's *Zen in the Art of Archery*.
What does Highet himself bring to the essay? Mark passages in which he makes important contributions and summarize them.

2. "Zen teachers," Highet observes, "seem to deny the power of language and thought
altogether" (paragraph 18). How, then, does Highet manage to write about Zen?

3. Highet says Zen is "a religion rather than a philosophy" (paragraph 22). How has he
led up to this conclusion? What definitions of religion and philosophy does it imply?

4. In his essay Highet addresses criticism of Zen only at the end, while Jean-Paul
Sartre, in "Existentialism" below, defends existentialism as he explains it. Consider the
differences these two approaches make in the content, organization, and tone of the
two essays. What might Highet's essay be like if he defended Zen throughout, Sartre's if
he addressed criticism of existentialism only at the end?

5. Write an essay in which you describe learning to perform a physical action. Pay particular attention to what you learned through language, what through action.

JEAN-PAUL SARTRE *Existentialism*

MAN IS NOTHING ELSE but what he makes of himself.
Such is the first principle of existentialism. It is also
what is called subjectivity, the name we are labeled
with when charges are brought against us. But
what do we mean by this, if not that man has a
greater dignity than a stone or table? For we
mean that man first exists, that is, that man first of all is the being who hurls
himself toward a future and who is conscious of imagining himself as being in
the future. Man is at the start a plan which is aware of itself, rather than a
patch of moss, a piece of garbage, or a cauliflower; nothing exists prior to this
plan; there is nothing in heaven; man will be what he will have planned to be.
Not what he will want to be. Because by the word "will" we generally mean a

From Sartre's classic 1947 statement of his philosophy, L'existentialisme est un human-
isme *(translated variously as* Existentialism, Existentialism and Humanism, *or* Existentialism and Human Emotions*). The version printed here was translated by Bernard
Frechtman.*

conscious decision, which is subsequent to what we have already made of ourselves. I may want to belong to a political party, write a book, get married; but all that is only a manifestation of an earlier, more spontaneous choice that is called "will." But if existence really does precede essence, man is responsible for what he is. Thus, existentialism's first move is to make every man aware of what he is and to make the full responsibility of his existence rest on him. And when we say that a man is responsible for himself, we do not only mean that he is responsible for his own individuality, but that he is responsible for all men.

The word "subjectivism" has two meanings, and our opponents play on the two. Subjectivism means, on the one hand, that an individual chooses and makes himself; and, on the other, that it is impossible for man to transcend human subjectivity. The second of these is the essential meaning of existentialism. When we say that man chooses his own self, we mean that every one of us does likewise; but we also mean by that that in making this choice he also chooses all men. In fact, in creating the man that we want to be, there is not a single one of our acts which does not at the same time create an image of man as we think he ought to be. To choose to be this or that is to affirm at the same time the value of what we choose, because we can never choose evil. We always choose the good, and nothing can be good for us without being good for all.

If, on the other hand, existence precedes essence, and if we grant that we exist and fashion our image at one and the same time, the image is valid for everybody and for our whole age. Thus, our responsibility is much greater than we might have supposed, because it involves all mankind. If I am a workingman and choose to join a Christian trade union rather than be a Communist, and if by being a member, I want to show that the best thing for man is resignation, that the kingdom of man is not of this world, I am not only involving my own case—I want to be resigned for everyone. As a result, my action has involved all humanity. To take a more individual matter, if I want to marry, to have children, even if this marriage depends solely on my own circumstances or passion or wish, I am involving all humanity in monogamy and not merely myself. Therefore, I am responsible for myself and for everyone else. I am creating a certain image of man of my own choosing. In choosing myself, I choose man.

This helps us understand what the actual content is of such rather grandiloquent words as anguish, forlornness, despair. As you will see, it's all quite simple.

First, what is meant by anguish? The existentialists say at once that man is anguish. What that means is this: the man who involves himself and who realizes that he is not only the person he chooses to be, but also a lawmaker who is, at the same time, choosing all mankind as well as himself, cannot help escape the feeling of his total and deep responsibility. Of course, there are many people who are not anxious; but we claim that they are hiding their anxiety, that they are fleeing from it. Certainly, many people believe that when they do something, they themselves are the only ones involved, and when someone

5

says to them, "What if everyone acted that way?" they shrug their shoulders and answer, "Everyone doesn't act that way." But really, one should always ask himself, "What would happen if everybody looked at things that way?" There is no escaping this disturbing thought except by a kind of double-dealing. A man who lies and makes excuses for himself by saying "not everybody does that" is someone with an uneasy conscience, because the act of lying implies that a universal value is conferred upon the lie.

Anguish is evident even when it conceals itself. This is the anguish that Kierkegaard[1] called the anguish of Abraham. You know the story: an angel has ordered Abraham to sacrifice his son; if it really were an angel who has come and said, "You are Abraham, you shall sacrifice your son," everything would be all right. But everyone might first wonder, "Is it really an angel, and am I really Abraham? What proof do I have?"

There was a madwoman who had hallucinations; someone used to speak to her on the telephone and give her orders. Her doctor asked her, "Who is it who talks to you?" She answered, "He says it's God." What proof did she really have that it was God? If an angel comes to me, what proof is there that it's an angel? And if I hear voices, what proof is there that they come from heaven and not from hell, or from the subconscious, or a pathological condition? What proves that they are addressed to me? What proof is there that I have been appointed to impose my choice and my conception of man on humanity? I'll never find any proof or sign to convince me of that. If a voice addresses me, it is always for me to decide that this is the angel's voice; if I consider that such an act is a good one, it is I who will choose to say that it is good rather than bad.

Now, I'm not being singled out as an Abraham, and yet at every moment I'm obliged to perform exemplary acts. For every man, everything happens as if all mankind had its eyes fixed on him and were guiding itself by what he does. And every man ought to say to himself, "Am I really the kind of man who has the right to act in such a way that humanity might guide itself by my actions?" And if he does not say that to himself, he is masking his anguish.

There is no question here of the kind of anguish which would lead to quietism, to inaction. It is a matter of a simple sort of anguish that anybody who has had responsibilities is familiar with. For example, when a military officer takes the responsibility for an attack and sends a certain number of men to death, he chooses to do so, and in the main he alone makes the choice. Doubtless, orders come from above, but they are too broad; he interprets them, and on this interpretation depend the lives of ten or fourteen or twenty men. In making a decision he cannot help having a certain anguish. All leaders know this anguish. That doesn't keep them from acting; on the contrary, it is the very condition of their action. For it implies that they envisage a number of possibilities, and when they choose one, they realize that it has value only because it is chosen. We shall see that this kind of anguish, which is the kind that existentialism describes, is explained, in addition, by a direct responsibility to the other men whom it involves. It is not a curtain separating us from action, but is part of action itself.

1. Søren Kierkegaard (1813–1855), Danish religious philosopher.

When we speak of forlornness, a term Heidegger[2] was fond of, we mean only that God does not exist and that we have to face all the consequences of this. This existentialist is strongly opposed to a certain kind of secular ethics which would like to abolish God with the least possible expense. About 1880, some French teachers tried to set up a secular ethics which went something like this: God is a useless and costly hypothesis; we are discarding it; but, meanwhile, in order for there to be an ethics, a society, a civilization, it is essential that certain values be taken seriously and that they be considered as having an *a priori*[3] existence. It must be obligatory, *a priori*, to be honest, not to lie, not to beat your wife, to have children, etc., etc. So we're going to try a little device which will make it possible to show that values exist all the same, inscribed in a heaven of ideas, though otherwise God does not exist. In other words—and this, I believe, is the tendency of everything called reformism in France—nothing will be changed if God does not exist. We shall find ourselves with the same norms of honesty, progress, and humanism, and we shall have made of God an outdated hypothesis which will peacefully die off by itself.

The existentialist, on the contrary, thinks it very distressing that God does not exist, because all possibility of finding values in a heaven of ideas disappears along with Him; there can no longer be an *a priori* Good, since there is no infinite and perfect consciousness to think it. Nowhere is it written that the Good exists, that we must be honest, that we must not lie; because the fact is we are on a plane where there are only men. Dostoievsky[4] said, "If God didn't exist, everything would be possible." That is the very starting point of existentialism. Indeed, everything is permissible if God does not exist, and as a result man is forlorn, because neither within him nor without does he find anything to cling to. He can't start making excuses for himself.

If existence really does precede essence, there is no explaining things away by reference to a fixed and given human nature. In other words, there is no determinism, man is free, man is freedom. On the other hand, if God does not exist, we find no values or commands to turn to which legitimize our conduct. So, in the bright realm of values, we have no excuse behind us, nor justification before us. We are alone, with no excuses.

That is the idea I shall try to convey when I say that man is condemned to be free. Condemned, because he did not create himself, yet, in other respects is free; because, once thrown into the world, he is responsible for everything he does. The existentialist does not believe in the power of passion. He will never agree that a sweeping passion is a ravaging torrent which fatally leads a man to certain acts and is therefore an excuse. He thinks that man is responsible for his passion.

The existentialist does not think that man is going to help himself by finding in the world some omen by which to orient himself. Because he thinks that man will interpret the omen to suit himself. Therefore, he thinks that man, with no support and no aid, is condemned every moment to invent man.

2. Martin Heidegger (1889–1976), German philosopher of existential phenomenology.
3. Without examination or analysis (Latin).
4. Fyodor Dostoyevsky (1821–1888), Russian novelist.

Ponge,[5] in a very fine article, has said, "Man is the future of man." That's exactly it. But if it is taken to mean that this future is recorded in heaven, that God sees it, then it is false, because it would really no longer be a future. If it is taken to mean that, whatever a man may be, there is a future to be forged, a virgin future before him, then this remark is sound. But then we are forlorn.

15   To give you an example which will enable you to understand forlornness better, I shall cite the case of one of my students who came to see me under the following circumstances: his father was on bad terms with his mother, and, moreover, was inclined to be a collaborationist,[6] his older brother had been killed in the German offensive of 1940, and the young man, with somewhat immature but generous feelings, wanted to avenge him. His mother lived alone with him, very much upset by the half-treason of her husband and the death of her older son; the boy was her only consolation.

The boy was faced with the choice of leaving for England and joining the Free French forces—that is, leaving his mother behind—or remaining with his mother and helping her to carry on. He was fully aware that the woman lived only for him and that his going off—and perhaps his death—would plunge her into despair. He was also aware that every act that he did for his mother's sake was a sure thing, in the sense that it was helping her to carry on, whereas every effort he made toward going off and fighting was an uncertain move which might run aground and prove completely useless; for example, on his way to England he might, while passing through Spain, be detained indefinitely in a Spanish camp; he might reach England or Algiers and be stuck in an office at a desk job. As a result, he was faced with two very different kinds of action: one, concrete, immediate, but concerning only one individual; the other concerned an incomparably vaster group, a national collectivity, but for that very reason was dubious, and might be interrupted en route. And, at the same time, he was wavering between two kinds of ethics. On the one hand, an ethics of sympathy, of personal devotion; on the other, a broader ethics, but one whose efficacy was more dubious. He had to choose between the two.

Who could help him choose? Christian doctrine? No. Christian doctrine says, "Be charitable, love your neighbor, take the more rugged path, etc., etc." But which is the more rugged path? Whom should he love as a brother? The fighting man or his mother? Which does the greater good, the vague act of fighting in a group, or the concrete one of helping a particular human being to go on living? Who can decide *a priori*? Nobody. No book of ethics can tell him. The Kantian[7] ethics says, "Never treat any person as a means, but as an end." Very well, if I stay with my mother, I'll treat her as an end and not as a means; but by virtue of this very fact, I'm running the risk of treating the people around me who are fighting, as means; and, conversely, if I go to join those

5. François Ponge (1899–1988), French surrealist poet.
6. After the defeat of France by Germany in 1940, a French government headquartered in Vichy collaborated with the Germans; the French National Committee of Liberation (Free French), headquartered in London, fought with the Allies against them.
7. Immanuel Kant (1724–1804), German philosopher.

who are fighting, I'll be treating them as an end, and, by doing that, I run the risk of treating my mother as a means.

If values are vague, and if they are always too broad for the concrete and specific case that we are considering, the only thing left for us is to trust our instincts. That's what this young man tried to do; and when I saw him, he said, "In the end, feeling is what counts. I ought to choose whichever pushes me in one direction. If I feel that I love my mother enough to sacrifice everything else for her—my desire for vengeance, for action, for adventure—then I'll stay with her. If, on the contrary, I feel that my love for my mother isn't enough, I'll leave."

But how is the value of a feeling determined? What gives his feeling for his mother value? Precisely the fact that he remained with her. I may say that I like so-and-so well enough to sacrifice a certain amount of money for him, but I may say so only if I've done it. I may say "I love my mother well enough to remain with her" if I have remained with her. The only way to determine the value of this affection is, precisely, to perform an act which confirms and defines it. But, since I require this affection to justify my act, I find myself caught in a vicious circle.

On the other hand, Gide[8] has well said that a mock feeling and a true feeling are almost indistinguishable; to decide that I love my mother and will remain with her, or to remain with her by putting on an act, amount somewhat to the same thing. In other words, the feeling is formed by the acts one performs; so, I cannot refer to it in order to act upon it. Which means that I can neither seek within myself the true condition which will impel me to act, nor apply to a system of ethics for concepts which will permit me to act. You will say, "At least, he did go to a teacher for advice." But if you seek advice from a priest, for example, you have chosen this priest; you already knew, more or less, just about what advice he was going to give you. In other words, choosing your adviser is involving yourself. The proof of this is that if you are a Christian, you will say, "Consult a priest." But some priests are collaborating, some are just marking time, some are resisting. Which to choose? If the young man chooses a priest who is resisting or collaborating, he has already decided on the kind of advice he's going to get. Therefore, in coming to see me he knew the answer I was going to give him, and I had only one answer to give: "You're free, choose, that is, invent." No general ethics can show you what is to be done; there are no omens in the world. The Catholics will reply, "But there are." Granted—but, in any case, I myself choose the meaning they have.

When I was a prisoner,[9] I knew a rather remarkable young man who was a Jesuit. He had entered the Jesuit order in the following way: he had had a number of very bad breaks; in childhood, his father died, leaving him in poverty, and he was a scholarship student at a religious institution where he was constantly made to feel that he was being kept out of charity; then, he

20

8. André Gide (1864–1951), French novelist and dramatist.
9. Sartre, who served in the French army during World War II, was a prisoner of war from 1940 to 1941.

failed to get any of the honors and distinctions that children like; later on, at about eighteen, he bungled a love affair; finally, at twenty-two, he failed in military training, a childish enough matter, but it was the last straw.

This young fellow might well have felt that he had botched everything. It was a sign of something, but of what? He might have taken refuge in bitterness or despair. But he very wisely looked upon all this as a sign that he was not made for secular triumphs, and that only the triumphs of religion, holiness, and faith were open to him. He saw the hand of God in all this, and so he entered the order. Who can help seeing that he alone decided what the sign meant?

Some other interpretation might have been drawn from this series of setbacks; for example, that he might have done better to turn carpenter or revolutionist. Therefore, he is fully responsible for the interpretation. Forlornness implies that we ourselves choose our being. Forlornness and anguish go together.

As for despair, the term has a very simple meaning. It means that we shall confine ourselves to reckoning only with what depends upon our will, or on the ensemble of probabilities which make our action possible. When we want something, we always have to reckon with probabilities. I may be counting on the arrival of a friend. The friend is coming by rail or streetcar; this supposes that the train will arrive on schedule, or that the streetcar will not jump the track. I am left in the realm of possibility; but possibilities are to be reckoned with only to the point where my action comports with the ensemble of these possibilities, and no further. The moment the possibilities I am considering are not rigorously involved by my action, I ought to disengage myself from them, because no God, no scheme, can adapt the world and its possibilities to my will. When Descartes[10] said, "Conquer yourself rather than the world," he meant essentially the same thing.

25 The Marxists to whom I have spoken reply, "You can rely on the support of others in your action, which obviously has certain limits because you're not going to live forever. That means: rely on both what others are doing elsewhere to help you, in China, in Russia, and what they will do later on, after your death, to carry on the action and lead it to its fulfillment, which will be the revolution. You even *have* to rely upon that, otherwise you're immoral." I reply at once that I will always rely on fellow-fighters insofar as these comrades are involved with me in a common struggle, in the unity of a party or a group in which I can more or less make my weight felt; that is, one whose ranks I am in as a fighter and whose movements I am aware of at every moment. In such a situation, relying on the unity and will of the party is exactly like counting on the fact that the train will arrive on time or that the car won't jump the track. But, given that man is free and that there is no human nature for me to depend on, I cannot count on men whom I do not know by relying on human goodness or man's concern for the good of society. I don't know what will become of the Russian revolution; I may make an example of it to the extent that at the present time it

10. René Descartes (1596–1650), French philosopher, scientist, and mathematician.

is apparent that the proletariat plays a part in Russia that it plays in no other nation. But I can't swear that this will inevitably lead to a triumph of the proletariat. I've got to limit myself to what I see.

Given that men are free and that tomorrow they will freely decide what man will be, I cannot be sure that, after my death, fellow-fighters will carry on my work to bring it to its maximum perfection. Tomorrow, after my death, some men may decide to set up Fascism, and the others may be cowardly and muddled enough to let them do it. Fascism will then be the human reality, so much the worse for us.

Actually, things will be as man will have decided they are to be. Does that mean that I should abandon myself to quietism? No. First, I should involve myself; then, act on the old saw, "Nothing ventured, nothing gained." Nor does it mean that I shouldn't belong to a party, but rather that I shall have no illusions and shall do what I can. For example, suppose I ask myself, "Will socialization, as such, ever come about?" I know nothing about it. All I know is that I'm going to do everything in my power to bring it about. Beyond that, I can't count on anything. Quietism is the attitude of people who say, "Let others do what I can't do." The doctrine I am presenting is the very opposite of quietism, since it declares, "There is no reality except in action." Moreover, it goes further, since it adds, "Man is nothing else than his plan; he exists only to the extent that he fulfills himself; he is therefore nothing else than the ensemble of his acts, nothing else than his life."

According to this, we can understand why our doctrine horrifies certain people. Because often the only way they can bear their wretchedness is to think, "Circumstances have been against me. What I've been and done doesn't show my true worth. To be sure, I've had no great love, no great friendship, but that's because I haven't met a man or woman who was worthy. The books I've written haven't been very good because I haven't had the proper leisure. I haven't had children to devote myself to because I didn't find a man with whom I could have spent my life. So there remains within me, unused and quite viable, a host of propensities, inclinations, possibilities, that one wouldn't guess from the mere series of things I've done."

Now, for the existentialist there is really no love other than one which manifests itself in a person's being in love. There is no genius other than one which is expressed in works of art; the genius of Proust is the sum of Proust's works; the genius of Racine is his series of tragedies.[11] Outside of that, there is nothing. Why say that Racine could have written another tragedy, when he didn't write it? A man is involved in life, leaves his impress on it, and outside of that there is nothing. To be sure, this may seem a harsh thought to someone whose life hasn't been a success. But, on the other hand, it prompts people to understand that reality alone is what counts, that dreams, expectations, and hopes warrant no more than to define a man as a disappointed dream, as miscarried hopes, as vain expectations. In other words, to define him negatively

11. Marcel Proust (1871–1922), French novelist; Jean Baptiste Racine (1639–1699), French dramatist who wrote only tragedies.

and not positively. However, when we say, "You are nothing else than your life," that does not imply that the artist will be judged solely on the basis of his works of art; a thousand other things will contribute toward summing him up. What we mean is that a man is nothing else than a series of undertakings, that he is the sum, the organization, the ensemble of the relationships which make up these undertakings.

30   When all is said and done, what we are accused of, at bottom, is not our pessimism, but an optimistic toughness. If people throw up to us our works of fiction in which we write about people who are soft, weak, cowardly, and sometimes even downright bad, it's not because these people are soft, weak, cowardly, or bad; because if we were to say, as Zola did,[12] that they are that way because of heredity, the workings of environment, society, because of bio-logical or psychological determinism, people would be reassured. They would say, "Well, that's what we're like, no one can do anything about it." But when the existentialist writes about a coward, he says that this coward is responsible for his cowardice. He's not like that because he has a cowardly heart or lung or brain; he's not like that on account of his physiological make-up; but he's like that because he has made himself a coward by his acts. There's no such thing as a cowardly constitution; there are nervous constitutions; there is poor blood, as the common people say, or strong constitutions. But the man whose blood is poor is not a coward on that account, for what makes cowardice is the act of renouncing or yielding. A constitution is not an act; the coward is de-fined on the basis of the acts he performs. People feel, in a vague sort of way, that this coward we're talking about is guilty of being a coward, and the thought frightens them. What people would like is that a coward or a hero be born that way.

From these few reflections it is evident that nothing is more unjust than the objections that have been raised against us. Existentialism is nothing else than an attempt to draw all the consequences of a coherent atheistic position. It isn't trying to plunge man into despair at all. But if one calls every attitude of unbelief despair, like the Christians, then the word is not being used in its original sense. Existentialism isn't so atheistic that it wears itself out showing that God doesn't exist. Rather, it declares that even if God did exist, that would change nothing. There you've got our point of view. Not that we believe that God exists, but we think that the problem of His existence is not the issue. In this sense existentialism is optimistic, a doctrine of action, and it is plain dis-honesty for Christians to make no distinction between their own despair and ours and then to call us despairing.

12. Émile Zola (1840–1902), French writer whose novels about a single family, *Les Rougon-Macquart*, probed the influences of heredity and environment.

QUESTIONS

1. "Existence precedes essence": this concept is central to Sartre's existential philosophy. What does he mean by it?

2. Sartre develops his essay by definition: existentialism, he says, enables us to understand the "actual content" of three terms: "anguish," "forlornness," and "despair" (paragraph 4). What are Sartre's definitions of these three terms? How does he distinguish among them?

3. Throughout his essay Sartre defends existentialism against criticism as he explains it, in contrast, for example, to Gilbert Highet, who, in "The Mystery of Zen" (p. 718), addresses criticism only at the end. Consider the differences these two approaches make in the content, organization, and tone of these two essays. What might Sartre's essay be like if he addressed criticism of existentialism only at the end, Highet's if he defended Zen throughout?

4. Sartre says, "when we say that a man is responsible for himself, we do not only mean that he is responsible for his own individuality, but that he is responsible for all men" (paragraph 1). Write an essay explaining how, in the framework of existentialist beliefs, this paradoxical statement is true.

AUTHORS

Edward Abbey (1927–1989)
American writer, essayist, and self-described "agrarian anarchist." Born in Pennsylvania, Abbey lived in the Southwest from 1948, when he arrived there to study at the University of New Mexico, until his death. A former ranger for the National Park Service, he took as his most pervasive theme the beauty of the Southwestern region and the ways it has been despoiled by government, business, and tourism. Abbey's books include the novels *Fire on the Mountain* (1963), *The Monkey Wrench Gang* (1975), and *Good News* (1980). He also published several collections of essays, among them *Desert Solitaire* (1968), *Abbey's Road* (1979), *Beyond the Wall: Essays from the Outside* (1984), and *One Life at a Time, Please* (1988).

André Aciman (b. 1951)
American essayist, memoirist, and scholar. Born in Alexandria, Egypt, to a Sephardic Jewish family of Turkish nationality, Aciman grew up among the various émigré communities of that city. Though French was spoken at home, Aciman attended English-language schools, first in Alexandria, and later, when his family moved to Italy in 1965, in Rome. In 1969, the family moved to the United States, where Aciman completed his B.A. at Lehman College and his Ph.D. in comparative literature at Harvard University. He is the author of *Out of Egypt* (1996), a memoir about his childhood as a secular Jew in Egypt in the 1950s and 1960s, for which he won the Whiting Award. He has also published *False Papers: Essays on Exile and Memory* (2001) and a novel, *Call Me by Your Name* (2007). In addition, he has coauthored and edited *Letters of Transit* (2000) and *The Proust Project* (2004). He currently teaches at the Graduate School and University Center of the City University of New York.

Marjorie Agosín (b. 1955)
Chilean American poet and activist. Born in Maryland, Agosín earned her B.A. at the University of Georgia and her M.A. at and Ph.D. at Indiana University. Much of her work deals with her family's Jewish-Chilean history. Members of Agosín's family were killed in the Holocaust, and those who escaped emigrated to Chile, where Agosín lived from the age of three months to sixteen years. She is the author of numerous books of poetry and memoir, including *Dear Anne Frank* (1998), a collection of bilingual poems; *A Cross and a Star: Memories of a Jewish Girl in Chile* (1997), a book about her mother; and *Always from Somewhere Else* (2000), a book based on Agosín's memories of her father. Other work includes *Secrets in the Sand: The Young Women of Juarez* (2006) and *Writings Towards Hope* (2006). A committed human rights activist, Agosín was awarded the Gabriela Mistral Medal of Honor for Life Achievement in 2002 by the government of Chile. She is currently a professor of Spanish at Wellesley College.

Philip Alcabes (b. 1954)
American epidemiologist and essayist. Alcabes completed his B.S. at Union College, his M.A. at the University of California, Berkeley, his M.P.H. at Columbia University, and his Ph.D. at Johns Hopkins University. He is a professor at the City University of New York, Hunter College. He has published in scholarly journals such as *JAMA*, the *American Journal of Epidemiology*, and the *New England Journal of Medicine*. Known for his willingness to take on the status quo on public health issues, Alcabes has written essays and Op-Eds for the *American Scholar*, *Newsday*, the *Chronicle of Higher Education*, and the *Washington Post*.

Maya Angelou (b. 1928)
African American writer, poet, playwright, actress, and singer. Born in St. Louis, Angelou attended public schools in Arkansas and California before studying music and dance. In a richly varied life, she has been a cook, streetcar conductor, singer, actress, dancer, teacher, and director, with her debut film *Down in the Delta* (1998). Author of several

volumes of poetry and ten plays (stage, screen, and television), Angelou may be best known for her poem "On the Pulse of Morning," which she read at the inauguration of President William Jefferson Clinton in 1993. *I Know Why the Caged Bird Sings* (1970), the first volume of her autobiography, is one of the fullest accounts of the African American woman's experience in contemporary literature. Angelou published her sixth volume of autobiography, *A Song Flung Up to Heaven*, in 2002.

Gloria Anzaldúa (1942–2004)
Chicana American lesbian-feminist poet and writer. Born on a ranch in southern Texas, Anzaldúa worked as an agricultural laborer as an adolescent until she went to Pan American University, the first woman from her family to attend college. She received an M.A. in English from the University of Texas, Austin, and taught writing at several colleges, including San Francisco State University; the University of California, Santa Cruz; and Vermont College. She was also active in the migrant workers' rights movement. Her most ambitious work, *Borderlands/La Frontera* (1987), explores the situation of "border women" like herself who grew up neither within their Mexican Indian heritage nor within the Anglo-American society that considered them outsiders. Her other works include the American Book Award–winning anthology *This Bridge Called My Back* (1981), *Making Face, Making Soul/ Haciendo Caras* (1990), and the novel *La Prieta* (1997).

Hannah Arendt (1906–1975)
German American political scientist and philosopher. Born in Hanover, Germany, and educated at the University of Heidelberg, Arendt began her academic career in Germany, but was forced to leave when Hitler came to power. Arriving in the United States in 1940, she became chief editor for a major publisher and a frequent lecturer on college campuses. Arendt taught at a number of American colleges and universities, finishing her career at the New School for Social Research in New York City. She published over a dozen books, most notably *The Origins of Totalitarianism* (1951), which traces the roots of Nazism back to nineteenth-century imperialism and anti-Semitism; *Eichmann in Jerusalem: A Report on the Banality of Evil* (1963), which suggests that both the Nazis and those

who passively stood by were responsible for the massive destruction of the Holocaust; and *On Revolution* (1965).

Isaac Asimov (1920–1992)
American biochemist, science writer, and novelist. Born in Russia, Asimov was educated in the United States and received a Ph.D. in biochemistry from Columbia University. In 1949 he became a member of the faculty at the School of Medicine, Boston University, where he taught biochemistry. An extraordinarily prolific author, Asimov published more than 250 books on topics as diverse as mathematics, astronomy, physics, chemistry, biology, mythology, Shakespeare, the Bible, and geography; his science fiction works include some of the most famous and influential in that genre. His books include *The Stars, Like Dust* (1951), *Science, Numbers and I* (1968), *ABC's of the Earth* (1971), *The Road to Infinity* (1979), *The Exploding Suns: The Secrets of Supernovas* (1985), and *The Tyrannosaurus Prescription* (1989).

Margaret Atwood (b. 1939)
Canadian novelist, poet, and literary critic. Born in Ontario, Atwood received degrees from the University of Toronto, Radcliffe College, and Harvard University. She began her career as a poet in the 1960s, and her later fiction builds on many of the feminist and survivalist themes she began exploring in her poetry. Well regarded by both critics and the general public, her novels include *The Edible Woman* (1969); *Surfacing* (1972); *Bodily Harm* (1982); *The Handmaid's Tale* (1986), which was made into a movie in 1990; *Cat's Eye* (1988); *The Robber Bride* (1993); *Alias Grace* (1996); *The Blind Assassin* (2000), winner of the Booker Prize; *Oryx and Crake* (2003); *The Penelopiad* (2005); and *The Tent* (2006).

Francis Bacon (1561–1626)
English civil servant, politician, statesman, and philosopher. Trained as a lawyer, Bacon served as a member of Parliament during the reign of Queen Elizabeth I. After her death, he found favor with King James I and advanced in government service to the position of lord chancellor. His career was cut short in 1621 when he was convicted of accepting bribes. Retired, he married and devoted the rest of his life to study and to writing philosophical works. Bacon's books include *The Advancement of Learning* (1605), *Novum Organum*

(1620), and *Essays* (1597, rev. 1612 and 1625).

Matt Bai (b. 1968)
American journalist and author. Bai is a contributing writer for the *New York Times Magazine*, where he covered the 2004 presidential election. He has also written for *Newsday* and the *Boston Globe*. He is currently writing a book about "this moment in democratic politics and a group of people who are trying to rebuild a democratic movement."

David Baltimore (b. 1938)
American biologist. Born in New York City, Baltimore attended Swarthmore College, where he earned his B.A., and Rockefeller University, where he earned his Ph.D. In 1975, he received the Nobel Prize for his discovery of reverse transcriptase, "a DNA polymerase enzyme that transcribes single-stranded RNA into double-stranded DNA." Reverse transcriptase is a key factor in the reproduction of HIV and other retroviruses. Baltimore is currently the Robert A. Millikan Professor of Biology at the California Institute of Technology. He is the president of the American Academy for the Advancement of Science and is an influential voice in national policy concerning recombinant DNA research and the AIDS epidemic.

Andrea Barrett (b. 1954)
American novelist and short-story writer. Born in Boston, Massachusetts, Barrett earned a B.A. in biology from Union College in Schenectady, New York, before briefly attending a Ph.D. program in zoology. Barrett's background in science is reflected in her work, which is identified as "historical fiction." Many of the characters in her work are scientists, both historical and fictional. Barrett has taught in the Warren Wilson College M.F.A. Program and has been a visiting writer and lecturer at several institutions and writers' conferences, including the Breadloaf Writers' Conference in Vermont and the New York State Summer Writers' Institute at Skidmore College. She currently teaches at Williams College in Massachusetts. She has published six novels: *Lucid Stars* (1988), *The Forms of Water* (1988), *Secret Harmonies* (1989), *The Middle Kingdom* (1991), *The Voyage of the Narwhal* (1998), and *The Air We Breathe* (2007), and two collections of short stories: *Ship Fever* (1996), for which she won the National

Book Award, and *Servants of the Map* (2002).

Daniel Bergner (b. 1960)
American journalist and writer. Bergner received his B.A. from Brown University and his M.F.A. from Columbia University's Fiction Writing Program. He has reported from many African countries, as well as from Afghanistan and Iraq. He is the author of *Moments of Favor* (1991), a novel that addresses the dangerous appeal of celebrity. His nonfiction works include *God of the Rodeo* (1999), which tells the stories of prisoners serving life sentences in Louisiana's Angola State Penitentiary and was named a *New York Times* Notable Book of the Year, and *In the Land of Magic Soldiers: A Story of White and Black in West Africa* (2003), a harrowing account of Sierra Leone, which won an Overseas Press Club Award and a Lettre-Ulysses Award and was named a *Los Angeles Times* Best Book of the Year. Bergner is a contributing writer for the *New York Times Magazine* and has written for *Harper's*, *Talk*, *Granta*, *Mother Jones*, and the *New York Times* Op-Ed page. His current book, about desire, will be published in September 2008.

Caroline Bird (b. 1915)
American journalist, public-relations specialist, and writer. Bird attended Vassar College, graduated from the University of Toledo, and received her master's from the University of Wisconsin (1939). She worked as a researcher at *Newsweek* and *Fortune* in the 1940s, then moved into public relations, which she left after twenty years to pursue writing full time. Bird is the author of a number of books focusing on feminist concerns: *Born Female: The High Cost of Keeping Women Down* (1968), *Everything a Woman Needs to Know to Get Paid What She's Worth* (1973), *The Case Against College* (1975), *The Good Years: Your Life in the Twenty-first Century* (1983), and *Lives of Our Own: Secrets of a Salty Old Woman* (1995).

Jennifer Britz (b. 1957)
American college admissions professional and writer. A native of Minnesota, Britz attended Carleton College and the University of Arizona, where she earned her B.A. and M.F.A. degrees. She has been the dean of admissions and financial aid at Kenyon College since July 2003. In 2005, she was named by the

Chronicle of Higher Education as one of ten "New Thinkers." Britz garnered national attention in 2006, when she wrote an Op-Ed piece for the *New York Times* that addresses the decreasing number of male college applicants and the ways in which this disequilibrium is affecting the admissions process.

Jacob Bronowski (1908–1974)
English mathematician, scientist, and writer. Born in Poland and educated in England, where he received a Ph.D. in mathematics from Cambridge University in 1933, Bronowski served as a university lecturer before entering government service during World War II. From 1950 until 1963 he was head of research for Britain's National Coal Board; from 1964 until his death he was a resident fellow at the Salk Institute, La Jolla, California. The author of many books, among them *Science and Human Values* (1956; 1965), *Nature and Knowledge* (1969), and *Magic, Science, and Civilization* (1978), Bronowski is also known for the thirteen-part television series "The Ascent of Man" (1973–74).

David Brooks (b. 1961)
Canadian author and news commentator. Brooks is a columnist for the *New York Times* and commentator on *The News Hour with Jim Lehrer*. He was previously the senior editor of the *Weekly Standard* and prior to that wrote and edited for the *Wall Street Journal*. He is the author of *Bobos in Paradise: The New Upper Class and How They Got There* (2000) and *On Paradise Drive: How We Live Now (And Always Have) in the Future Tense* (2004). His writing has been published in the *New Yorker*, the *New York Times Magazine*, *Forbes*, the *Washington Post*, *TLS*, *Commentary*, the *Public Interest*, and other magazines. Brooks was born in Toronto, grew up in New York City, and graduated from the University of Chicago in 1983 with a degree in history.

Anthony Burgess (1917–1993)
John Anthony Burgess Wilson, English novelist, playwright, and editor. Born in Manchester, England, and a graduate of Manchester University, Burgess was a lecturer and teacher of English until 1954, when he became an education officer in the Colonial Service, stationed in Malaya. He began writing while there, but when told in 1959 that he had a year to live, Burgess returned to

England and wrote five novels in one year. The diagnosis proved wrong, and Burgess lived to write several dozen more, including *A Clockwork Orange* (1962), which was made into a film by Stanley Kubrick; *Enderby Outside* (1968); *Earthly Powers* (1980); *The End of the World News: An Entertainment* (1984); *Any Old Iron* (1989); and *A Dead Man in Deptford* (1993). In addition, Burgess wrote critical studies, giving special attention to James Joyce and D. H. Lawrence.

Rachel Carson (1907–1964)
American marine biologist and writer. Born in Springfield, Pennsylvania, Carson received a B.A. from Pennsylvania College for Women (now Chatham College) and an M.A. from the Johns Hopkins University. She joined the U.S. Fish and Wildlife Service in 1936, and her early works on sea life, *Under the Sea Wind* (1941), *The Sea around Us* (1951), and *The Edge of the Sea* (1954), were highly acclaimed. Her most influential book, *Silent Spring* (1962), exposed the dangers of the use of pesticides, particularly DDT. This work led to a presidential commission that later banned the use of DDT in American agriculture. Carson is often referred to as the founder of the modern environmental movement. She was posthumously awarded the Presidential Medal of Freedom.

Judith Ortiz Cofer (b. 1952)
Puerto Rican American novelist, poet, and essayist. Born in Hormigueros, Puerto Rico, Cofer spent much of her childhood traveling between her Puerto Rican home and Paterson, New Jersey. Educated at Florida Atlantic University and Oxford University, Cofer is currently the Regents' and Franklin Professor of English and Creative Writing at the University of Georgia. *Silent Dancing* (1990) reflects her ongoing efforts to explore her bicultural and bilingual roots. Her other books include *The Latin Deli: Prose and Poetry* (1995), *Woman in Front of the Sun: On Becoming a Writer* (2000), *The Meaning of Consuelo* (2003), and the young adult novel *Call Me Maria* (2006).

Aaron Copland (1900–1990)
American composer, conductor, and writer. Born in New York City, Copland studied music theory and practice in Paris (1921–24), then returned to New York to compose, organize concert series,

publish American scores, and further the cause of the American composer. After experimenting with the adaptation of jazz to classical composition, Copland developed a distinctly American style. He incorporated American folk songs and legends into many of his works, including three ballet scores: *Billy the Kid* (1938), *Rodeo* (1942), and *Appalachian Spring* (1944), which won the Pulitzer Prize. His other popular works include *Twelve Poems of Emily Dickinson*, songs for voice and piano (1950); *Lincoln Portrait* (1942), for narrator and orchestra; and *Fanfare for the Common Man* (1942). Copland also wrote music criticism and essays.

Sara Corbett (b. 1975)

American journalist. Corbett is a contributing writer to the *New York Times Magazine*. She has a particular interest in stories about environmental health and has also written extensively on women's sports, including a book about the 1996 U.S. women's Olympic basketball team, *Venus to the Hoop* (1998).

Amy Cunningham (b. 1955)

American journalist and essayist. Cunningham studied English at the University of Virginia and has been a freelance writer since she graduated in 1977. She has written articles on cultural and feminist topics for magazines such as *Glamour*, *Mademoiselle*, and the *Washington Post Magazine*, as well as several on-line journals.

Debra Dickerson (b. 1960)

African American lawyer and essayist. Raised in St. Louis, Missouri, Dickerson has been an officer in the U.S. Air Force, a senior editor at *US News and World Report*, and a lawyer for the NAACP Legal Defense Fund. She is a Senior Fellow at the New American Foundation in Washington, D.C. Her writing has appeared in the *New Republic*, the *New York Times*, and the *Nation*, among other periodicals. Her books include the memoir *An American Story* (2000) and *The End of Blackness* (2004).

Joan Didion (b. 1934)

American novelist, essayist, and screenwriter. A native Californian, Didion studied at the University of California at Berkeley. After winning *Vogue* magazine's Prix de Paris contest for excellence in writing, she began working for the magazine. Didion rose to associate feature ed-

itor before leaving *Vogue* in 1963, the year her first novel, *Run River*, was published. Since then, she has written five more novels, the most recent of which is *The Last Thing He Wanted* (1996). A frequent contributor to magazines and literary reviews, Didion has published her essays in collections that include *Slouching towards Bethlehem* (1969) and *The White Album* (1979). *Salvador*, a work of reportage based on her visit to El Salvador in 1983, marked Didion's growing concern with politics, as did *Miami* (1987), an attempt to come to terms with the complexities of an American city, and her book *Political Fictions* (2001). Her recent works of nonfiction include *Fixed Ideas: America since 9.11* (2003), and *The Year of Magical Thinking* (2005), a book-length essay that chronicles the year following her husband's death, a period in which Didion's daughter, Quintana (who has since passed away), was gravely ill. In November 2005, it won the National Book Award for nonfiction.

Annie Dillard (b. 1945)

American nature writer, poet, and novelist. Born in Pittsburgh, Pennsylvania, Dillard received her B.A. and M.A. from Hollins College. A keen observer, she has published a wide variety of books, from the poetry collections *Tickets for a Prayer Wheel* (1974) and *Mornings Like This: Found Poems* (1995) to the personal narratives/explorations *Holy the Firm* (1977) and *For the Time Being* (1999), the memoir *An American Childhood* (1987), the book of theory *Living by Fiction* (1982), the essay collection *Teaching a Stone to Talk* (1982), and the novel *The Living* (1992), about pioneers on Puget Sound. In her Pulitzer Prize–winning nonfiction narrative *Pilgrim at Tinker Creek* (1974) Dillard recounts years she spent living in seclusion in the natural world. In *The Writing Life* (1989) she tells personal stories about being a writer. Her most recent work is *The Maytrees: A Novel* (2007).

John Donne (1572–1631)

English poet, essayist, and cleric. Born into a Roman Catholic family at a time when Catholicism was barely tolerated in England, Donne attended Oxford and Cambridge Universities, but could not receive a degree because he was not a member of the Church of England. Donne studied, although never practiced, law and, after quietly abandoning

Catholicism sometime during the 1590s, entered government service. In 1615 he became an Anglican minister, and in 1621 he was named dean of St. Paul's Cathedral. Due in part to the enthusiasm and wit he had cultivated as a writer of love poems, he was considered one of the greatest religious orators of his age. Donne's literary reputation rests on his poetry as well as on his devotions and sermons.

Frederick Douglass (1818–1895)
African American abolitionist, orator, and writer. Born a slave in Maryland, Douglass learned at a young age how to read and write, an amazing feat since it was against the law to teach literacy to a slave. In 1836 he escaped from his master and fled to the North with Anna Murray, a free black woman, whom he later married. Douglass soon became an important orator in the abolitionist movement and, with the publication of his first autobiography, *Narrative of the Life of Frederick Douglass* (1845), an international spokesman for freedom. Douglass founded the antislavery newspaper the *North Star* in 1847 and actively recruited black soldiers to join the Union Army at the outbreak of the Civil War. He continued his autobiography in *My Bondage and My Freedom* (1855) and *The Life and Times of Frederick Douglass* (1881; rev. 1892).

Lars Eighner (b. 1948)
American writer. Born in Corpus Christi, Texas, Eighner attended the University of Texas, in Austin, where he now lives. A self-described "skeptical Democrat," Eighner has worked in hospitals and drug-crisis programs. His book *Travels with Lizbeth* (1993), which describes his three years of surviving on the streets with his dog, was a best-seller. He has also published *Elements of Arousal* (1994), a how-to guide on writing gay erotica, and the comic novel *Pawn to Queen Four* (1995), about the gay subculture of a Texan town.

William Faulkner (1897–1962)
American novelist and short-story writer. Faulkner lived his whole life in his native Mississippi, apart from a short time in military service and a period spent writing screenplays in Hollywood. He attended the University of Mississippi, in the town of Oxford, and much of his writing depicts life in fictional Yoknapatawpha County, an imaginative reconstruction of the area near Oxford. With

the help of the author Sherwood Anderson, Faulkner published his first novel, *Soldier's Pay*, in 1926. His major novels include *The Sound and the Fury* (1929), *As I Lay Dying* (1930), *Sanctuary* (1931), *Light in August* (1932), and *Absalom! Absalom!* (1936). His short stories are included in the collections *These Thirteen* (1931), *Go Down, Moses and Other Stories* (1942), and *The Collected Stories of William Faulkner* (1950). He received the Nobel Prize for literature in 1949.

Benjamin Franklin (1706–1790)
American statesman, inventor, writer, and diplomat. Apprenticed at twelve to his brother, a printer, Franklin learned all aspects of the trade, from setting type to writing editorials. At twenty-four, he was editor and publisher of the *Pennsylvania Gazette*. In 1733 he began writing *Poor Richard's Almanack*, a collection of aphorisms and advice. He retired from business at forty-two to devote himself to study and research, but soon found himself involved in colonial politics. From 1757 until 1763 he was diplomatic representative for the colonies in England. He served as a member of the committee appointed to draft the Declaration of Independence, and later was minister to France and delegate to the Paris peace conference that officially concluded the Revolutionary War.

Paul Fussell (b. 1924)
American writer and teacher. After distinguished military service in World War II, Fussell earned a Ph.D. at Harvard University and became an instructor of English at Connecticut College. In 1955 he was hired by the University of Pennsylvania, where he is a professor emeritus of English. Fussell's early books deal with poetic theory and eighteenth-century literature. With the publication of *The Great War and Modern Memory* (1975) and *Abroad: British Literary Traveling between the Wars* (1980), his attention shifted to the twentieth century. In 1983 he published *Class: A Guide through the American Status System*. Two of his essay collections are *The Boy Scout Handbook and Other Observations* (1982) and *Thank God for the Atom Bomb and Other Essays* (1988). Fussell has also edited *The Norton Book of Travel* (1987) and *The Norton Book of Modern War* (1990).

William Golding (1911–1993)
English novelist. Educated at Marlborough Grammar School and Oxford Uni-

versity, Golding was a schoolmaster at Bishop Wordsworth's School, Salisbury, before becoming a novelist at forty-three. His novels are characterized by their darkly poetic tone, dense symbolism, and rejection of societal norms. His most famous work is *Lord of the Flies* (1954), a story of schoolboys marooned on an island, who revert to savagery. His other novels include *Pincher Martin* (1956), *The Spire* (1964), *The Pyramid* (1967), *Rites of Passage* (1980), *Close Quarters* (1987), and *Fire Down Below* (1989). In 1983 Golding received the Nobel Prize for literature.

Mary Gordon (b. 1949)
American novelist, literary critic, and memoirist. Gordon was born in Far Rockaway, New York. She received her B.A. from Barnard College in 1971 and her M.A. from Syracuse University in 1973. Her novels include *Final Payments* (1978), *The Company of Women* (1981), *Men and Angels* (1985), *The Other Side* (1989), *Spending* (1998), and *Pearl* (2005). She is the author of three memoirs: *The Shadow Man: A Daughter's Search for Her Father* (1996), *Seeing Through Places: Reflections on Geography and Identity* (2000), and *Circling My Mother: A Memoir* (2007). She has also published a collection of essays, *Good Boys and Dead Girls* (1991), along with poems, short stories, and other works of nonfiction. She is currently Millicent C. McIntosh Professor of Writing at Barnard College.

Al Gore (b. 1948)
American politician, environmentalist, and author. Gore was born in Washington D.C. Like his father, Gore served as a U.S. Representative (1977–85) and Senator (1985–93). Gore was Vice President for the two-term Clinton administration (1993–2000). As Vice President he was an important advocate for the North American Free Trade Agreement (NAFTA), deficit reduction, and improvements in government efficiency. Gore was the Democratic nominee for president in 2000, and won the popular vote while losing the electoral vote in one of the closest and most controversial elections in U.S. history. Gore is president of the American television channel Current TV and chairman of Generation Investment Management. He lectures widely on the topic of global warming and starred in the 2006 Academy Award–winning climate change documentary, *An Inconvenient Truth*. In 2007

Gore and the U.N.'s Intergovernmental Panel on Climate Change won the Nobel Peace Prize. Gore is the author of three best-selling books: *Earth in the Balance* (1992), *An Inconvenient Truth* (2006), and *The Assault on Reason* (2007).

Stephen Jay Gould (1941–2002)
American paleontologist, essayist, and teacher. Raised in New York City, Gould graduated from Antioch College and received a Ph.D. from Columbia University in 1967. That same year he joined the faculty of Harvard University as a professor of geology and zoology and taught courses in paleontology, biology, and the history of science. Witty and fluent, Gould demystified science for lay readers in essays written for a regular column in *Natural History* magazine. Many of his essays have been collected in *Ever Since Darwin* (1977), *Hen's Teeth and Horse's Toes* (1983), and *Eight Little Piggies* (1993). Gould's *The Mismeasure of Man* (1981), which questioned traditional ways of testing intelligence, won the National Book Critics Circle Award for essays and criticism. His last major study of Darwinian evolution, *The Structure of Evolutionary Theory*, appeared in 2002.

Lani Guinier (b. 1950)
African American law professor and writer. Born in Queens, New York, Guinier attended the Yale Law School with Bill and Hillary Clinton and now teaches at the University of Pennsylvania. President Clinton nominated her for assistant attorney general, but withdrew the nomination in response to protests over her alleged political views. Guinier has since written a book, *The Tyranny of the Majority* (1994), and numerous articles about the implications of this experience. Her other books include *Becoming Gentlemen* (1997), *Lift Every Voice* (1998), and *Who's Qualified?* (2001).

David Guterson (b. 1956)
American novelist and essayist. Born in Seattle, Washington, and educated at the University of Washington, Guterson taught high school for many years. Inspired by his own educational experience and that of his children, he has written numerous essays and a book, *Family Matters* (1993), in favor of homeschooling. He has also written a collection of stories, *The Country Ahead of Us, the Country Behind* (1989), and two novels, *Snow Falling on Cedars* (1994), which won the PEN/Faulkner Award in 1995,

and *East of the Mountains* (1999). Guterson is a contributing editor to *Harper's Magazine* and has also published in the *New York Times Magazine* and the *Utne Reader*. Often writing about everyday subjects such as sports or shopping malls, Guterson says that he has an "ethical and moral duty . . . to tell stories that inspire readers to consider more deeply who they are." Guterson's 2003 novel, *Our Lady of the Forest*, is about a fictional Marian apparition witnessed by a teenage girl in Washington.

Ernest Hemingway (1899–1961)
American novelist and short-story writer. Hemingway began his professional writing career as a journalist, reporting for newspapers in Kansas City and Toronto. In the 1920s he lived in Paris as a part of the American expatriate community, known as "the Lost Generation," which included Gertrude Stein, F. Scott Fitzgerald, and Ezra Pound. Hemingway's literary reputation rests on his short stories, collected in *In Our Time* (1925) and *Men without Women* (1927), and his novels, including *The Sun Also Rises* (1926), *A Farewell to Arms* (1929), and *For Whom the Bell Tolls* (1940). *The Old Man and the Sea* (1952) was the last work published during his lifetime. Hemingway received the Nobel Prize for literature in 1954.

Gilbert Highet (1906–1978)
Scottish American scholar, poet, writer, and teacher. Born in Glasgow, Scotland, Highet was educated at the University of Glasgow and Oxford University. From 1932 until 1936 he taught at St. John's College, Oxford; he then accepted an appointment at Columbia University, where he taught Greek and Latin literature for thirty years. Considered a master teacher, Highet communicated his enthusiasm for classical literature not only in the classroom, but also in a number of books. Of the fourteen he wrote, perhaps the most famous are *The Classical Tradition* (1949), *The Art of Teaching* (1950), and *The Anatomy of Satire* (1962).

John Holt (1923–1985)
American teacher and theorist of education. Born in New York City, Holt taught for many years in high schools in Colorado and Massachusetts and then at Harvard University and the University of California at Berkeley. His numerous books, based on his teaching experiences and centrally concerned with education, include *How Children Fail* (1964), *How*

Children Learn (1967), *The Under-Achieving School* (1967), *Freedom and Beyond* (1972), and *Escape from Childhood* (1984).

Langston Hughes (1902–1967)
African American poet, playwright, and fiction writer. Hughes emerged as a key figure in the Harlem Renaissance of the 1920s and 1930s. Encouraged by his fellow artists, he published his first collection of poems, *The Weary Blues*, in 1926. Although critical response was mixed, the degree of public acceptance achieved by Hughes with this and subsequent works enabled him to become one of the few African American modernist writers to support himself from his writing and lecturing. He published in his lifetime seventeen volumes of poetry, two novels, seven collections of short stories, and twenty-six plays.

Molly Ivins (1944–2007)
Mary Tyler Ivins, American columnist and writer. Born in California and raised in Houston, Texas, Ivins received a B.A. from Smith College and an M.A. in journalism from Columbia University. She worked on the staffs of the *Houston Chronicle*, the *Minneapolis Star Tribune*, the *Texas Observer*, and the *New York Times* and as a syndicated political columnist at the *Fort Worth Star-Telegram*. Ivins delighted in exposing politics at its worst and used humor to present serious issues such as gun control. Her articles appeared in *Mother Jones*, *Ms.*, the *Nation*, and the *Progressive*; collections include *Nothin' but Good Times Ahead* (1993) and *You Got to Dance with Them What Brung You* (1998). Her books included *Shrub: The Short but Happy Political Life of George W. Bush* (2000), *Bushwhacked: Life in George W. Bush's America* (2004), *Who Let the Dogs In?: Incredible Political Animals I Have Known* (2005), and, posthumously, *Bill of Wrongs: The Executive Branch's Assault on America's Fundamental Rights* (2007).

Thomas Jefferson (1743–1826)
American lawyer, architect, and writer; secretary of state to George Washington (1789–93), vice president to John Adams (1797–1801), and third president of the United States (1801–9). A learned man of significant accomplishments in many fields, Jefferson entered politics in his native Virginia, where he served in the House of Burgesses and eventually became governor (1779–81). In 1809 he

founded the University of Virginia, designing both the buildings and the curriculum. A fluent stylist, Jefferson wrote books on science, religion, architecture, and even Anglo-Saxon grammar. He is probably best known for writing the Declaration of Independence; preliminary drafts were done by a committee, which relied on Jefferson for the drafts and the final revision.

Jesus (c. 4 B.C.E.–c. 30 C.E.)
Jesus of Nazareth, first-century religious teacher. Source of the Christian religion and Savior in the Christian faith, Jesus spent his short public career in Palestine, preaching a message of repentance and conversion. One of his favorite teaching devices was the parable, a literary form with a long history, used extensively in rabbinical tradition.

Samuel Johnson (1709–1784)
English lexicographer, critic, moralist, and essayist. In spite of childhood poverty, poor eyesight, and scant advanced education, Johnson achieved renown in his day as a wit, a conversationalist, and an astute observer of the human experience. In 1737, having failed as a schoolmaster, he sought his fortune in London, where he soon found work contributing essays and poems to the *Gentleman's Magazine*. Johnson's literary career prospered as he wrote and published poems, plays, and essays. In 1750 he founded the *Rambler*, a popular periodical containing essays, fables, and criticism. One of the greatest prose stylists of the English language, Johnson prepared the monumental *Dictionary of the English Language* (1755) and wrote *Rasselas* (1759), a didactic tale, and *The Lives of the Poets* (1779–81).

Garrison Keillor (b. 1942)
American radio host, humorist, and writer. Born in Anoka, Minnesota, Keillor graduated from the University of Minnesota. He is the creator and host of the popular NPR radio program *A Prairie Home Companion*. He has won numerous awards, including a Grammy for best nonmusical recording (*Lake Wobegon Days*, 1987), and was inducted into the Music Broadcast Communications Radio Hall of Fame in 1994. He is the author of *Happy to Be Here* (1982), the bestselling *Lake Wobegon Days* (1985), *The Book of Guys* (1993), and the children's book *Cat, You Better Come Home* (1995). Recent books include *Wobegon Boy* (1997), *Minnesota Days: Our Heritage in Stories, Art, and Photos* (1999), and *Lake Wobegon Summer, 1956* (2001).

John Fitzgerald Kennedy (1917–1963)
American writer, orator, and thirty-fifth president of the United States. Born in Brookline, Massachusetts, Kennedy graduated *cum laude* from Harvard University. Before being elected to the House of Representatives at twenty-nine, he had received the Navy and Marine Corps Medal for his service in World War II and developed his senior thesis into a best-selling book, *Why England Slept* (1962). In 1952, after only six years in the House, Kennedy's family helped him campaign for the Massachusetts Senate election, which he narrowly won. The young senator's fame grew in the 1950s, and his eloquence and poise in televised debates against Richard Nixon helped Kennedy win the presidency in 1960. His inaugural address, calling for all citizens' participation in the affairs of their nation, is one of the best-known speeches in American history. On November 22, 1963, in Dallas, Texas, he was assassinated by Lee Harvey Oswald.

Jamaica Kincaid (b. 1949)
Caribbean American writer. Born in the West Indies, Kincaid moved to the United States when she was seventeen and worked as a domestic helper. Although she had barely the equivalent of a high school diploma, she took classes at the New School for Social Research and eventually became a staff writer for the *New Yorker*. Her books include *At the Bottom of the River* (1988), *A Small Place* (1988), *Lucy* (1990), *The Autobiography of My Mother* (1995), and *My Brother* (1997). Kincaid's interest in gardening has led to books on the subject, including *My Garden* (2001), a collection of essays. *Among Flowers: A Walk in the Himalayas* (2005) chronicles Kincaid's journey into the foothills of the Himalayas in search of rare plants to bring home to her Vermont garden.

Martin Luther King Jr. (1929–1968)
African American clergyman and Civil Rights leader. By the age of twenty-six, King had completed his undergraduate education, finished divinity school, and received a Ph.D. in religion from Boston University. The Montgomery, Alabama, bus boycott in 1956 marked his entry into public politics; blacks boycotted segregated buses, and King took a public stand in their support. Drawing on the

New Testament teachings of Jesus and the principles of passive resistance of Mahatma Gandhi, King advocated nonviolent protest to effect significant social change. In the years following the boycott, he became a major figure in the Civil Rights movement. In 1963, Birmingham, Alabama, perhaps the most segregated city in the South, became the focal point for violent confrontations between blacks and whites; 2,400 civil rights workers, King among them, were jailed. King then wrote his now-famous "Letter from Birmingham Jail." In 1964, at thirty-five, he became the youngest person ever to receive the Nobel Peace Prize. He was assassinated on April 14, 1968, in Memphis, Tennessee.

Maxine Hong Kingston (b. 1940)
Chinese American autobiographer and novelist. Born in California, the eldest of six children in a Chinese immigrant family, Kingston grew up in a culture in which English was a second language; friends and relatives regularly gathered at her family's laundry to tell stories in Chinese and reminisce about their native country. Graduating from the University of California at Berkeley, Kingston taught school in California and Hawaii and began publishing poetry, stories, and articles in a number of magazines, including the *New Yorker*, *New West*, the *New York Times Magazine*, *Ms.*, and the *Iowa Review*. Her books of reminiscence, which both won National Book Critics Circle Awards, are *The Woman Warrior: Memoirs of a Girlhood among Ghosts* (1973) and *China Men* (1980). She has also published a novel, *Tripmaster Monkey: His Fake Book* (1989).

Nicholas D. Kristof (b. 1959)
American journalist and political writer. Raised in Yamhill, Oregon, Kristof was educated at Harvard University and at Magdalen College, Oxford, where he was a Rhodes scholar. He specializes in East Asia and has written several books in that area, including *China Wakes: The Struggle for the Soul of a Rising Power* (1994) and *Thunder from the East: Portrait of a Rising Asia* (2000), both coauthored with his wife, Sheryl WuDunn. In 1990, Kristof and WuDunn were awarded the Pulitzer Prize for International Reporting, in recognition of their coverage of the pro-democracy student movement in China and the Tiananmen square protests that accompanied it.

Currently a columnist for the *New York Times*, Kristof has recently gained attention for his coverage of the crises in the Darfur region of the Sudan.

Elisabeth Kübler-Ross (1926–2004)
Swiss American psychologist. Born and educated in Switzerland, Kübler-Ross came to prominence in the United States, where she lived from 1958 until her death. Her work is largely a response to what she called "the horrifying experience of the [postwar European] concentration camps." She gave seminars and wrote about death and dying not only to better understand the process, but also to improve care for the terminally ill. Her books on the subject include the bestselling *On Death and Dying* (1969), *On Children and Death* (1983), *AIDS: The Ultimate Challenge* (1987), *The Wheel of Life: A Memoir of Living and Dying* (1997), and, with David Kessler, *Life Lessons: Two Experts on Death and Dying Teach Us about the Mysteries of Life and Living* (2000). *On Life after Death* (1995) retracts much of her earlier work.

Anthony Lane (b. 1962)
English book and film critic. Lane completed his undergraduate degree in English at Trinity College, Cambridge, where he also did graduate work on the poet T. S. Eliot. He worked as a freelancer and wrote book and film reviews for the *Independent* before joining the *New Yorker*, where he has been a film critic since 1993.

Aldo Leopold (1886–1948)
American essayist and environmentalist. Leopold graduated from Yale University's School of Forestry and worked as a forest ranger in the Arizona and New Mexico territories. A vocal member of the Forestry Service, he fought for legislation to protect ecosystems threatened by development of the land. Leopold opposed purely economic views of land use and worked to protect America's wilderness from exploitation. His essays and lobbying fostered many of the environmental protection acts in place today, and his 1933 book, *Game Management*, advanced his "conservation ethic," which argued for the intrinsic value of nature. In 1949 a collection of essays about the Wisconsin farm where he lived in later life was published posthumously as *A Sand County Almanac, and Sketches Here and There*.

Michael Levin (b. 1943)

American philosopher and educator. Educated at Michigan State University and Columbia University, Levin was a member of the Department of Philosophy at Columbia from 1968 until 1980. He is currently professor of philosophy at City College of the City University of New York. His research interests include ethics, philosophy, and the mind. The author of a number of scholarly articles, Levin has published *Metaphysics and the Mind-Body Problem* (1979), *Feminism and Freedom* (1987), *Why Race Matters: Race Differences and What They Mean* (1997), and *Sexual Orientation and Human Rights* (1999).

Abraham Lincoln (1809–1865)

American lawyer and orator, and sixteenth president of the United States. Born in Kentucky, Lincoln was a self-made and self-taught man. In 1830 his family moved to Illinois, where Lincoln prepared himself for a career in law. In 1834 he was elected to the first of four terms in the Illinois state legislature; in 1847, to the U.S. Congress. Elected president in 1860, Lincoln sought to preserve the Union amid the strife of the Civil War while he worked for the passage of the Thirteenth Amendment, which would outlaw slavery "everywhere and forever" in the United States. During his first term, Lincoln delivered the "Gettysburg Address" (1863) at the site of one of the Civil War's bloodiest battles. Reelected in 1864, he gave his Second Inaugural Address, an eloquent appeal for reconciliation and peace, in 1865. Lincoln was assassinated by the actor John Wilkes Booth on April 15, 1865.

Niccolò Machiavelli (1469–1527)

Florentine statesman and political philosopher. An aristocrat who held office while Florence was a republic, Machiavelli fell from favor when the Medicis returned to power in 1512. Briefly imprisoned, he was restored to an office of some influence, but he never regained his former importance. Machiavelli's most famous work, *The Prince* (1513), has exerted considerable literary and political influence within the Western tradition.

E. S. Maduro (pseudonym; DOB unknown)

American youth counselor and writer. E. S. Maduro is the pseudonym of the author of "Excuse Me While I Explode," one of twenty-six essays in *The Bitch in the House* (2003), a collection of pieces by women about their lives. The writer divides her time between New England and Central America.

Nancy Mairs (b. 1943)

American nonfiction writer and essayist. Married at nineteen, Mairs finished college, had a child, and earned an M.F.A. and a Ph.D. from the University of Arizona. The personal difficulties that inform her writing include six months spent in a state mental hospital, suffering from a near-suicidal mixture of agoraphobia and anorexia, and the later discovery that she suffered from multiple sclerosis. She found a dual salvation in writing and in Roman Catholicism, to which she converted in her thirties. Mairs's books include *Plain-text* (1986), *Carnal Acts* (1990), *Waist-High in the World: A Life among the Nondisabled* (1997), and *Troubled Guest: Life and Death Stories* (2001).

Scott McCloud (b. 1960)

American cartoonist and comics theorist. McCloud was born in Boston, Massachusetts. He is the creator of the science fiction/superhero comic book series *Zot!* His other print comics include *Destroy!!*, described as "a deliberately over-the-top, over-sized single-issue comic book, intended as a parody of formulaic superhero fights," and the graphic novel *The New Adventures of Abraham Lincoln* (1998). In 1993, he published *Understanding Comics*, a scholarly work on the definition, history, and methodology of comics, done entirely in comics form. It is widely considered one of the definitive works on the subject. He followed this study with *Reinventing Comics* (2000) and *Making Comics* (2006).

Bill McKibben (b. 1960)

American environmentalist and writer. Born in Lexington, Massachusetts, McKibben attended Harvard University, where he was president of the *Harvard Crimson* newspaper. From 1982 to 1987 he worked as a staff writer at the *New Yorker*, where his first book, *The End of Nature* (1989), a study of climate change intended for a nonspecialist audience, was serialized before publication. The main topics of his writing are global warming, alternative energy, and human genetic engineering. In 2007, he spearheaded one of the biggest demonstrations against global warming in U.S. history. His most recent book is *Deep*

Economy (2007), a work that McKibben describes as "challeng[ing] the prevailing view of our economy." His other books include *The Age of Missing Information* (1992), *Hope, Human and Wild: True Stories of Living Lightly on the Earth* (1995), *The Comforting Whirlwind: God, Job and the Scale of Creation* (2005), and *Wandering Home* (2005).

John McMurtry (b. 1939)
Canadian writer, teacher, and philosopher. Educated at the University of Toronto, McMurtry became a professional football player before earning his Ph.D. at the University of London. Now professor of philosophy at the University of Guelph, he has written several books, including *The Dimensions of English* (1970), *The Structure of Marx's World-View* (1978), *Understanding War* (1989), *Unequal Freedoms* (1998), *The Cancer Stage of Capitalism* (1999), and *Value Wars: Moral Philosophy and Humanity* (2002).

Jessica Mitford (1917–1996)
Anglo-American writer and social critic. Born into one of England's most famous aristocratic families, Mitford left for the United States shortly after completing her education in 1936. A naturalized American citizen (1944), she established herself as an investigative reporter with a talent for pungent social criticism. Her study of the American funeral industry, *The American Way of Death* (1963; 1998), was followed by *The Trial of Dr. Spock* (1969) and *Kind and Unusual Punishment: The Prison Business* (1973). She also wrote *Faces of Philip: A Memoir of Philip Toynbee* (1984) and the biography *Grace Had an English Heart* (1989). Her last work echoes her earliest—*The American Way of Birth* (1992).

N. Scott Momaday (b. 1934)
Native American poet, writer, and artist. Momaday grew up on reservations in the Southwest, but he was strongly influenced by the example and traditions of the Kiowa people of his native Oklahoma. He studied at the University of New Mexico and Stanford University before beginning a teaching career. Currently, Momaday is Regents' Professor of the Humanities at the University of Arizona. He has published several volumes of poetry, including *Angle of Geese and Other Poems* (1973) and *The Gourd Dancer* (1976); a Pulitzer Prize–winning novel, *House Made of Dawn* (1968); an autobiography, *The Names: A Memoir*

(1976); and a collection of Kiowa folktales, *The Way to Rainy Mountain* (1969). More recently, he has published *In the Presence of the Sun* (1992), a collection of stories and poems, and *The Man Made of Words: Essays, Stories, Passages* (1997).

Toni Morrison (b. 1931)
American writer and teacher. Born to working-class parents and raised in Lorain, Ohio, Morrison received her undergraduate education at Howard University before completing her master's degree at Cornell University. Her works, which center on the complexities of race and gender, have met with both critical and popular acclaim. By the time she won the Pulitzer Prize for *Beloved* in 1987, she had published four other novels: *The Bluest Eye* (1970), *Sula* (1973), *Song of Solomon* (1977), and *Tar Baby* (1981). After the publication of *Jazz* (1992) she received the Nobel Prize for literature in 1993. Morrison held teaching positions at Howard, Yale, and Rutgers Universities before moving to Princeton University, where she is currently a fellow in the Council of the Humanities. Her most recent novel, *Paradise*, was published in 1997. Her most recent novel is *Love* (2003).

John Muir (1838–1914)
American naturalist and writer. Muir's family emigrated from Scotland to the United States in 1849 and settled in Wisconsin. Muir was an avid student of nature and studied geology and botany at the University of Wisconsin, though he left without taking a degree. As a young man, Muir traveled widely in the western United States to study its flora and fauna. He became a vocal advocate for the preservation of forests, and his efforts in the last decade of the nineteenth century contributed to the creation of Yosemite National Park. His writings extol the natural beauty of the American West, and in his many magazine articles and popular books, such as *The Mountains of California* (1894) and *My First Summer in the Sierra* (1911), Muir shared his own fascination with the natural world with his readers.

Vladimir Nabokov (1899–1977)
Russian American fiction writer and educator. Born in Russia and educated at Trinity College, Cambridge, Nabokov came to the United States in 1940 to lecture at Stanford University and stayed

for twenty years. While teaching at Wellesley College and Cornell University, he wrote dozens of novels and contributed essays, stories, and poems to several American magazines. Although he was well known in literary circles, Nabokov did not achieve fame until 1958, when his controversial novel *Lolita* was published. *Lolita* earned Nabokov enough money so that he could retire to Switzerland and pursue the writing of fiction. His subsequent novels include *Pale Fire* (1962), *Ada* (1969), and *Look at the Harlequins!* (1974).

Gloria Naylor (b. 1950)

African American fiction writer and essayist. Born in New York City to parents from southern sharecropping families, Naylor was a member of the Jehovah's Witnesses as a teenager and young adult. When she suffered a nervous breakdown in 1975 and left the church, Naylor began to read works by other African American women and returned to school, earning a B.A. from Brooklyn College and an M.A. in Afro-American studies from Yale University. She has been a writer in residence at George Washington University, the University of Pennsylvania, New York University, and Princeton University and is the author of *The Women of Brewster Place* (1982), which won the American Book Award for Best First Novel; *Linden Hills* (1985); *Mama Day* (1988); *Bailey's Cafe* (1992); and *The Men of Brewster Place* (1998). Naylor's most recent work, *1996*, was published in 2005.

John Henry Newman (1801–1890)

English Roman Catholic prelate, poet, novelist, and theologian. Educated at Trinity College, Oxford, Newman became a priest in the Anglican Church. He was a major force in the Oxford movement, an effort to reestablish the authority and traditions of the Church of England. In 1845 Newman became a Roman Catholic; in 1846 he was ordained in Rome and returned to England. From 1852 on, he delivered not only sermons but also a number of influential lectures on education. The latter culminated in one of Newman's finest works, *The Idea of a University Defined and Illustrated* (1852), which ranks with his treatise *An Essay in Aid of a Grammar of Assent* (1870) as a classic statement of belief. Newman wrote two novels, *Loss and Gain* (1848) and *Callista* (1856); an explanation of his conversion, *Apologia*

Pro Vita Sua (1864); and a visionary poem, "The Dream of Gerontius" (1865). In 1879 he became a cardinal in the Roman Catholic Church.

George Orwell (1903–1950)

Pen name of Eric Blair, English journalist, essayist, novelist, and critic. Born in India and educated in England, Orwell was an officer in the Indian Imperial Police in Burma (1922–27), a part of his life that he later recounted in a novel, *Burmese Days* (1934). In 1927 he went to Europe to develop his writing talents. His first book, *Down and Out in Paris and London* (1933), depicts his years of poverty and struggle while working as a dishwasher and day laborer. Orwell's experiences fighting in the Spanish Civil War are the subject of his memoir, *Homage to Catalonia* (1938). Of his seven novels, *Animal Farm* (1945) and *Nineteen Eighty-Four* (1949), directed at totalitarian government, have become classics. Orwell published five collections of essays, including *Shooting an Elephant and Other Essays* (1950).

Alexander Petrunkevitch (1875–1964)

Russian-born zoologist and teacher. Petrunkevitch was educated in Russia and Germany before coming to the United States as a lecturer at Harvard University in 1904. In 1910 he joined the Department of Zoology at Yale University, where he became professor in 1917 and served until 1944. Petrunkevitch was an expert on the behavior of American spiders; his *Index Catalogue of Spiders of North, Central, and South America* (1911) and *An Inquiry into the Natural Classification of Spiders* (1933) are classic studies.

Plato (c. 428–c. 348 B.C.E.)

Greek philosopher and teacher. When Socrates died in 399 B.C.E., his student Plato went into exile. Plato returned in the 380s and founded a school, the Academy. He adopted the Socratic method of teaching, a technique of asking rather than answering questions. Although most of Plato's writings take the form of dialogues, he occasionally uses parables and allegories.

Michael Pollan (b. 1955)

American environmentalist and author. Pollan is Professor of Journalism and Director of the Knight Program in Science and Environmental Journalism at the University of California, Berkeley. He was educated at Bennington College, where he received his B.A., at Mansfield College at Oxford University, and at Columbia University, where he earned his M.A. in English and was awarded a President's Fellowship as a Ph.D. student. Pollan is a contributing writer for the *New York Times Magazine*, a former executive editor of *Harper's*, and the author of four books: *The Omnivore's Dilemma: A Natural History of Four Meals* (2006), *The Botany of Desire: A Plant's-Eye View of the World* (2001), *A Place of My Own* (1997), and *Second Nature: A Gardener's Education* (1991). His recent work has focused on the U.S. meat industry.

Katha Pollitt (b. 1949)

American essayist, journalist, and poet. Born in New York City, Pollitt earned a B.A. from Harvard University and an M.F.A. from Columbia University. She has written for the *Nation* since 1982, initially as the literature editor and then as a contributing editor; since 1992 she has been an associate editor. Pollitt's *Antarctic Traveler* (1982) won the National Book Critics Circle Award for poetry. Her poems have appeared in the *New Yorker*, the *New Republic*, and *Poetry*, and she has collected her essays in *Reasonable Creatures: Essays on Women and Feminism* (1994). She has published two collections of columns: *Subject to Debate: Sense and Dissents on Women, Politics, and Culture* (2001), and *Virginity or Death!: And Other Social and Political Issues of Our Time* (2006). Her most recent book is *Learning to Drive: And Other Life Stories* (2007).

Neil Postman (1931–2003)

American critic and educator. Postman received his B.S. from the State University of New York at Fredonia and his M.A. and Ed.D. from Columbia University. He was Paulette Goddard Chair of Media Ecology at New York University and chair of the Department of Communications Culture. His pedagogical and scholarly interests included media and learning, as is seen in many of his seventeen books, including *Amusing Ourselves to Death* (1985), *Conscientious Objections* (1988), *Technopoly: The Surrender of Culture to Technology* (1992), *The End of Education* (1995), and *Building a Bridge to the Eighteenth Century: How the Past Can Improve Our Future* (1999).

Anna Quindlen (b. 1953)

American journalist and novelist. Born in Philadelphia, Quindlen graduated from Barnard College and immediately began writing for the *New York Post*. Eventually she moved to the *New York Times*, where she was a regular columnist for over twenty years. Her columns allowed her to thrive by "taking things personally for a living," and they eventually earned her a Pulitzer Prize. They have been collected in *Living Out Loud* (1988) and *Thinking Out Loud: Thoughts on the Personal, the Political, the Public, and the Private* (1993). Quindlen resigned from the *New York Times* to spend more time writing fiction and has since published five novels: *Object Lessons* (1991); *One True Thing* (1994), which was made into a movie in 1998; *Black and Blue* (1998); *Blessings* (2002); and *Rise and Shine* (2006). *How Books Changed My Life* (1998) is Quindlen's memoir about the importance of reading. She currently writes a bi-weekly column for *Newsweek*.

Jonathan Rauch (b. 1960)

American journalist. A contributing editor for the *National Journal* in Washington, D.C., Rauch writes about the contemporary American political scene. His books include *The Outnation: A Search for the Soul of Japan* (1992), *Kindly Inquisitors: The New Attacks on Free Thought* (1993), *Demosclerosis: The Silent Killer of the American Government* (1994), and *Government's End: Why Washington Stopped Working* (2000). His essays have appeared in the *New Republic*, the *Atlantic Monthly*, the *New York Times*, and the *Wall Street Journal*.

Tom Regan (b. 1938)

American philosopher and teacher. After receiving a Ph.D. in philosophy from the University of Virginia, Regan taught at Sweet Briar College before joining the Department of Philosophy and Religion at North Carolina State University. He does research in theoretical and applied ethics, and his writing reveals his particular interest in environmentalism and animal rights. His works include *All That Dwell Within* (1982), *The Case for Animal Rights* (1983), *The Thee Generation: Reflections on the Coming Revolution* (1991), and *Defending Animal Rights* (2001).

Adrienne Rich (b. 1929)
American poet and essayist. Rich's most recent books of poetry are *The School Among the Ruins: Poems 2000–2004*, and *Fox: Poems 1998–2000* (Norton). A selection of her essays, *Arts of the Possible: Essays and Conversations*, was published in 2001. A new edition of *What Is Found There: Notebooks on Poetry and Politics*, appeared in 2003. She is a recipient of the Lannan Foundation Lifetime Achievement Award, the Lambda Book Award, the Lenore Marshall/Nation Prize, the Wallace Stevens Award, the Bollingen Prize in Poetry, and the National Book Foundation's 2006 Medal for Distinguished Contribution to American Letters, among other honors. She lives in California.

Mary Roach (b. 1959)
American essayist and journalist. Born in Hanover, New Hampshire, Roach attended Wesleyan University. She has written articles, essays, and columns for *Salon.com*, *Wired*, *Outside*, *GQ*, *Discover*, *Vogue*, and the *New York Times Magazine*, and has published two books. The first, *Stiff: The Curious Lives of Human Cadavers* (2003), explores the post-mortem fate of human bodies—from use in medical training, transportation safety research, and experiments by forensic scientists to cannibalism and various methods of burial or disposal. Her second book, *Spook: Science Tackles the Afterlife* (2005), explores efforts to find proof of a soul or afterlife. Roach maintains that she has "always gravitated toward the peculiar" in her writing.

Richard Rodriguez (b. 1944)
American essayist and teacher. The son of Mexican American immigrants, Rodriguez learned to speak English in a Catholic grammar school but later looked back with regret at the Spanish language he so willingly cast aside. He received a B.A. from Stanford University and an M.A. from Columbia University. Enrolled in the doctoral program in English literature at the University of California at Berkeley, Rodriguez won a Fulbright scholarship and attended the Warburg Institute in London (1972–73). He now works for the Pacific News Service and contributes commentaries to many journals and news programs. In *Hunger of Memory: The Education of Richard Rodriguez* (1982), he recounts his assimilation into mainstream American society. His second book, *Days of*

Obligation: A Letter to My Mexican Father (1992), describes his difficulties as a homosexual in America. His most recent books include *King's Highway* (1999), *Movements* (1999) and *Brown: The Last Discovery of America* (2002).

Scott Russell Sanders (b. 1945)
American writer and teacher. Born in Tennessee and educated at Brown and Cambridge Universities, Sanders has spent his entire teaching career in the Department of English at Indiana University at Bloomington, where he is now professor of English. He is best known for his nature writing and his depictions of American places and people, including *Wilderness Plots: Tales about the Settlement of the American Land* (1983), *Audubon's Early Years* (1984), *In Limestone Country* (1985), *Staying Put: Making a Home in a Restless World* (1993), and *Writing from the Center* (1995). *The Paradise of Bombs* (1987) is a collection of essays on violence in the United States. He published his most recent book, *A Private History of Awe*, in 2006.

Jean-Paul Sartre (1905–1980)
French playwright, novelist, critic, philosopher, and political activist. After earning an advanced degree in philosophy, Sartre became a provincial schoolmaster, then a playwright and writer of philosophical essays. Described by the *New York Times* as "a rebel of a thousand causes, a modern Don Quixote," Sartre was a major force in the intellectual life of post–World War II France. His philosophy of existentialism influenced generations of artists and thinkers. Steadfastly independent, Sartre refused both the Nobel Prize for literature (1964) and the Legion of Honor. His major works include *The Flies* (1943), *Being and Nothingness* (1943), *No Exit* (1944), and *Life Situations* (1977).

Chief Seattle (c. 1786–1866)
Native American leader. A fierce young warrior, Seattle (also Seathl or Sealth) was chief of the Suquamish, Duwamish, and allied Salish-speaking tribes of the Northwest. In the 1830s he converted to Christianity and became an advocate of peace. Local settlers honored him and his work by naming their town Seattle. When the Port Elliott Treaty of 1855 established reservations for Native Americans, Seattle signed the treaty and lived the rest of his life at the Port Madison Reservation. Because of his example, his

people did not become involved in the bloody warfare that marked the history of the territory from 1855 until 1870. His "Address" is a reply to a treaty proffered in 1854 by Governor Isaac Stevens, commissioner of Indian Affairs for the Washington Territory.

Richard Selzer (b. 1928)
American surgeon and essayist. Born in Troy, New York, Selzer earned his B.A. from Union College and his M.D. from Albany Medical College. He completed a surgical internship and residency at Yale University, where he remained as Assistant Clinical Professor of Surgery until 1985. His writing is informed and inspired by his experiences as a doctor and often focuses on patients. In a review of *Rituals of Surgery* (1973), Selzer's first collection of short stories, in the *Village Voice*, Judith Ramsey praised Selzer for his "deftness of style, his imaginative use of medical and surgical materials, and his clear narrative talent." Selzer has received numerous honors, including an American Medical Writers Award and a Guggenheim Fellowship. His books include *Mortal Lessons: Notes on the Art of Surgery* (1976), *Confessions of a Knife* (1979), a collection of twenty-four essays, roughly half of which are surgical memoirs, *Letters to a Young Doctor* (1982), and *Down from Troy: A Doctor Comes of Age* (1992), his autobiography. *The Exact Location of the Soul: New and Selected Essays* (2001) is his most recent work.

Lauren Slater (b. 1963)
American psychologist and author. Slater earned a B.A. in British and American literature from Brandeis, before completing her master's degree in psychology at Harvard University and her doctorate in psychology at Boston University. She is best known for *Opening Skinner's Box: Great Psychological Experiments of the Twentieth Century* (2004), a book in which she narrates psychology experiments as stories. Slater has written five other books: *Welcome to My Country* (1996), *Prozac Diary* (1998), *Lying: A Metaphorical Memoir* (2000), *Love Works Like This: Travels Through a Pregnant Year* (2003), and *Blue Beyond Blue: Extraordinary Tales for Ordinary Dilemmas* (2005).

Susan Sontag (1933–2004)
American writer, art critic, and filmmaker. Born in New York City, Sontag grew up in Tucson, Arizona, and Los Angeles. After graduating from high school at fifteen, she immediately started classes at the University of California at Berkeley, and later received degrees from the University of Chicago and Harvard University. Her collection of essays *Against Interpretation* (1966) established her reputation as a serious intellectual and critic, just as *Trip to Hanoi* (1968) established her reputation as a political and cultural critic. After a near-fatal bout with breast cancer, Sontag wrote *Illness as Metaphor* (1978), followed by *AIDS and Its Metaphors* (1988). She also wrote several films and plays and the novels *Volcano Lover* (1992) and *In America: A Novel* (2001). Her collection of essays, *Where the Stress Falls*, appeared in 2001.

Elizabeth Cady Stanton (1815–1902)
American feminist and women's rights activist. Born in Johnstown, New York, she married the prominent abolitionist Henry B. Stanton, and the two spent their honeymoon at the World's Antislavery Convention. Stanton joined Lucretia Mott and Susan B. Anthony to fight for women's rights. She cofounded the National Women Suffrage Association and was also one of the first women to try introducing legislation that would make divorce laws more sympathetic to women in abusive marriages. "The Declaration of Sentiments and Resolutions" grew out of the first American convention for women's rights, held in Seneca Falls, New York, in 1848.

Brent Staples (b. 1951)
African American journalist and writer. Born in Chester, Pennsylvania, Staples holds a Ph.D. in psychology from the University of Chicago. He is currently on the editorial board of the *New York Times*. His memoir, *Parallel Time: Growing Up in Black and White*, was published in 1994.

Fred Strebeigh (b. 1951)
American nonfiction writer and teacher. Born in New York City and raised in Nonquitt, Massachusetts, Strebeigh attended Yale University, where he now teaches nonfiction writing jointly in the English department and the School of Forestry and Environmental Studies. His work has appeared in the *Atlantic Monthly*, *Audubon*, the *New Republic*, *Reader's Digest*, *Smithsonian*, the *New York Times Magazine*, and *Sierra Magazine*.

Andrew Sullivan (b. 1963)

American editor and journalist. Sullivan is a former model who became an openly gay media personality when he was named the editor of the *New Republic* at age twenty-eight. His most influential work, *Virtually Normal: An Argument about Homosexuality* (1995), argues in favor of same-sex marriages, asserting that "gay marriage is not a radical step; it is a profoundly humanizing, traditionalizing step." He has also edited *Same-Sex Marriages, Pros and Cons: A Reader* (1997) and is the author of *Love Undetectable: Notes on Friendship, Sex, and Survival* (1998). Sullivan currently blogs for *The Atlantic Online*, *The Atlantic Monthly's* online presence.

Jonathan Swift (1667–1745)

Anglo-Irish poet, satirist, and cleric. Born to English parents who resided in Ireland, Swift studied at Trinity College, Dublin, then departed for London (1689). There he became part of the literary and political worlds, beginning his career by writing political pamphlets in support of the Tory cause. Ordained in the Church of Ireland (1695), Swift was appointed dean of St. Patrick's Cathedral, Dublin, in 1713 and held the post until his death. One of the master satirists of the English language, he wrote several scathing attacks on extremism, including *The Tale of a Tub* (1704), *The Battle of the Books* (1704), and *A Modest Proposal* (1729), but he is probably best known for his novel *Gulliver's Travels* (1726).

Lewis Thomas (1913–1993)

American physician, teacher, science writer, and humanist. Educated at Princeton University and Harvard Medical School, Thomas specialized in pediatrics, public health, and cancer research. From 1973 to 1980 he served as president of Memorial Sloan-Kettering Cancer Center in New York City. In 1970 Thomas began writing occasional essays for the *New England Journal of Medicine*. A number of these, gathered in *The Lives of a Cell* (1974), established Thomas's reputation as a science writer. Other collections of Thomas's writings are *The Medusa and the Snail* (1979), *The Youngest Science* (1983), *Late Night Thoughts on Listening to Mahler's Ninth Symphony* (1983), *Et Cetera, Et Cetera* (1991), and *The Fragile Species* (1992).

Henry David Thoreau (1817–1862)

American philosopher, essayist, naturalist, and poet. A graduate of Harvard University, Thoreau worked at a number of jobs—schoolmaster, house painter, employee in his father's pencil factory—before becoming a writer and political activist. He became a friend of Emerson's and a member of the Transcendental Club, contributing frequently to its journal, the *Dial*. Drawn to the world of nature, he wrote his first book, *A Week on the Concord and Merrimac Rivers* (1849), about a canoe trip with his brother. Thoreau's strong stance against slavery led to his arrest for refusing to pay the Massachusetts poll tax (an act of protest against government sanction of the Mexican War, which he viewed as serving the interests of slaveholders). His eloquent essay defending this act, "Civil Disobedience" (1849); his probing meditation on the solitary life, *Walden* (1854); and his speech "A Plea for Captain John Brown" (1859) are classic literary documents in the history of American life and thought.

Sallie Tisdale (b. 1957)

American nurse and essayist. A writer on health and medical issues, Tisdale has contributed to the *Antioch Review*, *Esquire*, the *New York Times Magazine*, the *New Republic*, *Vogue*, and *Harper's*. She has written several books, including *The Sorcerer's Apprentice: Tales of the Modern Hospital* (1986), *Lot's Wife* (1988), *Talk Dirty to Me* (1994), *The Best Thing I Ever Tasted: The Secret of Food* (2000), and *Women of the Way: Discovering 2,500 Years of Buddhist Wisdom* (2006).

Barbara Tuchman (1912–1989)

American historian. After graduating from Radcliffe College in 1933, Tuchman worked as a research assistant for the Institute of Pacific Relations, an experience that later found expression in *Stilwell and the American Experience in China* (1971), for which she won a Pulitzer Prize in 1971. During the 1930s and 1940s she wrote on politics for the *Nation*, covered the Spanish Civil War as a journalist in London, and after Pearl Harbor took a job with the Office of War Information in Washington, D.C. Critical and public acclaim followed the publication of *The Zimmerman Telegram* (1958) and *The Guns of August* (1962), both on the origins of World War I. Her other books include *The Proud Tower* (1966), *A Distant Mirror: The Calami-*

tous Fourteenth Century (1978), The
March of Folly (1984), and Practicing
History (1981), a collection of articles,
reviews, and talks.

Mark Twain (1835–1910)
Pen name of Samuel L. Clemens, American novelist, journalist, and humorist.
First apprenticed as a printer, Twain was
by turns a riverboat pilot, a gold prospec-
tor, and a journalist. He achieved fame
with his short story "The Celebrated
Jumping Frog of Calaveras County," published in 1867. Twain subsequently
wrote many articles, essays, and stories
and lectured widely. Several of his novels, including The Adventures of Tom
Sawyer (1876) and The Adventures of
Huckleberry Finn (1885), are classics.

John Updike (b. 1932)
American fiction writer, poet, and critic.
After graduating from Harvard University
and attending the Ruskin School of
Drawing and Fine Art at Oxford University, Updike joined the staff of the New
Yorker, beginning an association that
continues today. The winner of two
Pulitzer Prizes, he has described his subject as "the American Protestant small
town middle class." Updike's more than
forty books include collections of poetry,
such as The Carpentered Hen and Other
Tame Creatures (1958) and Seventy Poems (1972); collections of short stories,
such as The Music School (1966) and
Trust Me (1987); and novels, such as
Couples (1968) and his quintet of "Rabbit" works, from the novel Rabbit, Run
(1960) through the novella Rabbit
Remembered (2000). His recent publications include the collections More
Matter: Essays and Criticism (1999) and
Americana: And Other Poems (2001) and
the novels Seek My Face (2002), Villages
(2004), and Terrorist (2006).

Alice Walker (b. 1944)
African American poet, novelist, and essayist. Born and raised by sharecroppers
in rural Georgia, Walker was educated at
Spelman College and Sarah Lawrence
College. Afterward she worked as an editor for Ms. magazine and became active
in the Civil Rights movement. She received widespread fame for her Pulitzer
Prize–winning novel, The Color Purple
(1982) which has since been adapted for
both film and Broadway. Her other novels
include Meridian (1986), The Temple of
My Familiar (1989), Possessing the Secret
of Joy (1992), By the Light of My Father's

Smile (1998), The Way Forward Is with a
Broken Heart (2000), and Now Is the
Time to Open Your Heart (2005). Walker
has also published several volumes of poetry, collections of short stories, and nonfiction works, including Sent by Earth: A
Message from the Grandmother Spirit After the Bombing of the World Trade Center and Pentagon (2001) and We Are the
Ones We Have Been Waiting For (2006).
She lives in San Francisco and runs the
publishing company Wild Tree Press.

Henry Wechsler (b. 1932)
American research psychologist and educator. Wechsler was born in Warsaw,
Poland; his family immigrated to the
United States during World War II. He
received an A.B. from Washington and
Jefferson College and an M.A. and a
Ph.D. in social psychology from Harvard
University. Wechsler has contributed to
numerous books on medical and psychological topics and is currently a lecturer
of social psychology at Harvard. Since
1988 he has been the director of Harvard's Youth Alcohol-Drug Program in
the Department of Health and Social Behavior. Since 1990, Wechsler has studied
binge drinking and its effects with a team
of researchers at the Harvard School of
Public Health, including Sonia Castillo,
Andrea Davenport, Charles Deutsch,
George Dowdall, and Barbara Moeykens.

Eudora Welty (1909–2001)
American writer, critic, amateur painter,
and photographer. Born and raised in
Jackson, Mississippi, Welty retained her
deep attachment to the people and
places of the South. After graduating
from the University of Wisconsin in
1929 and studying for a year at Columbia University's School of Business, she
returned to Jackson and became a publicity agent for the Works Progress Administration, a New Deal social agency.
With the help of Robert Penn Warren
and Cleanth Brooks, she published several short stories that launched her literary career. Welty's work encompasses
various collections of short stories, including Collected Stories (1980); novel-
las and novels, including Delta Wedding
(1946), Losing Battles (1970), and The
Optimist's Daughter (Pulitzer Prize,
1972); two volumes of photographs; and
an acclaimed collection of critical essays,
The Eye of the Story (1978). Three lectures delivered at Harvard University
in April 1983 were published as One
Writer's Beginnings (1984).

E. B. White (1899–1985)

American poet, journalist, editor, and essayist. After graduating from Cornell University in 1921, White became a reporter, then an advertising copywriter before beginning a sixty-year career on the staff of the *New Yorker*. With Harold Ross, the magazine's founding editor, and Katharine Angell, its literary editor, White made the *New Yorker* the most important publication of its kind in the United States. He wrote poems and articles for the magazine and served as a discreet and helpful editor. Among his many books, three written for children earned him lasting fame: *Stuart Little* (1945), *Charlotte's Web* (1952), and *The Trumpet of the Swan* (1970). White revised and edited William Strunk's text *The Elements of Style*, a classic guide to writing.

Walt Whitman (1819–1892)

American poet and writer. Born on Long Island and raised in Brooklyn, New York, Whitman received scant formal education before going to work at age eleven in a newspaper office. He taught school from 1835 to 1840 and worked at several government posts during his lifetime, but Whitman considered himself primarily a writer, publishing poetry, stories, and newspaper articles from the age of nineteen. In 1855 he published *Leaves of Grass*, a series of twelve poems that most scholars consider his finest work. As it evolved through a number of editions, *Leaves of Grass* came to include well over 100 poems, including "Song of Myself," "Crossing Brooklyn Ferry," and "Out of the Cradle Endlessly Rocking." In his poetry and prose, Whitman celebrates the landscape and people of the United States. Although he was an ardent Democrat, he supported Lincoln; indeed, Lincoln was the subject of Whitman's moving elegy "When Lilacs Last in the Dooryard Bloom'd" (1865).

Patricia Williams (b. 1951)

American legal scholar and critic. Williams received her B.A. from Wellesley College and her J.D. from Harvard Law School. She is currently the James L. Dohr Professor of Law at Columbia Law School. Williams writes a column for the *Nation* titled "Diary of a Mad Law Professor." Her books include *The Alchemy of Race and Rights: A Diary of a Law Professor* (1991), *The Rooster's Egg* (1995), *Seeing a Color-Blind Future: The Paradox of Race* (1997), and *Open House: Of Family, Friends, Food, Piano Lessons, and the Search for a Room of My Own* (2004). She has received a MacArthur Foundation Fellowship, along with numerous other honors.

Terry Tempest Williams (b. 1955)

American writer, naturalist, and environmental activist. Named by the *Utne Reader* as one of their "Utne 100 Visionaries," Williams grew up surrounded by the vast desert landscape of her native Utah. Her ideas, she says, "have been shaped by the Colorado Plateau and the Great Basin, . . . then sorted out through the prism of my culture—and my culture is Mormon." Her first book, *Pieces of White Shell: A Journey to Navajoland* (1984), is a personal exploration of Native American myths. "The Clan of One-Breasted Women" became the final section of one of her best-known books, *Refuge: An Unnatural History of Family and Place* (1991). She has since written *An Unspoken Hunger: Stories from the Field* (1994), *Desert Quartet: An Erotic Landscape* (1995), and *Leap* (2000). Her most recent books are *Red: Passion and Patience in the Desert* (2001), a collection of essays that chronicle her attachment to the deserts of Utah, and *The Open Space of Democracy* (2004), an argument for a democratic way of life that integrates social, ecological, and spiritual values.

E. O. Wilson (b. 1929)

American biologist, naturalist, and scholar. Wilson was born in Birmingham, Alabama. He earned his B.S. and M.S. degrees at the University of Alabama and his Ph.D. from Harvard University. He is a world-renowned scientist with particular expertise in the study of ants, the focus of his early career and work. He has also discovered hundreds of new species and established sociobiology, which he defines as "the systematic study of the biological basis of all social behavior," as a new science field. Wilson is considered by many to be "the father of biodiversity." Among his many books are *Sociobiology: The New Synthesis* (1975), *Genes, Mind and Culture: The Coevolutionary Process* (1981), *The Future of Life* (2002), and *The Creation: A Meeting of Science and Religion* (2006). Wilson has twice won the Pulitzer Prize, once for *On Human Nature* (1979) and again for *The Ants* (with Bert Holldobler) (1991). He is currently the Pellegrino Research Professor in Entomology for the Department of Organismic and Evolutionary Biology at Harvard University.

Mary Wollstonecraft (1759–1797)
English social critic, essayist, and novelist. Wollstonecraft was one of the first people to present a well-developed, radical argument against the inequality between women and men in eighteenth-century England. After a troubled early life, she left home and started a school, which soon closed. By 1787, the year she began channeling her ideas into writing, she had suffered the devastating losses of both her mother and her best friend. In the years that followed, Wollstonecraft published essays, translations, novels, an anthology, and a children's book. Her *Vindication of the Rights of Men* (1790), which supported the principles of the French Revolution, was an instant success and established her reputation in literary and political circles. Her *Vindication of the Rights of Women* (1792) is an important early feminist treatise.

Virginia Woolf (1882–1941)
English novelist, critic, and essayist. The daughter of respected philosopher and writer Sir Leslie Stephen, Woolf educated herself by unrestricted reading in her father's library. She lived at the center of the Bloomsbury group, a celebrated collection of artists, scholars, and writers. Woolf, together with her husband, socialist writer Leonard Woolf, founded the Hogarth Press. Her work, both nonfiction and fiction, is marked by a resonant autobiographical voice. *A Room of One's Own* (1929), a historical investigation of women and creativity; *Mrs. Dalloway* (1925), *To the Lighthouse* (1927), and *The Waves* (1931), novels about artistic consciousness and the development of personality; and *The Common Reader* (1925) and *The Second Common Reader* (1932), collections of essays on topics as diverse as literature and automobiles, all reveal penetrating intelligence as well as innovations in narrative technique.

William Zinsser (b. 1922)
American journalist, writer, editor, and educator. After graduating from Princeton University in 1944 and serving in the army for two years, Zinsser joined the staff of the *New York Herald Tribune*, first as a features editor, then as a drama editor and film critic, and finally as an editorial writer. In 1959 he became a freelance writer, and in 1971 he joined the English faculty at Yale University, where he taught until 1979. Zinsser is the author of more than a dozen books, among them the well-known *On Writing Well: An Informal Guide to Writing Non-Fiction* (1976; 1998).

PERMISSIONS
ACKNOWLEDGMENTS

Pollitt: "Does a Literary Canon Matter?" by Katha Pollitt. Reprinted by permission of the author from the Sept. 23, 1991, issue of *The Nation*.

Postman: From *The End of Education* by Neil Postman. Copyright © 1995 by Neil Postman. Used by permission of Alfred A. Knopf, a division of Random House, Inc.

Quindlen: "Between the Sexes, a Great Divide" by Anna Quindlen was originally published in *The New York Times*. Copyright © 1988 by The New York Times Co. Reprinted by permission.

Rauch: "In Defense of Prejudice" by Jonathan Rauch. Copyright © 1995 by *Harper's Magazine*. All rights reserved. Reproduced from the May issue by special permission.

Regan: "The Case for Animal Rights," from *In Defense of Animals* by Tom Regan. Copyright © 1985 by Tom Regan. Reprinted by permission of Blackwell Publishing Ltd.

Rich: "Aunt Jennifer's Tigers." Copyright © 1993, 1951 by Adrienne Rich. "The Loser." Copyright © 1993, 1967, 1963 by Adrienne Rich. The lines from "Snapshots of a Daughter-in-Law." Copyright © 1993, 1967, 1963 by Adrienne Rich. "Orion." Copyright © 1993 by Adrienne Rich. Copyright © 1969 by W. W. Norton & Company, Inc. "Planetarium." Copyright © 1993 by Adrienne Rich. Copyright © 1971 by W. W. Norton & Company, Inc. From *Collected Early Poems: 1950–1970* by Adrienne Rich. "Taking Women Students Seriously" from *On Lies, Secrets and Silence: Selected Prose 1966–1978*. Copyright © 1979 by W. W. Norton & Company, Inc. Used by permission of the author and W. W. Norton & Company, Inc.

Roach: From *Stiff: The Curious Lives of the Human Cadavers* by Mary Roach. Copyright © 2003 by Mary Roach. Used by permission of W. W. Norton & Co., Inc.

Rodriguez: "Aria" from *Hunger of Memory* by Richard Rodriguez is reprinted by permission of David R. Godine, Publishers, Inc. Copyright © 1982 by Richard Rodriguez.

Sanders: "Looking at Women" from *Secrets of the Universe* by Scott Russell Sanders. Copyright © 1991 by Scott Russell Sanders. Reprinted by permission of Beacon Press, Boston. "Under the Influence," copyright © 1989 by *Harper's Magazine*. Reprinted from the November issue by special permission. All rights reserved. Lines from "My Papa's Waltz" by Theodore Roethke. Copyright 1942 by Hearst Magazines, Inc. from *The Collected Poems of Theodore Roethke*. Used by permission of Doubleday, a division of Random House, Inc.

Sartre: "Existentialism" from *Existentialism* by Jean-Paul Sartre. Reproduced by permission of Philosophical Library Publishers.

Selzer: "The Knife" from *Mortal Lessons: Notes on the Art of Surgery* by Richard Selzer. Copyright © 1974, 1975, 1976, 1987 by Richard Selzer. Reprinted by permission of Georges Borchardt, Inc., on behalf of the author.

Slater: "On Love" by Lauren Slater from *National Geographic* magazine, Feb. 2006, is reprinted by permission of the publisher.

Sontag: "A Century of Cinema" from *Where the Stress Falls*, copyright © 2001 by Susan Sontag, is reprinted by permission of The Wylie Agency.

Staples: "Why Colleges Shower Their Students with A's" was originally published in *The New York Times*. Copyright © 1998 by The New York Times Co. Reprinted by permission. "Black Men and Public Space" first appeared as "Just Walk On By" in *Ms.* magazine, Sept. 1986. Copyright © 1986 by Brent Staples. Reprinted by permission.

Strebeigh: "The Wheels of Freedom: The Bicycle in China" from *Bicyling* magazine, April 1991. Copyright © 1991 by Fred Strebeigh. Reprinted by permission of the author.

Sullivan: "What Is a Homosexual" from *Virtually Normal* by Andrew Sullivan. Copyright © 1995 by Andrew Sullivan. Reprinted by permission of Alfred A. Knopf, a division of Random House, Inc.

Thomas: "Notes on Punctuation" from *The Medusa and the Snail* by Lewis Thomas. Copyright © 1979 by Lewis Thomas. Used by permission of Viking Penguin, a division of Penguin Books USA, Inc.

Tisdale: "We Do Abortions Here" from *Harper's Magazine*, Oct. 1990. Copyright © 1990 by Sallie Tisdale. Reprinted by permission of the author.

Tuchman: From *A Distant Mirror* by Barbara W. Tuchman. Copyright © 1978 by Barbara W. Tuchman. Used by permission of Alfred A. Knopf, a division of Random House, Inc.

Updike: "Beer Can" from *Assorted Prose* by John Updike. Copyright © 1965 and renewed © 1993 by John Updike. "Moving Along" from *Just Looking* by John Updike. Copyright © 1989 by John Updike. Used by permission of Alfred A. Knopf, a division of Random House, Inc.

Walker: "Beauty: When the Other Dancer Is the Self" from *In Search of Our Mothers' Gardens: Womanist Prose*. Copyright © 1983 by Alice Walker. Reprinted by permission of Harcourt, Inc.

Wechsler et al.: "Too Many Colleges Are Still in Denial about Alcohol Abuse" from *The*

Genres Index